Electronic Commerce 2012

A Managerial and Social Networks Perspective

Global Edition

lia

Stanley Myles C. Seballos

COC-PHINMA Education Network, Philippines

PEARSON

Boston   Columbus   Indianapolis   New York   San Fran

Amsterdam   Cape Town   Dubai   London   Madrid   Milar   ito

Delhi   Mexico City   São Paulo   Sydney   Hong Kong

Dedicated to all who are interested in learning
about electronic commerce.

Editorial Director: Sally Yagan
Acquisitions Editor: Bob Horan
Senior Acquisitions Editor, Global Edition: Steven
 Jackson
Editorial Assistant, Global Edition: Emily Jones
Director of Editorial Services: Ashley Santora
Editorial Project Manager: Kelly Loftus
Editorial Assistant: Ashlee Bradbury
Director of Marketing: Maggie Moylan
Executive Marketing Manager: Anne Fahlgren
Marketing Manager, International: Dean Erasmus
Senior Managing Editor: Judy Leale
Production Project Manager: Ilene Kahn

Senior Operations Supervisor: Arnold Vila
Operations Specialist: Cathleen Petersen
Creative Director: Blair Brown
Sr. Art Director/Design Supervisor: Janet Slowik
Interior Designer: Jill Little
Cover Designer: Jodi Notowitz
Cover Image: © Павел Игнатов
Media Project Manager, Production: Lisa Rinaldi
Media Project Manager, Editorial: Allison
 Longley
Full-Service Project Management: Sharon
 Anderson/Bookmasters
Cover Printer: Lehigh-Phoenix Color/Hagerstown

The right of Efraim Turban, David King, Jae Lee, Ting-Peng Liang, and Deborrah C. Turban to be identified as
authors of this work has been asserted by them in accordance with the Copyright, Designs and Patents Act 1988.

*Authorised adaptation from the United States edition, entitled Electronic Commerce 2012, 7th Edition,
ISBN 978-0-13-214538-1 by Efraim Turban, David King, Jae Lee, Ting-Peng Liang and Deborrah C. Turban,
published by Pearson Education, publishing as Prentice Hall © 2012.*

ISBN: 978-0-27-376134-1

British Library Cataloguing-in-Publication Data
A catalogue record for this book is available from the British Library

10 9 8 7 6 5 4 3 2 1
15 14 13 12 11

Typeset in 10.5/12, Times New Roman by Integra Software Services
Printed and bound by Edwards Brothers in The United States of America

Contents in Brief

Contents

PART 2 EC Applications   133

CHAPTER 9   E-COMMERCE SECURITY AND FRAUD PROTECTION. 486

Online Chapter

PART 6—LAUNCHING ONLINE BUSINESSES AND EC PROJECTS

Online Files

Online Tutorials

Entering the second decade of the 21st century, we are experiencing one of the most important changes to our daily lives—the move to an Internet-based society. Internet World Statistics reported at the end of March 2011 that more than 2 billion people worldwide surf the Internet (per *ABC News* 2011). The number of Internet users worldwide using cell phone access to the Internet was more than 1.2 billion by April 2011 (out of 4.5 billion cell phone users). The number of those people using desktop Internet is also increasing. The advent of less expensive computers ($150 or less) closes the digital divide, and puts more people on the Internet (Ray 2010). All this contributes to the development and growth of the field of electronic commerce, the subject of this book.

Electronic commerce (EC) describes the manner in which transactions take place over networks, mostly the Internet. It is the process of electronically buying and selling goods, services, and information. Certain EC applications, such as buying and selling stocks and airline tickets on the Internet, are growing very rapidly, exceeding non-Internet trades. But EC is not just about buying and selling; it also is about electronically communicating, collaborating, and discovering information. It is about e-learning, e-government, social networks, and much more. EC is having an impact on a significant portion of the world, affecting businesses, professions, and of course, people.

The most important development in EC that happened since 2010 is the phenomenal growth of social networks, especially Facebook and Twitter, and the trend toward conducting EC in social networks. Also, related business models such as the one devised by Groupon are providing EC with major new areas of growth.

WHAT'S NEW IN THIS EDITION?

The following are the major changes in this edition:

- The number of chapters has been reduced from 18 to 15.
- We replaced the in-text and the online appendices and many online files with 12 tutorials.
- **New chapters.**
  - Social commerce is becoming a major element of EC. Chapter 7 is new, and describes this exciting field.
  - EC implementation is covered in Chapter 13 and deals mostly with cost–benefit analysis, EC systems development, and several other implementation issues such as Gartner's hype cycle and business process restructuring. Also, material from old Chapters 14 and 18 are included in Chapter 13.
- **Chapters with major changes.** Major changes have been made to the following chapters:
  - Chapter 1 now includes social commerce, new business models (e.g., Groupon), and other leading-edge EC-related topics.
  - Chapter 2 includes extensive coverage of Web 2.0 tools, virtual communities, social networks, virtual worlds, and the commercial applications of each.
  - Old Chapters 6 and 12 have been combined to make one unified chapter on order fulfillment and supply chain management (Chapter 11).
  - The m-commerce chapter (now Chapter 6) was extensively revised with the newest enterprise applications and l-commerce.
  - In all chapters, we have significantly expanded the use of social networking in relation to the chapter topics (e.g., real estate and travel in Chapter 3, e-government in Chapter 5).

▶ **Chapters with less significant changes.** All data in the chapters were updated. About 25 percent of all end-of-chapter material has been updated and/or expanded. Duplications were eliminated and explanations of exhibits have been made more understandable. New topics were added in many of the sections to reflect the Web 2.0 and social networking revolution.

NEW ONLINE TUTORIALS

The following tutorials are not related to any specific chapter. They cover the essentials of the technologies and provide a guide to additional resources.

T1—e-CRM
T2—Business Plan and Strategy
T3—RFID
T4—Smart Grid
T5—Supply Chain Management
T6—Mass Customization
T7—Cloud Computing
T8—Business Intelligence, Data, Text, and Web Mining
T9—Knowledge Management
T10—Online Collaboration
T11—EDI, Extranets, and XML
T12—Competition in Cyberspace

NEW FEATURES

The following new features were added to *all chapters*.

1. Topics for class discussion and debates—5 to 10 topics per chapter.
2. A class assignment that involves the opening case.
3. A class assignment that requires watching short videos (5 to 10 minutes) about a certain technology or a minicase followed by questions or some other engagement.
4. Video recommendations related to specific topics are suggested in the text.
5. Video recommendations with a short description are now available in the instructor's manual (3 to 5 per chapter).
6. Over 75 real-world short examples on specific topics and subtopics.
7. Learning objectives for the entire book.

BOOK'S LEARNING OBJECTIVES (OUTCOMES)

Upon completion of this book, the reader will be able to:

1. Define all types of e-commerce systems and describe their major business and revenue models.
2. Describe all the major mechanisms that are used in e-commerce.
3. Describe all methods of selling products and services online.
4. Understand all online business-to-business activities including procurement, auctions, and collaboration.
5. Describe EC activities other than trading online, such as e-government, e-learning/training, and e-collaboration.
6. Relate the support services of payment, security, order fulfillment, and so forth to e-commerce implementation.
7. Describe social networks, virtual worlds, and social software as facilitators of social commerce.

8. Describe the landscape of social commerce applications including social advertising and shopping, enterprise social commerce, social market research, and crowdsourcing.

9. Understand e-commerce strategy and describe its process and steps including justification, planning, implementation, and assessment.

10. Describe the options of acquiring or building EC systems.

11. Understand the legal, social, ethical, and business environments within which e-commerce operates.

12. Describe the global aspects of e-commerce as well as its use in SMEs and in developing countries.

FEATURES OF THIS BOOK

Several features are unique to this book.

MANAGERIAL ORIENTATION

Electronic commerce can be approached from two major aspects: technological and managerial. This text uses the second approach. Most of the presentations are about EC applications and their implementation. However, we do recognize the importance of the technology; therefore, we present the essentials of security in Chapter 9 and the essentials of infrastructure and systems development in Chapter 13. We also provide some detailed technology material in the 12 online tutorials on the book's website. Managerial issues are also provided at the end of each chapter.

REAL-WORLD ORIENTATION

Extensive, vivid examples from large corporations, small businesses from different industries and services, government, and nonprofit agencies from all over the world make concepts come alive. These examples show students the capabilities of EC, its cost and justification, and the innovative ways real corporations are using EC in their operations.

SOLID THEORETICAL BACKGROUND AND RESEARCH SUGGESTIONS

Throughout the book, we present the theoretical foundations necessary for understanding EC, ranging from consumer behavior to the economic theory of competition. Furthermore, we provide website resources, many exercises, and extensive references to supplement the theoretical presentations. At the end of each chapter, we provide a list of online resources.

MOST CURRENT CUTTING-EDGE TOPICS

The book presents the most current topics relating to EC, as evidenced by the many 2009 to 2011 citations. Topics such as social networking, e-learning, e-government, e-strategy, Web-based supply chain systems, collaborative commerce, mobile commerce, cloud computing, crowdsourcing, RFID, and f-commerce are presented from the theoretical point of view as well as from the application side.

INTEGRATED SYSTEMS

In contrast to other books that highlight isolated Internet-based systems, we emphasize those systems that support the enterprise and supply chain management. Social network–based systems are highlighted as are the latest innovations in global EC and in Web-based applications.

GLOBAL PERSPECTIVE

The importance of global competition, partnerships, and trade is increasing rapidly. EC facilitates exporting and importing, the management of multinational companies, and electronic trading around the globe. International examples are provided throughout the book. Our authors and contributors are from six different countries. Examples and cases come from over 20 countries.

INTERDISCIPLINARY APPROACH

E-commerce is interdisciplinary, and we illustrate this throughout the book. Major EC-related disciplines include accounting, finance, information systems, marketing, management, operations management, and human resources management. In addition, some nonbusiness disciplines are related, especially public administration, computer science, engineering, psychology, political science, and law. Finally, economics plays a major role in the understanding of EC.

EC FAILURES AND LESSONS LEARNED

In addition to EC success stories, we also present EC failures and, where possible, analyze the causes of those failures with lessons learned (e.g., in Chapters 12 and 13).

ORGANIZATION OF THE BOOK

The book is divided into 15 chapters grouped into 5 parts.

PART 1—INTRODUCTION TO E-COMMERCE AND E-MARKETPLACES

In Part 1, we provide an overview of today's business environment as well as the fundamentals of EC and some of its terminology (Chapter 1). A discussion of electronic markets and their mechanisms and impacts is provided in Chapter 2 where special attention is given to virtual communities and social (Web 2.0) software tools.

PART 2—EC APPLICATIONS

In Part 2, we describe EC B2C applications in three chapters. Chapter 3 addresses e-tailing and electronic service industries (e.g., travel, e-banking), as they relate to individual consumers. In Chapter 4 we examine the one-to-many B2B models including auctions, and the many-to-many models including trading exchanges. In Chapter 5 we present several interesting applications, such as e-government, e-learning, collaborative commerce, and consumer-to-consumer EC.

PART 3—EMERGING EC PLATFORMS

Chapter 6 explores the developing applications in the world of wireless EC (m-commerce, l-commerce, and pervasive computing). Finally, in Chapter 7 we explore the new world of social commerce.

PART 4—EC SUPPORT SERVICES

There are four chapters in this part. Chapter 8 is dedicated to market research and advertising. Chapter 9 begins with a discussion of the need to protect computer systems. It also describes various types of computer attacks including fraud, and then it discusses how to minimize these risks through appropriate security programs. Chapter 10 describes a major EC support service—electronic payments. Chapter 11 concentrates on order fulfillment, supply chain improvement, the role of RFID, CPFR, and the use of intelligent agents.

PART 5—E-COMMERCE STRATEGY AND IMPLEMENTATION

Chapter 12 discusses strategic issues in implementing and deploying EC. The chapter also presents global EC and EC for small businesses. Chapter 13 deals with implementation issues, concentrating on justification and cost–benefit analysis, system acquisitions and developments, and impacts of EC. Chapter 14 deals with legal, ethical, and societal issues concentrating on regulatory issues, compliance, and green IT.

ONLINE PART 6—LAUNCHING ONLINE BUSINESSES AND EC PROJECTS

Chapter 15 is unique; it describes how to build an e-business from scratch, as well as how to build a webstore. It takes the reader through all the necessary steps and provides guidelines for success.

LEARNING AIDS

The text offers a number of learning aids to the student:

▶ **Chapter Outlines.** A listing of the main headings ("Content") at the beginning of each chapter provides a quick overview of the major topics covered.

▶ **Learning Objectives.** Learning objectives at the beginning of each chapter help students focus their efforts and alert them to the important concepts to be discussed.

▶ **Opening Cases.** Each chapter opens with a real-world example that illustrates the importance of EC to modern corporations. These cases were carefully chosen to call attention to some of the major topics to be covered in the chapters. Following each opening case is a short section titled "What We Can Learn . . ." that links the important issues in the case to the subject matter of the chapter.

▶ **EC Application Cases.** In-chapter cases highlight real-world problems encountered by organizations as they develop and implement EC. Questions follow each case to help direct student attention to the implications of the case material.

▶ **Exhibits.** Numerous attractive exhibits (both illustrations and tables) extend and supplement the text discussion.

▶ **Review Questions.** Each section ends with a series of review questions about that section. These questions are intended to help students summarize the concepts introduced and to digest the essentials of each section before moving on to another topic.

▶ **Marginal Glossary and Key Terms.** Each key term is defined in the margin when it first appears. In addition, an alphabetical list of key terms appears at the end of each chapter and at the end of the book, with a page reference to the location where the term is discussed.

▶ **Managerial Issues.** At the end of every chapter, we explore some of the special concerns managers face as they prepare to do business in cyberspace. These issues are framed as questions to maximize readers' active engagement with them.

▶ **Chapter Summary.** The chapter summary is linked one-to-one with the learning objectives introduced at the beginning of each chapter.

▶ **End-of-Chapter Exercises.** Different types of questions measure students' comprehension and their ability to apply knowledge. Discussion Questions are intended to provoke individuals to express their thinking about relevant topics. Topics for Class Discussion and Debates promote discussions and develop critical-thinking skills. Internet Exercises are challenging assignments that require students to surf the Internet and apply what they have learned. Over 250 hands-on exercises send students to interesting websites to conduct research, investigate an application, download demos, or learn about state-of-the-art technology. The Team Assignments and Projects are challenging group projects designed to foster teamwork.

▶ **Closing Cases.** Each chapter ends with a comprehensive case, which is presented in somewhat more depth than the in-chapter EC Application Cases. Questions follow each case relating the case to the topics covered in the chapter.

▶ **List of Online Resources.** At the end of each chapter we provide a list of the chapter's online files with a brief description of their content. In addition we provide a list of URLs linked to relevant resources for the chapter.

USING WIKIPEDIA AS A REFERENCE

We increased substantially the number of references to Wikipedia. While at the beginning there were many criticisms of the quality of the online encyclopedia, the situation has been changed in the last five years. Wikipedia introduced significant quality assurance measures and its reliability is increasing (e.g., see en.wikipedia.org/ wiki/reliability_of_wikipedia). This entry includes many academic testimonials. Also see Davidson (2007).

The academic world's view of Wikipedia has improved during the last few years, as can be inferred from the increase in the number of citations in international scientific journals. A search in the *Science Direct* (2010) database (a large online collection of published scientific research papers produced by Elsevier) for academic and scientific journal articles that are citing Wikipedia in their references yields the following results from January through June 2010.

Year Article Published	No. of Articles Citing Wikipedia
Before 2003	0
2003	1
2004	9
2005	31
2006	133
2007	330
2008	451
2009	614
2010 (January–June 2010)	478

We see several advantages to using Wikipedia as a reference. The major ones are:

 ▶ The material there is constantly updated.
 ▶ Due to space limitation, the presentation in the book is frequently too short. The presentation in Wikipedia is comprehensive.
 ▶ The presentation in Wikipedia includes, in many cases, both the positive and negative aspects.
 ▶ The presentation in Wikipedia includes many references to academic and trade sources.

SUPPLEMENTARY MATERIALS

The following support materials are also available.

ONLINE INSTRUCTOR'S RESOURCE CENTER: PEARSONGLOBALEDITIONS.COM/TURBAN

This convenient online *Instructor's Resource Center* includes all of the supplements: Instructor's Manual, Test Item File, TestGen, PowerPoint Lecture Notes, and Image Library (text art).

The **Instructor's Manual**, written by Jon Outland, includes answers to all review and discussion questions, exercises, and case questions. The **Test Item File**, written by Lisa Miller, is an extensive set of multiple-choice, true-false, and essay questions for each chapter. It is available in Microsoft Word and TestGen.

The **PowerPoint Lecture Notes**, by Judy Lang, are oriented toward text learning objectives.

COMPANION WEBSITE: PEARSONGLOBALEDITIONS.COM/TURBAN

The book is supported by a companion website that includes:

 ▶ Online Chapter 15.
 ▶ Online tutorials.
 ▶ Bonus EC Application Cases and other features can be found in each chapter's online files.
 ▶ All of the Internet Exercises from the end of each chapter in the text are provided on the website for convenient student use.

ACKNOWLEDGMENTS

Many individuals helped us create this text. Faculty feedback was solicited via reviews and through individual interviews. We are grateful to them for their contributions.

Several individuals helped us with the administrative work. We thank Daphne Turban, Sarah Miller, and all these people for their dedication and superb performance shown throughout the project.

We also recognize the various organizations and corporations that provided us with permissions to reproduce material. Special thanks go to Dion Hinchcliffe for allowing us to use his figures and materials from his websites. Thanks also to the Pearson Prentice Hall team that helped us from the inception of the project to its completion under the leadership of Executive Editor Bob Horan. The dedicated staff includes Editorial Project Manager Kelly Loftus, Editorial Assistant Ashlee Bradbury, Production Managers Ilene Kahn and Lynn Savino, Art Director Janet Slowik, and Media Project Manager Allison Longley.

Last, but not least, we thank Judy Lang who, as coordinator and problem solver, contributed innovative ideas and also provided the necessary editing.

CONTENT CONTRIBUTORS

The following individuals contributed material for this edition.

- Linda Lai of the Macau Polytechnic Institute of China updated Chapter 3 and updated and contributed to Online Chapter 15.
- Carol Pollard of Appalachian State University updated Chapter 13.
- San Murugasen contributed to Chapter 7 and developed the cloud computing tutorial.
- Judy Lang of Lang Associates updated material in several chapters and conducted supported research.
- Kevin Waugh of Strategic Enterprise, LLC, updated Chapter 14.
- Stanley Myles C. Seballos of COC-PHINMA Education Network, Philippines, contributed the new illustrations and helped in updating several chapters.

REVIEWERS

We wish to thank the faculty who participated in reviews of this text and our other EC titles.

David Ambrosini, Cabrillo College
Timothy Ay, Villanova University
Deborah Ballou, University of Notre Dame
Christine Barnes, Lakeland Community College
Martin Barriff, Illinois Institute of Technology
Sandy Bobzien, Presentation College
Stefan Brandle, Taylor University
Joseph Brooks, University of Hawaii
Bruce Brorson, University of Minnesota
Clifford Brozo, Monroe College-New Rochelle
Stanley Buchin, Boston University
John Bugado, National University
Ernest Capozzolli, Troy State University
Mark Cecchini, University of Florida
Edward Cherian, George Washington University
Sandy Claws, Northern University
Jack Cook, State University of New York at Geneseo
Larry Corman, Fort Lewis College
Mary Culnan, Georgetown University
Chet Cunningham, Madisonville
   Community College
Ron Dickinson, Lincoln Memorial University
Roland Eicheleberger, Baylor University
Ted Ferretti, Northeastern University
Colin Fukai, Gonzaga University
Vickie Fullmer, Webster University
Dennis Galletta, University of Pittsburgh
Ken Griggs, California Polytechnic University
Varun Grover, University of South Carolina

Tom Gruen, University of Colorado
   at Colorado Springs
Norman Hahn, Thomas Nelson Community College
Harry Harmon, University of Central Missouri
James Henson, Barry University
Sadie Herbert, Mississippi Gulf Coast
   Community College
James Hogue, Wayland Baptist University
Brian Howland, Boston University
Chang Hsieh, University of Southern Mississippi
Paul Hu, University of Utah
Jin H. Im, Sacred Heart University
Bandula Jayatilaka, Binghamton University
Jeffrey Johnson, Utah State University
Kenneth H. Johnson, Illinois Institute
   of Technology
Robert Johnson, University of Connecticut
Morgan Jones, University of North Carolina
Charles Kelley, California Baptist University
Douglas Kline, Sam Houston State University
Mary Beth Klinger, College of Southern Maryland
Parag Kosalge, Grand Valley State University
Tanvi Kothari, Temple University
Joanne Kuzma, St. Petersburg College
Charles Lange, DeVry University
Carlton Lawrence, Colorado Technical University
Chunlei Liu, Troy State University
Byungtae Lee, University of Illinois at Chicago
Lakshmi Lyer, University of North Carolina

Joseph Maggi, Technical College of the Lowcountry

Ross Malaga, Montclair State University

Steve Mann, Humphreys College

Michael McLeod, East Carolina University

Susan McNamara, Northeastern University

Mohon Menon, University of South Alabama

Stephanie Miller, University of Georgia

Ajay Mishra, State University of New York at Binghamton

Bud Mishra, New York University

Robert Moore, Mississippi State University

Lawrence Muller, LaGuardia Community College, CUNY

Suzy Murray, Piedmont Technical College

Mohammed M. Nadeem, National University

William Nance, San Jose State University

Lewis Neisner, University of Maryland

Katherine A. Olson, Northern Virginia Community College

Ant Ozok, University of Maryland, Baltimore County

Somendra Pant, Clarkson University

Wayne Pauli, Dakota State University

Craig Peterson, Utah State University

Sarah Pettitt, Champlain College

Dien D. Phan, University of Vermont

H.R. Rao, State University of New York at Buffalo

Catherine M. Roche, Rockland Community College

Laraine Rodgers, University of Arizona

Jorge Romero, Towson University

Greg Rose, California State University at Chico

Linda Salchenberger, Loyola University of Chicago

George Schell, University of North Carolina at Wilmington

Sri Sharma, Oakland University

Daniel Shen, SUNY New Paltz

Seungjae Shin, Mississippi State University-Meridian

Sumit Sircar, University of Texas at Arlington

Elliot B. Sloane, Villanova University

Hongjun Song, University of Memphis

Kan Sugandh, DeVry Institute of Technology

Yi Sun, California State University, San Marcos

John Thacher, Gwinnett Technical College

Goran Trajkovski, Towson University

Dothang Truong, Fayetteville State University

Hiep Van Dong, Madison Area Technical College

Linda Volonino, Canisius College

Andrea Wachter, Point Park University

Ken Williamson, James Madison University

John Windsor, University of North Texas

Gregory Wood, Canisius College

Walter Wymer, Christopher Newport University

Hongjiang Xu, Butler University

Gene Yell, State University of New York at Utica-Rome

James Zemanek, East Carolina University

GLOBAL EDITION CONTRIBUTORS AND REVIEWERS

Pearson would like to acknowledge and thank the following people for their work on the Global Edition:

Amit Das, College of Business & Economics, Qatar University, Qatar

Dr. Ailsa Kolsaker, The Surrey Business School, University of Surrey, UK

Mark Hornshaw, University of Notre Dame Australia (Sydney), Australia

Hoda M. Hosny, The American University in Cairo, Egypt

Dr. Martin Rich, Faculty of Management, Cass Business School, City University London, UK

Prof. Dr. Swen Schneider, Department of Business and Law, FH Frankfurt am Main, Germany

Neerja Sethi, Nanyang Business School, Nanyang Technological University, Singapore

Vijay Sethi, Nanyang Business School, Nanyang Technological University, Singapore

Suku Sinnappan, Business, Technology and Management Group, Swinburne University of Technology, Australia

Joseph Chi-ho So, Hong Kong Community College, The Hong Kong Polytechnic University, Hong Kong

Dr. Xuemei Tian, Faculty of Higher Education, Swinburne University of Technology, Australia

Professor Doug Vogel, Department of Information Systems, City University of Hong Kong, Hong Kong

Hen Kai Wah, Faculty of Accountancy and Management, University Tunku Abdul Rahman, Malaysia

REFERENCES

ABC News. "2 Billion People Now Surfing the Net." January 27, 2011. abc.net.au/news/stories/2011/01/27/3122545.htm (accessed April 2011).

Davidson, C. "We Can't Ignore the Influence of Digital Technologies." *Chronicle of Higher Education*, March 23, 2007.

Ray, T. "Comcast Promises Broadband, $150 PC for Low Income Homes." *Tech Daily Trader*, December 27, 2010.

"Science Direct Indexed Papers." sciencedirect.com (accessed April, 2011).

CHAPTER 1

OVERVIEW OF ELECTRONIC COMMERCE

Content

Learning Objectives

Upon completion of this chapter, you will be able to:

1. Define electronic commerce (EC) and describe its various categories.
2. Describe and discuss the content and framework of EC.
3. Describe the major types of EC transactions.
4. Discuss e-commerce 2.0.
5. Describe social commerce and social software.
6. Understand the elements of the digital world.
7. Describe the drivers of EC as they relate to business pressures and organizational responses.
8. Describe some EC business models.
9. Describe the benefits of EC to organizations, consumers, and society.
10. List and describe the major limitations of EC.

NET-A-PORTER: DRESS FOR SUCCESS

Will a woman buy a $2,000 dress online without trying it on? Chic digital merchant Net-a-Porter (a UK online retailer, known as "the Net") bet on it and proved that today's women will purchase their dresses (for success) with a click on their iPhones, especially if the luxury clothing and accessories are international brands such as Jimmy Choo, Givenchy, or Calvin Klein.

The Opportunity

When talking about e-commerce (EC) most people think about buying online books, vitamins, CDs, or other commodity items. And this indeed was what people bought in the mid-1990s, when EC began. But in 2000,

Natalie Massenet, a fashion journalist and stylist, saw an opportunity because of the success of luxury online stores such as Blue Nile (see Chapter 2) and the fact that professional women are very busy and are willing to do more purchasing online.

The Solution

On one website, Massenet combined the efficiency of online shopping and the thrill of shopping at a chic boutique. In addition to selling items it designs in house, the Net sells merchandise from more than 300 top designers (which very few large physical stores can offer). The Net ships to 170 different countries (also something that physical stores cannot match). The offline cycle for designers has always been to show spring fashions in the fall and fall fashions in the spring so buyers would have six months lead time to buy for physical outlets. The online cycle for designers is much shorter, and therefore the Net can predict fashion trends quickly. Also, customers do not have to wait 4 to 6 months after a runway fashion show to buy a new style dress. The store offers same-day delivery (Chapter 3) in London and New York City.

The Net is running its own fashion shows in London and New York. The company also offers an online discount channel called the *Outnet*. The company uses EC and IT extensively. The Internet enables the company to offer a huge selection of items. The Internet also enables live fashion shows of top brands in real-time. Two giant flat screens in the company's headquarters track orders as they come in (with prices and locations) to motivate the staff. The over 2 million unique visitors that come

to the sites every week are also offered the company's online fashion magazine. Furthermore, the Net's collection is considered to be the best in the world.

Order fulfillment is very important for the Net, and it must be done quickly. The solution includes a global distribution system. For regular orders, the company uses UPS in the United States and DHL for the rest of the world. For rush orders in London and New York, the company uses its own delivery vehicles staffed by good-looking and well-mannered employees.

A key success factor for the Net is the ability to buy what customers want from designers. Both the Net and some designers collect new information over the Internet, including from social networks, so they can shorten the lead time of new merchandise to the market.

Yet another success factor for the Net is the superb customer service that is provided both online and in the physical stores. Finally, Massenet's knowledge of the fashion industry combined with her understanding of modern professional women's attitudes toward online shopping helped in the design and proper operation of the Net's site.

The company plans to take advantage of the social media environment that is changing the fashion industry (Rowe 2010).

The Results

In 2008, the company grossed $135 million for a $16.6 million profit. The company became profitable one year after being in business. The initial customers were friends and family followed by media executives, financers, and wealthy women. The company was so successful that luxury goods company Richemont purchased a major financial stake in the business.

During the economic crisis of 2009, the Net's total sales were up 45 percent, versus a 14 percent decrease for one of its major competitors (Neiman Marcus Direct, Web and paper catalog sales).

In June 2010 when the company celebrated its 10th anniversary, it opened a new website dedicated entirely to menswear, selling labels such as Ralph Lauren, YSL, Lanvin, and Burberry. With success comes competition, and the

Net's competitors include Bluefly (low prices), Shopbop (an Amazon.com company, but it lacks of the Net's prestige), and high-end department stores with their own online stores (Nordstrom, Neiman Marcus). But the Net has the highest prestige and growth rate. A major threat may come from eBay, which has been reaching out to high-end designers about creating their own virtual stores (hosted by eBay) where they can sell in fixed prices and also use auctions. Finally, note that in late 2010, Google entered the fashion field of e-commerce with its Boutiques.com. To stay on top of the competition, the Net is planning new ventures and expanding its business model even to include children's clothes.

Sources: Compiled from *en.wikipedia.org/wiki/Net-A-Porter* (accessed April 2011), Brodie (2009), Rowe (2010), *fashionablymarketing.me* (accessed April 2011), and *netaporter.com* (accessed April 2011).

Source: Courtesy of Net-a-Porter.com. Used with permission.

WHAT WE CAN LEARN . . .

The Net's case illustrates a story of a very successful Internet start-up company that is doing business almost exclusively online. Doing business electronically is one of the major activities of e-commerce (EC), the subject of this book. Selling online is a popular and very competitive activity. In this case, a business is selling to individual customers in what is known as business-to-customer (B2C). The case demonstrates several of the topics that you will learn in this chapter and throughout the book. These are:

a. You need to have the right idea, capitalizing on the capabilities of online business.

b. These capabilities include the ability to offer a very large number of products so that no single company in the physical world can even come close to your inventory. You can do it because your customer base is huge, and people can buy from anywhere at any time. You can also do it with less cost since you do not need physical stores.

c. Every company needs a business model that describes how the company operates, how it generates sales, how it provides value to the customers, and eventually provides profits to its owners. This model is a part of EC strategy and can be changed over time.

d. In online businesses customers cannot see the physical product, store, or sellers. Therefore, a good business needs to provide services such as superb customer care, a good return policy, detailed information about the products including a superb 3-D visual presentation of each product, and trust in the brand.

e. In a regular store you pay and pick up the merchandize. In an online business the product is shipped to you or to a pick-up location (the two physical stores in London and New York). Therefore, order fulfillment needs to be very efficient and timely.

f. There are a few barriers of entering an online business. Success brings out the imitators very quickly, therefore competitive strategy is a must, and it may lead to a change in the business model.

g. One advantage of EC is the ability to go global, which expands your customers' base. (The Net is selling in 170 countries.) This is part of today's business environment, which provides both threats and opportunities (these topics are discussed in this chapter).

h. Finally, an online business is a business first, and it must use all basic and critical success factors of a business, such as having a business strategy, operating an effective supply chain, having financial viability, providing superb customer service, providing a superb relationship with its business partners (notably the suppliers), and, perhaps most important, being innovative, creative, and open-minded in order to maintain a strategic advantage.

The Net case covers major topics related to B2C and doing business online in general. These topics are discussed throughout the book. Chapter 1 provides an introduction to the field and an overview of the book. The chapter also covers the digital economy, the business environment and drivers, benefits, and limitations of EC. Finally, the chapter introduces the emerging topics of social networks and social commerce.

1.1 ELECTRONIC COMMERCE: DEFINITIONS AND CONCEPTS

Let's begin by looking at what the management guru Peter Drucker had to say about EC in 2002:

> *The truly revolutionary impact of the Internet Revolution is . . . e-commerce—that is, the explosive emergence of the Internet as a major, perhaps eventually the major, worldwide distribution channel for goods, for services, and, surprisingly, for managerial and professional jobs. This is profoundly changing economics, markets and industry structure, products and services and their flow; consumer segmentation, consumer values and consumer behavior; jobs and labor markets. But the impact may be even greater on societies and politics, and above all, on the way we see the world and ourselves in it. (Drucker 2002, pp. 3–4)*

DEFINING ELECTRONIC COMMERCE

electronic commerce (EC)
The process of buying, selling, or exchanging products, services, or information via computer.

Electronic commerce (EC) is the process of buying, selling, transferring, or exchanging products, services, and/or information via computer networks, mostly the Internet and intranets. For an overview, see en.wikipedia.org/wiki/E-commerce. EC is often confused with e-business.

DEFINING E-BUSINESS

e-business
A broader definition of EC that includes not just the buying and selling of goods and services, but also servicing customers, collaborating with business partners, and conducting electronic transactions within an organization.

Some people view the term *commerce* as describing only buying and selling transactions conducted between business partners. If this definition of commerce is used, the term *electronic commerce* would be fairly narrow. Thus, many use the term *e-business* instead. **E-business** refers to a broader definition of EC, not just the buying and selling of goods and services, but also servicing customers, collaborating with business partners, conducting e-learning, and conducting electronic transactions within an organization. However, others view e-business as comprising those activities that do not involve buying or selling over the Internet, such as collaboration and intrabusiness activities; that is, it is a *complement* of the narrowly defined e-commerce. In this book, we use the broadest meaning of electronic commerce, which is basically equivalent to the broadest definition of e-business. The two terms will be used interchangeably throughout the text.

MAJOR EC CONCEPTS

Several other concepts are frequently used in conjunction with EC. The major ones are as follows.

Pure Versus Partial EC

EC can take several forms depending on the degree of digitization (the transformation from physical to digital) of: (1) the ordering system (order, payment), (2) the processing (e.g., create product/service), and (3) the shipment (delivery) method. The possible configurations of these three dimensions (Exhibit 1.1) determine different levels of EC. Each dimension may be physical or digital. These alternatives create eight cubes, each of which has three dimensions. In traditional commerce, all three dimensions of the cube are physical (lower-left cube); in pure EC, all dimensions are digital (upper-right cube). All other cubes include a mix of digital and physical dimensions.

If there is at least one digital dimension, we consider the situation EC, but only partial EC. For example, purchasing a computer from Dell's website or a book from Amazon.com is partial EC, because the merchandise is physically delivered. However, buying an e-book from Amazon.com or a software product from Buy.com is pure EC, because ordering, processing and delivery to the buyer are all digital.

EC Organizations

brick-and-mortar (old economy) organizations
Old-economy organizations (corporations) that perform their primary business offline, selling physical products by means of physical agents.

Purely physical organizations (companies) are referred to as **brick-and-mortar (old economy) organizations**, whereas companies that are engaged only in EC (pure or partial) are

EXHIBIT 1.1   The Dimensions of Electronic Commerce

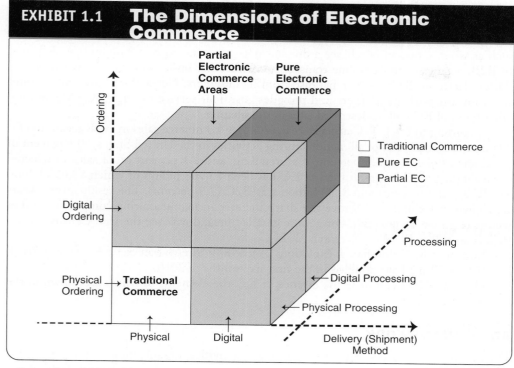

Source: Drawn by E. Turban.

considered **virtual (pure-play) organizations**. **Click-and-mortar (click-and-brick) organizations** are those that conduct some EC activities, usually as an additional marketing channel. Gradually, many brick-and-mortar companies (e.g., Sears, Walmart, Target) are changing to click-and-mortar ones (see the closing case about IKEA in Chapter 3).

ELECTRONIC MARKETS AND NETWORKS

EC can be conducted in an **electronic market (e-marketplace)** where buyers and sellers meet online to exchange goods, services, money, or information. Electronic markets are connected to sellers and buyers via the Internet or to its counterpart within organizations, an *intranet*. An **intranet** is a corporate or government network that uses Internet tools, such as Web browsers, and Internet protocols. Another computer environment is an **extranet**, a network that uses the Internet to link intranets of several organizations in a secure manner.

Section 1.1 ▶ REVIEW QUESTIONS

1. Define EC and e-business.
2. Distinguish between pure and partial EC.
3. Define click-and-mortar and brick and mortar organizations.
4. Define electronic markets.
5. Define intranets and extranets.

1.2   THE ELECTRONIC COMMERCE FIELD: CLASSIFICATION, CONTENT, AND A BRIEF HISTORY

The EC field is diversified so some classification can help. A good example of how a company effectively uses EC is Dell (Online File W1.1).

The Dell case demonstrates several ways that businesses can use EC to improve their bottom line. Dell is not the only company that is doing business online. Thousands of other

---

virtual (pure-play) organizations
Organizations that conduct their business activities solely online.

click-and-mortar (click-and-brick) organizations
Organizations that conduct some e-commerce activities, usually as an additional marketing channel.

electronic market (e-marketplace)
An online marketplace where buyers and sellers meet to exchange goods, services, money, or information.

intranet
An internal corporate or government network that uses Internet tools, such as Web browsers, and Internet protocols.

extranet
A network that uses the Internet to link multiple intranets.

companies, from retailers to hospitals, are moving in this direction. In general, selling and buying electronically can be either business-to-consumer (B2C) or business-to-business (B2B). In B2C, online transactions are made between businesses and individual consumers, such as when a person purchases a dress at net-a-porter.com or a computer at dell.com. In B2B, businesses make online transactions with other businesses, such as when Net-a-Porter electronically buys merchandise from its designers. Net-a-Porter also collaborates electronically with its partners and provides customer service online (e-CRM). Several other types of EC will be described later in this chapter.

According to the U.S. Census Bureau (2010), e-commerce sales in 2008 accounted for 39 percent of total sales of all manufacturing activities in the United States, 20.6 percent of merchant wholesalers, 3.6 percent of all retailing, and 2.1 percent of all sales in selected service industries. The grand total of EC has been $3,708 billion of which $3,416 billion was B2B (92.2 percent) and $288 billion was B2C (7.9 percent). The results over 5 years are shown in Exhibit 1.2. Notice the sharp increase in manufacturing compared to other sectors (e.g., see Tode 2009). For a more detailed breakdown, see the U.S. Census Bureau Report as well as Plunkett Research (2011).

Note that in China EC is exploding. According to eMarket Services News (2010), EC sales in China have doubled in the first six months of 2010.

These activities comprise the essence of EC, the elements of which are shown in the following framework.

AN EC FRAMEWORK

The EC field is a diverse one, involving many activities, organizational units, and technologies. Therefore, a framework that describes its contents can be useful. Exhibit 1.3 introduces one such framework.

As shown in the exhibit, there are many EC applications (top of exhibit), some of which are illustrated in Online File W1.1 about Dell; others will be shown throughout the book (see also en.wikipedia.org/wiki/E-commerce). To execute these applications, companies need

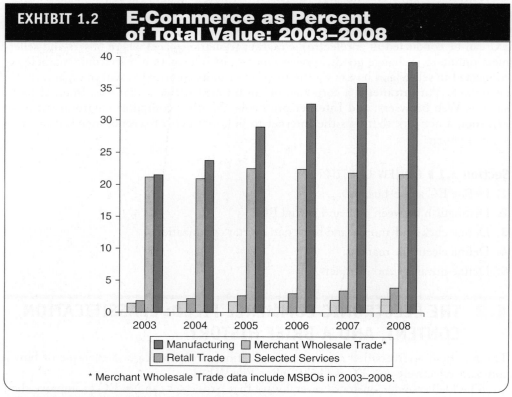

EXHIBIT 1.2 E-Commerce as Percent of Total Value: 2003–2008

Legend:
- Manufacturing
- Retail Trade
- Merchant Wholesale Trade*
- Selected Services

* Merchant Wholesale Trade data include MSBOs in 2003–2008.

Source: census.gov/estats (accessed December 2010).

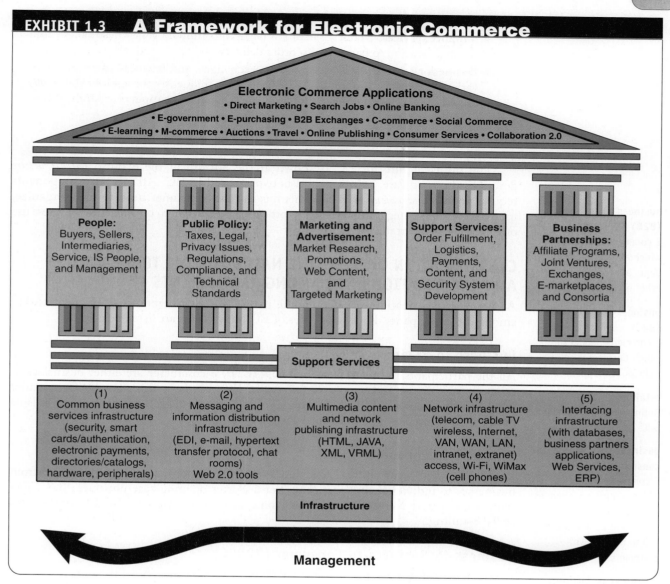

EXHIBIT 1.3   A Framework for Electronic Commerce

Electronic Commerce Applications
• Direct Marketing • Search Jobs • Online Banking
• E-government • E-purchasing • B2B Exchanges • C-commerce • Social Commerce
• E-learning • M-commerce • Auctions • Travel • Online Publishing • Consumer Services • Collaboration 2.0

People:
Buyers, Sellers,
Intermediaries,
Service, IS People,
and Management

Public Policy:
Taxes, Legal,
Privacy Issues,
Regulations,
Compliance, and
Technical
Standards

**Marketing and
Advertisement:**
Market Research,
Promotions,
Web Content,
and
Targeted Marketing

Support Services:
Order Fulfillment,
Logistics,
Payments,
Content, and
Security System
Development

**Business
Partnerships:**
Affiliate Programs,
Joint Ventures,
Exchanges,
E-marketplaces,
and Consortia

Support Services

(1)	(2)	(3)	(4)	(5)
Common business services infrastructure (security, smart cards/authentication, electronic payments, directories/catalogs, hardware, peripherals)	Messaging and information distribution infrastructure (EDI, e-mail, hypertext transfer protocol, chat rooms) Web 2.0 tools	Multimedia content and network publishing infrastructure (HTML, JAVA, XML, VRML)	Network infrastructure (telecom, cable TV wireless, Internet, VAN, WAN, LAN, intranet, extranet) access, Wi-Fi, WiMax (cell phones)	Interfacing infrastructure (with databases, business partners applications, Web Services, ERP)

Infrastructure

Management

the right information, infrastructure, and support services. Exhibit 1.3 shows that EC applications are supported by infrastructure and by the following five support areas (shown as pillars in the exhibit):

▶ **People.** Sellers, buyers, intermediaries, information systems and technology specialists, other employees, and any other participants comprise an important support area.

▶ **Public policy.** Legal and other policy and regulatory issues, such as privacy protection and taxation, which are determined by governments. Included as part of public policy is the issue of technical standards, which are established by government and/or industry-mandated policy-making groups. Compliance with regulations is an important issue.

▶ **Marketing and advertising.** Like any other business, EC usually requires the support of marketing and advertising. This is especially important in B2C online transactions, in which the buyers and sellers usually do not know each other.

> ▶ **Support services.** Many services are needed to support EC. These range from content creation to payments to order delivery.
> ▶ **Business partnerships.** Joint ventures, exchanges, and business partnerships of various types are common in EC. These occur frequently throughout the *supply chain* (i.e., the interactions between a company and its suppliers, customers, and other partners).

The infrastructure for EC is shown at the bottom of the exhibit. *Infrastructure* describes the hardware, software, and networks used in EC. All of these components require good *management practices*. This means that companies need to plan, organize, motivate, devise strategy, and restructure processes, as needed, to optimize the business use of EC models and strategies.

CLASSIFICATION OF EC BY THE NATURE OF THE TRANSACTIONS AND THE RELATIONSHIPS AMONG PARTICIPANTS

A common classification of EC is by the nature of the transactions or the relationship among the participants. The major types of EC transactions are listed below:

Business-to-Business (B2B)

business-to-business (B2B)
E-commerce model in which all of the participants are businesses or other organizations.

All the participants in **business-to-business (B2B)** e-commerce are either businesses or other organizations. Today, over 90 percent of EC volume is B2B. For Dell, the entire wholesale transaction is B2B. Dell buys all of its parts through e-commerce, and sells its products to businesses (and individuals) using e-commerce.

Business-to-Consumer (B2C)

business-to-consumer (B2C)
E-commerce model in which businesses sell to individual shoppers.

Business-to-consumer (B2C) EC includes retail transactions of products or services from businesses to individual shoppers. The Net-a-Porter opening case illustrates B2C. The typical shopper at Net-a-Porter or Amazon.com is an individual. This EC type is also called **e-tailing**.

e-tailing
Online retailing, usually B2C.

Business-to-Business-to-Consumer (B2B2C)

business-to-business-to-consumer (B2B2C)
E-commerce model in which a business provides some product or service to a client business that maintains its own customers.

In **business-to-business-to-consumer (B2B2C)** EC, a business provides some product or service to a client business. The client business maintains its own customers, who may be its own employees, to whom the product or service is provided. An example is godiva.com. The company sells chocolates directly to business customers. Those businesses may then give the chocolates as gifts to employees or to other businesses. Godiva may mail the chocolate directly to the recipients (with compliments of . . .). Another interesting example of B2B2C can be found at wishlist.com.au.

Consumer-to-Business (C2B)

consumer-to-business (C2B)
E-commerce model in which individuals use the Internet to sell products or services to organizations or individuals who seek sellers to bid on products or services they need.

The **consumer-to-business (C2B)** category includes individuals who use the Internet to sell products or services to organizations and individuals who seek vendors to bid on products or services for them. Priceline.com is a well-known organizer of C2B travel service transactions.

Intrabusiness EC

intrabusiness EC
E-commerce category that includes all internal organizational activities that involve the exchange of goods, services, or information among various units and individuals in an organization.

The **intrabusiness EC** category includes all internal EC organizational activities that involve the exchange of goods, services, or information among various units and individuals in that organization. Activities can range from selling corporate products to one's employees, to online training, and to collaborative design efforts.

Business-to-Employees (B2E)

The **business-to-employees (B2E)** category is a subset of the intrabusiness category in which an organization delivers services, information, or products to individual employees. A major category of employees is *mobile employees*, such as field representatives or repair services that go to customers. EC support to such employees is also called *business-to-mobile employees (B2ME)*.

Consumer-to-Consumer (C2C)

In the **consumer-to-consumer (C2C)** category consumers transact directly with other consumers. Examples of C2C include individuals selling residential property, cars, and so on in online classified ads. EBay's auctions are mostly C2C. The advertising of personal services over the Internet and the online selling of knowledge and expertise are other examples of C2C.

Collaborative Commerce

When individuals or groups communicate or collaborate online, they may be engaged in **collaborative commerce (c-commerce)**. For example, business partners in different locations may design a product together using collaborative software and online procedures (see Chapter 5).

E-Government

In **e-government** EC, a government entity buys or provides goods, services, or information from or to businesses (G2B) or from or to individual citizens (G2C). Governments can deal also with other governments (G2G).

The previous categories are illustrated in Exhibit 1.4.

Many examples of the various types of EC transactions will be presented throughout this book.

business-to-employees (B2E)
E-commerce model in which an organization delivers services, information, or products to its individual employees.

consumer-to-consumer (C2C)
E-commerce model in which consumers sell directly to other consumers.

collaborative commerce (c-commerce)
E-commerce model in which individuals or groups communicate or collaborate online.

e-government
E-commerce model in which a government entity buys or provides goods, services, or information from or to businesses or individual citizens.

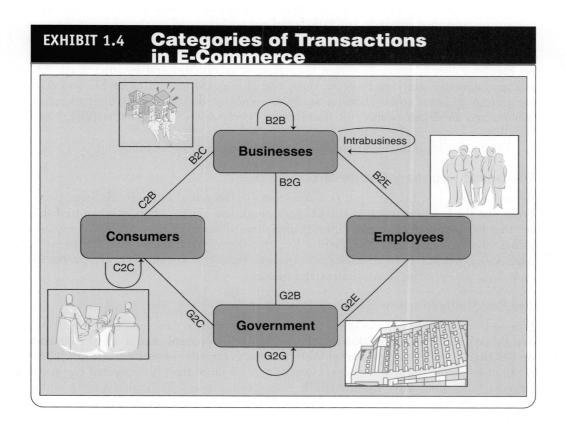

EXHIBIT 1.4   Categories of Transactions in E-Commerce

A BRIEF HISTORY OF EC

EC applications were first developed in the early 1970s with innovations such as *electronic funds transfer (EFT)* (see en.wikipedia.org/wiki/Guide_to_E-payments), whereby funds could be routed electronically from one organization to another. However, the use of these applications was limited to large corporations, financial institutions, and a few other daring businesses. Then came *electronic data interchange (EDI),* a technology used to electronically transfer routine documents, which later expanded from financial transactions to other types of transactions (see Online Tutorial T11 for more on EDI). EDI enlarged the pool of participating companies from financial institutions to manufacturers, retailers, services, and many other types of businesses. Such systems were called *interorganizational systems (IOS)* applications, and their strategic value to businesses has been widely recognized. More new EC applications followed, ranging from travel reservation systems to online stock trading.

The Internet began life as an experiment by the U.S. government in 1969, and its initial users were a largely technical audience of government agencies, academic researchers, and scientists. Some users started to place personal classifieds on the Internet. A major milestone in the development of EC was the introduction of the World Wide Web in the early 1990s. This allowed companies to have a presence on the Internet with both text and photos. When the Internet became commercialized and users began flocking to participate in the World Wide Web in the early 1990s, the term *electronic commerce* was coined. EC applications rapidly expanded. A large number of so-called dot-coms, or *Internet start-ups,* also appeared. One reason for this rapid expansion was the development of new networks, protocols, and EC software. The other reason was the increase in competition and other business pressures (see discussion in Section 1.5).

Since 1995, Internet users have witnessed the development of many innovative applications. Almost every medium- and large-sized organization in the world now has a website, and most large U.S. corporations have comprehensive portals through which employees, business partners, and the public can access corporate information. Many of these sites contain tens of thousands of pages and links. In 1999, the emphasis of EC shifted from B2C to B2B, and in 2001 from B2B to B2E, c-commerce, e-government, e-learning, and m-commerce. In 2005, social networks started to receive quite a bit of attention, as did m-commerce and wireless applications. As of 2009 EC added social commerce channels, in what is known as **f**-commerce—the commercial activities on Facebook (see Chapter 7). Given the nature of technology and Internet usage, EC will undoubtedly continue to grow, shift, and change. More and more EC successes are emerging. For a comprehensive ready-reference guide to EC including statistics, trends, and in-depth profiles of hundreds of companies, see Plunkett (2011) and en.wikipedia.org/wiki/E-commerce.

While looking at the history of EC, one must keep in mind the following.

The Interdisciplinary Nature of EC

Because EC is a new field, it is just now developing its theoretical and scientific foundations. From just the brief overview of the EC framework and classification, you can probably see that EC is related to several different disciplines. The major academic EC disciplines include the following: *accounting, business law, computer science, consumer behavior, economics, engineering, finance, human resource management, management, management information systems, marketing, public administration,* and *robotics.*

The Google Revolution

During its early years, EC was impacted by companies such as Amazon.com, eBay, AOL, and Yahoo!. However, since 2001 no other company has probably had more of an impact on EC than Google. Google related Web searches to targeted advertisements much better than its competitors did. Today, Google is much more than just a search engine; it employs many innovative EC models, it is involved in many EC joint ventures, and it impacts both organizational activities and individual lives. For more details, see Vise and Malseed (2008).

F-Commerce

Given the popularity of Facebook and the rapidly increasing commercial activities on the site, some believe that Facebook is revolutionizing e-commerce. Thus, they coin the term **f-commerce**, pointing to the increased role of Facebook in the e-commerce field as of 2009.

f-commerce
E-commerce activities conducted on Facebook or influenced by the site.

EC Failures

Starting in 1999, a large number of EC companies, especially e-tailing and B2B exchanges, began to fail (see disobey.com/ghostsites). Well-known B2C failures include eToys, Xpeditor, MarchFirst, Drkoop, Webvan, and Boo. Well-known B2B failures include Chemdex, Ventro, and Verticalnet. (Incidentally, the history of these pioneering companies is documented in David Kirch's "The Business Plan Archive" [businessplanarchive.org].) A survey by Strategic Direction (2005) found that 62 percent of dot-coms lacked financial skills, and 50 percent had little experience with marketing. Similarly, many companies failed to ensure they had the inventory and distribution setup to meet the fluctuating and increasing demand for their products. The reasons for these and other EC failures are discussed in Chapters 3, 4, and 11. In 2008, many start-ups related to Web 2.0 and social commerce started to collapse (per blogs.cioinsight.com/knowitall/content001/startup_deathwatch_20.html).

Does the large number of failures mean that EC's days are numbered? Absolutely not! First, the dot-com failure rate is declining sharply. Second, the EC field is basically experiencing consolidation as companies test different business models and organizational structures. Third, some pure EC companies, including giants such as Amazon.com, are expanding operations and generating increased sales. Finally, the click-and-mortar model seems to work very well especially in e-tailing (e.g., Sears, Walmart, Target, and Best Buy).

EC Successes

The last few years have seen the rise of extremely successful virtual EC companies such as eBay, Google, Facebook, Yahoo!, Amazon.com, VeriSign, AOL, and E*TRADE. Click-and-mortar companies such as Cisco, Target online, General Electric, IBM, Intel, and Schwab also have seen great success. Additional success stories include start-ups such as Alloy.com (a young-adults-oriented portal), Blue Nile (Chapter 2), Ticketmaster, Zappos (Application Case 1.1), Expedia, Net-a-Porter, and Campusfood (see Online File W1.2).

THE FUTURE OF EC

Today's predictions about the future size of EC, provided by respected analysts such as comScore, eMarketer.com, and Forrester, vary. For a list of sites that provide statistics on EC, see Chapter 3, Exhibit 3.1. For example, in 2008, 80 percent of Generation X (Internet users ages 33 to 44) shopped online. Of Generation Y (users ages 18 to 32) 71 percent shopped online. Interest in online shopping is considerably lower among the youngest and oldest groups; 38 percent of online teens buy products online, as do 56 percent of Internet users ages 64 to 72, and 47 percent ages 73 and older (reported by Jones and Fox 2009).

The number of Internet users worldwide was estimated to be around 2 billion in 2010, up from 1.5 billion in 2008 (Schonfeld 2009). According to IDC's Digital Marketplace Model and Forecast, 50 percent of all Internet users will shop online by 2009 (*IDC* 2008). EC growth will come not only from B2C, but also from B2B and from newer applications such as e-government, e-learning, B2E, and c-commerce. Overall, the growth of the field will continue to be strong into the foreseeable future. Despite the failures of individual companies and initiatives, the total volume of EC has been growing every year. With more people on the Internet more EC will come.

The rising price of petroleum, along with repercussions of the 2008–2010 financial meltdown, should motivate people to shop online and look for bargains where price comparison is easy and fast (e.g., try buy.com). Another important factor is the increase in mobile devices and especially smartphones. According to Weintraub (2010) the number of smartphones almost doubled from 2008–2009, and the number of mobile devices is overtaking PCs. This makes EC activities easier (from any place, any time).

Finally, EC is now entering its second phase of life as illustrated next.

CASE 1.1
EC Application

ZAPPOS: A SUCCESS STORY OF SELLING FOOTWEAR ONLINE

Zappos.com Inc. ("*Zappos.com;*" zappos.com) is an online retailer with one of the largest selection of shoes any-where—online or offline. It is owned by Amazon.com.

The Opportunity

Nick Swinmurn founded the company in 1999 after spending a day at a San Francisco mall looking for a pair of shoes and returning home empty-handed. If one store had the right style, it did not have the right color; the next store had the right color, but it did not have the correct size. Nick tried to locate the shoes he wanted online, but after a frustrating day of browsing, he discovered that he was unable to find online what he wanted.

Swinmurn discovered that there was no major online retailer that specialized in shoes. So, he decided to create a website that offered the very best selection in shoes in terms of brands, styles, colors, sizes, and widths.

The Solution

The company's strategy was to offer such a huge selection that the customers would say WOW! And by 2010 this selec-tion exceeded 3.4 million items (from over 1,300 vendors)—unmatchable by any online or offline store.

The company's initial business model was to sell only online, and only shoes. This model has evolved to also sell several related products, ranging from jewelry to clothes, (and even electronics and video games) and to also sell via a few physical outlets.

Believing that the speed at which a customer receives an online purchase plays a very important role in customer retention, Zappos constructed huge warehouses containing everything it advertises. The company offers free shipping with domestic orders and often delivers the next day.

In order to ensure fast order fulfillment, the company worked with Arup, a global firm of designers, engineers, planners, and business consultants providing a diverse range of professional services to its suppliers; designers; and other business partners around the globe. For example, the logis-tics designers worked with the Zappos warehouse automation team to design a world-class "direct-to-customer" fulfillment system. The high-speed material handling system (from FKI Logistex) is fully automated and housed in a Shepherdsville, Kentucky, 800,000 square foot warehouse. The system allows rapid delivery to customers no matter where they are located. The Zappos shopping experience also features extensive website search options and clear views of every product (see photo below). Unlike most other online retailers, Zappos does not offer an item for sale unless it is physically avail-able in its warehouse. Once the last size or color of a shoe is shipped out, it is no longer offered on the website. The moment a new style, size, or color is available in the ware-house, it instantly pops up on the website. This "live inventory" is made possible by a full-service photo lab in the fulfillment center, where digital photographs of each item are taken from a variety of angles and immediately uploaded to Zappos.com. The photo lab even includes a studio to shoot live human models for certain shoes, apparel, and accessories.

The company's culture is also a key to the success of the business. Without dedicated and excited employees, the company becomes an adequate company, not the best.

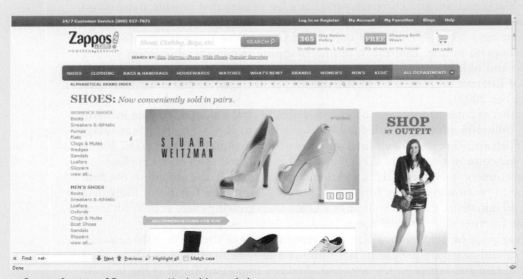

Source: Courtesy of Zappos.com. Used with permission.

(*continued*)

CASE 1.1 *(continued)*

The culture has matured over the life of the company to include 10 core values from which the company developed the culture, brand, and business strategies. These values can be found online at the company's website.

Zappos also realized that, along with the best selection, customer service is also a key success factor (see Hsieh 2010b). Therefore, Zappos operates under the theory that providing an excellent shopping experience (instead of maximizing profits) will be followed by sales growth.

The company's "WOW" philosophy of customer experiences and the huge selection are supplemented by 365-day free returns and 24/7 customer service. The company uses EC Web 2.0 mechanisms such as blogs, Tweets, discussion forums, e-newsletters, user-contributed videos by customers (watch at *Zappos.com/video-experience*), and more to create a community of loyal buyers and foster its relationship with its customers. The company now has a presence on Facebook and Twitter (e.g., see *twitter.zappos.com*).

The employees are members of an enterprise social network, (an in-house social network) and it is used to keep employees happy and, therefore, more productive. Employees are well trained to work as individuals, as well as in teams. The company provides EC mechanisms to foster individual and team work.

Doing business online requires a security system to protect customers' and vendors' data. Zappos provides encryption and other security measures to protect customer data.

The Results
Gross merchandise sales started at "almost nothing" in 1999 and doubled every year to reach more than $1 billion in 2008. The total number of employees grew from 3 in 1999 to over 1,500 in 2009.

By focusing on service and product selection that WOWs the customers, employees, and vendors, Zappos is on its way to fulfilling its vision that one day 30 percent of all retail transactions in the United States of shoes and related items will be sold online; and people will buy from the company with the best service and the best selection—Zappos will be that company. Zappos is facing strong competition (see list at *wikipedia.org*), but so far its competitive advantage has worked very well.

In July 2009, Amazon.com "acquired" Zappos. However, the Zappos brand continues to be separate from the Amazon.com brand. Zappos has access to many of Amazon.com's resources, but continues to build the brand and culture just as it has in the past. The Zappos mission remains the same: delivering happiness to all stakeholders, including employees, customers, and vendors. Zappos plans to continue to maintain its relationships with its vendors, and Amazon.com will continue to maintain its relationships it has with its own vendors.

Sources: Compiled from *zappos.com* (accessed April 2011), Hsieh 2010a and 2010b, *Logistics Online* (2008), Taylor (2008), *Wall Street Journal* (2009), and *en.wikipedia.org/wiki/Zappos.com* (accessed April 2011).

Questions

1. List the major critical success factors of the company.
2. Why was Amazon.com interested in the company?
3. What is "WOW" about?
4. Why did the company change its business model?
5. How is order fulfillment being done?
6. Access *wikihow.com/customize-your-shoes*. Discuss how such customization may affect Zappos's business.

Section 1.2 ▶ REVIEW QUESTIONS
1. List the major components of the EC framework.
2. List the major transactional types of EC.
3. Describe the major landmarks in EC history.
4. List some EC successes and failures.
5. Summarize the future of EC.

1.3 E-COMMERCE 2.0: FROM SOCIAL COMMERCE TO VIRTUAL WORLDS

The first generation of EC involved mainly trading, e-services, and corporate-sponsored collaboration. We are moving now into the second generation of EC, which we call e-commerce 2.0. It is based on Web 2.0 tools, social networks, and virtual worlds, the result of social computing.

SOCIAL COMPUTING

social computing
An approach aimed at making the human–computer interface more natural.

Social computing is computing that is concerned with the intersection of social behavior and information systems. It is performed with a set of tools that includes blogs, mashups, instant messaging, social network services, discussion forums, wikis, social bookmarking, and other *social software*, and marketplaces (see Chapter 2). Whereas traditional computing systems concentrate on supporting organizational activities and business processes and zero in on cost reduction and increases in productivity, social computing concentrates on improving collaboration and interaction among people and on user-generated content. It is a shift from traditional top-down management communication to a bottom-up strategy where individuals in communities become a major organizational power. In social computing and commerce, people can collaborate online, get advice from one another and from trusted experts, and find goods and services that their friends, whom they trust, recommend.

Example. Advances in social computing are affecting travel decisions and arrangements. Travelers share information and warn others of bad experiences at sites such as tripadvisor.com.

The premise of social computing is to make socially produced information available to all. This information may be provided directly, as when systems show the number of users who have rated a book or a movie (e.g., at amazon.com and netflix.com). Or, the information may be provided indirectly, as is the case with Google's page rank algorithms, which sequence search results based on the number of page hits. In all of these cases, information is produced by individuals and it is available to all, usually for free. Social computing is largely facilitated by Web 2.0 tools.

WEB 2.0

Web 2.0
The second generation of Internet-based services that lets people collaborate and share information online in new ways, such as social networking sites, wikis, communication tools, and folksonomies.

The term **Web 2.0** was coined by O'Reilly Media in 2004 to refer to a supposed second generation of Internet-based tools and services that let people generate and control content and collaborate and share information online in perceived new ways, such as social networking sites, wikis, communication tools, and folksonomies. O'Reilly Media, in collaboration with MediaLive International, used the phrase as a title for a series of conferences. Since then, it has become a popular, ill-defined, and often criticized buzzword in the technical and marketing communities.

O'Reilly (2005) divided Web 2.0 into the following four levels:

> ▶ Level 3 applications, the most "Web 2.0" oriented, exist only on the Internet, deriving their effectiveness from interhuman connections and from the network effects that Web 2.0 makes possible and growing in effectiveness as people make more use of them. O'Reilly offered eBay, Craigslist, Wikipedia, del.icio.us, Skype, Dodgeball, and AdSense as examples of level 3 applications.
>
> ▶ Level 2 applications can operate offline but gain advantages from going online. O'Reilly cited Flickr as an example, which benefits from its shared photo database and from its community-generated tag database.
>
> ▶ Level 1 applications operate offline but gain features online. O'Reilly pointed to Writely (now Google Docs & Spreadsheets) and iTunes (because of its music store portion) as examples.
>
> ▶ Level 0 applications work as well offline as online. O'Reilly offered the examples of MapQuest, Yahoo! Local, and Google Maps.

Karakas (2009) views Web 2.0 as a new digital ecosystem, which can be described through five C's: creativity, connectivity, collaboration, convergence, and community.

For more information on Web 2.0, see en.wikipedia.org/wiki/WEB_2.0. The major characteristics of Web 2.0 are presented in Online File W1.3. The major tools of Web 2.0 are described in Chapter 2, and the applications are described in most chapters. Also, browse Don Hinchcliffe's socialcomputingjournal.com for an open forum about the

Internet, society, collective intelligence, and the future. For Web 2.0 definitions, explanations, and applications see en.wikipedia.org/wiki/Web_2.0 and Chapter 7.

SOCIAL NETWORKS AND SOCIAL NETWORK SERVICES

The most interesting e-commerce application in recent years has been the emergence of social and enterprise social networks. Originating from online communities (Chapter 2), these networks are growing rapidly and providing for many new EC initiatives, revenue models, and business models. (See innovative.com for "new business models.")

A **social network** is a social structure composed of nodes (which are generally individuals, groups, or organizations) that are tied by one or more specific types of interdependencies, such as values, visions, ideas, financial exchange, friendship, kinship, dislike, conflict, or trade. The structures are often very complex.

In its simplest form, a social network can be described as a map of all relevant ties (connection) between the nodes. The network can also be used to determine the social capital of individual participants. These concepts are often displayed in a social network diagram, where nodes are the points and ties are the lines.

Participants in a *social network* congregate on a website where they can create their own homepage for free and on which they can write blogs and wikis; post pictures, videos, or music; share ideas; and link to other Web locations they find interesting. Social networkers chat using instant messaging and Twitter and tag the content they post with their own key words, which makes the content searchable and facilitates the conduct of people-to-people interactions and transactions.

social network
A category of Internet applications that help connect friends, business partners, or individuals with specific interests by providing free services such as photo presentation, e-mail, blogging, and so on using a variety of tools.

Social Networking Services

Social networking services (SNSs), such as LinkedIn and Facebook, provide a Web space for people to build their homepages, which the services organizations host for free, and they also provide basic communication and other support tools for conducting different activities. Social networks are people oriented. For example, a 15-year-old Filipino singer named Pempengco thought her music career was doomed after she lost a local singing competition in 2006, but YouTube gave her a "cyber" of a lifetime when a video clip of her singing Jennifer Holliday's "And I'm Telling You I Am Not Going" caught the attention of TV host Ellen DeGeneres and Grammy Award–winning producer David Foster. Initially, social networks were used for only social activities. Today, corporations are starting to have an interest in the business aspects of social networks (e.g., see linkedin.com, a network that connects businesses by industry, functions, geography, and areas of interest). For more on social networking, see De Jonge (2008) and en.wikipedia.org/wiki/Social_networking.

social networking service (SNS)
A service that builds online communities by providing an online space for people to build free homepages and that provides basic communication and support tools for conducting different activities in the social network.

Social Networking

We define **social networking** as the execution of any Web 2.0 activity, such as blogging and/or having a presence in a social network.

The following are examples of representative social network services:

▶ Facebook.com: The most visited social network website.
▶ YouTube.com and metacafe.com: Users can upload and view video clips.
▶ Flickr.com: Users share and comment on photos.
▶ Friendster.com: Provides a platform to find friends and make contacts.
▶ Hi5.com: A popular global social network.
▶ Cyworld.nate.com: Asia's largest social networking website.
▶ Habbo.com: Entertaining country-specific sites for kids and adults.
▶ MySpace.com: Facilitates socialization for people of all ages.

social networking
The creation or sponsoring of a social network service and any activity, such as blogging, done in a social network (external or internal).

ENTERPRISE SOCIAL NETWORKS

Business-oriented social networks can be public, such as LinkedIn.com. As such, they are owned and managed by an independent company. Another type of business-oriented social network is private, owned by corporations and operated inside them. These are known as *enterprise social networks.*

Example of an Enterprise Social Network

Carnival Cruise Lines sponsors a social networking site (carnivalconnections.com) to attract cruise fans. Visitors use the site to exchange opinions, organize groups for trips, and much more. It cost the company $300,000 to set up the site, but Carnival anticipates that the cost will be covered by increased business.

SOCIAL COMMERCE

social commerce
The e-commerce activities conducted in social networks and/or by using social software (i.e., Web 2.0 tools).

E-commerce activities are conducted in social networks by using social software (i.e., Web 2.0 tools) are referred to as **social commerce**. As of 2009, and rapidly increasing in 2010 and 2011, social commerce began to explode. We will return to social commerce in Chapter 7.

Here are some examples of social commerce.

> ▶ Dell computer claims to have made $6.5 million by selling computers on Twitter in two years (Nutley 2010). Also Dell generates ideas from community members (Idea Storm site).
>
> ▶ Procter & Gamble sells its Max Factor brand cosmetics through Facebook.
>
> ▶ Disney allows people to book tickets on Facebook without leaving the social network.
>
> ▶ PepsiCo gives a live notification when its customers are close to physical stores (grocery, restaurants, gas stations) that sell Pepsi products. Then PepsiCo sends them coupons and discount information using Foursquare (see Chapter 7).
>
> ▶ Starbucks is using extensive promotions on Facebook including generating ideas from the members via Starbucks Idea website (see Chapter 7 for details).
>
> ▶ Mountain Dew attracts video game lovers and sport enthusiasts via Dewmocracy contests. The company also uses the most dedicated community members to contribute ideas. The company used Facebook, Twitter, and YouTube to unite consumers through a common interest.
>
> ▶ Levi's advertises on Facebook by enabling consumers to autopopulate a "shopping cart" based on what their friends think they would like. There is also a video on YouTube to educate consumers on how to use Facebook to shop for and with their friends. (See web-strategist.com/blog/2010/04/30/social-commerce-breakdown-how-levis-and-facebook-prompt-your-friends-to-get-you-to-buy for details.)
>
> ▶ Wendy's uses Facebook and Twitter to award $50 gift cards to those who have the funniest and quirkiest responses to various challenges.

Overall, close to 1 million companies have had a presence on Facebook by summer 2010. For more applications see Chapter 7.

VIRTUAL WORLDS AND SECOND LIFE

virtual world
A user-defined world in which people can interact, play, and do business. The most publicized virtual world is Second Life.

A special class of social networking is the *virtual world.* A **virtual world**, also known as a *metaverse,* is a 3-D computer-based simulated environment built and owned by its residents. In addition to creating buildings, people can create and share cars, clothes, and many other items. Community members inhabit virtual spaces and interact via *avatars.* These avatars are usually depicted as textual, 2-D, or 3-D graphical presentations, although other forms are possible. The essentials of virtual worlds and the prime example, Second Life (secondlife.com), are presented in Chapter 2.

Until 2007, virtual worlds were most often limited to 3-D games, including massively multiplayer online games. More recently, they have become a new way for people to socialize, and even do business. For example, there.com focuses more on social networking activities, such as chatting, creating avatars, interacting, playing, and meeting people.

How Students Make Money in a Virtual World

If you cannot get a summer (or other) job, try a job in a virtual world. With summer jobs in short supply, more young people are pursuing money-making opportunities in virtual worlds. According to Alter (2008), a new breed of young entrepreneurs is honing their computer skills to capitalize on the growing demand for virtual goods and services.

Alter provides examples of six young and successful entrepreneurs:

▶ Mike Mikula, age 17, uses graphic design tools to build virtual buildings. His avatar in Teen Second Life, Mike Denneny, helps him to earn $4,000 a month as a builder and renovator of sites on Second Life.

▶ Ariella Furman, age 21, earns $2,000 to $4,000 a month using her avatar Ariella Languish in Second Life. She is a machinima, a filmmaker who works exclusively in Second Life. She directs avatars using a virtual producer and works in the virtual world for companies like IBM and Nestlé.

▶ John Eikenberry, age 25, earns $2,000 to $4,000 a month building Second Life neighborhoods, creating malls, coffee shops, and an auditorium over 16 landscaped acres called regions. His avatar is Lordfly Digeridoo in Second Life.

▶ Kristina Koch, age 17, is a character designer. Her avatar in Teen Second Life, Silver Bu, earns $600 to $800 a month using Second Life tools to add effects, such as shadows, to avatars. She and her boyfriend also design and sell virtual fairy wings and wizard's robes to dress avatars.

▶ Mike Everest, age 18, is a virtual hunter and trader, selling the skins of what he hunts. He also learned how to transform virtual ore into virtual weapons, which he sells. His avatar in the virtual world of Entropia Universe, Ogulak Da Basher, earns $200 to $1,000 a month. He is the family's primary money maker, and he was able to finance his brother's college education.

▶ Twins Andy and Michael Ortman, age 19, are inventors. Their avatars in Teen Second Life, Alpha Zaius and Ming Chen, earn about $2,500 a month each. The engineering majors work for Deep Think Labs, a virtual world development company based in Australia. They program Open Simulator, which allows companies and individuals to hold private meetings and training sessions in virtual environments similar to Second Life.

THE MAJOR TOOLS OF WEB 2.0

Web 2.0 uses dozens of tools such as wikis, RSS feeds, blogs, and microblogs (e.g., Twitter). You can transmit to a list of recipients short messages (up to 140 characters) via the Internet and wireless or wireline devices. As of 2009, Twitter became a major tool of Web 2.0 with diversified business applications. These are described in Chapter 2.

Section 1.3 ▶ REVIEW QUESTIONS

1. Define social computing and list its characteristics.
2. Define Web 2.0 and list its attributes.
3. Define social networks.
4. Describe the capabilities of social network services (SNSs).
5. Describe Facebook. Why is it so popular?
6. What is an enterprise social network?
7. Define social commerce.
8. Describe e-commerce activities on Facebook. Why is it referred to as **f**-commerce?
9. Define virtual worlds and list their characteristics.
10. Describe some ways for students with computer skills to make money from virtual worlds.

1.4 THE DIGITAL WORLD: ECONOMY, ENTERPRISES, AND SOCIETY

The digital revolution is upon us. We see it every day at home and work, in businesses, in schools, in hospitals, on the roads, in entertainment, and even in wars. Next, we describe three elements of the digital world: economy, enterprises, and society.

THE DIGITAL ECONOMY

digital economy

An economy that is based on digital technologies, including digital communication networks, computers, software, and other related information technologies; also called the *Internet economy,* the *new economy,* or the *Web economy.*

The **digital economy** refers to an economy that is based on digital technologies, including digital communication networks (e.g., the Internet, intranets, extranets, and VANs), computers, software, and other related information technologies. The digital economy is sometimes called the *Internet economy,* the *new economy,* or the *Web economy.* This platform displays the following characteristics:

- A vast array of digitizable products—databases, news and information, books, magazines, TV and radio programming, movies, electronic games, musical CDs, and software—are delivered over a digital infrastructure anytime, anywhere in the world, interconnected by a global grid (see Bisson et al. 2010). We are moving from analog to digital, even the media is getting digital (TVs as of February 2009).
- Consumers and firms conduct financial transactions digitally through digital currencies that are carried via networked computers and mobile devices.
- Microprocessors and networking capabilities are embedded in physical goods such as home appliances and automobiles.
- Information is transformed into a commodity.
- Knowledge is codified.
- Work and production are organized in new and innovative ways.

The term *digital economy* also refers to the convergence of computing and communications technologies on the Internet and other networks and the resulting flow of information and technology that is stimulating EC and vast organizational changes. This convergence enables all types of information (data, audio, video, etc.) to be stored, processed, and transmitted over networks to many destinations worldwide. Exhibit 1.5 describes the major characteristics of the digital economy.

The digital revolution accelerates EC mainly by providing competitive advantage to organizations. The digital revolution also enables many innovations, and new ones appear almost daily. The digital revolution provides the necessary technologies for EC and creates major changes in the business environment, as described in Section 1.5.

THE DIGITAL ENTERPRISE

digital enterprise

A new business model that uses IT in a fundamental way to accomplish one or more of three basic objectives: reach and engage customers more effectively, boost employee productivity, and improve operating efficiency. It uses converged communication and computing technology in a way that improves business processes.

The term *digital enterprise* has a number of interpretations. It usually refers to an enterprise, such as Net-a-Porter, Amazon.com, Google, Facebook, or Ticketmaster, that uses computers and information systems to automate most of its business processes. The **digital enterprise** is a new business model that uses IT in a fundamental way to accomplish one or more of three basic objectives: (1) reach and engage customers more effectively, (2) boost employee productivity, and (3) improve operating efficiency. It uses converged communication and computing technology in a way that improves business processes. The major characteristics of a digital enterprise are listed in Exhibit 1.6, where they are compared with those of a traditional enterprise.

A digital enterprise uses networks of computers to facilitate the following:

- All internal communication is done via an intranet, which is the counterpart of the Internet inside the company.
- All business partners are reached via the Internet, or via a group of secured intranets, called an extranet, or via value-added private communication lines.

EXHIBIT 1.5   Major Characteristics of the Digital Economy

Area	Description
Globalization	Global communication and collaboration; global electronic marketplaces and competition.
Digital system	From TV to telephones and instrumentation, analog systems are being converted to digital ones.
Speed	A move to real-time transactions, thanks to digitized documents, products, and services. Many business processes are expedited by 90 percent or more.
Information overload and intelligent search	Although the amount of information generated is accelerating, intelligent search tools can help users find what they need.
Markets	Markets are moving online. Physical marketplaces are being replaced by electronic markets; new markets are being created, increasing competition.
Digitization	Music, books, pictures, videos, and more are digitized for fast and inexpensive distribution.
Business models and processes	New and improved business models and processes provide opportunities to new companies and industries. Cyberintermediation and no intermediation are on the rise.
Innovation	Digital and Internet-based innovations continue at a rapid pace. More patents are being granted than ever before.
Obsolescence	The fast pace of innovation creates a high rate of obsolescence.
Opportunities	Opportunities abound in almost all aspects of life and operations.
Fraud	Criminals employ a slew of innovative schemes on the Internet. Cybercons are everywhere.
Wars	Conventional wars are changing to cyberwars.
Organizations	Organizations are moving to digital enterprises.

EXHIBIT 1.6   The Digital Versus Brick-and-Mortar Company

Brick-and-Mortar Organizations	Digital Organizations (Enterprises)
Selling in physical stores	Selling online
Selling tangible goods	Selling digital goods as well
Internal inventory/production planning	Online collaborative inventory forecasting
Paper catalogs	Smart electronic catalogs
Physical marketplace	Electronic marketplace
Use of telephone, fax, VANs, and traditional EDI	Use of computers, smartphones, the Internet, and extranets
Physical auctions, infrequently	Online auctions, everywhere, any time
Broker-based services, transactions	Electronic infomediaries, value-added services
Paper-based billing	Electronic billing
Paper-based tendering	Electronic tendering (reverse auctions)
Push production, starting with demand forecasting	Pull production, starting with an order (build-to-order)
Mass production (standard products)	Mass customization, build-to-order
Physical-based commission marketing	Affiliated, virtual marketing
Word-of-mouth, slow and limited advertisement	Explosive viral marketing, in particular in social networks
Linear supply chains	Hub-based supply chains
Large amount of capital needed for mass production	Less capital needed for build-to-order; payments can be collected before production starts
Large fixed cost required for plant operation	Small fixed cost required for plant operation
Customers' value proposition is frequently a mismatch (cost > value)	Perfect match of customers' value proposition (cost <= value)

corporate portal

A major gateway through which employees, business partners, and the public can enter a corporate website.

The vast majority of EC is done on computers connected to these networks. Many companies employ a **corporate portal**, which is a gateway for customers, employees, and partners to reach corporate information and to communicate with the company.

The major concern of many companies today is how to transform themselves into digital (or at least partially) enterprises so that they can take part in the digital economy. For example, Harrington (2006) describes why and how, as a CEO, he transformed the Thomson Corp. from a traditional $8 billion publishing business into an electronic information services provider and publisher for professionals in targeted markets. In five years, revenue increased over 20 percent and profit increased by more than 65 percent.

Note that the term *enterprise* refers to any kind of organization, small or large. An enterprise can be a manufacturing plant, a hospital, a university, a TV network or even an entire city. They are all moving toward being digitized.

THE DIGITAL SOCIETY

The final, and perhaps most important, element of the *digital world* is people and the way they live. Clearly, the digital society has changed contemporary life with regard to almost any activity we can think of—work, play, shopping, entertainment, travel, medical care, education, and much more. Almost every day new digital applications are developed. Just think about your digital camera, your digital TV, your digital car, and almost anything else. It is only natural that people are utilizing EC at an accelerating rate. Let's take a look at some examples:

> ▶ Kaboodle.com makes it easy to shop online as a community with your friends (see Chapter 7). You can share recommendations and discover new products and services with your community friends. Shopping at Kaboodle can be fun. You can discover many useful things from people with similar tastes and styles and discuss with them certain vendors and products. You can even enrich your life with a wish list.
>
> ▶ Google has developed cars that drive themselves automatically in traffic (autonomous vehicles). It might seem like an unusual project for Google, but it could actually have big benefits. The cars are running on Google's Android operating system. Safety is the project's main purpose. Google believes that the technology could nearly half the number of automobile-related deaths because computers are supposedly better at driving than humans in the right circumstances. There are other hypothetical benefits too. The vehicles' instant reaction time and 360-degree awareness allow them to drive closer together on the highway than humans can, reducing traffic congestion. They could be more careful when operating the gas, reducing fuel consumption. Another benefit would be the hour or so of daily commute time the car owner would save. Instead of driving, he or she could either be productive or entertained in the vehicle, doing work on a wireless Internet connection or watching television. Unfortunately, the most optimistic projection put this technology at least eight years away from market, though. Legal hassles are among the myriad problems; all of the current traffic laws assume that a human driver is present in the vehicle. A related smart car is being developed by GM (see Franklin 2009).
>
> ▶ As of 2008, high school girls are able to solicit feedback from their friends regarding 70 different prom dresses that were displayed by Sears on Facebook. This enabled Sears to extend the shopping experience into the social sphere.
>
> ▶ As of 2009, users can use *social smartphones* (e.g., the Android handset from Motorola) to connect quickly and easily to mobile features in social networks such as Facebook. For example, users can communicate directly in messages with networks members' friends who are on their phone contact lists.
>
> ▶ According to Farivar (2004), VIP patrons of the Baja Beach Club in Barcelona, Spain, can have RFID chips, which are the size of a grain of rice, implanted into

their upper arms, allowing them to charge drinks to a bar tab when they raise their arm toward the RFID reader. The RFID (see Online Tutorial T3) is a tiny tag that contains a processor and antenna; it can communicate wirelessly with a detecting unit in a reader over a short distance. "You don't call someone crazy for getting a tattoo," says Conrad Chase, director of Baja Beach Clubs International. "Why would they be crazy for getting this?"

▶ Dryers and washers in some college dorms are hooked to the Web. Students can punch a code into their cell phones or sign in at esuds.net and check the availability of laundry machines. Furthermore, they can receive e-mail alerts when their wash and dry cycles are complete. Once in the laundry room, a student activates the system by swiping a student ID card or keying in a PIN number. The system automatically injects premeasured amounts of detergent and fabric softener, at the right cycle time.

▶ Using his blog site (oneredpaperclip.blogspot.com), Kyle MacDonald of Canada was able to trade a red paper clip into a three-bedroom house. He started by advertising in the barter section of craigslist.org that he wanted something bigger or better for one red paper clip. In the first iteration, he received a fish-shaped pen, and he posted on Craigslist again and again. Following many iterations and publicity on TV, after one year, he traded for a house (MacDonald 2007).

▶ Camera-equipped cell phones are used in Finland as health and fitness advisors. A supermarket shopper using the technology can snap an image of the bar code on a packet of food. The phone forwards the code number to a central computer, which sends back information on the item's ingredients and nutritional value. The computer also calculates how much exercise the shopper will have to do to burn off the calories based on the shopper's height, weight, age, and other factors.

▶ Doggyspace.com allows dog lovers from around the globe to come together. You can build a page and a profile and post a video or photos to show off your dog, creating a social experience around the pets you care about. The site offers medical and other advice. Like in any other social network, people can create groups of friends (e.g., with the same type of dog) with whom to share their doggy experiences.

▶ A remote medical monitoring system can help with early diagnosis of heart failure. A person stands on a special bathroom scale that can wirelessly transmit data to a clinician's screen. A computer analyzes the weight change and triggers an alarm for a suspected anomaly that predicts possible trouble. A medical technician then calls the person to discuss medication, the need to see a doctor, and so forth. The system keeps patients healthier and cuts health care costs.

▶ Online dating and matching services are becoming more and more popular. Companies such as eHarmony, Match.com, JDate, and Yahoo! Personals are leading hundreds of other companies worldwide that are making matches. For example, Match.com has begun offering free profile and photo tips via an online video with Jay Manuel, of the television show *America's Next Top Model*. The company also sells services for $2 to $6 a month that offer advice on dating and ways to make profiles and photographs stand out. Match.com treats online dating as if the candidates are on stage and being viewed by thousands of prospects. It suggests spending some time backstage getting ready. Several companies can help you to get ready, mostly for free (e.g., dating-profile.com and e-cyrano.com).

▶ A Polish priest has installed an electronic reader in his church for schoolchildren to leave their fingerprints in order to monitor their attendance at mass. The pupils mark their fingerprints every time they go to church over three years and if they attend 200 masses they will be freed from the obligation of having to pass an exam prior to their confirmation. The pupils like the idea and also the priest who invented it. The students say that they do not have to stand in a line to get the priest's signature (confirming presence at the mass).

▶ Bicycle computers (by Bridgestone Cycle Co.) can automatically keep track of your travel distance, speed, time, and calorie consumption. Travel data are stored for 30 days, and you can transmit it to your computer. For cycling communities websites see bikewire.net and cyclingforum.com.

▶ Queen Elizabeth II opened several pages on Facebook telling people what she is doing every day. Her family and staff opened pages too.

▶ During his presidential campaign, Barack Obama purchased Internet ads featured in 18 video games through Microsoft's Xbox Live Service. His objective was to target young adult males, who are difficult to reach through traditional campaign advertising. It is estimated that this and similar activities netted him at least 2 percent of the vote. Some claim that without such tactics Obama would have lost the election.

▶ Champions of the World Series of Poker used to be people in their 50s and 60s who spent years playing the game to gain the experience needed to win. But in 2009, Joe Cada from the United States won the main event at the World Series of Poker, at the age of 21. Cada regularly plays about a dozen tournaments at a time online, or three at a time in heads-up cash games, which have allowed him to gain a vast amount of experience in a short period of time.

A comprehensive example of the use of several EC models in the 2008 Olympics is provided in Online File W1.4. One of the most interesting phenomena of the digital society is the change in the way that politicians interact with the public. This topic will be discussed in Chapter 5.

Section 1.4 ▶ REVIEW QUESTIONS

1. Define the digital revolution and list its components.
2. List the characteristics of the digital economy.
3. Define a digital enterprise.
4. Compare traditional and digital enterprises.
5. Describe the digital society.
6. Visit doggyspace.com and dogtoys.com. Compare the two sites and relate their contents to the digital society.

1.5 THE CHANGING BUSINESS ENVIRONMENT, ORGANIZATIONS' RESPONSE, AND EC SUPPORT

EC is driven by many technological, economic, and social factors. These are frequently related to global competition and rapid changes in the business environment.

THE CHANGING BUSINESS ENVIRONMENT

Economic, legal, societal, and technological factors and the trend for globalization have created a highly competitive business environment in which customers are becoming more and more powerful. These environmental factors can change quickly, vigorously, and sometimes in an unpredictable manner. Companies need to react quickly to both the problems and the opportunities resulting from this new business environment. Because the pace of change and the level of uncertainty are expected to accelerate, organizations are operating under increasing pressures to produce more products, faster, and with fewer resources. For example, the financial crisis of 2008–2010 has resulted in many companies going out of business or being acquired by other companies. It has also presented the opportunity for large banks, for example, to buy even larger ones. These business environment changes impact the manner in which companies operate, and many firms have restructured themselves and their information systems, as well as their EC initiatives.

Let's see how all of these impact organizational performance.

PERFORMANCE, BUSINESS PRESSURES, AND ORGANIZATIONAL RESPONSES AND EC SUPPORT

Most people, sports teams, and organizations are trying to improve their *performance*. For some, it is a challenge; for others, it is a requirement for survival. Yet for others it is the key to improved quality of life, profitability, or reputation.

Most organizations measure their performance periodically, comparing it to some metrics and to the organization's mission, objectives, and plans. Unfortunately, in business, performance often depends not only on what you do but also on what others are doing, as well as on what is happening in the business and physical environments. The *business environment* may create significant pressures that can impact performance in uncontrollable, or sometimes even in unpredictable, ways.

The Business Environment and Performance Impact Model

The model shown in Exhibit 1.7 illustrates how the business environment (left) creates pressures, problems, and opportunities that drive what organizations are doing in their business processes (the "Our Company" box). Other drivers are the organization's mission, goals, strategy, and plans. Business processes include competencies, activities, and responses to the environmental pressures that we call *critical response activities* or *solutions*. The business processes and activities result in measurable performance, which provides solutions to problems/opportunities, as well as feedback to the attainment of the mission, strategy, goals, and plans.

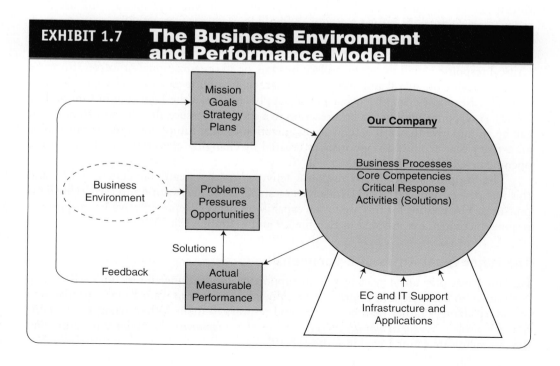

EXHIBIT 1.7 The Business Environment and Performance Model

EXHIBIT 1.8   Major Business Pressures

Market and Economic Pressures	Societal Pressures	Technological Pressures
Strong competition	Changing nature of workforce	Increasing innovations and new technologies
Global economy	Government deregulation, leading to more competition	Rapid technological obsolescence
Regional trade agreements (e.g., NAFTA)	Compliance (e.g., Sarbanes-Oxley Act)	Increases in information overload
Extremely low labor costs in some countries	Shrinking government subsidies	Rapid decline in technology cost versus labor cost (technology becomes more and more attractive)
Frequent and significant changes in markets	Increased importance of ethical and legal issues	
Increased power of consumer	Increased societal responsibility of organizations	
Political and government	Rapid political changes	
	Terrorism	

Notice that in Exhibit 1.7 EC and IT provide support to organizations' activities and to the resultant performance, countering the business pressures. Now, let's examine the two major components of the model: business pressures and organizational responses.

Business Pressures

In this text, business pressures are divided into the following categories: market (economic), societal, and technological. The main types of business pressures in each category are listed in Exhibit 1.8. (Note that some of the business environment conditions create opportunities.)

Organizational Response Strategies

How can organizations operate in such an environment? How can they deal with the threats and the opportunities? To begin with, many traditional strategies are still useful in today's environment. However, because some traditional response activities may *not* work in today's turbulent and competitive business environment, many of the old solutions need to be modified, supplemented, or discarded. Alternatively, new responses can be devised. Critical response activities can take place in some or all organizational processes, from the daily processing of payroll and order entry to strategic activities such as the acquisition of a company. Responses can also occur in the supply chain (see the Dell case in Online File W1.1). A response activity can be a reaction to a specific pressure already in existence, or it can be an initiative that will defend an organization against future pressures. It can also be an activity that exploits an opportunity created by changing conditions as shown in the opening case of Net-a-Porter.

   The Support of EC   Many response activities can be greatly facilitated by EC, and this fuels the growth of the field. In some cases, EC is the *only* solution to certain business pressures. The reasons for this are to the capabilities of EC. Representative EC-supported response activities are provided in Exhibit 1.9 and in Online File W1.5.

The Major Capabilities of E-Commerce

EC initiatives play an increasing role in supporting innovations and strategies that help companies to compete and flourish, especially companies that want to be proactive and introduce changes rather than be reactive and respond to them. What makes EC suitable for such a role is a *set of capabilities* and *technological developments*; the major capabilities and developments are summarized in Exhibit 1.10.

EXHIBIT 1.9   Innovative Organizational Responses

Response Strategy	Descriptions
Strategic systems	Improve strategic advantage in industry.
Agile systems	Increase ability to adapt to changes and flexibility.
Continuous improvements and business process management	Using enterprise systems to improve business processes. Introduce e-procurement.
Customer relationship management	Introduce programs to improve customer relationships using the Internet and EC models.
Business alliances and partner relationship management (PRM)	Create joint ventures, partnerships, e-collaboration, virtual corporations, and others for win-win situations—even with competitors.
Electronic markets	Use both private and public electronic markets to increase efficiency and effectiveness.
Cycle time reduction	Increase speed of operation and reduce time to market.
Empowering employees, especially on the front line (interacting with customers, partners)	Provide employees with computerized decision aids so they can make quick decisions on their own.
Mass customization in a build-to-order system	Produce customized products (services) rapidly at reasonable cost to many, many customers (mass) as Dell does.
Intrabusiness use of automation	Many intrabusiness activities, from sales force automation to inventory management can be improved with e-commerce and m-commerce.
Knowledge management	Appropriate creation, storage, and dissemination of knowledge using electronic systems, increases productivity, agility, and competitiveness.
Customer selection, loyalty, and service	Identify customers with the greatest profit potential; increase likelihood that they will want the product or service offering; retain their loyalty.
Human capital	Select the best employees for particular tasks or jobs, at particular compensation levels.
Product and service quality	Detect quality problems early and minimize them.
Financial performance	Better understand the drivers of financial performance and the effects of nonfinancial factors.
Research and development	Improve quality, efficacy, and where applicable, safety of products and services.
Social networking	Innovative marketing, advertising, collaboration, and innovation using the power of the crowd.

EXHIBIT 1.10   Major Capabilities That Contribute to the Growth of EC

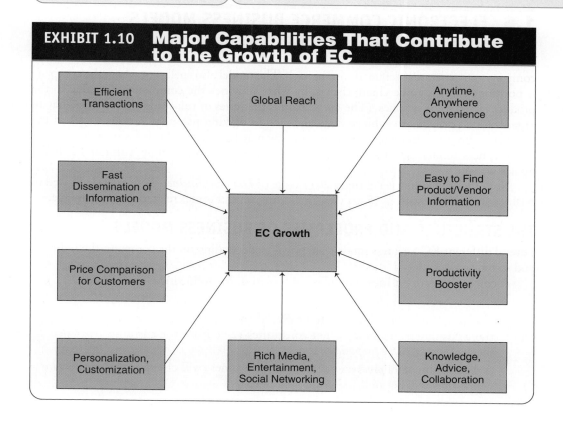

The essential capabilities that drive EC are the ability to

> ▶ Provide efficient and effective business transactions.
> ▶ Provide global reach for selling, buying, or finding business partners.
> ▶ Conduct business anytime, from anywhere, in a convenient way. For example, there are more than 250 million wireless subscribers in the United States (Burns 2007).
> ▶ Disseminate information rapidly, frequently in real time (e.g., the Beijing Olympics case, see Online File W1.4).
> ▶ Compare prices.
> ▶ Customize products and personalize services.
> ▶ Use rich media in advertisement, entertainment, and social networking.
> ▶ Receive experts' and other users' advice quickly.
> ▶ Collaborate in different ways, both internally and externally.
> ▶ Share information and knowledge.
> ▶ Increase productivity and performance, reduce costs, and compress time (e.g., by having smarter applications).
> ▶ Easily and quickly find information about vendors, products, and competitors.

Because EC technology is improving over time and decreasing in cost, its comparative advantage is continuously increasing, further contributing to the growth of EC.

Section 1.5 ▶ REVIEW QUESTIONS

1. List the components of the business environment performance model and explain the model.
2. List the major factors in today's business environment.
3. List some of the major response activities taken by organizations.
4. List and briefly discuss five capabilities of EC (consult Exhibit 1.8).

1.6 ELECTRONIC COMMERCE BUSINESS MODELS

One of the major characteristics of EC is that it enables the creation of new business models (Prahalad and Krishnan 2008). A **business model** is a method of doing business by which a company can generate revenue to sustain itself. The model also spells out where the company is positioned in the value chain; that is, by what activities the company adds value to the product or service it supplies. (The *value chain* is the series of value-adding activities that an organization performs to achieve its goals, such as making profit, at various stages of the production process.) In many cases one company may have several business models.

Business models are a subset of a business plan (see the Online Tutorial T2 at the book's website).

Note that the January-February 2011 issue of *Harvard Business Review* is dedicated to business model innovations (5 articles), including several topics related to e-commerce.

THE STRUCTURE AND PROPERTIES OF BUSINESS MODELS

Several different EC business models are possible, depending on the company, the industry, and so on.

A comprehensive business model is composed of the following elements:

> ▶ A description of the *customers* to be served and the company's relationships with these customers, including what constitutes value from the customers' perspective (*customers' value proposition*).
> ▶ A description of all *products* and *services* the business will offer and the markets in which they will be sold.

business model
A method of doing business by which a company can generate revenue to sustain itself.

- A description of the *business process* required to make and deliver the products and services including distribution and marketing strategies.
- A list of the *resources* required and the identification of which ones are available, which will be developed in-house, and which will need to be acquired (including human resources).
- A description of the organization's *supply chain*, including *suppliers* and other *business partners*.
- A list of the major competitors, their market share, and strengths/weaknesses.
- The competitive advantage offered by the business model.
- The anticipated organizational changes and any resistance to change.
- A description of the revenues expected (*revenue model*), anticipated costs, sources of financing, and estimated profitability (financial *viability*).

Models also include a *value proposition,* which is an analysis of the benefits of using the specific model (tangible and intangible), both the customers and the organization. A detailed discussion of and examples of business models and their relationship to business plans is presented in Online Tutorial T2.

This chapter presents two of the models' elements: *revenue models* and *value propositions.*

Revenue Models

A revenue model outlines how the organization, or the EC project, will generate revenue. For example, the revenue model for Zappos shows revenue from online sales of shoes. The major revenue models are:

- **Sales.** Companies generate revenue from selling merchandise or services on their websites. An example is when Net-a-Porter, Amazon.com, or Godiva sells a product online.
- **Transaction Fees.** A company receives a commission based on the volume of transactions made. For example, when a home owner sells a house, he or she typically pays a transaction fee to the broker. The higher the value of the sale, the higher the total transaction fee. Alternatively, transaction fees can be levied *per transaction.* With online stock trades, for example, there is usually a fixed fee per trade, regardless of the volume.
- **Subscription Fees.** Customers pay a fixed amount, usually monthly, to get some type of service. An example would be the access fee for AOL. Thus, AOL's primary revenue model is subscription (fixed monthly payments).
- **Advertising Fees.** Companies charge others for allowing them to place a banner on their sites (see Chapter 8).
- **Affiliate Fees.** Companies receive commissions for referring customers to others' websites. A good program is available at Amazon.com.
- **Licensing Fees.** Another revenue source is licensing fees (e.g., see datadirect-technologies.com). Licensing fees can be assessed as an annual fee or a per usage fee. Microsoft receives fees from each workstation that uses Windows NT, for example.
- **Other Revenue Sources.** Some companies allow people to play games for a fee or to watch a sports competition in real time for a fee (e.g., see espn.go.com).

A company uses its *revenue model* to describe how it will generate revenue and its *business model* to describe the *process* it will use to do so. Exhibit 1.11 summarizes five common revenue models.

The revenue model can be part of the value proposition or it may supplement it.

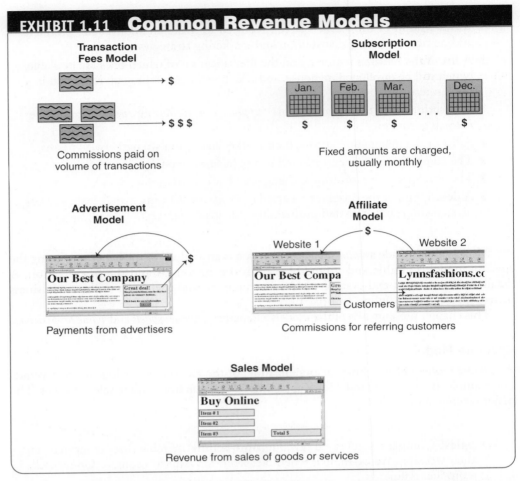

EXHIBIT 1.11 Common Revenue Models

Transaction Fees Model

Commissions paid on volume of transactions

Subscription Model

Jan.   Feb.   Mar.   ...   Dec.

Fixed amounts are charged, usually monthly

Advertisement Model

Our Best Company

Great deal!

Payments from advertisers

Affiliate Model

Website 1   Website 2

Our Best Compa   Lynnsfashions.co

Customers

Commissions for referring customers

Sales Model

Buy Online

Item # 1

Item #2

Item #3   Total $

Revenue from sales of goods or services

Innovative Revenue Models for Individuals. The Internet allows for innovative revenue models, some of which can be utilized even by individuals, as demonstrated by the following two examples.

Example 1: *Buy Low–Sell High.* This strategy has been known for generations, but now you have a real chance. How about buying stuff cheap on Craigslist (or other online classified sites) and resell it for a 50 to 200 percent profit in an auction on eBay? Try it, you might make money. Some people make it even bigger. The person who bought the domain name *pizza.com* for $20 in 1994 sold it for $2.6 million in April 2008 (one of the many he purchased).

Example 2: *Traffic Arbitrage.* This is a more complex implementation of buy low–sell high. Basically, you buy ad space on less expensive search engines (such as Microsoft's Ad Center). The search engine then directs traffic to your website via key words. Then you fill your personal website with Google's ads (see Chapter 8 for AdSense). When users come to your website and click on Google's ads, they are directed to advertisers' websites. The advertisers pay Google for the referrals, and Google shares the fees with you.

Value Proposition

value proposition
The benefits a company can derive from using EC.

Business models also include a value-proposition statement. A **value proposition** refers to the benefits, including the intangible, nonquantitative ones, that a company can derive from using the model. In B2C EC, for example, a value proposition defines how a company's product or service fulfills the needs of customers. The *value proposition* is an important part of the marketing plan of any product or service.

Specifically, how do e-marketplaces create value? Amit and Zott (2001) identify four sets of values that are created by e-business: search and transaction cost efficiency, complementarities, lock-in, and novelty. *Search and transaction cost efficiency* enables faster and more informed decision making, wider product and service selection, and greater economies of scale—cost savings per unit as greater quantities are produced and sold (e.g., through demand and supply aggregation for small buyers and sellers). *Complementarities* involve bundling some goods and services together to provide more value than from offering them separately. Lock-in is attributable to the high switching cost that ties customers to particular suppliers. *Novelty* creates value through innovative ways for structuring transactions, connecting partners, and fostering new markets.

Functions of a Business Model

Business models have the following functions or objectives:

> ▶ Describe the major business processes of a company.
>
> ▶ Describe the business models' (the venture's) positioning within the value network linking suppliers and customers (includes identification of potential complementors and competitors). Also, describe the supply and value chains.
>
> ▶ Formulate the venture's competitive strategy and its long-range plans.
>
> ▶ Articulate a customer value proposition.
>
> ▶ Identify a market segment (who will use the technology for what purpose; specify the revenue-generation process; where the company will operate).
>
> ▶ Define the venture's specific value chain structure.
>
> ▶ Estimate the cost structure and amount and profit potential.

TYPICAL EC BUSINESS MODELS

There are many types of EC business models. Examples and details of EC business models can be found throughout this text and in Rappa (2010). The following are five common models. Additional models are listed in Online File W1.6.

1. **Online direct marketing.** The most obvious model is that of selling products or services online. Sales may be from a *manufacturer* to a customer, eliminating intermediaries or physical stores (e.g., Dell Computer), or from *retailers* to consumers, making distribution more efficient (e.g., Net-a-Porter, Walmart online). This model is especially efficient for digitizable products and services (those that can be delivered electronically). This model has several variations (see Chapters 3 and 4) and it uses different mechanisms (e.g., auctions). It is practiced in B2C (where it is called *e-tailing*) and in some B2B types of EC.

2. **Electronic tendering systems.** Large organizational buyers, private or public, usually make large-volume or large-value purchases through a **tendering (bidding) system**, also known as a *reverse auction*. Such tendering can be done online, saving time and money. Pioneered by General Electric Corp., e-tendering systems are gaining popularity. Indeed, several government agencies mandate that most of their procurement must be done through e-tendering. (Details are provided in Chapter 4.)

3. **Electronic marketplaces and exchanges.** Electronic marketplaces existed in isolated applications for decades (e.g., stock and commodities exchanges). But as of 1996, hundreds of e-marketplaces (old and new) have introduced new methods and efficiencies to the trading process. If they are well organized and managed, e-marketplaces can provide significant benefits to both buyers and sellers. Of special interest are vertical marketplaces that concentrate on one industry. For details see Chapter 4.

4. **Viral marketing.** According to the viral marketing model (see Chapters 7 and 8), people use e-mail and social networks for spreading word-of-mouth advertising. Thus, an organization can increase brand awareness or even generate sales by inducing people to send influencing messages to other people or to recruit friends to join certain programs. It is basically Web-based *word-of-mouth* advertising, and it is popular in social networks.

5. **Group purchasing.** Group purchasing is a well-known offline method, especially for companies. It is based on the concept of quantity discounts ("cheaper-by-the-dozen"). The Internet model allows individuals to get together, so they can gain the large-quantity advantage. This model was not popular until 2010 when Groupon introduced

tendering (bidding) system
Model in which a buyer requests would-be sellers to submit bids; the lowest bidder wins.

a modified model in which people are grouped around special deals as illustrated in Case 1.2 and in Chapter 7.

Note that a company may use several EC models as demonstrated in the DFL closing case, Dell case (Online File W1.1), and the Beijing Olympic case (Online File W1.4).

CASE 1.2
EC Application
GROUPON

Groupon is a deal-of-the-day website combined with group buy, which is localized to major geographic markets in the United States and many other countries. As of January 2011, Groupon serves more than 160 markets in North America and 110 markets in Europe, Asia, and South America and has amassed 40 million registered users. Groupon was founded in November 2008 and is considered as the fastest-growing company, ever.

Groupon is projecting that the company is on pace to make $1 billion in sales faster than any other business. In 2010 the company rejected a $6 billion buyout offer from Google. Groupon is preparing for a $15 billion IPO in 2011. Groupon also owns a several international operations, all of which were originally deal-of-the-day services or similar to it, but then re-branded under the Groupon name after acquisition.

The Business Model and Transaction Process
The company offers one "Groupon" ("group coupon") per day in each of the markets it serves. The Groupon works as an assurance contract; if a certain number of people sign up for the offer, then the deal becomes available to all; if the predetermined minimum is not met, no one gets the deal that day. This reduces risk for retailers who can treat the coupons as quantity discounts, as well as sales promotion tools. Groupon makes money by getting a cut of each deal from the retailers. The process is illustrated in the exhibit below; it is a combination of group buy and deal flash models.

Groupon business strategy is to break into new markets by identifying successful local businesses, first by sending in an advance squad of employees to research the local market; when it finds a business with outstanding reviews, salespeople approach it and explain the business model and try to sign up the vendors. Groupon's promotional text for the deals has been seen as a contributing factor to the popularity of the site. Groupon uses social marketing sites such as Facebook to further promote the idea. The Groupon model shows the logic of why merchants are willing to offer 50 to 80% discount to volume shoppers. By fulfilling demand direct from consumers in aggregate, both large chains and SMBs can fulfill orders more efficiently and reduce sales and marketing expenses and overhead.

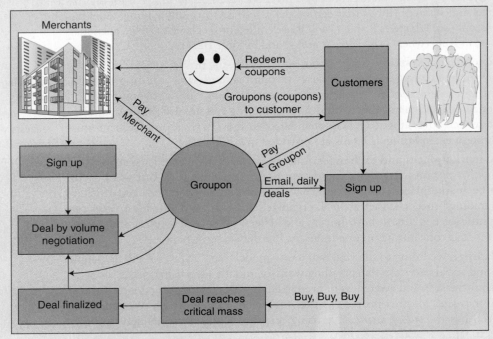

The Business Model and Process of Groupon

(continued)

Limitations of the Model

As will be described in Section 7.6 a small business can be temporarily swamped with too many customer orders creating the possibility that customers will be unsatisfied, or that there would not be enough product to meet the demand. GAP, a large clothing retailer, was able to handle 445,000 coupons in a national deal (although it experienced server problems at one point), but a smaller business could become suddenly flooded with customers. As will be described in Section 7.6 a restaurant in Hong Kong was unable to feed all its customers in a timely manner. One coffee shop in Portland was swamped with a stampede of over 1,000 customers on the first day of Groupon's sale. In response to similar problems, Groupon officials stated that "deal" subscriptions should be capped in advance to a reasonable number.

Benefits and Expansion

Groupon's model is a win-win one.

The major benefits to customers are:

▶ Deep discounts (50 to 90%)
▶ Discovery of new/specialized services products
▶ "Side" deals offered by Groupon
▶ Personalized deals
▶ Learn to know vendors in your area
▶ Can tell your friends/family

The major benefits to merchants are:

▶ Can sell larger quantities quickly
▶ Save advertising and marketing expenses
▶ Repeat customers (if they like the deal and the service)
▶ Lower customer acquisition cost

The Competition

As with any successful business, here too, there is a large number of companies that want to clone Groupon.

According to *en.wikipedia.org/wiki/Groupon* 200 similar sites have sprung up in North America with some sites even copying the color, font, and logo. Worldwide, there are over 500 similar sites. In China there are over 1,000 companies but they use a different business model. However, by January 2011, only one competitor, LivingSocial, has been described as a serious competitor; it received an investment from Amazon of $175 million. Other notable competitors include BuyWithMe, Jasmere.com, Weforia (Powered by Yellowbook), Groop Swoop, Groupalia, TownHog, TeamGrab.com, Agenzy.com, DailyQ.com, and eWinWin. Some sites, such as Dealradar, Dealery, Yipit, and SocialDealMap, collate deals from many other websites.

Groupon has been aggressively expanding its market into emerging markets. Recently, it acquired an Indian competitor, SoSasta.com, and is attempting to penetrate the Chinese market.

Facebook, Google, and Other Competitors

As described in the closing case in chapter 7, Facebook Deals is an attempt to enter this market. At the time this book was written it was difficult to assess the magnitude of this attempt. Google, after failing to acquire Groupon, created Google Offers in 2011 to complete with Groupon and the hundreds of smaller sites. At the time the book was written the impact of Google's efforts was not clear (see *groups.google.com/group/buy*).

Upcoming competitors include Yahoo!, eBay, Yelp, local and national newspapers, Craigslist, and large vendors (e.g., Dell).

Factors in the Competition

Given the large size of Groupon, its financial might, its many dedicated employees, its policies and strategies, and it is not going to be easy to compete with this company. Therefore, the competitors use strategies such as concentrating on a niche market (e.g., one product, one industry). Also, some concentrate on a small territory (e.g. a city) in which they have a competitive advantage. Similarly, group deals for certain communities (e.g., nurses, electrical engineers) may be very successful. For a discussion see *stratagroupbuy.com/another-group-buy-website*.

The success of Groupon was enabled by the ability of the company to create groups of buyers large enough to assure a quantity discount. Also, its relationship with the merchants is excellent (see an example of an interview at *lexicom/blog/2010/12/one-merchants-experience-with-groupon*).

Sources: Compiled from Carpenter (2010), *en.wikipedia.org/wiki/Groupon*, *grouponworks.com/merchant-services*, and *groupon.com/learn* (all accessed March 2011).

Questions

1. It is difficult to do business with Groupon. About 85% of merchants' suggestions are dismissed by Groupon. Why do you think Groupon is so strict and how will this policy impact the competition?

2. Some claim that Groupon is basically an e-mail list that charges advertisers to send out their coupons (called Groupons). Comment.

3. Why does Groupon use Facebook to promote its business, while Facebook is its competitor?

4. Read Carpenter (2010) and write a short essay on Groupon's chance of survival in the intensely competitive environment. Examine its revenue model and expansion plans.

5. Learn more about Groupon's order fulfillment (e.g., ability to handle volume, control of deliveries, and dealing with marketing and competitors). Write a report.

6. Research Groupon's global efforts. Start with Emma Hall's article "Groupon Clones in Europe Say They Offer Better Deals and Treatment of Merchants" at *adage.com/article/global-news/groupon-clones-europe-win-consumers-merchants/147689*.

7. Groupon uses classified ads for rental apartments. How does this fit with its business model?

8. Groupon now deals in B2B. Search the Internet and find out how it is being done.

Section 1.6 ▶ REVIEW QUESTIONS

1. What is a business model? Describe its functions and properties.
2. Describe a revenue model and a value proposition. How are they related?
3. Describe the following business models: direct marketing, tendering system, electronic exchanges, viral marketing, and social networking/commerce.
4. Identify some business models related to buying and those related to selling.
5. Describe how viral marketing works.

1.7 BENEFITS, LIMITATIONS, AND IMPACTS OF ELECTRONIC COMMERCE

Few innovations in human history encompass as many benefits as EC does. The global nature of the technology, the opportunity to reach hundreds of millions of people, its interactive nature, the variety of possibilities for its use, and the resourcefulness and rapid growth of its supporting infrastructures, especially the Web, result in many potential benefits to organizations, individuals, and society. These benefits are just starting to materialize, but they will increase significantly as EC expands. It is not surprising that some maintain that the EC revolution is as profound as the change that accompanied the Industrial Revolution.

THE BENEFITS AND IMPACTS OF EC

EC provides benefits to *organizations, individual customers,* and *society.* These benefits are summarized in Exhibit 1.12. Many benefits can be found in the list of EC resources in Online File W1.7.

EC as a Provider of Competitive Advantage

The business models created by EC and the benefits of the technology may result in significant changes in the way business is conducted. These changes may positively impact corporate operations resulting in a competitive advantage for the firms using EC. For a description and discussion see Online Tutorial T12.

THE LIMITATIONS AND BARRIERS OF EC

Barriers to EC can be classified as either technological or nontechnological. Representative major barriers are listed in Exhibit 1.13.

According to a 2006 study (Harmony Hollow Software 2006), the major barriers to EC are (1) resistance to new technology, (2) implementation difficulties, (3) security concerns, (4) lack of technology skills, (5) lack of potential customers, and (6) cost. Van Toorn et al. (2006) classified the barriers into: sectoral barriers (e.g., government, private sector, international organizations), internal barriers (e.g., security, lack of technical knowledge, and lack of time and resources), and external barriers (e.g., lack of government support). Van Toorn et al. (2006) also list the top barriers with regards to global EC: cultural differences, organizational differences, incompatible B2B interfaces, international trade barriers, and lack of standards. These limitations need to be addressed when implementing EC. One important area is that of ethics.

Ethical Issues

ethics
The branch of philosophy that deals with what is considered to be right and wrong.

Ethical issues can create pressures or constraints on EC business operations. Yet, ethical sites increase trust and help EC vendors. **Ethics** relates to standards of right and wrong, and *information ethics* relates to standards of right and wrong in information technology and EC practices. Ethical issues have the power to damage the image of an organization and morale of employees. Ethics is a difficult area, because ethical issues are not cut-and-dried. What is considered ethical by one person may seem unethical to another. Likewise, what is considered ethical in one country may be unethical in another. For further discussions of EC ethical issues see Chapter 14 and Gaskin and Evans (2010).

EXHIBIT 1.12 Benefits of E-Commerce

Benefit	Description
Benefits to Organizations	
Global reach	Locating customers and/or suppliers worldwide, at reasonable cost and fast.
Cost reduction	Lower cost of information processing, storage, distribution.
Facilitate problem solving	Solve complex problems that have remained unsolved.
Supply chain improvements	Reduce delays, inventories, and cost.
Business always open	Open 24/7/365; no overtime or other costs.
Customization/personalization	Make it to consumer's wish, fast and at reasonable cost.
Seller's specialization (niche market)	Seller can specialize in a narrow field (e.g., dog toys), yet make money.
Ability to innovate, use new business models	Facilitate innovation and enable unique business models.
Rapid time to market and increased speed	Expedite processes; higher speed and productivity.
Lower communication costs	The Internet is cheaper then VAN private lines.
Efficient procurement	Saves time and reduces costs by enabling e-procurement.
Improved customer service and relationship	Direct interaction with customers, better CRM.
Fewer permits and less tax	May need fewer permits and be able to avoid sales tax.
Up-to-date company material	All distributed material is up-to-date.
Help SME to compete	EC may help small companies to compete against large ones by using special business models.
Lower inventories	Using customization inventories can be minimized.
Lower cost of distributing digitizable product	Delivery online can be 90 percent cheaper.
Provide competitive advantage	Innovative business models.
Benefits to Consumers	
Inventory	Huge selection to choose from (vendor, products, styles).
Ubiquity	Can shop any time from any place.
Customized products/services	Can customize many products and/or services.
Cheaper products/services	Can compare and shop for lowest prices.
Instant delivery	Digitized products can be downloaded immediately upon payment.
Information availability	Easy finding what you need, with details, demos, etc.
Convenient auction participation	Do auctions any time and from any place.
No sales tax	Sometimes.
Enable telecommuting	Can work or study at home.
Electronic socialization	Can socialize online in communities yet be at home.
Find unique items	Using online auctions, collectible items can be found.
Comfortable shopping	Shop at your leisure without pushy sales clerks bothering you.
Benefits to Society	
Enable telecommuting	Facilitate work at home; less traffic, pollution.
More public services	Make education, health, etc., available for more people. Rural area can share benefits; more services for the poor.
Improved homeland security	Facilitate domestic security.
Increased standard of living	Can buy more and cheaper goods/services.
Close the digital divide	Allow people in developing countries and rural areas to accept more services and purchase what they really like.

Implementing EC use may raise ethical issues ranging from employee e-mail monitoring to invasion of privacy of millions of customers whose data are stored in private and public databases. In implementing EC, it is necessary to pay attention to these issues and recognize that some of them may limit, or even prohibit, the use of EC. An example of this can be seen in the attempted implementation of RFID tags (Online Tutorial T3) in retail stores due to the potential invasion of buyers' privacy.

Despite these barriers, EC is expanding rapidly. As experience accumulates and technology improves, the cost-benefit ratio of EC will increase, resulting in even greater rates of EC adoption.

EXHIBIT 1.13   Limitations of Electronic Commerce

Technological Limitations	Nontechnological Limitations
Lack of universal standards for quality, security, and reliability.	Security and privacy concerns deter customers from buying.
The telecommunications bandwidth is insufficient, especially for m-commerce, videos, and graphics.	Lack of trust in EC and in unknown sellers hinders buying.
Software development tools are still evolving.	People do not yet sufficiently trust paperless, faceless transactions.
It is difficult to integrate Internet and EC software with some existing (especially legacy) applications and databases.	Many legal and public policy issues, including taxation, have not yet been resolved or are not clear.
Special Web servers are needed in addition to the network servers, which add to the cost of EC.	National and international government regulations sometimes get in the way.
Internet accessibility is still expensive and/or inconvenient.	It is difficult to measure some of the benefits of EC, such as online advertising. Mature measurement methodologies are not yet available.
Order fulfillment of large-scale B2C requires special automated warehouses.	Some customers like to feel and touch products. Also, customers are resistant to the change from shopping at a brick-and-mortar store to a virtual store.
	In many cases, the number of sellers and buyers that are needed for profitable EC operations is insufficient.
	Online fraud is increasing.
	It is difficult to obtain venture capital due to the failure of many dot-coms.

WHY STUDY E-COMMERCE?

The academic area of e-commerce started around 1995 with only a few courses and textbooks. Today, many universities offer complete programs in e-commerce or e-business (e.g., majors in e-commerce, minors in e-commerce and certificate programs; see University of Virginia, University of Maine). Recently, e-commerce topics have been integrated into all functional fields (e.g., Internet marketing, electronic financial markets). The reason for this proliferation is that e-commerce is penetrating more and more into business areas, services, and governments.

However, there are also some very tangible benefits to increased knowledge of EC. First, your chances of getting a good (or better) job are higher. The demand for both technical and managerial EC skills is growing rapidly, and so are the salaries (e.g., see salary comparison sites such as salary.com, cbsalary.com, and monster.com). Second, your chances for promotion could be higher if you understand EC and know how to seize its opportunities. Finally, it gives you a chance to become a billionaire, like the founders of Google, Facebook, YouTube, Amazon.com and Yahoo!, or to make lots of money on eBay (see Joyner 2007). Even if you are not so lucky you can still make good money in Second Life (see Alter 2008 and Rymaszewski et al. 2008) or simply by selling on eBay, Yahoo!, Facebook, Craigslist, or your own website. And you can do it while you are a student, as Lily, Shu, and Adrian did (see Case 1.3).

Lily, Shu, and Adrian are not the only students engaged in making money from EC. Diane Keng, an entrepreneur from Cupertino Monte Vista High School in California, initiated three Web 2.0 successful start-up companies, making substantial money (see Fowler 2010).

There are many other opportunities for young people to make money from EC in addition to the examples in this book of Second Life and selling on eBay. Hunt (2010) suggests the following ways to earn extra cash online: (1) sell your craft; (2) make money from your talent; (3) be a nurse on call; (4) write, edit, or proofread; (5) design graphics and websites; (6) tutor kids or adults; (7) give advice; (8) provide customer service; (9) launch a blog; (10) give your opinion (for a fee); (11) search the Internet; and (12) do online tasks. Hunt also provides examples, URLs, and advice regarding scams.

Web 2.0 also creates many opportunities for full-time jobs. For a list and discussion, see Tice (2010).

CASE 1.3
EC Application

HOW COLLEGE STUDENTS BECOME ENTREPRENEURS

Stanford University students Lily Kim, Shu Lindsey, and Adrian Mak use computers and the Internet extensively. They also do extensive writing (on paper) and especially like using ultra thin pens with a tip half the width of the average ballpoint. They learned about these pens when they visited Japan. Because these pens were not available in U.S. stores, they purchased them online directly from Japan. When they showed the pens to their friends (an example of the power of social marketing), they found that there was great interest in such pens in the United States.

Sensing the opportunity, in 2004 they decided to use their $9,000 savings to open a business, called JetPens (*jetpens.com*), selling pens they imported from Japan to their classmates. To keep costs low, they used open source free software (from osCommerce) to build and run the store. Soon after they opened an online storefront, they began advertising their products via e-mail to other students. The number of registered users on the site grew rapidly. To meet the demand, they initially kept an inventory of pens in their bedrooms, but now they rent storage space.

They also have a small advertising budget for Google ads. By using smart key words, their store ranks at the top of search engine discoveries when a user searches for "Japanese pens." This strategy is called *search engine (site) optimization* (SEO) see Chapter 8 and *en.wikipedia.org/wiki/Search_engine_optimization*) for details.

In 2007, the owners expanded the product line by adding interesting office supplies, including a best-selling

eraser with 28 corners, which increased their sales volume to over 10,000 items per month. Other best sellers include a pen with a tip fine enough to write on a grain of rice, the Uni-ball Alpha Gel ballpoint pen with a squishy silicone-gel grip (this silicone gel is famous for keeping an egg from breaking when dropped from 5 feet), colorful and erasable gel pens that work just as well as pencils, and BeGreen environmentally friendly pens. To find friends and customers, they use Facebook, Flickr, Twitter, and YouTube and they have a discussion forum on the JetPens website.

By keeping a tight cap on operating expenses and using Internet advertising successfully, the young entrepreneurs have been able to do what many others have failed to do—generate a profit within two years, and grow by hundreds of percentage points every year.

Sources: Compiled from Blakely (2007) and *jetpens.com* (accessed April 2011).

Questions

1. Go to *jetpens.com* and examine the catalog and features of the site. What impresses you the most?

2. Evaluate the site's ease of use.

3. Do you think that a business like this can succeed as an independent offline-only store? Why or why not?

4. What is the purpose of the site's JetPress RSS Feed?

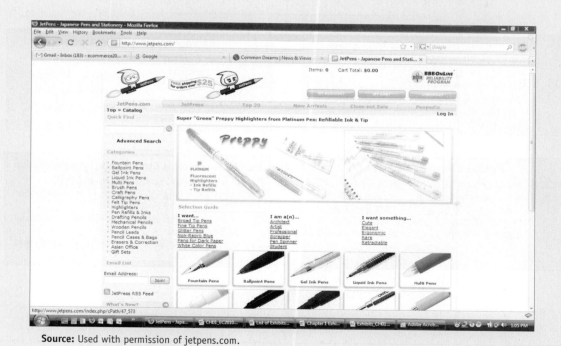

Source: Used with permission of jetpens.com.

Section 1.7 ▶ REVIEW QUESTIONS

1. Describe some EC benefits to organizations, individuals, and society.
2. List the major technological and nontechnological barriers and limitations to EC.
3. Describe some of the benefits of studying EC.
4. How can EC help entrepreneurship?

1.8 OVERVIEW OF THIS BOOK

This book is composed of 15 chapters grouped into five parts, as shown in Exhibit 1.14. Additional content, including 12 tutorials and online supplemental files for each chapter, is also available online at the book's website.

The specific parts and chapters of this textbook are as follows.

PART 1: INTRODUCTION TO E-COMMERCE AND E-MARKETPLACES

This section of the book includes an overview of EC and its content, benefits, limitations, and drivers, which are presented in Chapter 1. Chapter 2 presents electronic markets and their mechanisms, such as auctions, portals, and search engines. Chapter 2 also includes a presentation of Web 2.0 tools and environments.

PART 2: EC APPLICATIONS

This section includes three chapters. Chapter 3 describes e-tailing (B2C), including some of its most innovative applications for selling products online. It also describes the online delivery of services, such as banking, travel, and insurance. In Chapter 4, we introduce B2B

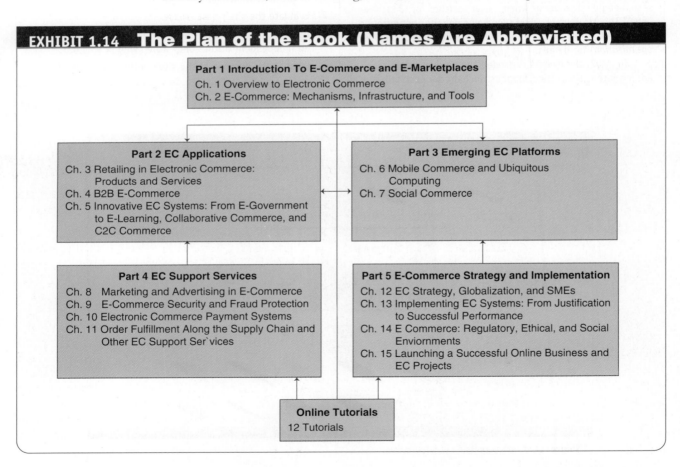

EXHIBIT 1.14 The Plan of the Book (Names Are Abbreviated)

Part 1 Introduction To E-Commerce and E-Marketplaces
Ch. 1 Overview to Electronic Commerce
Ch. 2 E-Commerce: Mechanisms, Infrastructure, and Tools

Part 2 EC Applications
Ch. 3 Retailing in Electronic Commerce: Products and Services
Ch. 4 B2B E-Commerce
Ch. 5 Innovative EC Systems: From E-Government to E-Learning, Collaborative Commerce, and C2C Commerce

Part 3 Emerging EC Platforms
Ch. 6 Mobile Commerce and Ubiquitous Computing
Ch. 7 Social Commerce

Part 4 EC Support Services
Ch. 8   Marketing and Advertising in E-Commerce
Ch. 9   E-Commerce Security and Fraud Protection
Ch. 10 Electronic Commerce Payment Systems
Ch. 11 Order Fulfillment Along the Supply Chain and Other EC Support Ser`vices

Part 5 E-Commerce Strategy and Implementation
Ch. 12 EC Strategy, Globalization, and SMEs
Ch. 13 Implementing EC Systems: From Justification to Successful Performance
Ch. 14 E Commerce: Regulatory, Ethical, and Social Enviornments
Ch. 15 Launching a Successful Online Business and EC Projects

Online Tutorials
12 Tutorials

EC and describe company-centric models (one buyer–many sellers, one seller–many buyers) as well as electronic exchanges (many buyers and many sellers).

E-government, e-learning, C2C, and knowledge management are the major subjects of Chapter 5.

PART 3: EMERGING EC PLATFORMS

This part includes two chapters. Chapter 6 deals with the topic of mobile commerce including location-based commerce. Chapter 7 provides a comprehensive coverage of social commerce.

PART 4: EC SUPPORT SERVICES

This part includes four chapters. Chapter 8 deals with market research, customer services, and online advertisement. Chapter 9 covers security and fraud protection.

Electronic payments are covered in Chapter 10, while order fulfillment and supply chain management are covered in Chapter 11.

PART 5: E-COMMERCE STRATEGY AND IMPLEMENTATION

This part includes four chapters: Chapter 12 deals with EC strategy, globalization, EC in SMEs, and EC impacts. In Chapter 13, we cover implementation issues starting with EC justification, business process management, technology adoption, and change management. Chapter 14 deals with legal, ethical, social, and compliance issues.

ONLINE TUTORIALS

Twelve short online tutorials supplement the text. These tutorials cover topics ranging from RFID to cloud computing. They are available at the book's website (pearsonglobaleditions.com/turban).

ONLINE CHAPTER SUPPLEMENTS

The final chapter, Chapter 15 (available online at the book's website pearsonglobaleditions.com/turban), deals with the process of launching an e-business and the introduction of EC projects and initiatives. A large number of online files organized by chapter number support the content of each chapter.

MANAGERIAL ISSUES

Many managerial issues are related to EC. These issues are discussed throughout the book and also are summarized in a separate section (like this one) near the end of each chapter. Some managerial issues related to this introductory chapter are as follows.

1. **Is EC real?** For those not involved in EC, the first question that comes to mind is, "Is it real?" We believe that the answer is an emphatic "yes." The Internet is already an integral part of our lives. Banking from home, trading stocks online, and buying goods from Amazon.com are now common practices for many people. The concern is not whether to start EC, but to what extent should it be developed and how to ensure the success of the e-business initiatives. Jack Welch, former CEO of General Electric, has commented, "Any company, old or new, that doesn't see this technology (EC) literally as important as breathing could be on its last breath" (McGee 2000).

2. **Why is B2B e-commerce so essential and successful?** B2B EC is essential for several reasons. First, some B2B models are easier to implement than B2C models. The volume and value of transactions is larger in B2B than in B2C, and the potential savings are larger and easier to justify in contrast to B2C, which has several major problems, ranging from channel conflict with existing distributors to fraud to a lack of a critical mass of buyers. Many companies can start B2B by simply buying from existing online stores and B2B exchanges or selling electronically by joining existing marketplaces or an auction house. The problem is determining *what* and *where* to buy or sell.

3. **Which EC business model should I choose?** Beginning in early 2000, the news was awash with stories about the failure of many dot-coms and EC projects. Industry consolidation often occurs after a "gold rush." About 100 years ago, hundreds of companies tried to manufacture cars, following Ford's success in the United States; only three survived. The important thing is to learn from the successes and failures of others, and discover the right business model for each endeavor. For lessons that can be learned from EC successes and failures, see Chapters 3 and 4.

4. **How can we exploit social commerce?** There are major possibilities here. Some companies even open their own social networks. Advertising is probably the first thing to consider. Recruiting can be a promising avenue as well. Offering discounted products and services should also be considered. Providing customer services and conducting market research can be a useful activity as well. Finally, the ultimate goal is associating the social network with commerce so that revenue is created.

5. **What are the top challenges of EC today?** The top 10 technical issues for EC (in order of their importance) are security, adequate infrastructure, virtualization, back-end systems integration, more intelligent software, cloud computing, data warehousing and mining, scalability, and content distribution. The top 10 managerial issues for EC are justification, budgets, project deadlines, keeping up with technology, privacy issues, unrealistic management expectations, training, reaching new customers, improving customer ordering services, and finding qualified EC employees. Most of these issues are discussed throughout this book.

SUMMARY

In this chapter, you learned about the following EC issues as they relate to the chapter's learning objectives.

1. **Definition of EC and description of its various categories.** EC involves conducting transactions electronically. Its major categories are pure versus partial EC, Internet versus non-Internet, and electronic markets versus company-based systems.

2. **The content and framework of EC.** The applications of EC, and there are many, are based on infrastructures and are supported by people; public policy and technical standards; marketing and advertising; support services, such as logistics, security, and payment services; and business partners—all tied together by management.

3. **The major types of EC transactions.** The major types of EC transactions are B2B, B2C, C2C, m-commerce, intrabusiness commerce, B2E, c-commerce, e-government, social commerce, and e-learning.

4. **E-commerce 2.0.** This refers to the use of social computing in business, often through the use of Web 2.0 tools (such as blogs, wikis), as well as the emergence of enterprise social networking and commercial activities in virtual worlds. Social and business networks attract huge numbers of visitors. Many of the visitors are young (future EC customers). Therefore, advertisers are willing to spend money on advertising, either to an entire group or to individuals (e.g., using Google's technology).

5. **Describe social commerce and social software.** Companies are beginning to exploit the opportunity of conducting business transactions in social networks and by using social software such as blogs. Major areas are advertising, shopping, customer service, recruiting, and collaboration.

6. **The elements of the digital world.** The major elements of the digital world are the digital economy, digital enterprises, and digital society. They are diversified and expanding rapidly.

7. **The drivers of EC.** EC is a major product of the digital and technological revolution, which enables companies to simultaneously increase both growth and profits. This revolution enables digitization of products, services, and information. The business environment is changing rapidly due to technological breakthroughs, globalization, societal changes, deregulation, and more. The changing business environment forces organizations to respond. Many traditional responses may not be sufficient because of the magnitude of the pressures and the pace of the changes involved. Therefore, organizations must frequently innovate and reengineer their operations. In many cases, EC is driven by the needs of organizations to perform well and even survive.

   EC provides strategic advantage so organizations can compete better. Also, organizations can go into remote and global markets for both selling and buying at better prices. Organizations can speed time-to-market to gain competitive advantage. They can improve the internal and external supply chain as well as increase collaboration. Finally, they can better comply with government regulations.

8. **The major EC business models.** The major EC business models include online direct marketing, electronic tendering systems, name-your-own-price, affiliate marketing, viral marketing, group purchasing, online auctions, mass customization (make-to-order), electronic exchanges, supply chain improvers, finding the best price, value-chain integration, value-chain providers, information brokers, bartering, deep discounting, and membership.

9. **Benefits of EC to organizations, consumers, and society.** EC offers numerous benefits to all participants. Because these benefits are substantial, it looks as though EC is here to stay and cannot be ignored.

10. **Limitations of e-commerce.** The major limitations of EC are the resistance to new technology, fear from fraud, integration with other IT systems may be difficult, costly order fulfillment, privacy issue, unclear regulatory issues, lack of trust in computers, difficulties to justify EC initiatives, and lack of EC skilled employees.

KEY TERMS

Brick-and-mortar (old economy) organizations	38	Consumer-to-consumer (C2C)	43	Intranet	39
Business model	60	Corporate portal	54	Social commerce	50
Business-to-business (B2B)	42	Digital economy	52	Social computing	48
Business-to-business-to-consumer (B2B2C)	42	Digital enterprise	52	Social network	49
Business-to-consumer (B2C)	42	E-business	38	Social networking	49
Business-to-employees (B2E)	43	E-government	43	Social networking services (SNSs)	49
Click-and-mortar (click-and-brick) organizations	39	Electronic commerce (EC)	38	Tendering (bidding) system	63
Collaborative commerce (c-commerce)	43	Electronic market (e-marketplace)	39	Value proposition	62
		E-tailing	42	Virtual (pure-play) organizations	39
		Ethics	66	Virtual world	50
		Extranet	39	Web 2.0	48
Consumer-to-business (C2B)	42	F-commerce	45		
		Intrabusiness EC	42		

DISCUSSION QUESTIONS

1. Compare brick-and-mortar and click-and-mortar organizations.

2. Why is buying with a smart card from a vending machine considered EC?

3. Explain how EC can reduce cycle time, improve employees' empowerment, and facilitate customer support.

4. Compare and contrast viral marketing with affiliate marketing.

5. Identify the contribution of Web 2.0. What does it add to EC?

6. Discuss the reasons companies embark on social commerce.

7. Distinguish an enterprise social network from a public one such as Facebook.

8. Carefully examine the nontechnological limitations of EC. Which are company-dependent and which are generic?

9. Why are virtual worlds such as Second Life related to EC?

10. Register at **ibm.com/ibm/ideasfromibm/us/ceo/20080505** and download IBM's study "The Enterprise of the Future" (IBM 2008). In one page, summarize how the enterprise of the future differs from today's enterprise.

TOPICS FOR CLASS DISCUSSION AND DEBATES

1. How can EC be a business pressure and an organizational response to other business pressure?

2. Debate: Does digital business eliminate the "human touch" in trading? And if "yes," is it really bad?

3. Why do companies frequently change their business models? What are the advantages? The disadvantages?

4. Debate: EC eliminates more jobs than it creates. Should we restrict its use and growth?

5. Debate: Will online fashion hurt fashion retailers?

INTERNET EXERCISES

1. Visit bigboxx.com and identify the services the company provides to its customers. What type of EC is this? What business model(s) does bigboXX use?

2. Visit amazon.com and locate recent information in the following areas:
   a. Find the five top-selling books on EC.
   b. Find a review of one of these books.
   c. Review the personalized services you can get from Amazon.com and describe the benefits you receive from shopping there.
   d. Review the products directory.

3. Visit priceline.com and zappos.com and identify the various business models used by both. Discuss their advantages.

4. Go to nike.com and design your own shoes. Next, visit office.microsoft.com and create your own business card. Finally, enter jaguar.com and configure the car of your dreams. What are the advantages of each activity? The disadvantages?

5. Try to save on your next purchase. Visit letsbuyit.com, kaboodle.com, yub.com, and buyerzone.com. Which site do you prefer? Why?

6. Enter espn.go.com, 123greetings.com, facebook.com and identify and list all the revenue sources on each of the companies' sites.

7. Enter lala.com and listen to some of the commercial-free digital songs offered (cost 10¢). What other digital products and services do they offer? Write a summary.

8. Enter philatino.com, stampauctioncentral.com, and statusint.com. Identify the business model(s) and revenue models they use. What are the benefits to sellers? To buyers?

9. Enter lowes.com. View the "design it" online feature and the animated "How Tos." Examine the Project Calculators and Gift Advisor features. Relate these to the business models and other EC features in this chapter.

10. Go to zipcar.com. What can this site help you do?

11. Enter digitalenterprise.org. Prepare a report regarding the latest EC models and developments.

12. Visit some websites that offer employment opportunities in EC (such as execunet.com and monster.com). Compare the EC salaries to salaries offered to accountants. For other information on EC salaries, check *Computerworld*'s annual salary survey, unixl.com, and salary.com.

13. Visit bluenile.com, diamond.com, and jewelry exchange.com. Compare the sites. Comment on the similarities and the differences.

14. Visit ticketmaster.com, ticketonline.com, and other sites that sell event tickets online. Assess the competition in online ticket sales. What services do the different sites provide?

15. Enter The Timberland Company (timberland.com) and design a pair of boots. Compare it to building your own sneakers at nike.com. Compare these sites to zappos.com/shoes.

16. Examine two or three of the following sites: prosper.com, swapthing.com, swaptree.com, peerflix.com, lala.com, swapvillage.com, bigvine.com, etc. Compare their business and revenue models.

TEAM ASSIGNMENTS AND PROJECTS

1. **Assignment for the Opening Case**

   Read the opening case and answer the following questions.

   a. Why would you buy (or not buy) from Net-a-Porter?
   b. Watch the video "The Future of Shopping" (youtube.com/watch?v=jDi0FNcaock). How would you integrate this development with Net-a-Porter?
   c. What are the advantages and disadvantages of the Net's physical stores?
   d. It is said that the Net is playing a significant role in transforming how designers reach customers. Explain why.
   e. Read the benefits of EC to customers (Section 1.7), which ones are most relevant here?
   f. What EC capabilities are helping the Net and its designers?
   g. Analyze the competition in the high-end fashion market.
   h. What is the importance of globalization in this case?
   i. Imitators are springing up on all sides. Even eBay and Amazon.com are expanding their fashion e-tailing efforts. What strategy do you suggest for the Net? (Hint: Read Brodie 2009 to get some ideas.)

2. Create an online group for studying EC or a particular aspect of EC that interests you. You can do this via Google Groups, a social network of your choice, or Yahoo! Groups. Each member of the group must have an e-mail account. Go to Yahoo! Groups

groups.yahoo.com and log in. At the bottom of the page, there is a section titled "Create your own Group."

Step 1: Click on "Start a Group."

Step 2: Select a category that best describes your group (use the Search Group Categories, or use the Browse Group Categories tool). You must find a category.

Step 3: Describe the purpose of the group and give it a name.

Step 4: Set up an e-mail address for sending messages to all group members.

Step 5: Each member must join the group (select "profile"); click on "Join this Group."

Step 6: Go to Word Verification Section; follow the instructions.

Step 7: Finish by clicking "Continue."

Step 8: Select a group moderator. Conduct a discussion online of at least two topics of the group's interest.

Step 9: Arrange for messages from the members to reach the moderator at least once a week.

Step 10: Find a similar group (use Yahoo!'s "find a group" and make a connection). Write a report for your instructor.

3. Each team will research two EC success stories. Members of the group should examine companies that operate solely online and some that extensively utilize a click-and-mortar strategy. Each team should identify the critical success factors for their companies and present a report to the other teams.

4. Each team selects a business-oriented social network such as LinkedIn, Xing, or Viadeo. Each team presents the essential capabilities of the site, the attributes, etc. Each team will try to convince other students why their site is superior.

5. Watch the video *Part 1-E-Commerce* (8 minutes) at youtube.com/watch?v=OY2tcQ574Ew.

   a. Update all the data shown in the video.
   b. What fundamental change is introduced by EC?
   c. What is the first mover advantage discussed in the video?
   d. Amazon.com and other companies that lost money during the time the video was made are making lots of money today; find out why.
   e. Identify all the EC business models discussed in the video.
   f. How can one conduct an EC business from home?
   g. EC is considered a disruptor. In what ways?

6. All class members that are not registered in Second Life need to register and create their avatars. Let each team address one of the following areas:

   - Trading virtual properties
   - Creating buildings, projects, stores
   - Shopping and retail outlets
   - Virtual jobs
   - Learning and training
   - Other topics

   a. Prepare a description of what is going on in that area.
   b. Have members' avatars interact with other avatars. Write a report about your experience.
   c. What can you learn from this project?

Closing Case

E-COMMERCE AT THE GERMAN SOCCER LEAGUE (BUNDESLIGA)

Soccer is one of the most popular games in the world. The international governing organization for soccer is FIFA (*fifa.com*) where 265 million people play in over 200 different countries. Most of these countries have their own national leagues where soccer teams compete against each other. One popular league is the Bundesliga, the German soccer league that consists of 18 different soccer clubs, including the European Champion's League winner FC Bayern München. Germany has 27,000 different soccer clubs that are all united under the Deutsche Fussball Liga (DFL) or German Soccer Association. Not just a popular sport, soccer is a multibillion-dollar industry, and the DFL, as well as individual clubs, are involved in merchandizing, advertising, and other marketing activities. E-commerce provides new opportunities for these activities.

Providing Information

The DFL website (*bundesliga.de/en/index.php*) targets several different groups: fans, sponsors, advertising customers, and officials from both big and small clubs who are also members of the DFL. The main objective, however, is to provide fans with general information including soccer-related news features, match and player statistics, as well as links to purchasing tickets online. The website provides historical records and tools for creating match forecasts and "what-if" analyses for future games on the website. Fans can also subscribe to a soccer newsletter that can be customized, for example, with information about the German Bundesliga and also news about other soccer leagues including the Premier League in the United Kingdom, Ligue 1 in France, Serie A in Italy, and La Liga in Spain. The association assists the sport in general and also represents smaller soccer clubs online. Additionally, the DFL provides internal information for other soccer club officials including details of rule changes and other administrative tools for officials. Information about the association and its partners, sponsors, and board members is also available.

In addition, instructions for potential partners are provided to help them understand how they can capitalize on advertising opportunities and how to issue co-branded credit or debit cards.

Videos and Online Games

The website *Bundesliga.de* hosts videos showing the best goals from the most recent games as well as commentary on topical news features. Games and online competitions are also available for fans to enjoy including fantasy leagues where fans can act as soccer managers for their favorite club or dream team—choosing the formation, selecting the team, and making the tactical changes as they play against other virtual managers. The role-playing game uses artificial intelligence by storing information about previous behaviors of the player and then using it to form the basis of future decisions. By adding media-rich content, fans are more likely to visit the site and so traffic to the website increases.

Information, Wireless News, and Social Networks

The DFL supports the broadcast of information to cell phones via SMS and to computers and mobile smartphones via RSS or Twitter. Fans can find out information about other soccer games while they are in a stadium watching a live match. Furthermore, the DFL has a presence on social network sites including Facebook and Twitter where fans can exchange comments and thoughts. The DFL website also serves as a mediation platform that, for example, acts as an agent for

establishing contact between fans who want to drive to an away game.

Fans can receive real-time local news including sport scores texted to their cell phones from several stadiums that are equipped with state-of-the-art wireless systems. Smartphones now allow users to go online and view games that are streamed in real time or view photos of stadiums that are shown on TV. Quick response codes allow smartphone users to receive a sales discount in the stadium by taking a picture of the discount code and then storing the information using an app (Mobile Tagging). The system also enables employees to process ticket sales quickly (Mobile Ticketing).

Online Shop

The DFL has decided not to host an online shop selling merchandise and tickets. Instead, it implemented an affiliate program where customers are referred to club websites or partner ticket distributors, such as Ticketmaster. In return, the DFL receives a small agency fee for the referral. The DFL also operates as a travel agency by selling rail and flight tickets online not only for fans but also for officials, business partners, and the soccer teams themselves who are travelling from game to game.

Sources: Compiled from www.bundesliga.de/en/ (accessed August 2011) and Mayar and Ramsey (2011)

Questions

1. Identify all of the applications and decide if they support B2B, B2C, or B2E.
2. How does playing online games on the DFL´s site relate to EC?
3. Compare the DFL information available on Facebook and Twitter.
4. Find additional DFL-related applications not cited in this case.
5. Why does Bundesliga.de not host a web shop?

ONLINE RESOURCES
available at pearsonglobaleditions.com/turban

Online Files

W1.1   Application Case: Dell—Using E-Commerce for Success

W1.2   Application Case: Campusfood.com—Student Entrepreneurs

W1.3   Major Characteristics of Web 2.0

W1.4   Application Case: Beijing 2008: A Digital Olympics

W1.5   Response Activities for Organizations

W1.6   Representative EC Business Models

W1.7   Basic Resources for E-Commerce

Other Resources

Online Files

Online Files organized by chapter number support the content of each chapter.

Online Tutorials

Twelve tutorials are available at the book's website

Miscellaneous Resources

(*pearsonglobaleditions.com/turban*).

Comprehensive Educational Websites

ecommerce-journal.com: Source for news, events, etc., about e-commerce.

libraries.rutgers.edu/rul/rr_gateway/research_guides/busi/ecomm. shtml: Electronic Resource Guide: Electronic Commerce offers resources and links to Internet statistics—see ClickZ Stats, Nielsen/NetRatings, U.S. Census Bureau, and comScore.

socialcomputingjournal.com: Social Computing Journal is an open forum with articles on the Internet, social commerce, collective intelligence, and all things Web 2.0.

webopedia.com: Online encyclopedia dedicated to computer technology.

whatis.techtarget.com/definition: Detailed definitions of most e-commerce and other technological topics.

Other resources for the entire book are provided in Online File W1.7.

REFERENCES

Alter, A. "My Virtual Summer Job." *SmallBiz.com*, May 21. 2008. smsmallbiz.com/profiles/My_Virtual_Summer_Job.html (accessed March 2011).

Bisson, P., et al. "The Global Grid." *McKinsey Quarterly*, June 2010.

Blakely, L. "Making Their Point." *Business 2.0*, April 23, 2007.

Brodie, J. "The Amazon of Fashion." *Fortune*, September 14, 2009.

Burns, E. "U.S. Wireless Subscriptions Surge Past 250 Million." *Clickz.com*, November 27, 2007. clickz.com/showPage.html?page=3627705 (accessed April 2011).

Carpenter, S. "A TC Teardown: What Makes Groupon Tick." May 2, 2010. techcrunch.com/2010/05/02/teardown-groupon (accessed February 2011).

De Jonge, A. *Social Networks Around the World*. North Charleston, SC: Booksurge Publications, 2008.

Drucker, P. *Managing in the Next Society*. New York: Truman Talley Books, 2002.

eMarket Services News. "eCommerce Doubles in China." September 21, 2010. emarketservices.com/start/News/International/news/e-Commerce-doubles-in-China.html?xz=0&cc=1&sd=1&ci=3077 (accessed April 2011).

Farivar, C. "New Ways to Pay." *Business 2.0*, July 1, 2004. forbes.com/forbes/2006/0508/122.html (accessed March 2011).

Fowler, G. "Teenage-Entrepreneurs: Personal Finance News from Yahoo! Finance." May 11, 2010. finance.yahoo.com/career-work/article/109472/teenage-entrepreneurs?mod=career-work (accessed November 2010).

Franklin, C. "Code, Networks Are the Key to Smarter Cars." *Information Week*, November 13, 2009.

Gaskin, S., and A. Evans. *Go! With Ethics in Cyberspace Getting Started*. Upper Saddle River, NJ: Prentice Hall, 2010.

Harmony Hollow Software. "What Are the Barriers of Implementing E-Commerce Solutions?" 2006. harmonyhollow.net/webmaster-resources/ecommerce/15604.php (accessed March 2011).

Harrington, R. "The Transformer" (an e-mail interview with *Baseline*'s editor-in-chief, J. McCormic). *Baseline*, April 2006.

Hickins, M. "Arizona Cardinals Score Technology Touchdown." *IT Infrastructure*, March 11, 2009.

Hsieh, T. "Why I Sold Zappos." *INC*, June 2010a.

Hsieh, T. "Zappos's CEO on Going to Extremes for Customers." *Harvard Business Review*, July–August 2010b.

Hunt, M. "Make Money Online." *Womansday.com*, October 1, 2010.

IBM. "IBM Global CEO Study: The Enterprise of the Future." IBM special study, 2008.

IDC. "IDC Finds More of the World's Population Connecting to the Internet in New Ways and Embracing Web 2.0 Activities." June 25, 2008. idc.com/getdoc.jsp?containerId=prUS21303808 (accessed April 2011).

Jones, S., and S. Fox. "Generations Online in 2009." *PewResearch.org*, January 8, 2009. pewresearch.org/pubs/1093/generations-online (accessed April 2011).

Joyner, A. *The eBay Billionaire's Club*. Hoboken, NJ: Wiley Publications, 2007.

Karakas, F. "Welcome to World 2.0: The New Digital Ecosystem." *Journal of Business Strategy*, 3, no. 4 (2009).

Khosrow-Pour, M. (Ed.). *E-Commerce Trends for Organizational Advancement*. Hershey, PA: Information Science Reference, 2010.

Khosrow-Pour, M. (Ed.). *Encyclopedia of E-Commerce, E-Government, and Mobile Commerce*. Hershey, PA: Idea Group Reference, 2006.

Logistics Online. "FKI Logistex 'Wows' Zappos.com with New Automated Order Fulfillment Center." March 23,

2008. **logisticsonline.com/article.mvc/FKI-Logistex-Wows-Zapposcom-With-New-Automate-00021** (accessed April 2011).

MacDonald, K. *One Red Paperclip: Or How an Ordinary Man Achieved His Dream with the Help of a Simple Office Supply.* New York: Three Rivers Press, 2007.

Mayar, V and Ramsey, G. *Digital Impact: The Two Secrets to Online Marketing Success*, Hoboken, New Jersey: John Wiley & Sons, 2011.

McCafferty, D. "How the NFL Is Using Business Technology and Information Technology Together." *Baseline*, August 8, 2008.

McGee, M. K. "Chiefs of the Year: Internet Call to Arms." *InformationWeek*, November 27, 2000.

Nutley, M. "Forget E-Commerce; Social Commerce Is Where It's At." *Marketing Week*, July 28, 2010. **marketingweek.co.uk/disciplines/digital/forget-e-commerce-social-commerce-is-where-its-at/3016388. article** (accessed November 2010).

O'Reilly, T. "What Is Web 2.0?" *OReillynet.com*, September 30, 2005. **oreillynet.com/pub/a/oreilly/tim/news/2005/09/30/what-is-web-20.html** (accessed March 2011).

Plunkett, J. W. *Plunkett's E-Commerce and Internet Business Almanac 2011.* Houston, TX: Plunkett Research, Ltd., March 2011.

Prahalad, C. K., and M. S. Krishnan. *The New Age of Innovation.* New York: McGraw-Hill, 2008.

Rappa, M. "Business Models on the Web." *Digitalenterprise. org*, **digitalenterprise.org/models/models.html** (accessed March 2011).

Rowe, R. "Facebook and Twitter Impact Fashion Industry." *Goshtv.net*, May 19, 2010. **goshtv.net/2010/05/19/facebook-and-twitter-impact-fashion-industry** (accessed April 2011)

Rymaszewski, M., et al. *Second Life: The Official Guide.* Indianapolis, IN: Wiley Publishers, Inc., 2008.

Schonfeld, E. "ComScore: Internet Population Passes One Billion; Top 15 Countries." *Techcrunch.com*, January 23, 2009. **techcrunch.com/2009/01/23/comscore-internet-population-passes-one-billion-top-15-countries** (accessed April 2011).

Strategic Direction. "DotCom Boom and Bust: The Secrets of E-Commerce Failure and Success." February 2005.

Taylor, B. "Why Zappos Pays New Employees to Quit—and You Should Too." *Harvard Business Publishing*, May 19, 2008. **blogs.harvardbusiness.org/taylor/2008/05/why_zappos_pays_new_employees.html** (accessed April 2011).

Tice, C., et al. "Emerging Jobs in Social Media." 2010. **hotjobs.yahoo.com/career-articles-emerging_jobs_in_social_media-1274** (accessed April 2011).

U.S. Census Bureau. "E-Stats: E-Commerce 2008." May 27, 2010. **census.gov/estats** (accessed April 2011).

Van Toorn, C., D. Bunker, K. Yee, and S. Smith. "The Barriers to the Adoption of E-Commerce by Micro Businesses, Small Businesses and Medium Enterprises." *Sixth International Conference on Knowledge, Culture, and Change in Organisations*, Prato, Tuscany, Italy, July 11–14, 2006.

Vise, D. A., and M. Malseed. *The Google Story: For Google's 10th Birthday.* New York: Delacorte Press, 2008.

Wall Street Journal. "Zappos CEO Posts Letter to Staff." July 22, 2009. **blogs.wsj.com/digits/2009/07/22/zappos-ceos-letter-to-staff** (accessed October 2009).

Weintraub, S. "The Numbers Don't Lie: Mobile Devices Overtaking PCs." *Fortune*, August 11, 2010. **tech. fortune.cnn.com/2010/08/11/the-great-game-mobile-devices-overtaking-pcs** (accessed April 2011).

CHAPTER 2

E- COMMERCE: MECHANISMS, INFRASTRUCTURE, AND TOOLS

Content

Learning Objectives

Upon completion of this chapter, you will be able to:

1. Describe the major electronic commerce (EC) activities and processes and the mechanisms that support them.

2. Define e-marketplaces and list their components.

3. List the major types of e-marketplaces and describe their features.

4. Describe electronic catalogs, search engines, and shopping carts.

5. Describe the major types of auctions and list their characteristics.

6. Discuss the benefits and limitations of e-auctions.

7. Describe bartering and negotiating online.

8. Describe virtual communities.

9. List the major Web 2.0 tools and their use in EC.

10. Describe social networks as an EC mechanism.

11. Understand virtual worlds and their use in EC.

12. Describe Web 3.0 and define Web 4.0.

WEB 2.0 TOOLS AT EASTERN MOUNTAIN SPORTS

Eastern Mountain Sports (EMS) (*ems.com*) is a medium-sized specialty retailer (with annual sales of $29.3 million) that sells goods in more than 64 physical stores in 12 states, through mail-order catalogs and online. Operating in a very competitive environment, the company uses leading-edge information technologies. EMS is now using a complementary set of Web 2.0 tools in order to increase collaboration, information sharing, and communication among stores and their employees, suppliers, and customers. Let's see how this works.

The Business Intelligence Strategy and System

During the past few years, the company has implemented a business intelligence (BI) system (see Online Tutorial T8) that includes business performance management and dashboards. (A *dashboard* is a graphical presentation of performance results). A BI system collects raw data from multiple sources, processes them into a data warehouse (or data mart), and conducts analyses that include comparing performance to operational metrics in order to assess the health of the business (see details in Turban et al. 2011).

The illustration below shows how the system works. Point-of-sale (POS) information and other relevant data, which are available on an IBM mainframe computer, are loaded into Microsoft's SQL server and into a database (see Online Tutorial T8). The data are then analyzed with Information Builders' WebFOCUS platform. The results are presented via a series of dashboards that users can view by using Web browsers.

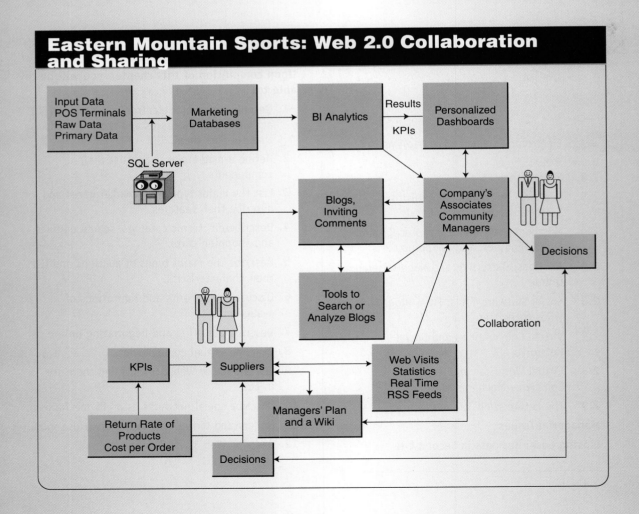

Eastern Mountain Sports: Web 2.0 Collaboration and Sharing

The Web 2.0 Collaboration, Sharing, and Communications System

The company created a multifunctional employee workbench called *E-Basecamp*. E-Basecamp contains all information relevant to corporate goals integrated with productivity tools (e.g., Excel) and role-based content customized to each individual user. Then, EMS added a set of Web 2.0 tools. The system facilitates collaboration among internal and external stakeholders. EMS uses 20 operation metrics (e.g., inventory levels and turns). These metrics also cover e-tailing, where e-commerce managers monitor Web traffic and conversion rates on an hourly basis. The dashboard shows deviations from targets by means of a color code. The system uses the Web 2.0 tools that are illustrated in the exhibit.

- **Wikis.** *Wikis* are used to encourage collaborative interaction throughout the company. Dashboard users are encouraged to post an hypothesis or request for help and then invite commentary and suggestions, almost like a notepad alongside the dashboard.

- **Blogs.** Blogs were created around specific data or a key metric. The blogs are used to post information and invite comment. Tools are then used to archive, search, and categorize blogs for easy reference. For example, store managers post an inquiry or explanation regarding sale deviations (anomalies). Keeping comments on blogs lets readers observe patterns they might have overlooked using data analysis alone.

- **RSS feeds.** RSS feeds (*en.wikipedia.org/wiki/RSS_feeds*) are embedded into the dashboards to drive more focused inquiries. These feeds are the base for information sharing and online conversations. For example, by showing which items are selling better than others, users can collectively analyze the transaction characteristics and selling behaviors that produce the high sales. The knowledge acquired then cascades throughout the organization.

Going to Business Partners Externally

Suppliers can monitor the return rate of a product on the dashboard and invite store managers to provide explanations and suggestions using wikis or blogs. The objective is to build a tighter bond with business partners. For instance, by attaching a blog to suppliers' dashboards, the suppliers can view current sales information and post comments to the blogs. Product managers use a wiki to post challenges for the next season (such as a proposed percentage increase in sales) and then ask vendors to suggest innovative ways to achieve these goals. Several of the customers and other business partners subscribe to RSS feeds.

Called *Extreme Deals*, blogs are also embedded into the EMS product life-cycle management (PLM) tool. This allows vendors to have virtual conversations with the product development managers.

The major impact of the Web 2.0 collaboration tools is that instead of having conversations occur in the hallway (where you need to be in the right place at the right time), conversations take place on blogs, wikis, and discussion forums where all interested parties can participate.

Sources: Compiled from Nerille (2007) and from *ems.com* (accessed November 2010).

WHAT WE CAN LEARN . . .

Eastern Mountain Sports was successful in bolstering communication and collaboration both among its own managers and with its suppliers. It did so with Web 2.0 tools: blogs, wikis, and RSS feeds. These tools facilitated the company's business processes and their existing information systems. Web 2.0 tools enhance the activities of e-commerce, business-to-employee (B2E) information sharing, B2B (as in this case), and e-tailing (business-to-consumer). The Web 2.0 tools are the newest mechanisms of EC and are introduced in this chapter (Section 2.4 and Sections 2.6–2.8) together with the more traditional mechanisms that support selling and buying online.

2.1 ELECTRONIC COMMERCE MECHANISMS: AN OVERVIEW

The many EC models and types of transactions presented in Chapter 1 are enabled by different mechanisms. To begin with, most B2C applications are conducted on the Internet. In addition, the generic enablers of any information system including databases, networks, security, software and server software, operating systems, hardware (Web servers), and hosting services need to be established. Then come the special EC enablers that are presented in this chapter such as electronic markets, shopping carts, and e-catalog services such as payment and order fulfillment, which are needed as well as CRM and streaming for rich media. Also, there are different methods for executing EC, such as buying at a fixed price or at an auction, and each method has a different support mechanism. In this chapter, the major EC mechanisms are described so that you will understand what they are when you read about them in the forthcoming chapters.

EC ACTIVITIES AND SUPPORT MECHANISMS

The EC trading activities are divided into six categories, which are listed on the left side of Exhibit 2.1. Each activity is supported by one or more EC mechanisms, which are

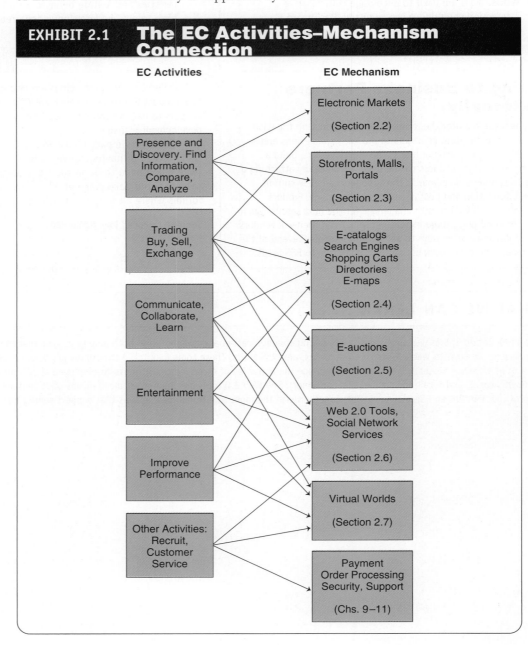

EXHIBIT 2.1   The EC Activities–Mechanism Connection

EC Activities

- Presence and Discovery. Find Information, Compare, Analyze
- Trading Buy, Sell, Exchange
- Communicate, Collaborate, Learn
- Entertainment
- Improve Performance
- Other Activities: Recruit, Customer Service

EC Mechanism

- Electronic Markets (Section 2.2)
- Storefronts, Malls, Portals (Section 2.3)
- E-catalogs Search Engines Shopping Carts Directories E-maps (Section 2.4)
- E-auctions (Section 2.5)
- Web 2.0 Tools, Social Network Services (Section 2.6)
- Virtual Worlds (Section 2.7)
- Payment Order Processing Security, Support (Chs. 9–11)

shown on the right side of Exhibit 2.1, along with the section number in this chapter, where they are presented. Additional mechanisms exist for special activities, such as payment (Chapter 10), security (Chapter 9), and order fulfillment (Chapter 11). Also standard IT technologies such as RFID, EDI, and extranets are described in Online Tutorials T3 and T11.

Next, we present one of the major processes in EC, which is online trading.

SELLERS, BUYERS, AND TRANSACTIONS

Typically, a seller (retailer, wholesaler, or a manufacturer) sells to customers. The seller buys from suppliers either raw materials (as a manufacturer) or components for assembly (as an assembler), or finished goods (as a retailer). This process is illustrated in Exhibit 2.2.

The selling company, shown as "Our Company," appears in the center of the exhibit. Internally, processes and transactions are conducted there in different functional departments and are supported by EC applications. The customers place orders (in B2C or B2B), and Our Company fulfills them. Our Company buys materials, products, services, and so on directly from suppliers, from distributors (B2B), or from the government (G2B) in a process called *e-procurement*. Sometimes intermediaries are involved in this process. Let's zero in on what happens during a typical purchasing process.

The Purchasing Process

Customers buy goods online in different ways. The most common way is purchasing from catalogs at fixed prices. Sometimes prices may be negotiated or discounted. Another way to determine price is *dynamic pricing*, which refers to nonfixed prices such as those in auctions or stock (commodity) markets. The buyers use the process illustrated in Exhibit 2.3.

The process starts with logging into a seller's website, registering (if needed), and entering into an online catalog or the buyer's "My Account." E-catalogs can be very large, so a search mechanism may be needed. Also, buyers usually like to compare prices. Some sellers (e.g., American Airlines) provide comparisons with competing vendors. Otherwise, the buyer may need to leave the site or do price comparisons *before* entering into the specific seller's store. If not satisfied, the buyer will abandon the site. If satisfied, the buyer will select an item and place it in a *shopping cart* (or bag). The buyer may return to the catalog to choose more items. Each selected item is placed in the shopping cart. When the shopping is completed, the buyer goes to a checkout page, where a shipment option is selected from a menu. Also, a payment option may be available. For example, newegg.com lets you pay by credit card, with PayPal, by check after billing, in installments, and so on. After checking all details for accuracy, the buyer *submits* the order.

The major mechanisms that support this process are described in Sections 2.3 and 2.4 of this chapter. The place where buying and selling occurs is called an *e-marketplace*, which we introduce next.

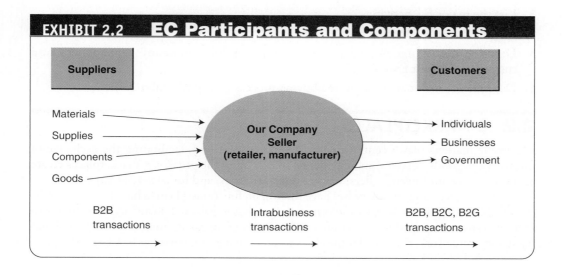

EXHIBIT 2.2 **EC Participants and Components**

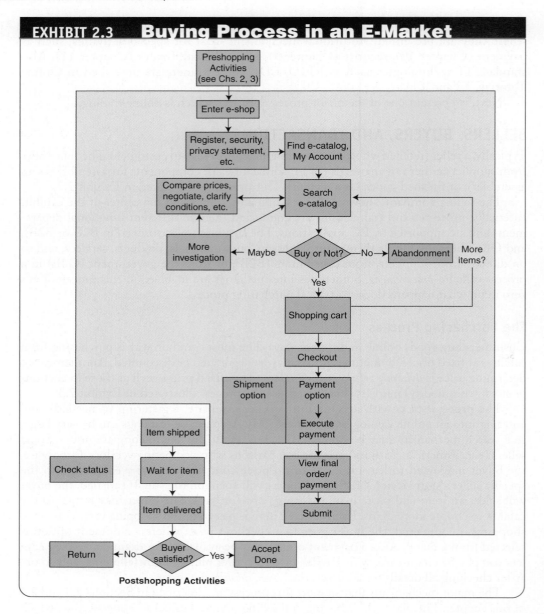

EXHIBIT 2.3   Buying Process in an E-Market

Section 2.1 ▶ REVIEW QUESTIONS

1. List the major EC activities.
2. List the major EC mechanisms.
3. Describe the selling–buying process among a selling company, its suppliers, and customers (consult Exhibit 2.2).
4. Describe the major activities in the buying process (consult Exhibit 2.3).

2.2 E-MARKETPLACES

Electronic markets play a central role in the digital economy, facilitating the exchange of information, goods, services, and payments. In executing the process, e-marketplaces create economic value for buyers, sellers, market intermediaries, and for society at large.

Markets (electronic or otherwise) have three main functions: (1) matching buyers and sellers; (2) facilitating the exchange of information, goods, services, and payments associated with market transactions; and (3) providing an institutional infrastructure, such as a legal and regulatory framework, that enables the efficient functioning of the market (see Exhibit 2.4).

EXHIBIT 2.4   Functions of a Market

Matching of Buyers and Sellers	Facilitation of Transactions	Institutional Infrastructure

• Determination of product offerings
  Product features offered by sellers
  Aggregation of different products
• Search (of buyers for sellers and
  of sellers for buyers)
    Price and product information
    Organizing bids and bartering
    Matching seller offerings with
      buyer preferences
• Price discovery
    Process and outcome in
    determination of prices
    Enabling price comparisons
• Others
    Providing sales leads
    Provide W2.0 tools
    Arrange auction
	• Logistics
	    Delivery of information, goods,
	      or services to buyers
	• Settlement
	    Transfer of payments to sellers
	• Escrow services
	• Trust
	    Credit system, reputations,
	      rating agencies such as
	      Consumer Reports and the
	      BBB, special escrow and online
	      trust agencies
	• Communication
	    Posting buyers' requests
	    Posting RFQs
	• Mechanisms: provide catalogs, etc.
		• Legal
		    Commercial code, contract law,
		      dispute resolution, intellectual
		      property protection
		• Regulatory
		    Rules and regulations, compliance,
		      monitoring, enforcement
		• Discovery
		    Provides market information
		      (e.g., about competition,
		      government regulations)

Sources: Compiled from Bakos (1998), from *E-Market Services* (2006), and from author's experience.

ELECTRONIC MARKETS

The major place for conducting EC transactions is the electronic market. An **e-marketplace** (also called *e-market, virtual market,* or *marketspace*) is a virtual market in which sellers and buyers meet and conduct different types of transactions. Customers exchange goods and services for money (or for other goods and services if bartering is used). The functions of an e-market are the same as those of a physical marketplace; however, computerized systems tend to make electronic markets much more efficient by providing more updated information and diverse support services to buyers and sellers such as rapid execution.

EC has increased market efficiencies by expediting and or improving the functions listed in Exhibit 2.4. Furthermore, EC has been able to significantly decrease the cost of executing these functions.

The emergence of *electronic* marketplaces, especially Internet-enabled ones, changed several of the processes used in trading and supply chains. These changes, driven by technology, resulted in many cases of:

e-marketplace
An online market, usually B2B, in which buyers and sellers exchange goods or services; the three types of e-marketplaces are private, public, and consortia.

> ❭ Greater information richness of the transactional and relational environment
>
> ❭ Lower information search time and cost for buyers
>
> ❭ Diminished information asymmetry between sellers and buyers
>
> ❭ Possibly less time between purchase and possession of physical products purchased in the e-marketplace (especially if the product can be digitized)
>
> ❭ Greater temporal proximity between time of purchase and time of possession of digital products purchased in the e-marketplace
>
> ❭ The ability of buyers, sellers, and the virtual market to each be in a different location
>
> ❭ The ability for EC to leverage capabilities with increased effectiveness and lower transaction and distribution costs, leading to more efficient "friction-free" markets

COMPONENTS OF AND THE PARTICIPANTS IN E-MARKETPLACES

marketspace
A marketplace in which sellers and buyers exchange goods and services for money (or for other goods and services), but do so electronically.

A **marketspace** includes electronic transactions that bring about a new distribution of goods and services. The major components and players in a marketspace are customers, sellers, products and services (physical or digital), infrastructure, a front end, a back end, intermediaries and other business partners, and support services. A brief description of each follows:

▶ **Customers.** More than 2 billion Internet surfers worldwide who surf the Web are potential buyers of the goods and services offered on the Internet. These consumers are looking for bargains, customized items, collectors' items, entertainment, socialization, and more. They are in the driver's seat. They can search for detailed information, compare, bid, and sometimes negotiate. Organizations are the largest consumers, accounting for more than 85 percent of EC volume and value activities.

▶ **Sellers.** Millions of storefronts on the Web are advertising and offering a huge variety of items. These stores are owned by companies, government agencies, or individuals. Every day it is possible to find new offerings of products and services. Sellers can sell directly from their websites or from public e-marketplaces.

digital products
Goods that can be transformed to digital format and delivered over the Internet.

▶ **Products and services.** One of the major differences between the marketplace and the marketspace is the possible digitization of products and services in a marketspace. Although both types of markets can sell physical products, they can also sell **digital products**, which are goods that can be transformed to digital format. However, marketspaces can instantly deliver the purchased product over the Internet. In addition to digitization of software, music, and airline tickets, it is possible to digitize dozens of other products and services, as shown in Online File W2.1. Digital products have different cost curves than those of physical products. In digitization, most of the costs are fixed, and variable costs are very low. Thus, profits will increase very rapidly as volume increases, once the fixed costs are paid.

▶ **Infrastructure.** The marketspace infrastructure includes electronic networks, hardware, software, and more.

front end
The portion of an e-seller's business processes through which customers interact, including the seller's portal, electronic catalogs, a shopping cart, a search engine, and a payment gateway.

▶ **Front end.** Customers interact with a marketspace via a **front end**. The major components of the front end can include the seller's portal, electronic catalogs, a shopping cart, a search engine, an auction engine, and a payment gateway.

▶ **Back end.** All the activities that are related to order aggregation and fulfillment, inventory management, purchasing from suppliers, accounting and finance, insurance, payment processing, packaging, and delivery are done in what is termed the **back end** of the business.

back end
The activities that support online order fulfillment, inventory management, purchasing from suppliers, payment processing, packaging, and delivery.

▶ **Intermediaries.** In marketing, an **intermediary** is typically a third party that operates between manufacturers and buyers. Intermediaries of all kinds offer their services on the Web. Some are manual, many are electronic. The role of these electronic intermediaries is frequently different from that of regular intermediaries (such as wholesalers or retailers), as will be seen throughout the text, especially in Chapters 3 and 4. For example, online intermediaries create and manage the online markets. They help match buyers and sellers, provide escrow services, and help customers and/or sellers institute and complete transactions. Physical intermediaries may be eliminated or their job be computerized as shown next.

intermediary
A third party that operates between sellers and buyers.

DISINTERMEDIATION AND REINTERMEDIATION

Intermediaries usually provide two types of services: (1) They provide relevant information about demand, supply, prices, and requirements and, in doing so, help match sellers and buyers; (2) They offer value-added services such as transfer of products, escrow, payment arrangements, consulting, or assistance in finding a business partner. In general, the first type of service can be fully automated and thus it is likely to be assumed by e-marketplaces, infomediaries, and portals that provide free or low-fee services. The second type requires expertise, such as knowledge of the industry, the products, and technological trends, and therefore it can only be partially automated.

Intermediaries that provide only (or mainly) the first type of service may be eliminated; this phenomenon is called **disintermediation**. An example is the airline industry and its push for selling electronic tickets directly by the airlines. As of 2004, most airlines require customers to pay $5 or more per ticket if they buy a ticket from an agent or by phone, which is equivalent to the agent's commission. This is resulting in the *disintermediation* of travel agents from the purchasing process. In another example, discount stockbrokers that only execute trades manually are disappearing. However, brokers who manage electronic intermediation are not only surviving but may also be prospering (e.g., Priceline and Expedia in travel and Ameritrade Corp. in stock trading). This phenomenon, in which disintermediated entities or newcomers take on new intermediary roles, is called *reintermediation* (see Chapter 3).

Disintermediation is more likely to occur in supply chains involving several intermediaries, as illustrated by Blue Nile in Case 2.1.

disintermediation
Elimination of intermediaries between sellers and buyers.

CASE 2.1

EC Application

HOW BLUE NILE INC. IS CHANGING THE JEWELRY INDUSTRY

Blue Nile Inc. (*bluenile.com*), a pure-play online e-tailer that specializes in diamonds and jewelry, capitalized on online diamond sales as a dot-com start-up in 1999. The company provides a textbook case of how EC fundamentally undercuts the traditional way of doing business.

The Opportunity

Using the B2C EC model—knocking out expensive stores and intermediaries and then slashing prices (up to 35 percent less than rivals to gain market share)—Blue Nile captured a high market share in a short time, making a sizable profit by inducing more people to buy online.

How did the start-up defy conventional wisdom that diamonds could not be sold online? Basically, Blue Nile offers a huge selection of diamonds and more information on diamonds than a jewelry expert offers in a physical store. In November 2010, Blue Nile offered about 70,000 round diamonds that could be used to build a customized wedding ring. No physical store can offer so many diamonds. It also features educational guides in plain English and provides independent (and trusted) quality ratings for every stone. A customer can look over a rating scale for cut, clarity, color, and so on and then conduct a price comparison with Diamond.com (*diamond.com*) and other online stores. Most important is the 30-day 100 percent

money-back guarantee (now an online industry standard). This provides customers a comfort level against fraud and gives Blue Nile a competitive edge against stores that take the stones back but charge a fee to do so. The company has a mobile website for iPhone and Android users (*m.bluenile.com* and *bluenile.com*). You can compare prices and quality while you search the inventory. The site provides a live chat, financing services, a build-your-own engagement ring, gift ideas, and much more.

The Results

Blue Nile sales reached $129 million in 2003 (a 79 percent increase over 2002), with a net income of $27 million. In 2007, sales exceeded $320 million (40 percent annual growth). The company became the eighth-largest specialty jewelry company in the United States and went public in 2004 (one of the most successful IPOs of 2004). While sales fell during the economic downturn in 2008, in 2009 the company rallied again with a 2.3 percent growth.

To sell $320 million in jewelry, a traditional retail chain needs 300 stores and close to 3,000 employees. Blue Nile does it with one 10,000-square-foot warehouse and 190 staffers. The company also bypasses the industry's tangled supply chain, in which a diamond may pass through five or more middlemen before reaching a retailer.

(continued)

CASE 2.1   (continued)

Blue Nile deals directly with original suppliers, such as Thaigem.com.

This is one reason why in the United States some 465 small jewelry stores closed in 2003 alone. The survivors specialize in custom-crafted pieces. Large rivals try to fight back, streamlining the supply chain, emphasizing customer service, and even trying to sell some products online as an additional channel.

The future seems to be clear, as summarized by Roger Thompson, a small jeweler in Lambertville, New Jersey, who said, "Anyone with half a brain, who wants a diamond engagement ring will go to the Internet." So, he stopped selling diamonds. In the meantime, grooms make proposals with Blue Nile rings, saving $3,000 to $5,000.

Note that the competition in the jewelry business is very strong, not only from jewelry retailers, but also from general e-tailers such as *overstock.com*, *ice.com*, and *amazon.com*.

Sources: Compiled from Rivlin (2007), *BusinessWeek Online* (2006), and *bluenile.com* (accessed December 2010).

Questions

1. Using the classification of EC (Section 1.2, Chapter 1), what can you say about Blue Nile?
2. In what ways is the company changing its industry?
3. What are the critical success factors of the company?
4. Research Blue Nile's affiliate marketing program via LinkShare. How does this program help Blue Nile?
5. Competition between Blue Nile and Amazon.com will continue to increase. In your opinion, which one will win? (Visit their websites and see how they sell jewelry.)
6. Compare the following three sites: *diamond.com*, *ice.com*, and *bluenile.com*.
7. Follow the performance of Blue Nile's stock since 2003 (symbol: NILE, go to *money.cnn.com*). Compare it to the performance of the market average. What is your conclusion?
8. Find all the ways you can pay at Blue Nile when you shop.

TYPES OF E-MARKETPLACES

On the Web, the term *marketplace* differs from the physical one. We distinguish two types of e-marketplaces: private and public.

sell-side e-marketplace
A private e-marketplace in which one company sells either standard and/or customized products to qualified companies.

buy-side e-marketplace
A private e-marketplace in which one company makes purchases from invited suppliers.

Private E-Marketplaces

Private e-marketplaces are those owned and operated by a single company. Dell, HP, and United Airlines sell from their websites. Private markets are either sell-side or buy-side. In a **sell-side e-marketplace**, a company, (e.g., Net-a-Porter or Cisco) will sell either standard or customized products to individuals (B2C) or to businesses (B2B); this type of selling is considered to be one-to-many. In a **buy-side e-marketplace**, a company purchases from many potential suppliers; this type of purchasing is considered to be *many-to-one*, and it is a B2B activity. For example, Raffles Hotel (Online File W2.2) buys its supplies from approved vendors that come to its e-market. Private marketplaces may be open only to selected members and are not publicly regulated. We will return to the topic of private e-marketplaces in Chapters 3 (B2C) and 4 (B2B).

Public E-Marketplaces

Public e-marketplaces are usually B2B markets. They often are owned by a third party (not a seller or a buyer) or by a group of buying or selling companies (referred to as a consortium), and they serve many sellers and many buyers. These markets also are known as *exchanges* (e.g., a stock exchange). They are open to the public and usually are regulated by the government or the exchange's owners. Public e-marketplaces are presented in detail in Chapter 4.

Section 2.2 ❯ REVIEW QUESTIONS

1. Define e-marketplace and describe its attributes.
2. What is the difference between a physical marketplace and an e-marketplace (marketspace)?

3. List the components of a marketspace.

4. Define a digital product and provide five examples.

5. Describe private versus public e-markets.

2.3 CUSTOMER SHOPPING MECHANISMS: STOREFRONTS, MALLS, AND PORTALS

Several kinds of interactions exist among sellers, buyers, and e-marketplaces. The major B2C mechanisms are *storefronts* and *Internet malls*. Let's elaborate on these, as well as on the gateways to e-marketplaces—portals.

ELECTRONIC STOREFRONTS

A **Webstore (storefront)** refers to a single company's website where products and services are sold (see the screen capture below). It is an electronic store that usually has an online shopping cart associated with it. Many Webstores target a specific industry and find their own unique corner of the market. The storefront may belong to a manufacturer (e.g., geappliances.com and dell.com), to a retailer (e.g., zappos.com and wishlist.com.au), to individuals selling from home, or to another type of business. Note that companies that sell services (such as insurance) may refer to their storefronts as *portals*. An example of a service-related portal is an online hotel reservation system, as shown in Online File W2.2.

A Webstore includes several mechanisms that are necessary for conducting online sales. These are known as a *merchant software suite*. The most common mechanisms are an *electronic catalog*; a *search engine* that helps the consumer find products in the catalog; an *electronic cart* for holding items until checkout; *e-auction facilities* where auctions take place; a *payment gateway* where payment arrangements can be made; a *shipment court* where shipping arrangements are made; and *customer services*, which include product and warranty information.

Microsites

Microsite refers to a page or pages that are meant to function as an auxiliary supplement to a primary website. It adds information, usually editorial or commercial, about the primary website.

Webstore (storefront)
A single company's website where products or services are sold and usually has an online shopping cart associated with it. Many Webstores target a specific industry and find their own unique corner of the market.

Source: Courtesy of Seeds of Change. Used with permission.

ELECTRONIC MALLS

In addition to shopping at individual storefronts, consumers can shop in electronic malls (e-malls). Similar to malls in the physical world, an **e-mall (online mall)** is an online shopping location where many stores are located. For example, Mall of Maine (emallofmaine.com) is an e-mall that aggregates products, services, and providers in the state of Maine. It contains a directory of vacation services and product categories and the vendors in each category. When a consumer indicates the category he or she is interested in, the consumer is transferred to the appropriate independent *storefront*. This kind of mall does not provide any shared services; it is merely a directory. Other malls, such as Choice Mall (choicemall.com), do provide some shared services.

TYPES OF STORES AND MALLS

There are several different types of stores and malls:

- **General stores/malls.** These are large marketspaces that sell all kinds of products. Examples are amazon.com, choicemall.com, walmart.com, spree.com, and the major public portals (yahoo.com and msn.com). All major department stores and discount stores also fall into this category.
- **Specialized stores/malls.** These sell only one or a few kinds of products, such as shoes, books, flowers, wine, cars, electronics, or pet toys. 1800flowers.com sells flowers and related gifts; cars.com sells cars; fashionmall.com/beauty.html specializes in beauty products; and cattoys.com sells cat toys. Visit newegg.com for computer electronics and endless.com or zappos.com for shoes and accessories.
- **Regional versus global stores.** Some stores, such as e-grocers or sellers of heavy furniture, serve customers that live nearby. For example, parknshop.com serves the Hong Kong community only; it will not deliver outside of Hong Kong. However, some local stores will even sell to customers in other countries if the customer is willing to pay shipping, insurance, and other costs (e.g., see hothothot.com).
- **Pure-play versus click-and-mortar stores.** Stores may be pure online (i.e., virtual or pure-play) organizations, such as Blue Nile, Amazon.com, Buy.com, Newegg.com, or Cattoys.com. They do not have physical stores. Others are physical stores that also sell online (e.g., Walmart with walmart.com, 1-800-Flowers.com with 1800flowers.com, and Woolworths with woolworths.com.au). This second category is called *click-and-mortar*. Both categories will be described further in Chapter 3.

WEB (INFORMATION) PORTALS

A *portal* is an information gateway that is used in e-marketplaces, e-stores, and other types of EC (e.g., in e-collaboration, intrabusiness, and e-learning). A **Web portal** is a single point of access, through a Web browser, to critical business information located inside (via intranet) and outside (via Internet) of an organization. Many Web portals can be personalized for the users. Note that wireless devices are becoming portals for both enterprise and Internet access. A schematic view of a portal is shown in Exhibit 2.5. Information sources (external and internal) are shown on the left side, and integrated and process data are shown as output on the monitor's screen. For more on portals, see en.wikipedia.org/wiki/Web_portal.

Portals present information from diverse sources in a unified way. Apart from the search engine standard, Web portals offer other services such as e-mail, news, stock prices, entertainment, shopping capabilities, and other features. Portals provide a way for enterprises to provide a consistent look and feel with access control and procedures for multiple applications that otherwise would have been different entities altogether.

EXHIBIT 2.5   How a Portal Works

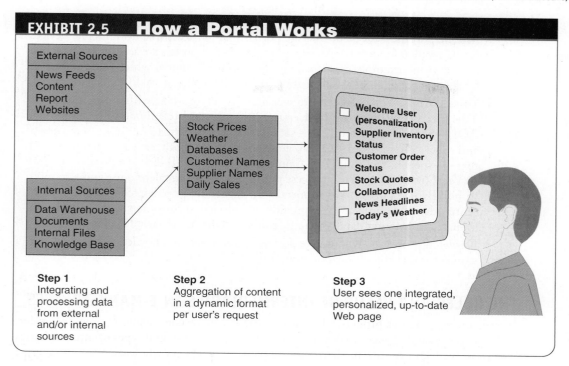

Step 1
Integrating and processing data from external and/or internal sources

Step 2
Aggregation of content in a dynamic format per user's request

Step 3
User sees one integrated, personalized, up-to-date Web page

Types of Portals

Portals can be described in many ways and assume many shapes. One way to distinguish among them is to look at their content, which can vary from narrow to broad, and their community or audience, which also can vary. The major types of portals are as follows:

▶ **Commercial (public) portals.** These portals offer content for diverse communities and are the most popular portals on the Internet. Although they can be customized by the user, they are still intended for broad audiences and offer fairly routine content, some in real time (e.g., a stock ticker and news about a few preselected items). Examples of such sites are yahoo.com, aol.com, and msn.com.

▶ **Corporate portals.** Corporate portals provide organized access to rich content within relatively narrow corporate and partners' communities. They also are known as *enterprise portals* or *enterprise information portals*. Corporate portals appear in different forms and are described in detail in Chapters 4 and 5. Examples of e-commerce portals can be found at sterlingcommerce.com.

▶ **Publishing portals.** These portals are intended for communities with specific interests. These portals involve relatively little customization of content, but provide extensive online search features and some interactive capabilities. Examples of such sites are techweb.com and zdnet.com.

▶ **Personal portals.** These target specific filtered information for individuals. They offer relatively narrow content and are typically very personalized, effectively having an audience of one. Personalized portals, or homepages, pioneered by Netvibes (netvibes.com) are an alternative to a regular Web portal. They are offered by Yahoo!, Google, and many more. Netvibes lets individuals assemble their favorite widgets (a *widget* is an element of user interface that displays an information arrangement changeable by the user, such as a window), websites, blogs, e-mail accounts, social networks, search engines, instant messenger, photos, videos, podcasts, and everything else they enjoy on the Web—all in one place. Today, Netvibes is a multilingual global community of users who are taking control of their digital lives by personalizing their Web experience. Netvibes is also a widget platform that is used by thousands of publishers around the world.

mobile portal
A portal accessible via a mobile device.

voice portal
A portal accessed by telephone or cell phone.

> ▸ **Mobile portals.** Mobile portals are portals that are accessible from mobile devices (see Chapter 6 for details). An increasing number of portals are accessible via mobile devices. One example of such a mobile portal is i-mode, which is described in Chapter 6. For additional information see en.wikipedia.org/wiki/On-Device-Portal.
>
> ▸ **Voice portals.** Voice portals are websites, usually portals, with audio interfaces. This means that they can be accessed by a standard telephone or a cell phone. AOLbyPhone is an example of a service that allows users to retrieve e-mail, news, and other content from AOL via telephone. It uses both speech recognition and text-to-speech technologies. Companies such as Tellme (tellme.com) and BeVocal (bevocal.com) offer access to the Internet from telephones, and also tools to build voice portals. Voice portals are especially popular for 1-800 numbers (enterprise 800 numbers) that provide self-service to customers with information available in Internet databases (e.g., finding flight status at delta.com).
>
> ▸ **Knowledge portals.** Knowledge portals enable access to knowledge by knowledge workers and facilitate collaboration.

THE ROLES AND VALUE OF INTERMEDIARIES IN E-MARKETPLACES

Intermediaries, such as brokers, play an important role in commerce by providing value-added activities and services to buyers and sellers. There are several types of intermediaries. The most well-known intermediaries in the physical world are wholesalers and retailers.

The two major types of *online intermediaries* are brokers and infomediaries.

Brokers

A *broker* in EC is a person or a company that facilitates transactions between buyers and sellers. The following are different types of brokers:

> ▸ **Buy/sell fulfillment.** A corporation that helps consumers place buy and sell orders (e.g., E*TRADE).
>
> ▸ **Virtual mall.** A company that helps consumers buy from a variety of stores (e.g., Yahoo! Stores).
>
> ▸ **Metamediary.** A firm that offers customers access to a variety of stores and provides them with transaction services, such as financial services (e.g., Amazon zShops).
>
> ▸ **Comparison agent.** A company that helps consumers compare prices and service at different stores (e.g., bizrate.com).
>
> ▸ **Shopping facilitator.** A company that helps consumers use online shops by providing currency conversion, language translation, payment features, delivery solutions, and potentially a user-customized interface (e.g., puntomio.com).
>
> ▸ **Matching services.** These match jobs to openings, buyers to products, dating candidates, and so forth.

Infomediaries

infomediaries
Electronic intermediaries that provide and/or control information flow in cyberspace, often aggregating information and selling it to others.

In cyberspace, some intermediaries provide and/or control information flow. These electronic intermediaries are known as **infomediaries**. The information flows to and from buyers and sellers via infomediaries. Infomediaries are websites that gather and organize large amounts of data and act as intermediaries between those who want the information and those who supply the information (see webopedia.com/TERM/I/infomediary.html). There are two types of infomediaries:

> ▸ The first type offers consumers a place to gather information about specific products and companies before making purchasing decisions (e.g., autobytel.com, cars.com, and bizrate.com).

▶ The second is not necessarily Web-based. It provides vendors with consumer information that will help the vendor develop and market products. The infomediary collects personal information from the buyers and sells that data to businesses.

Financial Standard performs both types of services, as illustrated in Case 2.2.

CASE 2.2
EC Application
FINANCIAL STANDARD

Financial Standard is a Sydney-based infomediary that provides trade news, investment analysis, and consulting services for a broad cross section of financial stakeholders including individual and corporate investors. These include superannuation trustees, financial planners, researchers, consultants, investment managers, and professional investors. They are also providers of education, employment, and human resources services for career-orientated aspirants of the financial industry. Financial Standard is a member of the Rainmaker Group which was founded in 1992.

The company derives its revenue from the provision of news, information, recruitment, and consulting services. More specifically, this entails the supply of current and developing financial and market news, strategic, tactical, and analytical information, and services for both company recruiters and job seekers. Information is gathered from sources including the government, legal systems, investment organizations, and banks. It also consults on matters ranging from financial strategy to human resource management. This is all available from a single, user-friendly source: the company website, at competitive rates.

Financial Standard operates a subscription-type business model. Subscriptions are charged for the base service, which includes website access and delivery of the *Financial Standard* newspaper. It is also a freemium business model however as customers are given free access to the website and to a limited amount of journal content, but a fee is required for the full or premium service.

Membership offers the following benefits among others:

▶ Access to the *Financial Standard* newspaper which offers trade news reviews, sector reviews, performance tables, market expectation surveys, and a black book of industry contacts—delivered fortnightly
▶ Access to the Financial Standard E-News Service—delivered daily
▶ Online access to news stories
▶ Financial Standard Best Practice seminar and workshop discounts
▶ Discounts on the Financial Standard Intelligence Reports

In addition to the *Financial Standard* newspaper, individual and corporate clients can subscribe to a number of quarterly journals through the website.

Consumers also can subscribe to the Financial Standard Intelligence Unit's (FSIU) Vantage Point, which is an additional source of balanced insights into investment and economic issues.

The Financial Standard service has the following objectives:

▶ **Provide a one-stop information service:** This is largely through the *Financial Standard* newspaper.
▶ **Achieve interactive and collaborative engagement with clients and partners:** This involves exploiting the features of Web 2.0 including blogs written by leading financial players, social networking, and videos provided by Rainmaker iTV on a range of topics including industry profiles and market updates.
▶ **Advance professional education:** The Financial Standard Continuous Professional Development Program addresses the requirement for development for financial professionals.
▶ **Help sustain the viability of the labor market in financial services:** Financial Standard provides global recruiting services for the banking, financial, and accounting sectors. Job seekers and employers can access a customized package of job postings, résumé databases, and brand advertising.

The success of Financial Standard is a result of its competitive differentiation. Its investment analysis is derived from an innovative combination of internal and external expertise and its service is less restrictive than others in giving access to its diverse range of content.

Sources: *financialstandard.com.au* (accessed July 2011) and *rainmaker.com.au* (accessed July 2011).

Questions

1. What are the specific elements that qualify Financial Standard as an infomediary?

2. Describe any significant differences between the terms *intermediary, infomediary,* and *portal.*

3. Outline four major categories of customer for Financial Standard, explaining in each case the specific benefits they obtain from the service.

4. As an information provider, what further additions to the services (if any) offered by Financial Standard would you recommend?

The advantage of infomediaries is usually that consumer privacy is protected and some infomediaries offer consumers a percentage of the fees they earn.

Distributors in B2B

A special type of intermediary in e-commerce is the B2B *e-distributor*. These intermediaries connect manufacturers with business buyers (customers), such as retailers (or resellers in the computer industry). **E-distributors** basically aggregate the catalogs or product information from many manufacturers, sometimes thousands of them, in one place—the intermediary's website. An example is W.W. Grainger (see grainger.com).

Changing Roles and Location of Intermediaries

Traditionally intermediaries acted mostly between two parties in a market (e.g., between a company and its suppliers, or a company and financial source). This was done along the supply chain as illustrated in Part A of Exhibit 11.4 (p. 590). In EC, intermediaries can be found frequently at the center of a hub (Part B of the exhibit).

> **e-distributor**
> An e-commerce intermediary that connects manufacturers with business buyers (customers) by aggregating the catalogs of many manufacturers in one place—the intermediary's website.

Section 2.3 ❯ REVIEW QUESTIONS

1. Describe electronic storefronts and e-malls.
2. List the various types of stores and e-malls.
3. What are information portals? List the major types.
4. List the roles of intermediaries in e-markets.
5. Describe e-distributors.
6. Describe the changing position and location of intermediaries in the supply chain.

2.4 MERCHANT SOLUTIONS: ELECTRONIC CATALOGS, SEARCH ENGINES, AND SHOPPING CARTS

To enable selling online, a website usually needs *EC merchant server software*. Merchant software includes many functionalities. One example is osCommerce, which is open-system software (see oscommerce.com and en.wikipedia.org/wiki/OsCommerce). Another example can be seen in the Yahoo! Merchant Solutions, at smallbusiness.yahoo.com/ecommerce. The basic functionality offered by such software includes electronic catalogs, search engines, and shopping carts, all intend to facilitate the electronic ordering process.

ELECTRONIC CATALOGS

Catalogs have been printed on paper for generations. Recently, electronic catalogs on CD-ROM and the Internet have gained popularity. **Electronic catalogs (e-catalogs)** consist of a products database, directory, and a presentation function. They are the backbone of most e-commerce sales sites. For merchants, the objective of electronic catalogs is to advertise and promote products and services. For the customer, the purpose of such catalogs is to locate information on products and services. Electronic catalogs can be searched quickly with the help of search engines, and they can be interactive. For example, *Change My Image* from Infinisys (en.infinisys.co.jp/product/cmimage/index.shtml) allows you to insert your photo and then change the hairstyle and color in the photo, so you see how you would look with a new hairstyle. Electronic catalogs can be very large; for example, the Library of Congress Web catalog (catalog.loc.gov) contains many millions of records as does Amazon.com's catalog.

Most early online catalogs were replications of text and pictures from printed catalogs. However, online catalogs have evolved to become more dynamic, customized, and integrated with selling and buying procedures, shopping carts, order taking, and payment. They may even include video clips. The tools for building them are being integrated with merchant suites and Web hosting (e.g., see smallbusiness.yahoo.com/ecommerce). Examples of a product catalog can be seen at jetpens.com—see Case 1.2 in Chapter 1).

> **electronic catalogs (e-catalogs)**
> The presentation of product information in an electronic form; the backbone of most e-selling sites.

Although used only occasionally in B2C commerce, customized catalogs are used frequently in B2B e-commerce. For a comprehensive discussion of online catalogs, see jcmax.com/advantages.html.

Online Catalogs Versus Paper Catalogs

Although online catalogs have significant advantages, such as lower cost, ease of updating, the ability to be integrated with the purchasing process, coverage of a wide spectrum of products, interactivity, customization, and strong search capabilities, they also have disadvantages and limitations. To begin, customers need computers and Internet access to view online catalogs. Second, some customers have difficulties finding what they want in many catalogs that are not user-friendly. However, as computer availability, Internet access, and user's competence continue to increase, the disadvantages will be minimized and many paper catalogs will be supplemented by, if not actually replaced by, electronic ones (like the famous Sears catalog). The number of print newspapers and magazines have diminished due to online ones, but the future of print will not disappear entirely. Paper catalogs probably will not disappear altogether either. There seems to be room for both media, at least in the near future. However, in B2B, paper catalogs may disappear more quickly, especially in the case where catalogs can be accessed by smartphones.

Example. RadioShack (radioshack.com) builds and maintains electronic catalogs based on its paper catalogs. The catalogs include search capabilities, the ability to feature large numbers of products, enhanced viewing capabilities, updating, and support. There are no paper catalogs. The same is true of Walmart, Best Buy, and most department stores.

EC SEARCH ACTIVITIES, TYPES, AND ENGINES

Search activities are popular in EC, and many tools for conducting searches are available. Consumers search inside one company's catalog, for example, to find a product or service, or they use Google or Bing to find companies that sell the product they need. Here we describe only the essentials for EC search. For the video "Google Commerce Search," see youtube.com/watch?v=gj7qrotOmVY. For a special Google search for e-commerce, see google.com/commercesearch and a description in Chapter 3. First, though, we look at three major types of searches.

Types of EC Searches

The three major types of EC searches are *Internet/Web search*, *enterprise search*, and *desktop search*.

> **Internet/Web Search.** This is the most popular search that involves any documents on the Web. According to Pew Internet and other statistical sites, finding information is one of the most frequent activities done on the Web.
>
> **Enterprise Search.** An enterprise search is the practice of identifying and enabling specific content across an enterprise, to be indexed, searched, and displayed to authorized users. It describes the application of search technology to information *within* an organization. This is in contrast to the other two main types of search environment: Internet/Web search and desktop search.
>
> **Desktop Search.** A desktop search is conducted by tools that search only the contents of a user's own computer files. The emphasis is on finding all the information that is available on the user's PC, including Web browser histories, e-mail archives, music, chats, photos, and word-processed documents. There are several search approaches to desktop search. For details see en.wikipedia.org/wiki/Desktop-search.

One main advantage of desktop search programs is that search results come up in a few seconds. A variety of desktop search programs are available, such as Spotlight from Apple Computer, XI Enterprise, and Google's Desktop (see desktop.google.com). Desktop search is very useful: It is an efficient productivity tool that helps to save time.

enterprise search
The practice of identifying and enabling specific content across the enterprise to be indexed, searched, and displayed to authorized users.

desktop search
Search tools that search the contents of a user's or organization's computer files, rather than searching the Internet. The emphasis is on finding all the information that is available on the user's PC, including Web browser histories, e-mail archives, and word-processed documents, as well as in all internal files and databases.

Each search method discussed here is accomplished by search engines and intelligent agents.

Search Engines

A **search engine** is a computer program that can access databases of Internet or intranet resources, search for specific information or key words, and report the results. For example, customers tend to ask for information (e.g., requests for product information or pricing) in the same general manner. This type of request is repetitive, and answering such requests is costly when done by a human. Search engines deliver answers economically and efficiently by matching questions with frequently asked question (FAQ) templates, which respond with "canned" answers.

Google, AltaVista, Lycos, and Bing are popular search engines. Portals such as AOL, Yahoo!, and MSN have their own search engines. Special search engines organized to answer certain questions or search in specified areas include Ask.com, Northern Light, Mama, and Looksmart. Thousands of different public search engines are available (see searchengineguide.com). Each of these tools excels in one area. These can be very specialized with different capabilities (see Martin 2008). In addition, thousands of companies have their own search engines on their portals or storefronts. For example, Endeca InFront (from endeca.com) is a special search engine for online catalogs.

Software (Intelligent) Agents

Unlike a search engine, a software (intelligent) agent can do more than just "search and match." It has capabilities that can be used to perform routine tasks that require intelligence. For example, it can monitor movements on a website to check whether a customer seems lost or ventures into areas that may not fit the customer's needs. If it detects such confusion, the agent can notify the customer and provide assistance. Software agents can be used in e-commerce to support tasks such as conducting complex searches, comparing prices, interpreting information, monitoring activities, and working as an assistant. Users can even chat or collaborate with intelligent agents as is done in Second Life, where the agents are avatars and some even "understand" a natural language interface. For definitions, classes, references, and links see en.wikipedia.org/wiki/Intelligent_agents.

Questions and Answers Online

Intelligent search engines can answer user questions. Some search engines focus on doing just that. A leading engine is Ask.com (a subsidiary of IAC). Ask.com has about 500 million answered questions in its databases. The Q&A service matches the questions to answers. For details see ask.com. A competing engine is Answers.com, answers.com, a question and answer (Q&A) site, which comprises WikiAnswers and ReferenceAnswers platforms to locate answers to users' questions. WikiAnswers is a community-generated social knowledge Q&A platform available in various languages, such as English, French, Italian, German, and Spanish, where people ask questions and the community answers them. *ReferenceAnswers* offers editorial content on various topics licensed from reference publishers.

Voice-Powered Search

To ease searching, especially when using a smartphone, Google introduced a voice-powered tool that allows you to skip the keyboard altogether. The first product was included as part of the iPhone's mobile search application. It allows you to talk into your phone, ask any question, and the results of your query are offered on your iPhone. In addition to asking questions by talking into your iPhone, you can also listen to search engine results. For example, the search engine Bing has a lyrics search feature that allows you to listen to more than 5 million full-length songs streaming through Microsoft's Tune music service.

Visual Shopping Search Engine

Using computer vision and machine learning technology, like.com (a Google company) provides a visual search engine that focuses on shoes, clothes, jewelry, and décor. (For other companies see searchme.com.)

The technology lets users see what terms like "red high-heeled pumps" and "floral patterned sleeveless dress" mean. It also created algorithms that explain to searchers whether those red pumps complement or clash with that dress they are buying. This type of search is a subset known as visual search (see en.wikipedia.org/Visual_search_engine, which is popular in mobile search engines).

SHOPPING CARTS

An **electronic shopping cart** (also known as *shopping bag* or *shopping basket*) is an order-processing technology that allows customers to accumulate items they wish to buy while they continue to shop. In this respect, it is similar to a shopping cart in the physical world. The software program of an electronic shopping cart allows customers to select items, review what has been selected, make changes, and then finalize the list. Clicking on "buy" and paying will trigger the actual purchase.

> **electronic shopping cart**
> An order-processing technology that allows customers to accumulate items they wish to buy while they continue to shop.

Shopping carts for B2C are fairly simple (visit amazon.com to see an example), but for B2B a shopping cart may be more complex. Shopping cart software is sold or provided for free as an independent component (e.g., networksolutions.com/e-commerce/index.jsp, zippycart.com, and easycart.com). It also is embedded in merchants' servers, such as smallbusiness.yahoo.com/ecommerce. Free online shopping carts (trials and demos) are available at volusion.com and 1freecart.com. For more on shopping carts, see en.wikipedia.org/wiki/Shopping_cart_software.

OTHER MECHANISMS IN MERCHANT SOFTWARE

Several other mechanisms exist such as the following.

Other Shopping Engines

Many other search engines are available to shoppers.

Example. Info.com (info.com) is a search platform that pulls together the best search tools. From a single search query, Info.com provides results from the leading search engines (e.g., Google, Bing, Yahoo!, Ask) and pay-per-click directories. Info.com is also partnered with other search providers to include comparison shopping and product reviews, a broad selection of news, health, pictures, eBay, jobs, white and yellow pages, tickets, flights, hotels, weather, maps, and directions. For example, Info.com has partnered with Become.com, a comparison shopping service, to make informed purchase decisions. It enables you to read product reviews, compare products, prices, and stores and buy from thousands of online merchants.

- **Audio.info.com/music.** Audio.com results are provided by *Yahoo! Audio* and *SingingFish*. To use Audio.com links, you need to have software tools installed on your computer.

- **Flights.info.com and Hotels.info.com.** Info.com offers real-time prices, availability, and other travel information from over 100 other online travel sites in one easy-to-use display, including prices and itineraries from 551 airlines and 91,000 hotels. Info.com's travel offering is powered by Kayak.com.

- **Health.info.com.** Health information from over 170,000 health and medical sites representing 130 million pages of content from the Internet including specialist medical reports and research studies. Health.info.com is powered by Healthline.com.

- **Research.info.com.** Research information covering 3 million topics comprising of clear and authoritative content drawn from over 100 high-quality titles, including "the deep" or "invisible Web" often not available to search engines. On the right hand side of the reference results page users are able to view Info.com's meta search results from all the leading search engines. Info.com's research content is powered by Answers.com.

- **Video.info.com.** View videos from hundreds of providers across the Web, including YouTube, AOL, Reuters, *BusinessWeek*, BBC, CNN, Hollywood.com, and *Rolling Stone*. Info.com users can search millions of videos by relevance, category, provider, or freshness. Video.info.com is powered by Pixsy.com.

- **Classified.info.com.** Access over 18 million classifieds from over 750,000 sites. In your area you can find exactly what you're looking for from autos, pets, rentals, houses, or used items. Classified.info.com is powered by Oodle.com.

Merchant software usually includes search engine submission, online tracking and reporting, product self-configuration, fraud screening and protection, and a payment gate. For an example see sunvirtual.com (see the "Merchant" account feature). Also see product configuration, which we will cover next.

Product Configuration

A key characteristic of EC is the ability to self-customize products and services, as done by Dell. Manufacturers need to produce customized products in economical and rapid ways so that the price of the products will be competitive. *Product configuration* systems support the acquisition of customer requirements while automating the order-taking process, and they allow customers to configure their products by specifying their technical requirements.

Section 2.4 ▶ REVIEW QUESTIONS

1. List and briefly describe the dimensions by which electronic catalogs can be classified.
2. List the benefits of electronic catalogs.
3. Explain how customized catalogs are created and used.
4. Compare search engines with software intelligent agents.
5. Describe an electronic shopping cart.
6. Describe voice- and vision-related search engines.
7. What is self configuration?
8. Compare and contrast Ask.com and Answers.com.

2.5 AUCTIONS, BARTERING, AND NEGOTIATING ONLINE

One of the most interesting market mechanisms in e-commerce is electronic auctions (Nissanoff 2006). They are used in B2C, B2B, C2C, G2B, and G2C.

DEFINITION AND CHARACTERISTICS

auction
A competitive process in which a seller solicits consecutive bids from buyers (forward auctions) or a buyer solicits bids from sellers (backward auctions). Prices are determined dynamically by the bids.

An **auction** is a market mechanism that uses a competitive process by which a seller solicits consecutive bids from buyers (forward auctions) or a buyer solicits bids from sellers (reverse auctions). Prices are determined dynamically by the bids. Auctions, an established method of commerce for generations, deal with products and services for which conventional marketing channels are ineffective or inefficient, and they ensure prudent execution of sales. For example, auctions can expedite the disposal of items that need to be liquidated or sold quickly. Rare coins, stamps, and other collectibles are frequently sold at auction. Auctions facilitate competition and market efficiency. A wide variety of online markets qualify as auctions using this definition. Auctions are very popular online mechanisms worldwide. For a comprehensive description, see en.wikipedia.org/wiki/Auction.

There are several types of auctions, each with its own specialties and procedures. (For details, see en.wikipedia.org/wiki/Online_auction_business_model.) They can be conducted in *public* auction sites, such as at eBay, or conducted in *private* auctions sites, which are by invitation only.

DYNAMIC PRICING

dynamic pricing
Prices that change based on supply and demand relationships at any given time.

One major characteristic of auctions is that they are based on dynamic pricing. **Dynamic pricing** refers to prices that are not fixed but that are allowed to fluctuate as supply and demand in a market change. In contrast, catalog prices are fixed, as are prices in department stores, supermarkets, and most electronic storefronts.

Dynamic pricing appears in several forms. Perhaps the oldest forms are negotiation and bargaining, which have been practiced for many generations in open-air markets.

TRADITIONAL AUCTIONS VERSUS E-AUCTIONS

Traditional, physical auctions are still very popular. However, the volume traded on e-auctions is significantly larger and continues to increase. Also, person-to-person auctions are done mostly online.

Limitations of Traditional Offline Auctions

Traditional offline auctions, regardless of their type, have several limitations. They usually last only a few minutes, or even seconds, for each item sold. This rapid process may give potential buyers little time to make a decision, so they may decide not to bid. Therefore, sellers may not get the highest possible price; bidders may not get what they really want, or they may pay too much for the items. Also, in many cases the bidders do not have much time to examine the goods. Bidders have difficulty learning about auctions and cannot compare what is offered at each location. Bidders must usually be physically present at auctions; thus, many potential bidders are excluded.

Similarly, it may be difficult for sellers to move goods to an auction site. Commissions are fairly high because a physical location must be rented, the auction needs to be advertised, and an auctioneer and other employees need to be paid. Electronic auctioning removes these deficiencies.

Electronic Auctions

The Internet provides an infrastructure for executing auctions electronically at lower cost, with a wide array of support services, and with many more sellers and buyers. Individual consumers and corporations both can participate in this rapidly growing and very convenient form of e-commerce. Forrester Research projects that the Internet auction industry will reach $65.2 billion in sales by 2010 (Edgar Online 2006).

Electronic auctions (e-auctions) are similar to offline auctions except that they are conducted online. E-auctions have been in existence since the 1980s over LANs (e.g., flowers; see Saarinen et al. 2006). Host sites on the Internet, which were started in 1995, serve as brokers, offering services for sellers to post their goods for sale and enabling buyers to bid on those items.

Major online auctions, such as eBay (see Online File W2.3), offer consumer products, electronic parts, artwork, vacation packages, airline tickets, and collectibles, as well as excess supplies and inventories being auctioned off by B2B marketers. Another type of B2B online auction is increasingly used to trade special types of commodities, such as electricity transmission capacities and gas and options (e.g., see ice.com). Furthermore, conventional business practices that traditionally have relied on contracts and fixed prices are increasingly being converted into auctions with bidding for online procurements. For online tools, see en.wikipedia.org/wiki/online_auction_tools. Some examples of innovative auctions are provided next.

electronic auctions (e-auctions)
Auctions conducted online.

INNOVATIVE AUCTIONS

Examples of innovative implementations of e-auctions are as follows:

▶ Every year, Warren Buffett, the famous U.S. stock investor and investment guru, invites a group of eight people to lunch with him. The eight pay big money for the pleasure. The money is donated to the needy in San Francisco. In the past, Buffett charged $30,000 per group. Since July 2003, Buffett has placed the invitation on an online auction (eBay). In 2003, bidders pushed the bid from $30,000 to $250,100. The winning bid in 2008 was $2,110,000. One of the winners commented that he was willing to pay whatever was needed so that he could express to Buffett his appreciation for investment guidance. Before the auction, he had no chance to be invited.

> ▶ A Harley-Davidson motorcycle autographed by celebrities and offered by talk-show host Jay Leno fetched $800,100 on eBay to benefit tsunami victims.
>
> ▶ JetBlue airlines started to auction flights in September 2008 on eBay. The initial offer was 300 flights and six vacation packages, with opening bids set between 5¢ and 10¢ (yes, cents). The flights are to more than 20 destinations, including four "mystery" JetBlue Getaways—vacation packages to undisclosed locations. The three-, five-, and seven-day auctions included one- and two-person round-trip, weekend flights in September from Boston, Chicago, New York, Orlando, Salt Lake City, Fort Lauderdale, or Southern California. Although no one was lucky enough to get a flight for 5¢ or 10¢, many auctions gave the winners a flight that was 10 to 20 percent cheaper than regular prices.

TYPES OF AUCTIONS

It is customary to classify auctions into the following major types based on how many buyers and sellers are involved.

One Buyer, One Seller

In this configuration, one can use negotiation, bargaining, or bartering. The resulting price will be determined by each party's bargaining power, supply and demand in the item's market, and (possibly) business environment factors.

One Seller, Many Potential Buyers

forward auction
An auction in which a seller entertains bids from buyers. Bidders increase price sequentially.

In this configuration, the seller uses a **forward auction**, an auction in which a seller entertains bids from multiple buyers. (Because forward auctions are the most common and traditional form, they often are simply called *auctions*.) The four major types of forward auctions are *English* and *Yankee* auctions, in which bidding prices increase as the auction progresses, and *Dutch* and *free-fall* auctions, in which bidding prices decline as the auction progresses. Each of these can be used for either liquidation or for market efficiency.

One Buyer, Many Potential Sellers

reverse auction (bidding or tendering system)
Auction in which the buyer places an item for bid (tender) on a request for quote (RFQ) system, potential suppliers bid on the job, with the price reducing sequentially, and the lowest bid wins; primarily a B2B or G2B mechanism.

name-your-own-price model
Auction model in which a would-be buyer specifies the price (and other terms) he or she is willing to pay to any willing and able seller. It is a C2B model that was pioneered by Priceline.com.

Two popular types of auctions in which there is one buyer and many potential sellers are reverse auctions (tendering) and name-your-own-price auctions.

Reverse Auctions. When there is one buyer and many potential sellers, a **reverse auction (bidding system or tendering)** is in place. In a reverse auction, the buyer places an item he or she wants to buy for a bid (or *tender*) on a *request for quote* (RFQ) system. Potential suppliers bid on the item, reducing the price sequentially (see Exhibit 2.6). In electronic bidding in a reverse auction, several rounds of bidding may take place until the bidders do not reduce the price further. The winning supplier is the one with the lowest bid (assuming that only price is considered). Reverse auctions are primarily a B2B or G2B mechanism. (For further discussion and examples, see Chapter 4 including its opening case).

The Name-Your-Own-Price Model. Priceline.com pioneered the **name-your-own-price model**. In this model, a would-be buyer specifies the price (and other terms) that he or she is willing to pay to any willing and able seller. For example, Priceline.com presents consumers' requests to sellers, who fill as much of the guaranteed demand as they wish at prices and terms requested by buyers. Alternately, Priceline.com searches its own database that contains vendors' lowest prices and tries to match supply against requests. Priceline.com asks customers to guarantee acceptance of the offer if it is at or below the requested price by giving a credit card number. This is basically a C2B model, although some businesses also use it (see en.wikipedia.org/wiki/Name_Your_Own_Price).

EXHIBIT 2.6   The Reverse Auction Process

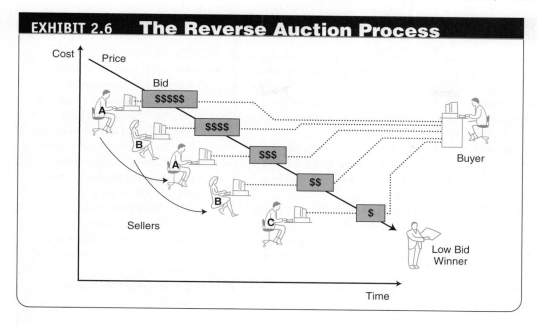

Many Sellers, Many Buyers

When there are many sellers and many buyers, buyers and their bidding prices are matched with sellers and their asking prices based on the quantities on both sides. Stocks and commodities markets are typical examples of this configuration. Buyers and sellers may be individuals or businesses. Such an auction is also called a **double auction** (see en.wikipedia.org/wiki/Double_Auction).

Penny Auctions

A *bidding fee auction*, also called a **penny auction**, is a new type of forward auction in which participants must pay a small nonrefundable fee each time she or he places a bid (usually in small increments above the previous bid). When time expires, the last participant to have placed a bid wins the item and also pays the final bid price, which is usually significantly lower than the retail price of the item. For a tutorial, see youtube.com/watch?v=MVzupKxlipY.

Because most bidders will receive nothing in return for their paid bids, some observers have stated that the fee spent on the bid is actually equivalent to a lottery or wager. The auctioneer receives income both in the form of the fees collected for each participant bidder and in the form of payment for the winning bid. Examples of companies are swoopo.co.uk, madbid.com, and quibids.com. At 100auctionsites.com/penny-auction.php, you can find a list of popular companies. Some companies allow the unsuccessful bidders to use all the bidding fees toward a purchase of items at regular prices. For additional information, see en.wikipedia.org/wiki/Penny_auction. Several other innovative auctions are available. For an interesting one, see global.dubli.com.

BENEFITS AND LIMITATIONS OF E-AUCTIONS

E-auctions are becoming important selling and buying channels for many companies and individuals. E-auctions enable buyers to access goods and services anywhere auctions are conducted. Moreover, almost perfect market information is available about prices, products, current supply and demand, and so on. These characteristics provide benefits to all.

Benefits of E-Auctions

The auction culture seems to revolutionize the way customers buy, sell, and obtain what they want. A listing of the benefits of e-auctions to sellers, buyers, and e-auctioneers is provided in Exhibit 2.7.

double auction
An auction in which multiple buyers and their bidding prices are matched with multiple sellers and their asking prices, considering the quantities on both sides.

penny auction
A formal auction in which participants pay a nonrefundable small fee for each bid. Bid level changes by small increments.

EXHIBIT 2.7 Benefits of E-Auctions

Benefits to Sellers	Benefits to Buyers	Benefits to E-Auctioneers
• Increased revenues from broadening bidder base and shortening cycle time. Can sell anywhere globally. • Opportunity to bargain instead of selling at a fixed price. Can sell any time and conduct frequent auctions. • Optimal price setting determined by the market (more buyers, more information). • Sellers can gain more customer dollars by offering items directly (saves on the commission to intermediaries; also, physical auctions are very expensive compared with e-auctions). • Can liquidate large quantities quickly. • Improved customer relationship and loyalty (in the case of specialized B2B auction sites and electronic exchanges).	• Opportunities to find unique items and collectibles. • Entertainment. Participation in e-auctions can be entertaining and exciting. • Convenience. Buyers can bid from anywhere, even with a cell phone; they do not have to travel to an auction place. • Anonymity. With the help of a third party, buyers can remain anonymous. • Possibility of finding bargains, for both individuals and organizations.	• Higher repeat purchases. Jupiter Research (*jupiterresearch.com*) found that auction sites, such as eBay, tend to garner higher repeat-purchase rates than the top B2C sites, such as Amazon.com. • High "stickiness" to the website (the tendency of customers to stay at sites longer and come back more often). Auction sites are frequently "stickier" than fixed-priced sites. Stickier sites generate more ad revenue for the e-auctioneer. • Easy expansion of the auction business.

Limitations of E-Auctions

E-auctions have several limitations. The most significant limitations are minimal security, the possibility of fraud, and limited participation.

Minimal Security. Some of the C2C auctions conducted on the Internet are not secure because they are done in an unencrypted environment. This means that credit card numbers could be stolen during the payment process. Payment methods such as PayPal (paypal.com) can be used to solve the problem (see Chapter 9). In addition, some B2B auctions are conducted over highly secure private lines.

Possibility of Fraud. Auction items are in many cases unique, used, or antique. Because the buyer cannot see the items, the buyer may get defective or false products. Also, buyers can commit fraud by receiving goods or services without paying for them. Thus, the fraud rate on e-auctions is relatively high. For a discussion of e-auction fraud and fraud prevention, see fraud.org/tips/internet/onlineauctions.htm. Lately several people warn about fraud in penny auctions sites. For examples of scams see tomuse.com/penny-auction-fraud-scam-cheat-bidders.

Limited Participation. Some auctions are by invitation only; others are open to dealers only. Limited participation may be a disadvantage to sellers, who usually benefit from as large a pool of buyers as possible. Buyers also may be unhappy if they are excluded from participation.

IMPACTS OF AUCTIONS

Because the trade objectives and contexts for auctions are very diverse, the rationale behind auctions and the motives of the different participants for setting up auctions are quite different. The following are some representative impacts of e-auctions.

Auctions as a Social Mechanism to Determine a Price

For objects that are not traded in traditional markets, such as unique or rare items, or for items that may be offered randomly or at long intervals, an auction creates a marketplace that attracts potential buyers, and often experts. By offering many of these special items at a single place and time and by attracting considerable attention, auctions provide the requisite exposure of purchase and sale orders, and hence liquidity of the market in which an optimal price can be determined. Typical examples are auctions of fine arts or rare stamps, as well as auctions of communications frequencies, Web banners, and advertising space. For example, wine collectors can find a global wine auction at winebid.com.

Auctions as a Highly Visible Distribution Mechanism

Some auctions deal with special offers. In this case, a supplier typically auctions off a limited number of items, using the auction primarily as a mechanism to gain attention and to attract those customers who are bargain hunters or who have a preference for the gambling dimension of the auction process. For example, airline seat auctions by Cathay Pacific, American Airlines, and Lufthansa fall into this category.

Auctions as an EC Component in a Business Model

Auctions can stand alone, or they may be combined with other e-commerce activities. An example of the latter is the combination of group purchasing with reverse auctions, as described in Online File W2.4.

Auctions for Profit for Individuals

As illustrated in Chapter 1, individuals can make money by selling things that they buy at bargain prices on eBay. If you are interested in learning how to do this, read Joyner (2007) and Weber (2008).

ONLINE BARTERING

Bartering, the exchange of goods and services, is the oldest method of trade. Today, it is done primarily between organizations. The problem with bartering is that it is difficult to match trading partners. Businesses and individuals may use classified ads to advertise what they need and what they offer in exchange, but they still may not be able to find what they want. Intermediaries may be helpful, but they are expensive (20 percent to 30 percent commissions) and very slow.

bartering
The *exchange* of goods and services.

E-bartering (electronic bartering)—bartering conducted online—can improve the matching process by attracting more partners to the barter. In addition, matching can be done faster, and as a result, better matches can be found. Items that are frequently bartered online include office space, storage, and factory space; idle facilities; and labor, products, and banner ads. (Note that e-bartering may have tax implications that need to be considered.)

e-bartering (electronic bartering)
Bartering conducted online, usually in a bartering exchange.

E-bartering is usually done in a **bartering exchange**, a marketplace in which an intermediary arranges the transactions. These exchanges can be very effective. Representative bartering websites include u-exchange.com, swapace.com, and barterdepot.com. The process works like this: First, the company tells the bartering exchange what it wants to offer. The exchange then assesses the value of the company's products or services and offers it certain "points" or "bartering dollars." The company can use the "points" to buy the things it needs from a participating member in the exchange.

bartering exchange
A marketplace in which an intermediary arranges barter transactions.

Bartering sites must be financially secure. Otherwise, users may not have a chance to use the points they accumulate. (For further details see virtualbarter.net and barternews.com.)

ONLINE NEGOTIATING

Dynamic prices also can be determined by *negotiation*. Negotiated pricing is commonly used for expensive or specialized products. Negotiated prices also are popular when large quantities are purchased. Much like auctions, negotiated prices result from interactions and bargaining among sellers and buyers. Negotiation also deals with nonpricing terms, such as the payment method, timing, and credit. Negotiation is a well-known process in the offline world (e.g., in real estate, automobile purchases, and contract work). In addition, in cases where there is no standard service or product to speak of, some digital products and services can be personalized and "bundled" at a standard price. Preferences for these bundled services differ among consumers, and thus they are frequently negotiated. A simple peer-to-peer (P2P) negotiation can be seen at ioffer.com. For more on negotiation in P2P money lending, see the ZOPA and Prosper case in Online File W7.1. *Online (electronic) negotiation* may be more effective and efficient than offline negotiation.

Section 2.5 ▶ REVIEW QUESTIONS

1. Define auctions and describe how they work.
2. Describe the benefits of electronic auctions over traditional (offline) auctions.
3. List the four types of auctions.
4. Distinguish between forward and reverse auctions.
5. Describe the "name-your-own-price" auction model.
6. Describe penny auctions.
7. List the major benefits of auctions to buyers, sellers, and auctioneers.
8. What are the major limitations of auctions?
9. List the major impacts of auctions on markets.
10. Define bartering and describe the advantages of e-bartering.
11. Explain the role of online negotiation in EC.

2.6 SOCIAL SOFTWARE TOOLS: FROM BLOGS TO WIKIS TO TWITTER

social software
A software product that enables people to rendezvous, connect, and collaborate through computer-mediated communication.

The Web 2.0 environment is usually associated with its software tools. **Social software** encompasses a range of software systems that allows users to interact and share data. This computer-mediated communication and collaboration has become very popular with social sites like Facebook, media sites like Flickr and YouTube, and commercial sites like Amazon.com and eBay. Many of these applications share characteristics like open application program interfaces (APIs), service-oriented design, and the ability to upload data and media. The terms *Web 2.0* and (for large-business applications) *Enterprise 2.0* are also used to describe this style of software. Major advocates of using these tools believe that they are the backbone to creating actual communities and social networks. The major social software tools are listed in Exhibit 2.8 and at en.wikipedia.wiki.org/social_software. For a comprehensive list, see Kathy Schrock's *Guide for Educators* at kathyschrock.net/web20. Also see D'Souza's guide at TeachingHacks.com, and category 5 at nzsocialmedia.ning.com. For a discussion of social media tools, tactics, and strategies, see Safko (2010).

The increased importance of social computing resulted in many innovative tools and services. Social networking, for example, is penetrating into enterprises and even becoming a B2B phenomenon. According to a Forrester survey, companies are spending money mostly on wikis, blogs, RSS, tagging, podcasting, and social networking (Farber 2008).

In this chapter, we will cover blogs, wikis, and microblogging (including Twitter) in this section and virtual worlds in Section 2.7.

BLOGGING (WEBLOGGING)

blog
A personal website that is open to the public to read and to interact with; dedicated to specific topics or issues.

The Internet offers the opportunity for individuals to publish on the Web using a technology known as *Weblogging*, or *blogging*. A **blog** is a personal website, or part of a website, open to the public, in which the owner expresses his or her feelings or opinions. Blogs can result in two-way communication and collaboration, group discussion, and so on. Blogs can be used on the Internet or internally within the enterprise. The totality of blogs is known as the *blogosphere*. For a comprehensive coverage of blogs, see en.wikipedia.org/wiki/Blog.

vlog (video blog)
A blog with video content.

Many blogs provide commentary or news on a particular subject; others function mostly as personal online diaries. A typical blog combines text, images, and links to other blogs, Web pages, and other media related to its topic. A **vlog (video blog)** is a blog with video content. Notice that almost 10,000 fake or spam blogs are created daily (out of

EXHIBIT 2.8   Social Networking Software Tools

Tools for Online Communication
- Instant messaging
- VoIP and Skype
- Text chat
- Collaborative real-time editors
- Internet forums
- Blogs, vlogs, microblogs (Twitter)
- Wikis
- Prediction markets

Types of Services
- Social network services
- Commercial and professional social networks
- Social network search engines
- Enterprise social networks
- Social guides
- Media sharing (YouTube) and Photos (Flickr)
- Social bookmarking
- Social citations
- Social libraries
- Virtual worlds and massively multiplayer online games (MMOGs)
- Nongame worlds
- Other specialized social applications
- Social games (Zynga, Electronic Arts)
- Politics and journalism
- Content management tools

Emerging Technologies
- Peer-to-peer social networks
- Virtual presence
- Mobile tools for Web 2.0

Tools for Individuals
- Personalization
- Customization
- Search
- Clipping tools
- RSS
- File-sharing tools

Web 2.0 Development Tools
- Mushups
- Web services

Sources: Compiled from *en.wikipedia.org/wiki/Social_software*, *en.wikipedia.or/wiki/List-of-social-software* (accessed November 2010), Weblogs, Inc. (2007), and author's experience.

150,000 to 200,000 total). The number of blogs is estimated to double every year. Most blogs are written in English and Japanese.

Building Effective Blogs

It is becoming easier and easier to build blogs. Programs from blogger.com, pitas.com, and other vendors are very user-friendly. Blog space is free; the goal is to make it easy for users to create their own blogs. *Bloggers* (the people who create and maintain blogs) are handed a fresh space on their website to write in each day. They can easily edit, add entries, and broadcast whatever they want by simply clicking "Send." Blogging software such as WordPress or Movable Type helps bloggers update their blogs easily. Bloggers also use a special terminology. See samizdata.net/blog/glossary.html for a dictionary of blog terms.

For the legal and social consequences of blogs, including the danger of defamation or liability, political dangers, relation to employment, and court cases, see en.wikipedia.org/wiki/Blog. For a blogger's legal guide, see eff.org/issues/bloggers/legal.

Commercial Uses of Blogs

The blog concept has transferred quickly to the corporate world. See Sloan and Kaihla (2006) for a survey of commercial uses of blogs.

Example: How Stonyfield Farm Uses Blogs. Stonyfield Farm is the third largest organic yogurt company in the world, producing more than 18 million cups of yogurt each month (see facebook.com/oikos) and generating more than $300 million in annual sales in 50 states. The company's core values are promoting healthy food and protecting the environment. It guarantees the use of only natural ingredients in its products and donates 10 percent of its profit each year to efforts that protect the earth (see the YouTube videos at stonyfield.com).

The company employs ""word-of-mouth" marketing approaches that are compatible with its grassroots "people-friendly" image. As of 2007, Stonyfield turned to blogs to further personalize its relationship with its customers and connect with even more people. The blogs provide the company with what the management calls a "handshake" with customers. Stonyfield publishes four different blogs on its website: (1) "Healthy Kids" encourages healthy food consumption in public schools; (2) "Strong Women Daily" features fitness, health tips, and stress-coping strategies; (3) "Baby Babble" provides a forum for child development and balancing work with family; and (4) "The Bovine Bugle" provides reports from organic dairy farms.

Stonyfield hires a journalist and almanac writer to post new content to each of the blogs daily, five days a week. When readers subscribe to the blogs, they receive automatic updates, and they can also respond to the postings. The blogs have created a positive response for the Stonyfield brand by providing readers with topics that inspire them and pique their interests. They are also, of course, persuaded to try and buy Stonyfield products (you can buy only shirts and toys at the company's online store). The management believes that blogs are an excellent method of public relations.

Potential Risks of Corporate Blogs

Some people see risks in corporate blogging. Two obvious examples are the risk of revealing trade secrets by insiders, and of making statements that are or could be considered as libel or defamation. Another risk is that bloggers can be biased against a company and tint its reputation. Many companies have corporate policies on internal blogging.

According to Flynn (2006), blog-related risks can be minimized by establishing a strategic *blog management* program that incorporates the three *E*'s of electronic risk management:

1. **Establish comprehensive, written rules and policies**. Make sure employees understand that all company policies apply to the blogosphere, regardless of whether employees are blogging at the office or from home.
2. **Educate employees about blog-related risks, rules, and regulations.** Be sure to address rights and privacy expectations, as well as the organization's blog-related risks and responsibilities.
3. **Enforce blog policy with disciplinary action and technology.** Take advantage of blog search engines to monitor the blogosphere and to keep track of what is being written about your company.

For a comprehensive discussion of corporate blogs, their risk, and how to mitigate this risk, see Cox et al. (2008).

MICROBLOGGING AND TWITTER

Microblogging is a form of blogging that allows users to write short messages (or an image, or embedded video) and publish them, either to be viewed by anyone or by a restricted group that can be chosen by the user. These messages can be submitted by a variety of means, including text messaging from cell phones, instant messaging, e-mail, MP3, or just on the Web.

The content of a microblog differs from that of a regular blog due to the limited space per message (usually up to 140 characters). Many provide short messages about personal matters.

The most popular service is Twitter; although in February 2009 more than 100 competitors were in existence.

TWITTER

Twitter is a free microblogging service that allows its users to send messages and read other users' messages and updates, otherwise known as **tweets**, which are text-based posts. These are displayed on the user's profile page and delivered to other users who have signed up to receive them. The sender can restrict delivery to those in his or her circle of friends (delivery to everyone being the default). Twitter is not a social network as many characterize it; it is actually a social media tool for broadcasting information. It is a service for communications and to stay connected through the exchange of quick frequent answers to questions such as "What are you doing?" For capabilities and details, see en.wikipedia.org/wiki/Twitter and twitternet.com. Twitter and its business applications are described in detail in Chapter 7 and in smbceo.com/2009/03/25/top-27-twitter-applications/.

As of November 2010, Twitter claims to have more than 120 million registered accounts. Twitter is becoming a useful enterprise tool. Socialtext (socialtext.com) offers a Twitter service for the enterprise (see en.wikipedia.org/wiki/Twitter).

Twitter is important because it:

▶ Provides a method for tapping into the brainwaves of people whose thoughts and opinions are valuable to a company or a person.

▶ Can help recipients to catch breaking news very quickly. It's the digital equivalent of word of mouth.

▶ Can allow people to communicate and network with other people they want to meet.

▶ Lets you keep track of colleagues, see what they're working on, and better understand what they do.

▶ Can serve as a messaging tool to quickly communicate with multiple contacts.

The Essentials of Twitter for Business

Twitter is a communications platform that helps businesses and their customers. As a business, you can use it to quickly share information with people interested in your company, gather real-time market intelligence and customer feedback, and build relationships with customers, partners, and other people who care about your company. As an individual user, you can use Twitter to tell a company (or anyone else) that you've had a great—or disappointing—experience with their business, offer product ideas, and learn about great offers.

Twitter can connect you to your customers right now, in a way that was never before possible. For example, let's say you work for a custom bike company. If you run a Twitter search for your brand, you may find people posting messages about how happy they are that your bike lets them ride in the French Alps—giving you a chance to share tips about cyclist-friendly cafés along their route.

Others may post minor equipment complaints or desired features that they would never bother to contact you about—providing you with invaluable customer feedback that you can respond to right away or use for future planning. Still others may twitter about

microblogging
A form of blogging that allows users to write messages (usually up to 140 characters) and publish them, either to be viewed by anyone or by a restricted group that can be chosen by the user. These messages can be submitted by a variety of means, including text messaging, instant messaging, e-mail, MP3, or just on the Web.

Twitter
A free microblogging service that allows its users to send and read other users' updates.

tweets
Text-based posts up to 140 characters in length posted to Twitter.

serious problems with your bikes—letting you offer customer service that can turn around a bad situation.

The Major Benefits of Twitter. One of Twitter's key benefits is that it gives you the chance to communicate informally and casually with customers on their terms, creating friendly relationships along the way—tough for corporations to do when using most other communication mediums. The conversational nature of twittering lets you build relationships with customers, partners, and other people important to your business. Beyond transactions, Twitter gives your constituents direct access to your employees and a way to contribute to your company; as marketers say, it shrinks the emotional distance between your company and your customers. Plus, the platform lends itself to integration with your existing communication channels, and strategies.

Example.   Suppose you run a big retail website. In addition to learning more about what your customers want, you can provide exclusive Twitter coupon codes, link to key posts on your blog, share tips for shopping online, and announce specials at store locations. And you can take things a step further by occasionally posting messages about fun, quirky events at your company, providing a small but valuable connection with the people in your company. For examples see business.twitter.com/twitter101 and click on best practices and case studies.

Examples of Twitter as Enterprise Tools (based on business.twitter.com/twitter101).

> ▸ Dell uses Twitter to disseminate information and interact with its customers. With over 80 Dell-branded Twitter accounts, the company found Twitter useful in expanding awareness of its products and increased sales.
>
> ▸ JetBlue has about 1 million followers on Twitter. The company uses Twitter for customer service and market research. The company found customers wanted JetBlue to see them as a resource for helping JetBlue deliver better service. The company posts questions and information to which people respond. Twitter helps tear down the artificial walls between customers and the company's employees.
>
> ▸ Tasti D-Lite offers guilt-free frozen treats in over 50 stores in New York. Twitter is being used to find out what customers are saying about the products and the competition. The company also mingles with customers on the customer's terms. Customers also help in problem solving (e.g., in delivery), and the company distributes paperless mobile coupons. Each store has its own Twitter account.
>
> ▸ Etsy is an online marketplace for buying and selling mostly handmade goods. Over 250,000 sellers offer handmade goods on the site. The sellers are using Twitter to promote their shops and products. The company monitors the tweets of the followers to harness the collective brains of the participating community. They use RSS feeds of the relevant blogs, alert followers to particularly creative products from specific sellers, share valuable tips, and alert people about upcoming events and promotion on the site. Monitoring community concerns is another activity as well as garnering feedback and ideas instantaneously, effectively creating focus groups from Etsy followers.
>
> ▸ Several companies analyze messages on Twitter to identify complaints. For example, Comcast reps are solving subscriber issues by reaching out to them on Twitter. Frank Eliason, a Comcast customer-service rep, has more than 13,000 followers on Twitter. Eliason believes his experience with Twitter can help sales forces handle their customers' complaints. For details, see pmtips.net/case-twitter-comcast-salesforce-case-study.
>
> ▸ Using Twitter makes it possible to predict the performance of Hollywood movies in their initial weeks at the box office. The accuracy rate of the preliminary tests is very precise and more accurate than the current gold standard, the Hollywood Stock Exchange, which is closely followed by the industry. These methodologies

can be applied to various products or even ad campaigns. For details see liberatemedia.com/blog/twitter-can-predict-movie-success.

▶ Pepsi is using Twitter to supplement a toll-free telephone number to share product feedback faster and in a more personal way. The company monitors and talks with customers and has reached a new audience that never bothered to call. Many of these people are very creative. The company also uses Twitter to handle complaints.

Note: The most popular Twitter application (out of many hundreds) is TweetDeck'it, which allows users to send and receive tweets and view profiles in Facebook, LinkedIn, MySpace, Google Buzz, and Foursquare. For details, see en.wikipedia.org/wiki/Tweetdeck. For more on Twitter, see Mangalindan (2010) and en.wikipedia.org/wiki/Twitter.

WIKIS

A **wiki (wikilog)** is a website that allows the easy creation and editing of any number of interlinked Web pages via a Web browser, using a simplified markup language or a WYSIWYG text editor. Wikis are typically powered by wiki software and are often used to create *collaborative wiki* websites, to power community websites, and to take personal notes. They are also used in corporate intranets and in knowledge management systems.

Wikis may exist to serve a specific purpose, and in such cases, users apply their editorial rights to remove material that is considered "off topic." Such is the case of the collaborative encyclopedia Wikipedia.

A wiki can be viewed as an extension of a blog. Whereas a blog usually is created by an individual (or maybe a small group) and may have an attached discussion board, a wiki (or *wikilog, wikiblog*) is essentially a blog that enables everyone to participate as a peer. Anyone may add, delete, edit, or change content. It is like a loose-leaf notebook with a pencil and eraser left in a public place. Anyone can read it, scrawl notes, tear out a page, and so on. Wikis can be implemented in many ways. One way is through a contribution by many, as in the case of Wikipedia (see Waters 2010). A similar concept is employed by the CIA in their "Intellipedia." For applications and guide see Chatfield (2009). A commercial use of a wiki was presented in the opening case. For a comprehensive list of wikis, see wikiIndex.org. For characteristics, e-commerce applications, resources, and more, see en.wikipedia.org/wiki/Wiki and Chatfield (2009).

wiki (wikilog)
A blog that allows everyone to participate as a peer; anyone may add, delete, or change content.

Business Applications of Wikis

In the opening case for this chapter, we illustrated the use of wikis for collaboration. And indeed wikis are getting to be an important enterprise collaboration tool. An interesting example is Wind Rivers, a software company that uses wikis extensively to support team work (see details at twiki.org/cgi-bin/view/Main/TWikiSuccessStoryOfWindRiver).

MECHANISM AIDS FOR WEB 2.0 TOOLS: TAGS, FOLKSONOMY, MASHUPS, AND SOCIAL BOOKMARKS

When you blog, you may see a notice that reads "Browse This Blog's Tags," followed by a list of key words. Tags are one of the most useful aids to Web 2.0 tools. (See en.wikipedia.org/wiki/Tag_(metadata) for details.)

Tags

A **tag** is a nonhierarchical key word or term assigned to a piece of information (such as an Internet bookmark, digital image, video clip, or any computer document). This kind of metadata (data about data) helps describe an item as a key word and allows it to be found by browsers when searching. Tags are chosen informally and personally by the item's

tag
A nonhierarchical key word or term assigned to a piece of information (such as an Internet bookmark, digital image, video clip, or any computer document).

creator or by its viewer, depending on the system. On a website in which many users tag many items, this collection of tags becomes a *folksonomy*.

Folksonomy

folksonomy (collaborative tagging, social tagging)
The practice and method of collaboratively creating, classifying, and managing tags to annotate and categorize content.

Folksonomy (also known as **collaborative tagging**, or **social tagging**) is the practice and method of collaboratively creating, classifying, and managing tags to annotate and categorize content. In contrast with traditional subject indexing, key words are generated not only by experts but also by creators and consumers of the content. Usually, freely chosen key words are used instead of a controlled vocabulary. *Folksonomy* (from *folk* and *taxonomy*) is a user-generated taxonomy. For additional information, see en.wikipedia.org/wiki/Folksonomy.

Mashups

mashup
Combination of two or more websites into a single website that provides the content of both sites (whole or partial) to deliver a novel product to consumers.

A **mashup** is essentially the combination of two or more websites into a single website that provides the content of both sites (whole or partial) to deliver enriched, improved, or a novel product or service to consumers. Mashups reach into the API for a given application and extract information, including Web page elements, and use them to launch a new application that adds value. The most popular type of mashup relates to maps (e.g., Google Maps, Yahoo! Maps), which can be combined with other data sources to produce interesting results.

For example, combining Google Maps and real estate information, Zillow (zillow.com) enables users to zoom in on a neighborhood of interest to see the environment and examine home values, home sales' history, and so on. For those who prefer to rent, Housing Maps (housingmaps.com) offers a combination of Craigslist rentals with Google Maps to show rental opportunities in nearly 40 regions across the United States. Other mashups combine travel, shopping, sports, news, video, and photo sites. An interesting site that tracks the mashup phenomenon is ProgrammableWeb (programmableweb.com), which offers a mashup dashboard showing all the latest mashup sites. One of its powerful tools is its "mashup matrix" (programmableweb.com/mashup), which presents approximately 200 websites in a grid with dots that highlight the intersection where two sites have been brought together in a mashup. At each intersection between sites, pop-up boxes list all mashups that have been created using the sites; in many cases, there are multiple sites at each intersection. For a more detailed discussion of mashups, refer to en.wikipedia.org/wiki/Mashup_(web_application_hybrid).

Social Bookmarking

social bookmarking
Web service for sharing Internet bookmarks. The sites are a popular way to store, classify, share, and search links through the practice of folksonomy techniques on the Internet and intranets.

Social bookmarking is a method for Internet users to store, organize, search, and manage bookmarks of Web pages on the Internet with the help of metadata.

In a social-bookmarking system, users save links to Web pages that they want to remember and/or share. These bookmarks are usually public and can be saved privately, shared only with specified people, groups, or networks, and so forth. People can usually view these bookmarks chronologically, by category or tags, or via a search engine. For details, see en.wikipedia.org/wiki/Social_bookmarking.

Stormhoek Winery, in Case 2.3, is a good example of a company that effectively uses multiple social tools.

Section 2.6 ▶ REVIEW QUESTIONS

1. Define blogs and bloggers.
2. Discuss the critical features that distinguish a blog from a user-produced regular Web page.
3. Describe the potential advantages and risks of blogs.
4. Discuss the commercial uses of blogs and wikis.
5. Define wikis.
6. Define tags, mashups, folksonomy, and social bookmarking.

CASE 2.3
EC Application
STORMHOEK WINERY EXCELS WITH WEB 2.0 TOOLS

Stormhoek Winery is a small winery in South Africa (*stormhoek.com*). Annual sales in 2005 were only $3 million, but with Web 2.0 technologies sales grew to $10 million in 2007 and are projected to reach $30 million in 2010. The company devised a marketing campaign called "100 Geek Dinners in 100 Days." One volunteer would host each dinner, which would be used as a Stormhoek wine tasting for several dozen guests in the United Kingdom and the United States. How can you get 100 people to host a wine tasting and how do you find 40 to 60 guests for each event? The answer: Web 2.0 technologies. Here is what the company did.

Blogging. The CEO of Orbital Wines, Stormhoek's parent company, in collaboration with a well-known blogger, Hugh Macleod, wrote dozens of blog entries about the events, soliciting volunteer hosts, including bloggers and wine enthusiasts.

Wiki. Each volunteer was provided with contact and location information on a wiki. The wiki technology was mainly used for customer relationship management (CRM). The wiki included wine-related cartoons and other entertainment and advertising.

Podcasts. Web-content feed (enabled by an RSS) was used to push information to participants' inboxes. Information included wine news, wine analyses, and descriptions of the 100 parties.

Video Links. The corporate blog supported video links. Bloggers could cut and paste embedded links to YouTube videos directly into an entry.

Shopping. The blog site acted as a portal to Stormhoek and included support for order placement and shopping carts for promotional "swag," such as posters and T-shirts.

Mashups. An interactive map was integrated into the wiki using mashup software. This allowed dinner hosts to display a map of the location of the event. Also, guests could click an event on the map to make a reservation, get a reservation confirmation, send a query to the host, and receive photos of the house and the hosts. The company's wiki also had a link to the host-blogger's homepage.

The home parties were attended by over 4,500 people, and the publicity enabled Stormhoek to triple its sales in

2 years (mainly in the United Kingdom). The only problem was a profusion of blog spam—random comments that were automatically posted by marketers for promotions. This required a daily purging and cleaning of the blog from unwanted postings.

The blogging resulted in word-of-mouth (viral) marketing publicity. The blogging was done by a professional blogger (Hugh Macleod at *gapingvoid.com*). The blog offered a free bottle of wine to any blogger who was of legal age and had blogged for 3 months. Macleod also organized the 100 dinners described earlier. Technorati like RSS pioneer Dave Winer have attended some of the dinners.

A final word: Stormhoek wine is really good! Viral marketing cannot sell bad wine.

Connection to Social Networks. In January 2011, Stormhoek was connected to social networks in the following ways:

▶ A dedicated group at Facebook
▶ A video channel at YouTube
▶ A photo and video collection at Flicker (Stormhoek's photo stream)
▶ RSS feed service
▶ Was followed on Twitter

Sources: Compiled from Bennett (2007), *Stormhoek.com/blog*, McNichol (2007), and *stormhoek.com* (accessed January 2008).

Questions

1. What was the corporate blog used for?
2. What were the hosts' blogs used for?
3. What capabilities were introduced by the mashups?
4. How did the wiki help in communication and collaboration?
5. Why do you think the Web 2.0 technologies were successful in increasing sales?
6. What is blog spam and why is it a problem?
7. How did viral marketing work here?

2.7 VIRTUAL COMMUNITIES AND SOCIAL NETWORKS

A *community* is a group of people with common interests who interact with one another. A **virtual community** is one in which the interaction takes place over a computer network, mainly the Internet. Virtual communities parallel typical physical communities, such as neighborhoods, clubs, or associations, but people do not meet face-to-face. Instead, they meet online. A virtual community is a social network organized around a common interest, idea, task, or goal; members interact across time, geographic, and organizational

virtual community
A group of people with similar interests who interact with one another using the Internet.

EXHIBIT 2.9   Types of Virtual Communities

Community Type	Description
Transaction and other business activities	Facilitate buying and selling (e.g., *ausfish.com.au*). Combine an information portal with an infrastructure for trading. Members are buyers, sellers, intermediaries, etc., who are focused on a specific commercial area (e.g., fishing).
Purpose or interest	No trading, just exchange of information on a topic of mutual interest. Examples: Investors consult The Motley Fool (*fool.com*) for investment advice; rugby fans congregate at the Fans Room at *nrl.com.au*; music lovers go to *mp3.com*.
Relations or practices	Members are organized around certain life experiences. Examples: *ivillage.com* caters to women and *seniornet.com* is for senior citizens. Professional communities also belong to this category. Examples: *isworld.org* is a space for information systems faculty, students, and professionals.
Fantasy/role playing	Members share imaginary environments. Examples: sport fantasy teams at *espn.com*; see *games.yahoo.com*, *horsderacegame.com/community/game_and_com*, and *facebook.com/pages/the-fantasy-gaming-community* for many more fantasy communities.
Social networks	Members communicate, collaborate, create, share, form groups, entertain, and more. Facebook.com is the leader.
Virtual worlds	Members use avatars to represent them in a simulated 3-D environment where they can play, conduct business, socialize, and fantasize.

boundaries to develop personal relationships. Virtual communities offer several ways for members to interact, collaborate, and trade (see Exhibit 2.9).

CHARACTERISTICS OF TRADITIONAL ONLINE COMMUNITIES AND THEIR CLASSIFICATION

Most virtual communities are Internet-based, known also as *Internet communities*.

Hundreds of thousands of communities exist on the Internet, and the number is growing rapidly. Pure-play Internet communities may have thousands, or even hundreds of millions, of members. By 2011, Facebook grew to 750 million members. This is one major difference from traditional purely physical communities, which usually are smaller. Another difference is that offline communities frequently are confined to one geographic location, whereas only a few online communities are geographically confined. For more information on virtual communities, see en.wikipedia.org/wiki/Virtual_community.

Types of Communities

The following are the major types of online communities.

> ▷ **Associations.** Many physical associations have a Web presence. These range from Parent–Teacher Associations (PTAs) to professional associations. An example of this type of community is the Australian Record Industry Association (aria.com.au). Another example is a retirement community (e.g. see myretirement.org).
>
> ▷ **Affinity portals.** These are communities organized by interest, such as hobbies, technical topic, vocations, political parties, or trade unions. MySpace changed its model in 2010 to become an entertainment social network.

Example: A Virtual World Community. In 2008, Sony launched a virtual community service for its PlayStation 3 (PS3) video game network with 8 million members. The 3-D service called Home allows users to create avatars, decorate homes, and interact and socialize with other users in a virtual world. Sony considers this an important part of the game-playing experience. Avatars can interact with each other, and users can play games with friends at a virtual arcade. The community is regional due to language and cultural considerations. As an extension, the service allows downloading of content and movies to PS3.

▶ **Ethnic communities.** Many communities are country or language specific.
▶ **Gender communities.** Women.com and ivillage.com, the two largest female-oriented community sites, merged in 2001 in an effort to cut losses and become profitable.
▶ **Catering to young people (teens and people in their early twenties).** Many investors see unusual opportunities here. Examples include alloy.com and bolt.com, which operates from the United States and concentrates on cell phone users.
▶ **Communities of practice.** These can be physical or virtual. Members are professionals and practitioners who share an area of practice (e.g., professors, physicians, dentists). Members also share knowledge in discussion groups. An example is Linux Online (inux.org), whose members develop code for the Linux operating system.
▶ **Neighborhood communities.** Some associations and newspapers have created websites for local communities. For example, at myadvertiser.com users can check out community events, share photos, and read local news and blogs about seven communities near Honolulu, Hawaii. Location-based companies such as Foursquare use this concept for their operation.
▶ **Social networks sites.** These are socially oriented online megacommunities, such as Facebook and LinkedIn, in which millions of members can express themselves, find friends, exchange photos, view videos, and more. In addition to general-interest communities such as Facebook, interest-based networks have also emerged, such as networks for dog lovers (e.g., doggyspace.com and dogster.com) and cat lovers (catster.com).
▶ **Virtual worlds.** These 3-D communities (see the next section) are adding many capabilities found on social networks (e.g., discussion groups).

Other Classifications of Virtual Communities

Virtual communities can be classified in several other ways.

Public Versus Private Communities. Communities can be designated as *public*, meaning that their membership is open to anyone. The owner of the community may be a privately held corporation or a public one. Most of the social networks, including Facebook, belong to the public category.

In contrast, *private* communities belong each to a company, an association, or a group of companies, and their membership is limited to people who meet certain requirements (e.g., work for a particular employer or work in a particular profession). Private communities may be internal (e.g., only employees can be members), or external (for customers).

Example: IBM's Virtual Universe Community. This is a private, internal community of over 8,500 individuals (in January 2011) who are active in virtual worlds. It was launched in 2006 with the goal of moving IBM into a range of new and profitable industries, from the creation of IBM hardware and software for virtual worlds to 24-hour virtual service desks staffed by avatars.

Classification Categories. Another option is to classify the members as *traders, players, just friends, enthusiasts,* or *friends in need.* A more common classification recognizes six types of Internet communities: (1) transaction, (2) purpose or interest, (3) relations or practices, (4) fantasy, (5) social networks, and (6) virtual worlds. For additional types of virtual communities and issues of participation and design of communities, see en.wikipedia.org/wiki/Virtual_community.

The most popular type of virtual community is the social network, the subject of our next section.

ONLINE SOCIAL NETWORKS

Let's first define social networks and then look at some of their services provided and capabilities.

A Definition and Basic Information

As you may recall, in Chapter 1 we defined a *social network* as a place where people create their own space, or homepage, on which they write blogs; post pictures, videos, or music; share ideas; and link to other Web locations they find interesting. In addition, members of social networks can tag the content they create and post it with key words they choose themselves, which makes the content searchable. The mass adoption of social networking websites points to an evolution in human social interaction.

A list of the characteristics and capabilities of social networks was provided in Section 1.3 of Chapter 1.

The Size of Social Network Sites

Social network sites are growing rapidly, with some having over 100 million members. For example, Facebook had 750 million members in June 2011. The typical annual growth of a successful site is 40 to 50 percent in the first few years and 15 to 25 percent thereafter. For a list of the major sites, including user counts, see en.wikipedia.org/wiki/List_of_social_networking_websites.

A Global Phenomenon

Although Facebook and MySpace attract the majority of media attention in the United States, they do have many members in other countries. Other social network sites are proliferating and growing in popularity worldwide. For example, Friendster (friendster.com) has gained traction in the Pacific Islands and Malaysia. Orkut (orkut.com) is the premier service in Brazil, Mixi (mixi.jp) has attained widespread adoption in Japan, LunarStorm (lunarstorm.se) has taken off in Sweden, Dutch users have embraced Hyves (hyves.nl), and Grono (grono.net) has captured Poland. Hi5 (hi5.com) has been adopted in smaller countries in Latin America, South America, and Europe. Additionally, previously popular communication and community services have begun implementing social networking features. For example, the Chinese QQ instant messaging service instantly became one of the largest social networking services in the world once it added profiles and made friends visible to one another (Boyd and Ellison 2007), and Cyworld conquered the Korean market by introducing homepages and buddies. Note that international entrepreneurs, inspired by the success of the largest social network sites and their capabilities, have created their own local knockoffs. Information about social networks is changing rapidly; therefore, to get the most up-to-date data, go to alexa.com, wikipedia.org, and comscore.com.

The following is a list of interesting representative social networking sites:

- Piczo.com is a teen-friendly site that is popular in Canada and the United Kingdom.
- Hi5.com is a global, multilanguage, social network popular in Asia and parts of Europe, Africa, and South America.
- Friendsreunited.co.uk connects alumni and helps in organizing reunions. Users can also find dating and employment opportunities.

- Iwiw.net is a Hungarian social networking site with a multilingual interface.
- Migente.com focuses on the American Latino community.
- Blackplanet.com focuses on African American issues and people.
- Grono.net is a Polish social networking site.
- Ning.com provides a platform for users to create their own social networks.

Social networking is strongly related to mobile devices and networks.

Representative Capabilities and Services Provided by Social Network Sites

Social network sites provide many capabilities and services such as:

- Users can construct a Web page that they can use to present themselves to the larger community.
- Users can create a circle of friends who are linked together.
- The site provides discussion forums (by subgroup, by topic).
- Photo, video, and document viewing and sharing (streaming videos, user-supplied videos) are supported.
- Wikis can be used to jointly create documents.
- Blogs can be used for discussion, dissemination of information, and much more.
- The site offers community e-mail and instant messaging (IM) capabilities.
- Experts can be made available to answer member queries.
- Consumers can rate and comment on products.
- Online voting may be available to poll member opinions.
- The site provides an e-newsletter.
- The site supports conference (group) chatting, combined with photo sharing.
- Message and bulletin board services are available for posting information to groups and anyone on the website.
- The site provides storage for content, including photos, videos, and music.
- Users can bookmark self-created content.
- Users can find other networks, friends, or topics of interest.

Not all networks have all these capabilities, but some have these and even more.

BUSINESS-ORIENTED SOCIAL NETWORKS

Business-oriented social networks also known as *professional social networks*, are social networks whose primary objective is to facilitate business. The prime example here is LinkedIn.com, which provides business connections and enables job finding and recruiting. (Linkedin's IPO in June 2011 was successful and offers hope for other social networking sites.) Another example is YUB. Yub.com is a huge online shopping mall with about 6 million items. Users can hang out at Yub.com with friends and meet others who are looking for discounts and bargains. Yet another example is craigslist.org, the classified ad super site, which offers many social-oriented features. Businesses are increasingly using business social networks as a means of growing their circle of business contacts and promoting themselves online. Because businesses are expanding globally, social networks make it easier to keep in touch with other contacts around the world. Specific cross-border EC platforms and business partnering networks now make globalization accessible even for small and medium-sized companies and for individuals.

business-oriented social networks
A social network whose major interest is business topics. Members are professional people. Such networks are used mostly for creating contacts, providing requirements, and enlisting members' support for problem solving and knowledge sharing.

Example of a Business-Oriented Social Network

Originating in Germany, Xing.com (xing.com) is a business network that attracts millions of executives, sales representatives, and job seekers from many countries, mostly in Europe. The site offers secure services in 16 languages. Users can visit the site to:

▶ Establish new business contacts.
▶ Systematically expand and manage their contacts' networks.
▶ Market themselves to employers in a professional business context.
▶ Identify experts and receive advice on any topic.
▶ Organize meetings and events.
▶ Control the level of privacy and ensure that their personal data are protected.

For more on Xing.com, take the site's "Guided Tour." Services also are available for mobile device users.

Some Capabilities of Business-Oriented Networks

With Web 2.0 tools, companies can engage users on a one-to-one basis in a way that old media, from flat websites to Super Bowl ads, was never able to accomplish. More direct communication is achieved by offering more ways for consumers to engage and interact. For example, a company can:

▶ Encourage consumers to rate and comment on products.
▶ Allow consumers to create their own topic areas and build communities (forums) around shared interests possibly related to a company's products.
▶ Hire bloggers or staff editors who can lead more company-formatted essays and discussions that allow, but are not driven by, customer comments.
▶ Provide incentives such as sweepstakes and contests for customers to get involved in new product (service) design and marketing campaigns.
▶ Encourage user-made videos about products/services and offer prizes for winning video ads, thus capitalizing on streaming videos.
▶ Provide interesting stories in e-newsletters.

BUSINESS MODELS AND SERVICES RELATED TO SOCIAL NETWORKING

Social networking sites provide innovative business models, ranging from customer reviews of food and night life in India (burrp.com) to users who dress up dolls that look like celebrities (stardoll.com). New revenue models are being created daily. Although some generate limited revenue, others succeed wildly. Lately, location-based commerce and group purchasing have become popular as described in Chapter 7.

Many communities attract advertisers. For example, Vivapets (vivapets.com) attracts pet lovers with Wikipedia-like contributions in its quest to catalog every pet breed. The site attracts hundreds of thousands of unique visitors per month. Obviously, pet food–related vendors are interested in placing ads there.

Social Network Analysis Software

Social network analysis software is used to identify, represent, analyze, visualize, or simulate network nodes (e.g., agents, organizations, or knowledge) and edges (relationships) from various types of input data (relational and nonrelational), including mathematical models of social networks. Various input and output file formats exist.

Network analysis tools enable researchers to investigate representations of networks of different forms and different sizes, from small (e.g., families, project teams) to very large. Visual representations of social networks are popular, and are important to understand network data and to convey the results of the analysis.

For details, see en.wikipedia.org/wiki/Social_network_analysis_software.

Xanga

Xanga (xanga.com) hosts blogs, photoblogs, and social networking profiles. Users of Xanga are referred to as "Xangans." Xanga's origins can be traced back to 1999, when it was launched as a site for sharing book and music reviews. It has since evolved into one of the most popular blogging and networking services on the Web, with an estimated 40 million users worldwide. (Xanga is very popular in Hong Kong, Macao, and Singapore.)

A *blogring* connects a circle of Weblogs with a common focus or theme. All Xanga users are given the ability to create a new blogring or join an existing one. Blogrings are searchable by topic. A list of blogrings that the user is associated with appears in a module, typically on the left side of the website. Each user is allowed a maximum of eight blogrings.

Digg

Digg (digg.com) is a community-based popularity website with an emphasis on technology and science articles (see en.wikipedia.org/wiki/Digg). The site expanded in 2008 to provide a variety of other categories, including politics and videos. It combines social bookmarking, blogging, and syndication with a form of nonhierarchical, democratic editorial control. Users submit news stories and websites, and then a user-controlled ranking system promotes these stories and sites to the front page. This differs from the hierarchical editorial system that many other news sites employ. When users read news items, they have the option to "digg it" or "digg that."

MOBILE SOCIAL NETWORKING

Mobile social networking refers to social networking where members converse and connect with one another using cell phones or other mobile devices. A current trend for social networking websites such as Facebook is to offer mobile services. According to comScore, the number of mobile subscribers accessing Facebook increased 112 percent between January 2009 and January 2010. Some social networking sites offer mobile-only services (e.g., ZYB, Brightkite, and Fon11).

There are two basic types of mobile social networks. The first type is companies that partner with wireless carriers to distribute their communities via the default start pages on cell phone browsers. For example, users can access MySpace via AT&Ts wireless network. The second type is companies that do not have such carrier relationships (also known as "off deck") and rely on other methods to attract users. Examples of this second type include MocoSpace (mocospace.com) and Mobikade (mobikade.com). For details, see en.wikipedia. org/wiki/Mobile-social-network.

Windows Live Spaces Mobile can be viewed as a mobile device with limited screen size and slow data connections. It allows users to browse and add photos, blog entries, and comments directly from their mobile devices. However, it has also introduced several other features to improve the user experience with handheld devices. For more information on Windows Live Spaces Mobile, see mobile.spaces.live.com and en.wikipedia.org/wiki/Windows_Live_Spaces_Mobiles.

Mobile social networking is especially popular in Japan, South Korea, and China, generally due to better data pricing (flat rates are widespread in Japan). In Japan, where 3G networks have achieved over 80 percent user penetration, the leaders in social networking are Mixi (mixi.jp) and Mobage-Town (mbga.jp). Numerous other mobile social networking sites have been launched in Japan. For statistics on exponential growth of mobile social networks, see comscore.com.

Experts predict that mobile social networks will experience explosive growth, increasing from about 200 million in 2011 to about 300 million in 2015.

Mobile Enterprise Networks. Several companies have developed (or fully sponsor) mobile-based social networks. For example, in 2007 Coca-Cola created a social network that could only be accessed by cell phones in an attempt to lure young people to its sodas and other products.

Mobile Community Activities

In many mobile social networks, users can use their mobile devices to create their profiles, make friends, participate in chat rooms, create chat rooms, hold private conversations, and

mobile social networking
Members converse and connect with one another using cell phones or other mobile devices.

share photos, videos, and blogs. Some companies provide wireless services that allow their customers to build their own mobile community and brand it (e.g., Sonopia at sonopia.com).

Mobile video sharing, which is sometimes combined with photo sharing, is a new technological and social trend. Mobile video-sharing portals are becoming popular (e.g., see myubo.com and myzenplanet.com). Many social networking sites are offering mobile features.

SOCIAL NETWORK SERVICES

Social network services are companies that host social communities. They are known in brief as social networks.

Social networks appear in a variety of forms, the most well-known, mostly social-oriented networks are Facebook and MySpace. LinkedIn is a business-oriented network. Covering both aspects via classified services is Craigslist, which is described in Case 2.4.

CASE 2.4

EC Application

CRAIGSLIST: THE ULTIMATE ONLINE CLASSIFIED COMMUNITY

If you want to find (or offer) a job, housing, goods and services, social activities, romance, advice, and much more in more than 570 cities in six languages and in more than 50 countries worldwide, go to Craigslist (*craigslist.org*). The site has much more information than you will find in all the newspapers in the individual cities it serves. For example, more than 1 million new jobs are listed, and Craigslist receives 80 million new classified ads every month. Each month there are more than 50 million visitors to the site in the United States alone. The site receives over 20 billion page views per month (per *alexa.com* and *compete.com*), making it the seventh most visited site in the English language. Craig Newmark, the founder of Craigslist, has said that everything is for sale on the site except the site itself. Although many other sites offer free classifieds, no other site even comes close to Craigslist.

In addition, Craigslist features 100 topical discussion forums with more than 120 million user postings. Every day, people in 700 cities worldwide check classified ads and interact on forums. Craigslist is considered by many as one of the few websites that could change the world because it is simply a free social-oriented, trusted, and useful notice board. For more information, see *craigslist.org/about/factsheet* and *en.wikipedia.org/wiki/Craigslist*.

Users cite the following reasons for the popularity of Craigslist:

▸ It gives people a voice.
▸ It promotes a sense of trust, even intimacy.
▸ It is consistent and champions down-to-earth values.
▸ It illustrates simplicity.
▸ It has social-networking capabilities.

▸ It can be used for free in most cases (you can post free ads except for business, for rent, or for sale ads in a few large cities; some employments ads; and for adult and therapeutic services).
▸ It is effective and well visited.

As an example of the site's benefits, we provide the personal experience of one of the authors, who needed to rent his condo in Los Angeles. The usual process would take two to four weeks and $400 to $700 in newspaper ads, plus ads in the local online sites for rent services, to get the condo rented. With Craigslist, it took less than a week at no cost. As more people discover Craigslist, the traditional newspaper-based classified ad industry will probably be the loser; ad rates may become lower, and fewer ads will be printed.

Craigslist charges for "help wanted" ads and apartment broker listings in some large cities. In addition, Craigslist may charge ad placers, especially when an ad has rich media features. Classified advertising is Craigslist's real money-making opportunity.

Concerns About Craigslist. Questions regarding the future of Craigslist have to do with the very hands-off mentality that made this site famous. Specifically, critics charge that users post illegitimate and possibly illegal ads on the site, and the Craigslist staff are unable to effectively police this practice. Some users have complained about questionable ads being posted, especially in the "jobs" section. This would include pyramid schemes and under-the-counter work. Craigslist also attracts criminals seeking to commit fraud by misleading the gullible into accepting false checks. The anonymity of Craigslist's users

(continued)

and the lack of ratings systems create an environment where deceitful users cannot be held accountable for their actions.

Another concern is that erotic services make up a significant portion of the total traffic on the site. There is a fear that many of the sexual encounters facilitated using Craigslist have been with underage girls. With the sheer volume of users and ads posted per day, such policing is not possible given the modest workforce of only 30 that the site employs. (On September 8, 2010, Craigslist closed its adult and erotic services sections.)

In addition, many supporters contend that attempts to control Craigslist may simply cause users to relocate to a different, less-regulated site. Surely the design of Craigslist shouldn't be too difficult to duplicate. However, its brand is extremely strong.

Sources: Compiled from *craigslist.org* (accessed November 2010), Clark (2009), Liedtke (2009), and *en.wikipedia.org/wiki/Craigslist* (accessed January 2011).

Questions

1. Identify the business model used by Craigslist.
2. Visit *craigslist.org* and identify the social network and business network elements.
3. What do you like about the site? What do you dislike about it?
4. Why is Craigslist considered a site that "changes the world"?
5. What are some of the risks and limitations of using this site?

Section 2.7 ▶ REVIEW QUESTIONS

1. Define virtual communities and describe their characteristics.
2. List the major types of virtual communities.
3. Define social network.
4. List some major social network sites.
5. Describe the global nature of social networks.
6. Define social network analysis.
7. Describe social networking.

2.8 VIRTUAL WORLDS AS AN ELECTRONIC COMMERCE MECHANISM

According to en.wikipedia.org/wiki/Virtual_world, a **virtual world** is a form of a computer-based simulated environment through which users can create an online community where they can interact with one another and use and create objects. Virtual worlds are intended for its users to inhabit and interact, and the term today has become largely synonymous with interactive 3-D virtual environments, where the users take the form of avatars visible to others graphically. In virtual worlds the *computer-simulated* world offers the use of visual stimuli that in turn can manipulate elements of the modeled world and thus create *telepresence,* to a certain degree. The modeled world may motivate situations and rules, based on the real world or on some fantasy world. Users can manipulate elements of the modeled world and thus experience telepresence to a certain degree. The virtual world appeared initially in massively multiplayer online games that depict a world very similar to the real world, with real world rules and real-time actions and communication. However, virtual worlds are not limited to games. Players can create a character to travel between buildings, towns, and even worlds to carry out business or leisure activities. In a virtual world, you can be anyone you want. You can build a dream house, decorate it, have a job, or fly a spaceship. For an overview, see Malaby (2009).

With the use of avatars, communication among users can include text, graphical icons, visual gestures, video clips, sound, and so forth.

AVATARS

Virtual worlds are populated with interactive animated characters—software agents with personalities known as *avatars.* **Avatars** are animated representations of humanlike

virtual world
A user-defined world in which people can interact, play, and do business. The most publicized virtual world is Second Life.

avatars
Animated computer characters that exhibit humanlike movements and behaviors.

movements and behaviors depicted as 2-D or 3-D graphical representation. Advanced avatars can "speak" and display behaviors such as gestures and facial expressions. They can be fully automated to act like robots. The purpose of avatars is to introduce believable emotions so that the computerized agents gain credibility with users. For example, the real estate giant RE/MAX uses hundreds of avatars as virtual sales agents. Many companies use avatars as tour guides or to staff virtual reception desks. For a demonstration of avatars in business, see meez.com.

Avatars are aimed at making the human–computer interface more natural. Thus, they are sometimes referred to as interactive *conversational characters*. They are being used extensively to support Internet chat with companies (e.g., LiveChat), representing the company's people. Instant-messaging programs such as Google Talk and Yahoo! Messenger support the use of avatars. Avatars can improve customer satisfaction and retention by offering personalized, one-to-one service. They also can help companies get to know their customers and support advertising.

Example. American TESOL Institute teaches and certifies qualified individuals to teach English worldwide. The company deploys multiple characters throughout its website. Visitors to the site are initially greeted by a VHost character who provides a quick overview of the company's services and training. In addition, characters have been added to two of the company's complimentary service offerings including the "Tip of the Week" and "Shakespeare's Corner." Soon after the company experienced increases in unique visits to the site and its services offering pages of *over 250 percent* and *57 percent*, respectively, as well as increases in its income. The characters also provide tips for ESL students to help them improve their conversational abilities.

For more on avatars, see en.wikipedia.org/wiki/Avatar_(computing), and of course you must see the 2009 movie *Avatar*.

BUSINESS ACTIVITIES AND VALUE IN VIRTUAL WORLDS

Virtual worlds provide an interesting platform for business activities. As businesses compete in the real world, they also compete in virtual worlds. Many companies and organizations now incorporate virtual worlds as a new form of advertising and sales. An example of this would be Apple Computer creating a virtual store within Second Life. This allows users to browse Apple's latest innovative products. You cannot actually purchase a product (yet), but having these "virtual stores" is a way for vendors to access a different customer demographic as customers examine products in 3-D and exchange opinions and recommendations.

There are several types of business activities in virtual worlds:

▶ Creating and managing a virtual business (see Terdiman 2008 for guidelines on how to do this)

▶ Conducting regular business activities (e.g., advertising, marketing, collaboration) within the framework of the virtual world

▶ Providing services for those who build, manage, or make money with virtual properties

For additional business activities, see Mahar and Martin-Mahar (2009), and Chapter 7.

For instance, in a cover story in *BusinessWeek*, Hof (2008) discusses the various opportunities for conducting business in Second Life. Specifically, he introduces seven residents who are making substantial amounts of money. These include the Anshe Chung avatar, known as the "Rockefeller of Second Life," who buys virtual land from Second Life, "develops" it, and sells or rents it globally. Her business has grown so rapidly that she employs (in 2010) 20 people to design and program the development project.

Following are two examples of how companies are using virtual worlds to bolster their physical businesses:

Example 1: Collaboration. More than 2,000 IBM employees signed up as members of Second Life, using the site to share ideas and work on projects. IBM holds an "alumni block party" in Second Life, allowing current and former employees from around the globe to get together in virtual meetings. IBM purchases islands for use as meeting places and technology showcases, and for experiments in virtual reality businesses. For example, IBM has set up a Sears appliance store as a virtual commerce demonstration project. IBM allows greater interactivity with products than a conventional store will allow. Users can, for example, customize appliances at Sears.

Example 2: Research and Marketing. Starwood Hotels constructed a prototype of the new Aloft brand hotels before they appeared in the real world in 2008. The company purchased two islands: Aloft, for the hotel prototype, and Argali, where visitors viewed the development project. Working from a preliminary architectural sketch, the designers began roughing out the layout, furnishings, and textures of the hotel, which were then refined in response to feedback from the *brick-and-mortar* architects and from Second Life residents who were invited to critique the design and layout. Then, the developers began remodeling the hotel in response to feedback from Second Life residents.

Using virtual worlds gives companies the opportunity to gauge customer reaction and receive feedback about new products or services. This can be crucial because it will give the companies insight into what the market and customers want from new products, which can give companies a competitive edge. For potential other activities, see Mahar and Martin-Mahar (2009). For more, see this chapter's closing case.

Virtual Shopping

Imagine you are going mall shopping with a gang of friends, even while you remain miles apart. In reality, you are all at your computer terminal, but on the screen you would be transported to a digital replica of the shopping center. As you walk by a sale at a virtual jeans store, Web cameras in the real store let you see how crowded it actually is, in case a popular item is selling out. Your avatar, set to your body's measurements, tries on the jeans and spins around to show them to your pals. You might buy the pants online or visit the physical store later. Either way, you'd have had a fun afternoon without leaving your home or workplace. Virtual shopping is gaining popularity (see Schuman 2007 and Chapter 7).

One type of virtual shopping is described next.

Trading Virtual Properties

As you will see in the closing case, trading virtual properties is a very popular activity in Second Life. Habbo Hotel (habbo.com) sells more virtual furniture worldwide than the giant Swedish retailer IKEA sells actual ones. The furniture is designed by teens on the site who decorate their Habbo rooms with the furniture. The kids are buying not only furniture but also clothes, bags, etc., for their avatars.

Section 2.8 ▶ REVIEW QUESTIONS

1. Define virtual worlds.
2. Describe avatars. Why do we use them?
3. List some business activities in virtual worlds. Categorize them by type.
4. Describe virtual shopping.

2.9 THE FUTURE: WEB 3.0 AND WEB 4.0

Web 2.0 is here. What's next? The answer is a still-unknown entity referred to as *Web 3.0*, the future wave of Internet applications. Some of the characteristics of Web 3.0 are already in the making. Based on nontechnological success factors and technological factors and trends, there is general optimism about the future of the Web and EC (Hempel 2009).

WEB 3.0: WHAT'S NEXT?

Web 3.0 will not be just about shopping, entertainment, and search. Web 3.0 will deliver a new generation of business applications that will see business and social computing converge on the same fundamentals as on-demand architecture is converging with consumer applications today. Thus, Web 3.0 is just not merely of passing interest to those who work on enterprise EC. The Web 3.0 era could radically change individuals' career paths as well as the organizations where they work, and it may even revolutionize social networking (see Laurent 2010, and Hempel 2009).

Web 3.0
A term used to describe the future of the World Wide Web. It consists of the creation of high-quality content and services produced by gifted individuals using Web 2.0 technology as an enabling platform.

According to en.wikipedia.org/wiki/Web_3, the next-generation Internet will not just be more portable and personal, it will also harness the power of people, making it even easier to zero in on precisely what you are looking for. Web 3.0 has the potential to usher in the following:

> ▶ Faster, far-flung connectivity; richer ways of interacting
> ▶ New Web Services that work entirely within a browser's window
> ▶ More powerful search engines
> ▶ More clout for everyday people and more user-friendly application-creation capabilities
> ▶ New artificial intelligence applications
> ▶ 10MB of bandwidth (instead of 1MB in Web 2.0, on average)
> ▶ More uses of 3-D tools
> ▶ Greater utilization of wireless and mobile social networks

Unlike Web 2.0 where key words are used to organize data into digestible nuggets for search engines, Web 3.0 will effectively categorize and present digital information to users in a visually improved manner that enhances interaction, analysis, intuition, and search functions. The key driver in this scenario is the concept of taxonomies—standardized and self-describing classifications with codified semantics that are related to one another via highly normalized and descriptive metadata, not by hyperlinks. For Web 3.0 to live up to its hype, it must contain a new magnitude of computer intelligence.

With Web 3.0, the Internet can finally realize elaborate and complex virtual worlds, where social interaction drives business operations. These worlds have been anticipated and talked about for years, but they have so far failed to materialize.

Web 3.0 and the Semantic Web

Semantic Web

An evolving extension of the Web in which Web content can be expressed not only in natural language, but also in a form that can be understood, interpreted, and used by intelligent computer software agents, permitting them to find, share, and integrate information more easily.

One of the major possible platforms of Web 3.0 technologies is the **Semantic Web** (see en.wikipedia.org/wiki/Semantic_Web). The Semantic Web is an evolving extension of the Web in which Web content can be expressed not only in natural language, but also in a form that can be understood, interpreted, and used by intelligent computer software agents, permitting them to find, share, and integrate information more easily. The technology is derived from W3C director Tim Berners-Lee's vision of the Web as a universal medium for data, information, and knowledge exchange. At its core, the Semantic Web comprises a philosophy, a set of design principles, collaborative working groups, and a variety of enabling technologies.

A similar view about the role of the Semantic Web is expressed by Borland (2007), who believes that the role of the Semantic Web in Web 3.0 is certain, and coming soon. Borland believes that new Web 3.0 tools (some of which are already helping developers "stitch" together complex applications) will improve and automate database searches, help people choose vacation destinations, and sort through complicated financial data more efficiently.

As of 2010 an experimental Semantic-Web browser is being developed that users can apply to display data, draw graphs, and so on. Another example would be "friend-of-a-friend" networks, where individuals in social networks provide data in the form of links between themselves and friends.

Example: A Virtual Music Factory. At a virtual music factory, you will be able to seamlessly shop and listen to music, receive staff recommendations, talk to fellow shoppers, and put your 3 terabyte music collection on the cloud (see cloud computing in Online Tutorial T7). Instead of combing through recommendations on various music shopping websites and doing countless searches to find newly recorded classical, pop, or jazz performances, you will be able to type a somewhat complex sentence into a Web 3.0 browser or talk to the computer, and get back highly customized, organized, and impeccably relevant results. The browser then would redirect you automatically to your favorite virtual music store where you would be able to download the recording and place a copy of it in your own personal cloud space so you could listen to it on-demand, via a Web-enabled mobile or other device anywhere anytime. Because your Web 3.0 browser would have learned your likes and dislikes, it would start to function as a trusted advisor, mentor, and personal assistant, and less like a search engine.

The Semantic Web could help visualize such complex networks and organize them to enable a deeper understanding of such communities' structures.

For more on Web 3.0 and the Semantic Web, see en.wikipedia.org/wiki/Web_3. For a video by Kate Ray, see Gain (2010).

Web 4.0

Web 4.0 is the next Web generation after Web 3.0. It is still an unknown entity. However, Coleman and Levine (2008) envision it as being based on islands of intelligence and on being ubiquitous. Exhibit 2.10 depicts the relationship of Web 4.0 to Web 1.0, 2.0, and 3.0.

Concerns

The following are a few concerns regarding the implementation of Web 3.0 and the future of EC.

▶ **Future threats.** According to Stafford (2006) and Laurent (2010), the following six trends may slow EC and Web 3.0, and even cripple the Internet.
▶ **Security concerns.** Shoppers as well as users of e-banking and other services worry about online security. The Web needs to be made safer.
▶ **Lack of net neutrality.** If the big telecommunications companies are allowed to charge companies for a guarantee of faster access, critics fear that small innovative Web companies could be crowded out by the Microsofts and Googles that can afford to pay more.
▶ **Copyright complaints.** The legal problems of YouTube, Craigslist, Wikipedia, and others may result in a loss of vital outlets of public opinion, creativity, and discourse.
▶ **Choppy connectivity.** Upstream bandwidths are still constricted, making uploading of video files a time-consuming task. Usable mobile bandwidth still costs a lot, and some carriers impose limitations on how Web access can be employed.

Web 4.0
The Web generation after Web 3.0. It is still an unknown entity. However, it is envisioned as being based on islands of intelligence and as being ubiquitous.

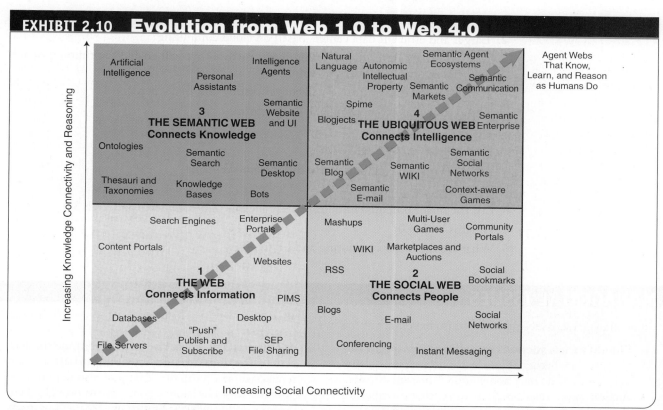

EXHIBIT 2.10 Evolution from Web 1.0 to Web 4.0

Source: M. Davis. "Semantic Wave 2008: Industry Roadmap to Web 3.0 and Multibillion Dollar Market Opportunities." Project 10X, 2008. *project10x.com/about.php* (accessed November 2010). Used with permission.

> ▶ **Language fitness.** There will be a need to reconsider the existing spoken languages with Web 3.0 taxonomies and schemes.
> ▶ **Standards.** There will be a need for architectural standards for Web 3.0.

Despite these concerns, Web 3.0 and e-commerce could thrive due to several innovations in the technological environment.

THE TECHNOLOGICAL ENVIRONMENT

The future of EC, Web 3.0, and Semantic Web is dependent on how far the relevant information technology has advanced. Two interesting predictions follow.

McKinsey & Company's Prediction

According to this prediction (Bughin et al. 2010), the following are the 10 tech-enabled business trends to watch:

Trend 1:   Distributed cocreation moves into the mainstream
Trend 2:   Making the network the organization
Trend 3:   Collaboration at scale
Trend 4:   The growing "Internet of Things" (pervasive computing)
Trend 5:   Experimentation and big data
Trend 6:   Wiring for a sustainable world
Trend 7:   Imagining anything as a service
Trend 8:   The age of the multisided business model
Trend 9:   Innovation coming from the bottom of the pyramid
Trend 10:   Producing public good on the information grid

Nicholas Carr's Predictions

In his free e-book, Nicholas Carr (2008) discusses the following trends:

1. More intelligent computers
2. Larger and efficient data centers based on cloud computing
3. Use of virtualization in computing infrastructure that will enable the running of any application on an external computing grid
4. Parallel processing grids that will cut processing cost by 90 percent
5. Utility and cloud computing will be the norm

Section 2.9 ▶ REVIEW QUESTIONS

1. What is Web 3.0, and how will it differ from Web 2.0?
2. Define Semantic Web.
3. List the major potential inhibitors and concerns of e-commerce and Web 3.0.
4. What is Web 4.0?
5. What are the major computing and IT trends?

MANAGERIAL ISSUES

Some managerial issues related to this chapter are as follows.

1. **Should we use auctions for selling?** A major strategic issue is whether to use auctions as a sales channel. Auctions do have some limitations, and forward auctions may create conflicts with other distribution channels. If a company decides to use auctions, it needs to select auction mechanisms and determine a pricing strategy. These decisions determine the success of the auctions and the ability to attract and retain visitors on the site. Auctions also require support services. Decisions about how to provide these services and to what extent to use business partners are critical to the success of high-volume auctions.

2. **Should we barter?** Bartering can be an interesting strategy, especially for companies that lack cash, need special material or machinery, and have surplus resources. However, the valuation of what is bought or sold may be hard to determine, and the tax implications in some countries are not clear.

3. **How do we select merchant software?** There are many products and vendors on the market. Small businesses should consider offers from Yahoo! or eBay since the software is combined with hosting and offers exposure to the vendor-managed e-market. The functionalities of the software must be examined as well as the ease of building webstores (see discussion in Chapter 13).

4. **How can we use Facebook and other social networks in our business?** There are many possibilities that are presented in Chapter 7, mostly in marketing and advertising. Any progressive organization should examine and experiment with social networking.

5. **How shall we start using Web 2.0 tools?** Start small: Determine whether a collaborative tool would benefit a team or group working on a specific project. People in the marketing department are often good first targets for information sharing with others because they are usually the ones tasked with sharing corporate information. Try establishing a wiki for a team's collaborative project. Some wikis are hosted on an internal server, whereas others are available as open source or via hosted service.

6. **Shall we take part in virtual worlds?** For many companies and applications, the technology is still immature and cumbersome. A good strategy is to observe what other companies, especially in the same industry, are doing in Second Life.

7. **How should we deal with Web 2.0 risks?** There are several possible risks, depending on the applications. The knowledge from unreliable participants may downgrade the credibility of knowledge from open sources. To protect the security get some outside legal advice. Use a risk expert for large projects to examine and evaluate the risks.

SUMMARY

In this chapter, you learned about the following EC issues as they relate to the chapter's learning objectives.

1. **Activities and mechanisms.** The major activities are information dissemination and presence, online trading, collaboration, entertainment, and search. The major mechanisms are marketplaces, storefronts, shopping carts, catalogs, search engines, Web 2.0 tools, and virtual worlds.

   Most of the activities are between sellers and buyers. But there are collaboration activities among supply chain members as well as among people within organizations. EC attempts to automate the interaction process for the above.

2. **E-marketplaces and their components.** A marketspace, or e-marketplace, is a virtual market that does not suffer from limitations of space, time, or borders. As such, it can be very efficient and effective. Its major components include customers, sellers, products (some digital), infrastructure, front-end processes, back-end activities, electronic intermediaries, other business partners, and support services.

   The role of intermediaries will change as e-markets develop: Some will be eliminated (disintermediation); others will change their roles and prosper (reintermediation). In the B2B area, for example, e-distributors connect manufacturers with buyers by aggregating electronic catalogs of many suppliers. New value-added services that range from content creation to syndication are mushrooming.

3. **The major types of e-marketplaces.** In the B2C area, there are storefronts and e-malls. In the B2B area, there are private and public e-marketplaces, which may be vertical (within one industry) or horizontal (across different industries). Exchanges are the platform for many buyers and sellers to meet and trade. Different types of portals provide access to e-marketplaces.

4. **Electronic catalogs, search engines, and shopping carts.** The major mechanisms in e-markets are electronic catalogs, search engines, software (intelligent) agents, and electronic shopping carts. These mechanisms, which are known as merchant suits, facilitate EC by providing a user-friendly and efficient shopping environment.

5. **Types of auctions and their characteristics.** In forward auctions, bids from buyers are placed sequentially, either in increasing mode or in decreasing mode. In reverse auctions, buyers place an RFQ and suppliers submit offers in one or several rounds. In name-your-own-price auctions, buyers specify how much they are willing to pay for a product or service, and an intermediary tries to find a supplier to fulfill the request.

6. **The benefits and limitations of auctions.** The major benefits for sellers are the ability to reach many buyers, to sell quickly, and to save on commissions to intermediaries. Buyers have an excellent access to auctions, a chance to obtain bargains and collectibles while

shopping from their homes. The major limitation is the possibility of fraud.

7. **Bartering and negotiating.** Electronic bartering can greatly facilitate the swapping of goods and services among organizations, thanks to improved search and matching capabilities, which is done in bartering exchanges. Software agents can facilitate online negotiation.

8. **The structure and role of virtual communities.** Virtual communities create new types of business opportunities—people with similar interests that congregate at one website are a natural target for advertisers and marketers. Using chat rooms, members can exchange opinions about certain products and services. Of special interest are communities of transactions, whose interest is the promotion of commercial buying and selling. Virtual communities can foster customer loyalty, increase sales of vendors that sponsor communities, and facilitate customer feedback for improved service and business.

9. **Web 2.0 tools.** The major tools discussed in this chapter are blogs, wikis, and Twitter. Web 2.0 tools are used for several purposes, most commonly to improve communication and collaboration, to initiate viral marketing (word of mouth), to create branding awareness, and to foster interpersonal relationships.

10. **Social networks as an EC mechanism.** These are very large Internet communities that enable the sharing of content, including text, videos, and photos, and promote online socialization and interaction. Hundreds of networks are popping up around the world, some of which are global, competing for advertising money. Millions of corporations advertise, entertain, and even sell on social networks.

Business-oriented communities concentrate on business issues both in one country and around the world (e.g., recruiting, finding business partners). Social marketplaces meld social networks and some aspects of business. Notable business-oriented social networks are LinkedIn and Xing. Also, some companies own private social networks, whereas others conduct business in public social networks, such as in Facebook. Enterprise social networks are those owned and operated inside one company. Their members are usually employees and retirees. They are used mainly for collaboration, knowledge creation and preservation, training, and socialization. Many large companies have such networks (e.g., IBM, Wells Fargo).

11. **Virtual worlds.** These environments provide entertainment, trading virtual property, discussion groups, learning, training, and much more. Everything is simulated, animated, and supported by avatars. Thousands of companies have established presences in virtual worlds, especially in Second Life, offering mainly dissemination of information and advertising.

12. **Web 3.0 and Web 4.0.** Web 3.0, the next generation of the Web, will combine social and business computing. It will be more portable and personal, with powerful search engines, increased clout, and greater connectivity with the wireless environment and on-demand applications. Knowledge management will be one of its main pillars. The Semantic Web will play a major role in Web 3.0 applications. Web 3.0 and its applications will depend on IT trends such as the developments in cloud computing, utility computing, parallel processing, and machine intelligence. Web 4.0 is a futuristic Web that will be built on ubiquitous and intelligent systems. It will connect "islands" of intelligence from different sources.

KEY TERMS

Term	Page	Term	Page	Term	Page
Auction	98	E-mall (online mall)	90	Search engine	96
Avatars	119	E-marketplace	85	Sell-side e-marketplace	88
Back end	86	Enterprise search	95	Semantic Web	122
Bartering	103	Folksonomy (collaborative tagging,		Social bookmarking	110
Bartering exchange	103	social tagging)	110	Social software	104
Blog	104	Forward auction	100	Tags	109
Business-oriented social networks	115	Front end	86	Tweet	107
Buy-side e-marketplace	88	Infomediary	92	Twitter	107
Desktop search	95	Intermediary	86	Virtual community	111
Digital products	86	Marketspace	86	Virtual world	119
Disintermediation	87	Mashup	110	Vlog (video blog)	104
Double auction	101	Microblogging	107	Voice portal	92
Dynamic pricing	98	Mobile portals	92	Web 3.0	121
E-bartering (electronic bartering)	103	Mobile social networking	117	Web 4.0	123
E-distributor	94	Name-your-own-price model	100	Web portal	90
Electronic auctions (e-auctions)	99	Penny auction	101	Webstore (storefront)	89
Electronic catalogs (e-catalog)	94	Reverse auction (bidding or		Wiki (wikilog)	109
Electronic shopping cart	97	tendering system)	100		

DISCUSSION QUESTIONS

1. Compare marketplaces with marketspaces. What are the advantages and limitations of each?

2. Discuss the competitive advantage of Craigslist in classifieds.

3. Discuss the value of a virtual world as an EC environment. Why does it attract users? Why does it attract companies? How can it provide a competitive advantage to a company that has a presence there? What are its limitations?

4. Discuss how wikis, blogs, and virtual worlds can be used to facilitate collaboration.

5. Discuss the reasons why Twitter is becoming so popular.

6. Discuss the potential risks of using Web 2.0 tools.

7. Discuss the need for portals in EC.

8. How do business-oriented networks differ from regular social networks such as MySpace?

9. What are the major characteristics of Web 2.0? What are some of the advantages of Web 2.0 applications?

10. Why are social marketplaces considered to be a Web 2.0 application?

11. Discuss the following statement: "Technically, you can put together a portal in a weekend, but culturally there are a slew of things to consider; therefore it takes much longer."

12. Discuss the pros and cons of selling cars via auctions. Why does GM auction only via its dealers on eBay?

TOPICS FOR CLASS DISCUSSION AND DEBATES

1. Compare and contrast competition in traditional markets with that in digital markets.

2. Explain why sell-side and buy-side marketplaces in the same company are usually separated, whereas in B2B exchanges they are combined.

3. Discuss the advantages of dynamic pricing strategy over fixed pricing. What are the potential disadvantages of dynamic pricing?

4. Discuss the opportunities that the faltering economy provides to social networking in assisting enterprises.

5. What is the advantage of a business using eBay instead of conducting auctions from its own site? Distinguish between C2C and B2B cases.

6. Should companies build in-house social networks for external activities or use existing public social networks (e.g., see Roberts 2008)?

7. Debate: Blogs and wikis are going to eliminate e-mail.

8. Debate: Should Craigslist and YouTube monitor and control what users publish there? Who will pay the cost?

9. Debate: Social network services, such as Visible Path, can provide social networking services for entire enterprises that are fairly secure. However, security may limit users' creativity and disrupt the business. Should a company use this service?

10. Debate: Some research suggests that the use of public social networks by employees can be good for a business, because employees develop relationships and share information, which increases productivity and innovation. Others say it is a waste of time and ban the use of Facebook, YouTube, and other such sites.

11. Debate the business value of social networking. As a start, read Tom Davenport's "Where's the Working in Social Networks" (**blogs.harvardbusiness. org/davenport/2007/10/wheres_the_working_in_ social_n.html**) and Brett Bonfield's "Should Your Organization Use Social Networking Sites" (**techsoup. org/learningcenter/internet/page7935.cfm**).

12. Debate: Facebook and Twitter compete for advertiser's money. Who has a better chance to get more ad money and why? (Consult Mangalindan 2010.)

INTERNET EXERCISES

1. Enter **etsy.com** and find all the EC mechanisms used. Prepare a report.

2. Examine how bartering is conducted online at **tradeaway.com**, **barterquest.com**, and **u-exchange. com**. Compare and contrast the functionalities and ease of use of these sites.

3. Enter **blogger.com** and find its capabilities. Then enter **blogsearch. google.com** and find what this site helps you to do. Write a report.

4. Enter **mfgquote.com** and review the process by which buyers can send RFQs to merchants of their choice.

Evaluate all the online services provided by the company. Write a report based on your findings.

5. Enter respond.com and send a request for a product or a service. Once you receive replies, select the best deal. You have no obligation to buy. Write a short report based on your experience.

6. Enter *Web 2.0 Journal* at web2.sys-con.com and find recent material on wikis, blogs, and Twitter. Write a report.

7. Enter dtsearch.com and find its capabilities. What type(s) of search it conducts (e.g., desktop, enterprise, general)?

8. Enter cars.com. List all services available to sellers and to buyers of cars. Compare it to carsdirect.com. Also, identify the revenue sources of the sites.

9. Enter ups.com.

   a. Find out what information is available to customers before they send a package.

   b. Find out about the "package tracking" system; be specific.

   c. Compute the cost of delivering a 10" × 20" × 15" box, weighing 40 pounds, from your hometown to Long Beach, California. Compare the fastest delivery against the lowest cost.

   d. Prepare a spreadsheet for two different types of calculations available on the site. Enter data to solve for two different calculators. Use Excel.

10. Register at Second Life, and enter the site.

    a. Find what IBM and Coca-Cola are doing on the site.

    b. Find out what three universities that you are familiar with are doing on the site.

    c. Write a report.

11. Create an avatar in Second Life. Let your avatar interact with avatars of some companies. Why do we consider an avatar as a mechanism for EC? Write a report.

12. Enter ca.com/us/products.aspx and register. Take the Clever Path Portal Test Drive. (Flash Player from Macromedia is required.) Then enter ibm.com and oracle.com/bea. Prepare a list of the major products available for building corporate portals.

13. Enter sap.com and find the key capabilities of its enterprise portals. List the benefits of using five of the capabilities its portals.

14. Enter networksolutions.com. View the shopping cart demo. What features impress you the most and why? What related services does it provide? Compare it to storefront.net and nexternal.com.

15. Compare the shopping malls of Yahoo!, amazon.com, and internetmall.net. Write a report.

16. Enter the website of a social network service (e.g., myspace.com or facebook.com). Build a homepage. Add a chat room and a message board to your site using the free tools provided. Describe the other capabilities available. Make at least five new friends.

17. Enter vivapets.com and dogster.com and compare their offerings.

18. Enter smartmobs.com. Go to blogroll. Find three blogs related to Web 2.0 and summarize their major features.

19. Access Hof's "My Virtual Life" (2008) at businessweek.com/print/magazine/content/06_18/b3982001.htm?chang=g1 and meet the seven residents in the slideshow. Prepare a table that shows the manner in which they make money, the required skills, and the reason they do it in Second Life.

20. Enter secondlife.com and find the commercial activities of the following avatars: Fizik Baskerville, Craig Altman, Shaun Altman, FlipperPA Peregrine, and Anshe Chung. Describe briefly what they represent.

21. Enter global.dubli.com and find how it works. Watch the video on the site. Compare the process to the one on eBay and to a penny auction.

22. Enter zippy.com and find the "13 Link Building Tactics for E-Commerce." Write a brief summary.

TEAM ASSIGNMENTS AND PROJECTS

1. Assignment for the Opening Case

   Read the opening case and answer the following questions.

   a. Why not just have meetings and send e-mails rather than use blogs, wikis, and RSS feeds?

   b. What are the benefits to EMS of combining its BI system with the Web 2.0 tools?

   c. In what ways is corporate performance bolstered?

   d. How can customers of the retail stores utilize the Web 2.0 tools?

   e. Can the company use any other Web 2.0 technologies? What and how?

2. Assign each group to a large e-tailer (e.g., Amazon.com, Walmart.com, Target.com, Dell.com, Apple.com, and HP.com). Trace the purchasing process. Look at the catalogs, search engines, shopping carts, Web 2.0 features, and any other mechanism that improves e-shopping. Make a presentation that will include recommendations for improving the existing process.

3. Enter en.wikipedia.org/wiki/Businesses_and_ organizations_in_Second_Life and view the list of businesses. Identify some virtual companies and explore several in depth. Then browse secondlife.com. Find what products (services) companies offer and how much they charge if they sell their products (services). Then, identify several companies that are related to real-world businesses (e.g., SL Bay auctions allow you to purchase real-world items with Linden dollars).

4. Build your own business in Second Life (SL). This can be each member or each group. Using the company cited in question 3, determine what business you want to build. Then obtain a copy of Terdiman's book (2008), or Mahar and Martin-Mahar (2009), or a similar book. Register at SL and go to work. In your project, do the following:

   a. Select a business category and develop a business strategy.
   b. Develop a business plan and model (see Online Tutorial T2) for your virtual enterprise.
   c. Choose where on SL to set up your business.
   d. Conduct a budget and cash flow analysis (see Appendix B in Terdiman 2008).
   e. Buy virtual land and other virtual properties.
   f. Develop marketing and advertising plans (examine the competition).
   g. Look for any possible revenues; make a pricing decision.
   h. Examine the possibility of running your business in "Teen SL."
   i. Plan all support services using the SL tools.
   j. Watch for legal issues and other risks; plan their mitigation.

   k. Build the business (using the SL tools).
   l. Build a supporting blog. How would you use it for viral marketing?

5. Watch the video "Online Communities: The Tribalization of Business" (Part 1 = 6:15 minutes, Parts 2 and 3 are optional) at youtube.com/watch?v=qQJvKyytMXU and answer the following questions:

   a. Why is the term tribalization used?
   b. What are virtual communities?
   c. How can traditional business benefit from online communities?
   d. What is the value of communities for the customers?
   e. Compare social vs. marketing frameworks.
   f. How are virtual communities aligned with the business?
   g. Discuss the issues of measurements, metrics, and CSFs.

Optional: View Parts 2 and 3 (6 and 10 minutes), and summarize the major topics discussed.

6. Watch the video "Auction, Work from Home, Home Business, Home Business Home, Auctions, Business Opportunity, shopping" 10 minutes at youtube.com/watch?v=rTLOKR_JCAc and answer the following questions:

   a. What is the business model of Dubli (esy.dubli.com)?
   b. Why do they concentrate on top brands?
   c. How does the system work?
   d. Relate the system to penny auctions and reverse auctions.
   e. What is Dubli's revenue model?

Closing Case

BUSINESS IN SECOND LIFE

In 2003, a 3-D virtual world called Second Life (SL) was opened to the public. The world is entirely built and owned by its residents. In 2003, the virtual world consisted of 64 acres. By 2010 it had grown to over 100,000 acres and was inhabited by millions of residents from around the planet (see secondlife.com). The virtual world consists of a huge digital continent, islands, people, entertainment, experiences, and opportunities.

Thousands of new residents join each day and create their own avatars through which they travel around the SL world meeting people, communicating, having fun, and buying virtual land and other virtual properties where they can open a business or build a personal space, limited only by their imaginations and their ability to use the virtual 3-D applications. Avatars have unique names and move around in imaginative vehicles including helicopters, submarines, and hot-air balloons.

Residents get some free virtual land (and they can buy more) where they build a house, a city, or a business. They can then sell the virtual properties or the virtual products or services they create. Residents can also sell real-world products or services. For example, Copeland and Kelleher (2007) report that more than 25,000 aspiring entrepreneurs trade virtual products or services at SL. Virtual goods entrepreneurs, landowners, in-world builders, and service providers generated user-to-user transactions totaling US$350 million in 2008 (Linden 2009). Stevan Lieberman, an attorney, is one of these people. He uses his expertise in intellectual property and the site to solicit work—mainly from programmers who are looking to patent their code. SL is managed by Linden Labs, which provides Linden dollars that can be converted to U.S. dollars. SL uses several Web 2.0 tools such as blogs, wikis, RSS, and tags (from *delicious.com*).

Virtual businesses succeed due to the owners' ingenuity, artistic ability, entrepreneurial expertise, and reputation.

Many organizations use SL for 3-D presentations of their products. Even governments open virtual embassies on "Diplomacy Island," located on the site. Many universities offer educational courses and seminars in virtual classrooms (see "EduIslands" on the SL site and Appendix A in Rymaszewski, et al. [2008]).

Roush (2007) describes how to combine SL with Google Earth. Such combinations enable investigation of phenomena that would otherwise be difficult to visualize or understand. Shopping for virtual goods is popular in SL. You can start at the GNUbie Store (bargain prices), New Citizens Incorporates (NCI), and Free Dove. SL friends will help you choose! You can shop outside SL (for real goods) yet pay Linden dollars, the currency of SL (see *xstreetsl.com*). For SL fashion selection, try *blog.secondstyle.com*. Also *sluniverse.com/php/shop* lets you quickly and easily search and shop for many items. You can even use a shopping cart on this site.

Note: We suggest you build your own virtual business in SL in order to experience real-life thrills. For suggestions on how to profit in SL see Chapter 1 in Rymaszewski, et al. (2008). You can work as a musician, hunter, financial speculator, or a writer. You can also work in many other virtual jobs—you are only limited by your imagination.

Example. For some time, real-world organizations have been taking a growing interest in SL. Educational institutions were the first to recognize the potential of the virtual world to act as a new communications, advertising, and learning platform, and they were quickly followed by corporations doing what most corporations do: Look for profit. Appendix C of Rymaszewski, et al. (2008) provides information about real-life brand presence and retail outlets in SL.

At the time of this writing, corporate activity in SL is still in its infancy. Although an impressive number of companies have made or are in the process of making a foray into the virtual world, many treat it as an experiment whose only sure payoff is the media publicity it generates in the real world. However, to others—perhaps more visionary—SL offers very tangible advantages: A visit to *work.secondlife.com* will educate you in-depth on how organizations utilize SL's virtual environment. For readers interested in the corporate take on the virtual world, Rymaszweski, et al. (2008) present three voices from three countries, representing companies in different fields of business.

The most common commercial activities in SL are:

- Advertising
- Joint designing and prototyping
- Market research
- Marketing and sales
- Corporate communication
- Broadcasting and entertainment
- Travel and tourism
- Training and e-learning

For details, see Chapter 7 and Robbins and Bell (2008).

An increasing number of businesses are using the virtual world. For example, IBM uses it as a location for meetings, training, and recruitment. American Apparel was the first major retailer to set up shop in SL. The Mexican Tourism Board and Morocco Tourism are examples of 3-D presentations of major tourist attractions. Many companies use SL as a hot place to go to try new business ideas (see Rosedale 2007). For example, you can test-drive a Toyota Scion, toymakers prototype toys, and anyone can become a virtual architect. For a comprehensive video see *blip.tv/file/242816*.

Sources: Compiled from Copeland and Kelleher (2007), Linden (2009), Robbins and Bell (2008), Rosedale (2007), and Rymaszewski, et al. (2008), Roush (2007), and *secondlife.com* (accessed April 2011).

Questions

1. Enter the SL site (*secondlife.com*) and identify EC activities there. (You need to register for free and create an avatar.)

2. Which types of transactions are observable at the site?

3. Which business models are observable at the site?

4. If you were a travel agent, how would you utilize the site?

5. Have your avatar communicate with five others. Write a report on your experience.

ONLINE RESOURCES
available at pearsonglobaleditions.com/turban

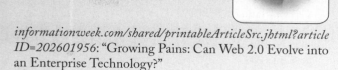

Online Files

W2.1   Examples of Digital Products

W2.2   Application Case: How Raffles Hotel Is Conducting E-Commerce

W2.3   Application Case: EBay: The World's Largest Auction Site

W2.4   Application Case: Reverse Mortgage Auctions in Singapore

Comprehensive Educational Websites

wiki.secondlife.com/wiki/Video_Tutorials: Learn SL in a fun, easy way.

vectec.org/resources: The Virginia Electronic Commerce Technology Center offers special reports, e-business news, and statistics.

allthingsweb2.com: An open directory for the interactive Web.

informationweek.com/shared/printableArticleSrc.jhtml?article ID=202601956: "Growing Pains: Can Web 2.0 Evolve into an Enterprise Technology?"

cioinsight.com/c/a/Past-News/5-Reasons-to-Deploy-a-Corporate-Social-Network: "Five Reasons to Deploy a Corporate Social Network."

bloombergmarketing.blogs.com: Diva Marketing Blog.

blogs.zdnet.com/Hinchcliffe: Dion Hinchcliffe's Enterprise 2.0 blog.

awarenessnetworks.com: Webinars on social media, Web 2.0, ROI, and marketing.

newsgator.com/enterprise20/Oct2008: Webinar on social computing deployment.

REFERENCES

Bakos, Y. "The Emerging Role of Electronic Marketplaces on the Internet." *Communications of the ACM* (August 1998).

Bennett, E. "Cleaning Up a Dirty Job. (Portal Software)." *Baseline*, February 2007.

Borland, J. "A Smarter Web." *Technology Review*, March–April 2007.

Boyd, D. M., and N. B. Ellison. "Social Network Sites: Definition, History and Scholarship." *Journal of Computer-Mediated Communication* (January 2007).

Bughin, J., M. Chui, and J. Manyika. "Clouds, Big Data, and Smart Access: Ten Tech-Enabled Trends to Watch." *McKinsey Quarterly*, August 2010. mckinseyquarterly. com/High_Tech/Strategy_Analysis/Clouds_big_data _and_smart_assets_Ten_tech-enabled_ business_trends_to_watch_2647 (accessed April 2011).

BusinessWeek Online. "Hot Growth Special Report 2006." May 2006. businessweek.com/hot_growth/2006/ company/10.htm (accessed April 2011).

Carr, N. "IT in 2018: From Turing's Machine to Computing Cloud." *Internet.com IT Management eBook*, New York: Jupitermedia Corp., 2008.

Chatfield, T. B. *The Complete Guide to Wikis*. Florida: Atlantic Publishing Group, 2009.

Clark, K. "Discover the Best of Craigslist." *L'Atelier*, March 10, 2009. atelier-us.com/internet-usage/article/ discover-the-best-of-craigslist (accessed April 2011).

Coleman, D., and S. Levine. *Collaboration 2.0*. Cupertino, CA: Happy About Info., 2008.

comScore. "Facebook and Twitter Access Via Mobile Browser Grows by Triple Digits in the Past Year." March 3, 2010. comscore.com/Press_Events/Press_ Releases/2010/3/Facebook_and_Twitter_Access_via_ Mobile_Browser_Grows_by_Triple-Digits (accessed April 2011).

Copeland, V. M., and K. Kelleher. "The New New Careers." *Business 2.0*, May 2007.

Cox, J. L., E. R. Martinez, and K. B. Quinlan. "Blogs on the Corporation: Managing the Risk, Reaping the Benefits." *Journal of Business Strategy*, 29, no. 3 (2008).

Davis, M. "Semantic Wave 2008: Industry Roadmap to Web 3.0 and Multibillion Dollar Market Opportunities." *Project 10X*, 2008. project10x.com/ about.php (accessed April 2011).

Edgar Online. "Growth of Online Commerce and Online Auction Market." March 17, 2006. sec.edgar-online. com/2006/03/17/0001047469-06-003660/ Section9.asp (no longer available online).

eMarket Services. "Why Use E-Markets?" *eMarket Services.com*, 2006. emarketservices.com/start/Knowledge/ eMarket-Basics/Why-use-eMarkets/index.html (accessed April 2011).

Farber, D. "2009: The Year of Enterprise Social Networks." *ZDNet*, February 14, 2008. blogs.zdnet.com/BTL/? p=7997 (accessed April 2011).

Flynn, N. *Blog Rules: A Business Guide to Managing Policy, Public Relations, and Legal Issues*. Saranac Lake, NY: AMACOM, 2006.

Gain, M. "What Is Web 2.0 and How Will It Impact PR?" May 12, 2010. matthewgain.com/2010/05/what-is-web-3-0-and-how-will-it-impact-pr/ (accessed April 2011).

Hempel, J. "Web 2.0 Is so Over, Welcome to Web 3.0." *Fortune*, January 8, 2009.

Hof, R. D. "My Virtual Life." *BusinessWeek*, May 1, 2008.

Joyner, A. *The eBay Billionaires Club*. Hoboken, NJ: Wiley & Sons, 2007.

Laurent, W. "Interface: Where We're Headed with Web 3.0." *Information Management Magazine*, July/August 2010.

Liedtke, M. "Study: Craigslist Revenue to Climb 23% to $100 Million." *Physorg.com*, June 10, 2009. physorg.com/news163824409.html (accessed April 2011).

Linden, M. "State of the Economy." *SecondLife.com*, April 9, 2009. blogs.secondlife.com/community/features/blog/tags/lindex (accessed April 2011).

Mahar, J., and S. Martin-Mahar. *The Unofficial Guide to Building Your Business in Second Life Virtual World: Marketing and Selling Your Product, Services, and Brand In-World*. New York: AMACOM, 2010.

Malaby, T. *Making Virtual Worlds: Linden Lab and Second Life*. NY: Cornell University Press, 2009.

Mangalindan, J. P. "Twitter's Business Model: A Visionary Experiment." *Fortune*, July 9, 2010.

Martin, R. "The Right Search Tool." *InformationWeek*, September 29, 2008.

McNichol, T. "Vin Du Blogger." *Business 2.0*, August 2007.

Nerille, J. "X-treme Web 2.0." *Optimize Magazine*, January 2007.

Nissanoff, D. *Future Shop: How the New Auction Culture Will Revolutionize the Way We Buy, Sell, and Get Things We Really Want*. New York: The Penguin Press, 2006.

O'Buyonge, A. A., and L. Chen. "E-Health Dot-Coms' Critical Success Factors." In M. Khosrow-Pour (Ed.), *Encyclopedia of E-Commerce, E-Government, and Mobile Commerce*. Hershey, PA: Idea Group Reference, 2006.

Rivlin, G. "When Buying a Diamond Starts with a Mouse." *New York Times*, January 7, 2007.

Robbins, S., and M. Bell. *Second Life for Dummies*. Hoboken, NJ: Wiley & Sons, 2008.

Roberts, B. "Social Networking at the Office." *HR Magazine*, March 2008.

Rosedale, P. "Alter Egos." *Forbes*, May 7, 2007.

Roush, W. "Second Earth." *Technology Review*, July/August 2007.

Rymaszewski, M., et al. *Second Life: The Official Guide*, 2nd ed. Indianapolis, IN: Wiley & Sons, 2008.

Saarinen, T., M. Tinnild, and A. Tseng (Eds.). *Managing Business in a Multi-Channel World: Success Factors for E-Business*. Hershey, PA: Idea Group, Inc., 2006.

Safko, L. *The Social Media Bible: Tactics, Tools and Strategies for Business Success*, 2nd ed. Hoboken, NJ: Wiley & Sons, 2010.

Schuman, E. "E-Commerce's New Dimension." *Baseline*, December, 2007.

Sloan, P., and P. Kaihla. "Blogging for Dollars." *Business 2.0*, September 2006.

Stafford, A. "The Future of the Web." *PC World*, November, 2006.

Terdiman, D. *The Entrepreneur's Guide to Second Life*. Indianapolis, IN: Wiley & Sons, 2008.

Turban, E., et al. *Business Intelligence: A Managerial Approach*, 2nd ed. Upper Saddle River, NJ: Prentice Hall, 2011.

Waters, R. "Fact and Friction." *Financial Times*, January 2–3, 2010.

Weber, S. *eBay 101: Selling on eBay for Part Time or Full Time Income*. Falls Church, VA: Web Books, 2008.

Weblogs, Inc. "The Social Software Weblog." 2007. socialsoftware.weblogsinc.com (accessed April 2011).

RETAILING IN ELECTRONIC COMMERCE: PRODUCTS AND SERVICES

Content

Learning Objectives

Upon completion of this chapter, you will be able to:

1. Describe electronic retailing (e-tailing) and its characteristics.

2. Classify the primary e-tailing business models.

3. Describe how online travel and tourism services operate and their impact on the industry.

4. Discuss the online employment market, including its participants, benefits, and limitations.

5. Describe online real estate services.

6. Discuss online stock-trading services.

7. Discuss cyberbanking and online personal finance.

8. Describe on-demand delivery of groceries and similar perishable products and services related to them.

9. Describe the delivery of digital products and online entertainment.

10. Discuss various online consumer aids, including comparison-shopping aids.

11. Describe disintermediation and other B2C strategic issues.

AMAZON.COM: THE WORLD'S LARGEST B2C E-STORE

The Opportunity

Amazon.com (*amazon.com*) reported that its annual profit for 2008 had doubled from 2007, with a 41 percent revenue increase, despite adverse U.S. and global economic conditions.

Entrepreneur Jeff Bezos faced an opportunity rather than a business problem. In the early 1990s, Bezos saw the huge potential for retail sales over the Internet and identified books as the most logical product for e-tailing. In July 1995, Bezos started Amazon.com, an e-tailing pioneer, offering books via an electronic catalog from its website. Over the years, the company has recognized that it must continually enhance its business models and online storefront by expanding its product selection, improving the customer experience, and adding services and alliances. In addition, the company recognized early on the importance of order fulfillment and warehousing. It has invested hundreds of millions of dollars in building physical warehouses designed for shipping small packages to hundreds of thousands of customers. Amazon.com's challenge was, and remains, how to succeed where many have failed—namely, how to sell consumer products online, at a profit, and show a reasonable rate of return on investment.

The Solution: Reaching Out to Customers

In addition to its initial electronic bookstore, Amazon.com has expanded its offerings to a vast array of products and services segmented into three broad categories: media (books, music, DVDs, etc.); electronics and other merchandise (including its new wireless reading device, Kindle 2; office supplies; cameras; toys; etc.); and other (nonretail activities, such as Web services, Amazon Enterprise Solutions, etc.). Key features of the Amazon.com superstore are easy browsing, searching, and ordering; useful product information, reviews, recommendations, and personalization; broad selection; low prices; secure payment systems; and efficient order fulfillment.

Amazon.com is known for its innovations. For example in 2010, Amazon Seller Product Suggestion Box provides transparency to sellers by recommending specific products for third-party sellers to sell on Amazon.com. The suggestions are based on customers' browsing history.

The Amazon.com website has a number of features that make the online shopping experience more enjoyable. For example, its "Gift Ideas" section features seasonally appropriate gift ideas and services. AmazonConnect allows customers to select their favorite authors, read about them, and then receive e-mails from some of those authors.

Amazon.com also offers various marketplace services. Amazon Auctions hosts and operates auctions on behalf of individuals and small businesses throughout the world. The Shops service hosts electronic storefronts for a monthly fee, offering small businesses the opportunity to have customized storefronts supported by the richness of Amazon.com's order-fulfillment processing. Customers can use Web-enabled cell phones, PDAs, or pocket PCs to access Amazon.com and shop anywhere, anytime (more than $1 billion of merchandise in 2009). Amazon.com also can be accessed via AT&T's #121 voice service. Amazon.com is recognized as an online leader in creating sales through customer intimacy and customer relationship management (CRM), which are cultivated by informative marketing front ends and one-to-one advertisements. In addition, sales are supported by highly automated, efficient back-end systems. When a customer makes a return visit to Amazon.com, a cookie file (see Chapter 8) identifies the user and says, for example, "Welcome back, Sarah Shopper," and then proceeds to recommend new books from the same genre of the customer's previous purchases and a range of other items. It also provides detailed product descriptions and ratings to help consumers make informed purchase decisions. The site has an efficient search engine and other shopping aids. Amazon.com has a superb warehousing system that gives the company an advantage over the competition.

Amazon.com is known for its strategy and acquisition of its successful competitors in niche markets (e.g., CDNow, Zappos). The company also acquired supplementary companies such as Alexa, Junglee, and DPReview (see *en.wikipedia.org/wiki/Amazon.com*).

Customers can personalize their accounts and manage orders online with the patented "1-Click" order feature. 1-Click includes an electronic wallet (see Chapter 10), which enables shoppers to place an order in a secure manner without the need to enter their address, credit card number, and other information each time they shop and allows customers to view their order status, cancel or combine orders that have not yet entered the shipping process, edit the shipping options and addresses on unshipped orders, modify the payment method for unshipped orders, and more.

In 1997, Amazon.com started an extensive associates program. By 2009, the company had more than 2 million partners worldwide that refer customers to Amazon.com. Partners that feature Amazon's products in their self-contained online store embedded directly within their partners' Web page can earn up to a 15 percent referral fee if the advertisement ends with a sale (see *affiliate-program.amazon.com*). Starting in 2000, Amazon.com has undertaken alliances with major "trusted partners" that provide knowledgeable entry into new markets. For example, clicking "Office Supplies" allows customers either to select from Amazon.com's office supplies or to browse those of Office Depot; clicking "Health and Personal Care" allows customers to benefit from great deals offered by Weight Watchers. In yet another extension of its services, in September 2001 Amazon.com signed an agreement with Borders Group Inc., providing Amazon.com's users with the option of in-store pick up for their merchandise at Borders' physical bookstores.

Amazon.com also is becoming a Web fulfillment contractor for national online chains such as Target. AmazonFresh is a grocery delivery service. Amazon MP3 allows downloads, some free, others for 69¢ per song. Amapedia is a wiki for user-generated content, a video on demand service for Amazon MP3.

AmazonConnect allows authors to post remarks on their book pages to customers who have bought their books. Amazon.com offers many Web 2.0 social shopping features (e.g., customers' reviews). It also acquired Woot.com, a company known for its social commerce activities.

The Results

In 1999, *Time* magazine named Bezos "Person of the Year," recognizing the company's success in popularizing online shopping. In January 2002, Amazon.com declared its first profit—for the 2001 fourth quarter. Since then, the company has remained profitable. Annual sales for Amazon.com have trended upward, driven largely by product diversification and its international presence. This pioneer e-tailer now offers over 17 million book, music, and DVD/video titles to some 20 million customers.

Despite the increased competition, Amazon.com has been holding its place as the number one B2C money-making EC site in the world. Given its warehouse system and order fulfillment, Amazon.com can offer very low prices. Add this to the high

customer satisfaction and the huge and superb selection of products and you can understand why Amazon.com is selling more than three times the products compared to its nearest competitor.

Amazon.com also offers several features for international customers, including over 1 million Japanese-language titles. Amazon.com maintained its position as the number one e-tailer in 2008, generating revenues of $19.2 billion, with a net income of $645 million. Amazon.com, the king of e-tailers, which has shown all others the potential of B2C EC, is increasing its profitability, even in economic crises.

Sources: Compiled from Reuters (2008), Dignan (2008), *en.wikipedia.org/wiki/Amazon.com*, and *amazon.com* (accessed April 2011).

WHAT WE CAN LEARN . . .

The case of Amazon.com, the most recognized name of all e-tailers in the world, demonstrates the evolution of e-tailing, some of the problems encountered by e-tailers, and the solutions that a company can employ to expand its business. It also is indicative of some key trends in Internet retailing. For example, there is fierce completion online. Amazon.com is successful there because of its size, innovations, personalization, and customer service. The biggest online retailer is still growing and becoming more dominant. E-tailing, as demonstrated by the Amazon.com case, continues its double-digit, year-over-year growth rate despite the global economic downturn. This is, in part, because sales are shifting away from physical stores and also because online shoppers are, in general, more affluent. However, some experts argue that online retailers will need to better understand customer behavior and preferences if they are to achieve a better convergence between technological capability and customer desires. In this chapter, we will look at the delivery of both products and services online to individual customers. We also discuss e-tailing successes and failures.

3.1 INTERNET MARKETING AND B2C ELECTRONIC RETAILING

The Amazon.com case illustrates how commerce can be conducted on the Internet. Indeed, the amount and percentage of goods and services sold on the Internet is increasing rapidly, despite the failure of many dot-com companies. According to *Internet Retailer* (2009), approximately 60 percent of adult U.S. Internet users shop online and/or research offline sales online. Similar figures are reported in several Western countries and in Taiwan, Malaysia, Australia, and New Zealand. With estimates of 228 million Internet users in the United States, this suggests that in 2009 there were approximately 139 million online shoppers. In 2010, online retail sales approached $200 billion, about 4 percent of all U.S. retail sales. This is up from less than 2 percent in 2000 and less than 3 percent in 2005. However, as the number of Internet users reaches saturation, the rate of increase of online shoppers may slow. On the other hand, the economic downturn may increase online shopping as a means of saving money. However, in some countries (e.g., Taiwan) shoppers are spending less. Still, one of the challenges for electronic retailers, therefore, is to increase the amount people spend online. As discussed in Chapter 1, companies have many reasons to market and sell their goods and services online. Innovative marketing models and strategies, and a deep understanding of online consumer behavior and preferences, will be required for sustained success in the competitive online environment. For statistics on EC in general and retail trade in particular, see census.gov/compendia/statab.

This chapter presents an overview of Internet retailing, its diversity, prospects, and limitations. Retailing, especially when conducted in a new medium, must be supported by an understanding of consumer buying behavior, market research, and advertising, topics that will be presented in Chapter 8. Let's begin our discussion of EC products and services with an overview of electronic retailing.

OVERVIEW OF ELECTRONIC RETAILING

A retailer is a sales *intermediary*, a seller that operates between manufacturers and customers. Even though many manufacturers sell directly to consumers, they usually do it to supplement their major sales through wholesalers and retailers. In the physical world, retailing is done in stores (or factory outlets) that customers must visit in order to make a purchase. Companies that produce a large number of products for millions of customers, such as Procter & Gamble, must use retailers for efficient distribution. However, even if a company sells only a relatively few products (e.g., Kodak), it still might need retailers to reach a large number of customers scattered in many locations.

Catalog (mail order) sales offer companies and customers a relief from the constraints of space and time: Catalogs free a retailer from the need for a physical store from which to distribute products, and customers can browse catalogs on their own time. Mail order retailers usually buy products from many manufacturers and then sell them via their aggregated catalog. With the ubiquity of the Internet, the next logical step was for regular and mail catalog retailing to move online. Retailing conducted over the Internet is called **electronic retailing (e-tailing)**, and those who conduct retail business online are called **e-tailers**. E-tailing can be conducted through catalogs with fixed prices as well as via auctions. E-tailing also makes it easier for a manufacturer (e.g., Dell.com) to sell directly to the customer, cutting out the intermediary. This chapter examines the various types of e-tailing and related issues.

The concept of retailing and e-tailing implies sales of goods and/or services to individual customers—that is, B2C EC. However, the distinction between B2C and B2B EC is not always clear. For example, Amazon.com sells books mostly to individuals (B2C), but it also sells to corporations (B2B). Amazon.com's chief rival in selling books online, Barnes & Noble (barnesandnoble.com), has a special division that caters only to business customers. Walmart (walmart.com) sells to both individuals and businesses (via Sam's Club). Dell sells its computers to both consumers and businesses from dell.com, Staples sells to both markets at staples.com, and insurance sites sell to both individuals and corporations.

SIZE AND GROWTH OF THE B2C MARKET

The statistics for the volume of B2C EC sales, including forecasts for future sales, come from many sources. Reported amounts of online sales *deviate substantially* based on how the numbers are derived, and thus it is often difficult to obtain a consistent and coherent picture of the growth of EC. Some of the variation stems from the use of different definitions and classifications of EC. For example, when tallying financial data, some analysts include the investment costs in Internet infrastructure, whereas others include only the value of the actual transactions conducted via the Internet. Another issue is how the items for sale are categorized. Some sources combine certain products and services; others do not. Some sources include online travel sales in the data for EC retail; others do not. Sometimes different time periods are used in the measurement. When reading data about B2C EC sales, therefore, it is very important that care is taken in interpreting the figures.

The sites listed in Exhibit 3.1 provide statistics on e-tailing as well as on other Internet and EC activities. Typical statistics used in describing e-tailing and consumer behavior

---

electronic retailing (e-tailing)
Retailing conducted online, over the Internet.

e-tailers
Retailers who sell over the Internet.

EXHIBIT 3.1   Representative Sources of EC Statistics

BizRate (*bizrate.com*)

Business 2.0 (*money.cnn.com/magazines/business2*)

comScore (*comscore.com*)

ClickZ Network (*clickz.com*)

Ecommerce Info Center (*ecominfocenter.com*)

eMarket (*emarket.com*)

Forrester Research (*forrester.com*)

Gartner (*gartner.com*)

Gomez (*gomez.com*)

InternetRetailer (*internetretailer.com*)

Nielsen Online (*nielsen-online.com*)

Shop.org (*shop.org*)

Ominture SiteCatalyst (*omniture.com*)

Pew Internet (*pewinternet.org*)

Yankee Group (*yankeegroup.com*)

U.S. Census Bureau (*census.gov/econ/estats*)

include Internet usage by demographic (online sales by age, gender, country, etc.); online sales by item; online sales by vendor; and buying patterns online.

WHAT SELLS WELL ON THE INTERNET

With approximately 170 million shoppers online in the United States in 2010, e-tailers appreciate the need to provide excellent choice and service to an ever-increasing cohort of potential customers. Hundreds of thousands of items are available on the Web from numerous vendors. Exhibit 3.2 shows the major categories that are selling well online. For some current trends in B2C, see Online File W3.1.

Developments in E-Commerce

The first-generation e-commerce sold books, software, and music—simple to understand items (known as commodity items) that are easy to ship to consumers. The second wave of online growth started in 2000 as consumers moved beyond simple transactions to research and purchase more complex products online (see Opening Case in Chapter 1, Net-a-Porter). Now in 2011, consumers are researching and purchasing online from categories like furniture, expensive jewelry, designer clothes, appliances, cars, flooring, big-screen TVs, and building supplies. Consumers are buying many services as well.

CHARACTERISTICS AND ADVANTAGES OF SUCCESSFUL E-TAILING

Many of the same basic principles that apply to physical retail success also apply to e-tail success. Sound business thinking, visionary leadership, thorough competitive analysis and financial analysis, and the articulation of a well-thought-out EC strategy are essential. So, too, is ensuring appropriate infrastructure, particularly a stable and scalable technology infrastructure to support the online and physical aspects of EC business operations. Newly required capabilities (e.g., capabilities in logistics and distribution) might need to be obtained through external strategic alliances. Offering quality merchandise at good prices coupled with excellent service, and cross-channel coordination and integration in which customers can almost seamlessly operate between the online and physical environments of a business are also important elements in successful e-tailing. In a sense, the online and traditional channels are not very different. However, e-tailers can offer expanded consumer services not offered by traditional retailers. For a comparison of e-tailing and retailing, including advantages, see Exhibit 3.3.

With all else being equal in the online environment, goods with the following characteristics are expected to facilitate higher sales volumes:

▶ High brand recognition (e.g., Lands' End, Dell, Sony)

▶ A guarantee provided by highly reliable or well-known vendors (e.g., Dell, Amazon.com, BlueNile.com)

EXHIBIT 3.2   What Sells Well on the Internet?

Category	Description
Travel	Online travel agents offer a range of services, including travel booking, hotel reservations, car rentals, and vacation packages (e.g., Priceline, Expedia).
Computer hardware and software	Dell, HP, and Gateway are major online vendors of computer hardware and software. Computer hardware and software is the largest category of products sold online.
Consumer electronics	Consumer electronics include digital cameras, printers, scanners, and wireless devices. Consumer electronics is the second largest category of products sold online.
Office supplies	B2C and B2B sales of office supplies are increasing rapidly, all over the world, as companies increasingly use the Internet to place orders for stationery and the like. Staples is the leader.
Sport and fitness goods	Sporting goods sell very well on the Internet. However, it is difficult to measure the exact amount of sales because only a few e-tailers sell sporting goods exclusively online (e.g., *fogdog.com*).
Books and music (CDs, DVDs)	Amazon.com and Barnesandnoble.com are the major sellers of books. However, hundreds of other e-tailers sell books on the Internet, especially specialized books (e.g., technical books, children's books).
Toys and hobbies	Many stores sell items for children, adults, and pets.
Health and beauty	A large variety of health and beauty products—from vitamins to cosmetics and fragrances—are sold online by most large retailers and by specialty stores.
Entertainment	This is another area where dozens of products, ranging from tickets to events (e.g., *ticketmaster.com*) to paid fantasy games are embraced by millions of shoppers worldwide.
Apparel and clothing	With the possibility of buying customized shirts, pants, and even shoes, the online sale of apparel also is growing. Guaranteed return policies and improved features on fitting clothing without first trying it on have increased customers' comfort zone for buying apparel online.
Jewelry	Online sales of jewelry are booming. With claims of prices about 40 percent less than would be paid in traditional stores, the trend toward online jewelry sales is likely to continue (see Case 2.1 Blue Nile, Chapter 2).
Cars	The sale of cars over the Internet is just beginning (people still like to "kick the tires"), but could be one of the top sellers on the Internet in the near future. Customers like order the build-to-capabilities, but even selling used cars online has advantages and is increasing rapidly. Support services such as financing, warranties, and insurance also are selling well online.
Services	Sales in service industries, especially travel, stock trading, electronic banking, real estate, and insurance, are increasing—more than doubling every year in some cases.
Food and drugs	Innovative delivery solutions help with food sales. Ordering prescription drugs online may save time and money. Many online pharmacies provide information about drug interactions. Some even e-mail alerts when a drug is recalled or a generic equivalent becomes available.
Pet supplies	Pet supplies are a new category in the top-seller list. As family pets become more and more integrated as members of the family, online spending on toys, edible treats, food, pet accessories, and veterinary products and services is soaring.
Others	Many other products, ranging from prescription drugs to custom-made shoes are offered on the Internet. Many items are specialized or niche products. Furniture, gifts, flowers, groceries, and more.

Sources: Compiled from *Biz Report* (2007), U.S. Census Bureau eStats (2010), Mulpuru et al. (2008), miscellaneous notes in *Internet Retailer* and *eMarketer*, and *census.gov/econ/estats* (accessed December 2010).

- Digitized format (e.g., software, music, e-books, or videos)
- Relatively inexpensive items (e.g., office supplies, vitamins)
- Frequently purchased items (e.g., groceries, prescription drugs)
- Commodities with standard specifications (e.g., books, CDs, airline tickets), making physical inspection unimportant
- Well-known packaged items that cannot be opened even in a traditional store (e.g., canned foods, chocolates, vitamins)

EXHIBIT 3.3   Retailing Versus E-Tailing

Factor	Retailers	E-Tailers
Physical expansion (when revenue increases as the number of visitors grows)	• Expansion of retailing platform to include more locations and space	• Expansion of e-commerce platform to include increased server capacity and distribution facilities
Physical expansion (when revenue does not increase as the number of visitors grows)	• May not need physical expansion • Expand marketing effort to turn "window shoppers" into effective shoppers	• May still need physical expansion to provide sustainable services • Expand marketing to turn "pane shoppers" into effective shoppers
Technology	• Sales automation technologies such as POS systems	• Front-end technologies • Benefit from browsing • Back-end technologies • "Information" technologies
Customer relations	• More stable due to nonanonymous contacts • More tolerable of disputes due to visibility • "Physical" relationships	• Less stable due to anonymous contacts • More intolerant of disputes due to invisibility • "Logical" relationships
Cognitive shopping overhead	• Lower cognitive shopping overhead due to easy-to-establish mutual trust	• Higher cognitive shopping overhead due to hard-to-establish mutual trust
Competition	• Local competition	• Global competition
Customer base	• Fewer competitors • Local area customers • No anonymity • Fewer resources needed to increase customer loyalty • Customers remain loyal for future purchases	• More competitors • Wide area customers • Anonymity • More resources needed to increase customer loyalty • Customers shift loyalty
Supply chain cost	• High, interruption	• Lower
Customization and personalization	• Expensive and slow	• Fast, efficient
Price changing and price discrimination	• Expensive to do, done not so often	• Inexpensive, anytime
Adaptability to market trends	• Slow	• Rapid

Sources: Compiled from Kwon and Lennon (2009), Ha and Stoel (2009), and author's experience.

Advantages of E-Tailing

E-tailing provides advantages both to sellers and buyers. The advantages of e-commerce described in Chapter 1 apply here too.

Major advantages to sellers are:

- Lower product cost, increasing competitive advantage.
- Reach more customers, many outside the vendor's region.
- Change price and catalogs quickly including visual presentation (price flexibility increases competitive advantage).

- ▶ Lower supply chain costs (see Chapter 11).
- ▶ Provide customers with a wealth of information, thus saving on customer service costs.
- ▶ React quickly to customers' needs, complaints, tastes, etc.
- ▶ Provide customization of products and services and personalization of customer care.
- ▶ Compete with larger companies.
- ▶ Better understand customers and interact with them.
- ▶ Engage customers in different activities.
- ▶ Reach customers who are not reachable with traditional methods of communication.

The major benefits to the buyers are:

- ▶ Pay less.
- ▶ Find products/services not available in local stores.
- ▶ Shop globally, compare prices and services.
- ▶ Shop anytime and from anywhere.
- ▶ Do not need to go to the store, waste time and gasoline, and be pressured.
- ▶ Find collectors' items.
- ▶ Buy in groups, buy with friends and do social shopping.

The next section examines the major business models that have proven successful in e-tailing.

Section 3.1 ▶ REVIEW QUESTIONS

1. Describe the nature of B2C EC.
2. What sells well in B2C?
3. What are the characteristics of high-volume products and services?
4. Describe the major trends in B2C.
5. Why is B2C also called e-tailing?
6. List the major characteristics of B2C.
7. What are the benefits of B2C?

3.2 E-TAILING BUSINESS MODELS

business model

A method of doing business by which a company generates revenue to sustain itself and achieves its goals.

In order to better understand e-tailing, let's look at it from the point of view of a retailer or a manufacturer that sells to individual consumers. The seller has its own organization and must also buy goods and services from others, usually businesses (B2B in Exhibit 3.4). As also shown in Exhibit 3.4, e-tailing, which is basically B2C (right side of the exhibit), is done between the seller (a retailer or a manufacturer) and an individual buyer. The exhibit shows other EC transactions and related activities that may impact e-tailing. Retailing businesses, like other businesses, are driven by a business model. A **business model** is a description of how an organization intends to generate revenue through its business operations. More specifically, it includes an analysis of the organization's customers, and from that a discussion is created on how that organization will achieve profitability and sustainability by delivering goods and services (value) to those customers.

In this section, we will look at the various B2C models and their classifications.

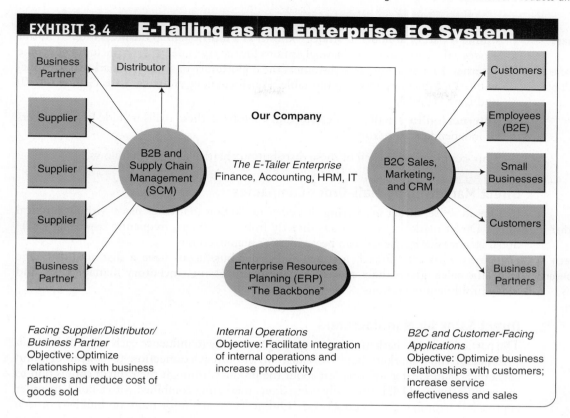

EXHIBIT 3.4   E-Tailing as an Enterprise EC System

CLASSIFICATION OF MODELS BY DISTRIBUTION CHANNEL

E-tailing business models can be classified in several ways. For example, some classify e-tailers by the scope of items handled (general purpose versus specialty e-tailing) or by the scope of the sales region covered (global versus regional), whereas others use classification by revenue sources. Here we will classify the models by the distribution channel used, distinguishing five categories:

1. **Direct marketing by mail-order retailers that go online.** Most traditional mail-order retailers, such as QVC, Sharper Image, and Lands' End, simply added another distribution channel—the Internet. Several of these retailers also operate physical stores, but their main distribution channel is direct marketing.

2. **Direct marketing by manufacturers.** Manufacturers, such as Dell, Nike, LEGO, Godiva, and Sony, market directly online from company sites to individual customers. Most of these manufacturers are click-and-mortar, also selling in their own physical stores or via retailers.

3. **Pure-play e-tailers.** These e-tailers do not have physical stores, only an online sales presence. Amazon.com is an example of a pure-play e-tailer.

4. **Click-and-mortar retailers.** These are of two sorts, depending on how the businesses were originally founded. Originally, click-and-mortar (also known as "brick-and-click") referred to traditional businesses that developed websites to support their business activities in some way (e.g., walmart.com and homedepot.com). For details, see en.wikipedia.org/wiki/Bricks_and_clicks. However, we are now seeing the reverse trend. A small number of successful e-tailers are now creating physical storefronts, leveraging the brand power of the online environment to support more traditional trading activities via stores. For example, Dell, a pioneer of e-tailing and one of the largest sellers of computers online, has also opened physical stores. Expedia.com opened physical kiosks for tourists, Net-a-Porter has two physical stores, and

multichannel business model

A business model where a company sells in multiple marketing channels simultaneously (e.g., both physical and online stores).

Zappos.com has opened three physical outlets. The idea of selling both online and offline is part of a model or strategy known as a **multichannel business model**. In this strategy the company offers several options for the customer to shop, including over the Internet. This strategy gives customers the opportunity to select the marketing channel with which they are most comfortable. For discussions and a case see Greene (2010) and Lewis (2010).

5. **Internet (online) malls.** As described in Chapter 2, these malls include large numbers of independent storefronts.

Our examination of each of these distribution channel categories follows.

Direct Marketing by Mail-Order Companies

direct marketing

Broadly, marketing that takes place without intermediaries between manufacturers and buyers; in the context of this book, marketing done online between any seller and buyer.

In a broad sense, **direct marketing** describes marketing that takes place without physical stores. Direct marketers take orders directly from consumers, frequently bypassing traditional intermediaries. Sellers can be retailers or manufacturers.

Firms with established, mature mail-order businesses have a distinct advantage in online sales, given their existing payment processing, inventory management, and order-fulfillment operations.

Direct Sales by Manufacturers

The parties in direct marketing have a great opportunity to influence each other. Sellers can understand their markets better because of the direct connection to consumers, and consumers gain greater information about the products through their direct connection to the manufacturers. Dell is primarily using direct marketing combined with a build-to-order approach, customizing its products (see Online Tutorial T6 for more on build-to-order). Case 3.1 describes the process by which customers can configure and order cars online from manufacturers.

The competitive advantages of a "pull" vehicle distribution process are:

1. Improved customer satisfaction and better pricing
2. Large cost savings in finished vehicle inventory carrying costs
3. Virtually real-time market feedback
4. A barrier to entry against foreign made cars
5. Better cash flow to the manufacturers

CASE 3.1

EC Application

SELLING CARS ONLINE: BUILD-TO-ORDER

The world's automobile manufacturers operate in complex enterprises with thousands of suppliers and millions of customers. Their traditional channel for distributing cars has been the automobile dealer, who orders cars and then sells them from their exhibition lot. When a customer wants a particular feature or color ("options") that is not in stock in the traditional system, the customer might have to wait weeks or even months until the "pipeline" of vehicles that has those particular options can go onto the production line.

In the traditional system, the manufacturers conduct market research in order to estimate which features and options will sell well, and then they make the cars they wish to sell. In some cases, certain cars are ultimately sold from stock at a loss when the market exhibits insufficient demand for a particular vehicle. The automakers have long operated under this "build-to-stock" environment, building cars that are carried as inventory during the outbound logistics process (ships, trucks, trains, and dealers' lots). General Motors (GM) estimates that it holds as much as $40 billion of unsold vehicles in its distribution channels. Other automakers hold large amounts as well.

Ford, GM, and Toyota, along with other automakers around the world, have announced plans to implement a

(continued)

CASE 3.1 (continued)

build-to-order program, much like the Dell approach to building computers. These auto giants intend to transform themselves from build-to-stock companies to build-to-order companies, thereby cutting inventory requirements in half, while at the same time giving customers the vehicles they want in a shorter period (e.g., one to two weeks).

Example: Jaguar

Jaguar car buyers can build a dream car online. At *jaguar.com*, consumers are able to custom configure their car's features and components, see it online, and price it, much as you can do with Dell's or HP's laptops and have it delivered to a nearby dealer. Using a virtual car on the website, customers can view in real time more than 1,250 possible exterior combinations out of several million, rotate the image 360 degrees, and see the price updated automatically with each selection of trim or accessories. After storing the car in a virtual garage, the customer can decide on the purchase and select a dealer at which to pick up the completed car. (Thus, conflicts with the established dealer network channel are avoided.) The website helps primarily with the research process—it is not a fully transactional site. The configuration, however, can be transmitted to the production floor, thereby reducing delivery time and contributing to increased customer satisfaction. Similar configuration systems are available from all the major car manufacturers.

Customers can electronically track the progress of the car creation, including visualization of the production process in the factory.

During the difficult economic times between 2008 and 2010, Detroit's build-to-forecast "push" distribution model has become unsustainable. A build-to-order "pull" distribution model is now a possible alternative to the build-to-forecast "push" system. The idea is to not ship a vehicle from its assembly plant until a retail customer pays for it. The proof-of-concept build-to-order model centralizes the completed vehicle inventory at the assembly plant and segments the market into "stock" vehicles and "special order" vehicles.

Sources: Compiled from *jaguar.com* (accessed April 2011), McElroy (2009), and Weiner (2006).

Questions

1. Why sell cars online?
2. Why is build-to-order an attractive strategy for a car manufacturer?
3. Why do customers like to configure their cars?
4. Compare a push versus a pull model.

The major success factor of this model is the ability to offer customized products at a reasonable cost. For how this is done, see Online Tutorial T6.

Pure-Play E-Tailers

Virtual (pure-play) e-tailers are firms that sell directly to consumers over the Internet without maintaining a physical sales channel. Amazon.com is a prime example of this type of e-tailer. Virtual e-tailers have the advantage of low overhead costs and streamlined processes. However, one drawback can be a lack of established infrastructure (including logistics) to support the online front-office activities. Virtual e-tailers can be *general purpose* or *specialized* e-tailers.

General e-tailers, such as Amazon.com, selling a vast range of goods and services online, capitalize on the Internet to offer such variety to a diverse group of customers geographically without the need to maintain a large physical retail network. Amazon.com and Buy.com are typical examples. Note that a general store may be composed of specialty stores. For example hayneedle.com includes over 200 specialty stores such as: furniture, seasonal gifts, yard and garden, etc. General purpose pure-play companies can be very large. Amazon.com is one example and so is Rakuten Ichiba, Japan's largest online mall that offers more than 50 million products made by over 33,000 merchants. In May 2010, the Japanese company acquired U.S.-based Buy.com. The combined company offers more than 60 million products made by over 35,000 merchants worldwide. The company had over 64 million registered members in Japan in 2009. In 2010, there are about 80 million registered members and sales approaching $4 billion.

Specialty e-tailers can operate in a very narrow market, as does CatToys.com (cattoys.com), described in Online File W3.2, or Rugman.com (rugman.com), which offers more than 12,000 Oriental and Persian rugs online. Blue Nile (Chapter 2) is

virtual (pure-play) e-tailers
Firms that sell directly to consumers over the Internet without maintaining a physical sales channel.

another example. Such specialized businesses would find it difficult to survive in the physical world because they would not have enough customers and could not hold the variety of stock.

Example. The Atlanta Falcons Club operates an online store, falcon365.com, where fans can purchase team merchandise. The store has an excellent navigation tool and powerful search engine at the front of the store, as well as a superb order fulfillment system that is integrated with the company's back office. For details, see ignify.com/ Atlanta_Falconc_eCommerce_ Case_Study.html.

Click-and-Mortar Retailers

A **click-and-mortar retailer** is a combination of both the traditional retailer and an online transactional website. Many click-and-mortar retailers started life as traditional storefronts with a physical retail presence only and over time adopted an online transactional capability as well (mortar-only to click-and-mortar). Another type of click-and-mortar business is a business that started online and then expanded to a physical storefront as well (click-only to click-and-brick; e.g., expedia.com).

Brick-and-mortar retailers conduct business in the physical world, in traditional brick-and-mortar stores. Traditional retailing frequently involves a single distribution channel, the physical store. In some cases, sellers also might operate a traditional mail-order business.

In today's digital economy, *click-and-mortar* retailers sell via stores, through voice phone calls to human operators, over the Internet through interactive websites, and via mobile devices. A firm that operates both physical stores and an online e-tail site is said to be a click-and-mortar business selling in a *multichannel business model*. Examples of retailers going from brick-only to brick-and-click are department stores, such as Macy's (macys.com) and Sears (sears.com), as well as discount stores, such as Walmart (walmart.com) and Target (target.com). It also includes supermarkets and all other types of retailing.

Retailing in Online Malls

There are two types of online malls: referring directories and malls with shared shopping services.

Referring Directories. This type of mall is basically a directory organized by product type. Catalog listings or banner ads at the mall site advertise the products or vendors. When users click on the product and/or a specific store, they are transferred to the storefront of the seller, where they then complete the transaction. Examples of referring directories can be found at bedandbreakfast.com. The stores listed in a directory either own the site collectively or they pay a subscription fee or a commission to the third party that advertises their logos. This type of e-tailing is basically a kind of affiliate marketing.

Malls with Shared Services. In online malls with shared services, a consumer can find a product, order and pay for it, and arrange for shipment. The hosting mall provides these services.

Ideally, the customer would like to go to different stores in the same mall, use one shopping cart, and pay only once. This arrangement is possible, for example, in Yahoo! stores (smallbusiness.yahoo.com/ecommerce). Other examples of malls with shared services are firststopshops.com and bing.com/shopping.

OTHER B2C MODELS AND SPECIAL RETAILING

Several other business models are used in B2C. They are discussed in various places throughout the book and by Wieczner (2010). Some of these models also are used in B2B, B2B2C, G2B, and other types of EC. A summary of these other models is provided in Exhibit 3.5.

---

click-and-mortar retailers
Brick-and-mortar retailers that offer a transactional website from which to conduct business.

brick-and-mortar retailers
Retailers who do business in the non-Internet, physical world in traditional brick-and-mortar stores.

EXHIBIT 3.5   Other B2C Business Models

Model Name	Description	Revenue Model	Location in Book
Transaction brokers	Electronically mediate between buyers and sellers. Popular in services, the travel industry, the job market, stock trading, and insurance (e.g., *Hotels.com*).	Transaction fees	Ch. 3
Information portals	Besides information, most portals provide links to merchants, for which they are paid a commission (affiliate marketing). Some provide hosting and software (e.g., *store.yahoo.com*), and some also sell.	Advertising, subscription fees, transaction fees	Chs. 3 and 4
Community portal and social networks	Combines community services with selling or affiliate marketing (e.g., *virtual communities.start4all.com*). Also see *facebook.com*.	Advertising, subscription, affiliate referral fees	Chs. 2 and 7
Content creators or disseminators	Provide content to the masses (news, stock data). Also participate in the syndication chain (e.g., *espn.com*, and *reuters.com*).	Advertising, subscription fees, affiliate referral fees	Chs. 7 and 8
Viral marketing	Use e-mail or SMS to advertise. Also can sell direct or via affiliates (e.g., Twitter).	Sales of goods and services	Chs. 2, 7, and 8
Market makers	Create and manage many-to-many markets (e.g., *chemconnect.com*); also auction sites (e.g., *ebay.com* and *dellauction.com*). Aggregate buyers and/or sellers (e.g., *ingrammicro.com*).	Transaction fees	Chs. 3 and 4
Make (build)-to-order	Manufacturers that customize their products and services via online orders (e.g., *dell.com*, *nike.com*, and *jaguar.com*).	Sales of goods	Online Tutorial T6
B2B2C	Manufacturer sells to a business, but delivers to individual customers (*godiva.com*).	Sales of goods and services	Ch. 4
Service providers	Offer online payments, order fulfillment (delivery), and security (e.g., *paypal.com* and *escrow.com*).	Sales of services	Chs. 8, 9, 10, and 11

B2C SOCIAL SHOPPING

B2C sites such as Amazon.com (amazon.com) and Netflix (netflix.com) provide consumers with rich social context and relevancy to the purchases that they are making. The participant companies have promoted three activities that shoppers can do collectively via wikis, blogs, and other online tools: find, collect, and share/recommend. These three acts comprise the phenomenon of several social shopping models such as online *group buying*.

Online Group Buying

In these depressed economic times, more people are using the Internet as a smart way to save money. Using online *group buying*, it is easy to quickly find enough people to enjoy the discount of large volume buying and/or share the freight and other costs. It is also easier to get larger discounts when more people take part in a group purchase (see Chapter 7 for details).

Such sites have a mechanism for intergroup feedback in that they allow users to leave a short review of the product they bought as well as the services obtained from the sellers. Meanwhile, other participants rely on group members who have previously rated the product/service and/or seller. B2C e-commerce relies on "word of mouth" among social network participants.

Examples of group aggregators are Groupon, Living Social, and BuyWithMe. Groups can be organized by potential buyers themselves. Other social shopping models are described next.

Personalized Event Shopping

event shopping
A B2C model in which sales are done to meet the needs of special events (e.g., a wedding, black Friday).

Some people like to be invited to special sales in person. You sign up to a product category and indicate how you want to be invited (e.g., Twitter, Facebook e-mail, etc.), then when there is a special sale ("*flash sale*") the system is activated and you receive your invitation (e.g., see Woot.com and its blog and discussion forum). This model is called **event shopping** and it may be combined with group purchasing (to lower your cost). Several start-ups are in this market: Groupon.com, Yipit and Deal Radar (for local deals), and MyNines and RowNine (for online flash sales). For details see Chapter 7 and Wieczner (2010). Two variations of this model are the private shopping clubs and group gifting online.

Private Shopping Clubs

private shopping club
A members-only shopping club, where members can buy goods at large discounts.

An online **private shopping club** is a members only shopping club, where members can buy goods at large discounts. The clubs organize events for their members that typically last two to six days. Because the clubs are private, members have to sign up before they are invited to see the goods and services on the special offers.

True private shopping clubs source their products directly from the brands and don't buy liquidation stock from retailers to assure quality and to protect the brand owners. Examples of clubs are Gilt in the United States (see Wieczner 2010) and KupiVIP in Russia.

Private shopping clubs can be organized in different ways. (e.g., see lockerz.com). For details, see Chapter 7 and en.wikipedia.org/wiki/Private_shopping_club.

Group Gifting Online

When an event such as a birthday, housewarming, or wedding comes up, sometimes a group of people decide it might be nice to give something as a group. But in reality, the hassles of trying to coordinate who is going to contribute, then selecting the gift and actually collecting the money and making the purchase is difficult. Luckily, Mother Necessity has brought the whole group gifting process online through sites like edivvy.com. For how you can set up a group gifting for a friend or family, see ehow.com/how_4788212_group_gift_online.html.

Location-Based E-Commerce

location-based e-commerce (l-commerce)
Delivery of e-commerce transactions to individuals in a specific location, at a specific time.

Location-based e-commerce (l-commerce) is a wireless based technology in which vendors send advertisements relevant to the location where customers are at a given time (using GPS for finding the location). The technology is a part of mobile commerce (Chapter 6). The model was unsuccessful until social networking emerged. Today companies such as Foursquare.com, Gowalla, MyTown, and Facebook Local provide l-commerce services. For details, see Chapters 6 and 8.

Shopping in Virtual Worlds

B2C in virtual worlds is also becoming popular. An example of this is the Dell Island in Second Life. Dell created a store on an island inside Second Life. Through the store it sells virtual computers for use in Second Life and real computers for use in real life, engaging users and fostering user interaction with each other and the products in the virtual world, which leads to purchases in the real world (see Chapter 7 and Brown 2009). Note that there are several hundreds of socially oriented start-ups employing the previously mentioned models and their innovative modifications. For some examples, see Wieczner (2010).

VIRTUAL VISUAL SHOPPING

For the first few years e-commerce was taking hold, it was challenging for sites to get close to delivering the in-store experience online. Eighty-five percent of all purchases are made at the shelf, making impulse buys a major money maker for brick-and-mortar retailers.

Many consumers embrace impulse buying because they get interesting products they'd never have bought without seeing them. Theoretically, shoppers in a 3-D Second Life–like environment could get the same experiences.

One aspect of 3-D is its ability to put dimensions and shape into a more physical context. A fully digitized depiction of a house interior could take the guesswork out of determining whether a large-screen television would fit in the intended space. Consider consumers shopping for a home entertainment system; the shoppers can enter a consumer electronics e-commerce site using a 3-D computer presentation and determine what they need based on seeing a system in a house similar to their own. Similarly, moving furniture around a room becomes a simple point and click, which allows consumers to see how the furniture will fit into their home before they buy. 3-D applications could take the guesswork out of buying and installing home entertainment systems, as well as home furnishings, decorating, renovations, and so forth.

Example. Can you imagine looking at a computer screen where you can see yourself in a piece of clothing you have selected. Exactly like in a fitting room. You can wave your hand to change the color of the outfit, wave your hand again and the dress can be shorter or longer. Another wave of your hand and another dress is on. A dream? Not really, it is coming! For an illustration, see the video at youtube.com/watch?v=rn_iPjGKd0M.

Section 3.2 ▶ REVIEW QUESTIONS

1. List the B2C distribution channel models.
2. Describe how traditional mail-order firms are transforming or adding online options.
3. Describe the direct marketing model used by manufacturers.
4. Describe virtual e-tailing.
5. Describe the click-and-mortar approach. Compare it to a pure e-tailing model.
6. Describe the different types of e-malls.
7. Describe B2C social shopping models.
8. Describe shopping in virtual worlds.
9. Describe visual virtual shopping.

3.3 TRAVEL AND TOURISM (HOSPITALITY) SERVICES ONLINE

Online travel services are provided by many vendors. Some major travel-related websites are expedia.com, travelocity.com, and priceline.com. Also all major airlines sell tickets and other services and so are travel vacation services (e.g., blue-hawaii.com); trains (e.g., amtrak.com); car rental agencies (e.g., autoeurope.com); hotels (e.g., marriott.com); commercial portals (e.g., cnn.com/travel); and tour companies (e.g., atlastravelweb.com). Publishers of travel guides such as Lonely Planet (lonelyplanet.com) provide considerable amounts of travel-related information on their websites, as well as selling travel services there. The competition is very fierce, but there is also collaboration. For example, hotels.com provides services to many sites. Thus, consumers find the same information and prices on many sites.

The revenue models of online travel services include direct revenues (commissions), revenue from advertising, lead-generation payments, consultancy fees, subscription or membership fees, revenue-sharing fees, and more. With such rapid growth and success, the travel industry seems to have matured beyond initial concerns such as trust, loyalty, and brand image. However, competition among online travel e-tailers is fierce, with low margins, little customer loyalty, and increasing commoditization of products and services. Thus, guaranteed best rates and various loyalty programs are likely to be popular ways of affecting customer behavior.

Three important trends will drive further changes in the online travel industry. First, online travel agents may try to differentiate themselves through customer-service messaging and other related services, presenting themselves as adding value to the customer.

Second, the number of travel meta search facilities, or "travel bots"—online sites or services that search through a range of related sites to find the best price or compare the value of travel products for a consumer—is likely to increase. Third, online travel companies are likely to increasingly use the growing phenomenon of social commerce to provide content to would-be travelers and also use these sites to study the behavior of potential customers (see the discussion later in this section and in Chapter 7).

SERVICES PROVIDED

Virtual travel agencies offer almost all the services delivered by conventional travel agencies, from providing general information to reserving and purchasing tickets, accommodations, and entertainment. In addition, they often provide services that most conventional travel agencies do not offer, such as travel tips, fare tracking (free e-mail alerts on low fares to and from a city and favorite destinations), experts' opinions, detailed driving maps and directions within the United States and several other countries (see infohub.com), and chat rooms and bulletin boards. In addition, some offer several other innovative services, such as online travel auctions.

SPECIAL SERVICES ONLINE

Many online travel services offer travel bargains. Consumers can go to special sites, such as those offering standby or last-minute tickets, to find bargain fares. Lastminute.com (lastminute.com) offers very low airfares and discounted accommodation prices to fill otherwise-empty airline seats and hotel rooms. Last-minute trips also can be booked on americanexpress.com, sometimes at a steep discount. Special vacation destinations can be found at priceline.com, stayfinder.com, and greatrentals.com. Flights.com (flights.com) offers cheap tickets and also Eurail passes. Travelers can access cybercaptive.com for a list of thousands of Internet cafés around the world. Similar information is available via many portals, such as Yahoo! and MSN. Search engines such as Google or Bing can also be helpful.

Also of interest are sites that offer medical advice and services for travelers. This type of information is available from the World Health Organization (who.int), governments (e.g., cdc.gov/travel), and private organizations (e.g., tripprep.com, medicalert.org, and webmd.com).

Other special services include:

- **Wireless services.** Many airlines (e.g., Cathay Pacific, Delta, and Qantas) allow customers with mobile devices with Internet access to check their flight status, update frequent flyer miles, and even book flights.
- **Advanced check-in.** Most airlines provide advanced online check-in. You can print your boarding pass within 24 hours prior to departure. Alternatively, you can use a smartphone to download the boarding pass into your cell phone and then submit your phone to the security people with an ID. The security has an electronic reader that can read the boarding pass from your smartphone and let you board the plane.
- **Direct marketing.** Airlines sell electronic tickets over the Internet. When customers purchase electronic tickets online (or by phone), all they have to do is print the boarding pass from their computer's printer or upon arrival at the airport enter their credit card at an *electronic kiosk* to get a boarding pass.
- **Alliances and consortia.** Airlines and other travel companies are creating alliances to increase sales or reduce purchasing costs. For example, some consortia aggregate only fares purchased over the Internet.

Social Travel Networks

Since 2005, online leisure travelers' use of social computing technologies, such as blogs, RSS, wikis, and user reviews, for researching travel has skyrocketed. Travelers are increasingly using sites like Facebook, YouTube, Twitter, IgoUgo.com, Flickr, Foursquare, and Trip Advisor to plan their trips, and talk about their experience afterward—both good and bad. Travel e-businesses, marketing executives, and managers realized that social computing was increasingly playing a larger role in corporate online strategy, even if all a company did was monitor what travelers were saying about a certain company in third-party forums. For example, Delta Airlines has a shop on Facebook that allows people to search, book, and pay for flights within Facebook. For details, see Marsden (2010).

As travelers forge connections and share information with like-minded travelers online, their needs and expectations change. They want more relevance and more correct information. Social computing has shifted online travel from passive selling to active customer engagement, which affects how travel companies and agents distribute and market their products. Several social networks have travel channels that cater to travelers. Examples of such networks are wikitravel.org and world66.com, which features a travel channel. Wikitravel was built in order to make it easy to share travel knowledge and let others share it. The site uses a wiki that allows any Internet reader to create, update, edit, and illustrate *any* article on the website. World66 believes that travelers are the best source of travel information. It is an open content travel guide, where people from all over the world can write about the places they love, hotels they stayed in, or restaurants where they have eaten. Every part of the travel guide can be directly edited. For a comprehensive resource, see tourism2-0.co.uk. Other social networks exclusively available for travelers are: Dopplr, Trip Wolf, Trip Say, Trip Hub, Driftr, Virtual Tourist, BootsnAll, Lonely Plant, Thorn Tree, and TripAdvisor. Case 3.2 shows an example of a social network for travelers.

For a discussion on how hotels are using social commerce, see hvs.com/article/4429/examples-of-how-hotels-are-using-social-media-a-guide-for.

CASE 3.2
EC Application

WAYN: A LIFESTYLE AND TRAVEL SOCIAL NETWORK

WAYN (which stands for "Where Are You Now?") is a social networking website (*wayn.com*) with a goal of uniting travelers from around the world. WAYN was launched in London in May 2003. It has grown from 45,000 to about 15 million members as of 2009, adding 20,000 new members each day. Approximately 2 million members are based in the United Kingdom. It also is strong in the United States, Canada, Australia, New Zealand, and countries in Western Europe.

As with many other social networking services, WAYN enables its users to create a personal profile and upload and store photos. Users can then search for others with similar profiles and link them to their profiles as friends. It also is possible to send and receive messages using discussion forums. Because it is designed for travelers, members are able to search for contacts based on a particular location. Using a world map, users can visually locate where each of their contacts is situated around the world. Users can also share experiences, tips, and memories with others. The goal of the service is for members to keep friends informed of where they are while traveling and, in turn, to be able to locate their friends.

In addition, users can send SMSs to any of their contacts worldwide, chat online using WAYN's Instant Messenger, plan trips, and notify their friends about them. Using WAYN, users can create discussion groups, ask for recommendations, and send smiley icons to all. Finally, chat bots (avatars) are dynamic and fully active, representing one of the best ways of meeting people in the WAYN community.

WAYN is one of the very few sites that did not lose new subscriptions after introducing fees for its premier membership service, making it one of the few social networking communities that managed to quickly become profitable.

WAYN is now popular in 220 countries, becoming a global brand. It is not aimed at any particular age group, but it seems to be most popular with the 18-to-25 age group. It also has a strong position among the 35-to-45-plus age group. Members can find out who will be traveling to their next intended destination, at the same time as they are. The WAYN VIP Club, which offers 100 free international SMSs per month, has the ability to create private forums and other benefits. WAYN can be followed on Facebook, Twitter, and on their founders' blog. WAYN's revenue model is based on advertisements. WAYN can be accessed on the go via several downloadable applications.

Sources: Compiled from Butcher (2008), *wayn.com* (accessed November 2010), and *en.wikipedia.org/wiki/WAYN* (accessed April 2011).

Questions

1. Visit *wayn.com*. What options do you find most exciting on the site?

2. Enter *wayn.com* and identify all advertisement options. List them and discuss three which would work best for you as a traveler.

3. Identify the mobile capabilities on the site.

4. Why has WAYN been so successful even though the site requires subscription fees?

Note: Travelers are happy to use Facebook, Twitter, and Foursquare to facilitate their travel; however, such inquiries (as used on WAYN) may create traffic jams in the social networking sites.

BENEFITS AND LIMITATIONS OF ONLINE TRAVEL SERVICES

The benefits of online travel services to travelers are enormous. The amount of free information is tremendous, and it is accessible at any time from any place. Substantial discounts can be found, especially for those who have time and patience to search for them. Providers of travel services also benefit: Airlines, hotels, and cruise lines are selling otherwise-empty spaces online. Also, direct selling saves the provider's commission and its processing. For tips on the limitations and hazards for the use of social travel, see Barish (2010).

Online travel services do have some limitations. First, the amount of time and the difficulty of using virtual travel agencies can be very large, especially for complex trips and for inexperienced Internet surfers. Second, complex trips or those that require stopovers might not be available online because they require specialized knowledge and arrangements, which may be better done by a knowledgeable, human travel agent. Therefore, the need for travel agents as intermediaries remains, at least for the immediate future.

CORPORATE TRAVEL

The corporate travel market is huge and its online portion has been growing rapidly in recent years. Corporations can use all the travel services mentioned earlier. However, many large corporations receive additional services from large travel agencies. To reduce corporate travel costs, companies can make arrangements that enable employees to plan and book their own trips. Using online optimization tools provided by travel companies, such as those offered by American Express (americanexpress.com/gcs/travel), companies can try to reduce travel costs even further. Travel authorization software that checks availability of funds and compliance with corporate guidelines is usually provided by travel companies such as American Express. Expedia via its Egencia company (egencia.com), Travelocity (travelocity.com), and Orbitz (orbitz.com) also offer software tools for corporate planning and booking.

Example: American Express's Business Travel Helps URS Inc. to Survive Hurricanes. URS is one of the largest engineering and architectural design firms in the world with close to 30,000 employees and 370 offices in more than 20 countries. URS spends $13 million on travel every year, and the firm is extremely security conscious.

With over 800 employees in the Gulf Coast during Hurricane Katrina, URS was confronted with its own internal crisis trying to identify and contact affected employees in a timely manner, including travelers in the region. The firm realized it needed an automated solution to quickly identify travelers impacted during times of crisis.

To solve the problem, URS implemented American Express Business Travel's TrackPoint system, an intuitive, Web-based system with a user-friendly interface that enables companies to quickly identify impacted travelers, pinpoint their locations, and review their itineraries. TrackPoint consolidates data from both online and traditional bookings and is automatically updated to keep information current as itineraries change.

Within two months of implementation, TrackPoint helped URS identify and assist over one hundred employees who were in the projected path of Hurricane Ernesto or were affected by the new Travel Security Administration's regulations in response to the failed London terrorist plot. In each situation, URS was able to contact travelers within 24 hours and provide updates on the current situation and give special instructions.

For further discussion, see B2B travel in Chapter 4 and acte.org.

A major issue emerged in 2009 when about 50 municipalities filed a class action suit against the online travel companies demanding the imposition of a fuel tax on the discounted fares (the travel companies pay a discount price). For details, see Bowling (2009). Another class action suit argued that online travel companies do not pay enough local occupancy taxes on hotel rooms they help fill.

Section 3.3 ▶ REVIEW QUESTIONS

1. What travel services are available online that are not available offline?
2. List the benefits of online travel services to travelers and to service providers.
3. How do social networks facilitate travel?
4. Describe corporate online travel services.

EXHIBIT 3.6 Traditional Versus Online Job Markets

Characteristic	Traditional Job Market	Online Job Market
Cost	Expensive, especially in prime space	Can be very inexpensive
Life cycle	Short	Long
Place	Usually local and limited if global	Global
Context updating	Can be complex, expensive	Fast, simple, inexpensive
Space for details	Limited	Large
Ease of search by applicant	Difficult, especially for out-of-town applicants	Quick and easy
Ability of employers to find applicants	May be very difficult, especially for out-of-town applicants	Easy
Matching of supply and demand	Difficult	Easy
Reliability	Material can be lost in mail	High
Communication speed between employees and employers	Can be slow	Fast
Ability of employees to compare jobs	Limited	Easy, fast

3.4 EMPLOYMENT PLACEMENT AND THE JOB MARKET ONLINE

The online job market connects individuals who are looking for a job with employers who are looking for employees with specific skills. An online job market is a very popular approach, and, increasingly, both job seekers and prospective employers are turning away from traditional print-based advertising and recruitment methods (or at minimum supplementing them) in preference of online advertisements and recruitment activities. In addition to online job ads and placement services available through specialized websites (such as careerbuilder.com), larger companies are increasingly building career portals on their corporate websites as a way of trimming recruitment costs and reducing the time to fill vacancies. Advantages of the online job market over the traditional one are listed in Exhibit 3.6.

THE INTERNET JOB MARKET

The Internet offers a rich environment for job seekers and for companies searching for hard-to-find employees. Nearly all *Fortune* 500 companies now use the Internet for some of their recruitment activities, and studies reveal that online resources are now the most popular way to find suitably qualified applicants for job vacancies. Online job recruitment revenues and volume overtook print ad classifieds and in 2008 were estimated to reach $6 billion (Fisher 2008). More than 40,000 online job boards are now operating in the United States. The U.S. market is dominated by three major players: Monster, Careerbuilder, and Yahoo! HotJobs, which together comprise about 55 percent of the market. Craigslist, LinkedIn, Twitter, and Facebook are also becoming important online recruitment sites.

The following parties use the Internet job market:

> **Job seekers.** Job seekers can reply to employment ads. Or, they can take the initiative and place their résumés on their own homepages or on others' websites, send messages to members of newsgroups asking for referrals, and use the sites of recruiting firms, such as careerbuilder.com, hotjobs.yahoo.com, and monster.com. For entry-level jobs and internships for newly minted graduates, job seekers can go to collegerecruiter.com. Job seekers can also assess their market value in different U.S. cities at wageweb.com and use the Web to compare salaries and conditions, obtain information about

employers, and get career advice. Passive job seekers, those just keeping an eye on opportunities, are using this medium, as well as those actively seeking new employment.

Job seekers can access via jobs.info.com to see millions of employment opportunities from over 500 websites, major job boards, the top 200 newspapers, hundreds of associations, and companies' career pages.

- **Employers seeking employees.** Many organizations, including public institutions, advertise openings on their websites. Others advertise job openings on popular public portals, online newspapers, bulletin boards, and with recruiting firms. The basic idea is to automate portions of the hiring process (e.g., see Webb 2009, and Weinstein 2009). For example, employers can conduct interviews and administer interactive intelligence, skills, and psychological tests on the Web. Forty percent of large U.S. firms are using computerized assessments to screen new hires or to identify up-and-comers for training and development (AlexFrankel.com 2008). The tests are designed to predict success by measuring behavioral or personality traits and comparing a candidate's profile with those of people who have succeeded in similar jobs. Trovix.com uses embedded intelligence to help manage the entire recruiting process. Its software agents emulate the human decision-making assessment of a candidate's qualifications. For companies such as Infosys that receives over 1 million job applications a year, the automation of the process by using such software is a must. Also see Yahoo!'s Resumix (at viviente.com/resumix/website). For more on how e-commerce can help in recruiting, see Webb (2009).

  A relatively new trend is to use new tools such as videos to meet and then interview candidates from remote locations. It may not be so simple. For details, see Park and Lombardi (2010). Also, there are virtual *job fairs*, where employers can conduct initial interviews; see Weinstein (2009).

- **Classified ads.** Classified ads for job openings and job seekers are available at craigslist.org, ebayclassifieds.com, webclassifieds.us, and in the online classified sections of many newspapers. Also, several social networks, including Facebook, allow posting of job openings.

- **Job agencies.** Hundreds of job agencies are active on the Web. They use their own Web pages to post available job descriptions and advertise their services in e-mails and at other websites. Job agencies and/or employers use newsgroups, online forums, bulletin boards, Internet commercial résumé services, and portals such as Yahoo! HotJobs and AOL. Most portals are free; others, such as MktgLadder (marketing-jobs.theladders.com), charge membership fees but offer many services.

- **Government agencies and institutions.** Many government agencies advertise openings for positions on their websites and on other sites; some are required by law to do so. In addition, some government agencies use the Internet to help job seekers find jobs elsewhere, as is done in Hong Kong, the Philippines, and Germany. As an initiative by the Australian Government, Jobsearch (jobsearch.gov.au), the largest free job board in Australia, offers free advertising to employers. It has over 1 million visitors per month, with an average of 80,000 jobs on offer at any one time. It links this online presence to an Australia-wide network of touchscreen kiosks. Employers are notified when a candidate's résumé matches an advertised job (*Workplace.gov.au* 2009). In Germany, the government created the "*virtual labor market*" that links unemployed workers with employers. For a comprehensive review and analysis, see computerworld.com/s/article/9032081/Honors_Program_Germany_s_Labor_Agency_Bundesagentur_f_r_Arbeit_.

Online Job Markets on Social Networks

In today's age of Web 2.0, the wide reach of social networking sites can get people hired faster. As demonstrated in Exhibit 3.7, job referral social networking sites (e.g., jobster.com and bluechipexpert.com) solve the problem of finding the right people for the job in hours. The sites provide job seekers opportunities to promote their areas of expertise as well as help them get "found" by employers. The added incentive of getting paid for every successful referral makes it even more worthwhile to join these networks. The site's algorithms enable headhunters to sort qualified applicants by different criteria. When an offer is made, the job referral site receives payment on behalf of the employees, including a referral fee. Social commerce has certainly found its niche in the online job recruitment industry. While recruits text message thank-yous to hiring managers, mostly not well received, some recruiters are offering Facebook "friend" invitations to candidates they have interviewed (Bowers 2008). Facebook has many features that help people find jobs (see facebook.com/urhired). A similar service is provided by LinkedIn.com. For an overview and examples, see Dickler (2009). The LinkedIn search engine can help employers quickly find the appropriate candidate. For more on social networking activities in recruiting, see Chapter 7.

Lately there has been an increased use of Twitter as an aid for job search. The following are possible activities:

a. Follow and read job search experts

b. Search for posted positions

c. Follow and read about people in your field

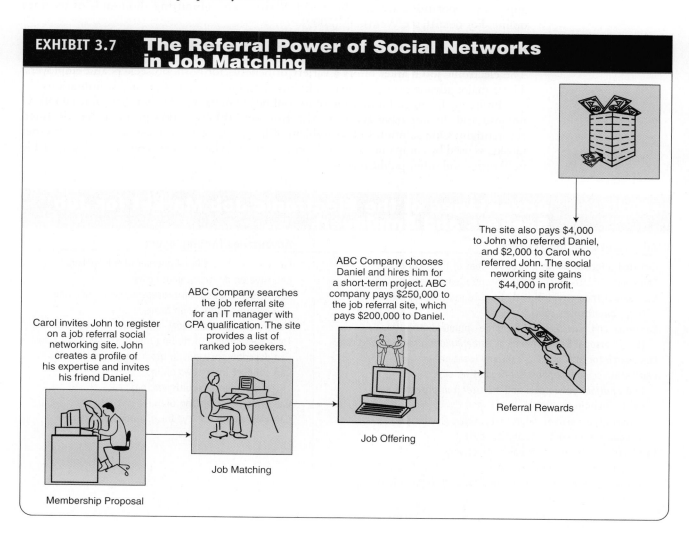

EXHIBIT 3.7   The Referral Power of Social Networks in Job Matching

Carol invites John to register on a job referral social networking site. John creates a profile of his expertise and invites his friend Daniel.

Membership Proposal

ABC Company searches the job referral site for an IT manager with CPA qualification. The site provides a list of ranked job seekers.

Job Matching

ABC Company chooses Daniel and hires him for a short-term project. ABC company pays $250,000 to the job referral site, which pays $200,000 to Daniel.

Job Offering

The site also pays $4,000 to John who referred Daniel, and $2,000 to Carol who referred John. The social neworking site gains $44,000 in profit.

Referral Rewards

   d. Engage, communicate with people and ask for help

   e. Connect with people at your target companies

   For details, see Needleman (2009) and Dickler (2009).

Global Online Portals for Job Placement

The Internet is very helpful for anyone looking for a job in another country. An interesting global portal for Europe is described in Online File W3.3. An interesting global site for placing/finding jobs in different countries is xing.com (see Internet Exercise 7). The electronic job market can also create high turnover costs for employers by facilitating employees' movement to better jobs. Finally, finding candidates online is more complicated than most people think, mostly due to the large number of résumés available online. To facilitate recruitment, top recruiters are seeking the benefits of using new tools like video to meet (interview) candidates from remote locations.

Virtual Job Fairs

Virtual job fairs as well as recruiting via social networks are new strategies for quickly finding qualified candidates at a reduced cost. These are done in virtual worlds, social networks, or the employers' websites.

   Example. KPMG, which operates in 145 countries, found a virtual job fair to be an efficient way to reach a global pool of job applicants. In 2008, the company decided that a virtual job fair in which each country staffs a "booth" would allow applicants to focus on a particular global office's opportunities, or to "stroll" the virtual floor, learning about and applying to positions around the world. Visitors are submitting thousands of résumés online. For details, see Weinstein (2009).

BENEFITS AND LIMITATIONS OF THE ELECTRONIC JOB MARKET

The electronic job market offers a variety of benefits for both job seekers and employers. These major advantages are shown in Exhibit 3.8. However, it also has few limitations.

   Probably the biggest limitation of the online job market is the fact that some people do not use and do not have access to the Internet, although this problem has declined substantially. One solution to the problem of limited access is the use of in-store Internet kiosks, as used by companies such as Home Depot or Macy's. Also, computers are available in libraries and other public places.

EXHIBIT 3.8	Advantages of the Electronic Job Market for Job Seekers and Employers
Advantages for Job Seekers	**Advantages for Employers**
Can find information on a large number of jobs worldwide	Can advertise to a large number of job seekers
Can communicate quickly with potential employers	Can save on advertisement costs
Can market themselves directly to potential employers (e.g., *quintcareers.com*)	Can reduce application-processing costs by using electronic application forms
Can write and post résumés for large-volume distribution (e.g., Personal Search Agent at *careerbuilder.com, brassring.com*)	Can provide greater equal opportunity for job seekers
Can search for jobs quickly from any location	Increased chance of finding highly skilled employees
Can obtain several support services at no cost (e.g., *hotjobs.yahoo.com* and *monster.com* provide free career-planning services)	Can describe positions in great detail
Can assess their market value (e.g., *wageweb.com* and *rileyguide.org* look for salary surveys)	Can conduct interviews online (using video teleconferencing)
Can learn how to use their voice effectively in an interview (*greatvoice.com*)	Can arrange for testing online
Can access newsgroups that are dedicated to finding jobs (and keeping them)	Can view salary surveys for recruiting strategies

Security and privacy are another limitation. Résumés and other online communications are usually not encrypted, so one's job-seeking activities might not be secure, and thus confidentiality and data protection cannot be guaranteed. It is also possible that someone at a job seeker's current place of employment (his or her boss) might find out that that person is job hunting. LinkedIn, for example, provides protection of privacy, enabling job seekers to determine who can see their résumé online.

Yahoo! Hotjobs advises online applicants how to avoid making these five mistakes: (1) not taking appropriate action, (2) ignoring the privacy setting, (3) staying silent, (4) being indiscrete, and (5) not updating your information.

Section 3.4 ▶ REVIEW QUESTIONS

1. What are the driving forces of the electronic job market?
2. What are the major advantages of the electronic job market to the candidate? To employers?
3. Why is LinkedIn so useful for job seekers and for employees? List the specific tools provided by EC to job seekers.
4. List the specific tools provided by recruiters.
5. What are the limitations of electronic job markets?

3.5 REAL ESTATE, INSURANCE, AND STOCK TRADING ONLINE

Online service industries are exploding on the Internet and are being embraced by customers. Internet and related technologies are more than just new distribution channels. They are a different way of providing these services. Some major services are presented in this and the following section.

REAL ESTATE ONLINE

Changes in real estate transactions are reaching a tipping point, beyond which the nature of the business will be altered.

To get some idea of the changes, consider the following statistics. Borrell Associates forecasts that by 2013, 33.1 percent of a projected $35.3 billion in real estate–related advertising will be spent online, compared with online's 19.6 percent market share in 2005. Online advertising by real estate–related companies and mortgage lenders grew by nearly 20 percent in 2007, but we see slower growth during the current economic downturn (*Ahorre.com* 2009). The increase in Internet real estate advertising is understandably influencing buying behavior. Studies by the National Association of Realtors (NAR) have shown that over 80 percent of real estate buyers begin their searches for properties on the Internet (*Realtors Magazine* 2009).

In the face of such increases in consumer knowledge and control of the early parts of the identification and purchase of properties, some U.S. realtors have tried to restrict public access to some of the databases of properties, such as the local Multiple Listing Services. In summary, e-commerce and the Internet are slowly but surely having an ever-increasing impact on the real estate industry. For example, despite the changes that are beginning to emerge, real estate agents have not been disintermediated. Home buyers today tend to use both real estate agents and the Internet. Thus, despite the fact that the Internet is shaking up the real estate industry, the emerging pattern is more complex than the simple disintermediation of agents, but their commission percentage starts to decline as more buyers find sales on the Internet.

Zillow, Craigslist, and Other Web 2.0 Real Estate Services

Craigslist and Zillow are examples of Web 2.0 free real estate services that have been intended to disintermediate unnecessary middlemen, such as newspaper classified advertising, and allow buyers to find information and do comparisons on their own.

Zillow (zillow.com) operates the "Make Me Move" function that allows users to see what is available on the market in detail, ask a question, get advice, and gather information on related services. Users can participate in a blog, start a discussion, and so forth. Home owners who may have no intention of moving, but who certainly would for the right price, can list information about their homes on "Make Me Move" so that gutsy buyers can try to make a deal. A home owner can post a "Make Me Move" price without exposing any personal information. Zillow then enables interested buyers to contact the owner through an e-mail "anonymizer." The service is free. The company also provides free listings for all home owners and realtors. Listings can include photos, and realtors can also create websites for each listing. Other Web 2.0 features of Zillow are a blog and a real estate wiki, which has hundreds of articles on buying, selling, financing, or any topic an owner/buyer might need. Wiki visitors can edit or comment on articles or create new articles. Zillow went public in July 2011 with a successful IPO.

Craigslist (craigslist.org) has become a powerhouse site for advertising real estate for sale and rent listings, with more and more agents turning to the site for added exposure to buyers looking online. Property listings are free to list on Craigslist in all markets except in some large cities, where brokers must pay a fee for listing. For more about real estate applications and services offered online, see realtor.com, real-estate-online.com, and auction.com.

INSURANCE ONLINE

An increasing number of companies use the Internet to offer standard insurance policies, such as auto, home, life, or health, at a substantial discount, mostly to individuals. Furthermore, third-party aggregators offer free comparisons of available policies. Several large insurance and risk-management companies (e.g., Allstate, State Farm, Progressive, GEICO) offer comprehensive insurance contracts online. Although many people do not trust the faceless insurance agent, others are eager to take advantage of the reduced premiums. For example, a visit to insurance.com will show a comparison of a variety of different policies. At answerfinancial.com, customers and businesses can compare car insurance offerings and then make a purchase online. At globaltravelinsurance.com, customers can book travel insurance. Another popular insurance site is insweb.com. Many insurance companies use a dual strategy, keeping human agents but also selling online. Like the real estate brokers, insurance brokers send unsolicited e-mails to millions of people. It is estimated that Web insurance transactions cost about 50¢ each to process, compared with up to $8 for those that are paper-based (McDougall 2007). The stiff competition will reduce the commission for the surviving agents.

Example. Aegon Group, a life and health insurance company, needed an effective way to distribute information about its life insurance products to existing and future customers. Using a specially designed EC portal designed by Online Insight, the company can provide general information, customer education, interactive decision purchasing tools, and much more in an easy and inexpensive way.

ONLINE STOCK TRADING

The commission for an online trade is between $1 and $19, compared with an average fee of $100 from a full-service broker and $25 from a non-Internet discount broker. With online trading, there are no busy telephone lines, and the chance for error is small, because there is no oral communication in a frequently noisy environment. Orders can be placed from anywhere, at any time, day or night, and there is no biased broker to push a sale. Furthermore, investors can find a considerable amount of free research information about specific companies or mutual funds. Many services provided to online traders include online statements, tax-related calculations, extensive research on industries, real-time news, and even tutoring on how to trade. (e.g., check etrade.com or finance.google.com).

Several discount brokerage houses initiated extensive online stock trading, notably Charles Schwab in 1995. Full-service brokerage companies, such as Merrill Lynch, followed in 1998–1999. As of 2009, 97 percent of stock trades in the United States are executed via electronic communications networks including the Internet (Stokes 2009).

How does online trading work? Let's say an investor has an account with Schwab. The investor accesses Schwab's website (schwab.com), enters an account number and password, and clicks stock trading. Using a menu, the investor enters the details of the order (buy, sell, margin or cash, price limit, or market order). The computer tells the investor the current (real-time) "ask" and "bid" prices, much as a broker would do over the telephone, and the investor can approve or reject the transaction. The flow chart of this process is shown in Exhibit 3.9.

Some companies, including Schwab, are now also licensed as exchanges. This allows them to match the selling and buying orders of their own customers for many securities in one to two seconds. Some well-known companies that offer online trading are E*TRADE, Ameritrade, Scottrade, and ShareBuilder.

E*TRADE is expanding rapidly into several countries, enabling global stock trading. As of 2009, E*TRADE started allowing customers to trade online in seven different countries, taking care of the currency exchange rate.

With the rapid pace of adoption of mobile handsets, mobile banking is becoming more and more popular. Mobile banking services enable users to receive information on their account balances via SMS and to settle payments for bills and purchase stocks. (see details in Chapter 6). See Online File W3.4 for more on investment information available online.

The Risk of Trading in an Online Stock Account

The major risk of online trading is security. Although all trading sites require users to have an ID and password, problems may still occur. Problems of this nature also can occur when conducting online banking, our next topic.

Section 3.5 ▶ REVIEW QUESTIONS

1. List the major online real estate applications.
2. What are the advantages of selling insurance online?
3. What are the advantages of online stock tracking?

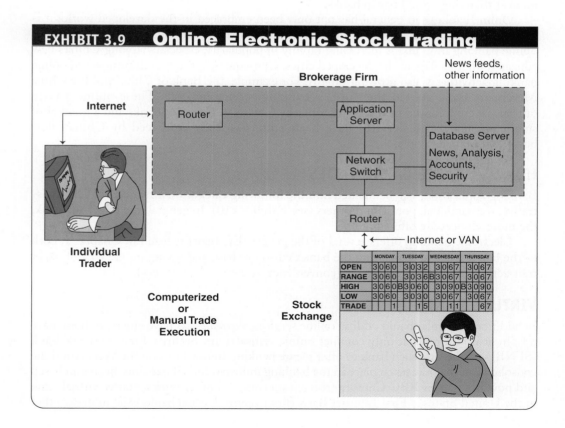

EXHIBIT 3.9   Online Electronic Stock Trading

3.6   BANKING AND PERSONAL FINANCE ONLINE

electronic (online) banking (e-banking)
Various banking activities conducted from home or the road using an Internet connection; also known as cyberbanking, virtual banking, online banking, and home banking.

Electronic (online) banking (e-banking), also known as cyberbanking, virtual banking, or home banking, includes various banking activities conducted via the Internet from home, business, or on the road rather than at a physical bank location. Consumers can use e-banking to check their accounts, pay bills online, secure a loan electronically, and much more. The credit crisis of 2007, banking collapses of 2008, and the resulting recession caused consumers to watch their spending more closely, fueling a desire for efficient but elegant online banking, bill pay, and personal finance management tools. Eight out of 10 households now bank online. Paying bills online is now a routine practice for Americans. Javelin's 2009 survey data indicates that 70 percent of households paid a bill online in the previous month either through a financial institution, a biller, or both (Javelin Strategy and Research 2009). Several sites help you with personal finance and budgeting. Examples are MINT.com, Geezeo.com, Kiplinger.com, and Wesabe.com

E-banking saves users time and money. For banks, it offers an inexpensive alternative to branch banking and a chance to enlist remote customers. Many physical banks now offer home banking services, and some use EC as a major competitive strategy. One such U.S. bank is Wells Fargo (wellsfargo.com). Another one is JPMorgan Chase. HSBC of UK/ Hong Kong offers savings CDs online as well as checking accounts in the United States. Many banks offer wireless services.

An emerging innovation in online banking is peer-to-peer (P2P) online lending. Two examples are Zopa in the United Kingdom (uk.zopa.com, and en.wikipedia.org/wiki/zopa) and Prosper (prosper.com, and en.wikipedia.org/wiki/prosper-marketplace) in the United States, which offer P2P online lending (see Chapter 7). Note that despite the global credit crunch of 2008–2010 and the fact that neither has a government-backed guarantee, Zopa and Prosper are enjoying solid growth For example, in the third quarter of 2008 new borrowers of Zopa increased by nearly 50 percent, to 3,700, compared with the previous quarter (Keegan 2008). The default rate of these P2P lenders is very low, because the borrowers and the lenders know each other through social networking. Disintermediation of the banks also allows the lenders to get higher interest and the borrowers to pay lower interest than they would pay in banks.

Online banking in general has not only been embraced in the developed world; it is becoming an enabling feature of business growth in the developing world. For example, online banking in China is increasing rapidly in popularity, especially among China's new educated middle class in the developed cities. Consequently, the overall turnover of online banking activities is also growing rapidly. For example, the Bank of China and the China Merchants Bank started their online banking service in 1998. These online service offerings were followed by online offerings by China's other major banks and a number of smaller banks. These services have been enthusiastically embraced by China's new business-oriented people.

HOME BANKING CAPABILITIES

Banking applications can be divided into the following categories: informational, administrative, transactional, portal, and others (see Exhibit 3.10). In general, the larger the bank, the more services are offered online.

Electronic banking offers several of the generic EC benefits listed in Chapter 1, both to the banks (such as expanding the bank's customer base and saving on the cost of paper transactions) and to the customers (convenience, sometimes lower fees).

VIRTUAL BANKS

In addition to regular banks adding online services, *virtual banks* have emerged; these have no physical location but only conduct online transactions. Security First Network Bank (SFNB) was the first such bank to offer secure banking transactions on the Web. Amid the consolidation that has taken place in the banking industry, SFNB has since been purchased and now is a part of RBC Centura (rbccentura.com). Another representative virtual bank in the United States is First Internet Bank (firstib.com). Virtual banks exist in many other

EXHIBIT 3.10 Online Banking Applications

Application Type	Information/Services Provided
Informational	General bank information and history
	Financial education information
	Employment information
	Interest rate quotes
	Financial calculators
	Current bank and local news
Administrative	Account information access
	Opening of new account online
	Applications for services
	Moving all banking online
	Personal finance software applications
Transactional	Account transfer capabilities
	Transfer funds housed at different financial institutions
	Bill-pay services
	Corporate services (e.g., cash management, treasury)
	Online insurance services
	Online brokerage services
	Real-time funds transfer
	Online trust services
Portal	Links to financial information
	Links to community information
	Links to local business
	Links to nonlocal businesses (and/or advertisers)
Others	Wireless capabilities
	Search function

Sources: Compiled from Acharya, et al. (2008) and Cash Edge (2006).

countries (e.g., bankdirect.co.nz). In some countries, virtual banks are involved in stock trading, and some stockbrokers are doing online banking (e.g., see etrade.com). More than 97 percent of the hundreds of pure-play virtual banks failed by 2003 due to a lack of financial viability. Many more failed during 2007–2010. The most successful banks seem to be of the click-and-mortar type (e.g., HSBC).

A word of caution about virtual banking: Before sending money to any cyberbank, especially those that promise high interest rates for your deposits, make sure that the bank is a legitimate one. Several cases of fraud already have occurred. For a discussion, see *Network World* (2010).

INTERNATIONAL AND MULTIPLE-CURRENCY BANKING

International banking and the ability to handle trades in multiple currencies are critical for international trading. Although some international retail purchasing can be done by providing a credit card number, other transactions may require international banking support. Examples of such cross-border support include the following:

- TradeCard and MasterCard have developed a multiple-currency system for global transactions (see tradecard.com).
- Bank of America (bankofamerica.com) and most other major banks offer international capital funds, cash management, trades and services, foreign exchange, risk management investments, merchant services, and special services for international traders.
- Fxall.com is a multidealer foreign exchange service that enables faster and cheaper foreign exchange transactions. Special services are being established for stock market traders who need to pay for foreign stocks (e.g., at Charles Schwab, Fidelity Finance, or E*TRADE).

ONLINE FINANCIAL TRANSACTION IMPLEMENTATION ISSUES

As one would expect, the implementation of online banking and online stock trading can be interrelated. In many instances, one financial institution offers both services. The following are some other implementation issues for online financial transactions.

Securing Financial Transactions

Financial transactions for home banking and online trading must be very secure. In Chapters 9 and 10, we discuss the details of secure EC payment systems. In Case 3.3, we give an example of how a bank provides security and privacy to its customers. For examples, look at the *Security Centers* of all major banks' sites (e.g., chase.com).

Imaging Systems

Many financial institutions (e.g., Bank of America, Wells Fargo, and Citibank) allow customers to view images of all of their incoming checks, invoices, and other related online correspondence. Image access can be simplified with the help of a search engine.

CASE 3.3

EC Application

SECURITY FOR ONLINE BANK TRANSACTIONS

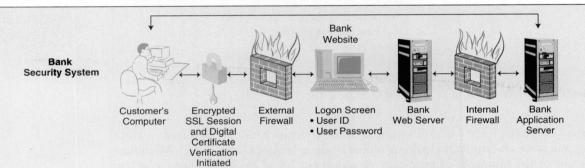

Banks provide extensive security to their customers. The following describes some of the safeguards provided.

Customers accessing a bank system from the outside must go through encryption provided by SSL (Secure Socket Layer) and digital certificate verification (see Chapters 9 and 10). The verification process assures users each time they sign on that they are indeed connected to their specific bank. The customer inquiry message then goes through an external firewall. Once the logon screen is reached, a user ID and a password are required. This information flows through a direct Web server and then goes through an internal firewall to the bank's application server.

Information is shared among a bank's family of partners only for legitimate business purposes. Sharing information with outside companies is done with extreme care.

Banks do not capture information provided by customers when conducting "what-if" scenarios using planning tools (to ensure privacy). Many banks use cookies to learn about their customers; however, customers can control both the collection and in some cases the use of such information. In addition, most banks provide suggestions on how users

can increase security (e.g., "Use a browser with 128-bit encryption.").

With the increased use of mobile devices the threat of security risks has increased. Banks are coming up with innovative solutions. For example, in January 2009 Bank of America introduced its "Safe Pass Card," a device that can generate a six-digit, one-time pass code that is necessary to complete an online transaction. The pass code is delivered via a text message to your mobile device.

Sources: Compiled from various security statements of online bank websites, including *co-operativebank.co.uk* (accessed April 2011) and *anz.com* (accessed April 2011).

Questions

1. Why is security so important for a bank?
2. Why is there a need for two firewalls?
3. Who is protected by the bank's security system—the customer, the bank, or both? Elaborate.
4. What might be the limitations of such a security system?

Fees Online Versus Fees for Offline Services

Computer-based banking services are offered free by some banks, whereas others charge $5 to $10 a month. Also, some banks charge fees for individual transactions (e.g., fee per check, per transfer, and so on). Financial institutions must carefully think through the pricing of online and offline services. Fee issues must take into account the costs of providing the different types of services, the organization's desire to attract new customers, and the prices offered by competitors. Many banks charge more for offline service in order to encourage customers to go online.

Risks

Online banks, as well as click-and-mortar banks, might carry some risks and problems, especially in international banking. The first risk that most people think of is the risk of hackers getting into their accounts. In addition, some believe that virtual banks carry *liquidity* risk (the risk of not having sufficient funds to pay obligations as they come due) and could be more susceptible to panic withdrawals. Regulators are grappling with the safeguards that need to be imposed on e-banking.

According to *Network World* (2010) online banking fraud in the United Kingdom alone exceeds $100 million in 2009 (an increase of 15 percent over 2008).

ONLINE BILLING AND BILL PAYING

The popularity of e-payment is growing rapidly. The number of checks the U.S. Federal Reserve System processes has been decreasing while the volume of commercial automated clearinghouse (ACH) transactions has been increasing. Many people prefer online payment of monthly bills such as mortgage payments, car loans, telephone, utilities, rent, credit cards, cable, TV, and so on. The recipients of such payments are equally eager to receive money online because online payments are received much more regularly and quickly and have lower processing costs.

Another method to pay bills over the Internet is electronic bill presentment and payments (EBPP). With this method, the consumer makes payments at each biller's website either with a credit card or by giving the biller enough information to complete an electronic withdrawal directly from the consumer's bank account. The biller makes the billing information available to the customer (presentment) on its website, by an e-mail, or the site of a billing hosting service. Once the customer views the bill, he or she authorizes and initiates payment at the site (a "no challenge" signifies an approval). The payment can be made with a credit/debit card or an ACH debit. The biller then initiates a payment transaction that moves funds through the payment system, crediting the biller and debiting the customer. See Chapter 10 for more about EBPP.

Online billing and bill paying can be classified as B2C, B2B, or C2C. This section has focused largely on B2C services, which help consumers save time and the payees save on processing costs. However, large opportunities also exist in B2B services, which can save businesses about 50 percent of billing costs. In Hong Kong, for example, Citicorp enables automatic payments by linking suppliers, buyers, and banks on one platform.

Taxes

One important area in personal finance is advice about and computation of taxes. Dozens of sites are available to help people in their federal tax preparations. Many sites will help people legally cut their taxes. The following list offers some sites worth checking:

- ▶ irs.gov: The official website of the Internal Revenue Service.
- ▶ webtax.com: A massive directory of tax-related information, research, and services.
- ▶ fairmark.com: A tax guide for investors.
- ▶ taxaudit.com: Offers advice on legally minimizing taxes and the chance of being audited by the IRS.

For a list of 20 best money websites in most areas discussed in Sections 3.5 and 3.6, see: money.cnn.com/galleries/2010/moneymag/1002/gallery.Best_money_websites.moneymag/index.html.

Section 3.6 ▶ REVIEW QUESTIONS

1. List the capabilities of online banking. Which of these capabilities would be most beneficial to you?

2. How are banks protecting customer data and transactions?

3. Describe a P2P loan system.

4. How are banking transactions protected?

5. List and briefly describe other major personal finance services available online.

3.7   ON-DEMAND DELIVERY OF PRODUCTS, DIGITAL ITEMS, ENTERTAINMENT, AND GAMING

This section examines B2C delivery issues related to on-demand items, such as perishable products, as well as the delivery of digitizable items, entertainment, and games.

ON-DEMAND DELIVERY OF PRODUCTS

Most e-tailers use common logistics carriers to deliver products to customers. They might use the postal system within their country or they might use private shippers such as UPS, FedEx, or DHL. Delivery can be made within days or overnight. Customers are frequently asked to pay for expedited shipments.

Some e-tailers and direct marketing manufacturers own a fleet of delivery vehicles and incorporate the delivery function into their business plans in order to provide greater value to the consumer, such as Net-a-Porter. These firms will either provide regular deliveries on a daily or other regular schedule or they will deliver items within very short periods of time, sometimes one hour. They might also provide additional services to increase the value proposition for the buyers. An online grocer, or **e-grocer**, is a typical example of a business in this category. Home delivery of food from restaurants is another example. In addition, several online groceries, office supplies, repair parts, and pharmaceutical products promise virtually instantaneous or at least same-day delivery of goods to consumers.

Whether the delivery is made by company-owned vehicles or it is outsourced to a carrier, an express delivery model is referred to as an **on-demand delivery service**. In such a model, the delivery must be done fairly quickly after an order is received. A variation of this model is same-day delivery. According to this model, delivery is done faster than "overnight" but slower than the 30 to 60 minutes expected with on-demand delivery of pizzas, fresh flowers, or blood. E-grocers often deliver using the same-day delivery model.

The Case of E-Grocers

In the United States, online grocery sales amounted to $7.3 billion in 2008 and are expected to reach $13.7 billion, 2 percent of total grocery sales, in 2012 (Mulpuru, et al. 2008). It is a very competitive market, and margins are very thin. Many e-grocers are click-and-mortar retailers that operate in the countries where they have physical stores, such as Woolworths in Australia (woolworths.com.au) and Albertsons (albertsons.com) in the United States. (For statistics on the grocery industry, see retailindustry.about.com.) Note that Amazon.com offers an online grocery service (called AmazonFresh.com) both in the United States and United Kingdom.

Today, it is possible to shop for groceries from smart phones (e.g., iPhone, PDA, BlackBerry).

Example: FreshDirect. FreshDirect is an online grocer (freshdirect.com) that delivers to residences and offices in the New York City metropolitan area. The company uses SAP AG software to process thousands of orders placed on its website every day. Orders are dispatched to the company's kitchen, bakery, and deli as well as to fresh storage rooms, produce ripening rooms, and production areas within the company's refrigerated facility. All order components are custom-cut, packaged, weighed, and priced. In the case of dry goods or frozen foods, items are picked from storage before being placed inside bins that travel along conveyors to the sorting and packaging area. There, products in a customer's order are scanned and gathered in corrugated fiberboard boxes. The boxes are labeled,

---

e-grocer
A grocer that takes orders online and provides deliveries on a daily or other regular schedule or within a very short period of time.

on-demand delivery service
Express delivery made fairly quickly after an online order is received.

recorded, and loaded into refrigerated delivery trucks. FreshDirect adopts a *just-in-time* manufacturing practice that reduces waste and improves quality and freshness (see en.wikipedia.org/wiki/just_in_time).

ONLINE DELIVERY OF DIGITAL PRODUCTS, ENTERTAINMENT, AND MEDIA

Certain goods, such as software, music, or news stories, can be distributed in a physical form (such as hard copy, CD-ROM, DVD, and newsprint), or they can be digitized and delivered over the Internet. For example, consumers can purchase online shrink-wrapped CD-ROMs containing software (along with the owner's manual and a warranty card) or pay for the software at a website and immediately download it onto their computers (usually through File Transfer Protocol [FTP], a fast way to download large files).

For sellers, the costs associated with the manufacture, storage, and distribution of physical products (DVDs, CD-ROMs, paper magazines, etc.) can be enormous. Inventory management also becomes a critical cost issue, and so does delivery and distribution. The need for retail intermediaries requires the establishment of relationships with channel partners and revenue-sharing plans. Direct sales of digital content through digital download, however, allow a producer of digital content to bypass the traditional retail channel, thereby reducing overall costs and capturing greater profits. However, retailers often are crucial in creating demand for a product through in-store displays, advertising, and human sales efforts, all of which are lost when the producer disintermediates the traditional channel.

A major revolution in the online entertainment industry occurred when Napster (en.wikipedia.org/wiki/Napster) introduced the P2P file-sharing of music. Another major phenomenon in the online delivery of entertainment is YouTube (see Chapter 7).

ONLINE ENTERTAINMENT

Online entertainment is growing rapidly and is now the most popular medium in the United States among young people between the ages of 8 and 17. There are many kinds of Internet entertainment. It is even difficult to precisely categorize them because there tends to be a mixture of entertainment types, delivery modes, and personal taste and choice in deciding whether something is entertainment or not. Some online entertainment can be regarded as interactive, in that the user can interact, often in a somewhat conversational way, with the software and thus change the outcome or shape the direction of the entertainment activity. PricewaterhouseCoopers (2008) forecasts that the global entertainment and media industry as a whole will reach $2.2 trillion in 2012. This includes online gaming, streaming video and audio, as well as mobile access to the entertainment field.

The major forms of traditional entertainment are television, film, radio, music, games, reading, and gambling. All of these are now available over the Internet. However, some have become much more popular in the new environment because the capabilities of modern technology mean that the experience can be enhanced for people who enjoy that activity. For example, online games offer multimedia experiences with colorful animations and sound and allow the player to affect the course and outcome of the game. For a more detailed summary of online entertainment, see Online File W3.5. For information on entertainment in the Web 2.0 environment and social networks, see Chapter 7.

Adult Entertainment

Online adult entertainment is probably the most profitable B2C model and accounts for a large percentage of Internet usage. Adult content sites succeed because they offer three things unavailable in an offline store: anonymity, instant gratification, and huge choice. This popularity may cause a problem for organizations. According to Nielsen Online, in October 2008 approximately a quarter of U.S. employees visited Internet porn sites during working hours, a 23 percent increase from October 2007 (Kuchment and Springen 2008). With little or no advertising effort to attract viewers, many of these sites are making good money. According to reports by market research firms that monitor the industry, such as Forrester, IDC, DataMonitor, Jupiter Media, and NetRating, viewers are willing to pay substantial fees to view adult sites.

Internet Gaming

Internet gaming is comprised of all forms of gaming, including arcade gaming, lotteries, casino gaming, promotional incentives, and so on. Between 2008 and 2010, online gambling revenue continued to increase despite bad economic times. A 2008 study by Baranzelli indicated that although the offline market is anticipated to produce only a modest average development rate of 2.2 percent until 2012, the online market is going to accomplish average expansion rates of 10.3 percent per annum until 2012, hitting a total market volume of $ 24.4 billion, or 6.3 percent of the gaming market (Baranzelli 2008). The ease of access and use of broadband services throughout the world in recent years has been vital to the expansion of online gaming.

Online Dating Services

Online dating is a dating system that allows people to make contact and communicate with each other over the Internet, usually with the objective of developing a personal romantic relationship. Online dating services usually provide unmoderated matchmaking over the Internet through the use of personal computers or cell phones. As a paid content category, online dating services are the third largest attractor of Internet users after music and games, carrying up to 10 percent of the online audience. According to one study (Jupiter Research 2007), online dating sites are projected to increase revenue from $900 million in 2007 to $1.9 billion in 2012, an increase of 16 percent annually over five years.

Section 3.7 ▶ REVIEW QUESTIONS

1. Describe on-demand delivery service.
2. Explain how e-grocers operate.
3. What are the difficulties in conducting an online for grocery business? Describe some solutions.
4. Describe digital goods and their delivery.
5. What are the benefits and the limitations of digital delivery of software, music, etc.?
6. What are the major forms of online entertainment? (See Online File W3.5.)

3.8 ONLINE PURCHASING-DECISION AIDS

Many sites and tools are available to help consumers with online purchasing decisions. Some sites offer price comparisons as their primary tool (e.g., pricerunner.com and shopzilla.com); others evaluate services, trust, quality, and other factors. Shopping portals, shopping robots ("shopbots"), business ratings sites, trust verification sites, friends' advice in social networks, and other shopping aids also are available. The major types are discussed next.

SHOPPING PORTALS

shopping portals
Gateways to webstores and e-malls; may be comprehensive or niche oriented.

Shopping portals are gateways to webstores and e-malls. Like any other portal, they can be comprehensive or niche-oriented. Comprehensive, or general-purpose, portals have links to many different sellers and present and evaluate a broad range of products. An example of a comprehensive portal is eCOST.com (ecost.com). Several public portals also offer shopping opportunities and comparison aids. Examples are shopping.com, shopping.yahoo.com, and bing.com/shopping. EBay is a shopping portal too because it offers shopping at fixed prices as well as auctions. All have clear shopping links from the main page of the portal, and they generate revenues by directing consumers to their affiliates' sites. Some of these portals even offer comparison tools to help identify the best price for a particular item. Several of these evaluation companies have purchased shopbots (see the following discussion) or other, smaller shopping aids and incorporated them into their portals.

Some shopping portals also offer specialized niche aids with information and links for purchasers of automobiles, toys, computers, travel, hospitals, or some other narrow area. Such portals also help customers conduct research. Examples include review.zdnet. com and shopper.cnet.com for computer equipment. Examples of sites for hospitals are: HealthGrades.com provides you with hospital ratings, hospitals' error rates, procedure costs, and more. HospitalCompare.hhs.gov provides comparisons of hospitals on 17 measures. The advantage of niche shopping portals is their ability to specialize in a certain line of products and carefully track consumer tastes within a specific and relevant market segment.

Helping Communities

Social communities can be very helpful for their members as shown in this book via several examples. Here is another one.

Yub.com (yub.com) is an online mall where you can meet people from around the world, hang out, discuss products and trends, and shop for more than 6 million products at the world's best online retailers. As part of the free service, you earn up to a 25 percent discount on every product you buy when you shop via Yub.com. When you join YubClub, you can earn up to a 34 percent discount on everything you buy. Like helping other people? The company gives some cash back to the Yubbers who help other shoppers. For more on helping communities such as Yelp see Chapter 7.

PRICE AND QUALITY COMPARISON BY SHOPBOT SOFTWARE AGENTS

Savvy Internet shoppers may bookmark their favorite shopping sites, but what if they want to find other stores with good service and policies that sell similar items at lower prices? **Shopping robots (shopping agents, shopbots)** are *shopping search engines* that scout the Web for consumers who specify search criteria. Different shopbots use different search methods. For example, mySimon (mysimon.com) searches the Web to find the best prices and availability for thousands of popular items. For example, sortprice.com provides a wide range of services (see Pitta 2009). Hotwire provides comparisons for travelers. Comparisons are not a simple task. The shopbot might have to evaluate different SKU (stock-keeping unit) numbers for the same item, because each e-tailer may have a different SKU rather than a standardized data-representation code. In addition to price, comparison sites such as pricegrabber.com include product details and features, product reviews from merchants and consumers, and additional information about the stores selling the item.

shopping robots (shopping agents, shopbots) Tools that scout the Web on behalf of consumers who specify search criteria.

Google Commerce Search 2.0

Google Commerce Search is a powerful search service for online stores. The server helps online retailers maximize sales, satisfaction, and usability by allowing customers to find exactly what they are looking for quickly and with no unnecessary navigation. Google Commerce Search delivers an optimal search experience to users.

For retailers, an innovative merchandising dashboard is a simple way to manage targeted promotions, ranking rules, and other success selling rules. Additional customization options make for a streamlined yet powerful online retail experience. For details, see google.com/commercesearch.

"Spy" Services

In this context, "spy" services are not the CIA or MI5. Rather, they are services that visit websites for customers, at their direction, and notify them of their findings. Web surfers and shoppers constantly monitor sites for new information, special sales, ending time of auctions, stock market updates, and so on, but visiting the sites to monitor them is time consuming. Several sites will track stock prices or airline special sales and send e-mails accordingly. For example, money.cnn.com, pcworld.com, and expedia.com will send people personalized e-mail alerts.

Of course, one of the most effective ways to spy on Internet users is to introduce cookies and spyware to their computers (see Chapter 8 for details.)

Wireless Shopping Comparisons

Users of mySimon, AT&T Digital PocketNet service, and other comparison sites have access to wireless shopping comparisons. Users who are equipped with an AT&T Internet-ready cell phone can find the service on the AT&T main menu; it enables shoppers to compare prices anytime from anywhere, including from any physical store. Comparisons can be accessed from all smartphones.

BUSINESS RATINGS SITES

Many websites rate various e-tailers and online products based on multiple criteria. Bizrate.com (bizrate.com), Consumer Reports Online (consumerreports.org), Forrester Research (forrester.com), and Gomez Advisors (gomez.com) are such well-known sites. Bizrate.com organized a network of shoppers that reports on various sellers and uses the compiled results in its evaluations. Note that different raters provide different rankings. Alexa Internet, Inc. (alexa.com) is a subsidiary company of Amazon.com that is best known for operating a website that provides information on Web traffic to other websites. Alexa ranks sites based on tracking information of users of its Alexa Toolbar for Internet Explorer and from integrated sidebars in Mozilla and Netscape.

Recommendations from Other Shoppers and Friends

referral economy
The effect upon sales of consumers receiving a referral or recommendation from other consumers.

In marketing, a **referral economy** is the effect of consumers receiving a referral or recommendation from other consumers on their buying actions. It occurs on the Internet via blogs, social networking sites (e.g., discussion forums, question and answer functions), and review sites where users recommend items to other users. Because these recommendations take place over the Internet, potential customers perceive that the referring users are genuine and the recommendation is noncommercial. Therefore the recommendation has a higher perceived value. Many advertising agencies have launched word-of-mouth marketing departments designed to create viral campaigns via the Internet or "sneezing" campaigns. *Sneezing* describes the attention-grabbing behavior of agencies that go out to consumer environments and boast about how great a brand or item is in order to spread the word. Sites such as Kaboodle aim to tap into the referral economy and drive purchase through users' personal recommendations.

Kaboodle. Established in 2005, Kaboodle is a social shopping community where people find, recommend, and share products. Kaboodle's powerful shopping tools allow people to organize their shopping through lists, find new items from people with similar tastes, get discounts on popular products, and find the best prices. Kaboodle is an entertaining community of people who love to shop. Community members create and join groups, share advice, feedback, and product suggestions, and personalize their profiles with polls and other widgets. The site has over 800,000 registered users who have added more than 8 million products to the site and boasts more than 12 million visitors per month.

TRUST VERIFICATION SITES

With so many sellers online, many consumers are not sure whom they should trust. A number of companies purport to evaluate and verify the trustworthiness of various e-tailers. One such company is TRUSTe (truste.com). The TRUSTe seal appears at the bottom of each TRUSTe-approved e-tailer's website. E-tailers pay TRUSTe for the use of the seal (which they call a "trustmark"). TRUSTe's 1,300-plus members hope that consumers will use the seal as an assurance and as a proxy for actual research into their conduct of business, privacy policy, and personal information protection.

Some comprehensive trust verification sites are VeriSign and BBBOnline. VeriSign (verisign.com) tends to be the most widely used. Other sources of trust verification include Secure Assure (secureassure.com), which charges yearly license fees based on a company's annual revenue. In addition, Ernst & Young, the global public accounting firm, has created its own service for auditing e-tailers in order to offer some guarantee of the integrity of their business practices.

OTHER SHOPPING TOOLS

Other digital intermediaries assist buyers or sellers, or both, with research and purchase processes. For example, escrow services (e.g., escrow.com and fortis-escrow.com) assist buyers and sellers in the exchange of items and money. Because buyers and sellers usually do not see or know each other, a trusted third party frequently is needed to facilitate the proper exchange of money and goods. Escrow sites may also provide payment-processing support, as well as letters of credit (see Chapter 10).

To organize store information in a standard, easy to see, and understandable format, vendors can use tools such as thefind.com. Shoppers can use the same tool to quickly find information about the vendors and products.

Other decision aids include communities of consumers who offer advice and opinions on products and e-tailers known as *mass reviews*. One such site is epinions.com, which has searchable recommendations on thousands of products. Pricescan.com is a price-comparison engine, pricegrabber.com is a comparison shopping tool that covers over 1 million products, and Onlineshoes.com specializes in all types of shoes.

Other software agents and comparison sites are presented in Online File W3.6.

Another shopping tool is a *wallet*—in this case, an *electronic wallet*, which is a program that contains the shopper's information. To expedite online shopping, consumers can use electronic wallets so that they do not need to reenter the information each time they shop. Although sites such as Amazon.com offer their own specialized wallets, Microsoft has a universal wallet in its Passport program (see Chapter 10 for details). For more on shopping aids, see Strauss and Frost (2008). Shopping aids are now expanding to social networking sites as shown in the case of Yelp.

Yelp

Yelp (yelp.com) is a search engine whose mission is to help people find local (in a specific city) qualified services ranging from mechanics to restaurants to hairstylists. It connects people and businesses. Community members, known as Yelpers, write reviews of the businesses and then rate them. Yelpers also find events and special offers and can chat with each other.

The site is also a place for businesses to advertise their products and services (paying fees to yelp.com). Help is accessible also via mobile devices and a blog. Yelp operates in 40 states, the United Kingdom, and France. It concentrates on *local search* for its visitors. A typical search includes what the user is seeking (e.g., a barber shop) and the location from which the search is to be performed, entered as a specific address, neighborhood, city/state combination, or zip code. Each listed business is evaluated by the community on a five-point rating scale. The listings include details such as the business address, hours of operation, accessibility, and parking. Site visitors can aid in keeping the business listings up to date, and business owners can directly update their own business's listing information with moderator approval.

Listings and related content are organized by city and a multi-tier categorization system. Content and listings can also be discovered through categorized reviews or via Yelp member profiles and their review lists. Maps leveraging Google Maps show reviewed businesses to further aid in business discovery. (Google was negotiating buying Yelp in November 2010 but the deal fell through in January 2011.)

Yelp contains many social networking features (ability to add friends, create groups, talk in forums, etc.). Adding social Web functionalities to user reviews creates a de-facto reputation system, whereby site visitors can see which contributing users are the most popular, respected, and prolific, how long each has been a member, and which have interests similar to theirs. Strong peer feedback mechanisms and the featured placement of popular reviews on the site and in local newsletters help motivate contributors. Yelp also applies a "First to Review" reward system to create a competition among contributing members, further motivating the creation of reviews and adding to the site's business coverage. For further information, see en.wikipedia.org/wiki/Yelp,_Inc.

Note: Some shopping aids can be used for both online and offline shopping. One such aid is the touch-screen PC and smart phones available in stores, where you can examine catalogs and place the order online, or shop in the store.

Section 3.8 ▶ REVIEW QUESTIONS

1. Define shopping portals and provide two examples.
2. What are shopbots?
3. Explain the role of business and website rating and site verification tools in the purchase-decision process.

4. Why are escrow services and electronic wallets useful for online purchases? Describe "spy" services in B2C EC.

5. How can a site motivate people to contribute opinions on products and vendors?

3.9 ISSUES IN E-TAILING AND LESSONS LEARNED

The following are representative issues and problems that need to be addressed when conducting B2C. These and others are discussed by Laseter, et.al. (2007), with some lessons learned from conducting B2C experiences.

DISINTERMEDIATION AND REINTERMEDIATION

disintermediation

The removal of organizations or business process layers responsible for certain intermediary steps in a given supply chain.

Disintermediation refers to the removal of organizations or business process layers responsible for certain intermediary steps in a given supply chain. As shown in part B of Exhibit 3.11, a manufacturer can bypass wholesalers and retailers, selling directly to consumers. Thus, B2C may drive regular retailers out of business. For a vivid case of such disintermediation, see the Blue Nile case in Chapter 2.

However, consumers might have problems selecting an online vendor; vendors might have problems delivering to customers; and both might need an escrow service to ensure the transaction. Thus, new types of intermediaries might be needed, and it might be provided by new or by traditional intermediaries. In such cases, the intermediaries fill new roles, providing *added value* and assistance. This process is referred to as **reintermediation**. It is pictured in part C of Exhibit 3.11. Thus, for the intermediary, the Internet offers new ways to reach new customers, new ways to bring value to customers, and perhaps new ways to generate revenues.

reintermediation

The process whereby intermediaries (either new ones or those that had been disintermediated) take on new intermediary roles.

The intermediary's role is shifting to one that emphasizes value-added services, such as assisting customers in comparison shopping from multiple sources, providing total solutions by combining services from several vendors, or providing certifications and

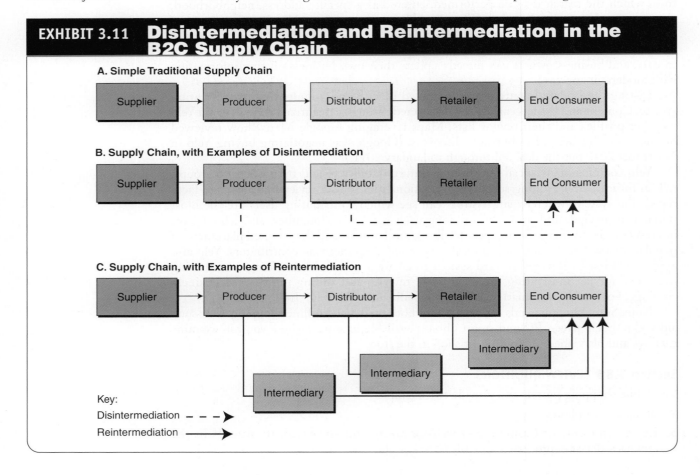

EXHIBIT 3.11   Disintermediation and Reintermediation in the B2C Supply Chain

A. Simple Traditional Supply Chain

Supplier → Producer → Distributor → Retailer → End Consumer

B. Supply Chain, with Examples of Disintermediation

Supplier → Producer → Distributor → Retailer → End Consumer

C. Supply Chain, with Examples of Reintermediation

Supplier → Producer → Distributor → Retailer → End Consumer
Intermediary   Intermediary   Intermediary

Key:
Disintermediation – – – ▶
Reintermediation ——————▶

trusted third-party control and evaluation systems. For instance, in cyberspace, new and used car sales businesses may require electronic intermediaries to assist buyers and/or sellers with additional information, special requirements, and so forth. There are new *reintermediaries in cyberspace*; intermediaries that have restructured their role in the purchase process. An example of the new roles of intermediaries is Edmunds (edmunds.com), which gives consumers a vast amount of information about cars, including price comparisons, ratings, the location of cars for sale, and the dealer's true costs online. Another example would be travel agents that can arrange complicated trips, provide longer periods for holding reservations, and arrange special tours and spot deals. Such companies can grow rapidly while other intermediaries decline.

CHANNEL CONFLICT

Many traditional retailers establish a supplemental marketing channel when they start selling online. (For a discussion about a situation known as *multichannel* marketing, see Kline 2010.) Similarly, some manufacturers have instituted direct marketing initiatives in parallel with their established channels of distribution, such as retailers or dealers. In such cases, *channel conflict* can occur. **Channel conflict** refers to any situation in which direct competition and/or damage caused by bypassing a former existing channel partner is perceived to have resulted from the introduction of a new, often online, channel. The extent of this conflict varies according to the nature of the industry and the characteristics of particular firms, but sometimes, a move to sell online can damage old, valued relationships between trading partners. Channel conflict can also be said to occur when a move to online trading simply moves a company's customers from their traditional stores to an online environment, thus cannibalizing the sales from the former and potentially negatively impacting the traditional outlets by rendering them less profitable. However, careful management and the adoption of sound strategies can deliver a number of synergies for click-and-mortar e-tailers, especially those associated with encouraging cross-channel cooperation and exploiting the unique strengths of each channel to maximize the experience for the customer. One model that can solve the conflict is to allow ordering and payment online, but the delivery is done at a physical store; see Chapter 11 for details. For how to manage multichannel situations, see Kline (2010).

channel conflict
Situation in which an online marketing channel upsets the traditional channels due to real or perceived damage from competition.

POSSIBILITY OF A PRICE CONFLICT AND DETERMINING THE RIGHT PRICE BY SELLERS

Pricing a product or service on the Internet, especially by a click-and-mortar company, is complicated. One reason is that prices need to be competitive both on the Internet and in the physical stores. Today's comparison engines will show the consumer the prices at many stores, for almost all commodity (or standard) products, for free or at almost no cost to the consumer. So, sellers may be forced to discount their online products. However, balanced against this is the fact that for some items, transaction costs for the sellers will decrease, then the cost of distribution will decrease, and supply chains may become more efficient and shorter, meaning that e-tailers might be able to compete in the aggressive online marketspace by providing low prices. In addition, the click-and-mortar e-tailer may be forced to offer online prices lower than the same company charges in its physical store. On the other hand, prices should be in line with the corporate policy on profitability and, in a click-and-mortar company, in line with the offline channel's pricing strategy. To avoid such internal price conflicts, some companies have created independent online subsidiaries, some with different names.

PRODUCT AND SERVICE CUSTOMIZATION AND PERSONALIZATION

The Internet also allows for easy self-configuration ("design it your way"). This creates a large demand for customized products and services. Manufacturers can meet that demand by using a *mass customization* strategy (see Online Tutorial T6). As indicated earlier, many companies offer customized products from their websites (e.g., see the Dell case in Online File W1.1).

One significant characteristic of many online marketing business models is the ability of the seller not only to offer customized products, but also to create an element of *personalization* services for each individual consumer.

Although pure-play e-tailing may be risky, e-tailing is growing rapidly as a complementary distribution channel to traditional stores and catalogs. In other words, the *click-and-mortar model is winning currently and all evidence suggests that this trend will continue* (see the closing case at the end of the chapter).

ONLINE COMPETITION

It is easy to start an online business and therefore millions of online businesses are competing among themselves and with traditional retailers. The competition is even stronger in areas where comparisons can be made online. The consumers are queens and kings! In many cases, prices are almost equal in all major sites. So customer service and other factors count. Rising competition is evidenced in many areas discussed in this chapter. Also see Laseter, et.al. (2007).

Example. In 2009, high-end retailer Saks, Inc., started "online private event" sales (e.g., for 36 hours) open only to those invited by e-mail. Each event concentrates on a certain category such as "discounted designer goods." This is done in order to compete with Web discounters. The topic of online competition is discussed in Chapters 12 and 13 and in Online Tutorial T12.

FRAUD AND OTHER ILLEGAL ACTIVITIES

A major problem in B2C is the increasing rate of online fraud. This can cause losses to both buyers and sellers. For a more detailed and thorough discussion of online fraud and how to minimize it, see Chapter 9.

LESSONS LEARNED FROM FAILURES AND LACK OF SUCCESS OF E-TAILERS

Like in the physical world, companies fail when doing business online. Online File W3.7 provides a sample of failed B2C companies. Some enduring principles can be distilled from the failures, and some of these "lessons learned" are discussed next.

Although thousands of companies have evolved their online strategies into mature websites with extensive interactive features that add value to the consumer purchase process, many other sites remain simple "brochureware" sites with limited interactivity. Many traditional companies are in a transitional stage. Mature transactional systems include features for payment processing, order fulfillment, logistics, inventory management, and a host of other services. In most cases, a company must replicate each of its physical business processes and design several more that can only be performed online. Today's environment includes sophisticated access to order information, shipping information, product information, and more through Web pages, touch-tone phones, Web-enabled cell phones, and PDAs over wireless networks. Faced with all of these variables, the challenges to profitably in implementing EC can be daunting.

A traditional brick-and-mortar store with a mature website that uses a successful click-and-mortar strategy is able to do the following:

- ▶ **Speak with one voice.** A firm can link all of its back-end systems to create an integrated customer experience. The online experience should be an extension of the experience encountered in traditional transactions.
- ▶ **Leverage the multichannels.** The innovative retailer will offer the advantages of each marketing channel to customers from all channels. Whether the purchase is made online or at the store, the customer should benefit from the presence of both channels.
- ▶ **Empower the customer.** The seller needs to create a powerful 24/7 channel for customer service, purchasing, and information. Through various information technologies, sellers can give customers the opportunity to perform various functions interactively, at any time. Such functions include the ability to find store locations, product information, and inventory availability online.

Section 3.9 ▶ REVIEW QUESTIONS

1. Define disintermediation.
2. Describe disintermediation and reintermediation.
3. Describe channel conflict and other conflicts that may appear in e-tailing.
4. Describe price determination in e-tailing. Under what circumstances might there be a conflict?
5. Explain personalization and customization opportunities in e-tailing. What are their benefits to customers?
6. What makes click-and-mortar companies successful?

MANAGERIAL ISSUES

Some managerial issues related to this chapter are as follows.

1. **What are the limitations of e-tailing? Where is e-tailing going?** In Korea, Internet retailing has become the second most important distribution channel, exceeding the national sales volume of all department stores. The question is what the limits of e-tailing will be. The large online order-related volume has grown faster than individual webstores and may slow Internet traffic. The market concentration has already happened, making the entrance barrier to new e-tailers very high. However, small businesses can easily start their online channel as part of a stable e-mall service platform when they find a niche opportunity. The opportunity can be cultivated by redefining the merchant's business plan with the addition of click-and-mortar strategies or of alliances with online and/or offline partners.

   Because many easy sources of funding have dried up and revenue models are being scrutinized, vendor consolidation will continue until a greater stability within the e-tailing sector occurs. Ultimately, there will likely be a smaller number of larger sellers with comprehensive general sites (e.g., Amazon.com) and many smaller, specialized niche sites (e.g., Net-a-Porter, Blue Nile).

2. **How should we introduce wireless shopping?** In some countries (e.g., Japan), shopping from cell phones is very popular. In other countries, mobile shopping is not popular, although the platform itself is available. Alternative channels and a culture of a variety of communication channels should be developed in different countries in order to develop mobile strategies. Also, because the younger generation prefers the mobile platform, the age effect on the platform should be monitored closely. Offering mobile shopping might not be simple or appropriate to all businesses, but it will certainly be dominant in the future.

3. **Do we have ethics and privacy guidelines?** Ethical issues are extremely important online as much as offline. In traditional systems, human agents play an important role in assuring the ethical behavior of buyers and sellers. Will online ethics and the rules of etiquette be sufficient to guide behavior on the Internet? Only time will tell. For example, as job-applicant information travels over the Internet, security and privacy become even more important. It is management's job to make sure that information from applicants is secure. Also, e-tailers need to establish guidelines for protecting the privacy of customers who visit their websites. Security and privacy must be high priorities.

4. **How will intermediaries act in cyberspace?** The role of online intermediaries has become more and more important. In the banking, stock trading, job market, travel industry, and book sales sectors, the Internet has become a most important service channel. These intermediary services create new business opportunities for sellers and intermediaries.

5. **Should we try to capitalize on social networks?** Many organizations and individuals began advertising or selling products and services on Facebook and other social networks. Although large companies are concentrating on advertising at the moment, some are experimenting with B2C sales (see Chapter 7). Social commerce may become an extremely important marketing channel and should be at least experimented with by many vendors.

6. **How should we manage multichannel marketing to avoid channel and/or price conflicts?** Managing multichannels requires a strategy on how to handle different types of transactions in the most appropriate and cost-effective channel. This needs to be done together with appropriate conflict management (see Kline 2010 for approaches).

7. **What are the major potential limitations of the growth of B2C EC?** First, it depends on the demand. Saturation effect may be strong. Second, the cost and availability of Internet access may influence growth. Third, cultural differences and habits may deter or accelerate e-shopping. Fourth, the ease of doing it is important, and fifth, the availability of payments and order fulfillment infrastructure are critical success factors.

SUMMARY

In this chapter, you learned about the following EC issues as they relate to the chapter's learning objectives.

1. **The scope and characteristics of e-tailing.** E-tailing, the online selling of products and services, is growing rapidly. Computers, software, and electronics are the major items sold online. Books, CDs, toys, office supplies, and other standard commodities also sell well. More successful are services that are sold online, such as airline tickets and travel services, stock trading, and some financial services.

2. **Classify e-tailing business models.** The major e-tailing business models can be classified by distribution channel—a manufacturer or mail-order company selling direct to consumers, pure-play (virtual) e-tailing, a click-and-mortar strategy with both online and traditional channels, and online malls that provide either referring directories or shared services. Social commerce facilitates group buying and location shopping.

3. **How online travel/tourism services operate.** Most services available through a physical travel agency also are available online. In addition, customers get much more information, much more quickly through online resources. Customers can even submit bids from travel providers. Finally, travelers can compare prices, participate in auctions and chat rooms, and view videos and maps. Lately, social travel is becoming popular, with travelers learning from each other or organizing joint trips.

4. **The online job market and its benefits.** The online job market is growing rapidly, with thousands and thousands of jobs matched with job seekers each day. The major benefits of online job markets for employers are the ability to reach a large number of job seekers at low cost, provide detailed information online, take applications online, and even to conduct tests. Also, using intelligent agents, résumés can be checked and matches made more quickly. Millions of job offers posted on the Internet help job seekers, who also can post their résumés for recruiters. Recruiting in social networks, especially LinkedIn and Facebook, is growing rapidly.

5. **The electronic real estate marketplace.** The online real estate marketplace is basically supporting rather than replacing existing agents. However, both buyers and sellers can save time and effort in the electronic market. Buyers can purchase distant properties much more easily and in some places have access to less expensive properties and services (insurance, mortgages, etc.). Eventually, commissions on regular transactions are expected to decline as a result of the electronic market for real estate, and more sales "by owner" will materialize.

6. **Online trading of stocks and bonds.** One of the fastest growing online businesses is the online trading of securities. It is inexpensive, convenient, and supported by a tremendous amount of financial and advisory information. Trading is very fast and efficient, almost fully automated, and moving toward 24/7 global trading. However, security breaches are possible, so tight protection is a must.

7. **Cyberbanking and personal finance.** Branch banking is on the decline due to less expensive, more convenient online banking. The world is moving toward online banking; today, most routine banking services can be done from home. Banks can reach customers in remote places, and customers can bank with faraway institutions. This makes the financial markets more efficient. Online personal finance applications, such as bill paying, monitoring of accounts, and tax preparation, also are very popular.

8. **On-demand delivery service.** On-demand delivery service is needed when items are perishable or when delivering medicine, express documents, or urgently needed supplies. One example of on-demand delivery is e-groceries; these may be ordered online and are shipped or ready for store pickup within 24 hours or less.

9. **Delivery of digital products.** Anything that can be digitized can be successfully delivered online. Delivery of digital products such as music, software, e-books, movies, and other entertainment online has been a success. Some print media, such as electronic versions of magazines or electronic books (see Chapter 5) also are having success when digitized and delivered electronically.

10. **Aiding consumer purchase decisions.** Purchase decision aids include shopping portals, shopbots and comparison agents, business rating sites, recommendations (including electronic ones), trust verification sites, and other tools. These include real-time mobile devices and extensive support from social networks.

11. **Disintermediation and other B2C strategic issues.** Direct electronic marketing by manufacturers results in disintermediation by removing wholesalers and retailers. However, online reintermediaries provide additional services and value, such as helping consumers make selections among multiple products and vendors. Traditional retailers may feel threatened or pressured when manufacturers decide to sell directly online; such direct selling can cause channel conflict. Pricing of online and offline products and services is also an issue that frequently needs to be addressed.

KEY TERMS

DISCUSSION QUESTIONS

1. Discuss the importance of comparison tools, product reviews, and customer ratings in online shopping.

2. Discuss the advantages of a specialized e-tailer, such as DogToys.com (dogtoys.com). Could such a store survive in the physical world? Why or why not?

3. Use Google to find the benefits of travel-related social networking sites. Discuss five of them. (Start with hotels.megawn.com/benefits-of-travel-related-social-networking-sites-2.)

4. Discuss the benefits of build-to-order (customization) to buyers and sellers. Are there any disadvantages?

5. Why are online travel services a popular Internet application? Why do so many websites provide free travel information?

6. Compare the advantages and disadvantages of online stock trading with offline trading.

7. Compare the advantages and disadvantages of distributing digitizable products electronically versus physical delivery.

8. Do you trust your personal data on social networks such as LinkedIn or Facebook? How do you protect your privacy?

9. Many companies encourage their customers to buy products and services online, sometimes "pushing" them to do it. Why?

10. Would you use monster.com or linkedin.com for recruiting or would you rather use a physical office of a traditional agency? Why?

TOPICS FOR CLASS DISCUSSION AND DEBATES

1. Discuss the advantages of established click-and-mortar companies such as Walmart over pure-play e-tailers such as Amazon.com. What are the disadvantages of click-and-brick retailers as compared with pure-play e-tailers?

2. Online employment services make it easy to change jobs; therefore, turnover rates may increase. This could result in total higher costs for employers because of increased costs for recruiting and training new employees and the need to pay higher salaries and wages to attract or keep existing employees informed. What can companies do to ease this problem?

3. Discuss each of the following as limiting factors on the growth of B2C EC: (a) Too much competition, (b) expensive technology, (c) need a computer to shop, (d) people need the social interaction of face-to-face shopping, (e) many people cannot afford Internet access, (f) the fear of fraud and security breaching.

4. How should a company handle channel conflict with its distributors?

5. Debate: Competition between pure play e-tailers (e.g., Amazon.com, Blue Nile) and traditional e-tailers that add the Web as a part of a multichannel (e.g., Walmart, HP, department stores) (e.g., see O'Connell 2009). Who may win? Under what assumptions?

6. Debate: Should online sales be an independent division in a click-and-mortar firm?

7. Debate: What is the future of Amazon.com?

INTERNET EXERCISES

1. Many consumer portals offer advice and ratings of products or e-tailers. Identify and examine two separate general-consumer portals that look at sites and compare prices or other purchase criteria. Try to find and compare prices for a digital camera, a microwave oven, and an MP3 player. Visit yippy.com. How can this site help you in your shopping? Summarize your experience. Comment on the strong and weak points of such shopping tools.

2. Visit landsend.com and prepare a customized order for a piece of clothing. Describe the process. Do you think this will result in better-fitting clothing? Do you think this personalization feature will lead to greater sales volume for Lands' End?

3. Make your résumé accessible to millions of people. Consult asktheheadhunter.com or careerbuilder.com for help rewriting your résumé. See monster.com for ideas about planning your career. Get prepared for a job interview and look at Tronix (by Monster) for interesting capabilities. Also, use the Web to determine what salary you can get in your profession in the city of your choice in the United States.

4. Visit move.com, decisionaide.com, or a similar site and compute the monthly mortgage payment on a 30-year loan at 5.5 percent fixed interest. Also check current interest rates. Estimate your closing costs on a $200,000 loan. Compare the monthly payments of the fixed rate with that of an adjustable rate for the first year. Finally, compute your total payments if you take the loan for 15 years at the going rate. Compare it with a 30-year mortgage. Comment on the difference.

5. Access the Virtual Trader game at virtualtrader.co.uk and register for the Internet stock game. You will be bankrolled with £100,000 in a trading account every month. You also can play investment games at investorsleague.com and etrade.com. Comment on your experiences.

6. Compare the price of a specific Sony digital camera at shopping.com, mysimon.com, bizrate.com, and pricescan.com. Which site locates the best deal? Where do you get the best information?

7. Enter xing.com and socialmediatoday.com and identify job-related help features. Prepare a list of support activities offered.

8. Enter Bazaarvoice (bazaarvoice.com) and find how consumers can engage in a dialog. Look at its Ask & Answer service. How is quality of content maintained? Write a report based on your findings.

9. Enter viviente.com/resumix/website, examine the capabilities of the tools, and write a report.

10. Enter lockerz.com and compare its feature with that of gilt.com and ideeli.com. What are the similarities? What are the differences?

11. Enter tripit.com and dopplr.com. How can these sites help travelers? How do they relate to social networks?

12. How can LinkedIn and Facebook help job seekers? How can they help employers?

13. Compare the sites yelp.com and epinions.com.

14. Visit hayneedle.com. What kind of a mall is this?

15. Compare the offering of JobServe to that of Aspire Media Group regarding solutions for recruitment. Distinguish services to employees from those to employers.

TEAM ASSIGNMENTS AND PROJECTS

1. **Assignment for the Opening Case**

   Read the opening case and answer the following questions.

   a. What are Amazon.com's critical success factors? Is its decision to offer a much broader selection of items a good marketing strategy? With the broader selection, do you think the company will dilute its brand or extend the value proposition to its customers?

   b. Amazon.com uses Zappos as a separate store. Does it make sense? Why or why not?

   c. Visit amazon.com and identify at least three specific elements of its personalization and customization features. Browse specific books on one particular subject, leave the site, and then go back and revisit the site. What do you see? Are these features likely to encourage you to purchase more books in the future from Amazon.com? Check the 1-Click feature and other shopping aids provided. List the features and discuss how they may lead to increased sales.

   d. With what type of companies does Amazon.com have alliances? Why?

   e. Check all the personalization features at the site. List their advantages.

   f. Find the non-B2C activities of Amazon.com. Why do they offer these services?

   g. Find some recent material on the marketing strategy of Amazon.com and discuss it.

h. Examine social networking activities at Amazon. com. What are their purposes?

i. Describe what an "astore" is.

2. Each team will investigate the services of two online car-selling sites (from the following list or other sites). When teams have finished, they should bring their research together and discuss their findings.

a. Buying new cars through an intermediary (autobytel. com, carsdirect.com, autoweb.com, or amazon. com)

b. Buying used cars (autotrader.com)

c. Buying used cars by auto dealers (manheim.com)

d. Automobile ratings sites (carsdirect.com and fuel economy.gov)

e. Car-buying portals (thecarportal.com and cars. com)

f. Buying collectors' cars (classiccars.com and anti quecar.com)

3. Each team (or team member) will review two or three travel-oriented, social-oriented networks (e.g., Zimbio, World 66, Virtual Tourist, BootsnAll, Eezeer, Trip Advisor, TrekCafe, Lonely Planet Thorn Tree, WAYN, and Budget Globetrotting). Compare their functionalities.

4. Each team will represent a broker-based area (e.g., real estate, insurance, stocks, employment). Each team will find a new development that has occurred in the assigned area over the most recent three months. Look for the site vendor's announcement and search for more information on the development with google.com or another search engine. Examine the business news at bloomberg.com. After completing your research, as a team, prepare a report on disintermediation in your assigned area.

5. Plan a wedding entirely online (geek-style). First, make a chart of the process. Do not forget the proposal itself, buy the ring, get music, use Twitter, and use a self-managed DJ. You want to save money and to use guest-generated content. You may start by looking at itworld.com/offbeat/68244/wedding-20-when-weddings-go-geek and by searching Google for "geek wedding."

6. Watch the video "Internet Marketing and E-Commerce with Tom Antion" (Part 1; Part 2 is optional); 9 minutes, youtube.com/watch?v=tc1u9eqpf68, and answer the following questions:

a. What revenue sources are cited?

b. What B2C revenue sources that you are aware of are not cited?

c. What are the two "affiliate" models? Compare these two models.

d. Why is eBay so great for selling?

e. Comment on the suggestions for products/services to be sold from your home.

f. What problems and limitations do you see for conducting business from your home?

7. View some videos about future retail shopping (both offline and online). Discuss what B2C e-commerce may look like in the future considering these developments (e.g., see Microsoft's future vision on retailing and several videos by Metro AG in Europe).

Closing Case

IKEA: THE CONVERGENCE OF THE VIRTUAL AND PHYSICAL WORLDS

IKEA is one of the most well-known do-it-yourself furniture companies; in 2010 it made $405 billion in sales. The company operates in more than 41 countries and has over 127,000 employees (see *ikea.com*). IKEA sells goods such as home furnishings, small appliances, and furniture. Most of IKEA's revenue comes from selling furniture that customers need to assemble on their own. However, IKEA also offers van rentals in addition to a delivery service that includes assembling customers' products on-site.

When companies use the Internet, the physical and the virtual world converge through an evolutionary process. In every industry, there are progressive as well as more conservative groups, and this causes some companies to be early adopters of technology and others to be latecomers. IKEA was an early adopter who gradually increased its usage of e-commerce tools.

When e-commerce was in its early stages, IKEA initially used it only for marketing purposes. The company stated in TV commercials and advertisements that it had an Internet homepage in order to highlight its progressive nature. As IKEA matured through the publishing and transaction stage, it began to offer full descriptions of its products, instruction manuals, and other downloadable items such as the current IKEA catalog. The customer can now also order directly from the IKEA Internet shop and can clearly view all the furniture. IKEA has begun to carry out online marketing by encouraging customers to sign up for catalogs, e-mails, and text messages (permission marketing).

In addition, to become more connected with the digital world, IKEA implemented affiliate programs with partners including Apple and *kitchenremodelinghelp.com*.

The site now enables customers to interactively connect with and contact the company through many channels. IKEA has created an avatar named Anna who answers users' questions. In addition to this, IKEA implemented an after-sales service, which includes a blogging platform for customers called "Jobbarbloggen." Here, employees can write about their work at IKEA. In addition, IKEA utilizes Web 2.0 tools including Twitter, RSS Feeds, and a Facebook link and "Like" button on its website.

IKEA now hosts a mobile site for smartphones where customers can write reviews, give recommendations, and provide ratings of products. In 2010, IKEA created an augmented reality app that provides customers with the product catalog and real-time planning tools for rooms such as the kitchen. Users can select a piece of furniture from the IKEA catalog and place it anywhere inside their chosen room. The app also gives customers access to different furniture inspirations via mobile video, restaurant recommendations, and a calorie burning table via a jogging app. The goal of these initiatives is to increase traffic to the IKEA website and therefore to increase sales. The next step for IKEA is to establish location-based real interaction to support every shopping situation via smartphones or to simulate real furniture shopping situations anytime and anywhere. Smartphones will adjust to the environment in which the phone is being used and will be able to detect customer behavior and emotions via sensors such as temperature and body heat.

A 3D image of the customers' body or a simulated avatar will be displayed on a smartphone to enable customers to walk around a simulated room featuring IKEA furniture. In the future using augmented reality, customers could use glasses or other more advanced body interfaces to support the shopping experience and to display ideas about how to arrange furniture in their homes. These developments using augmented reality aim to enable customers to use location- and situation-based services on their smartphones.

Sources: Hansmann (2011).

Questions

1. What kind of services can be purchased on *ikea.com*?

2. Compare buying furniture from *ikea.com* versus buying it from a physical furniture store close to where you live. Explore the difference between the shopper's experience. Does the emotional experience differ?

3. What are the options and features available for international customers on the IKEA website?

4. Study IKEA's affiliate program. How does it compare to that of Amazon.com? (See *kitchenremodelinghelp.com/affiliates.html*).

5. What are the benefits and risks of augmented reality?

ONLINE RESOURCES
available at pearsonglobaleditions.com/turban

Online Files

W3.1 Some Current Trends in B2C EC
W3.2 Application Case: CatToys.com, a Specialty E-Tailer
W3.3 Application Case: The European Job Mobility Portal (Eures CV Search) and Xing.com
W3.4 Investment Information
W3.5 Examples of Online Entertainment
W3.6 Representative Shopping Software Agents and Comparison Sites
W3.7 Lessons Learned from E-Tailing Failures

Comprehensive Educational Websites

investopedia.com: Resources for investing education (tutorials, videos, white papers).

bnet.com/topics/B2C: White papers, Webcasts, and other resources on B2c e-commerce.

digitsmith.com/ecommerce-definition.html: Definitions and types of e-commerce.

marketresearch.com/map/research/B2C/622.html: B2C research reports on e-commerce.

managementhelp.org/infomgnt/e_cmmrce/e_cmmrce.htm: Basic guide to e-commerce.

bitpipe.com: A comprehensive site for information on most topics in this chapter.

internetretailing.net: A very comprehensive site about e-tailing.

employmentguide.com: An easy search tool for finding jobs.

group-digests@linkedin.com: An online marketing group at LinkedIn.

silicon.com: Find white papers, news, and a job search (matching applicants and positions).

REFERENCES

Acharya, R. N., A. Kagan, and S. R. Lingam. "Online Banking Applications and Community Bank Performance." *International Journal of Bank Marketing* (October 2008).

Ahorre.com. "2009 Real Estate Internet Marketing." January 2009. ahorre.com/dinero/internet/marketing/2009_real_estate_internet_marketing (accessed December 2010).

AlexFrankel.com. "Personality Tests." January 15, 2008. alexfrankel.com/blog/?p=8 (requires authorization code).

Baranzelli, M. F. "Growing Revenue in Internet Gambling." *Online Casino Extra*, November 18, 2008. onlinecasinoextra.com/casino_news_1811.html (accessed April 2011).

Barish, M. "Social Networking and Travel: Do's and Don'ts." *RSS Feed*. gadling.com/2010/04/21/social-networking-and-travel-dos-and-donts (accessed April 2011).

Biz Report. "Toys Made in China off Christmas Shopping Lists." *BizReport.com*, November 14, 2007. bizreport.com/2007/11/toys_made_in_china_off_christmas_shopping_lists.html (accessed April 2011).

Bowers, T. "Hiring Manager: Step Away from the Facebook!" September 10, 2008. blogs.techrepublic.com.com/career/?p=398 (accessed April 2011).

Bowling, B. "Lawrence County Joins Tax Movement Against Online Hotel Businesses." *Tribune Review*, September 9, 2009.

Brown, K. "Social Media Marketing: B2C Success Stories." *SlideShare.net*, April 2009. slideshare.net/pixelpointpress/social-media-marketing-b2c-success-stories-1251538 (accessed April 2011).

Butcher, M. "WAYN Said to Be Close to Sale. The Price? $200m. The Buyer? AOL." *Tech Crunch*, January 16, 2008. eu.techcrunch.com/2008/01/16/wayn-said-to-be-close-to-sale-the-price-200m-the-buyer-aol (accessed April 2011).

Cash Edge. "Cash Edge Survey Confirms Consumer Demand for Value Added Online Banking Services." *News Blaze*, October 12, 2006. newsblaze.com/story/2006101206005100005.pz/topstory.html (accessed April 2011).

Compete Inc. "Compete Releases Top 25 Retail Web Sites for July 2009." August 27, 2009. competeinc.com/news_events/pressReleases/238 (accessed April 2011).

Dickler, J. "I Found My Job on Twitter." *CNNMoney*, May 12, 2009. money.cnn.com/2009/05/12/news/economy/social_networking_jobs (accessed April 2011).

Dignan, L. "Retail Stinks, but Amazon Doesn't; E-Tailer Delivers Strong Fourth Quarter." *ZDNet*, January 29, 2009. blogs.zdnet.com/BTL/?p=11928 (accessed April 2011).

Fisher, A. "30 Best Web Sites for Job Hunters." *Fortune*, May 9, 2008. money.cnn.com/2008/05/07/news/economy/best.websites.fortune/index.htm (accessed April 2011).

Greene, M.V. "Many Channels, One Customer." *Stores*, June 2010.

Ha, S., and L. Stoel. "Consumer E-Shopping Acceptance: Antecedents in a Technology Acceptance Model." *Journal of Business Research* (2009).

Hansmann, U., et al. *Pervasive Computing: The Mobile World*, Germany: Springer, 2011.

Internet Retailer. "60% of Internet Users Shop Online, Make 36 Purchases a Year, Study Says." 2009. internetretailer.com/internet/marketing-conference/46151-60-internet-users-shop-online-making-36-purchases-year-study-says.html (accessed April 2011).

Internet Retailer. "Walmart's New In-Store Pick-Up Service Might Not Be Fast, But It's Free." March 6, 2007. internetretailer.com/2007/03/06/wal-mart-s-new-in-store-pick-up-service-might-not-be-fast-but (accessed April 2011).

Javelin Strategy and Research. "2009 Online Banking and Bill Payment Forecast: Active Users Grow While Bill Pay Overtakes Biller Direct." 2009. javelinstrategy.com/brochure-150 (accessed April 2011).

Jupiter Research. "Online Dating in 2007." *Market Research*, February 2, 2007. findarticles.com/p/articles/mi_m0EIN/is_2007_Feb_12/ai_n17218532 (accessed April 2011).

Keegan, V. "Zopa Shows Banks How to Do It Right." *The Guardian*, November 13, 2008. browse.guardian.co.uk/search?search=Zopa+Shows+Banks+How+to+Do+It+Right&search_target=%2Fsearch&fr=cb-guardian (accessed April 2011).

Kline, C. "Delivering Exceptional Customer Experience in a Multichannel World." *CRMBuyer.com*, July 12, 2010. crmbuyer.com/story/70386.html?wlc=1291140890 (accessed April 2011).

Kuchment, A., and K. Springen. "The Tangled Web of Porn in the Office." *Newsweek*, November 29, 2008. newsweek.com/id/171279 (accessed April 2011).

Kwon, W. S., and S. J. Lennon. "What Induces Online Loyalty? Online Versus Offline Brand Images." *Journal of Business Research* (vol. 62, no. 5, 2009).

Laseter, T. M., D. Mollenkopf, E. Rabinovich, and K. Boyer. "Critical Issues in Internet Retailing." *MIT Sloan Management Review* (Spring 2007).

Lewis, L. "Open-Shelf Solution," *Stores*, March 2010.

Maestri, N. "Walmart.com Offers 'Thousands' of Wiis from Monday." *Reuters*, December 7, 2008. reuters.com/article/technologyNews/idUSTRE4B60852008 1207 (accessed April 2011).

Marsden, P. "Delta Opens F-Commerce Store for the Mile High Club." *Social Commerce Today*, August 16, 2010.

McDougall, P. "Web Lets Insurers Cut Costs, Improve Service." *InformationWeek*, September 17, 2007.

McElroy, J. "An Intriguing Build-to-Order Concept." *Autoline*, June 11, 2009. autolinedetroit.tv/journal/?p= 4395 (accessed April 2011).

Mulpuru, S., C. Johnson, B. McGowan, and W. Scott. "U.S. eCommerce Forecast: 2008 to 2012." Forrester Research, January 18, 2008. forrester.com/Research/ Document/ Excerpt/0,7211,41592,00.html (accessed April 2011).

Needleman, S. E. "A New Job Just a Tweet Away." *Wall Street Journal*, September 8, 2009.

Network World. "Online Banking Fraud Losses Rise to Nearly £60." networkworld.ccom/news/2010/031110-online-banking-fraud-losses-rise.html (accessed April 2011).

O' Connell, V. "Saks Challenges Web Discounters." *Wall Street Journal*, October 29, 2009.

Park, H., and M. Lombardi. "The Video-Enabled Talent Scout." *E-Commerce Times*, January 21, 2010. ecommerce times.com/rsstory/69157.html (accessed April 2011).

Pitta, D. A. (Ed.). "Internet Currency." *Journal of Consumer Marketing*, vol. 26 #4, 2009.

PricewaterhouseCoopers. "Global Entertainment & Media to Reach $2.2T in 2012, Driven by Digital, Mobile." *Marketing Charts*, June 20, 2008. marketing charts. com/television/global-entertainment-media-toreach-22t-in-2012-driven-by-digital-mobile-5012 (accessed April 2011).

Realtors Magazine. "Market Research by Industry." 2009. realtor.org/wps/wcm/connect/752953004bbaa1ca950 bdff09f174b6c/Research+Book.pdf?MOD=AJPERE S&CACHEID=752953004bbaa1ca950bdff09f174b6c (accessed April 2011).

Reuters. "Amazon Net Profit Doubles, Helped by Asset Sale." July 23, 2008. reuters.com/article/pressReleasesMolt/ idUSWNAB207520080723 (accessed April 2011).

Stokes, J. "The Matrix, but with Money: The World of High-Speed Trading." *ARS Technica*, July 27, 2009. arstechnica.com/tech-policy/news/2009/07/-it-sounds-like-something.ars (accessed April 2011).

Strauss, J., and R. Frost. *E-Marketing*. Upper Saddle River, NJ: Prentice Hall, 2008.

Taipei Times. "Online Group Buying—A Great Way to Save Money." March 26, 2009. taipeitimes.com/ News/lang/archives/2009/03/26/2003439407 (accessed April 2011).

U.S. Census Bureau. *e-Stats 2008.* Released May 27, 2010. census.gov/econ/estats/2008/2008reportfinal.pdf (accessed April 2011).

Webb, A. "Hiring Help." *Training Magazine*, September 2009.

Wieczner, J. "The Mall Goes High-Tech." *Smart Money*, November 2010.

Weiner, M. (2006) "The 5-Day Car: Ordered on Monday—Delivered on Friday." *Ilipt.org*, February 28, 2006. fraunhofer.de/fhg/Images/magazine_2-2006_28_tcm6-64704.pdf (accessed April 2011).

Weinstein, M. "Virtual Handshake." *Training Magazine*, September 2009.

Workplace.gov.au. "A Job Seekers Guide to Jobsearch." 2009. workplace.gov.au/NR/rdonlyres/F1CE1A17-0AEC-4630-8351-CCD24CA15247/0/GuidetoAJS_final.pdf (accessed April 2011).

B2B E-COMMERCE

Content

Learning Objectives

Upon completion of this chapter, you will be able to:

1. Describe the B2B field.
2. Describe the major types of B2B models.
3. Discuss the models and characteristics of the sell-side marketplace, including auctions.
4. Describe the sell-side intermediaries.
5. Describe the characteristics of the buy-side marketplace and e-procurement.
6. Explain how reverse auctions work in B2B.
7. Describe B2B aggregation and group purchasing models.
8. Describe other procurement methods.
9. Define exchanges and describe their major types.
10. Describe B2B portals.
11. Describe third-party exchanges.
12. Describe how B2B can benefit from social networking and Web 2.0.
13. Describe Internet marketing in B2B, including organizational buyer behavior.

BRANAS ISAF COMPETES BY USING E-TENDERING

Branas Isaf, based in Corwen, North Wales, United Kingdom is a small company that provides care for children with behavioral problems. One of the major strengths of the company is its training division, which provides both bespoke training and vocational qualifications.

The Problem

Over the last two years, the company has doubled in size to 25 employees. Approximately 80 percent of the company's business comes from the private sector, with a remainder coming from the public sector. These customers include privately owned care companies, foster homes, private schools, as well as residential child care facilities, both in England and in Wales (about 1,000 in total).

Branas Isaf's major competitive advantages are that it is able to deliver its training programs at realistic rates, but at the same time can tailor these programs to its customers' needs—

for instance by delivering on-site training. These strategies enable it to compete with large organizations such as colleges.

Branas Isaf frequently bids on jobs, especially in the public sector where tendering is mandatory. Furthermore, many of its customers are moving the tendering process to the Internet. Thus, to maintain its competitive advantage, Branas Isaf decided to participate in e-tendering. (Later on in this chapter we will explain how companies, such as Branas, organize the jobs for which they solicit bids.)

This case describes Branas's experience in its first electronic bid.

The Solution

The government mandated that the specific bid be done via the eTendering System for the Government Work Based Learning Programme. Branas followed the following steps on the eTendering portal:

1. Electronically submitted a pre-qualification questionnaire.
2. Accepted the terms and conditions of Bravo Solution eTraining System.
3. Received online supplier guidance material.
4. Created a user name; received a password.
5. Found the specific invitation to tender (ITT) on which they wanted to bid online.
6. Pressed the "Express Interest" button—moved automatically to "My ITTs."

7. Downloaded all the necessary documents for the specific bid.
8. Made a decision to bid and pressed the "Reply" button.
9. Accessed the project's details, found and filled out a questionnaire.
10. Submitted the tender electronically and uploaded all necessary attachments. (It is possible to update it or change it until the deadline.)

Sending and receiving messages are embedded in the portal with e-mail alerts. Acceptance notification also is done via an e-mail alert. Once the bid is accepted by the system, a winner icon is displayed. The entire process with sample screen shots is available free online at *eproc.org/site/guides/EPROC_csp_ Branas_Isaf_Training.pdf*.

The Results

Since its inception in late 2007, the practice of e-tendering at Branas has been grown rapidly. Branas employees have become experts in using the computerized system. While the cost to Branas declined only slightly, the opportunity for such a small company to compete with the very large competitors increased significantly.

Furthermore, since most nonprofit organizations and many for-profit ones mandate eTendering, bidders have

no choice but to use the system. Also, Branas understands that eTendering is clearly more efficient for Branas's customers as well as being a more sustainable way of doing business. All in all, Branas was able to maintain its competitive advantage and continue to grow rapidly.

Sources: Compiled from eProc.org (2010), *branas.co.uk* (accessed November 2010), and *etenderwales.bravosolution.com* (accessed November 2010).

WHAT WE CAN LEARN . . .

B2B e-commerce, which constitutes over 90 percent of all EC volume, is composed of different types of marketplaces and methods. E-tendering is a major procurement method for companies that want to buy products or services via a reverse auction approach. This case demonstrates how a seller can participate in a tendering process that is conducted on the Web. We describe this approach from the buyers' perspective in Section 4.6 (buy-side). As far as a seller like Branas is concerned, there may not be many benefits to participating in an electronic tendering system versus a manual one, but from the buyer's point of view the benefits are enormous (see Section 4.6). In addition to e-tendering, we describe in this chapter all the major EC buying and selling B2B methods as well as types of B2B marketplaces and portals. Finally, we relate B2B to social networking and to Internet marketing.

4.1 CONCEPTS, CHARACTERISTICS, AND MODELS OF B2B E-COMMERCE

B2B, as noted in Chapter 1, is the leading EC activity in terms of volume. B2B EC has some special characteristics as well as specific models, components, and concepts. The major ones are described next.

BASIC B2B CONCEPTS AND PROCESS

Business-to-business e-commerce (B2B EC), also known as *eB2B* (*electronic B2B*), or just B2B, refers to transactions between businesses conducted electronically over the Internet, extranets, intranets, or private networks. Such transactions may take place between a business and its supply chain members, as well as between a business, a government, and any other business. In this context, a *business* refers to any organization, private or public, for profit or nonprofit. The major characteristic of B2B is that companies attempt to electronically automate trading transactions or communication and collaboration processes in order to improve them. Note that B2B commerce can be done without the Internet.

Key business drivers for B2B (some of which were shown in the opening case) are the need to reduce cost; to gain competitive advantage; the availability of a secure broadband Internet platform and private and public B2B e-marketplaces; the need for collaboration between suppliers and buyers; the ability to reduce delays, and the emergence of effective technologies for intra- and interorganizational systems' integration.

> **business-to-business e-commerce (B2B EC)**
> Transactions between businesses conducted electronically over the Internet, extranets, intranets, or private networks; also known as eB2B (electronic B2B) or just B2B.

THE BASIC TYPES OF B2B TRANSACTIONS AND ACTIVITIES

The number of sellers and buyers and the form of participation used in B2B determine the four basic B2B transaction types:

1. **Sell-side.** One seller to many buyers.
2. **Buy-side.** One buyer from many sellers.
3. **Exchanges.** Many sellers to many buyers.
4. **Supply chain improvements and collaborative commerce.**

The last category includes activities other than buying or selling among business partners, for example, supply chain improvements, communicating, collaborating, and sharing of information for joint design, planning, and so on (see Chapter 11).

Exhibit 4.1 illustrates these four B2B types. A brief explanation follows.

THE BASIC TYPES OF B2B E-MARKETPLACES AND SERVICES

The following are the descriptions of three basic types of B2B e-marketplaces.

One-to-Many and Many-to-One: Private E-Marketplaces

In one-to-many and many-to-one markets, one company does either all the selling (*sell-side market*) or all the buying (*buy-side market*). Because EC is focused on a single company's buying or selling needs, this type of EC is also referred to as **company-centric EC**. Company-centric marketplaces—both sell-side and buy-side—are discussed in Sections 4.2 through 4.7.

In company-centric marketplaces, the individual sell-side or buy-side company has complete control over who participates in the selling or buying transaction, and over the supporting information systems. Thus, these marketplaces are essentially *private*. They may be at the sellers' or buyers' websites or hosted by a third party (intermediary).

> **company-centric EC**
> E-commerce that focuses on a single company's buying needs (many-to-one, or buy-side) or selling needs (one-to-many, or sell-side).

Many-to-Many: Public Exchanges

In many-to-many e-marketplaces, many buyers and many sellers meet electronically for the purpose of trading with one another. There are different types of such e-marketplaces, which are also known as **exchanges (trading communities, trading exchanges)**. We will use the term *exchanges* in this book. Exchanges are usually owned and run by a third party or

> **exchanges (trading communities, trading exchanges)**
> Many-to-many e-marketplaces, usually owned and run by a third party or a consortium, in which many buyers and many sellers meet electronically to trade with each other.

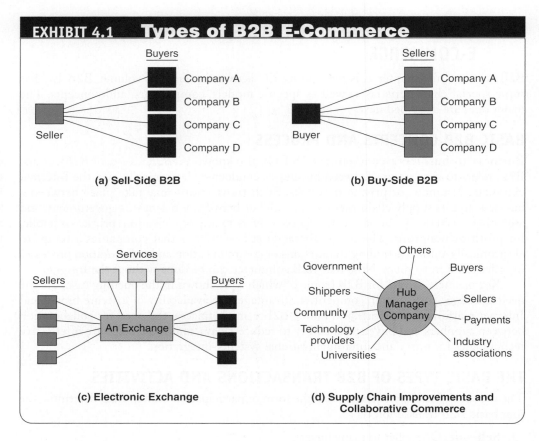

EXHIBIT 4.1   Types of B2B E-Commerce

(a) Sell-Side B2B

(b) Buy-Side B2B

(c) Electronic Exchange

(d) Supply Chain Improvements and Collaborative Commerce

public e-marketplaces
Third-party exchanges open to all interested parties (sellers and buyers).

by a consortium. They are described in more detail in Section 4.8. **Public e-marketplaces** are open to all interested parties (sellers and buyers).

Supply Chain Improvers and Collaborative Commerce

B2B transactions are conducted frequently along segments in the supply chain. Therefore, B2B initiatives need to be examined in light of other supply chain activities such as manufacturing, procurement of raw materials shipments, and logistics.

Businesses deal with other businesses for purposes beyond just selling or buying. One example is that of *collaborative commerce*, which is communication, joint design, planning, and information sharing among business partners (see Chapters 5 and 11).

MARKET SIZE AND CONTENT OF B2B

Market forecasters estimate that by 2012 the global B2B market (online and offline) could reach $15 trillion. The U.S. Census Bureau estimates B2B online sales to be 20 to 40 percent of the total B2B volume depending on the type (39 percent in manufacturing as shown in Exhibit 1.2). Chemicals, computer electronics, utilities, agriculture, shipping and warehousing, motor vehicles, petrochemicals, paper and office products, and food are the leading items in B2B. According to the authors' experience and several sources, as of 2011, the dollar value of B2B comprises at least 85 percent of the total transaction value of e-commerce, and in some countries it is over 90 percent.

The B2B market, which went through major consolidation in 2000–2002, is growing rapidly. Note that different B2B market forecasters use different definitions and measurement methodologies. Because of this, predictions frequently change and statistical data from different sources often differ. Therefore, we will not provide any more estimates here. Data sources that can be checked for the latest information on the B2B market are provided in Chapter 3 (Exhibit 3.1).

B2B EC is now in its fifth generation, as shown in Exhibit 4.2. This generation includes collaboration with suppliers, buyers, government, and other business partners, internal and external supply chain improvements, and expert (intelligent) sales systems. Just

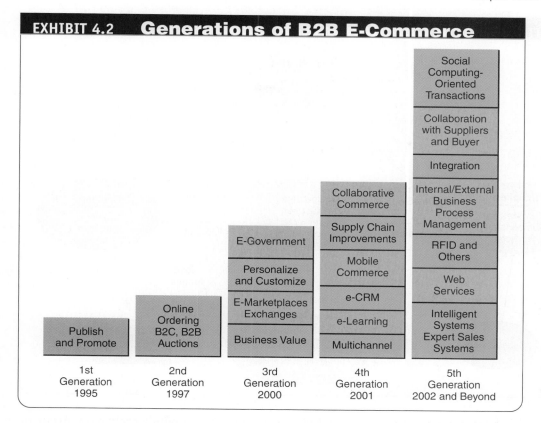

EXHIBIT 4.2   Generations of B2B E-Commerce

starting is B2B social commerce, which could usher in the sixth generation of B2B. Note that older generations coexist with new ones. Also, some companies are still using only EC from early generations. This chapter focuses on topics from the second and third generations. Topics from the fourth and fifth generations are presented in Chapters 5 through 8.

The B2B field is very diverse depending on the industry, products and services transacted, volume, method used, and more. The diversity can be seen in Exhibit 4.3 where we distinguish five major components: Our company that may be manufacturer, retailer, service provider, and so forth is shown in the center. It has suppliers (on the left) and customers (on the right). Our company operations are supported by different services (bottom), and we may work with several intermediaries (top of exhibit).

B2B CHARACTERISTICS

Here we examine various qualities by which B2B transactions can be characterized.

Parties to the Transaction: Sellers, Buyers, and Intermediaries

B2B commerce can be conducted *directly* between a *customer* and a *manufacturer* or it can be conducted via an **online intermediary**. The intermediary is a third party entity that brokers the transactions between the buyer and seller; it can be a virtual intermediary or a click-and-mortar intermediary. See Papazoglou and Ribbers (2006) for details. Some of the electronic intermediaries for individual consumers mentioned in Chapter 3 also can be referenced for B2B by replacing the individual consumers with business customers. Consolidators of buyers or sellers are typical B2B activities conducted by intermediaries.

Types of B2B Transactions: How Do Firms Buy?

B2B transactions are of two basic types: *spot buying* and *strategic sourcing*. **Spot buying** refers to the purchasing of goods and services as they are needed, usually at prevailing market prices, which are determined dynamically by supply and demand. The buyers and the sellers may not even know each other. Stock exchanges and commodity exchanges (oil, sugar, copper, corn, etc.) are examples of spot buying. In contrast, **strategic (systematic) sourcing** involves purchases based on *long-term contracts,* and the parties know each other.

online intermediary
An online third party that brokers a transaction online between a buyer and a seller; may be virtual or click-and-mortar.

spot buying
The purchase of goods and services as they are needed, usually at prevailing market prices.

strategic (systematic) sourcing
Purchases involving long-term contracts that usually are based on private negotiations between sellers and buyers.

EXHIBIT 4.3   The Components of B2B

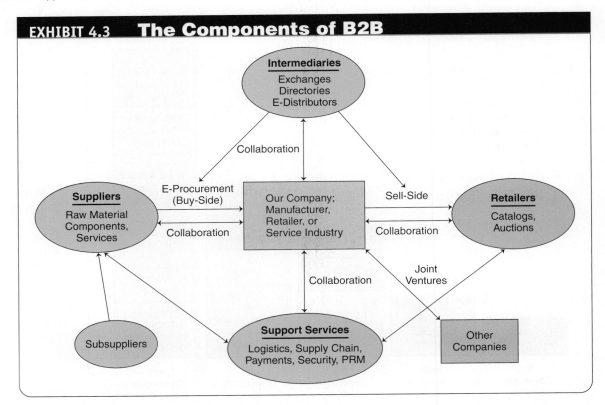

Spot buying can be conducted most economically on public exchanges. Strategic purchases can be supported more effectively and efficiently through direct buyer–seller offline or online negotiations, which can be done in private marketplaces or private trading rooms in public exchanges.

Types of Materials Traded: What Do Firms Buy?

Two major types of materials and supplies are traded in B2B: *direct* and *indirect*. **Direct materials** are materials used in making the products, such as steel in a car or paper in a book. The characteristics of direct materials are that their use is usually scheduled and planned for. They usually are not shelf items and are frequently purchased in large quantities after extensive negotiation and contracting.

Indirect materials are items, such as office supplies or light bulbs, that support operation and production. They are usually used in **maintenance, repair, and operation (MRO)** activities. Collectively, they are also known as *nonproduction materials*.

The Direction of the Trades

B2B marketplaces can be classified as *vertical* or *horizontal*. **Vertical marketplaces** are those that deal with one industry or industry segment. Examples include marketplaces specializing in electronics, cars, hospital supplies, steel, or chemicals. **Horizontal marketplaces** are those that concentrate on a service or a product that is used in all types of industries. Examples are office supplies, PCs, or travel services.

The types of materials traded and the types of B2B transactions define the B2B marketplaces. One classification is:

- Systematic sourcing and indirect materials = MRO hubs (horizontal markets for MRO)
- Systematic sourcing and direct materials = Vertical markets for direct material
- Spot sourcing and indirect materials = Horizontal markets for spot sourcing
- Spot sourcing and direct materials = Vertical markets (B2B exchanges)

The various characteristics of B2B transactions are presented in summary form in Exhibit 4.4.

---

direct materials
Materials used in the production of a product (e.g., steel in a car or paper in a book).

indirect materials
Materials used to support production (e.g., office supplies or light bulbs).

MRO (maintenance, repair, and operation)
Indirect materials used in activities that support production.

vertical marketplaces
Markets that deal with one industry or industry segment (e.g., steel, chemicals).

horizontal marketplaces
Markets that concentrate on a service, material, or a product that is used in all types of industries (e.g., office supplies, PCs).

EXHIBIT 4.4 Summary of B2B Characteristics

Parties to Transactions Direct, seller to buyer or buyer to seller Via intermediaries B2B 2C: A business sells to a business, but delivers to individual consumers	**Types of Transactions** Spot buying Strategic sourcing
Types of Materials Sold Direct materials and supplies Indirect (MROs)	**Direction of Trade** Vertical Horizontal
Number and Form of Participation One-to-many: Sell-side (e-storefront) Many-to-one: Buy-side Many-to-many: Exchanges Many, connected: Collaborative, supply chain	**Degree of Openness** Private exchanges, restricted Private exchanges, restricted Public exchanges, open to all Private (usually), can be public

SUPPLY CHAIN RELATIONSHIPS IN B2B

In the various B2B transaction types, business activities are frequently conducted along the supply chains of a company. The supply chain process consists of a number of interrelated subprocesses and roles. These extend from the acquisition of materials from suppliers, to the production of a product or service, to packaging and moving the final product to distributors and retailers. The process ends with the eventual purchase of a product by the end consumer. E-commerce B2B can make supply chains more efficient and effective or it can change the supply chain completely, eliminating one or more intermediaries.

Historically, many of the segments and processes in the supply chain have been managed through paper transactions (e.g., purchase orders, invoices, and so forth). B2B applications are offered online so they automate the processes and can serve as supply chain enablers that enable distinct competitive advantages (see Chapter 11 for a discussion).

SERVICE INDUSTRIES ONLINE IN B2B

In addition to trading products between businesses, services also can be provided electronically in B2B. Just as service industries such as travel, banking, insurance, real estate, and stock trading can be conducted electronically for individuals, as described in Chapter 3, they can also be conducted electronically for businesses. The major B2B services are:

▶ **Travel and hospitality services.** Many large corporations arrange their travel electronically through corporate travel agents. To further reduce costs, companies can make special arrangements that enable employees to plan and book their own trips online. For instance, American Express Business Travel offers several tools to help corporate travel managers plan and control employee travel. In addition to traditional scheduling and control tools, it offers the following EC-based tools:

  ▶ *TrackPoint* enables travel managers, as well as schedulers and controllers, to pinpoint a traveler's whereabouts at any time.

  ▶ *Travel Alert* and *Info Point* are information services that provide details about specific travel destinations. They are available free of charge to American Express Business Travel Clients.

  ▶ *Travel Insight Plus* consulting service identifies specific opportunities for savings in air travel expenditures for a given organization. The consulting study compares the client company's air travel expenditures against that of its true peers—other organizations that travel similar routes, over similar periods, with comparable volumes. Savings are identified through two key comparisons: the difference between the client and peer group's average spending on a route as well as highlighting the number of peers that are paying a lower average fare than the client's.

▶ *American Express* also offers a social network online.

▶ *Egencia* egencia.com and Expedia, Inc. partner with companies around the globe to maximize travel program utilization and savings. Backed by global market expertise, Egencia creates and manages programs designed to meet clients' goals.

Egencia combines expert travel agents, industry-leading technology, and unparalleled access to the best inventory of available services in the marketplace. Experienced account management, easy-to-use online tools and full-service travel agents help businesses plan, manage, and control travel, while maximizing the value of a company's corporate travel investment. The tools and services deliver greater control, visibility, and insight into a company's program—from managing corporate travel policy and expenses to 24/7 access to real-time analytics and reporting.

Expedia, Travelocity, Orbitz, and other online travel services provide similar services both B2C and B2B.

▶ **Real estate.** Commercial real estate transactions can be large and complex. Therefore, the Web might not be able to completely replace existing human agents. Instead, the Web can help businesses find the right properties, compare properties, and assist in negotiations. Some government-run foreclosed real estate auctions are open only to corporate real estate dealers and are conducted online.

▶ **Financial services.** Internet banking is an economical way of making business payments, transferring funds, or performing other financial transactions. For example, electronic funds transfer (EFT) is popular with businesses as are electronic letters of credit. Transaction fees over the Internet are less costly than any other alternative method. To see how payments work in B2B, see Chapter 10. Businesses can also purchase insurance online, both from pure online insurance companies and from click-and-mortar ones.

▶ **Banking and online financing.** Business loans can be solicited online from lenders. Bank of America, for example, offers its commercial customers a matching service on IntraLoan (the bank's global loan syndication service), which uses an extranet to match business loan applicants with potential lending corporations. Several sites, such as garage.com, provide information about venture capital. Institutional investors use the Internet for certain trading activities.

▶ **Other online services.** Consulting services, law firms, health organizations, and others sell enterprise knowledge and special services online. Many other online services, such as the purchase of electronic stamps (similar to metered postage, but generated on a computer), are available online (see stamps.com). Also, recruiting and staffing services are done online.

PARTNER AND SUPPLIER RELATIONSHIP MANAGEMENT

Successful e-businesses carefully manage partners, prospects, and customers across the entire value chain, most often in a 24/7 environment. For benefits and methods, see Markus (2006). Therefore, one should examine the role of solution technologies, such as call centers and collaboration tools, in creating an integrated online environment for engaging e-business customers and partners. The use of such solutions and technology appears under two names: customer relationship management (CRM) and partner relationship management (PRM).

Corporate customers may require more services than individual customers need. For example, corporate customers need to have access to the supplier's inventory status report so they know what items a supplier can deliver quickly. Customers also may want to see their historical purchasing records, and they may need private showrooms and trade rooms. Large numbers of vendors are available for designing and building appropriate B2B relationship solutions. The strategy of providing such comprehensive, quality e-services for business partners is sometimes called **partner relationship management (PRM)**.

In the context of PRM, business customers are only one category of business partners. Suppliers, partners in joint ventures, service providers, and others also are part of the B2B community in an exchange or company-centric B2B initiative. PRM is particularly important to companies that conduct outsourcing. Companies with many suppliers, such as the automobile companies, may create special programs for them. Such programs are called **supplier relationship management (SRM)**.

THE BENEFITS AND LIMITATIONS OF B2B

The benefits of B2B are for buyers, sellers, or for both, and they depend on which model is used. In general, though, the major benefits of B2B (the beneficiaries are marked after each benefit (S = seller, B = buyer, J = joint) are that it:

> Creates new sales opportunities (S)
> Eliminates paper and reduces administrative costs (J)
> Expedites processing and reduces cycle time (J)
> Lowers search costs and time for buyers to find products and vendors (B)
> Increases productivity of employees dealing with buying and/or selling (J)
> Reduces errors and improves quality of services (J)
> Makes product configuration easier (B)
> Reduces marketing and sales costs (S)
> Reduces inventory levels and costs (J)
> Enables customized online catalogs with different prices for different customers (J)
> Increases production flexibility, permitting just-in-time delivery (S)
> Reduces procurement costs (B)
> Facilitates customization via configuration (J)
> Provides for efficient customer service (B)
> Increases opportunities for collaboration (J)

B2B EC development has limitations as well, especially regarding channel conflict and the operation of public exchanges. Also, personal face-to-face interactions may be needed but unavailable. These will be discussed in Chapter 11.

The development of B2B might eliminate the distributor or the retailer, which could be a benefit to the seller and the buyer (though not a benefit to the distributor or retailer). In previous chapters, such a phenomenon is referred to as *disintermediation* (Chapters 2 and 3). The benefits and limitations of B2B depend on such variables as who is buying, what items and what quantities, who are the suppliers, how often a company buys, and so forth.

In the remainder of the chapter, we will look at the various components of Exhibit 4.3 (p. 184) as well as the major types of B2B structural models (sell-side, buy-side, exchanges) as well as at transaction models (e.g., auctions) and other B2B topics.

Section 4.1 ❯ REVIEW QUESTIONS

1. Define B2B.
2. Discuss the following: spot buying versus strategic sourcing, direct materials versus indirect materials, and vertical markets versus horizontal markets.
3. What are company-centric marketplaces? Are they public or private?
4. Define B2B exchanges.

partner relationship management (PRM)
Business strategy that focuses on providing comprehensive quality service to business partners.

supplier relationship management (SRM)
A comprehensive approach to managing an enterprise's interactions with the organizations that supply the goods and services it uses.

5. Relate the supply chain to B2B transactions.
6. Describe PRM and SRM.
7. List the benefits and limitations of B2B.

4.2 ONE-TO-MANY: SELL-SIDE E-MARKETPLACES

A major portion of B2B is selling in what is known as B2B marketing. A variety of methods exist.

SELL-SIDE MODELS

sell-side e-marketplace
A Web-based marketplace in which one company sells to many business buyers from e-catalogs or auctions, frequently over an extranet.

In the B2C model, a manufacturer or a retailer sells electronically directly to consumers from a *storefront* or *webstore*. In a B2B **sell-side e-marketplace** a business sells products and services to business customers electronically, frequently over an extranet. The seller can be a manufacturer selling to an intermediary such as a wholesaler, or to a retailer, or to an individual business. Intel, Cisco, and Dell are examples of such sellers. Or the seller can be a distributor selling to retailers or businesses (e.g., W.W. Grainger, to be presented in Section 4.3). In either case, sell-side e-marketplaces involve one seller and many potential buyers. In this model, both individual consumers and business buyers might use the same private sell-side marketplace (e.g., dell.com), or they might use a public marketplace. Exhibit 4.5 shows the different configuration of sell-side B2B marketplaces. The arrows indicate online or offline possible directions. The exhibit shows some, but not all, of the possible intermediaries. For example, there could be value-added-retailers (VARs) who add some services and then sell the improved product or service to customers.

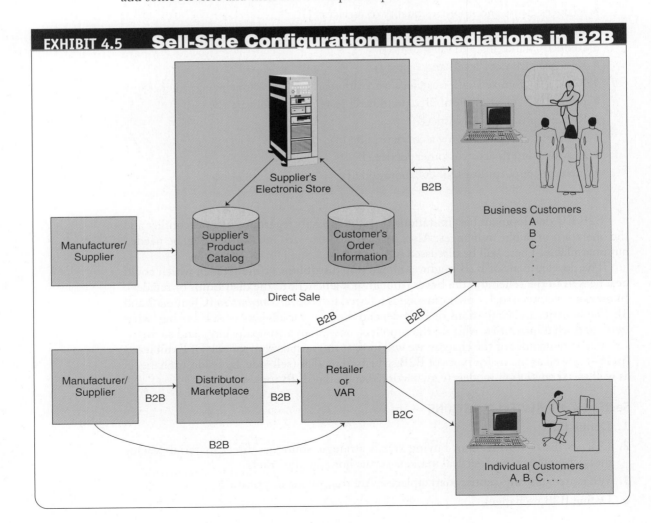

EXHIBIT 4.5   Sell-Side Configuration Intermediations in B2B

The architecture of this B2B model is similar to that of B2C EC. The major differences are in the process. For example, in B2B, large customers might be provided with customized catalogs and prices. Usually, companies will separate B2C orders from B2B orders. One reason for this is that B2C and B2B orders have different *order-fulfillment processes* (see Chapter 11), different delivery (transportation) systems, and different pricing models (i.e., wholesale versus retail pricing). Also, in B2B we use technologies such as EDI and XML (Online Tutorial T11), which are not usually used in B2C.

The one-to-many model has three major marketing methods: (1) selling from *electronic catalogs*; (2) selling via *forward auctions*; and (3) one-to-one selling, usually under a *negotiated* long-term contract. Such one-to-one negotiating is familiar: The buying company negotiates price, quantity, payments, delivery, and quality terms with the selling company. We describe the first method in this section and the second method in Section 4.4.

B2B Sellers

Sellers in the sell-side marketplace may be click-and-mortar manufacturers or intermediaries (e.g., distributors or wholesalers). The intermediaries may even be pure online companies, as in the case of bigboXX.com.

Customer Service

Online sellers can provide sophisticated customer services. For example, General Electric receives over 20 million calls a year regarding appliances. Although most of these calls come from individuals, many come from businesses. By using the Internet and automatic-response software agents (autoresponders), GE has reduced the cost of handling such calls from $5 per call when done by phone to $0.20 per electronically answered call. Patton (2006) estimated in general that a call handled by a human agent costs $2 to $10. If answered automatically (e.g., autoresponder, interactive voice response), the cost is between $.02 and $.20.

We now turn our attention to the most common sell-side method—selling online from the company's electronic catalogs.

SALES FROM CATALOGS: STOREFRONT

Companies can use the Internet to sell directly from their online catalogs. A company may offer one catalog for all customers or a *customized catalog* for each large customer (possibly both). For example, Staples, an office-supply vendor, offers its business customers personalized software catalogs of about 100,000 products and pricing at stapleslink.com.

Example. Microsoft sells over $20 billion of software annually to its distributors and larger customers. Using Microsoft's extranet-based order-entry tool (MOET), buyers can check availability of products, make transactions, and look up the status of orders. The online orders are automatically fed into the customer's SAP applications. The extranet handles over 1 million transactions per year. The system significantly reduces the number of phone calls, e-mails, and incorrect product shipments.

Many companies use a multichannel marketing strategy where one channel is e-commerce.

Brady Corporation offers a multichannel system as shown in Case 4.1.

Selling from catalogs is done by hundreds of thousands of companies worldwide.

In selling online to business buyers, manufacturers might encounter a similar problem to that of B2C, namely conflict with the regular distribution channels, including corporate dealers (channel conflict). To avoid conflicts, some companies advertise online, but sell only in physical stores. An example is Gregg's Cycles (greggscycles.com). The company sells only peripheral products, such as parts and accessories, to individual consumers online. In addition, Gregg's Cycles provides a locator where customers can buy its core product—bicycles—at brick-and-mortar stores.

CASE 4.1

EC Application

BRADY CORPORATION USES CATALOGS AND MULTICHANNELS TO SELL

Brady Corporation (bradycorp.com) produces products and people identification items, selling over 150,000 different products to more than 500,000 customers worldwide through direct catalog and other distribution channels.

The Problem

With 9,000 employees worldwide and more than 150,000 products, the company needed an e-catalog to localize these products in several languages, currencies and measurements, that could serve customers both efficiently and swiftly. The company was using Excel data to build the firm's online catalog. This method was labor intensive as there was no way to make global data changes, forcing staff to manually update details on a given product in multiple locations in the company's e-catalogs. Also, the system did not provide the means needed for storing product attributes, making it difficult to provide timely information vital to customers' purchasing decisions online. Another problem was the less than user-friendly setup at the Excel-based e-catalog. It was difficult for customers to find information for the products they needed, so most of them turned to Brady's direct sales team, call centers, or even distribution partners to find the best products for their needs. Brady knew that customer satisfaction could only be improved through better search and navigation of the catalog and its product information.

The Solution

Brady chose FullTilt's Product Information Management Solution to store and organize its product data and attributes in a central repository for easy access and updating. By centralizing all product information in a single repository and creating a consistent set of product information that could be edited and exported for online use, the company was able to allow authorized users around the globe to edit product information locally, yet maintain the accuracy and consistency of the product information.

If a product exists multiple times in the catalog, a change made in one place is automatically made in all the other locations. Users can also visually check the product description against product images maintained in the database, providing an extra layer of defense against data errors. New product

information is automatically imported from the marketing department, doing away with unnecessary manual steps. Updated information is uploaded to *bradyid.com*, Brady's e-commerce website, via an export file. The system is so easy to use that Brady only needs two e-commerce content managers to maintain and update the system at the SKU level. To meet the challenge of site navigation and search, Brady chose Endeca's Information Access Platform (IAP) to deliver the necessary product information from the FullTilt internal system. Using Endeca's Guided Summarization technique, the catalog is able to support featured products, make suggestions, and offer related information based on customer exploration of the site. In this way, customers can investigate options and select products best suited to their needs. The site offers an efficient ordering system as well as distributors' location maps and directions.

The Results

The platform resulted in reduced costs by decreasing the number of people needed to build and maintain the system, by expediting deployment of accurate and up-to-date custom catalogs, and by enabling more efficient catalog maintenance. The Endeca Platform provided a single source of product information and resulted in an 84 percent increase in conversions (the ratio of the number of customers who visited the site and those that went on to buy), more than 25 percent increase in leads for sales, and double-digit increase in online sales also materialized.

Sources: Compiled from *FullTilt* (2004), *Endeca* (2008), and *bradid.com* (accessed December 2010).

Questions

1. Why did Brady need an e-catalog?
2. Why was the Excel-based catalog useless?
3. What are the benefits of the new e-catalog? To customers? To Brady?
4. What did Endeca's product contribute?

Customization and Self-Configuration

As with B2C EC, B2B direct sales offer an opportunity for efficient customization.

Example: Cisco Systems. Cisco Systems (cisco.com) is the world's leading producer of routers, switches, and network interconnection services. Cisco's portal has evolved over several years, beginning with technical support for customers and developing into one of the world's largest B2B direct sales sites.

Cisco provides online tools for self-configuration, pricing, ordering, and so on. Today, Cisco offers about a dozen Internet-based applications to both end-user businesses and reseller partners. Cisco also provides a superb communication system to its business partners and employees as described in Online File W4.1. Business customers can self-configure customized products, get price quotes, and submit orders, all online.

For an example of another successful B2B portal which enables greater efficiency in the ordering process, read about Haier in Case 4.2.

Benefits and Limitations of Online Sales from Catalogs

Successful examples of the B2B online direct sales model include manufacturers, such as Dell, Intel, IBM, and Cisco, and distributors, such as Ingram Micro (which sells to value-added retailers; the retailer adds some service along with the product). Sellers that use this model can be successful as long as they have a superb reputation in the market and a large enough group of loyal customers.

Although the benefits of direct online sales are similar to that of B2C, there also are limitations. One of the major issues facing direct sellers is how to find buyers. Many companies know how to advertise in traditional channels but are still learning how to contact would-be business buyers online. Also, B2B sellers may experience channel conflicts with their existing distribution systems. Another limitation is that if traditional electronic data interchange (EDI)—the computer-to-computer direct transfer of business documents—is used, the cost to the customers can be high, and they will be reluctant to go online. The solution to this problem is the transfer of documents over extranets (see Online Tutorial T11) and an Internet-based EDI (see Online Tutorial T11). Finally, the number of business partners online must be large enough to justify the system infrastructure and operation and maintenance expenses.

COMPREHENSIVE SELL-SIDE SYSTEMS

Sell-side systems must provide several essential functionalities that enable B2B vendors to efficiently execute sales, provide superb customer service, allow integration with existing IT systems, and provide integration with non-Internet sale systems. Here is an example of such a system provided by Sterling Commerce (an AT&T Company) to Best Buy.

CASE 4.2
EC Application
THE HAIER GROUP

The Haier Group is a multinational consumer electronics and home appliances company headquartered in Qingdao, Shandong, China. Although it faced bankruptcy in the early 1980s, by 2010 it had transformed into a global brand producing 6.1 percent of white goods worldwide (see *www.haier.net/products/index.asp* for details).

Haier's strategy aims at brand recognition and product competitiveness based on a robust corporate structure. Its strategic business networks encompass design, procurement, production, distribution, and after-sales functions.

Haier was quick not only to appreciate the competitive potential of the Internet and specifically e-commerce, but also to understand the need for significant levels of business process reengineering in order to meet changing customer needs. It also made the most of emerging technologies. Logistics is a good example of where Haier has excelled. Haier's logistics are comprised of three networks: the global supply chain resources network, a global user resource network, and a computer information network.

Haier relies on its B2B trade portal (*ihaier.com*) to generate profit and reduce costs. This portal includes a global supply chain that engages primary suppliers and helps to maintain close relationships with partners, exercise stricter control over logistics and production, reduce operating costs, and improve service quality. There are four key modules on the website: product customization, smart shopping, online ordering, and user design recommendations. Underlying all this are Haier's three *zero goals*: zero storage (no physical warehousing), zero distance (goods supplied from anywhere and at anytime), and zero business capital (goods made to order).

Haier also created a B2C site, (*www.eHaier.com*) which enables customers to make online orders.

Systems supporting Haier's portals include just-in-time and computer integrated manufacturing systems (CIMS), which enable mass customization and flexible production; SAP; which generates daily production line data; and CRMs, which provide information that responds to both market and customer needs.

In pursuing the benefits of e-business, Haier has reengineered its entire business operation to accommodate the supply chain management provided by iHaier. This included streamlining processes to reduce costs and increase efficiency. It plans to expand its e-commerce platform significantly to enable the growth of its electronics business.

Sources: *haier.com.au* (accessed August 2011), *haier.net/index.htm* (accessed August 2011), and *ritamcgrath.com/ee/images/uploads/Haier_Report.pdf* (accessed August 2011).

Questions

1. What are the benefits of the trading portal (B2B) for Haier and for its customers?

2. Would Haier be able to operate efficiently without SAP? If not, why not?

3. What is the connection between Haier's B2B and B2C portal?

4. Do you agree that Haier's successful transformation to e-business can be explained by its adoption of advanced technologies and information systems?

Note: To answer these questions you will need to use the sources above and your own independent research.

Example. Best Buy is known for its retail stores, but the company is a major supplier to small and medium businesses (only large companies can buy directly from manufacturers because they buy very large quantities). Customers include educational institutions, government entities, and SMEs that buy relatively small quantities at a time.

Sterling provided a system to Best Buy with the following capabilities:

> ▶ Search capabilities with search by key word, price range, category, manufacturer, and platform
> ▶ Side-by-side, feature-by-feature product comparisons
> ▶ Customer account-specific pricing, coupon, promotion redemption, and gift cards
> ▶ Suggestions for additional items such as accessories and warranties
> ▶ Up-to-date inventory availability with Best Buy's distribution partners such as Ingram Micro
> ▶ Order status and second level status information that not only tracks shipping and invoices, but also the specifics of "in process" orders (e.g., with fulfillment partner, acknowledged, partially acknowledged, on backorder, or partial backorder)
> ▶ Gives the call center interface key information for cross selling, upselling, and details for offering discounts

These capabilities resulted in the following benefits for Best Buy:

▶ Make it easier for business customers to do business with Best Buy
▶ Deliver business customers
▶ Enable sales operation to control pricing and promotions, and review daily operations
▶ Facilitate the fulfillment of products with third parties through an automated fulfillment

Cellular Accessories for Less (CAFL) is another example of how e-commerce solutions benefit sellers. The solution includes a variety of tools that provide useful capabilities for the buying customers, as well as for the sellers.

Example. Cellular Accessories for Less (CAFL) is a Los Angeles–based B2B seller of accessory products for wireless/cellular phones and personal digital assistants (PDAs). To meet customer requirements, CAFL must provide all the correct protocols and products' properties so the products are easy to be evaluated, compared, and ordered. The rapid pace of change in the cellular phone industry—with up to 10 new phones introduced every week—makes accurate, updated information even more crucial.

To enhance the company's competitive position, CAFL is using several products from Ariba Inc. including Ariba Supplier Network, Ariba Ready, and Ariba Express Content. Finally, Ariba PunchOut allows CAFL's customers to instantly click out of the CAFL website for extensive content on products, functionalities, and compatibility, then pop back to the Ariba Supplier Network to complete the transactions. Up-to-the-minute alerts and hyperlinks with detailed specifications further enhance accuracy. And automatic updates eliminate the redundant processes typically required to match catalogs and website content.

Through Ariba's Procurement solutions, new CAFL buyers can access Express Content and take advantage of discounted pricing, technical readiness, and faster service. Customers can now easily share negotiated price discounts throughout the organization, maximize use of approved vendors, reduce processing expenses, and simplify transactions. CAFL now maintains strong relationships with its customers without as many phone discussions.

Section 4.2 ▶ REVIEW QUESTIONS

1. What are buy-side and sell-side transactions? How do they differ?
2. List the types of sell-side B2B transaction models.
3. Distinguish between the use and nonuse of intermediaries in B2B sell-side transactions.

4. Describe customer service in B2B systems.

5. Describe the direct online B2B sales process from catalogs.

6. Discuss the benefits and limitations of direct online B2B sales from catalogs.

7. List some of the benefits that B2B software can provide to sellers. (Hint: Consult the Best Buy example.)

4.3 SELLING VIA DISTRIBUTORS AND OTHER INTERMEDIARIES

Manufacturers can sell directly to businesses, and they do so if the customers are large buyers. However, frequently they use intermediaries to distribute their products to a large number of smaller buyers. The intermediaries buy products from many manufacturers and aggregate them into one catalog from which they sell to customers or to retailers. Now, many of these distributors also are selling online via storefronts.

Some well-known online distributors for businesses are SAM's Club (of Walmart), Avnet, and W.W. Grainger (Case 4.3). Most e-distributors sell in horizontal markets, meaning that they sell to businesses in a variety of industries. However, some specialize in one industry (vertical market), such as Boeing PART (see Online File W4.2). Most intermediaries sell at fixed prices; however, some offer quantity discounts, negotiated prices, or conduct auctions.

CASE 4.3

EC Application

W.W. GRAINGER AND GOODRICH CORPORATION

W.W. Grainger has a number of websites, but its flagship is *grainger.com*. In 2009, of Grainger's over $7 billion in annual sales, more than $1.7 billion was generated from e-commerce, with the majority of those sales placed through *grainger.com*.

More than 900,000 brand-name products from more than 3,000 suppliers are offered at *grainger.com* (versus 400,000 that can be seen at the physical stores), and a growing number of Grainger's 1.8 million customers from 150 countries are ordering online. The website continues the same kind of customer service and wide range of industrial products provided by Grainger's traditional offline business with the additional convenience of 24/7 ordering, use of search engines, and additional services.

This convenience is what first attracted Goodrich Corporation in Pueblo, Colorado. In 2000, it found *grainger.com* to be one of the most convenient and easy purchasing sites to use. The purchasing agent of this relatively small Goodrich plant of approximately 250 employees used to call in an order to a supplier, give the salesperson a part number, and wait until the price could be pulled up. Goodrich's purchaser now can place orders online in a matter of minutes, and the purchaser's display has Goodrich's negotiated pricing built in.

Goodrich can get just about anything it needs from *grainger.com*. Grainger interfaces with other suppliers, so if Goodrich needs something specific that Grainger does not normally carry, Grainger will research and find the items through Grainger's sourcing team. Consolidating their purchases through Grainger provided better prices.

Goodrich has achieved additional savings from the tremendous decrease in paperwork that has resulted from buying through *grainger.com*. Individuals in each department now have access to purchasing cards, which allow them to do some of their own ordering. Before, the central purchasing department had to issue purchase orders for every single item. Now, employees with purchasing cards and passwords can place orders according to the spending limits that have been set up based on their positions.

In 2002, the Goodrich Pueblo operation spent $200,000 for purchases from *grainger.com*, which reflected a 10 to 15 percent savings on its purchases. As a result, Goodrich signed a company-wide enterprise agreement that allows every Goodrich facility in the country to order through *grainger.com*, with an expected savings of at least 10 percent.

Sources: Compiled from *en.wikipedia.org/wiki/W._W._Grainger* (accessed January 2011), *grainger.com* (accessed January 2011), and Lucas (2005).

Questions

1. Enter *grainger.com* and review all of the services offered to online buyers. Prepare a list of these services.

2. Explain how Goodrich's buyers save time and money.

3. What other benefits does Goodrich enjoy by using *grainger.com*?

4. How was desktop purchasing (see details in Section 4.7) implemented at Goodrich Corporation?

Section 4.3 ▶ REVIEW QUESTIONS

1. What are the advantages of using intermediaries in B2B sales?
2. What types of intermediaries exist in B2B?
3. Compare an e-distributor in B2B to Amazon.com. What are the similarities? What are the differences?

4.4 SELLING VIA E-AUCTIONS

Auctions are gaining popularity both as B2B buying and as sales channels. Some major B2B auction issues are discussed in this section.

USING AUCTIONS ON THE SELL SIDE

Many companies use *forward auctions* to liquidate their unneeded products or capital assets. In such a situation, items are usually displayed on an auction site (private or public) for quick disposal. Forward auctions offer the following benefits to B2B sellers:

▶ **Revenue generation.** Forward auctions support and expand online and overall sales. Forward auctions also offer businesses a new venue for quickly and easily disposing of excess, obsolete, and returned products (e.g., see liquidation.com).

▶ **Cost savings.** In addition to generating new revenue, conducting auctions electronically reduces the costs of selling the auctioned items. These savings also help increase the seller's profits.

▶ **Increased "stickiness."** Forward auctions give websites increased "stickiness," namely, potential buyers stay there longer. Stickiness is a characteristic that describes customer loyalty to a site that eventually results in higher revenue.

▶ **Member acquisition and retention.** All bidding transactions result in additional registered members, who are future business contacts. In addition, auction software aids enable sellers to search and report on virtually every relevant auction activity. Such information can be used for future analysis.

Forward auctions can be conducted in two ways. A company can conduct its forward auctions from its own website or it can sell from an intermediary auction site, such as liquidation.com or ebay.com. Let's examine these options.

AUCTIONING FROM THE COMPANY'S OWN SITE

For large and well-known companies that frequently conduct auctions, such as GM, it makes sense to build an auction mechanism on the company's own site. Why should a company pay a commission to an intermediary if the intermediary cannot provide the company with added value? Of course, if a company decides to auction from its own site, it will have to pay for infrastructure and operate and maintain the auction site. Note that if the company already has an electronic marketplace for selling from e-catalogs, the additional cost for conducting auctions might not be too high. However, a significant added value that could be provided by intermediaries is the attraction of many potential buyers to the auction site.

USING INTERMEDIARIES IN AUCTIONS

Several intermediaries offer B2B auction sites (e.g., see asset-auctions.com and liquidation.com). Some companies specialize in government auctions while others focus on surplus stock auctions (e.g. swipebids.com). An intermediary might conduct private auctions for a seller, either from the intermediary's or the seller's site. Or a company might choose to conduct auctions in a public marketplace, using a third-party hosting company (e.g., eBay, which has a special "business exchange" for small companies).

Using a third-party hosting company for conducting auctions has many benefits. The first is that no additional resources (e.g., hardware, bandwidth, engineering resources, or IT personnel) are required. Nor are there any hiring costs or opportunity costs associated with the redeployment of corporate resources. B2B auction intermediary sites also offer fast time-to-market: They enable a company to have a robust, customized

CASE 4.4
EC Application

HOW VICFORESTS SELLS TIMBER THROUGH AN ONLINE AUCTION PLATFORM

VicForests, a state-owned business in Victoria, Australia, is responsible for the harvest, regeneration, and sale of timber from Victoria's public forests. Approximately one-third of Victoria's timber (21.2356 square miles) is supplied by VicForests under strict environmental guidelines.

Since April 2006, VicForests has used a B2B online auction system, the Forest Auction Platform, to sell its product. The auctions can be selling auctions, where bidders compete until the highest bid is reached, or buying auctions, where the price is reduced competitively. The company has the option of adopting either method, dependant on various factors such as stock levels, dispensing immediacy, and buyer/seller interest. Descriptive catalogs are released beforehand and participation is subject to prior bidder certification by VicForests which ensures that bidders adhere to a number of terms and conditions.

Tradeslot, an established electronics company, designs and operates the Forest Auction Platform. Technology and auction support services include bidder training, mock auctions, auction management, and stakeholder feedback.

Auction results and benefits include:

- Operating cost reductions, efficiency, transparency, and substantial revenue increases. The first auction resulted in a 40 percent increase in revenue and the average auction results in more than a 17 percent increase.
- A platform capable of assessing optimal allocations among 3 million options in real time.
- Allowance for both price and non-price factors (e.g., incumbency quality) translating them into *factored bids*.

Sources: *vicforests.com.au/index.htm* (accessed August 2011), *forestauctions.com* (accessed August 2011), and *www.tradeslot.com* (accessed August 2011).

Questions

1. What are the benefits of implementing the Forest Auction Platform for the Victorian government?

2. What benefits does the Forest Auction Platform offer buyers?

3. How has the development of automated online auction platforms changed the historical negotiating relationship between buyer and seller?

4. What are the advantages and disadvantages (if any) of employing an intermediary such as Tradeslot to design and conduct online auctions?

auction up and running immediately. Without the intermediary, it can take a company weeks to prepare an auction site in-house.

Another benefit of using intermediaries relates to billing and collection efforts, which are handled by the intermediary rather than the selling company. For example, intermediaries calculate merchant-specific shipping fees and charge customers for shipping of auctioned items. These services are not free, of course. They are provided as part of the merchant's commission to the intermediary: a cost often deemed worth paying in exchange for the ease and value of the services provided.

For an example of using an intermediary in B2B auction services, see liquidity servicesinc.com. For another example of a successful auction service, read about VicForests in Case 4.4.

EXAMPLES OF B2B FORWARD AUCTIONS

The following are examples of B2B auctions:

- Whirlpool Corp. sold $20 million in scrap metal in a single auction via asset-auctions.com, increasing the price received by 15 percent.
- Sam's Club (samsclub.com) auctions thousands of items (especially electronics) at auctions.samsclub.com. Featured auctions include the current bid, the number of bids, and the end date.
- Resort Quest, a large vacation rental company, uses auctionanything.com to auction rental space.
- At GovernmentAuctions.org (governmentauctions.org), businesses can bid on foreclosures, seized items, abandoned property, and more.
- Yahoo! conducts both B2C and B2B auctions of many items.

Section 4.4 ▶ REVIEW QUESTIONS

1. List the benefits of using B2B auctions for selling.
2. List the benefits of using auction intermediaries.
3. What are the major purposes of forward auctions, and how are they conducted?

4.5   ONE-FROM-MANY: E-PROCUREMENT AT BUY-SIDE E-MARKETPLACES

buy-side e-marketplace
A corporate-based acquisition site that uses reverse auctions, negotiations, group purchasing, or any other e-procurement method.

When a buyer goes to a sell-side marketplace, such as Cisco's, the buyer's purchasing department sometimes has to manually enter the order information into its own corporate information system. Furthermore, manually searching webstores and e-malls to find and compare suppliers and products can be slow and costly. As a solution, large buyers can open their own marketplaces called buy-side e-marketplaces, and invite sellers to browse and offer to fulfill orders. The term *procurement* is used to refer to the purchase of goods and services by organizations. It is usually done by *purchasing agents*, also known as *corporate buyers*.

INEFFICIENCIES IN TRADITIONAL PROCUREMENT MANAGEMENT

procurement management
The planning, organizing, and coordinating of all the activities relating to purchasing goods and services needed to accomplish the organization's mission.

Procurement management refers to the planning, organizing, and coordinating of all the activities pertaining to the purchasing of the goods and services necessary to accomplish the mission of an enterprise. It involves the B2B purchase and sale of supplies and services, as well as the flow of required information and networking systems. Approximately 80 percent of an organization's purchased items, mostly MROs, constitute 20 to 25 percent of the total purchase value. Furthermore, a large portion of corporate buyers' time is spent on non-value-added activities, such as entering data, correcting errors in paperwork, expediting delivery, or solving quality problems.

The procurement process may be lengthy and complex due to the many activities performed. The following are the major activities that may be evidenced in a single purchase:

▶ *Search for items* using search engines, catalogs, showrooms, and sales presentations.
▶ *Learn details of items and terms* using comparison engines and quality reports and research the items and vendors.
▶ *Negotiate or join group purchasing* using intelligent software agents (if available).
▶ *Sign agreement or contract* using contract management; arrange financing, escrow insurance, etc.
▶ *Create specific purchasing order(s)* using computerized system. Determine when and how much to order each time. Authorize corporate buyers.
▶ *Arrange packing, shipments, and deliveries* using electronic tracking, RFID, etc.
▶ *Arrange invoicing, payments, expense, management, and purchasing budgetary control* using software packages.

An example of the traditional procurement process is shown in Exhibit 4.6, and it is often inefficient. For example, for high-value items, purchasing personnel spend a great deal of time and effort on procurement activities. These activities include qualifying suppliers, negotiating prices and terms, building rapport with strategic suppliers, and carrying out supplier evaluation and certification. If buyers are busy with the details of the smaller items (usually the MROs), they do not have enough time to properly deal with the purchase of the high-value items.

maverick buying
Unplanned purchases of items needed quickly, often at non-prenegotiated higher prices.

Other inefficiencies also may occur in conventional procurement. These range from delays, to paying too much for rush orders. One procurement inefficiency is maverick buying. This occurs when a buyer makes unplanned purchases of items needed quickly, which results in buying at non-prenegotiated, usually higher, prices.

To correct the situation, companies reengineer their procurement systems, implement new purchasing models, and, in particular, introduce e-procurement. Let's elaborate first about the procurement methods.

EXHIBIT 4.6   A Traditional Procurement Process

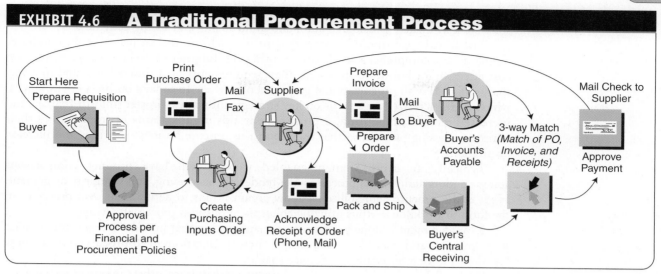

Source: Ariba.com, February 2001. Courtesy of Ariba Inc.

PROCUREMENT METHODS

Companies use different methods to procure goods and services depending on what and where they buy, the quantities needed, how much money is involved, and more. Each method has its own process benefits and limitations. To minimize the inefficiencies described earlier, companies automate activities in the process. This is the major objective of e-procurement. The major procurement methods include the following:

▶ Conduct bidding in a system in which suppliers compete against each other. This method is used for large-ticket items or large quantities (Section 4.6).

▶ Buy directly from manufacturers, wholesalers, or retailers from their catalogs, and possibly by negotiation (Sections 4.2 through 4.4).

▶ Buy at private or public auction sites in which the organization participates as one of the buyers (Section 4.6).

▶ Buy from the catalog of an intermediary (e-distributor) that aggregates sellers' catalogs (Section 4.7).

▶ Buy from an internal buyer's catalog, in which company-approved vendors' catalogs, including agreed-upon prices, are aggregated. This approach is used for the implementation of *desktop purchasing*, which allows the requisitioners to order directly from vendors, bypassing the procurement department (Section 4.7).

▶ Join a group-purchasing system that aggregates participants' demand, creating a large volume. Then the group may negotiate prices or initiate a tendering process (Section 4.7).

▶ Buy at an exchange or industrial mall (Section 4.8).

▶ Collaborate with suppliers to share information about sales and inventory, so as to reduce inventory and stock-outs and enhance just-in-time delivery. (See Chapters 5 and 11 on collaborative commerce.)

E-PROCUREMENT CONCEPTS

e-procurement (electronic procurement)
The electronic acquisition of goods and services for organizations via the Internet, EDI, etc.

E-procurement (electronic procurement) is the business-to-business purchase of supplies, work, and services through the Internet (or private network, such as EDI).

Typically, e-procurement websites allow qualified and registered buyers in a company to look for suppliers. It also allows placing a request for suppliers to bid on a job (see the opening case). Transactions can be initiated and completed electronically. Ongoing purchases may qualify customers for volume discounts or special offers. E-procurement software may make it possible to automate some buying and selling activities.

The broad spectrum of e-procurement is much more than just making purchases online. It is a comprehensive platform—using the Internet to make it easier, faster, and cost effective for businesses to source their requirements on a timely basis, and in a way that is aligned with organizational goals and objectives. In today's business environment, which is characterized by a focus on key strategic initiatives, shorter time-to-market, and increased global competition, e-procurement aids organizations in streamlining their entire purchasing process, so that they can focus on core business activities and increase profitability.

Typically an e-procurement-enabled website will have product comparisons across vendors and various processes like tendering, auctioning, and vendor management. High-end e-procurement solutions allow organizations to define their own processes in the form of workflows—thus utilizing concepts of business process modeling.

E-procurement is done with a software application that includes features for supplier management and complex auctions. A new generation of e-procurement is now "on-demand" or a Software as a Service (SaaS).

Some of these activities are done in private marketplaces, others in public exchanges.

THE GOALS AND PROCESS OF E-PROCUREMENT

As stated earlier, e-procurement automates activities in the purchasing process frequently via the Web. The aim is to control, simplify, and automate the purchase of goods and services from multiple suppliers.

Improvements to procurement have been attempted for decades, usually by using information technologies. The real opportunity for improvement lies in the use of e-procurement, the electronic acquisition of goods and services for organizations. For comprehensive coverage and case studies, see zdnet.com/topics/e-procurement. The general e-procurement process (with the exception of tendering) is shown in Exhibit 4.7.

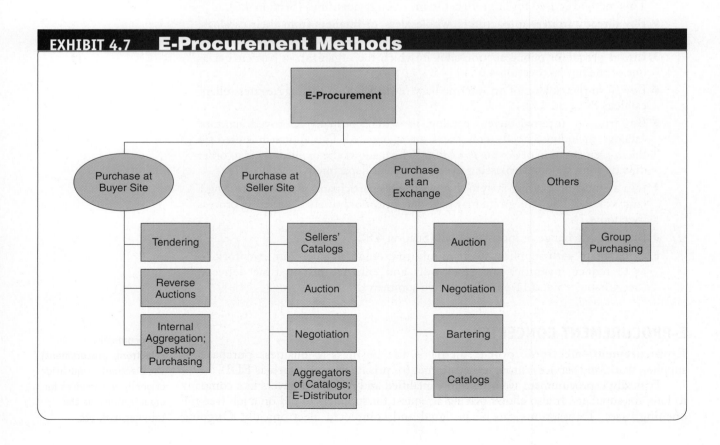

EXHIBIT 4.7   E-Procurement Methods

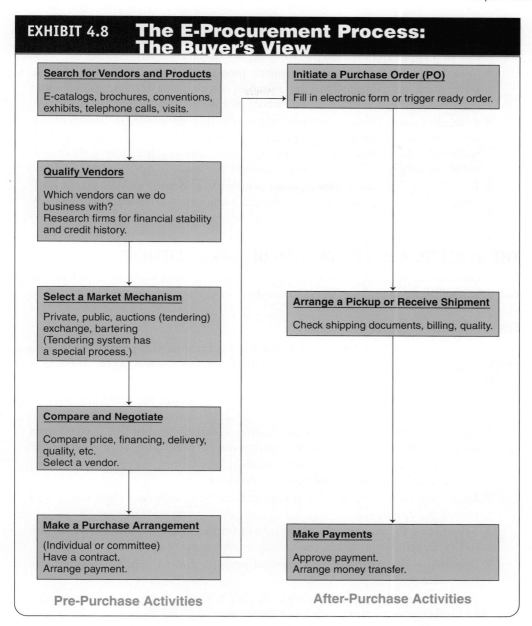

EXHIBIT 4.8   The E-Procurement Process: The Buyer's View

Search for Vendors and Products

E-catalogs, brochures, conventions, exhibits, telephone calls, visits.

Qualify Vendors

Which vendors can we do business with?
Research firms for financial stability and credit history.

Select a Market Mechanism

Private, public, auctions (tendering) exchange, bartering
(Tendering system has a special process.)

Compare and Negotiate

Compare price, financing, delivery, quality, etc.
Select a vendor.

Make a Purchase Arrangement

(Individual or committee)
Have a contract.
Arrange payment.

Initiate a Purchase Order (PO)

Fill in electronic form or trigger ready order.

Arrange a Pickup or Receive Shipment

Check shipping documents, billing, quality.

Make Payments

Approve payment.
Arrange money transfer.

Pre-Purchase Activities   After-Purchase Activities

Types of E-Procurement

E-procurement methods can be organized into four segments: (1) Buy at own website, (2) buy at sellers' store, (3) buy at exchanges, and (4) buy at others' e-market sites. Each segment includes several activities, as illustrated in Exhibit 4.8. Some of these will be described in Sections 4.8 through 4.9.

According to en.wikipedia.org/wiki/E-procurement, the seven main types of e-procurement are as follows:

▶ **E-sourcing.** Identifying new suppliers for a specific category of purchasing requirements using Internet technology.

▶ **E-tendering.** Sending requests for information and prices to known suppliers and receiving the suppliers' responses and bids using Internet technology.

▶ **E-reverse auctioning.** Using Internet technology to buy goods and services from a number of known or unknown suppliers.

> **E-informing.** Gathering and distributing purchasing information both from and to internal and external parties using Internet technology.
>
> **Web-based ERP (electronic resource planning).** Creating and approving purchasing requisitions, placing purchase orders, and receiving goods and services by using a software system based on Internet technology.
>
> **E-market sites.** Buying communities access favored suppliers' products and services, add products to shopping carts, create requisitions, seek approval, receive purchase orders, and process electronic invoices, integrating them into suppliers' supply chains and buyers' financial systems.
>
> **E-MRO (maintenance, repair, and operating).** The same as Web-based ERP except that the goods and services ordered are non-product-related MRO supplies.

THE BENEFITS AND LIMITATIONS OF E-PROCUREMENT

E-procurement has the ability of taking supply chain management to the next level, providing real-time intelligence to the suppliers as to the status of a customer's needs.

The Benefits of E-Procurement

By automating and streamlining the laborious routines of the purchasing function, purchasing professionals can focus on more strategic purchases, *achieving the following goals and benefits*:

> - Increasing the productivity of purchasing agents (providing them with more time and reducing job pressure), possibly reducing purchasing agents' overhead.
> - Lowering purchase prices through product standardization, reverse auctions, volume discounts, and consolidation of purchases.
> - Improving information flow and management (e.g., supplier's information and pricing information).
> - Minimizing the purchases made from noncontract vendors thereby reducing the risk of maverick buying and controlling inventory more effectively.
> - Improving the payment process and savings due to expedited payments (for sellers).
> - Establishing efficient, collaborative supplier relations due to high transparency and information sharing with business partners.
> - Improving the manufacturing cycle for suppliers.
> - Ensuring delivery on time, every time.
> - Slashing order-fulfillment and processing times by leveraging automation.
> - Reducing the skill requirements and training needs of purchasing agents.
> - Reducing the number of suppliers.
> - Streamlining the purchasing process, making it simple and fast (may involve authorizing requisitioners to perform purchases from their desktops, bypassing the procurement department).
> - Control parts' inventory more effectively at the buyers' end.
> - Streamlining invoice reconciliation and dispute resolution.
> - Reducing the administrative processing cost per order by as much as 90 percent by reducing purchasing overheads and brokerage fees (e.g., GM achieved a reduction from $100 to $10).
> - Finding new suppliers and vendors that can provide goods and services faster and/or less expensive (improved sourcing).

- Integrating budgetary controls into the procurement process.
- Minimizing human errors in the buying or shipping processes.
- Monitoring and regulating buying behavior.

The Limitations and Challenges of E-Procurement

Unfortunately there are some limitations and risks for e-procurement:

- The cost may be too high (TCO).
- It may be difficult to get suppliers to cooperate electronically.
- The system may be too complex (e.g., when it is traditional EDI, see Online Tutorial T11), sometimes involving different standards).
- It may be difficult to have internal and external integration.
- The technology needs to be updated frequently.

For additional benefits, see Saryeddine (2004). For software, see eprocurementsoftware. org. For the e-procurement process and implementation, see Online File W4.3. For an example of its use in government, see eprocurement.nc.gov.

Section 4.5 ▶ REVIEW QUESTIONS

1. Define the procurement process.
2. Describe the inefficiencies of traditional procurement.
3. List the major procurement methods.
4. Define e-procurement and list its goals.
5. List the major e-procurement segments and some activities in each.
6. List the benefits of e-procurement.

4.6 REVERSE AUCTIONS AT BUY-SIDE E-MARKETPLACES

A major method of e-procurement is using reverse auctions. Recall from our earlier discussion that a *reverse auction* is a tendering system in which suppliers are invited to bid on the fulfillment of an order and the lowest bid wins. In B2B usage of a reverse auction, a buyer may open an electronic market on its own server and invite potential suppliers to bid on the items the buyer needs. The "invitation" to such reverse auctions is a form or document called a **request for quote (RFQ)**. Traditional tendering usually implied one-time sealed bidding, whereas an e-reverse auction opens the auction to competing *sequential bidding*. See en.wikipedia.org/wiki/Reverse_auction for a comprehensive overview of reverse auctions.

Governments and large corporations frequently mandate reverse auctions, which may provide considerable savings. The electronic process is faster and administratively much less expensive. It also can benefit buyers in locating the cheapest possible products or services.

request for quote (RFQ)
The "invitation" to participate in a tendering (bidding) system.

CONDUCTING REVERSE AUCTIONS

As the number of reverse auction sites increases, suppliers will not be able to manually monitor all relevant tendering sites. This problem has been addressed with the introduction of online directories that list open RFQs. Another way to solve this problem is through the use of monitoring software agents. Software agents also can aid in the bidding process itself. Examples of agents that support the bidding process are auctionsniper.com and auctionflex.com.

Alternatively, third-party intermediaries may run the electronic bidding, as they do in forward auctions (e.g., see gxs.com). Auction sites such as govliquidation.com, liquidation.com, and asset-auctions.com also belong to this category. Conducting reverse auctions in B2B can be a fairly complex process. This is why an intermediary may be beneficial.

The reverse auction process is demonstrated in Exhibit 4.9. As shown in the exhibit, the first step is for the would-be buyer to post bid invitations. When bids arrive, contract and purchasing personnel for the buyer evaluate the bids and decide which one(s) to accept.

E-Tendering by Governments

Most governments must conduct tendering when they buy or sell goods and services. Doing this manually is slow and expensive. Therefore, many are moving to e-reverse auctions.

GROUP REVERSE AUCTIONS

To increase their bargaining power and get price discounts, companies, like individuals, can buy in a group.

B2B reverse auctions can be done in a private exchange or at an aggregator's site for a group of buying companies. Such *group reverse auctions* are popular in South Korea and usually involve large conglomerates. For example, the LG Group operates the LG MRO Auction for its members, and the Samsung Group operates iMarketKorea, as described in the closing case of this chapter. This practice is popular in the health care industry in the

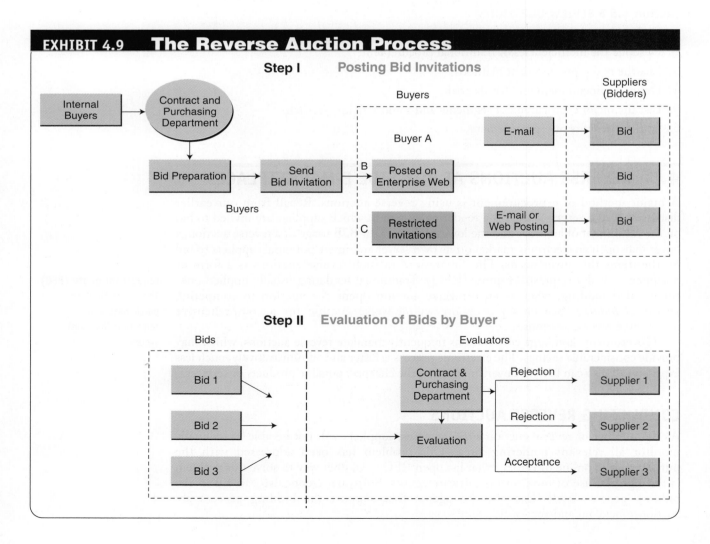

EXHIBIT 4.9   The Reverse Auction Process

United Kingdom, the United States, and other countries where hospitals are banding together to buy their supplies at a low price due to the high volume.

Section 4.6 ▶ REVIEW QUESTIONS

1. Describe the manual tendering system.
2. How do online reverse auctions work?
3. List the benefits of Web-based reverse auctions.
4. Describe group reverse auctions.

4.7 OTHER E-PROCUREMENT METHODS

Companies also have implemented other innovative e-procurement methods. Some common ones are described in this section.

AN INTERNAL PURCHASING MARKETPLACE: AGGREGATING SUPPLIERS' CATALOGS AND DESKTOP PURCHASING

Large organizations have many corporate buyers (purchasing agents) that are usually located in different departments and locations. For example, Bristol-Myers Squibb Corporation has more than 3,000 corporate buyers located all over the world. These agents buy from a large number of suppliers. The problem is that even if all purchases are made from approved suppliers, it is difficult to plan and control procurement when many buyers purchase individually in different locations. In many cases, to save time, buyers engage in *maverick buying*, which is, unplanned, emergency-type buying, and buyers usually pay more in such a case. In addition, an organization needs to control the purchasing budget. This situation is especially serious in government agencies and multinational entities where many buyers and large numbers of purchases are involved.

One effective solution to such a procurement problem is to aggregate the catalogs of all approved suppliers, combining them into a single internal electronic catalog. Prices are negotiated in advance or determined by a tendering, so that the buyers do not have to negotiate each time they place an order. By aggregating the suppliers' catalogs on the buyer's server, it is also easier to centralize and control all procurement. Such an aggregation of catalogs is also called an **internal procurement marketplace**.

internal procurement marketplace
The aggregated catalogs of all approved suppliers combined into a single internal electronic catalog.

Benefits of Internal Aggregated Catalogs

Corporate buyers can use search engines to look through internal aggregated catalogs to quickly find what they want; check prices, availability, and delivery times; and complete electronic requisition forms. Another advantage of such aggregation is that a company can reduce the number of suppliers it uses. For example, Caltex, a multinational oil company, reduced the number of its suppliers from over 3,000 to 800. Such reduction is possible because the central catalog enables buyers at multiple corporate locations to buy from remote, but fewer, sellers. Buying from fewer sellers typically increases the quantities bought from each, lowering the per unit price.

Example. MasterCard International aggregates more than 10,000 items from the catalogs of approved suppliers into an internal electronic catalog. The goal of this project is to consolidate buying activities from multiple corporate sites, improve processing costs, and reduce the supplier base. Payments are made with MasterCard's corporate procurement card. The system is used by all corporate buyers (about 3,000). MasterCard is continually adding suppliers and catalog content to the system (see MasterCard 2006).

Finally, internal catalogs allow for easy financial controls. As buyers make purchases, their account balances are displayed. Once the budget is depleted, the system will not allow new purchase orders to go through. Therefore, this model is especially popular in public institutions and government entities. The implementation of internal purchasing marketplaces is frequently done via a process known as *desktop purchasing*.

Desktop Purchasing

desktop purchasing
Direct purchasing from
internal marketplaces
without the approval of
supervisors and without
the intervention of a
procurement department.

Desktop purchasing implies purchasing by purchasing employees without the approval of supervisors and without the intervention of a procurement department. This is usually done by using a *purchasing card (P-card)* (see Chapter 10). Desktop purchasing reduces the administrative cost and the cycle time involved in purchasing urgently needed or frequently purchased items of small dollar value. This approach is especially effective for MRO purchases.

For example, Microsoft built its internal marketplace (MS Market) for the procurement of small items. The aggregated catalog that is part of MS Market is used by Microsoft employees worldwide, whose purchasing totals over $4 billion annually. The system has drastically reduced the role and size of the procurement departments at Microsoft.

The desktop-purchasing approach also can be implemented by partnering with external private exchanges. For instance, Samsung Electronics of South Korea, a huge global manufacturer and its subsidiaries, has integrated its iMarketKorea exchange (see the closing case at the end of this chapter) with the e-procurement systems of its buying agents. This platform can also be easily linked with *group purchasing*, which is described next.

GROUP PURCHASING

group purchasing
The aggregation of orders
from several buyers into
volume purchases so that
better prices can be
negotiated.

Many companies, especially small ones, are moving to *group purchasing*. With **group purchasing**, orders from several buyers are aggregated into volume purchases so that better prices can be negotiated. The model is similar to the one we described for B2C. Two models are in use: internal aggregation and external (third-party) aggregation.

Internal Aggregation of Purchasing Orders

Large companies, such as GE, spend billions of dollars on MROs every year. Company-wide orders, coming from GE companies and subsidiaries, for identical items are aggregated using the Web and are replenished automatically. Besides economies of scale (lower prices for large purchases) on many items, GE saves on the administrative cost of the transactions, reducing transaction costs from $50 to $100 per transaction to $5 to $10. With 5 million transactions annually at GE, this is a substantial savings.

External Aggregation for Group Purchasing

Many SMEs would like to enjoy quantity discounts but have difficulty finding others to join group purchasing to increase the procurement volume. Finding partners can be accomplished by an external third party such as BuyerZone (buyerzone.com), HIGPA (higpa.org), or the United Sourcing Alliance (usa-llc.com). The idea is to provide SMEs with better prices, selection, and services by aggregating demand online and then either negotiating with suppliers or conducting reverse auctions. The external aggregation/group purchasing process is shown in Exhibit 4.10. Groupon modified its business model so it can also be used in B2B group purchasing.

Several large companies, including large CPA firms, software companies such as EDS and Ariba, provide similar aggregation services, mainly to their regular customers. Yahoo! and AOL also offer such services. A key to the success of these companies is a critical mass of buyers. An interesting strategy is for a company to outsource aggregation to a third party. For example, energysolutions.com provides group buying in the energy industry.

Group purchasing, which started with commodity items such as MROs and consumer electronic devices, has now moved to services ranging from travel to payroll processing and Web hosting. Some aggregators use Priceline's "name-your-own-price" approach. Others try to find the lowest possible price (see njnonprofits.org/groupbuy.html). In many cases groups of buyers use reverse auctions to get lower prices.

BUYING AT SELLERS' SITES

Section 4.3 described how companies use e-distributors as a sales channel (recall the case of W.W. Grainger). When buying small quantities, purchasers often buy from an e-distributor. If they buy online, it is considered e-procurement. Another option for the e-procurement is to buy at a B2B exchange in one of several available methods. These methods are described in the next section. In all of these options, one may automate some activities in the process such as the generation of a purchasing order (e.g., see esker.com).

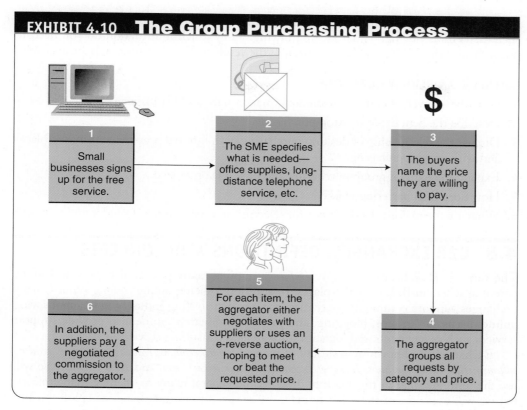

EXHIBIT 4.10   The Group Purchasing Process

1. Small businesses signs up for the free service.
2. The SME specifies what is needed—office supplies, long-distance telephone service, etc.
3. The buyers name the price they are willing to pay.
4. The aggregator groups all requests by category and price.
5. For each item, the aggregator either negotiates with suppliers or uses an e-reverse auction, hoping to meet or beat the requested price.
6. In addition, the suppliers pay a negotiated commission to the aggregator.

Purchasing Direct Goods

Until 2001, most B2B e-procurement implementations took place in the sell-side of large vendors (e.g., Cisco, Intel, and IBM) and in the procurement of MROs. In general, MROs comprise 20 to 50 percent of a company's purchasing budget. The remaining 50 to 80 percent of corporate purchases are for *direct materials* and *services*. Therefore, most companies would reap great benefits in using e-purchasing to acquire direct goods: Buyers would be able to purchase direct goods more quickly, reduce unit costs, reduce inventories, avoid shortages, and expedite their own production processes. Sourcing direct materials typically involves more complex transactions requiring negotiation and *collaboration* between the seller and buyer and greater information exchange. This leads us to collaborative commerce, which will be discussed in Chapters 5 and 11.

ACQUISITION VIA ELECTRONIC BARTERING

Bartering is the exchange of goods or services without the use of money. The basic idea is for a company to exchange its surplus for something that it needs. Companies can advertise their surpluses in classified ads and may find a partner to make an exchange, but in many cases a company will have little success in finding an exact match on its own. Therefore, companies usually ask an intermediary to help.

A bartering intermediary can use a manual search-and-match approach or it can create an electronic bartering exchange. With a **bartering exchange**, a company submits its surplus to the exchange and receives points of credit, which the company can then use to buy items that it needs. Popular bartering items are office space, idle facilities and labor, products, and even banner ads. Examples of bartering companies are u-exchange.com and itex.com.

SELECTING AN APPROPRIATE E-PROCUREMENT SOLUTION

Having many procurement methods, consultants, and software makes the selection of the right method(s) difficult. Ariba.com provides an innovative score sheet with which companies can evaluate vendors based on the described success factors. The success factors are grouped by cost reduction, increased agility, managing complete commerce, and fulfilling tactical requirements. The score sheet is available at eeiplatform.com/2539/ariba-selecting-the-right-eprocurement-solution.

bartering exchange
An intermediary that links parties in a barter; a company submits its surplus to the exchange and receives points of credit, which can be used to buy the items that the company needs from other exchange participants.

When organizations make such decisions, these decisions may be influenced by factors such as: Who is buying? What are you buying? How much information do you need to make the decision? What is the reputation of the vendors? What testimonials are available?

Section 4.7 ▶ REVIEW QUESTIONS

1. Describe a buyer-operated procurement marketplace and list its benefits.
2. Describe the benefits of desktop purchasing.
3. Discuss the relationship of desktop purchasing with internal procurement marketplaces and with group purchasing.
4. Explain the logic of group purchasing and how it is organized.
5. How does B2B bartering work?
6. What are the major considerations for selecting an e-procurement vendor and solution?

4.8 B2B EXCHANGES: DEFINITIONS AND CONCEPTS

The term *B2B exchange* or simply *exchange* implies many potential buyers and many potential sellers in B2B e-marketplaces. In addition to being online trading venues, many exchanges support community activities, such as distributing industry news, sponsoring online discussion groups, blogging, and providing research. Some also provide support services such as payments and logistics software and consulting services.

Exchanges are known by a variety of names: *e-marketplaces, trading exchanges, trading communities, exchange hubs, Internet exchanges, Net marketplaces,* and *B2B portals.* We will use the term *exchange* in this book to describe the general many-to-many e-marketplaces, but we will use some of the other terms in more specific contexts (e.g., see epiqtech.com/others-B2B-Exchanges.htm).

Despite their variety, all exchanges share one major characteristic: Exchanges are electronic trading-community meeting places for many sellers and many buyers, and possibly for other business partners, as shown in Exhibit 4.11. At the center of every exchange is a market maker that operates the exchange and, in some cases, may also own it.

Exchanges can be horizontal (serving many industries) or vertical serving one or few connected industries (e.g., see chemconnect.com and Online File W4.4).

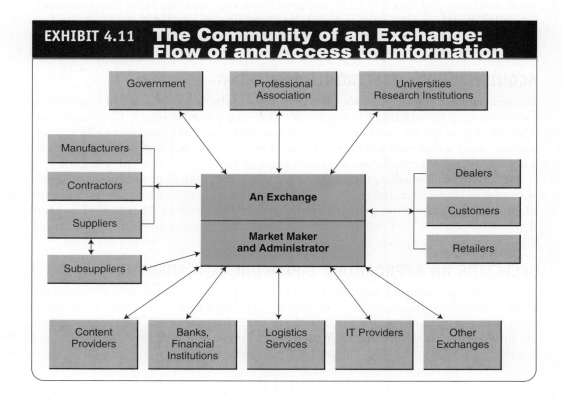

EXHIBIT 4.11 The Community of an Exchange: Flow of and Access to Information

In an exchange, just as in a traditional open-air marketplace, buyers and sellers can interact and negotiate prices and quantities. Generally, free-market economics rule the exchange community.

Functions of Exchanges

Exchanges have the following three major sets of functions:

1. **Matching buyers and sellers.** The matching of buyers and sellers includes such activities as:
   - Establishing product offerings
   - Aggregating and posting different products for sale
   - Providing price and product information
   - Organizing bids, bartering, and auctions
   - Matching supplier offerings with buyer preferences including qualification and registration
   - Enabling price and product comparisons
   - Supporting negotiations and agreements between buyers and suppliers
   - Providing directories of buyers and sellers
   - Maintaining security and anonymity

2. **Facilitating transactions.** Facilitating transactions by optimizing the purchasing and sales processes includes the following activities:
   - Providing the trading platform and mechanisms such as arranging logistics of delivering information, goods, or services to buyers
   - Providing catalogs and their management
   - Providing billing and payment information, insurance, logistics, and escrow
   - Defining terms and other transaction values including negotiation
   - Inputting searchable information including industry news
   - Granting exchange access to users and identifying company users eligible to use the exchange
   - Collecting transaction fees and providing the necessary software and its integration, including EDI, XML, etc.
   - Providing analysis and statistics
   - Registering and qualifying buyers and suppliers
   - Maintaining appropriate security over information and transactions
   - Arranging for group (volume) purchasing

3. **Maintaining exchange policies and infrastructure.** Maintaining institutional infrastructure involves the following activities:
   - Ascertaining compliance with commercial code, contract law, export and import laws, and intellectual property law for transactions made within the exchange
   - Maintaining technological infrastructure to support volume and complexity of transactions, providing auction management
   - Providing interface capability to standard systems of buyers and suppliers
   - Obtaining appropriate site advertisers and collecting advertising and other fees

Services Provided by Exchanges

Exchanges provide many services to buyers and sellers. The types of services offered depend on the nature of the exchange. For example, the services provided by a stock exchange are completely different from those provided by a steel or food exchange or by an intellectual property or patent exchange. However, most exchanges provide the services shown in Exhibit 4.12. For example, IBM administers an exchange for patents, and the Planet Eureka exchange matches ideas of investors with buyers.

OWNERSHIP OF B2B EXCHANGES

Exchanges, portals, and directories are usually owned by a third-party operator. This arrangement is preferred by both sellers and buyers. Alternatively, exchanges may be

EXHIBIT 4.12   Services in Exchanges

The Exchange and Its Services

Sellers

A
B
C
D
•
•
•

- Buyer–seller registration, qualification, coordination
- Catalog management (conversion, integration, maintenance)
- Communication/protocol translation (EDI, XML, CORBA)
- Sourcing—RFQ, bid coordination (product configuration, negotiation)
- Security, anonymity
- Software: groupware, workflow
- Integration with members' back-office systems
- Auction management
- News, information, industry analysis
- Support services (financing, payment, insurance, logistics, tax, escrow, order tracking)
- Administration—profiles, statistics, etc.

Buyers

X
Y
Z
•
•
•

owned by a few vary large sellers or buyers. This kind of arrangement is referred to as a *consortium*.

Third-Party Independent Marketplaces

Third-party exchanges are electronic intermediaries. The intermediary not only presents catalogs, but tries to *match* buyers and sellers and encourages them to make transactions by providing electronic trading floors and rooms.

Third-party exchanges are characterized by two contradicting properties. On the one hand, they are *neutral* because they do not favor either sellers or buyers. On the other hand, because they do not have a built-in constituency of sellers or buyers, they sometimes have a problem attracting enough buyers and for sellers to attain financial viability. Therefore, to increase their financial viability, these exchanges try to team up with some partners, such as large sellers or buyers, financial institutions that provide payment schemes, and logistics companies that fulfill orders.

A thriving example of a third-party exchange is Intercontinental Exchange.

Intercontinental Exchange (ICE). Intercontinental Exchange is an Internet-based B2B exchange that operates marketplaces that trade commodities contracts and over-the-counter (OTC) energy and commodity features as well as related derivative financial products. While the company's original focus was energy products, recent acquisitions have expanded its activity into "soft" commodities (sugar, cotton, and coffee), foreign exchange, and equity index futures. For details, see en.wikipedia.org/wiki/IntercontinentalExchange.

ICE is linked electronically to all its customers (members). Trading is global and is done 24/7. Currently, ICE is organized into three business lines:

▶ **ICE Markets.** Futures, options, and OTC markets. Energy futures are traded via ICE Futures Europe; soft commodity futures/options are handed by ICE Futures U.S.

▶ **ICE Services.** Electronic trade confirmations and education.

▶ **ICE Data.** Electronic delivery of market data, including real-time trades, historical prices, and daily indices.

ICE offers market participants a range of trading and risk management services globally:

1. Benchmark futures contracts

2. Risk management via a global central counterparty clearinghouse

3. Integrated access to global derivatives markets

4. Leading electronic trading platform

5. Transparency and regulation

6. Independence governance

Intercontinental Exchange owns several exchanges such as ChemConnect (see Online File W4.4).

Consortium Exchanges

A **consortium trading exchange (CTE)** is an exchange formed and operated by a group of major companies in one industry. They can be suppliers, buyers, or both. The major declared goal of CTEs (also called consortia) is to provide industry-wide transaction services that support buying and selling. These services include links to the participants' back-end processing systems as well as collaborative planning and design services. Examples of consortia exchanges are Avendra (hospitality industry), OceanConnect (shipping), and Elemica (chemical oil).

Note that some consortia have hundreds of members in the same industry (e.g., Elemica) and as such the consortia can be fairly independent in their operation. Also note that exchanges provide a unique combination of market information, industry expertise, e-commerce solutions, and an active network of trading partners.

consortium trading exchange (CTE)
An exchange formed and operated by a group of major companies in an industry to provide industry-wide transaction services.

DYNAMIC PRICING IN B2B EXCHANGES

The market makers in both vertical and horizontal exchanges match supply and demand in their exchanges, and this matching determines prices, which are usually *dynamic* and are based on changes in supply and demand. **Dynamic pricing** refers to a rapid movement of prices over time and possibly across customers. Stock exchanges are the prime example of dynamic pricing. Another good example of dynamic pricing occurs in auctions, where prices vary all the time.

The typical process that results in dynamic pricing in most exchanges includes the following steps:

dynamic pricing
A rapid movement of prices over time and possibly across customers, as a result of supply and demand matching.

1. A company posts a bid to buy a product or an offer to sell one.
2. An auction (forward or reverse) is activated.
3. Buyers and sellers can see the bids and offers but might not always see who is making them. Anonymity often is a key ingredient of dynamic pricing.
4. Buyers and sellers interact with bids and offers in real time. Sometimes buyers join together to obtain a volume discount price (group purchasing).
5. A deal is struck when there is an exact match between a buyer and a seller on price, volume, and other variables, such as location or quality.
6. The deal is consummated, and payment and delivery are arranged.

ADVANTAGES, LIMITATIONS, AND THE REVENUE MODEL OF EXCHANGES

Exchanges have several benefits, including making markets more efficient, providing opportunities for sellers and buyers to find new business partners, cutting the administrative costs of ordering MROs, and expediting trading processes. They also facilitate global trade and create communities of informed buyers and sellers.

Despite these benefits, beginning in 2001, exchanges started to collapse, and both buyers and sellers realized that they faced the risks of exchange failure or deterioration. In the case of exchange failure, the risk is primarily a financial one—of suddenly losing the market in which one has been buying and selling and, therefore, having to scramble to find a new exchange or to find buyers and sellers on one's own. In addition, finding a new place to trade is an operational risk. Buyers also risk potentially poor product performance and receipt of incomplete information from degraded exchanges, which is a risk the sellers may face, too. The potential benefits and risks of B2B exchanges for buyers and for sellers are summarized in Exhibit 4.13. As the exhibit shows, the benefits outnumber the risks.

Revenue Models

Exchanges, like all organizations, require revenue to survive. Therefore, an exchange's owners, whoever they are, must decide how they will earn revenue. The potential sources of revenue for exchanges are similar to those discussed in Chapter 1. They include: transaction fees, membership fees, service fees, advertising fees, and auction fees. In addition, exchanges offer software, computer services, management consultation, etc., for which they receive revenue from buyer and sellers.

EXHIBIT 4.13   Potential Gains and Risks in B2B Exchanges

	For Buyers	For Sellers
Potential gains	• One-stop shopping, huge • Search and comparison shopping • Volume discounts • 24/7 ordering from any location • Make one order from several suppliers • Huge, detailed information • Access to new suppliers • Status review and easy reordering • Community participation • Fast delivery • Less maverick buying • Better partner relationship management	• New sales channel • No physical store is needed • Reduced ordering errors • Sell 24/7 • Community participation • Reach new customers at little extra cost • Promote the business via the exchange • An outlet for surplus inventory • Can go global more easily • Efficient inventory management • Better partner relationship management
Potential risks	• Unknown vendors; may not be reliable • Loss of customer service quality (inability to compare all services)	• Loss of direct CRM and PRM • More price wars • Competition for value-added services • Must pay transaction fees (including on seller's existing customers) Possible loss of customers to competitors

Section 4.8 ▶ REVIEW QUESTIONS

1. Define B2B exchanges and list the various types of exchanges.
2. List the major functions of exchanges and the services they provide.
3. What is dynamic pricing? How does it work?
4. List the potential advantages, gains, limitations, and risks of exchanges to buyers.
5. List the major advantages and limitations to sellers.
6. List the major ownership types in B2B exchanges.
7. Define consortium trading exchanges.

4.9   B2B PORTALS AND DIRECTORIES

B2B marketplaces tend to have two complimentary facilities: portals and directories.

AN OVERVIEW

Portals as defined in Chapter 2 are gateways to information.

B2B portals
Information portals for businesses.

B2B portals are information portals for businesses. They usually include *directories* of products offered by each seller, lists of potential buyers and what they want, and other industry or general information. Buyers then visit sellers' sites to conduct their transactions. The portal may get a commission for referrals, or derive revenue from advertisements. Thus, information portals sometimes have a difficult time generating sufficient revenues. Because of this, many information portals are beginning to offer, for a fee, additional services that support trading, such as escrow and shipments. An example of a B2B portal is MyBoeingFleet (myboeingfleet.com), which is a Web portal for airplane owners, operators, and MRO operators. Developed by Boeing Commercial Aviation Services, MyBoeingFleet provides customers (primarily businesses) direct and personalized access to information essential to the operation of Boeing airplanes.

vortals
B2B portals that focus on a single industry or industry segment; "vertical portals."

Like exchanges, information portals may be horizontal (e.g., Alibaba.com, described later in this chapter), offering a wide range of information about different industries. Or they may be vertical, focusing on a single industry or industry segment. Vertical portals often are referred to as **vortals**. Portals can be limited to directory services as will be described later in this chapter. But let us first look at the various types of corporate portals.

CORPORATE (ENTERPRISE) PORTALS

Corporate portals facilitate collaboration with suppliers, customers, employees, and others. This section provides in-depth coverage of corporate portals, including their support of collaboration and business process management.

Corporate Portals: An Overview

A **corporate (enterprise) portal** is a gateway to a corporate website and other information sources that enables communication, collaboration, and access to company information. In contrast with public commercial portals such as Yahoo! and MSN, which are gateways to general information on the Internet, corporate portals provide a single point of access to information and applications available on the intranets and extranets of a specific organization. Companies may have separate portals for outsiders and for insiders. (For an overview of applications and vendors, see en.wikipedia.org/wiki/Enterprise_portal.)

Today's business environment demands a new approach—one where customers can ask or voice concerns and employees can answer in real time, improving service delivery and product innovation. The Web presence may be the only way customers and partners engage with companies and one of the primary ways employees get work done. Companies need to make those interactions count. With a good portal such as the IBM WebSphere Portal (combined with IBM Lotus collaboration software) companies can create a security-rich Web portal that delivers a single point of personalized interaction, promoting collaboration and communication, increasing customer loyalty, and giving competitive advantage. For a discussion, see 01.ibm.com/software/websphere/portal and IBM.com (2009).

Corporate portals offer employees, business partners, and customers an organized focal point for their interactions with the firm. Through the portal, these people can have structured and personalized access to information across large, multiple, and disparate enterprise information systems, as well as the Internet. A schematic view of a corporate portal is provided in Exhibit 4.14. It illustrates the features and capabilities of a typical portal.

corporate (enterprise) portal
A major gateway through which employees, business partners, and the public can enter a corporate website.

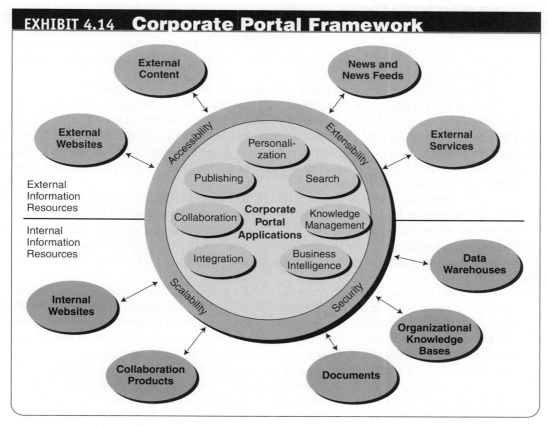

EXHIBIT 4.14 Corporate Portal Framework

Source: Compiled by N. Bolloju, City University of Hong Kong, from Aneja et al. (2000) and Koundadis (2000).

Examples

The following are examples of corporate portals.

P&G. The IT division of P&G developed a system for sharing documents and information over the company's intranet. The scope of this system later expanded into a global knowledge catalog to support the information needs of tens of thousands of its employees worldwide. Although the system helped provide required information, it also led to information overload. To solve this problem, P&G developed a corporate portal that provides personalized information to each employee. P&G's corporate portal provides P&G's employees with marketing, product, and strategic information and with industry news documents numbering more than 1 million Web pages. The corporate portal can be accessed through a Web browser without having to navigate through all of the different divisions' websites. Employees can gain access to the required information through customized preset views of various information sources and links to other up-to-date information.

DuPont. DuPont implemented an internal portal to organize millions of pages of scientific information stored in information systems throughout the company. The initial version of the portal was intended for daily use by more than 550 employees to record product orders, retrieve progress reports for research products, and access customer-tracking information. However, today, DuPont uses the portal for its 60,000 employees in 30 business units in 70 countries.

Staples. The corporate portal for Staples, an office supply company, was launched in February 2000. It was immediately used by the company's 3,000 executives, knowledge workers, and store managers; by 2006, most of its employees were registered users. The portal serves as the interface to Staples' business processes and applications. It offers e-mail, scheduling, headlines on articles about the competition, new product information, internal news, job postings, and newsletters. The portal is used by top management as well as by managers of contracts, procurement, sales and marketing, human resources, and retail stores and by the company's three B2B websites.

Types of Corporate Portals

Corporate portals are either generic or functional. Generic portals are defined by their audience (e.g., suppliers, employees). Functional portals are defined by the functionalities they offer. See BEA Systems (2006) for an interesting array of both generic and functional portal applications.

The following five generic types of portals can be found in organizations.

Portals for Suppliers and Other Partners. Using such portals, suppliers can manage the inventories of the products that they sell to each specific customer online. They can view what they sold to the portal owner and for how much. They can see the inventory levels of the portal owner, and reorder material and supplies when they see that an inventory level is low using vendor managed inventory strategy (see Chapter 5); they can also collaborate with corporate buyers and other staff.

An example of a partners' portal is that of Samsung Electronic America's Digital IT. The company must keep in touch with over 110,000 resellers and distributors. As part of its partner relationship management (PRM), Samsung developed a portal that enables it to personalize relationships with each partner (e.g., conduct promotions, provide special pricing, etc.). The portal helped to increase sales by 30 percent; related expenses dropped by 25 percent.

Customer Portals. Portals for customers serve businesses' customers. Customers can use these customer-facing portals to view products and services and to place orders, which they can later track. They can view their own accounts and see what is going on in almost real time. They can pay for products and services, arrange for warranties and deliveries, and much more. These portals include a personalized part (e.g., under "My account"). For example, UNICCO Service Company, a cleaning, maintenance, and other services company, established a B2B customer portal, myUNICCO (my.unicco.com), for about 200 business customers who use the portal to track work quality, invoice processing, and compliance with contracts. The portal integrates many disparate software applications. It is also used by about 1,500 employees.

Employee Portals. Such portals are used for training, dissemination of company news and information, discussion groups, and more. Employee portals also are used for self-service activities, mainly in the human resources area (e.g., reporting change of address forms, filing expense reports, registering for classes, and requesting tuition reimbursement). Employees' portals are sometimes bundled with supervisors' portals in what are known as *workforce portals* (e.g., Workbrain Enterprise Workforce Management, workbrain.com).

Example.   Shuffle Master is a casino equipment maker that depends on a large sales team that needed accurate and timely information. The company tried various enterprise software packages. However, they did not "talk" to each other; information was stale and not useful. The solution was an information portal for the employees built using Microsoft SharePoint server software that pulls data on demand from more than 60 databases, integrating them in one portal.

Executive and Supervisor Portals. These portals enable managers and supervisors to control the entire workforce management process—from budgeting to workforce scheduling. For example, Pharmacia (a Pfizer company) built a portal for its executives and managers worldwide, the Global Field Force Action Planner, which provides a single, worldwide view of the company's finances and performance. Business goals and sales figures are readily available on a consistent and transparent basis, allowing corporate management to evaluate and support field offices more effectively. Country managers also can share best practices with their peers and learn from other action plans, helping them to make better decisions.

Mobile Portals. Mobile portals are portals accessible via mobile devices, especially cell phones and PDAs. Many mobile portals contain noncorporate information such as in DoCoMo's i-mode. (See the description of i-mode in Chapter 6.) Large corporations have mobile corporate portals or they offer access to their regular portals from wireless devices.

mobile portals
Portals accessible via mobile devices, especially cell phones and PDAs.

The Functionalities of Portals

Whoever their audience, the functionalities of portals range from simple information portals that store data and enable users to navigate and query those data, to sophisticated collaborative portals that enable collaboration.

Several types of functional portals exist: *Business intelligence portals* are used mostly by middle- and top-level executives and analysts to conduct business analyses and decision-support activities. For example, a business intelligence portal might be used to generate ad hoc reports or to conduct a risk analysis. *Intranet portals* are used mostly by employees for managing fringe benefits and for self-training. *Knowledge portals* are used for collecting knowledge from employees and for disseminating collected knowledge. (For an example of a business intelligence and knowledge management portal, see Kesner 2003.)

information portals
Portals that store data and enable users to navigate and query these data.

collaborative portals
Portals that allow collaboration.

Corporate Portal Applications and Issues

Typical portal applications include knowledge bases and learning tools; business process support; customer-facing (frontline) sales, marketing, and services; collaboration and project support; access to data from disparate corporate systems; personalized pages for various users; effective search and indexing tools; security applications; best practices and lessons learned; directories and bulletin boards; identification of experts; news; and Internet access.

One of the most useful features of B2B is the directory that is displayed in the corporate portal or offered by an independent, third-party company.

Directory Services and Search Engines

The B2B landscape is huge, with hundreds of thousands of companies online. Therefore, specialized search engines are becoming a necessity in many industries due to the information glut. The most useful search engines are those concentrating on vertical searches. Examples of vertical search engines and their services can be found at globalspec.com. In contrast to vertical searches, products such as Google Search provide search capabilities on many topics within one enterprise or on the Web in general. But search engines by themselves may not be sufficient. Directories contain large amounts of information that can be searched manually or with the directory search engine.

Directory services can help buyers and sellers manage the task of finding specialized products, services, and potential partners. Here are some examples.

Thomas Register and ThomasNet

The *Thomas Register of American Manufacturers* is a directory of about 650,000 distributors, manufacturers, and service companies within 67,000 plus industrial categories in 28 countries and in 9 languages (in November 2010). The company stopped publishing its print products in 2006 due to declining circulations as Internet searches eroded the products' usability. Thomas then moved its database online as ThomasNet (thomasnet.com). ThomasNet has expanded the paper-based information to provide not only product and company information, but also online catalogs, computer-aided design (CAD) drawings, news, press releases, forums, and blogs. The company derives its revenue from advertisement. For details, see thomasnet.com/fag.html. A similar information-only service is provided by Manufacturing.net (manufacturing.net).

Alibaba.com

Another intermediary that started as a pure information portal offering a directory of companies, but now is moving toward becoming a trading exchange as well, is Alibaba.com (alibaba.com). Launched in 1999, Alibaba.com initially concentrated on China. Today it includes a large, robust community of international buyers and sellers who are interested in direct trade without an intermediary. Initially, the site was a huge posting place for classified ads. Alibaba.com is also discussed in Online Chapter 15. Today, Alibaba.com has several complementary markets, as described in Case 4.5.

CASE 4.5

EC Application

ALIBABA.COM

Alibaba.com Limited is a global leader in business-to-business (B2B) e-commerce and the flagship company of Alibaba Group. Founded in 1999, Alibaba.com makes it easy for millions of buyers and suppliers around the world to do business online through three marketplaces: an international trade marketplace (*alibaba.com*) for importers and exporters (in English); a Chinese marketplace (*alibaba.com.cn*) for domestic trade in China; and, through an associated company, a Japanese language marketplace (*alibaba.co.jp*), which facilitates trade to and from Japan. Together, its marketplaces form a community of 50 million registered users from more than 240 countries including over 100,000 suppliers in 6000 different categories. Headquartered in Hangzhou, Alibaba.com has offices in more than 40 cities across Greater China as well as in Europe and the United States. Alibaba.com offers trade information in both breadth and depth and matches buyers and sellers 24/7.

Alibaba China (*alibaba.com.cn*) is China's largest online Chinese-language marketplace for domestic trade. With more than 31.6 million registered users, Alibaba China is a trusted community of members who regularly meet, chat, search for products, and do business online. Trust and safety are fundamental to e-commerce. Paid suppliers on Alibaba.com must pass an authentication and verification process conducted by an independent third party. Only those that have been successfully verified by the third party can obtain an Alibaba "TrustPass." Information such as the company's business registration, name, address, and the applicant's relationship with the business entity are verified. Alibaba.com's experience shows that over 85 percent of its buyers prefer to do business with verified members only.

Alibaba International (*alibaba.com*) is an English-language global trade marketplace, serving mostly small and medium-sized enterprises (SMEs) in the international trade community. Alibaba.com offers a broad range of products and services to both suppliers and buyers. Basic features, such as standard supplier storefronts, product listings, and communication tools, are available for free. It also offers paid membership packages to verified suppliers. The subscription fee includes authentication and verification of the member's identity, which is performed by a third-party credit reporting agency. Alibaba.com is prospering from a business model dedicated to serving a vital, but disadvantaged, segment of China's economy: SMEs. Alibaba for China offers simple and efficient Internet solutions for such companies. Just as in the international marketplace, customers pay an annual subscription fee for membership, which entitles them to post trade offers and products online.

In addition, Alibaba Group owns and maintains the following:

▶ *Yahoo.china.cn* is a leading Chinese-language portal. It offers search tools, an interactive community, and one of the most popular e-mail services in China. In 2008, it acquired China's leading classified listing website, Koubei.com, which then became Yahoo! Koubei.

▶ *Taobao.com* is China's largest Internet retail site. Taobao has 120 million registered users, and more than 1.6 million

(continued)

sellers have opened stores on the site. The annual transaction volume on Taobao (gross merchandise volume, or GMV) reached nearly $15 billion in 2008, expanding at a 3-year compound annual growth rate of more than 150 percent and exceeding the largest retailer in China in transaction volume. Alimama (*alimama.com*), an online advertising exchange and affiliate network for more than 400,000 publishers in China, was merged into Taobao in 2008. Taobao offers services similar to LinkedIn and more.

▶ *Alipay.com* is China's leading third-party online payment platform. It enables individuals and businesses to execute payments online in a safe and secure manner. In August 2007, Alipay launched an online payment solution to help merchants worldwide sell directly to consumers in China, cooperating with more than 300 global retail brands and supporting transactions in 12 major foreign currencies.

▶ *Alisoft.com* offers an Internet-based business management solution. It develops, markets, and delivers Internet-based business management software to SMEs in China. It commands more than 40 percent of the Software as a Service (SaaS) model, offering enterprise management tools, such as e-mail, customer support software, and information management software, and basic financial management tools, such as invoicing and bookkeeping.

To understand the capabilities of Alibaba.com, we need to explore its marketplace (take the online multimedia tour!).

The Database

The center of Alibaba.com is its huge database, which is basically a horizontal information portal with offerings in a wide variety of product categories. The portal is organized into 44 major industry categories (as of 2009), including agriculture, apparel and fashion, automobiles, and toys. Each industry category is further divided into subcategories (over 700 in total). For example, the toy category includes items such as dolls, electrical pets, and wooden toys. Each subcategory includes classified postings organized into four groups: sellers, buyers, agents, and cooperation. Each group may include many companies. The postings are fairly short. Note that in all cases a user can click an ad for details. Some categories have thousands of product postings; therefore, a vertical search engine is provided to users to facilitate them in redefining the search words. The search engine works by country, type of advertiser, and age of the postings.

Reverse Auctions and Negotiations

Alibaba.com also allows buyers to post RFQs. Would-be sellers can then send bids to the buyer, conduct negotiations, and accept a purchase order when one is agreed upon (all via the exchange). The RFQ process can be fully automated, partially automated, or done entirely manually. (To see how the process works, go to "My trade activity" and take the tour, initiate a negotiation, and issue a purchase order.)

Features and Services

Alibaba.com provides the following major community features: free e-mail, instant messenger Trade Manager, Trust Service, FAQs, tutorials for traders, free e-mail alerts, news (basically related to importing and exporting), trade show information, legal information, arbitration, forums and discussion groups, trade trends, and so on. In addition, a member can create a personalized company Web page as well as a "product showroom"; members also can post their own marketing leads (where to buy and sell). Premium membership packages also provide premium storefronts, priority listing, dedicated training, and customer service, as well as a range of value-added services, including Product Showcase (private product showroom), Traffic Analyzer™, Buyer GPS™, Biz Trends, Buyer Country Locator, and company e-mail accounts. Additional services are added to increase the company's revenue stream.

The Revenue Model

In order to attract buyers, sourcing on Alibaba.com is always free. Although it offers a number of tools and services for free, Alibaba.com offers a paid membership service to suppliers. Income is generated through paid memberships and value-added services. Alibaba.com competes with several global exchanges that provide similar services (e.g., see *asialinks.com* and *globalsources.com*).

In November 2008, Alibaba.com launched its new entry-level product—the Gold Supplier Starter Pack—designed for exporters that plan to shift their business online to achieve efficiencies in the current economic environment. The product, priced at $2,900 per year, offers basic storefront display and unlimited product listings. The original premium membership has been updated to enjoy more premium website features, such as additional Virtual Showrooms, which will enable suppliers to substantially increase the visibility of their key products. Companies must obtain third-party authentication and verification under the Quality Supplier Program before they can purchase the Gold Supplier Starter Pack. Alibaba.com was strong enough to sustain losses until 2003, when it made a $12 million profit. Since then, profits have grown very rapidly. Total revenue for 2010 was $833.5 million, a 43 percent increase over 2009.

Social Networks

Alibaba is crafting social-networking platforms specifically to complement two of its core operations. The beta version of a website with Facebook-style applications and a Twitter-style feed is being added to *taobao.com*, Alibaba's auction and retail website with 120 million registered users. A more professional platform similar to LinkedIn is being added to Alibaba.com, the group's business-to-business e-commerce operation.

The entertainment-based platform for Taobao in particular combines standard social-networking functions with original features that promote online purchases. It goes a step beyond efforts to mix e-commerce and social networking using the platform of companies like Amazon.com and Facebook.

(continued)

CASE 4.5 *(continued)*

Going Public with an IPO

Alibaba.com's founder, Jack Ma, took the company public in November 2007, and used the $1.7 billion collected from the IPO to deploy its business model on a full scale in order to show that e-commerce in China can make money. The influx of capital allowed Alibaba to continue building its customer base by offering the bulk of its services at no charge. And that may prove a winning strategy.

Sources: Compiled from Chandler (2007), Fletcher (2009), *alibaba.com* (accessed November 2010), Alibaba.com (2009a), and Alibaba.com (2009b).

Questions

1. Why did hundreds of large corporations rush to invest in Alibaba's IPO?
2. Trace Alibaba.com's revenue sources.
3. List the major services provided by Alibaba.com.
4. Why is it using social networking?
5. Some say that Alibaba will outshine Amazon.com and eBay. Why?

Section 4.9 ▶ REVIEW QUESTIONS

1. Define B2B portals.
2. Distinguish a vortal from a horizontal portal.
3. List the major types of corporate portals.
4. Describe some directory services in B2B.

4.10   B2B IN WEB 2.0 AND SOCIAL NETWORKING

Although a large number of companies conduct social networking that targets individual consumers (B2C), there is also some activity in the B2B arena. However, the potential in B2B is large, and new applications are added daily. The opportunities of B2B social networking depend on the companies' goals and the perceived benefits and risks involved (search b2bonline.com for more information).

E-COMMUNITIES IN B2B

B2B applications may involve many participants: buyers and sellers, service providers, industry associations, and others. In such cases, the B2B market maker needs to provide community services, such as chat rooms, bulletin boards, and possibly personalized Web pages.

E-communities are connecting personnel, partners, customers, and any combination of the three. E-communities offer a powerful resource for e-businesses to leverage online discussions and interaction in order to maximize innovation and responsiveness (e.g., see Case 4.5 on Alibaba.com). It is therefore beneficial to study the tools, methods, and best practices of building and managing B2B e-communities. Although the technological support of B2B e-communities is basically the same as for any other online community (see Chapter 2), the nature of the community itself and the information provided by the community are different.

B2B e-communities are mostly communities of transactions and, as such, members' major interests are trading and business-related information gathering. Most of the communities are associated with vertical exchanges; therefore, their needs may be fairly specific. However, it is common to find generic services such as classified ads, job vacancies, announcements, industry news, and so on. Communities promote partnering. The newest variation of these communities is the business-oriented or professional social networks such as LinkedIn, which are discussed in Chapters 2 and 7.

THE OPPORTUNITIES OF SOCIAL COMMERCE IN B2B

Companies that use B2B social networking may experience the following advantages:

▶ Discover new business partners.
▶ Enhance their ability to learn about new technologies, competitors, and the business environment.

> Find more sales prospects.

> Solve problems by using the "answer" function in LinkedIn and other networks.

> Improve participation in industry association activities (including lobbying).

> Create brand awareness.

> Create buzz about upcoming product releases.

> Advertise products and services and promote new ones.

> Drive traffic to their online Web properties in hopes of enticing users to engage with their sites, products, or solutions. Also word of mouth may increase traffic.

> Create social communities to encourage discussions among business partners (e.g., suppliers) about their products and/or act as a feedback mechanism about their products/services (for business improvements).

> Use social networks, such as Facebook and LinkedIn, to recruit new talent. Some HR departments are using social networks to obtain more insight into potential new hires.

For more opportunities, see Schaefer (2010).

More uses of B2B social networking are seen in *enterprise social networking*, which are private social networks within the enterprise. We cover the topic briefly in Chapter 7.

THE USE OF WEB 2.0 TOOLS IN B2B

More companies are using blogs, wikis, RSS feeds, video ads, and other tools in B2B EC. For example, Eastern Mountain Sports uses blogs, RSS feeds, and wikis to communicate and collaborate with suppliers and distributors (see the opening case in Chapter 2). Thousands of other companies are using (or experimenting with) these tools. For a study on the utilization of Web 2.0 tools in B2B EC, see New Media Institute (2006). On using YouTube for B2B, see Bannan (2010); and on using Twitter, see Maddox (2010b).

SOCIAL NETWORKING IN B2B

The importance of social networks has yet to be fully realized in the B2B marketplace. According to a 2006 study by KnowledgeStorm, 77 percent of respondents had little or no interaction with social networks (KnowledgeStorm 2006). Of the social networks frequented by business and EC professionals, LinkedIn (linkedin.com) was the most well known (see Case 7.1, p. 373). Does this mean that B2B buyers and sellers are antisocial? Well, not really; it just means that because social networks are still fairly new they have not been used much for B2B applications. It may also indicate that there is a need for more B2B social network sites. Also, it is difficult to demonstrate tangible benefits from the use of B2B social networks, so firms may be reluctant to invest in them.

Businesses can use B2B social networking to improve knowledge sharing, collaboration, and feedback. Furthermore, social networking sites may also prove beneficial in aiding troubleshooting and problem-solving efforts. Companies (especially small ones), are using LinkedIn's Answers, for example, for problem solving. B2B participants need to look into social networking as part of their overall EC strategy, otherwise they may miss an opportunity to reach the B2B audience and differentiate themselves from the competition.

By the end of 2010, social networking is playing a much more important role in B2B. According to a 2010 study by Regus, both small and large businesses are using social networks quite successfully to find and retain new business (reported by *BizReport* 2010). A few highlights of the study include:

> 50 to 75 percent of companies globally use social networks for various networking functions.

> 40 percent of businesses worldwide have found new customers via social networks.

> 27 percent of companies include social networking activity to both acquire and retain customers in the marketing budget.

The main uses of social networks are: Keeping in contact with business contacts; meeting with special interest groups; learning useful business intelligence; organizing, managing, and connecting with customer groups.

According to eMarketer (2008), B2B advertising on social networking sites will grow from $15 million in 2007 to $240 millions in 2012 (about a 13-fold increase). The same report attempted to answer the following key questions:

▶ How much will marketers spend on social network advertising aimed at a business audience?

▶ What types of B2B advertising can businesses do on social network sites?

▶ Why are companies creating social networks to market to business customers, vendors, distributors, and channel partners?

▶ What are the challenges of developing such networks?

Now companies are using social media analysis in B2B (see Booker 2010).

EXAMPLES OF OTHER ACTIVITIES OF B2B SOCIAL NETWORKS

The following are examples of some social-network-oriented B2B activities:

▶ **American Express-sponsored Business Travel Social Network.** In October 2008, American Express launched an online social network, Business Travel ConneXion (BTX, businesstravelconnexion.com), for the corporate travel industry. American Express hopes that BTX will be a dynamic network that will harness the collective intelligence of the business industry. It is designed for travel professionals who wish to become more informed and better equipped to optimize their travel and entertainment programs. The site offers an array of tools—blogs, photo albums, videos, galleries, community calendars, mobile alerts, a friends list, and the ability to form subgroups—to leverage the power of social networking. For details, see Greengard (2008).

▶ **Corporate profiles on social networks.** LinkedIn and Facebook include substantial information on companies and their individual employees. In fact, employees' profiles can be part of a company's brand. For example, IBM currently has approximately 120,000 employees registered on LinkedIn; Microsoft has around 35,000 as of November 2010. In addition, some sites feature company profiles, with comments by employees and customers.

Success Stories

BtoB's Interactive Marketing Guide (available at btobonline.com) provides the following example of successful applications:

▶ **Arketi Group.** Created and sponsors a B2B marketing community on LinkedIn, and is known for its 500 ongoing discussions.

▶ **Cisco Systems.** Uses Facebook to aggregate Twitter, Flickr, YouTube, blogs, and RSS feeds from one interface. With about 40,000 fans, daily postings include vlogs from the CEO and social events (e.g., Halloween photos).

▶ **Hewlett-Packard Co. (HP).** The company uses *viral videos* (Chapters 7 and 8) to promote renewals of Care Pack Service agreements. A three-video series follows Alex, an IT guy, and his interaction via science fiction with the renewal process.

▶ **Reed Business Information.** The company uses LinkedIn-generated content in a community of "Automation and Control Engineering." With about 5,000 members globally, the community focuses on members' needs for specific expertise and members' advice. Over 100 ongoing discussion groups encourage engagement and participation.

▶ **Deloitte.** The company uses Facebook as a brand-building strategy to shift its image from an old accounting firm to a technology-based innovator. Over 25,000 fans are engaged in discussions of how better to serve customers' needs.

STRATEGY FOR B2B SOCIAL NETWORKING

Gaffney (2007) makes the following strategy suggestions for B2B social networking:

> ▶ **Participate.** Executives should become bloggers and social media participants. For example, an executive should create a LinkedIn profile (or another community) and post a few blog entries on industry-specific websites.
>
> ▶ **Monitor.** Social media monitoring is a big business. If you decide not to go with an automated report on how your company is mentioned in social media, assign an internal team to report on it.
>
> ▶ **Use existing applications.** Companies can find their own software applications to create a private B2B network or work with one of the public networks.

Eventually, companies will be able to use social networking more efficiently and decide what information should be made available to the entire network or to a more focused section of it. Companies want their employees to be more engaged on a long-term basis, which is precisely the direction in which enterprise social networking is moving. Success stories of the following five companies: SAP, United Linen (a small laundry service), Forrester Research, Kinaxis, and Expert Laser services are discussed by Pergolino (2010). These companies use mostly blogs, social networks, and Twitter to conduct media campaigns (e.g., using blogs and videos). Additional strategy tips are provided by Gillin (2010).

THE FUTURE OF B2B SOCIAL NETWORKING

Products such as Google's OpenSocial may spark interest from the B2B community with regard to social networking. OpenSocial is a programming standard that lets developers create applications that can run on a wide range of social networking platforms. More important, OpenSocial promises users the choice of which social networks they want to use for their applications. Marketers are working now toward social and search integration. For the results of a study on this topic, see Maddox (2010a).

Businesses must embrace social networking in order to understand the needs and wants of their prospects and clients. Establishing trust with business partners and generating brand awareness will force B2B companies to become more involved in social commerce in general and social marketing in particular.

Section 4.10 ▶ REVIEW QUESTIONS

1. List some of the opportunities for corporations to use social networking in B2B EC.
2. What are some of the benefits of social networking for B2B EC?
3. List some Web 2.0 social software B2B applications.
4. Describe some of the applications of B2B in social networks.
5. Discuss the strategies for B2B social networking.
6. Define e-communities in B2B.

4.11 B2B INTERNET MARKETING

B2B marketing refers to marketing by manufacturers and wholesalers along the sell-side of the supply chain.

Major differences exist between B2B and B2C EC with respect to the nature of demand and supply and the trading process. Here we discuss the corporate purchaser's buying behavior and some of the marketing and advertising methods used in B2B EC. More discussion of this topic is provided in Chapter 8 and in blog.marketo.com that provides tutorials and tips as a guide to successful B2B social marketing, and B2B marketing optimization guides. For meeting and managing B2B demand, see "Creating and

B2B marketing
Marketing by manufacturers and wholesalers along the sell-side of the supply chain.

Managing Demand in B2B Marketing," a white paper from Demandbase.com (available for download at demandbase.com/white_papers.html).

ORGANIZATIONAL BUYER BEHAVIOR

Although the number of organizational buyers is much smaller than the number of individual consumers, their transaction volumes are by far larger, and the terms of negotiations and purchasing are more complex. In addition, the purchasing process itself usually is more complex than the purchasing process of an individual customer. Also, the organization's buyer may be a group. In fact, decisions to purchase expensive items are usually made by a group. Therefore, factors that affect individual consumer behavior and organizational buying behavior are quite different.

A Behavioral Model of Organizational Buyers

The behavior of an organizational buyer is described by the model illustrated in Exhibit 4.15. A B2B module includes the organization's purchasing guidelines and constraints (e.g., contracts with certain suppliers) and the purchasing system used. Interpersonal influences, such as authority, and the possibility of group decision making must be considered.

THE MARKETING AND ADVERTISING PROCESSES IN B2B

The marketing and advertising processes for businesses differ considerably from those used for selling to individual consumers. For example, traditional (offline) B2B

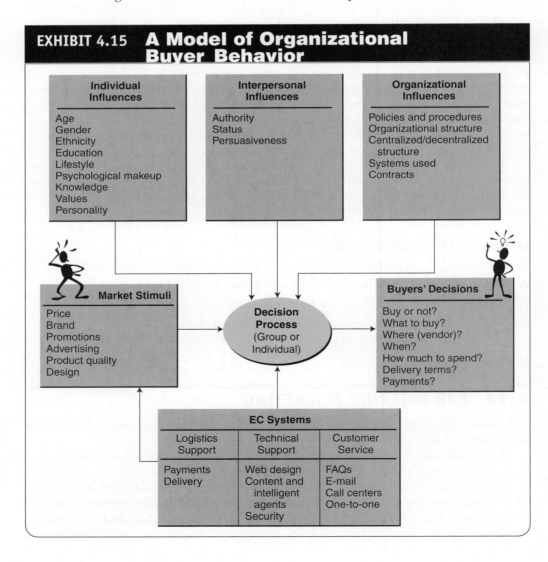

EXHIBIT 4.15 A Model of Organizational Buyer Behavior

marketers use methods such as physical trade shows, advertisements in industry magazines, paper catalogs, and salespeople who call on existing customers and potential buyers.

In the digital world, these approaches may not be effective, feasible, or economical. Therefore, organizations use a variety of online methods to reach business customers. Popular methods include online directory services, matching services, the marketing and advertising services of exchanges, cobranding or alliances, affiliate programs, online virtual trade shows, online marketing services (e.g., see digitalcement.com), or e-communities. Several of these methods are discussed next.

METHODS FOR B2B ONLINE MARKETING

When a B2C niche e-tailer seeks to attract its audience of skiers, musicians, or cosmetic customers, it may advertise in traditional media targeted to those audiences, such as magazines or television shows, or use Internet ads. The same is true in B2B when trade magazines and directories are used. But when a B2B vendor wants to grow by adding new customers or products, it may not have a reliable, known advertising channel. How can it reach new customers?

Targeting Customers

A B2B company, whether a provider of goods or services, an operator of a trading exchange, or a provider of digital real-time services, can contact all of its targeted customers individually when they are part of a well-defined group. For example, to attract companies to an exchange for auto supplies, one might use information from industry trade association records or industry magazines to identify potential customers.

Another method of bringing new customers to a B2B site is through an affiliation service, which operates just as a B2C affiliate program does. A company pays a small commission every time the affiliate company "drives traffic" to the payer's site.

An important part of any marketing effort is advertising. Several of the advertising methods that will be presented in Chapter 8 are applicable both to B2C and B2B. For example, an ad server network provider, such as DoubleClick (doubleclick.com, now a Google company), can be used to target customers in B2B2C EC.

AFFILIATE PROGRAMS, MARKET RESEARCH, AND DATA MINING

Several additional methods and approaches can be used in B2B marketing and advertising. Here we examine three popular methods: affiliate programs, infomediaries, and online data and text mining services.

Affiliate Programs

B2C affiliation services were introduced in Chapter 1. There are several types of affiliate programs. With the simplest type, which is used extensively in B2C EC, an affiliate puts a banner of another vendor, such as amazon.com, on its site. When a consumer clicks the vendor's banner, the consumer is taken to that vendor's website, and a commission is paid to the affiliate if the customer makes a purchase or just for clicking on the vendor site. Examples include the Netflix opening case in Chapter 8. The same method works for B2B.

With B2B, additional types of affiliate programs are possible. Schaeffer Research (schaeffersresearch.com), for example, offers financial institutions a content alliance program in which content is exchanged so that all obtain some free content. For more on B2B affiliate programs, see en.wikipedia.org/wiki/Affiliate_marketing.

B2B Market Research

One of the major objectives of market research is to provide tactics and strategies for EC advertising, as described in Chapter 8. For the use of data mining in B2B market research, see Online File W8.4.

A final note: In marketing we use the classical 4Ps (product, price, place and promotion). Dunay (2010) argues that the 4Ps are good mostly for B2C. For B2B, he proposes 4Cs: content, connection, communication, and conversion.

Section 4.11 ▶ REVIEW QUESTIONS

1. Distinguish between organizational buyers and individual consumers.
2. Describe B2B EC marketing and advertising methods.
3. Explain how affiliate programs and data mining work in B2B EC.
4. What can market research and data mining do to help in B2B?

MANAGERIAL ISSUES

Some managerial issues related to this chapter are as follows.

1. **Which B2B model(s) should we use for e-procurement?** When evaluating the various upstream B2B models, we need to match the suitable e-procurement goals with solution strategies depending upon whether the purchases are direct material or indirect material. Four typical goals that should be distinguished are organizational operational efficiency, minimum price, minimum inventory and stock-outs, and low purchase administrative cost. For each of these goals, the appropriate solution and system should be designed accordingly. Many third-party portal sites have provided mismatched solutions and failed their business. Handling many small and medium suppliers that do not have sophisticated systems is a challenging goal.

2. **Which B2B model(s) should we use for online B2B sales?** A key issue for B2B sales is how to reconcile with the multiple buyers who adopt different EDI and ERP systems. The Enterprise Application Integration (EAI) solution transforms the internal data of multiple EDI formats used by different buyers. The integration of various types of EDI standards with ERP solutions is another challenge to overcome.

   In addition to contract management, B2B marketers use auctions, liquidations, and social networks to increase sales.

3. **Which exchange should we join?** One of the major concerns of management is selecting exchanges in which to participate. At the moment, most exchanges are not tightly connected, so there may be a substantial start-up effort and cost for joining multiple exchanges. This is a multicriteria decision situation that should be analyzed carefully. A related issue is whether to join a third-party public exchange or a consortium or to create a private exchange. Companies must take very seriously the issues listed in Exhibit 4.13 (p. 210). The risks of joining an exchange must be carefully weighed against the expected benefits. Joining an exchange may require a restructuring of the internal supply chain, which may be expensive and time consuming. Therefore, this possibility must be taken into consideration when deciding whether to join an exchange.

4. **Which solutions and vendor(s) should we select?** Vendors normally develop and deploy the B2B applications, even for large organizations. Two basic approaches to vendor selection exist: (1) Select a primary vendor such as IBM, Microsoft, or Oracle. This vendor will use its software and procedures and add partners as needed. (2) Use an integrator that will mix and match existing products and vendors to create "the best of breed" for your needs. See Chapter 13 for details.

5. **What is the organizational impact of B2B?** The B2B system will change the role of the procurement department by redefining the role and procedures of the department. The function of the procurement department may be completely outsourced. A procurement policy portfolio is necessary to balance strategic sourcing items and spot purchasing items and to design a supply relationship management system.

6. **What are some ethical issues in B2B?** Because B2B EC requires the sharing of proprietary information, business ethics are a must. Employees should not be able to access unauthorized areas in the trading system, and the privacy of trading partners should be protected both technically and legally. Control of partner relationship management is important in this regard.

7. **How shall we manage the suppliers?** Global suppliers can be evaluated periodically with regard to price, quality, and timely delivery. A supplier relationship management system (see Online Tutorial T1) can support the evaluation of suppliers. Management must decide whether to negotiate a quantity discount or to compel the suppliers to compete in reverse auctions.

8. **Which type of social network should we use— private (proprietary) or public?** There are successes and failures in both types. Some large companies have both types (e.g., Toyota, Coca-Cola, Disney). In most cases it is better to go with public networks such as LinkedIn and Facebook (see the discussion in Chapter 7).

9. **Can we use B2C marketing methods and research in B2B?** Some methods can be used with adjustments; others cannot. B2B marketing and marketing research requires special methods (see Chapter 8).

SUMMARY

In this chapter, you learned about the following EC issues as they relate to the chapter's learning objectives.

1. **The B2B field.** The B2B field comprises e-commerce activities between businesses. B2B activities account for 77 to 95 percent of all EC. B2B e-commerce can be done by using different models.

2. **The major B2B models.** The B2B field is very diversified. It can be divided into the following segments: sell-side marketplaces (one seller to many buyers), buy-side marketplaces (one buyer from many sellers), and trading exchanges (many sellers to many buyers). Each segment includes several business models. Intermediaries play an important role in some B2B models.

3. **The characteristics and models of sell-side marketplaces.** Sell-side B2B EC is the online direct sale by one seller (a manufacturer or an intermediary) to many buyers. The major technology used is electronic catalogs, which also allow for efficient customization, configuration, and purchase by customers. In addition, forward auctions are becoming popular, especially for liquidating surplus inventory. Sell-side auctions can be conducted from the seller's own site or from an intermediary's auction site. Sell-side activities can be accompanied by extensive customer service. E-commerce allows customization of products and services in personalized catalogs.

4. **Sell-side intermediaries.** The role of intermediaries in B2B primarily is to provide value-added services to manufacturers and business customers. Intermediaries can also aggregate buyers and conduct auctions. Intermediaries can also be the distributors that aggregate catalogs of many sellers.

5. **The characteristics of buy-side marketplaces and e-procurement.** Today, companies are moving to e-procurement to expedite purchasing, save on item and administrative costs, and gain better control over the purchasing process. Major procurement methods are reverse auctions (bidding system); buying from storefronts and catalogs; negotiation; buying from an intermediary that aggregates sellers' catalogs; internal marketplaces and group purchasing; desktop purchasing; buying in exchanges or industrial malls; and e-bartering. E-procurement offers the opportunity to achieve significant cost and time savings.

6. **B2B reverse auctions.** A reverse auction is a tendering system used by buyers to get better prices from suppliers competing to fulfill the buyers' needs. Auctions can be done on a company's website or on a third-party auction site. Reverse auctions can dramatically lower buyers' costs, both product costs and the time and cost of the tendering process.

7. **B2B aggregation and group purchasing.** Increasing the exposure and the bargaining power of companies can be done by aggregating either the buyers or the sellers. Aggregating suppliers' catalogs into an internal marketplace gives buying companies better control of purchasing costs. In desktop purchasing, buyers are empowered to buy from their desktops up to a set limit without the need for additional approval. They accomplish this by viewing internal catalogs with pre-agreed-upon prices with the suppliers. Industrial malls specialize in one industry (e.g., computers) or in industrial MROs. They aggregate the catalogs of thousands of suppliers. A purchasing agent can place an order at an industrial mall, and shipping is arranged by the supplier or the mall owner. Buyer aggregation through group purchasing is very popular because it enables SMEs to get better prices on their purchases. In addition to direct purchasing, items can be acquired via bartering.

8. **Other procurement methods.** Common procurement methods include: internal marketplaces and desktop purchasing, buying at e-auctions, group purchasing, buying from distributors, bartering, and buying at exchanges.

9. **Exchanges defined and the major types of exchanges.** Exchanges are e-marketplaces that provide a trading platform for conducting business among many buyers, many sellers, and other business partners. Types of public e-marketplaces include B2B third-party trading exchanges, and consortium trading exchanges. Exchanges may be vertical (industry oriented) or horizontal. They may target systematic buying (long-term relationships) or spot buying (for fulfilling an immediate need).

10. **B2B portals.** B2B portals are gateways to B2B community-related information. They are usually of a vertical structure, in which case they are referred to as *vortals*. Some B2B portals offer product and vendor information and even tools for conducting trades, sometimes making it difficult to distinguish between B2B portals and trading exchanges.

11. **Third-party exchanges.** Third-party exchanges are owned by an independent company and usually operate in highly fragmented markets. They are open to anyone and, therefore, are considered public exchanges. They try to maintain neutral relations with both buyers and sellers.

12. **B2B in Web 2.0 and social networks.** Although there are considerable B2C social networking activities, B2B activities are just beginning. A major success has been seen in the use of blogs and wikis to collaborate with suppliers and customers. Large companies use social networking to create and foster business relationships. Smaller companies use social networking for soliciting

experts' opinions. Other companies use it for finding business partners, cultivating business opportunities, recruiting employees, and finding sales leads.

13. **B2B Internet marketing methods and organizational buyers.** Marketing methods and marketing research in B2B differ from those of B2C. A major

reason for this is that the buyers must observe organizational buying policies and frequently conduct buying activities as a committee. Organizations use modified B2C methods such as affiliate marketing. Buying decisions in B2B may be determined by a group, and purchasing is controlled by rules and constraints.

KEY TERMS

B2B marketing	219	E-procurement (electronic procurement)	197	Online intermediary	183
B2B portals	210			Partner relationship management (PRM)	187
Bartering exchange	205	Exchanges (trading communities, trading exchanges)	181	Procurement management	196
Business-to-business e-commerce (B2B EC)	181	Group purchasing	204	Public e-marketplaces	182
Buy-side e-marketplace	196	Horizontal marketplaces	184	Request for quote (RFQ)	201
Collaborative portals	213	Indirect materials	184	Sell-side e-marketplace	188
Company-centric EC	181	Information portals	213	Spot buying	183
Consortium trading exchange (CTE)	209	Internal procurement marketplace	203	Strategic (systematic) sourcing	183
Corporate (enterprise) portal	211	Maverick buying	196	Supplier relationship management (SRM)	187
Desktop purchasing	204	Mobile portals	213	Vertical marketplaces	184
Direct materials	184	MRO (maintenance, repair, and operation)	184	Vortals	210
Dynamic pricing	209				

DISCUSSION QUESTIONS

1. Explain how a catalog-based sell-side e-marketplace works and describe its benefits.

2. Discuss the advantages of selling through online auctions over selling from catalogs. What are the disadvantages?

3. Discuss the role of intermediaries in B2B. Distinguish between buy-side and sell-side intermediaries.

4. Discuss and compare all of the mechanisms that group-purchasing aggregators can use.

5. Should desktop purchasing only be implemented through an internal marketplace?

6. Suppose a manufacturer uses an outside company to deliver material purchases or finished products. How can the manufacturer use an exchange for this job?

7. Compare and contrast a privately owned exchange with a private e-marketplace.

8. Compare external and internal aggregation of catalogs.

9. Relate social commerce to B2B group buying.

TOPICS FOR CLASS DISCUSSION AND DEBATES

1. Discuss B2B opportunities in social networking.

2. Discuss the risks in B2B social networking.

3. Discuss how globalization impacts B2B.

4. Relate B2B to the four Ps of marketing (product, pricing, placement, and promotion).

5. Discuss potential channel conflicts in B2B and how to deal with them.

6. What is the contribution of Alibaba.com to global trade? What are the potential limitations?

7. Debate: Some say that exchanges must be owned by a third-party intermediary and that consortium should not be allowed.

8. Debate: It is better to use the 4 Cs for B2B versus the 4 Ps.

INTERNET EXERCISES

1. Enter **gxs.com** and review GXS Express's bidding process. Describe the preparations a company would have to make in order to bid on a job. Find the use of EDI at the site.

2. Enter **sterlingcommerce.com** and **centredaily.com**. Find the products/services they have for the B2B sell- and the buy-sides. How do they support mobile and social commerce?

3. Examine the following sites: **ariba.com**, **trilogy.com**, and **ibxeurope.com**. Review their products and services. Match a B2B business model with the services in each site.

4. Visit **supplyworks.com** and **procuri.com**. Examine how each company streamlines the purchase process. How do these companies differ from **ariba.com**?

5. Visit **ebay.com** and identify all of the activities related to its small business auctions. What services are provided by eBay? Enter eBay's Business Industrial area (**business.ebay.com** or **ebay.com** and select "wholesale"). What kind of e-marketplace is this? What are its major capabilities?

6. Enter **ondemandsourcing.com** and view the demo. Prepare a list of benefits to small and medium-sized organizations.

7. Enter **bitpipe.com** and find recent B2B vendor reports related to e-procurement. Identify topics not covered in this chapter.

8. Visit **iasta.com**, **purchasing.com**, and **cognizant.com**, and examine the major tools they sell for conducting various types of e-procurement. List and analyze each tool.

9. Visit **converge.com**. What kind of exchange is this? What services does it provide? How do its auctions work?

10. Enter **thebuyinggroup.com**, **tidewatergpo.com**, and other group purchasing sites. Report on B2B group buying activities.

11. Enter **blog.marketo.com** and find eight recent successful applications of social B2B. Prepare a list of topics covered at the site. Write a brief summary about the content, including tips and guides, and lessons learned.

12. Go to **alibaba.com** and sign up as a member (membership is free). Create a product and post it. Tell your instructor how to view this product.

13. Compare the services offered by **globalsources.com** with those offered by **alibaba.com**. Assuming you are a toy seller, with which one would you register? Why? If you are a buyer of auto parts, which one would you join and why?

14. Enter **dir.yahoo.com/Business_and_Economy/Business_to_Business**. Prepare a list of resources about exchanges and B2B directories.

15. Enter **smallbusiness.yahoo.com/ecommerce** and summarize the sell-side case.

16. Enter **eprocurement.nc.gov**. What e-procurement methods does it provide? What are the benefits of each method?

TEAM ASSIGNMENTS AND PROJECTS

1. **Assignment for the Opening Case**

   Read the opening case and answer the following questions.

   a. Discuss the drivers of e-tendering for Branas.
   b. Given the small size of the company, was it an advantage or disadvantage to participate?
   c. Is the process of e-tendering simple or complex? Explain.
   d. Why do buyers choose e-tendering instead of regular tendering?
   e. What are the benefits for a small company such as Branas?

2. B2B marketing and sales methods are competitive. Go to **btobonline.com** and find archived Webcasts on B2B marketing (e.g., from Adobe, Citrix [GoToMeeting],

   and Unica). Each team views one Webcast, summarize its essentials and comment on the lesson learned.

3. Each team should explore a different e-procurement method and prepare a summary paper for a class presentation. The paper should include the following about the e-procurement method:

   a. The mechanisms and technologies used
   b. The benefits to buyers, suppliers, and others (if appropriate)
   c. The limitations
   d. The situations for which each method is recommended

   Hint: Look at vendors' systems. For example, check the e-procurement modules in Oracle 11i.

4. Form two teams (A and B) of five or more members. On each team, person 1 plays the role of an assembly company that produces television monitors. Persons 2 and 3 are domestic parts suppliers to the assembling company, and persons 4 and 5 play foreign parts suppliers. Assume that the TV monitor company wants to sell televisions directly to business customers. Each team is to design an environment composed of membership in exchanges they can use and present its results. A graphical display is recommended.

5. Enter b2bonline.com and find the "10 Great B-to-B Sites" for the last three years. Read the comments and visit these sites. Each team prepares a statement of why they think seven of these 10 sites are so great. The sites for 2010 are: Accenture, Airclic, Dropbox, Fright Center, Interaction Design Association, iStockphoto, Mack Trucks, SAS Institute, Show Group, and Tyco.

6. Enter gtnexus.com and examine its offerings. Prepare a report on how exchanges can benefit from its services. How does GT Nexus facilitate supply chains? Can it help e-marketplaces?

Closing Case

IMARKETKOREA

Established in 2000, iMarketKorea (iMK) is South Korea's largest e-marketplace (exchange) specializing in MRO items for various industries and direct materials for the electronics industries. iMK's e-catalog includes over 1 million items. In 2008, sales revenues were $722 million, with 180,000 monthly purchase orders. IMK was originally established as the online procurement sourcing company of Samsung Group in 2000; since then it has expanded its customer groups to various industries, including manufacturing, finance, retail, universities, and hospitals. Since its inception, the company has grown rapidly (an average annual growth rate of 23 percent).

From a market for Samsung's 45 affiliated companies, iMK has grown to serve approximately 350 companies in 2008. Currently, 70 percent of customers are Samsung related, whereas 30 percent are non-Samsung related. Many of the newly added customers are not Samsung affiliates, including some from outside South Korea. The site offers Korean, English, and Japanese options to registered users.

Initially, iMK concentrated on acting as a procurement agent to the Samsung companies. By 2007, however, the company shifted its mission to become a B2B procurement service provider, providing end-to-end procurement and logistics services for a variety of industries.

Among its most popular services for buyers are payments, deliveries, purchasing, budget management, internal approval processes, inventory management, storage, and more. In addition, iMK helps to smooth its customers' supply chains (e.g., process improvement and workflow management). iMK also supports connectivity to enterprise systems (e.g., ERP, legacy systems). The system architecture and the major participants are shown in the following exhibit.

iMK's business model is interesting because IMK does not charge fees for its services, but rather shares in the reduced costs with its buying customers. In this manner,

iMK removes the risk from the customer side. iMK pursues a 3S leadership strategy: sourcing, service, and system leadership. The strategic sourcing suites that iMK provides include SRM, Sourcing DSS, and e-catalog collaboration tools. They include features such as the following:

▶ Tools to calculate "total cost of ownership" (for purchasing)

▶ Strategic sourcing processes

▶ A scorecard grading system tool to perform a formal evaluation of suppliers (assessment, selection, monitoring)

▶ Knowledge sharing about best practices of procurement

▶ B2B auctions (forward and reverse, either as supporting the entire process or in helping customers take charge of the major activities, helping only with procedural matters during the auction)

▶ Spend management analysis and control tools

▶ Collaborative e-sourcing tools

▶ Decision support and optimization models for buyers

▶ Contract management features

▶ Integration of suppliers by selecting those who are reliable and sound and who are able to provide value (price matters, too, of course), leading to long-term strategic relationships (win-win situation)

▶ Risk assessment and management

▶ Item standardization for inventory and cost reduction at the suppliers' level, enabling better cataloging and faster and easier search (e.g., simultaneous search of many items)

▶ Analyzes replies to RFQs quickly, considering large amount of computerized information and knowledge

▶ Joint process improvement, attempting to reduce supplier's TCO (providing suppliers with a comprehensive program of how to do it)

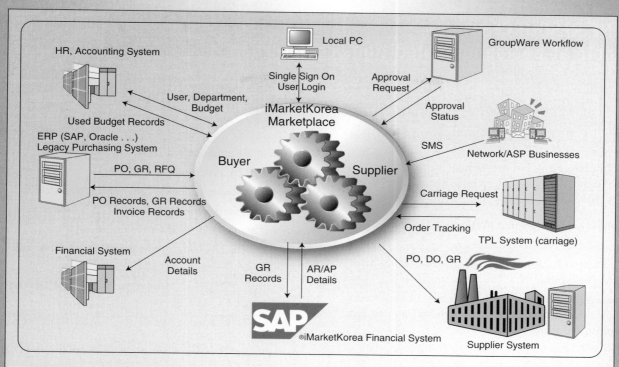

Source: iMarketKorea, "Purchasing Innovation: Value Proposition," 2011. *imarketkorea.co.kr/en_HD/DC9553ED_IMK_homepage_en_200408.pdf* (accessed January 2011).

The following are some recent iMK initiatives:

▶ An alliance with the Japanese Samitomo Corp. (a top online trading company), kicking off global business expansion. iMK is already exporting MROs to 12 countries.

▶ IMK exported over $87 million in MROs in 2008, plus $18 million in direct materials (a 37 percent increase from 2007).

▶ In collaboration with Woori Bank, iMK opened B2C and B2B2C channels for selling gifts over the Internet to the bank's employees.

The results speak for themselves. iMK's customers have experienced the following benefits:

▶ On-time delivery has increased from 72 percent to 94.5 percent.

▶ Average lead time has been reduced from 5.3 to 3.31 days.

▶ Catalog search speed has increased 40 percent.

▶ 12 to 18 percent savings in purchase prices.

▶ 30 to 50 percent savings in process costs.

▶ 5 to 15 percent savings in inventory management costs.

▶ 40 to 60 percent savings in reduced inventory.

All these savings have contributed to the success and growth of iMK and helped it have a successful IPO in the Korean stock market in 2010.

Sources: Compiled from iMarketKorea (2006), iMarketKorea (2005), Lee and Lee (2007), and *imarketkorea.com* (accessed February 2009).

Questions

1. How do the support services benefit the exchange?

2. Relate this case to desktop purchasing.

3. Write a summary of the benefits of the exchange to buyers.

4. Write a summary of the benefits of the exchange to sellers.

5. Compare iMK to Alibaba.com. What are the similarities and the differences?

6. Much of iMK's success is attributed to the understanding of the Korean culture and business environment. Given that iMK wants to expand internationally, what could be some of its stumbling blocks?

7. Check the recent news and press releases (last 6 months) at *imarketkorea.com*. Identify expansion patterns.

ONLINE RESOURCES
available at pearsonglobaleditions.com/turban

WWW

Online Files

W4.1 Application Case: Cisco System's Connection Online

W4.2 Application Case: Boeing's Spare PART Marketplace

W4.3 Implementing E-Procurement

W4.4 Application Case: ChemConnect: The World Commodity Chemical Exchange

Comprehensive Educational Websites

b2btoday.com: Full of B2B resources.

btobonline.com: Guides, Webcasts, videos, blog, white paper, and much more.

optimizeandprophesize.com: Jonathan Mendez's blog covering many topics including analytics, applications, landing page optimization, and social media.

silicon.com: Case studies, publications.

btob.com: B2B topics, news, software, etc.

netb2b.com: B2B magazine.

ibm.com/software/success/cssdb.nsf/topstoriesFM?OpenForm& Site=tivoli: Case studies from IBM.

business.com: B2B, procurement, and more.

eproc.org: All about e-procurement, guides, resources, etc.

internet.com: Diversified resources.

procurement.com.au: Comprehensive resources.

blog.marketo.com: A comprehensive blog site on B2B marketing.

REFERENCES

Alibaba.com. "Alibaba.com Announced Full Year 2008 Results." 2009a. news.alibaba.com/specials/aboutalibaba/aligroup/index.html (accessed November 2010).

Alibaba.com. "Alibaba Group: Company Overview." 2009b. news.alibaba.com/specials/aboutalibaba/aligroup/index.html (accessed November 2010).

Aneja, A., C. Rowan, and B. Brooksby. "Corporate Portal Framework for Transforming Content Chaos on Intranets." *Intel Technology Journal* (Q1, 2000).

Bannan, K. J. "10 Great B2B Sites." September 13, 2010. btobonline.com/article/20100913/309139988/10-great-b-to-b-sites (accessed October 2010).

BEA System. "State of the Portal Market 2006: Portals and the New Wisdom of the Enterprise." ebizq.net/white_papers/7140.html (accessed December 2010).

BizReport. "Survey: Small Businesses Find Success with Social Networking." July 9, 2010. bizreport.com/2010/07/survey-small-businesses-find-success-with-social-networking.html (accessed December 2010).

Booker, E. "The Case for Sentiment Analysis in B2B Settings." November 2010. clarabridge.com/ClarabridgeBlog/tabid/189/EntryId/59/The-Case-for-Sentiment-Analysis-in-B2B-Settings.aspx (accessed December 2010).

Bush, D. "e-Sourcing Does Not Equal Reverse Auction." *E-Sourcing Forum*, March 24, 2006. esourcingforum.com/index.php?s=e-Sourcing+Does+Not+Equal+Reverse+Auction (no longer available online).

Chandler, C. "China's Web King." *Fortune*, November 23, 2007.

Commonwealth of Pennsylvania. "Pennsylvania's Surplus Property Programs." 2006. portal.state.pa.us/portal/server.pt?open=512&objID=1395&&PageID=256271&level=4&css=L4&mode=2&cached=true (accessed December 2010).

Dunay, P. "The 4 C's of B2B Marketing." January 2010. pauldunay.com/4-cs-of-b2-marketing (accessed November 2010).

eMarketer. "B2B Marketing on Social Networks." August 2008. emarketer.com/Report.aspx?code=emarketer_2000516 (accessed December 2010).

Endeca. "Delivering a Consistent and Intuitive Online Catalog." 2008. endeca.com/resource-center-case-studies.htm (accessed December 2010).

Eproc.org. "Sustainable Electronic Procurement Case Study: Branas Isaf Training." eproc.org/site/guides/EPROC_csp_Branas_Isaf_Training.pdf (accessed December 2010).

Fletcher, O. "China's Alibaba Adds Social Networking to E-Commerce." *PC World*, August 4, 2009.

Fulltilt. "Brady Goes Fulltilt to Streamline E-Catalog Production." 2004. Case study (no longer available online).

Gaffney, J. "Social Media Stepping Up as Source for Connecting B2B Networks." 2007. demandgenreport.com/archives/feature-articles/89-social-media-stepping-up-as-source-for-connecting-b2b-networks.html (accessed December 2010).

Gillin, P. "B-to-B Firmly in Social Media." *Btobonline*, April 12, 2010. btobonline.com/apps/pbcs.dll/article?

AID=/20100412/FREE/304129965/1077/img2010# seenit (accessed December 2010).

Greengard, S. "Flying High with Social Networking." *Baseline*, November 2008.

IBM. "Drive Better Business Outcomes through Web Portals." White paper, *EPF14013-USEN-00*. December 2009.

IBM. "Whirlpool's B2B Trading Portal Cuts per Order Cost Significantly." White Plains, NY: IBM Corporation Software Group, Pub. G325-6693-00, 2000.

iMarketKorea. "iMarketKorea Enters into Strategic Business Cooperation Agreement with Sumitomo Corporation Japan." January 25, 2006. imarketkorea.co.kr/en_HD/ menu_05001-19view.jsp (accessed December 2010).

iMarketKorea. "iMarketKorea Opens Woori Bank e-Shop." December 19, 2005. imarketkorea.com/en_HD/menu_ 05001-17view.jsp (accessed December 2010).

Kesner, R. M. "Building a Knowledge Portal: A Case Study in Web-Enabled Collaboration." *Information Strategy: The Executive Journal* (Winter 2003).

KnowledgeStorm. "Emerging Media Series: Online Video, Social Networks, and Wikis?" November 9, 2006. knowledgestorm.com/sol_summary_85553.asp (accessed December 2010).

Koundis, T. "Business Intelligence for Intelligent Business." *DM Review Magazine*, February 2000.

Lee, Z., and D. S. Lee. "Transition from a Buyer's Agent to a Procurement Service Provider in B2B iMarketKorea." In J. K. Lee, et al., *Premier E-Business Cases from Asia*. Singapore: Prentice Hall and Pearson Education South Asia, 2007.

Lucas, H. C. *Information Technology: Strategic Decision Making for Managers*. Hoboken, NJ: Wiley & Sons, 2005.

Maddox, K. "Marketers Working toward Social, Search Integration." August 16, 2010a. btobonline.com/apps/ pbcs.dll/article?AID=/20100816/FREE/308169984/11 08/FREE (accessed December 2010).

Maddox, K. "Twitter Debuts New Ad Platform; B-to-B Marketers Still Deciding if Promoted Tweets Should Be Part of Social Media Mix." *BtoB*, May 2010b. highbeam. com/doc/1G1-225731735.html (accessed November 2010).

Markus, L. "The Golden Rule." *CIO Insight*, July 2006.

MasterCard. "MasterCard Purchasing Card Program." *Mastercard.com*, 2006. mastercard.com/us/business/ en/pdf/MC%20Sell%20Sheet%20Purchasing%2005 3006.pdf (accessed February 2011).

Microsoft. "Case Study: Eastman Chemical." 2000. microsoft.com/casestudies/Case_Study_Detail.aspx ?casestudyid=4000002678 (accessed December 2010).

New Media Institute. "Is the B2B Marketplace Utilizing Online Video, Social Networks, and Wikis?" November 13, 2006. newmedia.org/articles/is-the-b2b-marketplace- utilizing-online-video-social-networks—wikis.html (accessed December 2010).

Papazoglou, M., and P. Ribbers. *Building B2B Relation- ships—Technical and Tactical Implementations of E-Business Strategy*. Hoboken, NJ: Wiley & Sons, 2006.

Patton, S. "Answering the Call." *CIO.com*, June 1, 2006. cio.com.au/article/180389/answering_call (accessed December 2010).

Pergolino, M. "5 B2B Social Media Success Stories." May 16, 2010. blog.marketo.com/blog/2010/05/b2b-social- media-success.html (accessed July 2010).

Saryeddine, R. *E-Procurement: Another Tool in the Tool Box*. Ottawa, Ontario, Canada: The Conference Board of Canada, 2004.

Schaefer, N. *Windmill Networking: Understanding, Leveraging, and Maximizing LinkedIn*. Scotts Valley, CA: BookSurge Publishing, 2010.

INNOVATIVE EC SYSTEMS: FROM E-GOVERNMENT TO E-LEARNING, COLLABORATIVE COMMERCE, AND C2C COMMERCE

Learning Objectives

Upon completion of this chapter, you will be able to:

1. Describe various e-government initiatives.

2. Describe e-government activities and implementation issues including e-government 2.0 and m-government.

3. Describe e-learning, virtual universities, and e-training.

4. Describe e-books and their readers.

5. Describe knowledge management and dissemination as an e-business.

6. Describe and discuss online advisory systems.

7. Describe collaborative e-commerce.

8. Describe collaboration 2.0.

9. Describe C2C activities in e-commerce.

Content

KNOWLEDGE SHARING AS A STRATEGIC ASSET AT CATERPILLAR INC.

Caterpillar Inc. (CAT) is a large global manufacturer of heavy construction and mining equipment and a service provider for its products. It is also a major financial services provider.

The Problem

CAT has about 100,000 employees and sells through over 220 dealerships in about 200 countries. The company has experienced explosive growth, more than doubling its size from 2003 to 2006. Reaching so many employees in so many locations and in different countries and time zones had become a major challenge for the company. In addition, there were many newcomers, as well as new and improved products and services; therefore, CAT needed to train and retrain employees and dealers.

One of the biggest challenges facing any organization, let alone a large global one with a tightly integrated dealer network, is how to enable learning across an extended enterprise that includes employees, dealers, suppliers, and customers.

Another problem was a knowledge drain. By early 2000, nearly half of CAT's senior leadership team and the general employee population were eligible to retire. Also, the industry is very competitive (e.g., competition from Japan is very intense), so employees and dealers need to have the skills and knowledge to compete and succeed as a leader in the twenty-first-century workforce.

The Solution

The company spends more than $100 million a year on training. It created a learning infrastructure that includes three major elements: governance, a learning technology infrastructure (mainly Web-based), and an alignment strategy to create a lifelong culture of learning in accord with the firm's business goals. To do so Caterpillar created Caterpillar University (CAT U) to meet its training and learning needs. CAT U uses a universal virtual team collaboration system and tool, a synchronous online learning management system (LMS), and a *knowledge network*.

Caterpillar's LMS is a worldwide platform that supports both employees and dealers. The LMS has a learner-centric user interface that allows individual users to experience it in a customized fashion. It dynamically constructs each individual's learning plan on his or her desktop and directs the learner in executing the plan.

CAT U enables e-learning through its knowledge management system—the Caterpillar Knowledge Network. Caterpillar employees, dealers, suppliers, and customers exchange information, share knowledge, ask questions, and contact subject-matter experts around the world through 4,000 communities of practice organized around specific business-related topics. The knowledge network provides a deep mine of searchable data, giving users access to information created everywhere, anytime, in every area of the organization.

The company also uses the CAT Knowledge Network to help preserve the knowledge of retiring executives and experts. Approximately 10,000 experts have been identified and listed. These experts' searchable "expert descriptions" serve as expertise locators for users within Caterpillar and throughout its value chain. Thus, users can search online for experts by area of expertise and ask their advice.

In addition, the knowledge network includes "lessons learned," which capture past experiences in a formal template and are searchable too. The knowledge network also includes a discussion bulletin board and collaboration tools.

The network is now organized as a social network and thus it is a powerful tool for making personal connections. Users no longer have to rely on a personal network built through years of experience and various job assignments; instead, they rely on a keyword search in the knowledge network. This allows a wheel-loader engineer in China, for instance, to quickly locate a transmission software expert in Europe.

Synchronous online learning allows the virtual delivery of learning across the globe. In this setting, a live instructor interacts with dispersed learners who are attending virtual classes. Online learning saves time and money by allowing information to be distributed quickly and by reducing travel costs. CAT U is conducting about 2,100 classes using synchronous online learning, and more than 300,000 meetings are conducted each year using virtual collaboration systems.

The Results

Caterpillar's knowledge sharing technology enables its employees to quickly build both competence and confidence. In addition, the technology infrastructure is an important contributor to business sustainability by dramatically reducing travel and other expenses and increasing employee productivity. By aligning learning needs and corporate strategies at the divisions and enterprise levels, Caterpillar is able to improve enterprise performance by providing the right skills and knowledge through learning. This increases people's engagement and discretionary efforts, which lead to better performance. Engagement is the extent to which employees commit, rationally or emotionally, to the organization, how hard they work as a result of this commitment, and how long they intend to stay. This all provides strategic advantage and leads to a bottom-line benefit, because better enterprise performance results in increased profitability. (In 2006, the system received the prestigious ASTD Excellence in Practice Award, a U.S. National Award.) Finally, the

knowledge-sharing platform is so successful that its software and procedures have been sold to other companies.

Sources: Compiled from Glynn (2008), Boehle (2007), and *jointeamcaterpillar.com* (accessed April 2011).

WHAT WE CAN LEARN . . .

E-learning is an EC application that helps organizations, including universities, teach and retrain a large number of learners to ensure that they can grow and handle their jobs effectively. E-learning at Caterpillar is based in part on the knowledge and best practices accumulated by employees over the years. This knowledge is managed and shared in a knowledge management (KM) system, and it is accessible to learners and problem solvers electronically. Learning is facilitated by a collaborative system and tools. E-learning, KM, and collaborative commerce are three innovative systems introduced in this chapter. Other innovative systems described in this chapter are e-government, e-books, and consumer-to-consumer EC.

5.1   E-GOVERNMENT: AN OVERVIEW

Electronic government, or *e-government,* is a growing e-commerce application that encompasses many topics. This section presents the major ones.

DEFINITION AND SCOPE

e-government
E-commerce model in which a government entity buys or provides goods, services, or information to businesses or individual citizens.

As e-commerce matures and its tools and applications improve, greater attention is being given to its use in improving the business of public institutions and governments (country, state, county, city, etc.). **E-government** is the use of information technology in general, and e-commerce in particular, to provide citizens and organizations with more convenient access to government information and services, and to provide effective delivery of public services to citizens, business partners, and those working in the public sector. It also is an efficient and effective way of conducting governments' business transactions with citizens and businesses, and transacting effectively within governments themselves. See Shark and Toporkoff (2008) and en.wikipedia.org/wiki/E-Government for details.

In this book, the term *e-government* is used in its broader context—the bringing together of governments, citizens, and businesses in a network of information, knowledge, and commerce. In this broader view, e-government offers an opportunity to improve the efficiency and effectiveness of the functions of government and to make governments more transparent to citizens and businesses by providing access to more of the information generated by government, as well as facilitating transactions with and within governments.

Several major categories fit within this broad definition of e-government: government-to-citizens (G2C), government-to-business (G2B), government-to-government (G2G), internal efficiency and effectiveness (IEE), and government-to-employees (G2E). The performance objectives of the first four categories are provided in Exhibit 5.1. For a description of the range of e-government activities in the United States, see whitehouse.gov/omb/egov.

GOVERNMENT-TO-CITIZENS

government-to-citizens (G2C)
E-government category that includes all the interactions between a government and its citizens.

The **government-to-citizens (G2C)** category includes all the interactions between a government and its citizens that can take place electronically. As described in the closing case about the government of New Zealand, G2C can involve dozens of different initiatives. The basic idea is to enable citizens to interact electronically with the government from anywhere and sometimes at any time. G2C applications enable citizens to ask questions of government agencies and receive answers, pay taxes, receive payments

EXHIBIT 5.1   Categories of E-Government Performance Objectives

G2C	G2B
• Create easy-to-find single points of access to government services for individuals. • Reduce the average time for citizens to find benefits and determine eligibility. • Increase the number of citizens who use the Internet to find information on recreational opportunities. • Meet the high public demand for information. • Improve the value of government to citizens. • Expand access to information for people with disabilities. • Make obtaining financial assistance from the government easier, cheaper, quicker, and more comprehensible.	• Increase the ability for citizens and businesses to find, view, and comment on rules and regulations. • Reduce the burden on businesses by enabling online tax filing. • Reduce the time to fill out export forms and locate information. • Reduce time for businesses to file and comply with regulations. • Make transactions with the government easier, cheaper, quicker, and more comprehensible.
G2G	**IEE**
• Decrease response times for jurisdictions and disciplines to respond to emergency incidents. • Reduce the time to verify birth and death entitlement information. • Increase the number of grant programs available for electronic application. • Share information more quickly and conveniently between the federal and state, local, and tribal governments. • Improve collaborations with foreign partners, including governments and institutions. • Automate internal processes to reduce costs within the federal government by disseminating best practices across agencies. • Plan IT investments more effectively. • Secure greater services at a lower cost. • Cut government operating costs.	• Increase availability of training programs for government employees. • Reduce the average time to process clearance forms. • Increase use of e-travel services within each agency. • Reduce the time for citizens to search for federal jobs. • Reduce time and overhead costs to purchase goods and services throughout the federal government.

Sources: U.S. Government (2003), Lee, et al. (2005), and Hyperion (2007).

and documents, and schedule services, such as employment interviews and medical appointments. For example, in many U.S. states, residents can renew driver's licenses, pay traffic tickets, and make appointments for vehicle emission inspections and driving tests—all online. Governments also can disseminate information on the Web, conduct training, help citizens find employment, and much more. Government services to citizens are provided via citizen portals. The services will vary depending on the country, on the level (city, county, country), and on the users' skills in using computers. For the diversity of services, see the Hong Kong case in Online File W5.1.

The basic features of government websites are "how to contact us" information, links to other sites, publications, and databases. The major areas of G2C activities are social services, tourism and recreation, research and education, downloadable forms, discovery of government services, information about public policy, and advice about health and safety issues. G2C is available now in many countries on mobile/wireless devices.

An interesting application is the use of the Internet by politicians, especially during election periods. For example, the French political parties pursued millions of voters in the blogosphere for the 2007 presidential election. In the United States, during the

2008 presidential election, both major-party candidates sent e-mail messages and tweets to potential voters, and had comprehensive information portals. Aspiring politicians are using blogs to promote themselves. Many continue to use blogs after being elected. Social networks, especially Facebook, MySpace, and Web 2.0–based communication platforms such as Twitter and YouTube are being used to reach the voters directly, especially young voters. For example, Facebook had many thousands of candidate profiles for the November 2010 U.S. elections. All the major-party presidential candidates had profiles on several social networks for the 2008 election. President Obama even created a social network site (my.barackobama.com) and had pages on MySpace, Facebook, LinkedIn, and Second Life, and he used Twitter much earlier than his competitors who followed with similar activities. In South Korea, politicians log on to the Internet to recruit voters, because many people who surf the Internet rarely read newspapers or even watch TV. The major target audience of these politicians is 20- to 30-year-olds, the vast majority of whom surf the Internet. Pasdaq, the Seoul-based over-the-counter stock exchange, in Korea offers an Internet political game that simulates the stock market and measures the popularity of some 300 politicians by allowing players to buy and trade "stocks" in these politicians. In its first year, over 500,000 users signed up. Some politicians even make decisions based on citizens' opinions collected on the Internet.

Another area of G2C activity is in solving constituents' problems. The government (or a politician) can use CRM-type software to assign inquiries and problem cases to the appropriate staff member (as shown in the New Zealand case, at the end of the chapter and in e.govt.nz). Workflow CRM software can then be used to track the progress of the problems' resolution.

Note that over 20 countries block some websites for political, social, or other reasons (e.g., China, Iran, Syria). For more on G2C, see enusa.gov/Citizen/Topics/All_Topics.shtml. An example of C2G is electronic tax filing. Two popular examples of G2C are provided next.

Electronic Voting

Voting processes inherently are subject to errors and also could be subject to manipulation and fraud. In many countries, there are attempts to "rig" the votes; in others, the losers want to recount. Voting may result in major political crises, as happened in several countries. Problems with the U.S. 2000 and 2004 presidential elections have accelerated the trend toward electronic voting.

Voting encompasses a broad spectrum of technological and social processes and problems that must be systematically addressed—from registration and voter authentication to the casting of ballots and subsequent tallying of results (see Exhibit 5.2). Electronic voting automates some or all steps in the process.

Fully electronic voting systems have raised considerable controversy because of a variety of factors, such as the proprietary nature of the software, the weakness of the certification criteria, the difficulties of black-box testing to provide full assurances of correctness, the general secrecy of the evaluation process, vendor-commissioned evaluations, and the lack of any mechanism whereby independent recounting of the ballots and auditing of the vote totals can be performed.

The first country to use fully computerized balloting was Brazil. In the United States, electronic systems have been in use since 1980, mainly for scanning the marked ballots; large-scale implementation of touchscreen systems occurred only in 2008. It is interesting to note that several states (e.g., California, Nevada) require that touchscreen machines be able to produce a printed record. A good voting machine should show the voter what he or she has entered and ask for confirmation, much like when purchasing a book online from Amazon.com, transferring funds, or buying stocks.

From a technology point of view, election fraud could be carried out by changing a computer program to count votes for a specific candidate twice or not to count votes for another at all. Therefore, security and auditing measures are the key to the success of e-voting. However, considering the amount of fraud that occurs with traditional, non-e-voting systems and the fact that e-security is improving (see Epstein 2007), e-voting eventually could be the norm. For more information on e-voting, see en.wikipedia.org.wiki/Electronic_voting, eff.org/issues/e-voting, and notablesoftware.com/evote.html.

EXHIBIT 5.2   The Process of E-Voting

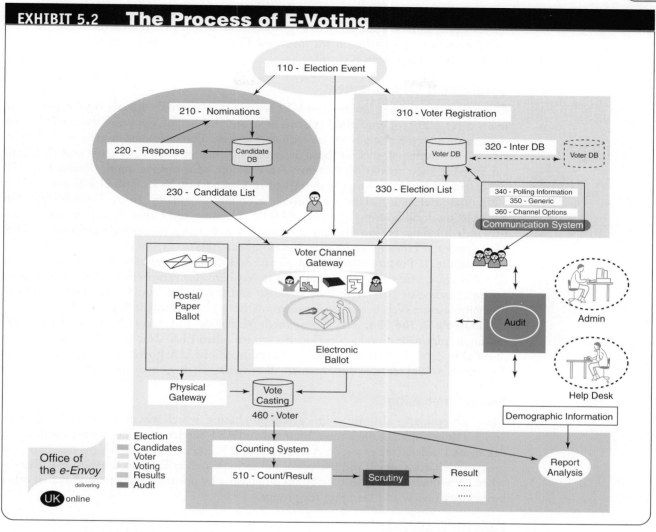

Source: e.govt.nz/plone/archive/resources/conferences/gartner/al-meeting-20040510/chapter29.html?q=archive/resources/conferences/gartner/al-meeting-20040510/chapter29.html (accessed July 2011).

Electronic Benefits Transfer

One e-government application that is not new is electronic benefits transfer (EBT), which has been available since the early 1990s and now in use in many countries. The U.S. government, for example, transfers over $1,000 billion in benefits to its citizens annually. In 1993, the U.S. government launched an initiative to develop a nationwide EBT system to deliver government benefits electronically. Initially, the attempt was made to deliver benefits to recipients' bank accounts. However, more than 20 percent of these transfers go to citizens who do not have bank accounts. To solve this problem, the government initiated the use of smart cards (see Chapter 10). Benefit recipients can load electronic funds onto the cards and use the cards at automated teller machines (ATMs), point-of-sale locations, and grocery and other stores, just like other bank card users do. The advantage is not only the reduction in processing costs (from about 50 cents per paper check to 2 cents for electronic payment) but also the reduction of fraud. With biometrics (see Chapter 9) coming to smart cards and PCs, officials expect fraud to be reduced substantially. For more information on EBT in government, see fns.usda.gov/snap/ebt. These activities are similar to those conducted in B2B (see Chapter 4).

GOVERNMENT-TO-BUSINESS

Governments seek to automate their interactions with businesses. Although we call this category **government-to-business (G2B)**, the relationship works two ways: government-to-business and business-to-government. Thus, G2B refers to e-commerce in which

government-to-business (G2B)
E-government category that includes interactions between governments and businesses (government selling to businesses and providing them with services and businesses selling products and services to the government).

government sells products to businesses or provides them with services, as well as to businesses selling products and services to government. Two key G2B areas are e-procurement and the auctioning of government surpluses. For other U.S. G2B initiatives, see usa.gov/Business/Business_Gateway.shtml.

Government E-Procurement

Governments buy large amounts of MROs and other materials directly from suppliers. In many cases, RFQ (or tendering) systems are mandated by law. For years, these RFQs were done manually; the systems are now moving online. These systems employ reverse (buy-side auction systems), such as those described in Chapter 4. Governments provide all the support for such tendering systems. An example of a reverse auction used for G2B procurement in Hong Kong is described in Online File W5.1 and at info.gov.hk. For additional information about such reverse auctions, see gsa.gov. In the United States, for example, the local housing agencies of HUD (Housing and Urban Development), which provides housing to low-income residents, are moving to e-procurement (see U.S. Department of Housing and Urban Development 2008).

Example 1: Procurement at GSA. GSA's website (gsa.gov) uses technologies such as demand aggregation and reverse auctions to buy items for various units of the federal government (see also governmentauctions.org and liquidation.com). The agency seeks to apply innovative Web-based procurement methods to government buying.

Example 2: The SBA. The Procurement Marketing and Access Network of the Small Business Administration has developed a service called PRO-Net (pro-net.sba.gov). It is a searchable database that contracting officers in various U.S. government units can use to find products and services sold by small, disadvantaged, or women-owned businesses.

Group Purchasing

Many governments also use online group purchasing, which was described in Chapters 1 and 3. For example, in the United States, the eFAST service conducts reverse auctions for aggregated orders (see gsa.gov). A related aspect is *quantity discount* where suppliers post group-purchasing offers, and the prices fall as more orders are placed. Another activity is when government buyers initiate group purchasing by posting product requests that other buyers may review and then join the groups.

Forward E-Auctions

Many governments auction equipment surpluses or other goods, ranging from vehicles to foreclosed real estate. These auctions are now moving to the Internet. Governments can auction from a government website or they can use third-party auction sites such as ebay.com, bid4assets.com, or governmentauctions.org. The U.S. General Services Administration (GSA) in the United States operates a property auction site online (auctionrp.com) where real-time auctions for surpluses and seized goods are conducted. Some of these auctions are restricted to dealers; others are open to the public (see governmentauctions.org).

GOVERNMENT-TO-GOVERNMENT

government-to government (G2G)
E-government category that includes activities within government units and those between governments.

The **government-to-government (G2G)** category consists of EC activities between units of governments, including those within one governmental body. Many of these are aimed at improving the effectiveness or the efficiency of the government operation. Here are a few examples from the United States:

▶ **Intelink.** Intelink is an intranet that contains classified information that is shared by the numerous U.S. intelligence agencies.

▶ **Federal Case Registry (Department of Health and Human Services).** This service helps state governments locate information about child support, including data on paternity and enforcement of child-support obligations. It is available at acf.hhs.gov/programs/cse/newhire/fcr/fcr.htm.

For more examples of G2G services, see govexec.com, socialsecurity.gov/gso/gsowelcome.htm, and the closing case about e-government in New Zealand.

GOVERNMENT-TO-EMPLOYEES AND INTERNAL EFFICIENCY AND EFFECTIVENESS

Governments are introducing various EC models internally. Two areas are illustrated next.

Government-to-Employees (G2E)

Governments are just as interested as private-sector organizations are in providing electronically services and information to their employees. Indeed, because employees of federal and state governments often work in a variety of geographic locations, government-to-employee (G2E) applications may be especially useful in enabling efficient communication and collaboration.

Example: G2E in the U.S. Navy. The U.S. Navy uses G2E to improve the flow of information to sailors and their families. Because long shipboard deployments cause strains on Navy families, the Navy is continuously seeking ways to ensure that quality-of-life services and information reaches Navy personnel and their loved ones all over the world. Examples of quality-of-life services include self-help, deployment support, stress management, parenting advice, and relocation assistance.

To help Navy families, the Navy developed Lifelines. Lifelines uses the Internet, simulcasting, teleconferencing, cable television, and satellite broadcasting to reach overseas personnel. The Navy has found that certain media channels are more appropriate for different types of information. Lifelines regularly features live broadcasts, giving forward-deployed sailors and their families welcome information and, in some cases, a taste of home. On the Web, several thousands of people access the Lifelines portal each day. The portal covers dozens of topics ranging from jobs to recreation.

The government provides several other e-services to Navy personnel. Notable are online banking, personal finance services, and insurance. Education and training also are provided online. The Navy provides mobile computing devices to sailors while they are deployed at sea. The handheld devices offer both entertainment and information to Navy personnel on active duty. For details, see lifelines.navy.mil.

> **government-to employees (G2E)**
> E-government category that includes activities and services between government units and their employees.

Internal Efficiency and Effectiveness (IEE)

Governments have to set an example of efficiency and effectiveness of their operation in order for them to inspire citizens and businesses to do the same. Unfortunately, only few governments (or units within government) attempt to do it. E-commerce provides an opportunity to significantly improve operations.

The following internal initiatives provide tools for improving the effectiveness and efficiency of government operations. Mostly, the processes are intrabusiness applications implemented in various government units. For example, the U.S. Office of Management and Budget provides the following services:

> ▶ **E-payroll.** Consolidates systems at more than a dozen processing centers across the government.
>
> ▶ **E-records management.** Establishes uniform procedures and standards for agencies in converting paper-based records to electronic files.
>
> ▶ **E-training.** Provides a repository of government-owned courseware.
>
> ▶ **Enterprise case management.** Centralizes justice litigation case information.
>
> ▶ **Integrated acquisition.** Agencies share common data elements to enable other agencies to make better informed procurement, logistical, payment, and performance-assessment decisions.
>
> ▶ **Integrated human resources.** Integrates personnel records across government.
>
> ▶ **One-stop recruitment.** Automates federal government information on career opportunities, résumé submission and routing, and assessment. Streamlines the federal hiring process and provides up-to-the-minute application status for job seekers.

Improving *homeland security* is also an IEE activity. The government is using different EC-related systems to improve security. For more information on security in e-government, go to dhs.gov/index.shtm.

IMPLEMENTING E-GOVERNMENT

Like most other organizations, government entities want to move into the digital era. Therefore, one can find a large number of EC applications in government organizations. This section examines some of the trends and issues involved in implementing e-government. These are summarized in Online File W5.2. Note that one of the major implementation problems is the mind-set of many governments that favors maintaining control over the use of data and knowledge (remember that knowledge is power).

THE TRANSFORMATION TO E-GOVERNMENT

The transformation from traditional delivery of government services to full implementation of online government services may be a lengthy process. The business consulting firm Deloitte & Touche conducted a study that identified six stages in the transformation to e-government. These stages do not have to be sequential, but frequently they are, with a seventh stage added by the authors as shown in Online File W5.2.

All major software companies provide tools and solutions for conducting e-government. One example is Cognos (an IBM Company; ibm.com/software/data/cognos/solutions/government). The company also provides free white papers.

E-GOVERNMENT 2.0 AND SOCIAL NETWORKING

Government 2.0
How government makes use of Web 2.0 technologies to interact with citizens and provide government services.

According to Baumgarten and Chui (2009), government agencies often fail to meet users' needs despite spending enormous amounts on Web-based initiatives. By employing Web 2.0 tools, new business models, and embracing social networks and user participation, government agencies can raise the effectiveness of their online presence. Such initiatives are referred to as **Government 2.0**. For extensive coverage of this topic, see egov.vic.gov.au/government-2-0.html. Government agencies around the world are now experimenting with social networking tools as well as with their own pages and presence on public social networking sites. Governments are using Web 2.0 tools mainly for collaboration, dissemination of information, e-learning, and citizen engagement. An interesting example is the initiatives going on in New Zealand, where social networking tools are being used extensively both for internal as well as external use (see this chapter's closing case about New Zealand's e-government).

The Promise of Government 2.0

According to an Australian Government 2.0 task force report (finance.gov.au/publications/gov20taskforcereport/index.html), by embracing Government 2.0 governments can:

▶ Improve the quality and responsiveness of services in areas like education, health, and environmental management, and at the same time deliver these services with greater agility and efficiency.

▶ Cultivate and harness the enthusiasm of citizens, letting them more fully contribute to their well-being and that of their community.

▶ Make democracy more participatory and informed.

▶ Unlock the immense economic and social value of information and other content held by governments to serve as a precompetitive platform for innovation.

▶ Revitalize the public sector and make government policies and services more responsive to people's needs and concerns by:

▶ Providing government with the tools for a much greater level of community engagement

> ▶ Allowing the users of government services much greater participation in their design and continual improvement of these services

> ▶ Involving communities of interest and practice outside the public sector, which offer unique access to expertise, local knowledge, and perspectives, in policy making and delivery

> ▶ More successfully attracting and retaining bright, enthusiastic citizens to the public service workforce by making their work less hierarchical, more collaborative, and more intrinsically rewarding.

Some people believe that social networking will replace the current portal-based e-government and that the trend is clearly away from the "one-stop" passive portal. Government initiatives are very diversified with the Web 2.0 approach. For example, many governments own islands on Second Life on which they present diplomatic issues and advertise tourist attractions. With such initiatives, it is important to have strict security, accountability, and compliance functionality in place, which has proven challenging when implementing wikis and blogs. Government experts encourage efforts to experiment with social networking but suggest that such pilots have to remain very well-focused and somewhat isolated from mainstream processes for at least the first two years. However, products such as Atlassian, which integrates with Microsoft SharePoint, have more than enough "control" to satisfy most government security requirements.

Note that politicians are using social networking extensively. For example, during the 2008 U.S. presidential election, Democratic candidate Barack Obama created pages at Facebook and LinkedIn, where he received thousands of connections and responses to his question, "What ideas do you have to keep America competitive in the years ahead?" Many of the responses were very interesting and insightful. Obama also created a LinkedIn interest group. One of the keys to Obama's success was that his LinkedIn profile was set up much like a "regular person" in tone and language, fitting with his strategy of not appearing to be an old-school Washington insider.

For an extensive list of resources on social networks in governments including reports, applications, and policies, see egov.vic.gov.au/government-2-0/government-2-0-getting-started-in-the-social-web.html. E-government software and solutions are provided by most large software vendors (e.g., see Adobe.com's Government white paper; Cisco systems; IBM/Cognos's solutions for government; Microsoft). For extensive coverage of e-government, see wisegeek.com/what-is-e-government.htm.

M-GOVERNMENT

Mobile government (m-government) is the wireless implementation (mobile platform) of e-government applications (see en.wikipedia.org/wiki/M-government) mostly to citizens (e.g., Government of Canada Wireless Portal), but also to businesses. M-government uses wireless Internet infrastructure and devices. It is a value-added service, because it enables government to reach a larger number of citizens and is more cost-effective than other IT applications; it is convenient to users as well (per Trimi and Sheng 2008). In addition, governments employ large numbers of mobile workers who can be supported by wireless devices.

Example: Public Buses in Honolulu. An example is the city government-run bus-location system in Honolulu, Hawaii. Using your cell phone you can find the estimated arrival time of any of the buses at more than 4,000 bus stops. Buses are equipped with GPSs (Chapter 6) that transmit the bus location every two minutes. The system then calculates the estimated arrival time for each stop.

Proponents of m-government argue that it can help make public information and government services available "anytime, anywhere" and that the ubiquity of these devices mandates their employment in government functions. An example of such beneficial use of mobile technologies would be the sending of a mass alert to registered citizens via short message service (SMS) in the event of an emergency.

mobile government (m-government)
The wireless implementation of e-government mostly to citizens but also to businesses.

The Benefits of M-Government

The major benefits of m-government are:

▶ Cost reduction
▶ Increased efficiency
▶ Transformation/modernization of public sector organizations
▶ Added convenience and flexibility for users
▶ Better services to the citizens
▶ Ability to reach a larger number of people through mobile devices than would be possible using wired Internet only (e.g., in the event of an emergency)

Some Implementation Issues

Representative issues are:

▶ Wireless and mobile networks and related infrastructure, sufficient to support the increasing demand as well as software, must be developed.
▶ To increase citizen participation and provide citizen-oriented services, governments need to offer easy access to m-government information in several forms.
▶ Mobile phone numbers and mobile devices are relatively easy to hack, and wireless networks are vulnerable because they use public airwaves to send signals.
▶ Many countries have not yet adopted legislation for data and information practices that spell out the rights of citizens and the responsibilities of the data holders (government).

Applications

Several wireless applications suitable for e-government are presented in Chapter 6. Notable are B2E applications, especially for field employees, and B2C information discovery, such as the U.S. Government 511 National Parks and travel system. Another example is the city of Bergen, Norway, which provides extensive wireless portable tourism services. For a comprehensive list of emerging applications, see Trimi and Sheng (2008) and Khosrow-Pour (2010).

For other implementation issues, success stories, applications, benefits, and more, see egov4dev.org/mgovernment, mgovernment.org, and m-government.info.

Section 5.1 ▶ REVIEW QUESTIONS

1. Define e-government.
2. What are the four major categories of e-government services?
3. Describe G2C.
4. Describe how e-voting works.
5. Describe the two main areas of G2B activities.
6. How does government use EC internally and when dealing with other governments?
7. Describe e-government social networking activities. What are some potential benefits?
8. Describe m-government and its implementation issues.

5.2   E-LEARNING, E-TRAINING, AND E-BOOKS

The topic of e-learning is gaining much attention, especially because world-class universities such as MIT, Harvard, and Stanford in the United States and Oxford in the United Kingdom are implementing it. Exhibit 5.3 shows the forces that are driving the transition from traditional education to online learning. E-learning also is growing as a method for training and information delivery in the business world and is becoming a major e-business activity. In this section, we will discuss several topics related to e-learning.

EXHIBIT 5.3   The Drivers of E-Learning

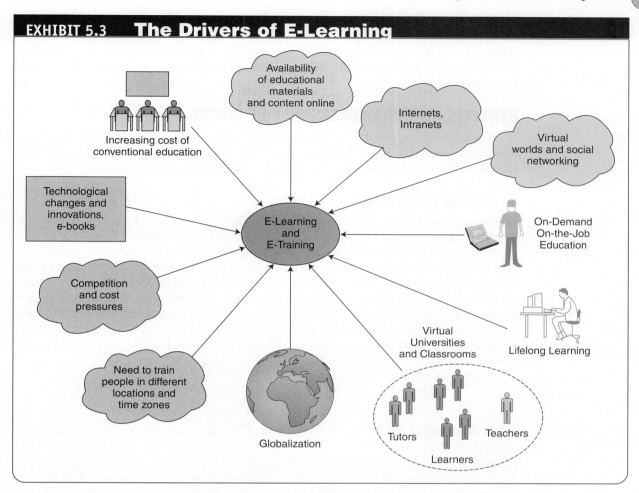

THE BASICS OF E-LEARNING: DEFINITIONS AND CONCEPTS

E-learning is the online delivery of information for purposes of education, training, or knowledge management (see elearnmag.org). It is a Web-enabled system that makes knowledge accessible to those who need it, when they need it, anytime, anywhere. It appears in a variety of formats, ranging from virtual classrooms to mobile learning. For an overview on how e-learning works, including its major concepts, tools, delivery systems, and benefits, see Oblinger (2010).

According to Wikipedia (en.Wikipedia.org/wiki/E-learning), e-learning can refer to any method of computer-enhanced learning. This could be as simple as the extension of traditional mail-order distance learning, where CD-ROMs are used for media-rich interaction with the student. Alternatively, it can be extended all the way to fully interactive, institution-wide "managed learning environments" in which students communicate with professors and classmates, in a similar manner to what occurs in face-to-face delivered courses. E-learning may include the use of Web-based teaching materials and hypermedia in general, multimedia CD-ROMs, learning and teaching portals, discussion boards, collaborative software, e-mail, blogs, wikis, chat rooms, computer-aided assessments, educational animation, simulations, games, learning management software, electronic voting systems, and more (possibly a few of these combined).

E-learning is also broader than the term *online learning*, which generally refers to purely Web-based learning. The term *m-learning* has been proposed when the material is delivered wirelessly to cell phones or PDAs.

E-learning can be useful both as an environment for facilitating learning at schools and as an environment for efficient and effective corporate training (see the Cisco case in Online File W5.3).

e-learning
The online delivery of information for purposes of education, training, or knowledge management.

Technological advances, such as simulations, virtual worlds, and open source software have reshaped the e-learning landscape. Rapid development tools enable organizations to create e-learning environments quickly and easily. Comprehensive sites about e-learning, including videos and PowerPoint presentations, are available at e-learningcenter.com and e-learningcentre.co.uk.

BENEFITS AND DRAWBACKS OF E-LEARNING

E-learning has many benefits both to the teaching institutions and to the learners. These benefits are presented in the following discussion and in Wagner (2008) and in Oblinger (2010). However, it also has several drawbacks, thus making it a controversial topic.

Benefits of E-Learning

E-learning can be a great equalizer: By eliminating barriers of time, distance, and socioeconomic status, it can enable individuals to take charge of their own lifelong learning. In the information age, skills and knowledge need to be *continually updated* and refreshed to keep up with today's fast-paced business environment. E-learning of new content will help organizations and countries rapidly adapt to the demands of the Internet economy by training their workers and educating their citizens. E-learning can save money, reduce travel time, increase access to experts, enable large numbers of students to take classes simultaneously, provide on-demand education, and enable self-paced learning. It can be taken any place and any time. It also may make learning less frustrating by making it more interactive and engaging.

Additional benefits of e-learning are as follows:

- **Learning and training time reduction.** E-learning can reduce training time by up to 50 percent.
- **Large number and diversity of learners.** E-learning can provide training to a large number of people from diverse cultural backgrounds and educational levels even though they are at different locations in different time zones.
- **Innovative teaching.** Ability to provide innovative methods such as special engagement, interaction with experts, interaction with learners in other countries, etc.
- **Measurement and assessment of progress.** Ability to assess progress in real time, find areas of difficulties, and design remedial work.
- **Cost reduction.** The cost of providing a learning experience can be reduced by 50 to 70 percent when classroom lectures are replaced by e-learning sessions.
- **Higher content retention due to self-paced learning.** E-learning students usually are self-initiated and self-paced. Their motive for acquiring more knowledge may be to widen their scope of view or to develop career skills. Such self-motivation may result in content retention that could be 25 to 60 percent higher than with traditional lecturer-led training.
- **Richness and quality.** Using videos and other multimedia, it is possible to present even difficult content in an interesting and easy to understand manner. Using top instructors, quality delivery can be assured.
- **Flexibility and self-paced.** E-learners are able to adjust the time, location, content, and speed of learning according to their own personal schedules. For example, if necessary, they can refer back to previous lectures without affecting the learning pace of other students. This allows students to learn at the most suitable pace (personalized learning).
- **Updated and consistent material.** It is almost impossible to economically update the information in textbooks more frequently than every two or three years; e-learning can offer just-in-time access to timely information. Delivery of

e-learning may be more consistent than that of material presented in traditional classroom learning, because variations among teachers are eliminated.

▶ **Ability to learn from mobile devices.** This helps to learn in any place and any time as well as to provide support to learners.

▶ **Expert knowledge.** In contrast with the knowledge of a single instructor in the classroom, e-learning may include the knowledge of several experts, each of which prepares a course module in his or her area of expertise.

▶ **Fear-free environment.** E-learning can facilitate learning for students who may not wish to join a face-to-face group discussion or participate in class. This kind of behavior usually is attributed to their fear of showing in public what they consider lack of knowledge. E-learning can provide a fear-free and privacy-protected environment in which students can put forth any idea without fear of looking ignorant or stupid. This increases the retention of material and the learner's satisfaction.

Tutoring services that once required face-to-face settings can now be profitably handled online and offshored to low-cost countries such as India. For more discussion of the benefits of e-learning, see about-elearning.com/e-learning-advantages-and-disadvantages.html and elearnmag.org. For current topics, see icl-conference.org and its International Conference.

Drawbacks and Challenges of E-Learning

Despite the numerous benefits, e-learning does have some drawbacks, such as the following:

▶ **Need for instructor retraining.** Some instructors are not competent in teaching by electronic means and may require retraining. It costs money to provide such training.

▶ **Equipment needs and support services.** Additional funds are needed to purchase multimedia tools to provide support services for e-learning creation, use, and maintenance.

▶ **Lack of face-to-face interaction and campus life.** Many feel that the intellectual stimulation that takes place through instruction in a classroom with a "live" instructor cannot fully be replicated with e-learning.

▶ **Assessments and examinations.** In the higher education environment, one criticism is that professors may not be able to adequately assess student work completed through e-learning. There is no guarantee, for example, of who actually completed the assignments or exams.

▶ **Maintenance and updating.** Although e-learning materials are easier to update than traditionally published materials, there are practical difficulties (e.g., cost, instructors' time) in keeping e-learning materials up-to-date. The content of e-learning material can be difficult to maintain due to the lack of ownership of and accountability for website material. In addition, no online course can deliver real-time information and knowledge in the way a "live" instructor can.

▶ **Protection of intellectual property.** It is difficult and expensive to control the transmission of copyrighted works downloaded from the e-learning platform.

▶ **Computer literacy.** E-learning cannot be extended to those students who are not computer literate or do not have access to the Internet.

▶ **Student retention.** Without some human feedback, it may be difficult to keep some students mentally engaged and enthusiastic about e-learning over a long period of time.

According to Rossett and Marsh (2010), the top constraints for corporate e-learning are: (1) too costly; (2) difficult to persuade people to learn in new ways; (3) insufficient technological support; (4) employee hesitation to contribute to social network, if one is involved; (5) customers and clients of companies that provide e-training (like Cisco) prefer classroom instruction.

Advanced technologies can reduce some of these drawbacks. For example, some online products have features that help stimulate student thinking. Biometric controls can be used to verify the identity of students who are taking examinations from home, offsetting the assessment drawback. However, these features add to the costs of e-learning.

From the learner's perspective, the challenge is simply to change the mind-set of how learning typically takes place. Learners must be willing to give up the idea of traditional classroom training, and they must come to understand that continual, lifelong learning will be as much a part of normal work life, past the college years, as voice mail and e-mail. From the teaching perspective, all learning objects must be converted ("tagged") to a digital format. This task can be difficult. Finally, another challenge for e-learning systems is the updating of the knowledge in them—who will do it and how often? Also, who will pay the cost of the updating? For ways to prevent e-learning failures, see Online File W5.4.

DISTANCE LEARNING AND ONLINE UNIVERSITIES

distance learning
Formal education that takes place off campus, usually, but not always, through online resources.

The term **distance learning** also known as *distance education*, refers to formal education that takes place off university campuses, often from home. It is a process that creates and provides access to learning when the teaching system and the learners are separated by time and distance, or both. In other words, distance learning is the process of creating an educational experience of equal quality for learners to best suit them outside the classroom. Sometimes students do meet in a physical location in order to know each other or take examinations. Distance learning is becoming widely used in universities and institutions around the globe. With the recent trend of technological advances, distance learning is becoming more recognized for its potential in providing individualized attention and communication with students internationally. The most widely cited pedagogical theory of distance education is that of *transactional distance*. For details, see en.wikipedia.org/wiki/ Distance_education.

The concept of long distance learning is not new. Educational institutions have been offering mail correspondence courses and degrees for decades. What is new, however, is the application of IT in general, and the Web in particular, to expand the opportunities for distance learning to the online environment. Neal (2007) describes the role of the Web 2.0 tools in distance learning in higher education, surveying implementation issues in terms of technology, course content, and pedagogy.

Virtual Universities

virtual universities
An online university from which students take classes from home or other offsite locations, usually via the Internet.

The concept of **virtual universities**, online universities from which students take classes from home or an offsite location via the Internet, is expanding rapidly. Hundreds of thousands of students in dozens of countries, from the United Kingdom to Israel to Thailand, are studying in such institutions. A large number of existing universities, including Stanford University and other top-tier institutions, offer online education of some form; for example, MIT is offering its entire 1,800 course curriculum online. Over 1.5 million independent learners (students, professors, self-learners) log on to the MIT OpenCourseWare site each month. Some universities, such as University of Phoenix (phoenix.edu), California Virtual Campus (cvc.edu), and the University of Maryland (umuc.edu/online_ed.shtml), offer hundreds of courses and dozens of degrees to students worldwide, all online. See distancelearn.about.com for more distance learning resources and online universities. For a list of the top online MBA programs in the world, see onlinedegrees.com/Online-MBA-Degrees.html. To help you match your objectives with an online university, go to a comparison engine such as NexTag (nextag.com).

The virtual university concept allows universities to offer classes worldwide. Moreover, integrated degrees may soon appear by which students can customize a degree that will best fit their needs and take courses at different universities. Several other virtual schools include hkvu.ust.hk/hkvu, waldenu.edu, and trainingzone.co.uk. Note that many schools and industries use e-learning as a supplementary channel to support traditional classrooms.

THE ENGKEY – ROBOT ENGLISH TEACHER

Source: The Korea Institute of Science and Technology. Used with permission.

Innovations in E-Learning

There are many innovations in e-learning, one of which is shown in the following example.

Example: E-Learning via Robots. As of December 2010, 29 robots, each 3.3-feet tall, started to teach English in Korea. Developed by the Korea Institute of Science and Technology (KIST), the robots are teaching English in Korean elementary schools (see above photo).

The robots are wheeled around the classroom via remote control, speaking to the students, reading books to them, and dancing to music by moving their head and arms. The robots, which display the face of a Caucasian "teacher" as an avatar, are controlled remotely by teachers of English in the Philippines who can see and hear the children via a remote control system.

Cameras detect the Filipino teachers' facial expressions and instantly reflect them on the robot's avatar face. Well-educated, experienced Filipino teachers are far cheaper than their counterparts elsewhere, including South Korea. Apart from reading books, the robots use pre-programmed software to sing songs and play educational games with the children. The kids seem to love it because the robots are cute and interesting. The students are more active in participating; especially shy ones who are afraid of speaking out to human teachers. But some adults have also expressed interest, saying they may feel less nervous talking to robots than a real person. Some robots are sent to remote rural areas of South Korea shunned by foreign English teachers.

KIST scientists have held pilot programs in Korean schools since 2009. The program to develop robots that teach English, math, science, and other subjects at different levels cost between $5,000 and $8,000. The robots largely back up human teachers, but will eventually have a bigger role. Robots do not complain about their salary, working hours, health insurance, sick leave, and severance packages; nor do they leave for a better-paying job in another country. Upkeep of the robots includes repairs and upgrades.

ONLINE CORPORATE TRAINING

Like educational institutions, a large number of business organizations are using e-learning on a large scale. Many companies offer online training, as Cisco does. Some, such as Barclays Bank, COX Industries, Toyota, and Qantas Airways, call such learning centers "universities." For example, new employees at IBM Taiwan Corp. are given Web-based "electronic training," and KPMG Peat Marwick offers e-learning to its customers in such universities. A 2008 study found that nearly one-third of corporate training content is now delivered electronically (per Rossett and Marsh, 2010).

Corporate training is driven by multiple factors and is often done via intranets and corporate portals. It has several variations, one of which is on-demand online training, which is offered by companies such as Citrix Systems (citrix.com). However, in large corporations with multiple sites and for studies from home, the Internet is used to access the online material. Vendors and success stories of online training and educational materials can be found at convergys.com and brightwave.co.uk. For how online training works, see Wallace (2007).

Examples of Corporate Training

The following are two examples of successful e-training:

▶ Cable and Wireless is a UK-based global telecommunications company that employs close to 15,000 people in over 80 countries. One of its major e-training projects was in business continuity of operations (see Chapter 9). Every employee, in every country, must be ready for when disaster strikes. The key benefits of such training are:
  ▶ Customers know that their business is in safe hands.
  ▶ Reduction of overall business risks in case of disasters.
  ▶ Compliance with future business continuity legislation.
  ▶ Employees know what to do, how to minimize business impacts, and who to contact in the event of an emergency or crisis.
  ▶ Rapid development just 13 weeks from beginning to end.
  ▶ Raises awareness about where business continuity information is stored.
▶ Using e-learning (packaged by Brightware) allowed Cable and Wireless to rapidly deploy and reuse the training. The package was tailored to audience learning styles, by giving the learners the opportunity to learn in a variety of ways (e.g., using videos; interactive briefings; individual progress assessment; podcasting, portable devices, and e-books). In addition to retraining all employees, the program is also used for training new employees. The company uses its own LMS for the delivery of training programs. For further details, see brightwave.co.uk/case-studies/cable-andwireless-uses-an-innovative-e-learning-approach-for-business-continuity-training.
▶ The University of Toyota (UOT), a division of Toyota Motor Sales, was established in 1999 to develop and deliver training for its many thousands of employees and dealership associates. In addition to classroom training, UOT is developing dozens of e-learning courses per year, all distributed via a commercially available learning management system (LMS). External vendors produce the majority of these courses. UOT uses a single set of development standards, benchmarks, purchasing specifications, and best practices to ensure standardization and quality of the work of its many vendors. This also helps in avoiding duplications and encourages the dissemination of new information among vendors. A major task was to coordinate all e-training efforts. Because each division (e.g., Lexus, Scion, etc.) is fairly independent in managing training, UOT arranges a corporate e-learning team from all divisions to work together with the vendors and the IT units. The best practices of each division are observed and shared among all the divisions. These efforts have been more than successful (Morrison 2008). The training is done via the UOT website (called E-source). Ease of use and clarity are achieved via standardization, and detailed instructions are sent via a bimonthly e-mail bulletin. E-learning eliminates delays in the deployment of new courses and increases learners' satisfaction.

SOCIAL NETWORKS AND E-LEARNING

social learning
Learning, training, and knowledge sharing in social networks and by using social software tools for learning.

Since its inception, social networking has been interrelated with learning (e.g., see Mason and Rennie 2008; Kidd and Chen 2009). A new term, **social learning**, has been coined to describe the learning, training, and knowledge sharing in social networks derived from using social software tools for learning (see Bingham and Conner 2010). Well-constructed social environments provide an excellent opportunity to model high-tech learning in a safe online environment, making it possible for employees and/or students to share their experiences with others. Thus, several companies are using social networking for training and development (e.g., see advancinginsights.com and Wang and Ramiller 2009).

Some students use Facebook, MySpace, LinkedIn, and so forth, to connect with other learners. For example, learners can get together and study or hold a discussion online. Unfortunately the clutter and distractions found on these networks can make it difficult to focus on learning. Therefore, some users are seeking virtual spaces geared to more specific needs, such as study or discussion.

Several social networks (or communities) are dedicated to learning and training (e.g., see e-learning.co.uk). For example, in 2008 Wi5Connect launched CommSocial, a Web 2.0 network platform, to fully leverage social networking's unique power to create "social communities" that can produce business value. The company also launched LearnSocial, which integrates social networking with LMS. Another example of a social network for learning is learnhub.com. Study Curve (studycurve.com) combines social networking and learning for middle schoolers through adults. Users can find experts to answer questions and rate the quality of their contributions.

According to Derven (2009), social networking technology provides many creative means that can affect learning. These include:

▶ **Link learners before and/or after a format learning event.** It provides for discussion collaboration and problem solving.

▶ **Engage next generation learners.** Generation X and Millenial workers use Web 2.0 tools extensively for interacting among themselves and with others. Organizations can reach out to this group and use social networks for training.

▶ **Provide content before a face-to-face learning event.** This can expedite classroom delivery.

▶ **Provide links to resources related to new learning content.**

▶ **Determine future training needs and issues.**

▶ **Reinforce and sustain learning.**

▶ **Use as a coaching and mentoring tool.**

Many universities combine e-learning and social networks; also numerous professors have blogs and wikis for their classes.

Bingham and Conner (2010) explain why social media is the ideal solution to some of the most pressing educational challenges organizations face today, such as a widely dispersed workforce and striking differences in learning styles, particularly across generations. They definitively answer common objections to using social media as a training tool and show how to win over even the most resistant employees. Then, using examples from a diverse group of organizations including Deloitte, IBM, TELUS, and others, Bingham and Conner help readers sort through the array of technological options available and decide when and how to use each one to achieve key strategic goals.

LEARNING IN VIRTUAL WORLDS AND SECOND LIFE

A number of interesting learning initiatives have been implemented in virtual worlds, especially in Second Life (SL). Users can participate in simulations, role-plays, construction projects, and social events (see Robbins and Bell 2008 and Chapter 7 for details). Learners can use virtual worlds to explore ancient civilizations, gothic castles, or fantasy worlds. These places can be springboards to fiction writing, sociology studies, and historical reenactments.

Many people see SL and other virtual worlds as an opportunity to carry out learning projects that would be impossible in the real world because of constraints such as geography or cost. Others see it as a chance to engage a younger generation of learners, many of whom are impatient with traditional forms of education and training. Many see it as a way to advance the practice of learning itself, creating new pedagogies and extending and modifying old ones. Therefore, many refer to SL as the classroom of the future.

Learning in virtual worlds also offers the possibility of collaboration. With the growth in bandwidth, online games are not only multiplayer, but massively multiplayer when played on the Internet, and some games are educational. For example, managerial training is no longer a matter of a learner interacting with a learning program. Now learners can interact with each other as well, across dispersed teams and communities of practice around the globe. This further extends the range of the types of learning that can, theoretically, take place in an online environment like SL. Learning a foreign language, team building, and leadership all benefit from group interaction. In addition, students report that they are learning more in SL than they would in the traditional classroom.

Learning in virtual worlds in general, and in SL in particular, is growing rapidly, with many activities and projects. Scores of universities have set up campuses on SL's islands, where classes meet and students interact in real time. They hold chat discussions and create multimedia presentations. Education-related SL applications are demonstrated in Online File W5.5. For a comprehensive list of resources, see the SL education wiki at simteach.com/wiki/index.php?title=Second_Life_Education_Wiki.

VISUAL INTERACTIVE SIMULATION

An effective technology for e-training and e-learning is *visual interactive simulation* (VIS), which uses computer graphic displays to present the impact of decisions. It differs from regular graphics in that the user can adjust the decision-making process and see the results of the interventions. Some learners respond better to graphical displays, especially when they are done interactively. For example, VIS was used to examine the operations of a physician clinic environment within a physician network in an effort to provide high-quality, cost-effective health care in a family practice. The simulation system identified the most important input factors that significantly affected performance. These inputs, when properly managed, led to lower costs and higher service levels.

VIS can represent a static or a dynamic system. Static models display a visual image of the result of one decision alternative at a time. Dynamic models display systems that evolve over time, and the evolution can be presented by animation. The learners can interact with the simulated model, watch the results develop over time, and try different activities or decision strategies.

Such systems provide the following major potential benefits:

- Shorten learning time.
- Aid in teaching how to operate complex equipment.
- Enable self-paced learning, any place, any time.
- Aid in memorization.
- Lower overall training costs.
- Record an individual's learning progress and improve on it.

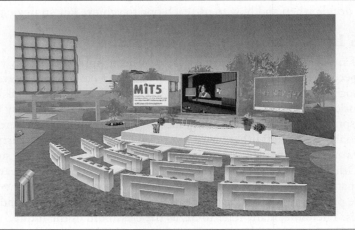

Source: Image by Jo Kay, via Flickr at: www.flickr.com/photos/33002318@N00/466962751. Used with permission.

EXHIBIT 5.4   SimMagic Trainee Progress Chart

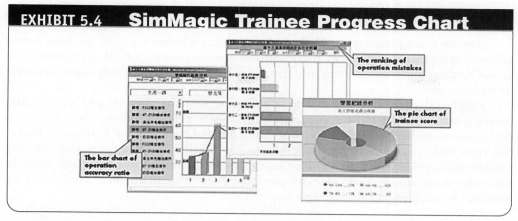

Source: Courtesy of HamaStar Technology. Used with permission.

Example. Several companies provide the necessary software and learning procedures for VIS. One product is SimMAGIC from HamaStar Technology Co. in Taiwan (hamastar.com.tw). Exhibit 5.4 provides a trainee progress chart.

Visual interactive simulation can facilitate learning on-demand.

Learning On-Demand

A newly emerging trend, **learning on-demand** or "*just-in-time learning*," is provided to an employee while the work is being done (in terms of troubleshooting or performance support). In a learning on-demand environment, courses, references, help files, documents, Webcasts, audios, videos, books, and presentations are all made available when and where a worker needs them.

In addition, learning on-demand can be complemented by more formal training methods made available in an integrated environment that features blended learning. The employee (or his or her manager) decides which training methods and/or tools use enabling "self-directed learning." For a comprehensive discussion, see Allen and Seaman (2009). Software for learning on-demand is provided by major vendors such as SAP, Adobe, IBM, and Citrix. For a seminar on "How to Build an On-Demand Training Program," go to infozone.clomedia.com/gotomeeting. For a national survey, see Allen and Seaman (2009).

E-LEARNING MANAGEMENT

A **learning management system (LMS)** consists of software applications for the administration, documentation, tracking, and reporting of training programs, classroom and online events, e-learning programs, and training content. According to Ellis (2009), a robust LMS should be able to:

▶ Centralize and automate administration.
▶ Use self-service and self-guided services.
▶ Assemble and deliver learning content rapidly.
▶ Consolidate training initiatives on a scalable Web-based platform.
▶ Support portability and standards.
▶ Personalize content and enable knowledge reuse.

Many companies (e.g., Saba, SumTotal) provide methodologies, software, hardware, and consultation on e-learning and its management. For examples, see Colvin-Clark and Mayer (2008) and Wagner (2008). For more on LMS, see en.wikipedia.org/wiki/Learning_Management_Systems.

One of the most effective tools for learning management is Blackboard (which was combined with WebCT). A brief description follows.

Example: Blackboard. Blackboard Inc. is the world's largest supplier of course management system software to educational institutions. There is a good chance that you

learning on-demand
Learning provided to an employee while the work is being done (in terms of troubleshooting or performance support). In a learning on-demand environment, courses, references, help files, documents, Webcasts, audios, videos, books, and presentations are all made available when and where a worker needs them.

learning management system (LMS)
Software applications for the administration, documentation, tracking, and reporting of training programs, classroom and online events, e-learning programs, and training content.

will use the Blackboard framework when using this textbook. These products provide the Internet software needed for e-learning.

How do these products work? A publisher places a book's content, teaching notes, quizzes, and other materials on Blackboard in a standardized format. Instructors can access modules and transfer them into their own Blackboard sites, which can be accessed by their students.

Blackboard offers a complete suite of enterprise software products and services that power a total "e-education infrastructure" for schools, colleges, universities, and other education providers. Blackboard's two major lines of business are Course & Portal Solutions and Commerce & Access Solutions. The Blackboard Connect service provides millions nationwide with time-sensitive information—via voice, text, e-mail and more. It uses mass communication to alert its users' communities and enhance their safety by keeping them informed, involved, and prepared.

A professor can easily incorporate a book's content into the software that is used by thousands of universities worldwide. As of 2009, Blackboard also delivers corporate and government employee training programs in every major region of the world that increase productivity and reduce costs. For details, see blackboard.com and en.wikipedia.org/wiki/Blackboard_Inc.

Moodle. An alternative to Blackboard is an open source system called Moodle (see moodle.org and en.wikipedia.org/wiki/Moodle).

IMPLEMENTING E-LEARNING AND E-TRAINING

One facility that is used in industry is the learning center. A *learning center* is a focal point for all corporate training and learning activities, including online ones. Some companies have a learning center dedicated only to online training. However, many companies combine online and offline activities. In industry, an increasing number of companies are using e-learning for teaching all skills, including managerial ones (see Roberts 2008). For additional information about e-learning, see trainingmag.com, elearnmag.org, and astd.org/lc.

Some Representative E-Learning Tools

Many e-learning tools are available (e.g., see the directories of products and services at trainingmag.com and at e-learningcentre.co.uk/eclipse/vendors/social.htm). One of the facilitators of e-learning is Web 2.0 technologies, such as blogs and wikis. The following are several examples of the use of Web 2.0 in e-learning:

▶ IBM Workplace Collaborative Learning 2.0 software (ibm.com/software/workplace/collaborativelearning) is a Web-based tool that can be customized to fit a company's training needs. It uses customer-supplied job profile information to deliver role-based learning resources right to the users' desktops.

▶ ComputerPREP (computerprep.com) offers almost 400 e-learning products, including a comprehensive library of Web-based classroom, distance-learning, and self-study curricula. Students can even combine products from different categories to customize their learning environments.

▶ Macromedia offers tools for wireless devices at adobe.com/software.

▶ eCollege (ecollege.com) offers an e-learning platform that includes free collaboration tools.

▶ Camtasia studio offers many e-learning tools, some of which instructors and students can use to create video tutorials (see techsmith.com/camtasia).

For additional information about e-learning, see trainingmag.com, elearnmag.org, and learningcircuits.org.

E-learning content can be facilitated with the aid of e-books, our next topic, and it is related to knowledge management (Section 5.3).

electronic book (e-book)
A book in digital form that can be read on a computer screen or on a special device.

ELECTRONIC BOOKS (E-BOOKS)

An **electronic book (e-book)** is a book in digital form that can be read on a computer screen, including handheld computers or on a dedicated device known as an e-reader. A major event in electronic publishing occurred on March 24, 2000, when Stephen King's book *Riding the Bullet* was published exclusively online. For $2.50, readers were able to purchase the e-book at Amazon.com and other e-book providers. Several hundred thousand copies were sold in a few days. However, the publishing event did not go off without a problem. Hackers breached the security system and distributed free copies of the book online. There are several types of e-books as well as e-readers. Note that Kindle and some other e-readers enable users to wirelessly download books, blogs, magazines, and newspapers.

Publishers of e-books have since become more sophisticated, and the business of e-publishing has become more secure. E-books can be delivered and read in various ways:

> ▶ **Via Web access.** Readers can locate a book on the publisher's website and read it there. The book cannot be downloaded. It may be interactive, including links and rich multimedia.
> ▶ **Via Web download.** Readers can download the book to a PC.
> ▶ **Via a dedicated reader.** The book must be downloaded to a special device, an e-reader such as Amazon's Kindle 3.0 or Sony PRS-200.
> ▶ **Via a general-purpose reader.** The book can be downloaded to a general-purpose device, such as a Palm Pilot.
> ▶ **Via a Web server.** The contents of a book are stored on a Web server and downloaded for print-on-demand (which is discussed later in this book).

Most e-books require some type of payment. Readers either pay before they download a book from a website, or they pay when they order the special CD-ROM edition of a book. Today, Amazon.com offers hundreds of thousands of e-books, newspapers (including international ones), and much more. All are cheaper than the hard-copy version (e.g., new releases of books may cost $10 or less).

Devices for Reading E-Books

The major device used to read an e-book is an e-reader. Most e-readers are lightweight (about 10 ounces) and convenient to carry. The major readers are listed and compared at the-ebook-reader.com. During 2010 there was a price war among all the major e-reader manufacturers.

Several other aids are available to help readers who want to read large amounts of material online. For example, ClearType from Microsoft and CoolType from Adobe can be used to improve screen display, colors, and font sizes.

Advantages and Limitations of E-Books

For e-books to make an impact, they must offer advantages to both readers and publishers. Otherwise, there would be little incentive to change from the traditional format. E-books, like other books, can be used for pleasure reading and as textbooks to support learning.

The advantages of e-books are:

> ▶ Ability to store hundreds of books on a small mobile device (7" to 10"). (External storage can hold much more.)
> ▶ Lower cost to buyers.
> ▶ Searchable text—you can show links, and connect easily to the Web.
> ▶ Instant delivery via downloads from anywhere. You can get information when needed and quickly.
> ▶ Portability—they go where you go. You can read on the train, plane, boat, or when standing and waiting in line.

- Easy integration of content.
- Durability—they are built stronger than a traditional book, and most users will find it harder to lose or leave somewhere unintentionally.
- Ability to enlarge the font size for easy reading.
- Media rich (audio, video, etc.), which make them easy to copy.
- Ease of reproduction and distribution (which can be a problem for maintaining intellectual property rights).
- Minimal cost for printing out a hard copy.
- Easy updating and reprinting.
- Almost no wear and tear.
- Easy to find out-of-print books.

The primary advantage that e-books offer publishers is lower production, marketing, and distribution (sale) costs, which have a significant impact on the price of books (e-textbooks are about 50 percent cheaper than print versions). Other advantages for publishers are lower updating and reproduction costs; the ability to reach many readers; and the ease of combining chapters from several books, to create customized textbooks so professors can use materials from different books by the same publisher in one course.

E-books also can reduce some of the physical burdens of traditional books. A number of studies have shown that 6 out of 10 students ages 9 to 20 report chronic back pain related to heavy backpacks filled with books. Some schools have eliminated lockers for safety reasons, causing students to carry heavy backpacks not only to and from school, but all day long. A number of schools are experimenting with eliminating textbooks altogether and using an Internet-based curriculum or school materials on CD-ROMs.

According to en.wikipedia.org/wiki/E-book, as of 2009, new marketing models for e-books were being developed and dedicated reading hardware was being produced. In the United States, as of September 2009, the Amazon Kindle model and Sony's PRS 500 were dominant e-reading devices. By March 2010, the Barnes & Noble Nook was selling more units than the Kindle. In August 2010, Amazon released Kindle 3.0, which is still battling for best e-reader with Nook. On January 27, 2010, Apple launched the iPad and announced agreements with five of the six largest publishers that would allow Apple to distribute e-books. However, many publishers and authors have not endorsed the concept of electronic publishing, citing issues with demand, piracy, and proprietary devices. For e-readers, news, reviews and comparisons, see the-e-book-reader.com.

In July 2010. Amazon.com reported sales of e-books for its proprietary Kindle outnumbered sales of hardcover books for the first time ever during the second quarter of 2010, saying it sold 140 e-books for every 100 hardcover books, including hardcovers for which there was no digital edition. In July, this number had increased to 180 Kindle e-books per 100 hardcovers. In January 2011 Amazon.com reported that it sold more e-books than paperback books. The American Publishing Association estimated that e-books represented 8.5 percent of sales as of mid-2010.

Of course, e-books have some *limitations*: They require hardware and software that may be too expensive for some readers; some people have difficulty reading large amounts of material on a computer screen; batteries may run down; and there are multiple, competing software and hardware standards. Several of these obstacles may be lessened in time.

Despite the limitations, e-books have become very popular as sophisticated e-readers reached the market. For a comparison of e-books and printed books, see en.wikipedia.org/wiki/E-book.

Section 5.2 ▶ REVIEW QUESTIONS

1. Define e-learning and describe its drivers and benefits.
2. List some of the major drawbacks of e-learning and describe how they can be prevented.

3. Describe virtual universities and distance learning.

4. Define e-training and describe how it is done.

5. Describe the connection between learning and social networking.

6. Describe learning in virtual worlds.

7. List some e-learning tools, and describe Blackboard and visual interactive simulation (VIS).

8. Describe e-books.

9. What is an e-reader? What are its major capabilities?

10. List the major advantages and limitations of e-books.

5.3 KNOWLEDGE MANAGEMENT, ADVISORY SYSTEMS, AND ELECTRONIC COMMERCE

The term *knowledge management* is frequently mentioned in discussions of e-learning. Why is this? To answer this question, you first need to understand what knowledge management is.

AN OVERVIEW OF KNOWLEDGE MANAGEMENT

Knowledge management and e-learning both use the same "coin of the realm"—knowledge. Whereas e-learning uses that "coin" for the sake of individual learning, knowledge management uses it to improve the functioning of an organization or groups of people. Knowledge is one of the most important assets in any organization, and thus it is important to capture, store, and apply it. These are the major purposes of knowledge management. Thus, **knowledge management (KM)** refers to the process of capturing or creating knowledge, storing and protecting it, updating it constantly, disseminating it, and using it whenever necessary (see Online Tutorial T9 and Awad and Ghaziri 2010).

Knowledge is collected from both external and internal sources. Then it is examined, interpreted, refined, and stored in what is called an *organizational knowledge base*, the repository for the enterprise's knowledge. A major purpose of an organizational knowledge base is to allow for *knowledge sharing*. Knowledge sharing among employees, with customers and with business partners, has a huge potential payoff in improved customer service, the ability to solve difficult organizational problems, shorter delivery cycle times, and increased collaboration within the company and with business partners. Furthermore, some knowledge can be sold to others or traded for other knowledge.

KM TYPES AND ACTIVITIES

Organizational knowledge is embedded in the following resources: (1) human capital, which includes employee knowledge, competencies, and creativity; (2) structured capital (organizational capital), which includes organizational structure and culture, processes, patents, and the capability to leverage knowledge through sharing and transferring; and (3) customer and partner capital, which includes the relationship between organizations and their customers and other partners.

This organizational knowledge must be properly managed, and this is the major purpose of KM. KM has the following major tasks:

> **Create knowledge.** Knowledge is created as people determine new ways of doing things or develop know-how. Sometimes external knowledge is brought in.

> **Capture knowledge.** Existent knowledge must be identified as valuable and be represented in a reasonable way.

> **Refine knowledge.** New knowledge must be placed in context so that it is actionable. This is where human insights (tacit qualities) must be captured along with explicit facts.

knowledge management (KM)
The process of capturing or creating knowledge, storing it, updating it constantly, disseminating it, and using it whenever necessary.

> **Store knowledge.** Useful knowledge must then be stored in a reasonable format in a knowledge repository so that others in the organization can access it.
> **Manage knowledge.** The knowledge must be kept current. It must be reviewed to verify that it is relevant and accurate. If not, it must be updated.
> **Disseminate knowledge.** Knowledge must be made available in a useful format to anyone in the organization who needs it, and authorized to access it anywhere and anytime.

These tasks can be viewed as a cyclical process, as shown in Exhibit 5.5. The objective of e-commerce is to automate KM activities as well as to use the stored knowledge.

For a comprehensive list of KM activities and tools, see Online Tutorial T9, en.wikipedia.org/wiki/Knowledge_management, kmworld.com, brint.com, Holsapple (2003), and Awad and Ghaziri (2010).

KNOWLEDGE SHARING

Knowledge is of limited value if it is not updated and shared. The ability to share knowledge decreases its cost per user and increases its effectiveness for greater competitive advantage. Thus, a major purpose of KM is to increase knowledge sharing. Shared knowledge can also decrease risk and uncertainty and facilitate problem solving. KM is about sharing a company's knowledge repository, but increasingly it is also about sharing the information stored in people's heads. An example of a knowledge-sharing system at Infosys Technologies is provided in Case 5.1.

Software Tools for Knowledge Sharing

There are many software knowledge-sharing tools. These are considered by some as "knowledge sharing technologies." In this chapter and book, we cover the following:

> Collaborative commerce tools
> Expert and expertise location systems
> Knowledge management systems
> Social networks and Web 2.0 tools (Chapters 2 and 7)

EXHIBIT 5.5   The Knowledge Management System Cycle

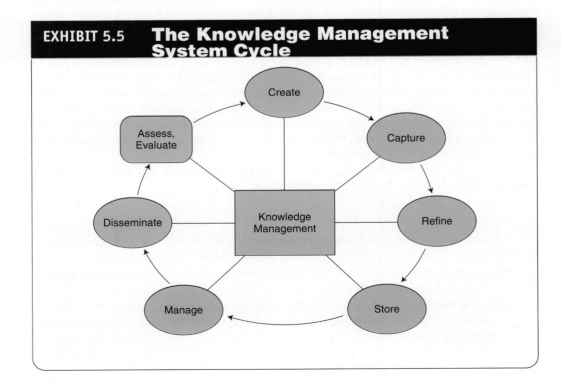

CASE 5.1
EC Application

KNOWLEDGE MANAGEMENT AT INFOSYS TECHNOLOGIES

The Problem

Infosys Technologies, a global software services company based in India, is a worldwide leader in technology outsourcing and consulting. With over 23,000 employees and globally distributed operations, Infosys develops IT solutions for some of the largest corporations in the world. During the past 12 years, Infosys has experienced annual growth of 30 percent. Infosys faced a challenge of keeping its large employee base up-to-date, staying ahead of both its competitors and clients, and ensuring that the lessons learned in one part of the organization were available to its consultants so they could reuse the knowledge accumulated in the company. The company's motto is "Learn once, use anywhere." The company's vision is that every instance of learning within Infosys should be available to every employee at any place and any time. But how does an organization turn such a vision into a reality?

The Solution

Infosys Technologies' effort to convert each employee's knowledge into an organizational asset started in the early 1990s and it is still going on today. In the early 1990s, Infosys launched its *bodies of knowledge (BOK)* initiative, which involved encouraging employees to provide written accounts of their experiences across various topics, such as technologies, software development, and living abroad. These experiences were then shared in hard-copy form with all other employees. This early effort ballooned into a full-fledged KM effort supported by e-mail, bulletin boards, and various knowledge repositories. In 1996, a corporate intranet was developed to make BOKs, in HTML format, easily accessible to all. In 1999, Infosys began an organization-wide program to integrate the various knowledge initiatives. A central *knowledge portal* was created, called KShop, and the KM group developed the technology infrastructure, while the local groups were encouraged to maintain their own content on KShop.

The composition of KShop consisted of different content types—BOKs, case studies, reusable artifacts, and downloadable software—each with its own homepage. Content was carefully categorized by the KM group to ensure that as the amount of content increased, it would still be possible for people to quickly find what they needed.

In early 2000, Infosys had a very functional KM system; however, patronage by employees remained low. The KM group therefore initiated a reward program to increase both use and knowledge contribution. The program gave employees who contributed to KShop knowledge currency units (KCUs) that could be accumulated and exchanged for monetary rewards or prizes.

As you can see, KM initiatives are much more than the implementation of technology tools to allow employees to create or document knowledge. Infosys's KM initiatives involved processes to organize knowledge, to categorize knowledge, and to rate knowledge usefulness, as well as strategies to encourage knowledge contribution sharing and reuse.

The Results

Within a year of the introduction of the incentive KCU program, 2,400 new knowledge assets had been contributed to KShop by some 20 percent of Infosys's employees. (By 2010, there were 75,000 knowledge assets in the corporate central knowledge repository.) However, as the volume of content increased, so, too, did problems relating to finding the needed information. Moreover, the sizable growth in contributions taxed the limited number of volunteer reviewers, who served an important quality-control function. The KM group therefore modified the KCU's incentive program. The group developed a new KCU program that rated the usefulness of knowledge from the perspective of the users of the knowledge, rather than the reviewers. And, to increase accountability, the KM group requested tangible proof to justify any high ratings. Finally, the KM group raised the bar for cashing in KCU points for monetary awards.

The KM project enabled the company to sustain its competitiveness and market leadership (Suresh and Mehesh 2008).

Sources: Compiled from *infosys.com* (accessed April 2011), Mehta, et al. (2007), Suresh and Mehesh (2008), and Garud and Kumaraswamy (2005).

Questions

1. Why are consulting organizations such as Infosys interested in KM?
2. Identify the benefits of the system to the company.
3. Identify the KM cycle in this case.
4. Why is a reward system beneficial? Compare the old and new reward systems.

HOW IS KNOWLEDGE MANAGEMENT RELATED TO E-COMMERCE?

To better perform their EC tasks, organizations need knowledge, which is provided by KM. For example, EC strategic planning needs considerable amounts of knowledge. To mitigate this problem, e-commerce can proactively incorporate KM processes to facilitate quick access to different types of knowledge.

For example, by analyzing database marketing data in a timely manner, organizations can learn about their customers and generate useful knowledge for planning and decision making. For these activities to be successful in both B2B and B2C, appropriate knowledge is needed to interpret information and to execute operational activities.

Core KM activities for companies doing EC should include the following electronically supported activities: identification, creation, capture and codification, classification, distribution, utilization, and evolution of the knowledge needed to develop products and partnerships. *Knowledge creation* involves using various computer-based tools and techniques to analyze transaction data and generate new ideas. *Knowledge capture and codification* includes gathering new knowledge and storing it in a machine-readable form. *Knowledge classification* organizes knowledge using appropriate dimensions relating it to its use. *Knowledge distribution* is sharing relevant information with suppliers, consumers, and other internal and external stakeholders through electronic networks—both public and private. *Knowledge utilization* involves appropriate application of knowledge to problem solving. *Knowledge evolution* entails updating knowledge as time progresses.

Some managers believe that a major EC-related role of KM is linking EC and business processes. Specifically, knowledge generated in EC contributes to the enhancement of three core processes: CRM, SCM, and product development management. For more on KM-enabling technologies and how they can be applied to business unit initiatives, see kmworld.com, brint.com/km, and knowledgestorm.com.

KM AND SOCIAL NETWORKS

A major place of knowledge creation is in online communities. This is done by a process known as *crowdsourcing* or the *wisdom of the crowd* and *communities of practice* (see Chapter 7). This area has several variations. One variety is limited within a single company (see the Knowledge Network in the Caterpillar opening case). Another is a public community whose members are interested in a common topic. Yet another type is a combination of the two. The major purposes of such communities are:

▶ **Knowledge creation.** The creation of knowledge for a specific problem or area. Individuals are asked to contribute to a solution or offer valuable advice. For example, IBM, GE, and other companies have communities of employees and business partners who contribute to idea generation and problem solving.

▶ **Knowledge sharing.** Members share knowledge by telling other members where to find knowledge of interest to the community.

Web 2.0 applications help aggregate corporate knowledge and simplify the building of repositories of best practices, as demonstrated by the following example.

Example: IBM's Innovation Jam. IBM has long used communities for idea generation and problem solving. One of its best-known communities is the Innovation Jam, an online brainstorming session. This community of over 150,000 employees and members of business partners tries to move the latest technologies to the market. IBM has been hosting online brainstorming sessions since 2001. For example, in July 2006, IBM invited employees, partners, and customers to contribute ideas about a certain new product. Within 72 hours, more than 50,000 ideas were posted. These ideas were then winnowed down by using sophisticated analytical software. Of the remaining, several ideas were implemented for a substantial savings.

Virtual meetings where IBM employees can participate in Innovation Jam launches are conducted in SL. IBM's CEO has even created an avatar to represent him. Topics that have been explored by Innovation Jams recently include new technologies for water filtration, 3-D Internet, and branchless banking. For more on IBM's Innovation Jams—the process, example of topics, and results, as well as the use of virtual worlds, see Bjelland and Wood (2008) and en.wikipedia.org/wiki/IBM_Virtual_Universe_Community.

DEPLOYING KM TECHNOLOGIES

Knowledge management as it relates to EC and IT is not easy to implement. Currier (2010) lists the following reasons by declining order of importance: ROI difficult to measure, training end-users, insufficient budget, defining strategies, employee resistance, finding the right products, ensuring security, customization is too difficult, maintaining quality of output, lack of management commitment, executing strategies, implementation is disruptive, lack of IT commitment, techs are not mature enough, and employee privacy issues.

ONLINE ADVICE AND CONSULTING

Another use of knowledge online is offering advice and consulting services. The online advice and consulting field is growing rapidly as tens of thousands of experts of all kinds sell (or provide for free) their expertise over the Internet. The following are some examples:

▶ **Medical advice.** Companies such as WebMD (webmd.com) and others (see liveperson.com) provide health advice and some consultations with top medical experts. Consumers can ask specific questions and get answers from specialists in a few days. Health sites also offer specialized advice and tips for travelers, for pet owners, and more.

▶ **Management consulting.** Many management consulting companies are selling their accumulated expertise from their organizational knowledge bases. A pioneer in this area was Accenture (accenture.com). Other management consultants that sell knowledge online are Aberdeen (aberdeen.com) and Forrester Research (forresterresearch.com). Because of their high consultation fees, such services mainly are used by corporations.

▶ **Legal advice.** Delivery of legal advice to individuals and businesses by consultation services has considerable prospects. For example, Atlanta-based law firm Alston & Bird coordinates legal counseling with 12 law firms for large health care companies and for many other clients.

▶ **Gurus.** Several sites provide diversified expert services, some for free. One example is guru.com, which provides businesses with an efficient platform to connect and perform transactions with freelance professionals locally, nationally, and globally. As of 2009, it had more than 1 million registered members and over 250,000 active freelancer profiles. Expertise is also advertised at elance.com—companies find, hire, manage, and pay contractors online. On Elance, companies can gain instant access to tens of thousands of rated and tested professionals who offer technical, marketing, and business expertise. Of special interest is scientificamerican.com/sciammag, which offers advice from science experts. Some of the most popular services that offer information from experts are answers.com (previously GuruNet), answers.yahoo. com, catholic.com, healthanswers.com, wineanswers.com, and many more. Some provide answers for free; others charge fees for premium services.

▶ **Financial advice.** Many companies offer extensive financial advice. For example, Merrill Lynch Online (totalmerrill.com) provides free access to some of the firm's research reports and analyses. Regarding wealth management, see bloomberg.com and money.cnn.com.

▶ **Social networks.** Several social networks allow users to post questions and get answers. For business-oriented questions, go to linkedin.com.

▶ **Other advisory services.** Many other advisory services are available online—some for free and others for a fee. For example, guestfinder.com makes it easy for people who work in the media to find guests and interview sources.

One word of caution about advice: It is not wise to risk your health, your money, or your legal status on free or even for-fee online advice. Always seek more than one opinion, and carefully check the credentials of any advice provider.

FINDING EXPERTISE AND/OR EXPERTS ELECTRONICALLY AND THE USE OF EXPERT LOCATION SYSTEMS

Expert advice can be provided within an organization in a variety of ways. Human expertise is rare; therefore, companies attempt to preserve it electronically in corporate knowledge bases. Users may look for human experts to answer their problems or they may search electronically for expertise that is stored in knowledge bases.

People who need help may post their problems on corporate intranets (e.g., using discussion forums or blogs), or on public social networks such as LinkedIn (linkedin. com) that has an "answers to questions" space and capability, and ask for help. Similarly, companies may ask for advice on how to solve problems or exploit an opportunity. Answers may generate hundreds of useful ideas within a few days. It is a kind of brainstorming.

Automated Question-Answer Systems

In addition to advice provided by humans, an increasing number of applications attempt to provide automated answers to users' questions. The expertise finding system described in the following section is an example of such a system. The user asks a question and the computer tries to find an answer that matches the question. The goal of an **automated question-answer (QA) system** is to locate, extract, and provide specific answers to user questions expressed in natural language. A subset of this attempt is *automated decision making* in which the question is about a specific routine decision situation (e.g., to approve a loan request or reject it).

A *QA system* differs from *frequently asked questions (FAQ)* in that the content of an FAQ is fairly structured and limited in its size, concentrating on "frequently asked questions." Also, FAQ posts questions to choose from while in QA users ask the unstructured questions in a natural language.

To begin, the computer needs to understand the question (natural language understanding), then the computer needs to search for a matching answer. There are several methods for computers to find the answers to such questions. One method is based on the use of Artificial Intelligence (AI) by using intelligent agents such as expert systems. This approach concentrates mostly on automated problem solving and is not related to Web search.

Live Chat with Experts

Live chats with experts are becoming popular. For example, you can chat with physicians of different specialties. You can do it in many other disciplines.

Example 1: Moontoast. Moontoast (moontoast.com) is an online *knowledge marketplace*, where experts exchange information with *seekers* (those looking for information) via a live video chat session, for a prearranged fee. All members of Moontoast can list services they can provide as experts and book sessions with seekers, whether they are professionals in that service or partake in it recreationally. Seekers can then search Moontoast to find services that interest them and schedule video conferences with the relevant expert.

Example 2: Search Engines Advice. Answers.com and Ask.com belong to a special category of search engines that has a huge collection of questions with appropriate answers. The engine tries to match a question made in natural language with appropriate answers; see the discussion in Chapter 2.

Expert Location Systems

Expert/expertise location systems (ELS) are interactive computerized systems that help employees find and connect with colleagues—whether they are across the country or across the organization—in order to solve specific, critical business problems in a short time. Expertise location systems are designed to:

▶ Identify people with expertise and link them to those with questions or problems.

▶ Identify potential staff for projects requiring specific expertise.

▶ Link people to information about experts.

▶ Assist in career development.

▶ Provide support for teams and communities of practice.

For benefits, limitations, and risks, see kmedge.org/wp/snel-whentouse.html.

Software for such systems is made by companies such as AskMe, RightNow Technologies, and Tacit Knowledge Systems, Inc. For example, Realcom's AskMe, a software solution for deploying employee knowledge networks, enables organizations to fully leverage employee knowledge and expertise to drive innovations and improve bottom-line performance. The solution is the result of AskMe's collaboration, experience, and success with real-world customer deployments. For benefits, features, and demonstrations, see realcom-inc.com. Most expert location systems work in a similar manner, exploring knowledge bases for either an answer to the problem (if it exists there) or locating qualified experts. The generic process is shown in Exhibit 5.6.

EXHIBIT 5.6 AskMe's Expert Location System

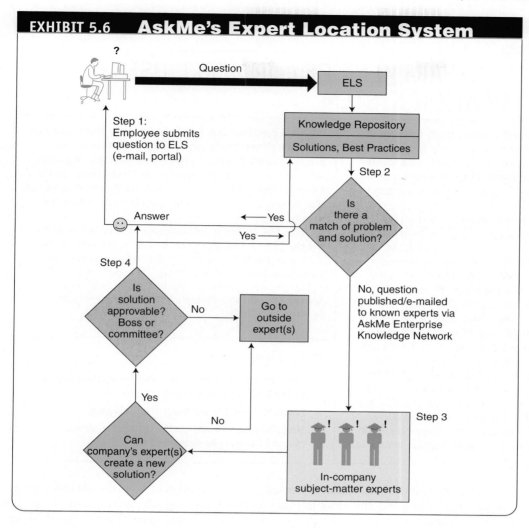

The four steps of the process are:

1. An employee submits a question to the ELS.

2. The software searches its database to see if an answer to the question already exists. If it does, the information (research reports, spreadsheets, etc.) is returned to the employee. If not, the software searches documents and archived communications for an "expert."

3. Once a qualified expert candidate is located, the system asks if he or she is able to answer the question from a colleague. If so, the expert submits a response. If the expert is unable to respond, he or she can elect to pass on the question. The question is then routed to the next appropriate expert until one responds.

4. After the response is sent, it is reviewed for accuracy by a corporate advisor and sent to the person who made the query. At the same time, the question and its response are added to the knowledge database. This way, if the question comes up again, it will not be necessary to seek real-time assistance from a human expert.

Case 5.2 demonstrates how such a system works for the U.S. government.

Seeking Expertise in Social Networks

Seeking expertise (and experts) is becoming a very popular social activity. People post their problems on bulletin boards, forums, and blogs and wait for responses. The New Zealand closing case describes several initiatives of this nature. One of the features of LinkedIn is the free "LinkedIn Answers," where users ask questions for the community with which he or she is connected, to receive an answer.

CASE 5.2

EC Application

HOW THE U.S. DEPARTMENT OF COMMERCE USES AN EXPERT LOCATION SYSTEM

The U.S. Commercial Service Division at the Department of Commerce (DOC) conducts approximately 200,000 counseling sessions a year involving close to $40 billion in trade. The division employs many specialists who frequently need to do research or call on experts to answer a complex question posed by a U.S. corporation.

For example, a U.S.–based software company called Brad Anderson, a DOC specialist, for advice. The software company wanted to close a deal with a customer in Poland, but the buyer wanted to charge the U.S. company a 20 percent withholding tax, a tax it attributed to Poland's admission into the European Union. Was the tax legitimate?

To find out, Anderson turned to the DOC Insider, an expertise location system (from AskMe). After typing in his question, Anderson first found some documents that were related to his query, but they did not explain the EU tax code completely. Anderson next asked the system to search the Commercial Service database for a "live" expert, and within seconds, he was given a list of 80 people in the DOC who might be able to help him. Of those, he chose the six people he felt were most qualified and then forwarded to them his query.

Before the DOC Insider was in place, Anderson says, it would have taken him about three days to get an answer to the same question. "You have to make many phone calls and deal with different time zones," he says. Thanks to the expertise location system, however, he had three responses within minutes, a complete answer within an hour, and the sale went through the following morning. Anderson estimates that he now uses the system for roughly 40 percent of the work he does.

The DOC Insider is an invaluable tool. Anderson thinks the tool is vital enough to provide it to other units at the agency. In the first nine months the system was in place, it saved more than 1,000 man hours.

Sources: Compiled from D'Agostino (2004) and *realcom-inc.com* (accessed April 2011).

Questions

1. What are the benefits of the expertise location system to the DOC and similar organizations?

2. Review Exhibit 5.6 and relate it to this case.

3. What, in your opinion, are the limitations of this system? Can they be overcome? How?

In many organizations, social networking and the location of expertise are converging. Some organizations use the same internal social networking site, intranet, or portal for internal expertise location as they do for communication and general networking. Many consider expertise location to be an extension of knowledge management, in that the goal is to capture and reuse the skills and experience of internal staff members in order to increase competitive advantage. For discussion and details of when to use social networking for expert location, see kmedge.org/wp/snel-whentouse.html.

Section 5.3 ▶ REVIEW QUESTIONS

1. Define knowledge management.

2. Discuss the relationship between KM and EC.

3. Describe online advisory services.

4. Describe expert location systems and their benefits.

5. Relate social networks to providing advice.

5.4   COLLABORATIVE COMMERCE

collaborative commerce (c-commerce)
The use of digital technologies that enable companies to collaboratively plan, design, develop, manage, and research products, services, and innovative EC applications.

Collaborative commerce is an e-commerce technology that can be used to improve collaboration within and among organizations, frequently in supply chain relationships.

ESSENTIALS OF COLLABORATIVE COMMERCE

Collaborative commerce (c-commerce) refers to the use of digital technologies mostly online, that enable companies to collaboratively plan, design, develop, manage, and research products, services, and innovative EC applications. An example would be a manufacturer that is collaborating electronically with a supplier that designs a product or a part for the manufacturer. C-commerce implies communication, information sharing, and collaborative planning done electronically by using tools such as groupware, blogs, wikis, and specially designed EC collaboration tools. In the supply chain case, the major benefits are cost reduction, increased revenue, faster move of goods, and better customer retention. These benefits are the result of fewer stock-outs, less exception and rush-order processing, reduced inventory throughout the supply chain, lower material costs, increased sales volume, and increased competitive advantage.

THE ELEMENTS AND PROCESSES OF C-COMMERCE

The elements of processes of c-commerce vary according to situations. For example, in many cases collaboration involves a manufacturer (or assemblers) with its suppliers, designers, and other business partners as well as its customers and possibly government, usually along the supply chain. The major elements of the collaboration are illustrated in Exhibit 5.7. Notice that the collaboration is based on the analysis of internal and external data that are made visible via a portal. On the left side of the exhibit, we show the cyclical process of collaborative commerce. The people involved in this cycle use the information in the displays as well as the interactions among the major groups of participants. The elements of c-commerce can be arranged in different configurations, one of which is a hub.

COLLABORATION HUBS

A popular form of c-commerce is the *collaboration hub*, which is often used by the members of a supply chain. A collaboration hub (c-hub) is the central point of control for an e-market. A single c-hub, representing one e-market owner, can host multiple *collaboration spaces* (c-spaces) in which trading partners use c-enablers to exchange data with the c-hub.

collaboration hub (c-hub)
The central point of control for an e-market. A single c-hub, representing one e-market owner, can host multiple collaboration spaces (c-spaces) in which trading partners use c-enablers to exchange data with the c-hub.

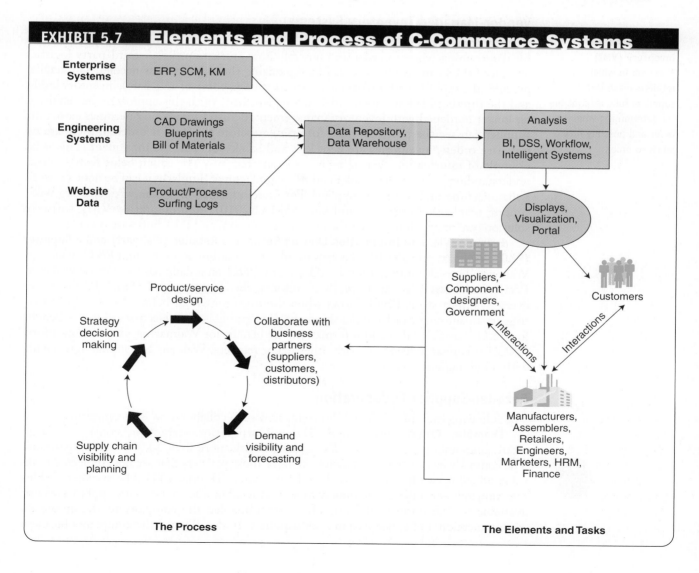

EXHIBIT 5.7 Elements and Process of C-Commerce Systems

The Process   The Elements and Tasks

C-commerce activities usually are conducted between and among supply chain partners. For discussion and examples, see Chapter 11. There are several varieties of c-commerce, ranging from joint design efforts to joint demand forecasting. Collaboration can be done both between and within organizations. For example, a collaborative platform can help in communication and collaboration between headquarters and subsidiaries or between franchisers and franchisees of the company. The platform provides services such as e-mail, message boards, chat rooms, and online corporate data access around the globe, no matter the time zone. Note that collaboration with business partners involves extensive sharing of data and information (see Healey 2010) as shown in the following examples.

REPRESENTATIVE EXAMPLES OF COLLABORATIVE COMMERCE

Leading companies such as Dell, Cisco, and HP use collaborative commerce strategically, enabling sophisticated business models while transforming their value chains. They also have implemented collaboration initiatives along the supply chain (see Chapter 11) such as e-procurement. Other collaboration EC initiatives were done to streamline operations, reduce overhead, and maintain or enhance margins in the face of intense competition. For example, Dell implemented end-to-end integrated configuration and ordering for its PC, a single enterprise middleware backbone, and multi-tier collaborative planning. This has enabled Dell to support the make-to-order business model with best-in-class speed and efficiency. Cisco supports a virtual business model focusing on time-to-market and customer satisfaction. Cisco has integrated its order process with back-end processes, implemented purchase order automation, and enabled collaborative product development.

Vendor-Managed Inventory Systems

vendor-managed inventory (VMI)
A system in which retailers make their suppliers fully responsible for determining when to order and possibly how much to order.

With **vendor-managed inventory (VMI)**, retailers make their suppliers fully responsible for determining when to order and possibly how much to order. A third-party logistics provider (3PL) can also be involved by organizing the shipments as needed. The retailer provides the supplier with real-time information (e.g., point-of-sale data), inventory levels, and the threshold below which orders are replenished. With this approach, the retailer is no longer burdened with inventory management, demand forecasting becomes easier, the supplier can see the potential need for an item before the item is ordered, there are no purchase orders, inventories are kept low, and stock-outs become infrequent. This is an example of information sharing and it is supported by VMI, which helps foster a close understanding between the retailer and the manufacturer. Similarly, it can be done between a manufacturer and its major suppliers. For more information, see en.wikipedia.org/wiki/vendor_managed_inventory, and Spychalska (2010). Representative VMI software solutions are provided by sockeyebusinesssolutions.com and JDA Software (jda.com).

Example: VMI and Information Sharing Between a Retailer (Walmart) and a Supplier (P&G). Walmart provides P&G access to sales information on every item P&G makes for Walmart. The sales information is collected by P&G on a daily basis (or made visible to P&G) from every Walmart store. By monitoring the inventory level of each P&G item in every Walmart store, P&G knows when the inventories fall below the threshold that triggers an automatic order and a shipment. Everything is done electronically. The benefit for P&G is accurate demand information; the benefit for Walmart is adequate inventory. P&G has similar agreements with other major retailers; Walmart has similar agreements with other major suppliers.

Retailer-Supplier Collaboration

The following example of Target illustrates how such collaboration is accomplished.

Example: Target Corporation. Target Corporation (targetcorp.com) is a large retail conglomerate. It conducts EC activities with more than 20,000 trading partners. The company has an extranet-based system for those partners that are not connected to its value-added network (VAN)–based EDI (see Online Tutorial T11). The extranet enables the company not only to reach many more partners but also to use many applications not available on the traditional EDI. The system enabled the company to streamline its communication and collaboration with suppliers. It also allowed the company's business

EXHIBIT 5.8   Target's Extranet

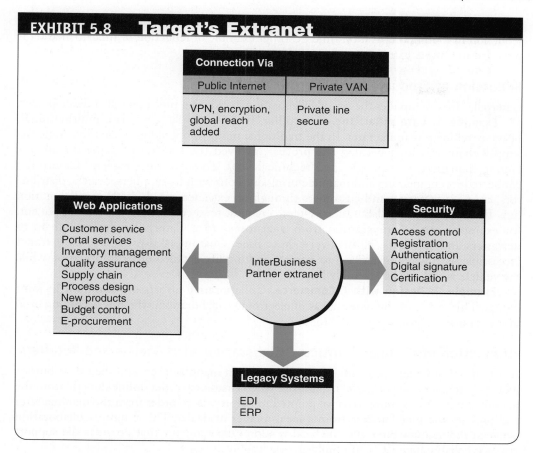

customers to create personalized Web pages, as shown in Exhibit 5.8. Target now has a website called Partners Online (partnersonline.com), which it uses to communicate with and provide an enormous amount of information to its partners.

Reducing Transportation and Inventory Costs

Cost reduction in transportation and inventory through collaboration are illustrated in this example of Unilever.

Example: The Case of Unilever. Unilever (unilever.com) is a large global manufacturer of leading brands in food, home care, and personal care. Its 30 contract carriers deliver 250,000 truckloads of shipments every day. Unilever's Web-based database, the Transportation Business Center (TBC), is shared with the contract carriers, providing them with site-specification pickup and delivery requirements. TBC also helps Unilever organize and automate its carrier selection processes based on contract provisions and commitments. When a primary carrier is unable to accept a shipment, TBC automatically recommends alternative carriers.

Reduction of Design Cycle Time

The case of Clarion Malaysia demonstrates cycle time reduction through collaboration.

Example: Clarion Malaysia. Clarion Malaysia, part of the global company Clarion Group, employs approximately 700 people in Malaysia. It manufactures audio electronic systems for cars.

Working with IBM through the implementation of a computer aided design (CAD) system and collaborative product cycle management (PLM) technologies, Clarion has slashed its time-to-market from 14 months to about 9 months, while at the same time improving the quality of the products because more time can be spent in yielding superior designs. The application of the latest information technology has also supported much closer cooperation with and responsiveness to customers throughout the design process, better use of materials through the deployment of 3-D modeling, and a 60 percent reduction in tooling preparation time. Another example of reduction of time-to-market is provided in Online File W5.6.

Reduction of Product Development Time

Caterpillar Inc. exemplifies the use of collaboration in reducing time in product development.

Example 1: Caterpillar, Inc. Caterpillar, Inc. (caterpillar.com) is a multinational, heavy-machinery manufacturer. In the traditional mode of operation, cycle time along the supply chain was long because the process involved the transfer of paper documents among managers, salespeople, and technical staff. To solve the problem, Caterpillar connected its engineering and manufacturing divisions with its suppliers, dealers, distributors, overseas factories, and customers through an extranet-based global e-collaboration hub. By means of the collaboration system, a request for a customized tractor component, for example, can be transmitted from a customer to a Caterpillar dealer and on to designers and suppliers, all in a very short time. Customers also can use an extranet (accessible with wireless devices) to retrieve and modify detailed order information while the vehicle is still on the assembly line.

Example 2: Design with C-Commerce. Collaborative efforts are common in joint design. This is one of the oldest areas of electronic collaboration, which is becoming even more popular due to EC Web 2.0 tools.

Elimination of Channel Conflict: Collaboration with Dealers and Retailers

As discussed in Chapters 3 and 4, a conflict between manufacturers and their distributors, including retailers and/or dealers, may arise when customers order online directly from the manufacturer. One solution that we pointed to before was to order from the manufacturer and pick up the merchandize from a local retailer or dealer. This requires collaboration between the manufacturer and the local vendor. One company that provides the support for such collaborative EC is JG Sullivan (see jgsullivan.com).

The company's product known as "Collaborative E-Commerce Platform" is a way for manufacturers who sell primarily through a retailer channel to offer their products for sale online in a manner which does not impact the retailer-consumer relationship.

Starting from the manufacturer's site, consumers research and select the product they wish to purchase. If needed, they can customize it (e.g., cars, appliances). The consumers add the product to the shopping cart on the manufacturer's site. When they are ready to check out, they are first asked for their ZIP code and presented with a list of retailers near them. The consumers select a retailer from the list, and their order is transferred from the manufacturer's site to the retailer's site for the rest of the order fulfillment to occur. The software leverages the strengths of the manufacturer and the local dealer. The local dealers need to be involved to deliver products, install (if needed), service, and haul away old products. Obviously, the manufacturer and the dealers must work together, and they do it electronically.

Example: Whirlpool Corp. The world's largest manufacturer of major home appliances had a problem: channel conflict. Consumers were coming to the Whirlpool.com website ready to buy an appliance directly from Whirlpool (some products can be customized, see the closing case in Chapter 11). Whirlpool's nationwide network of dealers was not happy. And besides, some appliances (e.g., a dishwasher, washing machines) are not the kind of thing you can have drop-shipped to someone's house—you need to install the new one, haul away the old one, service the product in the future, the kind of thing that adds value to a local dealer's business.

JG Sullivan's system was installed globally, making customers happy and making dealers happy too since their marketing and sales experiences decreased significantly, and allowed Whirlpool to know their customers better.

IMPLEMENTING C-COMMERCE

Leading companies such as Dell, Cisco, and HP use collaborative commerce strategically, enabling sophisticated business models while transforming their value chains. They also have implemented e-procurement and mature collaboration techniques to streamline operations, reduce overhead, and maintain or enhance margins in the face of intense competition. For example, Dell implemented an end-to-end integrated configuration and ordering system, a single enterprise middleware backbone, and multitier collaborative planning. These enabled Dell applications to support a make-to-order business model with best-in-class speed and efficiency. Cisco chose to support a virtual business model focusing on time-to-market and customer satisfaction. Cisco also has integrated its order process with back-end processes, implemented purchase order automation, and enabled collaborative product development.

BARRIERS TO C-COMMERCE

Despite the many potential benefits, c-commerce is moving ahead fairly slowly in many companies except some very large ones. Reasons cited in various studies include technical factors involving a lack of internal integration, standards, and networks; security and privacy concerns, and some distrust over who has access to and control of information stored in a partner's database; internal resistance to information sharing and to new approaches; and lack of company skills to conduct c-commerce. Gaining agreement on how to share costs and benefits can also prove problematic.

A big stumbling block to the adoption of c-commerce has been the lack of defined and universally agreed-upon standards. New approaches, such as the use of XML and its variants and the use of Web Services, could significantly lessen the problem of standards. Also, the use of collaborative Web 2.0 tools that are based on open source could be helpful.

Finally, global collaboration may be complicated by additional barriers ranging from language incompatibility to cultural misunderstandings. According to Currier (2010), the following are the major challenges faced when deploying collaboration technologies (listed by declining order of importance): Insufficient budget, training end users, ROI difficult to measure, employee resistance, lack of management commitment, defining strategies, finding the right products, ensuring security, disruptions during implementation, difficulty in customizing, maintaining quality of output, executing strategies, inexperienced techs, lack of IT commitment, and employee privacy issues.

Overcoming Barriers to Collaboration

Specialized c-commerce software tools may break down some of the barriers to c-commerce. In addition, as companies learn more about the major benefits of c-commerce—such as smoothing the supply chain, reducing inventories and operating costs, and increasing customer satisfaction and the competitive edge—it is expected that more companies will rush to jump on the c-commerce bandwagon. Finally, it is essential to have a collaborative culture within and among organizations. For how to do this, see Hansen (2009). One area in which c-commerce is conducted is consumer-to-consumer e-commerce, which is presented in the next section.

Collaboration Processes and Software   A large number of propriety methods and supportive communication and collaborative software are available to support c-commerce. These will be briefly introduced in Online Tutorial T10.

Section 5.4 ▶ REVIEW QUESTIONS

1. Define c-commerce.
2. List the major types and characteristics of c-commerce.
3. Describe some examples of c-commerce.
4. Describe the elements and process of c-commerce.
5. List some major barriers to c-commerce. How can a company overcome these limitations?

5.5 CONSUMER-TO-CONSUMER ELECTRONIC COMMERCE

consumer-to-consumer (C2C) EC
E-commerce model in which consumers sell directly to other consumers.

Consumer-to-consumer (C2C) EC, which is sometimes referred to as *peer-to-peer (P2P) exchanges,* involves all transactions between and among individual consumers. These transactions can also include third parties, such as eBay or a social network site, that organize, manage, and facilitate the C2C network. C2C networks may include classified ads, music and file sharing, career and job websites (e.g., linkedin.com and careerone. com.au), and also personal services, such as dating websites (e.g., match.com).

In C2C EC, consumers sell goods and/or services to other consumers. There are millions of sellers with different items to sell and an equally large number of buyers. Finding each other may take a long time and can even incur high costs to both buyers and sellers, and this is why intermediaries such as eBay or Craigslist are so important. They simply mediate between consumers who want to buy and sell. Some take small cuts of a seller's profit as a fee for bringing customers to the sellers.

C2C EC has given online shopping and trading a new dimension. Although this sort of trading is prevalent in the offline world (classified newspaper ads, garage sales, etc.), it was not expected to take off online due to problems with trust because of the anonymity of the traders. This problem was solved by using a third-party payment provider (e.g., PayPal), and in escrow or insurance services provided by eBay and others. One advantage of C2C EC is that it reduces the cost to buyers. It also gives many individuals and small business owners a low-cost way to sell their goods and services.

Social networks have become a popular place for C2C activities such as selling products and services via classified ads, and on Facebook and other social networks' pages. People are sharing or selling music, bartering, selling virtual properties, and providing personal services.

E-COMMERCE: C2C APPLICATIONS

EC has redefined the traditional structure of business by giving small firms and individuals the same opportunities to conduct business as large corporations do. As a result, many websites have been created that encourage and assist with c-commerce activities between individual people. We cover several representative applications next.

C2C Auctions

A very successful example of a C2C application is auctions. In dozens of countries, selling and buying on auction sites is exploding. Most auctions are managed by intermediaries (the most well-known is eBay). Consumers can visit auctions at general sites such as ebay.com or auctionanything.com or they can use specialized sites, such as bidz.com, which focuses on exclusive and brand name jewelry. In addition, many individuals are conducting their own auctions with the use of special software. For example, greatshop.com provides software to create C2C reverse auction communities online.

Classified Ads

People sell to other people every day through classified ads. Internet-based classified ads have several advantages over newspaper classified ads. They offer a national, rather than a local, audience, and they can be updated and quickly and easily. This greatly increases the supply of goods and services available and the number of potential buyers. One of the most successful sites of C2C classified ads is Craigslist (see Chapter 2). Another example is iclassifieds2000.com, which contains a list of about 500,000 cars, compared with the much smaller number you might find in any local newspaper. Classified ads also include apartments for rent across the United States (powered by forrent.com) and personal ads (powered by match.com). Yet, another example is freeclassifieds.com. Both Google and Yahoo! are expanding their online classifieds. Many newspapers also offer their classified ads online. In some cases, placing an ad on one website brings it automatically into the classified sections of numerous partners. This increases ad exposure at no additional cost. To help narrow the search for a particular item, on some sites shoppers can use search engines.

Classified ads appear in thousands of websites including popular social networks such as Facebook and LinkedIn.

Personal Services

Numerous personal services are available on the Internet (lawyers, handy helpers, tax preparers, investment clubs, dating services). Some are in the classified ads, but others are listed in specialized websites (e.g., hireahelper.com) and directories. Some are free, some charge a fee. Be very careful before purchasing any personal services. Fraud or crime could be involved (e.g., a lawyer online may not be an expert in the area professed or may not be a lawyer at all). Online advising and consulting, described in Section 5.3, also are examples of personal services.

File-Sharing Utilities: Napster and Others

It all started in 2001. By logging onto services such as Napster, people were able to download files that others were willing to share. Such *P2P networks* enabled users to search other members' hard drives for a particular file, including data files created by users or copied from elsewhere. Digital music and games were the most popular files accessed. Then came the movies and videos. Napster had more than 60 million members in 2002 before it was forced to stop its service due to copyright violations.

The Napster server functioned as a directory that listed the files being shared by other users. Once logged into the server, users could search the directory for specific songs and locate the file owner. They could then directly access the owner's computer and download the songs they had chosen. Napster also included chat rooms to connect its millions of users.

However, a U.S. federal court found Napster to be in violation of copyright laws because it enabled people to obtain music files without paying the creators of the music for access to their material. Following this ruling, in March 2002, Napster closed its free services. Napster continued to operate on a small scale, with users paying a fee for file sharing and Napster passing along part of the fee to copyright owners.

A number of free file-sharing programs still exist. For example, an even purer version of P2P is Gnutella (gnutella.com), a P2P program that dispenses with the central database altogether (downloadable software) in connecting the peer computers. To access games over P2P networks, try trustyfiles.com. Despite the temptation to get "something for nothing," remember that downloading copyrighted materials for free may be against the law; violators are subject to penalties if caught.

C2C Activities in Social Networks and Trading Virtual Properties

C2C activities in social networks include the sharing of photos, videos, music, and other files; trading of virtual properties; and much more. It is usually legal to do it. Trading virtual properties is very popular in virtual worlds, especially in SL (Chapters 2 and 7).

Section 5.5 ▶ REVIEW QUESTIONS

1. Define C2C e-commerce.
2. Describe the benefits of C2C.
3. Describe the major e-commerce applications.
4. Define file sharing.
5. How is C2C practiced in social networking?

MANAGERIAL ISSUES

Some managerial issues related to this chapter are as follows.

1. **What are the e-government opportunities?** If an organization is doing business with the government, eventually some or all of its activities may be moved online. Organizations may find new online business opportunities with the government because governments are getting serious about going online; some even mandate it as a major way to conduct B2G and G2B.

2. **How do we design the most cost-efficient government e-procurement system?** Several issues are involved and questions may be raised: How much can the governmental e-procurement system save on procurement costs? How can it enhance the transparency of the procurement process and prevent illegal bribery? How should the online and offline procurement systems be designed? How should the portfolio of auctions and desktop purchasing be constructed? Can the government use commercial B2B sites for procurement? Can businesses use the government procurement system for their own procurement? Would the boundary between G2B and B2B blur as the channel of procurement? This must be considered in an effective design.

3. **How do we design the portfolio of e-learning knowledge sources?** There are many sources of e-learning services. The e-learning management team needs to design the portfolio of the online and offline training

applications, and the internal and external knowledge sources (paid and nonpaid sources). The internal knowledge management system is an important source of training materials for large corporations, whereas external sources could be more cost-effective for small corporations. Obviously, justification is needed and goes hand-in-hand with the selection of supporting tools (see West 2007). For illustrative case studies, see *brightwave.co.uk*.

4. **How do we incorporate social networking–based learning and services in our organization?** With the proliferation of social networking initiatives in the enterprise comes the issue of how to integrate these with the enterprise system, including CRM, KM, training, and other business processes. An issue is how to balance the quality of knowledge with the scope of knowledge.

5. **What will the impact be of the e-book platform?** If the e-book is widely adopted by readers, the distribution channel of online book sales may be disruptive. This new platform may cannibalize the offline book retail business. Also, there is the need for protection of the intellectual property of digital contents that is easy to copy and distribute.

6. **How do we connect our expert location system and social networking initiatives?** Expert location systems and knowledge management systems can be developed to assist in finding experts both internally and externally. This service can be linked with a job matching portal and professional social networks (e.g., LinkedIn).

7. **How difficult is it to introduce e-collaboration?** Dealing with the technology may be the easy part. Tackling the behavioral changes needed within an organization and its trading partners may be the greater challenge. Change management requires an understanding of the new interdependencies being constructed and the new roles and responsibilities that must be adapted in order for the enterprise and its business partners to collaborate. Finally, e-collaboration costs money and needs to be justified. This may not be an easy task due to the intangible risks and benefits involved.

8. **Can we capitalize on C2C EC?** Individual and small businesses cannot utilize many C2C activities unless businesses provide secure payment services such as *paypal.com* or an escrow service. Businesses may consider sponsoring C2C activities in order to increase viral marketing and advertising.

9. **How much can be shared with business partners?** Can they be trusted? Many companies are sharing forecast data and actual sales data. But when it comes to allowing real-time access to product design, inventory, and interface to ERP systems, there may be some hesitation. It is basically a question of security and trust. The more information that is shared, the better the collaboration. However, sharing information can lead to the giving away of trade secrets. In some cases, there is a cultural resistance against sharing (some employees do not like to share information even within their own organization). The value of sharing needs to be carefully assessed against its risks.

10. **Who benefits from vendor-managed inventory?** The vendor-managed inventory (VMI) system in collaborative planning, forecasting, and replenishment (CPFR) requires the supplier side to take the highest responsibility without the guarantee of sales. However, small suppliers may not have the ability to systematically manage inventory well. In this case, the large buyer will need to support the inventory management system on behalf of the suppliers. Sensitive issues must be agreed upon when initiating VMI. One such issue is who takes responsibility for unsold items due to the wrong demand forecast.

SUMMARY

In this chapter, you learned about the following EC issues as they relate to the chapter's learning objectives.

1. **E-government activities.** Governments, like any other organization, can use EC applications for great savings and increased effectiveness. Notable applications are e-procurement using reverse auctions, e-payments to and from citizens and businesses, auctioning of surplus goods, and electronic travel and expense management systems. Governments also conduct electronic business with other governments. Finally, governments can facilitate homeland security with EC tools.

2. **Implementing e-government to citizens, businesses, and its own operations.** Governments worldwide are providing a variety of services to citizens over the Internet. Such initiatives increase citizens' satisfaction and decrease government expenses in providing customer service applications including electronic voting. Governments also are active in electronically trading with businesses. Finally, EC is done within and between governments. E-government's growth can be strengthened through the use of wireless systems in what is described as mobile or m-government. E-government 2.0 is becoming increasingly popular with tools such as wikis, blogs, and Twitter.

3. **E-learning and training.** E-learning is the delivery of educational content via electronic media, including the Internet and intranets. Degree programs, lifelong learning topics, and corporate training are delivered by thousands of organizations worldwide. A growing area

is distance learning via online university offerings. Some are virtual; others are delivered both online and offline. Online corporate training also is increasing and is sometimes conducted at formal corporate learning centers. Implementation is done in steps starting with just presence and ending with activities on social networks. New e-readers contain easy-to-read text, search capabilities, and many other functions. Add to this the low cost of books and the capability of storing many books on a small device and you can understand the increased popularity of the device.

4. **E-books and their readers.** There is increased interest in e-books due to their many benefits (Amazon.com sells more e-books than hardcover ones). There is intense competition among e-reader manufacturers, and their capabilities have increased while their prices have declined. E-books are used both for pleasure reading and for studying. E-books can be read on iPads and other portable devices.

5. **Knowledge management and dissemination as an e-business.** Knowledge has been recognized as an important organizational asset. It needs to be properly captured, stored, managed, and shared. Knowledge is critical for many e-commerce tasks. Knowledge can be shared in different ways; expert knowledge can be provided to nonexperts (for a fee or free) via a knowledge portal or as a personal service (e.g., via e-mail).

6. **Online advisory systems.** Online advisory systems of all kinds are becoming popular. Some are for free while most charge money. Users must be careful as to the quality of the advice. Social networks and portals provide a variety of services. In addition, these systems are in active use with many organizations.

7. **C-commerce.** Collaborative commerce (c-commerce) refers to a planned use of digital technology by business partners. It includes planning, designing, researching, managing, and servicing various partners and tasks, frequently along the supply chain. C-commerce can be between different pairs of business partners or among many partners participating in a collaborative network.

8. **Collaboration 2.0.** Collaboration with Web 2.0 tools and in social networks adds a social dimension that could improve communication, participation, and trust. There are many new tools, some of which are being added to traditional collaboration tools. Better collaboration may improve supply chain operation, knowledge management, and individual and organizational performance.

9. **C2C activities.** C2C consists of consumers conducting e-commerce with other consumers, mainly in auctions (such as at eBay), classified ads, matching services, and file sharing.

KEY TERMS

Automated question-answer (QA) systems	258	Electronic book (e-book)	250	Knowledge management (KM)	253
Collaboration hub (c-hub)	261	Expert location systems (ELS)	258	Learning management system (LMS)	249
Collaborative commerce (c-commerce)	260	Government 2.0	238	Learning on-demand	249
Consumer-to-consumer (C2C) EC	265	Government-to-business (G2B)	235	Mobile government (m-government)	239
Distance learning	244	Government-to-citizens (G2C)	232	Social learning	246
E-government	232	Government-to-employees (G2E)	237	Vendor-managed inventory (VMI)	262
E-learning	241	Government-to-government (G2G)	236	Virtual universities	244

DISCUSSION QUESTIONS

1. Discuss the advantages and disadvantages of e-government using social networking versus the traditional e-government portal.

2. Discuss the advantages and shortcomings of e-voting.

3. Discuss the advantages and disadvantages of e-books.

4. Discuss the advantages of e-learning in the corporate training environment.

5. In what ways does KM support e-commerce?

6. Some say that B2G is simply B2B. Explain.

7. Compare and contrast B2E with G2E.

8. Which e-government EC activities are intrabusiness activities? Explain why they are intrabusiness.

9. Identify the benefits of G2C to citizens and to governments.

10. Relate IBM's Innovation Jam to KM and social networks.

11. Relate KM to learning, to e-publishing, and to C2C.

12. It is said that c-commerce signifies a move from a transaction focus to a relationship focus among supply chain members. Discuss.

TOPICS FOR CLASS DISCUSSION AND DEBATES

1. Discuss the advantages of e-learning for an undergraduate student and for an MBA student.

2. Discuss the advantages of expert location systems over corporate databases that contain experts' information and knowledge. What are the disadvantages? Can they be combined? How?

3. Discuss the benefits of using virtual worlds to facilitate learning. What are the limitations? The disadvantages?

4. Discuss possible strategies to facilitate c-commerce.

5. Will e-universities replace universities?

6. Debate: E-books will replace traditional paper books.

7. Debate: Why aren't all firms embracing KM?

8. Debate: The pros and cons of electronic voting.

INTERNET EXERCISES

1. Enter tamago.us and nextag.com and learn how they operate. What content do they offer? Write a report.

2. Enter e-learningcentre.co.uk, elearnmag.org, and elearningpost.com. Identify current discussion issues and find two articles related to the effectiveness of e-training. Write a report. Also prepare a list of the resources available on these sites.

3. Enter adobe.com and find the tutorials and tools it offers for e-learning, knowledge management, and online publishing.

4. Identify a difficult business problem. Post the problem on elance.com, linkedin.com, and answers.com. Summarize the offers you received to solve the problem.

5. Enter blackboard.com and en.wikipedia.org/wiki/Blackboard and find the major services provided by the company, including its community system. Write a report.

6. Enter oecd.org and identify the studies conducted by the Organisation for Economic Co-operation and Development (OECD) on the topic of e-government. What are the organization's major concerns?

7. Enter fcw.com and read the latest news on e-government. Identify initiatives not covered in this chapter. Check the B2G corner. Then enter gcn.com. Finally, enter estrategy.gov. Compare the information presented on the three websites.

8. Enter procurement.org and govexec.com. Identify recent e-government procurement initiatives and summarize their unique aspects.

9. Enter insight24.com and opentext. com and find the most recent and most popular videos about knowledge management. Also use the search engines of YouTube and Google. Prepare a list of five and view one in each category. Prepare a report.

10. Enter infozone.clomedia.com/gotomeeting and find the Webinar titled "How to Build an On-Demand Training Program" sponsored by Citrix Online. View it (45 minutes) and write a report on what it is and what the benefits are.

11. Enter amazon.com, bn.com, and sony.com and find the latest information about their e-readers. Compare their capabilities and write a report. (Consult ebookreader.com.)

12. Enter wi5connect.com and find what products it has for learning in social networking. Prepare a list of capabilities of each product.

13. Enter kolabora.com or mindjet.com. Find out how collaboration is done. Summarize the benefits of the site to the participants.

14. Enter vignette.com or share360.com and read the company vision for collaborative commerce. Then view the demo. Explain in a report how the company facilitates c-commerce.

15. Enter guru.com and elance.com and compare their offerings. Which one would you prefer to post your skills on and why?

16. Find two companies that enable C2C (or P2P) e-commerce. (Try tamango.us, egrovesys.com/application-development/c2c-ecommerce-solution.html, etc.) Comment on their capabilities.

17. Enter collaborate.com and read about recent issues related to collaboration. Prepare a report.

18. Enter vignette.com or cybozu.com and read the company vision for collaborative commerce. Then view the demo. Explain in a report how the company facilitates c-commerce.

TEAM ASSIGNMENTS AND PROJECTS

1. **Assignment for the Opening Case**

   Read the opening case and answer the following questions.

   a. Explain why knowledge sharing is considered a strategic asset for the company.

   b. Explain how thousands of "communities of practice" operate and how they relate to CAT's Knowledge Network.

   c. How does CAT provide e-learning? Why is it needed?

   d. Identify the enterprise social network(s) at CAT. Find material about their operation.

   e. Relate this case to the topic of finding expertise discussed in this chapter.

2. Each team is assigned a different country. Explore the e-government offerings of that country. Each team will make a presentation to convince the class that its country's offerings are the most comprehensive. (Exclude Hong Kong and New Zealand.)

3. Create four teams, each representing one of the following: G2C, G2B, G2E, and G2G. Each team will prepare a plan of its major activities in a small country, such as Holland, Denmark, Finland, or Singapore. A fifth team will deal with the coordination and collaboration of all e-government activities in each country. Prepare a report.

4. View the video: "Panel Discussion on Collaborative Commerce" (Pt.1) @ Ariba LIVE 2011 (12:37 minutes) at **youtube.com/watch?v=bucxXpDvWDI**. Answer the following questions: (For Part 1; Optional–Part 2)

   a. What benefits do the buyers see? Relate these benefits to collaborative commerce.

   b. How is EC used to support c-commerce?

   c. How can buyer/supplier relationships be fostered with c-commerce?

   d. Run a similar panel discussion in class. If possible ask large buyers to attend and take part.

   e. How is bringing business partners online accomplished?

   f. What role does Ariba play? (Check their website.)

   g. What did you learned in this video about the benefits of c-commerce and e-commerce?

5. View the video: "E-learning Debate 2010—Highlights" (4.5 minutes) at **youtube.com/watch?v= Q42flb1Fnck**. Debate the pros and cons regarding the value of e-learning.

   a. List all of the pro and all the con statements from the video.

   b. For each statement have two teams (or individuals) explain why each agrees or disagrees with the statement.

   c. Add several pro and con statements from what you learned in class or discovered on the Web.

   d. Repeat assignment "b" for item "c."

   e. Jointly prepare a summary. The use of a wiki is advisable.

6. Have each team represent one of the following sites: **netlibrary.com**, **ebooks.com**, and **cyberread.com**. Each team will examine the technology, legal issues, prices, and business alliances associated with its site. Each team will then prepare a report answering the question, "Will e-books succeed?"

7. Have teams explore KM videos and other resources at **portal.brint.com** and **kmworld.com**. Also search YouTube and Google's video search. Relate them to two KM topics of this chapter. Prepare a report.

8. Each team is assigned a question-and-answer company (e.g., **answers.com**, **ask.com**). Check the company's offerings including social networking/games. Compare it to **moontoast.com**. Make a presentation.

Closing Case

SOCIAL NETWORKING INITIATIVES BY THE NEW ZEALAND GOVERNMENT

For such a small country, the New Zealand government is very active in implementing new technologies. As of 2008, it has created a number of e-government social networking initiatives.

Cross-Government Initiatives

A number of Web 2.0 initiatives have been implemented to help various government agencies and their employees work together:

▶ **Shared Workspaces.** A suite of online tools that supports information sharing and interagency collaboration, enabling specialist groups and networks to share expertise, experience, and good practices. Over 250 shared workspaces are used in 50 agencies by over 5,000 employees. The major tools are blogs and wikis.

▶ **E-Initiatives Wiki.** An online library of IT projects across government that allows those working on similar projects to share information and experience.

▶ **TWiki.** The Ministry of Education's collaborative website for people from various agencies in the tertiary education sector.

▶ **Principals Electronic Network.** An interactive online community of school principals and school leaders, established as a space for reflection and discussion and to facilitate learning from colleagues' knowledge and expertise.

▶ **Best Practices Forum.** A blog that seeks to provide leadership around best practices in significant work programs, including online authentication, strategy and policy, and Web standards.

▶ **Research e-Labs.** A blog that explores Web trends, open source software, and technology in government. It aims to publish practical technical research and case studies and generate conversations on related topics.

▶ **Sustainable living forums.** A forum provided by government for people to discuss sustainable living and eco-building experiences.

Public Engagement

Most of the government's social networking initiatives have been developed by agencies for the purpose of engaging with the public. The following are key examples:

▶ **Police Act wiki.** An initiative by the New Zealand Police to encourage public contributions to inform the drafting of the new Policing Act. The wiki was one of a number of initiatives undertaken by the New Zealand Police to enable people to participate in the project. The experiment resulted in thousands of visits and a huge number of ideas and suggestions from the public during a short time. All were posted publicly online, and this material was provided to the special committee considering submission on the bill about the police act.

▶ **National Library of New Zealand.** The National Library has created a number of initiatives. Create Readers is a blog about youth literature and literacy that is run by school services staff around the country. On the Library TechNZ blog, Web development staff share their thoughts about work progress on the National Library's technology. The 2007 New Zealand Poet Laureate has a blog where she shares her own poetry news and events. In addition, portions of the National Library's image collection are posted on Flickr with the aim of helping people discover new material.

▶ **Web Standards wiki.** A collaborative space in which to share knowledge and make suggestions on the New Zealand Government Web Standards. These standards exist to ensure that government websites are accessible regardless of a user's computer literacy level, Web browser, mobile device, or connection speed.

▶ **Participation Project wiki.** A vehicle for collaborative policy making developed by the State Services Commission. This wiki attracted comments from more than 1,200 people over eight days during the process of developing the Guide to Online Participation—far more input than had ever been received from a conventional public forum.

▶ **NZAID field blog.** A forum for staff of New Zealand's international aid and development agency to write about their experiences as they travel on New Zealand–funded projects and to discuss issues relevant to development work.

▶ **Ministry for Culture and Heritage.** The Ministry for Culture and Heritage offers Lively, a blog for "everyone involved in New Zealand's cultural sector," with topics such as identity, social media, and cultural research. New Zealand History Online discussion forums offer community forums on specific topics. Selected images of New Zealand from Te Ara, the Encyclopedia of New Zealand, are posted on Flickr, where users can comment and post their own photos.

▶ **Ministry for the Environment.** The Ministry for the Environment offers a discussion forum where visitors can post comments on topics related to energy, water, rubbish, and reducing adverse impacts on the environment. It also offers a website for people to show (and share with others) their videos about what sustainability means to them. The videos are posted on the Ministry for the Environment's YouTube page. The Sustainability Challenge group in Facebook encourages people to post ideas about steps that can be taken to reduce adverse impacts on the environment.

▶ **Ministry of Youth Development.** The Ministry's ID360 short-film competition provides an opportunity for young people to tell their stories through films about what identity and diversity mean to them. The films are posted on YouTube with links from the Ministry's website, and the public are invited to vote and comment on them. The Ministry also offers an online forum and a blog for young people to discuss various topics and ideas about community participation.

▶ **Families Commission.** The Families Commission set up "The Couch" to hear the views of New Zealanders on issues relating to families. It is part of a wider community engagement program in which the commission seeks feedback from families, as well as community groups and organizations, through forums and meetings. The responses from polls and questionnaires help in advocacy work to improve services and support for families, and improve advice on proposed government policies.

▶ **ePetitions.** A Wellington City Council initiative to allow anyone to make suggestions relevant to Council business via the Internet and for others to endorse them. Petitioners can provide links to background information to support their cases.

▶ **Audio visual wiki.** An Archives of New Zealand initiative to enable the public to view films online, add information about the content or context of the films, and discuss them with other users.

Other Agency-Related Social Media Initiatives

Agencies are also using social networking tools in collaboration with nongovernment organizations. In some instances, intermediaries are using them on behalf of agencies; in others, an agency's relationship with the service being provided is not made explicit. The following are examples of such initiatives:

- **Wikipedia.** Nearly every New Zealand government agency has a listing on this site (many of which are quite extensive). However, these public profiles may not have been created, monitored, or managed by New Zealand government agencies.

- **Facebook.** New Zealand government has a presence on Facebook, mostly for dissemination of information.

- **Second Life.** In 2010, the government was planning a presence in Second Life for tourist advertisement and some educational activities.

- **Business online discussion groups.** Discussion groups accessed via *business.govt.nz* are in fact hosted by a private company, which in turn has relationships with the various subject experts who comment on postings.

- **LG Online Groups.** A Web forum and shared workspace for local government personnel to communicate about best practices and seek responses to general inquiries.

- **100% Pure New Zealand.** A layer on Google Earth provided by Tourism New Zealand. Google Earth provides geographic information by combining satellite imagery, maps, terrain information, and 3-D building imagery.

Anyone can write articles in Wikipedia or post photos in Panoramio, videos in YouTube, or comments in Google Earth Community and "geotag" them with coordinates so they appear in the Google Earth layer. This enables a user to browse other people's comments, photographs, and posts about a particular place.

Sources: Compiled from New Zealand E-Government (2008a and 2008b).

Questions

1. Given the richness of New Zealand's offerings, do you believe that the portal style of e-government will be replaced by a social networking style?

2. What are the benefits of the internal initiatives?

3. Comment on the connections to YouTube, Flickr, and Facebook.

4. Why do wikis and blogs play such an important role in many of these initiatives?

5. Which initiatives are related to e-learning? To c-commerce? In what ways?

6. Enter *e.govt.nz* and identify new initiatives in EC as of January 2010.

ONLINE RESOURCES
available at pearsonglobaleditions.com/turban

Online Files

W5.1   Application Case: E-Government in Hong Kong (1998 to 2009)

W5.2   Key Issues and Trends of E-Government Development and Implementation

W5.3   Application Case: E-Learning at Cisco Systems

W5.4   Preventing E-Learning Failures

W5.5   Education-Related Activities in Second Life

W5.6   Fila's Collaboration Software Reduces Time-to-Market and Product Cost

Comprehensive Educational Websites

ASTD.org: American Society for Training and Development's website.

egov.gov: Official e-government site of the U.S. government.

egov.vic.gov.au: A major resource center on e-government.

e-learningcentre.co.uk: A vast collection of selected and reviewed links to e-learning resources.

forums.e-democracy.org: A portal focused on e-democracy.

icl-conference.org: Annual conference on e-learning.

kmworld.com: A collection of KM solutions.

knowledgemanagement.wordpress.com: Best collection of KM-related material.

metakm.com: A portal for KM.

mgovernment.org: A mobile government consortium.

the-ebook-reader.com: All about e-readers (e.g., comparisons).

tools.kmnetwork.com: A portal for KM tools and techniques.

portal.brint.com: A portal for KM.

updates.zdnet.com/tags/e-government.html: White papers, case studies, technical articles, and blog posts relating to e-government.

wwwords.co.uk/elea: An e-learning journal and comprehensive portal.

REFERENCES

Allen, E., and J. Seaman. "Learning on Demand: Online Education in the United States." 2009. sloanconsortium.org/publications/survey/pdf/learning_ondemad.pdf (accessed April 2011).

Awad, E. M., and H. Ghaziri. *Knowledge Management*, 2nd ed., Hershey, PA: International Technology Group, 2010.

Baumgarten, J., and M. Chui. "E-Government 2.0." *McKinsey Quarterly*, Summer 2009.

Bingham, T., and M. Connor. *The New Social Learning*. Alexandria, VA: ASTD Press, 2010.

Bjelland, O. M., and R. C. Wood. "An Inside View of IBM's Innovation Jam." *MIT Sloan Management Review* (Fall 2008).

Boehle, S. "Caterpillar's Knowledge Network." *ManagementSmart.com*, October 16, 2007. managesmarter.com/msg/content_display/training/e3iff0e5ee8955eaff00d02da7d36a5b662 (accessed April 2011).

Colvin-Clark, R., and R. E. Mayer. *e-Learning and the Science of Instruction*, 2nd ed. San Francisco: Pfeiffer/Wiley & Sons, 2008.

Currier, G. "Sharing Knowledge in the Corporate Hive." *Baseline*, May/June 2010.

D'Agostino, D. "Expertise Management: Who Knows About This?" *CIO Insight*, July 1, 2004.

Derven, M. "Social Networking: A Force for Development?" *Training and Development*, July 2009.

Ellis, R. K. (Ed.). "A Field Guide to Learning Management Systems." American Society for Training and Development (ASTD), 2009.

Epstein, J. "Electronic Voting." *Computer*, August 2007.

Garud, R., and A. Kumaraswamy. "Vicious and Virtuous Circles in the Management of Knowledge: The Case of Infosys Technologies." *MIS Quarterly* (March 1, 2005).

Glynn, C. E. "Building a Learning Infrastructure." *Training and Development*, January 2008.

Hansen, M. *The Best IT-Business Books of 2009*. Boston: Harvard Business Press, 2009.

Healey, M. "Data Sharing," *Informationweek.com*, June 21, 2010.

Holsapple, C. W. (Ed.). *Handbook on Knowledge Management*. Heidelberg, Germany: Springer Computer Science, 2003.

Hyperion. "Federal Government—Additional Details." 2007. hyperion.com/solutions/federal_division/legislation_summaries.cfm (no longer available online).

Kidd, T., and I. Chen. *Wired for Learning*. Charlotte, NC: Information Age Publication, 2009.

Khoshrow-Pour, M. (Ed.). *E-Commerce Trends for Organizational Advancement*. Hershey, PA: IGL Global, 2010.

Lee, S. M., X. Tan, and S. Trimi. "Current Practices of Leading E-Government Countries." *Communications of the ACM*, 48, no. 10 (October 2005).

Mason, R., and F. Rennie. *E-Learning and Social Networking Handbook: Resources for Higher Education*. New York: Routledge Pub., 2008.

Mehta, N., S. Oswald, and A. Mehta. "Knowledge Management Program of Infosys Technologies." 2007. knowledgemanagement.wordpress.com/2007/11/26/the-knowledge-management-program-of-infosys-technologies (accessed April 2011).

Morrison, M. "Learner E-Learning: The University of Toyota Case." *Training* (January 2008).

Neal, L. "Predictions for 2007." *eLearn Magazine*, January 12, 2007. elearnmag.org/subpage.cfm?article=42-1&section=articles (accessed March 2011).

New Zealand E-Government. "Networking Government in New Zealand: Agency Initiatives." 2008a. e.govt.nz/resources/research/progress/agency-initiatives/chapter9.html (accessed April 2011).

New Zealand E-Government. "Networking Government in New Zealand: Web 2.0 Networking Tools." 2008b. e.govt.nz/resources/research/progress/agency-initiatives/chapter6.html (accessed April 2011).

Oblinger, L. A. "How E-Learning Works." *Howstuffworks.com*. communication.howstuffworks.com/elearning.html (accessed April 2011).

Robbins, S., and M. Bell. *Second Life for Dummies*. Hoboken, NJ: Wiley, 2008.

Roberts, B. "Hard-Facts About Self Skills E-Learning." *HR Magazine*, January 2008.

Rossett, A., and J. Marsh. "E-Learning: What's Old Is New Again." *Training and Development*, January 2010.

Shark, A., and S. Toporkoff. *Beyond e-Government and e-Democracy: A Global Perspective*. Scotts Valley, CA: BookSurge Publishing, 2008.

Spychalska, D. *Vendor Managed Inventory: Exploring Objectives, Benefits and Shortcomings of the Business Concept*. Saarbrucken, Germany: LAP–Lambert Academic Publishing, 2010.

Suresh, J. K., and K. Mehesh. "Managing the Knowledge Supply Chain at Infosys." *Knowledge Management Review* (September/October 2008).

Trimi, S., and H. Sheng. "Emerging Trends in M-Government." *Communications of the ACM* (May 2008).

U.S. Department of Housing and Urban Development. *FY 2008 Performance and Accountability Report*. November 2008. hud.gov/offices/cfo/reports/hudpar-fy2008.pdf (accessed March 2011).

Wagner, E. "Delivering on the Promise of E-Learning." Adobe Systems, Inc., San Jose, California, white paper #95010203, May 2008.

Wallace, J. "How Online Training Works." *HowStuffWorks.com*, July 23, 2007. communication.howstuffworks.com/how-online-training-works.htm (accessed April 2011).

Wang, P., and N. C. Ramiller. "Community Learning in Information Technology Innovation." *MIS Quarterly*, 33, no. 4 (December 2009): 709–734.

West, E. "Rapid E-Learning." Adobe Systems, Inc., San Jose, California, white paper, 2007.

CHAPTER 6

MOBILE COMMERCE AND UBIQUITOUS COMPUTING

Content

Learning Objectives

Upon completion of this chapter, you will be able to:

1. Discuss the value-added attributes, benefits, and fundamental drivers of m-commerce.

2. Describe the mobile computing infrastructure that supports m-commerce (devices, software, services).

3. Describe the four major types of wireless telecommunications networks.

4. Discuss m-commerce applications in banking and financial services.

5. Describe enterprise applications.

6. Describe consumer and personal applications of m-commerce including entertainment.

7. Understand the technologies and potential applications of location-based m-commerce.

8. Define and describe ubiquitous computing and sensory networks.

9. Describe the major implementation issues from security and privacy to barriers of m-commerce.

HERTZ GOES MOBILE ALL THE WAY

The Problem

The car rental industry is very competitive, and Hertz (*hertz.com*), the world's largest car rental company, competes against hundreds of companies in 8,400 locations in 146 countries. The competition focuses on customer acquisition and retention. In the last few years, competition has intensified, and profits in the industry have been drifting downward. Hertz has pioneered some mobile commerce applications to increase its competitiveness. This system is now part of the company's national wireless network that can check credit cards, examine your rental history, determine which airline to credit your loyalty mileage to, and more.

The Solution

Here are some major mobile projects:

- **Super easy and quick rentals.** Upon making a reservation, each renter receives an e-mail confirmation on the booking. Upon arrival to a city, the renter receives a text message indicating the car's license plate and location on the lot. To unlock and engage the vehicle, members simply need to sweep their card over the car's radio frequency identification system (RFID). In some locations, Hertz's curbside attendant greets you, confirms your reservation, and transmits your name wirelessly to the rental booth. The rental booth employee advises the curbside attendant about the location of your car. All you need to do is go to the slot where the car is parked and drive away.

- **Instant returns.** A handheld device connected to a database via a wireless system expedites the car return transaction. Right in the parking lot, the lot attendant uses a handheld device that automatically calculates the cost of the rental and prints a receipt for the renter. You check out in less than a minute, and you do not have to enter the rental booth at all.

- **NeverLost Onboard.** Some Hertz cars come equipped with an onboard GPS system, which provides route guidance in the form of turn-by-turn directions to many destinations. The information is displayed on a screen with computer-generated voice prompts. An electronic mapping system (a GIS) is combined with the GPS, enabling you to see where you are and where you are going. Also, consumer information about the locations of the nearest hospitals, gas stations, restaurants, and tourist areas is provided on the map.

- **Additional customer services.** Hertz's customers can view Hertz's location guide, driving directions, emergency telephone numbers, city maps, shopping guides, and even reviews of restaurants, hotels, and entertainment on NeverLost. This content is available to Hertz's club members also at home where they can load the app into their smartphones, PDAs, and other wireless devices.

- **Car locations.** Hertz is experimenting with a GPS-based car-locating system. This will enable the company to know the location of a rental car at any given time, and even how fast it is being driven. Although the company promises to provide discounts based on your usage pattern, this capability is seen by many as an invasion of *privacy*. On the other hand, some may feel safer knowing that Hertz knows where they are at all times.

- **Public service.** Hertz partners with HopStop to help city dwellers via mobility solutions. These solutions are available on desktop computers as well, and they include carpool sharing, information about renting by the hour, and comparisons of public transportation versus renting a car. The service is available in 26 major markets and provides door-to-door walking and mass-transit directions to city residents and tourists. HopStop also offers point-to-point directions and the locations of nearby subway and bus stops, remotely on mobile devices via an array of mobile applications, including iPhone applications and a mobile site at *m.hopstop.com*.

- **Wi-Fi connection.** High-speed Internet access is available in Hertz's rental areas in all major airports served by Hertz in the United States.

The Results

Despite the economic problems of 2008–2011, Hertz was able to remain number one in the car rental industry. Its earnings, which declined in 2008 and 2009, rebounded in 2010. Hertz did better than most of its competitors. Its share price bottomed out in 2009, but more than tripled in 2010. The company is expanding operations and maintaining an excellent reputation among customers thanks in part to its mobile applications.

Sources: Compiled from *hertz.com* (accessed April 2011), Goodwin (2010), and Butcher (2010).

WHAT WE CAN LEARN . . .

The Hertz case illustrates several applications in the transportation industry that help improve both customer service and the company's operations. The applications run on mobile devices and are supported by a wireless network. (Both topics are discussed in Section 6.2.)The mobile technology is based on a set of unique attributes (Section 6.1) enabling the use of many applications (Sections 6.3 through 6.6).

The Hertz case is only one example of the impact of emerging mobile and wireless technologies on commerce and electronic commerce (EC). In this chapter, we will explore a number of these emerging mobile and wireless technologies as well as their potential applications in the commercial and societal arenas. The chapter also deals with location-based services and ubiquitous computing, which are cutting-edge technologies.

6.1   MOBILE COMMERCE: CONCEPTS, LANDSCAPE, ATTRIBUTES, DRIVERS, APPLICATIONS, AND BENEFITS

BASIC CONCEPTS AND THE LANDSCAPE

Mobile commerce (m-commerce), also known as m-business, is the ability to conduct business using a mobile device. Mobile commerce includes any business activity conducted over a wireless telecommunications network. Activities include B2C, B2B, m-government, and m-learning transactions as well as the transfer of information, money, and services via wireless mobile devices. Like regular EC applications, m-commerce can be done via the Internet, via private communication lines, or over other computing networks. M-commerce is a natural extension of e-commerce. Mobile devices create an opportunity to deliver new services to existing customers and to attract new customers. However, the small screen size and slow bandwidth of most mobile computing devices have limited the consumer interest. So even though the mobile computing industry recognizes the potential for B2C m-commerce applications, the number of existing applications is still small, but growing, and consumer uptake has been slow. However, this situation is changing mostly thanks to 3G and 4G networks and to devices such as the iPhone and iPad, as well as to the proliferation of a slew of smartphones. Thus, it is expected that the *strategic value* of mobile systems will increase significantly. For a discussion, see Scornavacca and Barnes (2008). In this chapter, we consider some of the distinguishing attributes and key drivers of m-commerce, the technical issues underpinning m-commerce, and some of the major m-commerce applications. The overall landscape of m-commerce is summarized in Exhibit 6.1.

mobile commerce (m-commerce; m-business)
Any business activity conducted over a wireless telecommunications network or from mobile devices.

Note that in the exhibit the enabling technologies (e.g., devices, networks) are on the left side and the resulting capabilities and attributes are in the middle. These provide the foundation for the applications that are shown on the right side of the exhibit. In this section, we describe the attributes and provide an overview of the applications. In Section 6.2, we present the technologies.

THE ATTRIBUTES OF M-COMMERCE

Generally speaking, many of the EC applications described in this book also apply to m-commerce. For example, online shopping, Internet banking, e-stock trading, e-entertainment, and online gambling are all gaining popularity in wireless B2C. Auction sites are starting to use m-commerce (e.g., sending a text message alert when an auction is about to close), governments encourage m-government (Chapter 5) and wireless collaborative commerce in B2B EC is emerging. There are some key attributes that offer the opportunity for development of new applications that are possible only in the mobile environment. The attributes include:

EXHIBIT 6.1   The Landscape of Mobile Computing and M-Commerce

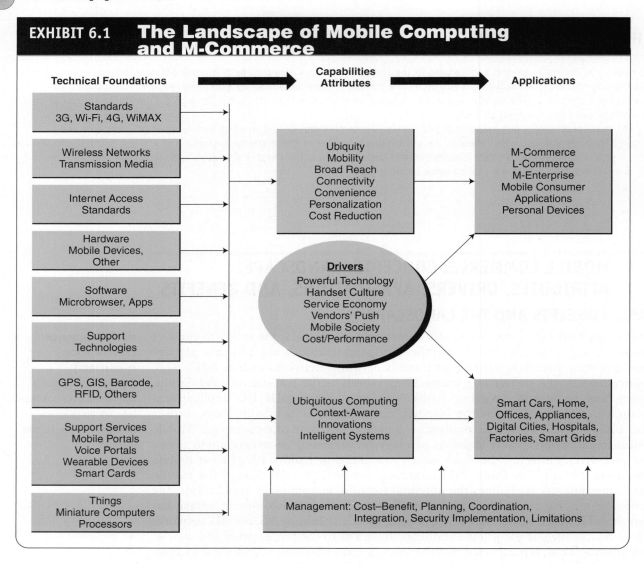

> **Ubiquity.** *Ubiquity* means being available at any location at any time. A wireless mobile device such as an iPhone and iPad can deliver information when it is needed, regardless of the user's location (as long as Internet access is available). Ubiquity creates easier information access in a real-time environment, which is highly valued in today's business and competitive markets.

> **Convenience.** It is very convenient for users to operate in the wireless computing environment. Mobile computing devices' functionality and usability are increasing while their physical size remains small. Unlike traditional computers, mobile devices are portable, can be set in a variety of monitoring modes, and most devices feature instant connectivity (i.e., no need to wait for the device to boot up). Thus, mobile devices enable users to connect easily and quickly to the Internet, intranets, other mobile devices, and online databases.

> **Interactivity.** In comparison with the desktop computing environment, transactions, communications, and service provision are immediate and highly interactive in the mobile computing environment. Businesses in which customer support and delivery of services require a high level of interactivity with the customer are likely to find more value added in mobile computing.

> **Personalization.** Mobile devices are truly personal computing devices. Whereas a computer in a home, in a library, at work, or in an Internet café may be used by a number of people, mobile devices are almost always owned and operated by a single individual. This enables true consumer personalization—the delivery of information, products, and services designed to meet the needs of individual consumers. For example, users planning or taking a trip can be sent travel-related information for retrieval when and where they want it (see the Hertz opening case).

> **Localization.** Knowing where a user is physically located at any particular moment is key to offering relevant mobile advertisement or services in real time. Such services are known as location-based m-commerce (see Section 6.7). Localization may be general—for example, targeting everyone in a certain location (e.g., all shoppers at a shopping mall) or, even better, it may be targeted so that users get messages that depend both on where they are and on what their preferences are, thus combining personalization and localization.

Mobile vendors and carriers can differentiate themselves in the competitive marketplace by offering new, exciting, and useful services based on these attributes. These value-adding attributes can be the basis for businesses to better deliver the value proposition they offer to customers.

DRIVERS OF M-COMMERCE

In addition to the value-added attributes just discussed, the development of m-commerce is being driven by the following technological, business, social, and economic factors:

> **Widespread availability of more powerful mobile devices.** By the end of 2010, worldwide mobile telephone subscriptions exceeded 4 billion. By 2011, the overall penetration is forecasted to be over 75 percent. Mobile devices are increasing in power, functionality, and features (e.g., color screens, GPS locators, Internet access) that support m-commerce. Thus, the potential mass market for conducting m-commerce has emerged. These devices are supported by powerful operating systems (OS). According to *IT Business Edge* (2010), mobile devices and applications are one of the top 10 strategic technologies for 2011. This is based on a Gartner Inc. estimate that by the end of 2010, 1.2 billion people will carry handsets (e.g., smartphones with Internet access whose numbers are growing by more than 50 percent annually) capable of rich, mobile commerce, providing an ideal environment for the convergence of mobility and the Web. In a few years, the primary means of accessing the Internet will be through highly portable smart mobile devices, and not via desktops or laptop PCs. This means that m-commerce could be the primary platform for conducting e-commerce.

> **The handset culture.** A closely related driver is the widespread use of cell phones especially among the 12- to 25-year-old age group. The young users will constitute a major online buying force once they begin to make and spend reasonable amounts of money. The culture is that of both individuals and organizations. People say that cell phones are now part of their lifestyle. Because the quality of applications and devices has improved over the years, customers are increasingly choosing to interact with companies via their mobile devices. This has led companies to push out applications as a competitive tool to improve relationships and gain advantage over competitors whose interfaces are purely desktop browser-based.

> **The service economy.** The transition from a manufacturing to a service-based economy is encouraging the development of mobile-based services, especially when customer service is a differentiator in highly competitive industries. Time-starved, but resource-rich, individuals are willing to pay more for mobile services

that perform a range of tasks at their convenience (e.g., locating a restaurant or dry cleaner in close proximity to the user's position, or mobile banking that allows users to pay bills online from their cell phones).

▶ **Vendor's push.** Both mobile communication network operators and manufacturers of mobile devices are advertising the many potential applications of m-commerce so that they can push new technologies, products, and services to buyers. These companies are spending a lot on advertising to encourage businesses to "go mobile" or "mobilize your business." Also, the competition among vendors and products creates more innovative applications.

▶ **The mobile workforce and mobile enterprise.** Some workers (such as salespeople and field service employees) have always worked away from an office. Increasingly, other segments of the workforce also are "going mobile." This is being driven by social trends in the workplace such as telecommuting, employers' concerns about security, employees' desires for improved work–life balance, and a general questioning of where knowledge workers need to be located to best conduct their work. In addition to facilitating mobile employees, companies have a large number of applications inside the enterprise where employees move around.

A most widely recognized benefit of increased mobility is the productive use of travel time. Workers who commute long distances, and especially executives who travel frequently, want to make more productive use of the time that they spend in public transportation vehicles or in airport lounges.

▶ **Improved price/performance.** The price of wireless devices and of per-minute pricing of mobile services continues to decline even as available services and functionality are increasing. This is leading to improvements in the price/performance ratio, enticing new owners into the market and encouraging existing owners to increase consumption of services and to upgrade their handsets.

▶ **Improving bandwidth.** To properly conduct m-commerce, sufficient bandwidth is needed to transmit the desired information via text, picture, voice, video, or multimedia. Theoretically, the 3G communications technology supported by newer smartphones (e.g., the iPhone) is providing a data rate of up to 2 Mbps. Empirically, 3G transmission speeds are much slower, with actual rates somewhere between .1 and .5 Mbps. This is in comparison to standard Wi-Fi, which is close to 56 Mbps. However, the arrival of 3.5G and 4G provides better capabilities.

These attributes and drivers of m-commerce underlie most of the mobile applications.

AN OVERVIEW OF THE APPLICATIONS OF M-COMMERCE

There are thousands of different m-commerce applications (called in short *apps*). Many of these are described in Chapters 3 through 5. Some can be executed on either desktop or mobile devices. Others can be done only on mobile devices. We categorized these applications by the framework used by Motorola Corp. (motorola.com/Business/US-EN/Enterprise+Mobility).

According to this framework, enterprise applications are created to meet specific business needs. These needs have some generic aspects as well as industry-specific aspects (see Exhibit 6.2). The four needs are:

1. **Field mobility**—the support of the workforce
2. **Fleet mobility**—the support to vehicles in order to minimize downtime and increase utilization
3. **Warehouse management**—the improvement of the operations inside warehouses
4. **Direct store delivery (DSD) route accounting**—the increased accuracy by managing inventory properly and delivering goods as well as to make the most of presales and merchandise calls

EXHIBIT 6.2   M-Commerce Applications and Their Classifications

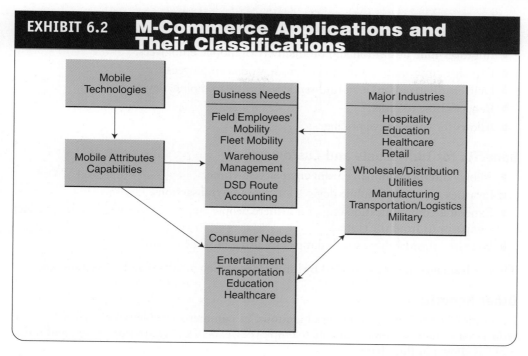

These needs can exist in any industry, and drive the use of m-commerce. The major industries that use m-commerce are: hospitality, education, health care, retail, wholesale and distribution, utilities, manufacturing and transportation, and logistics. Each of the industries and its needs can be divided into 3 to 10 subcategories for which Motorola (and other vendors) provide solutions.

To simplify our presentation, we divided the applications in this chapter into the following categories adding consumer applications to the framework:

▶ Banking and financial services—Section 6.3

▶ Mobile enterprise applications—Section 6.4

▶ Consumer services and entertainment—Section 6.5

▶ Location-based mobile commerce, which adds a dimension to the previously mentioned applications—Section 6.6

▶ Ubiquitous computing applications—Section 6.7

Mobile commerce is an important new way of thinking about e-commerce due to the anytime, anywhere communications phenomena that is redefining the way in which business is conducted. This chapter as well as Olariu and Tiliute (2011) addresses the paradigm shift away from traditional e-commerce to mobile commerce by discussing the technique and applications in the field from a managerial point of view. A related application area is that of ubiquitous computing (see Head and Li 2009).

THE BENEFITS OF M-COMMERCE

M-commerce has many benefits both to organizations and individuals.

Benefits for Organizations

▶ Increases sales due to ease of ordering from anywhere, anytime.

▶ Allows location-based commerce for more sales and revenue (Section 6.6).

▶ Provides an additional channel for advertising and distribution of coupons (wider reach).

- Improves customer satisfaction through real-time apps.
- Reduces training time and help desk resources.
- Improves time utilization and productivity of mobile employees.
- Expedites information flow to and from mobile employees.
- Delivers digitized products and services directly to mobile devices.
- Reduces time to order.
- Allows for competitive pricing.

Benefits for Individuals and Customers

- Allows Internet commerce from any place, anytime.
- Provides a choice of mobile devices for the same transactions.
- Expedites communication (e.g., find where people are, get fast answer; can do product comparisons from the stores).
- Increases affordability over desktop computing in some countries.

These advantages are accompanied by limitations, which are discussed in Section 6.8.

Other Benefits

In addition to the benefit of being ubiquitous, m-commerce enables true personalization, reduces cost, increases time available to employees, expedites business processes, and much more as shown in this chapter.

Section 6.1 ▶ REVIEW QUESTIONS

1. Define m-commerce.
2. Briefly describe the five value-added attributes of m-commerce.
3. List and briefly describe eight major drivers of m-commerce.
4. Describe the framework of m-commerce applications.
5. What are the major categories of m-commerce applications?
6. Describe the landscape of m-commerce.
7. What are the major benefits of m-commerce?

6.2   TECHNICAL INFRASTRUCTURE: COMPONENTS AND SERVICES OF MOBILE COMPUTING

The technology that supports m-commerce is very diversified. Here we concentrate only on the major technology items.

OVERVIEW OF MOBILE COMPUTING

wireless mobile computing (mobile computing)
Computing that connects a mobile device to a network or another computing device, anytime, anywhere.

In the traditional computing environment, users require a desktop computer and cable connections (wire line) to networks, servers, and peripheral devices such as printers. This situation has limited the use of computers to fixed locations and has created difficulties for people who either want or need to be connected anytime, anywhere. For instance, salespeople, field service employees, law enforcement agents, inspectors, utility workers, and executives who travel frequently can be more effective if they can use information technology while at their jobs in the field or in transit. A solution to this situation is **wireless mobile computing** (**mobile computing**), which enables a real-time connection between a mobile device and computing networks, or to another computing device—anytime, anywhere. M-commerce is conducted mainly via the mobile Web. Note: A *mobile web* refers to the use of Internet-connected applications, or browser-based access to the Internet from a mobile device.

An extensive hardware and software infrastructure underlies mobile computing. First, there are the mobile devices (e.g., smartphones) that enable a user to connect to a

EXHIBIT 6.3   Mobile Computing Basic Terminology

Bluetooth. A chip technology wireless standard designed for temporary, short-range connection (data and voice) among mobile devices and/or other devices (see *bluetooth.org*).

Global Positioning System (GPS). A satellite-based tracking system that enables the determination of a GPS device's location. (See Section 6.6 for more on GPS.)

Personal Digital Assistant (PDA). A small portable computer, such as BlackBerry handhelds and the pocket PC devices from companies like Research In Motion or Palm.

Short Messaging Service (SMS). A technology for sending short text messages (up to 160 characters) on cell phones. SMS messages can be sent or received concurrently, even during a voice or data call. Used by hundreds of millions of users, SMS is known as "the e-mail of m-commerce." Some companies offer multilanguage text creation.

Smartphones. Internet-enabled cell phones that can support mobile applications. These "phones with a brain" are becoming standard devices. They include WAP microprocessors for Internet access and the capabilities of PDAs as well. The iPhone is the most popular example of a smartphone.

WiMAX. A wireless technology based on the IEEE 802.16-2004 standard, designed to provide Internet access across metro areas to fixed (not moving) users. It is considered wireless broadband technology.

Wireless Application Protocol (WAP). A technology that offers Internet browsing from wireless devices.

Wireless Local Area Network (WLAN). A broad term for all 802.11 standards. Basically, it is a wireless version of the Ethernet networking standard.

For an extensive list of other terms, see *harvest.cals.ncsu.edu/index.cfm?showpage=291* and *webopedia.com/Mobile_Computing*.

mobile network. Next, there are those components that support the wireless connection, (e.g., network access points and Wi-Fi), as well as parts of the infrastructure that support the delivery of services over the connection (e.g., GPS locators). Finally, there are those components that support m-commerce activities in the same way they support typical e-commerce activities. For example, a Web server, database server, and enterprise application server offer the same services to a wireless device as they do to a wired computer, with one significant exception. Certain characteristics of mobile devices—small screens, reduced memory, limited bandwidth, and restricted input capabilities—mean that hardware and software designers need to anticipate special requirements. Mobile systems need to be designed accordingly.

This section briefly discusses the major technologies of mobile computing systems. But before you continue we suggest you review the basic terminology in Exhibit 6.3.

MOBILE DEVICES

A few years ago, a computer was basically a computer, a cell phone was basically a phone, and a personal digital assistant (PDA) was essentially a stand-alone personal information manager (calendar, contacts, calculator, and the like). Today, all of these devices are converging so that it is difficult from a functional perspective to tell them apart.

Mobile devices come in all shapes and sizes—laptops, thin-and-light notebooks, tablet computers, ultra portables, and ultra-mobile PCs (UMPCs). Most of these have the same basic capabilities (e.g., support for audio and video, e-mail, Internet browsers, and Wi-Fi connections) and run essentially one of the few operating systems. What distinguishes one type of mobile computer from another is its physical footprint. Thin notebooks weigh 2 to 5 pounds and have 15 to 21 inch displays. In comparison, ultra portables weigh less than 3 pounds and have smaller screens. Most of the major computer manufacturers (HP, Apple, Dell, ASUS, Toshiba, ACER, and Lenovo) produce thin notebooks and ultra portables. In contrast, few of the major computer makers currently produce UMPCs. Although UMPCs are also full-blown computers, they tend to have much smaller footprints—either no standard keyboard or much smaller keyboards, weigh between 1 and 2 pounds, and have much smaller screens (5 to 6 inches). Apple, Samsung, OQO, and ASUS are some of the manufacturers offering UMPCs.

Mobile devices can be large. Take the Dell M6500 mobile workstation as an example. It is a 17 inch powerful computer (cost over $5,000) and competes with nonmobile workstations. Similar products are available from HP and Lenovo.

Personal Digital Assistants

personal digital assistant (PDA)
A stand-alone handheld computer principally used for personal information management.

Originally, a personal digital assistant (PDA), also known as a *palmtop*, was a stand-alone handheld computer that provided access to a user's address book and calendar and supported calculation and desktop applications such as word processing and spreadsheets. Most of the original PDAs were able to be synchronized with a user's desktop computer. This enabled a user to read e-mails offline. Over time, most PDAs have added support for wireless connectivity to the Internet through Wi-Fi. In this way, a PDA can be used to browse the Web and read and send e-mail in real time. Most PDAs also provide multimedia support for audio and video.

The leading producers of PDAs are Research In Motion (BlackBerry; rim.com), Palm, Inc. (palm.com), and Hewlett-Packard (hp.com). From a hardware perspective, most PDAs have small screens (2.5 to 4 inches) and small memories up to 256 MB of RAM. As of 2011, hardware included small keyboards with thumb wheels or a virtual keyboard on the screen, and expansion slots for memory cards (SD or compact flash) that offer additional storage or access to other applications. From a software perspective, most PDAs either run the Palm Operating System (OS) or Microsoft's Windows Mobile operating system. For new capabilities of the BlackBerry, see Garcia (2010).

Smartphones

smartphone
A mobile phone with PC-like capabilities.

Basically, a smartphone is a mobile phone with Internet access and PDA-like or PC-like functionality, including e-mail, Web browsing, multimedia capabilities, address book, calendar, calculator, support for reading Word and PDF documents, a digital camera, and so forth. Unlike PDAs, there is a wide variety of smartphone manufacturers. For an overview, see Garcia (2009). Note that smartphones get "smarter" with time by adding capabilities (see Rash, 2010b). There is also a wide variety of operating systems, including Symbian, Linux, Palm OS, Windows Mobile, Apple OS/X, Google Android, and RIM BlackBerry (and forthcoming Google's Chrome OS). Like PDAs, smartphones have small screens, keyboards, memory, and storage. Most smartphones have Internet access.

There are an increasing number of brands on the market with new capabilities appearing daily, especially with the ultra-fast 4G smartphones. For business applications of smart phones see Del Rey (2010).

Tablets

Another category of mobile devices is *tablet computers,* which received a major boost in 2010 with the introduction of the Apple iPad and its competitors.

The *iPad* is particularly marketed as a platform for audio and visual media such as e-books, periodicals, movies, music, and games, as well as Web content. At about 1.5 pounds (680 grams), its size and weight are between those of most contemporary smartphones and laptop computers.

The iPad runs the same operating system as the earlier Apple's iPod Touch and iPhone. It can run its own applications as well as ones developed for the iPhone. The iPad uses a Wi-Fi data connection to browse the Internet, load and stream media, and install software. Some models also have a 3G wireless data connection, which can connect to GSM 3G data networks. The device is managed and synced by iTunes on a personal computer via a USB cable.

Other Mobile Devices

Many other mobile devices exist. Here is a representative list:

▶ **Smartbooks.** Smartbooks are low-cost, ultraportable devices that are a blend of smartphone and laptop, and typically come with always-on mobile connectivity (e.g., from ASUS computers).

▶ **Wearable devices.** Mobile employees who work on buildings, electrical poles or other difficult-to-climb places may be equipped with a special form of mobile wireless computing device called a wearable device. People wear these devices on their arms, clothes, or helmets. Examples of wearable devices include:

  ▶ **Screen.** A computer is mounted on a safety hat, in front of the wearer's eyes, or on a hand, displaying information to the worker.

  ▶ **Camera.** A camera is usually mounted on a safety hat. Workers can take digital photos and videos and transmit them instantly to a portable computer nearby. (Photo transmission is made possible via Bluetooth technology.)

  ▶ **Touch-panel display.** In addition to the wrist-mounted keyboard, mobile employees can use a flat-panel screen, attached to the hand, which responds to the tap of a finger or stylus.

  ▶ **Keyboard.** A wrist-mounted keyboard enables typing by the other hand. (Wearable keyboards are an alternative to voice recognition systems, which are also wireless.)

  ▶ **Speech translator.** For those mobile employees who do not have their hands free to use a keyboard, a wearable speech translator is handy.

  ▶ **Watch-like device.** Such a device is carried on the arm like a watch and can display information or be used as a cell phone. Swatch and Microsoft offer such watches. You can get news, weather, and so forth from Microsoft's MSN broadcasts.

  One area where wearables are in extensive use is warehouses. Employees usually wear such devices on their hands (see Section 6.4). We suggest you watch a video from Motorola to view how such wearables are used (business.motorola.com/enterprisemobility/video/ENG.html).

  Future wearable devices may include smartbooks, sensors, and so forth, which will have sensitive screens with built-in processors. An example is the WaveFace machine, which has touch, voice, and gesture recognition capabilities. For further information, see en.wikipedia.org/wiki/wearable_computing.

▶ **RFID (radio frequency identification).** This wireless technology is used to identify items that are tagged with a code (like a bar code). For details, see Online Tutorial T3.

▶ **Scanners.** These are available in many shapes and sizes. An example is Symbol MC909X-K, which is a rugged pocket PC/bar code scanner. For others, see collectivedata.com/mobile.html.

▶ **Mobile browsers (microbrowsers),** is a Web browser designed for use on a mobile device. Mobile browsers are optimized to display Web content most effectively for small screens on portable devices. Mobile browser software must be small and efficient to accommodate the low memory capacity and low bandwidth of wireless handheld devices. Websites designed for access from these browsers are referred to as *wireless portals*.

  Mobile Web browsers differ greatly in terms of features offered and operating systems supported. The best can display most websites and offer page zoom and keyboard shortcuts. While some devices don't offer much of a choice in which mobile Web browsers you can use, many new devices are running operating systems like Windows Mobile that has several different mobile Web

mobile browser (microbrowser)
Web browser designed for use on a mobile device optimized to display Web content most effectively for small screens on portable devices.

browsers built for it. Representative examples are Symbian WebKit, Opera Mobile, Skyfire, Firefox Mobile, and Microsoft IE for mobile.

Mobile browsers connect to the Internet through a cellular network or a wireless LAN (local area network). Some mobile browsers can display regular HTML sites, while others can only display websites that have been specially formatted for mobile browsers. Content optimized for mobile browsers is typically text-based or low-graphic and may be written in languages that were designed for mobile computing such as WML (wireless markup language) or CHTML (compact HTML).

▸ **Dashtop mobile.** Dashtop mobile equipment refers to wireless mobile devices mounted on the vehicle dashboard. Dashtop mobile equipment includes satellite radios, GPS navigation, OnStar, mobile TV, HD radio, vehicle tracking system, and Broadband Wireless Access (BWA) devices. Currently, the dashtop mobile devices are mostly satellite-based wireless technology. Except for OnStar and BWA devices, most of them are in the stage of passive one-way communications equipment.

However, fast-evolving mobile technology is on the threshold of turning dashtop mobile equipment into full-duplex multimedia gadgetry on the strength of fast-growing broadband infrastructure, including expanding WiMAX networks. Growing indications show that convergence into an all-in-one dashtop mobile device is an ultimate destination. For more information, see en.wikipedia.org/wiki/Dashtop_mobile.

Clearly, many mobile devices and especially PDAs and smartphones appear to be converging toward the same endpoint—a small-footprint, handheld mobile device that combines all the capabilities of these devices in one package.

MOBILE COMPUTING SOFTWARE AND SERVICES

Although mobile devices present a variety of software challenges, they also offer a number of software-enabled services that aren't found in the desktop or even mobile computer worlds. These services provide a foundation for many of the applications described later in the chapter. Included among these services are messaging, location-based services, and voice-support services.

Mobile Portals and Content Providers

mobile portal
A gateway to the Internet optimized for mobility that aggregates and provides content and services for mobile users.

A **mobile portal** is a gateway to the Internet optimized for mobility that aggregates and provides content and services for mobile users. These portals offer services similar to those of desktop portals such as Yahoo! and MSN (see en.wikipedia.org/wiki/Mobile_portal for an additional discussion of portals). An example of a pure mobile portal (whose only business is to be a mobile portal) is zed.com from Sonera in Finland. The world's most well-known mobile portal, with over 60 million members, mostly in Japan, is i-mode from NTT DOCOMO.

The services provided by mobile portals include news, sports, e-mail, entertainment, and travel information; restaurants and event information; leisure-related services (e.g., games, TV and movie listings); community services; and stock trading. A sizable percentage of the portals also provide downloads and messaging, music-related services, and health, dating, and job information. Mobile portals frequently charge for their services. For example, you may be asked to pay 50 cents to get a weather report over your mobile phone. Alternatively, you may pay a monthly fee for the portal service and get the report free anytime you want it. In Japan, for example, i-mode generates revenue mainly from such subscription and advertisement fees.

short message service (SMS)
A service that supports the sending and receiving of short text messages on mobile phones.

Short Message Service

Short message service (SMS), frequently referred to as *text messaging*, or simply *texting*, is a service that supports the transmittal of short text messages (up to 140 to 160 characters) between mobile phones residing on a cellular telephone network. Their cost is very low compared to the charge per minute on cell phones. The limited message length means users often use acronyms to convey the message in shorthand text. Examples include "how are you" becomes "how r u," or "hru," and "great" becomes "gr8." Texting has been immensely popular in Asia and Europe for some time. In the United States, adoption of SMS has been slower than in other parts of the world, but it is catching up.

Texting is getting more popular in the United States thanks to the iPhone and Twitter. In 2010, the total global user base for SMS text messaging passed 4 billion, and 72 percent of all mobile phone subscribers worldwide use SMS text messaging. More than half of all Americans are active users of SMS text messaging, catching up with the average European SMS text messaging usage levels (*Quasi News* 2010).

Multimedia Messaging Services

Multimedia messaging service (MMS) is the emerging generation of wireless messaging, delivering rich media, including video and audio, to mobile phones and other devices. MMS is an extension of SMS (for a larger fee). It allows longer messages and utilizes a special protocol for displaying media content. MMS enables the convergence of mobile devices and personal computers because MMS messages can be sent between PCs, PDAs, and mobile phones that are MMS enabled.

multimedia messaging service (MMS) The emerging generation of wireless messaging; MMS is able to deliver rich media.

Location-Based Services

Location-based services use the *global positioning system (GPS)* or other positioning techniques to find the location of customers and clients and deliver in real time ads about products and services. It also is used in emergency services (see Section 6.6).

Voice-Support Services

The most natural mode of human communication is voice. Voice recognition and voice synthesizing in m-commerce applications offer advantages such as hands- and eyes-free operation, better operation in dirty or moving environments, faster input (people talk about two-and-a-half times faster than they type), and ease-of-use for disabled people. Most significantly, increased use of voice-support services exploits the built-in audio capabilities of many mobile devices and reduces their dependence on less-than-satisfactory input solutions, such as handwriting recognition, keypads, or virtual touchscreen keyboards.

IVR Systems. Voice support applications such as **interactive voice response (IVR)** systems enable users to interact with a computerized system to request and receive information and to enter and change data using a telephone, including cell phones. These systems have been around since the 1980s but are becoming more functional and widespread as artificial intelligence–based voice-recognition capabilities continue to improve.

interactive voice response (IVR) A voice system that enables users to request and receive information and to enter and change data through a telephone to a computerized system.

Voice Portals. The highest level of voice support services is a **voice portal**, a website with an audio interface that can be accessed through a telephone call. A visitor requests information by speaking, and the voice portal finds the information on the Web, translates it into a computer-generated voice reply, and provides the answer by voice. For example, tellme.com and bevocal.com allow callers to request information about weather, local restaurants, current traffic, and other handy information. IVR and voice portals are likely to become important ways of delivering m-commerce services over audio.

voice portal A website with an audio interface that can be accessed through a telephone call.

WIRELESS TELECOMMUNICATIONS NETWORKS

All mobile devices need to connect with a telecommunications network or with other devices. How they do this depends on the purpose of the connection, the capabilities and location of the device, and what connection options are available at the time. Included among the various networks are (1) personal area networks for device-to-device connections up to 30 feet, (2) wireless local area networks for medium-range connections up to 300 feet, (3) wireless metropolitan networks for connections up to 30 miles, and (4) wireless wide area networks for connecting to a network with cellular phone coverage. Details are:

personal area network (PAN)

A wireless telecommunications network for device-to-device connections within a very short range.

Bluetooth

A set of telecommunications standards that enables wireless devices to communicate with each other over short distances.

wireless local area network (WLAN)

A telecommunications network that enables users to make short-range wireless connections to the Internet or another network.

Wi-Fi (wireless fidelity)

The common name used to describe the IEEE 802.11 standard used on most WLANs.

WiMAX

A wireless standard (IEEE 802.16) for making broadband network connections over a medium-size area such as a city.

▶ **Personal area networks.** A personal area network (PAN) is suitable for mobile users who need to make very short-range device-to-device wireless connections within a small space, typically a single room. The most common way to establish a PAN is with Bluetooth. Bluetooth is a set of telecommunications standards that enables wireless devices to communicate with each other over short distances of up to 60 feet (20 meters). Bluetooth can be used to pair a number of different devices—wireless keyboards with tablet PCs, PDAs with computers for easy data synchronization, and digital cameras with printers. Bluetooth also can link more than two devices, as is done in connectBlue's operating-room control system (connectblue.se). Equipment that monitors a patient's heartbeat, ECG, respiration, and other vital signs can be linked via Bluetooth, eliminating obstructive and dangerous cables and increasing the portability of the equipment. For additional information, see bluetooth.com and bluetooth.org.

▶ **Wireless local area networks and Wi-Fi.** As its name implies, a wireless local area network (WLAN) is equivalent to a wired LAN, but without all the cables. Most WLANs run on a telecommunications standard known as *IEEE 802.11* (e.g., 802.11g), which is commonly called Wi-Fi (wireless fidelity). Exhibit 6.4 explains how Wi-Fi works. It outlines the processes and components underlying Wi-Fi. At the heart of a WLAN is a wireless access point that connects a wireless device to the desired network. The wireless device communicates with the access point by a wireless network card installed by the user or by the manufacturer of the device. In turn, the access point has a wired connection to the Internet in the same manner as a wired LAN cable. Most public hotspots located in airports, hotels, restaurants, and conference centers rely on Wi-Fi. Similarly, many home owners have installed Wi-Fi to enable Internet connectivity throughout their homes without the need to retrofit the house with cables. Online File W6.1 describes the growing use of Wi-Fi by the traveling public.

▶ **Municipal Wi-Fi networks (WMAN).** By using a large number of connected hotspots, one can create a wireless city. This is known as a *city-wide* or *municipal Wi-Fi network*. For example, on August 16, 2006, Google created a network of 380 access points posted on light poles throughout the city of Mountain View, California. Residents of Mountain View just had to choose the "Google WiFi" signal and sign into their Google accounts with their user ID and password to access the Web through the free Wi-Fi service. These networks also are known as *grid* or *mesh networks* (see Online File W6.2). Throughout the United States, there have been a number of municipal Wi-Fi projects. Most of these, like Philadelphia, Pennsylvania's "Wireless Philadelphia" project, have experienced cost and schedule overruns only to provide much less coverage than originally envisioned. Philadelphia's system was purchased by the city government for pennies on the dollar and will be for government use only (*Whyy.org* 2010).

▶ **WiMAX.** Instead of relying on a mesh or grid of multiple access points, like in municipal Wi-Fi, networks, WiMAX (Worldwide Interoperability for Microwave Access) provides relatively fast (e.g., 70 Mbps) broadband access over a medium-sized area of up to 31 miles (50 kilometers). WiMAX works somewhat like a cell phone. More specifically, WiMAX coverage is divided into a series of overlapping areas called *cells*. Each of these cells provides broadband Internet coverage within a given geographical area. At the center of each cell is a tower with a base station that is connected to the Internet using high-speed lines. A tower broadcasts radio signals over a set radio frequency called a *spectrum*. Unlike Wi-Fi, the spectrum is restricted to companies who have licensed its usage (e.g., Sprint). This provides wider and more reliable coverage. In order to access a WiMAX network, a device (e.g., UMPC) requires a built-in or external card. WiMAX is gaining popularity in a number of municipal areas throughout the world. The WiMAX Forum (wimaxforum.org) provides detailed information about WiMAX capabilities and usage.

▶ **Wireless wide area networks.** A **wireless wide area network (WWAN)** offers the broadest wireless coverage. WWANs rely on the same network technologies as cell phones. This means that a user with a mobile computer and a WWAN card can access the Internet regionally, nationally, or even globally, depending on the coverage of the wireless service provider the user is accessing. WWANs can be distinguished by their speed (e.g., 2G versus 3G versus 4G networks), by the communication protocols they use (e.g., the time division multiple access [TDMA] protocol used in 2G networks versus the code division multiple access [CDMA] designed for 3G networks), and the cellular standards on which they are based (e.g., much of the world utilizes the Global System for Mobile Communications [GSM] and Personal Digital Cellular [PDC] in Japan).

wireless wide area network (WWAN)
A telecommunications network that offers wireless coverage over a large geographical area, typically over a cellular phone network.

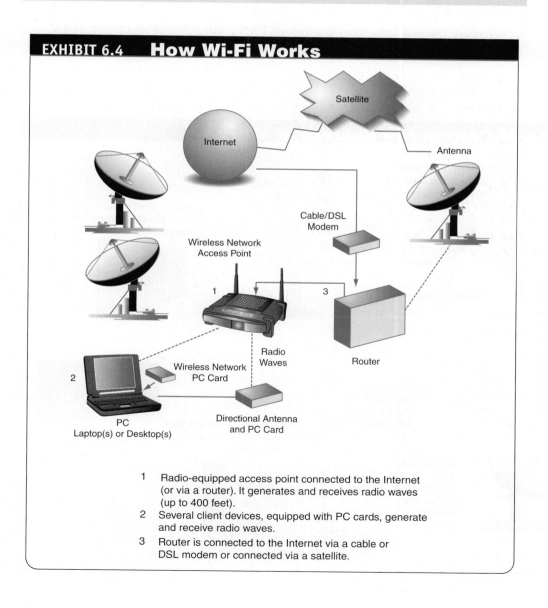

EXHIBIT 6.4   How Wi-Fi Works

1 Radio-equipped access point connected to the Internet (or via a router). It generates and receives radio waves (up to 400 feet).
2 Several client devices, equipped with PC cards, generate and receive radio waves.
3 Router is connected to the Internet via a cable or DSL modem or connected via a satellite.

Information about WWANs can be found at the websites of the various service providers (e.g., sprint.com) and at the sites of various mobile or cellular associations (e.g., gsmworld.com).

PUTTING IT ALL TOGETHER

The previously mentioned software, hardware, and telecommunications are put together by a management system to support wireless electronic trading as shown in Exhibit 6.5. The exhibit shows the flow of information from the user (Step 1) to the conclusion of the transaction (Step 9).

Section 6.2 ▶ REVIEW QUESTIONS

1. Briefly describe some of the key differences and similarities among the major mobile devices.
2. Why is it difficult to develop software and services for mobile devices?
3. Briefly describe the types of messaging services offered for mobile devices.
4. Define mobile portal and voice portal.
5. Distinguish between MSM and MSS.
6. Define IVR.
7. What are the distinguishing features of PANs, WLANs, WMAN, WiMAX, and WWANs?

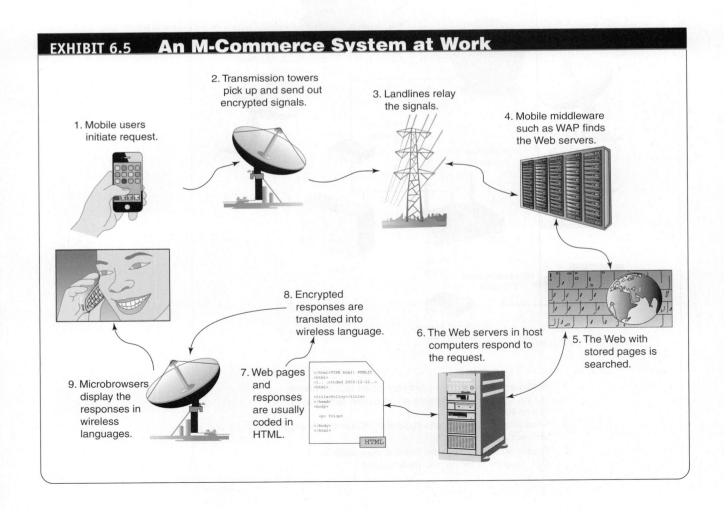

EXHIBIT 6.5   An M-Commerce System at Work

1. Mobile users initiate request.
2. Transmission towers pick up and send out encrypted signals.
3. Landlines relay the signals.
4. Mobile middleware such as WAP finds the Web servers.
5. The Web with stored pages is searched.
6. The Web servers in host computers respond to the request.
7. Web pages and responses are usually coded in HTML.
8. Encrypted responses are translated into wireless language.
9. Microbrowsers display the responses in wireless languages.

6.3 MOBILE FINANCIAL APPLICATIONS

Most mobile financial services are basically mobile versions of their wireline counterparts, but they have the potential to turn a mobile device—cellular phone or personal digital assistant—into a powerful business tool, replacing bank branches, ATMs, and credit cards by letting a user conduct financial transactions anytime, anywhere. We divided these services into two broad categories: mobile banking and other financial services. The topic of mobile payment is described in Chapter 10.

MOBILE BANKING

Mobile banking (also known as m-banking) is a term used to describe the performance of banking activities such as balancing checks, account transactions, payments, credit applications, etc., via a mobile device. Until 2011, mobile banking was most often performed via SMS or the mobile Web. The influx of smartphones and PDAs, Apple's initial success with iPhone and iPad, and the rapid growth of phones based on Google's Android system have led to the increased use of special client application programs (apps) downloaded to a mobile device for conducting mobile banking. For details and a conceptual model, see en.wikipedia.org/wiki/Mobile_banking.

mobile banking
Performing banking activities such as balance checks, account transactions, payments, credit applications, etc., via a mobile device.

Throughout Europe, the United States, and Asia, an increasing percentage of banks are offering mobile access to financial and account information.

Examples. Most banks deploy mobile services through a variety of channels, although the Internet and SMS are the most widely used. A blog written by Brandon McGee (brandonmcgee.blogspot.com) provides links to a number of banking websites throughout the world that provide financial services. Take, for instance, the Chase Mobile services offered by J.P.Morgan Chase Bank. On the one hand, customers can access their accounts at chase.com via the browser on their smartphones in much the same way they would access their accounts from their desktop or laptop computers. On the other hand, customers can send Chase Mobile shorthand SMS text messages to inquire about their balances (BAL), payment due dates (DUE), or transaction histories (TRANS).

American Express offers a version of their website for mobile phones. A free trial is available at americanexpress.com.

Historically, the uptake of mobile banking has been relatively low. This is beginning to change. Much of the change is being driven by the world economic crisis of 2008–2010. Bank and financial services' customers are utilizing their smartphones and cell phones to obtain up-to-the minute financial information and to perform up-to-the-minute transactions. For example, MONILINK, the United Kingdom's mobile money network, which is used by most of the UK high-street banks, reported in October 2008 that customers had used the network for approximately 1 million transactions, a substantial increase over the previous months (*M2 Presswire* 2008). In April 2010, Berg Insight estimated that users of m-banking and related services doubled between 2008 and 2009 to 55 million and would double again in 2010. The number of mobile users should reach close to 1 billion by 2015 (reported by *mobiThinking.com* 2010).

OTHER FINANCIAL-RELATED MOBILE APPLICATIONS

There are several other financial-related mobile applications (see mint.com/blog/trends/the-future-of-mobile-finance). Next are two examples.

Mobile Stock Trading

Several brokerage companies offer extensive mobile services and stock trading tools.

Example: E*TRADE Mobile. E*TRADE enables customers to trade anytime and anywhere from their smartphones. In late 2010, it introduced E*TRADE Mobile Pro for the iPad.

Using the E*TRADE software and the iPad, users can:

- Get real-time news and charts.
- Trade stocks (regular market sessions and extended hours).
- Check their stock watch lists and portfolios.

▶ Access and manage their accounts.

▶ Prepare year-end tax documents.

▶ Stream live CNBC TV financial programs.

For about $10 you can buy MobFinance software (for BlackBerry and Symbian devices). MobFinance is a powerful real-time stock tracking software and mobile stock portfolio management software that enables users to monitor portfolios by retrieving stock quotes and live charts directly from their mobile phones from 57 stock exchanges all over the world (including the United States, United Kingdom, China, India, Canada, Germany, and Australia). Free services are available from Google and Yahoo!. Both employ a search engine that provides real-time stock market information and financial news and research data.

Real Estate

The real estate market can be an ideal place for mobile commerce since real estate brokers are on the move and so are the customers. Most realtors offer a photo gallery for each property on a desktop. These pictures can also be seen on the mobile screen, but m-commerce can do more than that. Let's look at the examples.

Example 1: Mobile Video Marketing Platform at Partners Trust. Partners Trust Estate is a brokerage firm for high-end properties that in 2010 launched an interactive mobile campaign to help buyers find their dream properties. The mobile marketing video platform from Mogreet (mogreet.com) delivers relevant, timely, and informative mobile video tours directly to buyers' mobile devices. The service allows for real estate associates to better connect with their customers by giving them the ability to view video tours, be the first to know about new properties on the market, check for open houses, and receive local information about schools and neighborhoods directly on their mobile devices.

Each Partners Trust real estate associate has individual keywords for each property listing number, which are marketed across various channels, including sign riders, print advertisements (e.g., the *Los Angeles Times*), and through Partners Trust social media. By simply texting these keywords (for example: text RonS1 to 21534) and opting-in to the service, customers will instantly receive relevant text and video information about this listing, including exclusive access to a sneak peek of a virtual tour of the property before it is released to the public via the MLS service. For consumers, this gives serious home buyers the tools to find their dream homes, and customers get the upper hand in finding the newest inventory. For details, see prnewswire.com/news-releases/partners-trust-real-estate-brokerage—acquisitions-launches-mogreets-mobile-video-marketing-platform-to-enable-home-buyers-to-see-mobile-video-tours-111378279.html.

Example 2: Using Augmented Realty. Using augmented reality (en.wikipedia,org/wiki/augmented_reality), some companies in Europe allow you to open your mobile phone, point at certain buildings in a city (e.g., Paris), and in seconds you can see the property's value per square meter superimposed over a live image of the building streamed through the phone's camera. It could be the new frontier for on-demand property search.

This application, engineered by Layar, a company based in Amsterdam, uses augmented reality technology to harness a phone's camera, global positioning system (GPS) (see Section 6.7), and compass to locate buildings. Elements like statistics and 3-D images are essentially layered over a live picture so that the user gets a single view of all available information. For details, see Macintosh (2010).

Several other mobile real estate applications are being developed combining Google Maps and Google Earth with mobile applications. Note that some people object to other people taking photos of their houses on the basis that it is an invasion of privacy.

Section 6.3 ▶ REVIEW QUESTIONS

1. Describe some of the services provided by mobile banking.

2. List some of the benefits that you can derive as a customer from e-banking.

3. Describe mobile stock trading applications.

4. Describe mobile applications in real estate.

6.4 MOBILE ENTERPRISE SOLUTIONS: FROM SUPPORTING THE WORKFORCE TO IMPROVING INTERNAL OPERATIONS

The majority of mobile applications are enterprise-related.

DEFINING MOBILE ENTERPRISE

Mobile technology is rapidly moving us from the information age into the age of boundless communication, collaboration, and work. However, the success of today's cutting-edge mobile technologies will not be determined merely by their new features. Rather, the way companies integrate these technologies into their day-to-day business operations will determine their success or failure. Such integration can be done in hundreds of different ways depending on the industry, the mobile models, and the organizational culture. In the previous sections we introduced several examples, including the Hertz opening case, in what we call "mobile enterprise applications" or in short "mobile enterprise." This term refers to mobile applications in enterprises (to distinguish from consumer-oriented applications, such as mobile entertainment). Obviously, there are many mobile enterprise applications as illustrated in Section 6.1, Exhibit 6.2 (p. 281).

A Working Definition of Mobile Enterprise.

Mobile enterprise refers to mobile applications conducted by enterprises to improve the operations of the employees, the facilities, and the supply chains, within the enterprise and with its business partners. For a comprehensive description of mobile enterprise including guidelines for implementation, best practices, and case studies, see Unhelkar (2009). The term is also known as *enterprise mobility*.

Note: The term *mobile enterprise* is also used to describe a Web-based mobile cloud computing business solution, leveraging the Internet infrastructure to deliver Software as a Service to businesses. It consists of a collection of online interactive business applications (e.g., see Motorola 2007). For details, see en.wikipedia.org/wiki/Mobile_Enterprise.

mobile enterprise
Application of mobile computing inside the enterprise (e.g., for improved communication among employees).

THE FRAMEWORK AND CONTENT OF MOBILE ENTERPRISE APPLICATIONS

In addition to Motorola's framework that we introduced in Section 6.1, there are several other proprietary frameworks and classifications used by other vendors. For example, AT&T Mobile Enterprise Application Platform includes the following three categories:

- **The sales application** provides organizations with a complete view across all facets of a customer relationship—accounts, opportunities, contacts, tasks, and more—from an easy-to-use mobile application running on an AT&T device. Benefits include: improved business processes, increased sales productivity, improved customer retention, improved visibility, and overall reporting accuracy.

- **The support application** empowers IT support technicians with real-time access anywhere to time-sensitive, actionable incident and problem management information. Benefits include: increased field support team productivity, reduced operational costs by improving first-call fix rates, improved customer visibility of service status, and significant ROI based on capital expense reduction.

- **The service application** provides field service workers with bidirectional access to real-time customer, inventory, and other job-related information. Benefits include all those for the support applications, plus enhanced parts usage information, which helps reduce inventory costs.

Although B2C m-commerce gets considerable publicity in the media, for most organizations the greatest benefit from m-commerce is likely to come from applications within the enterprise mostly supporting the mobile workforce employees who spend a substantial part of their workday away from corporate premises.

mobile worker
Any employee who is
away from his or her
primary work space at
least 10 hours a week
or 25 percent of the
time.

MOBILE WORKERS

A **mobile worker** is usually defined as any employee who is away from his or her primary work space at least 10 hours a week (or 25 percent of the time). In 2008, there were more than 150 million workers in the United States, of which approximately 50 million or one-third could be classified as mobile. Using the definition of mobile workers, IDC forecasted that in 2010 there would be approximately 1 billion mobile workers worldwide (CIO Zone 2010). This represents about a third of the total workforce. In the United States alone, it estimates that 75 percent of the workforce will be mobile. This represents a major shift.

Examples of mobile workers include members of sales teams, traveling executives, telecommuters, employees working in corporate yards or warehouses, and repair or installation employees who work at customers' sites or in the field. These individuals need access to the same office and work applications and data as their nonmobile counterparts. The following discussion examines mobile devices and technologies that can be used to support mobile workers and the issues that arise in providing this support. For details, see Motorola (2007).

MOBILE WORKFORCE AND M-COMMERCE SUPPORT

Workforce mobility is not a new phenomenon. What is new is the magnitude of the phenomenon and its explosive growth. Therefore, there is growing recognition within enterprises that a mobile workforce requires technology support and can benefit from specialized mobile solutions and devices. For a comprehensive report, see Gargiulo (2009).

Toward this end, companies are providing a substantial percentage of their employees with a wide range of mobile devices, including BlackBerry's voice-enabled PDAs, Wi-Fi-enabled laptops, iPhones, and iPads, all with enterprise applications. The percentage of mobile devices used in one company varies depending on the industry, as well as on the company's size.

Benefits of Mobile Workforce Support

As with other IT investments, many enterprises cite "enhancing productivity and reduced costs" as the main reasons for the widespread deployment of mobile devices and applications within their organizations. Mobile solutions—devices and applications—provide mobile workers with real-time access to enterprise data and applications. Such support can reduce, for example, the time required in the field to process orders or to service customers' requests. Mobile solutions can also automate existing paper and pen processes and workflows. This can ensure, for instance, that processes are completed in a uniform fashion with minimal data entry errors or data loss.

Some of the solutions that are widely used by the three segments cited previously include the following:

▶ **Sales force automation.** Generally speaking, sales force automation (SFA) systems help guide and automatically record the various stages of the sales process. These stages run the gamut from managing contacts with customers and prospects, tracking sales leads, forecasting sales, and managing orders. Providing mobile access to a company's SFA system can help keep its mobile sales personnel better informed about new product launches, product information, pricing schedules, order status, manufacturing schedules, inventory levels, and delivery schedules. Sales staff can enter sales meetings with the most current and accurate information, perhaps even checking sales and product information during the meeting itself. When it is time to close a deal, the salesperson can wirelessly check production schedules and inventory levels to confirm product availability and even specify a delivery date. This real-time available-to-promise/capacity-to-promise (ATP/CTP) capability reduces the potential for delayed or canceled sales. It also can mean more competitive and realistic offers to prospects and customers. Online File W6.3 provides a detailed example of the use of SFA at a major UK retail manufacturer, the Hillarys Corp.

▶ **Field force automation (FFA).** One group of inherently mobile employees are those involved in delivery and dispatch services, as well as services aimed at equipment and service repair, including transportation (e.g., delivery of food, oil, newspapers, and cargo; courier services; tow trucks; taxis), utilities (e.g., gas, electricity, phone, water), field services (e.g., computer, office equipment, home repair), health care (e.g., visiting nurses, doctors, social services), and security (e.g., patrols, alarm installation). FFA, also called *field service management (FSM)*, is designed to support this segment of the mobile workforce.

An important part of field force management is *dispatching of employees*. This includes the automation of work orders. Tools such as the BlackBerry include software for improving dispatching (e.g., see the case of Centra Windows Ltd. at blackberry.com/go/success).

▶ **Mobile office applications.** According to a worldwide survey of 375 top business executives conducted by the Intelligence Unit of *The Economist* magazine (*Economist* 2007), e-mail, calendaring, and keeping in touch with colleagues via messaging are the most popular mobile applications. Looking to 2013, these applications are expected to maintain their popularity with a few minor changes. Executives feel that mobile voice-over-IP (VoIP) and videoconferencing will increase in importance. They also anticipate greater use of mobile customer relationship management (CRM) by their sales and services teams. Finally, mobile collaboration is increasing, facilitated by microblogging (Twitter), blogging, wikis, and social networking, such as discussion forums and use of the answer (ask) function.

▶ **Mobile CRM (e-CRM) and PRM.** E-CRM is discussed in detail in Online Tutorial T1. *CRM* is an industry term that encompasses methodologies and software that help an enterprise manage customer relationships in an organized fashion. Usually, an extensive database of customer information, including customer contact information, is at the center of a CRM system. In a CRM system, information is entered and accessed by a range of employees through the company, including sales, marketing, customer service, human resources, product engineering and manufacturing, and accounting and finance personnel. A similar system exists for business partners, known as partner relationship management or PRM. These systems are now going mobile.

Challenges of Mobile Workforce Support

Even though most enterprises recognize the need to provide mobile workers with specialized applications and devices, there are many nuts-and-bolts challenges involved in delivering mobile solutions to mobile workers. The challenges include issues from both the solution providers' and users' point of view: Representative issues are:

▶ **Network coverage gaps and interruptions.** Imagine all the places where your cell phone doesn't work or works poorly—in tunnels, in remote locations, large buildings and warehouses, hospitals and health care facilities, and rural areas, to name just a few. Now imagine trying to do critical work in these locations. Not only do these dead spots cause interruptions, but they also result in poor performance for both devices and applications. Improvement in technology reduces this problem with time.

▶ **Internetwork roaming.** Cellular networks and devices are designed to support roaming from one cell or network to the next. As users roam or move from one cell or network to another, performance and latency issues can arise. Not only can roaming result in performance and latency issues, but it can also result in application crashes and can force users to reenter lost or corrupt data.

▶ **Device and network management.** While mobile workers see the gaps, interruptions, and poor performance as major frustrations, the teams charged with planning and implementing these mobile solutions are more concerned with managing and securing network access to enterprise data and solutions. This can present a substantial challenge, especially if there are many disparate mobile devices.

▶ **Bandwidth management.** As the number of mobile workers and mobile solutions increases, so does network traffic. Unless the increases are well understood and planned for in a systematic fashion, there can be substantial contention for network bandwidth. *Note:* These problems are lessening with time due to technological improvements.

Other Categories of Mobile Applications

In addition to the mobile workforce, there is a support related to improvements in supply chains, such as in logistics and warehouse management. In Chapter 11, we will describe mobile support to the supply chain. Mobile fleet and transportation management is another fertile area for mobile enterprise applications. Next we present two mobile enterprise areas: Fleet and transportation management, and mobile applications in warehousing.

For implementation issues related to mobile employees, see Gargiulo (2009). Many of the applications are based on wireless communication; see Rash (2010a) for details. For a study on how employees use smartphones at IBM, see Ahmad and Orton (2010).

FLEET AND TRANSPORTATION MANAGEMENT

One of the more successful applications of m-commerce is fleet management. Many companies own fleets of cars and trucks that need to be managed properly. There are several activities and tools that can be used to maximize the vehicles and driver usage, increase efficiencies, and meet customer expectations. For details, see Motorola (2007).

Example. Procter & Gamble, a global company with a presence in 80 countries, is using a vehicle management system (VMS) in its fleets of industrial trucks. For example, in the Germany plants the system helps improve workplace safety and security by restricting vehicle access to trained, authorized operators, providing electronic vehicle inspection checklists, and sensing vehicle impacts. The wireless VMS also helps reduce fleet maintenance costs by automatically uploading vehicle data, reporting vehicle problems electronically, scheduling maintenance according to actual vehicle usage rather than by calendar, minimizing manual data entry, and helping determine the optimal economic time to replace equipment. In addition, a wireless VMS helps improve supply chain productivity by establishing accountability for the use of equipment, ensuring equipment is in the proper place at the right time, streamlining material handling workflow, and providing unique metrics on equipment utilization. P&G is able to configure the system such that the drivers can continue using their existing employee identification badges, and the system can communicate over P&G's existing wireless network using advanced Wi-Fi security protocols.

The following are some other representative areas of applications.

Fleet Maintenance

By capturing and managing vehicle data across the enterprise, companies can reduce truck maintenance costs and optimize fleet utilization. They can save time and increase data accuracy by replacing hard-copy work orders with mobile computers and RFID systems. Companies can use vehicle-performance data, made available by reading the truck's bar code or RFID tag, to plan maintenance activities. This will minimize downtime by ensuring fixes are made exactly when needed.

Tracking People and Vehicles

Using GPS, companies can track the location of their vehicles in real-time and assist drivers to solve problems. This can enhance safety and increase operational efficiency. For example, drivers can be directed to the least expensive gas stations on their routes. This is usually supplemented with a two-way radio communication system where cell phones do not work (no signals). Using Google Maps, all premier fleet owners have the ability to accurately track their fleet vehicles anytime, anywhere, and in any view—street, satellite, terrain, and more.

Companies can also track fleet usage and assure compliance with government and company regulations. Representative vendors are Motorola and FleetMatics. For additional information, see motorola.com/Business/US-EN/Business+Solutions/Product+Solutions/ Fleet+Managementmotorola.com/business/us-en/business+solutions/product+solutions/ fleetmanagement.

How the Tracking System Works. Fleet management information is delivered from the vehicle via satellite communication, ensuring that data is uninterrupted by land obstructions or lack of terrestrial transmission towers. All mobile resource data is received, stored, and analyzed at the Network Operations Center, as illustrated in Exhibit 6.6.

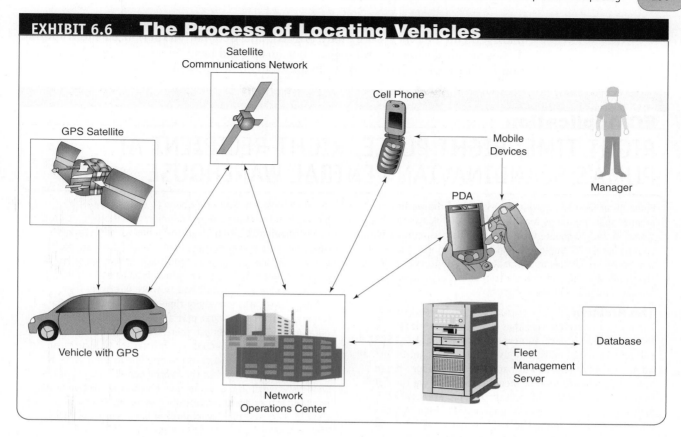

EXHIBIT 6.6   The Process of Locating Vehicles

Vehicle telematic data is accessed by logging on to Fleet Central via a Web browser from any computer or mobile device. From this application, reports are generated, commands issued, alerts set, and all monitoring is performed. An optional two-way, in-cab message display terminal allows near real-time communications between the driver and the fleet manager or the dispatcher. A description of such a system by Fleet Management Solutions is available at fleetmanagementsolutions.com/frontend/overview.aspx.

Transportation Management

Transportation management includes the fleet maintenance and vehicle tracking described earlier. In addition it includes several other tasks. Recall the Hertz opening case and all the applications there. Mobile devices are used extensively in airports and by airlines, traffic control systems, public bus systems, and more (see the NextBus case in Online File W6.4).

Mobile Fleet Management for iPad. An interesting application is the fleet management tool that runs on the iPad. The tool has been used for shuttle fleet management. Managers can use this myFleet iPad app to:

- View real-time vehicle location.
- Access ridership reports.
- Manage SMS alerts anytime, anywhere.

For details, see blog.goosenetworks.com/content/myfleet-mobile-fleet-management-apple-ipad.

MOBILE APPLICATIONS IN WAREHOUSES

Warehouses are important components in the supply chain. They exist in most organizations either as part of their plants, or as in the case of retailers as independent storage entities. The smooth operation of the warehouse is critical for supply chains and manufacturing efficiencies as shown in Online File W6.5.

Handheld devices are playing a major role in increasing the efficiency of warehouse management. But they were bulky, rugged, and frequently experienced interruptions. Today, mobile devices are still rugged, but smaller and much more effective. One application is illustrated in Case 6.1 about Puma's warehouse in Sweden.

CASE 6.1
EC Application
RIGHT TIME, RIGHT PLACE, RIGHT RECIPIENT AT PUMA'S SCANDINAVIAN CENTRAL WAREHOUSE

Puma AG of Germany (*puma.com*) is one of the world's premier sporting goods brands. Over 18,000 sports items are stored in 39,370 square feet in its Swedish warehouse. With approximately 70 employees and two work shifts, the warehouse dispatches approximately 30,000 items a day. The items are shipped directly to retailers around Sweden, Norway, Finland, and the Baltic states.

The Problem
The number of stored items has grown and with it the size of the warehouse. In fact, turnover has increased from USD32 million to USD160 million in just six years. Up until 2007, all warehouse management was handled using a paper-based system. Synchronization between restocking from the buffer to picking was inefficient, and the number of incorrect deliveries and complaints was unacceptably high. A lack of organization in handling this had a negative effect on all divisions within the company from customer service and the returns department all the way up to the top management team. In 2006, the warehouse received a corporate directive to reduce paper flow and make the warehouse management system more efficient. Intermec Inc.'s handheld computers played a key role in the process of switching from paper-based to automatic warehouse management.

The Solution
Puma's new warehouse management is completely automated. It uses a Cisco-compatible compact handheld computer (the Internet CN3). Picking of incoming and outgoing deliveries and inventory control are conducted using bar codes and handheld computers synched with a wireless network via a central server.

The Results
Just a week after the handheld computers were deployed, the number of complaints dropped substantially with a simultaneous reduction in the time it took to handle them, and there were very few incorrect deliveries (99 percent accuracy).

Now, Puma can organize incoming and outgoing deliveries in a completely different manner than before. Advance planning and scheduling are very important in this industry. Since shops often have limited storage space, Puma was able to synchronize the deliveries with the warehouses needs. The deliveries do not come either too early or too late.

For Puma, where there is a relatively high proportion of part-time staff, the automated system has been a real asset. Familiarity with and deep knowledge of the warehouse are not prerequisites in order for Puma staff to work productively. Today, the Internet CN3 handheld computer automatically identifies the correct bay and confirms that the scanned goods correspond with the orders.

Previously, in order for goods to be restocked, the pickers had to inform the truck driver, which often resulted in staff having to sit and wait for goods to be restocked. Now, the system checks that there is a sufficient supply of goods available for picking at all times. If not, an order is automatically sent to a truck, which fetches them from the buffer. Previously, the staff had to write out every item number, which was incredibly time-consuming. Today the terminals take care of that part as well as storing all the data. Around the warehouse there are 17 Cisco Wi-Fi access points. These are connected to a central server, which can be viewed by warehouse staff in their handheld computers' Web windows. At various times the central server releases orders wirelessly, which the users receive on their respective units. Long order lists are automatically divided up among two or three pickers and then synchronized back together at the end. This expedites order fulfillment.

Today, Puma's people work using personal handheld computers that they have signed for, which also helps instill them with a sense of responsibility for servicing and maintenance of the machines. In addition, the users have been actively involved in the units' system development. Applications, options, and buttons have been shaped to a large extent by the users' stated needs and preferences. The "to ask" button featured on the terminals is a prime example of this. Previously, when an item ended up on the floor, it was seldom, if ever, picked up by a staff member since they did not know where to put it. Today, the employees can scan the items with their handheld computers, the screen then displays the item's correct location in the warehouse, and the staff members can put the items back in their proper place.

Puma is looking forward to further enhancements to the system. It is hoped that IP-telephony—using smartphones and making calls over the existing access points—may be the next step in the development of the system. At present though, everyone (including customers) is extremely happy with the warehouse system and the possibilities that it has presented.

Sources: Compiled from Intermec (2010), *puma.com* (accessed January 2011), and *en.wikipedia.org/wiki/Puma_AG* (accessed February 2011).

Questions

1. What drove Puma to use a mobile system?
2. What are the components of the system?
3. What are the benefits to the company? To the employees? To the customers?

Typical Mobile Devices Used in Warehouses

The following is a list of mobile activities and the tools that are usually used in warehouses:

- ▶ **Vehicle mount solutions.** Equipping forklifts with wireless computers, rugged bar code readers, and RFID readers allows employees to scan the bar codes to find where parts are locationed, and receive notifications.
- ▶ **Handheld solutions.** The same devices that are mounted on vehicles are wearable on hands. These are used to track and trace assets, manage inventories, and help improve inventory accuracy.
- ▶ **Hands-free and voice solutions.** These devices provide freedom of movements and enable multitasking. They include the use of mobile voice mail (e-mail plus voice communication in one device), digital two-way radio communication and VoIP capabilities. All are used to better manage inventory and locate items quickly with real-time information.
- ▶ **Other solutions.** Cold storage and freezer solutions are usually wireless, RFID applications (see Chapter 11 and Online Tutorial T3), cross docking solutions. These are very effective in the warehouse. For a detailed description of all of these solutions, see motorola.com/Business/US-EN/Business+ Solutions/Industry+Solutions/ Manufacturing/Materials+and+Warehouse+Management_US-EN.

OTHER ENTERPRISE MOBILE APPLICATIONS

Hundreds of other mobile applications exist. For examples, see motorola.com/Business/ US-EN/Enterprise+Mobility.

One area is security (see the discussion of *sensory systems* in Section 6.7). Another security area is surveillance via smartphones (see Parks 2010). A popular area is that of medical care in clinics, physicians' offices, and hospital. For an interesting case study in Union Hospital in Hong Kong, see motorola.com/web/Business/Products/Mobile_Computers/ MC55/_Documents/Static_File/CS_UnionHos_210410-d4.pdf (click on industry, then Healthcare, then case study). The major applications there are: patient identification, instant data access and input, investigative tests, and information security. Also, see the "mobilizing Biz Apps at Mobileenterprise.com" (case study, Maryland's Fredrick Memorial Hospital).

iPad in the Enterprise

Apple's iPad is now moving to the enterprise. Initially the iPad was used as a communication and collaboration device connected to existing systems (see apple.com/iPad/Business). But, according to Carr (2010) many companies are using iPads for many business applications especially in hotels, financial services, construction, and manufacturing. In addition, the iPad is replacing paper menus in restaurants. For example, sandwich and pastry chain Au Bon Pain uses iPads for tabletop ordering. Travelers in New York's John F. Kennedy International Airport can order foods from iPad menus while they wait for their flight. Payment can be made via the iPad as well.

Section 6.4 ▶ REVIEW QUESTIONS

1. Describe the major segments of the mobile workforce. How quickly is this workforce growing?
2. What are some of the common benefits of mobile SFA, FFA, and CRM?
3. What are some of the challenges that companies incur when they try to implement solutions for a mobile workforce?
4. Describe the use of mobile applications on fleet management.
5. How can wireless systems increase productivity in a warehouse?

6.5 MOBILE ENTERTAINMENT AND OTHER CONSUMER SERVICES

Mobile entertainment applications have been around for years, but only recently they expanded rapidly due to developments in wireless devices and technology. Consumer applications started in the 1990s, but really took off after 2000. This section will describe mainly mobile entertainment and briefly discuss some other areas of consumer services.

OVERVIEW OF MOBILE ENTERTAINMENT

There is some debate about what actually constitutes mobile entertainment and which of its segments falls under the rubric of m-commerce. For example, if you purchase a song on the Web and download it to your PC, then copy it to your MP3 player, is this a form of mobile entertainment? What if you copy it to your smartphone rather than an MP3 player? What if you buy it and download it directly from the Web to your smartphone? What if you buy it and download it from the Web directly to an iPod? What if the song was free? There are many similar "what ifs." By strict definition, mobile entertainment is any type of leisure activity that utilizes *wireless telecommunication* networks, interacts with wireless service providers, and usually incurs a fee upon usage. Given that it requires wireless telecommunications, the implication is that mobile entertainment involves devices that operate over these networks.

mobile entertainment
Any type of leisure activity that utilizes wireless telecommunication networks, interacts with service providers, and incurs a cost upon usage.

Based on research findings (Juniper Research 2008), it is estimated that the global market for mobile entertainment will jump from worldwide revenues of approximately $21 billion in 2008 to $65 billion in 2012.

To put these figures into context, PricewaterhouseCoopers (2008) forecasted that online and offline global entertainment and the media industry as a whole will reach $2.2 trillion in 2012. Thus, mobile entertainment will be about only 3 percent of the overall entertainment market (i.e., $65 billion versus $2.2 trillion). But the online segment is growing much, much faster than the offline one.

This section discusses some of the major types of mobile entertainment, including mobile music and video, mobile gaming, and mobile gambling. This discussion is preceded by a look at the mobile entertainment market in general. Mobile entertainment in social networks is covered in Chapter 7.

MOBILE MUSIC AND VIDEO PROVIDERS

When you think of digital and mobile music and video, the first thing that comes to mind is Apple and iTunes. Apple is the clear leader in the digital distribution of music and video. Since 2001, Apple has offered consumers the ability to download songs and videos from the Apple iTunes store. iTunes customers are purchasing billions of songs annually. In 2010, Apple's customers are also downloading videos at the rate of 70,000 a day. At the end of 2007, Amazon.com, the largest online store, launched their Amazon MP3 and Amazon Video On Demand, a digital download service for music and video, respectively. Other major providers of music online are Walmart.com, Google (with its YouTube), MySpace, and Facebook. Note that cell phones today can display analog TV (popular in developing countries) using chips from Telegent systems. Smartphones can display anything that is being offered on the Internet. For details, see venturebeat.com/2010/12/01/telegent-ships-100mth-chip-for-tv-on-mobile-phones. Note that Dish Network extends remote streaming to the iPad through its remote app, and Netflix has a free iPhone app for its monthly subscribers to search and watch selections from their video library while on the go.

MOBILE GAMES

A wide variety of mobile games have been developed to meet the needs and styles of different types of players. They can be classified in several ways:

- **Technology.** Embedded, SMS/MMS, Web browsing, J2ME, BREW, native OS
- **Number of players.** Solo play or multiplay (from few to many)

- **Genre.** Action, logic/puzzle/skill, sports and racing, arcade, role playing, card and casino, movie, adult, and lifestyle
- **Social network-based.** Using smartphones people can play games available in social networks, such as Farmville in Facebook. Note that Zynga, the largest social game company (see Chapter 7) acquired Newtoy, a mobile game company. Similarly Japan's DeNA acquired iPhone game maker ngmoco:). Such acquisitions are aimed to increase mobile gaming.

Several blogs provide information and discussion about the current state of the mobile gaming market, including various game offerings, as well as the technologies and platforms used to develop the games. One of the best is mobilegames.blogs.com. For an overview, see en.wikipedia.org/wiki/mobile_gaming.

According to Soh and Tan (2008), the demand for mobile games is fueled by three main factors:

- Increasing mobile device penetration rates in many countries, especially Finland, Japan, Korea, and Sweden; many users of mobile devices are potential consumers of mobile games
- The ability of mobile devices to deliver quality video and audio continues to improve significantly, making such devices suitable for playing mobile games
- The improving ability of wireless networks to handle broadband transmission, allowing users of mobile devices to download larger and more compelling mobile games

The potential size and growth of the overall market (according to Soh and Tan, 2008) is very large. The wireless gaming industry in the Asia-Pacific region alone is growing 40 percent annually. This explains the large number of companies involved in creating, distributing, and running mobile games. Some put the estimate of the number of game developers, aggregator-distributors, publishers, and portals at close to 2,000 enterprises. Many of these reside in the United States and Europe.

Hurdles for Growth

Although the market is growing rapidly, especially in China and India, game publishers are facing some major hurdles such as lack of standards, different software and hardware, and increasing costs. The coming generation of games requires advanced capabilities of the higher-end handsets and 3G networks. The adoption of these handsets and networks has not been as fast as originally anticipated. Finally, there was a belief that game advertising would generate revenues to offset the costs. The ad spending in mobile games has remained low, but it is growing fast. With the widespread use of smartphones, the potential audience for mobile games is substantially larger than the market for other platforms, PlayStation and Game Boy included. Because of the market potential, Nokia has entered the mobile gaming world, producing not only the phone/console but also the games that are delivered on memory cards. It also develops and markets near-distance multiplayer gaming (over Bluetooth) and wide-area gaming using cellular networks.

To address these hurdles, some of the more established game publishers such as Sega Corporation, as well as many start-ups, are focusing attention on Apple's iPhone and iPad and on similar devices. As mobile devices become an indispensable component of everyday life, the market for mobile gaming is likely to continue to increase well into the future.

MOBILE GAMBLING

Unlike some of the other forms of mobile entertainment, the mobile gambling market has some unique hurdles. First, mobile gambling requires two-way financial transactions. Not only must bettors or gamblers have a way of paying for their online bets, but the online gambling establishment must also have a way of paying off the bettor or gambler if they win. Second, online gambling sites face major trust issues. Gamblers and bettors have to believe that the site is trustable and fair, that they have a chance of winning, and that they are not being ripped off. Finally, the legislative and regulatory picture is very unclear. Most existing gambling legislation was passed prior to the advent of the Web and is outdated. Even if it isn't outdated, the legislative picture is like a patchwork quilt with some forms of gambling barred in certain territories but not in others.

From a legal standpoint, the United Kingdom has some of the least stringent regulations. This is one of the reasons that the United Kingdom is the largest market in terms of gross wagers, accounting for 52 percent of all wagers in 2007. In the future, the United Kingdom's overall percentage is likely to decline as the markets in other countries, such as Australia, China, and other Southeast Asian countries, where online gambling is also legal, grow over the next five years. It is also one of the reasons that online gambling is not projected to grow much in the near term.

Some countries have attempted to prohibit online gambling altogether or to control the type of online gambling that takes place by making it illegal to operate an online gambling site or a particular type of online gambling site within their jurisdictions. This has simply created a business opportunity for other countries that have encouraged online gambling sites to operate within their borders and have licensed them to do so.

Within the United States, some states have laws that ban gambling on the Internet outright, including Illinois, Indiana, Kentucky, Louisiana, Massachusetts, Michigan, Nevada, New Jersey, New York, Oregon, South Dakota, Washington, and Wisconsin. Additionally, attorneys general in Florida, Kansas, Minnesota, Oklahoma, and Texas have issued opinions that Internet gambling is illegal in their states. In the other states, online gambling is not directly prohibited, but it is controlled by federal statutes.

MOBILITY AND SPORTS

In Chapter 1, we described the use of mobile devices during the Beijing 2008 Olympics (Online File W1.4). There are many other mobile applications that relate to sports (e.g., see the closing case about the DFL in Chapter 1).

Here are some representative examples of unique mobile applications in sports:

- Nike and Apple introduced an iPod shoe called Nano that can provide real-time feedback on distance, time, and calories burned during a workout. A sensor and a receiver embedded in the shoe provide a wireless connection to the iPod, with workout information stored on the device and displayed on the screen. Runners can get audible feedback through the headphones, and data stored on the Nano can be downloaded to an iPad or PC after a run. In addition to these functions, the Nike+iPod system delivers music and commentary to help joggers make it through their workouts. Nike is offering free workout-related podcasts that include advice from marathon runner Alberto Salazar and inspiration from bicycling champion Lance Armstrong. The company also is planning to unveil a collection of jackets, tops, shorts, and armbands designed for the Nike+iPod Sport Kit and iPad. A similar service is offered by BonesinMotion.com together with Sprint. It uses a GPS to turn mobile phones into exercise tracking devices.

- Personalized live sport events can be viewed on mobile devices. The user can select the event. In the future systems will be able to predict users' preferred events during live sports competitions. Streaming live sports to mobile devices is becoming very popular. Unfortunately, you may be asked to pay some fee for use.

- Levi Strauss has a new line of jeans specifically geared toward iPod users. The $200 trousers come complete with headphones, a joystick, and even a docking cradle.

- ESPN's SportsCenter offers a cell phone dedicated to sports with Sanyo. You can get quick access to news and your favorite teams. Video clips of up to 30 seconds are available and so is a built-in camera. To alleviate waiting time, sports trivia are offered. Alerts are sent by request.

- Tickets to sporting (and other entertainment) events can be sent today to smartphones by their sellers. Users are then able to use their tickets immediately, by presenting their phones at the venue. The same technology is used for distribution of coupons, boarding passes for airplanes, etc.

- The Slipstream/Chipotle bike team uses BlackBerry Pearl wireless devices to let the manager schedule drug tests with just a few hours' notice. The team also tracks its riders' biological profiles for sharp changes that might indicate doping. This makes it virtually impossible to cheat since the riders are connected to the managers via the BlackBerry 24/7.

▶ *Invisible* is a term that characterizes a device manufactured and sold by Fitsense Technology (fitsense.com), a Massachusetts developer of Internet sports and fitness monitors. With this 1 ounce device that is clipped to a shoelace, runners are able to capture their speed and the distance they have run. The device transmits the data via a radio signal to a wrist device that can capture and transmit the data wirelessly to a desktop computer for analysis. Along the same lines, Champion Chip (championchip.com), headquartered in the Netherlands, has developed a system that keeps track of the tens of thousands of participants in very popular long-distance races. The tracking system includes miniature transponders attached to the runners' shoelace or ankle bracelets and antenna mats at the finish line that use radio frequencies to capture start times, splits, and finish times as the runners cross them.

▶ Eventbrite, an event ticketing and social commerce company, offers the Eventbrite Easy Entry, an iPhone application that enables event organizers to seamlessly check-in attendees, eliminating the hassle of manual and otherwise cumbersome and time-consuming processes. The new app can be downloaded for free at the iTunes store: itunes.apple.com/us/apple/eventbrite-easy-entry/id368260521?mt=8. Organizers can leverage Eventbrite's intelligence, analytics, and reporting capabilities to maintain an on-going, comprehensive view into key reporting metrics.

SERVICE INDUSTRY CONSUMER APPLICATIONS

A large number of mobile applications are in use in the different service industries. Here are two examples.

Health Care

Mobile devices are everywhere as illustrated next:

▶ Your physician can submit an order of medicine for you from a handheld device directly to the pharmacy. In addition, your physician can order tests, access medical information, scan billable items—all from the patient's bedside.

▶ Remote patient monitoring not only monitors patient vital signs but also can adjust medical equipment while moving throughout the health care facility.

▶ The managing, tracking, and verifying of blood for transfusion can be validated by mobile devices to reduce errors.

▶ A variety of devices and methods including wireless broadband and narrow band two-way radio equipment are used for clinical communication.

For more applications see motorola.com/Business/US-EN/Business+Solutions/ Industry+Solutions/Healthcare.

Hospitality Management

Many applications from travel and tourism (discussed earlier) to safety in hotel rooms exist. Examples are: two-way radio communication, wireless hotspot solutions, food safety, parking lot management, asset location and management, guest services, safety and security on the premises, entertainment, inventory management, and much more. For details, see motorola.com/Business/US-EN/Business+Solutions/Industry+Solutions/Hospitality. One area in hospitality that benefits from a wireless system is restaurant operations.

Example: Dolphin Fast Food. Dolphin Fast Food operates 19 Burger King franchises in Minnesota. To streamline operations and control costs while meeting the needs of customers, staff, and regulators, the company uses a sophisticated wireless system. The company has both public Wi-Fi for its customers and a corporate wireless network for its management. The company realized that it must offer Wi-Fi so its customers can use their mobile devices while dining. The same Wi-Fi enables managers to be more productive by enabling them to work on mobile devices while in the dining room. The corporate wireless systems give managers on-site access to back office PCs, printers, and video surveillance systems. The Internet access is protected by a VPN (see Chapter 9). The service to customers includes the blocking of content that is inappropriate for family-themed restaurants. The system is secured to allow protection of credit card transactions. The wireless infrastructure serves the POS terminals, but as a separate entity. All the wireless systems are well protected against malware attacks (see Chapter 9). For the deployment of the system and the security tools used, see Dolphin (2010).

Note: In full-service restaurants there are several additional applications such as taking orders on handheld devices where the orders go directly to the kitchen and to the cashiers, and a device for advising waiting customers to come when their tables are ready.

Public Safety and Crime Prevention

There are many mobile devices and methods for improving public safety. For example, mobile camera systems are used to fight motor vehicle theft and identify unregistered cars. The cameras can read license plate numbers of parked and even moving cars, comparing numbers to a database. For example, the cameras are used in Vietnam to find illegal taxi operators.

Other Industries

Mobile systems and applications can be found in all industries. For example, the METRO GROUP closing case gives some applications in retailing. Extensive applications can be found in m-government and m-learning (see Chapter 5). Homeland security applies many devices as do the transportation industry and the military. In agriculture wireless devices can guide tractors to work even in the dark.

Section 6.5 ▶ REVIEW QUESTIONS

1. Briefly describe the growth patterns of the various segments of mobile entertainment.
2. Discuss the basic components of the mobile music market.
3. What are some of the key barriers to the growth of the mobile games market?
4. Discuss some of the key legal issues impeding the growth of mobile gambling.
5. Describe the use of mobility in sports.
6. Describe some consumer service industry mobile applications.

6.6 LOCATION-BASED MOBILE COMMERCE

location-based m-commerce (l-commerce)
Delivery of m-commerce transactions to individuals in a specific location, at a specific time.

Location-based m-commerce (l-commerce) refers to the use of GPS-enabled devices or similar technologies (e.g., triangulation of radio- or cell-based stations) to find where a customer or client is and provide advertising and sometimes deliver coupons and services to him or her based on the customer's location. Location-based services are attractive to both consumers and businesses alike. From a consumer's (or business user's) viewpoint, localization offers safety (emergency services can pinpoint the mobile device owner's exact location), convenience (a user can locate what is nearby without consulting a directory, pay phone, or map), and increased productivity (time can be optimized by determining points of interest within close proximity). From a business supplier's point of view, location-based m-commerce offers an opportunity to provide services that more quickly or precisely meet a customer's needs. A major application is the use in social networks, which is described in Chapter 7.

The services provided through location-based m-commerce focus on five key factors:

1. **Location.** Determining the basic position of a person or a thing (e.g., car or boat)
2. **Navigation.** Plotting a route from one location to another
3. **Tracking.** Monitoring the movement of a person or a thing (e.g., a package or vehicle)
4. **Mapping.** Creating maps of specific geographical locations
5. **Timing.** Determining the precise time at a specific location

For example, WeatherBug (weather.weatherbug.com) and Send Word Now (sendwordnow.com) have combined some of these five services to ensure the safety of customers, employees, and stores during weather emergencies.

The newest development of l-commerce is known as **real-time location systems (RTLS)**, which are used to track and identify the location of objects in real time (see Malik 2009, and en.wikipedia.org/wiki/Real-time_location_system). Similar to RFID, these systems use readers to receive wireless signals from tags attached to items or people. A real-time location system is one of a number of technologies that detect the current geolocation of a target, which may be anything from a vehicle to an item in a manufacturing plant to a person. RTLS-capable products are used in an ever-increasing number of sectors including supply chain management (SCM), health care, the military, retail, recreation, and postal and courier services. RTLS is typically embedded in a product, such as a mobile phone or a navigational system. Most such systems consist of wireless nodes—typically tags or badges—that emit signals, and of readers that receive those signals. Current real-time location systems are based on wireless technologies, such as Wi-Fi, Bluetooth, ultra wideband, RFID, and GPS. One application, vehicle tracking, was describe in Section 6.4.

real-time location systems (RTLS)
Systems used to track and identify the location of objects in real time.

L-COMMERCE INFRASTRUCTURE

L-commerce rests on an infrastructure made up of five basic components, which include the following:

1. **Mobile devices.** These are tools used to request information. Location-based devices can be divided into two categories: single purpose or multipurpose. Single-purpose devices include such things as onboard navigation systems, toll boxes, transceivers, and GPS location devices. Multipurpose devices can be mobile phones, smartphones, PDAs, laptops, tablet PCs, and the like.

2. **Communication network.** The network that transfers user data and service requests from the mobile terminal to the service providers, and then the requested information is transferred back to the user.

3. **Positioning component.** In order to process or service a user's request, the user's position has to be determined. This can be done either through a mobile network or by using a global positioning system (GPS).

4. **Service or application provider.** Providers are responsible for servicing a user's request. Services can include such things as finding routes, searching yellow pages or other information sources based on the user's location, etc.

5. **Data or content provider.** Service providers usually rely on geographic data or location-based information to service user requests. More often than not, the location data or information is maintained by a third party, not the service provider.

The five components work together as illustrated in Exhibit 6.7.
Here is how the LBS system works:

1. Using a cell phone equipped with GPS, the user expresses his or her wish by clicking on a function (e.g., find me the nearest gas station).

2. The service finds where the user is located (finding the location of the GPS).

3. Via the mobile communication network, the request is routed to an application server, which activates a search.

4. The search will go to a database, find the nearest gas station, and check if it is reachable from the user's location at the given time.

5. Using a GIS, the service will deliver the reply to the user, if necessary with a map and driving directions.

EXHIBIT 6.7 LBS Components Creating a System

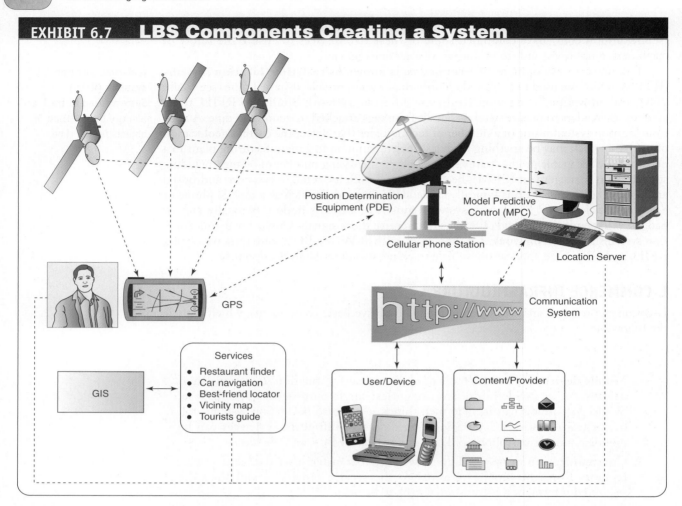

Geolocation

LBS is related to the concept of *geolocation*. **Geolocation** is the process of automatically identifying a Web user's physical location without that user having to provide any information. Geolocation works on all Web browsers, requires no plug-ins or cookies, and is already used by many of the world's most successful websites.

Yunker (2009) describes how companies are using geolocation to greatly improve the user experience across languages and borders—resulting in increased click-through rations and conversions rates (see Chapter 8).

L-commerce is distinguished from general m-commerce by the *positioning component* and the *geographical information systems* on which the various location-based services or applications rest.

The GPS: Positioning Component

Usually, the *positioning component* of an l-commerce system is either network-based or terminal-based. **Network-based positioning** relies on base stations to find the location of a mobile device sending a signal or sensed by the network. For example, the location of a mobile phone can be determined by knowing the location of the nearest mobile phone antenna (base station). In **terminal-based positioning**, the device calculates the location from signals received from the base stations. This is how the well-known global positioning system (GPS) works.

The **global positioning system (GPS)** is based on a worldwide satellite tracking system that enables users to determine exact positions anywhere on the earth. GPS was developed by the U.S. Defense Department for military use, but its high value for civilian use was immediately recognized, and the technology was released into the civilian domain, initially for use by commercial airlines and ships. In recent years, GPS

geolocation
The process of automatically identifying a Web user's physical location without that user having to provide any information.

network-based positioning
Relies on base stations to find the location of a mobile device sending a signal or sensed by the network.

terminal-based positioning
Calculating the location of a mobile device from signals sent by the device to base stations.

global positioning system (GPS)
A worldwide satellite-based tracking system that enables users to determine their position anywhere on the earth.

locators have become a part of the consumer electronics market and today are used widely for business and recreation. Online File W6.4 provides an example of the use of GPS for tracking buses.

GPS is supported by 24 U.S. government satellites. Each satellite orbits the earth once every 12 hours on a precise path at an altitude of 10,900 miles. At any point in time, the exact position of each satellite is known, because the satellite broadcasts its position and a time signal from its onboard atomic clock, which is accurate to one-billionth of a second. Receivers on the ground also have accurate clocks that are synchronized with those of the satellites.

GPS locators may be stand-alone units or embedded into a mobile device including cell phones. At any given time, a GPS locator can receive signals from at least three satellites. Using the fast speed of the satellite signals (186,272 miles, or 299,775 kilometers, per second; the speed of light), the system can determine the location (latitude and longitude) of any GPS locator, to within 50 feet (15 meters) by triangulation, using the distance from the GPS locator to three satellites to make the calculation of a location (longitude or latitude). A fourth satellite can also be used to determine elevation, although not to the same degree of accuracy as a location. Advanced forms of GPS can pinpoint a location within a centimeter. GPS software then computes the latitude and longitude of the receiver. More information on how the GPS system works is available at trimble.com/gps, McNamara (2008), and electronics.howstuffworks.com/gadgets/travel/gps.htm.

In 1999, the European Union (EU) proposed the construction of an alternative global navigation satellite system called *Galileo*. Unlike the U.S. GPS, Galileo is a civilian system, not a military system. As envisioned, Galileo would consist of 30 satellites orbiting at a distance of 14,429 miles, or 23,222 kilometers, above the earth and would provide positioning to within about a meter. Although the European Union and European Space Agency agreed to fund the project in 2002, the project has been beset by budgetary problems. In April 2008, the EU transportation ministers of 27 countries reached an agreement on funding. Under this agreement, the system will supposedly be operational by 2013 (Parlamentul European 2008). In 2010, Japan started work on its own system, which will be ready in 2014.

Note: GPS applications can help you get a date based on proximity and convenience (see sites such as Grindr or Skout). For details see Sutter (2010).

Location-Based Data

Location-based services and l-commerce revolve around a series of location-based questions or queries. One way to categorize these questions is the following (Steiniger, et al. 2006):

> ▸ **Locating.** Where am I? Where is a specific object or person?
> ▸ **Navigating.** How do I get to a specific address, place, position, or person?
> ▸ **Searching.** Where is the nearest or most relevant object or person?
> ▸ **Identifying.** What, who, or how much is here or there?
> ▸ **Event checking.** What happens here or there?

Using Data Collections. GPS-enabled smartphones and other devices help to collect large amounts of data. These can be used in decision making to save millions of dollars; see Feldman (2010).

Geographical Information Systems

The data, information, and processes needed to service location-based queries are usually handled by a *geographical information system (GIS)*. A geographical information system (GIS) captures, stores, analyzes, manages, and presents data that refer to or is linked to a location for supporting decision making. For example, suppose a person is using his or her mobile phone to ask an online directory service to provide a list of Italian restaurants that are close by. In order to service this query, the directory service would need access to a GIS containing information about local restaurants by geographical coordinates and type. GIS applications are tools that allow users to create interactive queries (user-created searches),

geographical information system (GIS)
A computer system capable of integrating, storing, editing, analyzing, sharing, and displaying geographically referenced (spatial) information.

EXHIBIT 6.8	**Location-Based Applications and Services**

Category	Examples
Advertising	Banners, advertising alerts
Billing	Road tolling, location-sensitive billing
Emergency	Emergency calls, automotive assistance
Games	Mobile games, geocaching
Information	Infotainment services, travel guides, travel planner, mobile yellow pages, shopping guides
Leisure	Buddy finder, instant messaging, social networking
Management	Facility, infrastructure, fleet, security, environmental
Navigation	Directions, indoor routing, car park guidance, traffic management
Tracking	People/vehicle tracking, product tracking

Sources: Compiled from Steiniger, et al. (2006) and en.wikipedia.org/wiki/Location-based_service (accessed July 2011).

analyze spatial information, edit data, maps, and present the results of all these operations. Geographic information science is the science underlying the geographic concepts, applications and systems. For more on GIS, see en.wikipedia.org/wiki/Geographical_information_ system and DeMers (2009).

LOCATION-BASED SERVICES AND APPLICATIONS

Exhibit 6.8 provides an overview of the main categories of location-based services and applications.

location-based service (LBS)

An information service accessible from and to mobile devices through a mobile network utilizing the ability to make use of the geographical position of the mobile device to deliver a service to the user.

A **location-based service (LBS)** is an information service, accessible from and to mobile devices through a mobile network and utilizing the ability to make use of the geographical position of the mobile device to deliver a service to the user.

LBS services can be used in a variety of contexts, such as health, marketing, personal life, etc. LBS services include services to identify a location of a person or object, such as discovering the nearest banking cash machine or the whereabouts of a friend or employee. LBS services also work in parcel tracking (e.g., by the USPS or FedEx) and vehicle tracking services (to be describe later in this section). LBS can include mobile commerce when taking the form of coupons or advertising directed at customers based on their current location (see Chapter 7). They also include personalized weather services and even location-based games.

Some examples of location-based services are:

▶ Recommending social events in a city to tourists and residents.

▶ Finding the nearest business or service, such as an ATM or restaurant.

▶ Providing turn-by-turn navigation to any address.

▶ Locating people on a map displayed on the mobile device.

▶ Delivering alerts, such as notification of a sale, or warning of a traffic jam.

▶ Asset recovery (combined with active RF) to find, for example, stolen assets.

▶ Network security: Wi-Fi Protected Access (WPA) can limit the physical area from which a user can connect to restrict access based on the user's location.

▶ Inventory and asset tracking: RFID technologies are widely used for asset and inventory tracking. RFID tags communicate wirelessly with RFID readers throughout the enterprise (Chapter 11 and Online Tutorial T3).

Personnel Tracking. Different technologies are used for on-site personnel and workers tracking in the field. Systems that track field workers are typically GPS-enabled mobile phones. On-site personnel tracking systems often use RFID technology, such as RFID-enabled badges (Sections 6.4 and 6.5).

For additional information, see en.wikipedia.org/wiki/Location-based_service.

The following examples illustrate some of the myriad of l-commerce services currently in use.

Example 1: Navigation. One of the major problems in many cities is the lack of sufficient parking spaces. This is the situation in Paris, France, where as many as 20 to 25 percent of all vehicles may circulate the city, looking for a parking space at certain times of the day. This causes traffic jams and wastes gasoline. At the end of 2006, Orange, a large mobile telecommunications company, and its partners organized a system that allows drivers to quickly find empty parking spaces in nearby parking garages. Here is how it works: The 120 participating garages collect information electronically about open parking spaces. The information is updated over the Internet to a central server at Orange. Drivers contact the Orange server with their cell phones. Orange can determine the location of the driver either through the location of the antenna being used to make the cell phone call or, if the driver's phone is equipped with a GPS, through the coordinates provided by the GPS (*Taipei Times* 2006). China TransInfo Technology Group (Chinatransinfo.com) developed a similar system that advises drivers of empty parking sports in a parking lot via visual displays.

Example 2: Product and Assets Tracking. UltraEX, a U.S. West Coast company that specializes in same-day deliveries of items such as emergency blood supplies and computer parts, equips all of its vehicles with @Road's GPS receivers and wireless modems. In addition to giving dispatchers a big-picture view of the entire fleet, @Road helps UltraEX keep clients happy by letting them track the location and speed of their shipments on the Web in real time using smartphones. This service shows customers a map of the last place the satellite detected the delivery vehicle, and it calculates how fast it was traveling. Drivers use AT&T's Mobile Data Service to communicate with dispatch, and drivers who own their vehicles are unable to falsify mileage sheets because @Road reports exact mileage for each vehicle. Product tracking includes inventory tracking (see Chapter 11).

Example 3: Operations Management. The Mexican company CEMEX is the third largest cement producer in the world. Concrete is mixed en route to construction sites and must be delivered within a certain time period or it will be unusable. Rather than waiting for orders, then preparing the delivery schedules, and then sending out the deliveries as most companies do, CEMEX has trucks fitted with GPS patrolling the roads at all times, waiting for orders; this allows the company to guarantee delivery within 20 minutes of the agreed-upon time. Real-time data on each truck's position are available not only to company managers but also to clients and suppliers, enabling them to plan their schedules to fit in with the next available truck. Digital maps help locate the customers and the trucks, allowing the use of shortcut routes.

Example 4: Vehicle Location. Automatic vehicle location (AVL) is a means for automatically determining the geographic location of a vehicle and transmitting the information to a request. Most commonly, the vehicle location is determined by using GPS, and the transmission mechanism is a satellite, terrestrial radio, or cellular connection from the vehicle to a radio receiver, satellite, or nearby cell tower. Other options for determining actual location, for example in environments where GPS illumination is poor, are dead reckoning (i.e., inertial navigation or active RFID systems) or cooperative RTLS systems. Combinations of these systems may be applied. An example is the use of GPS to locate buses in the San Francisco Bay area (see the NextBus case in Online File W 6.4). For additional information, see en.wikipedia.org/wiki/Automatic_vehicle_location.

Example 5: Finding Your Friends. Want to know where your friends are in real time? The mobile market is swarming with social networking start-ups in partnership with the cell phone behemoths who think they can provide you with the answer to this question (see Chapter 7). One of the start-ups is Loopt. Loopt has signed deals with many of the major mobile operators including Sprint Nextel, T-Mobile, Verizon, AT&T, and Boost. Loopt utilizes a cell phone's embedded GPS positioning to show users where friends are located and what they are doing via detailed, interactive maps on their mobile phones. Loopt helps friends connect on the fly and navigate their social lives by orienting them to people, places, and events.

automatic vehicle location (AVL)
A means for automatically determining the geographic location of a vehicle and transmitting the information to a request.

Other Innovative Examples

New and innovative applications appear almost daily. Here are some examples:

- Luxor casino in Las Vegas can detect when guests land at the airport and turn on their cell phones. Also, the hotel can determine when guests leave the hotel, luring them back with mobile incentives and pitches.
- GlobalPetFinder (globalpetfinder.com) is a device weighing 5 ounces that snaps onto your pet's collar. If Fido wanders outside the "virtual fence" you set up, you'll receive a text alert and the pet's whereabouts on your phone. Monthly monitoring fees start at $17, plus there's a one-time $35 activation charge.
- KnowledgeWhere Mobile service (knowledgewhere.com), Kamida's Socialight (socialight.com), and Proxpro (proxpro.com) are applying LBSs to social networking. Socialight lets people publish pictures, words, sound, and video tagged to specific locales.
- Papa John's customers with GPS-enabled cell phones can track their pizza delivery status on a street-by-street basis (trackmypizza.com).

Added Value Created by Location-Based Services

According to Steiniger, et al. (2006), the following services are enabled by LBS technology:

- **Resource tracking with dynamic distribution.** Taxis, service people, rental equipment, doctors, fleet scheduling.
- **Resource tracking.** Objects without privacy controls, using passive sensors or RF tags, such as packages and train boxcars.
- **Finding someone or something.** Person by skill (doctor), business directory, navigation, weather, traffic, room schedules, stolen phone, emergency calls.
- **Proximity-based notification (push or pull).** Targeted advertising, buddy list, common profile matching (dating), automatic airport check-in.
- **Proximity-based actuation (push or pull).** Payment based upon proximity (EZPass, toll watch).

Social Location-Based Marketing

social location-based marketing
Marketing activities that are related to social behavior and are related to social networking activities.

Social location-based marketing is where social media tools give users the option of sharing their location, and hence give businesses the opportunity to deliver targeted offers and messages to consumers and collect data about their preferences and behavior. For more information see the video: "The Future of M-Commerce - Did You Know?" (5 minutes); youtube.com/watch?vquO-sxqFYcE.

The major players in this new business model are Foursquare, Facebook Places, Plyce, and Gowalla. Complete coverage is provided in Chapter 7.

BARRIERS TO LOCATION-BASED M-COMMERCE

What is holding back the widespread use of location-based m-commerce? Several factors come into play, including the following:

- **Lack of GPS in mobile phones.** In 2010, only about 20 percent of mobile phones were sold with GPS. This means that most of the mobile phones in existence lack the feature. Although it is possible to locate a mobile device with other means and GPS-enabled phones are increasing in popularity, this still inhibits the overall adoption of location-based services.
- **Accuracy of devices.** Some of the location technologies are not as accurate as people expect them to be. A good GPS provides a location that is accurate up to

50 feet (15 meters). Less expensive, but less accurate, locators can be used to find an approximate location within 1,640 feet (500 meters).

▶ **The cost–benefit justification.** For many potential users, the benefits of location-based services do not justify the cost of the devices or the inconvenience and time required to utilize the service. After all, many seem to feel that they can just as easily obtain information the old-fashioned way.

▶ **Limited network bandwidth.** Wireless bandwidth is currently limited; it will be improved as 4G technology spreads. As bandwidth improves, applications will improve, which will attract more customers.

▶ **Invasion of privacy.** When "always-on" cell phones are a reality, many people will be hesitant to have their whereabouts and movements tracked throughout the day, even if they have nothing to hide. This issue will be heightened when our cars, homes, appliances, and all sorts of other consumer goods are connected to the Internet and have a GPS device embedded in them.

Section 6.6 ▶ REVIEW QUESTIONS

1. Describe the key elements of the l-commerce infrastructure.
2. What is GPS? How does it work?
3. What are some of the basic questions addressed by location-based services?
4. How are location-based services being integrated with social networking?
5. Define geographical information systems. How do they relate to LBS?
6. Describe social location-based marketing.
7. List some services enabled by LBS.

6.7 UBIQUITOUS (PERVASIVE) COMPUTING AND SENSORY NETWORKS

Many experts believe that the next major step in the evolution of computing will be *ubiquitous (pervasive) computing*. In a ubiquitous computing environment, almost every object has processing power and a wired or wireless connection to a network. It is a model of human computer interaction. This section provides an overview of ubiquitous computing and briefly examines a number of related applications in the areas of sensor network technologies.

OVERVIEW OF UBIQUITOUS COMPUTING

Ubiquitous computing is a comprehensive field that includes many topics (e.g., see en.wikipedia.org/wiki/ubiquitous_computing and Krumm 2009). Here we present only the essentials that are related to EC.

Definitions and Basic Concepts

Ubiquitous computing (ubicom) is invisible, everywhere computing; it is computing capabilities that are being embedded into the objects around us, which may be mobile or stationary. In contrast, mobile computing is usually represented by devices—handheld computers, handset phones, headsets, and so on—that users hold, carry, or wear. Ubiquitous computing is also called *embedded computing*, *augmented computing*, or *pervasive computing*. Sometimes a distinction is made between pervasive and ubiquitous computing. The distinction revolves around the notion of mobility. **Pervasive computing** is embedded in the environment but typically not mobile. In contrast, ubiquitous computing combines a high degree of mobility with a high degree of embeddedness. So, for example, most smart appliances in a smart home represent wired, pervasive computing, and mobile objects with embedded computing, such as in clothes, cars, and personal communication systems, represent ubiquitous computing. In this chapter, however, we treat pervasive and ubiquitous as equivalent terms and we use them interchangeably. *Ubiquitous computing* describes

ubiquitous computing (ubicom)
Computing capabilities that are being embedded into the objects around us, which may be mobile or stationary.

pervasive computing
Computing capabilities embedded in the environment but typically not mobile.

the way in which current technological models, based upon three base designs: smart devices (mobile, wireless service), smart environments (of embedded system devices), and smart interaction (between devices), relate to and support a computing vision for a greater range of computer devices, used in a greater range of (human, ICT, and physical) environments and activities. Poslad (2009) details the rich potential of ubiquitous computing, the challenges involved in making it a reality, and the prerequisite technological infrastructure. Additionally, the book discusses the application and convergence of several current major and future computing trends.

The idea of pervasive computing has been around for years. Mark Weiser first articulated the term in 1988 at Xerox's computer science laboratory, the Palo Alto Research Center (PARC). Weiser and his colleagues were attempting "to conceive a new way of thinking about computers, one that takes into account the human world and allows the computers themselves to vanish into the background." According to Weiser, pervasive computing is the opposite of virtual reality. In virtual reality, the user is immersed in a computer-generated environment. In pervasive computing, the user is immersed in an invisible "computing is everywhere" environment—in cars, clothes, homes, the workplace, and so on.

Invisible Computing. Weiser did not mean to imply that pervasive computing devices would not be seen but, rather, that, unlike a desktop or handheld computer, these embedded computers would not intrude on our consciousness. As he observed, "The most profound technologies are those that disappear . . . they weave themselves into the fabric of everyday life until they are indistinguishable from it." Think of electric motors. They exist in the devices all around us, but they are invisible to us, and we do not think about using them. This is Weiser's vision for pervasive computing. The user will not think about how to use the processing power in the object; rather, the processing power automatically helps the user perform the task. An example from EC is an intelligent agent that calls your attention to incorrect data entry.

Principles of Pervasive Computing

Underlying the embeddedness of pervasive computing are four principles that will define its development:

> ▶ **Decentralization.** The decentralization of computing that began with the transition from the centralized mainframe computer to the personal computer will continue in pervasive computing. Indeed, computing devices in the future will not be computers but tags, sensors, badges, and commonplace objects all cooperating together in a service-oriented infrastructure.
>
> ▶ **Diversification.** Computing devices will evolve from a fully functional one-computer-does-all paradigm to one in which specialized, diversified devices will suit the requirements of an individual for a specific purpose. A person may own several devices that slightly overlap in functionality, but each will be the preferred tool for each specific purpose.
>
> ▶ **Connectivity.** The independent pervasive computing devices—tags, sensors, badges—will be seamlessly connected to the network or to each other. Open, common standards will be required to achieve this level of connectivity and interoperability.
>
> ▶ **Simplicity.** These devices must be designed for simplicity of use. Intuitive interfaces, speech recognition, one-handed operation, instant on, and always connected are a few of the requirements for high, but simple, usability.

Context-Aware Computing

context-aware computing
Application's ability to detect and react to a set of environmental variables that is described as context (which can be sensor information or other data including users' attitudes).

Context-aware computing centers on the concept of using information about an end user's environment, activities, connections and preferences that can improve the quality of interaction with that end user, by reacting to what the system knows and senses, such as the provision of EC advertising. The end user may be a customer, business partner, or employee.

A contextually aware system anticipates the user's needs (or finds it by asking) and serves up the most appropriate and customized content, product, or service. Gartner Inc. predicts that by 2013, more than half of *Fortune* 500 companies will have some context-aware computing initiatives, and by 2016, one-third of worldwide mobile consumer marketing will be context-awareness-based. Gartner considers this as one of the top 10 technologies and trends that will be strategic for most organizations in 2011. For details, see itbusinessedge.com/slideshows/show.aspx?c=85144&slide=8. Context awareness devices and applications are an extension of LBS (Section 6.6). However, context devices know something about people, not only their location. It can also be used without LBS.

Example. Your context device "knows" it's noon. It also knows (via accelerometer data) that you have not moved from your desk for the last couple of hours. Because it "knows" you need to have lunch at 12:30 (the device reads your tagged calendar entries), it will remind you when you should leave. As soon as you move the device, it displays the list of places where you have had lunch the last couple of weeks. The device generates the latest consumer rating of the restaurants offered. At the same time, it also highlights restaurants located within walking distance that will allow you to be back in time for your scheduled 2 p.m. meeting. Finally, the device can check the weather conditions (take an umbrella? taxi?) and may find for you the current waiting time at the suggested restaurants.

Carnegie Mellon University is a leader in the research regarding business applications of this technology. For more, see Frank (2010).

Internet of Things

Early forms of ubiquitous information and communication networks are evident in the widespread use of mobile devices. These devices have become an integral and intimate part of everyday life around the globe. Developments are underway to take this phenomenon even further by embedding short-range mobile transceivers into a wide array of gadgets and everyday items, enabling new forms of communication between people and things and between the things themselves. This will add a new dimension to anytime, anyplace connectivity (Krumm 2006). The dimension is *anything* connectivity. The Internet will become an *Internet of Things (IoT)*. For business applications of the Internet of Things, see Rogers-Nazarov (2009).

In order for there to be an IoT, there has to be a way to (1) uniquely identify the things, (2) enable detection of changes in the physical status of those things (e.g., temperature or location), (3) embed intelligence in the things themselves, and (4) enable things to communicate either with one another or with people via the Internet. This is where radio frequency identification (RFID), sensor networks, smart objects, and Internet standards such as the Internet Protocol (IP) come into play.

SMART APPLICATION: GRID, HOMES, CARS, AND MORE

Pervasive computing, with its tiny devices and tags, including RFID tags and sensors, is the key to many smart applications. Some examples are presented next.

Smart Grid

A **smart grid** is an electricity network managed by utilizing digital technology. According to Wikipedia, a smart grid delivers electricity from suppliers to consumers using two-way digital communications to control appliances at consumers' homes; thus, it saves energy, reduces costs, and increases reliability and transparency. It overlays the ordinary electrical grid with an information and net metering system that includes smart meters. Smart grids are being promoted by many governments as a way of addressing energy independence, global warming, and emergency resilience issues. See Online Tutorial T4 for a comprehensive overview of the smart grid.

smart grid
An electricity network managed by utilizing digital technology.

The grid encompasses myriads of local area networks that use distributed energy resources to serve local loads and/or to meet specific application requirements for remote power users or a premium power, and for customers it distinguishes critical loads and provides protection. For details, see Violino (2009).

The U.S. Department of Energy provides substantial information about the smart grid (see oe.energy.gov/smartgrid.htm). A smart grid is made possible by applying sensing,

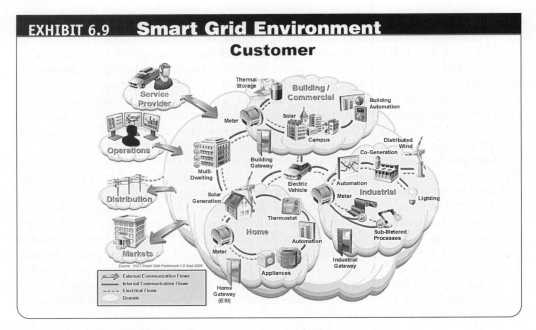

EXHIBIT 6.9   Smart Grid Environment

Source: National Institute of Standards and Technology, U.S. Department of Commerce *nist.gov/smartgrid/upload/FinalSGDoc2010019-corr010411-2.pdf* (accessed March 2011).

measurement, and control devices with two-way communication to electricity production, transmission, distribution, and consumption. Also parts of the power grid communicate information about grid condition to system users, operators, and automated devices, making it possible to dynamically respond to changes in grid environmental conditions (see Exhibit 6.9).

The major features of the grid are: smart meters, smart charging, self-healing from power disturbance events, and active participation by consumers in demand response. A smart meter tracks a customer's usage continuously throughout the day and uses wireless technology to automatically transmit the data in real time to the utility company. This automated meter reading technology makes it possible for regulators to set prices that vary at different times of the day and encourage or discourage consumption based on the relative cost of power production and periods of peak energy demand. Smart grids enable the use of smart homes and appliances. For more information, see Online Tutorial T4 and smartgrid1.blogspot.com/2009/07/cnet-news-faq-what-smart-grid-means-to.html.

Smart Homes and Appliances

In a smart home, the home computers, televisions, lighting and temperature controls, home security system, and other appliances within the home can "talk" to each other via the Internet or a home intranet. These linked systems can be controlled through various devices (see Park, et al. 2009).

In the United States, tens of thousands of homes are already equipped with home-automation devices, and there are signs that Europe is also warming to the idea. Currently, home automation systems support a number of different tasks:

> ▶ **Lighting.** Users can program their lights to go on and off or dim them to match their moods and needs for comfort and security.
>
> ▶ **Energy management.** A home's HVAC (heat, ventilation, and air-conditioning) system can be programmed for maximum energy efficiency and controlled with a touch panel or a telephone.
>
> ▶ **Water control.** WaterCop (watercop.com) is a device that relies on a series of strategically placed moisture-detection sensors. When a moisture level rises in one of these sensors, it assumes a water leak has occurred and sends a wireless signal to the WaterCop control unit, which turns off the main water supply.

> ◗ **Home security and communication.** The window blinds, garage doors, front door, smoke detectors, and home security system all can be automated from a network control panel. These can all be programmed to respond to scheduled events (e.g., when the home owner goes on vacation). Home security can be connected to sensors to monitor the health of disable or sick people (see hookelehealth.com).
>
>   Sensors can also be used at home to detect intruders, keep an eye on working appliances and much more.
>
> ◗ **Home entertainment.** Users can create a multisource audio and video center around their house that can be controlled with a touch pad or remote. For example, if a person has a DVD player in the master bedroom but wants to see a movie in a child's room, with the click of a remote the signal can be directed to the child's room.
>
> ◗ **Smart appliances.** An Internet-ready appliance that can be controlled by a small handheld device or desktop computer via a home phone intranet (wireline or wireless) or the public Internet.

One organization that is focused on smart appliances is the Internet Home Alliance (internethomealliance.com). The alliance is made up of a number of appliance manufacturers (e.g., Best Buy) and vendors specializing in home automation (e.g., Lutron Electronics). The mission of the alliance is to accelerate the process of researching, developing, and testing new home products and services that require a broadband or persistent connection to the Internet.

Smart and Driverless Cars

The average automobile on the road today contains at least 20 microprocessors that are truly invisible. They are under the hood, behind the dash, in the door panels, and on the undercarriage. Microprocessors control the entertainment system, decide when the automatic transmission should shift gears, remember seat position for different drivers, and control the inside temperature. Car computers often operate independently, but some swap data among themselves—a growing trend. They require little maintenance and operate under extreme temperature, vibration, and humidity. The onboard microprocessors are also used to diagnose problems. One example is the "Smart" brand (from Daimler AG in Germany). The automotive industry is in the process of testing a variety of experimental systems to improve auto safety in areas such as collision avoidance, computer vision for cars, vehicle stability, and driver monitoring. For example, General Motors (GM), in partnership with Delphi Automotive Systems, has developed an Automotive Collision Avoidance System that employs radar, video cameras, special sensors, and GPS to monitor traffic and driver actions in an effort to reduce collisions with other vehicles and pedestrians. Franklin (2009) provides a comprehensive review of all the challenges and solutions related to smart cars.

There is also a growing trend to connect car microprocessors to mobile networks and to the Internet to provide emergency assistance, driving directions, e-mail, and other services. GM's OnStar system (onstar.com), for example, uses cellular telephone and satellite technology to connect a vehicle with a 24-hour service center. Some of the services provided by OnStar include automatic air-bag deployment notification, route support to guide drivers to their destinations, stolen vehicle tracking, and remote unlocking of doors.

OnStar is the forerunner of smart cars of the future. The next generation of smart cars is likely to provide even more automated services, especially in collision prevention and emergency situations. For instance, although OnStar automatically notifies the service center when a vehicle's air bags have been deployed and immediately contacts emergency services if the drivers and passengers are incapacitated, OnStar cannot provide detailed information about a crash. Newer systems are under development that will automatically determine the impact speed, whether the car has rolled over, and whether the driver and passengers were wearing seat belts. Information of this sort might be used by emergency personnel to determine the severity of the accident and what types of emergency services will be needed.

316   Part 3: Emerging EC Platforms

There are many experiments underway with self-driven cars, which are usually electrical cars. The following are some examples.

Google Driverless Car. The *Google driverless car* is a project at Stanford University that includes a robotic vehicle named Stanley (which won the 2005 DARPA Grand Challenge and its $2 million prize from the U.S. Department of Defense). The system includes information gathered for Google Street View with artificial intelligence software that combines input from video cameras inside the car, a LIDAR sensor on top of the vehicle, radar sensors on the front of the vehicle, and a position sensor attached to one of the rear wheels helps locate the car's position on the map. As of 2010, Google has tested several vehicles equipped with the system, driving 1,000 miles (1,600 kilometers) without any human intervention, in addition to 140,000 miles (230,000 kilometers) with occasional human intervention. The only accident occurred when one of the cars was rear-ended while stopped at a red light. Google anticipates that the increased accuracy of its automated driving system could help reduce the number of traffic-related injuries and deaths, while utilizing energy and space on roadways more efficiently. For details, see en.wikipedia.org/wiki/Google_driverless_car.

Self-Driven Road Train. The SARTRE project, which stands for Safe Road Trains for the Environment (sponsored by Volvo), aims to provide *semiautonomous* cars on highways that can travel in *convoys* and have the aim of cutting down congestion while improving safety. Every time the cars are on the road, each convoy will be led by an expert driver and would follow a set route as well as having a fixed speed, in enabling drivers to choose the convoy they wish and join it for at least a part of their journey. Once a car starts moving in a convoy, a special onboard computer will take over the steering and the acceleration, following cars in front autonomously and providing the drivers with the chance to put their feet up and read a newspaper, talk on the phone, or drink a cup of tea. As soon as they are ready to exit, drivers can then take control of their vehicle and leave the convoy at the next exit. For details, see fastcompany.com/1708789/road-trains-en-route-in-europe-five-car-convoys-in-2011 and news.carrentals.co.uk/self-driven-road-trains-near-completion-34225707.html.

RADIO FREQUENCY IDENTIFICATION (RFID)

radio frequency identification (RFID)
A short-range radio frequency communication technology for remotely storing and retrieving data using devices called *RFID tags* and *RFID readers*.

In the world of EC and m-commerce, a number of pervasive computing initiatives revolve around the use of RFID. Simply put, **radio frequency identification (RFID)** is a short-range radio frequency communication technology for remotely storing and retrieving data using devices called *RFID tags* and *RFID readers*. Most RFID tags have a small footprint. They can be embedded or attached to virtually any object—products, people, animals, or vehicles. The essentials of RFID are presented in Online Tutorial T3 together with its major operations. Applications in supply chain management are presented in Chapter 11.

WIRELESS SENSOR NETWORKS

A question facing many companies interested in becoming more efficient is "How can we sense the important events in the real world and quickly respond with actions that lead to success?" *Real-world awareness* is a concept used to describe the ability (of a company) to sense information in real time from people, IT sources, and physical objects—by using technologies like RFID and sensors—and then respond quickly and effectively.

Sensor Network Basics

sensor network
A collection of nodes capable of environmental sensing, local computation, and communication with its peers or with other higher performance nodes.

At the core of real-world awareness are *sensor networks*. A **sensor network** is a collection of nodes, sometimes as small as millimeters in length or diameter, capable of environmental sensing, local computation, and communication with its peers or with other higher performance nodes. Each node consists of (1) a sensor capable of detecting one or more environmental conditions (e.g., temperature, humidity, vibration, and chemical concentration), (2) a microprocessor for storing and processing data and information, and (3) a weak radio that transmits and receives data and information. The nodes are dispersed throughout some environment of interest (such as a manufacturing plant) and communicate via a *mesh network* in which information is passed bucket-brigade style along the network to a gateway node that transmits the information to a central computer for processing or storage. Today, communications among the nodes are mostly by wireless rather than wired networks. For an overview see en.wikipedia.org/wiki/wireless_sensor_network.

The term *smart item* or *smart object* is sometimes applied to the nodes of a sensory network where they are embedded into physical goods, items, or assets (such as apparel). The reason the term *smart* is applied is because the nodes have embedded intelligence. More accurately, the microprocessor in a node enables it to potentially make autonomous decisions and carry out autonomous actions based on a combination of the logic embedded in the node and the sensory data it receives. In most applications, however, it is better to think of the network of nodes as being collectively *smart* rather than the separate nodes being individually smart.

When coupled with a physical sensing device, active RFIDs can serve as nodes in a sensor network. However, most sensors and sensor networks are based on other technologies. These technologies are provided by companies such as Crossbow Technology, Ember, and Dust Networks.

Example: Dust Networks. The name of the company is taken from the concept of *smartdust*, which is used to describe a network of tiny wireless microelectromechanical systems (mems) sensors, robots, or devices installed with wireless communications that can detect (for example) light, temperature, or vibration. The concept was introduced by one of the founders of the company, Kris Pister, at the University of California, Berkley. The idea was that the wireless sensors would be so small that they could be sprinkled like dust throughout a building, home, or an industrial facility—or even in a forest or a field. The networks provided by Dust Networks are called *SmartMesh* and they consist of miniature wireless sensors called *motes*. The term *mote* is frequently used to connote the nodes in a sensor network. Currently, motes are about 12 millimeters squared (not quite dust) and can run on microbatteries for years. Dust Networks has focused on selling its products to industrial automation companies for tasks such as monitoring pipelines, valves, tanks for oil refineries, natural gas plants, and product facilities.

Smart Sensor Applications

Although computer-based instrumentation has existed for a long time, the density of instrumentation made possible by a shift to mass-produced intelligent sensors and the use of pervasive networking technology give wireless sensor networks a new kind of scope that can be applied to a wide range of uses.

Connected World magazine (connectedworldmag.com), one of the few publications dedicated to covering the machine-to-machine communication market, has constructed a list of more than 180 applications of sensor networks. In addition to this listing, *M2M* also provides a listing of the major sensor network vendors, as well as key resources for sensor networking (*M2 Presswire 2008*).

Another way to differentiate the applications of sensor networks is to categorize the type of monitoring being done by the network. Essentially, there are three types of monitoring:

▶ Monitoring space
▶ Monitoring things
▶ Monitoring the interactions of things with each other and the encompassing space

The first category includes environmental and habitat monitoring, precision agriculture, indoor climate control, surveillance, treaty verification, and intelligent alarms. Online File W6.6 provides an example of this category. The second includes structural monitoring, condition-based equipment maintenance, medical diagnostics, urban terrain mapping, and traffic flow (see INRIX in Case 6.2). The most dramatic applications involve monitoring complex interactions, including wildlife habitats, disaster management, emergency response, ubiquitous computing environments, asset tracking, health care, and manufacturing process flow. Online File W6.7 provides a sample of applications in all these categories.

CASE 6.2

EC Application

SENSORS AT INRIX SOLVE TRANSPORTATION PROBLEMS

Predictive analysis is used to predict traffic congestion levels hours or even days in advance, with almost 90 percent accuracy. INRIX (*inrix.com*) is a company that provides such predictions for a subscription fee. The predictive analysis is done with a mass of data obtained from the environment and government sources, including:

- Real-time traffic flow and incident information collected by items installed on highways (tool-tag readers, cameras, radar units, and magnetic sensors embedded in the pavement)
- Speed and location data collected by global positioning system (GPS) units of vehicles owned by participating trucking and delivery companies and by many GPS owners
- Weather forecasts and conditions
- Other events (e.g., road construction schedules, school calendars, sports, concerts, other scheduled special events)

INRIX's proprietary predictive algorithms combine these data to create a snapshot of traffic flows and expected congestion and road conditions over the next hours and days. Obviously, each city requires its own unique model and database. In 2010, INRIX offered this prediction in 20 countries. This service is combined with digital maps (see *teleatlas.com*, the provider of information to GIS companies such as MapQuest). Also, INRIX partners with cell phone operators, traditional satellite broadcasters, and in-car navigation services. In the Seattle area, where INRIX is located, the company delivers traffic information via smartphones and electronic boards on sections of highways, using color codes for signals. The phones also display estimated time for the roads to

be either clear or become jammed. By 2011, the company covered 260,000 miles of highways in North America with real-time traffic flow.

The INRIX system suggests automated decisions such as the following:

- Best route for a delivery van
- Ideal time to go or leave work (for those on a flex schedule) or go to a meeting
- How to reroute a trip to avoid an incident that just occurred
- Pricing of highways based on traffic condition

The following are some of the technologies in use for sensing and controlling traffic:

- Magnetic loop detectors in the road surface
- Closed-circuit TV cameras monitoring traffic conditions
- Information about traffic conditions provided by radio and on the Internet in real time
- Freeway access ramps controlled by the traffic lights

The system also provides a real-time picture of what is going on along freeways. The information is sold to companies and individuals, but some is broadcast free by Clear Channel Radio's Total Network.

If you live in 1 of 16 states in the United States along the I-95 corridor, you can enjoy the INRIX Traffic U.S. service for free (e.g., via "travel" time signs).

Sources: Compiled from Jonietz (2005/2006), *inrix.com* (accessed April 2011), and Barke (2005).

PRIVACY ISSUES IN UBIQUITOUS COMPUTING

For ubiquitous systems to be widely deployed, it is necessary to overcome many of the technical, ethical, and legal barriers associated with mobile computing (see Section 6.8) as well as a few barriers unique to ubiquitous, invisible computing. Poslad (2009) provides a comprehensive list of technical challenges, social and legal issues, and economic concerns (including finding appropriate business models) in deploying pervasive computing systems. Poslad also cites research challenges, such as component interaction, adaptation and contextual sensitivity, user interface interaction, and appropriate management mechanisms.

Among the nontechnical issues confronting the deployment of pervasive computing, the prospective loss of individual privacy seems to be at the forefront. In some cases, privacy groups have expressed concern that the tags and sensors embedded in items, especially retail items, make it possible to track the owners or buyers of those items. Although this is a possibility, the larger problem is that the information produced by tags, sensors, and other devices in various networks has the potential to threaten an individual's privacy if misused or mishandled.

With privacy issues, the principle of consent often applies. By law, there are limits to how data may be used by or supplied to third parties. For instance, if you make a purchase with a loyalty card, the information generated during the purchase belongs to the authority that issued the card, which can do what it likes with the data since it was obtained legally and with the explicit and implicit consent of the cardholder. Similarly, if you fill out an online survey in exchange for an online research article, then the information belongs to the enterprise sponsoring the survey and, again, it can do whatever it wants with the information, since you have given your consent by participating.

With ubiquitous computing, the privacy issue is not as straightforward. In most cases, the data are collected in an unobtrusive and invisible fashion. Even though most of the data is low-level, if retained and analyzed it could compromise individual privacy. More importantly, if the data can be tied to specific individuals or groups of individuals, there is often no way for the individual(s) to opt out or provide consent. In the near term, the applications where privacy issues are most likely to arise are medical, retail, and transport systems. For example, equipping the elderly or impaired with wearable devices for monitoring movement, vital signs, usage of facilities and equipment, etc., and transmitting this information regularly over a sensor network can provide the means for people to live safely on their own or with minimal assistance.

In order to protect the privacy of individuals, privacy must be designed into the tags, nodes, and networks, and not addressed only in a post hoc fashion. Basically, systems can be engineered in such a way that the data that it gathered are limited to that which is needed to carry out the desired function and nothing else. Identity data can be discarded or disguised to the maximum extent so that specific users cannot be identified unless there is an absolute need.

Section 6.7 ▶ REVIEW QUESTIONS

1. Define pervasive computing.
2. List four principles of pervasive computing.
3. What is the Internet of Things?
4. Describe the smart grid and the role of sensors there.
5. Describe a smart home.
6. What are the major characteristics of smart cars? Of driverless cars?
7. Describe some of the applications of sensor networks.
8. In what ways can pervasive computing impinge on an individual's right to privacy?

6.8 IMPLEMENTATION ISSUES IN MOBILE COMMERCE: FROM SECURITY AND PRIVACY TO BARRIERS OF M-COMMERCE

Despite the vast potential for mobile commerce to change the way many companies do business, several barriers are either slowing down the spread of m-commerce or leaving many m-commerce businesses and their customers disappointed or dissatisfied. The major barriers to enterprise mobile computing are security, performance, availability, cost–benefit, lack of clear strategy (see Gold 2008), difficulty integrating with in-house IT, and the difficulty in customizing applications. In this section, we examine some of these barriers, starting with the issue of the security of mobile communications and mobile computing systems.

M-COMMERCE SECURITY AND PRIVACY ISSUES

In 2004, Cabir became the first known worm capable of spreading through mobile phones. The worm arrives in the phone's messaging in-box in the guise of a file named *caribe.sis*. When an unsuspecting recipient clicks on the file, the worm activates and is sent to other devices via Bluetooth. The same is true for other malicious code, such as Brador and Redbrowser (Laudermilch 2006). More attacks on phones are a possibility in the future. However, to date, the worm has not been launched on a widespread basis.

Most Internet-enabled cell phones in operation today have their operating systems and other functional software "burned" into the hardware. This makes them incapable of storing applications and, in turn, incapable of propagating a virus, worm, or other rogue program from one phone to another. However, as the capabilities of cellular phones increase and the functionality of PDAs and cell phones converge, the threat of attack from malicious code will certainly increase. Although m-commerce shares some of the same security issues as general e-commerce (see Chapter 9), there are some differences between the two.

The basic security goals of confidentiality, authentication, authorization, and integrity (Chapter 9) are just as important for m-commerce as they are for e-commerce, but they are more difficult to ensure. Specifically, m-commerce transactions almost always pass through several networks, both wireless and wired. An appropriate level of security must be maintained on each network, in spite of the fact that interoperability among the various networks is difficult. Similarly, post-transactional security issues of auditing and nonrepudiation are more difficult because cell phones do not yet have the capability to store the necessary software.

In general, many of the processes, procedures, and technologies used for e-commerce security and for general organizational computer security also apply to m-commerce security. Passwords, encryption, active tokens, and user education are all cases in point. However, given the unique nature of mobile security, special security measures for m-commerce may also be required. For example, to prevent the theft of a mobile device, a user might carry a "wireless tether" that sounds a warning if a device is left behind or carried away. Wi-Fi networks have their own built-in security system known as *wired equivalent privacy (WEP)*, which is, as the name suggests, similar to encryption protocols used on wired networks. The approaches to m-commerce security are discussed in more detail in Online File W6.8.

TECHNOLOGICAL BARRIERS TO M-COMMERCE

When mobile users want to access the Internet, the *usability* of the site is critical to achieve the purpose of the visit and to increase user stickiness (the length of time and degree to which users remain at a site). However, current devices have limited usability, particularly with respect to pocket-size screens or data input devices. In addition, because of the limited storage capacity and information access speed of most smartphones and PDAs, it is often difficult or impossible to download large files to these devices. However, this problem is lessening with the passage of time.

Mobile visitors to a website are typically paying premium rates for Internet connections and are focused on a specific goal (e.g., conducting a stock trade). For visitors to find exactly what they are looking for easily and quickly, the navigation systems have to be fast and designed for mobile devices. Similarly, the information content needs to meet the user's needs. Other technical barriers related to mobile computing technology include limited battery life and transmission interference with home appliances. These barriers and others are listed in Exhibit 6.10. Note that with the passage of time the technological barriers are decreasing, especially with the iPhone and iPad.

FAILURES IN MOBILE COMPUTING AND M-COMMERCE

As with many new technologies, there have been many failures of applications as well as collapse of entire companies in m-commerce. It is important to anticipate and plan for possible failures as well as to learn from them.

Example: Northeast Utilities. According to Hamblen (2001), Northeast Utilities (located in Berlin, Connecticut), which supplies energy products and services to 1.2 million customers, embarked on a wireless project in 1995 in which its field inspectors used wireless devices to track spills of hazardous material and report them to headquarters in real time. After spending a year and a half and $1 million, the project failed. The reasons for the failure can be seen in the following lessons learned:

- Do not start without appropriate infrastructure.
- Do not start a full-scale implementation; use a small pilot for experimentation.
- Pick up an appropriate architecture. Some users don't need to be persistently connected, for example.
- Talk with a range of users, some experienced and some not, about usability issues.
- Users must be involved; hold biweekly meetings if possible.
- Employ wireless experts if you are not one.
- Wireless is a different medium from other forms of communication. Remember that some people are not used to the wireless paradigm.

Having learned from these "lessons" and correcting the deficiencies, Northeast made its next wireless endeavor a success. Today, all field inspectors carry rugged wireless laptops, which are used to conduct measurements related to electricity transformers, for example. Then the laptops transmit the results, in real time, to chemists and people who prepare

EXHIBIT 6.10 Technical Limitations of Mobile Computing

Limitation	Description
Insufficient bandwidth	Sufficient bandwidth is necessary for widespread mobile computing, and it must be inexpensive. It will take a few years until 3G and WiMAX are available in many places. Wi-Fi solves some of the problems for short-range connections.
Security standards	Universal standards are still under development. It may take 3 or more years for sufficient standards to be in place.
Power consumption	Batteries with long life are needed for mobile computing. Color screens and Wi-Fi consume more electricity, but new chips and emerging battery technologies are solving some of the power consumption problems.
Transmission interferences	Weather and terrain, including tall buildings, can limit reception. Microwave ovens, cordless phones, and other devices on the free, but crowded, 2.4GHz range interfere with Bluetooth and Wi-Fi 802.11b transmissions.
GPS accuracy	GPS may be inaccurate in a city with tall buildings, limiting the use of location-based m-commerce.
Potential health hazards	Potential health damage from cellular radio frequency emission is not known yet. Known health hazards include cell phone addiction, thumb-overuse syndrome, and accidents caused by people using cell phones while driving.
Human–computer interface	Screens and keyboards are too small, making mobile devices uncomfortable and difficult for many people to use.
Complexity	Too many optional add-ons (e.g., battery chargers, external keyboards, headsets, microphones, cradles) are available. Storing and using the optional add-ons can be a problem.

government reports about hazardous material spills. In addition, time is saved because all the information is entered directly into proper fields of electronic forms without having to be transcribed. The system is so successful that it has given IT workers the confidence to launch other applications such as sending power-outrage reports to managers via smartphones and wireless information to crews repairing street lights.

For smart ways to avoid mistakes and encourage enterprise mobility success, see Goldschlag (2008).

ETHICAL, LEGAL, PRIVACY, AND HEALTH ISSUES IN M-COMMERCE

The increasing use of mobile devices in business and society raises new ethical, legal, and health issues that individuals, organizations, and society will have to resolve.

One workplace issue is the isolation that mobile devices can impose on a workforce. The introduction of desktop computing invoked a profound change on social interaction in the workplace, illustrated by the walled cubicles featured in Dilbert cartoons. Some workers had difficulty adjusting to this new environment and sought to replace face-to-face interactions with texting interactions, prompting organizational policies against the forwarding of nonbusiness-related texting and IM messages that are used in m-commerce.

The truly personal nature of the mobile device also raises ethical and legal issues in the workplace. Most employees have desktop computers both at home and at work, and they can easily separate business and personal work accordingly. However, it is not so easy to separate work and personal life on a cell phone, unless one is willing to carry two phones or two PDAs. And if an organization has the right to monitor e-mail communications on its own network, does it also have the right to monitor voice communications on a company-owned cell phone?

The widespread appearance of mobile devices in society has led to the need for cell phone etiquette, the creation of "cell free" zones in hospitals and airport lounges, and

National Cell Phone Courtesy Month. For an insightful essay into the impact of cell phones in work and social spaces, see Australian Mobile Telecommunications Association (2008).

A widely publicized potential, but not yet proven, health issue is the damage from cellular radio frequency emissions. Cell phone addiction also is a problem. A study by Seoul National University found that 30 percent of South Korean high school students reported addiction effects, such as feeling anxious when they did not have their phones with them. Many also displayed symptoms of repetitive stress injury from obsessive text messaging (Rosen 2006).

Other ethical, legal, and health issues include the ethics of monitoring staff movements based on GPS-enabled devices or vehicles, maintaining an appropriate work–life balance when work can be conducted anywhere at any time, and the preferred content of an organizational policy to govern the use and control of personal mobile computing devices in and out of the workplace. Finally, there is the issue of privacy infringement and protection.

Privacy. Violation of privacy is one of the major issues related to the use of mobile computing technologies, especially LBS, tracing, RFID, and context aware applications (see Chapter 14 for a discussion of privacy issues).

For steps for creating a mobile strategy that mitigates these issues to take advantage of the power of mobility, see AT&T (2010).

MOBILITY MANAGEMENT

With an increasing number of people using mobile devices for many applications, management of mobility has become an important and challenging task. For example, Greengard (2011) suggest organizing mobility management under the security and control of IT, concentrating on data instead of on devices and employees. Also, there is a need for security policy, governance, and zero tolerance on specific relevant issues. For guidelines on device management strategy see Dreger and Moerschel 2010.

Section 6.8 ▶ REVIEW QUESTIONS

1. How is m-commerce security similar to e-commerce security? How is it different?
2. Discuss the role that usability plays in the adoption of m-commerce.
3. Discuss a few of the technical limitations of m-commerce.
4. Describe some lessons learned from the failures of m-commerce.
5. Describe the potential impact of mobile devices on legal, health, and privacy issues.

MANAGERIAL ISSUES

Some managerial issues related to this chapter are as follows.

1. **What is your m-commerce strategy?** M-commerce is an amalgamation of three basic market segments: support for internal business processes; an extension of existing e-business services that touch customers, suppliers, and other partners; and an extension of Web-based consumer services to a rapidly growing population of smartphone users. The key to success in the m-commerce world is to define your overall e-commerce and m-commerce business strategy, determine which segments are critical to the strategy and the order in which they need to be addressed, and which of the available mobile technologies will support the strategy and critical segments (consult Gold 2008).

2. **What is your implementation timetable?** Mobile technologies and applications are undergoing rapid change. It seems like every six months new technologies and opportunities emerge. In this accelerated and changing environment, the challenge is to craft an m-commerce strategy that can take advantage of rapidly changing market conditions while at the same time ensuring that choice of mobile solutions and technologies is "future proof."

3. **Are there any clear technical winners?** Among mobile devices, the answer is yes. The all-in-one devices, such as smartphones, have surged to the forefront of the mobile device market and will likely stay there. Tablet devices are very popular as well. Among the other components of the mobile infrastructure (e.g., wireless networks such as WiMAX, Wi-Fi, and 3G) the answer is no. There is still a confusing multiplicity of standards, devices, and supporting hardware. The key is to select a well-architected platform and infrastructure that can support the existing range of services while at the same time enabling adoption of future technologies as they emerge.

4. **Which applications should be implemented first?** Although there is something of a "cool factor" associated with various m-commerce applications, especially location-based services, mobile applications must be judged like any other business technology—ROI, cost–benefit analysis, cost reductions, and efficiency. Toward these ends, many of the more mundane internal applications supporting the mobile workforce, fleets, and warehouses have resulted in the highest returns. Regardless, the application of mobile technology must be based on a realistic view of each situation to determine whether the technology is suitable or not. Recall that the m-commerce platform is the most preferred by younger generations. It is important to understand why Japan and Korea have a much higher penetration in m-commerce while other countries with the same level of mobile telecommunication infrastructure do not have a similar level of penetration (consult Gold 2008). Implementation includes the topic of mobile devices management (see Oliver 2008).

SUMMARY

In this chapter, you learned about the following EC issues as they relate to the chapter's learning objectives.

1. **What is m-commerce, its value-added attributes, and fundamental drivers?** M-commerce is any business activity conducted over a wireless telecommunications network. M-commerce is a natural extension of e-commerce. M-commerce can help a business improve its value proposition to customers by utilizing its unique attributes: ubiquity, convenience, interactivity, personalization, and localization. Currently, m-commerce is being driven by the large number of users of mobile devices; a developing "cell phone culture" among youth; demands from service-oriented customers; vendor marketing; declining prices; a mobile workforce; improved performance for the price; and by the increasing bandwidth.

2. **What is the mobile computing environment that supports m-commerce?** The mobile computing environment consists of two key elements: mobile devices and wireless networks. Although mobile computing devices vary in size and functionality, they are rapidly moving toward an all-in-one device that is overcoming some of the limitations associated with poor usability, such as small screen size, limited bandwidth, and restricted input capabilities. Even with their limitations, mobile devices offer a series of support services, principally SMS, voice, and location-based services, which differentiate m-commerce from e-commerce.

3. **Which type of networks support mobile devices?** Mobile devices connect in a wireless fashion to networks or other devices at a personal, local, metropolitan, or wide area levels. Bluetooth (personal), cellular phone networks (WWAN), and wireless LANs (like Wi-Fi) are well-known technologies that are well established in the wireless marketplace. In contrast, municipal and WiMAX (metropolitan) are less well-known and are vying for a broader foothold in the wireless marketplace.

4. **Financial applications.** Many EC applications in the financial services industries (such as e-banking) can be conducted with wireless devices. Most mobile financial applications are simply versions of their wireline counterparts, and they are conducted via SMS or the mobile Web system. Mobile banking and mobile payments are good examples of this activity. Increasingly, banks throughout the world are enabling their customers to use mobile devices to check balances, monitor transactions, obtain account information, transfer funds, locate brands or ATMs, and sometimes pay bills.

5. **Mobile enterprise solutions.** Business applications such as mobile office applications, sales force automation (SFA), field force automation (FFA), mobile CRM, inventory management, and wireless job dispatch offer the best opportunities for a high return on investment (ROI) for most organizations, at least in the short run. All of these applications are focused on supporting the mobile worker (someone who is away from his or her primary work space at least 10 hours a week or 25 percent of the time), although the applications are aimed at different segments of the mobile workforce (i.e., mobile professionals, mobile field force, and mobile specialty workers).

6. **Consumer and personal applications and mobile entertainment.** One of the fastest growing markets in m-commerce is mobile entertainment. Mobile entertainment encompasses mobile music, games, gambling, adult services, and specialized user-generated content. Among these, mobile music is the largest. Mobile gambling is one of the smallest, although it is the fastest growing in spite of the legal restrictions placed on it by various government bodies. Also growing is mobile sports applications. Service industries using mobile applications include: health care, hospitality, public safety, crime prevention, and homeland security.

7. **Location-based commerce.** Location-based commerce (l-commerce) refers to the use of positioning devices, such as GPS, to find where a customer or client is and

deliver products and services based on his or her location. The services provided by l-commerce companies tend to focus on one or more of the following factors: location, navigation, tracking, mapping, and timing. These services rest on five basic components: mobile devices, communication networks, positioning components, service and application providers, and data or content providers. Among these, the position and data components, especially geographical information system (GIS), are critical. Although l-commerce has been widely hailed, several factors impede its widespread use, including the accuracy of the mobile devices, the cost of most applications in relation to the benefits, limited network bandwidth, and the potential invasion of privacy.

8. **Ubiquitous computing and sensory systems.** The *Internet of Things* is upon us and so are cutting-edge and futuristic systems that involve many embedded and invisible processors. These systems appear in several formats, notably the context aware one, and they enable intelligent and useful applications. They are interrelated with sensory systems and provide for smart applications such as smart electric grids, smart homes, smart buildings, smart cars, and many more.

9. **Security and other implementation issues.** Even though potential benefits of m-commerce applications may be substantial, their implementation faces a number of challenges, including technical interruptions and gaps in network coverage; problems caused by Internet work roaming; performance problems created by slow mobile networks and applications; managing and securing mobile devices; and managing mobile network bandwidth. The mobile computing environment offers special challenges for security, including the need to secure transmission over the open air and through multiple connecting networks. The biggest technological changes relate to the usability and changes of devices. Finally, ethical, legal, and health issues can arise from the use of m-commerce, especially in the workplace.

KEY TERMS

Automatic vehicle location (AVL)	309	Mobile enterprise	293	Short message service (SMS)	286
Bluetooth	288	Mobile entertainment	300	Smart grid	313
Context-aware computing	312	Mobile portal	286	Smartphone	284
Geographical information system (GIS)	307	Mobile worker	294	Social location-based marketing	310
Geolocation	306	Multimedia messaging service (MMS)	287	Terminal-based positioning	306
Global positioning system (GPS)	306	Network-based positioning	306	Ubiquitous computing (ubicom)	311
Interactive voice response (IVR)	287	Personal area network (PAN)	288	Voice portal	287
Location-based m-commerce (l-commerce)	304	Personal digital assistant (PDA)	284	Wi-Fi (wireless fidelity)	288
Location-based service (LBS)	308	Pervasive computing	311	WiMAX	288
Mobile banking	291	Radio frequency identification (RFID)	316	Wireless local area network (WLAN)	288
Mobile browser (microbrowser)	285	Real-time location systems (RTLS)	305	Wireless mobile computing (mobile computing)	282
Mobile commerce (m-commerce; m-business)	277	Sensor network	316	Wireless wide area network (WWAN)	289

DISCUSSION QUESTIONS

1. Discuss how m-commerce can expand the reach of EC.

2. Which of the m-commerce limitations listed in this chapter do you think will have the biggest near-term negative impact on the growth of m-commerce? Which ones will be minimized within five years? Which ones will not?

3. Discuss the difference between a smart car, an ALV, and a semiautonomous car in a convoy.

4. View the video "Ben E. Keith video case study" at motorola.com/Business/US-EN/Business+Solutions/Industry+Solutions/Manufacturing/Materials+and+Warehouse+Management_US-EN and identify all mobile devices used in the warehouse. List their contribution. (The video is 4.24 minutes.)

5. Discuss the factors that are critical to the overall growth of mobile banking.

6. What is the relationship between mobile sales force automation, mobile field force automation, and mobile CRM?

7. Why are many of the more popular mobile gambling sites located on small island countries?

8. How are GPS and GIS related?

9. Discuss the advantages of m-commerce over wired EC.

TOPICS FOR CLASS DISCUSSION AND DEBATES

1. Discuss the potential benefits and drawbacks of conducting m-commerce on social networks.

2. Investigate the business opportunities of context aware computing and discuss the benefits, potential CSFs, and the privacy issue.

3. Discuss the strategic advantage of m-commerce.

4. Google acquired AdMob in part as a response to Apple's iAds. Discuss the strategic implications of AdMob versus iAds.

5. Debate: Debate the issue of employee whereabouts tracking. Related to this is the privacy issue in tracking people and cars. Discuss the pros and cons. For a start, read Elias (2010).

6. Debate: Debate the issue of a company's right to open all e-mail and voice communications done during work hours on the company's devices.

INTERNET EXERCISES

1. Research the status of 3G and the future of 4G by visiting 3gnewsroom.co.uk (you can find information on 4G by searching for the term at the site by going to verizon.com and to en.wikipedia.org/wiki/4G). Prepare a report on the status of 3G and 4G based on your findings.

2. You've been asked to put together a directory of Wi-Fi hotspots in your local area. There are a number of sites, such as hotspot-locations.com, that offer search capabilities for finding hotpots in a given area. Construct a list of sites that offer this feature.

3. Most of the major social networking sites provide mobile capabilities. The same is true for newer start-ups like Loopt and GyPSii. Compare and contrast the types of social networking capabilities provided by the major sites (e.g., Facebook) and the start-ups.

4. Juniper Research has created a variety of white papers dealing with different segments of the mobile entertainment market (e.g., mobile games). Go to juniperresearch.com and download a white paper dealing with one of these segments. Use the white paper to develop a written summary of the market segment you selected—the size of the market, the major vendors, the factors encouraging and impeding its growth, and the future of the market segment.

5. Enter gpshopper.com. What sorts of products and services do they provide? One of their products is Slifter. Go to slifter.com and run nearbynow.com. Compare the products and services it provides with those offered by GPShopper.

6. Find information about Google Maps for mobile devices. Also review the capabilities of Google SMS and other related Google applications. Relate Google Maps to l-commerce. Write a report on your findings.

7. Enter marketwatch.com/iphoneinstall and download the software; if you do not own an iPhone find what this software can do for you. Write a report.

8. Enter thefango.com and find examples of services provided to customers. Write a report.

9. Provide a general description of the EPC identification standard. What role do EPCglobal (epcglobalinc.org) and Auto-ID Labs (autoidlabs.org) play in this standard? EPCglobal has developed a set of policies for the use of EPCs. What are these policies and how are they enforced?

10. Enter fleetmatics.com and find its major tracking systems for fleets (vehicles) and summarize its capabilities and benefits.

11. Enter ehow.com/how and Google find information on "how to locate a cell phone with GPS." Why do you need this capability?

TEAM ASSIGNMENTS AND PROJECTS

1. **Assignment for the Opening Case**

   Read the opening case and answer the following questions.

   a. Do you really need the NeverLost GPS (cost $8/day) when you can get almost the same information with a smartphone like the iPhone (or iPad) and a portable GPS? Why or Why not?

   b. Which of the applications can be considered a mobile enterprise and which can be considered mobile customer service?

c. Identify finance and marketing-oriented applications in this case.

d. What are the benefits of offering the system to Hertz?

e. As a renter how do you feel about Hertz knowing where you are at all times?

2. Each team should examine a major vendor of mobile devices (Nokia, Kyocera, Motorola, Palm, BlackBerry, etc.). Each team will research the capabilities and prices of the devices offered by each company and then make a class presentation, the objective of which is to convince the rest of the class to buy that company's products.

3. Each team should explore the commercial applications of m-commerce in one of the following areas: financial services, including banking, stocks, and insurance; marketing and advertising; travel and transportation; human resources management; public services; and health care. Each team will present a report to the class based on their findings. (Start at wirelessresearch.eu.)

4. Each team should take one of the following areas—homes, cars, appliances, or other consumer goods, such as clothing—and investigate how embedded microprocessors are currently being used and will be used in the future to support consumer-centric services. Each team will present a report to the class based on its findings.

5. Learn about smartphones by visiting vendors' sites such as Nokia, RIM, Apple, Samsung, Motorola, and others. List the capabilities that the various devices from these vendors offer for supporting m-commerce. In the future, what sorts of new capabilities will be provided by smartphones?

6. Download Steiniger, et al. (2006). Find new applications in the report's existing categories. Also find new categories of applications.

7. A utility company had its service technicians scattered across several states, and work orders were being dispatched manually through a paper-based system that was prone to errors and delays. The company found that it was difficult to track the activities of field staff. Once employees collected their work orders and were on the road, the company lost track of their location and job status at any given time. For example, a technician, might have been performing low-priority work at one location while a nearby technician was struggling alone to complete high-priority orders. The company had no easy way of reassigning its resources. As a consultant, prepare a proposal for the company that covers how to solve the problem with wireless m-commerce.

8. View the video "The Technology Advances Fuelling M-Commerce Today" (8 minutes) at youtube.com/watch?v=398EztRwPiY and answer the following questions:

a. What EC services are provided by m-commerce?

b. Discuss the role of m-commerce in retailing.

c. Discuss the lack of m-commerce strategy vs. its wide acceptance.

d. Why is m-commerce such a fragmented market?

e. Why do retailers spend much of their IT budget on m-commerce?

f. Discuss the impact of m-commerce on competition among retailers.

g. What are the difficulties in managing mobile technology?

h. Examine the position of mobile payment on the Hype Cycle (see Chapter 13).

i. What are the advantages of mobile payments?

j. Research the major methods and vendors of m-payments.

Closing Case

HASSLE-FREE SHOPPING AT THE METRO GROUP FUTURE STORE

The METRO GROUP Future Store

The METRO GROUP is a leading retail group employing 290,000 people in 2,100 stores including Real, Media Market, Saturn, and Galeria Kaufhof. It operates in 33 countries in Europe, Africa, and Asia. In 2008 the METRO GROUP reopened its real,- Future Store (future-store.org/) in Toenisvorst, Germany. The Future Store initiative aims to develop new technologies for the retail sector in order to improve customers' shopping experiences. More than 90 partners including IBM, Intel, and Cisco are working with the METRO GROUP as part of this initiative to test new products, business processes, and procedures. The technological innovations used in the real,- Future Store in Toenisvorst show how technology is changing the way we will shop in the future.

The Importance of RFID and Handheld Scanners

The real,- Future Store makes use of self-checkout systems that require the use of handheld scanners by customers who scan their products independently. This is a very good cost-saving system as the store only requires one or two cashiers for approximately four point-of-sale stations. However, the drawback for the customer is the extra amount of time it takes the customer to find and scan the product barcodes. The use of RFID (radio-frequency identification) tags could solve this problem and make the shopping experience easier for the customer. Today, retailers like Walmart insist that their suppliers use RFID tags on every pallet of goods, but the tags are not yet included on single products. Since 2006, selected METRO suppliers have been tagging palettes to improve their logistics and warehouse management. METRO has also considered using RFIDs to check packages of meat for their freshness by including a small computer chip with an antenna in the packaging. RFIDs would help to ensure that only fresh packages of meat and sausages are stocked according to their demand. The use of RFID tags could also be beneficial for the supply chain management of frozen products if sensors were incorporated to check variables such as temperature. The tags would enable companies to monitor the expiration date of each product and therefore when to replace it.

The METRO GROUP also encourages networking between employees and suppliers to maintain efficiency in the supply chain. All parties have access to an extranet, which improves communication, the exchange of information, and collaboration by sharing virtual workspaces with employees and teams around the world. Suppliers have access to software systems where they can check the planning status, delivery dates, and palette rescheduling, and employers know where goods are located at all times.

Mobile Shopping and Data Mining

Customer convenience is critical and therefore the METRO GROUP implemented a variety of m-commerce technologies in the Toenisvorst store. One example is the "real,- app" which provides customers with the option to create a mobile shopping list, find directions to the closest store, and take advantage of weekly special offers and cooking recipes. Customers also have the ability to scan the barcode of a product and add it to their shopping list via their cell phone. Customers can also send the shopping list to the retailer who will pack and bag the items. Another service offered by the METRO GROUP is the Mobile Shopping Assistant (MSA). This app for Andriod and iPhone cell phones enables customers to automatically scan products and provides up-to-date price information and the total price of their purchases. The MSA also has a "Search" function, which enables customers to find groups of products more conveniently within the store. Customers then have the option to pay for their shopping via their smartphone. Smartphones are equipped with NFC (near field communication), which is a standard for transferring data over short distances to a payment terminal.

The MSA provides the METRO GROUP with the added benefit of collecting data about the purchased products and the customers' shopping routes. Specifically it provides information about how long a customer stands in front of products, what products were put in their bags, and which ones they put back on the shelf. The collected data can be used for data mining based on individual customer profiles, and then enriched with other customers' shopping habits to provide real-time suggestions for customers by sending them additional advertisements to their cell phones. The "real,-body coach" is another mobile application offered by the METRO GROUP that calculates the calories of customers' shopping choices and offers recipes based on product choices and the necessary calorie intake for the customer.

The devices offered in the Toenisvorst store improve the automation of the business processes and make shopping more convenient for customers. Results indicate that customers are more satisfied and visit more often.

Sources: Compiled from Krafft and Mantrala (2008) and Reyes (2011).

Questions

1. What are the pros and cons of compiling data about customers and their shopping habits?
2. Why are RFIDs such an advantage for the retailing and logistics industry?

ONLINE RESOURCES
available at pearsonglobaleditions.com/turban

Online Files

W6.1 Wi-Fi and the Traveling Public

W6.2 Wi-Fi Mesh Networks, Google Talk, and Interoperability

W6.3 Application Case: Mobile Sales Solution Results in £1 Million Revenue Boost at Hillarys

W6.4 Application Case: NextBus: A Superb Customer Service

W6.5 Warehouse Management Systems: Mobile Solutions

W6.6 Application Case: Wi-Fi Sensor Net Aids Winemakers

W6.7 Representative Wireless Industrial Sensor Network Applications

W6.8 Security Approaches for Mobile Computing

Comprehensive Educational Websites

bitpipe.com: A library of white papers, product literature, Webcasts, and case studies on information technology.

brandon-mcgee.blogspot.com: Brandon McGee's blog on mobile banking and e-payment system.

ecommercetimes.com/perl/section/m-commerce: A huge collection of articles on m-commerce.

gs1.org/epcglobal: An integrated system of global standards for accurate identification and communication of information regarding products, assets,

iab.net: Interactive Advertising Bureau—standards, guidelines, and best practices of interacting advertising.

ipso-alliance.org: Technical information, resource library, meetings, and events on enabling the Internet of Things.

juniperresearch.com/viewreports.php?category=70&amp=2: A collection of reports on m-commerce.

mobile-weblog.com/50226711/mobile_commerce.php: A collec-tion of articles on mobile technologies including gadgets, tr

mobileenterprisemag.com: A collection of articles, reports, whitepapers and events on the mobile enterprise.

mobilemarketer.com: Articles, guides, and blogs on mobile media and commerce.

mobilemarketingwatch.com: Best practices and industry guidelines on mobile computing.

searchmobilecomputing.techtarget.com/resources: News, articles, white papers, blogs, and tutorials on mobile computing.

trimble.com/gps: A tutaorial on GPS technology.

wimaxforum.org: An industry-led, not-for-profit organization formed to certify and promote the compatibility and interoper-ability of broadband wireless pro

REFERENCES

Ahmad N., and P. Orton. "Smartphones Make 1 B11 Smarter, But Not as Expected." *Training and Development (T-D)*, January 2010.

AT&T. "Three Steps for Creating a Mobile Strategy." White paper AR-1500-01, September 21, 2010.

Australian Mobile Telecommunications Association. "The Impact of the Mobile Phone on Work/Life Balance." March 2008. **apo.org.au/research/impact-mobile-phone-worklife-balance-final-report** (accessed January 2011).

Barke, J. "Traffic Tamin." *Technology Review*, October 3, 2005.

Bonkoo, T. "Grocery Stores Providing a New Way of Shopping to Customers: Handheld Device Allows Customer to Forgo Long Line." *Associated Content Media*, January 18, 2007. **associatedcontent.com/article/284899/grocery_stores_providing_a_new_way.html** (accessed January 2011).

Business Wire. "IDC Predicts the Number of Worldwide Mobile Workers to Reach 1 Billion by 2011." January 15, 2008. **findarticles.com/p/articles/mi_m0EIN/is_2008_Jan_15/ai_n24230213** (accessed January 2011).

Butcher, D. "Hertz Breaks Multichannel Location-Based Campaign to Increase Car Rentals." *Mobile Marketer*, November 23, 2010. **mobilemarketer.com/cms/news/advertising/8206.html** (accessed January 2011).

Carr, D. F. "iPad in the Enterprise." *Information Week*, December 6, 2010.

CIO Zone. "IDC: Mobile Workers Will Pass 1 Billion in 2010." February 24, 2010. **ciozone.com/index.php/Mobile-and-Wireless/IDC-Mobile-Workers-Will-Pass-1-Billion-in-2010.html** (accessed January 2011).

Del Rey, J. "Does Your Business Need an App?" *Inc. com*, December 1, 2010. **inc.com/magazine/20101201/does-your-business-need-an-app.html** (accessed April 2011).

DeMers, M. N. *GIS for Dummies*. Hoboken, NJ: Wiley & Sons, 2009.

Dolphin, G. "Will There Be WiFi with That?" *Baseline*, May/June 2010.

Dreger, R., and G. Moerschel. "Watch Out." *Information Week*, May 3, 2010.

Economist. "Business in Motion: Managing the Mobile Workforce." *Economist Intelligence Unit*, 2007. **graphics. eiu.com/ebf/PDFs/Business_in_motion_April%20200 7_FINAL.pdf** (accessed January 2011).

Elias, P. "Discovery of GPS Tracker Becomes Privacy Issue." *Yahoo! News*, October 16, 2010. **news.yahoo. com/s/ap/20101017/ap_on_re_us/us_gps_tracking_w arrants** (accessed January 2011).

Feldman, J. "Location Data: More Valuable, Easier to Access." *InformationWeek*, October 30, 2010. **infor- mationweek.com/news/mobility/business/showArtic le.jhtml?articleID=228000281** (accessed January 2011).

Frank, O. "Goodbye Smartphones; Hello Predictive Context Device." *Advertising Age*, May 25, 2010. **adage. com/print?article_id=144077** (accessed January 2011).

Franklin, C., Jr. "Code, Networks Are the Key to Smarter Cars." *InformationWeek*, November 13, 2009. **informa tionweek.com/news/internet/web2.0/showArticle.jhtm l?articleID=221601545** (accessed January 2011).

Garcia, A. "New BlackBerrys Make Good Choices." *eWeek*, January 4, 2010.

Garcia, A. "Smartphones: The Next Generation." *eWeek*, July 6, 2009.

Gargiulo, T. L. "The Top Ten Strategies for Managers of Mobile Workers." *Human Capital Review* (January 2009). **humancapitalreview.org/content/default.asp?Article_I D=551** (accessed January 2011).

Gold, J. E. "Strategic Approach to Enabling Mobile Business Applications." *SearchMobileComputing.com*, July 1, 2008. **searchmobilecomputing.techtarget.com/feature/Enabl ing-mobile-business-applications-A-strategic- approach** (accessed January 2011).

Goldschlag, D. "How CIOs Can Encourage Innovative Enterprise Mobility—Top Mistakes to Avoid." *eWeek*, August 25, 2008. **eweek.com/c/a/Mobile-and-Wireless/ How-CIOs-Can-Encourage-Innovative-Enterprise- MobilityTop-Mistakes-to-Avoid** (accessed January 2011).

Goodwin, A. "Hitting the Road with Hertz's NeverLost GPS." *CNET.com*, August 18, 2010. **reviews.cnet.com/ 8301-13746_7-20014027-48.html** (accessed November 2010).

Greengard, S. "Can IT Manage Mobility?" *Baseline*, January/February 2011.

Hamblen, M. "Get Payback on Wireless." *Computer World*, January 1, 2001.

Head, M., and E. Y. Li. *Mobile and Ubiquitous Commerce: Advanced E-Business Methods*. Advances in Electronic Business (Aebus) Book Series, New York: Information Science Reference, 2009.

Intermec. "Puma Increases the Efficiency of its Central Scandinavian Warehouse." **intermec.com/learning/ content_library/case_studies/csPuma.aspx** (accessed January 2011).

IT Business Edge. "The Top 10 Technologies and Trends That Will Be Strategic for Most Organizations in 2011." **itbusinessedge.com/slideshows/show.aspx?c=85144&s lide=3** (accessed January 2011).

Jonietz, E. "Traffic Avoidance." *Technology Review* (December 2005/January 2006).

Juniper Research. "Mobile—Let Me Entertain You." 2008. **wirelessmobile-jobsboard.com/pdf/Mobile_Enter- tainment~White_Paper.pdf** (accessed January 2011).

Krafft, M., and Mantrala, M. (ed.). *Retailing in the 21st Century: Current and Future Trends*, Germany:Springer, 2008.

Krumm, J. *Ubiquitous Computing Fundamentals*. London: Chapman & Hall, 2009.

Laudermilch, N. "Will Cell Phones Be Responsible for the Next Internet Worm?" *InformIT*, April 28, 2006. **informit.com/articles/article.aspx?p=465449** (accessed January 2011).

M2 Presswire. "MONILINK: MONILINK Reaches One Million Account Enquiries per Month." November 11, 2008. **ip-pbx.tmcnet.com/news/2008/11/11/3778246. htm** (accessed January 2011).

Macintosh, S. "Portable Real Estate Listings—But with a Difference." *New York Times*, March 26, 2010.

Malik, A. *RTLS for Dummies*. Hoboken, NJ: Wiley & Sons, 2009.

McNamara, J. *GPS for Dummies*, 2nd ed. Hoboken, NJ: Wiley & Sons, 2008.

METRO. "METRO Group and Real—Open the Store of the Future." May 2008. **metro-link.com/metro-link/ html/en/15449208/index.html** (accessed January 2011).

mobiThinking.com. "Global Mobile Statistics 2010." April 21, 2010. **mobithinking.com/mobile-marketing-tools/ latest-mobile-stats** (accessed January 2011).

Motorola. "Synchronizing the Distribution Supply Chain with Mobility." White paper, 2007. **motorola.com/ supplychainmobility**.

Olariu, S., and D. E. Tiliute. *Handbook of Mobile Commerce*. New York: Chapman & Hall, 2011.

Oliver, M. *Mobile Device Management for Dummies*. New York: Wiley & Sons, 2008.

Park, J. H., C.-H. Hsu, and H. R. Arabnia. "Intelligent Systems and Smart Homes." *Information Systems Frontiers*, 11, no. 5 (November 2009).

Parks, L. "Eagle Eyes at Golf Mill: Mall's Wireless Surveillance System Reduces Cost, Improves Access." *Stores*, March 2010.

Parlamentul European. "Getting Galileo into Orbit by 2013." April 16, 2008. **europarl.europa.eu/sides/get_ Doc.do?language=EN&type=IM-PRESS&refer- ence=20080414BKG26528** (accessed January 2011).

Poslad, S. *Ubiquitous Computing: Smart Devices Environments and Interactions*. Hoboken, NJ: Wiley & Sons, May 2009.

PricewaterhouseCoopers. "Global Entertainment & Media to Reach $2.2T in 2012, Driven by Digital, Mobile." *Marketing Charts*, June 20, 2008. **marketingcharts.com/ television/global-entertainment-media-to-reach-22t- in-2012-driven-by-digital-mobile-5012** (accessed January 2011).

Quasi News. "2010 Survey Shows 'More People Doing More Things on Their Cell Phones.'" January 12, 2010. **qwasi.com/news/tag/text-message-statistics** (accessed January 2011).

Rash, W. "Enterprise Wireless: It's All About Work." *eWeek*, July 19, 2010a.

Rash, W. "Smartphones Get Even Smarter." *eWeek*, January 4, 2010b.

Reyes, P. *RFID in the Supply Chain*, USA: McGraw Hill, 2011.

Rogers-Nazarov, A. "The Internet of Things." September 5, 2009. **internetevolution.com/document.asp?doc_id= 181268** (accessed January 2011).

Rosen, C. "Our Cell Phones, Ourselves." *The New Atlantis*, May 29, 2006. **thenewatlantis.com/publications/our-cell-phones-ourselves** (accessed January 2011).

Scornavacca, E., and S. J. Barnes. "The Strategic Value of Enterprise Mobility: Case Study." *Information, Knowledge, Systems Management*, 7, no. 102 (2008).

Soh, J. O. B., and B. C. Y. Tan. "Mobile Gaming." *Communications of the ACM*, 51, no. 3 (March 2008).

Steiniger, S., M. Neun, and A. Edwardes. "Lecture Notes: Foundation of Location-Based Services."2006. **geo.unizh.ch/publications/cartouche/lbs_ lecturenotes_steinigeretal2006.pdf** (accessed January 2011).

Sutter, J. D. "With New GPS Dating Apps, It's Love the One You're Near." August 6, 2010, **articles.cnn.com/ 2010-08-06/tech/gps.dating.apps_1_apps-grindr-skout?_s=PM:TECH** (accessed April 2011).

Taipei Times. "New GPS Parking Hits the Spot for Paris." November 21, 2006.

Unhelkar, B. *Mobile Enterprise Transition and Management*. New York: CRC Press, 2009.

Violino, B. "No More Grid-Lock." *Informationweek.com*, November 16, 2009.

Whyy.org. "Second Chance for Wireless Philadelphia." May 25, 2010. **whyy.org/cms/news/regional-news/ 2010/05/25/second-chance-for-wireless-philadel-phia/3898** (accessed January 2011).

Yunker, J. "Going with Global Geolocation." White paper 83.138.162.138, Quova, Inc., 2009.

Zimmerman, K. A. "Beyond Bells and Whistles." *Grocery Headquarters*, May 2007.

SOCIAL COMMERCE

Content

Learning Objectives

Upon completion of this chapter, you will be able to:

1. Understand the Web 2.0 revolution, its characteristics and the context of social media.

2. Describe the fundamentals of social commerce, its drivers and landscape.

3. Describe the major models of social shopping.

4. Explain how advertising and promotions are conducted in social networking environments.

5. Understand how market research is conducted in social networking environments.

6. Describe how customer service, customer support, and CRM can be facilitated by social networking.

7. Describe the major social commerce activities that can be conducted within and by enterprises.

8. Define crowdsourcing and describe its use in social commerce.

9. Describe the commercial applications conducted in virtual worlds in general and in Second Life in particular.

10. Review the social commerce activities and relationship with e-entertainment and gaming.

11. Describe and discuss the major implementation issues of social commerce including strategy, security, and ROI.

12. Understand the major risks, concerns, and barriers of deploying social commerce applications.

HOW STARBUCKS DRIVES MILLIONS TO ITS COFFEE SHOPS USING SOCIAL MEDIA

Starbucks is the world's largest coffeehouse and services chain with over 16,000 stores in 50 countries. In addition, Starbucks sells coffee in its online store (*starbucksstore.com*).

The Problem

Starting in 2007 the company's operating income declined sharply (from over $1 billion in 2007 to $504 million in 2008 and $560 million in 2009). It was not only the economic slow-down, but increased competition (e.g., from Green Mountain Coffee Roasters), which was growing even during the recession.

The Solution

Starbucks is a very technology-savvy company, which appeals to younger people. It even offers free unlimited Wi-Fi in all its U.S. and Canadian company-owned stores. The company also has one of the best social media strategies. The focus is geared toward the needs, wants, and likes of existing customers and building on those relationships to help gain new customers.

Starbucks' major social media activities are centered on its private site, My Starbucks Idea, and on Facebook, but it has a presence in all major social networks. My Starbucks Idea (*mystarbucksidea.com*) is a forum for consumers to make suggestions, ask questions, and vent their frustrations. This community of about 200,000 registered members can discuss ideas and collaborate on creating new ones. The consumer-generated ideas range from thoughts on rewards cards, eliminating paper cups, ways to foster community within the brick-and-mortar Starbucks locations, and requests to revive drink flavors. The brand keeps the community in the loop with its "Ideas in Action" blog, where staffers write about new developments and announce community contest winners. For example, one recent post announced the return of salted caramel hot chocolate after several members expressed disappointment at its discontinuation. The blog also provides statistics on ideas generated by category (over 105,000 by January 2011). The company may provide incentives for idea generation. For example, in June 2010, Starbucks offered $20,000 for ideas for the reuse of its cups.

Facebook Over 19 million people like Starbucks on Facebook. One of the most popular sites on Facebook as of January 2011 is *facebook.com/starbucks*. The company is offering perhaps the best online purchasing experience on Facebook to date, and also offers mobile commerce dimensions.

Fully integrated into Facebook, Starbucks practices social commerce, known as *f-commerce* (see the closing case). Users can also reload their (virtual) Starbucks mobile card with a payment card in order to pay for drinks with their cell phone, or load cash onto the Starbucks plastic payment card. Users can also surprise their Facebook friends by reloading their friends' cards.

Starbucks started using social commerce on Facebook in 2007 and since then has actively used Facebook events, discussions, and notes in conjunction with well-coordinated ad campaigns to drive traffic both to its physical and online stores.

LinkedIn Starbucks has a profile on the site with 36,000 followers (January 2011). It provides business data about the company, shows new hires (managerial positions), and advertises managerial offerings.

Twitter In January 2011 there were 1,234,985 followers (Follow@starbucks) on Twitter organized in 18,025 lists (e.g., @starbucks/friends). Each "list" has its own followers and tweets. Whenever the company has some new update or campaign it ignites a conversation on Twitter. So things hit Twitter before they appear anywhere else, and it is good enough to create buzz and evoke sentiments from Twitter users, frequently creating word-of-mouth publicity.

YouTube and Flicker Starbucks runs campaigns and has a presence on both sites (*youtube.com/starbucks* and *flicker.com/starbucks*). There is also a selection of videos and photos for view. This social media marketing campaign has been very effective for Starbucks.

Early Adoption of Foursquare—a Failure Not all Starbucks social media projects were a success. The company decided to be an early adopter of geolocation by working with Foursquare (Section 7.4). It simply did not work, and the project ended in mid-2010. As an early adopter, Starbucks did not fully understand how to use the site effectively for its social media needs (see Teicher 2010 for an analysis of the reasons). Now that it has a better understanding of the opportunities, Starbucks may decide to try geolocation again with Facebook's Places, or may revive the Foursquare project.

Starbucks Digital Network Starbucks Digital Network offers exclusive content to all of its in-store customers. It is designed for all major mobile devices including the iPad and smartphones. The network's content features news, entertainment, business, health, and even local neighborhood information channels. Foursquare and LinkedIn have already signed partnership deals along with the *New York Times*, iTunes, and WSJ.com.

Starbucks has been active in the conversational aspects of social marketing through posts on its wall and information for fans via news feeds—whether it be content, questions, or updates aimed at stimulating discussion around the brand. On top of that, the company has invested in advertising in engagement ads on Facebook's homepage and elsewhere on Facebook to drive traffic to its page.

Results

According to Bryson-York (2010), Starbucks turned around sales by interacting effectively between the digital and the physical worlds. In 2010, operating income almost tripled ($1.437 billion versus $560 million in 2009) and so did the stock price. Earnings are projected to double by 2013.

The company's social media initiative was rewarded in 2008 by Forrester Research with a Groundswell Award, recognizing it as an excellent example of using social media to embrace customers. Finally, do not discount the popularity of a site that has exceeded the popularity of pop icon Lady Gaga on Facebook.

Sources: Compiled from Bryson-York (2010), Marsden (2010a), and Walsh (2010).

WHAT WE CAN LEARN . . .

The opening case illustrates how a large company utilizes social networks and Web 2.0 tools to build relationships with its customers. A central activity is to involve customers in improving operations by soliciting ideas and discussing them. It is a large electronic suggestion box, but it is visible to everyone on the company's private social network. In addition, there is a presence on the most visited public social networks. The major objective is to increase flow of visitors both to the physical and the virtual sites. Using special promotions and rewards, Starbucks attracted record visitors considerably improving revenue and profits since embarking on social media projects. Utilizing social media for marketing, advertisement, customer service, market research, and collaboration are the major topics of this chapter. Other topics deal with social entertainment, which Starbucks practices, as well as implementation issues.

7.1 THE WEB 2.0 AND SOCIAL MEDIA REVOLUTIONS

This chapter deals with the newest area of EC—social commerce, which is based on Web 2.0 concepts and tools. First, let's review Web 2.0.

WEB 2.0 AND ITS CHARACTERISTICS

In Chapters 1 and 2, we introduced the essentials of Web 2.0. Here is some additional material.

Representative Characteristics of Web 2.0

The major characteristics of Web 2.0 are presented in Online File W1.3 (Chapter 1). Other important features of Web 2.0 that are related to social commerce are the technology's dynamic content, rich user experiences, metadata, scalability, open source basis, and user's freedom (e.g., Net neutrality).

Most Web 2.0 applications also have a rich, interactive, user-friendly interface based on Ajax (Asynchronous JavaScript) and XML; see details at en.wikipedia.org/wiki/AJAX_Programming, Online Tutorial T10, or on a similar framework. Ajax is an effective and efficient Web development technique for creating *interactive* Web applications. The intent is to make Web pages feel more responsive by exchanging small amounts of data with the server behind the scenes so that the entire Web page does not have to be reloaded each time the user makes a change. This is meant to increase the Web page's interactivity, loading speed, and usability. Web 2.0 is closely related to the concept of user-generated content.

User-Generated Content

User-generated content (UGC), also known as *consumer-generated media*, refers to various kinds of media content that are produced by end users and are publicly available.

Notice that the term UGC is used in the definition of Web 2.0 and it is also used for a wide range of applications including problem solving, news, creation of ads, gossip, and entertainment.

user-generated content (UGC)
Various kinds of media content that are produced by end users and are publicly available.

Sometimes UGC can constitute only a portion of a website. For example, on Amazon.com the majority of content is prepared by administrators, but reviews of the products being sold are submitted by regular visitors to the site. Often UGC is partially or totally monitored by website administrators to avoid offensive content or language, copyright infringement issues, or simply to determine if the content posted is relevant to the site's general theme. For details about UGC, see en.wikipedia.org/wiki/User-generated_content. With regards to commercial applications, UGC is used in preparing ads (see Section 7.4), Wikipedia and similar collective intelligence projects (see Section 7.8), and social entertainment (Section 7.10).

With an increase in user-generated content on the Web, the user (or consumer) is in control. As a result, traditional push marketing strategies may not work. Consumers want to be associated with friends and family. They want to visit and participate in online "environments" where there is a certain amount of trust and an interest shared by the community.

New Business Models

The characteristics of Web 2.0, described previously, enable the creation of new and improved business models. These models include several social shopping business models, models to attract customers, and models to perform other social-related networking.

WELCOME TO THE WEB 2.0 REVOLUTION

Web 2.0 tools (social software) and social networks are changing the way people communicate, collaborate, work, and live; the change is very rapid and significant, so we can classify it as a *revolution*. It is no longer all about idly surfing, searching, reading, listening, or watching. It is about sharing, socializing, collaborating, and most of all creating. To get an overview of this revolution, read Fraser and Dutta (2008) and watch the video "Social Media Revolution 2" (youtube.com/watch?v=1FZ0z5Fm-Ng).

Here are some interesting statistics:

> ▶ Since March 2010, there were more Internet visits to Facebook than to Google (number one in the United States).
> ▶ According to Meeker et al. (2010), social networks are the new kings of communication, replacing e-mail (as of November 2007).
> ▶ Facebook's membership exceeded 750 million (worldwide in June 2011), aiming at $1 billion in annual revenue.
> ▶ The first "Funny or Die" comedy user-generated video, "The Landlord," had 70 million viewers in its first 6 months.
> ▶ Groupon, the leader in group-buy social shopping, a start-up, had annual revenues of $500 million in its second year. This prompted Google to offer $6 billion to acquire the site in October 2010. Groupon *rejected* the offer.
> ▶ According to hostway.co.uk (news item from January 11, 2011) half of the large and medium UK businesses already use social networks, and 60 percent plan to invest in new social networking projects in 2011.
> ▶ As of 2009, there are about five times more national and international conferences on Web 2.0–related topics than on e-commerce in general.
> ▶ Nielsen Company reported an 82 percent increase in the time spent on social networks (per person) in December 2009 versus December 2008.
> ▶ Over 25 percent of U.S. social networks' Internet page views occur at Facebook.
> ▶ According to Bernoff and Li (2008), about 25 percent of all Internet users are engaged in social activities. This percentage is increasing rapidly. For more statistics, see digital.venturebeat.com/2010/02/22/Nielsen-facebook-twitter.

SOCIAL MEDIA, SOCIAL MARKETING, SOCIAL CAPITAL, AND SOCIAL MEDIA MARKETING

Four interrelated concepts are part of the foundation of social commerce: social media, social marketing, social capital, and social media marketing.

Social Media

In this book, we use the word *media* to mean digital words, sounds, and pictures that are shared via the Internet. **Social media** refers to the online media platforms and tools that people use for social interactions and conversations, mainly to share opinions, experiences, insights, and perceptions with each other. Social media can take many different forms, including text, images, audio, or video. The key is that *users*, rather than organizations, produce, control, use, and manage content, often at little or no cost. Social media is a powerful force of democratization; the network structure enables communication and collaboration on a massive scale. Social media uses Web 2.0 technologies to turn communication into interactive dialogues. Kaplan and Haenlein (2010) define social media as "a group of Internet-based applications that build on the ideological and technological foundations of Web 2.0, which allows the creation and exchange of user-generated content." Businesses also view social media as consumer-generated media.

> **social media**
> The online platforms and tools that people use to share opinions, experiences, insights, perceptions, and various media, including photos, videos, and music, with each other.

Here are some additional definitions of social media:

- ▶ Any website or Web service that utilizes a "social" or "Web 2.0" philosophy. This includes blogs, social networks, social news, wikis, etc.
- ▶ Software tools that allow individuals and groups to generate content (text, video, audio, etc.) and engage in peer-to-peer sharing, publishing conversations, and exchange of content in a social environment.
- ▶ Social media is media designed to be disseminated through social interactions, created by using highly accessible and scalable publishing techniques.

A common thread running through all the definitions of social media is a blending of technology and social interactions for the co-creation of value. For details about social media, see socialcomputingjournal.com, en.wikipedia.org/wiki/social_media, and Safko and Brake (2009).

Exhibit 7.1 depicts the emergence and rise of mass media, comparing traditional media with social media. It describes the tools of social media (e.g., blogs, video blogs, etc.) as being under the consumer's control. With social media, content is produced and consumed by the users. Social media can be used as a platform through which marketing is conducted in what is known as *social media marketing*.

Social Marketing

Social marketing combines social policy and marketing practices to achieve a set of social behavioral goals within a target audience. This idea was developed in 1971 when Kotler and Zaltman (1971) began to use traditional marketing tools to sell concepts and behavioral practices instead of products. Notice that business (commercial) marketing attempts to discover what needs consumers may have and then offers those products that meet the consumers' perceived needs. In contrast, social marketing researchers attempt to discover what problems/needs the public or community may have and then seek to determine what behavioral changes would be necessary to remedy the problems. Health promotion is one of the largest sectors that utilize this type of marketing by encouraging positive health choices among consumers without offering a specific product. For details, see en.wikipedia.org/wiki/Social_marketing.

> **social marketing**
> A combination of social policy and marketing practices to achieve a set of social behavioral goals within a target audience.

Social marketing must not be confused with social media marketing; however, some of its characteristics can be found in social media marketing (see Answers.com 2011).

EXHIBIT 7.1   The Emergence and Rise of Mass Social Media

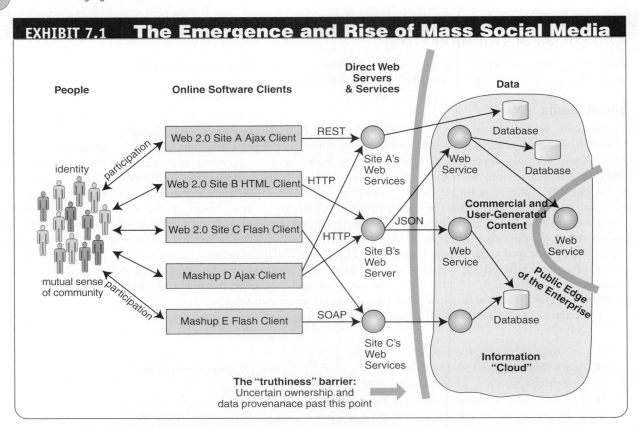

Source: D. Hinchcliffe, Web 2.0 Blog, *web2.wsj2.com*. Used with permission from Don Hinchcliffe.

social capital

A sociological concept that refers to connections within and between social networks. The core idea is that social networks have value. Just as physical capital or human capital can increase productivity (both individual and collective), so do social contacts affect the productivity of individuals and groups.

Example. The Georgia Department of Medical Assistance's campaign, called PeachCare for Kids, focused on marketing children's health care insurance (citing names of insurance companies) for working families. The campaign made affordable comprehensive medical care available to over 300,000 children. It was only partially supported by the Internet.

Social Capital

Social capital is a sociological concept, which refers to connections within and between social networks. Though there are many related definitions (search "define social capital" at Google), which have been described as "something of a cure-all" for the problems of modern society, they tend to share the core idea that social networks have value. Just as physical capital or human capital can increase productivity (both individual and collective), social contacts can also affect the productivity of individuals and groups. For details, see en.wikipedia.org/wiki/social_capital.

Social Media Marketing

social media marketing (SMM)

A term that describes use of social media platforms such as networks, online communities, blogs, wikis, or any other online collaborative media for marketing, market research, sales, CRM, and customer service. It may incorporate ideas and concepts from social capital, Web 2.0, social media, and social marketing.

Social media marketing (SMM) is a term that describes the use of social media platforms such as networks, online communities, blogs, wikis, or any other online collaborative media for marketing, market research, sales, CRM, and customer service. It may incorporate ideas and concepts from social capital, Web 2.0, social media, and social marketing. It is an online marketing strategy based on the utilization of online social media configurations. For example, social media can build brands because it amplifies and accelerates word of mouth.

Note that social media is concerned with communication and collaboration while SMM is concerned with marketing activities done via social media. SMM seeks to achieve branding and marketing communication goals through customers' participation in various social media. For details, see Borges (2009), Safko and Brake (2009), and Handley, et al. (2010).

According to en.wikipedia.org/wiki/Social_media_marketing, social media marketing programs usually center on efforts to create content that attracts attention and encourages readers to share it with their social network friends. This way, a corporate message spreads from user to user and presumably resonates because it is coming from a trusted source (i.e., word-of-mouth marketing), as opposed to coming from the brand or company itself.

Major Categories of Social Media. According to Kaplan and Haenlein (2010), the following are the six different types of social media: Collaborative projects, blogs and microblogs, content communities, social network sites, virtual game worlds, and virtual communities.

SOCIAL NETWORKS AND SOCIAL NETWORKING

As described in Chapters 1 and 2, Web 2.0 includes social software tools (e.g., wikis, blogs) and social network sites (e.g., Facebook). We also introduced the concept of *social networking*, which refers to activities done using social software tools (e.g., blogging), or social networking features (e.g. media sharing). We also introduced in Chapter 2 the concept of *mashups*, which facilitate a combination of two or more social software tools and/or social networks.

The Social Networking Space

The social networking space can be categorized as follows:

- **Leisure-oriented sites.** Socially focused public sites, open to all users
  - Facebook, MySpace, Orkut, Hi5
- **Professional networking sites.** Sites focusing on business networking
  - LinkedIn
- **Media sharing sites.** Sites focusing on the distribution and consumption of user-generated multimedia content, such as video and photos
  - YouTube, Flickr
- **Virtual meeting place sites.** Sites that are essentially a 3-D virtual world, built and owned by its residents (the users)
  - Second Life
- **Communication sites.**
  - Blogs: Blogger, LiveJournal, Open Diary, TypePad, WordPress, Vox, Expression Engine, Xanga
  - Microblogging/presence applications: Twitter, Plurk, Tumblr, Yammer, Qaiku
- **Collaboration sites.**
  - Wikis: Wikimedia, PBworks, Wetpaint
- **Social bookmarking (or social tagging):** Delicious, StumbleUpon, Google Reader, CiteULike
- **Social news:** Digg, Mixx, Reddit, NowPublic
- **Social network aggregation.**
  - NutshellMail, FriendFedd
- **Events.**
  - Upcoming, Eventful, Meetup.com
- **Enterprise-owned sites.** These are private sites owned by companies such as Starbucks, Disney, or Dell.

For a list of social networking websites, see en.wikipedia.org/wiki/List_of_social_networking_websites.

Note that in each of these you may find social software tools and socially oriented applications (APPs). Also note that due to mashups, it is possible to have content from several sites combined. For instance, a Facebook page might pull in photos from Flickr, updates from Twitter, the latest story on the presidential campaign from the *New York Times*, and much more. The Web is no longer simply a source of information, but it is a consortium of people's thoughts and actions.

Social media and networking are becoming new technological skills that influence the way that people exchange information so much so that social networking is quickly becoming a desirable job skill. For a discussion, see Harris and Rae (2009).

The Social Graph

social graph

A term coined by Mark Zuckerberg of Facebook, which originally referred to the social network of relationships between users of the social networking service provided by Facebook. The idea was for Facebook to benefit from the social graph by taking advantage of the relationships between individuals that Facebook provides, to offer a richer online experience. This definition was expanded to refer to a social graph of all Internet users.

The **social graph** is a term coined by Mark Zuckerberg of Facebook, which originally referred to the social network of relationships between users of the social networking service provided by Facebook. It has been described as a "global mapping of everybody and how they're related." The term was used to explain the Facebook Platform, which was introduced in 2007. The idea was for Facebook to benefit from the social graph by taking advantage of the relationships between individuals that Facebook provides, to offer a richer online experience. This definition was expanded to refer to a social graph of all Internet users.

The social graph describes the relationships between individuals online, as opposed to the concept of a social network, which describes relationships in the real world. The two concepts are very similar, but some minor differences do exist. For example, the social graph is digital, and more importantly, it is defined explicitly by all connections involved.

Facebook is helping people and websites with the construction of the social graph. To date, Facebook's social graph has been underused by brands. It's not surprising. The concept is quite complicated, and it also challenges what we think and know about social media marketing. For details, see en.wikipedia.org/wiki/Social_graph.

Using Social Media in the Enterprise

According to an *InformationWeek* survey of business technology experts, the most useful Web 2.0 tools in Enterprise 2.0 are instant messaging (69 percent), collaborative tools (61 percent), integrated search tools (56 percent), unified communication (49 percent), wikis (47 percent), and mashups (43 percent). Also of importance were Ajax, RSSs, blogs, and presence awareness (30 to 40 percent each). The experts identified the following major concerns with Enterprise 2.0: security issues (64 percent), lack of expertise (56 percent), integration with existing IT systems (52 percent), and difficulty in proving ROI (51 percent) (Hoover 2007).

Recognizing the importance of the social media revolution, many companies are building social media departments (see Gillette 2010).

Section 7.1 ▶ REVIEW QUESTIONS

1. Differentiate Web 2.0 from the traditional Web.
2. List five major characteristics of Web 2.0 and briefly discuss them.
3. What is user-generated content? Why is it an important concept?
4. Why is Web 2.0 considered a revolution?
5. Define social media, social marketing, social capital, and social media marketing.
6. Distinguish between social networking and social network sites.
7. List the major social networking spaces.
8. Describe the social graph.

7.2 THE FUNDAMENTALS OF SOCIAL COMMERCE AND SOCIAL NETWORKING

Social commerce is currently the hottest topic of e-commerce. A 2010 survey (Leggatt 2010) found that in July 2010 there were over 700,000 small businesses with Facebook Fan pages and close to 850,000 in February 2011, and LinkedIn's network exceeds 90 million members. Furthermore, almost 70 percent of all companies worldwide use some social networking. Clearly, this is a phenomenon that no business can ignore (see Marsden 2011).

Since the field of *social commerce* (SC) is very new and emerged from different academic and practical disciplines, it has different dimensions, and even definitions, the major of which are described next.

SOME DEFINITIONS OF SOCIAL COMMERCE

Social commerce (SC), also known as *social business,* refers to the delivery of e-commerce activities and transactions through social networks and/or via Web 2.0 software. Thus, it can be considered as a subset of e-commerce that involves using social media to assist in e-commerce transactions and activities. It also supports social interactions and user contributions. In essence, it is a combination of commerce and social activities. Stephen and Tuobia (2010) define SC as a form of Internet-based social media that allows people to participate actively in the marketing and selling of products and services in online marketplaces and communities. They distinguish *social shopping* that connects customers from *social commerce* that connects sellers. Their SC definition assumes sellers to be individuals and not corporations. Dennison, et al. (2009) provide an IBM definition that social commerce is the concept of word of mouth applied to e-commerce and it is the marriage of a retailer's products and the interaction of shoppers with content. Marsden (2009a) collected 22 different definitions of SC that include several of SC's properties (such as word of mouth, trusted advice, buying with the help of friends).

Note that the definitions of SC reflect the idea of community-level participation and socioeconomic impacts in e-commerce. *Social commerce* can also be defined as a subset of e-commerce that involves using social media, the online media that supports social interaction and user contributions, to assist in the online buying and selling of products and services. Social commerce is a place where people can collaborate online, get advice from trusted individuals, find goods and services, and then purchase them. For additional discussion, see bazaarvoice.com/resources/social-commerce?src=swf.

THE EVOLUTION OF SOCIAL COMMERCE

Social commerce emerged from the integration of several fields that are shown in Exhibit 7.2.

A major emphasis of SC is its marketing and sales orientation, and therefore SC is related to the concept of *social marketing,* which was initiated in 1970 as an approach to planned social change for improving the quality of life (Section 7.1). Social marketing has

social commerce (SC)
The delivery of e-commerce activities and transactions through social networks and/or via Web 2.0 software.

EXHIBIT 7.2   The Major Roots of Social Commerce

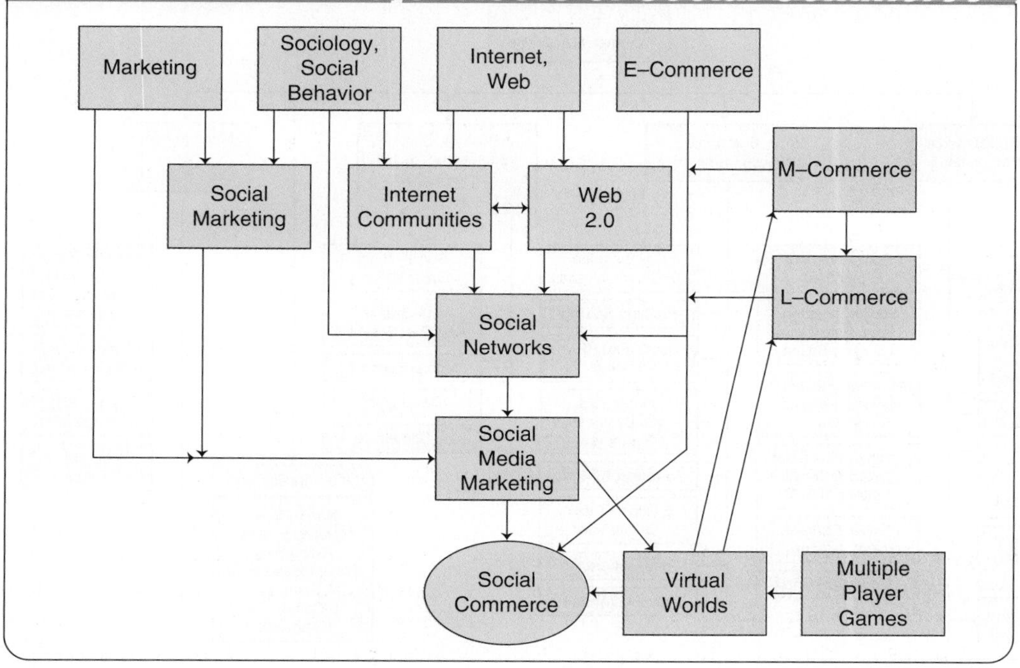

been developed as academic and practical fields that include commerce activities (see answers.com/topic/social-marketing for comprehensive coverage).

Another root of SC is the area of commercial applications of Web 2.0, which includes activities in social networks and the use of social software such as blogs and wikis. Mobile commerce is also a major ingredient of SC. First, SC models such as location-based are conducted on mobile devices, as are many SC applications. Most of all, it is the handheld culture that perfectly matched with social commerce. Other roots of SC are communication and collaboration theories, virtual communities, and virtual worlds. Finally, a major root is the field of e-commerce (or e-business) with its different business models.

THE LANDSCAPE OF SOCIAL COMMERCE

The landscape of social commerce is very diversified. Most of the activities center around the e-marketing, advertisement, and sales areas, usually expressed as *social media marketing* activities. However, several other areas are emerging in the field especially activities within organizations that are referred to as *enterprise social commerce*. We illustrate the landscape in Exhibit 7.3 and describe only some of the areas now. A discussion of the other activities of the exhibit is provided in the forthcoming sections of this chapter and throughout the book.

Note that a major area of activities is *social shopping* and *advertising* (e.g., see Solis and Kutcher 2010). However, there are several other emerging areas as illustrated in Sections 7.5 and 7.10.

For definitions of some of the major SC elements, see enterpriseirregulars.com/23628/the-2010-social-business-landscape. For a discussion, see Marsden (2011) and his presentation at socialcommercetoday.com/new-presentation-social-commerce-opportunities-for-brands.

THE POTENTIAL BENEFITS OF SOCIAL COMMERCE

Most of the benefits of SC are related to advertising, marketing, and collaboration activities. The major benefits are summarized in Exhibit 7.4.

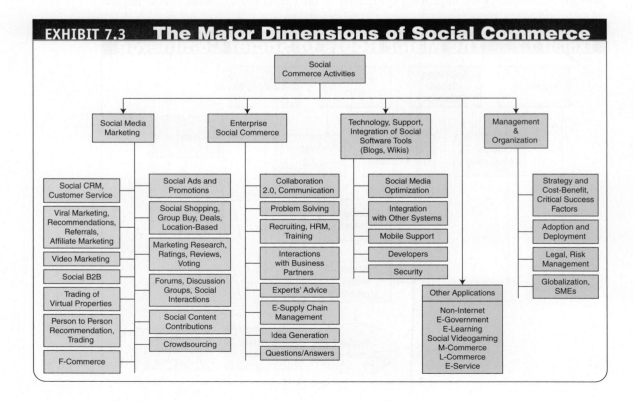

EXHIBIT 7.3   The Major Dimensions of Social Commerce

EXHIBIT 7.4   The Benefits of Social Commerce

Benefits to customers
- Pay less for products and services (group buy, special deals).
- Better and faster vendors' response to complaints, since customers can complain in public (on Twitter, Facebook, or even YouTube).
- Unhappy customers can reach millions millions through crowdsourcing. (Power!)
- Be engaged, develop relationship with vendors.
- Customers can assist other customers (e.g., in Forums).
- Customers' expectations can be met in fully and quickly.
- Customers can find out quickly about new staff.
- Can easily search, link, chat, and buy while being in the social network's page.
- Better self-service is possible.

Benefits to vendors
- Save money on customer service (e.g., smaller call centers).
- Can test new products/ideas quickly and inexpensively.
- Learn a lot about the customers.
- Identify problems quickly; assess magnitude, alleviate anger.
- Compare items/services to competitors.
- Can learn from the customers' experience, get feedback.
- Turn user-generated content into user-generated commerce.
- Increase retail sales—when customers discuss products in a community or via Twitter.
- Increase trust via direct conversations.
- Improve customer service and increase loyalty.
- Create better marketing campaigns and brand awareness.
- Improve product/design (e.g., a test bed for products); match with customer needs.
- Use low-cost user-generated content.
- Get free advertisement (e.g., viral advertisement).
- Increase traffic to site, increase sales and profit.
- Target advertisements more accurately.
- Improve operations due to accurate demand forecast.
- Increase revenue via better customer acquisition and retention.
- Reduce marketing and advertisement expenses.
- Identify brand advocates—use and reward them.
- Create viral advertisements—happy customers will share feelings with their friends.
- Create a community of fans for your brand.

Several surveys conducted in the last three years (e.g., Leggatt 2010) confirmed that social commerce results in significant monetary and strategic benefits to businesses.

Benefits to Retailers

Retailers stand to benefit from social commerce in several important ways.

▶ Consumers can provide feedback on the design of proposed or existing products, on marketing and advertising campaigns, and on how well customer service and support are performing, which can lead to improvements and innovations by manufacturers and retailers.

▶ Word-of-mouth marketing (i.e., *viral marketing*) is free advertising that can increase the visibility of niche retailers and products.

▶ Increased website traffic, a common effect of social media marketing (recall the Starbucks case) and viral marketing, inevitably brings more revenue dollars with it.

▶ Increased sales can come from harnessing techniques based on personal preferences such as collaborative filtering and targeted advertisement (Chapter 8). At a more advanced level, retailers strive for a higher degree of relevance in matching the knowledge of one person to someone of similar interests who has a need to know (the "twinsumer" concept). The twinsumer trend involves consumers looking for the best of the best, the first of the first, the most relevant of the relevant. Using collaborative filtering to create recommendations (e.g., Netflix, Amazon.com), these consumers connect with and listen to their *taste twins*—fellow consumers somewhere in the world who think and consume the way they do.

▶ Over 40 percent of businesses globally found new customers via social networks (Leggatt 2010).

▶ Over 27 percent of companies invest in social networking in order to acquire and retain customers (Leggatt 2010).

For a comprehensive presentation of social commerce impacts on retailing, see IBM's white paper by Dennison, et al. (2009).

These potential benefits encourage companies to at least experiment with social commerce. Successful applications are introduced in Sections 7.3 through 7.9, and a comprehensive list is available at Bazaarvoice (2011).

New or Improved Business Models

Social networking sites provide innovative business models; some are new while others are not successful as regular EC models (e.g., group buying). These models range from customer reviews of food and night life in India (mumbai.burrp.com) to users who dress up dolls that look like celebrities (stardoll.com). Several start-ups created new business models. For example, Joost.com invented a P2P service that sends broadcast-quality video over the Internet. New revenue models are being created daily.

An example of a new business model that has emerged from Web 2.0 is the accumulation of the "power of the crowd," or *crowdsourcing* (Section 7.8). The potential of such business models is very large. For example, wikia.com is using a crowdsourcing community in an attempt to develop a superior search mechanism. If it can create a successful one, Google may be in trouble.

MOBILE SOCIAL NETWORKING AND COMMERCE

Mobile commerce (Chapter 6) is spreading in social networks and social commerce applications.

mobile social networking

Members converse and connect with one another using cell phones or other mobile devices.

Mobile social networking refers to social networking where members converse and connect with one another using cell phones or other mobile devices. A current trend for social networking websites such as Facebook is to offer mobile services. Some social networking sites offer mobile-only services (e.g., Brightkite [brightkite.com]).

There are two basic types of mobile social networks. The first type is companies that partner with wireless carriers to connect with their communities via the default start pages on cell phone browsers. For example, users can access MySpace via AT&T wireless (wireless.att.com). The second type is companies that do not have such carrier relationships (also known as "off deck") and consequently they rely on other methods to attract users. Examples of this second type include MocoSpace (mocospace.com) and Peperonity (peperonity.com).

Example 1. Windows Live Spaces Mobile can be viewed on mobile devices even with limited screen sizes and slow data connections. It allows users to browse and add photos, blog entries, and comments directly from their mobile devices. Moreover, it has introduced several other features to improve the user experience with handheld devices.

For more information on Windows Live Spaces Mobile, see mobile.spaces.live.com and en.wikipedia.org/wiki/Windows_Live_Spaces_Mobiles.

Example 2. Coca-Cola created a social network that is only accessible via cell phones. The network is aimed at youngsters under the Sprite brand. Members can set profiles, meet friends, etc. The idea is to use the site mainly for advertisement. To attract visitors, the company offers free content (music and video clips). The free access requires a PIN found under Coca-Cola bottle lids.

With the current software, interactions within mobile social networks are not limited to exchanging simple text messages on a one-to-one basis. In many cases, they are evolving toward the sophisticated interactions of Internet social networks with graphics, voice, and videos.

CONCERNS AND LIMITATIONS OF CONDUCTING SOCIAL COMMERCE

Although social commerce presents many opportunities for organizations, its implementation may involve some potential risks and possibly complex integration and organizational issues. Representative risk factors are: difficulties in justification, security and privacy issues, possibilities of fraud, integration with existing IT systems, legal concerns, quality of UGC, and a waste of time by community members. For details, see Section 7.11.

Section 7.2 ▶ REVIEW QUESTIONS

1. Define social commerce.
2. List some major origins of social commerce (per Exhibit 7.2).
3. List the major blocks in the landscape of social commerce.
4. List five benefits of social commerce to the consumer and five to vendors.
5. Describe mobile social commerce.

7.3 SOCIAL SHOPPING: CONCEPTS, BENEFITS, AND MODELS

Shopping is a natural area for social networks to become involved in. Although shopping in social networks is only beginning to grow, it has enormous potential. In this section, we cover the essentials of social shopping.

DEFINITIONS, CONCEPTS, AND BENEFITS OF SOCIAL SHOPPING

Shopping is by nature, a fairly social activity. **Social shopping** (also known as Sales 2.0) is a method of e-commerce where shoppers' friends become involved in the shopping experience. It is about sharing the act of shopping with others. Social shopping attempts to use technology to mimic the social interactions found in physical malls and stores. Social shopping is the combination of social media and e-commerce. In essence, it is taking all of the key aspects of the social Web—friends, groups, voting, comments, discussions, reviews, etc., and focusing them on shopping. In other words it is like bringing your friends with you on the Web while you shop.

An overview of selling in social networks is provided by Jefferies (2008) and the authors who cite the following drivers:

social shopping
A method of e-commerce where shoppers' friends become involved in the shopping experience. Social shopping attempts to use technology to mimic the social interactions found in physical malls and stores.

▶ The huge number of people visiting social networks
▶ Pressure to increase top-line revenue growth
▶ Efforts to improve overall sales productivity
▶ Need to compete with increasing customer and prospect knowledge of products and competitive differentiators (the emergence of the *social customer*)
▶ The recommendations/suggestions made by friends
▶ The huge discounts available
▶ The society-oriented shopping models
▶ The ease of shopping while you are inside a social network
▶ The ease of communicating with friends in real-time using Twitter and cell phones

For more on social shopping, see dbpedia.org/page/Social_commerce and blog.comtaste.com.

Concepts and Content of Social Shopping

Social shopping is done in social networks (e.g., Facebook), in vendors' socially oriented stores, in stores of special intermediaries (such as Groupon.com), and more. The buyers are *social customers* that trust and/or enjoy social shopping. As will be seen later in this section, there is a wide range of social shopping models utilizing many of the Web 2.0 tools as well as social communities. The nature of shopping is changing especially for brand name clothes and related items. For example, popular brands including Gap, Shopbop, InStyle, and Lisa Klein are joining communities on Stylehive to help promote the season's latest fashion collections. Net savvy shoppers are logging onto sites like ThisNext to create profiles and blog about their favorite products in social communities. By tagging each item, everything becomes indexable; what this means is your search *within* these sites can yield some targeted results instead of a random set of picking from the online webstore.

Social shopping is the next opportunity for brands and consumers to connect and enjoy products in a new way. Social shopping communities help shoppers connect with each other based on tastes, location, age, gender, etc. Create a wish list, publish it on a social-oriented portal, and start attracting friends and fellow shoppers with similar interests. Sites such as ThisNext even offer a "'shopcasting'" feature where users can share their findings on their own blogs using a simple plug-in. Finally, Facebook and other social networks offer incredible opportunities for advertising, shopping, market research, and customer service.

There are two basic practices of social commerce:

1. Add social software (e.g., blogs) and features (e.g., polling) to existing commerce sites.
2. Add e-commerce functionalities (e.g., e-catalog, shopping cart) to social media and network sites.

Why Shoppers Go Social

Many shoppers like to hear from others prior to purchasing. They do it via the concept of communal shopping.

communal shopping
A method of shopping where the shoppers enlist others to participate in the purchase decision.

Communal shopping is a method of shopping where the shoppers enlist others to participate in the purchase decision. This added participation empowers the shoppers by giving them additional points of view. Having multiple opinions and ideas from other people provides the shopper with a more encompassing examination of the product/service.

Another factor that comes from *communal shopping* is boosted confidence in the decision to buy or not to buy. With a group contributing to the purchase decision, the shoppers are more likely to feel like they have properly inspected the product or service. This confidence allows the shoppers to reach a decision faster than if they had to look at the product/service from all angles on their own, and evaluate each aspect deemed important. For details, see en.wikipedia.org/wiki/Communal_shopping.

The Roles in Social Commerce

Gartner Inc. conducted a study on social commerce (as per *Techshout.com* 2010) in which it identified the following roles in social media and e-commerce:

▶ **Connector.** Connectors perform a bridging function between disparate groups of people. They have contacts in different social groups and enjoy introducing people to each other. Connectors come in two types: (1) Heavy connectors, who have varied but tight circles of friends and family; (2) Light connectors, with ties that are much weaker and less frequent.

▶ **Salesman.** Salesmen have extensive social connections, but their defining characteristics are their propensity to persuade people to do things, buy certain products, and act in certain ways.

▶ **Seeker.** Seekers connect with other people in order to find out the information, skills, and obligations they need to conduct their daily lives. When seekers go shopping, they tend to seek advice from experts who tell them which are the best gadgets to buy, where to get them, and at what prices.

▶ **Maven.** Mavens are knowledge exchanges brokers. They are experts in particular areas, and other people go to mavens for advice. Firms should remember that mavens are just as happy spreading negative commentary about a product or company as a positive message.

▶ **Self-sufficient.** These people prefer to find out for themselves what they need to know in order to satisfy their needs. This group of people can be a tough market to target because they are relatively impermeable to viral influences and bandwagon effects.

▶ **Unclassified.** Two-thirds of the population did not definitively fall into any of these social network categories.

The major influences are salesmen, connectors, and mavens.

Benefits of Social Shopping

Many of the benefits of social commerce (Exhibit 7.4, p. 341) apply to social shopping. Additional benefits are:

▶ You can discover products/services you never knew existed (e.g., see thisnext. com).

▶ You can interact with vendor (brand) representatives (e.g., feature available at stylehive.com/blog).

▶ Your confidence and trust in online shopping increases.

▶ You can get super deals via group buying, daily specials, and more. Join Groupon just to see the super deals.

▶ You can exchange shopping tips with your friends, fans, and others.

▶ You can build and share wish lists.

▶ You can have camaraderie shopping with peers with similar tastes.

▶ You can learn from others' experience.

▶ You can get simplified comparisons, even in real-time.

Kasteler (2009) elaborates on these benefits and provides a list of several dozen start-ups. So, before you go shopping, consult social shopping sources such as tkg.com/social-shopping.

Note that social shopping sites may generate revenue from advertising, commission on actual sales, sharing customer's information with retailers, and affiliate marketing.

THE MAJOR MODELS OF SOCIAL SHOPPING

A large number of social shopping models have appeared in recent years. Some are extensions of EC generic models; others are unique to social shopping. We arranged them into the following groups:

▶ Social recommendations, ratings and reviews, comparisons, and conversations

▶ Group buying and shopping together

▶ Deal purchases (flash sales), such as daily deals

> ◗ Shopping communities and clubs
> ◗ Peer-to-peer models (e.g., money lending)
> ◗ Location-based shopping (presented in Section 7.4)
> ◗ F-commerce; shopping at Facebook (see this chapter's closing case)
> ◗ Shopping with Twitter
> ◗ Other innovative models

To see the diversity of social commerce, see the slide presentation on social shopping at slideshare.net/oukearts/transforming-retail-into-social-commerce-retail-ceo-briefing-strategy-boutique-thaesis. Also, see Shih (2011).

Note: Both Facebook and Twitter are providing activities with some or all of these models directly and indirectly. For Twitter, see business.twitter.com/twitter101.

RATINGS AND REVIEWS, SOCIAL RECOMMENDATIONS, ADVICE, COMPARISONS, AND CONVERSATIONS

Prior to a purchase, customers like to collect information such as what brand to buy, from which vendor, and at what price. Online customers do it by using shopping aids described in Chapter 3 (e.g., comparison agents), looking at sites such as Epinions, and they do research at other sources. Today, it is done also by examining and participating in social networking. According to Gartner Inc. (per *Techshout.com* 2010), the majority of online customers already rely on social networks to guide them in purchase decisions. In the social commerce environment, shoppers resort to friends, fans, followers, and experienced customers. In this age of peer-to-peer engagement through social media, vendors recognize that their customers' voices can be their strongest marketing tool. Therefore, they want to hear what the customers say. A variety of SC models and tools is available for this purpose. We present two categories here.

Ratings and Reviews

Rating and reviews by friends, even by people that you do not know (hopefully experts) and by independent third-party evaluators of a product or service, are usually available in social shopping, and you also have an opportunity to contribute and discuss. The tool set includes:

> ◗ **Customer ratings and reviews.** Feedback from real customers, either integrated into an e-commerce product page, a social network page, a customer review site, and/or in customer news feeds (e.g., Amazon.com, iTunes, Buzzillions, Epinions). Customer ratings can be summarized by votes or polls.
> ◗ **Expert ratings and reviews.** The view from the independent voice of authority, professional, or prosumers, either integrated into an e-commerce product page, a social network page, a product review site, an online magazine, and/or in news feeds (e.g., Metacritic).
> ◗ **Sponsored reviews.** Paid-for reviews, either customer bloggers or experts on social media platforms (e.g., SponsoredReviews, PayPerPost).
> ◗ **Conversational marketing.** People converse via e-mail, blog, live chat, discussion groups, and tweets. Monitoring conversations may yield rich data for market research and customer service.
> ◗ **Video product review.** Reviews can be generated by using videos (see expotv.com and socialeyes.com).
> ◗ **Customer testimonials.** Customer stories typically published to an e-commerce site, allowing comments and discussion (e.g., Bazaarvoice "Stores").

Example. Maui Jim (mauijim.com), the fastest-growing polarized sunglass maker in the world, recently used Bazaarvoice's Ratings & Reviews to allow customers to contribute five-point ratings and authentic product reviews on the company's entire line of advanced-protection, fashion-forward sunglasses and accessories.

Maui Jim has long had a loyal following of satisfied customers. Word-of-mouth marketing has always been a key driver of sales for Maui Jim, because people love to recommend the products to friends, and Bazaarvoice's Ratings & Reviews is a great way to extend the customers' voices across the Web—allowing people to share their authentic opinions on the products and help each other make more informed purchase decisions.

Maui Jim is offering product ratings and reviews functionality on product detail, category, and collection landing pages, inviting customers to share their credible opinions on the style, fit, and performance of specific sunglass models. The reviews are integrated into site search functionality to ensure that customers searching for a particular product will see its star rating in the search results. Maui Jim also invites people to submit reviews via opt-in e-mail campaigns, and has seen a huge response to this outreach with thousands of customers submitting reviews.

Discussion. Ratings and reviews are a cornerstone of social commerce since 1995 (e.g., at Amazon.com) and a proven solution for boosting traffic volume, conversions (conversion from surfing a site to buying, see Chapter 8), and average order value. Reviews may result in word-of-mouth marketing through social influence, promoting purchase decisions with credible information. New developments in ratings and reviews are *review syndications* (to social networks), *contrast reviews* (showing positive and negative reviews), *tagged reviews* (tagging reviews with keywords), *video reviews, geotagged mobile reviews,* and story-based *customer testimonials.* Bazaarvoice (bazaarvoice.com) measured the impact of ratings and reviews as boosting conversion by up to 25 percent. Interestingly negative reviews appear not to have a detrimental effect on sales; we do not live in a five-star world, and shoppers do not expect it.

Social Recommendations and Referrals

These are closely related to ratings and reviews and are sometimes integrated with them.

The in-store analogy for this category is asking a fellow shopper for advice. Traditional online product review companies such as Amazon.com, Bazaarvoice, and Power Reviews have helped many consumers, but currently shoppers emphasize obtaining advice from and giving advice to friends and even strangers. Up-and-coming social shopping start-ups such as ShopSocially, Blippy, Swipely, and Bee Bargains now encourage *conversations* about purchases. The product recommendations come from people you know and arguably are more trustworthy than reviews by strangers. It will be interesting to see if this kind of model for product recommendation will eventually replace traditional website recommendations, and for what products, services, and price ranges customers will stay with the traditional methods. Recommendations and referrals are available within online social circles. There are many vendors that provide infrastructure and services for soliciting recommendations.

Examples. ThisNext (thisnext.com) is a social commerce site where people *recommend* their favorite products so others can discover what is best to buy online. It blends two powerful elements of real-world shopping otherwise lost for online consumers: word-of-mouth recommendations from trusted sources and the ability to browse products in the way that naturally leads to discovery. ThisNext has also developed a suite of distribution tools for bloggers, online communities, and e-commerce sites.

Another special site, productwiki.com, collects product reviews from people all over the world. Users can edit and change the product information.

Sometimes they are integrated in social shopping portals that bundle rating and reviews with recommendations and also provide shopping tools. A prime example is provided in Kaboodle. Note that Kaboodle is also considered a shopping community (which we will discuss later).

Common recommendation methods are:

> ▶ **Share with your network (social bookmarking).** Recommended products, deals, and tips are bookmarked and syndicated to friends, fans, and followers.
> ▶ **Referral programs.** Rewarding customers and partners for referring new customers (e.g., vente-privee, Gilt, Amazon Affiliates)
> ▶ **Social recommendations.** Personal shopping recommendations based on profile similarities to other customers (e.g., Apple Genius Recommendations, Amazon Recommendations, Netflix Cinematch, Honk)
> ▶ **Innovative methods.** Companies such as Honk and StyleFeeder automate personal recommendations based on algorithms comparing similarities between customer purchasing histories and profiles.

Discussion. Whereas ratings and reviews are usually visible to all, recommendations and referrals are personalized endorsements designed to realize value for customers and advocates. Often they take the form of online versions of traditional customer-get-customer and referral-rewards programs (e.g., Sky's Introduce a Friend) but can also use syndication tools via Twitter and Facebook to share recommendations with friends, fans, and followers. Note that reviews, ratings, and recommendations are useful not only to shoppers but also to vendors. See Section 7.5 for how these are being monitored and analyzed.

GROUP BUYING, DEAL PURCHASING, AND SHOPPING TOGETHER

The group buying model that was introduced in Chapter 1 was unpopular and seldom used in many countries, including the United States. However, in other countries (e.g., China) group buying has had some success. The problem with this model was the difficulty to organize the group, even with an intermediary. Furthermore, even if a group was organized, the negotiations about discounts could have been difficult, unless a very large volume was negotiated. In order to rally shoppers, group-shopping sites like Groupon, LivingSocial, and BuyWithMe offer major discounts or special deals during a short time frame. The start-up companies act as intermediaries to negotiate the deals with vendors. Group buying is closely associated with special deals (flash sales).

Deal Purchases (Flash Sales)

Short term deals are being practiced offline usually for people who are already in a store, or vendors advertise a sale for a day, or for several days. There are several variations of this model and it frequently is offered with other models (e.g., with group buying, as it is the case of Groupon, see Case 1.2, p. 64).

The deal purchase may be offered only in one city or state. For example, LivingSocial asks people to sign up for a deal at a restaurant, spa, or an event in a given city. You can click on "today's deal" or on "past deal" (some are active). The deals are e-mailed to anyone that signs up with LivingSocial. If you like it, you click on an icon and receive the deal the next day. After you buy the deal, you get a unique link to share with your friends. If you find three or more people willing to buy that specific deal using your link, then your deal is free. A common strategy of flash sale sites is to focus on an industry. For example, Gilt.com focuses on designer apparel, jewelry, bags, and upscale home furnishing.

Woot (an Amazon.com company) offers community information related to its deals. For example, there is a "discussion on today's deal," a Woot blog, top past deals, deal news, and what percentage of community members bought which product and what quantities of the products. Testimonials by members are also available. Woot is known as a favorite place for gadget geeks. Thus, Woot is not only a brand, but also a culture. Other interesting flash sale companies are Jetsetter and One King's Lane. Companies like Groupon, LivingSocial, and Woot run the promotions for the deals in major metropolitan areas. Discounts of 50 percent are common, and sometimes they reach 80 percent.

As stated earlier, it is common to combine group buys and a flash deal, and it can be done on Facebook.

Example. Vinobest Inc. (vinobest.com) uses Facebook for group buy/flash deals. Vinobest, a French group-buy wine merchant launched in June 2010, uses a flash sale application on Facebook. Vinobest offers expert oenologist opinion and sommelier selections for group-buy deals on wine. Unlike many other discount sale sites, Vinobest offers active pricing—the more people who buy, the cheaper the wine is. Extending flash sales to Facebook provides an ideal environment for recruiting friends into group-buy deals (member-get-member referrals are rewarded with vouchers for future purchases).

Group Buying in China

The Chinese elevated enthusiastic group buying for everything from cars to clothes to an art form long before sites like Groupon existed. About 1,200 companies are active all over China. For example, Lashou.com operates in more than 100 cities around China. The process however is different than in Western countries.

Example. Years ago Chinese Internet users started getting together online to organize as a group to buy the same car from the same dealer in order to get a quantity negotiated discount, and this team-buying concept quickly spread to other categories like computers. A group leader would coordinate the group's requirements and bargain with prospective dealers to close the sale. Sometimes the leader will bring the entire buying group to the negotiation. In fact, a group of Ford Focus buyers got into a shoving match at a Ford dealership when employees reportedly reneged on the agreed price, and the prospective buyers uploaded footage of the melee to video sites (e.g., see vimeo.com/8619105).

Since then group buying has soared. About 10 million Chinese used Groupon-like sites in October 2010, up from just 5 million in January 2010, according to iResearch Consulting Group. Today, all major Chinese Internet groups launched or plan to launch group buying and flash deals. These include Baidu, SINA, Tencent, and Alibaba. For details, see Madden (2010) and watch the video cnn.com/video/data/2.0/video/business/2011/01/26/yoon.china.coupon.gen.cnn.html.

Real-Time Online Shopping Together

In real-time online shopping, shoppers can log on to a site and either connect with Facebook or another social network, or invite their friends and family via Twitter, smartphone, or e-mail. They can then shop online together *at the same time*, discussing products and getting each other's opinion on services.

Some real-time shopping providers, such as DoTogether, and Wet Seal, have taken advantage of Facebook's *social graph* and integrated their shopping service right into the social network. You can simply log in to Facebook, install the app, and invite your friends via a chat or message to join on the virtual retail journey.

Shopping Together Sites. Dozens of sites facilitate shopping together models. For example, Select2gether allows you to join a conversation in a chat room; create a wish list; shop online in real-time with your friends; find inspirations, ideas, and advice; start a live showroom with your friends; and get access to the latest products the site specializes in (e.g., fashion-related). For details, see select2gether.com/clipper/login. Note that you can do many of these activities on Facebook. Wet Seal enables multiple people to shop together online. This is particularly applicable to fashion, where real-time opinions are important.

A variation of flash sales is "location-based" deals. We will present this topic in Section 7.4.

SHOPPING COMMUNITIES AND CLUBS

Community platforms, forums, and online clubs connect people with each other and sometimes to experts and businesses.

The analogy to shopping communities in real life is a club, where people join to spend time (and money) to talk about books, knitting, wine, etc., with like-minded people. Given just how many different kinds of clubs exist offline and how successful existing shopping communities have been to date especially for the fashion industry, we expect to see an emergence of shopping communities ranging from travel to adventure sports, among a myriad of other interests. We anticipate more interactions among real friends, not just "friends" on shopping communities.

Communities and common forum features are (per Marsden 2009b):

> ▶ **User forums.** People offering each other support and solving each others' task or product problems—members are typically customers and/or partners (e.g., Apple discussions, Threadless forums, P&G's Beinggirl)
>
> ▶ **User galleries.** People sharing and discussing video and image content with each other and with the gallery host, around a particular theme (e.g., Burberry's Art of the Trench)
>
> ▶ **Idea boards.** Online suggestion boards for constructive feedback, often with voting and commenting features (e.g., My Starbucks Idea, Dell's IdeaStorm)
>
> ▶ **Q&A forums.** New-style FAQs harnessing user contributions to answer common questions in a structured format (e.g., Bazaarvoice's Ask & Answer, PowerReviews' AnswerBox)
>
> ▶ **Brand communities.** Private communities of customers/partners, usually with a loyalty or advisory purpose
>
> ▶ **Comprehensive (multipurpose communities).** These communities have been primarily fashion-related (e.g., Stylefeeder, Polyvore, and Stylehive). Kaboodle is probably the most well-known community.

Private Online Shopping Clubs and Retail by Invitation

Private online shopping clubs originated in France in 2001 with the launch of vente-privee.com, which now has more than $1 billion in annual revenue. Here's how the model works: Shopping clubs host sales for their members that last just a few days and usually feature luxury brands at heavily discounted prices. Club organizers hosts three to seven sales per day, using usually e-mail messages to entice club members to shop at more than 70 percent off retail—but quickly, before the product runs out.

Luxury brands happily partner with online shopping clubs, as they offer a means to dispose of special-run, sample, overstock, or liquidation goods, while relative exclusivity of the clubs avoids diminishing a brand's image. On the consumer side, shopping clubs cater to the increasing number of brand-conscious but value-driven consumers.

The key to the business model's success is that not everyone is allowed to shop. The members-only model serves myriad purposes. Partially, it is a marketing device that makes members feel like VIPs; but it also helps the clubs manage growth.

Examples of Private Clubs. Some private clubs are Beyond the Rack (Canada), Gilt Groupe, Ruelala, BuyVIP (Europe), Ideeli, and One Kings Lane.

Discussion. Forums and communities are effective, popular, and useful. They can be integrated into social networking platforms to allow personal messaging and status updates to create an increased sense of community. They facilitate purchasing decisions primarily by allowing members to share trusted information with each other and the host. P&G has calculated that its Beinggirl forum is four times as effective as TV advertising. Innovations in this space include idea boards—online suggestion and discussion boards to capture constructive feedback, and user-powered Q&A forums for customer support in a moderated, guarded, and structured environment.

Kaboodle, a Unique Social Community

Kaboodle is the largest *social community*. It is a free service that lets users collect information from the Web and store it on a Kaboodle list that can be shared with others. The site's primary use is to simplify shopping by making it easier for people to find items they're interested in, in a catalog and by allowing users to share recommendations with one another using Kaboodle *lists* and *groups*. Kaboodle lists, however, can also serve a variety of purposes besides just shopping. They can be used for planning vacations, sharing research for work or school, sharing your favorite bands with friends, and basically anything else you might want to collect and share information about. Kaboodle makes it easy to create lists by offering downloadable Web browser buttons that directly add items to your list from the website you're browsing. When adding items to your list, Kaboodle also automatically adds a summary of the Web page you have saved. By allowing users to invite people as friends, Kaboodle makes it easy to connect with other people and share lists with friends as well.

Some Capabilities of Kaboodle. The "Our Add" Kaboodle button simplifies the online shopping experience because once you have it, you simply click on it whenever you see a product anywhere online, and you'll automatically upload a snapshot of the item, its price and other product information, and a link about where to buy it to one of your Kaboodle lists. Then, you can find it again anytime you want. You can also discover deals, amazing new products, express your unique style, connect with others, and share their discoveries, blog, create shopping lists, and more.

PopPicks, which is members-only, partners with a retailer each week to feature a collection of products. The Kaboodle community is then invited to vote for the products they like best. After four days of voting, the most liked products are made available to Kaboodle members at steeply discounted prices for four days or until the inventory is sold out.

OTHER INNOVATIVE MODELS

There are hundreds of start-ups in social commerce. Even Facebook is introducing services like "places" and "deals," which are described in this chapter's closing case. Here are some representative examples:

  ▶ **Find what your friends are buying.** This service is offered for example by clubfurniture. com, a site that sells direct home furnishings from its North Carolina factory. The button labeled "See What Your Friends Are Buying" allows users to log onto Facebook, Twitter, LinkedIn, or another social site of their choice. From there, they can view a list of their friends, friends of friends, or neighbors in the same zip code who have made purchases at clubfurniture.com. The widget also pulls up a list of repeat customers, which can bolster the comfort level of potential shoppers.

  ▶ **Filtering consumers reviews.** Example: TurboTax, a division of Intuit, launched a website called FriendsLikeYou.com that allows consumers to check boxes about their particular tax situation (own or rent a home, have children or not, previous tax prep method, etc.), and then filter reviews on TurboTax products to see only those written by "people like them." In other words, consumers can quickly filter reviews to include only those from people who have similar tax and income situations. Then, quickly find the right TurboTax product for their needs. From the FriendsLikeYou.com site, consumers can also click through to Facebook, Twitter, or MySpace and read reviews on TurboTax products written by members of their social network. In addition, anyone who reviews a TurboTax product, whether on FriendsLikeYou.com or on the main TurboTax.com website, can automatically publish their reviews to any of those three social networks, in one click.

  ▶ **Virtual gifts.** Similar to trading in virtual properties and gifts in Second Life, there is a rapidly increased market on social networks for virtual gifts. Facebook sells virtual gifts in its marketplace and Friendster.com on its Facebook page.

  ▶ **Getting help from friends.** The TurnTo model involves partnering with websites to have them carry a TurnTo button. When registered users click on it, a drop-down list shows which of their friends can advise them on that purchase. In January 2010, TurnTo announced that the partnership had helped JomaShop, ChristianCinema, and eParty boost sales during the 2009 holiday season. To help friends help friends, you may go to sites such as ShopSocially. You can post a question, share a purchase, and much more.

  ▶ **Shopping without leaving Facebook.** There are several avenues to turn Facebook Fan pages into retail outlets, so fans do not have to leave Facebook. Payment is one issue; security is another.

Example. When Pampers offered its new line of Pampers Cruisers through a storefront on its Facebook Fan page in April 2010, the limited supply of 1,000 packages for $9.99 each sold out in less than an hour. Thousands of eager would-be diaper-purchasers who missed out were offered the chance to preorder the Cruisers from online retailers

Amazon.com, BabiesRUs.com, and physical stores. That Pampers can create buzz for a diaper is indeed testimony to the power of Facebook and social media as business marketing tools. For how you can deal on Facebook, see Boatman (2010) and this chapter's closing case, which includes several other references.

▶ **Crowdsourcing shopping advice.** You can get advice from many people (the crowd, Section 7.8) as is done by Cloud Shopper. Cloud Shopper aims to organize the way people solicit advice. Users can browse products (pulled from Amazon.com), and select those they'd like to start a conversation about. They can either create a Facebook Wall Post asking for comments on that specific item or compile a list—let's say, "possible gifts for Suzie"—and share it with friends and friends of friends. When friends click on the Facebook link, they're directed to a commenting section where they can review each product. Products that users like are kept in a tabbed section for others to browse.

▶ **Helping bloggers sell products.** OpenSky helps bloggers monetize their businesses by making it easy for them to sell products directly to readers and earn a cut of the resulting sales. Bloggers choose what and when to sell; for example, it makes sense for makeup or fashion-focused bloggers to sell clothes and cosmetics to readers that they have established a rapport with over many months or years. OpenSky does some of the administrative work by signing on retailers, facilitating orders, and tracking purchases. It also uses a proprietary matching process to connect products and supplies to the most appropriate potential sellers.

▶ **Event shopping.** There are many sites that will help you, with the assistance of your friends, to shop for a special event (e.g., a wedding). Many variations exist. For example, Wendy's provides gift cards for Boneless Wings to consumers who organize viewing parties on Facebook.

SOCIAL MARKETPLACES AND DIRECT SALES

social marketplace

An online community that harnesses the power of one's social networks for the introduction, buying, and selling of products, services, and resources, including one's own creations. Also may refer to a structure that resembles a social network but is focused on individual members.

The term **social marketplace** is derived from *social networking* and *marketplaces*. Thus, a social marketplace essentially acts like an online intermediary that harnesses the power of one's social networks for introducing, buying, and selling products and services and mobilizing resources for social networking. Ideally, a social marketplace should enable the marketing of members' own creations.

Examples of social marketplaces include:

▶ **Craigslist.** Craigslist (craigslist.org) can be considered a social network marketplace in that it provides online classifieds in addition to supporting social activities (meetings, dating, events) (see Chapter 2).

▶ **Fotolia.** Fotolia (fotolia.com) is a social marketplace for a huge community of creative people who enjoy sharing, learning, and expressing themselves through images, forums, and blogs. Members provide royalty-free stock images that other individuals and professionals can legally buy and share.

▶ **Flipsy.** Anyone can use Flipsy (flipsy.com) to list, buy, and sell books, music, movies, and games. It was created to fill the need for a free and trustworthy media marketplace. Flipsy does not charge commissions in order to foster increased trading. Payment processing is handled by a third party, such as PayPal.

▶ **Listia.** Listia (listia.com) is an online auction marketplace where users swap virtual currency for free stuff. Beyond using typical online marketplace functionalities, Listia users share products by commenting on items for sale and share auctions with friends via Facebook Connect and Twitter.

Direct Sales from Social Networks

There is an increased volume of direct sales, mostly via Facebook (see this chapter's closing case). Here are some examples:

Example: How Musicians Sell Online via Social Networks. Many musicians and other artists used to front money to make their own CDs, T-shirts, and other items that may or may not sell. Now there is a social commerce solution. A new free Web-based platform (by Audiolife) gives artists a portable store, an e-commerce infrastructure to directly *monetize their fans*. It allows artists to publish items without mass producing them; merchandise is then produced on-demand.

Artists can download, personalize, and post the e-commerce portable store on sites like Facebook, Twitter, and MySpace to attract fans to place orders. Each order, even for one item, is then sent to vendors who manufacture the product and send it directly to the fans.

Audiolife only makes money when items sell. During 2010 Audiolife powered close to 70,000 storefronts worldwide, including ones for famous artists such as the Pussycat Dolls and George Benson. About 300 to 500 new online stores are publishing daily. For details, see sfvbj.com/news/2010/mar/29/ cash-strapped-musicians-empowered-tech-company/?print.

WHAT COMPONENTS TO EXPECT IN A SOCIAL SHOPPING SITE

Depending on the social shopping model, on the product offering–related information, and on the related information systems, one may find a diversity of components in a site. According to an IBM white paper (Dennison, et al. 2009) the following are major components that provide customers' experiences:

▶ **Shopper show-and-tell.** Blogs, photos, and components enable shoppers to share their product experiences, which helps provide informative perspectives for prospective shoppers making purchasing decisions about the product.

▶ **Product page discussion.** Ratings, reviews, recommendations, and comments power Q&A-type experiences around products, enabling shoppers and staff to interact around product features, benefits, and use cases.

▶ **Project journals.** Photos, user profiles, and blogs enable shoppers to establish product journals that chronicle the use of products.

▶ **How-to guides.** User, employee, and expert-created articles and videos provide shoppers with valuable information on product usage and provide retailers with a wealth of informational reference content.

B2B Social Networking

Topics unique to B2B social marketers include cost justification, prospecting and lead generation, matching tools to the sales funnel, B2B search engine optimization, social media monitoring, social media policy development, long-term client relationships, gaining stakeholder support, and building a more transparent organization. For a comprehensive guide, see Gillin and Schwartzman (2011). Also you can attend a podcast on the topic available at ontherecordpodcast.com/pr/otro/default.aspx. Finally, consult *B2BMagazine.com*.

Example: SAP. The SAP Community Network—a B2B social networking initiative nearly 2 million members strong and growing at a monthly pace of 30,000 new members, spanning 200 countries and territories worldwide—has been recognized as one of the most successful business-to-business social networking sites in the world.

SAP's B2B social networking formula has resulted in 6,000 posts per day, 1 million unique visitors per month, and 200,000 contributions by celebrating imperfection, profiting from surrender, improving product performance through user ratings, and building deeper professional relationships through personal interactions.

Zwilling (2011) presents location-based service (LBS) opportunities for B2B including:

▶ **Strategic partnership.** If your B2B contacts are frequenting other noncompetitive local businesses, LBS data could point you to more lucrative business partnerships. "Coopetition," or strategic cooperation with a competitor, is another angle.

▶ **Sponsorships and advertising.** If your B2B contacts check in regularly at certain types of locations (entertainment venues, stores, etc.) then you may want to consider potential sponsorships or advertising opportunities with that business or venue.

▶ **Incentives or rewards.** Knowing what your contacts like to do will give you insights on ways you can reward them. If you see a large percentage of your contacts checking into coffee shops each morning, you may want to consider gift cards as a possible reward for an upcoming incentive program.

▶ **Event marketing.** Are you seeing a lot of your contacts attending certain business events? Whether it is a local tweet-up or a major conference, this knowledge could be useful to help you plan what events you should sponsor or where you should set up your next booth.

▶ **Lead generation.** Identify potential new relationships. See who is checking into your business. See who checks into your competition. See who checks into the business events that your existing contacts attend.

▶ **Thought leadership.** If you know your contacts' real-life interests, you could use that information in your marketing efforts; however, there is a fine line between value delivery and privacy invasion.

▶ **Branded entertainment.** Leave tips where your contacts go (maybe similar to what History Channel does on Foursquare). Create a trip in Gowalla (see what Whole Foods or TOMS Shoes is doing) or create a society in Whrrl (check out *USA Today*'s society).

▶ **Understand competition.** Understand how users are physically interacting with your competition, and if so, what they are doing before and after those visits. If you notice any trends, you may be able to position your brand to cut off a potential visit before it happens.

▶ **Stronger nurturing and relationship building.** During lead nurturing, you could use LBS data to better understand your contacts' interests and use them to your advantage. LBS data can not only give you information to drive the relationship, but you can also use it to identify your sales reps with similar interests and partner them with the prospect.

Socially-Oriented Person to Person (P2P) Selling, Buying, Renting, or Bartering

When individuals trade online, they may do it with some social elements. For example, some consider Craigslist to be a socially oriented virtual community. Here are some more examples:

P2P Lending. P2P money lending is growing rapidly enabling people to lend money to each other. In the process they get to know each other. For details, see Online File W7.1. Another start-up created a community of people that rent goods to people in need, usually for the short term. SnapGoods helps these people to connect over the Internet.

SnapGoods is one of the many sites that have sprung up to facilitate offline sharing. Some sites have a narrow, obvious focus (like SwapBabyGoods.com) while others are more obscure (Neighborhood Fruit helps people share what's growing in their yards or find fruit trees on public land). All of the sites are encouraging *collaborative consumption*—in other words, peer-to-peer sharing or renting. The trend is taking off partly as a result of the recession. There is a green aspect as well, since sharing helps cut down on overall use of resources. But one of collaborative consumption's most surprising benefits turns out to be *social*. In an era when we may not know the people down the street from us, sharing things—even with strangers we have just met online—allows us to make meaningful connections.

Several variations exist. Some people share cars, others invite travelers to stay free in their homes, and much more. Even Google is providing a service that connects borrowers and lenders of money. Lending Tree is another company that allows prospective borrowers to get quick offers from multiple lenders.

Social Shopping in the Near Future

Imagine this scenario: A vendor (store) will ask you to use Facebook Connect (see the closing case in this chapter) to connect to your mobile service, as soon as you step into a physical store. By doing so, you can receive customized recommendations on your phone and on digital displays. Expect that your friends who have been in that store will digitally indicate which clothes are right for you. Expect digital displays to recommend what's best for you based on what friends "'like'" (see how Levi's is doing it on the Web at Levi's 2010), then walk in and find what you want. What about the risks? Expect privacy to be less important to Millennials who do not mind sharing their experiences with others (without revealing a person's full identity on an in-store screen). See a related video from Cisco about this at youtube.com/watch?v=jDi0FNcaock.

For example, when you walk into a dressing room in a department store, the mirror reflects your image, but you can also see images of an apparel item you like and celebrities wearing it, on an interactive display. A webcam also projects an image of the consumer wearing the item on a website, for everyone to see. This creates an interaction between the consumers inside the store and their social network outside the store. The technology behind this system uses RFID (see Online Tutorial T3). You can watch a video of how a smart dressing room works at youtube.com/watch?v=0VII-xdg5Ak&feature=related.

Section 7.3 ▶ REVIEW QUESTIONS

1. Define social shopping and describe its drivers.
2. List the major benefits of social shopping.
3. List the major models of social shopping. Briefly describe their function.
4. Describe ratings, reviews, and recommendations.
5. How are ratings and reviews being conducted?
6. Relate recommendations to social reviews and ratings.
7. Describe social marketplaces and direct sales.
8. Define group buying. How does it work with flash deals? (Hint: Groupon.)
9. Define social communities and social clubs as they relate to marketing. How do they work?
10. Describe Kaboodle.
11. Define social marketplaces. What is going on there?
12. What is the future of social shopping?

7.4 SOCIAL ADVERTISING: FROM VIRAL ADVERTISING TO LOCATION-BASED ADVERTISEMENT/MARKETING

The major current revenue source for social commerce vendors is advertising. The reason is that seeing the large number of visitors in the networks, and the amount of time they spent there, made advertisers willing to pay a great deal for placing ads and running promotions in social networks. Like other SC activities, advertising is done both in public as well as in private company-owned social networks.

Many advertisers are placing ads now on Facebook, YouTube, LinkedIn, MySpace, or Twitter. Although social media campaigns may have a small impact on actual online retail sales, it may have huge benefits with regard to increasing brand awareness.

Facebook features hundreds of thousands of third-party software applications on its site. One popular application area is travel. For example, one specific application is "Where I've Been," a map that highlights places where users have visited or hope to visit. You can plan trips, organize group travel, and find and rate free in-home accommodations (e.g., Couchswap). This information can be sold to travel-oriented vendors, who in turn advertise their products to Facebook members.

SOCIAL ADS AND SOCIAL APPS

Most ads in social commerce are branded content paid by advertisers. These come in two major categories: *social ads* and *social apps*.

▶ **Social ads.** Placing advertisement in paid-for media space on social media platforms such as Facebook, YouTube, and Twitter, as well as on blogs and forums

▶ **Social apps.** Creating branded online applications that support social interactions and user contributions (e.g., Nike+)

Social ads and apps stimulate purchase decisions through the social intelligence mechanisms of "consistency" and (in the case of apps) reciprocity. By clicking on an e-commerce link embedded in an app or ad, the user signifies an intention to make a purchase. Social apps also use reciprocity; social applications may solve people's problems (e.g., motivation and performance tracking in the case of Nike+). Social ads are far simpler to deploy, and are less dependent on insight and creativity—they require a compelling reason to click. For example, fast-food chain Chick-fil-A ran a successful Facebook free-sample engagement ad campaign; clicking on the ad revealed a form to receive a mail coupon. The downside of social ads is that they have low *click-through rates* (see the description in Chapter 8).

VIRAL (WORD-OF-MOUTH) MARKETING

viral marketing

Word-of-mouth (WOM) method by which customers promote a product (service) by telling others (frequently their friends) about it.

Viral marketing refers to a word-of-mouth (WOM) method by which customers promote a product (service) by telling others (frequently their friends) about it. Viral marketing (and advertising) has many variations (see Chapter 8) and it plays a major role in e-commerce and social commerce.

Young adults are especially good at viral marketing. If members like a certain product or service, word-of-mouth advertising will work rapidly. What they like can spread very quickly—sometimes to millions of people at a minimal cost to companies' advertisers. For example, YouTube conducted almost no advertising in its first few months, but millions joined because of WOM. For the "power of WOM," see bazaarvoice.com/resources/stats.

Viral Blogging

viral blogging

Viral (word-of-mouth) marketing done by bloggers.

Many retailers are capitalizing on WOM marketing by bloggers. See the example at livingstonbuzz.com. When viral marketing is done by bloggers, it is referred to as **viral blogging**. Viral blogging can be very effective with the use of tools such as Twitter (e.g., see business.twitter.com/twitter101/case_dell).

Example 1. An example of viral marketing on social networks is the story of Stormhoek Vineyards (stormhoek.com). The company first offered a free bottle of wine to bloggers. About 100 of these bloggers posted voluntary comments about the winery on their own blogs within six months. Most had positive comments that were read by their readers and by other bloggers.

The Stormhoek example raises an interesting question: Can bloggers be bought? The criticism is that bloggers are not required to disclose that they are being paid (or get gifts) for their endorsements. Companies can pay bloggers directly to endorse products or do it via an intermediary, such as PayPerPost.

Example 2. PayPerPost (payperpost.com) runs a marketplace where advertisers can find bloggers, video bloggers, online photographers, and podcasters who are willing to endorse advertisers' products.

A company with a product or a service to advertise registers with PayPerPost and describes what it wants. A sneaker company, for example, might post a request for people willing to write a 50-word blog entry about their sneakers or upload a video of themselves playing basketball wearing the sneakers. The company also says what it is willing to pay the bloggers for such posting.

Bloggers create the blog post (or whatever content is requested) and inform PayPerPost, which checks to see that the content matches what the advertiser asked for, and PayPerPost arranges payment. Note that the PayPerPost bloggers *are* required to disclose that they are being paid for their posting.

LOCATION-BASED ADVERTISEMENT AND SOCIAL NETWORKS

In Chapter 6, we introduced the concept of location-based advertising and marketing as a business model for m-commerce. The model is based on knowing where a customer is via a GPS on her or his cell phone. Once you know that a person is near a certain business, the vendor of this business can send a text, e-mail, or even a telephone call offering discounted products, coupons, or services. This business model was not too successful. The customers were not interested and those with GPS shut it off for privacy concerns.

The situation changed with the introduction of social networks. The nature of location-based marketing changed to being social, entertaining, and rewarding; advertisement came as an add on service. The major players in this area are Foursquare, Gowalla, and Facebook's Places—all are based on geolocation and geosocial networks.

Geosocial Networks

Geosocial networking is a type of social networking in which geographic services and capabilities such as geocoding and geotagging are used to enable additional social dynamics. User-submitted location data or geolocation techniques can allow social networks to connect and coordinate users with local people or events that match their interests. Geolocation on Web-based social network services can be IP-based or use hotspost triangulation. For mobile social networks, texted location information or mobile phone tracking can enable location-based services to enrich social networking. This technology is based on the concept of geolocation.

Geolocation. Geolocation is the identification of the real-world geographic location of an Internet-connected computer, mobile device, website visitor, or other. Geolocation data can include information such as country, region, city, postal/zip code, latitude, longitude, and time zone (see en.wikipedia.org/wiki/Geolocation).

geosocial networking
A type of social networking in which geographic services and capabilities such as geocoding and geotagging are used to enable additional social dynamics.

geolocation
The identification of the real-world geographic location of an Internet-connected computer, mobile device, website visitor, or other.

The Technology for Location-Based Social Networks

The basic idea is that users who have a GPS-enabled smartphone can let their friends know where they are. Users can also find places recommended by people they know, or to check in remotely at stores, clubs, bars, and restaurants.

Most social commerce applications involve advertisement. However, some involve sales. We will address the commercial applications.

How LBS Works. Typically, geolocation apps do two things: They report your location to other users, and they associate real-world locations (such as restaurants and events) to your location. Geolocation apps that run on mobile devices provide a richer experience than those that run on desktop PCs because the relevant data you send and receive changes as your location changes.

Many smartphones today have a GPS chip inside, and as described in Chapter 6, the GPS uses satellite data to calculate your exact position (usually when you are outdoors and the sky is clear). When a GPS signal is unavailable, geolocation apps can use information from cell towers to triangulate your approximate position, a method that isn't as accurate as GPS. Some geolocation systems use GPS and cell phone site triangulation (and in some instances, local Wi-Fi networks) in combination, to zero in on the location of a specific device (e.g., cell phone). This arrangement is called Assisted GPS (A-GPS).

From Foursquare to Facebook Places

Several start-ups are competing fiercely in the geolocation market. In 2011, the major one is Foursquare.

How Foursquare Works. Foursquare works with all major smartphones. (If no app exists for your smartphone, you can always use the Foursquare mobile website instead.) Foursquare can find your location with your permission, and thus tell your friends where they can find you. Foursquare provides a map, marking your location as "checking in." A detailed explanation of how Foursquare works and how to join it are provided at electronics.howstuffworks.com/foursquare.html.

You can check in to cafés, bars, restaurants, parks, offices, and pretty much anyplace else. Once your friends know where you are, they can recommend places for you to go or things for you to do and see nearby, or stores to visit. The service gives you points for each check-in; and you can earn various virtual badges that are tracking your progress toward Foursquare elitehood status. Thus, you have an incentive to provide information (and permission) to the company.

Foursquare also provides games and other incentives to encourage users to digitally "check in" to a specific location. The check-in shows up on Twitter, Facebook, and other social networks. Foursquare has a huge list of participating vendors all over the globe.

The most frequent visitor to each location is called a "mayor," receiving free gifts (as a mayor of McDonald's in your vicinity you will get a free Big Mac). In addition, every participant may get special discounts, coupons, and prizes. Foursquare also allows retailers to reward social sharing behavior. Foursquare on an Android phone shows your profile info, together with badges (rewards) that you have earned and the last place you checked in. All these help to increase customer loyalty (see Clifford 2010).

Competition: Gowalla, Brightkite, and Facebook Places. The competitors try to clone Foursquare and provide some extra services. For example, Gowalla allows trading the virtual badges you earn and even exchange some for free gifts from the sponsoring vendors. Facebook created its own network called Places (see the closing case).

Strategy for Small Businesses

According to Van Grove (2010), a small business can offer the following location-based deals: (1) verified check-in rewards, (2) social bar codes, (3) group deals, (4) challenge-based rewards, and (5) opt-in deals. For details, see mashable.com/2010/09/04/location-based-small-business-deals.

Privacy Concerns

There are some privacy concerns regarding finding the location of people or showing their profiles and shopping habits. Some sites, like Facebook, have been scrutinized for allowing users to "tag" their friends via e-mail while checking in. Google's new project, Buzz, is an automatic application that requires users to opt-out. If they do not, profiles displaying their social information will be open to all Gmail users.

Opt-in Versus Op-out. An "opt-in" is a permission-based network that requires a user to join or sign up. The host is then given permission to access the user's information and to contact him or her. An "opt-out" network is defaulted to have the user included in a group. Users must remove themselves from the network if they wish not to be included.

Examples of Successful Location-Based Applications

There are many new applications for LBS.

Example 1: AJ Bombers (Small Business). According to Chaffey (2010), AJ Bombers, a specialty burger bar in Milwaukee, attributed a sale increase of 110 percent to Foursquare. It has 1,400 people on its Foursquare page who have checked in 6,000 times during 3 months. The mayor gets a free burger.

Engagement also increased through people who add a tip to the restaurant's Foursquare page. They are rewarded with a free cookie when they show it to a waiter or cashier. The sales increase figure is based on a single campaign, which saw 161 check-ins (February 2010), a 110 percent sales increase when compared to a normal Sunday. Joe Sorge, owner of the restaurant, promoted an AJ Bombers-branded "Swarm Badge" to his Foursquare-using regulars. Such a customer badge is awarded to users who check in at a location where at least 50 other users are simultaneously checked in.

Example 2: Designers, Manufacturers, and Retailers Collaborate with Foursquare. Fashion designer Cynthia Rowley; Lovely Bride, an upscale bridal boutique in Manhattan; and dress manufacturer, The Dessy Group, collaborate by using a location-based service to promote fashion. The location-based component of this campaign was part of an aggressive online marketing campaign that merged direct e-mail, blogger outreach, and short-lead digital PR efforts. What made this campaign so interesting was that a digital marketing agency that coordinated the project had just two weeks to pull it off. Within the first three days, they laid out a strategy to leverage and cross promote all parties involved through a series of online and offline tactics. They created a fictional character—the Cynthia Rowley Bridesmaid (@CRBridal)—on Twitter and laid out "check-in locations" that fit the target demographic of the line. The check-in locations were selected together with Lovely Bride (the retailer). Each of the parties involved had their own social media profiles on Facebook and Twitter, as well as their own company blogs. The @CRBridal Twitter account was selected to be the hub of the information for the line launch, publicity, and social conversations. Each party also used their individual Twitter and Facebook accounts to carry the message to each of their audiences. Lovely Bride and Dessy created blog posts that focused on certain elements of the campaign. For the complete story and the astonishing success, see Wright (2010).

USING YOUTUBE AND OTHER SOCIAL PRESENTATION SITES FOR ADVERTISING

As we will see in Chapter 8, using videos for advertisement is becoming a major successful strategy. Sellers can bring their products to life and improve their visitor experience by adding video footage to their product pages on social networks, or their corporate portal. Product images are important, but a full motion video of products can really help vendors to sell. For example, 3dCart's YouTube video integration lets you easily search YouTube directly from your online store's control panel, select a video—whether it's a product review, demonstration, or viral commercial—and instantly display it on your product page. The major reason for such advertisement is the viral effect.

Viral Videos

In Chapter 8 we will describe the use of videos for advertisement, mostly via their viral impact. Here we will briefly describe how viral videos work with social commerce. Perhaps nowhere is social media more powerful than when a video goes viral, because it is funny, or shocking, or just interesting. Millions of people send it to millions of their friends and acquaintances, and as a result, huge groups actively watch an ad for a specific brand over and over. Of course, big brands dominate here. Think of the biggest viral videos of 2010 and names such as Old Spice (P&G), IKEA, Samsung, AXE (Unilever), and Evian come to mind. However, there are definitely many exceptions here. Great viral campaigns have come in 2010 from the Australian Tourism Board and from DC Shoes. An amazing ad came from a previously unknown organization—Sussex Safer Roads.

A **viral video** is any video that is passed electronically, from person to person, regardless of its content. Social networks are an ideal place to disseminate such videos. A *viral video* is one that becomes popular through the process of Internet sharing, typically through video sharing websites and/or e-mail. Viral videos often contain humorous content and include televised comedy sketches and amateur video clips. Some eyewitness events have also been caught on videos and have "gone viral." With the proliferation of smartphones with cameras, many videos are being shot by amateurs on these devices and sent immediately to friends and family. The availability of inexpensive video editing and publishing tools allows video shot on mobile phones to be edited and distributed virally, by e-mail or website, and between phones by Bluetooth or MMS. These consumer-shot videos are typically noncommercial, intended for viewing by friends or family. However, the same technology can be used by advertisers. For examples of some of the best viral videos, see baselinemag.com.

viral video
Any video that is passed electronically, from person to person, regardless of its content.

Why It Works. When you see an interesting video on YouTube, you tend to post the link on Twitter, Facebook, or share it by e-mailing friends. They pass it on to their friends, and the effect just multiplies and your message spreads rapidly, resulting in massive exposure. This approach does not even have to be expensive. For a discussion, see atlantaonlinemarketing. org/ youtube-viral-marketing-tips-it-is-going-to-blow-you-away.

Interesting examples are available at blog.socialmaximizer.com/youtube-business-use-cases and at youtubetrafficsystem.net.

USING TWITTER AS AN ADVERTISING AND MARKETING TOOL

Twitter and some other microblogging sites have social networking capabilities mostly because of their list of fans and friends. Sellers can reach out to these friends to create strong WOM.

According to Learmonth (2011), Twitter is becoming a little more of a business. The company launched its first ad product—"promoted tweets"—in 2010 and netted $45 million in ad dollars. That was due in part to the enthusiasm among brands like Virgin America, Coke, Ford, and Verizon to give the untried format a whirl. Learmonth estimates the ad revenue to be $150 million in 2011 and $250 million in 2012. Companies can tweet about their business and product offerings, including promotions. Then you can get your Twitter followers (and their followers) to come to your store. Twitter might be an abstract concept for many business owners, but it should not be overlooked since this powerful tool can help to create ads resulting in more sales for online business. The social commerce software suites (e.g., from 3dCart) help merchants reach their Twitter followers by posting "tweets" when the merchants add new products or create promotions. For successful examples, see twitter.com/SimplySpeakers and twitter.com/slgpublishing. It is extremely important to send interesting tweets and advertise as a "by-product" and not as the major topic of the tweet. Remember, people on Twitter want to know "what are you doing?" A smart advertiser must conceal the ad in the answer. Reminder: You can upload pictures to share as well as video. If your messages look like commercials, tweeters will go away. Twitter is already the world's third-largest social-networking platform (about 200 million registered users) and may reach 1 billion followers in a few years, according to MacMillan (2010), which may help the microblogging site compete with Facebook in attracting advertisements.

Twitter, whose users send more than 100 million short messages daily, said in September 2010 that it will open to more advertisers after a successful trial with leading brands including Starbucks Corp., ESPN, and Coca-Cola. Social networking sites are increasingly targeting marketer's ad budgets as a main source of revenue as the sites boast millions of users. Twitter is starting to try different types of monetizing methods. These sites have a lot of traffic, and a lot of people using them, but it is not easy to monetize because you do not know who is watching. For details, see MacMillan (2010). Note that only one of Twitter's competitors is really successful. It is an Asian mobile social network, Mig33, that is sending twice as many messages a day as Twitter (see mig33.com).

Finally here are some more ways one can advertise on Twitter (see business.twitter.com):

> ▶ Industry analysts, journalists, bloggers, and other influencers from most sectors of the economy are well-represented on Twitter. Tweet content of your own that could interest them (i.e., not just your marketing materials). Tweeting about content they post and engaging in dialog is a great way to get these people talking, and also writing about your company. It is less formal, more "social," and usually more effective than "cold" outreach.

> ▶ Staying in touch with customers on Twitter is not only more real-time than many other techniques, it is also far more cost-effective than direct mail, attending trade shows, picking up the phone, or even maintaining a customer newsletter. It is not that Twitter can replace other touch points completely of course, but it can reduce the required cost and frequency of high-touch interactions.

> ▶ It is very likely that your customers, prospects, and key influencers are already having conversations about your industry, your competition, and quite possibly your company on Twitter. If you are not participating in that conversion, you're missing valuable intelligence, business opportunities, and possibly even the opportunity to prevent damage to your firm's reputation. An example is American Apparel, which is using Twitter to solicit and discuss ideas for ads (see business.twitter.com/twitter101/case_americanapparel).

OTHER INNOVATIVE WAYS TO ADVERTISE IN SOCIAL MEDIA

A major objective of social advertisement is to increase traffic to the digital and or physical sites as described in the Starbucks' opening case. There are many innovative ways to do it. 3dCart (3dcart.com) lists the following:

> ▶ Use a company Facebook Page, including a store that attracts fans and lets them "meet" other customers. Then advertise in your Facebook store (see this chapter's closing case).

> ▶ Tweet the online store and stories to your customers.

⟩ Integrate ads into YouTube videos.

⟩ Add a social bookmarking to your product's page for easy return.

⟩ Embrace mobile apps.

⟩ Use social e-mail marketing on Facebook (see facebook.com/sociale-mailmarketing).

⟩ Add a Facebook "Like" button with its sponsored story to your product (e.g., Gatorade brand scored 1.2 million conversations in six months using their "'Mission Control'" campaign).

For details, see 3dcartblog.com/7-social-commerce-tools-to-increase-traffic.

Example 1: Mercedes-Benz. Mercedes-Benz launched a "Tweet Race," which challenges four teams to drive across the country to Dallas, Texas, where the 2011 Super Bowl was played in February 2011. Each team collected Twitter followers with the help of a celebrity coach. Each tweet or retweet earned the team points, as did other activities, such as photographing other Mercedes cars during the road trip. Whichever team had the most points by the end of the trip was declared the winner.

Example 2: Facebook's Sponsored Story. In January 2011, Facebook added an interesting feature called *sponsored story*. When a member chats with friends and one of them notifies that she or he "checked into" a place or "like it," say at Starbucks, a boxed "sponsored story" will appear with the logo of Starbucks (fee paid to Facebook). Furthermore, the name Starbucks will also appear in the user's news feed (another fee paid to Facebook). This feature has a few variations (e.g., uploaded photos). The users have the option to delete the boxed advertisement. This kind of advertisement can increase WOM as well. For details, see adage.com/digital?article_id=148452.

The Changing Rules of Branding

The December 2010 issue of *Harvard Business Review* is dedicated to the new rules of branding introduced by social media. Four articles there discuss how social networks can help you build—or destroy—your brand.

Using Blogs

Blogs are Web 2.0 tools. Most people think of a blog as an online journal. However, for business owners a blog can be a powerful advertisement tool to keep customers "in the loop" about a store's news about upcoming products and updates. Merchants can use a blog to post ideas about how new products can be used, or offer customers updates about new features within a store. Blogs can be added to a company's Facebook page (and other social networks) as well as to the company's in-house store. In addition, companies can place click-on banners on bloggers' pages.

Special Advertising Campaigns

Some retailers have successfully used the fall back-to-school season as a social networking focus. For example, in fall 2008, JCPenney created an online game called Dork-Dodge for girls in Facebook. Players had to navigate their way past undesirable boyfriends to get to their dream date. The retailer also had an interactive video (a modern-day take on the movie *The Breakfast Club*) where users could choose clothes from JCPenney for the actors. Similarly, Sears had a fall 2008 marketing campaign that featured actress Vanessa Hudgens from *High School Musical* playing various characters to show the different styles that could be put together with clothing from Sears.

Shoppers at Sears.com have the option of sharing prom dresses with their Facebook friends using a feature called Prom Premier 2011. Sears supplemented the option with an ad campaign placed on Facebook. Sears is using the program to test the benefits of melding EC with social networking. The company is monitoring the clickstream at the site using Web analytic tools.

Mobile Advertising

Mobile advertising is a rapidly developing area. It refers to advertisements on cell phones and other mobile devices. The competition for mobile ad revenue is intensifying, especially with the increased use of cell phones with access to the Internet. Recently, watching video clips has become popular on cell phones. Advertisers are starting to attach ads to these video clips (see Chapter 8). Finally, advertisers use microblogging, especially Twitter, to reach large audiences. According to Patel (2011), a Nielsen study of iPhone users compared Apple's iAds involving Campbell Soup Company as an advertiser against similar TV ads. The researcher found that those exposed to one of Campbell's iAd campaigns were more than twice as likely to recall it as those who had seen similar TV ads. Indeed the 5-week study showed that consumers shown an iAd remembered the brand "Campbell's" five times more often than TV ad respondents, and the ad messaging three times more often. For details about this study, see adage.com/print?article_id=148630.

Section 7.4 ▶ REVIEW QUESTIONS

1. Describe advertisement in social commerce.
2. Define social ads and social apps.
3. Define viral marketing.
4. Describe viral blogging.
5. Define geolocation and geosocial networks.
6. How does location-based advertising work?
7. Describe how Foursquare works.
8. List some concerns of LBS advertising.
9. Describe viral videos.
10. How is Twitter used for advertisement?
11. Describe mobile advertisement.

7.5 MARKET RESEARCH AND STRATEGY IN SOCIAL NETWORKS

Market research is an important activity in e-commerce (see Chapter 8). Social commerce provides superb opportunities to conduct such research. In addition, it is necessary to conduct research on social commerce itself. Much of this research is done in social networks or by using social software. The diversity of the field can be seen in Exhibit 7.5.

USING SOCIAL NETWORKING FOR MARKET RESEARCH

Traditionally, marketers used demographics (compiled by market research firms) as one of the main tools to identify and target potential customers. Factors such as a person's age, sex, and where they do social networking provide a new opportunity to assess markets in near real time. One major area is viral marketing. Word of mouth has always been one of the most powerful marketing methods—people more often than not use the products that their friends like and recommend. Social media sites can provide this type of data on numerous products and services. Want to find the best laptop computer? Doing a traditional Google search will not get you far. Why? Because you will not get a recommendation. More than likely, you will get a list of review sites.

If you do search in a social networking site, you will find a list of what people think are the best product(s). Because of the open nature of social networking, merchants can easily find their customers and see what they do online and who their friends are. Friends of the merchant's customers are an excellent target market. It may not be easy to conduct social-oriented market research. If you set up a Facebook profile and ask to become a friend with an existing customer, you may or may not be accepted. However, if members like your products (see the Starbucks opening case), they will become your friends. Through this one connection, you have the opportunity to identify their friends and other contacts.

However, it is not a good idea to make unsolicited requests for friendships on these websites. You'll probably get rejected as well as banned from contacting that person again.

EXHIBIT 7.5   A Framework for Social Commerce Market Research

However, if you can come up with good, interesting content, you can send it along to your friends list. If the friends like your information, they will ultimately value you.

There are several ways of doing such research, depending on your products, research budget, and research objective. You may hire a consultant (e.g., Buzzle.com), or you may join a market research-oriented group on LinkedIn and ask for help there. Market research is one step in the strategy needed for success in social commerce. Decker (2010) and Shih (2011) recommend that marketers go through the following seven-step process:

1. Craft messages and decide the social platforms (social networking pages, blogs, forums, etc.) where you can get people talking about your brand, products, or services online.

2. Let these conversations unfold, but also encourage participation through promotions, contests, ratings, and reviews, user-generated content (photo and video) uploads, and whatever else drives social interactions.

3. Analyze the conversations to find out what people are saying and why, to spot trends, and to find out exactly what customers want (as will be described next).

4. Deliver products, services, and promotions that meet the wants and needs of your customers.

5. Continue to get customer feedback, and integrate these findings with sophisticated analytics and marketing measurement tools to calculate the exact return on investment of social programs (see the discussion at the end of this section).

6. Use conversational marketing as a source for market research. How are consumer conversations and other user-generated content analyzed?

7. Find other opportunities for conducting social-based market research.

FEEDBACK FROM CUSTOMERS: CONVERSATIONAL MARKETING

Companies are starting to utilize Web 2.0 tools to get feedback from customers. This trend is referred to as *conversational marketing*. In Chapter 8, we describe customer feedback via questionnaires, focus groups, and other methods. However, Web 2.0 enables customers to supply feedback via blogs (e.g., see bloombergmarketing.blogs.com/Bloomberg_marketing), wikis, online forums, chat rooms, and social networking sites.

Companies are finding that these tools not only generate faster and cheaper results than traditional focus groups, but also foster closer customer relationships. For example, Macy's quickly removed a metal toothbrush holder from its product line after receiving several complaints about it online. Companies like Dell are also learning that conversational marketing including ideas from its in-house social network is less expensive and yields quicker results than focus groups. The computer maker operates a feedback site called IdeaStorm, where it allows customers to suggest and vote on improvements in its offerings.

With *enterprise feedback management*, companies are interested not only in collecting information, but also in the interaction between customers and company employees and in properly distributing customer feedback throughout the organization.

According to Gogoi (2007), retailers know that customers, especially the younger and more Net-savvy ones, want to be heard, and they also want to hear what others like them say. Increasingly, retailers are opening up their websites to customers, letting them post product reviews, ratings, and in some cases photos and videos. The result is that *customer reviews* are emerging as a prime place for online shoppers to visit.

Illustrative Examples

Example 1. Cookshack (and many other companies that operate online forums) invites customers to ask and answer questions about barbecue sauces, beef smokers, barbecue ovens, and cooking techniques (forum.cookshack.com/groupee). The community helps save money by freeing up customer service personnel who used to answer such questions by phone or e-mail. The community also fosters customer loyalty.

Example 2. Del Monte, through its "I Love My Dog" program, gathers data from pet owners that can help shape its marketing decisions. Its private social network helps Del Monte make decisions about products, test-market campaigns, understand buying preferences, and generate discussions about new items and product changes.

According to an eVoc Insights study (Gogoi 2007), 47 percent of consumers consult reviews before making an online purchase, and 63 percent of shoppers are more likely to purchase from a site if it has ratings and reviews. Negative reviews not only help the retailer address a defect or poorly manufactured item, they also help decrease the number of returns. People are less likely to return an item due to personal expectation because reviews give realistic views of a product and its characteristics. These market research studies help companies to devise strategies.

SOCIAL ANALYTICS AND SOCIAL INTELLIGENCE IN SOCIAL COMMERCE

In Sections 7.2 and 7.3 we described how consumers write reviews and ratings and how they conduct conversations.

Customer sentiment expressed on Twitter, Facebook, wikis, RSS feeds, blogs, and other tools represent a potential gold mine for companies. The full view of customers is meant to help create personalized customer experiences and improve customer relations (Section 7.6). These activities generate a considerable amount of data that needs to be analyzed so that management can conduct better marketing campaigns, product design, and service offerings. In addition monitoring Weblogs and analyzing them can be used as a basis for marketing advertising strategies in general (see Chapter 8). The data monitoring and collection, its analysis, and the resultant strategic decisions are combined in a process known as social intelligence (in analogy with business intelligence, see Online Tutorial T8).

SOCIAL ANALYTICS FOR SOCIAL INTELLIGENCE IN SOCIAL COMMERCE

Social analytics describes the process of measuring, analyzing, and interpreting the results of interactions and associations among people, topics, and ideas. These interactions may occur on social software applications used in the workplace, in internally or externally facing communities or on the social Web. Social analytics is an umbrella term that includes a number of specialized analysis techniques such as social filtering, social network analysis, sentiment analysis, and social-media analytics. Social network analysis tools are useful for examining social structure and interdependencies as well as the work patterns of individuals, groups, or organizations. Social network analysis involves collecting data from multiple sources, identifying relationships, and evaluating the impact, quality, or effectiveness of a relationship. Social analysis is frequently done in social commerce to check what is going on in communities, what costumers are talking about and much more. Here we present only the topic of analyzing consumer conversations and user-generated content.

Social Intelligence and Its Components

Social intelligence refers to the ability of humans to interact with each other effectively. Social intelligence is what a company needs to maintain meaningful, productive relationships with its current and potential customers, employees, partners, and any other relevant group interacting with the organization as well as with each other through social channels. The process of deploying social intelligence is not merely interactions; it is the ability to find hidden values in the social interactions and taking appropriate actions based on the findings. Learning the hidden value and meaning of social data is achieved using social analytics, but social intelligence takes it a step beyond by unlocking this value and generating actionable insights that impact business strategy. From a technical perspective social intelligence refers to the tools and practices companies use to aggregate and analyze social data, which is collected by social media monitoring tools and social analytics engines, with existing data, such as from social reviews, social conversations, or social CRM. This aggregated data is then integrated with systems of records and real-time analytics engines. This process brings forth previously unknown or seemingly unimportant or unrelated details about the business' customers, products, campaigns and even competitors. The end result: actionable insights.

ANALYZING CONSUMER CONVERSATIONS AND OTHER USER GENERATED CONTENT

According to Jayanti (2010), owing to their untainted, unfiltered, and unbiased nature, online consumer conversations have the potential to help marketers discover the right questions for conducting market research and to understand emerging issues, follow brand sentiments, benchmark companies against major competitors, detect damaging issues or rumors, spur product development, gather product suggestions, and discover alternate uses and enhancements volunteered by consumers. This requires appropriate analysis.

Such analysis can provide companies (vendors) with an entirely new and holistic view of consumer opinions and the important role they play throughout the purchase funnel, and in overall brand health. For example, a brand marketer will be able to understand how consumer reviews of their newly launched product indicate a successful launch campaign or early warning signs of negative sentiments that will impact sales of the product. Vendors will also be able to compare these online reviews to those conversations occurring across other social media platforms in order to understand the interplay between the two. One approach is to use data, text, and Web mining.

Tools for Mining Social Media for Consumer Trends

There are many ways to analyze what is going on in social networks and in conducting social networking activities. Generic e-commerce tools such as Web mining and text mining (e.g., Turban, et al. [2011a] and Online Tutorial T8) can be used here too. There are several other tools for doing data, text, and Web mining in social networks.

Example 1. IBM SPSS Modeler is a predictive analytics software tool that measures trends in consumer views of products and services. Modeler also analyzes emoticons and common texting slang terms. The software covers 180 verticals including life sciences, banking/insurance, and electronics. There are 400,000 industry-specific terms that can be analyzed (e.g., floating rate is understood as relevant to mortgage loan). The software can be used to analyze text gathered from *social media sources*, including Twitter, Facebook, blogs, wikis, and RSS feeds. Other major vendors for analytic tools are Clarabridge, Attensity, SAS, and SAP.

Example 2. Wendy's International uses software to sift through over 500,000 customer messages the fast-food chain collects each year. Using Clarabridge text analytics software, Wendy's analyzes comments from its online notes, e-mails, receipt-based surveys, and social media. Before, the company used a combination of spreadsheets and keyword searches to review comments in what it describes as a slow and expensive manual approach. The new software lets Wendy's track customer experiences at the store level within minutes.

Example 3. Bazaarvoice and Nielsen joined forces and are conducting complex analyses. Their clients can automatically feed all consumer-generated ratings and reviews collected by Bazaarvoice into Nielsen's My BuzzMetrics, where the data can be easily analyzed through a customizable dashboard. Clients can also receive custom analytic reports, which include customers' rating and review data from Bazaarvoice as well as the ability to benchmark their data against other social media data harvested by Nielsen. Using the combined method can help vendors know who their most vocal and influential customers are. Also, the analysis can address questions such as: Does the customers' feedback represent a larger trend that product design and marketing must address? Do some negative reviews or blog posts indicate an emerging brand reputation threat that needs to be stopped now?

CONDUCTING MARKET RESEARCH USING THE MAJOR SOCIAL NETWORKS

Market research can be conducted within the framework of social network sites, in situations where social software tools are deployed as well as where social presentation sites such as Twitter, YouTube, and Flicker are involved. Here are a few representative examples.

Using Facebook for Market Research

As you'll see in the closing case, Facebook is doing or enabling more and more commerce activities. Here are some relevant suggestions for merchants for conducting market research by using Facebook:

▶ Get feedback from your Facebook fans (and their friends if possible) on any advertising campaign, market research, improvement in product/process, etc. It is like using a free focus group! There are a couple of ways you can set this up. You can simply do a status update with a link to the material to be checked by the fans. Facebook will pull all the images that appear on that page and will allow you to choose which thumbnail to use. Or you can set up a poll (either as its own tab or in the Boxes section) and drive people to that page through a status update. People love sharing their opinions, and people value companies that care about their customers' opinions. (You may use Facebook's voting tool as well.)

▶ Do the same for any change, including discontinuing an advertisement, deleting a product/service, etc.

▶ Test market messages. Provide two or three options and ask fans which one they prefer and why. Tell the fans that you love their contributions.

▶ Use Facebook for survey invitations (i.e., to recruit participants). Essentially, turn Facebook into a giant panel, and ask Facebook users to come and participate in a survey. Facebook offers a self-service model for displaying ads, and ads can be invitations to come and take a survey (not just playing FarmVille). Facebook also allows you to target your audience very specifically based on traditional demographic models (age, gender, sex, etc.). For step-by-step instructions on how to recruit users to take a Facebook survey, see researchaccess.com/2010/06/social-media-research-using-facebook-for-survey-invitations-and-market-research.

Using Twitter for Market Research

Twitter is a rich source of instantly updated information. It is easy to stay updated on an incredibly wide variety of topics. Just follow @marketresearch. The fact that customers, prospects, and industry thought leaders are all using Twitter makes it a valuable tool for monitoring the topics and concerns being discussed. This is a great potential source of new product/service enhancement ideas as well as topics for blog posts, white papers, or other content. Here is what you can do:

▶ Visit search.twitter.com. Enter a company's Twitter name. Not only can you follow what companies are saying, you can also follow what *everyone is saying to them*. It's like hacking into their e-mail database, only completely legitimate. Monitoring @ replies to your competitors and their employees will help you develop your own Twitter strategy by allowing you to see (a) what they are doing, and, more importantly, (b) what people think about it. You can also find the company's response.

▶ Take advantage of the tools that enable you to find people in the industries they operate in. Use search.twitter.com to monitor industry-specific keywords. Check out twellow.com. This site automatically categorizes a Twitter user into one to three industries based on their bio and tweets, and allows users to set up to 13 categories or industries themselves manually.

▶ Want to see what topic is on most people's minds today? Look at the chart on TweetStats: It will show you the most frequently used words so you can be a part of those conversations. For other instructions, see ehow.com/how_5066590_use-twitter-conduct-market-research.html.

Customer Feedback with Twitter. An increasing number of companies are utilizing Twitter to solicit information from customers and interact with them. Several examples can be found at business.twitter. com/twitter101. They include Dell (connecting with customers), JetBlue (learning about customers), Teusner Wines (gathering feedback, sharing information), and Pepsi (fast response time in dealing with complaints).

Using LinkedIn for Market Research

There are many ways one can use LinkedIn for doing market research. One way is to post a question (e.g., solicit advice) regarding the topic of issue you are interested in. You may get a better result if you go to a specific LinkedIn group. For a comprehensive list of LinkedIn discussion groups related to market research, go to quirks.com/resources/market_research_linkedin.aspx.

PUTTING IT ALL TOGETHER

Companies can use several networks, including an in-house one, to run marketing research.

Example: Mountain Dew. Mountain Dew has done a great job in the past appealing to consumers who were looking for high-caffeine beverages, mostly video game lovers and extreme sports enthusiasts. Yet the brand sought to unite all of its customers into one community with its Dewmocracy contests, which let consumers pick the newest flavor.

Several brands have used social networks like Facebook to help pick new flavors, but Mountain Dew is slowly expanding its scale from the most-dedicated fans to the public-at-large. The first step of its market research involved sending seven flavors of soda to 50 Dew fanatics, who were also given cameras and told to debate and show their love (or dislike) for the brand on a video. The cameras were a great idea because it made the social media effort more personable. Rather than just looking at static images or tweets, Dew fans could see like-minded fanatics in action. One young man proved his allegiance by brushing his teeth with the soda. After narrowing the seven flavors to three, Mountain Dew turned to its Dew Labs Community, a 4,000-person group of passionate soda fans. Those fans then created nearly every element of the three sodas, including color, name, packaging, and marketing campaigns. After that process was complete, the three flavors were made available in stores for a limited time, with the general public electing a winner via online voting.

What Dew did was a little different from Starbucks and Dell, described earlier. Whereas these two brands set up sites soliciting ideas from all consumers, Dew began its promotion by reaching out to its most dedicated, loyal consumers offline, and then gave that offline community a place to assemble its testimonials and feedback. The Dewmocracy campaign used Facebook, Twitter, and YouTube just like the other brands used these social networks to unite consumers through a common interest. For details, see Hespos (2010).

Section 7.5 ▶ REVIEW QUESTIONS

1. How can a social network be used to conduct market research?
2. How is conversational marketing used for market research?
3. Describe social analytics.
4. Define and describe social intelligence.
5. What is data, text, and Web mining used for?
6. What can be mined in social media?
7. How is Facebook used for market research?
8. How is Twitter used for market research?

7.6 SOCIAL CUSTOMER SERVICE AND CRM

The customer service profession is undergoing significant transformation, as both the way that customer service professionals do business and the way that customers interact with companies adapt to a newly connected world. So-called "social" technologies have vastly altered both the expectations of customers and the capabilities of corporations.

At first one may think that there is not much connection between customer service and social commerce. The opposite is true.

HOW SOCIAL NETWORKING IMPROVES CUSTOMER SERVICE

It is said that one angry tweet can torpedo a brand, but one tweet can correct a problem (Bernoff and Schadler 2010). Let's examine how Facebook helped to change policy for one company.

Example: How Facebook's Chorus Ended the Instrument Luggage Ban at Qantas Airline of Australia. Qantas airlines had a policy that required large musical instruments to be stored in the cargo hold, sometimes causing damages to the instruments. In fall 2010, after suffering $1,200 damage to her saxophone, Jamie Oehlers of Australia organized a Facebook campaign to persuade the airline to reverse the policy. When one person complains, he or she will get a nice letter, but the policy will not change. But when more than 8,700 people joined forces on Facebook (including members of the country's symphony orchestras), posting stories and pictures of instruments that had been damaged in the cargo hold, and saying they will boycott the airline, Qantas was listening carefully. Qantas announced that they listened to their customers and changed the policy. The new policy allows small musical instruments as carry-on baggage (*Taipei Times* 2011).

This story is not unique; similar stories appear in the media frequently. In another example [Olson (2009)], Maytag (washing machines) only paid attention to a customer after she tweeted her nightmare experience with the company. Within a day, her problem had been solved. In the past, customers' complaints usually received low attention (or no attention) even when customers threatened to publish the complaint on the Internet. But today, when you say, "I will organize a campaign against you on Facebook, or on Twitter," you can be sure someone will listen.

Methods and Guidelines for Service

Customers are now empowered! The question then becomes: How does a company serve the social media customer?

Companies are looking for an answer to this question not only because they are afraid of the negative comments posted by social network members, but also because they see an opportunity to involve customers proactively to reduce problems by improved customer service (Baker 2010). Furthermore, companies can improve customers' loyalty, make their own customer service people happier, and get more respect from customers. Customer service and CRM is practiced in organizations by several departments, and these organizations need to integrate new guidelines with the traditional ones. See Ogneva (2010), Bernoff and Schadler (2010), and mashable.com/social-customer-service.

HOW TO SERVE THE SOCIAL CUSTOMERS

The empowered customers are referred to as **social customers**. These are customers that are members of social networks, do social shopping, and understand their rights and how to use the wisdom and power of the crowds and communities to their benefit. Social customers are choosing how they interact with companies and companies' brands, and this poses a challenge: a challenge of data volume, dynamic channels, and elevated expectations. The social customer is vested and participatory, and has active involvement within the business ecosystem, not just as purchasers but as advocates and influencers as well. Individuals are influenced by friends, friends' friends, and friends' friends' friends. Merchants must understand how these customers (and their numbers are increasing exponentially) differ from conventional customers, and provide them with appropriate customer service. Procedures, guidelines, and software are available for social CRM.

Social CRM

Customer relationship management (CRM) is a customer service approach that focuses on building long-term and sustainable customer relationships that add value both to the customers and the merchants. When delivered online it is referred to as e-CRM (Online Tutorial T1). The first generation of e-CRM focused heavily on data, task, and transaction management. CRM was, and is, internally focused, with an emphasis on specific processes, such as customer service, sales, and marketing touchpoints, and optimization of those processes.

What Is Social CRM?

Social CRM (SCRM) is a customer engagement strategy in support of companies' defined goals and objectives toward optimizing the customer experience. Success requires a focus on people, processes, and technology associated with customer touchpoints and interactions.

SCRM is an extension of CRM, not a replacement, and among the important benefits is that it adds benefits to the users (increased adoption) and the customers. It is the one part of the social business strategy that addresses how companies need to adapt to the *social* customer and the expectations these customers have with respect to companies they do business with. SCRM was evolved from CRM (and e-CRM) in a process that is illustrated in Exhibit 7.6. For a detailed presentation of this process and an overview of social CRM, download the "Guide to Understanding Social CRM" at chessmediagroup.com/ resource/guide-to-understanding-social-crm and Lieberman (2010). For a survey about the extent of the use of social CRM, see Techdirt Insight Community (2008).

---

social customers
Members of social networks who do social shopping and understand their rights and how to use the wisdom and power of crowdsourcing and communities to their benefit.

customer relationship management (CRM)
A customer service approach that focuses on building long-term and sustainable customer relationships that add value both to the customers and the merchants.

social CRM (SCRM)
A customer engagement strategy in support of companies' defined goals and objectives toward optimizing the customer experience. Success requires a focus on people, processes, and technology associated with customer touch-points and interactions.

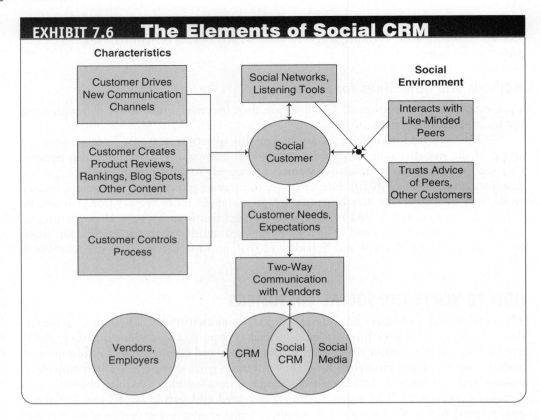

EXHIBIT 7.6   The Elements of Social CRM

Social CRM in the Enterprise and B2B Environments

Similar to how Facebook and Twitter have changed the way people communicate and interact within personal social networks, salespeople need comparable applications that facilitate collaboration within enterprise social networks and increase their sales effectiveness. They need applications that support the way they work to increase their efficacy in the critical activities that underline their daily business routines. For an overview of the challenges salespeople face, the growing social commerce trend in the enterprise, and the drivers for a new breed of social applications that complement traditional CRM systems to help salespeople close more deals quickly, see Techdirt Insight Community (2008).

Social CRM offers the following benefits:

▶ Provides for business collaboration at its best.
▶ Provides focused, intuitive, and easy-to-use applications.
▶ Puts contextual data only a fingertip away.
▶ Enables users to find sales leads quickly and easily.
▶ Converts leads to opportunities with more effective campaigns.
▶ Enables finding the right messages to win deals.

For details, visit oracle.com/socialCRM. For a comprehensive case study, see Egeland (2009).

IMPLEMENTATION OF SOCIAL CUSTOMER SERVICE AND CRM

There are many models and methods for implementing social customer service.
Example: How Safeway Provides Social Customer Service. Safeway, a large grocery chain, has a customer club. Members can get in-store discounts. Members also get e-mails

with coupons and a description of what is on sale as well as an online newsletter with health news and recipes, shopping tips, etc. To extend this service, Safeway invites you to become a Facebook Fan and follow the company on Twitter. This way you will be the first to know about exclusive promotions and savings. Plus, you'll be able to connect and share with other Safeway shoppers.

Also, you can visit the company's blog, *Today at Safeway!* Team members are posting items from Floral, Bakery, and other departments throughout the store. You can hear from Safeway's experts about nutrition, environmental sustainability, and more.

The Safeway blog is a free way to promote active discussion among the Safeway community. All comments are moderated by Safeway and will not be posted if they contain offensive language, private or personal information, hateful or violent content, personal attacks, self-serving or promotion of goods, sites, or services. Members are asked to post only original content.

How Social CRM Works—Problems and Solutions

The following five real-world examples are based on Gago (2010).

1. **Cordiant. The Problem:** Cordiant, an enterprise software company, needed a better way to coordinate the needs of individuals involved in the product requirements process.

   The Solution: They created an online community where employees, developers, customers, and partners can collaborate about product development. The feedback was very positive, resulting in 15 successful collaborative product releases.

2. **Linksys. The Problem:** Linksys, a Cisco division, needed to reduce costs while upholding high levels of customer support.

   The Solution: The company partnered with Lithium (a social CRM consultant) to create an online support community. The deployment of the community increased self-service participation, which reduced the need for costly phone support. Linksys reported savings in the millions.

3. **Enterasys. The Problem:** Enterasys Networks has hundreds of employees stationed around the globe. It required a social networking tool that would eliminate geographical boundaries and let its employees communicate in real time.

   The Solution: Enterasys decided to deploy Salesforce.com's Chatter (see Online Tutorial T10) application. The company experienced improved service performance, thanks to real-time collaboration on service issues. Additionally, the sales team was able to work more closely together and close a record number of deals in the first quarter after implementing Chatter.

4. **H&R Block. The Problem:** H&R Block wanted to find out what their customers were talking about in order to anticipate problems that arose.

   The Solution: The company decided to use Radian6's social monitoring technology to achieve its goal. The trend analysis tool allowed the company to drill down into community conversations and see which topics were creating the most buzz. This gave better insight, enabling H&R Block to be more proactive in their customer service.

5. **Pepperdine University. The Problem:** Pepperdine University was looking for a better way to encourage collaboration among students, staff, and faculty.

   The Solution: The University partnered with Yammer Inc. to create a Twitter-like environment where users can interact and communicate in real-time and with more transparency. The university saw a significant increase in community participation and collaboration.

SOME MORE ADVANCED APPLICATIONS

There are many advanced applications to better serve customers.

Example 1: How Best Buy Used Twitter to Provide Real-Time Customer Service. Best Buy is a large appliances retailer. Best Buy wanted to be a source for customers beyond their experience in the stores. The company developed a unique way to connect with customers through their Twitter's @twelpforce account to provide real-time customer service.

Best Buy empowered the "blue shirt" members of its Geek Squad tech support service and corporate employees to staff its @twelpforce, and any Best Buy employee working on company time, can provide answers by using an @ reply to the customer. About 4,000 employees signed up to answer questions. By tagging their tweets with Twelpforce, the answer is sent through the @twelpforce account, allowing anyone to search the feed for topics they are researching. Between December 15, 2010, and February 1, 2011, @twelpforce provided over 38,000 answers to customer inquiries.

Example 2: A Lesson in Customer Service. In December 2010, Groupon featured a discount to a restaurant delivery service in Tokyo for the New Year. The promotion was wildly successful as more than 500 "Groupons" were sold. Unfortunately, the restaurant was not prepared for the success and was unable to accommodate all the orders. Deliveries were late, and many of them were in "terrible condition."

Andrew Mason, the CEO of Groupon, took on the responsibility. He acknowledged that he contracted to an organization that was not prepared to deal with the volume of the Groupon promotion. Groupon refunded money back to the customers who bought the coupons and gave away vouchers for future business. Groupon also created a video that featured a public apology about the incident. It was sincere and informative, explaining exactly what happened and held nothing back.

For additional examples, see thesocialcustomer.com.

Social Networking Helps Customer Service in Small Companies

Most of the examples provided so far dealt with large companies. What about the small ones? Obviously there are some applications the SMEs cannot afford. But many others they can.

Example. Teusner Wines (teusner.com.au) is a small boutique winery (three employees) in Australia. Using Twitter, the company's one-person marketing department:

- Initiates online conversations about wine with influential people in the wine business.
- Sends tweets to people he found talking about Teusner Wines, praising them for trying the wines.
- Starts to build trust with customers via conversations.
- Invites people to tour the winery and taste the wines with an excellent response.
- Advises potential customers in the United States and Canada where they can buy the wine.
- Collects real-time feedback from customers.
- Encourages customer-to-customer conversations.
- Posts customer reviews on Twitter.
- Shares all information.

All this was done in a tiny company at virtually no cost. For details, see business. twitter.com/twitter101/case_teusner.

Section 7.6 ▶ REVIEW QUESTIONS

1. Define social customers and describe their properties.
2. Why and how are customers empowered by social networks?
3. What are the needs of social customers?
4. How are these needs fulfilled?
5. Describe social CRM; how does it differ from traditional CRM?

7.7 ENTERPRISE APPLICATIONS: FROM COMMUNITY BUILDING TO COLLABORATION

Social computing and networking is rapidly spreading in organizations with new applications of social commerce appearing regularly. Driven by f-commerce and the exponential growth of Twitter and LinkedIn, corporations are rushing to get involved and they do it in several innovative ways, as will be described in this section. According to IDC's Social

Business Survey (Valentine 2010), 57 percent of U.S. companies implemented enterprise social media for business purposes by 2010. This can fundamentally alter how businesses interact with employees, customers, and partners. The enterprise social platform market is forecasted to reach nearly $2 billion a year. A core concept in enterprise social applications is business networks.

A BUSINESS NETWORK

A *business network* is a group of people who have some kind of commercial or business relationship; for example, the relationships between sellers and buyers, buyers among themselves, buyers and suppliers, and professionals and their colleagues. Such networks of people can form **business social networks**, a business network that is built on social relationships, and can exist offline or online. Business social networking can take place outside the traditional corporate physical environments. For example, public places such as airports or golf courses provide opportunities to make new face-to-face business contacts if an individual has good social skills. Similarly, the Internet is also proving to be a good place to network. The most popular business-oriented social network service is LinkedIn (see Case 7.1).

business social network
A social network whose primary objective is to facilitate business connections and activities.

CASE 7.1
EC Application

LINKEDIN: THE BUSINESS-ORIENTED SOCIAL NETWORK

LinkedIn is a global business-oriented social networking site (in six languages) mainly used for professional networking. By February 2011, it had more than 90 million registered users spanning 200 countries around the world. LinkedIn can be used to find jobs, people, potential clients, service providers, subject experts, and other business opportunities. The company became profitable in 2010 with revenue exceeding $200 million and a net income of over $2.5 million. The company went on the stock market in 2011.

A major purpose of LinkedIn is to allow registered users to maintain a list of contacts of people they know and trust in business (see *en.wikipedia.org/wiki/LinkedIn*). The people in each list are called *connections*. Users can invite anyone, whether they are a LinkedIn user or not, to become a connection. When people join, they create a profile that summarizes their professional accomplishments. The profile makes it possible to find and be found by former colleagues, clients, and partners, even years after people left an organization and worked for other companies.

A *contact network* consists of users' direct connections, each of their connections' connections (called second-degree connections), the connections of second-degree connections (called third-degree connections), and so forth. The contact network makes it possible for a professional to gain an introduction to someone he or she wishes to know through a mutual, trusted contact. LinkedIn's officials are members and have hundreds of connections each (see Elad [2008] and *linkedin.com*).

The "gated-access approach," where contact with any professional requires either a preexisting relationship or the intervention of a contact of theirs, is intended to build trust among the service's users. LinkedIn participates in the EU Safe Harbor Privacy Framework.

The searchable LinkedIn groups feature allows users to establish new business relationships by joining alumni, industry, or professional, and other relevant, groups. It has close to 100,000 groups in its directory.

LinkedIn is especially useful in helping job seekers and employers find one another. Job seekers can list their résumés, search for open positions, check company profiles, and even review the profiles of hiring managers. Job seekers can also discover inside connections with existing contacts who can introduce them to a specific hiring manager. They can even see who has viewed their profiles.

Companies can use the site to post jobs and find and recruit employees, especially those who may not be actively searching for a new position.

Smart Ways to Use LinkedIn
LinkedIn is known mostly as a place for recruitment, job search, and making connections. However, there are many opportunities for doing marketing, advertising, sales, and more. For a list, see *linkedintelligence.com/smart-ways-to-use-linkedin*.

As of January 2007, LinkedIn featured "LinkedIn Answers." As the name suggests, the service is similar to Answers.com or Yahoo! Answers. The service allows LinkedIn users to ask questions for the community to answer. LinkedIn Answers is free. The identity of the people asking and answering questions is known, so further communication is possible.

In mid-2008, LinkedIn launched LinkedIn DirectAds as a form of sponsored advertising. It is similar to Google's AdWords. For a comparison with AdWords, see *shoutex.com/blog/linkedin-directads-vs-google-adwords-2*.

LinkedIn has also joined forces with the financial news site CNBC. The deal integrates LinkedIn's networking

(continued)

CASE 7.1 (continued)

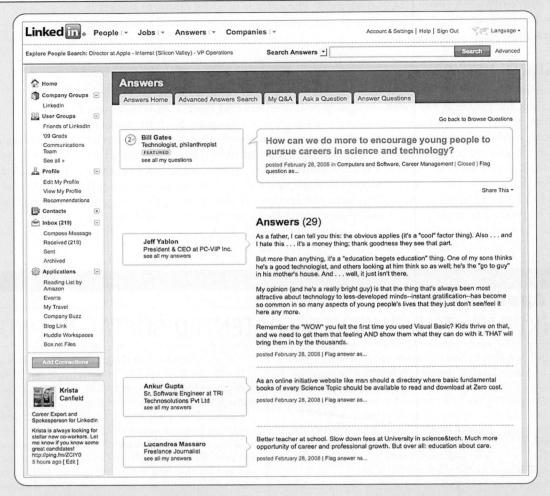

Source: LinkedIn.com. Used with permission.

functionality into CNBC.com, allowing LinkedIn users to share and discuss financial and other news with their professional contacts. Community-generated content from LinkedIn, such as survey and poll results, are broadcast on CNBC, and CNBC provides LinkedIn with programming, articles, blogs, financial data, and video content. CNBC is able to draw insights from LinkedIn's global user base to generate new types of business content for CNBC to broadcast.

In January 2011, LinkedIn announced the company's plan to raise money on the stock market as an IPO. The shares of Monster, a major online recruiting company, plunged more than 100 percent on January 28 due to fear that LinkedIn would take business from Monster. In June 2011, LinkedIn successfully launched its IPO.

Mobile Applications
A mobile version of the site was launched in February 2008, which offers access to a reduced feature set over a mobile device. The mobile service is available in six languages: Chinese, English, French, German, Japanese, and Spanish.

The following are some useful resources on LinkedIn: *blog. linkedin.com*, *mylinkedinpowerforum.com*, and *linkedinsearch. com/search*.

Sources: Compiled from Elad (2008), *en.wikipedia.org/wiki/LinkedIn*, and *linkedin.com* (both accessed February 2011).

Questions

1. Enter *linkedin.com* and explore the site. Why do you think the site is so successful?

2. What features are related to recruiting and job finding?

3. How does LinkedIn Answers work? Try to use it by posting a query. Report the results.

4. Conduct an investigation to find the revenue model of the company.

5. Several companies have attempted to clone LinkedIn with little success. Why do you think LinkedIn is dominating?

Commercial activities related to social networks are on the rise. An increasing number of people and companies are engaged in *business-oriented social networking*, which refers to business activities, especially marketing and operations, by which business opportunities are created through social networks of businesspeople. For example, people might offer to help others find sales connections rather than "cold-calling" on prospects (see en.wikipedia.org/wiki/Business_networking).

THE BENEFITS OF ENTERPRISE BUSINESS SOCIAL NETWORKING

Social networking appeals to business users for many reasons. The software makes it easy to find people and information, understand the relationships and communication patterns that make a company tick, and create a common culture across large organizations.

The major reasons to use or deploy business social networking are:

▶ To build better customer and employee relationships
▶ To increase revenue
▶ To facilitate recruiting and retention
▶ To increase business and marketing opportunities
▶ To build and nurture a community
▶ To reduce operation and travel costs
▶ To improve knowledge management (increase speed and access to knowledge)
▶ To gain expert advice (internally and externally)
▶ To improve knowledge management
▶ To reduce communication and improve collaboration

The introduction of a social networking site inside of a large enterprise enables a new method of communication between colleagues, encouraging both personal and professional sharing inside the protected walls of a company intranet. Professionals use internal social networking to build stronger bonds with others and to reach out to employees they do not know. Their motivations in doing this include connecting on a personal level with coworkers, advancing their careers with the company, and campaigning for their projects.

Social networking can be done by businesses either in public or in private social networks.

For details of these and other benefits, see Bughin and Chui (2010) and the slideshow at **cioinsight.com/c/a/Past-News/5-Reasonsto-Deploy-a-Corporate-Social-Network**.

BUSINESS-ORIENTED PUBLIC SOCIAL NETWORKING

Social networking activities can be conducted both in public and/or private social networking sites. For example, LinkedIn is a business-oriented public network, whereas Facebook is primarily a public social network for social-oriented activities. However, Facebook allows its members to conduct business-oriented activities. "My Starbucks Idea" is an example of a private social network.

The following are some examples of business-oriented public social networks:

▶ **Ryze.** Similar to LinkedIn, with Ryze (ryze.com) users create profiles that can be viewed and invite friends and business associates into special-interest "tribes."
▶ **The Business Social Network.** A social network site (thebusinesssocialnetwork.com) that connects businesspeople who want to make connections and identify businesses with similar goals, products, or services. It is a clone of LinkedIn, operating mainly in the United Kingdom.
▶ **Yammer.** Yammer (yammer.com) is a clone of Facebook for business. It is used by more than 1.5 million people in over 90,000 companies. It is mainly a communication and collaboration helper.

▶ **Viadeo.** Viadeo (viadeo.com) is a network of several million professionals, mostly in Europe and China. Its primary use is for connecting with business contacts. It is a clone of LinkedIn, with an emphasis on localization.

▶ **APSense.** APSense (apsense.com) is a business social network where people get paid to come together to share their business through networking, and deciding, exploring, and creating quality business content. Users build their own social networks by inviting their friends to APSense. Friends of friends can also be placed in users' networks.

Several other networks similar to LinkedIn are: Wealink (wealink.com) in China, Rediff Connexions (connexions.rediff.com) in India, International Jobs and Internships (ihipo.com) in Mexico, and Moikrug (moikrug.ru) in Russia. There are other public business-oriented networks that focus on entrepreneurs.

ENTREPRENEUR NETWORKS

Some business-oriented public network concentrates on entrepreneurial activities. A few examples are listed next.

▶ **Biznik** (biznik.com). Biznik is a community of entrepreneurs and small business owners dedicated to helping each other succeed through the premise that collaboration beats competition. The site embraces people who are building real businesses and sharing ideas, not just looking for their next job. All Biznik members use their real names and provide real data. Biznik editors review profiles for compliance with this policy. It is the place where honest conversations about small business and entrepreneurship are taking place. Biznik is not just online; it includes localized face-to-face meetings in order to build real, lasting business relationships.

▶ **E. Factor** (efactor.com). Over 750,000 members in 153 countries and 99 industries use this global network made by and for entrepreneurs. Members connect with like-minded people and with investors.

▶ **Startup Nation** (startupnation.com). Starting and running a new business is not always straightforward. There are plenty of things that can go wrong. Having a community of start-up owners and experts to rely on for those situations can be very helpful. That is what Startup Nation is all about.

▶ **Entrepreneur Connect** (econnect.entrepreneur.com). Entrepreneur Connect is one of the best portals for small businesses and start-ups. It not only has a lot of useful information for business owners, but it also has a great community for you to take advantage of to connect with fellow business owners from around the globe.

ENTERPRISE PRIVATE SOCIAL NETWORKS

An increasing number of companies have created their own in-house, private social networks for their employees, former employees, business partners, and/or customers. Such networks are considered to be "behind the firewall," and are often referred to as *corporate social networks*. Such networks come in several formats, depending on their purpose, the industry, the country, and so forth.

Taxonomy of Social Enterprise Applications

The following terms are frequently used in enterprise networking. Most will be discussed in this chapter.

1. **Networking and community building.** Networking and community building among employees, executives, business partners, and other stakeholders—both within and outside an organization—who might be mobile, geographically dispersed across several functional silos, regions, and nations, using social networks, blogs, and microblogs such as Twitter.

2. **Crowdsourcing.** Gathering ideas, insights, and feedback from crowds—customers and the public—using tools such as Salesforce's Ideas, Uservoice, and Getsatisfaction (Section 7.8).

3. **Social collaboration.** Collaborative work and problem solving using wikis, blogs, instant messaging, collaborative office, and other special purpose Web-based collaboration platforms such as Laboranova.

4. **Social publishing.** Employees and others creating, either individually or collaboratively, and posting contents—photos, videos, presentation slides, and documents—into a member's or a community's accessible content repository such as YouTube, Flicker, SlideShare, and DocStoc.

5. **Social views and feedback.** Getting feedback and opinions from the community on specific items, as witnessed on LinkedIn, Facebook, YouTube, Flicker, Amazon, and Yahoo!.

6. **Social intelligence and social analytics.** Monitoring, analyzing, and interpreting conversations, interactions, and associations among people, topics, and ideas to gain insights. Social analytics techniques include social filtering, social network analysis, and sentiment analysis. Social network analysis tools are useful for examining social structure and interdependencies, understanding relationship and work patterns of individuals and groups, and for discovering people and expertise.

Characteristics of Enterprise Social Networks

Social networks have gone behind the firewalls of enterprises. Businesses are now using dedicated social network–like platforms for communication, networking, and *community building* among their employees and business partners.

These enterprise social networks let employees display their profiles and connect with one another, integrating the workforce in unforeseen ways. By enabling connections among employees, a company can establish virtual teams, bring new employees up to speed, improve collaboration, and increase retention among people who hadn't felt a strong sense of belonging (Brandel 2008). Easier, quicker, and closer connections among people in an enterprise facilitates natural and better cross divisional collaboration leading to greater innovation. Employees can interact with other people on a social level that's typically absent in large organizations or when people work remotely.

Guidelines for Effective Social Networking

The following are representative examples for guidelines created for effective enterprise social networking:

- Allow employees to collaborate and communicate in an employee-driven system (e.g., see this chapter's closing case).
- Promote the use of enterprise wikis via demonstrations.
- Set up internal blogs and incorporate them into internal directories so users can see who has a blog.
- Set up enterprise social bookmarking systems so users can see what sort of content their colleagues are tagging.
- CIOs should be involved from the beginning to make sure the right infrastructure and tools are in place.

For additional information, see socialcomputingjournal.com; for a demo on enterprise social networking, see news.zdnet.com/2422-19178_22-246969.html. For additional tips and sources, see Kolakowski (2009).

An Example of Enterprise Networks

In the opening case, we introduced Starbucks' private network. Many other companies have enterprise networks of all kinds. Here is an example:

Example: IBM'S SocialBlue (formerly Beehive). IBM's SocialBlue is an internal social networking site that gives IBM employees a rich connection to the people they work with on both a personal and a professional level. SocialBlue helps employees make new connections, track current friends and coworkers, and renew contacts with people they have worked with in the past. When employees join SocialBlue, they get a profile page. They can use the status message field and the free-form "About Me" section on their profile page to let other people at IBM know where they are, what they are doing, and even what they are thinking. Employees can use SocialBlue to find out what team members they spent late nights with a couple of years ago working toward a deadline are doing now by checking out their coworkers' profiles.

Employees can also use SocialBlue to post photos, create lists, and organize events. If users are hosting an event, they can create an event page in SocialBlue and invite people to attend. The page can be a place to spread the buzz about the event and get people talking about it through the comments feature.

Users can create top-five lists, called "hive fives," to share their thoughts on any topic they are passionate about. For example, they can add a "hive five" list that outlines their ideas about their projects, and then invite their team members to examine the list and voice their opinions.

SocialBlue can also come in handy when preparing for conference calls. If users do not know the other people on the call, they can check out the participants' SocialBlue profiles beforehand and find out if they have common interests, either work-related or recreational, or if they have colleagues in common.

In addition to the social goal, the SocialBlue team created the site to help IBM employees to meet the challenge of building relationships that are vital to working in large, distributed enterprises. SocialBlue can help IBM employees discover people with common interests or the right skills for a project. Learning more about someone—personally and professionally—facilitates making contact and might entice people to learn about ongoing projects and activities beyond their immediate project.

SocialBlue is related to IBM's Innovation Jam project cited later in this section and in Chapter 5.

How Enterprise Social Networking Helps Employees

Enterprise social networking can help employees in one or more of the following ways (Shuen 2008):

1. **Quick access to knowledge, know-how, and "know-who."** As people list their skills, expertise, and experience, as well as what previous employees know, enterprise social networks can help simplify the job of locating people with specified knowledge and skills. This is particularly useful inside multidivisional and multinational organizations.

2. **Expansion of social connections and broadening of affiliations.** Enterprise social networks help to get managers and professionals to know people better by interacting with them in online communities and keeping up with their personal information. This can decrease the social distance in a company.

3. **Self-branding.** People can get creative in tailoring their profiles the way they want to be known. It helps them to build their own personal brand within the corporation.

4. **Referrals, testimonials, and benchmarking.** Enterprise social networks can help employees prepare and display referrals and testimonials about their work and also to benchmark them with their colleagues.

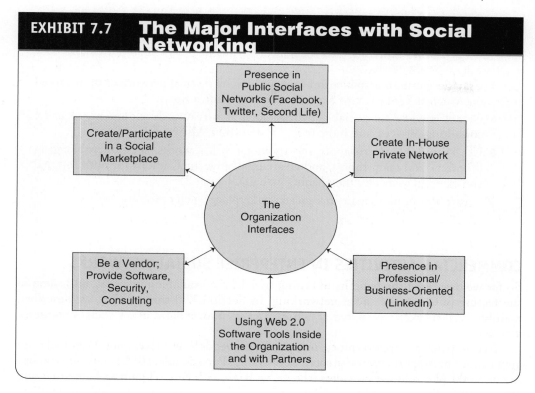

EXHIBIT 7.7   The Major Interfaces with Social Networking

Support Services for Enterprise Social Networks

Businesses can use a variety of services to support their social networking. Two examples follow.

Example 1. Socialcast (socialcast.com) is an online private social network platform that enterprises can deploy to let employees create their profiles and use them to facilitate collaboration and communication with coworkers. Employees can share ideas, questions, status updates, links, documents, and more—all at no charge. By opting for premium hosted or behind-the-firewall deployments, companies can add enhanced security options, directory sync, single sign on, and analytical tools. While the basic version of Socialcast is free, premium hosted services cost just $3 to $5 per user per month.

Example 2. Socialtext (socialtext.com) is a vendor of enterprise social software, providing an integrated suite of Web-based applications including social networking tools such as wikis, Weblogs, microblogging, directories, and group and personal dashboards using OpenSocial widgets and collaboration tools. It features authentication, authorization, and access control. Businesses use Socialtext to tap the power of their people by keeping them connected to each other, to the businesses strategy, and to new opportunities.

HOW COMPANIES INTERFACE WITH SOCIAL NETWORKS AND NETWORKING

Enterprises can interface with public and/or private social networks in several ways. The major interfaces are shown in Exhibit 7.7 and are described next.

▶ Use existing public social networks, such as Facebook or MySpace, or virtual worlds, such as Second Life, to create pages and microcommunities; advertise products or services; and post requests for advice, job openings, and so forth.

▶ Create an in-house private social network and then use it for communication and collaboration among employees and retirees or with outsiders (e.g., customers, suppliers, designers). Employees can create virtual rooms in their company's social networks where they can deploy applications to share information or collaborate (e.g., see wiki.oracle.com).

▶ Conduct business activities in a business-oriented social network or professional one (such as LinkedIn, or Sermo) or sponsor such a site.

▶ Create services for social networks, such as software development, security, consulting services, and more (e.g., Oracle, IBM, Microsoft).

▶ Use Web 2.0 software tools, mostly blogs, wikis, workspaces, microblogging (Twitter), and team rooms, and create innovative applications for both internal and external users (see the opening case in Chapter 2).

▶ Create and/or participate in a social marketplace (such as fotolia.com).

COMMERCIAL ACTIVITIES IN ENTERPRISE SOCIAL NETWORKS

So far we described the benefits of "going social," the available interfaces, and some of the feature of enterprise social networking. In Sections 7.3 through 7.6, we described mainly social marketing–related activities. Let us now explore other social commerce activities.

Recognizing the opportunities, many software vendors are developing Web tools and applications to support enterprise social networking. For example, IBM Lotus is encouraging its 5,000-plus solution providers who are working with Notes/Domino, Sametime, and other Lotus software to add Lotus Connections to their product lineups, building applications based on social networking technology. Microsoft's popular SharePoint now includes several Web 2.0 tools.

Representative areas and examples of enterprise social networking activities follow.

SOCIAL HUMAN RESOURCE MANAGEMENT

The HRM department in many organizations uses applications in social networks mainly in the areas of recruiting and training. For example, Deloitte Touche Tohmatsu set up a social network to assist its human resources managers in downsizing and regrouping teams. Hoover's has established a social network that uses Visible Path's technology to identify target business users for relationship building and to reach specific users.

Finding, Recruiting, and Training Workers

Both recruiters and job seekers are moving to a new recruiting platform—the online social networks. Enterprise recruiters are scanning online social networks, blogs, and other resources to identify and find information about potential employees. If job seekers are online and active, there is a good chance that they would be seen by recruiters. On social networks there are many so-called passive job seekers—people who are employed but would take a better job only if it came along. So it is important that both the active and passive job seekers maintain a good profile online that truly reflects them, at least in LinkedIn and Facebook.

Training. Several companies use enterprise social networking, and virtual worlds in particular, for training purposes. For example, Cisco is trying to use its virtual campus in Second Life for product training and executive briefings. IBM runs management and customer interaction training sessions in Second Life, too. Bernoff and Schadler (2010) provide an example of video training at Black & Decker using user-generated videos. The videos help to reduce training time.

Most of the public social networks, especially the business-oriented ones, facilitate recruiting and job finding. For example, recruiting is a major activity at LinkedIn and was the driver for the site's development (Case 7.1, p. 373). To be competitive, companies must look at the global market for talents, and they can use global social networking sites to find it. Large companies are using their in-house social networks to find in-house talents for vacant positions. For more on recruitment and job finding in social networks, see Chapter 3.

According to Gunelius (2010) 73 percent of all U.S. companies use social networks to recruit and hire new employees. Of these, 80 percent use LinkedIn, 55 percent use Facebook, and 45 percent use Twitter. The success rate is very high on LinkedIn (90%), moderate at Facebook (27.5%), and low at Twitter (14.2%).

LinkedIn, Facebook, MySpace, and Craigslist provide job listings, competing with online companies such as Monster. Many other social networks offer job listings as well.

One interesting example is Salesforce.com (salesforce.com). The CRM software company has partnered with Facebook to allow Salesforce.com customers to build applications on its Force.com platform inside Facebook. For example, a company's HRM employees could embed an announcement about an open position within their Facebook pages, and then use their social connections to search out new employees for their company.

MANAGERIAL PROBLEM SOLVING, INNOVATIONS, AND KNOWLEDGE MANAGEMENT

Managers are consistently engaged in decision making and problem solving; some of the problems are difficult to solve and require specialized knowledge. Thus, a major task in an organization is knowledge management including discovering and preserving knowledge of experts as well as knowledge dissemination. A major task in problem solving is idea generation.

Idea Generation and Problem Solving

Bernoff and Li (2008) suggest deployment of social networking for research and development, getting insight from conversations, and using the inputs to encourage innovations.

Example: IBM's Innovation Projects. As a technology leader, IBM created several innovation centers around the world. It also has several social commerce-oriented projects such as:

▶ **IBM Innovative Jam.** A social network of experts that can be used for idea generation and problem solving (Bjelland and Wood 2008).

▶ **ThinkPlace.** A virtual space where anyone in IBM can collaborate around ideas. ThinkPlace is an open intranet forum where ideas can be suggested, commented on by volunteers, modified, rated, sorted, and routed in the presence of any viewer. IBMers worldwide can submit ideas for how to improve any business, consulting, administrative, or engineering process; go after a market opportunity; or even address a societal challenge. Once an idea is posted in ThinkPlace, it is immediately available for comments by others, including suggesting ways to further develop and implement the idea. For details, see Majchrzak, et al. (2009).

▶ **SmallBlue.** SmallBlue, an opt-in social network analysis tool, provides business intelligence of who knows what, who knows whom, and who knows what about whom within IBM. It helps employees visualize their own network of connections by analyzing one's own and others' e-mail and instant message transcripts to determine the social network and infer and share expertise. For details, see Majchrzak, et al. (2009).

Problem-Solving Sites

Here are two examples of problem-solving professional sites:

▶ HP deployed an in-house private social network for IT people, called "48 upper." The site offers almost all the features that currently are being offered by existing social networks (e.g., Facebook), but it is equipped with HP system management tools. The site comes with an entirely new campaign for promoting information exchange. The site offers IT workers a platform on the Web for troubleshooting and discussing day-to-day IT problems. This information creates a library of information that is useful for other IT workers.

▶ Pharmaceutical company Pfizer has struck a partnership deal with Sermo, a social-networking site for licensed physicians, to make the way it reaches doctors more efficient. The collaboration creates open and transparent discussion between pharmaceutical professionals and the 30,000 physicians using Sermo. Sermo, launched in September 2006, is an online community where doctors exchange knowledge with each other.

An elaborate discussion on the role of discussion forums, blogs, and wikis for conversational knowledge management (KM) can be found in Wagner and Bolloju (2005). Other examples of these applications include experts' discovery and mapping communities of expertise.

Consider the following examples of social networking for KM and expert location:

▶ InnoCentive (innocentive.com) is a social network with over 150,000 participating scientists that specializes in solving science-related problems (for cash rewards).

▶ Northwestern Mutual Life created an internal social network where over 7,000 financial representatives share captured knowledge (using Awareness.com blogging software).

▶ Caterpillar created a knowledge network system for its employees and dealers, and it even markets the software to other companies.

Companies also are creating *retiree corporate social networks* to keep retirees connected with each other and with the organization. These people possess huge amounts of knowledge that can be tapped for productivity increases and problem solving (e.g., Alumni Connect from SelectMinds). With 64 million "baby boomers" retiring within the next 10 years, preserving their knowledge is a critical task.

Social Networking and Organizational Knowledge

Businesses are using the Web 2.0 tools to harness the collective intelligence of the firm. For many businesses, it is also important to keep records of the knowledge produced by its employees, as well as the context in which those knowledge and ideas were developed. Social networking tools can serve as a memory of an organization by recording conversations among its employees when facing a problem and finding solutions. Social networks are increasingly being seen as places where knowledge can be stored and then shared.

Example. Absolutely! is a new type of knowledge management software (KMS) that combines benefits of a traditional KMS with that of collaboration and engagement of wikis, blogs, forums, and social networks. It lets employees collaborate on creating and editing a knowledge base that may include documents, spreadsheets, photos, videos, interactive flow charts, and diagrams. Employees become not just passive recipients of information and users of knowledge, but active contributors to organizational knowledge.

USING WEB 2.0 TOOLS FOR MANAGERIAL TASKS

Collaboration drives business value by enabling people to work smarter together. Wikis and other social software tools can be effectively used by all types and sizes of enterprises for a wide range of tasks and activities, such as preparing reports, proposals, manuals, and other documents; developing policies; creating meeting agendas and minutes; doing analysis and reviews; gathering and refining new ideas; developing new products (e.g., see Wilderman 2010); brainstorming strategies; and more. Collaboration in social networking is done both internally, among employees from different units working in virtual teams for example, and externally, when working with suppliers, customers, and other business partners. Collaboration is done for example in forums and other types of groups and by using wikis and blogs. For details on collaboration in social networks, see Coleman and Levine (2008) and Online Tutorial T10. For using collaboration 2.0 in the enterprise, see Turban, et al. (2011b).

Using Blogs and Wikis Inside the Enterprise

In Chapter 2, we provided some examples of blogs and wikis used within enterprises. For examples of how wikis are used within enterprises, see Online File W7.2. The use of these tools is expanding rapidly. Jefferies (2008) reports on a study that shows that 71 percent of the best-in-class companies use blogs and 64 percent use wikis for the following applications:

> ▶ Project collaboration and communication (67%)
> ▶ Process and procedure document (63%)
> ▶ FAQs (61%)
> ▶ E-learning and training (46%)
> ▶ Forums for new ideas (41%)
> ▶ Corporate-specific dynamic glossary and terminology (38%)
> ▶ Collaboration with customers (24%)

For business blogging strategies, see Chaney (2010).

Questions and Answers in Social Networks

In the LinkedIn case, we described its "answer" function in which individuals and companies can post questions and the community provides them with answers. A similar service was described in Chapter 2, and earlier in this chapter we cited InnoCentive as a network for providing a solution for a fee. Many other professional networks and groups provide (for fee or free) advice and supporting material for decision making. For example, the medical social network "Sermo" provided for Q&A and for a discussion of problems and solutions.

A Suite of Tools for Social Collaboration

Laboranova (laboranova.com) is a project under the European Union's Sixth Framework Programme designed to support innovators, teams, and companies engaged in the development and management of innovative ideas and concepts. Its methods and tools can guide the users through the process of the early-stage innovation, starting with team building, generation and management of knowledge, ideas and concept, and idea evaluation and selection. It consists of a suite of Web 2.0 tools for embracing social innovation and collaboration. The tools include InnoTube, which operates like a private YouTube for business; and Melodie, which creates visual maps of concepts or idea submitted by its users, so that other users can comment or elaborate on the initial ideas. The tools are especially useful for collaborative design. For example, using the tools, car makers Fiat and Alfa Romeo were able to reduce the design time on a new model from six months to just one.

Section 7.7 ▶ REVIEW QUESTIONS

1. Define a business network and an enterprise social network.
2. List various categories of enterprise applications in social networks.
3. What are the benefits of enterprise social networking for companies? For employees?
4. Define public business-oriented network. Provide an example.
5. What is an entrepreneur network?
6. What are the major features of effective enterprise social networking?
7. Describe IBM's SocialBlue.
8. List all the ways that an organization can interface with social networking.
9. List social networking applications in HRM.
10. How can social networking facilitate problem solving?
11. Relate social networking to knowledge management.

7.8 CROWDSOURCING: COLLECTIVE INTELLIGENCE FOR PROBLEM SOLVING AND CONTENT CREATION

Another interesting class of social commerce activities relates to the concept of crowdsourcing.

DEFINITIONS, MAJOR CONCEPTS, AND BENEFITS

crowdsourcing
The act of outsourcing tasks, traditionally performed by an employee or contractor, to an undefined, large group of people or community (a "crowd"), through an open call.

The term *crowd* refers to any group of people such as a corporation or the entire general public. It is frequently considered a large group.

Crowdsourcing harnesses crowds to solve problems, innovate, and get work done. Crowdsourcing, a term coined by *Wired* magazine writer Jeff Howe in June 2006 (Howe 2008), embraces freelancers, volunteers, customers, and low-paid amateurs to create content, solve problems, or even do research and development. It presumes that a large number of enthusiasts can outperform a small group of experienced professionals (Libert and Spector 2007).

According to Wikipedia (en.wikipedia.org/wiki/Crowdsourcing), crowdsourcing is channeling the experts' desire to solve a problem and then freely sharing the answer with everyone.

Crowdsourcing is a distributed problem-solving and production process. In the classic use of the term, problems are broadcasted to an unknown group of solvers in the form of an open call for solutions. Users also known as the crowd typically form into online communities, and the crowd submits solutions. The crowd may also sort through the solutions, finding the best ones. These best solutions are then owned by the entity that broadcast the problem in the first place—the *crowdsourcer*—and the winning individuals in the crowd are sometimes rewarded. In some cases, this labor is well compensated, either monetarily, with prizes, or with special recognition. In other cases, the only rewards may be kudos or intellectual satisfaction. Crowdsourcing may produce solutions from amateurs or volunteers working in their spare time, or from experts or small businesses who were unknown to the initiating organization. Crowdsourcing is usually conducted as a Web-based activity. More than just brainstorming or ideation, crowdsourcing uses proven techniques to focus on innovation, creativity, and problem-solving capacity of a crowd on topics of vital interest to the host organization. An overview of crowdsourcing is provided in Howe's video "Crowdsourcing" (youtube.com/watch?v=F0-UtNg3ots).

Crowdsourcing Models

Howe (2008) has classified applications of crowdsourcing into the following four categories:

1. **Collective intelligence.** People solving problems and providing new insights and ideas leading to product, process, or service innovations.
2. **Crowd creation.** People creating various types of content and sharing with others for free or for a small fee.
3. **Crowd voting.** People giving their opinion and ratings on ideas, products, or services, as well as parsing, evaluating, and filtering information presented to them.
4. **Crowd supporting and funding.** People contributing and supporting endeavors for social causes, which might include volunteering their effort and time, offering donations, and microfinancing.

Chaordix Corp. classifies crowdsourcing into the following three models:

1. **Secretive.** Individuals submit ideas, and the winner is selected by the company. Ideas are not visible to all participants.
2. **Collaborative.** Individuals submit ideas, the crowd evolves ideas, and the crowd picks winner. Ideas are visible to all participants.

3. **Panel Selects.** Individuals submit ideas, the crowd evolves ideas, a panel selects finalists, the crowd votes for the winner.

Benefits of Crowdsourcing

The major perceived benefits of crowdsourcing include the following:

> ▶ Problems can be explored at comparatively little cost, and often very quickly.
>
> ▶ Payment is by results or even omitted.
>
> ▶ The organization can tap a wider range of talent than might be present in its own organization.
>
> ▶ By listening to the crowd, organizations gain firsthand insight on their customers' desires.
>
> ▶ The community may feel a brand-building kinship with the crowdsourcing organization, which is the result of an earned sense of ownership through contribution and collaboration.
>
> ▶ Crowdsourcing taps into the global world of ideas, helping companies work through a rapid design process.

Crowdsourcing also has the potential to be a problem-solving mechanism for governments and nonprofit use. Urban and transit planning are prime areas for crowdsourcing. One project to test crowdsourcing's public participation process for transit planning in Salt Lake City has been underway from 2008 to 2009. Another notable application of crowdsourcing to government problem solving is the Peer to Patent Community Patent Review project for the U.S. Patent and Trademark Office.

Smart companies and organizations have begun recognizing the value of tapping into the wisdom of the crowd to capture the best answers and the most innovative ideas.

THE PROCESS OF CROWDSOURCING

The process of crowdsourcing differs from application to application depending on the models discussed earlier, and on the specific problem to be solved. However, the following steps exist in most applications even though the details of the execution differ. The major steps are:

> 1. Identify the issue (problem) you want to investigate or solve.
>
> 2. Identify the target crowd.
>
> 3. Broadcast to the unknown crowd.
>
> 4. Engage the crowd in an innovative and creative process (e.g., idea generation).
>
> 5. User-generated content is then submitted. (This may include submission of opinions, voting, new ideas, suggestions, and so forth).
>
> 6. Evaluate the submitted material—by the initiator of the request or by the crowd (voting on the submitted content or on a few finalists selected by the company).

Example. In 2008, Starbucks introduced mystarbucksidea.com, a social media site designed to solicit ideas and feedback from its customers. The site was built around four key themes:

▶ **Sharing.** Community members can post ideas for Starbucks' products, services, community contributions, or changes in operations.

▶ **Voting.** Anyone can create an electronic suggestion box. One of the things that make mystarbucksidea.com special is that members can vote on the ideas. This helps the company prioritize ideas that are most likely to be attractive to most of its customers.

▶ **Discussing.** In addition to voting, members can provide feedback by commenting on the ideas of others. Designated "idea partners" (company employees) participate in these discussions, answer questions, and provide insights.

▶ **Seeing.** Community members can track an idea's progress toward implementation. A running tally of the votes (thumbs up or thumbs down) is displayed next to each entry. Next, ideas are tagged by the company with one of four status icons: "under review," "reviewed," "in the works," and "launched." This feedback demonstrates responsiveness.

Since its inception the project has collected many ideas and solved many problems. It generated ideas for the betterment of the participants as well.

The MIT Guide for Collective Intelligence

collective intelligence (CI)
The capacity of human communities to evolve toward higher order complexity and harmony, through such innovation mechanisms as variation-feedback-selection, differentiation-integration-transformation, and competition-cooperation-coopetition.

Malone, et al. (2010) conducted a detailed analysis on what they call **collective intelligence (CI)**, which is an application of crowdsourcing for problem-solving idea generation and innovations. The researchers attempted to answer the question: How can you get the crowds to do what your business needs done? Their major findings are in Malone et al. (2010).

SUCCESSFULLY DEPLOYED CROWDSOURCING SYSTEMS: SOME REPRESENTATIVE EXAMPLES

The following are some representative examples of implemented crowdsourcing systems.

▶ **Dell** through its popular "Idea Storm" (ideastorm.com) website lets customers vote for which features and products they want to see in the marketplace. For example, the Linux community asked for a UBUNTU box, which Dell created and launched.

▶ **Procter & Gamble,** which employs more than 9,000 scientists and researchers in corporate research and development, has many different problems. Researchers post their problems at InnoCentive (innocentive.com), offering cash rewards to problem solvers. P&G also uses other open innovation service providers and platforms such as NineSigma (ninesigma.com), YourEncore (yourencore.com), and yet2.com (yet2.com).

▶ **Amazon Mechanical Turk** (mturk.com) is a platform where information on tasks (known as HITs—human intelligence tasks) to be carried out is posted by enterprises and individuals. Individuals can take up the tasks of their interest, perform the tasks, and get paid for doing the work.

▶ **Threadless** (threadless.com) is an online community-based clothing retailer that sells T-shirts that are designed by and rated by its users. The most popular designs are then printed.

▶ **LEGO,** the toy maker, through its LEGO click (legoclick.com) reached out to the public for new ideas relating to toys and technology. The users can share their ideas through tweets or post them on LEGO's Facebook page.

▶ **Toyota** through its Ideas for Good (toyota.com/ideas-for-good) program invites public suggestions on how the brand's technology can be used for good in unexpected ways.

▶ **Facebook** used crowdsourcing to translate its site into several other languages. Volunteers in France and Germany did the job in a few weeks.

▶ **iStockPhoto** allows amateur photographers to upload their images and sell them as stock photos.

- **Goldcorp** is a Canadian mining company that was struggling financially and unable to find gold on its land in northern Ontario. The company puts all its geological data online, asked for help on where the gold was located, and put up $500,000 in prize money for accurate suggestions. Thousands of submissions came from people all over the world, including people using 3-D computer modeling techniques. Using the suggestions found $3 billion worth of gold on the property, and Goldcorp became one of Canada's biggest mining companies.

- **Cambrian House** is a crowdsourcing community that pioneered the technology to tap crowds for the best software ideas. To power open innovation in other businesses, they developed a *crowdsourcing platform*, Chaordix, which has the technology to harness a crowd for breakthrough ideas. See en.wikipedia.org/wiki/Cambrian_House for details.

- **Frito-Lay**, makers of Doritos tortilla chips, has harnessed crowdsourcing for creating its award-winning 2010 Super Bowl advertisement (Frito-Lay 2010).

- **TrendHunter** provides the Trend Report, which focuses on insight, predictions, market research, fashion, design, pop culture, retail, and e-commerce. These reports are used by CEOs, entrepreneurs, and the media. To create the 2011 annual Trend Report, TrendHunter crowdsourced the trends and filtered the response. According to the company, in preparing its trend report, it made use of the collective insights of 40,000 trend hunters, 92,000 crowdsourced articles, and 360,000,000 page views of data (trendreports.com/2011-Trend-Report).

- **Wikipedia** is considered by many as the "granddaddy" of crowdsourcing, and it is certainly the world's largest crowdsourcing project as shown in Case 7.2.

CASE 7.2
EC Application

WIKIPEDIA

Wikipedia is an online, user-generated encyclopedia. Wikipedia started as an offshoot of Nupedia, a free, online encyclopedia being written by experts. To speed up the production of articles, two members of the Nupedia team, Larry Sanger and Jimmy Wales, had an idea of allowing anybody to edit entries, using "wiki" technology. The result quickly eclipsed Nupedia. Since then, Wikipedia has become an astonishing success story. On paper, the idea that volunteers could collectively produce the largest and most popular encyclopedia the world has ever seen sounds implausible. Surely reference work is usually compiled by experts, yet Wikipedia now has over 17 million articles, 3.5 million of them in English (the rest are in 270 other languages), and its popularity—it is the fifth most visited site on the Web, and is used by around 400 million people each month—shows how much people value it. As well as being a useful reference work, Wikipedia is also the most striking example of the idea that a crowd of volunteers working together online can collectively produce something valuable.

The Wikipedia case shows how the crowdsourcing model works. It shows how the wisdom of the masses could be harnessed. This success inspired many other crowdsourcing projects.

The Problem

Wikipedia is a free nonprofit online collaborative encyclopedia. It compiled more knowledge than any other source and it is the fifth most visited site worldwide. In January 2010, it had over 17 million articles in over 270 languages and generated some 80 million hits per day. By comparison, Wikipedia is 100 times bigger than the *Encyclopedia Britannica*, which contains only 120,000 articles. In November 2010, over 411 million people visited Wikipedia (18 percent more than a year earlier).

Wikipedia's greatest strength is also its biggest weakness. Users create the content; but sometimes people with no special expertise in their chosen topics or people with malicious agendas post so-called "facts." For instance, once a contributor to an article on Pope Benedict substituted the Pontiff's photo with that of Emperor Palpatine from the *Star Wars* films. According to Farrell (2007), Microsoft paid experts to write information in Wikipedia about the company that was later found to be inaccurate.

In another, more serious incident, a contributor made the accusation that distinguished journalist and long-time civil rights advocate John Seigenthaler had been involved in the assassinations of President John Kennedy and his brother Bobby Kennedy. The contributor practically fabricated the

(continued)

CASE 7.2   *(continued)*

entire article. Seigenthaler pursued legal action against the anonymous Wikipedia contributor, via the poster's IP address, and charged the unidentified accuser with defamation. For Seigenthaler, Wikipedia is "populated by volunteer vandals with poison-pen intellects" and should not be permitted to exist in its current form.

Another problem is invasion of privacy. Even if information about a certain individual or company is correct (i.e., it is not defamatory), the individual may not want the information to be made public. Because most contributors do not ask permission from those they are writing about, an invasion of privacy occurs. Yet, another problem is that the bulk of Wikipedia is written by only 1,400 of its more than 100,000 contributors (see Blodget 2009), introducing possible influence and biases.

The Solution

In order to avoid false or misleading entries, the Wikimedia Foundation, which operates Wikipedia, along with several other wiki initiatives (such as Wikibooks), has promoted several measures to improve the quality of Wikipedia articles. The first step was the creation of a more formal advisory board. The second step was to empower system administrators to block access to the site to certain users who repeatedly vandalized entries. Next, the process of handling complaints was improved. Finally, Wikipedia posted notes regarding the quality of entries and the need for improvements.

Ultimately, the owners plan to change the site to Wikipedia 2.0 and are considering the following three options:

1. The editing of mediocre Wikipedia articles by experts in the specific field; especially the use of quality art editors to improve Wikipedia's humanities coverage.
2. The creation of original articles from the ground up. According to Larry Sanger, one of Wikipedia's cofounders, this could provide a more distinctive culture that will provide more pride in the articles. In this case, the name of the site may change to *citizendium*.
3. Make the users' policy more interactive. Wikipedia is asking readers to notify the company whenever they read inaccurate or incomplete content.

The Results

While the Seigenthaler issue was debated in fall 2005, early quality measures were instituted, and the site's founder, Jimmy Wales, appeared on CNN together with Seigenthaler in December 2005. During this time, traffic to Wikipedia nearly tripled, mostly due to the publicity of the CNN presentation and the subsequent publicity in newspapers and TV. Yet, problems still exist, with continued complaints against both inaccurate content and privacy invasion. And, after years of enormous growth, the rate of editing articles, new account registration, user blocks, article protection and deletion, and uploads have all declined. In addition, in 2008 Google launched a potential Wikipedia competitor with its service called Knol.

Note: While Wikipedia is a nonprofit venture that solicits financial support from the public, its sister site Wikia.com is a for-profit venture.

Many companies are now using a similar concept internally; for example, the pharmaceutical company Pfizer implemented an internal wiki, called Pfizerpedia, to accumulate knowledge about its pharmaceutical products and research. Many other companies use the wisdom of its employees to create corporate knowledge bases.

The Wikipedia case illustrates both the benefits to society and the problems of content created by volunteers.

Sources: Compiled from Blodget (2009), Farrell (2007), and Temple (2011).

Questions

1. Wikipedia is a nonprofit organization. Search and find its revenue model.
2. What drives Wikipedia?
3. Discuss the issue of quality—the problems and solutions.
4. Research the problem of copyright.
5. Research the relationship between Wikipedia and Wikia.

ISSUES AND CONCERNS IN IMPLEMENTING CROWDSOURCING

Along with all the success stories and the logic that "two heads are better than one" and the crowd is better than individuals come those that point to the other side of the coin. The fact is that not all crowdsourcing applications succeed. Bell (2009) and others raise the issues of what is true crowdsourcing: There may be no crowd in crowdsourcing. There are usually only virtuosos, usually uniquely talented, highly trained people in the crowd who have worked for decades in a field. Frequently, these innovators have been funded through failure after failure; however, from their fervent brains spring new ideas. The crowd has nothing to do with it.

1. In crowdsourcing a problem is broadcasted to a large number of people with varying forms of expertise. Then, individuals motivated by obsession, competition, money, or all three apply their individual talents to create a solution.
2. The vast majority of Wikipedia's content is the product of relatively few motivated individuals. After articles are created, they are curated—corrected, improved, and extended by many different people. Only some articles are indeed group creation.

3. There is no crowd of open source developers ready to attack every problem. In fact, most open source projects are the product of one obsessed individual (e.g., Linus Torvalds in Linux) who wrote the software to meet his own needs. Often this individual was joined by other programmers who shared the founder's vision and, under his or her direction, created great software.

4. The Netflix $1,000,000 contest (see Chapter 8) is a prime example of individual (or a small group) virtuosity at work. One team was clearly in the lead and then a consortium of teams that had worse performance joined together and combined their innovations to create an algorithm that won the contest. For most of the contest, individuals toiled to figure out a solution. At the end, a consortium was formed. None of the invention happened through a crowd.

According to Bell (2009) there is only one true crowdsourcing case, Jigsaw. Jigsaw, the community-created database of 16 million business contacts, is indeed crowdsourcing. Tens of thousands of people have added business contacts to Jigsaw's database so they can earn points and get access to business contacts entered by others. Jigsaw sells this data to companies, generating millions in revenue. The other businesses usually cited as successful cases of crowdsourcing such as InnoCentive, Threadless, Spreadshirt, and StockPhoto, are really versions of Wikipedia, that is, aggregations of the inventions of individual virtuosos. Other large projects like Linux, are virtuoso creations around which consortiums of experts have gathered.

While IBM and other companies hail the success of crowdsourcing as an idea generation tool, some question it. For example, with respect to Starbucks, Moore (2010) questions how many of the ideas the company says its customers generated really came from the community, suggesting that most of the implemented ideas were already under consideration by the company. Some critics say the overwhelmingly positive tone of the message postings and the relative lack of negativity suggests the possibility of censorship runs against the cultural norms of the social Web. Others suggest that if Starbucks was really interested in engaging people, it would be taken more seriously by participating in conversations at existing websites where people talk about the company (see starbucksgossip.typedpad.com).

Other concerns and issues frequently cited are:

▶ How accurate is content created by nonexperts in the crowd? How does the site maintain accuracy?

▶ How is crowd-created content being updated? How can we be sure that content is relevant?

▶ Should the crowd be limited to only experts? How do we do that?

▶ How do we maintain the number of contributors in the crowd? (Wikipedia's number of regular contributors dropped from 54,000 in March 2007, to 35,000 in September 2010.)

▶ The business case to justify crowdsourcing may be fuzzy due to unstructured information.

▶ The crowd may submit too many ideas, most are worthless. It costs too much money to evaluate all of them. During the BP oil spill in 2010, there were over 20,000 suggestions submitted on how to stem the flow of oil, but the problem was very technical so there were lots of poor suggestions. The company, which was under time pressure, had to evaluate all of them.

▶ Content contributors may violate copyrights, intentionally or unintentionally. How to guard against it can be a major issue.

▶ The quality of decisions depends on the composition of the crowd. Best decisions may come if the crowd is made up of diverse opinions and ideologies. But in many cases, you do not know the mix in advance.

▶ One of the opponents of crowdsourcing even said: "The IQ of a crowd equals the lowest individual IQ divided by the number of people in the crowd."

Conclusion. It is not as simple to successfully implement crowdsourcing as many people think.

To overcome all of these concerns, crowdsourcers need guidelines and rules, some of which need to be imposed on the crowd. Some interesting guidelines are provided by Lowitt (2010). We compiled samples in Online File W7.3. Also see Howe (2008) and Bell (2009).

Crowds are made up of individuals, and individuals differ dramatically from one another in their expertise, skills, and ability to come up with creative solutions. So, the quality of the responses from the crowd might vary considerably—from excellent and practical to bad or impractical ones. Hence, crowd responses have to be analyzed and filtered to separate the good from the bad. Perhaps the best filter for crowd-created ideas is the crowd itself—voting by the crowd on (shortlisted) ideas.

The individuals making up the crowd have limited resources—time, attention, physical resources, and knowledge—to address the posted problems. So, for crowdsourcing success, the problem posted should be addressable or solvable by individuals. In other words, tasks should be "'crowd-friendly'"—simple, modular, independent, and require less resources (Feller 2010).

And, as the crowd is distributed, problem solving and task completion should take place independently and asynchronously. Crowdsourcing systems should let individuals act and respond independently and facilitate effectively aggregation and integration and possibly ranking of the responses. Finally, as seen in the examples of successful applications, crowdsourcing can be used by small organizations and by entrepreneurs. For a discussion and tips, see entrepreneurs.about.com/od/beyondstartup/a/Tips-On-Effective-Use-Of-Crowdsourcing.

TOOLS FOR CROWDSOURCING

To launch crowdsourcing initiatives, businesses and developers can make use of crowdsourcing tools and platforms such as Salesforce.com's Ideas platform (salesforce.com/salesforceideas), NineSigma (ninesigma.com), InnoCentive (innocentive.com), YourEncore (yourencore.com), yet2.com (yet2.com), Uservoice (uservoice.com), Getsatisfaction (getsatisfaction.com), and IdeaScale (ideascale.com).

Hypios: A Marketplace for Crowdsourcing

Hypios (hypios.com) is a multinational social network of over 150,000 problem solvers. As a problem solver individual or research organization, you can: create a profile, make professional contacts, and connect with colleagues, peers, and friends. If you are a problem solver and only want to solve problems on Hypios, you choose what information you share on your profile and decide who can see it. Hypios is compatible with other social networks, like Facebook, so you can share your Hypios, activity with your contacts on other social networks. You can develop your own networks or join one of the many networks that already exist on Hypios. Import your contacts and stay connected to the social networks most important to you. You can meet with people who share your interest, and follow your friends' activities. After seeing what your friends are working on, you can decide to either compete (friendly competition) or to collaborate with them on solving a problem. If you are interested, watch the video "Become a Solver" on the site. Problems to be solved are broadcasted on hypios.com/problems (citing fees, solutions needed, time frame, etc.). Solvers and solutions are ranked by peers. As a market organizer, Hypios provides a service to solution seekers. Hypios combines intelligent crowdsourcing and expert identification. Applying advanced Semantic Web and machine-learning technologies, Hypios identifies problem solvers based on publicly available data on the Internet. It then invites these solvers to compete to solve specific research and development (R&D) challenges in their areas of expertise.

Section 7.8 ▶ REVIEW QUESTIONS

1. Define crowdsourcing; provide four examples.
2. List Howe's four categories of applications.
3. What are the major benefits of crowdsourcing? (List five to seven benefits.)
4. Describe the crowdsourcing process.
5. List some issues and concerns regarding crowdsourcing implementation.
6. Why is Wikipedia considered crowdsourcing?

7.9 SOCIAL COMMERCE: APPLICATIONS IN VIRTUAL WORLDS

Virtual worlds (see Chapter 2) such as Second Life—computer-based 3-D simulated environments, which look like real places—are an attractive platform for online social and professional interactions, community building, commerce, education, and training. As briefly described in Chapter 2, users can navigate and move around in the world using their avatars, which they can also use for communication and other activities. Virtual worlds also have provisions for buying and selling virtual goods paying for them with their own virtual currency. Thus, virtual worlds are attractive environments for real-time interactive communication, collaboration, and commerce (see en.wikipedia.org/wiki/Virtual_world).

Businesses can make use of virtual worlds not just to entertain their customers and prospects but also to engage them in an experience hitherto unavailable in a real world (see Reeves and Read 2009). The use of multiple senses in a virtual world can make the resulting users' experience more effective and fulfilling. As a result, virtual worlds continue to attract a growing number of users. For instance, according to a Second Life posting, as of February 2011, Second Life has over 22 million registered user accounts (unique residents) who spend more than 115 million hours a month on the site. Businesses can make effective use of this growing devoted user base. In doing so, they can leverage features and spaces as illustrated next. For opportunities and concerns, see en.wikipedia/wiki/Second_life.

THE FEATURES AND SPACES OF VIRTUAL WORLDS

Virtual worlds have a set of properties or features that provide the capabilities to conduct business there.

The Features That Businesses Can Leverage

▶ **Shared space.** The world allows many users to participate at once and engage in discussions and collaborative activities.

▶ **3-D visualization (graphical user interface).** The world depicts spaces visually, ranging in style from 2-D "cartoon" imagery to more immersive 3-D environments.

▶ **Immediacy.** Interaction takes place in real time, and users experience the results of their actions immediately.

▶ **Interactivity.** The world allows users to alter, develop, build, or submit customized content.

▶ **Persistence.** The world's existence continues regardless of whether individual users are logged in or not.

▶ **Socialization and community formation.** The world provides opportunities for socializing with other users and allows and encourages the formation of in-world social groups like teams, guilds, clubs, groups, housemates, and neighborhoods.

IBM, Walmart, Toyota, Sears, Wells Fargo, and many other companies have experimented with virtual worlds for testing designs, customer service, employee training, and marketing. Businesses are exploring the best way to leverage the new technology beyond holding staff meetings and collaborating with clients in virtual worlds and to attract more users to their virtual worlds' properties and activities.

THE LANDSCAPE OF VIRTUAL WORLD COMMERCIAL APPLICATIONS

Marketers, governments, retailers, vendors, small and large businesses (IT and non-IT), and individuals now have a new commerce avenue—virtual worlds—to explore and from which to benefit. The potential of virtual worlds, particularly when they are integrated with other

IT and business systems, is huge. A virtual world is a new platform to reach out particularly to a younger generation of customers that grew up on video games, and, more importantly, to engage them in their pursuits. For sellers, it might mean building powerful communities of fans for their products and services. For other businesses, particularly global ones, business with employees working at different locations worldwide who are becoming more technology-savvy, it might be about leveraging and embracing virtual worlds for improving teamwork and productivity, enhancing collaboration, fostering customer-led innovation, and strengthening relationships with customers and business partners.

Virtual worlds can be viewed as a set of the following multidimensional spaces: social space, entertainment space, transaction space, experimental and demonstration space, collaboration space, agents space, and fantasy space.

The Seven Dimensions of Virtual Worlds

The followings are brief descriptions of the seven spaces (for details, see Daden Ltd. 2010):

1. **Social space.** Place where users' avatars can meet, discuss, share information and views, and socialize.
2. **Entertainment space.** Place where avatars (and their owners) can play games, see movies, and attend concerts, and enjoy in a near-real 3-D environment.
3. **Transaction space.** Marketplace where one can conduct business and financial transactions, sell and buy available virtual goods as well as some real goods at a virtual shop front.
4. **Experimental/demonstration space.** Place where real-world environments, products, and services can be simulated for experimentation, demonstration, training, and evaluation.
5. **Collaboration space.** Place for collaboration, innovation, and new product development.
6. **Smart agents space.** Place where software agents, on your behalf, can seek information and engage with other agents to fulfill or facilitate transactions.
7. **Fantasy space.** Dream world where you can do things that are not feasible or not realizable in the real world.

One can arrange for the use of one or more of these seven spaces in innovative ways for business, education, medical, political, and other uses. Business applications of virtual worlds are varied and their use depends on the type of business in which a company is engaged, in the organizational objectives, and the target user profiles.

THE MAJOR CATEGORIES OF VIRTUAL WORLD APPLICATIONS

It is common to classify major applications into 19 categories (adapted from Murugesan 2008, Reeves and Read 2009, and wikipedia.org):

1. **Storefronts and online sales.** Companies have set up storefronts in virtual worlds to enable customers to have a more immersive experience by trying out products, including dresses and shoes, in the online world before they buy them. This requires furnishing a salesroom with possibilities to examine 3-D representations of products, peruse information, dress avatars, and/or complete a purchase through links to a secure trading site. In addition, there are markets for virtual goods (e.g., see Second Life). To learn how to shop in virtual worlds, you may go to secondlife.com/shop/learn.
2. **Front offices or help desks.** Virtual worlds can act as a front office for customer service. The customer service personnel, avatars of real employees, can spend

their entire day on the virtual world site. For instance, if you would like to inquire about a product or service a company offers, you can walk into the virtual office of the company in the virtual world.

3. **Advertising and product demonstrations.** Marketers and advertisers are placing signs and banners promoting products or services at various locations in virtual worlds to reach the world's growing number of virtual residents. Marketers are using virtual worlds to provide 3-D demonstrations of products that might be viewed by potential customers. Businesses are using avatars in virtual worlds to demonstrate the installation of an appliance such as a refrigerator or home theater after purchase by a consumer. Or it could be used for showing how to care for a plant in terms of watering or winter care.

   There are several advantages for using it. An example of this would be Apple creating an online store within Second Life. This allows the users to browse the latest and innovative products. You cannot actually purchase a product, but having these "virtual stores" is a way of accessing a different clientele and customer demographic. Before, companies would use an advertising company to promote their products. With the introduction of the prospect of commercial success within a virtual world, companies can reduce cost and time constraints by keeping this in-house. An obvious advantage is that it reduces any costs and restrictions that could come into play in the real world. For details and options, see wiki.secondlife.com/wiki/Advertising_in_Second_Life.

4. **Content creation and distribution.** Virtual worlds can serve as a channel for delivering music, games, art, and other forms of interactive content. Through virtual worlds, one can reach and immerse participants and involve them as viewers and contributors.

5. **Meetings, seminars, and conferences.** Virtual worlds are being used as a venue for individuals to virtually meet, participate, and interact through their avatars. Such interactive meetings with other participants open up immediate interaction between participants. Also these virtual meetings avoid travel, saving time and money.

6. **Training.** Another promising use for virtual worlds is interactive and/or collaborative training. Trainees can learn by doing and through simulation, and role-play. For example, a hotel chain is training receptionists in virtual lobbies. Some other companies are developing applications that can help them train staff on how to deal with a hostage or an emergency situation such as accidents and natural disasters; the Maryland Department of Transportation has replicated the Interstate 95 highway in a virtual world to train emergency workers under different scenarios by creating traffic accidents, and to watch their responses that might include closing exits, rerouting traffic, and rescuing the injured. Another area where this can be used is military training (e.g., flight and battlefield simulations). For details, see Heiphetz and Woodill (2009).

7. **Education.** Universities are using virtual worlds as a new immersive and interactive medium or platform that is useful for interacting with students and conducting courses.

8. **Recruiting.** A growing number of recruiters and companies are recruiting employees at virtual worlds. All the activities of recruitment, ranging from providing job details to conducting virtual interviews with candidates, are conducted at the recruiter's virtual office. This mode of recruiting is gaining acceptance by technology-savvy graduates and job seekers. The U.S. military is using virtual world simulations and examples to bolster recruiting.

9. **Tourism promotion.** Government agencies and tourist operators are using virtual worlds to promote their tourism destinations by providing tourists 3-D virtual immersive experiences of real places and activities of their interest.

10. **Museums and art galleries.** Many artists and agencies are setting up virtual museums and galleries to showcase their creations and to promote sales. They also use virtual worlds to stage musical and other performances.

11. **Information points.** Virtual worlds are used as sophisticated information kiosks. It can act as an extremely powerful, interactive, and dynamic online resource or brochure.

12. **Data visualization and manipulation.** Interactive data visualization and manipulation in the virtual environment is an interesting new application of interest to enterprises and professionals. For instance, the software *Glasshouse* by Green Phosphor (greenphosphor.com) lets one export data from either a spreadsheet or database query to a virtual world and presents the user with a 3-D representation of the data in a virtual world environment for the user to explore it interactively. A user's avatar can then manipulate the visualization of the data by drilling down into it, re-sorting it, or moving it around to see it from many different angles.

13. **Renting virtual world land and buildings.** One can earn money by selling or renting buildings and lands in strategic locations in virtual worlds and by engaging in the "real estate" business in the virtual world.

14. **Platform for social science research.** Virtual worlds are also a good platform for doing experimental social science research to observe how people behave or react (through their avatars) in structured and unstructured situations, and also to study customer behavior in virtual worlds.

15. **Market research.** Using virtual worlds as a tool allows companies to test user reaction and give them feedback on new products. This can be crucial as it will give the companies an insight as to what the market and customers want from new products, which can give them a competitive edge.

16. **Platform for design.** Many companies show products, the architecture photos of buildings, hotels, shows, etc., in 3-D for viewers to contribute opinions. For example, Dow Chemical Co. planned and designed its customer hospitality and business center on Second Life.

    The replica of the 36,000 square foot ballroom included the customer center walls and furnishings, and applied a variety of graphic theme approaches. Clients were able to log in to Second Life and, using avatars, walk freely around the virtual ballroom to evaluate layout and design.

17. **Providing CRM to employees and a platform for socialization.** Companies use virtual worlds for providing CRM to employees and/or customers. For example, Sun Microsystems created an island in Second Life dedicated for the sole use of their employees. This is a place where people can go and seek help, exchange new ideas, or advertise a new product. In addition to the traditional fantasy worlds, there are many commercial community-focused virtual worlds that emphasize socializing rather than gaming. These worlds offer a more open-ended experience and are strongly influenced by the culture of text-based chat rooms.

18. **Commercial gaming.** Commercial gaming worlds tend to focus on a singular fictional theme and consistently follow formal conventions such as character-focused avatars, progression through an interactive narrative storyline, and a series of competitive events.

19. **Virtual trade shows.** A *virtual tradeshow* (sometimes called a *virtual tradefair*) is a type of virtual event run in a virtual world. It can be considered the online equivalent of a traditional tradeshow or exhibition, but exhibitors and visitors connect with one another via the virtual world on the Internet regardless of the geographic location, to exchange valuable information.

For a description of virtual showrooms, see Online File W7.4 and Yu (2010).

Applications in Virtual Worlds

The following is an example of applications used in virtual worlds.

> **Example: Sony's Home for a Virtual Community of Gamers.** Sony's Home virtual world is a gathering place for PlayStation gamers. It has attracted over 17 million users worldwide. The community of gamers can play hundreds of games, attend a number of events, and buy lots of virtual goods. Visitors can create animated avatars and wander among virtual sites such as shopping malls, movie theaters, or game arcades. It has become a big digital online marketplace for video game fans. Gamers who own PlayStation 3 consoles are the only ones who can enter into Home, and they spend a lot of hours and money in Home. The engagement level at Home is higher than the engagement in standard social games or generic virtual worlds.
>
> Sony's Home offers free-to-play games within the virtual environment and houses over 235 games and 7,000 virtual items, available either for free or purchase. It staged 600 community events in 2010. According to Sony, Home's virtual goods and microtransaction business model makes it easy for Sony to make money. It serves also as a testing ground for other kinds of business models, such as in-game advertising and sponsorships (*Techfused.com* 2010).

Many scientific organizations that are seeing their budgets shrink are exploring ways to reduce the number of their physical meetings by holding virtual meetings at Second Life. Proponents see it as a win-win scenario, saving not only time and money but also improve the environment (see sciencemag.org/content/331/6013/27.summary).

For a review of other examples of how businesses and organizations are using virtual worlds to make the world greener, refer to *The Green Book: An Enterprise Guide to Virtual Worlds*, published by Association of Virtual Worlds (associationofvirtualworlds.com).

Additional Virtual World Applications Around the Globe

Here are a few other representative examples of applications.

- **Hanacity** (hanacity.com). Hana Bank of Korea uses a virtual world to educate its future customers, children ages 10 to 15. Its virtual world teaches children about money management, economics, career selection, and investment strategies.
- **MinyanLand** (minyanland.com). This site teaches children finance by showing them how to rent apartments, upgrade homes, and invest in the stock market. Hanacity and MinyanLand illustrate how a virtual world can turn information and education into a rich virtual experience.
- **Wells Fargo Stagecoach Island** (wellsfargo.com/stagecoachisland). In this virtual world created by Wells Fargo bank, members can explore, learn principles of smart money management, and make friends.
- **MeetMe** (meet-me.jp). To make their retail shopping experience more exciting, this virtual world takes visitors on a shopping trip and tour of Tokyo.
- **New Belgium Brewing** (newbelgium.com). The brewery has added a virtual component to its regular website. In this virtual world, visitors can take an interactive tour of the brewery.
- **Project Gamerz** (projectgamerz.com). This virtual world, created for the British Police, fosters a sense of safety and community among teens. This is an example of how virtual worlds can be used by law enforcement agencies to educate the community.

> **Toyota Metapolis** (metapolis.toyota.co.jp/about/map.html). This Japanese-language virtual world presents virtual cars, events, and a Toyota museum. This is an example of a brand utilizing a virtual environment to enrich customer experiences.
> **Aloft** (starwoodhotels.com/alofthotels/index.html). Aloft, the global brand of Starwood hotels and resorts, tested the design of its hotels on Second Life. The company uses the feedback collected from more than a million visitors to create the ultimate destination sensation.
> **Ty Girlz** (tygirlz.com). This virtual world for girls encompasses fashion, chat, games, and shopping that can be unlocked only by using a secret code found on the real-world Ty Girlz dolls. This application links a real-world toy with a virtual world environment.

Trading Virtual Goods and Properties

There are a lot of business opportunities in buying and selling virtual goods. Sales are done from electronic catalogs, classifieds, and auctions (e.g., see usd.auctions.secondlife.com). This is done with virtual money that can be converted to real money. The tax and contract/legal issues are not clear (e.g., see en.wikipedia.org/wiki/Second_Life) so be careful.

The major products/services in this category are:

1. **Land.** The big money is in land buying and selling, renting and developing.
2. **Retail.** Once you rent or buy store space, you can set up vending displays where people can shop while you sleep.
3. **Manufacturing.** Good builders can always make money by building and selling houses, jewelry, weapons, furniture, shoes, and so on.
4. **Scripting.** Good scripters are as in demand as builders. Examples of scripted items are doors that open and TV sets that work.
5. **Fashion.** Second Life fashionistas are deadly serious about their style. Don't expect to make a fortune, but a number of clothing and hair designers make their primary real-life incomes in Second Life.
6. **The sex industry.** Those new to Second Life sometimes start out as strippers or escorts. (Yes, there are animations for these activities.) In this capacity, you may be able to earn the capital to start more lucrative and respectable ventures. New nightclubs and strip clubs open and close, but the best turn profits.

For details and tips on how to do virtual trading, see Kurfiss (2011).

Potential Problems. A group of virtual landowners online have filed a class action lawsuit against Second Life, claiming the company broke the law when it rescinded their ownership rights. The plaintiff says a change in the terms of service forced them either to accept new terms that rescinded their virtual property ownership rights, or else be locked out of the site.

For further discussion on making money in virtual worlds, see (Business and Marketing Author 2011) and work.com/doing-business-in-second-life-1285.

THE MAJOR DRIVERS OF SOCIAL COMMERCE IN VIRTUAL WORLDS

The key factors that drive business applications in virtual worlds are:

> **Resemblance to the real-world environment.** Businesses want to exploit this virtual social platform that resembles the real-world environment for internal activities and for customer-facing applications: new product development, marketing, basic business operations, and customer service. For users it provides a more engaging, interactive experience resembling the real world.

▶ **Immersive online environment of choice by the younger generations.** As an outgrowth of online gaming, virtual worlds provide an immersion entertainment of choice for the younger generations. These digital generation users are comfortable with the virtual world concepts and their interfaces and even attend virtual universities. For large enterprises and even SMEs, it is an open space where organizations and people can meet and influence others through advertising and other activities and expand and retain their customer base.

▶ **New means of navigation and discovery.** Virtual worlds' 3-D representations make it easier to discover and move through items of interest than do pages on the conventional 2-D Web, which involves a relatively flat arrangement. And virtual worlds support the creation of more visually impressive sites with new types of incentives to visit.

▶ **Better online meeting spaces and collaborative platforms.** Virtual worlds can be better online meeting spaces and collaboration platforms than other computerized communication environments such as instant messaging. Participants can locate each other, congregate in groups, and roam between conversations.

▶ **Interactive environment for education and training.** A few different activities, as highlighted in Exhibit 7.8, can be used to enrich training and education in several areas.

EXHIBIT 7.8	**The Use of Virtual Worlds to Facilitate Learning**
Activity	**Description**
Simulation	Users can manipulate simulated scenarios and see results. Creating a virtual business is a popular activity.
Distance Learning	Virtual world can be used as a remote working, learning, and/or collaboration space. It is also used for team-building, collaborative learning and collaborative problem solving. Key means of interaction and teaching-learning are speech, text chat, posters, and whiteboards.
Class Meetings	Learning institutions offer a large number of virtual classes (many in Second Life). Students can explore, share, and work with teachers via their avatars.
Exploration	The virtual world is a good platform for explorative learning. It can be used to create an environment or an exhibit which the user can explore in the same way that they might do in real world. The information is communicated by the environment to the user/avatar visually, by text or other media.
Visualization	Visualization is a key learning enabler. The virtual world can be used to visualize a process or set of data which the user then explores or uses as the basis for further analysis or decision making.
Imaginative Scenarios	For study and to gain experience, in virtual world, one can create environments which would just not be possible or safe in real life, like walking on the moon or inside volcano and flying through clouds in space. This can be combined with simulation and exploration.
Information Dissemination	Many organizations, governments, and universities provide updated interactive information, which can be used to learn topics such as geography, public administration, hospitality management, and technology.

Sources: Compiled from Daden (2010), Murusegan (2008), Terdiman (2008), and *secondlife.com* (accessed May 2011).

CONCERNS AND LIMITATIONS OF COMMERCIAL ACTIVITIES IN VIRTUAL WORLDS

Though virtual worlds were expected to become a major platform for commerce, business, and social activities, they haven't reached widespread appeal and adoption yet. Despite their promise, virtual worlds present several challenges and constraints that developers, businesses, and users must be aware of. Virtual worlds such as Second Life are not easy to use, they are resource intensive, and software needs to be installed and updated, which for many users, is too cumbersome and/or expensive. Furthermore, the software usually has a long learning curve and substantial hardware requirements—limiting widespread adoption. There are also issues relating to in-world business practices, laws, taxation, ethics, performance, and reliability. And there are technology limitations, including congestion, accessibility, interface, security, bugs, and quality assurance.

According to en.wikipedia.org/wiki/Second_Life, there is considerable fraud and violation of intellectual property on Second Life. Wikipedia provides examples of fraud and suggestions for protection.

Like most other online applications, virtual worlds are susceptible to several different types of security threats. For instance, Second Life has been attacked several times by groups of residents who created objects that harass other residents, disrupt, or damage the system. Some Second Life residents have created objects such as "Grey Goo," which overwhelms the servers by infinitely reproducing themselves; orbiters, which throw an avatar up so high that it cannot get back down in a reasonable time frame without teleporting, and cages were created, which surround avatars and prevent them from moving.

As more companies seek ways to do their work in virtual environments, however, Second Life has introduced a behind-the-firewall service for enterprise customers. The Second Life Enterprise environment provides users an added layer of security and the ability to scale an avatar community. It also offers purchase of templates and other 3-D environments for their Second Life Enterprise world.

For guidelines dealing with most of these concerns, see Mahar and Mahar (2009).

Section 7.9 ▶ REVIEW QUESTIONS

1. What are the features of virtual worlds that businesses can make use of in deploying their virtual world applications?

2. From a business application perspective, virtual worlds can be visualized as a multidimensional space. Briefly describe different dimensions of virtual world space.

3. Outline a few examples of business applications of virtual worlds.

4. Discuss different ways of making real or virtual money in virtual worlds (see also Chapters 1 and 2).

5. What kind of educational and training activities do virtual worlds such as Second Life support?

6. What are the major concerns and limitations of virtual worlds?

7.10 ENTERTAINMENT, MULTIMEDIA SHARING, AND SOCIAL GAMES

The rich media capabilities of Web 2.0 technologies, the ability to engage millions of people who are interested in online entertainment, the availability of innovative tools, and the creative and collaborative nature of Web 2.0 all facilitate entertainment. Web 2.0 tools also are aiding in the proliferation of on-demand entertainment. This section describes some of the entertainment-centered social networks as well as other issues related to entertainment in social commerce. Note that a major issue with such social networks is copyright violations; a topic we discuss in detail in Chapter 14.

ENTERTAINMENT AND SOCIAL NETWORKS

A large number of social networks and communities are fully or partially dedicated to entertainment. In fact, MySpace seems to be morphing into an entertainment portal.

MySpace is the second most visited online video site after YouTube. It has a licensing agreement with Sony BMG and other large media companies that gives its members free access to streaming videos, music, and other entertainment in MySpace Music. The companies share in the ad revenue. MySpace is also offering free voice chat in collaboration with Skype.

The following are representative examples of the use of Web 2.0 applications for entertainment.

Mixi

Mixi, Inc. (mixi.co.jp) is a popular invitation-only social networking service in Japan. The focus of mixi is on "community entertainment"; that is, meeting new people by way of common interests. Users can send and receive messages, write in a diary, read and comment on others' diaries, organize and join communities, and invite their friends to join. Mixi Station, a client program that detects songs being played in iTunes and Windows Media Player, uploads songs automatically to a communally accessible list in the "Music" section.

The word *mixi* is a combination of *mix* and *I*, referring to the idea that the user, "I," "mixes" with other users through the service. As of March 2011, the site had about 22 million members and over 1 million small communities of friends and interests. For details, see (en.wikipedia.org/wiki/Mixi).

Last.fm

Last.fm (last.fm) is an Internet radio station and music recommendation system. In May 2007, CBS purchased Last.fm in order to extend its online reach. The system builds a detailed profile of each member's musical preferences. Based on this profile, Last.fm recommends artists similar to members' favorites and features their favorite artists and songs on a customizable Web page comprising the songs played on its stations selected via collaborative filtering (Chapter 8), or recorded by a Last.fm plug-in installed into its users' music-playing application.

Last.fm users can build their musical profiles in two ways: by listening to their personal music collection on a music player application with a special plug-in or by listening to the Last.fm Internet radio service. Songs played are added to a log from which musical recommendations are calculated. Last.fm calls this automatic track logging *scrobbling*. The user's page also displays recently played tracks, allowing users to display them on blogs or as forum signatures.

Regular membership is free; premium membership is $5 per month. The site, which operates in 10 major languages, has won several Best Community awards.

Pandora

Similar to Last.fm, Pandora (pandora.com) is a site for music lovers. The site runs entirely within a Web browser (unlike Last.fm, which requires a plug-in) and relies on people to suggest new music. As users select and listen to songs on Pandora and give them a thumbs-up or thumbs-down, the site also offers new songs that music evaluator experts have determined to be similar in style. Users can search for a particular artist, song, or genre and Pandora will create an entire personalized "radio station" full of similar music. In July 2011, Pandora launched its IPO with relative success.

Internet Series and Movie Streaming

Internet series are similar to soap operas on TV. The number of Internet series is increasing, and some are already on DVDs. Examples include *Broken Trail*, *Soup of the Day*, and *Floaters*.

Hulu (hulu.com). Hulu offers commercial-supported streaming video of TV shows and movies from NBC, Fox, and many other networks and studios. Due to copyright laws, Hulu videos were offered only to users in the United States and few other countries. Hulu provides video in Flash video format, including many films and shows. In addition, some TV shows and movies are now offered in high definition. It is similar to Google Sites, Fox Interactive Media, and Yahoo! Sites. Hulu incorporated social networking features into its offerings, called Hulu Friends. It gives users the opportunity to set up profiles, share favorite episodes of hit shows (e.g., *The Office*, *24*). Hulu Friends allows integration with Facebook, MySpace, Digg, and Delicious, along with Gmail, Yahoo!, and Hotmail. When it comes to online video, and culture touchstones like hit TV shows, people like communities, they like to share what they're downloading. Adding community features enables Hulu to build a community for its users within its own borders.

Moontoast. Moontoast lets fans listen, share, and buy entertainment without leaving Facebook. This creates a seamless experience for the fans, gives the selling artist more control, and puts more profits in the artist's pocket. The application, with no sign-up or subscription costs, lives on an artist's Facebook page and lets fans play, share, and buy music tracks and albums from an easy-to-use interface customizable for each artist. Moontoast Impulse gives forward-thinking artists a simple and effective way to not only participate but to maximize and monetize their social presence. It gives both established and up-and-coming artists an easy entry into social commerce, and could prove to be a game-changer for artists who see the potential of engaging with and selling to their fans direct.

Funny-or-Die. Funny-or-Die is a comedy video website. Unlike other viral video sites, members of Funny-or-Die are encouraged to vote on videos that they view, as being "Funny" or "Die." The video then gets a score of the total percent of people who voted the video "Funny." If the video receives an 80 percent or greater "Funny" rating after 100,000 views, it gets an "Immortal" ranking. If the video receives a 20 percent or less "Funny" rating after 1,000 views, it is relegated to the Crypt section of the site. For details, see en.wikipedia.org/wiki/Funny_or_Die.

MOBILE WEB 2.0 DEVICES FOR ENTERTAINMENT AND WORK

Several mobile devices have been designed with blogs, wikis, and other P2P services in mind. Here are some examples.

iPhone and Its Clones

The iPhone (from apple.com) was introduced in 2007. It is an all-in-one smartphone (see the following photo of the iPhone 3G). It is considered a disruptor in the cell phone market. Soon after the iPhone's release, Samsung announced a similar smartphone, BlackBerry introduced the Storm, and Google launched the Android Google phone. These smartphones are marketed by cell phone carriers such as AT&T and Verizon. The competition among these new smartphones is intense, and new capabilities appear frequently.

The iPhone is also a personal media player, offering all the capabilities of an iPod, with music and video playback, plus the benefits of a high-resolution widescreen display for watching movies and videos. It is a touchscreen smartphone with full-blown Internet communication capabilities; a quad-band, EDGE-capable mobile phone; and it has a "brain" (i.e., PAD capabilities), making it simple and easy to use. It also has a camera, a headset jack, and a built-in speaker. It also supports online multiplayer gaming.

The iPhone also has a sleep/wake button, and a proximity sensor turns off the screen when users hold the phone to their heads. It features automatic-orientation adjustment, switching between portrait and landscape modes on-the-fly. The iPhone boasts virtually no dedicated controls; instead, everything is driven using a new (patented) multitouch screen that Apple claims is far more accurate than previous touch-sensitive displays. New capabilities appear with every new version. For additional details, see apple.com/iphone and en.wikipedia.org/wiki/iphone.

The iPhone lets companies such as Apple and Google "merge without merging" by delivering Google services through Apple hardware.

MULTIMEDIA PRESENTATION AND SHARING SITES

Multimedia sharing can be done in several ways, and it is used for entertainment, advertising, training, and socialization. The following are the major types of sharing with representative companies:

▶ **Photography and art sharing:** Flickr, Photobucket, Picasa, deviantArt, SmugMug, Zoomr, BetweenCreation
▶ **Video sharing:** YouTube, sevenload, Viddler, Vimeo, Dailymotion. Metacafe, Nico Nico Douga, Openfilm, TubeMogul
▶ **Livecasting:** Justin.tv, Livestream, OpenCU, Skype, Stickam, Ustream

iPhone 3G

- ▶ **Music and audio sharing:** ccMister, Last.fm, MySpace Music, ReverbNation.com, ShareTheMusic, The Hype Machine
- ▶ **Presentation sharing:** Scribd, SlideShare
- ▶ **Media and entertainment platforms:** Cisco Eos
- ▶ **Virtual worlds:** Second Life, the Sims Online, Forterra
- ▶ **Game sharing:** Miniclip, Kongregate

Note that many of these have some features of social networks, and therefore are referred to as social networks.

SOCIAL GAMES

A social game or *social gaming* is a video game played in a social network. Generally speaking, these are "massively" multiplayer online games (known as MMOG or MMO),

social game
A video game played in a social network.

which are capable of supporting hundreds or thousands of players simultaneously. By necessity, they are played on the Internet, and feature at least one persistent world. They are, however, not necessarily games played on personal computers. Most of the newer game consoles, including the PSP, PlayStation 3, Xbox 360, Nintendo DSi, and Wii, can access the Internet and may therefore run MMO games. Additionally, mobile devices and smartphones based on such operating systems as Android, iOS, webOS, and Windows Mobile are seeing an increase in the number of MMO games available.

MMOGs can enable players to cooperate and compete with each other on a large scale, and sometimes to interact meaningfully with people around the world. They include a variety of gameplay types, representing many video genres. Social games are very popular (played by 20 percent of all Internet users, at least once a week). Some games require fees for enhanced features. The rest are free.

Games on Social Networks

The origin of the term "social games" comes from the distribution platform of the games; they run on social networks. So the term is usually read as *social (network) games*. It has little or nothing to do with how *social* the games are. However some games have social components such as gift-giving, lending help, and other asynchronous message-passing like notes, visiting your friends' pets, etc.

For a game to be more social it should facilitate and encourage communication about the game outside the game, run on or integrated with social network and use that network to enhance game play between players, and utilizes players' *social graph* to provide enhanced game experiences. Social games on Facebook (and there are thousands of them) could involve millions of players.

Examples of Popular Games on Facebook. There are several thousand games you can choose from on Facebook. The most popular ones, per Facebook (February 2011) were:

1. CityVille (96,509,000 monthly active users)
2. FarmVille (51,334,000)
3. TexasHoldEm Poker (37,900,000)
4. Frontierville (21,116,000)
5. Café World (15,800,000)
6. Mafia Wars (14,880,000)

To learn more, go to museumstuff.com/learn/topics/Social_network_game. To find friends and share gaming experiences on the Web you may go to the following sites: gamerDNA, Raptr, WeGame, UGAME, and Rupture.

Example: SCVNGR—A Game for "Checking In" in LBS. SCVNGR is a social location-based gaming platform for mobile phones. The application has both a consumer and enterprise component. Companies, educational institutions, and organizations can build challenges, the core unit of their game, at places on SCVNGR from the Web. The service also supports SMS.

By going places and doing challenges, players can earn points. They are also able to broadcast where they are and what they are up to on Facebook and Twitter. By doing challenges, players can unlock badges and real-world rewards, such as discounts or free items.

Conclusions: The Business Aspects

To understand the variety of games and their properties and commercial possibilities, we suggest you watch the video "Social Media Games: Worldwide Gamification Is the New Paradigm for Life and Business" (youtube.com/watch?v=xCWsgBHY_VU). The video presents opportunities in advertising, marketing, and training fields among others. Also, visit the site of Zynga, the major player in the field (zynga.com). In 2011, Zynga had about 250 million visitors each month (It took Facebook 4.5 years to reach the same level of visitors reached by Zynga in 2.5 years) and its revenue is estimated to be over $500 million a year, and growing rapidly (see Helft 2010). As far as revenues, Facebook games provide very little per person per month. Electronic Art, a Zynga's competitor, has some games that generate three to five times more per game. However, Zynga has significantly more players. Both companies now have gone mobile. For example, FarmVille for iPad and iPhone are available.

A final note: Not all games are fun or commerce oriented. Some have a true socio-educational purpose. For example, a Philippine-made Facebook game called Alter Space aims to educate the public on how to reduce pollution. Specifically, it educates the players about the concepts of carbon footprints and cleaner and renewable sources of energy and how being responsible and mindful of their activities could help achieve this end. For details, see facebook.com/AlterSpaceGame and Online File W7.5.

Section 7.10 ▶ REVIEW QUESTIONS

1. Relate entertainment to social commerce.
2. Describe Mixi, Last.fm, and Pandora.
3. Describe eFan, Hulu, Moontoast, and Funny or Die.
4. Relate the iPhone to entertainment on the Web.
5. Define social games; what types do you recognize?
6. Describe social games in social networks.
7. What are some of the business (commerce) aspects of social games?

7.11 JUSTIFICATION, RISKS, OTHER IMPLEMENTATION ISSUES, AND STRATEGY

Implementing social commerce faces problems similar to that of implementing other e-commerce applications (see Chapter 13). In this chapter, we cover only some relevant topics. We concentrate here on the following topics:

- ▶ Justification, cost–benefit, and ROI
- ▶ The risk of deploying social commerce systems
- ▶ Other implementation issues
- ▶ The strategy for successful implementation (including CSF)
- ▶ Revenue generation strategy

For an overview of SC implementation, see Dawson (2009).

THE COMPLEXITY OF SOCIAL COMMERCE IMPLEMENTATION

In Exhibit 7.3 (p. 340) we illustrated the diversity of the SC field. To illustrate the potential complexity of the field, the concept of the "social marketing compass," was developed by Brian Solis and can be found at briansolis.com/2009/10/introducing-the-social-compass (see Solis and Kutcher 2010 and Solis 2009 for details). The compass includes four components, which are listed in Online File W7.6 with their subcomponents.

JUSTIFICATION, COST–BENEFIT, AND ROI OF SOCIAL COMMERCE SYSTEMS

Even though the tangible (direct) cost of many social commerce projects is very low, the total cost can be very high due to the cost of the risks that may materialize (e.g., very negative conversations on some products). Therefore, it is wise to justify such systems including the risks. The methodology to do just that is the same as for any other EC systems, and it is presented in Chapter 13. Soat (2009) suggests starting with the following questions:

1. Are the competitors investing in social networking?
2. What will be the expected ROI?

3. What kind of network will you choose (e.g., private versus public)? What type of networking should you do?

4. How deep within the organization is social networking allowed to penetrate?

5. Is it necessary to have a corporate policy on social networking?

6. What can social media teach the company about internal collaboration?

7. What is next? What related projects are needed (e.g., mobility)?

Only when answers to these questions are clear can you start with the cost–benefit and quantitative justification.

It is also advisable to look at the reasons why companies use social commerce. Soat (2009) report a study done by Deloitte that shows the following business objectives of social networking (in decline order of importance):

- Generate more word of mouth
- Increase customer loyalty
- Bring outside ideas into the organization
- Improve customer support quality
- Increase sales
- Improve public relations effectiveness
- Improve partner relationship
- Business model innovation
- Reduce customer acquisition cost

These objectives relate to those reported in Sections 7.2 and 7.3. To justify SC projects, a company needs to decide which of these objectives it wants to attain and how important it is. Then, assess the potential contribution of social networking to the attainment of each objective as a part of the justification. Note that many of the objectives are intangible, which make the analysis difficult.

Measuring Social Commerce ROI

The following five-step cyclical process is based on Hayward (2009) and on the generic business performance management cycle provided in Chapter 13.

1. Decide on the goals and objectives.

2. Plan how the goals will be achieved.

3. Put the plan into action—implementation and execution.

4. Measure results.

5. Revisit, refine, adjust, and possibly redeploy. Revisit the goals and objectives and continue down the cycle.

Related to the measurements is the use of metrics. Companies such as Radiant6, Brandwatch, and Sentiment Metrics are active in this area.

For a discussion on how to measure ROI in social commerce, see Solis (2010) who also analyzes the difficulties in such a measurement.

Using Metrics

In executing the measurement step cited previously, it is common to compare the measured results against some standards or metrics. The comparisons can result in improving the marketing strategy. O'Neill (2010), Solis (2010), and Stuart (2009) suggest 10 metrics that are related to marketing. The metrics are:

1. Track traffic for finding leads (e.g., sources, changes over time).
2. Find the engagement duration.
3. Bounce rate (how quickly a visitor leaves your site).
4. Membership (numbers and their composition).
5. Activity levels (by type).
6. Conservation levels (by type).
7. Brand and company/product mentions (reputation); positive and negative comments in all social networking activities.
8. Loyalty and sharing; are social members really interacting in the network repeatedly, sharing content and links, mentioning your brands, evangelizing? How many members reshare? How often do they reshare? (Several possible measures can be used here.)
9. Extent of virality. Social members might be sharing Twitter tweets and Facebook updates relevant to your company, but is this info being reshared by their networks? How soon afterward are they resharing? How many friends of friends are resharing your links and content?
10. Blog interaction (several measures).

Bernoff and Li (2008) developed success metrics for the Social Web in each of the following categories: Marketing, sales, customer support, operations, and research and development. Most are quantitative.

Each of these may have several variations and measures. For more on social media metrics, see Stuart (2009), and Bonson and Flores (2010). Related to metrics is the area of *social analytics,* which evaluates what you measure; see Howard (2010).

In justifying SC initiatives, it is necessary to look at the potential risks and try to assess them as well (e.g., see Steinhart 2011). These risks are discussed next.

RISK FACTORS AND ANALYSIS

Although social commerce presents many opportunities for organizations, its implementation may involve some potential risks and possibly complex implementation issues (Steinhart 2009). Concerns and issues are related to companies engaged in social commerce activities as well as to individuals who participate in them.

Interfacing with social networks is not without risks. Aligning a product or a company with sites where content is user-generated and not edited or filtered has its downside. Another risk is that the company needs to be willing to accept negative reviews and feedback. If a company has really positive customer relationships and strong feedback and is willing to have customers share the good, but possibly some bad, as well as the ugly, it is a good candidate for social networking. If, however, the company worries about what its customers would say, the product or business might not be ready for social networking.

Another key consideration is the 20–80 rule, which posits that a minority of individuals (20 percent) contribute most of the content (80 percent) to blogs, wikis, and similar tools. For example, approximately 1,000 of Wikipedia's millions of contributors write most of its content (see money.cnn.com/2007/02/21/magazines/business2/nextnet_intro.biz2/index.htm).

In an analysis of thousands of submissions over a three-week period on audience in voting sites such as Digg and Reddit, the *Wall Street Journal* reported that one-third of the stories that made it to Digg's homepage were submitted by 30 contributors (out of 900,000 registered members), and that one single person on Netscape, going by the online name "Stoner," was responsible for 13 percent of the top posts on that site. Such distribution may result in biases.

Finally, the use of Web 2.0 applications may present a security risk. In 2011, the top eight security risks included insufficient authentication controls, phishing, and information leakage (see readwriteweb.com/archives/top_8_web_20_security_threats.php).

The following are representative issues that are frequently cited by companies:

▶ Wrong justification due to the difficulties cited earlier
▶ Legal risks (viruses, malware, etc.; see Chapter 9)
▶ Security threats
▶ Invasion of privacy (see Chapters 9 and 14)
▶ Social fraud (see Chapter 9)
▶ Violation of intellectual property and copyright (see Chapter 14)
▶ Employees' reluctance to participate
▶ Data leakage (corporate strategic information)
▶ Poor or biased quality of users' generated content
▶ Cyberbullying/cyberstalking and employee harassment
▶ Misuse and waste of time and other resources (loss of productivity)
▶ Risk to the reputation of the company (loss of credibility) due to users' conversations and bloggers' discussions (see Gaines-Ross 2010 and McGillicuddy 2007)

Risk to Users

In addition to risk to companies, there are some risks to users, mostly in the areas of fraud and privacy violation. As a result, some users abandon social networks. For a discussion, see della Cava (2010). For an overview of personal risk and how you can protect yourself, see netsecurity.about.com/od/newsandeditorial2/a/socialpredators.htm.

A discussion of the major risks is available at Online File W7.7 with supportive references. Also see Stroud (2010) and Turban, et al. (2012) for a description and ways to mitigate these risks.

OTHER IMPLEMENTATION ISSUES

Several other implementation issues are generic. The major ones are discussed in Chapter 13 including:

▶ Adoption of technology.
▶ Technical factors including integration with EC and IT existing systems, both internally and along the supply chain (Chapter 11). Also, payment systems in social networks can be an issue.
▶ Implementing B2B social networks.
▶ The issues of social software selection, adoption, usage patterns, and motivations for using (see comparesocialsoftware.com).
▶ Corporate culture and social commerce project implementation.
▶ Information flow.

Social networks and Twitter conversations and the one-way messages (from one source to a large audience) results in a very high level of information flow. Thus, it may be difficult for users and/or companies to find what is really going on. One solution is provided by Spindex, a Microsoft tool that can pull together a user's social streams from multiple social networks. This also enables the personalization of social information.

For further details, see ontherecordpodcast.com/pr/otro/B2B-social-networking.aspx, and Gillin and Schwartzman (2011). Each of these topics can be very complex and essential to the success of social networking. An interesting implementation issue particular for SC is managing a company's reputation.

Support Services

Social commerce needs support systems like any other EC. The major support systems are:

▶ Payments (as outlined in Chapter 10); also Facebook currency and payments (see the closing case), Twitter's virtual currency, (Goldman 2009), and payments in Second Life.
▶ Order fulfillment—this is identical to EC; see Chapter 11.

▶ Security—similar to EC; see Chapter 9.

▶ System development and business plans—similar to EC; see Chapters 13 and 15.

REPUTATION SYSTEM MANAGEMENT

Companies considering social networking invariably ask, "But wait, suppose somebody posts something negative? What do we do then?" That's the dilemma of meeting customers where they congregate online. For example, when you create a Facebook business page, by default the service allows other members of the service—potentially including disgruntled customers or sleazy competitors—to post notes to your Facebook Wall, or comment on what you've posted.

Yet, if you turn off the feature that lets others write on your Wall, people may wonder what you are afraid of. You will also be foreclosing the possibility of having great customer fan conversations take place, perhaps marketing your products and services better than you could do yourself. You can delete posts, but that may only encourages the post author to scream louder about being censored. Most social media marketing experts advise deleting only the most offensive posts, and trying to address the rest as constructively as possible.

One way to look at reputation systems is to design them properly so that there will be more opportunities for positive comments. Furthermore, a properly designed site will attract the proper visitors and facilitate proper trust and interactions. Thus, instead of looking at negatives, reputation systems should:

▶ Build trust.

▶ Promote quality.

▶ Facilitate member matching.

▶ Sustain loyalty.

For comprehensive coverage, see Dellarocas (2010). For how a company deals with the reputation issue, see the example that follows.

Example: Social Commerce Strategy at Rosetta Stone. Rosetta Stone is a maker of software for language translation. It is mostly a B2B organization. To get the most out of social media, Rosetta Stone uses a strategy and a software to control its customer interaction at Facebook. The strategy involves both human intervention and an investment in software to help monitor its social networking presence. Specifically, the company software helps to monitor Wall posts and respond to them appropriately.

Fans of facebook.com/RosettaStone who post questions on the Wall are likely to get a prompt answer because the Facebook page is integrated with customer service software from Parature Inc. The Parature for Facebook module adds a support tab to the page, where customers can submit a request for help that goes into the system as a standard support item.

The software helps by scanning Wall posts and flagging those that require a company response, as opposed to those that represent fans of the page talking among themselves. Through the PayPal application programming interface, customer service representatives are also able to post a response to the Wall that will be logged in the Parature issue tracking database. The customer service software is also integrated with Facebook chat. All this is done without leaving Facebook, so it is very convenient. Also, the Parature software is pretty accurate in flagging the posts that need help.

For details, see facebook.com/RosettaStone and Carr (2010).

A STRATEGY FOR SC SUCCESS OF IMPLEMENTATION

To succeed in social commerce projects' implementation, especially in medium and large companies, a process needs to be properly planned with a development strategy. A popular strategy involves four steps:

1. Learn and understand the environment inside and outside the organization.

2. Experiment with a small-scale project so you can observe and learn.

3. Assess the results of the experiment.

4. Develop or abandon the project.

Similar steps are offered by Gombert (2010): Evaluate opportunities, prepare a plan, engage your audience, and measure results.

There are many ways to execute this strategy (e.g., see Chapter 12). For example, a strategy that integrates the social Web with your own website and e-commerce plan will drive revenue growth, expand brand awareness, and increase customer loyalty and satisfaction. Implementing a social media strategy is not without potential pitfalls, but these challenges can be turned into a strong foundation for your success. The strategist's goal is to build a community on and off your website around your brand and use that community to increase awareness, drive revenue, and increase loyalty to your company. This kind of marketing is the key to your company's success, and the brand message needs to be distributed consistently across all of your digital channels from your website and e-commerce channel to micro-messaging on Twitter, or to post on a Facebook group. Participation in these channels has to be efficient and timely; missing opportunities to inform and educate potential buyers can have disastrous effects.

Examples

Here are three examples of how small businesses are using social networks:

1. The photographer and owner of Studio Seven, Lydia Schuster, started her business solely on the belief Facebook would work for her. She was looking at her friends list and she had more than 600 friends. She had always gotten a lot of really good feedback from any photos she posted on Facebook on her personal page. She then started her Facebook business page, and to attract customers, she offered some incentives such as the first person who responded would get a free sitting fee. She started receiving more fans, and her photos received thousands of votes. Schuster said she thinks people look at Facebook pages for photographers now instead of their websites.

2. Virginia McCoskrie, owner of Smockingbirds, started a weekly giveaway on her Facebook page. People need to comment on photos to enter their names into a drawing. Since she started doing the drawing, she had more people as fans of her business page, and her business grew dramatically.

3. Center Court Office Supplies uses its Facebook page to update its customers on what is new in the store and promotions being offered. It is able to decide on and run promotions quickly and the networking aspect has helped the small store.

Success in SMEs

According to several reports (e.g., Leggatt 2010), even small companies can succeed in social commerce. We demonstrated it throughout this chapter. For examples and discussions, see Moran (2010).

Some Other Strategy Issues

There are several strategic issues that companies may need to address. Here are some questions:

▶ Which is better for social media marketing: Facebook, Twitter, or others? (See Treese (2008) and an analysis at jazzou.com/index.php?option=com_content&task=view& id=451.)

▶ How do you select a social network site(s) to advertise or sell there?

▶ Do you have an internal private network or not?

▶ How do you generate constant traffic to your SC site? (See 10 ways at socialmediatoday. com/kieshaeasley/269512/10-ways-generate-constant-traffic?utm.)

▶ What small businesses can and cannot do with social networking?

▶ How can you have a sufficient number of fans and friends and have them participate?

Small Number of Followers. As you will see next, Walmart opened a private social network and spent a lot of money to get real-world actors and actresses and did lots of publicity. The fans did not show. The company had to close the site. This is one of the biggest challenges for almost all brands. Unless you are a brand that has been around for decades or who has a national reputation and presence like Starbucks, Coca-Cola, and McDonald's, you are not going to have millions of fans.

Hiring a consultant to help is not a bad idea, but it may be expensive for small and medium companies. Reading books, surfing the Internet, and placing questions of what to do on LinkedIn "Answers" and other Q&A sites can help.

Some Policies and Guidelines

Dozens of experts provide answers for these and similar strategy questions, and provide guidelines for success in specific areas of social commerce (e.g., marketing, security, policy). Several examples can be found at Dupre-Barnes and Barnes (2009). For 57 different social media policies and guidelines, see socialmediatoday.com/davefleet/151761/57-social-media-policy-examples-and-resources and itbusinessedge.com/commerce/?c=707. You can also learn from failures.

Example: Walmart's In-House Social Network. Although many companies have benefited significantly from enterprise social networking (e.g., Nike, Coca-Cola, and Sony), there have been some failures. For example, Walmart's enterprise networking effort was a complete failure.

For the largest retailer in the world, creating its own social network seemed to be natural and simple, but it was not. In 2007, Walmart launched a social network in order to bolster its image with younger consumers. The company hired professional actresses and actors to pose as teens on the site, but they were not convincing. Also, in an attempt to avoid future lawsuits, Walmart allowed parents to control page content. The young viewers were turned off. Because the number of visitors was very small, Walmart pulled down the site after a short period.

For the example of Starbucks' Foursquare failure, see Teicher (2010).

For other examples of failures, see the white paper "The Five Biggest Blunders with Enterprise Social Networks" at socialtext.com.

Internet Use and Social Commerce Policies

One of the major risks both in EC and SC is employees' abuse of the Internet. Many employees use it during working hours for personal use. One solution is to issue strict Internet use policies, and enforce them. For a discussion see Chapter 14.

Adoption Strategies

Many companies, consultants, vendors, and researchers provide tips, guidelines, and recipes for success. For example, Dion Hinchcliffe offers adoption strategies at ideamamaadnetwork. com/blog/2010/03/06/developing-social-media-innovation-strategy.

Bernoff and Schadler (2010) introduced a concept they call HERO (Highly Empowered and Resourceful Operative) that integrates managers and IT support for customer service into a framework of how to deal with dissatisfied customers, and how to handle the risks of networking. For comprehensive coverage of this topic, see Online Chapter 15 and Shih (2011).

REVENUE-GENERATION STRATEGIES IN SOCIAL NETWORKS

The following are some interesting ways social networks generate revenue: (1) offer premium service to individuals for a monthly or per service fee, (2) partner with organizations that pay a monthly service fee, and (3) create affiliations with physical venues where members can meet (e.g., meetup.com). Physical venues, such as coffee shops, may pay a fee to be affiliated with the social network.

Exhibit 7.9 illustrates how Web 2.0 applications can generate revenue. It shows users' contributions and the relationships among people, advertising, and Web 2.0 tools, such as mashups. The Web applications may generate revenue via subscription fees and advertisements. To learn more about how blogs can bring in big money, see Weber (2007).

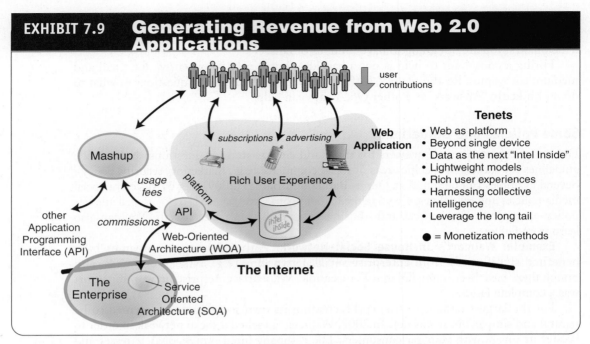

EXHIBIT 7.9   Generating Revenue from Web 2.0 Applications

Source: D. Hinchcliffe, Web 2.0 Blog, *web2.wsj2.com*. Used with permission from Don Hinchcliffe.

Increased Revenue and Its Benefits

Web 2.0 tools can generate revenue growth, user growth, and increased resistance to competition in indirect ways, which, in turn, lead to increased subscriptions, advertising, and commission revenue.

The strategic use of online communities can increase revenue and profit. Case 7.3 describes some of the potential revenue sources created by EC in social networks.

CASE 7.3
EC Application
REVENUE SOURCES AT YOUTUBE

Some experts think that Google paid too much for YouTube, especially in light of its copyright-related legal problems (see Online File W7.8). However, Google may actually have gotten a bargain. Consider the following:

▸ **Two-minute YouTube clips were just the start.** As television comes to the Internet, dozens of companies are competing to become the networks of tomorrow. Whichever networks attract the most viewers will inevitably attract vast numbers of advertisers as well. YouTube's ad revenue in 2007 alone has been valued at $200 million by *eMarketer* and Citigroup. And wherever there's video programming, viewers will be seeing more video ads. One forecast from *eMarketer* predicts that overall video advertising on the Web (including video ads replacing banners on regular Web pages) will reach $4.6 billion in 2013, a sevenfold leap from the 2006 total of $410 million (SeekingAlpha 2009).

▸ **Brand-created entertainment content.** In 2005, Nike produced a pseudo-home video of soccer star Ronaldinho practicing while wearing his new Nike Gold shoes. In one week, the clip was downloaded 3.5 million times on YouTube (worldwide), providing Nike with tremendous exposure to its core, mostly young male, audience. As the younger generation moves away from traditional TV, it is shifting its attention to YouTube and similar offerings.

▸ **User-driven product advertising.** User-generated videos could be leveraged in a similar manner to product placement on TV. For example, although not intentional, a 17-year-old girl's use of Logitech's Webcam featured in a short clip on YouTube where she talks about the breakup with her boyfriend greatly contributed to awareness of Logitech's offerings. The product placement trend is also expanding across the blogosphere, with Nokia promoting its new smartphone through the 50 most influential bloggers in Belgium and establishing a blogger-relationship blog.

▸ **Multichannel word-of-mouth campaign.** When Chevrolet decided to combine its *Apprentice* Tahoe campaign with an

(continued)

CASE 7.3   *(continued)*

online consumer-generated media (CGM) campaign, it did not anticipate the additional viral impact of YouTube. On the Chevrolet site, users could create their own customized video commercial, complete with text and background music. Environmentalists took the opportunity to produce spoof videos and published them on YouTube. However, the word-of-mouth advertising Chevrolet received on YouTube was ultimately beneficial to Chevrolet. The Chevrolet site generated 4 million page views, 400,000 unique visitors, and 22,000 ad submissions in just six months.

Sources: Compiled from Sahlin and Botello (2007), SeekingAlpha (2009), and *youtube.com* (accessed March 2011).

Questions

1. List the different advertising models on YouTube.
2. List the success factors from these cases.
3. How do users benefit from using YouTube?

THE FUTURE OF SOCIAL COMMERCE

In determining justification and strategy, we need to look into the future. Many researchers and consultants are speculating on the future (e.g., adage.com/digitalnext/post? article_id=143145, Shih (2011), and siliconprairienews.com/2010/07/lava-row-s-nathan-wright-predicts-future-of-social-media). The predictions are diverse, ranging from SC will dominate EC to "it is a buzz word and will disappear soon." Given the popularity of Facebook, Twitter, Groupon, YouTube, social games, social shopping, and social advertisement, it is difficult to side with the pessimistic predictions. It looks as if mobile social commerce will be a major area of growth as well as several of the social shopping and advertisement models. In the enterprise area, there is a trend to have a "social as a service" rather than an application approach (due to the influence of cloud computing, see Online Tutorial T7).

Conclusion: IBM's Watson and Social Commerce

There are many opinions on what the future of SC will be. Instead of presenting them, we decided to end this chapter by looking at IBM's Watson supercomputer. In February 2011, IBM's Watson won a *Jeopardy* 3-day tournament against two world champions. To achieve this victory, researchers fed Watson 200 million pages of text—about 1 million books—ranging from encyclopedias to movie scripts to newspapers to children's book abstracts. With its ability to store all that data, Watson then mines it to formulate contextual relationships. IBM says Watson's deep Q&A technology could be applied in diverse fields such as e-commerce, health care, legal, education, and government. Now assuming you could afford the hardware and information resources, imagine if you had your own personal Watson (one day such capabilities will be affordable), what will you be able to do in social commerce?

Here are a few personal social apps:

▶ **Personal shopping aid.** A combination of sales engine, e-commerce, and decision making, Watson can look at what is currently in your closet, learn what colors flatter your skin tone, and make recommendations on what clothes to buy. Hook it up to stores and you can peruse recommended selections at your favorite stores or at the best deal that Watson can find for you, and with a credit card, Watson can take care of finalizing the purchase.

▶ **Investing helper.** As your new portfolio manager, Watson can sift through SEC filings, sort through the wealth of financial analysis and reports and make educated decisions on exactly where you should be investing your money; who else has the time or patience to read those prospectus reports?

▶ **Language translator.** You may recall that in EC we need language translation for translating Web pages to other languages. We need it also for translating a natural human language to a language a computer can understand. Today's machine language is not so good. Watson, with its far more sophisticated natural language processing capabilities can provide superb machine translation.

▶ **Customer service.** Why should companies outsource call centers to India or China? Buy a slice of Watson and it can handle the tech support without worrying about routing users through tier 1, 2, or 3 levels of support. It will know about outages, can get monitoring data, and knows whether other people had recently complained about the same thing. You can be sure the service will be consistent, top quality, and available in real time.

▶ **Q&A service.** Watson will provide the best answers to any business, medical, legal, or personal question you have. It will answer any question and subsequent subquestions.

▶ **Matchmaking.** Watson can match sellers and buyers, products and markets, job seekers and jobs, partners to bartering, P2P lending participants. Any match you can think of. What about a partner in life? Move over, Match.com, eHarmony, and OKCupid. Watson has all the information about what you like, knows the type of people you have been attracted to in the past, and can balance it against what you are looking for, to find you that perfect date for the weekend or a soul mate.

Section 7.11 ▶ REVIEW QUESTIONS

1. List some major implementation issues.
2. List some difficulties in SC justification.
3. Solis's Compass includes four components. List two in each category and briefly describe them (consult Online File W7.6).
4. List and briefly describe three risk factors (consult Online File W 7.7).
5. List the major elements in a successful implementation strategy for social commerce.

MANAGERIAL ISSUES

Some managerial issues related to this chapter are as follows.

1. **How will social commerce impact businesses?** The impacts of social marketing can change the manner in which many shoppers make purchasing decisions. The impact may be so strong that the entire manner in which companies do business with social customers will be changed, with significant impacts on procedures, people, organizational structure, management, and business processes. Strong impact will be felt in advertising, viral marketing, collaboration, and brand recognition. The impact will also be strong on delivering customer service, conducting market research, and organizing collaboration.

2. **Should we explore Web 2.0 collaboration?** Consider whether your corporate culture is ready to experiment with social collaboration tools and social networks. Work with your corporate-learning or organization-development department to find areas likely for experimentation. Also explore the opportunities to collaborate with your business partners (e.g., in joint design). Consider blogs, wikis, and virtual worlds as well as the social network sites you want to use.

3. **Ethical and etiquette issues.** When working with social systems, it is important not to offend anyone. For example, some users may object to any commercial material. So spamming is a no-no. Some user-generated content is not copyrighted formally—do not steal it. Companies should not covet their competitor's blog. And no one should place unfounded information to make the competitors look bad. Do not sell anything unless users opt in; remember, people may come

there only for social objectives. For more guidelines, see *bristoleditor.wordpress.com*.

4. **What are the ethical issues that may be involved in deploying social commerce?** Social commerce can lead to several ethical issues such as privacy and accountability. In addition, mistakes can cause harm to others as well as the company. Another important ethical issue is human judgment, which is frequently a key factor in social commerce. Human judgment may be subjective or corrupt, and therefore, it may lead to unethical consequences. Companies should provide an ethical code for system builders and users. There are ethical issues related to the implementation of idea generation and other problem solving–related considerations. The actions performed in a simulated virtual world can be unethical, or even illegal. The issue is: Should an organization employ productivity-saving devices that are not ethical? Another ethical issue is the use of knowledge extracted in crowdsourcing from people. A related issue is: Should a company compensate an employee when knowledge that he or she contributed is used by others? This issue is related to the motivation issue. It is also related to privacy. Should people be informed as to who contributed certain knowledge?

5. **Do we need to sponsor a social network?** Although sponsoring a social network might sound like a good idea, it may not be simple to execute. Community members need services, which cost money to provide. The most difficult task is to find an existing community that matches your business. In many cases, the cost of a social

network may be justified by its contribution to advertising. However, the social network service providers needs to create various revenue models to maintain sustainable services. Creating revenue is the most challenging issue to social network service providers.

6. **How should we deal with social commerce risks?** There are several possible risks, depending on the applications. The knowledge from unreliable participants may downgrade the credibility of knowledge from open sources. To protect the security of the open system, consult your internal security experts and get some outside legal advice. Use a consultant for large projects to examine and evaluate the risks. Weighing the benefits of social media against security concerns is a major strategy issue (see Tucci 2010).

7. **Should we have an in-house social network? How do we get the employees to use it?** This is a debatable issue. Although most companies should probably opt to go into a successful public social network service,

there are cases where an in-house service can be much more beneficial. Large companies may use both. It is probably most advantageous to build the knowledge management system using both internal sources and external sources. For how to induce employees to contribute and use social networks, see Healey (2010).

8. **Is it wise for a small business to be on Facebook?** It depends on the business and on what you are trying to achieve. It could be helpful for those that need to constantly reach customers and/or suppliers. Facebook, at present, may not be helpful for direct sales. Just having a presence costs little and therefore should be considered. A major issue for SMBs is the loose security in social networks. See Shih (2011) for comprehensive coverage of this topic.

9. **What shall I do now?** Consult *ehow.com* and receive instructions on many topics such as how to advertise on social networks and how to make money there.

SUMMARY

In this chapter, you learned about the following EC issues as they related to the chapter's learning objectives.

1. **The Web 2.0 revolution and social media.** Web 2.0 is about the innovative application of existing technologies. Web 2.0 has brought together the contributions of millions of people and has made their work, opinions, and identity matter. The consequences of the rapid growth of person-to-person computing, such as blogging, are currently hard to understand and difficult to estimate. User-created content is a major characteristic of Web 2.0, as is the emergence of social networking. Social media implements Web 2.0 tools for social interactions, conversations, and sharing ideas, in many different ways.

2. **Fundamentals, drivers, and the landscape of social commerce.** Social commerce refers to conducting EC in social networks and using social networks. It is a comprehensive field comprised mostly of social media marketing (advertising, market research, and customer service). It also includes social networking, social entertainment, social CRM, and crowdsourcing. It is driven by the existence of giant social networks, social customers, Web 2.0 tools, and competition among vendors.

3. **Major models of social shopping.** The major models are: group buy, which is frequently combined with daily deals; providing reviews, recommendations, ratings, and conversations; shopping clubs and communities; location-based shopping; peer-to-peer trading; f-commerce, and shopping with Twitter. Groupon, Foursquare, Gilt, Kaboodle, and hundreds of other start-ups are active participants. Competition is getting strong, and

success is visible mostly in Facebook, Groupon, and Foursquare.

4. **How advertisement and promotions are conducted in social networking.** The major driver of SC is the money spent by advertisers who see a huge potential market. Advertising can be done in many ways. Using word of mouth is free, but it can be dangerous (negative comments). The use of banner ads and other paid models generate billions for social networks (mostly to Facebook). Large numbers of advertising apps exist. Also bloggers can provide positive (sometime negative) comments. LBS combines geolocation with advertisements and coupons (in the right time and place). Many companies developed special campaigns that engage community members in activities (play games, vote, generate ideas, etc.). Advertisement on Twitter and YouTube is becoming popular.

5. **Conducting market research.** Monitoring conversations, communication that is done directly with customers using Twitter, participation in discussion groups, using the answer function of LinkedIn and others all provide information to merchants that can be used to improve marketing and advertising plans, provide personalization, and do relevant analysis. Another area is customer feedback regarding new/improved products and services. Companies are getting almost free feedback from customers and suggestions about how to improve operations (e.g., Starbucks).

6. **Conducting customer service and CRM.** Customers are empowered by social networks and so they can get

attention quickly for problem resolution. Organizing a Facebook complaint blitz is not difficult. Customers can make suggestions for improvements and vote on them. Letting customers help themselves and each other is offered via social networking while reducing merchant expenses. Customers can become more loyal because they work closer with vendors. Social networking provides innovative ideas for improved and speedy customer service (e.g., Twitter can be very helpful).

7. **Major enterprise social commerce activities.** Collaboration and communication as well as community building are currently the major activities. Problem solving via idea generation and expertise finding are getting more and more important. Related to this is knowledge creation and management. Recruiting, training, and other HRM activities are practiced by many. Also, some companies allow P2P activities. Several companies use the enterprise social network for interactions with customers, suppliers, and other business partners.

8. **Crowdsourcing and social networking.** Crowd-sourcing is used mostly for idea generation, voting, and problem identification. Content creation and updating projects such as translating the Facebook website to French and German by volunteers falls into this category.

9. **Commercial application of virtual worlds.** The major P2P activity is trading or renting virtual goods. Companies conduct virtual meetings, training, testing designs, conduct advertisement, provide customer service (e.g., receptionists, call center help), recruitment, trade shows, market research, providing commercial games, and more.

10. **Social commerce, entertainment, and gaming.** Rich media, user-created content, and groups and subgroups with common interests open many possibilities for a second generation of online entertainment. Add to this the wireless revolution and the increased capabilities in mobile devices to support Web 2.0 tools and social networking activities and you will discover a new and exciting world of online entertainment.

11. **Implementing social commerce.** Implementing social commerce issues and procedures are similar to those of generic EC and IT (see Chapter 13). They can be divided into technical issues (e.g., security, system integration, scalability, appropriate design), and nontechnical (e.g., justification, employee resistance to contribute and use, lack of management support, lack of resources, risk mitigation, and training). Companies need to conduct a cost–benefit analysis of each project, including risk mitigation. Implementation is an important step in corporate strategy toward social networking and social network participation.

12. **Risks and concerns in deploying social commerce.** There are several potential risks in deploying social networking projects in organizations and/or when using public social networks. The major risks and concerns are: invasion of privacy, opening the gate for hackers, misuse of time and computing resources, revealing organizational confidential information, introducing inappropriate or inaccurate content, possibility of negative reviews, and the possibility of biased content by few contributors who contribute a lot of the content (including bloggers).

KEY TERMS

Business social network	373	Mobile social networking	342	Social media	335
Collective intelligence (CI)	386	Social capital	336	Social media marketing	
Communal shopping	344	Social commerce (SC)	339	(SMM)	336
Crowdsourcing	384	Social customer	369	Social shopping	343
Customer relationship		Social CRM (SCRM)	369	User-generated content	
management (CRM)	369	Social game	401	(UGC)	333
F-commerce	417	Social graph	338	Viral blogging	356
Geolocation	357	Social marketing	335	Viral marketing	356
Geosocial networking	357	Social marketplace	352	Viral video	359

DISCUSSION QUESTIONS

1. How do public business-oriented networks and private enterprise social networks differ?

2. Discuss the potential business use of Twitter (by major categories).

3. What are some of the risks companies may face if they decide to use public social networks?

4. Discuss the role of crowdsourcing in idea generation and market research.

5. How can marketers use social networks for viral marketing?

6. Why are advertisers so interested in social networks?

7. Compare group buying to shopping together.

8. Identify and discuss Facebook's revenue model.

9. Corporate social networking: Booster or time-waster? What are the pitfalls of enterprise social networking? Discuss.

10. Review any two Socialcast user case studies at socialcast.com/resources/customer_stories.html and discuss the following:

    a. What benefits the companies that embraced Socialcast have realized.

    b. Lessons learned from these cases.

11. Review the features of Socialtext (socialtext.com). Discuss how you would make use of this platform in a small enterprise in retail, manufacturing, or financial services.

12. Enter youtubetrafficsystem.net. Watch the video case "How Sam Got to the Top" (video 3). Discuss how Sam drove 3.5 million viewers to watch his fitness video.

13. What real value do virtual worlds present to commercial users and businesses?

14. Enter thesocialcustomer.com. Pick five posts and discuss each briefly.

15. How can crowdsourcing reduce risks to merchants?

TOPICS FOR CLASS DISCUSSION AND DEBATES

1. The crowdsourcing model works well with designers like this: (1) Come up with something that you need designing for. (2) Turn it into a competition between amateur and professional designers. (3) Decide on a winner, either by vote or executive decision. This is all at little to no cost for the person looking for the design. Now, think about the future of the graphic industry in general. What will be the fate of large design firms that are competing for the business of high-profile clients when the clients are now paying tiny, one-time fees to amateur designers? Is basing your business on crowdsourcing a viable model? Discuss.

2. Discuss the business value of social networking. As a start, read Tom Davenport's "Where's the 'Working' in Social Networks" (blogs.harvardbusiness.org/davenport/2007/10/wheres_the_working_in_social_n.html) and Brett Bonfield's "Should Your Organization Use Social Networking Sites" (techsoup.org/learning-center/internet/page7935.cfm).

3. What are the potential major legal issues that business applications in virtual worlds might encounter? Refer to online resources, including the Virtual World Law blog virtualworldlaw.com.

4. Idea generation by the employees or customers using crowdsourcing is becoming popular. Some say it is only an electronic suggestion box. Others disagree. Discuss.

5. Despite the promise of virtual worlds and the increased computing and graphic capabilities of personal computers, high-speed Internet access, and corporate interest in exploiting these worlds, why have virtual worlds not taken off, been adopted, or used widely. (Compare for example with Facebook, Twitter, blogs, or wikis.) What aspects hinder their adoption? What are the critical success factors? Discuss.

6. Read the Bernoff and Schadler article "Empowered: In a World Where One Angry Tweet Can Torpedo a Brand, Corporations Need to Unleash Their Employees to Fight Back." Then, discuss the top strategies employed by Best Buy including Twelpforce. Also discuss how other companies empower employees.

7. Debate: Should companies build in-house social networks for external activities (e.g., marketing, CRM) or use existing public social networks?

8. Debate: Some research suggests that the use of public social networks by employees can be good for a business, because employees develop relationships and share information, which increases productivity and innovation. Others say it is waste of time and ban the use of Facebook, YouTube, and other such sites.

9. Debate: Do Facebook privacy concerns really require government regulations? (Consult Prince 2010.)

10. Debate the pros and cons of the following: In order to control content and employee time, Manchester United and other companies do not allow employees to generate any content on its private social network site nor on public ones (e.g., Facebook).

INTERNET EXERCISES

1. Enter the website of a social network service (e.g., myspace.com or facebook.com). Build a homepage. Add a chat room and a message board to your site using the free tools provided. Describe the other capabilities available. Make at least five new friends.

2. Enter vivapets.com and dogster.com and compare their offerings.

3. Enter twitter.com, facebook.com, and linkedin.com and list the major sources of revenue for each.

4. Enter xing.com and linkedin.com and compare their functionalities (capabilities). Also, enter ryze.com and view the video tutorial on networking. Compare Ryze's capabilities with those of LinkedIn.com. Write a report.

5. Enter chicstar.com. Why is it an online entertainment service? What are the benefits to viewers? Compare this site to starz.com.

6. Enter advertising.com. Find the innovative/scientific methods that are offered and related to social commerce.

7. Enter the paulgillin.com blog and find information related to enterprise applications of social commerce technologies. Write a report.

8. Enter pandora.com. Find out how you can create and share music with friends. Why is this a social commerce application?

9. Enter webkinz.com and compare its activities to that of facebook.com. Enter nielsen-online.com and find the average stay time on both social network sites.

10. Enter smartmobs.com. Go to the blogroll. Find three blogs related to social commerce, and summarize their major features.

11. Enter mashable.com and review the latest news regarding social networks and network strategy. Right a report.

12. Enter usocial.com and softcity.com. Identify all the methods/tools they offer to increase social engagement/marketing and advertising. Write a report.

13. Enter comblu.com. Explore its products and discuss the role of a social marketing dashboard.

14. Enter secondlife.com and find the commercial activities of the following avatars: Fizik Baskerville, Craig Altman, Shaun Altman, FlipperPA Peregrine, and Anshe Chung. Describe briefly what they represent. Relate this to social commerce.

15. Enter crmbuyer.com/edpick/69895.html and identify five strategies suggested for improved customer service.

16. Enter thisnext.com. What are the features of the site. What do you like? dislike?

17. Enter en.wikipedia.org/wiki/Mixi and look at mixi's features that are similar to those offered by other social networks. Relate it to online entertainment.

18. Enter ning.com. Explore its capabilities and discuss how it is related to social network sites.

19. Enter fordstory.com. Find what is going on there. Also, watch the Fiesta video. Write a report.

20. Enter bazaarvoice.com. Summarize its major services. Examine SocialConnect and TweetConnect in particular.

21. Enter blippy.com and find the services it provides to customers.

22. Enter ehow.com and find "How to Use Twitter to Conduct Market Research." Follow instructions on a topic related to social commerce. Write a report.

TEAM ASSIGNMENTS AND PROJECTS

1. **Assignment for the Opening Case**

   Read the opening case, find some new material about Starbucks and social commerce and answer the following questions:

   a. Why is Starbucks putting such an emphasis on social media?

   b. List the specific social networking activities done by the company.

   c. What are the differences and similarities between Starbucks' own social network and its pages on Facebook, LinkedIn, and other social networks?

   d. Why did Starbucks fail with Foursquare?

   e. How are ideas generated at My Starbucks Idea? By whom?

   f. What did you learn about social media strategy?

2. Each group is assigned to a social network that has business activities on it (e.g., LinkedIn, Xing, f-commerce, Second Life, etc.). Each group will identify all social advertising and marketing on the sites. In addition, the group will register with Hellotxt (hellotxt.com) to find out what is going on in their chosen site with regard to recent business activities (use the dashboard). Write a report and make a class presentation.

3. Facebook is increasingly offering marketing tools (e.g., Open Graph, Social Plug-ins). Identify all the tools offered. Each group concentrates on the implication in one of the following areas: advertising and search engine optimization (SEO), shopping, market research, customer service, CRM, and others. Make a class presentation.

4. Your group signs in to secondlife.com and creates an avatar(s). Each member is assigned to explore a certain business area (e.g., virtual real estate, educational activities, tourism). Make sure the avatar interacts with other people's avatars. Write a report.

5. Each group adopts one or two of the following companies that actively advertise and engage on Facebook and Twitter: Coca-Cola, Starbucks, Ford, Pepsi, Disney,

Victoria's Secret, iTunes, Toyota, Sony, or P&G. Find what advertisement methods they use and how they do their campaigns.

6. Watch the tutorial video "Doing Business in Second Life" (blip.tv/file/24281), and answer:

   a. What can you do commercially on SL?
   b. How much will it cost you?
   c. How can you attract people to your SL page?
   d. What can you do there that you cannot do on Facebook or Twitter?
   e. What are the major benefits to companies? Consumers?
   f. What is the downside?
   g. What are IBM, Dell, and Coke doing in SL?

7. Enter ehow.com/how_4630584_advertise-second-life-event.html and read the article "How to Advertise a 'Second Life' Event." Follow the instructions and advertise a restaurant of your choice. Write a report.

Relate your work to the following SL features: affiliate program, Second Life Marketplace, blogs, and forums. Also look at secondlife.com/shop/learn. Write a report.

8. Have the group research the issue of "How Levi's and Facebook Prompt Your Friends to Improve Your Buying Experience." Start with web-strategist.com/blog/2010/04/30/social-commerce-breakdown-how-levis-and-facebook-prompt-your-friends-to-get-you-to-buy. Find out why Levi's is considered to be at level 6 or 7 while most brands are still at level 1. See also store.levi.com.

9. The class will investigate group buying in China and India. What is the prospect for group buying in Asia? (Start with Madden's article "China Pioneers Group Buying Discounts Without Groupon" at joomabc.com/website-clone/news/item/45-china-pioneers-group-buying-discounts-without-groupon).

Closing Case

F-COMMERCE: BUSINESS ACTIVITIES ON FACEBOOK

The story of Facebook is well known. If you do not know it, you may start by watching the 2010 movie *Social Network*, read the "Person of the Year" article in *Time* (December 27, 2010–January 3, 2011), or read Kirkpatrick (2011) and Shih (2011). With more than 750 million active users (growing by many thousands everyday), Facebook has become a very desirable place to advertise, sell, and conduct other social commerce activities. For an overview, see: "Using Facebook for Business" at the free Facebook Guide Book, *mashable.com/guidebook/facebook/*.

From E-Commerce to F-Commerce

Facebook is a social service or utility site that helps people communicate more efficiently with their friends, families, and coworkers. As a social utility, it changes the dynamics of relationships, how we communicate with one another, and how we discover, share, and learn (Grossman 2010/2011). Facebook and Social Media are redesigning the information super highway, forever altering how information flows and processes, and how people connect. It has become clear that the future of business is social, and it is giving rise to a new genre of connected consumers who are becoming influential in their own right.

As a platform, Facebook invites businesses to build a presence and design an engagement architecture that introduces a new opportunity to grow in prominence and connections; thus Facebook is defining and socializing the next era in business (see Shih 2011).

Facebook represents an important platform to engage and activate the social commerce. F-commerce is the ability to execute transactions in Facebook without leaving the network and by integrating Facebook into traditional site-based e-commerce platforms. And, more importantly, it ties each transaction to the *social graph*. What makes f-commerce different than e-commerce is the social experience. People are able to discuss products before, during, and after the sale within the Facebook environment. Facebook apps include advanced analytics that help understand consumer behavior on social networks. Traditional webstores will not disappear nor will physical stores, but f-commerce is becoming an important channel for retailers of all sizes and kinds.

f-commerce
The ability to execute transactions in Facebook without leaving the network or leveraging the open graph by integrating Facebook into traditional site-based e-commerce platforms. It ties each transaction to the social graph.

Example 1. Levi's introduced a "Friends Store" on its websites, which showcases the jeans that your friends have liked and also allows you to share the jeans you like with your friends. This introduces a *peer-to-peer* influence model where we influence and are influenced by those we trust. Levi's is betting that the more we interact within its Friends Store, the more people will be introduced to its jeans through the interactions. Doing so creates a bridge between the Web and social Web, content, and relationships.

Example 2. Ford Motors set a new standard in 2011 when it officially introduced its new Explorer model exclusively on its Facebook store rather than via the traditional industry auto show. Designed specifically for Facebook, Ford told a human story, by the people who helped create the new line of Explorer.

According to Marsden (2010b) 67 percent of all companies surveyed already use Facebook to drive customers to their EC sites, 44 percent use Facebook apps for product launches and promotions, and 26 percent build EC applications (e.g., webstore) on Facebook itself.

F-Commerce Strategy of Organizations

As part of your social commerce strategy, you should include a Facebook Page for your business, and use it to advertise your store. Many customers currently have a personal Facebook account and may become "fans" of your business in order to check on your products, be entertained there, or meet other customers with similar interests on your store page.

By adding the Facebook apps (for buying) to your Facebook page, you can easily link your online store directly to your Facebook Fan Page within its own tab. Select which products to display and advertise as home specials or "On Sale." What is more, you can empower your affiliates with the ability to create their own online stores within their Facebook pages and choose which of your products will be displayed. This can be done easily with commercial apps. Since the launch of Facebook Store, hundreds of thousands of vendors have brought millions of Facebook fans into their online stores.

Presence of Facebook

It is not a question of who is on Facebook, but who is not. Almost all large, medium, and many small companies are on Facebook. That includes many government organizations. You can even find the Queen of England there.

Advertisement: Methods and Benefits

Most of Facebook's revenue comes from advertising (about $2 billion in 2010, and an estimate of $4 billion in 2011).

Facebook has more display ads than Yahoo!, AOL, Microsoft, and Fox Interactive. There are several ways to advertise on Facebook; here are some alternatives (some are free for advertisers).

Facebook Connect. Facebook Connect is the most powerful way to get your audience to share your content. Not only has it removed the obstacle of remembering friends' e-mail addresses, but it has also created a socially acceptable broadcast communication channel for individuals. Facebook Connect helps bring traffic to merchants' websites (assuming the merchants know how to attract people to stay there).

Using the Facebook "Like" Button. Adding a Facebook "Like" button lets a user share content with a friend. For example, you can list your products and let your customers advertise your products for you on their Facebook pages. Their friends can see this and perhaps take enough of an interest in the item to become your customers as well! With 3dCart, for example, adding the Facebook "Like" button is a breeze. It is like a social bookmark.

Facebook Ads. Facebook allows merchants or individuals to create their own ads. See "Guide to Facebook Ads" (*facebook.com/advertising*), to achieve the following benefits:

Reach Your Target Customers

▸ Connect with more than 750 million potential customers.

▸ Choose your audience by location, age, and interests.

▸ Test simple image and text-based ads and use what works.

Deepen Your Relationships

▸ Promote your Facebook Page or website.

▸ Use the "Like" button to increase your ads and apps influence.

▸ Build a community around your business.

Control Your Budget

▸ Set the daily budget you are comfortable with.

▸ Adjust your daily budget at anytime.

▸ Choose to pay only when people click (CPC) or see your ad (CPM).

Facebook Page. Inside Facebook, any user can set up a Facebook Page. As a result, users often set up Facebook Pages for products, companies, or brands they like as a place to earnestly express their passion. Brand owners have to figure out how to respond, and how to advertise there. However, as Facebook Pages are becoming more widely adopted, a new type of "Page squatting" is starting to arise: creating a Facebook Page with the intent of selling ad space on it.

Facebook Apps. There are hundreds of thousands of applications developed by software companies. They let Facebook members and friends conduct many business-related activities. For example, you can conduct P2P trade, get advice on how to invest in stocks, and much more. For details, see *facebook.com/AppStore*. One popular area is advertisement.

Advertising Through Apps. An example of an application is the game FarmVille. FarmVille has over

80 million users. The power of such an application on Facebook and its advertising is unheard of. Organizations can create in-game items that help the user's farm (with their own logos), and every person who visits that farm will see these items, and the advertisement of the company on that person's farm. This is an effective marketing strategy because not many people see it as "commercial" but rather the company helping you in the game.

Other Advertising Methods. A variety of methods can be seen on Facebook. All the methods cited in Section 7.4 and in Chapter 8 can be used. For example, Glenview State Bank (in Illinois) organized a photo loading contest in which the top five users contributed photos (selected by the bank) that were voted on by fans and their friends on the bank's Facebook Page. Other representative methods are:

▶ Add a Facebook "Like" button or "Share to Facebook" button to individual product pages. The popular Like button is outshining the Share button.

▶ Add third-party sharing buttons, such as ShareThis, AddThis, or a branded version.

▶ For how to advertise on Facebook, see *ehow.com/how_ 2238669_advertise-facebook.html* and Shih (2011).

Selling on Facebook

There are several models of selling on Facebook (e.g., see Zarrella and Zarrella, 2011). We describe only a few here.

▶ Build a Facebook Webstore. This option is an alternative to a full-scale f-commerce effort, but still allows for Facebook shopping. By pulling a product feed into a Facebook Page tab, shoppers can browse products and share with friends, but are directed to the company's e-commerce site to purchase.

▶ This is the simplest model, usually from banner ads (Chapter 8). You are then taken from Facebook to the vendor's store.

▶ Use *Facebook Marketplace* (*facebook.com/marketplace*). It is a kind of classified ad section (housing, jobs). You can also "give it away," "ask for a product/service," and buy and sell among friends.

▶ Sell virtual gifts at Facebook's own store. This is a big multimillion-dollar business.

▶ Use Facebook Mall World. This is a place for people to build boutiques and sell virtual items. For details, see *apps.facebook.com/mallworldgame*.

▶ Use an integrated model. Combine ads and selling; this approach involves advertising that leads to selling.

Example: P&G Facebook Campaign Store for the Old Spice Man. Facebook supported and capitalized on P&G's Old Spice Man campaign. Here is how it worked: you saw the ad, you engaged with the promotion, and you could buy the merchandise. All without leaving Facebook, P&G also sold out 1,000 packs of diapers in 1 hour on Facebook.

P&G has launched an Amazon.com-powered application on Facebook (in the United Kingdom), which lets people comment on and like Max Factor products, as well as purchase them.

▶ **Facebook Places (for mobile).** This is similar to LBS (Section 7.4). You can find local deals (in addition to connect with friends nearby and share where you are). For details, see *facebook.com/places*.

▶ **Facebook Deals.** The Facebook marketing platform Wildfire, a specialist in plug-and-play Facebook apps for running promotions, has launched a Special Deal, which is similar to Groupon. Facebook deals allow companies that have a verified Places Page offer customers who check in to their stores a special gift or discounts. For example, Gap is one of the most well-known early cases. The apparel company gave away free jeans to the first 10,000 users who "checked in" on November 5, 2010, and a 40 percent off discount for other users throughout that day.

▶ **End-to-end Facebook store within a fan page.** Users shop and buy products fully within Facebook.

Example 1. Delta Airlines launched a Facebook store application enabling users to search, book, and pay for flights without having to leave the social networking site: a smart move for an airline that markets itself as being "the world's largest Wi-Fi equipped fleet."

Example 2. Disney sold cinema tickets for *Toy Story 3* across Facebook. The company is expanding the service.

Shopping Tools on Facebook

Facebook provides several tools to assist shoppers. It also allows developers to offer other apps. Here are some representative examples:

▶ **Facebook credit.** This is a private currency. People buy it from Facebook and use it to pay for games and products and services they buy on Facebook. (Facebook gets a 30 percent cut for the credit transactions.)

▶ **Open graph and social graph.** The open graph is a protocol that enables you to integrate your Web pages into the social graph (Section 7.2). For details, see *developers.facebook.com/docs/reference/api*.

▶ **Product recommendations.** Facebook teamed up with Amazon.com to provide product recommendations and upcoming birthday reminders.

▶ **Merchant shopping aids.** Facebook allows developers to create shopping apps directly on merchants' fan pages, making these pages points of sale, not just advertisements. Such shopping aids (known as *shoplets*), exist in many stores (e.g., 1-800Flowers.com, Nine West), and they are Flash-based.

- **Social bar.** Everywhere you go online your friends can be with you, forever connected.

- **Docs.com.** A partnership with Microsoft that allows Microsoft office docs to be shared with your Facebook friends.

- **"Presence" location-based data.** Facebook handed out an RFID tag that allows you to swipe it at kiosks to indicate your location on every friend's page.

- **Sponsored stories.** Facebook has a tool that enables advertisers to pay to "sponsor" comments people make about businesses, places, or products at Facebook. A Sponsored Stories tool allows advertisers to take word-of-mouth recommendations and promote them to eye-catching notices on Facebook's user pages. It is not a message saying you should buy this thing or you should come to this website. It is your friend that is saying "Look, I did this and I want to tell you about it," or "I like this." Sponsored Stories are updates or location "check-ins" that Facebook members post to be seen by friends and are only shared with those in a person's chosen circle of contacts at the online community. For details, see Lazerow (2011).

Some Interesting Apps for Supporting E-Commerce on Facebook

Hundreds of apps were created to support shopping on Facebook. For a representative list, see *tomuse.com/sell-on-facebook-ecommerce-shopping-cart-storefront-app*. One of the popular ones is Payvment.

Payvment and Its Social Mall. Payvment is a comprehensive e-commerce storefront solution that lets you create your own custom store to sell your products directly from Facebook. You can easily add new product listings, create categories, upload product images, add custom HTML, and more. Product listings can be edited and changed at any time, and inventory is automatically tracked. One particularly cool feature is the synchronization of the shopping cart with your own website. Payvment is available for a free download at *facebook.com. payvment*.

Payvment offers a relatively simple way to add a free shopping cart application to your Facebook Fan Page. Facebook allows payment through PayPal. Payvment tries to address the issue of shopping cart abandonment with its universal cart. Leave an item in a Payvment cart with one retailer, and it will show up as you shop with another Payvment retailer.

Payvment provides four primary e-commerce features on Facebook:

- **Open Cart Network.** A shopping cart that is networked between participating retailers.

- **Fan incentive pricing.** Ability to offer fan discounts via its Facebook Fan Incentive Pricing option.

- **Search.** Shopping discovery and search tool.

- **Customer interaction.** Ability for any Facebook user to go to a storefront and add comments and reviews.

Payvment's Social Mall. Payvment created the previously mentioned platform for businesses to open shop on what it calls a social mall (or social shopping mall). In February 2011, the first month of opening, Facebook signed over 50,000 retailers, mostly small retailers and many are independent clothing manufacturers. Initially, there were 1.2 million items on display.

The mall starts with a display of products that friends in your Facebook network have liked and recommended. That will help shoppers find items they might not have known about before. It's like going shopping with your friends.

You can search inside the mall by different categories, such as clothing or electronics, and buy products without leaving Facebook. You can also search within some stores. The mall also lets shoppers fill up the same shopping cart and use the same credit card, even if the products come from different sellers. The platform figures out the split and sends the money to the merchants.

Payvment does not charge retailers or customers to get into the mall and is not taking a cut of sales. The company hopes to cash in later by helping in the discovery of products and brands and collecting money from advertisers.

Issues Regarding F-Commerce

The following are representative issues and concerns about f-commerce.

- Privacy protection is not so good, even though it is being improved (e.g., see Prince 2010).

- Effectiveness of the advertisement. Facebook's users click on advertisement banners significantly less than in most other websites. It seems that Facebook users spend their time communicating with friends and therefore have their own attention diverted away from advertisements. An exception may be video ads.

- Too many buttons can confuse or irritate users.

- Devalues your message. Some businesses are engaged on Facebook, Twitter, LinkedIn, and a host of other social platforms. If you add too many of these buttons in your e-mail, it could lower the value of your message by being viewed as a distraction.

- Integrating Facebook into e-mail marketing campaigns. Instead of using buttons, you can share a message or a link on Facebook. This may not be easy to do. Consult. *facebook.com/share.php?u=*.

- Small businesses can advertise and sell on Facebook. The major issues for these are:

  - How to get started on Facebook
  - How to grow your presence and fan base

▶ How small businesses are using Facebook to improve customer service, generate leads, and increase sales

▶ How to create an interactive community of fans for your product or service

For full coverage, see Shih (2011) and a Webcast available at *myventurepad.com/clarashih/31508/using-facebook-grow-your-business*. For criticisms of retailing on Facebook, see Ferner (2011).

Sources: Compiled from Shih (2011), Grossman (2010/2011), Zarrella and Zarrella (2011), Lazerow (2011), Ferner (2011), *en.wikipedia.org/wiki/Facebook*, and *facebook.com* (all accessed March 2011).

Questions

1. Why conduct business on Facebook?

2. List five major advertising options on Facebook.

3. What is the purpose of the "Like" button?

4. How are product recommendations generated on Facebook?

5. How can person-to-person transactions be conducted on Facebook?

6. What tools are provided by Facebook to facilitate selling and buying?

7. What are "Sponsored Stories"? Who benefits? How?

8. What are some of the implementation issues?

9. Enter *donnygamble.com/social-commerce* and read the article "Social Commerce: How Facebook Will Change Online Shopping Forever." Explain the blogger's opinion.

10. There are several hundreds of travel apps on Facebook. Identify some of them.

11. Find "Where I've Been" and discuss its popularity.

ONLINE RESOURCES
available at pearsonglobaleditions.com/turban

Online Files

W7.1   Application Case: Social Money Lending: Zopa and Prosper

W7.2   How Wikis Are Used

W7.3   Seven Guidelines for Achieving Success in Crowdsourcing

W7.4   The Essentials of Virtual Trade Shows and Trade Fairs in Virtual Worlds

W7.5   How to Educate People to Reduce Pollution: The Alter Space Game

W7.6   Solis's Compass Components

W7.7   Potential Social Commerce Risks

W7.8   Application Case: YouTube and Company—A Whole New World

Comprehensive Educational Websites

awarenessnetworks.com: Webinars on social media, Web 2.0, ROI, and marketing.

blogs.zdnet.com/Hinchcliffe: Dion Hinchcliffe's Enterprise Web 2.0 blog.

blogs.newsgator.com/daily/2009/08/boost-social-computing-adoption-on-sharepoint-battelle-customer-story.html: Register here for a Webinar on social computing deployment.

bloombergmarketing.blogs.com/Bloomberg_marketing: Diva Marketing Blog.

britopian.com/author/admin: Social media blog by Michael Brito.

c21org.typepad.com/21st_century_organization/virtual_worlds: Trends, thought leaders, and workable models for the 21st century organization.

cioinsight.com/c/a/Past-News/5-Reasons-to-Deploy-a-Corporate-Social-Network: "Five Reasons to Deploy a Corporate Social Network."

darmano.typepad.com: In David Armano's personal blog; logic and emotion exist at the intersection of business, design, and the social Web.

dotmocracy.org/sites/dotmocracy.net/files/dotmocracy_handbook_2-02_lowrez.pdf: Dotmocracy: A guidebook.

ft.com/intl/connected-business: How businesses of all sizes use IT and IT services.

gauravbhalla.com: Insights on customer driven strategies.

informationweek.com/news/202601956: "Growing Pains: Can Web 2.0 Evolve into an Enterprise Technology?"

intuitcollaboratory.comom: Videos on Intuit's Collaboratory innovation program collaboration.

jvwr.org: *Journal of Virtual World Research*.

mashable.com: A very comprehensive social media resource center.

slideshare.net/oukearts/transforming-retail-into-social-commerce-retail-ceo-briefing-strategy-boutique-thaesis: Comprehensive slideshow (178 slides) about transforming retail into social commerce.

socialcast.com/resources/customer_stories.html: Socialcast Customer Case Studies.

socialcast.com/resources/videos.html#overview: Basics of Socialcast.

socialcomputingjournal.com: Open forum for insights and perspectives on the future of the Web and business.

socialcast.s3.amazonaws.com/corporate/downloads/socialcast_cookbook.pdf: The Socialcast Cookbook.

socialtext.com/products/resources.php: Socialtext is an endless source of products/services.

thesocialcustomer.com/submitform/tscebook030810: Free e-book on the social customer experience.

thesocialmediaguide.com/social_media/social-media-glossary: A social media glossary.

video.forbes.com/fvn/thought-leaders/open-services-innovations?partner=contextual: Video on open service innovation, crowdsourcing for innovation.

what-is-crowdsourcing.com: An open source platform where anyone can contribute their thoughts on crowdsourcing history, trends, and developments, and can promote the movement.

wiki.secondlife.com/wiki/Second_LifeWork?FAQs: A comprehensive source of answers to questions.

REFERENCES

Answers.com. "Social Marketing." answers.com/topic/social-marketing (accessed January 2011).

Baker, P. "Social Media Adventures in the New Customer." April 30, 2010. crmbuyer.com/story/69895.html?wlc=1299604941 (accessed March 2011).

Bazaarvoice.com. "Social Commerce Stories." bazaarvoice.com/blog/category/social-commerce-stories (accessed March 2011).

Bell, D. *The Crowdsourcing Handbook—THE How To on Crowdsourcing, Complete Expert's Hints and Tips Guide by the Leading Experts, Everything You Need to Know About Crowdsourcing.* Brisbane, Australia: Emerio Pty Ltd., 2009.

Bernoff, J., and C. Li. "Harnessing the Power of the Oh-So-Social Web." *MIT Sloan Management Review*, 49, no. 3 (2008).

Bernoff, J., and T. Schadler. "Empowered: In a World Where One Angry Tweet Can Torpedo a Brand, Corporations Need to Unleash Their Employees to Fight Back." *Harvard Business Review* (July–August 2010).

Bjelland, O. M., and R. C. Wood. "An Inside View of IBM's Innovation Jam." *MIT Sloan Management Review* (Fall 2008).

Blodget, H. "Who the Hell Writes Wikipedia, Anyway?" *Business Insider*, January 3, 2009. businessinsider.com/2009/1/who-the-hell-writes-wikipedia-anyway (accessed March 2011).

Boatman, K. "Let Your Fans Shop Without Leaving Facebook." April 12, 2010. inc.com/internet/articles/201004/facebook.html (accessed March 2011).

Bonson, E., and F. Flores. "Social Media Metrics and Corporate Transparency." *Online*, July/August 2010.

Borges, B. *Marketing 2.0: Bridging the Gap Between Seller and Buyer Through Social Media Marketing.* Tucson, AZ: Wheatmark Pub., 2009.

Brandel, M. "The New Employee Connection: Social Networking Behind the Firewall." *Computer World*, August 11, 2008. computerworld.com/s/article/322857/The_new_employee_connection_Social_networking_behind_the_firewall (accessed March 2011).

Bryson-York, E. B. "Starbucks Gets Its Business Brewing Again with Social Media." February 22, 2010. adage.com/digitalist10/article?article_id=142202 (accessed March 2011).

Bughin, J., and M. Chui. "The Rise of the Networked Enterprise: Web 2.0 Finds Its Payday." December 10, 2010. mckinseyquarterly.com/article_print.aspx?L2=18$L3=30&ar=2716 (accessed December 2010).

Business and Marketing Author. "Second Life—Different Methods to Make Cash in the Second Life Virtual World." January 7, 2011. onlinebusinessand-marketingclub.com/?p=2937 (accessed March 2011).

Carr, D. F. "Business Strategy on Facebook." *Baseline Magazine*, February 2010.

Chaffey, D. "Social Location-Based Marketing." October 20, 2010. smartinsights.com/digital-marketing-strategy-alerts/social-location-based-mar (accessed March 2011).

Chaney, P. "Business Blogging: Is There a Right or Wrong Way?" *Social Media Today*, February 17, 2010. socialmediatoday.com/SMC/175462 (accessed February 2010).

Clifford, S. "Linking Customer Loyalty with Social Networking." *New York Times*, April 28, 2010. nytimes.com/2010/04/29/business/media/29adco.html (accessed March 2011).

Coleman, D., and S. Levine. *Collaboration 2.0.* Cupertino, CA: Happy About Info, 2008.

Daden Ltd. "Virtual Worlds and Serious Business." 2010. daden.co.uk/downloads/Virtual_Worlds_and_Serious_Business.pdf (accessed March 2011).

Daden, B. "Virtual Worlds for Education and Training," A white paper, April 2010. daden.co.uk/downloads/Virtual_Worlds_for_Training_and_Education_01d2.pdf (accessed May 2011).

Dawson, R. *Implementing Enterprise 2.0: A Practical Guide to Creating Business Value Inside Organizations with Web Technologies.* Charleston, SC: Create Space, 2009.

Decker, S. "Social Commerce 101: Leverage Word of Mouth to Boost Sales." February 9, 2010. clickz. com/clickz/column/1711352/social-commerce-101-leverage-word-mouth-boost-sales (accessed March 2011).

della Cava, M. "Some Ditch Social Networks to Reclaim Time, Privacy." *USA Today*, February 10, 2010. usatoday.com/tech/webguide/internetlife/2010-02-10-1Asocialbacklash10_CV_N.htm (accessed March 2011).

Dellarocas, C. "Online Reputation Systems: How to Design One That Does What You Need." *MIT Sloan Management Review* (Spring 2010).

Dennison, G., S. Bourdage-Braun, and M. Chetuparambil. "Social Commerce Defined." IBM white paper, #23747, November 2009.

Dupre-Barnes, N., and F. R. Barnes. "Equipping Your Organization for the Social Networking Game." *Information Management*, November/December 2009.

Egeland, B. "One Case for Twitter- Comcast/Salesforce Case Study." July 25, 2009. pmtips.net/case-twitter-comcast-salesforce-case-study (accessed March 2011).

Elad, J. *LinkedIn for Dummies.* Hoboken, NJ: Wiley & Sons, 2008.

Farrell, N. "Microsoft Rumbled over Wikipedia Edits." *Inquirer*, January 24, 2007. theinquirer.net/inquirer/news/1013427/microsoft-rumbled-over-wikipedia-edits (accessed March 2011).

Feller, J. "Crowdsourcing: Behind the Buzzword." *Cutter IT Journal Email Advisor*, December 15, 2010.

Ferner, M. "Adgregate CEO Rebuts Criticisms of Retailing on Facebook." January 18, 2011. practicalecommerce.com/articles/2527-Notable-Views-Adgregate-CEO-Rebuts-Criticisms-of-Retailing-on-Facebook (accessed March 2011).

Fraser, M., and S. Dutta. *Throwing Sheep in the Boardroom: How Online Social Networking Will Transform Your Life, Work and World.* Hoboken, NJ: Wiley & Sons, 2008.

Frito-Lay. "Four Consumer-Created Doritos Ads Crash the Super Bowl, Now Face the Pros in Attempt to Win $5 Million Prize." fritolay.com/about-us/press-release-20100207.html (accessed March 2011).

Gago, B. "6 Social CRM Thought Leaders." April 29, 2010. genius.com/marketinggeniusblog/3815/6-crm-thought-leaders.html (accessed March 2011).

Gaines-Ross, L. "Reputation Warfare." *Harvard Business Review* (December 2010).

Gillette, F. "Twitter, Twitter, Little Stars." *Bloomberg Businessweek*, July 19–July 25, 2010.

Gillin, P., and P. Schwartzman. *Social Marketing to the Business Customer: Listen to Your B2B Market, Generate Major Account Leads, and Build Client Relationships.* Hoboken, NJ: Wiley & Sons, 2011.

Gombert, P. "4 Steps to Social Media Success." *E-Commerce Times*, April 29, 2010.

Gogoi, P. "Retailers Take a Tip from MySpace." *BusinessWeek Online*, February 13, 2007. businessweek.com/bwdaily/dnflash/content/feb2007/db20070213_626293_page_2.htm (accessed March 2011).

Goldman, D. "Twitter Whacks 'Mafia' Opportunity." June 23, 2009. money.cnn.com/2009/06/23/technology/twitter_140mafia_game_profit/?postversion=2009062316 (accessed March 2011).

Grossman, L. "Time Person of the Year—Mark Zuckerberg." *Time*, December 27, 2010–January 3, 2011.

Gunelius, S. "Social Networks, the Newest Recruiting Tool." July 15, 2010. blogs.forbes.com/work-in-progress/2010/07/15/social-network-recruiting-tool-linkedin-facebook (accessed March 2011).

Handley, A., et al. *Content Rules: How to Create Killer Blogs, Podcasts, Videos, Ebooks, Webinars (and More) that Engage Customers and Ignite Your Business (New Rules Social Media Series).* Hoboken, NJ: Wiley & Sons, 2010.

Harris, L., and A. Rae. "Social Networks: The Future of Marketing for Small Business." *Journal of Business Strategy*, 30, no. 5 (2009).

Hayward, M. "Measuring Social Media ROI: Does Size Matter?" April 14, 2009. socialcomputingjournal.com/viewcolumn.cfm?colid=794 (accessed March 2011).

Healey, M. "Socially Challenged." *InformationWeek*, September 2010.

Heiphetz, A., and G. Woodill. *Training and Collaboration with Virtual Worlds: How to Create Cost-Saving, Efficient and Engaging Programs.* New York: McGraw-Hill, 2009.

Helft, M. "Will Zynga Become the Google of Games?" July 24, 2010. nytimes.com/2010/07/25/business/25zynga.html?_r=1&ref=game-systems-acc (accessed March 2011).

Hespos, T. "How to Use Social Media to Unite Lonely Customers, Build Brand Loyalty." *AdAge*, October 20, 2010. adage.com/article/digitalnext/social-media-unite-lonely-consumers-build-brand-loyalty/146578 (accessed March 2011).

Hinchcliffe, D. "The 2010 Social Business Landscape." *Enterprise Irregulars*, August 12, 2010. dachisgroup.com/2010/08/the-2010-social-business-landscape (accessed March 2011).

Hoover, J. N. "Enterprise 2.0." *InformationWeek*, February 26, 2007.

Howard, R. "Collaboration: Putting Social Technology to Work." *InfoManagement Direct*, April 29, 2010. information-management.com/infodirect/2009_162/socil_technology_crm_customer_relationship_management-10017772-1.html (accessed March 2011).

Howe, J. *Crowdsourcing: Why the Power of the Crowd Is Driving the Future of Business.* New York: Crown Business, 2008.

Jayanti, R. "A Netnographic Exploration: Listening to Online Consumer Conversations." *Journal of Advertising Research* (June 2010).

Jefferies, A. "Sales 2.0: Getting Social about Selling." October 30, 2008. technewsworld.com/story/web20/64968.html?wlc=1225731395&amp%3Bwlc=1226960577 (accessed March 2011).

Kaplan, A., and M. Haenlein. "Users of the World, Unite! The Challenges and Opportunities of Social Media." *Business Horizons*, January 15, 2010.

Kasteler, J. "Why You Should Get Involved with Social Shopping." *E-Commerce 2.0*, July 28, 2009. searchengineland.com/why-you-should-get-involved-with-social-shopping-e-commerce-20-22995 (accessed January 2011).

Kirkpatrick, D. *The Facebook Effect: The Inside Story of the Company That Is Connecting the World.* New York: Simon & Schuster, 2011.

Kolakowski, N. "7 Things Needed for an Enterprise Social Network." *eWeek*, March 12, 2009. eweek.com/c/a/Messaging-and-Collaboration/7-Things-Needed-for-an-Enterprise-Social-Network-24589 (accessed March 2011).

Kotler, P., and G. Zaltman. "Social Marketing: An Approach to Planned Social Change." *Journal of Marketing*, 35 (1971).

Kurfiss, D. "Guide to Doing Business in Second Life." February 9, 2011. work.com/doing-business-in-second-life-1285 (accessed February 2011).

Lazerow, M. "Facebook Takes People-Centric Ads to the Next Level." January 27, 2011. adage.com/digitalnext/post?article_id=148490 (accessed January 2011).

Learmonth, M. "Study: Twitter Ad Revenue Grow to $150M in 2011." January 24, 2011. adage.com/digitalnext/post?article_id=148425 (accessed January 2011).

Leggatt, H. "Survey: Small Businesses Find Success with Social Networking." July 9, 2010. bizreport.com/2010/07/survey-small-businesses-find-success-with-social-networking.html (accessed March 2011).

Libert, B., and J. Spector. *We Are Smarter Than Me: How to Unleash the Power of Crowds in Your Business.* Philadelphia: Wharton School Publishing, 2007.

Lieberman, M. "Guide to Understanding Social CRM." White paper, 2010. slideshare.net/JacobMorgan8/guide-to-understanding-social-crm (accessed March 2011).

Lowitt, E. "3 Rules for Crowdsourcing Your Sustainability Projects." *GreenBiz.com*, December 20, 2010. greenbiz.com/blog/2010/12/20/3-rules-crowdsourcing-your-sustainability-projects (accessed March 2011).

MacMillan, D. "Twitter Targets 1 Billion Users, Challenging Facebook for Ads." October 12, 2010. businessweek.com/print/technology/content/oct2010/tc20101012_048119.htm (accessed March 2011).

Mahar, J., and S. M. Mahar. *The Unofficial Guide to Building Your Business in the Second Life Virtual World: Marketing and Selling Your Product, Services, and Brand In-World.* New York: AMACOM, 2009.

Majchrzak, A., L. Cherbakov, and B. Ives. "Harnessing the Power of the Crowd with Corporate Social Networking Tools: How IBM Does It." *MIS Quarterly Executive*, 8, no. 2 (2009).

Malone, T. W., R. Laubacher, and C. Dellarocas. "The Collective Intelligence Genome." *MIT Sloan Management Review* (Spring 2010).

Marsden, P. "Commerce Gets Social: How Your Networks Are Driving What You Buy." January 6, 2011. socialcommercetoday.com/speed-summary-wired-feb-2011-cover-story-on-social-co (accessed February 2011).

Marsden, P. "Starbucks F-Commerce + M-Commerce = New Gold Standard." May 7, 2010a. socialcommercetoday.com/starbucks-f-commerce-m-commerce-new-gold-standard (accessed February 2011).

Marsden, P. "Simple Definition of Social Commerce." November 17, 2009a. socialcommercetoday.com/social-commerce-definition-word-cloud-definitive-definition-list (accessed March 2011).

Marsden, P. "The 6 Dimensions of Social Commerce: Rated and Reviewed." December 22, 2009b. socialcommercetoday.com/the-6-dimensions-of-social-commerce-rated-and-reviewed (accessed March 2011).

Marsden, P. "Survey Says: 76% of Marketers Plan to Use Facebook for Social Commerce." July 15, 2010b. socialcommercetoday.com/survey-says-76-of-retailers-plan-to-use-facebook-for-social-commerce (accessed March 2011).

McGillicuddy, S. "Managing Online Reputation Growing Problem for Businesses." November 7, 2007. searchcio.techtarget.com/news/1280689/Managing-online-reputation-growing-problem-for-businesses (accessed March 2011).

Meeker, M., S. Devitt, and L. Wu. "Morgan Stanley Internet Trends." 2010. morganstanley.com/institutional/techresearch/pdfs/Internet_Trends_041210.pdf (accessed March 2011).

Moore, C. "Crowdsourcing for Good—Some Examples to Watch." August 13, 2010. chaordix.com/blog/2010/08/13/crowdsourcing-for-good---some-examples-to-wat (accessed March 2011).

Moran, G. "Going Social." *Entrepreneur*, January 2010.

Murugesan, S. S. "Harnessing the Power of Virtual Worlds: Exploration, Innovation, and Transformation—PART I & II." *Cutter Business Intelligence Executive Reports*, March and May 2008.

Ogneva, M. "How to: Better Serve the Social Media Customer." June 29, 2010. mashable.com/2010/06/29/social-customer-service (accessed February 2011).

Olson, P. "A Twitterati Calls Out Whirlpool." September 2, 2009. forbes.com/2009/09/02/twitter-dooce-may-tag-markets-equities-whirlpool.html (accessed February 2010).

O'Neill, N. "The 10 Social Media Metrics Your Company Should Monitor." February 24, 2010. thesocialworkplace.com/2010/02/25/nick-oneill-the-10-social-media-metrics-your-company-should-monitor (accessed March 2011).

Patel, K. "Apple, Campbell's Say IADs Twice as Effective as TV." *AdAge*, February 3. 2011. adage.com/print?article_id=148630 (accessed March 2011).

Prince, B. "Facebook Privacy Concerns Don't Stop Risky Behavior on Social Networks." April 5, 2010. eweek.com/c/a/Security/Facebook-Privacy-Concerns-Dont-Stop-Risky-Behavior-on-Social-Networks-884390 (accessed March 2011).

Reeves, B., and L. Read. *Total Engagement: Using Games and Virtual Worlds to Change the Way People Work and Businesses Complete.* Boston: Harvard Business School Press, 2009.

Safko, L., and D. Brake. *The Social Media Bible: Tactics, Tools and Strategies for Business Success,* 2nd ed. Hoboken, NJ: Wiley & Sons, 2009.

Sahlin, D., and C. Botello. *YouTube for Dummies.* Hoboken, NJ: Wiley & Sons, 2007.

SeekingAlpha. "eMarketer Top 10 Predictions for 2009." January 9, 2009. seekingalpha.com/article/114028-emarketer-top-10-predictions-for-2009 (accessed March 2011).

Shih, C. *The Facebook Era: Tapping Online Social Networks to Market, Sell, and Innovate,* 2nd ed. Upper Saddle River, NJ: Prentice Hall, 2011.

Soat, J. "Anti-Social Behavior." *InfoSecurity Professional*, 2, no. 6 (2009). isc2.org/uploadedFiles/(ISC)2_Member_Content/Member_Resources/infosecpromag2009.pdf (accessed March 2011).

Shuen, A. *Web 2.0: A Strategy Guide.* Sebastopol, CA: O'Reilly Media, 2008.

Solis, B. "Introducing the Social Compass." October 8, 2009. briansolis.com/2009/10/introducing-the-social-compass (accessed March 2011).

Solis, B. "ROI: How to Measure Return on Investment in Social Media." February 22, 2010. briansolis.com/2010/02/roi-how-to-measure-return-on-investment-in-social-media (accessed March 2011).

Solis, B., and A. Kutcher. *Engage: The Complete Guide for Brands and Businesses to Build Cultivate, and Measure Success in the New Web.* Hoboken, NJ: Wiley & Sons, 2010.

Stephen, A. T., and O. Toubia. "Driving Value from Social Commerce Networks." *Journal of Marketing Research* (April 2010).

Steinhart, M. "Web 2.0: Worth the Risk?" White paper. securecomputing.com/swat (accessed February 2011).

Stroud, R. "Reducing Social Media Risks." *Baseline*, November/December 2010.

Stuart, D. "Social Media Metrics." *Online*, November/December 2009.

Taipei Times. "Facebook Chorus Ends Instrument Luggage Ban." January 4, 2011. Taipei"times.com/News/lang/archives/2011/01/04/2003492593 (accessed March 2011).

Techdirt Insight Community. "Sales 2.0: How Businesses Are Using Online Collaboration to Spark Sales." September, 19, 2008. oracle.com/us/products/applications/Siebel/018829.pdf (accessed March 2011).

Techfused.com. "Sony's Home Virtual World Hits 17M Users and Finds a Business Model in Virtual Goods." December 15, 2010. techfused.com/sony%e2%80%99s-home-virtual-world-hits-17m-users-and-finds-a-business-model-in-virtual-goods (accessed March 2011).

Techshout.com. "Gartner Analyzes Social Networking Influence on Purchase Decisions." July 31, 2010. techshout.com/internet/2010/31/gartner-analyzes-social-networking-influence-on-purchase-decisions (accessed March 2011).

Teicher, D. "What Marketer Can Learn from Starbucks' Foursquare Stumble." July 27, 2010. adage.com/digitalnext/article?article_id=145108 (accessed March 2011).

Temple, J. "Wikipedia Celebrates 10th Anniversary." January 14, 2011. articles.sfgate.com/2011-01-15/business/27030632_1_wikipedia-wikimedia-foundation-john-seigenthaler (accessed March 2011).

Terdiman, D. *The Entrepreneur's Guide to Second Life.* Indianapolis, IN: Wiley & Sons, 2008.

Treese, W. "Social Network? Which One?" *Networker*, March 2008.

Tucci, L. "Monitoring the Benefits of Social Media, and the Risks." April 15, 2010. searchcio.techtarget.com/news/1510020/Monitoring-the-benefits-of-social-media-and-the-risks (accessed March 2011).

Turban, E., et al. *Business Intelligence: A Managerial Approach,* 2nd ed. Upper Saddle River, NJ: Prentice Hall, 2011a.

Turban, E., T. P. Liang, and S. Wu. "Collaboration 2.0." *Journal of Group Decisions and Negotiation* (April 2011b).

Turban, E., N. Bolloju, and T. P. Liang. "Enterprise Social Networks." *Organizational Computing and Electronic Commerce*, 2012.

Valentine, V. "IDC: Social Web to Penetrate the Enterprise." January 28, 2010. information-management.com/news/idc_social_media_to_penetrate_the_enterprise-10017067-1.html (accessed March 2011).

Van Grove, J. "5 New Ways Small Business Can Offer Location-Based Deals." September 4, 2010. mashable.com/2010/09/04/location-based-small-business-deals (accessed March 2011).

Wagner, C., and N. Bolloju. "Supporting Knowledge Management in Organizations with Conversational Technologies: Discussion Forums, Weblogs, and Wikis." *Journal of Database Management*, 16, no. 2 (2005).

Walsh, M. "Starbucks Surpasses 10 Million Fans, Closing in on Lady Gaga." July 14, 2010. mediapost.com/publications/?fa=Articles.showArticle&art_aid=131970 (accessed March 2011).

Weber, S. *Plug Your Business.* Falls Church, VA: Weber Books, 2007.

Wilderman, R. "Using Social Computing to Build Differentiated Product Development Processes." May 28, 2010. blogs.forrester.com/roy_wildeman/10-05-28-using_social_computing_build_differentiated_product_development_processes (accessed March 2011).

Wright, M. "The Cynthia Rowley Foursquare Case Study." September 26, 2010. fashionablymarketing.me/2010/09/cynthia-rowley-foursquare-study (accessed January 2011).

Yu, R. "Companies Turn to Virtual Trade Shows to Save Money." January 5, 2010. usatoday.com/travel/news/2010-01-04-virtual-trade-shows_N.htm (accessed March 2011).

Zarrella, D., and A. Zarrella. *The Facebook Marketing Book.* Sebastopol, CA: O' Reilly Media, 2011.

Zwilling, M. "Location-Based Services Are a Bonanza for Startups." January 31, 2011. blogs.forbes.com/martinzwilling/2011/01/31/location-based-services-are-a-bonanza-for-startups (accessed January 2011).

MARKETING AND ADVERTISING IN E-COMMERCE

Content

Learning Objectives

Upon completion of this chapter, you will be able to:

1. Describe the factors that influence consumer behavior online.

2. Understand the decision-making process of consumer purchasing online.

3. Discuss the issues of e-loyalty and e-trust in electronic commerce (EC).

4. Describe segmentation and how companies are building one-to-one relationships with customers.

5. Explain how consumer behavior can be analyzed for creating personalized services.

6. Describe consumer market research in EC.

7. Describe the objectives of Web advertising and its characteristics.

8. Describe the major advertising methods used on the Web.

9. Describe mobile marketing concepts and techniques.

10. Describe various online advertising strategies and types of promotions.

11. Describe some implementation topics.

NETFLIX INCREASES SALES USING MOVIE RECOMMENDATIONS AND ADVERTISEMENTS

Netflix (*netflix.com*) is the world's largest online movie rental and subscription company, with more than 20 million members in 2011. Rental is done by sending DVDs in the mail and by streaming video. Netflix members can choose from a huge selection of movies and TV episodes streamed over the Internet to PCs, Macs, and TVs and watch them immediately. Among the expanding base of devices streaming Netflix videos are Microsoft's Xbox 360, Nintendo's Wii, and Sony's PS3 consoles; an array of Blu-ray disc players, Internet-connected TVs, home theater systems, digital video recorders, and Internet video players; Apple's iPhone, iPad, and iPod touch, as well as Apple TV and Google TV. In all, more than 200 devices that stream from Netflix are available in the United States and a growing number are available in Canada. The company's appeal and success are built on providing the most comprehensive selection of DVDs, an easy way to choose movies, recommendations of what to see based on user tastes, and fast, free delivery. Netflix distributes millions of DVDs each day.

The Problem

Because of the large number of titles, customers often had difficulty determining which ones they wanted to watch. In many cases, they would choose the most recent and popular titles, which meant that Netflix had to maintain more copies of the same title. In addition, some less popular titles were not renting well, even though they matched certain customers' preferences. For Netflix, matching titles with customers yet maintaining the right level of inventory is critical.

A second major problem facing Netflix is the competitive nature of the movie rental business.

Netflix competes against Blockbuster and other rental companies, as well as against companies offering downloads of movies and videos. In 2008, Blockbuster started offering online movie rental subscriptions, including the most recent movies, increasing the direct competition with Netflix. Other online content providers such as Apple iTunes and Google also became direct competitors. Another issue is that there is a clear trend that more and more viewers watch videos online. Hence, Netflix unveiled its "watch instantly" service, free for subscribers, to attract Internet users.

The Solution

Netflix reacted successfully to the first problem by offering a recommendation service called *Cinematch*. This software agent uses data mining tools to sift through a database of more than 3 billion film ratings, as well as through customers' rental histories. Using proprietary formulas, Cinematch recommends rentals to individuals. It is a personalized service, similar to the one offered by *amazon.com* that recommends books to customers. The recommendation is accomplished by comparing an individual's likes, dislikes, and preferences against people with similar tastes by using a variant of collaborative filtering (described later in this chapter). With the recommendation system, Netflix tells subscribers which DVDs they probably would like. Cinematch is like the geeky clerk at a small movie store who sets aside titles he knows you will like and suggests them to you when you visit the store.

Netflix subscribers can also invite one another to become "friends" and make movie recommendations to each other, peek at one another's rental lists, and see how other subscribers have rated movies using a social network called *FriendsSM*. All these personalized functions make the online rental store very customer friendly.

To improve Cinematch's accuracy, in October 2006 Netflix began a contest offering $1 million to the first person or team to write a program that would increase the prediction accuracy of Cinematch by 10 percent. The company understands that this will take quite some time; therefore, it is offering a $50,000 Progress Prize each year the contest runs. After more than two years of competition, the grand prize went to the "Bellkor's Pragmatic Chaos" team, a combination of two runner-up teams.

Netflix is advertising extensively on the Web using several advertising techniques, especially placing static banner ads on reputed sites, permission e-mail, blogs, social networks, classifieds, Really Simple Syndication (RSS), and more.

The Results

As a result of implementing its Cinematch system, Netflix has seen very fast growth in sales and membership. The benefits of Cinematch include the following:

- **Effective recommendations.** Approximately 60 percent of Netflix members select their movies based on movie recommendations tailored to their individual tastes.

- **Customer satisfaction.** More than 90 percent of Netflix members say they are so satisfied with the Netflix service that they recommend the service to family members and friends.

- **Finance.** Netflix has experienced a significant growth in membership and financial performance. Its members have doubled since the financial tsunami in 2008 to over 20 million by January 2011, and stock prices have skyrocketed from below $40 per share in 2008 to around $280 per share in July 2011.

- **Ratings.** Netflix has more than 3 billion movie ratings from members. The average member has rated about 200 movies.

- **Rental habits.** Netflix members say they rent twice as many movies per month than they did prior to joining the service. Netflix members add 2 million movies to their queues (movies they want to get) every day.

The domain Netflix.com attracted about 250 million visitors in 2010, according to a Compete.com survey. This is about 10 times the number of visitors to Blockbuster.com (*Compete.com* 2011).

Cinematch has become the company's core competence. Netflix's future relies heavily on Cinematch's making accurate recommendations and subscribers' accepting them, which is why the company strives to increase its accuracy.

Sources: Compiled from *Compete.com* (2011), Flynn (2006), *en.wikipedia.org/wiki/Netflix*, and *netflix.com* (both accessed March 2011).

WHAT WE CAN LEARN . . .

This case illustrates that the use of online marketing is quite different from traditional marketing. In particular, Netflix uses intelligent agents to make personalized movie recommendations to gain a substantial advantage over its competitors. Netflix's Cinematch is designed to increase sales, customer satisfaction, and loyalty. The case also identifies some of the most popular advertising methods that are used in online EC. These topics are the main subjects of this chapter, which also covers market research, trust, and consumer behavior online.

8.1 LEARNING ABOUT CONSUMER BEHAVIOR ONLINE

Companies are operating in an increasingly competitive environment. Therefore, they treat customers so as to lure them to buy their goods and services. Finding and retaining customers are major critical success factors for most businesses, both offline and online. One of the key elements in building effective customer relationships is an understanding of consumer behavior online.

A MODEL OF CONSUMER BEHAVIOR ONLINE

For decades, market researchers have tried to understand consumer behavior, and have summarized their findings in various models. The purpose of a consumer behavior model is to help vendors understand how a consumer makes a purchasing decision. If a firm understands the decision process, it may be able to influence the buyer's decision, for example, through advertising or special promotions.

Before examining the consumer behavior model's variables, let's describe who the EC consumers are. Online consumers can be divided into two types: individual consumers (who get much of the media attention) and organizational buyers, who do most of the actual shopping in cyberspace in terms of dollar volume of sales. Organizational buyers include governments, private corporations, resellers, and public organizations. Purchases by organizational buyers are generally used to add value to materials or products. Also, organizational buyers may purchase products for resale without any further modifications. We discussed organizational purchasing in detail in Chapter 4 (e-procurement) and will focus on individual consumers in this chapter.

The purpose of a consumer behavior model (for individuals) is to show factors that affect consumer behavior. Exhibit 8.1 shows the basic elements of a consumer behavior model. The model is composed of two major parts: *influential factors* and the *consumer decision process*.

▶ **Influential factors.** Five dimensions are considered to affect consumer behavior. They are *consumer characteristics*, *environmental characteristics*, *merchant and intermediary characteristics* (which are at the top of the diagram and are considered uncontrollable from the seller's point of view), *product/service characteristics* (which include market stimuli), and *EC systems*. The last two are mostly controlled by the sellers. Exhibit 8.1 illustrates the major variables in each influential dimension.

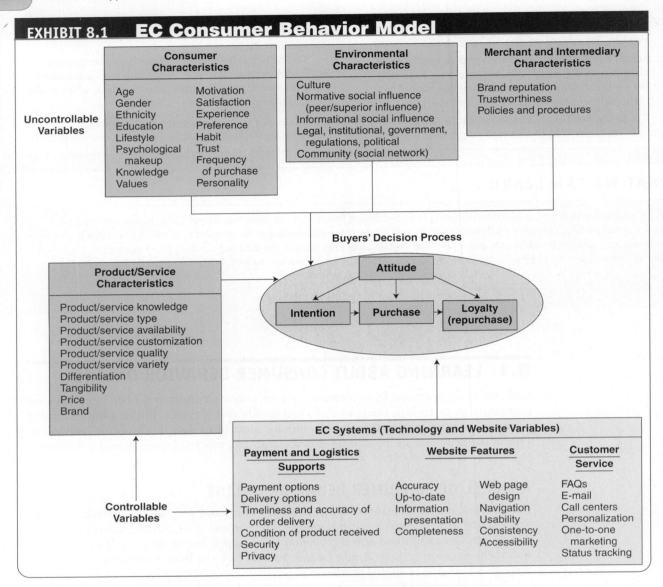

EXHIBIT 8.1   EC Consumer Behavior Model

▶ **The attitude-behavior decision process.** The consumer decision process usually starts with a positive attitude and ends with the buyer's decision to purchase and/or repurchase. A *favorable attitude* would lead to a stronger *buying intention*, which in turn would result in the *actual buying behavior*. Previous research has shown that the linkages among the previously mentioned three constructs are quite strong. For example, Ranganathan and Jha (2007) found that past online shopping experiences have the strongest associations with online purchase intention, followed by customer concerns, website quality, and computer self-efficacy. Therefore, developing a positive consumer attitude plays a central role in the final purchase decision.

The Major Influential Factors

These factors fall into the following categories:

Personal Characteristics. Personal characteristics, which are shown in the top-left portion of Exhibit 8.1, refer to *demographic* factors, individual *preferences*, and *behavioral* characteristics. Several websites provide information on customer buying habits online (e.g., emarketer.com, clickz.com, and comscore.com). The major demographics that such sites track are gender, age, marital status, educational level, ethnicity, occupation, and household income, which can be correlated with Internet usage and EC data. Males and females have been found to perceive information differently depending on their levels of purchase confidence and internal knowledge (Barber, et al. 2009). A recent survey by Crespo and Bosque (2010) shows that shopping experience has a significant effect on consumer attitude and intention to purchase online.

Psychological variables such as personality and lifestyle characteristics are also studied by marketers. These variables are briefly mentioned in several places throughout the text. The reader who is interested in the impact of lifestyle differences on online shopping may see Wang, et al. (2006).

Product/Service Factors. The second group of factors is related to the product/service itself. Whether a consumer decides to buy is affected by the nature of the product/service in the transaction. These may include the price, quality, design, brand, and other related attributes of the product.

Merchant and Intermediary Factors. Online transactions may also be affected by the merchant that provides the product/service. This group of factors includes merchant reputation, size of transaction, trust in the merchant, and so on. For example, people feel more secure when they purchase from Amazon.com (due to its reputation) than from a no-name seller. Other factors such as marketing strategy and advertising can also play a major role.

EC Systems. The EC platform for online transactions (e.g., security protection, payment mechanism, and so forth) offered by the merchant may also have effects. EC design factors can be divided into motivational and hygiene factors. Motivational factors were found to be more important than hygiene factors in attracting online customers (Liang and Lai 2002). Perceived usability is highly related to user preference for commercial websites (Lee and Koubek 2010).

Motivational Factors. Motivational factors are the functions available on the website to provide direct support in the transactional process (e.g., search engine, shopping carts, and multiple payment methods).

Hygiene Factors. Hygiene factors are functions available on the website whose main purpose is to prevent possible trouble in the process (e.g., security and product status tracking).

Environmental Factors. The environment in which a transaction occurs may affect a consumer's purchase decision. As shown in Exhibit 8.1, environmental variables can be grouped into the following categories:

Social Variables. People are influenced by family members, friends, coworkers, and "what's in fashion this year." Therefore, social variables (such as customer endorsement, word of mouth) play an important role in EC. Of special importance in EC are Internet communities (see Chapter 7) and discussion groups, in which people communicate via chat rooms, electronic bulletin boards, tweeting, and newsgroups. These topics are discussed in various places in the text.

Cultural/Community Variables. It makes a big difference in what people buy if a consumer lives near Silicon Valley in California or in the mountains in Nepal. Chinese shoppers may differ from French shoppers, and rural shoppers may differ from urban ones.

Other Environmental Variables. These include aspects such as available information, government regulations, legal constraints, and situational factors.

Section 8.1 ▶ REVIEW QUESTIONS

1. Describe the major components and structure of the consumer online purchasing behavior model.
2. List some major personal characteristics that influence consumer behavior.
3. List the major environmental variables of the purchasing environment.
4. List and describe five major merchant-related variables.
5. Describe the relationships among attitude, intention, and actual behavior in the behavior process model.

8.2 THE CONSUMER PURCHASING DECISION-MAKING PROCESS

Consumer behavior is a major element in the process of consumers' decisions to purchase or repurchase.

A GENERIC PURCHASING-DECISION MODEL

From the consumer's perspective, a general purchasing-decision model consists of five major phases (Hawkins and Mothersbaugh 2010). In each phase, we can distinguish several activities and, in some, one or more decisions. The five phases are (1) need identification, (2) information search, (3) evaluation of alternatives, (4) purchase and delivery, and (5) postpurchase activities. Although these phases offer a general guide to the consumer decision-making process, one should not assume that every consumer's decision-making process will necessarily proceed in this order. In fact, some consumers may proceed to a point and then revert to a previous phase, or they may skip a phase altogether. The phases are discussed in more details next.

product brokering
Deciding what product to buy.

merchant brokering
Deciding from whom (from what merchant) to buy a product.

> ▶ **Need identification.** The first phase occurs when a consumer is faced with an imbalance between the actual and the desired states of a need. A marketer's goal is to get the consumer to recognize such imbalance and then convince the consumer that the product or service the seller offers will fill this gap.
>
> ▶ **Information search.** After identifying the need, the consumer searches for information on the various alternatives available to satisfy the need. Here, we differentiate between two decisions: what product to buy (**product brokering**) and from whom to buy it (**merchant brokering**). These two decisions can be separate or combined. In the consumer's search for information, catalogs, advertising, promotions, and reference groups could influence decision making. During this phase, online product search and comparison engines, such as shopping.com, buyersindex.com, and mysimon.com, can be very helpful. (See decision aids in Chapter 3.)
>
> ▶ **Evaluation of Alternatives.** The consumer's information search will eventually generate a smaller set of preferred alternatives. From this set, the would-be buyer will further evaluate the alternatives and, if possible, negotiate terms. In this phase, a consumer will use the collected information to develop a set of criteria. These criteria will help the consumer evaluate and compare alternatives. For online consumers, the activities may include evaluation of product prices and features.
>
> ▶ **Purchase and delivery.** After evaluating the alternatives, the consumer will make the purchasing decision, arrange payment and delivery, purchase warranties, and so on.
>
> ▶ **Postpurchase activities.** The final phase is a postpurchase phase, which consists of customer service and evaluation of the usefulness of the product. Customer services and consumer satisfaction will result in positive experience and word of mouth (e.g., "This product is really great!" or "We really received good service when we had problems."). If the customer is satisfied with the product and services, loyalty will increase and repeat purchases will occur afterward.

Several other purchasing-decision models have been proposed. A classic model for describing consumer message processing is the Attention-Interest-Desire-Action (AIDA) model. It argues that consumer processing of an advertising message (part of the information search phase) includes the following four stages:

1. **A—Attention (Awareness).** The first step is to attract the attention of the customer.

2. **I—Interest.** A message may raise customer interest by demonstrating features, advantages, and benefits.

3. **D—Desire.** Customers may be convinced that they want and desire the product or service and that it will satisfy their needs.

4. **A—Action.** Finally, the consumer will take action toward purchasing.

   Now, some researchers also add another letter to form AIDA(S), where:

5. **S—Satisfaction.** Customer satisfaction will generate higher loyalty and lead to repurchase after using a product/service.

A recent version of AIDA is the AISAS model proposed by the Dentsu Group that is tailored to online behavior. The model replaces "*decision*" with "*search*" and adds "*share*" to show the increased word-of-mouth effect on the Internet. It indicates that consumers go through a process of Attention-Interest-Search-Action-Share in their online decision process. This model is particularly suitable for social commerce that is gaining momentum due to the increased popularity of social media.

CUSTOMER DECISION SUPPORT IN WEB PURCHASING

The preceding generic purchasing-decision model was widely used in research on consumer-based EC. In the Web-based environment, decision support is available in each phase. The framework that is illustrated in Exhibit 8.2 shows that each of the phases of the purchasing model can be supported by both a consumer decision support system (CDSS) that facilitates the process and Internet and Web aiding facilities. The CDSS facilities support the specific decisions in the process. Generic EC technologies and analytics provide the necessary mechanisms as well as enhanced communication and collaboration tools. Specific implementation of this framework and explanations of some of the terms are provided throughout this chapter and the entire text. The planner of B2C marketing needs to consider the Web purchasing models in order to better influence the customer's decision-making process (e.g., by effective one-to-one advertising and marketing).

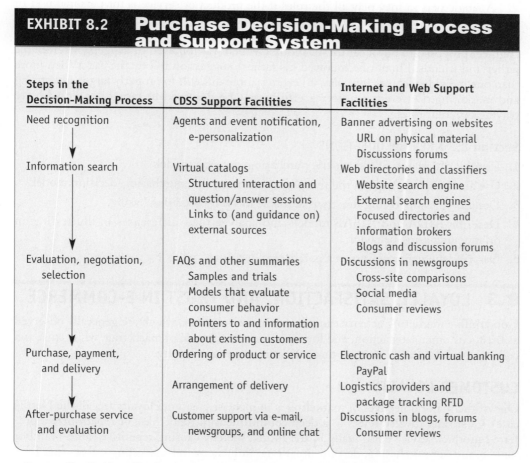

EXHIBIT 8.2   Purchase Decision-Making Process and Support System

Steps in the Decision-Making Process	CDSS Support Facilities	Internet and Web Support Facilities
Need recognition	Agents and event notification, e-personalization	Banner advertising on websites URL on physical material Discussions forums
Information search	Virtual catalogs Structured interaction and question/answer sessions Links to (and guidance on) external sources	Web directories and classifiers Website search engine External search engines Focused directories and information brokers Blogs and discussion forums
Evaluation, negotiation, selection	FAQs and other summaries Samples and trials Models that evaluate consumer behavior Pointers to and information about existing customers	Discussions in newsgroups Cross-site comparisons Social media Consumer reviews
Purchase, payment, and delivery	Ordering of product or service Arrangement of delivery	Electronic cash and virtual banking PayPal Logistics providers and package tracking RFID
After-purchase service and evaluation	Customer support via e-mail, newsgroups, and online chat	Discussions in blogs, forums Consumer reviews

Sources: Compiled from O'Keefe and McEachern (1998) and Hawkins and Mothersbaugh (2010).

Online File W8.1 shows a model for a website that supports buyer searching and decision making. This model revises the generic model by describing a purchasing framework. The model is divided into three parts. The first includes three stages of buyer behavior (see the top of the exhibit): identify and manage buying criteria, search for products and merchants, and compare alternatives. Below these activities are boxes with decision support options that support the three top boxes (such as product representation).

The second part of the model (on the right) has a box that includes price, financial terms, shipping, and warranty negotiations. These become relevant when alternatives are compared. The third part at the bottom of the exhibit cites major concerns.

PLAYERS IN THE CONSUMER DECISION PROCESS

Several different people may play roles in various phases of the consumer decision process. The following are five major roles:

1. **Initiator.** The person who first suggests or thinks of the idea of buying a particular product or service.
2. **Influencer.** A person whose advice or view carries some weight in making a final purchasing decision.
3. **Decider.** The person who ultimately makes a buying decision or any part of it—whether to buy, what to buy, how to buy, or where to buy.
4. **Buyer.** The person who makes an actual purchase.
5. **User.** The person who consumes or uses a product or service.

A single person may play all the roles if the product or service is for personal use. In this case, the marketer needs to understand and target that individual. In many situations, however, different people may play different roles, For example, a newly graduated engineer proposed to buy a car for his mother, which was followed by suggestions from his father and friends. Finally, he followed his father's suggestion to buy the car. When more than one individual comes into play, it becomes more difficult to properly target advertising and marketing. Different marketing efforts may be designed to target people who are playing different roles.

Section 8.2 ▶ REVIEW QUESTIONS

1. List the five phases of the generic purchasing-decision model.
2. Use an example to explain the five phases in the generic purchasing-decision model.
3. Describe the supporting functions available in Web-based purchasing.
4. Describe AIDA and AISAS models and analyze their differences in illustrating an online purchasing behavior.
5. Describe the major players in a purchasing decision.

customer loyalty
A deep commitment to repurchase or repatronize a preferred product/service continually in the future, thereby causing repetitive same-brand or same brand-set purchasing, despite situational influences and marketing efforts that have the potential to cause switching behavior.

8.3 LOYALTY, SATISFACTION, AND TRUST IN E-COMMERCE

Good online marketing activity can generate positive effects, which are generally observed as trust, customer satisfaction, and loyalty. *Loyalty* is the goal of marketing, while trust and customer satisfaction are factors that may affect customer loyalty.

CUSTOMER LOYALTY

One of the major objectives of marketing is to increase customer loyalty (recall the Netflix case). Customer loyalty refers to a deep commitment to repurchase or repatronize a preferred product/service continually in the future, thereby causing repetitive same-brand or same brand-set purchasing, despite situational influences and marketing efforts that have the potential to cause switching behavior. Customer acquisition and retention is a critical success factor in e-tailing. The expense of acquiring a new customer can be more than $100; even for Amazon.com, which has a huge reach, it is more than $15. In contrast, the cost of maintaining an existing customer at Amazon.com is $2 to $4.

Attracting and retaining loyal customers remains the most important issue for any selling company, including e-tailers. Increased customer loyalty can result in cost savings to a company in various ways: lower marketing and advertising costs, lower transaction costs, lower customer turnover expenses, lower failure costs such as warranty claims, and so on. Customer loyalty also strengthens a company's market position because loyal customers are kept away from the competition. In addition, customer loyalty can lead to high resistance to competitors, a decrease in price sensitivity, and an increase in favorable word of mouth.

It is interesting to note that companies have found that loyal customers end up buying more when they have an optional website from which to shop. For example, W.W. Grainger, a large industrial-supply company, found that loyal B2B customers increased their purchases substantially when they began using Grainger's website (grainger.com). (See Chapter 4 for more information.) Also, loyal customers may refer other customers to a site, especially with word of mouth in social networks. Therefore, it is important for EC companies to increase customer loyalty. The Web offers ample opportunities to do so.

E-Loyalty

E-loyalty refers to a customer's loyalty to an e-tailer or a manufacturer that sells directly online, or to loyalty programs delivered online or supported electronically. Companies can foster e-loyalty by learning about their customers' needs, interacting with customers, and providing superb customer service. Another source of information is colloquy.com, which concentrates on loyalty marketing.

e-loyalty
Customer loyalty to an e-tailer or loyalty programs delivered online or supported electronically.

In an online environment, merchant ratings can be the source of interpersonal communication and are obtained from other consumers, not just friends and family. It is interesting to note that positive customer reviews have considerable impact on repurchase intention. It is not the total number of reviews that influences customer repurchase intention, but the percentage of positive reviews. This increases e-loyalty. (For reviews and recommendations in social networks, see Chapter 7.)

Also, online ratings and word of mouth may undermine the effects of competitors' low prices. For example, Amazon.com has higher prices than Half.com, but Amazon.com is still preferred by many customers. The difference is that Amazon.com has customer reviews and other personalization services, and Half.com does not.

Many factors may affect customer loyalty and e-loyalty. A typical model is to check the relationship quality between retailers and their customers, which often is composed of trust, satisfaction, and commitment. Satisfaction and trust are particularly important because they will lead to commitment. For example, a recent study by Cyr (2008) found that e-loyalty is affected by trust and satisfaction across different cultures. Hence, we shall further discuss these two factors.

SATISFACTION IN EC

Satisfaction is one of the most important success measures in the B2C online environment. Customer satisfaction is associated with several key outcomes (e.g., repeat purchase, positive word of mouth, and so on) and it can lead to higher customer loyalty. A survey indicates that 80 percent of highly satisfied online consumers would shop again within two months, and 90 percent would recommend Internet retailers to others. However, 87 percent of dissatisfied consumers would permanently leave their Internet retailers without any complaints (Cheung and Lee 2005).

Satisfaction has received considerable attention in studies of consumer-based EC. For example, ForeSee Results, an online customer satisfaction measurement company, developed the American Customer Satisfaction Index (ACSI) (theasci.org) for measuring customer satisfaction with EC. The Customer Respect Group (customerrespect.com) also provides an index to measure customers' online experiences. The Customer Respect Index (CRI) includes the following components: simplicity, responsiveness, transparency, principles, attitude, and privacy.

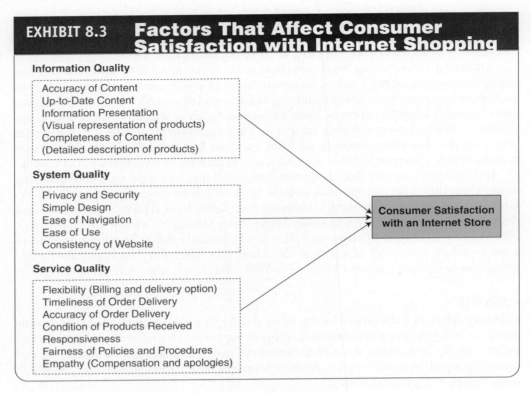

EXHIBIT 8.3   Factors That Affect Consumer Satisfaction with Internet Shopping

Information Quality

Accuracy of Content
Up-to-Date Content
Information Presentation
(Visual representation of products)
Completeness of Content
(Detailed description of products)

System Quality

Privacy and Security
Simple Design
Ease of Navigation
Ease of Use
Consistency of Website

Service Quality

Flexibility (Billing and delivery option)
Timeliness of Order Delivery
Accuracy of Order Delivery
Condition of Products Received
Responsiveness
Fairness of Policies and Procedures
Empathy (Compensation and apologies)

Consumer Satisfaction with an Internet Store

Researchers have proposed several models to explain the formation of satisfaction with online shopping. For example, Cheung and Lee (2005) proposed a framework for consumer satisfaction with Internet shopping by correlating the end-user satisfaction perspective with the service quality viewpoint. The framework is shown in Exhibit 8.3.

The ability to predict consumer satisfaction can be useful in designing websites as well as advertising and marketing strategies. However, website designers should also pay attention to the nature of website features including navigational, visual, and information design (Cyr 2008). Different features have different impacts on customer (dis)satisfaction. If certain website features, such as reliability of content, loading speed, and usefulness fail to perform properly, customer satisfaction will drop dramatically. In contrast, if features such as those make the usage enjoyable, entertaining, and useful, they could result in a significant jump in customer satisfaction.

TRUST IN EC

trust
The psychological status of willingness to depend on another person or organization.

Trust is the psychological status of depending on another person or organization to achieve a planned goal. When people trust each other, they have confidence that their transaction partners will keep their promises. However, both parties in a transaction assume some risk. In the electronic marketplace, sellers and buyers do not meet face to face. The buyer can see a picture of the product but not the product itself. Promises of quality and delivery time can be easily made—but will they be kept? To deal with these issues, EC vendors need to establish high levels of trust with current and potential customers. Trust is particularly important in global EC transactions due to the difficulty of taking legal action in cases of a dispute or fraud and the potential for conflicts caused by differences in culture and business environments.

In addition to sellers and buyers trusting each other, both must have trust in the EC computing environment and in the EC infrastructure. For example, if people do not trust the security of the EC infrastructure, they will not feel comfortable about using credit cards to make EC purchases.

EC Trust Models

Trust in e-commerce is often called **online trust**. Several models have been put forth to explain the factors that may affect online trust. For example, Lee and Turban (2001) examined the various aspects of EC trust and developed the model shown in Online File W8.2. According to this model, the level of trust is determined by numerous variables (factors) shown on the left side and in the middle of the exhibit. The exhibit illustrates the complexity of trust relationships, especially in B2C EC.

A newer model expands previous ones to include internal and external factors. Internal factors are directly related to online services provided by the vendor, and external factors are those that have indirect relationships (Salo and Karjaluoto 2007).

How to Increase Trust in EC

Consumer trust is fundamental to successful online retailing; it is considered the "currency" of the Internet. The following are representative strategies for building consumer trust in EC.

Improve Your Website. The most important factor that affects online trust is the quality of the website. Cyr (2008) found that the navigational, visual, and information design of a website affect consumer trust. Gregg and Walczak (2010) reported a positive relationship between website quality and trust. Higher perceived website quality induces higher trust and price premium based on a survey of 701 eBay users. Therefore, how to design the EC website that delivers high-quality information and navigational experience is a key to increase consumer trust in the website.

Affiliate with an Objective Third Party. This approach aims at building consumer trust by affiliating the customer with trusted third parties. Internet stores can put hypertext links on their websites to trusted targets, including reputable companies or well-known portals. These reputable companies are able to transfer brand equity to the Internet stores because companies with brand names facilitate trust. Internet stores can also use third-party seals of approval such as TRUSTe (truste.com) and BBBOnline (bbbonline.org), the online version of the Better Business Bureau. Escrow providers and reputation finders (e.g., cyberalert.com and cymfony.com) also are useful. These agencies provide business-critical intelligence on how brands are being used on the Internet as well as research about spying on businesses.

Working against EC trust are stories about fraud on the Internet, especially when unknown parties are involved. Reputation systems that were described in Chapter 7 can impact trust either positively or negatively.

Establish Trustworthiness. Trustworthiness can be achieved through three key elements: *integrity, competence*, and *security*. Integrity conveys an overall sense of the ability of the Internet store to build an image of strong justice and fulfill all the promises that have been made to the customers (i.e., offering a money-back guarantee with the products and clearly stating the guarantee policy on the website). Another indicator of trustworthiness is an Internet store's competence. Stores can promote the perception of competence by delivering a professional website. Finally, EC security mechanisms can help solidify trust. Dell was the first PC manufacturer to launch an online secure shopping guarantee to online shoppers making purchases at its website.

Other Methods for Facilitating Trust

Several other methods are used to facilitate trust on the Web. For example, tying cognitive style to communication with customers (Urban, et al. 2009, discussed later in the chapter) is designed to build trust. Another method is that of reputation.

Reputation-Based Systems. Reputation is the opinion of the public toward a person, a group of people, or an organization. It is an important factor in many fields, such as business, online communities, and social status. **Reputation-based systems** are used to establish trust among members of online communities where parties with no prior knowledge of each other use the feedback from their peers to assess the trustworthiness of the peers in the community. For details, see en.wikipedia.org/wiki/Reputation and p2pfoundation.net/Reputation. For a comprehensive overview and how to design a reputation system, see Dellarocas (2010). Also, see the discussion in Chapter 7 regarding reputation in social commerce situations.

online trust
The belief that an online website or other digital entities can deliver what they promise so that the recipient trusts them.

reputation-based systems
Systems used to establish trust among members of online communities where parties with no prior knowledge of each other use the feedback from their peers to assess the trustworthiness of the peers in the community.

A major player in this area is Yelp.com, which aggregates reviews that contain highly subjective judgments. Its system enables similarly minded users to spot each other.

Online Word of Mouth. Due to the increased social activities on the Internet, online word of mouth is also influencing trust level. A study by Awad and Ragowsky (2008) found that online word-of-mouth quality affects online trust and its effect varies across genders. In general, males value their ability to post online, whereas females value the responsive participation of other consumers. Online word of mouth may occur in different forms, such as consumer online feedback and participation in social media forums. Hence, fostering positive word of mouth is an effective strategy to build stronger trust in a website.

Section 8.3 ▶ REVIEW QUESTIONS

1. Describe customer loyalty and e-loyalty.
2. Describe the use of business intelligence and analytical software for e-loyalty.
3. Describe the issue of trust in EC and how to increase it.
4. What influences consumer satisfaction online? Why do companies need to monitor it?
5. How can trust be increased in EC?
6. Define reputation-based systems and relate them to trust in EC.

8.4   MASS MARKETING, MARKET SEGMENTATION, AND RELATIONSHIP MARKETING

One of the greatest benefits of EC is its ability to match products (services) with individual consumers (recall the Netflix case). Such a match is called *one-to-one marketing*, a part of the relationship marketing that treats each customer in a unique way to fit marketing and advertising with the customer's profile and needs. Let's first see how the one-to-one approach evolved from traditional marketing approaches.

FROM MASS MARKETING TO ONE-TO-ONE MARKETING

Three basic approaches are used in marketing and advertising: mass marketing, market segmentation, and one-to-one marketing.

Mass Marketing and Advertising

Marketing efforts traditionally were targeted to everyone (the "masses"). For example, using a newspaper or TV ad usually means one-way interpersonal communication to those who see it. Such an effort may be effective for brand recognition or for introducing a new product or service. It can be conducted on the Internet as well. Putting banner ads on an Internet portal to send messages to everyone who accesses the website is a typical example of mass marketing.

Example. In 2005, Ford Motor Company unveiled a roadblock approach on the Internet to promote its F-150 truck. (A "roadblock" refers to running a commercial on all major TV channels at exactly the same time, so viewers cannot switch channels to escape the commercial.) On the day of the launch, Ford placed static banner ads for 24 hours on the three leading Internet portals—AOL, MSN, and Yahoo!—introducing a 3-month campaign. Some 50 million Web surfers saw Ford's banner. Millions of them clicked on the banner, pouring onto Ford's website at a rate that reached 3,000 per second. Ford claimed that the traffic led to a 6 percent increase in sales over the first three months of the campaign.

Market Segmentation

market segmentation
The process of dividing a consumer market into logical groups for conducting marketing research and analyzing personal information.

Market segmentation refers to the practice of promoting a product or service to a subset of customers or prospects. For example, cosmetic products may put their advertisements in female magazines. This implies that the market is segmented by the gender of consumers. One advantage of market segmentation is that advertising and marketing efforts can match segments better than the "mass," providing a better response rate. Also, the expense of reaching the segments may be lower, and marketing efforts can be faster (e.g., e-mails are sent to fewer people, or banner ads are placed on fewer websites). The Internet enables more effective market segmentation, but it also improves close relationship marketing, or one-to-one marketing.

Criteria for Market Segmentation. For effective market segmentation, the following are common criteria that companies use:

> **Geographic.** Region; size of city, county, or Standard Metropolitan Statistical Area (SMSA); population density; climate; language.
>
> **Demographic.** Age, occupation, gender, education, family size, religion, race, income, nationality, urban (or suburban or rural).
>
> **Psychological (lifestyle).** Social class, lifestyle, personality, activities, VALS typology (see strategicbusinessinsights.com/vals/presurvey.shtml).
>
> **Cognitive, affective, behavioral.** Attitudes, benefits sought, loyalty status, readiness stage, usage rate, perceived risk, user status, innovativeness, usage situation, involvement, Internet shopping experience.
>
> **Profitability.** Valued customers are placed in a special category.
>
> **Risk core.** Low-risk customers are in a special category.

Statistical and data mining methods are often used to identify valuable segments for promotion or advertising. Modern companies assign a variety of segments to their customers, often dynamically defining segments and temporarily regrouping customers for specific campaigns. By segmenting customers, companies could begin more specialized communications about their products. Much of this relies on the company's understanding its business strategies to the extent that they know their most desirable segments. A simple way to do segmentation online is to go to a specialized website or portal and advertise to its visitors. For example, by going to ivillage.com, you reach mostly women. Advertising in Internet communities and social networks usually provides you with market segmentation. Increasingly, advertising is being placed on social networking sites (such as Facebook). Note that U.S. spending on social network advertising is growing rapidly (see Chapter 7, Section 7.4). Some Weblogs that focus on specific niches (e.g., paidcontent.org or fark.com) have received a generous amount of dollars from advertisers.

Relationship Marketing

Relationship marketing is different from traditional marketing in that it focuses on building long-term relationships with customers. In order to do so, the seller must have a much deeper understanding of its customers, from segmentation to individuals. As consumers began purchasing online, more data became available about them. Data analysts began associating products with the customers who were buying them. And it was through these analytic activities that companies began to understand that their customer data could be valuable for one-to-one marketing.

relationship marketing
Marketing method that focuses on building a long-term relationship with customers.

Although segmentation can focus on a group of customers, it may not be good enough because most of the competitors can adopt similar strategies. It may be advisable, therefore, to shift the target for marketing from a group of consumers to each individual. Instead of selling a single product to as many customers as possible, marketers are trying to sell as many products as possible to one customer—over a long period of time. To do this, marketers need to concentrate on building unique relationships with individual customers on a one-to-one basis. **One-to-one marketing**, one approach to relationship marketing, is a way for marketing departments to get to know their customers more intimately by understanding their preferences and then providing personalized advertisement and marketing to offers, thus increasing the odds of retaining customers.

one-to-one marketing
Marketing that treats each customer in a unique way.

One-to-one means not only communicating with customers as individuals, but possibly developing custom products and tailored messages based on the customer's explicit and implicit needs as well. It relies on a two-way dialog between a company and its customers in order to foster a true relationship, and allows customers to express desires that the company can help fulfill. The major characteristics of one-to-one marketing as compared to mass marketing and market segmentation are illustrated in Exhibit 8.4.

EXHIBIT 8.4   From Mass Marketing to Segmentation to One-to-One

Factor	Mass Marketing	Market Segmentation	Relationship Marketing (One to One)
Interactions	Usually none, or one-way	Usually none, or with a sample	Active, two-way
Focus	Product	Group (segment)	Customer-focused (one)
Recipient	Anonymous	Segment profiles	Individuals
Campaigns	Few	More	Many
Reach	Wide	Smaller	One at a time
Market Research	Macro in nature	Based on segment analysis or demographics	Based on detailed customer behaviors and profiles

HOW ONE-TO-ONE RELATIONSHIPS ARE PRACTICED

Although some companies have had one-to-one marketing programs for years, it may be much more beneficial to institute a corporate-wide policy of building one-to-one relationships around the Web. This can be done in several ways. For example, Exhibit 8.5 shows a possible one-to-one marketing cycle. The whole process includes four stages: identification of customer preference, differentiation of products/services, interaction with customers, and customization (personalized service). The process can start at any point in the cycle.

EXHIBIT 8.5   The One-to-One Marketing Cycle

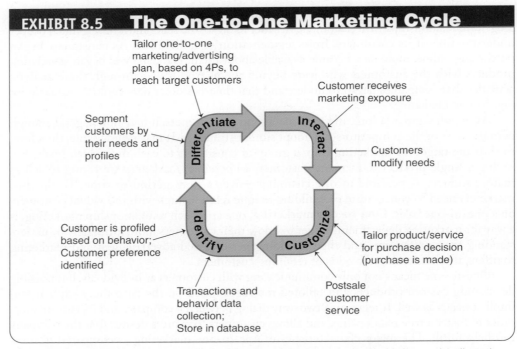

Sources: Compiled from Greenberg (2009), *en.wikipedia.org/wiki/personalized-marketing* (accessed April 2011), and author's experience.

For new customers, it usually starts with "Customer receives marketing exposure" (at the top right side of exhibit). The customer then decides on how to respond to the marketing exposure and makes the purchase decision (e.g., whether to buy the product online or offline; if online, whether to buy as an individual or to use group purchasing). When a sale is made, customer information is collected (lower left corner) and then placed in a database. Then, a customer's profile is developed, and the so-called four Ps of marketing (product, place, price, and promotion) are planned based on the profile, on a one-to-one basis. For example, appropriate advertisements are prepared and sent to the target customer, which will hopefully lead to another purchase by the customer. All of this can, and should, be done in the Web environment. For a new theory that incorporates customer feelings as a quality measure see Ziv (2010).

One of the benefits of doing business over the Internet is that it enables companies to better communicate with customers and better understand customers' needs and buying habits. These improvements, in turn, enable companies to enhance and frequently personalize their future marketing efforts. For example, Amazon.com can e-mail customers announcements of the availability of books in their areas of interest as soon as they are published; Expedia.com will ask consumers where they are likely to fly to and then e-mail them information about special discounts to their desired destinations. Details on these key concepts that are part of *personalization* are discussed in Section 8.5.

Section 8.4 ▶ REVIEW QUESTIONS

1. Define and describe mass marketing.
2. Define market segmentation. How is segmentation done?
3. Define one-to-one marketing. What are its advantages?
4. Describe the one-to-one marketing cyclical process.
5. How is the knowledge of a customer profile used by the advertisers?

8.5 PERSONALIZATION AND BEHAVIORAL MARKETING

Internet marketing facilitates the use of market segmentation and one-to-one marketing. Here we address three key issues related to one-to-one marketing: *personalization*, *behavioral targeting*, and *collaborative filtering*.

PERSONALIZATION IN E-COMMERCE

Personalization refers to the matching of services and advertising content to individuals based on their preferences. The matching process is based on what a company knows about the individual user. This knowledge is usually referred to as a *user profile*. The **user profile** defines customer preferences, behaviors, and demographics. It can be generated by getting information directly from the user; observing what people are doing online through the use of tools such as a **cookie**—a data file that is placed on a user's hard drive by a remote Web server, frequently without disclosure or the user's consent, that collects information about the user's activities at a site; building profiles from previous purchase patterns; performing marketing research (see Section 8.6 and the Netflix case); and making inferences.

Once a customer profile is constructed, a company can match the profile with a database of products, services, or ads. Manual matching is time-consuming and expensive; therefore, the matching process is usually done by software agents. One-to-one matching can be applied through several different methods. One well-known method is *collaborative filtering* (discussed later in this section).

Many vendors provide personalization tools that help in customer acquisition and retention. Examples of such vendors are Omniture (omniture.com) and Magnify 360 (magnify360.com).

Cookies in E-Commerce

The use of cookies is a well-known method that enables the identification of customers' future visits on the same computers (see en.wikipedia.org/wiki/cookies for more on cookies).

personalization
The matching of services, products, and advertising content with individual consumers and their preferences.

user profile
The requirements, preferences, behaviors, and demographic traits of a particular customer.

cookie
A data file that is placed on a user's hard drive by a remote Web server, frequently without disclosure or the user's consent, which collects information about the user's activities at a site.

Are cookies bad or good? The answer is "both." When users revisit Amazon.com or other sites, customers are greeted by their first name. How does Amazon.com know a user's identity? Through the use of cookies! Vendors can provide consumers with considerable personalized information if they use cookies that signal a consumer's return to a site. A variation of cookies is known as *e-sugging* ("SUG-ing," from "selling under the guise of research"). For example, consumers who visit travel sites may get more and more unsolicited travel-related e-mails and pop-up ads.

Cookies can provide marketers with a wealth of information, which then can be used to target ads to them. Thus, marketers get higher rates of "click-through," and customers can view the most relevant information. Cookies can also prevent repetitive ads because vendors can arrange for a consumer not to see the same ad twice. Finally, advanced data mining companies, such as NCR and Sift, can analyze information in cookie files so companies can better meet their customers' needs.

However, some people object to cookies because they do not like the idea that "someone" is watching their activity on the Internet. Users who do not like cookies can disable them. However, some consumers may want to keep the friendly cookies. For example, many sites recognize a person as a subscriber so that they do not need to register. Internet Explorer (IE) gives users control over third-party cookies. (Go to "Internet Options" under "Tools" and select "Private tab," click "Advanced," and put a check mark next to "Override automatic cookie handling." Then, direct IE to accept cookies.) For additional information, see en.wikipidia.org/wiki/cookies and cookiecentral.com.

Using Personalized Techniques to Increase Sales

Amazon.com makes recommendations on the basis of a customer's browsing and buying history, on items viewed or purchased by customers who have bought the product being viewed, and on items that seem related to the product being viewed. On Amazon.com, reviews, recommendations, and rankings become an essential part of browsing and shopping experiences. Another company, MotherNature.com (mothernature.com) is using data and text mining to analyze each site visit based on the customer's preferences and buying habits. It is able to track everything from the success rate of online promotions to trends that can be used in site personalization. Personalized services can be facilitated when the companies know more about their customers. Such information is provided, for example by rapleaf.com.

BEHAVIORAL MARKETING AND COLLABORATIVE FILTERING

One of the most popular ways of matching customers with ads is by using technologies based on customer behavior on the Web. We discuss here the essentials of this approach, which is known as *behavioral targeting*, and provide brief information on one method for doing it.

Behavioral Targeting

behavioral targeting
Targeting that uses information collected about an individual's Web-browsing behavior, such as the pages they have visited or the searches they have made, to select an advertisement to display to that individual.

Behavioral targeting uses information collected about an individual's Web-browsing behavior, such as the pages they have visited or the searches they have made, in order to select an advertisement to display to that individual. Many vendors believe that this can help them deliver online advertisements to users who then would be influenced by the ads. Behavioral targeting can be used on its own or in conjunction with other forms of targeting, such as using factors like location of the customers, demographics, or the surrounding content. Google is reported to test its "interest-based advertising" to make ads more relevant and useful. Representative vendors of behavioral targeting tools are Predictad.com, Adlink.com, Adaptlogic.com, Boomerang.com, Criteo.com, and Valueclick.com. For more information, see en.wikipedia.org/wiki/behavioral_targeting.

Collaborative Filtering

collaborative filtering
A market research and personalization method that uses customer data to predict, based on formulas derived from behavioral sciences, what other products or services a customer may enjoy; predictions can be extended to other customers with similar profiles.

It would be useful if the company could predict what products or services are of interest to a customer without asking the customer directly. **Collaborative filtering** is a method that attempts to do just that; it uses the preferences and activities of customers with similar characteristics to build user profiles of new customers and make product recommendations to them. Many personalization systems are based on collaborative filtering (e.g., backflip.com and choicestream.com). The statement "Those who bought this item also bought the following items:" is a typical statement generated by collaborative filtering, which intends to persuade a consumer by pointing to preferences of other consumers.

Other Methods

In addition to collaborative filtering, other methods for identifying users' profiles are:

Rule-Based Filtering. A company asks consumers a series of yes/no or multiple-choice questions. The questions may range from personal information to the specific information the customer is looking for on a specific website. Certain behavioral patterns are predicted using the collected information. From this information, the collaborative filtering system derives behavioral and demographic rules such as, "If customer age is greater than 35, and customer income is above $100,000, show Jeep Cherokee ad. Otherwise, show Mazda6 ad."

Content-Based Filtering. With this technique, vendors identify customer preferences by the attributes of the product(s) they intend to buy. Based on user preferences, the vendor's system will recommend additional products with similar attributes to the user. For instance, the system may recommend a text-mining book to customers who have shown interest in data mining, or recommend more action movies after a consumer rented one.

Activity-Based Filtering. Filtering rules can also be built by watching the users' activities on the Web.

For more about personalization and filtering, see en.wikipedia.org/wiki/collaborative_filtering.

Legal and Ethical Issues in Collaborative Filtering

Information often is collected from users without their knowledge or permission. This raises several ethical and legal issues, including invasion of privacy issues. Several vendors offer permission-based personalization tools. With these, companies request the customer's permission to receive questionnaires and ads. (See Chapter 14 for more on privacy issues, and Section 8.10 for information about permission marketing.)

In November 2010, Facebook announced the possibility of rolling out a Web-based advertising network that targets ads based on the recipients' behavior and the behavior of their Facebook friends. Privacy groups are not happy and are trying to pressure Facebook to cancel the project.

Social Psychology and Morphing in Behavioral Marketing

Social psychology is the branch of psychology that deals with how people think about, influence, and relate to one another. Research has found that shoppers do what is popularly known as "thinslicing" when they are out shopping. *Thinslicing* is a style of thinking (psychologists call it *heuristic-thinking*) that involves ignoring most of the information available, and instead using (slicing off) a few salient information cues, often social in nature, along with a set of simple, but usually smart mental rules of thumb to make intuitive decisions. Psychologists have identified six universal heuristics (mental rules of thumb) that shoppers use to process thin-sliced information. These are social proof (follow the crowd), authority (follow the authority), scarcity (scarce stuff is good stuff), liking (follow those you like), consistency (be consistent), and reciprocity (repay favors). *Social shopping tools are powerful because they harness these heuristics to make purchase decisions more likely.* For details, see Marsden (2009).

One level that social psychology reflects is *social shopping* (see Chapter 7); social shopping harnesses the human capacity for *social learning*—learning from the knowledge and experience of others we know and/or trust. This social learning faculty is part of our *social intelligence*, the ability to understand and learn from each other and profit from social situations. But social shopping tools also work at a more fundamental level, by playing to cognitive biases in how people are influenced by other people when shopping.

Use of Customer Database Marketing

Personalized services are often based on information the merchant gets from commercial database marketing services (e.g., see Strauss and Frost 2009). A unique example of such services is Rapleaf.

Example. Rapleaf (rapleaf.com) is a database marketing start-up. Acting primarily as a B2B firm, Rapleaf's database of consumer information helps businesses segment customers, understand consumer penetration across social media, plan online marketing campaigns, find influential customers for customer relationship management, and investigate fraud.

The company provides businesses with information about the reputation of individual customers. It is like credit card verification. But the information provided (e.g., demographic) on each customer enables merchants to provide personalized services. Individuals can see their own level of reputation (and hopefully improve it), and they can better understand their online footsteps. For how the company collects information, what they know about you, how they use the information, and what privacy concerns exist, see Steel (2010).

Section 8.5 ❯ REVIEW QUESTIONS

1. Define personalization.
2. List some benefits of personalization.
3. Describe cookies in EC.
4. Define behavioral targeting.
5. Define collaborative filtering.
6. Explain how one-to-one advertising is done with cookies and behavioral targeting.
7. Describe how social psychology and cognitive style influence shopping decisions.
8. Describe how customer database information can facilitate personalization.

8.6 MARKET RESEARCH FOR E-COMMERCE

In order to sell products well, it is important to conduct proper market research to find information and knowledge about consumers and products. The market researcher's goal is to discover marketing opportunities and issues, to establish marketing plans, to better understand the purchasing process, and to evaluate marketing performance. On the Web, its purpose is also to investigate the market and behavior of online customers. (e.g., see Strauss and Frost 2009). Market research includes gathering information about topics such as the economy, industry, firms, products, pricing, distribution, competition, promotion, and consumer purchasing behavior. Here we focus on the latter. In Chapter 12, we will look at some other market research topics: the need to research the market, the competition, the technology, the business environment, and more.

OBJECTIVES AND CONCEPTS OF MARKET RESEARCH ONLINE

Investigation of EC markets can be conducted through conventional methods or it can be done with the assistance of the Internet. Although telephone or shopping mall surveys will continue, interest in Internet research methods is on the rise. Market research that uses the Internet frequently is faster and more efficient and allows the researcher to access a more geographically diverse audience than those found in offline surveys (see FAQs at casro.org). Also, on the Web, market researchers can conduct a very large study much more cheaply than with other methods. Even telephone surveys can cost as much as $50 per respondent. This may be too expensive for a small company that needs several hundred respondents. An online survey will cost a fraction of a similarly sized telephone survey and can expedite research considerably, as shown in Case 8.1 about P&G. The increased sample size in online surveys can theoretically increase the accuracy and the predictive capabilities of the results. Hewson et al. (2003) provide a comprehensive review of online market research technologies, methods, tools, issues, and ethical considerations.

CASE 8.1
EC Application

INTERNET MARKET RESEARCH EXPEDITES TIME-TO-MARKET AT PROCTER & GAMBLE

For decades, Procter & Gamble (P&G; *pg.com*), Johnson & Johnson, and Colgate-Palmolive have been competitors in the market for personal care products. Developing a major new product from concept to market launch used to take more than 5 years. First, a concept test was conducted: The companies sent product photos and descriptions to potential customers, asking whether they might buy the product. If the feedback was negative, they tried to improve the product concept and then repeated the previous concept test. Once positive response was achieved, sample products were mailed out, and the customers were asked to fill out detailed questionnaires. When customers' responses met the companies' internal hurdles, the companies would start with mass TV advertising.

However, thanks to the Internet, it took P&G only 3½ years to get Whitestrips, a teeth-brightening product, onto the market and to a sales level of $200 million a year—considerably quicker than it had taken in the past with other oral care products. In September 2000, P&G threw out the old marketing test model and instead introduced Whitestrips on the Internet, offering the product for sale on P&G's website. The company spent several months studying who was coming to the site and buying the product and collecting responses to online questionnaires, which was much faster than the old mail ones.

The online research, which was facilitated by data mining conducted on P&G's huge historical data (stored in a data warehouse) and the new Internet data, identified the most enthusiastic groups. These included teenage girls, brides-to-be, and young Hispanic Americans. Immediately, the company started to target these segments with appropriate advertising. The Internet created a product awareness of 35 percent, even before any shipments were made to stores. This buzz created a huge demand for the product by the time it hit the shelves.

In 2006, P&G began using on-demand solutions from RightNow Technologies (*rightnow.com*), including survey tools that execute opinion polls among selected segments of consumers who have opted into the company's market research programs.

As of 2008, P&G started to experiment with feedback collected at Facebook and other social networks. Such an information solicitation can be beneficial for successful promotion of products since people can spread the word around by word of mouth.

From these experiences, P&G learned important lessons about flexible and creative ways to approach product innovation and marketing. The whole process of studying the product concept, segmenting the market, and expediting product development has been revolutionized. As of 2009, all major competitors established groups on Facebook, developed islands in Second Life, and use LinkedIn and Twitter to communicate and learn from customers. They shorten the time-to-market and get better information from customers, as shown at Johnson & Johnson (see the closing case of this chapter) and in Ploof (2009).

Sources: Compiled from *TMCnet* (2006), Buckley (2002), and *pg.com* (accessed March 2011).

Questions

1. How did P&G reduce time-to-market?
2. How were data mining techniques used?
3. What research methods were used?
4. Why do P&G and similar companies market on social networks such as Facebook and LinkedIn?

What Are Marketers Looking for in EC Market Research?

By looking at a personal profile that includes observed behaviors on the Web, it is possible for marketers to explain and predict online buying behavior. For example, companies want to know why some customers are online shoppers whereas others are not. Major factors that are used for predicting customer online purchasing behavior are (in descending order of importance): product information requested, number of related e-mails, number of orders made, products/services ordered, and gender.

Typical questions that online market research attempts to answer are: What are the purchase patterns for individuals and groups (market segmentation)? What factors encourage online purchasing? How can we identify those who are real buyers from those who are just browsing? How does an individual navigate—do consumers check information first or do they go directly to ordering? What is the optimal Web page design? Knowing the answers to questions such as these helps a vendor to advertise properly, to price items, to design the website, and to provide appropriate customer service. Online market research can provide such data about individuals, groups, and the entire organization.

Internet-based market research is often done in an interactive manner, allowing personal contact with customers, and it provides marketing organizations with a greater ability to understand the customer, the market, and the competition. For example, it can identify early shifts in product and customer trends, enabling marketers to identify new trends and marketing opportunities and to develop products that customers really want to buy. It also tells management when a product or a service is no longer popular. To learn more about market research on the Web, see the tutorials at webmonkey.com. For examples of results of market research, see Plunkett (2010).

REPRESENTATIVE MARKET RESEARCH APPROACHES

Of the many market research approaches, we selected some that are more useful for EC.

Market Segmentation Research

For years, companies used direct mail to contact customers. However, they frequently did so regardless of whether the products or services were appropriate for the specific individuals on the company's mailing list. For example, a retailing company may need to send out four mailings to 1 million customers each year. The cost of the direct mailings is $1.25 million or $1.25 per customer. Assuming that only 1 percent responds, this means the cost per responding customer is $125. Obviously, this type of direct marketing usually is not cost-effective.

One way to reduce the cost is to conduct market segmentation to increase the response rate. A consumer market can be segmented in several ways, for example, by geography, demographics, psychographics, and benefits sought, as discussed earlier. For EC markets, Brengman, et al. (2005) proposed segmenting Internet shoppers based on their Web-usage-related lifestyle, themes of Internet usage, Internet attitude, and psychographic and demographic characteristics. The researchers identified four online shopping segments (tentative shoppers, suspicious learners, shopping lovers, and business users) and four online nonshopping segments (fearful browsers, positive technology muddlers, negative technology muddlers, and adventurous browsers). By isolating and identifying combinations of attributes that make markets, prospects, and customers unique, marketers use strategies developed to appeal to targeted segments. One segment that is being targeted is the so-called Internet generation, or NetGen, the generation that has been raised with the power of the Internet. Internet marketing and advertising is more appropriate for the NetGen than traditional advertising.

Market segmentation can be done with the aid of tools such as data modeling and data warehousing. Using data mining and Web mining (see Online Tutorial T8), businesses can look at consumer buying patterns to slice segments even finer. This is not an easy process, and it requires considerable resources and computer support. Most successful market segmentation stories involve large companies. For example, Royal Bank of Canada segments its 10 million customers at least once a month to determine credit risk, profitability, and so on. This market segmentation has been very successful: The response to Royal Bank of Canada's advertising campaigns has increased from 3 to 30 percent. Market segmentation can be very effective in the Web environment, especially when used with appropriate statistical tools. For more on market segmentation surveys, see sric-bi.com/VALS/presurvey.shtml.

To perform online marketing, it is necessary to know what the customer wants or needs. Such information can be collected by the following approaches:

- Soliciting information from customers online (e.g., via interviews, questionnaires, use of focus groups, or blogging).
- Observing what customers are doing on the Web by transaction logs and cookies.
- Using data mining or collaborative filtering techniques to analyze available data.

Data Collection and Analysis

Specific methods for collecting online data include e-mail communication with individual customers, moderated focus groups conducted in chat rooms, questionnaires placed on websites, and tracking customers' movements on the Web. A typical Internet-based market research process is shown next.

Steps in Collecting Market Research Data.

1. Define the research issue and the target market.
2. Identify newsgroups and Internet communities to study.
3. Identify specific topics for discussion.
4. Subscribe to the pertinent groups; register in communities.
5. Search discussion group topic and content lists to find the target market.
6. Search e-mail discussion group lists.
7. Subscribe to filtering services that monitor groups.
8. Read FAQs and other instructions.
9. Visit chat rooms.

Content of the Research Instrument.

1. Post strategic queries to groups.
2. Post surveys on a website.
3. Offer rewards for participation.
4. Post strategic queries on a website.
5. Post relevant content to groups, with a pointer to a website survey.
6. Post a detailed survey in specific e-mail questionnaires.
7. Create a chat room and try to build a community of consumers.

Target Audience of the Study.

1. Compare audience with the target population.
2. Determine each segment's reason for wanting the product/service.
3. Determine market characteristics and trends.
4. Determine editorial focus.
5. Determine content.
6. Determine what Web services to create for each type of audience.

Note: This process is based on Kennaugh (2009) and Moisander and Valtonen (2006). Professional pollsters and marketing research companies frequently conduct online voting polls (e.g., see cnn.com and acnielsen.com). For example, comScore (comscore.com) offers reporters access to "apples-to-apples" comparisons that measure the entire network of sites owned by each major Internet portal or vendor (e.g., Google, Fox Interactive Media, Yahoo!, Viacom Digital, MSN). For how market research is organized, see the comScore example.

Example: Market Research by comScore, Inc. The comScore Media Metrix provides Internet audience measurements for advertising agencies, publishers, marketers, and financial analysts. It is using proprietary data collection technology and online data solicitation methodology. The comScore Media Metrix counts unique visitors across the digital world daily. Powered by a global panel of consumers, the comScore Media Metrix 2.0 delivers highly accurate and comprehensive audience ratings and estimates. This provides an accurate demographic view of Internet users, allowing websites to analyze their online efforts and compare them to that of competitors. Media Metrix 2.0 targets specific online audiences to improve advertising and marketing performance (more clicks, better conversions); it uses accurate and detailed demographic data to improve sales and partnership proposals; identifies and studies competitors' online activities in order to formulate strategies for gaining market share, providing a complete view of users' online efforts, and allowing for strategic and sound decisions; and utilizes panel-based methodology to provide greater insights into the online behavior of consumers.

The comScore Video Metrix enables clients to understand the rapidly growing online video market and effectively target advertising in this dynamic and evolving medium (video ads are discussed later in this chapter). The Video Metrix identifies and counts the total unique viewers and the number of videos viewed, duration, and videos seen per viewer. Inside Research (insideresearch.com) has recognized comScore as the fastest growing global market research firm. As the provision of online video content continues to grow, it is vital for the industry to have a comparative measure of all the competing entities in this segment of the Internet advertising market. For details, see en.wikipedia.org/wiki/ComScore.

Online Surveys

An online survey is a major method for collecting EC data. It has many advantages, including lower overall preparation and administration costs, greater speed in survey distribution and collection, better control of the questionnaire filling process (which may lead to fewer response errors, more complete responses, and easier follow-up), and more flexibility in the questionnaire design. However, online surveys also have some weaknesses, including potential lack of anonymity, data privacy and security concerns, technological competency variation of the potential respondents, and being impersonal. For a comprehensive review, see Sue and Ritter (2007).

Web-Based Surveys. A special type of online survey is placing the questions on the Web and inviting potential customers to reply. For example, Mazda North America used a Web-based survey to help design its Miata line. Web surveys may be passive (a fill-in questionnaire) or interactive (respondents download the questionnaires, add comments, ask questions, and discuss issues).

Several tools for Web-based surveys are available. For example, Super Survey (supersurvey.com) provides online surveys with 50 templates and 20-plus question types to create customized surveys. Surveys can be created in any language, including multibyte languages such as Chinese and Arabic. Advanced validation protocols, randomization, and filtering options help to ensure the integrity of survey results. For free software, see freeonlinesurveys.com.

Online Focus Groups. Several research firms create panels of qualified Web regulars to participate in online focus groups. For example, NPD Group's panel (npd.com) consists of a pod of 15,000 consumers recruited online and verified by telephone. NPD recruits participants in advance by telephone and takes the time to help them connect to the Internet, if necessary. Use of preselected focus group participants helps to overcome some of the research problems (e.g., small sample size and partial responses) that sometimes limit the effectiveness of Web-based surveys. Toluna Onlin (us.toluna.com/Default.aspx) picks users from its own database and then calls them periodically to verify that they are who they say they are. For more on online surveys, see info.com/conductingonlinesurveys.

Hearing Directly from Customers

Instead of using focus groups, a company may ask customers directly what they think about a product or service. Companies can use chat rooms, newsgroups, blogs, wikis, podcasts, and electronic consumer forums to interact with consumers. For example, toymaker LEGO used a market research vendor to establish a direct survey on an electronic bulletin board where millions of visitors read each other's comments and share opinions about LEGO toys. The research vendor analyzed the responses daily and submitted the information to LEGO. Netflix is using this approach extensively by inducing customers to report their likes and dislikes, as described earlier in this chapter. Software tools that can be used to hear directly from customers include those from Future Media Architects, Inc. (fma.com), Satmetrix (satmetrix.com), Betasphere (voconline.com), InsightExpress (insightexpress.com), and Survey (survey.com). Finally, as described in Chapter 7, social networks provide several opportunities to hear directly from customers.

Data Collection in the Web 2.0 Environment

Collecting data in the Web 2.0 environment provides new and exciting opportunities. Here are some methods:

- **Polling.** People like to vote (e.g., *American Idol*), expressing preferences (see the Netflix case). They provide opinions on products, services, and so forth. It is popular in social networks.
- **Blogging.** Bloggers can raise issues or induce others to express opinions.
- **Chatting.** Community members love to chat in public chat rooms. By following what goes on there, you can collect current data.
- **Live chat.** Here, you can collect interactive data from customers in real time.
- **Chatterbots.** These can be partially interactive. You can analyze logs of communications. Sometimes, people are more honest when they chat with an avatar.
- **Collective wisdom (intelligence).** This is a kind of community brainstorming. Researchers can find out what arguments people are having and the degree of the disagreements.
- **Find expertise.** Expertise is frequently found in the Web 2.0 environment, many times for free (e.g., the answer function of LinkedIn).
- **Folksonomy.** This social tagging makes data easier to find and access.
- **Data in videos, photos, and other rich media.** Places where these media are shared contribute to valuable data collection.
- **Discussion forums.** Subgroups in social networks use a discussion format where members exchange opinions on many topics.

Observing Customers' Movements Online

To avoid some of the problems of online surveys, especially the giving of false or biased information, some marketers choose to learn about customers by observing their behavior rather than by asking them questions. Many marketers keep track of consumers' Web movements by using methods such as transaction logs (log files) or cookie files.

Transaction Logs. A **transaction log** records user activities at a company's website. A transaction log is created from the computer log file of user actions that have occurred. With log file analysis tools, it is possible to get a good idea of where visitors are coming from, how often they return, and how they navigate through a site. The transaction-log approach is especially useful if the visitors' names are known (e.g., when they have registered with the site). In addition, data from the shopping cart database can be combined with information in the transaction log to reveal more insights.

Note that as customers move from site to site, they establish their **clickstream behavior**, a pattern of their movements on the Internet, which can be seen in their transaction logs. Both ISPs and individual websites are capable of tracking a user's clickstream.

Cookies, Web Bugs, and Spyware. Cookies and Web bugs can be used to supplement transaction-log methods. As discussed earlier, cookies allow a website to store data on the user's PC; when the customer returns to the site, the cookies can be used to find what the customer did in the past. Cookies are frequently combined with **Web bugs**, tiny graphics files embedded in e-mail messages and on websites. Web bugs transmit information about the user and his or her movements to a monitoring site.

Spyware is software that gathers user information through an Internet connection without the user's knowledge. Originally designed to allow freeware authors to make money on their products, spyware applications are typically bundled together with freeware that is downloaded onto users' machines. Many users do not realize that they are downloading spyware with the freeware. Sometimes the freeware provider may indicate that other programs will be loaded onto the user's computer in the licensing agreement (e.g., "may include software that occasionally notifies users of important news"). Spyware stays on the user's hard drive and continually tracks the user's actions, periodically sending

transaction log
A record of user activities at a company's website.

clickstream behavior
Customer movements on the Internet.

Web bugs
Tiny graphics files embedded in e-mail messages and in websites that transmit information about users and their movements to a Web server.

spyware
Software that gathers user information over an Internet connection without the user's knowledge.

information on the user's activities to the owner of the spyware. It typically is used to gather information for advertising purposes. Users cannot control what data are sent via the spyware, and unless they use special tools, they often cannot uninstall the spyware, even if the software it was bundled with is removed from the system. Effective tools for fighting spyware include Ad-Aware (lavasoft.com), Spykiller (spykiller.com), and Webwasher Spyware from Secure Computing (securecomputing.com). For more on spyware and banners, see Online File W8.3.

Representative vendors that provide tools for tracking customers' movements are Tealeaf Technology, Inc. (tealeaf.com, log files), Acxiom Corp. (acxiom.com, data warehousing), and Stat Counter (statcounter.com, real-time tracking).

The use of cookies and Web bugs is controversial. Many believe that they invade the customer's privacy (see privacyfoundation.org). Tracking customers' activities without their knowledge or permission may be unethical or even illegal.

Web Analytics and Mining. Web analytics services and software have grown beyond simply reporting which page was clicked and how long a visitor stayed there. They now offer more advanced functions that retailers are finding indispensable. For example, options from Coremetrics (coremetrics.com) and others are enabling retailers to make site adjustments on the fly, manage online marketing campaigns and e-commerce initiatives, and track customer satisfaction. Also, if a company redesigns its website, it can gain almost instant feedback on how the new site is performing. Web analytics can be done on a customer-by-customer or prospect-by-prospect basis, helping marketers decide which products to promote and merchandisers achieve a better understanding of the nature of demand. For tutorials on data mining and Web mining, see autonlab.org/tutorials; also watch the video "Beginning Analytics" at youtube.com/watch?v=Hdsb_uH2yPU&feature=channel.

clickstream data

Data that occur inside the Web environment; they provide a trail of the user's activities (the user's clickstream behavior) in the website.

Clickstream Analysis. **Clickstream data** are data generated in the Web environment; they provide a trail of a user's activities (the user's clickstream behavior) in a website. These data include a record of the user's browsing patterns: every website and every page of every website the user visits; how long the user remains on a page or site; in what order the pages were visited; and even the e-mail addresses of mail that the user sends and receives. By analyzing clickstream data, a firm can find out, for example, which promotions are effective and which population segments are interested in specific products. The list of information provided by clickstream data is available in Online File W8.4.

Several companies offer tools that enable such an analysis. For example, WebTrends 7 and higher features several advanced tools for analyzing clickstream data (e.g., see webtrends.com).

In addition, clickstream data can be maintained in a clickstream database or data warehouse for further analysis. Despite storing many terabytes of clickstream data and investing heavily in Web analytic tools, very few companies understand how to use the data effectively.

Web mining

Data mining techniques for discovering and extracting information from Web documents; explores both Web content and Web usage.

Web Mining. Web mining refers to the use of data mining techniques for discovering and extracting information from Web documents. Web mining explores both Web content and Web usage. The usage analysis is derived from clickstream data. Web mining has the potential to change the way we access and use the information available on the Web.

LIMITATIONS OF ONLINE MARKET RESEARCH AND HOW TO OVERCOME THEM

One problem with online market research is that too much data may be available. To use data properly, one needs to organize, edit, condense, and summarize it. However, such a task may be expensive and time-consuming. One solution to this problem is to automate the process by using data warehousing and data mining. The essentials of this process, known as *business intelligence*, are provided in Online Tutorial T8, and in Turban, et al. (2011).

Some of the limitations of online research methods are accuracy of responses, loss of respondents because of equipment problems, and the ethics and legality of Web tracking. In addition, focus group responses can lose something in the translation from an in-person group to an online group. A researcher may get people online to talk to each other and play off of each other's comments, but eye contact and body language are two interactions of traditional focus group research that are lost in the online world. However, just as it hinders the two-way assessment of visual cues, Web research can actually offer some participants the anonymity necessary to elicit an unguarded response. Finally, a major limitation of online market research is the difficulty in obtaining truly representative samples.

Concerns have been expressed over the potential lack of representativeness in samples of online users. Online shoppers tend to be wealthy, employed, and well educated. Although this may be a desirable audience for some products and services, the research results may not be extendable to other markets. Although the Web-user demographic is rapidly diversifying, it is still skewed toward certain population groups, such as those with convenient Internet access (at home or work). Another important issue concerns the lack of clear understanding of the online communication process and how online respondents think and interact in cyberspace.

BIOMETRIC MARKETING

One problem with Web analytics, Web mining, clickstream data, and so on is the representativeness. That is, we observe and follow a computer, not knowing who is actually moving the mouse. Many households have several users; thus, the data collected may not represent any one person's preferences (unless, of course, we are sure that there is one and only one user, as in the case of smart phones). A potential solution is suggested by Pons (2006) in the form of biometric marketing.

A **biometric** is one of an individual's unique physical or behavioral characteristics that can be used to identify an individual precisely (e.g., fingerprints; see the list in Chapter 9). By applying the technology to computer users, we can improve security and learn about the user's profile precisely. The question is how to do it. Indeed, there are programs by which users identify themselves to the computer by biometrics, and these are spreading rapidly. Utilizing the technology for marketing involves social and legal acceptability. For these reasons, advertisers are using methods that target individuals without knowing their profiles. An example is search engine–based methods, such as AdWords used by Google (see Section 8.8).

biometrics
An individual's unique physical or behavioral characteristics that can be used to identify an individual precisely (e.g., fingerprints).

Section 8.6 ▶ REVIEW QUESTIONS

1. Describe the objectives of market research.
2. Define and describe market segmentation.
3. Describe how market research is done online and the methods used by comScore.
4. Describe the role of Weblogs and clickstream analysis.
5. Define cookies, Web bugs, and spyware, and describe how they can be used in market research.
6. Describe how the issue of privacy relates to online market research.
7. Describe the limitations of online market research.
8. Describe how biometrics and cell phones can improve market research and advertising.

8.7 WEB ADVERTISING

Advertising on the Web plays an extremely important activity in e-commerce. Internet advertising is growing very rapidly, especially B2C, and companies are changing their advertising strategies to gain a competitive edge. Since the Internet provides interactivity, online ads are also useful for brand building directly through response ads. Online ad revenue reached a record high of $12.1 billion in the first quarter of 2010 in the United States alone, which is a 11.3 percent increase from the previous year. Spending is expected to increase rapidly on all types of online advertising methods, including social commerce. In this chapter we concentrate on generic Web advertising. We covered social networking advertisement in Chapter 7. For more information, see Tuten (2008).

OVERVIEW OF WEB ADVERTISING

Advertising is an attempt to disseminate information in order to affect buyer–seller transactions. Traditional advertising was impersonal, one-way mass communication that was paid for by sponsors. Telemarketing and direct mail ads were attempts to personalize advertising to make it more effective. These direct marketing approaches worked fairly well but were expensive and slow and seldom truly one-to-one interactive. The cost–benefit was poor. For example, say a direct mail campaign costs about $1 per person and has a response rate of only 1 to 3 percent. This makes the cost per responding person in the range of $33 to $100. Such an expense can be justified only for high-ticket items (e.g., cars).

One of the problems with direct mail advertising was that the advertisers knew very little about the recipients. Market segmentation by various characteristics (e.g., age, income, gender) helped a bit but did not solve the problem. The concept of **interactive marketing** enables marketers and advertisers to interact directly with customers, but it was not so effective when it was done by phone.

On the Internet, a consumer can click an ad to obtain more information or send an e-mail to ask a question. The customer can conduct live chat with the merchant, or with peers in a social network chat room. Besides the two-way communication and e-mail capabilities provided by the Internet, vendors also can target specific groups and individuals on whom they want to spend their advertising dollars. The Internet enables truly one-to-one advertising. A comparison of mass advertising, direct mail advertising, and interactive online advertising is shown in Online File W8.5. An example of cultivating customer relationships and e-loyalty on a one-to-one basis can be found in the case in Online File W8.6.

The two major business models for advertising online are (1) using the Web as a channel to advertise a firm's own products and services and (2) making a firm's site a public portal site and using captive audiences to advertise products offered by other firms (usually using affiliate marketing, see Chapter 1 and Section 8.10). For example, the audience might come to a P&G website to learn about Tide, but they might also get additional ads for products made by Coca-Cola.

The Advertising Cycle

With closed-loop campaign management, companies are treating advertising as a cyclical process, as shown in Exhibit 8.6. The cyclical process entails carefully planning a campaign

interactive marketing
Online marketing, facilitated by the Internet, by which marketers and advertisers can interact directly with customers, and consumers can interact with advertisers/vendors.

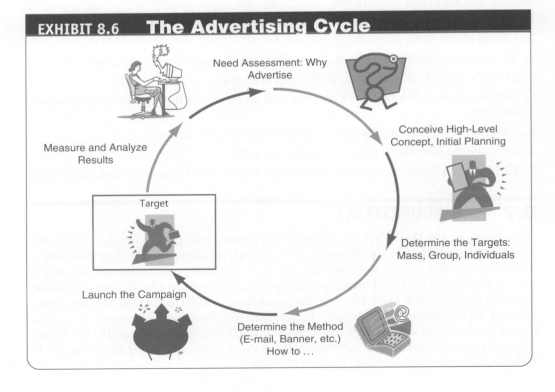

EXHIBIT 8.6   The Advertising Cycle

- Need Assessment: Why Advertise
- Conceive High-Level Concept, Initial Planning
- Determine the Targets: Mass, Group, Individuals
- Determine the Method (E-mail, Banner, etc.) How to …
- Launch the Campaign
- Target
- Measure and Analyze Results

to determine who the target audience is and how to reach that audience. Then, analyzing a campaign after its completion assists a company in understanding the campaign's success. This new knowledge is then used when planning future campaigns.

Before we describe the various steps in the cycle as it is implemented in Web advertising, let's learn some basic advertising terminology.

SOME BASIC INTERNET ADVERTISING TERMINOLOGY

The following list of terms and their definitions in the marginal glossary will be of use as you read about Web advertising.

▶ Ad views
▶ Button
▶ Page
▶ Click (ad click)
▶ CPM (cost per mille, i.e., thousand impressions)
▶ Conversion rate
▶ Click-through rate/ratio (CTR)
▶ Hit
▶ Visit
▶ Unique visit
▶ Stickiness

WHY INTERNET ADVERTISING?

The major traditional advertising media are television, newspapers, magazines, and radio. However, the market is changing as many consumers are spending more time on the Internet (about 25 percent annual growth) and using mobile devices. Internet advertising is getting more attention. The estimates for 2011 range from $42 billion to $106 billion, depending on how you define what you measure.

Companies advertise on the Internet for several reasons. To begin with, television viewers are migrating to the Internet. Worldwide, Internet users are spending significantly less time watching television and more time using the Internet. This trend will continue, especially as Internet-enabled cell phones are becoming commonplace. In addition, many Internet users are well educated and have high incomes. These Internet surfers are a desired target for many advertisers.

Advertising Online and Its Advantages

The major advantages of using the Internet over mass advertising are precise targeting, interactivity, rich media (grabs attention), cost reduction, efficiency, and eager customer acquisition. In comparison to traditional media, the Internet is the fastest growing communication medium by far. Worldwide, the number of Internet users surpassed 1 billion in 2005; and 2 billion Internet in 2011 (per physorg.com/news/2011-01-internet-users-worldwide-billion.html). Of course, advertisers are interested in a medium with such potential reach, both locally and globally.

Other reasons why Web advertising is growing rapidly include:

▶ **Cost.** Online ads are sometimes cheaper than those in other media. In addition, ads can be updated at any time with minimal cost.
▶ **Richness of format.** Web ads can effectively use the convergence of text, audio, graphics, video, and animation. In addition, games, entertainment, and promotions can be easily combined in online advertisements. Also, services such as mysimon.com enable customers to compare prices and, using a PDA or cell phone, do it at anytime from anywhere.

Marginal glossary

ad views
The number of times users call up a page that has a banner on it during a specific period; known as *impressions* or *page views*.

button
A small banner that is linked to a website; may contain downloadable software.

page
An HTML (Hypertext Markup Language) document that may contain text, images, and other online elements, such as Java applets and multimedia files; may be generated statically or dynamically.

click (ad click)
A count made each time a visitor clicks on an advertising banner to access the advertiser's website.

CPM (cost per mille, i.e., thousand impressions)
The fee an advertiser pays for each 1,000 times a page with a banner ad is shown.

conversion rate
The percentage of clickers who actually make a purchase.

click-through rate/ratio (CTR)
The percentage of visitors who are exposed to a banner ad and click on it.

hit
A request for data from a Web page or file.

visit
A series of requests during one navigation of a website; a pause of a certain length of time ends a visit.

unique visit
A count of the number of visitors entering a site, regardless of how many pages are viewed per visit.

stickiness
Characteristic that influences the average length of time a visitor stays in a site.

> ▶ **Personalization.** Web ads can be interactive and targeted to specific interest groups and/or individuals; the Web is a much more focused medium.
> ▶ **Timeliness.** Internet ads can be fresh and up-to-the-minute.
> ▶ **Location-based.** Using wireless technology and GPS, Web advertising can be location based; Internet ads can be sent to consumers whenever they are in a specific time and location (e.g., near a restaurant or a theater).
> ▶ **Linking.** It is easy to link from an online ad to a storefront—one click does it.
> ▶ **Digital branding.** Even the most price-conscious online shoppers are willing to pay premiums for brands they trust. These brands may be click-and-mortar brands (e.g., P&G) or dot-coms such as Amazon.com. British Airways places many Internet banner ads; however, these ads are not for clicking on to buy: They are all about branding, that is, establishing British Airways as a brand.

Traditional Versus Online Advertisement

Each advertising medium, including the Internet, has its advantages and limitations. Online File W8.7 compares the advantages and limitations of Internet advertising against traditional advertising media. Pfeiffer and Zinnbauer (2010) compared traditional advertising against Internet advertising (including social networks, Chapter 7). They concluded that not only is Internet advertisements more cost efficient, but the business impact of Internet ads is larger than traditional ads.

The combination of television–Web synergy can help attract more attention than either medium on its own. It has been found that a TV campaign increases brand awareness by 27 percent, whereas a combined TV and online campaign increases it by 45 percent. A TV campaign increases intent to purchase by 2 percent, whereas a combined TV and online campaign increases it by 12 percent.

The impact of Internet ads on newspaper viability is devastating. Many newspapers are disappearing, merging, or losing money. One solution is to increase their digital ads, as the *New York Times* is doing (see Vanacore 2010).

Section 8.7 ▶ REVIEW QUESTIONS

1. Define Web advertising and the major terms associated with it.
2. Describe the reasons for the growth in Web advertising.
3. Describe emerging Internet advertising approaches.
4. List the major benefits of Web advertising.
5. Draw and explain the advertising cycle.
6. What is the impact of online advertising on newspapers, TV, and billboard viability?

8.8   ONLINE ADVERTISING METHODS

A large number of online advertising methods exist. Next, we discuss a few major categories of ads.

MAJOR CATEGORIES OF ADS

Ads can be classified into three major categories: *classified*, *display*, and *interactive*.

Classified Ads. These usually use text, but lately may include photos. The ads are grouped according to classification (e.g., cars, rentals). They are the least expensive.

Classified ads can be found on special sites (e.g., craigslist.org and superpages.com), as well as on online newspapers, exchanges, and portals. In many cases, posting regular-size classified ads is free, but placing them in a larger size, in color, or with some other noticeable features is done for a fee. For examples, see traderonline.com and advertising.microsoft.com.

Display Ads. These use graphics, logos, colors, or special designs. They are an illustrated advertisement. The ads are usually not classified. Display ads are popular offline in billboards, yellow pages, and movies. They are becoming very popular on the Internet. All major search advertising companies (e.g., Google, Yahoo!, Microsoft, AOL) are leveraging their online positions in search advertising into the display ad business.

Interactive Ads. These use online or offline interactive media to communicate with consumers and to promote products, brands, and services. It is done through mediated means involving mutual action between consumers and producers. This is most commonly performed through the Internet, often using video content as a delivery medium.

In each of these categories there are several variations. For example, banner ads are a type of display ad. Some methods can be listed in more than one category. The major methods are presented next.

BANNERS

A **banner** is a graphic display that is used for advertising on a Web page (embedded in the page). A banner ad is linked to an advertiser's Web page. When users "click" the banner, they are transferred to the advertiser's site. Advertisers go to great lengths to design a banner that catches consumers' attention. Banners often include video clips and sound. Banner advertising including pop-up banners is the most commonly used form of advertising on the Internet.

There are several sizes and types of banners. The sizes are standardized by IAB and they are measured in pixels. For examples and details, see en.wikipedia.org/wiki/Web_banner. **Keyword banners** appear when a predetermined word is queried from a search engine. They are effective for companies that want to narrow their target audience. **Random banners** appear randomly, not as a result of some action by the viewer. Companies that want to introduce new products (e.g., a new movie or CD) or promote their brand use random banners. Static banners are always on the Web page. Finally, pop-up banners appear when least expected, as will be described later.

If an advertiser knows something about a visitor, such as the visitor's user profile, or area of interest, it is possible to match a specific banner with that visitor. Obviously, such targeted, personalized banners are usually most effective.

In the near future, banner ads will greet people by name and offer travel deals to their favorite destinations. Such *personalized banners* are being developed, for example, by Dotomi (dotomi.com). Dotomi delivers ads to consumers who opt-in to view its system. Initial results show a 14 percent click-through rate, which measures the success of a banner in attracting visitors to click, versus 3 to 5 percent with nonpersonalized ads.

A **live banner** is a banner ad that is created dynamically (or whose content is created dynamically) at the time of display, instead of being preprogrammed with fixed content. Live banners function the same way as traditional Web banners, except that the banner content is variable and may even update in real time. Live banners usually employ animation together with text, images, graphics, sounds, and video to catch the viewer's attention. For details and examples, see en.wikipedia.org/wiki/Live_banner.

Benefits and Limitations of Banner Ads

The major benefit of banner ads is that, by clicking on them, users are transferred to an advertiser's site, frequently directly to the shopping page of that site. Another advantage of using banners is the ability to customize them for individual surfers or a market segment of surfers. Also, viewing of banners is common, because in many cases customers are forced to see banner ads while waiting for a page to load or before they can get the free information or entertainment that they want to see (a strategy called *forced advertising*, and it is banner spam). Finally, banners may include attention-grabbing multimedia.

The major disadvantage of banners is their cost. If a company demands a successful marketing campaign, it will need to allocate a large percentage of its advertising budget to

banner
On a Web page, a graphic advertising display linked to the advertiser's Web page.

keyword banners
Banner ads that appear when a predetermined word is queried from a search engine.

random banners
Banner ads that appear at random, not as the result of the user's action.

live banner
A banner ad that is created dynamically (or whose content is created dynamically) at the time of display, instead of being preprogrammed with fixed content.

place banners on high-volume websites. Another drawback is that a limited amount of information can be placed on the banner. Hence, advertisers need to think of a creative but short message to attract viewers.

However, it seems that viewers have become somewhat immune to banners and simply do not notice them as they once did. The click-through rate has been declining over time. Because of these drawbacks, it is important to decide where on the screen to place banners (e.g., right side is better than left side, top is better than bottom). Companies such as QQ.com and Taobao.com in China have built behavior labs to track eye movements of consumers to understand how screen location and Web page design may affect viewer attention. For more on the efficient use of banner ads, see Online File W8.8.

POP-UP AND SIMILAR ADS

One of the most annoying phenomena in Web surfing is the increased use of pop-up, pop-under, and similar ads. A **pop-up ad**, also known as *ad spawning*, appears due to the automatic launching of a new browser window when a visitor enters or exits a website, when a delay occurs, or when other triggers cause the display. A pop-up ad appears in front of the active window. A **pop-under ad** is an ad that appears underneath (in back of) the current browser window. When users close the active window, they see the ad. Pop-ups cover the user's current screen and may be difficult to close. Pop-up and pop-under ads are controversial: Many users strongly object to this advertising method, which they consider to be intrusive. Most browsers provide an option that allows the viewer to block pop-up windows. Legal attempts have also been made to control pop-ups because they are basically a form of spam.

Several other tactics, some of them very aggressive, are being used by advertisers, and their use is increasing. These tactics may be accompanied by music, voice, and other rich multimedia. For details, see en.wikipedia.org/wiki/Popup_ad.

E-MAIL ADVERTISING

E-mail marketing is a form of direct marketing that uses e-mail as a means of communicating commercial messages to an audience. E-mail marketing may occur in different forms and for different purposes:

> Adding advertisements to e-mail messages sent by other companies to their customers. This is known as **e-mail advertising**.
> Sending e-mail messages with the purpose of enhancing the relationship of a merchant with its current or previous customers, to encourage customer loyalty and repeat business.
> Sending e-mail messages with the purpose of acquiring new customers or convincing current customers to purchase something immediately.
> Sending e-mail messages for commercial purposes via microblogs or other social media.

Sending company or product information to people or companies that appear on mailing lists has become a popular way to advertise on the Internet. E-mail messages may be combined with brief audio or video clips to promote a product; some messages provide links that users can click on to make a purchase. Sending coupons and special offers is done by all major retailers, including department stores and supermarkets. Airlines, banks, educational institutions, and anyone else who can get your e-mail will send you e-mail ads. You may recall from Chapters 1 and 7 that Groupon and similar companies base their business on e-mail, but so do spammers, scammers, and phishers. E-mail continues to enjoy popularity among consumers and is acknowledged as a legitimate and relied-upon marketing channel.

---

pop-up ad

An ad that appears in a separate window before, after, or during Internet surfing or when reading e-mail.

pop-under ad

An ad that appears underneath the current browser window, so when the user closes the active window the ad is still on the screen.

e-mail marketing

A form of direct marketing which uses e-mail as a means of communicating commercial messages to an audience.

e-mail advertising

Adding advertisements to e-mail messages sent to customers.

The Major Advantages and Limitations of E-Mail Advertisement

The major advantages of e-mail advertising are:

> ▶ It is a low-cost method with a measurable return on investment (proven to be high when done properly). E-mail marketing is often reported as second only to search marketing as the most effective online marketing tactic.
>
> ▶ Advertisers can reach substantial numbers of e-mail subscribers who have opted in (i.e., consented, see Chapter 14) to receive e-mail communications on subjects of interest to them. (See en.wikipedia.org/wiki/E-mail_marketing.)
>
> ▶ Over half of Internet users check or send e-mail on a typical day. So ads reach customers quickly.
>
> ▶ E-mail is an interactive medium that can combine advertising and customer service.
>
> ▶ E-mail ads can include a direct link to any URL, so they act like banners. A consumer may be more likely to respond to e-mail messages related to discounts or special sales.

Limitations. Using e-mail to send ads (sometimes floods of ads) without the receivers' permission is considered spamming.

The quantity of e-mail that consumers receive is exploding. In light of this, marketers employing e-mail must take a long-term view and work toward motivating consumers to continue to read the messages they receive. As the volume of e-mail increases, consumers' tendency to screen and block messages will rise as well. Today most e-mail services permit users to block messages from specific sources or automatic filter certain ads to junk mail.

Implementing E-Mail Advertising

A list of e-mail addresses can be a very powerful tool for a company, helping it to target a group of people that it knows something about. In many cases, the mailing list is based on membership and loyalty programs, such as the airlines' frequent-flyer program. For information on how to create a mailing list, consult groups.yahoo.com (the service is free) or topica.com.

E-mail can also be sent to mobile devices. Mobile phones, in particular, offer advertisers a real chance to advertise interactively and on a one-to-one basis with consumers—anytime, anyplace. In the future, e-mail ads will be targeted to individuals based not only on their user profiles but also on their physical location at any point in time. See Chapter 6 for a description of this concept, known as *l-commerce*.

E-Mail Hoaxes. E-mail hoaxes are very popular; some of them have been going on for years (e.g., Neiman Marcus's cookie recipe, the Nigerian treasure, the Koran and the Iraq invasion). Some of these are scams. For details, see ftc.gov and Chapter 9.

Fraud. Fraud is also a consideration. For example, a person may receive an e-mail stating that his or her credit card number is invalid or that his or her MSN service will be terminated unless another credit card number is sent in reply to the e-mail. For protection against such fraudulent practices, see scambusters.org and Chapters 9 and 14.

E-Mail Advertising Methods. E-mail advertising can be done in many different ways, as shown in Online File W8.9.

SEARCH ENGINE ADVERTISEMENT

Search advertising is a method of placing online advertisements on Web pages that show results from search engine queries. Search engines are a good mechanism for most people to find information and, therefore, a good platform for online advertising. Note that search advertising includes mobile search and social network search (see Adhikari 2010). The two major forms of search engine advertising are listing URLs and keyword advertising.

search advertising
A method of placing online advertisements on Web pages that show results from search engine queries.

URL Listing

Most search engine providers allow companies to submit their Internet addresses, called URLs (Universal Resource Locators), for free, so that these URLs can be searched electronically. Search engine spiders crawl through each site, indexing its content and links. The site is then included as a candidate for future searches. Because there are quite a few search engines, advertisers who use this method should register URLs with as many proper search engines as possible. In some cases, URLs may be searched even if they are not submitted.

The major advantage is that the listing can be very relevant to the content of search. This is the key to Google's success as we will describe later.

The second major advantage of using search engines as an advertising tool is that it is free. Anyone can submit a URL to a search engine and be listed. Searchers for a company's products will most likely receive a list of sites that mention the products, including the company's own site. Search engine advertisement has become the most popular online advertising method, mainly thanks to Google.

However, the URL method has several drawbacks. The major one is location on the list provided by the search engine. Search engines maintain a huge amount of Web pages and get even larger because it is the collection size that attracts users to create value. Hence, the chance that a specific site will be found and placed at the top of a search engine's display list (say, in the first 10 items) is very slim. (See the discussion of search engine optimization that follows.) Furthermore, even if a company's URL makes it to the top, others can quickly displace it. Second, different search engines index their listings differently; therefore, making the top of several lists is difficult. The searcher may have the correct keywords, but if the search engine indexed the site listing using the "title" or "content description" in the meta-tag, then the effort could be fruitless. A meta-tag is a coding statement (in HTML) that describes the content of a Web page and is used by search engines in indexing. Finally, if a search engine includes your company/product on the list, you have to pay if you want to include an ad there.

Keyword Advertising

Search advertisement is delivered (and also sold) on the basis of keywords entered by users in their search. A keyword may consist of one or several words. Search engines build indexes of Web pages using WebCrawler. When the publisher of a Web page arranges with a search engine firm to have ads served up on that page, the search engine applies its indexing technology to associate the content of that page with keywords.

Google has created a new advertising technology by linking an advertisement with the user's keywords. Advertisers choose the keywords to which their advertisements will link. Advertisements appear on the screen along with the search results when the chosen keywords are searched. This can substantially increase the likelihood that the advertisement will be viewed because of its high relevance to user interests. This innovation has resulted in the great success of Google. In a single year, more than 1.5 million U.S. marketers used Google as their advertising channel. In fact, more than 90 percent of Google's revenue is generated from this creative technology. Furthermore, Google allows the advertisers to bid for the order of appearance in the sponsored section, on the first page that shows the results of a search (see discussion on paid inclusion later in this section).

Advertisers who pay more will appear higher on the list. Payments are based on several metrics such as CPM (defined earlier).

Search Engine Optimization (SEO)

Since putting a Web page at the top of search listings is very competitive, many marketers are trying to outsmart the ranking algorithm and find shortcuts that can lead to a better position in the search results. This is the basic idea of search engine optimization. Search engines use algorithms to determine the position of a Web page in a search result based on certain criteria, such as popularity (e.g., the click-through rate) or centrality. Ads with poor click-through rates can be pushed down to the bottom of the first page of search results or onto subsequent pages. Even though advertisers are only paying for a click through, the algorithms assigning ad positions based on ad popularity provide incentives for optimizing keyword selection and other cost control measures. For methods and details, see en.wikipedia.org/wiki/Search_advertising.

Search engine optimization (SEO) is the process of improving the visibility of a website or a Web page in a search engine via the free (unpaid) search results. Other forms of search engine marketing (SEM) target paid listings. In general, the earlier (or higher on the page) and more frequently a site appears in the search result list, the more visitors it will receive from the search engine's users. SEO may target different kinds of search, including image search, local search, video search, and industry-specific vertical search engines. Companies can try to optimize by themselves. For how to do it, see Grappone and Couzin (2011). However, sometimes it may be wise to use a professional *optimizer*.

The optimizer needs to consider how search engines work, what people search for, the actual search terms typed into search engines, and which search engines are preferred by their targeted audience. The optimizer then can tailor the ads and the keywords accordingly. The optimizer, which can be a company person or a consultant, can use algorithms (such as Google analytics) to do the tailoring. The process of SEO with optimization is illustrated in Exhibit 8.7. For further details, see en.wikipedia.org/wiki/Search_engine_optimization.

Paid Inclusion (Sponsored Ad). Another solution is to buy keyword ads on the page that contain the search engine's results of a search. This is referred to as *paid inclusion* or sponsored search.

Example. Enquiro.com (a Meditative company; enquiro.com) specializes in search engine advertising and optimization. The company offers news, white papers, case studies, and more on its website (ask.enquiro.com). It specializes in both B2C and B2B applications. For details, see enquiro.com/services. The company connects site optimization with Web analytics, site analysis and auditing, keyword search, and clients' objectives and needs. For the relationship diagram, see enquiro.com/services/search-engine-optimization.php.

Finally, ads that appear on the side and top of the search results are attention-grabbers, but they are expensive (see AdWords, later in this section). Several companies provide services that optimize Web content so that a site has a better chance of being discovered by a search engine—for example, Web Position from WebTrends (webtrends.com). More tips for improving a site's listing in various search engines can be found at searchenginewatch.com.

search engine optimization (SEO) The craft of increasing site rank on search engines; the optimizer uses the ranking algorithm of the search engine (which may be different for different search engines) and best search phrases, and tailors the ad accordingly.

EXHIBIT 8.7   The Process of Search Engine Optimization

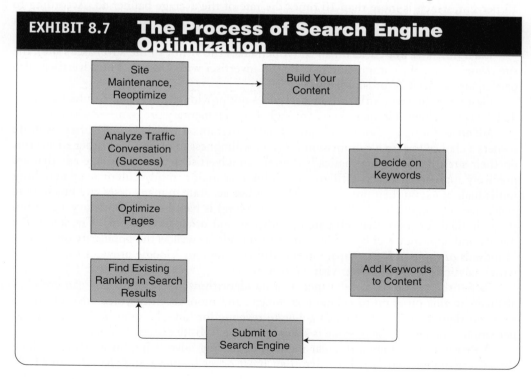

GOOGLE: THE ONLINE ADVERTISING KING

No other EC company can match the success of Google and its meteoric rise. Google is considered by many to be not only changing the Internet but also the world. Google uses several varieties of search engine advertising methods that are generating billions of dollars in revenue and profits. For a comprehensive discussion of Google, see en.wikipedia.org/wiki/Google.

Google derived almost all of its revenue from its advertising programs. Google has implemented various innovations in the online advertising market that helped make them one of the biggest brokers in the market. Using the behavioral marketing method of its subsidiary DoubleClick, Google can determine user interests and target advertisements so they are relevant to their context and the user who is viewing them. *Google Analytics* allows website owners to track where and how people use their website, for example by examining click rates for all the links on a page. Google advertisements can be placed on third-party websites in a two-part program. Google's AdWords allows advertisers to display their advertisements in the Google content network, through either a cost-per-click or cost-per-view program. The sister service, Google AdSense, allows website owners to display these advertisements on their website and earn money every time ads are clicked.

Google's Major Advertisement Methods: AdWords and AdSense

Google uses its Internet search technology to serve advertisements based on website content, the user's geographical location, and other factors. The major methods are AdWords and AdSense.

AdWords. AdWords is a self-service ad server that uses relevance-ranking algorithms similar to the ones that make the search engine so effective. Advertisers tell Google how much they want to spend and then "buy" pertinent keywords. When Web surfers type in a term that matches the advertiser's keyword, the advertiser is listed in a banner near the search results with the heading "Sponsored Links." Each time a user clicks the advertiser's banner ad, Google subtracts the cost-per-click from the advertiser's prepaid account; when the account's daily ad budget is depleted, Google stops displaying the ad.

The system is easy to use and remarkably effective. The click-through rate is about 15 percent, which is more than 10 times the rate of the average banner ad. According to industry experts, many Google advertisers have experienced a 20 to 25 percent increase in online sales.

Each time a visitor clicks on an ad (which takes the visitor to the advertiser's site), the site owner shares the commission paid by the advertiser with Google. The advertisers also participate in the AdWords program.

Despite its success, AdWords by itself does not provide the best one-to-one targeting. This may be achieved in many cases through a complementary program—AdSense.

AdSense. Google's AdSense is an affiliate program in which Google offers website owners a chance to earn a commission for their willingness to place ads of other advertisers on their sites. AdSense automatically delivers an advertiser's text and image ads that are precisely matched to each affiliate site. This is a major improvement over matching individuals based on their preferences, which is less accurate in many cases and much more expensive. The matching (called *contextual matching*) is based on a proprietary algorithm (Google filed for more than 60 patents on these and other innovations). The key is the quality and appearance of both the pages and the ads, as well as the popularity of the site. Hundreds of thousands participate in the affiliate program. Google provides the affiliates with analytics that help convert visitors to customers.

AdSense uses Google's relevance-scoring algorithms. Website owners can enroll as affiliates in this program to enable text, image, and more recently, video advertisements to be on their websites. These ads generate revenue for Google on either a per-click or per-impression basis. The revenue is shared with the website owners (affiliates).

AdSense has become a popular method of placing advertising on websites because the advertisements are less intrusive than most other banners, and the content of the advertisements is often more relevant to the website. For an example of a site using AdSense, see *RTC Magazine* (rtcmagazine.com). Google's success is attributed to the quality of the matches, the large number of advertisers in its network, the ability to use ads in many languages, and the ability to understand the content of websites. Characteristics and demographics of the visitors that Google knows are considered in the match. This is also true of Google's competitors (e.g., MSN, with its AdCenter methodology). Similar programs are offered by eBay and Yahoo! (see eBay AdContex and Yahoo!'s Content Match). The closer the match, the less intrusive the ad is to the visitor, and the better the chance of the visitor clicking on the ad.

For additional information, see adwords.google.com/select, google.com/adsense, and en.wikipedia.org/wiki/AdSense.

VIRAL MARKETING AND ADVERTISING

Viral marketing (viral advertising) refers to electronic word-of-mouth marketing (WOM) in which customers promote a product or service by telling others about it. This can be done by e-mails, by text messaging, in conversations facilitated in chat rooms, via instant messaging, by posting messages in newsgroups, and in electronic consumer forums. It is especially popular in social networks (see Chapter 7, Section 7.4). Having people forward messages to friends, asking them, for example, to "check out this product," is an example of viral marketing. This marketing approach has been used for generations, but now its speed and reach are multiplied by the Internet. This ad model can be used to build brand awareness at minimal cost, because the people who pass on the messages are paid very little or nothing for their efforts. The process is analogous to the spread of computer (or regular) viruses using a self-replication process. Viral promotions may take the form of video clips, interactive Flash games, advergames, e-books, brandable software, images, or text messages.

Viral marketing has long been a favorite strategy of online advertisers pushing youth-oriented products. For example, advertisers might distribute a small game program or a video embedded within a sponsor's e-mail that is easy to forward. By releasing a few thousand copies of the game to some consumers, vendors hope to reach hundreds of thousands of others. Viral marketing also was used by the founder of Hotmail, a free e-mail service that grew from zero to 12 million subscribers in its 18 initial months and to more than 50 million subscribers in about 4 years. Each e-mail sent via Hotmail carried an invitation for free Hotmail service. Also known as *advocacy marketing*, viral marketing, if properly used, can be effective, efficient, and relatively inexpensive. eWOM can also influence consumer product judgment (see Lee and Youn 2009). For further details, see en.wikipedia.org/wiki/Viral_marketing and en.wikipedia.org/wiki/Types_of_viral_campaigns, and learnmarketing.net/viralmarketing.htm.

According to a 2010 survey done in Chinese markets, word of mouth has become an important factor to consumers' purchasing decisions. In 2010, 64 percent of respondents said that word of mouth influenced their purchasing decisions, while in 2008 only 56 percent of consumers cared about word of mouth. Incidentally, online search was also found to be an important factor for people before they make the final purchase decision, other than traditional TV advertisement (see Atsmon and Magni 2010).

A major development in viral marketing is viral videos, which is discussed under video ads later in this chapter, as well as in Chapter 7 (for social networks).

One of the downsides of a viral strategy is that several e-mail hoaxes have been spread this way. Viral marketing has also been criticized by consumers because of a concern over unsolicited e-mails, which many see as an invasion of privacy. For details about viral marketing, see McColl (2010).

VIDEO ADS

Video ads are growing rapidly, mainly due to the popularity of YouTube and similar sites. Online video is growing at nearly 40 percent annually while TV viewing continues to fall. For monthly statistics, see comscore.com and marketingcharts.com. Video ads appear all over the Web, both as unsolicited pop-ups, or when you give permission to see a demo or information about a product. Video ads became very popular in the Web 2.0 environment and social networking (see Section 7.4 in Chapter 7).

viral marketing (viral advertising)
Word-of-mouth marketing by which customers promote a product or service by telling others about it.

The major reason for the popularity of video is that almost everyone who uses the Internet now watches online videos. Two other factors that have spurred the rapid growth of online video include the increasing availability of broadband Internet access and Web 2.0 technology that allows user interaction with and control of content. Online video is outpacing traditional TV in the contest for viewers' eyeballs.

There are primarily two approaches to incorporating videos in e-commerce: (1) per-product videos that are embedded in product details pages, providing additional information about the product; and (2) editorial-style videos that show products in context, allowing consumers to discover products and trigger purchases. Many retailers have started to add product-specific videos to their e-commerce sites. For a complete overview of video marketing and advertising, see Jarboe (2009). A third approach is to have a pop-up video before you see other videos you came to the site to view. Some allow you to skip the introductory videos but many do not. According to a Cisco survey, most large online retailers are using videos to sell products. Forrester Research found that most major retailers are making product videos central to their marketing strategies. According to clickz.com/clickz/stats/2031513/online-video-percent U.S. users spent 45 percent more time viewing online videos in January 2011 than in January 2010. Hulu is reported to have generated 783 million video ad impressions in July 2010. For a detailed overview of video advertising, see IAB (2008a). This report also includes a classification of all types of video ads as shown in Exhibit 8.8.

Some of the leading companies in this area are YouTube, Metacafé, VEVO, Hulu, Tremor Media Video Network, Adap.tv, and SPOTXchange.

Two-minute YouTube clips were just the beginning as television comes to the Internet to become the network of tomorrow. For example, Diggnation (see digg.com) is a weekly tech/Web culture show based on the top social bookmarking news stories site. Diggnation drew about 250,000 viewers a week in 2008 and was among the most popular free video podcasts on Apple's iTunes service—alongside offerings from ABC, the BBC, and CNN. Revision 3 (revision3.com) appeals to niche audiences interested in the geek culture; its advertisers can target their messages to smaller, more relevant groups of buyers.

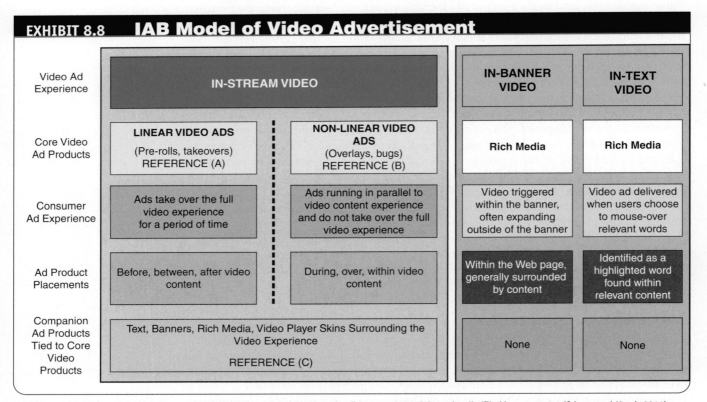

EXHIBIT 8.8   IAB Model of Video Advertisement

Video Ad Experience	IN-STREAM VIDEO		IN-BANNER VIDEO	IN-TEXT VIDEO
Core Video Ad Products	LINEAR VIDEO ADS (Pre-rolls, takeovers) REFERENCE (A)	NON-LINEAR VIDEO ADS (Overlays, bugs) REFERENCE (B)	Rich Media	Rich Media
Consumer Ad Experience	Ads take over the full video experience for a period of time	Ads running in parallel to video content experience and do not take over the full video experience	Video triggered within the banner, often expanding outside of the banner	Video ad delivered when users choose to mouse-over relevant words
Ad Product Placements	Before, between, after video content	During, over, within video content	Within the Web page, generally surrounded by content	Identified as a highlighted word found within relevant content
Companion Ad Products Tied to Core Video Products	Text, Banners, Rich Media, Video Player Skins Surrounding the Video Experience REFERENCE (C)		None	None

Source: Interactive Advertising Bureau. "A Digital Video Advertising Overview." January 2008. iab.net/media/file/dv-report-v3.pdf (accessed March 2011). Used with permission.

Consumer-Generated Videos

Many companies are trying to use user-generated videos for their online and even for TV commercials.

YouTube has emerged as the largest advertising platform for video ads. By one estimate, it has approximately 8 million videos and is growing at the rate of about 1 million videos a year. YouTube is already allowing marketers from brands like Wendy's and Dove to upload videos to YouTube, just like anybody else. YouTube also began adding conventional ads to some of its videos and splitting the revenue with users who provide the content. Google's AdSense ad distribution network also offers ad-supported video clips.

For example, KFC is among the companies that are using consumer-generated videos and combining several of them to tell a story. Then, they show the story as an ad. For another example, homemade videos of the foam eruptions that come from dropping Mentos into a two-liter bottle of Diet Coke became a huge hit on video sites (see eepybird.com/dcm1.html).

Example: Crash the Super Bowl. Doritos and Pepsi joined forces in 2010 to offer a grand prize of up to $2 million to solicit user-generated video ads (crashthesuperbowl.com). Wining videos were broadcasted at the Super Bowl. It attracted more than 2,000 submissions, and 3 million online viewers evaluated the submissions. This resulted in a huge advertising effect.

Interactive Videos

The term **interactive video** usually refers to a technique used to blend user interaction and videos. The interaction is controlled by a computer for entertainment, advertisement, or educational activities. Interactive videos started with videodisks and CD-ROMs and migrated to the Web. Since 2005, interactive video has increased online as the result of a number of factors including:

> ▶ The rise in numbers of users accessing the Internet at broadband speeds
> ▶ The addition of video as a media type of Flash

interactive video
A technique used to blend user interaction and videos.

Because users are often reluctant to pay for online content, it is perhaps unsurprising that many of the new online interactive videos (including all the examples given next) are either sponsored content or part of advertising campaigns.

Video Click Throughs. A few interactive video technologies have been developed in the last few years (e.g., by VideoClix.com and by Clickthrough.com) that utilize a new way of encoding videos, allowing users to click on any person, place, or object in the video.

Customizable Online Interactive Videos. Customizable videos allow the users to adjust some variables and then play a video customized to the user's particular preferences. However, the user does not actually interact with the video while it is playing. For examples of this form of video, see en.wikipedia.org/wiki/Interactive_video.

Live Interactive Video. In live interactive videos, you can see certain events in real time, and sometimes interact with those in the video. For example, GE delivered a live Webcast, presenting the company's annual report to investors in a banner ad, in real time. Viewers could interact with the presenters, asking questions or making comments. GE also invited its business partners for the viewing.

Example: Interactive Dressing Room. Knickerpicker.com created the first of its kind (in the United Kingdom): an interactive online video dressing room (for lingerie). It is loaded with all the leading designers' brands. The animated models appear with your selected brands, and you can control their movement (e.g., turn them around). For details, see knickerpicker.com.

Viral Videos

The term **viral video** refers to a video clip that gains widespread popularity through the process of Internet sharing, typically through e-mail or IM messages, blogs, and other media-sharing websites. Popular sites that embody this concept include YouTube (youtube.com), AOL Comedy (comedy.aol.com/viralvideos), and VEOH (veoh.com). The marketing potential of viral video has yet to be fully explored, but companies that offer viral video services to businesses are beginning to emerge, and companies are beginning to utilize public social networks to produce exponential increases in brand awareness.

viral video
A video clip that gains widespread popularity through the process of Internet sharing, typically through e-mail or IM messages, blogs, and other media-sharing websites.

Viral videos are those that their viewers like (or dislike) so much that they spread the word about them, quickly across the Internet via e-mail and social networks, drawing sometimes millions of viewers in a short time, creating all kinds of buzz for the brands that appear in the short clips (see adage.com for a periodic list of videos). If the reactions are positive, the buzz can be useful, but negative reactions can hurt the brand (see the discussion on reputation systems in Chapter 7). *Baseline* magazine provides a list of the 10 best viral marketing videos.

Video campaigns can be facilitated by blog coverage. For example, with the help of bloggers, Toyota's Swagger Wagon, and Google's Chrome Speed Test, had about 2 million views in their first week in May 2010 Google is also offering revenue-sharing to individual authors if their videos go viral to encourage more entertainment and high-quality video content.

ADVERGAMING

advergaming
The practice of using computer games to advertise a product, an organization, or a viewpoint.

Advergaming is the practice of using games, particularly computer games, to advertise or promote a product, an organization, or a viewpoint. Web-enabled game consoles, especially those in social networks (see Chapter 7, Section 7.9), are giving advertisers new ways to target the young generation. Advergaming normally falls into one of three categories:

1. A company provides interactive games on its website in the hope that potential customers will be drawn to the game and spend more time on the website or simply become more product (or brand) aware. The games themselves usually feature the company's products prominently. An example is shown at Intel's website (itmanager3.intel.com/en-us/default.aspx).

2. Games are published in the usual way, but they require players to investigate further. The subjects may be commercial, political, or educational. Examples include America's Army (americasarmy.com/downloads), intended to boost recruitment for the U.S. Army.

3. With some games, advertising appears within the actual game. This is similar to subtle advertising in films, whereby the advertising content is within the "world" of the movie or game. An example is cashsprint.com, which puts advertising logos directly on the player's racing vehicle and around the racetrack.

Example. In 2006, Cadillac tried a novel approach to get young male car buyers excited about its tricked-out V-series collection of luxury vehicles. Irrespective of advertising in magazines, TV commercials, or online display ads, the automaker took its campaign to Xbox (xbox360.com). Through an arrangement with Xbox live, customers were invited to download and put through their paces three virtual V-series cars in a popular high-speed driving game called *Project Gotham Racing 3*. Within six months, more than 240,000 players snagged the game. This Cadillac success story offers a beacon of hope at a time when advertisers are struggling to get the attention of a mass audience.

Advergames promote repeat traffic to websites and reinforce brands in compelling ways. Users choose to register to be eligible for prizes that can help marketers collect customer data. Gamers may invite their friends to participate, which could assist promotion from word-of-mouth or viral marketing. For further discussion, see en.wikipedia.org/wiki/Advergaming and adverblog.com.

AUGMENTED REALITY ADVERTISEMENT

augmented reality (AR)
A live direct or indirect view of a physical, real-world environment whose elements are *augmented* by computer-generated sensory input, such as sound or graphics.

Augmented reality (AR) is a term for a live direct or indirect view of a physical, real-world environment whose elements are *augmented* by computer-generated sensory input, such as sound or graphics. The technology functions by enhancing one's current perception of reality. Thus, it is utilized by advertisers and marketers, especially in the fashion industry.

Examples of Applications in Advertisement. Marketers started to use AR to promote products via interactive AR applications. At the 2008 L.A. Auto Show, Nissan unveiled the concept vehicle Cube and presented visitors with a brochure that, when held against a

Webcam, showed alternate versions of the vehicle. In August 2009, Best Buy ran a circular with an augmented reality code that allowed users with a Webcam to interact with the product in 3-D. The 2009 December issue of *Esquire* was dedicated to AR and its applications. In 2010, Walt Disney used mobile AR to connect a movie experience to outdoor advertising. Burger King used it in a promotion for its $1 burgers. When you held a piece of paper with a Burger King logo on it up to the Webcam, the program would recognize the logo, and the piece of paper would turn into a burger. You could move it around and even lift the bun up to reveal the contents of the burger. Watchmaker, Tissot, did something similar where you print out a piece of paper and wear it like a watch—the program then would recognize it and would place a virtual copy of the watch onto your wrist. You could choose whatever model or color watch and it would change instantly on your wrist as you turned and rotated your wrist.

One area that is using this technology is retailers in clothing, fashion, and jewelry where visualization is critical. For example, Fashionista Corp. combines AR and motion capture with real-time merchandize recommendations. It allows shoppers to "try on" clothing and share their favorite looks with family and friends in real time.

Virtual Dressing Rooms.   These are becoming popular (e.g., see Amato-McCoy 2010)—you can dress an avatar, or you can dress yourself when a Webcam is used to enter your photo. Fashionista provides technology for the latter applications.

ADVERTISING IN CHAT ROOMS AND FORUMS

Vendors frequently sponsor chat rooms. The sponsoring vendor places a chat link on its site, and the chat vendor does the rest (e.g., talkcity.com), including placing the advertising that pays for the session. The advertising in a chat room merges with the activity in the room, and the user is conscious of what is being presented.

Advertisers sometimes use online fantasy sports (e.g., available at Yahoo!) to send ads to specific sports fans (e.g., fans of the National Football League or Major League Baseball). According to *eMarketer* (2006), online fantasy sports attract millions of visitors every month.

As illustrated in Chapter 7, vendors also advertise to members of social networks. Sites such as Facebook offer targeted advertising opportunities, and vendors usually offer discounts to members on advertised products. Ads also link users to other sites that might be of interest to community members.

The main difference between an advertisement that appears on a static Web page and one that comes through a chat room is that the latter allows advertisers to cycle through messages and target the chatters again and again. Also, advertising can become more thematic in a chat room. An advertiser can start with one message and build upon it to a climax, just as an author does with a good story.

Chat rooms also are used as one-to-one connections between a company and its customers. For example, Mattel Corp. sells about one-third of its Barbie dolls to collectors. These collectors use a chat room to make comments or ask questions that are then answered by Mattel's staff.

Section 8.8 ▶ REVIEW QUESTIONS

1. Define banner ads and describe their benefits and limitations.
2. Describe banner swapping and banner exchanges.
3. Describe the issues surrounding pop-ups and similar ads.
4. Explain how e-mail is used for advertising.
5. Describe advertising via classified ads.
6. Describe the search engine optimization technique.
7. Describe Google's AdWords and AdSense.
8. Describe video ads and their growing popularity.
9. Define advergaming and describe how it works.
10. Describe augmented reality advertisement.

8.9 MOBILE MARKETING AND ADVERTISING

The ratio of mobile handsets to desktop and laptop computers is approximately two to one and growing. This represents a huge opportunity for online mobile marketing and advertising. Not only has the opportunity been heightened by current technological development and the other drivers discussed in Chapter 6, but it has also been spurred by the higher response rates to mobile marketing campaigns when compared to more traditional or even nonmobile online campaigns. For an overview of the field, see Dushinski (2009).

MAJOR CONCEPTS

Mobile marketing and advertising is a subset of m-commerce (Chapter 6). Its major elements are described next.

Defining Mobile Marketing

mobile marketing
Conducting marketing on or with a mobile device.

Although there are various definitions for the concept of mobile marketing, a commonly accepted definition does not exist. Mobile marketing is broadly defined as the use of the mobile medium as a means of marketing communication or distribution of any kind of promotional or advertising messages to customers through wireless networks. A working definition of **mobile marketing** refers to conducting marketing on or with a mobile device. The Mobile Marketing Association offers the following definition: "A set of practices that enables organizations to communicate and engage with their audience in an interactive and relevant manner through any mobile device or network." For a description, see Krum (2010).

Mobile marketing is a set of practices that enables organizations to communicate and engage with their audience in an interactive and relevant manner through any mobile device or network. Mobile marketing includes sales, market research, customer service, and advertisement, all supported by mobile computing. Note that with mobile marketing you can create and run your own text message marketing campaigns like a contest or customers voting, as well as sending coupons and promotions. You can make ads interactive since mobile computing provides a direct link between vendors and consumers. Both can send and receive text messages (e.g., see where2getit.com/solutions/mobile-locator). According to (en.wikipedia.org/wiki/M-commerce), companies have reported that they see a better response from mobile marketing campaigns than from traditional marketing campaigns.

The Process of Mobile Advertisement

Mobile advertising ranges from simple text messaging to intelligent interactive messages. The key parts of a mobile advertising system include the advertisers, a mobile ad network, mobile operators, and mobile devices. These parts are used in the advertising process.

Exhibit 8.9 shows how a mobile advertising system can work. In this example, a company creates and submits a small banner ad to a mobile advertising network and selects the location, time, and category as the ad promotion criteria. The mobile advertising submits these ads to multiple mobile networks and keeps track of the transmission, selection, and response to these ads. The mobile system operators review the capabilities of the customers' mobile devices in their network to determine which devices can receive and respond to the mobile ads.

Mobile Sales. Catalog merchants can accept orders from customers electronically, via the customer's mobile device. In some cases, the merchant may even deliver the catalog electronically. Some merchants provide mobile websites that are customized for the smaller screen and limited user interface of a mobile device. For details, see mobilestarterstore.com/index.php?.

Note: By November 2010, only 12 percent of the 500 major e-tailers had adapted their sites for purchasing by mobile phones. However, this number is growing (Cell-Phone-Plans.net 2010).

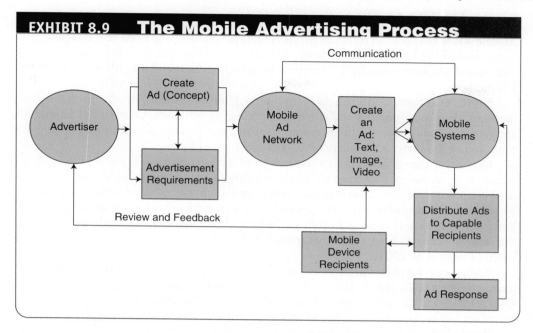

EXHIBIT 8.9   The Mobile Advertising Process

IMPLEMENTING MOBILE ADVERTISING AND MARKETING

Mobile advertising (m-advertising) is a form of advertising done via mobile devices. Some see mobile advertising as closely related to online Internet advertising, though its reach is far greater. Currently, most mobile advertising is targeted at mobile phones, and according to en.wikipedia.org/wiki/List_of_countries_by_number_of_mobile_phones_in_use, there are over 5 billion mobile phones in the world as of 2010. For an overview and a video, see advertising.microsoft.com/mobile-advertising.

The major activities in m-commerce center around the advertisement of brands and specific products, which are done by many methods, including campaigns. For a comprehensive description, see IAB (2008b). For the use of mobile devices in supermarkets, see the METRO GROUP closing case in Chapter 6.

Advertisers and the media increasingly account for the fast growing mobile market, though it remains at around only 1 percent of total advertising spent in the United States. A major booster to mobile advertisements are the success of the iPhone and other smartphones and the iPad (see Clifford 2010).

Mobile Interactive Advertising

Mobile interactive advertising refers to advertising or marketing messages delivered to portable devices, either via synchronized download or wirelessly. Although this broad definition potentially includes ads delivered to laptops, media players, and other classes of portable devices, in practice the most interesting and potentially revolutionary part of the mobile interactive advertising market lies in delivering messages to non-PC devices—primarily mobile phones, but also including portable media players and game devices. For details, see IAB (2008b).

An extension of interactive services is the use of Apple's iAds. The iAd platform is built directly into the iPhone's OS interface. Apple is looking to change the nature of advertising by conducting the ad experience within apps rather than within searches. This may improve the quality of the advertising as well. How does that work, you ask? Apple believes that the flaw of both standard online advertising and TV advertising is a lack of interaction and emotion. Traditional ads keep users within an app, rather than redirecting users to a browser window. In contrast, when you click on an iAd advertisement, it fills the screen so you can explore the ad.

mobile advertising (m-advertising)
Ads sent to and presented on mobile devices.

Types of Mobile Ads

Mobile ads may appear in different forms. The most popular one is short messages. Other forms include multimedia advertising, advertising within mobile games, ads in mobile videos, and ads during mobile TV receipts. The methods are similar to the generic Internet ads methods.

Short Messages. SMS ads are commercial messages sent in the form of short messages. It is quite popular and currently dominating the market but mobile banner ads are growing rapidly due to the increased popularity of smartphones and mobile applications and to the better technology of 4G networks.

One advantage of SMS is that while even in a conference, users are able to send and receive brief messages unobtrusively, while enjoying privacy. Even in such environments as in a restaurant, café, bank, travel agency office, and so on, the users can enjoy some privacy by sending and receiving brief text messages in an unobtrusive way. A major drawback, however, is that short messages often interrupt the user and hence a study indicates that the receiver tends to hold a negative attitude unless there is incentive or it is permission-based (Tsang, et al. 2004).

Several major mobile operators around the world launched their own mobile advertising portals (e.g., D2 in Japan, the joint venture of Japan's largest mobile operator NTT DOCOMO and Dentsu, Japan's largest ad agency). The effectiveness of a mobile ad campaign can be measured in a variety of ways, similar to that of wireline computers.

Mobile Video Ads. An interesting application is digital ads atop 12,000 taxis in various U.S. cities. The ads also include public service announcements. The technology comes from Vert (vert.net).

Vert displays live content and advertising messages very effectively by targeting specific zip codes, neighborhoods, and individual city blocks. Ads can be scheduled for specific times during the day (e.g., promote coffee during the morning commute). Ads are beamed to Vert-equipped taxis like a cell phone signal. GPS satellites pinpoint where the cab is traveling, allowing ads to change from block to block.

Location-Based Ads. Another interesting application is to deliver ads to mobile devices in the nearby area. Most smartphones and high-end mobile devices support GPS to detect locations. Location-sensitive businesses can take advantage of this feature to deliver location-based ads. A good example is a Google map that can show nearby convenient stores, gas stations, hotels, and restaurants when a location is searched. Some of these are paid ads (see Chapter 7 for details).

Viral Mobile Marketing

Mobile computing can be an interactive mass media, similar to that of the Internet itself. Thus, advertisers are eager to utilize *viral marketing* methods, by which one recipient of an advertisement on a mobile device will forward that message to a friend(s). Known also as "word of mouth," viral marketing allows users to become part of the advertising experience. At the bare minimum mobile ads with viral abilities can become powerful interactive campaigns. At the extreme, they can become engagement marketing experiences.

Mobile Marketing and Advertising Campaigns

According to a review of leading mobile marketing literature (Becker 2006), the analysis of 55 campaigns run by companies such as Coca-Cola and BMW, and

VERT Intelligent Displays: Advertising Used Atop Taxi Cabs

Source: Courtesy of Vert Incorporated.

interviews with 44 mobile marketing thought leaders, four basic classes of online campaigns have emerged. The classes include:

1. **Information.** Programs providing information about products, points of interest, news, weather, traffic, horoscopes, and related content.
2. **Entertainment.** Programs that "produce value to the customers" and provide amusement and emotional triggers through videos, music, games, personalization ringtones, wallpapers, and so forth.
3. **Raffles.** Programs that provide prizes such as digital content or physical goods.
4. **Coupons.** Programs that offer monetary incentives (like discounts), trial packages, or free services.

These classes focus on each of the Internet campaign objectives that fell into one of the following six categories:

1. **Building brand awareness.** Increase customers' ability to recognize and recall a brand in purchase and consumption situations.
2. **Changing brand image.** Change the perception of the brand by customers.
3. **Promoting sales.** Stimulate quicker or greater purchase of a product or service.
4. **Enhancing brand loyalty.** Increase consumers' commitment to repurchase the brand.
5. **Building customer databases.** Collect data about the mobile device, data network, or profiles of customers.
6. **Stimulating mobile word of mouth.** Encourage customers to pass ads from customer to customer via their mobile devices.

Obviously, these are the same types of campaigns and objectives underlying traditional marketing approaches.

Recent mobile marketing campaigns conducted by retailers were very successful, as illustrated next.

Representative Examples of Mobile Advertising

There are many examples of successful mobile ads; here are some:

Example 1: Fleming's 100. When designing the mobile platform for "Fleming's 100," the company's award-winning list of 100 wines served by the glass, adding the mobile restaurant locator was a strategic extension of the functionality that would enhance the customer experience. The site m.flemings100.com can be accessed by using Web-enabled mobile devices and it shows wine labels and robust descriptions of each of the 100 wines that make up "Fleming's 100." Location of restaurants with their menus can be found by using a zip code search. The site premiered in June 2009 and since then continues to receive heavy traffic, with 25 percent of visitors directly accessing the mobile site and 75 percent being directed from mobile search. No matter where Fleming's guests are traveling, they are now able to find quickly and easily the nearest Fleming's, as well as the perfect wine to round out their dining experience.

Example 2: Dolce & Gabanna (D&G). In 2008, Dolce & Gabanna ran a mobile campaign on the Nokia Media Network. The goal of the campaign was to promote awareness of D&G's overall brand and its teen-focused fashion catalog. Part of the campaign involved a game called "Dee&Gee," which could be downloaded from the D&G mobile website. Once at the site, consumers could also view the D&G teen catalog and download D&G-branded examples of wallpaper. The response to the D&G campaign was a 10 percent click-through rate (CTR). According to Nokia, this is typical. CTRs generally range from 2 percent to 20 percent. This may seem low, but it is consistently and substantially higher than similar online or traditional media ads. It is one of the main reasons for the growing interest in mobile advertising.

MOBILE MARKETING IMPLEMENTATION GUIDELINES

Although organizations such as the Direct Marketing Association have established codes of practice for Internet marketing, including the use of mobile media, most industry pundits agree that they are not well suited for the dynamic nature of mobile commerce. In response, the mobile media industry has established a set of guidelines and best practices for mobile advertising. The Global Code of Conduct from the Mobile Marketing Association (MMA) (mmaglobal.com/codeofconduct.pdf) is indicative of the types of practices promoted by the industry. The basic principles of the code include:

▶ **Notice.** Informing users of the marketer's identity or products and services offered and the key terms and conditions that govern an interaction between the marketer and the user's mobile device.

▶ **Choice and consent.** Respecting the right of the user to control which mobile messages they receive by obtaining consent (opt-in) and implementing a simple termination (opt-out) process.

▶ **Customization and constraint.** Ensuring that collected user information is used to tailor communication to the interests of the recipient and is handled responsibly, sensitively, and in compliance with applicable law. Mobile messages should be limited to those requested by the user and provide value such as product and service enhancements, contests, requested information, entertainment, or discounts.

▶ **Security.** Implementing reasonable technical, administrative, and physical procedures to protect user information from unauthorized use, alteration, disclosure, distribution, or access.

▶ **Enforcement and accountability.** The MMA expects its members to comply with the MMA Privacy Code of Conduct and has incorporated the code into applicable MMA guidelines, including the U.S. Consumer Best Practice (CBP) guidelines. Until the code can be enforced effectively by a third-party enforcement organization, mobile marketers are expected to use evaluations of their practices to certify compliance with the code.

Debunking Mobile Advertising Myths. Several myths slow the expansion of mobile advertising. Arvapally (2010) offers facts to debunk the following myths: smaller screen, smaller effect.

TOOLS TO SUPPORT MOBILE ADVERTISEMENT

Large numbers of applications, tools, and methods are available to support advertisement in m-commerce. There are hundreds of thousands of applications (apps) just for the iPhone.

Example: iPhone App—a Locator. The iPhone Locator enables companies to have their branded logos appear on users' iPhones. When a consumer searches for a company website on an iPhone it will automatically redirect them to the iPhone Locator. Users simply enter zip code or city/state to get locations as well as driving directions. A branded logo is then easily added to their iPhone home screen by clicking on the + sign at the bottom of the device.

Consumers download their branded iPhone applications through the Apple iTunes store or directly from their iPhone "App Store" that includes features like: find a location, find a product, coupons, events, and so forth. The advertiser's logos appear as an icon on the iPhone to help promote the advertiser's branding. The advertiser's branded app will auto-detect the consumer's location using the built-in iPhone GPS when searching for a vendor's location. For details, see where2getit.com/solutions/mobile-locator.

MOBILE AD TRENDS

Several predictions are made on the future of mobile ads. In general, they are extremely optimistic. According to a mobile trend series (sponsored by Samsung), the following are the current five important trends advertisers need to watch:

1. Continued importance of SMS
2. Experimenting with rich media
3. Mobile versus mobile apps
4. Interest in Geolocation (see Chapters 6 and 7)
5. The growth of mobile video

For details, see mashable.com/2010/08/19/mobile-advertising-trends.

Section 8.9 ▶ REVIEW QUESTIONS

1. Define mobile marketing (at least three definitions). Why are there several definitions?
2. What drives mobile advertisement?
3. What is the role of SMS in mobile ads?
4. Define mobile interactive advertisement.
5. Describe the process of mobile advertising.
6. Define viral marketing.
7. What are the similarities and differences between traditional media and mobile marketing/ads campaigns?
8. Summarize the basic principles of the Global Code of Conduct from the Mobile Marketing Association.

8.10 ADVERTISING STRATEGIES AND PROMOTIONS

Several advertising strategies can be used over the Internet. In this section, we will present some major strategies and implementation concerns.

PERMISSION ADVERTISING

One of the major issues in one-to-one advertising is the flooding of users with unwanted (junk) e-mail, banners, pop-ups, and so forth. One of the authors of this book experienced a flood of X-rated ads via the e-mail. Each time such an ad arrived, he blocked receipt of further ads from this source. That helped for a day or two, but then the same ads arrived from another e-mail address. Most e-mail providers can place software agents to identify and block such junk mail. This problem, the flooding of users with unsolicited e-mails and other types of ads, is referred to as **spamming**. Spamming typically upsets consumers and, when blocked, may keep useful advertising from reaching them. (Spamming is described in Chapters 9 and 14).

One solution used by advertisers is **permission advertising** or *permission marketing* (or the *opt-in approach*), in which users register with vendors and agree to accept advertising (see returnpath.net). For example, the authors of this book agreed to receive a large number of e-commerce newsletters, knowing that some would include ads. This way, we can keep abreast of what is happening in the field. We also agreed to accept e-mail from research companies, newspapers, travel agencies, and more. These vendors push, for free, very valuable information to us. The accompanying ads pay for such services. Note that Netflix asks permission to send users recommendations, but it does not ask whether it can use historical purchasing data to create recommendations.

spamming
Using e-mail to send unwanted ads (sometimes floods of ads).

permission advertising
Advertising (marketing) strategy in which customers agree to accept advertising and marketing materials (known as *opt-in*).

OTHER ADVERTISING STRATEGIES

Several advertising strategies exist both for wired and wireless systems. Some representative ones are described next.

Affiliate Marketing and Advertising

affiliate marketing
A marketing arrangement by which an organization refers consumers to the selling company's website.

We introduced the concept of *affiliate marketing* in Chapters 1 and 3—the revenue sharing model in which an organization refers consumers to the selling company's website. **Affiliate marketing** is used mainly as a revenue source for the referring organization and as a marketing tool for the sellers. However, the fact that the selling company's logo is placed on many other websites is free advertising as well. Consider Amazon.com, whose logo can be seen on more than 1 million affiliate sites! Moreover CDNow (a subsidiary of Amazon.com) and Amazon.com both are pioneers in the "get paid to view" or "listen to" commercials also used in affiliate marketing.

affiliate network
A network that acts as an intermediary between publishers (affiliates) and merchant affiliate programs.

Affiliate Networks. An **affiliate network** acts as an intermediary between publishers (affiliates) and merchant affiliate programs. It allows website publishers to more easily find and participate in affiliate programs that are suitable for their websites (and thus generate income from those programs), and allows websites offering affiliate programs (typically online merchants like Amazon.com) to reach a larger audience by promoting their affiliate programs to all the publishers participating in the affiliate network.

Most affiliate networks enable merchants to offer publishers a share of any revenue that is generated by the merchant from visitors to the publisher's site, or a fee for each visitor on the publisher's site that completes a specific action (making a purchase, registering for a newsletter, etc.). The majority of merchant programs have a revenue sharing model, as opposed to a fee-per-action model.

For merchants, affiliate network services and benefits may include tracking technology, reporting tools, payment processing, and access to a large base of publishers. For affiliates, services and benefits can include simplifying the process of registering for one or more merchant affiliate programs, reporting tools, and payment aggregation. Affiliates are generally able to join affiliate networks for free, whereas there is generally a fee for merchants to participate. Examples of networks are: Google Affiliate Network and LinkShare.

Ads as a Commodity (Paying People to Watch Ads)

With the ads-as-a-commodity approach, people are paid for time spent viewing an ad. This approach is used at mypoints.com, click-rewards.com, and others. At MyPoints.com, interested consumers read ads in exchange for payment from the advertisers. Consumers fill out data on personal interests, and then they receive targeted banners based on their personal profiles. Each banner is labeled with the amount of payment that will be paid if the consumer reads the ad. If interested, the consumer clicks the banner to read it, and after passing some tests as to its content, is paid for the effort. Readers can sort and choose what they read, and the advertisers can vary the payments to reflect the frequency and desirability of the readers. Payments may be cash (e.g., $0.50 per banner) or product discounts. This method is used with smartphones, too. For further details, see en.wikipedia.org/wiki/Online_advertising and en.wikipedia.org/wiki/Payment_conventions.

Selling Space by Pixels

Million Dollar Homepage (milliondollarhomepage.com) was created by 21-year-old student Alex Tew in the United Kingdom. The website sold advertising space on a first page grid, much as real estate is sold, displaying a total of 1 million pixels at $1 per pixel. The site was launched in August 2005 and sold out by January 13, 2006. Within a short time, people started to sell pixels in other countries (e.g., milliondollarhomepage.com.au, one of several Australian sites). Also, people who bought pixels at $1 each were selling them at higher prices through auctions. This is an innovative way of owning ad space because once you buy it, it's there forever. Incidentally, MillionDollarHomepage.com has been subjected to a distributed denial-of-service (DDoS) attack (Chapter 9) by malicious hackers who have caused the site to be extremely slow to load or completely unavailable. Blackmailers at first asked for $5,000 to avert an attack on the site. The DDoS attack was launched after they declined to pay, and the hackers then demanded $50,000 to stop attacking. A further refusal to pay prompted the attackers to deface the site, replacing the regular page with a message stating: "Don't come back, you sly dog!" The police solved the problem.

Personalized Ads

The Internet has too much information for customers to view. Filtering irrelevant information by providing consumers with customized ads can reduce this information overload. The heart of e-marketing is a customer database, which includes registration data and information gleaned from site visits. The companies that advertise via the one-to-one approach use the database to send customized ads to consumers. Using this feature, a marketing manager can customize display ads based on user profiles. The product also provides market segmentation.

Another model of personalization can be found in **Webcasting**, a free Internet news service that broadcasts personalized news and information as well as e-seminars. Users sign into the Webcasting system and select the information they would like to receive, such as sports, news, headlines, stock quotes, or desired product promotions. The users receive the requested information along with personalized ads based on their expressed interests and general ads based on their profile.

Webcasting
A free Internet news service that broadcasts personalized news and information, including seminars, in categories selected by the user.

Ad Exchanges

An *advertising exchange* is an open and transparent marketplace that facilitates the buying and selling of online media advertising inventory from multiple ad networks. It matches the need of advertisers and the capacity of ad providers. Advertising exchanges may use auctions (bids) to sell ads and directly connect advertisers and publishers. We have seen increased interest because of their transparency. Exchanges enable advertisers to bid for the type of ad and demographic that they would like to reach. For details, see en.wikipedia.org/wiki/Ad_exchange.

Advertisement as a Revenue Model

Many of the dot-com failures from 2000 to 2002 were caused by a revenue model that contained advertising income as the major or a major revenue source. Many small portals failed, but several large ones are dominating the field: Google, Facebook, AOL, Yahoo!, and MSN. However, even these heavy-traffic sites only started to show a significant profit after 2004. Too many websites are competing for the advertising money. Thus, almost all portals are adding other sources of revenue.

However, if careful, a small site can survive by concentrating on a niche area. For example, nflrush.com is doing well. It pulls millions of dollars in advertising and sponsorship by concentrating on NFL fans. The site provides comprehensive and interactive content, attracting millions of visitors. An important component in a revenue model is the pay-per-click (PPC) formula.

Pay per click (PPC) is a popular Internet advertising payment model where advertisers pay their host only when the ad is clicked on. PPC is the sum paid by an advertiser to search engines and other Internet publishers for a single click on their advertisement, which directs one visitor to the advertiser's website. With search engines, advertisers typically bid on keyword phrases relevant to their target market. Content sites commonly charge a fixed price per click rather than use a bidding system.

pay per click (PPC)
A popular Internet advertising payment model where advertisers pay their host only when the ad is clicked on.

In contrast to the generalized portal, which seeks to drive a high volume of traffic to one site, PPC implements the so-called affiliate model, which provides purchase opportunities wherever people may be surfing. Among PPC providers, Google AdWords, Yahoo! Search marketing, and Microsoft adCenter are the three largest network operators, and all three operate under a bid-based model. Cost per click (CPC) varies depending on the search engine and the level of competition for a particular keyword. For tips on how to economize the cost of using PPC, see Leibowitz (2009). For further information, refer to en.wikipedia.org/wiki/Pay_per_click.

Choose-Your-Own-Ad Format

This is a 2010 model that lets viewers pick up their own ad, known as *AdSelector*. This model has been in use mostly for online videos with YouTube leadership. The AdSelector is used by publishers like Hulu and Yahoo! For details, see Learmonth (2010).

The publishers allow consumers to decide which ads show up in video clips they view online. According to a research study from Vivaki, users are twice as likely to click on an ad when given a choice, as opposed to when one is selected for them.

ONLINE EVENTS, PROMOTIONS, AND ATTRACTIONS

In the winter of 1994, the term *EC* was hardly known, and people were just starting to discover the Internet. One company, DealerNet, which was selling new and used cars from physical lots, demonstrated a new way of doing business: It started a virtual car showroom on the Internet. It let people "visit" dozens of dealerships and compare prices and features. At that time, this was a revolutionary way of selling cars. To get people's attention, DealerNet gave away a car over the Internet.

This promotion received a lot of offline media attention and was a total success. Today, such promotions are regular events on thousands of websites. Contests, quizzes, coupons (see coolsavings.com), and giveaways designed to attract visitors are as much a part of online marketing as they are of offline commerce. Some innovative ideas used to encourage people to pay attention to online advertising are provided in Online File W8.8.

Live Web Events for Advertising

Live Web events (concerts, shows, interviews, debates, Webcasts, videos), if properly done, can generate tremendous public excitement and bring huge crowds to a website. Some of the best practices for successful live Web events are:

- Carefully planning content, audience, interactivity level, preproduction, and schedule
- Executing the production with rich media if possible
- Conducting appropriate promotion via e-mails, affinity sites, and streaming media, as well as conducting proper offline and online advertisement
- Preparing for quality delivery
- Capturing data and analyzing audience response so that improvements can be made

A global event can allow a product to debut in disparate locations. For example, Cisco Systems unveiled one of its products (ASR 1000 router) with the flair of an in-person event in 2008. It was covered by an e-mail campaign and traditional media coverage but also by content distribution to bloggers and by ads on social networking sites such as Facebook. The company bought banner ads on prominent sites to drive traffic to marketing materials on their site. It also built a game around the new product and invited top prospects to take part in telepresence sessions that put them at a virtual table. The events and the marketing campaign created a strong response.

LOCALIZATION

localization
The process of converting media products developed in one environment (e.g., country) to a form culturally and linguistically acceptable in countries outside the original target market.

Localization is the process of converting media products and advertisement material developed in one environment (e.g., a country) to a form culturally and linguistically acceptable outside the original target market. It is usually done by a set of internationalization guidelines. Web page translation (Chapter 12) is just one aspect of internationalization. However, several other aspects also are important. For example, a U.S. jewelry manufacturer that displayed its products on a white background was astonished to find that this display might not appeal to customers in some countries where a blue background is preferred.

If a company aims at the global market (and there are millions of potential customers out there), it must make an effort to localize its Web pages. This may not be a simple task because of the following factors:

> Many countries use English, but the English used may differ in terminology, spelling, and culture (e.g., United States versus United Kingdom versus Australia).

> Some languages use accented characters. If text includes an accented character, the accent will disappear when converted into English, which may result in an incorrect translation.

> Hard-coded text and fonts cannot be changed, so they remain in their original format in the translated material.

> Graphics and icons look different to viewers in different countries. For example, a U.S. mailbox resembles a European trashcan.

> When translating into Asian languages, significant cultural issues must be addressed, for example, how to address older adults in a culturally correct manner.

> Dates that are written mm/dd/yy (e.g., June 8, 2012) in the United States are written dd/mm/yy (e.g., 8 June 2012) in many other countries. Therefore, "6/8" would have two meanings (June 8 or August 6), depending on the location of the writer.

> Consistent translation over several documents can be very difficult to achieve. (For free translation in six languages, see freetranslation.com.)

INTELLIGENT AGENTS APPLICATIONS

Intelligent agents (also called *software agents*) are computer software designed for performing certain tasks automatically. They have been widely used in e-commerce to overcome information overload on the Internet. In general, they can be used to facilitate the consumer in all stages of the purchasing process. Exhibit 8.10 shows a framework for classifying different types of software agents based on the six stages in the purchase decision process. A more detailed description of software agents is available in Online File W8.10.

Major types of EC agents include:

> Agents that support needs identification
> Agents that support product brokering
> Agents that support merchant brokering
> Agents that support purchase and delivery
> Agents that support after-sales service and evaluation

For a general discussion of intelligent and software agents, see Chapter 11, Section 11.5.

DEVELOPING AN ONLINE ADVERTISING PLAN

Putting advertisements online has been a competitive necessity for most businesses these days. With so many different media and advertising methods available, a challenge is to develop an effective advertising plan within budget constraints. A life cycle process composed of six steps to build and maintain an advertising plan is illustrated in Exhibit 8.11. The details of the steps and the references are provided in Online File W8.11.

Section 8.10 ▶ REVIEW QUESTIONS

1. Describe permission advertising.
2. Describe video ads and their explosion.
3. Discuss the process and value of affiliate marketing.
4. How does the ads-as-a-commodity strategy work?
5. Describe other kinds of online advertising methods.

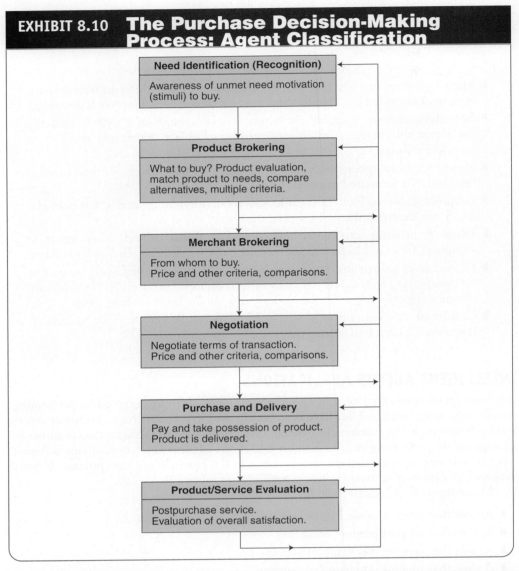

EXHIBIT 8.10   The Purchase Decision-Making Process: Agent Classification

Need Identification (Recognition)
Awareness of unmet need motivation (stimuli) to buy.

Product Brokering
What to buy? Product evaluation, match product to needs, compare alternatives, multiple criteria.

Merchant Brokering
From whom to buy.
Price and other criteria, comparisons.

Negotiation
Negotiate terms of transaction.
Price and other criteria, comparisons.

Purchase and Delivery
Pay and take possession of product.
Product is delivered.

Product/Service Evaluation
Postpurchase service.
Evaluation of overall satisfaction.

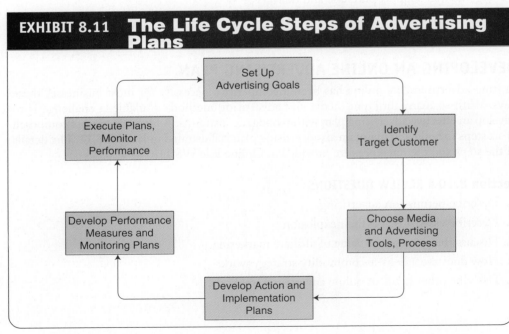

EXHIBIT 8.11   The Life Cycle Steps of Advertising Plans

Set Up Advertising Goals

Identify Target Customer

Choose Media and Advertising Tools, Process

Develop Action and Implementation Plans

Develop Performance Measures and Monitoring Plans

Execute Plans, Monitor Performance

6. Describe ad exchanges.

7. What is localization? What are the major issues in localizing Web pages?

8. Describe choose-your-own-ad format.

9. Describe the five-step process life cycle for an advertising plan.

MANAGERIAL ISSUES

Some managerial issues related to this chapter are as follows.

1. **Do we focus on value-creating customers?** Understanding customers, specifically what they need and how to respond to those needs, is the most critical part of consumer-centered marketing. This was not possible before the solutions for database marketing, one-to-one marketing, and customer relationship marketing became available. What tools do we use to satisfy and retain customers, monitor the entire process of marketing, sales, maintenance, and follow-up services? Do we focus these resources effectively to the VIP customers who contribute to enhancing the corporate value?

2. **Which Internet marketing/advertising channel do we use?** An increasing number of online methods are available from which to choose. These include banners, search engines, video ads, blogging, social networks, and more. Angel (2006) proposed a methodology for Internet marketing channel selection that might be adopted to assess these alternatives with a matrix for selection and implementation.

3. **What metrics do we use to guide advertisers?** A large amount of information has been developed to guide advertisers as to where to advertise, how to design ads, and so on. Specific metrics such as CPM (cost per thousand impressions), click-through rate, stickiness, and actual purchase rate may be used to assess the effectiveness of advertising and calculate the ROI from an organization's online advertising campaign. The metrics can be monitored by third-party monitoring companies. For example, industry standards for measuring mobile ad delivery were developed by the Mobile Marketing Association and IAB in 2010/2011.

4. **What is our commitment to Web advertising?** Once a company has committed to advertising on the Web, it must remember that a successful program is multifaceted. It requires input and vision from marketing, cooperation from the legal department, and strong technical leadership from the corporate information systems (IS) department. A successful Web advertising program also requires coordination with non-Internet advertising and top management support.

5. **Should we integrate our Internet and non-Internet marketing campaigns?** Many companies are integrating their TV and Internet marketing campaigns. For example, a company's TV or newspaper ads direct the viewers/readers to the website, where short videos and sound ads, known as *rich media*, are used. With click-through ratios of banner ads down to less than 0.5 percent at many sites, innovations such as the integration of offline and online marketing are certainly needed to increase click-through rates/ratios.

6. **Who will conduct the market research?** B2C requires extensive market research. This research is not easy to do, nor is it inexpensive. Deciding whether to outsource to a market research firm or maintain an in-house market research staff is a managerial concern. If a company owns a large-scale customer database, the research on the internal database itself can be an important market research tool, and data mining techniques will be helpful.

7. **Should we use intelligent agents?** Any company engaged in EC must examine the possibility of using intelligent agents to enhance customized service, and possibly to support market research and match ads with relevant consumers. Commercial agents that conduct collaborative filtering and basket analysis are available on the market at a reasonable cost.

8. **Should we use mobile coupons?** Consumers and advertisers are curious about mobile coupons, but current challenges and limited current consumer usage mean mobile coupons do not need to be an immediate priority. Advertisers should not feel the pressure to launch a nationwide coupon effort in the near future, but they should be laying the groundwork today for a solution that will integrate with existing loyalty programs. Forrester Research Corp. recommends applying its mobile POST analysis (for free) to determine which approach to mobile couponing is right for you.

9. **What ethical issues should we consider in online marketing?** Several ethical issues relate to online advertising. One issue that receives a great deal of attention is spamming (Chapters 9 and 14). Another issue is the selling of mailing lists and customer information. Some people believe that not only does a company need the consent of customers before selling a list, but also that the company should share the profits with customers derived from the sale of such lists. Using cookies without an individual's consent is considered by many to be an unethical issue. The negative impacts of advertising need to be considered.

SUMMARY

In this chapter, you learned about the following EC issues as they relate to the chapter's learning objectives.

1. **Factors influencing online consumer behavior.** Consumer behavior in EC is similar to that of any consumer behavior, but it has some unique features. It is described in a stimuli-based decision model that is influenced by factors that include the consumer's personal characteristics, environmental characteristics, product/service features, merchant and intermediary, and the EC systems (logistics, technology, and customer service). All of these characteristics and systems interact to influence the decision-making process and produce an eventual buyer decision.

2. **The online consumer decision-making process.** The goal of marketing research efforts is to understand the consumers' online decision-making processes and formulate an appropriate strategy to influence their behavior. For each step in the process, sellers can develop appropriate strategies. The Attention-Interest-Desire-Action model can help us design ad and marketing efforts for different purposes. The Attention-Interest-Search-Action-Share (AISAS) model is tailored to the online behavior in the decision process. This model is particularly suitable for social commerce.

3. **Increasing loyalty and trust.** Customers can switch loyalty online easily and quickly. Therefore, enhancing e-loyalty (e.g., through e-loyalty programs) is a must. Similarly, trust is a critical success factor that must be nourished. Creating loyalty is difficult since customers can switch easily to competitors. Building trust is very difficult since people do not know or see each other. Trust is influenced by many variables.

4. **Market segmentation and building one-to-one relationships with customers.** In segmentation, attention to advertising and marketing is given to a segment (e.g., female customers, customers in a certain country) for improving marketing effectiveness. EC offers companies the opportunity to build one-to-one relationships with customers that are not possible in other marketing systems. Product customization, personalized service, and getting the customer involved interactively (e.g., in feedback, order tracking, and so on) are all practical in cyberspace. In addition, advertising can be matched with customer profiles so that ads can be presented on a one-to-one basis.

5. **Online personalization.** Using personal Web pages, customers can interact with a company, learn about products or services in real time, or get customized products or services. Companies can allow customers to self-configure the products or services they want. Customization also can be done by matching products with customers' profiles. Personalization includes recommendation of products (services) and delivering content that customers want.

6. **EC consumer market research.** Several fast and economical methods of online market research are available. The two major approaches to data collection are (1) soliciting voluntary information from the customers, and (2) using cookies, transaction logs, or clickstream data to track customers' movements on the Internet and find what their interests are. Understanding market segmentation by grouping consumers into categories is also an effective EC market research method. However, online market research has several limitations, including data accuracy and representation of the statistical population by a sample.

7. **Objectives and characteristics of Web advertising.** Web advertising attempts to attract surfers to an advertiser's site. Once at the advertiser's site, consumers can receive information, interact with the seller, and in many cases, are easily given a chance to place an order. With Web advertising, ads can be customized to fit groups of people with similar interests (segmentation) or even individuals (one-to-one). In addition, Web advertising can be interactive, is easily updated, can reach millions at a reasonable cost, and offers dynamic presentation and rich multimedia.

8. **Major online advertising methods.** Banners are the most popular online advertising method. Other frequently used methods are pop-ups and similar ads, e-mail (including e-mail to mobile devices), classified ads, registration of URLs with search engines, and advertising in chat rooms. Some of these are related to search results obtained through search engines such as keyword advertising (especially Google). Social network communities provide new opportunities for marketing by enabling segmentation, viral marketing, user-generated ads, and more. Advertising in videos is gaining popularity as well.

9. **Mobile marketing.** With the explosion of mobile devices comes the opportunity for reaching individuals wherever they are at any time. Despite the small screen size, advertisers use clever designs to show not only banners but video ads as well. Mobile ads are designed for the young generation and some of these are interactive. The young generation is especially active in viral advertisement.

10. **Various advertising strategies and types of promotions.** The major advertising strategies are ads associated with search results (text links), affiliate marketing, pay incentives for customers to view ads, viral marketing, ads customized on a one-to-one basis, and online events and promotions. Web promotions are similar to offline

promotions. They include giveaways, contests, quizzes, entertainment, coupons, and so on. Customization and interactivity distinguish Internet promotions from conventional ones. It is also important that marketing projects need to be localized to meet different cultures.

11. **Implementation topics.** In permission marketing, customers are willing to accept ads in exchange for special (personalized) information or monetary incentives.

Ad management deals with planning, organizing, and controlling ad campaigns and ad use. Ads can be localized to culture, country, and so forth. Market research can be facilitated by feedback from bloggers, chats in social networks, recommendations of friends, polling of members' opinions, and so forth. Advertising is enhanced by user-generated ad content, viral marketing, better segmentation, and reading affinity with small groups.

KEY TERMS

Ad views	453	E-mail advertising	456	Pop-up ad	456
Advergaming	464	E-mail marketing	456	Product brokering	432
Affiliate marketing	472	Hit	453	Random banners	455
Affiliate network	472	Interactive marketing	452	Relationship marketing	439
Augmented reality (AR)	464	Interactive video	463	Reputation-based systems	437
Banner	455	Keyword banners	455	Search advertising	457
Behavioral targeting	442	Live banner	455	Search engine optimization (SEO)	459
Biometrics	451	Localization	474	Spamming	471
Button	453	Market segmentation	438	Spyware	449
Click (ad click)	453	Merchant brokering	432	Stickiness	454
Clickstream behavior	449	Mobile advertising		Transaction log	449
Clickstream data	450	(m-advertising)	467	Trust	436
Click-through rate/ratio (CTR)	453	Mobile marketing	466	Unique visit	454
Collaborative filtering	442	One-to-one marketing	439	User profile	441
Conversion rate	453	Online trust	437	Viral marketing (viral advertising)	461
Cookie	441	Page	453	Viral video	463
CPM (cost per mille,		Pay per click (PPC)	473	Visit	453
i.e., thousand impressions)	453	Permission advertising	471	Web bugs	449
Customer loyalty	434	Personalization	441	Web mining	450
E-loyalty	435	Pop-under ad	456	Webcasting	473

DISCUSSION QUESTIONS

1. How can you describe the process of the purchase decision when the customer is online and looking for an iPhone? What can an online store do to attract this customer to purchase from the store?

2. Why is personalization becoming an important element in EC? What techniques can be used to learn about consumer behavior? How can it be used to facilitate customer service? Give an example.

3. View the videos "Wherever You Want to Go" (from BMW), "One Million Heineken Hugs," and Burger King's "Sign and Race," and also read about them. Write a report on what made them so successful.

4. Discuss why banners are popular in Internet advertising. What kinds of products may be suitable for banners and what may not?

5. Discuss the advantages and limitations of listing a company's URL with various search engines.

6. How might a chat room be used for advertising?

7. Is it ethical for a vendor to enter a chat room operated by a competitor and pose queries?

8. Explain why online ad management is critical. What are the major concerns for a company managing its own online ad program?

9. Explain the advantages of using chatterbots. Are there any disadvantages? (See Online File W8.10.) Find information on their influence on online consumer shopping behavior

10. Discuss the benefits of using software agents in marketing and advertising. To determine whether a bargaining agent online (an agent that can interact with potential customers to settle a discount price) can help the online shop's sales, see Online File W8.10.

11. Discuss SRI Consulting's VALS tool. Enter strategic businessinsights.com/vals/presurvey.shtml. View their activities and discuss how they can facilitate online market segmentation.

12. When you buy a banner ad, you actually lease space for a specific time period. At milliondollarhomepage.com, you buy space forever. Compare and discuss.

13. Discuss the advantages and limitations of three methods of data collection about individual consumers.

14. Discuss the benefits of video ads in the social networking environment.

TOPICS FOR CLASS DISCUSSION AND DEBATES

1. Discuss the similarities and differences between data mining, text mining, and Web mining for online market research. (Hint: To answer this question, you will need to read Online Tutorial T8.)

2. Some say that people come to social networks to socialize and they will not accept ads. Others say that people do not mind the ads, but they ignore them. Discuss.

3. What strategic implications do you see for companies that use videos, mobile devices, and social networks as platforms for advertising? Discuss.

4. Debate: Will traditional advertisement (TV, newspapers, billboards) practically disappear in the future?

5. Debate: Netflix.com, amazon.com, and others view historical purchases as input in their recommendation systems. Some believe that this is an invasion of privacy.

INTERNET EXERCISES

1. Enter netflix.com/Affiliates?hnjr=3. Describe the value of the program as a marketing channel.

2. Surf homedepot.com and check whether (and how) the company provides service to customers with different skill levels. Particularly, check the "kitchen and bath design center" and other self-configuration assistance. Relate this to market research.

3. Examine a market research website (e.g., acnielsen.com or claritas.com). Discuss what might motivate a consumer to provide answers to market research questions.

4. Enter mysimon.com and share your experiences about how the information you provide might be used by the company for marketing in a specific industry (e.g., the clothing market).

5. Enter marketingterms.com and conduct a search by keywords as well as by category. Check the definitions of 10 key terms in this chapter.

6. Enter 2020research.com, infosurv.com, and marketing sherpa.com and identify areas for market research about consumer behavior.

7. Enter selfpromotion.com and find some interesting promotion ideas for the Web.

8. Enter selfpromotion.com and nielsen-online.com. What Internet traffic management, Web results, and auditing services are provided? What are the benefits of each service? Compare the services provided and their costs.

9. Enter adweek.com, wdfm.com, ad-tech.com, adage.com, and other online advertising websites to find new developments in Internet advertising. Write a report based on your findings.

10. Enter clairol.com to determine your best hair color. You can upload your own photo to the studio and see how different shades look on you. You can also try different hairstyles. This site also is for men. How can these activities increase branding? How can they increase sales?

11. Enter n-us.nielsen.com/tab/industries/media and view the demos on e-market research. Then go to clickz.com and find its offerings. Summarize your findings.

12. Enter hotwire.com and espn.com. Identify all the advertising methods used on each site. Can you find those that are targeted advertisements? What revenue sources can you find on the ESPN site? (Try to find at least seven.)

13. Enter omniture.com. How does it help with site optimization? What other services does it provide?

14. What resources do you find to be most useful at targetmarketingmag.com, clickz.com, admedia.org, marketresearch.com, and wdfm.com? Describe useful information for online marketing that you have found from these websites.

15. Enter thisnext.com/shopcast. Write a report relating this product to marketing and advertising.

16. Enter zoomerang.com and learn how it facilitates online surveys. Examine the various products, including those that supplement the surveys. Write a report.

17. Enter pewinternet.org and pewresearch.org. What research do they conduct that is relevant to B2C? To B2B? Write a report.

18. Enter loomia.com. Describe their recommendation engines. Compare this with the recommendation engine of amazon.com.

19. Enter whattorent.com and compare its recommendation system to Netflix. Write a brief report comparing the two.

TEAM ASSIGNMENTS AND PROJECTS

1. **Assignment for the Opening Case**

   Read the opening case about Netflix and answer the following questions:

   a. In your opinion is the recommendation of videos via Cinematch the major success factor of Netflix? Why or why not?

   b. Netflix is moving to downloading instead of physical shipping. But there, the company faces more competition. What are some CSFs for Netflix in this area?

   c. Netflix uses traditional banner ads for the mass audience. Is this wise? Any suggestions for improvement?

   d. Track the performance of the company stock. Is there a justification to the high price to earnings (P/E) ratio?

   e. What problems can the streaming of movies to TVs and PCs solve?

2. Apple is encroaching onto Google's turf by buying Quattro Wireless, a mobile advertising company and by initiating the iAd project. Research the reason for Apple's venture into the field and the Apple-Google battle.

3. Enter harrisinteractive.com, infosurv.com and similar sites. Have each team member examine the free marketing tools and related tutorials and demos. Each team will try to find a similar site and compare the two. Write a report discussing the team's findings.

4. Each team will choose one advertising method and conduct an in-depth investigation of the major players in that part of the ad industry. For example, direct e-mail is relatively inexpensive. Visit the-dma.org to learn about direct mail. Then visit ezinedirector.com, plattformad.com/media/overview, and similar sites. Each team will prepare and present an argument as to why its method is superior.

5. In this exercise, each team member will enter uproar.com or similar sites to play games and win prizes. What could be better? This site is the destination of choice for game and sweepstakes junkies and for those who wish to reach a mass audience of fun-loving people. Relate the games to advertising and marketing.

6. Let the team try the services of constantcontact.com. Constant Contact offers a turnkey e-mail marketing package solution. In less than 5 minutes, you can set up an e-mail sign-up box on your website. As visitors fill in their names and e-mail addresses, they can be asked to check off topics of interest (as defined by you) to create targeted groups.

   Constant Contact provides a system for creating custom e-mail newsletters that can be sent to your target users on a predetermined schedule. The site manages your mailings and provides reports that help you assess the success of your efforts. Pricing is based on the number of subscribers—less than 50 and the service is free. Write a report summarizing your experiences.

7. Watch the video of Google's CEO Eric Schmidt (8:19 minutes) at iab.net/video/videos/view/431 and answer the following questions:

   a. What is the vision for the mobile area?

   b. What is the brand advertisement? How may it change?

   c. What are the changes that mobile advertising brings to display ad advertising?

   d. What are the value-added benefits to customers?

   e. What is the vision for advertising?

   f. What are the impacting changes?

   g. How does the mobile revolution contribute to closing the digital divide?

8. Enter autonlab.org and download tools for conducting data mining analysis (these downloads are free). Get data on customer shopping and analyze it. Write a report.

9. Watch the video "Beginning Analytics: Interpreting and Acting on Your Data," at youtube.com/watch?v=Hdsb_uH2yPU and answer the following questions:

   a. To what metrics does the video refer?

   b. How can Google analytics be used?

   c. What can analytics contribute to competitive intelligence?

   d. Why is the average time on site so important?

   e. What decisions can be supported by analytics?

   f. What have you learned from this video?

Closing Case

JOHNSON & JOHNSON USES NEW MEDIA MARKETING

The Problem

Johnson & Johnson is the world's largest medical and health care product company. It has more than 100,000 employees worldwide. A major problem facing the company is that most of its products are under tight government regulations regarding their production and marketing. In the Internet age, it is important for the company to use online communication tools to reach and support its customers. In the past several years, Johnson & Johnson has adopted an open-minded strategy for new media and achieved significant performance improvement.

Using New Media Channels

Through the use of new media, Johnson & Johnson has grown in online strategies over the years. Some of their strategies are introduced next:

▶ **Web 1.0 Stage.** In 1996, Johnson & Johnson advertised in the cyberworld for the first time in the company's 110-year history by using *jnj.com*. This Web 1.0 website presented a simple online brochure to promote the company's products.

▶ **Web 2.0 Stage.**

1. **Kilmer House (First Blog).** In 2006, the company introduced its first Web 2.0 adverting tools after using Web 1.0 for over 10 years. Kilmer House was named after the company's first science director, Dr. Frederick Barnett Kilmer. The goal for the blog is to "offer a way to tell some of the stories about the early days and history of Johnson & Johnson, and the people who worked here." The blog was a perfect way for the company to enter the Web 2.0 era.

2. **JNJ BTW (Second Blog Web 2.0).** In 2007, the company launched its second blog after a year of Kilmer House. This blog promised to become "the voice of the company." What JNJ BTW became is a place where the company joins the online conversation about subjects that are related to Johnson & Johnson, and it's a place to offer public education about health care.

3. **JNJ health Channel on YouTube.** Through the company's first three new media channels, Johnson & Johnson has gained the experience of producing good content without violating regulatory rules. In May 2008, the company quickly launched two JNJhealth test videos: "Ask Dr. Nancy—Prostate Cancer" and "Obesity and Gastric Bypass Options." The latter video chronicles a teenage girl's (patient Chelsey Lewis) experience undergoing gastric bypass surgery—highlighting why she chose to have the surgery and what it was like afterward. The videos have been viewed over 200,000 times

and have 390 comments so far. For Johnson & Johnson it has turned out to be a great tool for interacting with consumers. After these two videos were tested, this site was officially launched on June 30, 2008.

4. **Twitter and Facebook.** In March 2009, the company launched its Twitter channel, and the site was monitored and updated by Marc Monseau, the editor of the JNJ BTW blog. In April 2009, the company created its first Facebook Group. The page contains biographical information about the company. Twitter and Facebook also serve as a "bridging communicative tool" to integrate viewers into JNJ BTW for further details about Johnson & Johnson.

▶ **Mobile Advertising Campaign.**   Johnson & Johnson also integrated several mobile advertising campaigns from 2007 to 2009.

1. **Johnson & Johnson ACUVUE campaign with IM.** In 2007 in response to research that has shown that 85% of daily contact lens wearers use instant messaging (IM) to stay in touch with their friends and that Asian people who use IM react highly to images that are friendly, cute, and fun, the company worked with Microsoft Digital Advertising Solutions to create a game called Saving Momo highlighted in a Theme Pack for IM users to download. The theme pack includes wallpapers, display pictures, and emoticons highlighting the Johnson & Johnson's ACUVUE brand.

2. **Using a multichannel mobile campaign.** In 2008, the company used in-call audio ads, SMS, and mobile websites to create a new way to send out advertising messages to its target audiences. The company used VoodooVox In-Call Networks to attract target audiences to fill out a form on the company's Wireless Application Protocol (WAP) page. Once an audience user fills out the form, MindMatics, a German mobile services provider, alerts VoodooVox on the behalf of J&J, and it sends a free trial offer of One-Day ACUVUE Moist Lenses to consumers to try.

3. **Johnson & Johnson's Zyrtec and iPhone 2.0.** Zyrtec is an over-the-counter allergy medication that generated $315.9 million of sales in 2008. In 2009, Johnson & Johnson conducted a mobile advertising campaign with The Weather Channel (TWC) putting a banner ad on the TWC application for iPhone users to download for free. TWC reaches more than 38 million users online each month, and it is the most popular online weather source in North America. The special feature for the banner ad is that it won't stop the application even after a user clicks the banner ad.

Therefore, the mobile advertising created a win-win situation for both the consumers and the brand, combining the latest forecast with an increased awareness of the brand.

Results

The intensive campaigns on various new media have resulted in significant performance improvements financially and managerially.

1. Robert Hapler, director of video communication for Johnson & Johnson, explained the ROI (return on investment) of using new media: "There is certainly a subjective ROI in the terms of our reputation. Look at some of the comments on our Nursing videos. . . . Management that I report to is extremely positive about the channel, particularly the large amount of views (over 700,000) and cost (essentially $0). Also, YouTube provides an excellent metric, including views over time, trends, most popular videos, even viewer retention rates. I provide this data to the senior management department, and sometimes to the operating companies, when applicable."

2. Mobile advertising has shown positive results with minimum effort over the years. In 2007, ACUVUE's one-month campaign recorded nearly 300,000 Theme Pack downloads and 200,000 game plays of Saving Momo. The campaign drove sales, improved the brand engagement within the target markets, and had a positive viral impact on the brand. In 2008, Johnson & Johnson used the In-Call Network as another option to engage consumers, which made it easier for users to get a free trial of ACUVUE.

3. The Zyrtec campaign reached more than 3 million downloads in the first three months after it was launched. The Weather Channel remained the number one download for iPhone users in the Apple Store. Mobile advertising has been seen as "a medium with real reach" because of its direct interaction between the brand and consumers.

Sources: Butcher (2008), Butcher (2009), Microsoft (2007), and Ploof (2009).

Questions

1. Identify the online advertising actions adopted by Johnson & Johnson and relate them to the methods described in the chapter.

2. Search the Internet to find more details about Johnson & Johnson's marketing activities on YouTube.

3. Search the Internet to find more details about Johnson & Johnson's marketing activities on Facebook and Twitter.

4. Search the Internet to find more details about Johnson & Johnson's marketing activities on mobile devices.

5. Outline the major benefits from Johnson & Johnson's online marketing activities.

ONLINE RESOURCES
available at pearsonglobaleditions.com/turban

Online Files

W8.1 Online Buyer Decision Making Process
W8.2 EC Trust Model
W8.3 Spyware
W8.4 The List of Information Provided by Clickstream Data
W8.5 From Mass Advertising to Interactive Advertising
W8.6 Application Case: 1-800-Flowers.com Uses Data Mining to Foster Customer Relationship Management
W8.7 Advantages and Limitations of Internet Advertising
W8.8 How to Attract Web Surfers
W8.9 E-Mail Advertising Methods
W8.10 Software Agents in Marketing and Advertising Applications
W8.11 The Life Cycle of an Online Advertising Plan

Comprehensive Educational Websites

cio.com/white-papers: Index of white papers by topic offered by CIO.com.
clickz.com/stat: EC statistics.
ecommercetimes.com: News and analysis.
ecommerce-guide.com/news/research: Comprehensive collection of resources.
emarketer.com: Statistics, news, products, laws.
internet.com: Many resources (for small business, in particular).
lib.unc.edu/reference/busecon/ecommerce.html: List of EC resources.
marketresearch.com: E-commerce market research reports (for free).
scribd.com: Comprehensive resource collection.
wilsonweb.com: Case studies, articles, tutorials, videos, and more; the research room may require fees.

REFERENCES

Adhikari, R. "Search Marketing 2010: Everyone Will Have to Work Harder." *Ecommerce Times,* February 22, 2010. ecommercetimes.com/rsstory/69389.html (accessed March 2011).

Amato-McCoy, D. M. "That's So "You." *Stores,* April 2010.

Angel, G. "The Art and Science of Choosing Net Marketing Channels." *E-Commerce Times,* September 21, 2006. ecommercetimes.com/story/53141.html (accessed November 2010).

Atsmon, Y., and M. Magni. "China's Internet Obsession." *McKinsey Quarterly* (March 2010).

Awad, N. F., and A. Ragowsky. "Establishing Trust in Electronic Commerce Through Online Word-of-Mouth: An Examination of Across Genders." *Journal of Management Information Systems* (Spring 2008).

Barber, N., T. Dodd, and N. Kolyesnikova. "Gender Difference in Information Search: Implications for Retailing." *Journal of Consumer Marketing,* 26, no. 6 (2009).

Becker, M. "Academic Review: Mobile Marketing Framework Overview." *Mobile Marketing,* 2006. mmaglobal.com/articles/academic-review-mobile-Marketing-framework-overview (accessed January 2011).

Brengman, M., M. Geuens, S. M. Smith, W. R. Swinyard, and B. Weijters. "Segmenting Internet Shoppers Based on Their Web-Usage-Related Lifestyle: A Cross-Cultural Validation." *Journal of Business Research,* 58 (2005).

Buckley, N. "E-Route to Whiter Smile." *Financial Times,* August 26, 2002.

Butcher, D. "Johnson & Johnson Breaks Multichannel Mobile Campaign." November 10, 2008. mobilemarketer.com/cms/news/advertising/2075.html (accessed March 2011).

Butcher, D. "Johnson & Johnson's Zyrtec Runs Mobile Banner Campaign on App." March 31, 2009. mobilemarketer.com/cms/news/advertising/2938.html (accessed March 2011).

Cell-Phone-Plans.net. "Going Mobile in Order to Grow—Big Commerce." November 2010. cell-phone-plans.net/blog/cell-phone-applications/going-mobile-in-order-to-grow-big-commerce (accessed April 2011).

Cheung, C. M. K., and M. K. O. Lee. "The Asymmetric Impact of Website Attribute Performance on User Satisfaction: An Empirical Study." *e-Service Journal* 3, no. 3 (2005).

Clifford, S. "Advertisers Show Strong Interest in Publishers Programs for Apple iPad." *New York Times,* March 26, 2010.

Compete.com. "Site Comparison: Netflix Versus Blockbuster." February 2, 2011. siteanalytics.compete.com/netflix.com+blockbuster.com/?metric=uv (accessed March 2011).

Crespo, A. H., and I. R. D. Bosque. "The Influence of the Commerce Features of the Internet on the Adoption of E-Commerce by Consumers." *Electronic Commerce Research and Development,* 9 (2010).

Cyr, D. "Modeling Website Design Across Cultures: Relationships to Trust, Satisfaction, and E-Loyalty." *Journal of Management Information Systems* (Spring 2008).

Dellarocas, C. "How to Design One That Does What You Need." *MIT Sloan Management Review* (Spring 2010).

Dushinski, K. *The Mobile Marketing Handbook: A Step-by-Step Guide to Creating Dynamic Mobile Marketing Campaigns.* Dayton, TN: Cyberbook, 2009.

eMarketer. "Social Network Ad Space: Sorry, Sold Out!" November 3, 2006.

Flynn, L. J. "Like This? You'll Hate That (Not All Web Recommendations Are Welcome)." *New York Times,* January 23, 2006.

Grappone, J., and G. Couzin. *Search Engine Optimization (SEO): An Hour a Day,* 3rd ed. Hoboken, NJ: Sybex, 2011.

Greenberg, P. *CRM at the Speed of Light: Social CRM 2.0 Strategies, Tools, and Techniques Engaging Your Customers,* 4th ed. New York: McGraw-Hill, 2009.

Gregg, D. G., and S. Walczak. "The Relationship Between Website Quality, Trust, and Price Premiums at Online Auctions." *Electronic Commerce Research,* 10 (2010).

Hawkins, D. I., and D. L. Mothersbaugh. *Consumer Behavior: Building Marketing Strategy,* 11th ed. Boston: McGraw-Hill, 2010.

Hewson, C., et al. *Internet Research Methods.* London: Sage, 2003.

IAB. "A Digital Video Advertising Overview." *Interactive Advertising Bureau,* January 2008a.

IAB. "A Mobile Advertising Overview." *Interactive Advertising Bureau,* July 2008b.

Jarboe, G. *YouTube and Video Marketing: An Hour a Day.* Hoboken, NJ: Sybex, 2009.

Kennaugh, C. "Collect Data for Your Marketing Strategy." *Microsoft.com,* 2009. office.microsoft.com/en-us/help/HA011415001033.aspx (accessed April 2009).

Krum, C. *Mobile Marketing: Finding Your Customers No Matter Where They Are.* New York: Que Publishing Co., 2010.

Learmonth, M. "Vivaki Predicts $100M Market for Choose-Your-Own-Ad Format." May 24, 2010. adage.com/print?article_id=144032 (accessed March 2011).

Lee, S., and R. J. Koubek. "The Effects of Usability and Web Design Attributes on User Preference for e-Commerce Websites." *Computers in Industry,* 61, no. 4 (May 2010).

Lee, M., and E. Turban. "Trust in B2C Electronic Commerce: A Proposed Research Model and Its Application." *International Journal of Electronic Commerce,* 6, no. 1 (2001).

Lee, M., and S. Youn. "Electronic Word-of-Mouth (eWOM): How eWOM Platforms Influence Consumer Product Judgment." *International Journal of Advertising,* 28, no. 3 (2009).

Leibowitz, B. "10 Pay per Click Steps to Reduce Costs and Increase Conversions Using Google AdWords." June 20, 2009. site-reference.com/articles/10-Pay-Per-Click-

Steps-to-Reduce-Costs-and-Increase-Conversions-using-Google-AdWords (accessed April 2011).

Liang, T. P., and H. J. Lai. "Effect of Store Design on Consumer Purchase: An Empirical Study of Online Bookstores." *Information & Management*, 39, no. 6 (2002).

Marsden, P. "How Social Commerce Works: The Social Psychology of Social Shopping." *Social Commerce Today*, December 6, 2009. socialcommercetoday.com/how-social-commerce-works-the-social-psychology-of-social-shopping (accessed March 2011).

McColl, P. *Viral Explosions! Proven Techniques to Expand, Explode, or Ignite Your Business or Brand Online.* Richmond, VA: Career Place, 2010.

Microsoft. "Johnson & Johnson Acuvue Case Study." November 27, 2007. advertising.microsoft.com/asia/SupportCenter/ResearchLibrary.aspx?pageid=2586&Adv_CaseStudyID=1319 (accessed March 2011).

Moisander, J., and A. Valtonen. *Qualitative Marketing Research: A Cultural Approach.* Thousand Oaks, CA: Sage, 2006.

Pfeiffer, M., and M. Zinnbauer. "Can Old Media Enhance New Media?" *Journal of Advertising Research* (March 2010).

Ploof, R. *Johnson & Johnson Does New Media.* e-book, June 15, 2009. ronamok.com/ebooks/jnj_case_study.pdf (accessed March 2011).

Plunkett, J. W. *Plunkett's E-Commerce & Internet Business Almanac 2010.* Houston, TX: Plunkett Research, 2010.

Pons, A. P. "Biometric Marketing: Targeting the Online Consumer." *Communications of the ACM*, August 2006.

Ranganathan, C., and S. Jha. "Examining Online Purchase Intentions in B2C E-Commerce: Testing an Integrated Model." *Information Resource Management Journal*, 20, no. 4 (2007).

Salo, J., and H. Karjaluoto. "A Conceptual Model of Trust in the Online Environment." *Online Information Review*, 31, no. 5 (2007).

Steel, E. "A Web Pioneer Profiles Users by Name." *Wall Street Journal*, October 28, 2010.

Strauss, J., and R. Frost. *E-Marketing*, 5th ed. Upper Saddle River, NJ: Prentice Hall, 2009.

Sue, V. M., and L. A. Ritter. *Conducting Online Surveys.* Thousand Oaks, CA: Sage Pub., 2007.

TMCnet. "Procter & Gamble Applies Right Now to Deliver Superior Consumer Experience." August 30, 2006. tmcnet.com/viewette.aspx?u=http%3a%2f%2fwww.tmcnet.com%2fusubmit%2f2006%2f08%2f30%2f1846211.htm&kw=4 (accessed March 2011).

Tsang, M., S. C. Ho, and T. P. Liang. "Consumer Attitudes Toward Mobile Advertising: An Empirical Study." *International Journal of Electronic Commerce.* (Spring 2004).

Turban, E., et al. *Business Intelligence: A Managerial Approach,* 2nd ed. Upper Saddle River, NJ: Prentice Hall, 2011.

Tuten, T. L. *Advertising 2.0: Social Media Marketing in a Web 2.0 World.* Westport, CT: Praeger, 2008.

Urban, G. L., J. R. Hauser, G. Liberali, M. Braun, and F. Sultan. "Morph the Web to Build Empathy Trust and Sales." *MIT Sloan Management Review* (Summer 2009).

Vanacore, A. "Web Ad Sales Help New York Times Co. Halt Declines." *New York Times,* July 22, 2010.

Wang, E. T. G., H. Y. Yeh, and J. J. Jiang. "The Relative Weights of Internet Shopping Fundamental Objectives: Effect of Lifestyle Differences." *Psychology and Marketing*, 23, no. 5 (2006).

Ziv, U. "Viewing Customer Relationships Through a New Lens." April 20, 2010. ecommercetimes.com/story/69810.html (accessed March 2011).

E-COMMERCE SECURITY AND FRAUD PROTECTION

Learning Objectives

Upon completion of this chapter, you will be able to:

1. Understand the importance and scope of security of information systems for EC.

2. Describe the major concepts and terminology of EC security.

3. Learn about the major EC security threats, vulnerabilities, and technical attacks.

4. Understand Internet fraud, phishing, and spam.

5. Describe the information assurance security principles.

6. Identify and assess major technologies and methods for securing EC access and communications.

7. Describe the major technologies for protection of EC networks.

8. Describe various types of controls and special defense mechanisms.

9. Describe consumer and seller protection from fraud.

10. Describe the role of business continuity and disaster recovery planning.

11. Discuss EC security's enterprisewide implementation issues.

12. Understand why it is not possible to stop computer crimes.

Content

HOW SEATTLE'S HOSPITAL SURVIVED A BOT ATTACK

The Problem

On a cold Sunday afternoon, many calls reached the computer help desk at Seattle's Northwest Hospital and Medical Center. PCs were running very slow (the hospital staff requested help), and documents wouldn't print, but no one could help. On Monday morning, as more employees came to work and logged onto their PCs, the problem spread. Finally, many PCs froze entirely.

By 10 a.m., all 50 people in the hospital's information technology (IT) department had been summoned, but their efforts made little difference. Strange things started happening. Operating-room doors stopped opening, and doctors' pagers wouldn't work. Even computers in the intensive care units were shut down.

Everybody was very frightened; hospital communications began to break down. What happened? Northwest was under attack by a *botnet,* a malicious computer code that infected the hospitals' computers and was controlled, in this case, by a 19-year-old Californian, Christopher Maxwell, and two juveniles. The trio exploited a flaw in Microsoft Windows that let them install pop-ups on the hospital's computers. As the bad code coursed through the network, the hospital's computers started turning into bots. These new bots, in turn, scanned the network, looking for new victims to infect, and the network become clogged with traffic. This kind of attack is known as a *zombie army* (Section 9.3), where computers are set up to attack other computers in the same or other organizations. Initially, Northwest's IT team tried to halt the attack by shutting off the hospital from the Internet. Even though the bots were now contained internally, they still infected PCs faster than the team could clean them.

The Solution

By Monday afternoon, the IT department had figured out which malware the bots were installing on the PCs and wrote a script, directing the PCs to remove the bad code. By Tuesday, Computer Associates—Northwest's antivirus vendor—figured out exactly which malware Maxwell had used to get into the network and wrote an antivirus program that blocked new code from coming in. The attack eventually harmed 150 out of 1,000 PCs—all of which had to have their hard drives wiped clean and their software reinstalled, at an estimated cost of $150,000.

The attack's aftermath lasted for weeks. As computers stopped working, hospital workers relied on *backup systems*—people and paper. Extra workers were brought in to help carry out tasks by hand. Lab results, for instance, were run by a person from the lab to the patients' bedsides on different floors rather than transmitted electronically. To save time, elective surgeries were postponed. Every day, department managers met several times to make sure the new security routines were holding and no patients were being endangered.

The Results

The hospital's network is now protected by CA's Pest Patrol, which blocks adware and spyware (Section 9.3), and Cisco MARS, an intrusion detection system (Section 9.3). The Windows flaw that the attacks slipped through has also been fixed.

Northwest wasn't Maxwell and crew's only prey. Among their other victims were the U.S. Department of Defense and Colton Joint Unified School District in California, according to court papers. Maxwell pleaded guilty to conspiracy and intentionally causing damage to a protected computer. He was sentenced in August 2006 to 37 months in federal prison. He also was ordered to pay $115,000 to cover the hospital's direct expenses.

Sources: Compiled from Kawamoto (2006) and O'Hagan (2006).

WHAT WE CAN LEARN . . .

Information systems inside organizations can be attacked by criminals who may not even benefit financially from the attacks. This attack was done via the Web, by using a virus hidden in pop-up ads. This is only one of the many methods used to attack information systems in organizations, disturbing their internal operations. Other attack methods interfere with online trading and other forms of e-commerce. In addition to criminal attacks, information systems may be attacked by natural disasters, human errors, equipment malfunction, and more. In this chapter, we concentrate on e-commerce attacks and on the defense against them. The chapter also covers the topic of fraud in EC and how to protect against it.

9.1 THE INFORMATION SECURITY PROBLEM

If you examine different lists of management concerns regarding the use of EC (and IT), the information security issue is and has been among the top concerns. Security is considered to be the backbone of doing business over the Internet. Security-breaching incidents involving all types of organizations (including high-level, secure government agencies such as the CIA, FBI, and the military) appear on the news frequently. Few organizations or individuals have not experienced some security breaches in their computerized systems. The damages of security breaches, including crimes, can be substantial and sometimes life-threatening, as was demonstrated in the opening case. Securing data, transactions, and privacy, and protecting people (buyers and sellers) is of utmost importance in conducting EC of any type.

information security
Protecting information and information systems from unauthorized access, use, disclosure, disruption, modification, perusal, inspection, recording or destruction.

Information security means protecting information and information systems from unauthorized access, use, disclosure, disruption, modification, perusal, inspection, recording, or destruction. In this chapter, we will provide an overview of the information security problems and solutions as they relate to EC and IT. In this section we look at the nature of the security problems, the magnitude of the problems, and the essential terminology and strategy used in dealing with these issues.

WHAT IS EC SECURITY?

Computer security refers to the protection of data, networks, computer programs, computer power, and other elements of computerized information systems (see en.wikipedia.org/wiki/Computer_security). It is a very broad field due to the many methods of attack as well as the many modes of defense. The attacks and defense of computers can affect individuals, organizations, countries, or the entire Web. Computer security aims to prevent or at least minimize the attacks. We classify computer security into two categories: *generic*, relating to any information system (e.g., encryption), and *EC-related*, such as buyers' protection. This chapter covers both, but it emphasizes the EC-related side. Attacks on EC websites, *identify theft* of both individuals and organizations, and a large variety of fraud schemes, such as phishing, are described in this chapter as well.

The Status of Computer Security in the United States

Several private and government organizations try to assess the status of computer security in the United States annually. Notable is the annual CSI report, which is described next.

CSI Computer Crime and Security Survey
Annual security survey of U.S. corporations, government agencies, financial and medical institutions, and universities conducted by the Computer Security Institute.

No one really knows the true impact of online security breaches because, according to the Computer Security Institute (CSI, gocsi.com), only 27 percent of businesses report to legal authorities about computer intrusions. For the 2010 survey, known as the **CSI Computer Crime and Security Survey**, see Richardson (2010). This is an annual security survey of U.S. corporations and government agencies; financial, medical, and other institutions; and universities, conducted by the Computer Security Institute. Highlights from the 2010/2011 Security Survey, which was based on responses from over 500 participants, include the following summary points:

▶ Malware infection continues to be the most commonly seen attack.
▶ Fewer financial frauds were reported than in previous years, with only 8.7 percent saying they had seen this type of incident.
▶ Tools that improve visibility into networks, Web applications, and endpoints were ranked among the highest on information security and information technology managers' wish lists, including better log management, security information and event management, security data visualization, and security dashboards.
▶ Of the approximately half of respondents who experienced at least one security incident last year, 45.6 percent of them reported they had been the subjects of at least one targeted attack.

▶ When asked what actions were taken following a security incident, 18.1 percent of respondents stated that they notified individuals whose personal information was breached, and 15.9 percent stated that they provided new security services to users or customers.

▶ Respondents generally said that regulatory compliance efforts have had a positive effect on their organization's security programs.

Information security has been ranked consistently as one of the top management concerns in the United States. The major specific topics cited in various studies as most important in information security are illustrated in Exhibit 9.1.

In addition to organizational security issues, there is also the issue of personal security.

Personal Security

As you will see in Section 9.4, fraud is aimed mostly against individuals. In addition, loose security may mean danger of personal safety due to sex offenders who can find victims on the Internet, fraud and identity theft, and cyberbullying (Chapter 14).

National Security

Protection of the U.S. computer networks is in the hands of the Department of Homeland Security (DHS), which coordinates government policies for thwarting cyberthreats. It includes the following programs:

▶ **Cyber Security Preparedness and the National Cyber Alert System.** Computer users can stay up-to-date on cyberthreats through this program.
▶ **U.S.-CERT Operations.** Analyzes and combats cyberthreats and vulnerabilities.
▶ **National Cyber Response Coordination Group.** Comprising 13 federal agencies, it coordinates the federal response to incidents.
▶ **CyberCop Portal.** Coordination with law enforcement helps capture and convict those responsible for cyber attacks.

On February 9, 2009, President Obama ordered the DHS to review U.S. government cybersecurity plans.

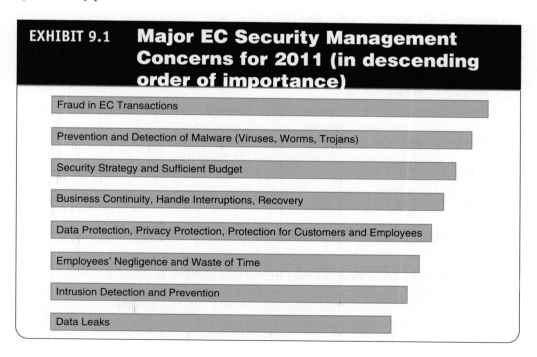

EXHIBIT 9.1   Major EC Security Management Concerns for 2011 (in descending order of importance)

- Fraud in EC Transactions
- Prevention and Detection of Malware (Viruses, Worms, Trojans)
- Security Strategy and Sufficient Budget
- Business Continuity, Handle Interruptions, Recovery
- Data Protection, Privacy Protection, Protection for Customers and Employees
- Employees' Negligence and Waste of Time
- Intrusion Detection and Prevention
- Data Leaks

Security Risks for 2011–2012

According to *Baseline*, *eWeek*, and security vendors, the major security risks for the near future are:

> ▶ Cyberespionage and cyberwars (discussed below).
> ▶ Attacks on mobile assets including smartphones and other mobile devices (Chapter 6). A particular target is the enterprise iPhone.
> ▶ Attacks on social networks and social software tools (Chapters 7 and 12). User-contributed content is a major source of malware.
> ▶ Cybergang consolidation—underground groups are multiplying and getting bigger, especially in Internet fraud.
> ▶ Attacks on new technologies such as cloud computing and virtualization.
> ▶ Attacks on Web applications.

For more information, see sans.org/top-cyber-security-risks/ and CSI Computer and Security Survey 2010 (gocsi.com/survey).

Cyberwars, Cyberespionage, and Cybercrimes Across Borders

In July 2009, suspected North Korean hackers launched a cyber attack against some of the most important government offices in the United States and South Korea, including the White House, the Pentagon, the New York Stock Exchange, and the Presidential Blue House in Seoul.

The attack took out some of South Korea's most important websites, including those of the defense ministry, the national assembly, and South Korea's top Internet portal, Naver. All in all the websites of 11 organizations had either gone down or had access problems. The attack also targeted the U.S. Joint Strike Fighter project (only a few files were stolen).

According to a CNN report (cnn.com/2009/TECH/03/29/ghostnet.cyber.espionage), nearly 1,300 computers in more than 100 countries have been attacked and have become part of a computer espionage network apparently based in China. Computers—including machines at NATO, governments, and embassies—were infected with software that lets attackers gain complete control of them. Researchers have dubbed the attacking network as GhostNet. The network can not only search a computer but also see and hear the people using it. GhostNet is capable of taking full control of infected computers, including searching and downloading specific files, and covertly operating attached devices, including microphones and Web cameras.

It resembles an attack that began a week earlier on government websites in the United States, including some that are responsible for fighting cybercrime. These are not isolated cases of cross-border cyber attacks. In February 2011, the U.S. security firm McAfee Inc. reported that Chinese hackers stole sensitive data from oil companies in the United States, Taiwan, Greece, and Kazakhstan. These attacks started in November 2009 and are increasing in magnitude. The attacks, which are still going on, are done via e-mails containing a virus sent to tens of thousands of recipients.

Types of Attacks

The attacks can be classified into two major categories:

1. **Corporate espionage that plagues businesses around the world.** Many attacks targeted energy-related companies. The fact that oil companies were targeted might speak more to the value of their inside information than any attempt to cause damage to pipelines (McAfee 2011). A separate report in 2010 from McAfee and the Center for Strategic and International Studies in Washington found that more than half of

the 600 operators of power plants and other infrastructure surveyed said their networks were infiltrated by sophisticated adversaries.

2. **Political espionage and warfare.** Political espionage and even wars are increasing in magnitude.

   Examples. In December 2010, the Iranian nuclear program was attacked via computer programs rumored to be created by the United States and Israel. The attack was fairly successful causing major physical damage to the nuclear program, delaying it by months or even years. The attack was perpetrated using a sophisticated computer worm named Stuknet. It was used as a weapon created by a state to achieve a goal that it otherwise may have achieved only by multiple cruise missiles. For the implications of such warfare, see Dickye, et al. (2010).

   According to the AP and the *New York Times*, in March 2009, a cyber spy network based mainly in China hacked into classified documents from government and private organizations in 103 countries, including the computers of the Dalai Lama and Tibetan exiles.

   Cyberwars are expected to grow in number and sophistication and hit larger targets. For example, in 2010, Google's network infrastructure was attacked repeatedly in China causing Google to discuss the possibility of leaving China. Also, in 2010, Estonia signed an agreement with NATO to create a joint cyber defense as a result of an alleged attack by Russia that caused great financial harm to Estonia via a cyberwar attack (see Murphy 2010 for details).

   A final note: The motive for cross-border attacks can be financial. In January 2011, a hacker breached several government, military, and educational websites from across the globe, and put on sale the administrative access to high-profile sites such as the official Italian government website, the Department of Defense PharmacoEconomic Center, and even the U.S. Army, Communications-Electronics Command. The hacker put on sale dot-gov, dot-mil, and dot-edu websites from across the globe at a price range of $55 to $499. The hacker was also offering personal information from the hacked sites at $20 for 1,000 records. For a detailed discussion on cyberwars and the state of defense readiness in the United States, see Prince (2011b).

   International organized crime syndicates, Al-Quaida groups, and other cybercriminals electronically steal hundreds of millions of dollars every year. Cybercrime is easier and safer than selling drugs, dealing in black market diamonds, or robbing banks. In addition, online gambling offers easy fronts for international money laundering operations.

THE DRIVERS OF EC SECURITY PROBLEMS

Security problems are the results of several drivers. Here, we describe four major ones: the *Internet's vulnerable design*, the *shift to profit-induced crimes*, the *Internet underground economy*, and the *dynamic nature of EC systems and the role of insiders*.

The Internet's Vulnerable Design

It is important to recognize that the Internet and its network protocols were never intended for use by untrustworthy people or criminals. They were designed to accommodate computer-to-computer communications in a closed and trusted community. However, the system evolved into an any-to-any means of communication in an open community. As you know, that community is global in scope, mostly unregulated, and out of control. Furthermore, the Internet was designed for maximum efficiency without regard for security or the integrity of a person sending a message or requesting access. Error checking to ensure that the message was sent and received correctly was important at that time but not user authentication or access control. The Internet is still a fundamentally insecure infrastructure.

Virtually every Internet application relies on the reliable operation of *domain name system* (DNS) services. The **domain name system (DNS)** translates (converts) domain names (e.g., pearson.com and fbi.gov) to their numeric IP addresses. An **IP address** is an address that identifies your computer on a network or Internet. The lack of source authentication and data integrity checking in DNS operations leave nearly all Internet services vulnerable to attacks.

Domain Name System (DNS)
Translates (converts) domain names to their numeric IP addresses.

IP address
An address that uniquely identifies each computer connected to a network or the Internet.

The Shift to Profit-Induced Crimes

There is a clear shift in the nature of the operation of computer criminals (see Symantec 2008, 2009). In the early days of e-commerce, many hackers simply wanted to gain fame or notoriety by defacing websites or "gaining root," that is, root access to a network. The opening case illustrates a criminal who did not attack systems to make a profit. Today, criminals are profit-oriented, and there are many more of them. Most popular is the theft of personal information such as credit card numbers, bank accounts, Internet IDs, and passwords. According to Privacy Rights Clearinghouse, approximately 250 million records containing personally identifiable information were involved in security breaches in the three years between April 2005 and April 2008 (reported by Palgon 2008). Today the number is much higher.

Examples. The following are some examples:

> ▶ Eisenmann (2009) provides an example of hackers who stole medical records at Sunnylake Hospital attempting blackmail. The hospital almost paid the demanded extortion money to avoid problems.
> ▶ In May 2009, hackers broke into some Facebook member accounts and sent messages to the members' friends, urging them to click on fake websites that look like the Facebook homepage. By doing so, the friends unwittingly gave their passwords to the hackers. The purpose was to spread spam advertisements or to steal their identities. This strategy is known as a *phishing attack* and will be described in Section 9.4 along with identity theft and fraud.
> ▶ In December 2010, Gawker media's servers were compromised resulting in security breaches in several of its subsidiaries. One and one half million names and passwords were stolen.
> ▶ Names, e-mail addresses, and phone numbers of an estimated 1.6 million jobseekers were accessed from Monster.com's résumé database in August 2007. Though widely described as a hacking, the data were actually accessed by attackers using legitimate user names and passwords, possibly stolen from professional recruiters or human resources personnel who were using Monster.com to look for job candidates.
> ▶ An intrusion access to corporate data occurred at discount retail conglomerate TJX (see Online File W9.1).

Laptop computers are stolen for two reasons: selling the hardware and trying to find valuable data on the machine.

A major driver of data theft and other crimes is the ability to profit from the theft. Stolen data are sold today in a huge illegal marketplace described next.

The Internet Underground Economy

Internet underground economy
E-markets for stolen information made up of thousands of websites that sell credit card numbers, social security numbers, other data such as numbers of bank accounts, social network IDs, passwords, and much more.

The **Internet underground economy** refers to the e-markets for stolen information. Thousands of websites sell credit card numbers, social security numbers, e-mail addresses, bank account numbers, social network IDs, passwords, and much more. For a comprehensive description, see McCormick and Gage (2005). Their report describes the structure of the market, the different members and their roles, the attack methods, and what can be done to avoid problems. Stolen credentials are sold for less than a dollar to several hundred dollars each to spammers or to criminals who are using them to send spam or conduct illegal financial transactions such as transferring money to their accounts or paying with someone else's credit card. For example, in August 2008, the FBI arrested a Countrywide employee who stole more than 2 million customer records and sold them on the underground market. The Internet security company Symantec released a comprehensive report that provides statistical data about the Internet underground economy (Symantec 2008). The Symantec report provides information on how cybercriminals are getting organized in Russia and other countries. According to this report, about 30 percent of all the transactions in this market deal with stolen credit cards. The value of all unsold items is estimated to be $275 million, while the potential worth of just the credit cards and banking information for sale is $7 billion. Forty-one percent of the underground economy is in the United States, while 13 percent is in Romania. The report also covers the issue of software piracy, which is estimated to be more than $100 million annually. For highlights of the report, see Symantec (2008). Criminals use several methods to steal the information they sell. One popular method is *keystroke logging*.

Keystroke Logging. Keystroke logging (keylogging) is a method of capturing and recording user keystrokes. Such systems are also highly useful for both law enforcement and for law breaking—for instance, by providing a means to obtain passwords or encryption keys and thus bypassing other security measures. Keylogging methods are widely available on the Internet. For more information, see en.wikipedia.org/wiki/Keystroke_logging.

keystroke logging (keylogging)
A method of capturing and recording user keystrokes.

The Dynamic Nature of EC Systems and the Role of Insiders

EC systems are changing all the time due to a stream of innovations. With changes often come security problems. In recent years, we have experienced many security problems in the new areas of social networks and wireless systems (some will be explored later in this chapter). Note also that almost half of the security problems are caused by insiders. New employees are being added frequently to organizations and so are the threats they bring.

Example. An insider let two criminals into London's office of Sumitomo Mitsui Bank, where the criminals tampered with the computer system, gaining access to the asset holdings of companies such as Toshiba. Then they tried to steal hundreds of millions of dollars from the bank and its corporate customers. They attempted to electronically transfer $323 million from accounts in the bank to their own account. Fortunately the attempt failed. Otherwise it would have been the biggest theft of its kind (*Taipei Times* 2009).

WHY IS AN E-COMMERCE SECURITY STRATEGY NEEDED?

Computer security in its simplest form can be divided into three categories: *threats, defenses,* and *management.* As you will see in Sections 9.3 and 9.4, there are many potential threats. In general, we divide these threats into two categories: unintentional and intentional. The intentional threats (including fraud) are known as *cybercrimes* when they are performed on the Web. These change frequently as the criminals become more sophisticated.

The defense (Sections 9.5 through 9.10) is changing too and is improving in response to new attack methods and to new technological innovations. Yet, neither cybercrime nor cybercriminals can be stopped (see Section 9.10). As in the physical world, Internet security systems cost money, sometimes a considerable amount. Therefore, one of management's tasks is to determine how much to invest in EC security. In addition, management is responsible for a variety of security programs across the enterprise. This requires a strategy.

The Computer Security Strategy Dilemma

The defense of information systems and EC is getting more difficult. The attackers change their strategies and attack methods all the time. For example, according to Cisco's "Cyber Crime Trends": Cisco's 2010 Annual Security Report (cisco.com/en/US/prod/collateral/vpndevc/security_annual_report_2010.pdf), cybercriminals and hackers have taken up new targets. They have shifted their focus from Windows PCs to other operating systems (e.g., Google Android) and mobile platforms such as smartphones and tablets. In addition, incidences of "money mulling" (use of unsuspecting people to help with money transfer) scams have grown. Users are also still vulnerable to the many ways these cybercriminals attempt to lure them into traps. This is creating new security challenges for companies struggling to adapt to the evolving security landscape while dealing with tight budgets. Cybercriminals are continuing to find new and creative ways to exploit networks, systems, and human vulnerabilities to steal information or do damage.

business continuity plan
A plan that keeps the business running after a disaster occurs. Each function in the business should have a valid recovery capability plan.

cybercrime
Intentional crimes carried out on the Internet.

cybercriminal
A person who intentionally carries out crimes over the Internet.

exposure
The estimated cost, loss, or damage that can result if a threat exploits a vulnerability.

fraud
Any business activity that uses deceitful practices or devices to deprive another of property or other rights.

malware (malicious software)
A generic term for malicious software.

phishing
A crimeware technique to steal the identity of a target company to get the identities of its customers.

risk
The probability that a vulnerability will be known and used.

social engineering
A type of nontechnical attack that uses some ruse to trick users into revealing information or performing an action that compromises a computer or network.

spam
The electronic equivalent of junk mail.

Information security departments with big workloads and small budgets are not able to optimize their EC security program for efficiency. Endless worms, spyware, data piracy, and other crimes keep them working reactively rather than strategically; they address security concerns according to attackers' schedules instead of their own. Finally, the defense is difficult because it is easy to learn to attack.

Learning How to Attack. The security problem is getting complicated because you do not need to be an expert to launch an ordinary attack. Attack toolkits are inexpensive, and some are given for free. For details, see Prince (2011a) and Symantec (2010).

According to Wong (2010), in China there are hacker training centers that openly recruit thousands of members online and provide them with cyber attack lessons and malicious software (for free). The Chinese police are trying to fight these hackers. In February 2010, the police shut down the Black Hawk Safety Net training center that had 12,000 paid subscribers who paid $1 million to learn how to hack. In addition, 170,000 people signed up for free membership and software.

As a result, security costs and efforts by organizations reacting to crises and paying for damages are greater than if they had an EC security strategy. This is the underlying reason why a comprehensive EC security is necessary.

Section 9.1 ▶ REVIEW QUESTIONS

1. Define computer security.
2. List the major findings of the CSI 2010 survey.
3. Describe the vulnerable design of the Internet.
4. Describe some profit-induced computer crimes.
5. Define the Internet underground economy.
6. Describe the dynamic nature of EC systems.
7. What makes EC security management so difficult? What is the dilemma?

9.2   BASIC E-COMMERCE SECURITY ISSUES AND LANDSCAPE

In order to better understand security problems, we need to understand some basic concepts in EC and IT security. We begin with some basic vocabulary frequently used in dealing with security issues.

BASIC SECURITY TERMINOLOGY

In the opening case and in Section 9.1, we introduced some key concepts and security terms. We begin this section by introducing alphabetically the major terms needed to understand EC security issues:

▶ **Business continuity plan**
▶ **Cybercrime**
▶ **Cybercriminal**
▶ **Exposure**
▶ **Fraud**
▶ **Malware (malicious software)**
▶ **Phishing**
▶ **Risk**
▶ **Social engineering**
▶ **Spam**
▶ **Vulnerability**
▶ **Zombie**

Definitions of these terms can be found in the margin glossary of this chapter, in webopedia.com/terms, and in cert.org (look for the glossary).

EXHIBIT 9.2   The EC Security Battleground

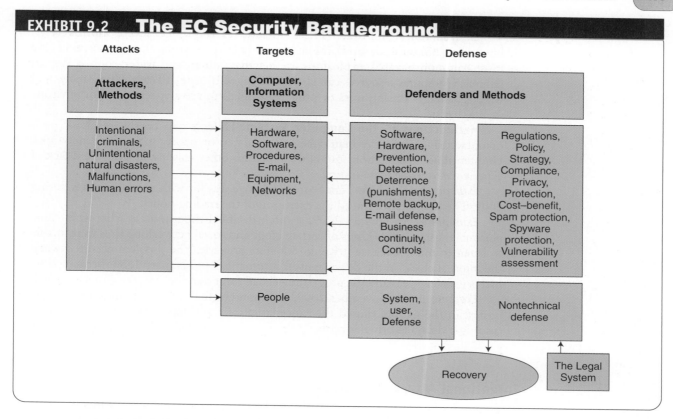

THE EC SECURITY BATTLEGROUND

The essence of EC security can be viewed as a battleground between attackers and defenders and their security requirements. This battleground includes the following components, as shown in Exhibit 9.2:

- ▶ The attacks, the attackers, and their strategies
- ▶ The assets that are being attacked (the targets) in a vulnerable area
- ▶ The security defense, the defenders and their methods and strategy

THE THREATS, ATTACKS, AND ATTACKERS

Information systems including EC are vulnerable to both unintentional and intentional threats.

Unintentional Threats

Unintentional threats fall into three major categories: human error, environmental hazards, and malfunctions in the computer system.

Human Error. Human errors can occur in the design of the hardware or information system. It can also occur in programming, testing, data collection, data entry, authorization, and instructions. Errors can be a result of negligence, inexperience, or misunderstanding (for example, not changing passwords creates a security hole).

Example. In November 2008, Jefferson County, West Virginia, released a site search engine that gave a new meaning to "open records." The engine exposed social security numbers and other personal information belonging to about 1.6 million citizens. It was a clear programming error made by a person.

vulnerability
Weakness in software or other mechanism that threatens the confidentiality, integrity, or availability of an asset (recall the CIA model). It can be directly used by a hacker to gain access to a system or network.

zombies
Computers infected with malware that are under the control of a spammer, hacker, or other criminal.

Environmental Hazards. These include earthquakes, severe storms (e.g., hurricanes, blizzards, or sand), floods, power failures or strong fluctuations, fires (the most common hazard), explosions, radioactive fallout, and water-cooling system failures. Computer resources can also be damaged by side effects such as smoke and water. Damages during wars or property vandalism are a special kind of environmental hazards.

Malfunctions in the Computer System. Defects can be the result of poor manufacturing, defective materials, and outdated or poorly maintained networks. Unintentional malfunctions can also happen for other reasons, ranging from lack of experience to inadequate testing.

Example 1. The New York Stock Exchange was hit with several glitches during 2009. The interference forced the extension of the trading hours.

Example 2. In January 2009, a glitch disabled thousands of Microsoft Zune personal music players. Users of certain blogs and social networking sites were unable to listen to music because it would not start properly. The problem occurred when the internal clock on the device moved automatically to January 1, but because 2008 had been a leap year and the programmers had forgotten about it, the glitch occurred.

Example 3. In November 2009, a computer glitch at the Atlanta airport, the busiest in the nation, caused the cancellation of most departing flights, leading to cascading delays at other airports up the East Coast and elsewhere in the country.

Intentional Attacks and Crimes

Intentional attacks are done by criminals. Types of intentional attacks include theft of data; inappropriate use of data (e.g., manipulating inputs); theft of laptops and equipment and/or programs; deliberate manipulation in handling, entering, processing, transferring, or programming data; vandalism or sabotage directed to the computers or its information systems; malicious damage to computer resources; destruction from viruses and similar attacks; miscellaneous computer abuses; and Internet fraud. Many are provided in Sections 9.3 and 9.4.

The Criminals and Methods

hacker
Someone who gains unauthorized access to a computer system.

cracker
A malicious hacker, such as Maxwell, in the opening case, who may represent a serious problem for a corporation.

Intentional crimes carried out on the Internet are called *cybercrimes*, which are done by *cybercriminals* (*criminals* for short) that include hackers and crackers. Hacker describes someone who gains unauthorized access to a computer system. A cracker is a *malicious hacker*, such as Maxwell, in the opening case, who may represent a serious problem for a corporation.

Criminals use a variety of methods for the attacks. Some are done with computers as a weapon; some are done against the computing assets depending on the target. For an interesting evolution of the term *hacker* and hacking, see en.wikipedia.org/wiki/Hacker.

Hackers and crackers may implicate unsuspecting people, including insiders, in their crimes. For example, unsuspecting people, referred to as "mules," are used to transfer stolen money. In a strategy called *social engineering* (Section 9.4), criminals trick unsuspected people into giving them information or access that they should not have. Social engineering is a collection of tactics used to manipulate people into performing actions or divulging confidential information. Notorious hacker Kevin Mitnick, who served time in jail for hacking, used social engineering as his primary method to gain access to computer systems. One recent popular method is *scareware,* in which criminals persuade users to download malicious files disguised as security applications.

THE TARGETS OF THE ATTACKS IN VULNERABLE AREAS

As seen in Exhibit 9.2 the targets can be people, machines, or information systems. Attacking people mainly involves fraud, aiming to steal money or other assets such as real estate. But computers are also used to harass people (e.g., cyberbullying), to damage their reputation, to violate their privacy (Chapter 14), and so forth.

Vulnerable Areas Are Being Attacked

Any part of an information system can be attacked. PCs can be stolen or be attacked by viruses and other malware. Users are subject to fraudulent actions. Databases can be attacked by unauthorized access, and data can be copied and stolen. Networks can be attacked, and information flow can be stopped or altered. Terminals, printers, and any other pieces of equipment can be damaged in many ways. Software and programs can be manipulated. Procedures and policies may be altered, and much more. Attacks are done on *vulnerable* areas.

Vulnerability Information. Vulnerabilities create *risk*, which is the probability that this weakness will be known and can be exploited. MITRE Corporation publishes a list of vulnerabilities called *common vulnerabilities and exposures (CVE)* (cve.mitre.org). In 2006, MITRE reported that four of the top five reported vulnerabilities were within Web applications. *Exposure* can result if a threat exploits a vulnerability.

Examples.   Three medical data breaches occurred in May 2008. Unauthorized peer-to-peer (P2P) file sharing led to a data breach at Walter Reed Army Medical Center that exposed the personal data of 1,000 patients. Patients at Staten Island University Hospital in New York were told that a computer with their medical records was stolen. Information on patients of the University of California San Francisco Medical Center was accidentally made accessible to everyone on the Internet.

Attacking E-Mail. One of the easiest places to attack is e-mail, since it travels via the unsecured Internet. One example is the ease with which Sarah Palin was hacked in March 2008. For a list of top attack areas, see Online File W9.2 and sans.org/top-cyber-security-risks/summary.php.

Attacking Cell Phones and Wireless Systems. This is becoming popular with the explosive growth of mobile computing since they are more vulnerable than wired systems.

The Vulnerability of RFID Chips. These chips are everywhere including credit cards and U.S. passports. They are designed to be read contactless, which is also their vulnerability. When you carry one in your wallet or pocket then anyone with a reader that can be close to you can read the RFID information. For a presentation, see the video "How to Hack RFID-enabled credit card for $8" at youtube.com/watch?v=vmajlKJlT3U. For protecting yourself, see blogs.techrepublic.com.com/security/?p=613&tag=nl.e101.

The Vulnerabilities in Business IT and EC Systems

According to Sullivan (2011), the following are the common vulnerabilities:

- **Technical Weaknesses**
  - Unencrypted communications
    - Man-in-the-middle attack
    - Replay attack
  - Insufficiently patched OSS and applications
  - Insufficient use of antivirus and personal firewalls
  - Weak boundary security
  - Poor application security

- **Organizational Weaknesses**
  - End-user training and security awareness
    - End-user training myths
  - Lax security with mobile devices
  - Inappropriate use of business computers and network services

Many areas can be vulnerable, some of which, such as RFID, we do not even think about.

SECURITY SCENARIOS AND REQUIREMENTS IN E-COMMERCE

Defending against attacks and attackers is done by using information security tactics.

The Content of Information Security

EC security involves more than just preventing and responding to cyber attacks and intrusions. Consider, for example, the situation in which users connect to a webstore to obtain some product literature. In return, the users are asked to "register," by filling out an electronic form providing information about themselves or their employers before receiving the literature. In this situation, what kinds of security issues may arise?

From the User's Perspective.

▶ How can the user know whether the Web server is owned and operated by a legitimate company?

▶ How does the user know that the Web page and form have not been compromised by spyware or other malicious code?

▶ How does the user know that a dishonest employee won't intercept and misuse the information?

From the Company's Perspective.

▶ How does the company know the user will not attempt to break into the Web server or alter the pages and content at the site?

▶ How does the company know that the user will not try to disrupt the server so that it is not available to others?

From Both Parties' Perspectives.

▶ How do both parties know that the network connection is free from eavesdropping by a third party "listening" on the line?

▶ How do they know that the information sent back and forth between the server and the user's browser has not been altered?

Such questions illustrate the kinds of security issues that arise in an EC transaction. For transactions involving e-payments, additional types of security issues must be confronted (see Chapter 10 for details).

EC Security Requirements

To protect EC transactions, we use the following set of requirements:

authentication
Process to verify (assure) the real identity of an individual, computer, computer program, or EC website.

authorization
Process of determining what the authenticated entity is allowed to access and what operations it is allowed to perform.

nonrepudiation
Assurance that online customers or trading partners cannot falsely deny (repudiate) their purchase or transaction.

▶ **Authentication. Authentication** is a process to verify (assure) the real identity of an entity, which could be an individual, software agent, computer program, or EC website. For transmissions, authentication verifies that the sender of the message is who the person or organization claims to be.

▶ **Authorization. Authorization** is the process of determining what an authenticated entity is allowed to access and what operations it is allowed to perform. Authorization of an entity occurs after authentication.

▶ **Auditing.** When a person or program accesses a website or queries a database, various pieces of information are recorded or logged into a file. The process of recording information about what was accessed, when, and by whom is known as *auditing.* Audits provide the means to reconstruct what specific actions have occurred and may help EC security investigators identify the person or program that performed unauthorized actions.

▶ **Availability.** Technologies such as load-balancing hardware and software help ensure availability.

▶ **Nonrepudiation.** Closely associated with authentication is **nonrepudiation**, which is the assurance that online customers or trading partners will not be able to falsely deny (repudiate) their purchase, transaction, or other obligation. Nonrepudiation involves several assurances, including providing:

▶ the sender of data with proof of delivery

▶ the recipient (EC company) with proof of the sender's identity

Authentication and nonrepudiation are potential defenses against phishing and identity theft. To protect and ensure trust in EC transactions, *digital signatures*, or *digital certificates*, are often used to validate the sender and time stamp of the transaction so it cannot be later claimed that the transaction was unauthorized or invalid. A technical overview of digital signatures and certificates and how they provide verification is provided in Section 9.6. Unfortunately, phishers and spammers have devised ways to compromise certain digital signatures.

THE DEFENSE: DEFENDERS, STRATEGY, AND METHODS

Security should be everyone's business. However, in general, the information system department and security vendors provide the technical side while management provides the administrative aspects. Such activities are done via security and strategy that users need to follow.

EC Defense Programs and Strategy

An **EC security strategy** consisting of multiple layers of defense is available. Such a strategy views EC security as the process of deterring, preventing, and detecting unauthorized use of the organization's brand, identity, website, e-mail, information, or other assets and attempts to defraud the organization, its customers, and employees. **Deterring measures** refer to actions that will make criminals abandon their idea of attacking a specific system (e.g., the possibility of losing a job, for insiders). **Prevention measures** help stop unauthorized users (also known as *intruders*) from accessing any part of the EC system (e.g., by requiring a password). **Detection measures** help determine whether intruders are attempting or attempted to break into the EC system, whether they were successful, whether they are still damaging the system, and what they may have done.

Information Assurance. Making sure that a shopping experience is safe and secure is a crucial part of improving the buyer experience. The ultimate goal of EC security is often referred to as *information assurance*. **Information assurance (IA)** is the protection of information systems against unauthorized access to or modification of information whether in storage, processing, or in transit; protection against denial of service to authorized users; and those measures necessary to detect, document, and counter threats (see details in Section 9.5).

The Possible Punishment

A part of the defense is to deter criminals by punishing them heavily if they are caught, as in the opening case. Judges now are giving more and larger punishments. For example, in March 2010 a federal judge gave Albert Gonzales 20 years in prison for his role in stealing millions of credit card numbers and selling them. Such severe sentences send a powerful message to hackers and help the defense. Unfortunately in many cases the punishment is too light to deter the criminals.

Defense Methods and Technologies

There are hundreds of defense methods, technologies, and vendors that can be classified in different ways. We introduce them in Sections 9.5 through 9.10.

RECOVERY

In security battles, there are winners and losers in each episode, but no one can win the war. As we will discuss in Section 9.10, there are many reasons for this. On the other hand, after a security breach, organizations and individuals usually recover. Recovery is especially critical in cases of a disaster or a major attack, and it must be speedy. Organizations need to continue their business until the information systems are fully restored, and they need to restore them fast. This is done by using a *business continuity and disaster recovery plan* (Section 9.9).

Because of the complexity of EC and network security, this topic cannot be covered in a single chapter or even a book. Those readers interested in a more comprehensive discussion should see the *Pearson/Prentice Hall Security Series* of security books and search Amazon.com.

EC security strategy
A strategy that views EC security as the process of preventing and detecting unauthorized use of the organization's brand, identity, website, e-mail, information, or other asset and attempts to defraud the organization, its customers, and employees.

deterring measures
Actions that will make criminals abandon their idea of attacking a specific system (e.g., the possibility of losing a job for insiders).

prevention measures
Ways to help stop unauthorized users (also known as "intruders") from accessing any part of the EC system.

detection measures
Ways to determine whether intruders attempted to break into the EC system; whether they were successful; and what they may have done.

information assurance (IA)
The protection of information systems against unauthorized access to or modification of information whether in storage, processing, or transit, and against the denial of service to authorized users, including those measures necessary to detect, document, and counter such threats.

Section 9.2 ▶ REVIEW QUESTIONS

1. List five major EC security terms.
2. Describe the major unintentional security hazards.
3. List five examples of intentional EC security crimes.
4. Describe the security battleground, who participates, and how. What are the possible results?
5. Define hacker, cracker, and social engineering.
6. List all security requirements and define authentication and authorization requirements.
7. What is nonrepudiation?
8. Describe deterring, preventing, and detecting in EC security systems.
9. What is a security strategy, and why it is needed?

9.3 TECHNICAL ATTACK METHODS: FROM VIRUSES TO DENIAL OF SERVICE

Criminals use many methods to attack information systems and users. Here, we cover some major representative methods.

It's helpful to distinguish between two types of attacks—*technical* (which we discuss in this section) and *nontechnical* (which we discuss in Section 9.4).

TECHNICAL AND NONTECHNICAL ATTACKS: AN OVERVIEW

Software and systems knowledge are used to perpetrate *technical attacks*. A computer virus is an example of a technical attack.

Nontechnical attacks are those in which a perpetrator uses some form of deception or persuasion to trick people into revealing information or performing actions that can compromise the security of a network. We include in these financial fraud, spam, *social engineering, phishing,* and other fraud methods. The goals of social engineering are to gain unauthorized access to systems or information. Phishing attacks rely on social engineering. The major nontechnical methods are described in Section 9.4.

THE MAJOR TECHNICAL ATTACK METHODS

Hackers often use several software tools readily and freely available over the Internet together with tutorials on how to use them, in order to learn of vulnerabilities as well as attack procedures. Although some of the free tools require expertise, novice hackers can easily use many of the other tools. The major attack methods are illustrated in Exhibit 9.3 and are described briefly next.

EXHIBIT 9.3	**The Major Technical Security Attack Methods (in descending order of importance)**

Malware (Virus, Worm, Trojan)

Unauthorized Access

Denial-of-Service Attacks

Spam and Spyware

Hijacking (Servers, Pages)

Botnets

MALICIOUS CODE: VIRUSES, WORMS, AND TROJAN HORSES

Malware (or *malicious software*) is software designed to infiltrate or damage a computer system without the owner's informed consent or even knowledge. Malware is a general term used by computer professionals to mean a variety of forms of hostile, intrusive, or annoying software or program codes.

Software is considered malware based on the perceived intent of the creator rather than any particular features. Malware includes computer viruses, worms, Trojan horses, most rootkits, spyware, dishonest adware, crimeware, and other malicious and unwanted software.

Viruses

A **virus** is a piece of software code that inserts itself into a host, including the operating systems; running its host program activates the virus. A virus has two components. First, it has a propagation mechanism by which it spreads. Second, it has a payload that refers to what the virus does once it is executed. Sometimes a particular event triggers the virus's execution. For instance, Michelangelo's birth date triggered the Michelangelo virus. On April 1, 2009, the entire world was waiting for a virus named Conficker (see Brooks 2009). Fortunately only limited attacks were reported. Some viruses simply infect and spread. Others do substantial damage (e.g., deleting files or corrupting the hard drive).

Web-based malware is very popular today, such as criminal attack blogging tools, plug-ins, Flash, etc.

> ▮ **E-mail with virus** could infect a system reading e-mail and subsequently spread throughout the entire organization. (Do not open unknown attachments and do not get lured in by messages such as "just for you" and "here you have.")
>
> ▮ **Network viruses** could enter through unprotected ports, compromising the whole network.
>
> ▮ **Web-based viruses** could compromise a system during browsing and subsequently affect other internal systems. (Do not download free software unless you are 100 percent sure what it is.)

Note that virus attacks are the most frequent computer attacks. The process of a virus attack is illustrated in Exhibit 9.4.

For tutorials and information about viruses, see microsoft.com/protect/computer/basics/virus.mspx.

virus
A piece of software code that inserts itself into a host, including the operating systems, in order to propagate; it requires that its host program be run to activate it.

Worms

Note that in the Microsoft tutorials you will learn how to identify a computer virus, how to know if you are infected, and how to protect yourself against viruses. Special variations of viruses are worms and Trojan horses.

Unlike a virus, a **worm** can spread itself without any human intervention. Worms use networks to propagate and infect a computer or handheld device (e.g., cell phone) and can even spread via instant messages. Also, unlike viruses that generally are confined within a target computer, a worm's ability to self-propagate can degrade network performance. Worms consist of a set of common base elements: a warhead, a propagation engine, a payload, a target-selection algorithm, and a scanning engine. The *warhead* is the piece of code in a worm that exploits some known vulnerability. A huge number of worms have been spread all over the Internet.

In December 2008, the Koobface worm attacked Facebook, MySpace, and other social networks. It created bogus links that looked innocent, but when you clicked them, it gave hackers access to sensitive personal data.

Macro Viruses and Microworms. A **macro virus (macro worm)** is executed when the application object that contains the macro is opened or a particular procedure is executed. Because worms spread much more rapidly than viruses, organizations need to proactively track new vulnerabilities and apply system patches as a defense against their spread.

Trojan Horse. A **Trojan horse** is a program that appears to have a useful function but contains a hidden function that presents a security risk. The name is derived from the

worm
A software program that runs independently, consuming the resources of its host in order to maintain itself, that is capable of propagating a complete working version of itself onto another machine.

macro virus (macro worm)
A macro virus or macro worm is executed when the application object that contains the macro is opened or a particular procedure is executed.

Trojan horse
A program that appears to have a useful function but that contains a hidden function that presents a security risk.

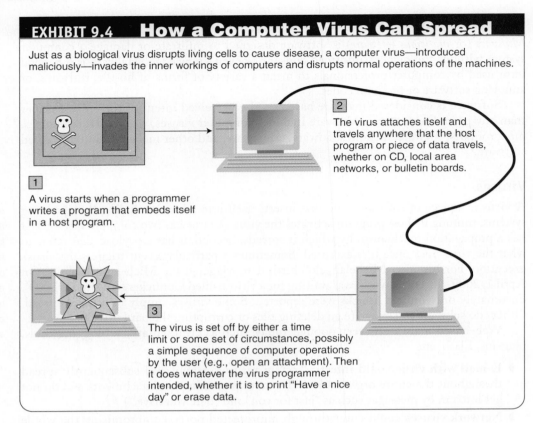

EXHIBIT 9.4   How a Computer Virus Can Spread

Just as a biological virus disrupts living cells to cause disease, a computer virus—introduced maliciously—invades the inner workings of computers and disrupts normal operations of the machines.

1 A virus starts when a programmer writes a program that embeds itself in a host program.

2 The virus attaches itself and travels anywhere that the host program or piece of data travels, whether on CD, local area networks, or bulletin boards.

3 The virus is set off by either a time limit or some set of circumstances, possibly a simple sequence of computer operations by the user (e.g., open an attachment). Then it does whatever the virus programmer intended, whether it is to print "Have a nice day" or erase data.

Trojan horse in Greek mythology. Legend has it that during the Trojan War the city of Troy was presented with a large wooden horse as a gift to the goddess Athena. The Trojans hauled the horse inside the city gates. During the night, Greek soldiers who were hiding in the hollow horse opened the gates of Troy and let in the Greek army. The army was able to take the city and win the war.

There are many variations of Trojan horse programs. The programs of interest are those that make it possible for someone else to access and control a person's computer over the Internet. This type of Trojan horse has two parts: a server and a client. The *server* is the program that runs on the computer under attack. The *client* program is the program used by the person perpetrating the attack. For example, a dangerous Trojan is Zeus, which spreads by a large botnet. It uses keystroke logging to steal financial information (see Falliere and Chien 2009). Another example, the Girlfriend Trojan, is a server program that arrives in the form of a file that looks like an interesting game or program. When the unsuspecting user runs the program, the user unknowingly installs the Trojan program. The installed program executes every time the user turns on the attacked computer. The server simply waits for the associated client program to send a command. This particular Trojan horse enables the perpetrator to capture user IDs and passwords, to display messages on the affected computer, to delete and upload files, and so on. Trojan threads are spread in many ways (e.g., under the guise of Verizon messages). Two examples follow:

Example 1. Spyware researchers at Webroot Software uncovered a stash of tens of thousands of stolen identities from 125 countries that they believe were collected by a new variant of a Trojan program the company named *Trojan-Phisher-Rebery* (Roberts 2006). The Rebery malicious software is an example of a **banking Trojan**, which is programmed to come to life when computer owners visit one of a number of online banking sites.

Example 2. Bank of America has more than 20 million customers online and processes more transactions online than it does in all of its physical banking centers. According to Gage (2006), Ahlo, a Miami wholesaler of ink and toner cartridges, sued Bank of America for being responsible for an unauthorized transfer of more than $90,000 from Ahlo's account to a bank in Latvia. A Coreflood Trojan infected the company's PC. The Trojan

banking Trojan
A Trojan that comes to life when computer owners visit one of a number of online banking or e-commerce sites.

was spread by a phishing attack—fraudulent e-mails that tricked bank customers into giving up their account information and infecting their computers with malware that logged keystrokes. (The bank does not discuss individual phishing attempts but posted information on its website, bofa.com/privacy/pdf/fin_security.pdf, to educate customers about online fraud.) In 2010, researchers developed antivirus products that are based on cloud technologies that were successful in blocking Trojans. However, in 2011 Microsoft discovered a Chinese Trojan called Bohu that neuters cloud-based products.

Note that as of 2008, criminals moved from e-mail attacks (e.g., viruses, spam) to sophisticated Web-based attacks. Targeting weaknesses in server-based applications such as Web 2.0 tools and client-side browser plug-ins including Flash has allowed malware to be installed when a user simply visits a Web page.

Denial of Service

A **denial-of-service (DoS) attack** is an attack in which a large number of requests for service or access to a site bombard a system, which causes it to crash or become unable to respond in time. In a DoS attack, an attacker uses specialized software to send a flood of data packets to the target computer, with the aim of overloading its resources. Many attackers rely on software created by other hackers, which is available over the Internet for free, rather than developing it themselves. A common method is the use of *zombie PCs* to launch DoS attacks. Some of the cyberwar attacks on the United States and Korean institutions (see Section 9.1) involved DoS. DoS attackers also target social networks, especially Facebook and Twitter (see Bradley 2009).

DoS attacks can be difficult to stop. Fortunately (or unfortunately), they are so commonplace that over the past few years, the security community has developed a series of steps for combating these costly attacks. For a comprehensive coverage, see en.wikipedia.org/wiki/Denial_of_service_attack.

denial-of-service (DoS) attack
An attack on a website in which an attacker uses specialized software to send a flood of data packets to the target computer with the aim of overloading its resources.

Web Server and Web Page Hijacking

Page hijacking is achieved by creating a rogue copy of a popular website that shows contents similar to the original. Once there, an unsuspecting user is redirected to malicious websites. Spammers can use this technique to achieve high rankings in result pages for certain keywords; so, more people will come to the site. Scammers and phishers can use the rogue copy to steal information and even money. For details, see en.wikipedia.org/wiki/Web_page_hijacking.

page hijacking
Creating a rogue copy of a popular website that shows contents similar to the original to a Web crawler. Once there, an unsuspecting user is redirected to malicious websites.

Botnets

A **botnet** refers to a huge number (as many as hundreds of thousands) of hijacked Internet computers that have been set up to run autonomously and automatically. It can be used to forward traffic, including spam and viruses (recall the opening case), to other computers on the Internet. An infected computer is referred to as a *computer robot*, or *bot*. Botmasters, or bot herders, control botnets. The combined power of these coordinated networks of computers can scan for and compromise other computers and perpetrate DoS or other attacks. Botnets are used in scams, spams, and frauds. Botnets appear in different forms (e.g., see the opening case) and can be worms or viruses. Notable botnets include Srizbi, Cutwail, Torpig, and Conficker.

Example. At the beginning of 2004, MyDoom, an e-mail virus, infected several hundreds of thousands of PCs around the world. Like many other e-mail viruses, this virus propagated by sending an official-looking e-mail message with a zip file attached. When the victim opened the zip file, the virus automatically found other e-mail addresses on the victim's computer and forwarded itself to those addresses. However, there was more to MyDoom than simple propagation. When the victim opened the zip file, the virus code also installed a program on the victim's machine that enabled the intruders to automatically launch a DoS attack. For more details, see en.wikipedia.org/wiki/Mydoom.

botnet
A huge number (e.g., hundreds of thousands) of hijacked Internet computers that have been set up to forward traffic, including spam and viruses, to other computers on the Internet.

Malvertising

Malvertising might sound like a fancy kind of virtual game, but it is really a fake online advertising designed to trick you into downloading malicious software onto your computer.

The most common kind of fake ad is for *security software* that you do not need and that could harm your computer. This is often called "rogue security software" or "scareware."

A final word: If you get an e-mail that congratulates you on winning a large amount of money and asks you "Please view the attachment," don't!!!

Section 9.3 ▶ REVIEW QUESTIONS

1. Describe the difference between a nontechnical and a technical cyber attack.
2. What are the major forms of malicious code?
3. What factors account for the increase in malicious code?
4. Define a virus and explain how it works.
5. Define worm and Trojan horse.
6. Define DoS. How are DoS attacks perpetrated?
7. Define server and page hijacking.
8. Describe botnet attacks.

9.4 NONTECHNICAL METHODS: FROM PHISHING TO SPAM

As discussed in Section 9.1, there is a shift to profit-related Internet crimes. These crimes are conducted with the help of both technical methods, such as malicious code that can steal confidential information from your online bank account, and nontechnical methods, such as social engineering.

SOCIAL ENGINEERING AND FRAUD

Social engineering is the act of psychologically or socially manipulating people into performing actions or divulging confidential information. While similar to a confidence trick or simple fraud, the term typically applies to trickery or deception for the purpose of information gathering, fraud, or computer system access; in most cases the attacker never comes face-to-face with the victim. The major social engineering methods are: phishing (several submethods), pretexting, and diversion theft. For details, see en.wikipedia. org/wiki/Social_engineering_(security). Once information is obtained from a victim (e.g., via phishing) it is used for committing a crime as shown in Exhibit 9.5.

As you can see in the exhibit, phishers (or other criminals) obtain confidential information by methods ranging from social engineering to physical theft. The stolen

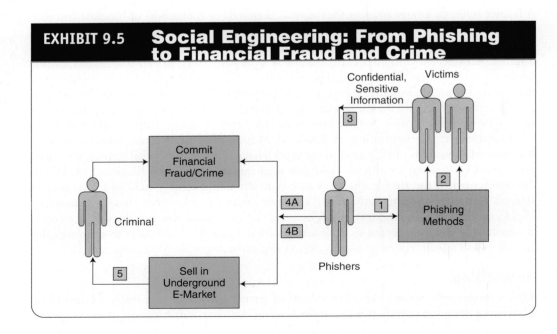

EXHIBIT 9.5 Social Engineering: From Phishing to Financial Fraud and Crime

information (e.g., credit card numbers, social security numbers) is used by thieves to commit financial fraud or is sold in the underground Internet marketplace to another set of criminals, who then use the information to conduct financial crimes. In this section, we will describe how such systems work with phishing.

SOCIAL PHISHING

In the field of computer security, *phishing* is defined as the criminal, fraudulent process of attempting to acquire confidential information such as user names, passwords, and credit card details by masquerading as a trustworthy entity such as a well-known bank, credit card company, a friend, a large social network, or a telecommunication company. This is done usually via e-mail or IM. Phishing typically directs users to enter details at a fake (e.g., hijacked) website that looks and feels almost identical to a legitimate one. Even when using server authentication, it may require skill to detect that the website is fake. For a discussion of what is phishing and how to recognize it, see ehow.com/how_5361193_recognize-phishing-scams.html.

Online shoppers and those conducting transactions electronically are attractive targets because they typically have higher incomes. Phishers, electronic shoplifters, con artists, and scammers stalk online shoppers because these cyber cons want shoppers' money or their confidential information—today's most valuable form of international currency.

Selling stolen information, like selling any stolen goods, can be profitable and unstoppable. Unfortunately, potential e-commerce customers list "too much risk of fraud," and "I don't trust online merchants" as their primary reasons for not shopping online. Of the total fraud complaints reported to the FTC, Internet-related fraud complaints accounted for 79 percent in 2008 (McMillan 2009b). Not only do concerns about cyber cons stunt EC growth, but defending against these cons and compensating for damages also significantly increases the costs of conducting EC. As companies try to expand their e-business in countries where the legal systems are underdeveloped, opportunities for fraud expand with it, making it difficult to conduct EC.

Example. German phishers sent out messages pretending to come from a utility company that provides an electronic invoice as an Adobe PDF file. This social engineering trick worked. Many customers clicked the link to download an "important document," which contained a Trojan horse. The program gave the phishers control of the infected computers. The Trojan monitored every Internet connection and keystroke, and reported passwords back to the Trojan's creator.

Sophisticated Phishing Methods

Phishing is a major provider of information used for financial fraud on the Internet. Exhibit 9.6 illustrates a typical phishing process called "drive-by downloads," a top Web threat (Symantec 2009). For other methods, see en.wikipedia.org/wiki/Phishing. For the latest phishing tactics and their potential impact on business, see VeriSign (2009).

For an overview of social phishing, its process, techniques, and the damage, see Jagatic, et al. (2007).

FRAUD ON THE INTERNET

Phishing is a first step that leads to many fraud schemes (recall Exhibit 9.5, p. 504). An environment where buyers and sellers cannot see each other breeds fraud. Fraud is a problem for online retailers and customers alike. However, even though actual losses per incident are rising, the rate of those losses is flattening out. In other words, the threat actually may be lessening—somewhat. Online merchants reject roughly 4 percent of incoming orders because of suspicion of fraud. An estimated 1 percent of accepted orders turn out to be fraudulent. As an adjustment to a slowing economy, merchants shifted fraud-fighting priorities since 2008, dropping the unaccepted orders from 4.2 percent to 2.9 percent. Among online orders from *outside* the United States and Canada, 2.7 percent of the orders were fraudulent. That rate is three times higher than the rate associated with orders from the United States and Canada (Marketing Charts 2009).

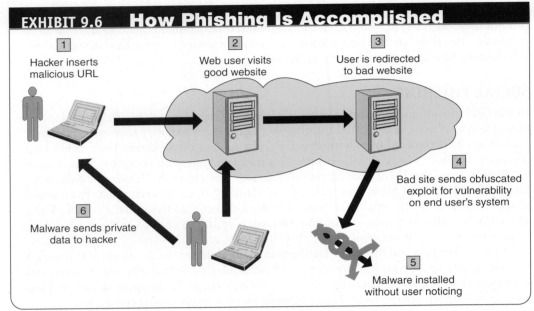

EXHIBIT 9.6   How Phishing Is Accomplished

1. Hacker inserts malicious URL
2. Web user visits good website
3. User is redirected to bad website
4. Bad site sends obfuscated exploit for vulnerability on end user's system
5. Malware installed without user noticing
6. Malware sends private data to hacker

Source: Symantec, "Web-Based Attacks," ©2009. Used with permission.

During the first few years of EC, many types of financial crime came to light, ranging from the online manipulation of stock prices to the creation of a virtual bank that disappeared with the investors' deposits. Internet fraud has grown even faster than the Internet itself. The following examples demonstrate the scope of the problem. Also, visit the Open Directory Project at dmoz.org/Society/Issues/Fraud/Internet for a comprehensive collection of fraud resources.

Examples of Typical Online Fraud Attacks

The following are some characteristic fraud attacks perpetrated on the Internet.

▶ Phishers uses spam e-mails or pop-up messages to deceive victims into disclosing credit card numbers, bank account information, social security numbers, passwords, or other sensitive information. Typically, the e-mail or pop-up message claims to be from a business or organization that the recipient may deal with; for example, an ISP, bank, online payment service, or even a government agency.

▶ Hawaiian Airlines issued a public alert in 2010 to warn of a fraudulent e-mail being circulated. The e-mail is labeled "Your airplane ticket." It appeared as a notice of a new ticketing service and informed the recipient that a new account had been opened in their name and a complimentary discounted ticket had been charged to their credit card. The e-mail contained an attachment designed to look like an electronic ticket, but instead it was contaminated by a virus. The e-mail also contained references to log-in, password, and credit card information, which Hawaiian would never include in an e-mail to customers.

▶ In March 2011 Google's apps were attacked; Google pulled out dozens of apps from its Android marketplace. These were infected with malware capable of rooting devices and stealing data. The infected apps included: Spider Man, Super Sex Positions, Photo Editor, and other popular apps. Phone owners who have downloaded the apps should wipe and "reset" their phones to their original state. Luckily, Google was able to quickly contain the malware, even if it was in remote locations.

▶ When one of the authors advertised online that he had a house to rent, several "doctors" and "nurses" from the United Kingdom and South America applied.

They agreed to pay a premium for a short-term lease and said they would pay with a cashier's check. They asked if the author would accept checks for $6,000 to $10,000 and send them back the balance of $4,000 to $8,000. When advised that this would be fine, but that the difference would be returned only after their checks had cleared, none of the would-be renters followed up.

▶ People get e-mails reporting for money to help stranded friends (scammers find their names). Money usually is to be sent to a UK address.

▶ Extortion rings in the United Kingdom and Russia pried hundreds of thousands of dollars from online sports betting websites. Any site refusing to pay protection fees was threatened with zombie computers using DoS attacks.

▶ Fake escrow sites take advantage of the inherent trust of escrow sites, stealing buyers' deposits. Dozens of fake escrow sites on the Internet have convincing names like "Honest-Escrow.net" and use ads such as "Worried about getting scammed in an Internet auction? Just use an escrow service like us."

A typical e-mail that looks like an official Yahoo! Request is shown in the box below:

YAHOO ACCOUNT
VERIFICATION ALERT!!! (KMM69467VL55834KM)
Dear Valued Member,

Due to the congestion in all Yahoo Accounts, Yahoo would be shutting down all unused Accounts. You will have to confirm your E-mail by filling out your Login Information below after clicking the reply button, or your account will be suspected for security reasons . . .

Yahoo! ID Card

Name: . . . .
Yahoo! ID: . . . .
Yahoo! Mail Address: . . . .
Password: . . . .

Member Information
Gender: . . . .
Birth Date: . . . .
Occupation: . . . .
Country: . . . .

If you are a Yahoo! Account Premium subscriber, we will refund the unused portion of your Premium subscription, if any . . . The refund will appear as a credit via the billing method we have on file for you. So please make sure that your billing information is correct and up-to-date. For more information, please visit billing.yahoo.com.
After following the instruction on this sheet your account will not be interrupted and will continue as normal.
We appreciate your being a Yahoo! Account user.

Sincerely,

Yahoo! Customer Support

More examples of Internet fraud and typical scams are provided in Online File W9.3 and in voices.washingtonpost.com/securityfix/web_fraud_20.

Types of Scams. The following are some representative types of scams (per spam laws.com/scams.html): Literary scams, poetry scams, jury duty scams, chain letters and e-mail scams, lottery scams, Nigerian scams, work at home scams, credit card scams, IRS e-mail scams, Vector Marketing scams, PayPal scams, missing persons scams, envelope stuffing scams, work from home scams, and free vacation scams. Many more can be found at the website.

Identity Theft and Identify Fraud

identity theft

Fraud that involves stealing an identity of a person and then the use of that identity by someone pretending to be someone else in order to steal money or get other benefits.

Identity theft refers to stealing an identity of a person; that information is then used by someone pretending to be someone else in order to steal money or get other benefits. The term is relatively new and is actually a misnomer, since it is not inherently possible to steal an identity, only to use it. The person whose identity is used can suffer serious consequences when he or she is held responsible for the perpetrator's actions. In many countries, specific laws make it a crime to use another person's identity for personal gain. Identity theft is the number one concern of EC shoppers, according to the U.S. Federal Trade Commission (ftc.gov). According to 2010 statistics, identity fraud affects over 10 million Americans each year, for a loss of over $50 billion, growing about 20 percent annually.

Identity theft is somewhat different from *identity fraud*, which is related to the unlawful usage of a "false identity" to commit fraud. Identity fraud activities include:

▶ Financial identity theft (using another's identity to obtain goods and services)
▶ Business/commercial identity theft (using another's business name to obtain credit)
▶ Criminal identity theft (posing as another when apprehended for a crime)
▶ Money laundering

Example. No one is immune from identity theft, even the sheriff of Merced County, California. On March 11, 2009, while the sheriff's deputies were searching the home of a woman accused of forging checks, they discovered on her computer the copied signature of their boss. Investigators said the woman lifted the sheriff's signature from a standard check given to departing inmates to reimburse them for pocket money confiscated during booking. She had uploaded the signature to a check-writing program. She used the checks to pay for services she received.

For additional information, see en.wikipedia.org/wiki/Identity_theft.

CYBER BANK ROBBERIES

Cyberattacks can happen to individuals and organizations including banks.

Example. An international computer-crime ring that was broken up in October 2010 siphoned about $70 million from over 400 bank accounts of small businesses, municipalities, and churches. Authorities in the United States, United Kingdom, the Netherlands, and Ukraine have detained or charged more than 100 people. According to the FBI, the organization running the hacking ring included computer-code writers in Ukraine, and the mule-network operators ("mules" are those recruited to move stolen funds via bank accounts opened with fake names) spread out across the United States, United Kingdom, and Ukraine. Victims were mostly in the United States, though some bank accounts were also targeted in the United Kingdom, the Netherlands, and Mexico.

The thieves used iterations of Zeus (a Trojan horse, described earlier that has become the weapon of choice for most cyber bank robbers) to steal hundreds of thousands of dollars at a time—the result of focusing on business accounts instead of individual consumers. Investigators said the transactions attempted could have led to losses of up to $220 million. The thieves particularly focused on small and medium businesses because of their poorly protected systems, which are often found at smaller companies (see Wagley 2010).

In addition to stealing bank accounts, criminals steal checks as well.

Example. Secureworks.com uncovered the following check fraud operations (per Prince 2010): Russian cybercriminals used malware, money mules and sophisticated technical methods to get their hands on data from check image repositories run by services that archive checks on behalf of businesses. The cybercriminals used a network of 2,000 computers in a scam to steal check information. The scammers used the names and addresses of 2,884 job seekers who responded to recruit e-mails as well as account information and check templates of five companies. The attackers then downloaded images of the checks used by businesses along with bank routing numbers, account-holder names, and other information.

Next, the scammers used off-the-shelf commercial check printing software to print counterfeit checks, which were given to money mules to deposit in their personal banking accounts. The mules were also tasked with wiring the deposited money to bank accounts in St. Petersburg, Russia, where the money might have been transferred, then converted into cash. The "mules" initially thought they were signing up for legitimate jobs. People became suspicious when they got the second set of instructions that said, "now you are going to wire the money to St. Petersburg."

Other Financial Fraud

Stock market fraud is a common area where swindlers are active. Other areas include the sale of bogus investments, phantom business opportunities, and other "get rich quick" schemes. In addition, foreign-currency-trading scams are increasing on the Internet because most online currency exchange shops are not licensed. For many examples of financial fraud, see Symantec (2009).

SPAM AND SPYWARE ATTACKS

E-mail spam also known as *junk e-mail* or just *spam,* is a subset of spam that involves nearly identical messages sent to numerous recipients by e-mail. A common synonym for spam is *unsolicited bulk e-mail.* Over 90 percent of messages on corporate networks in April 2009 were e-mail spam. An estimated worldwide total of *62 trillion spam e-mails* were sent in 2008. Globally, annual spam energy use totals 33 billion kilowatt-hours (KWh). That's equivalent to the electricity used in *2.4 million homes in the United States,* with the same GHG emissions as 3.1 million passenger cars using 2 billion gallons of gasoline. (McMillan 2009a). E-mail spam has grown steadily since the early 1990s to several billion messages a day. Spam has frustrated, confused, and annoyed e-mail users. Laws against spam have been sporadically initiated. The total volume of spam (more than 120 billion e-mails per day as of March 2011) has leveled off slightly in recent years and is no longer growing exponentially. But the amount received by most e-mail users has decreased mostly because of better automatic filtering. Approximately 80 percent of all spam is sent by fewer than 200 spammers. Botnets, networks of virus-infected computers, are used to do it. Since the cost of the spam is borne mostly by the recipient, spam is effective e-mail advertising.

e-mail spam
A subset of spam that involves nearly identical messages sent to numerous recipients by e-mail.

E-mail addresses are collected from chat rooms, websites, newsgroups, and viruses that harvest users' address books. Much spam is sent to invalid e-mail addresses. ISPs have attempted to recover the cost of spam through lawsuits against spammers, although they have been mostly unsuccessful in collecting damages despite winning in court. An example of how spam is used for stock market fraud is provided in Case 9.1.

Typical Examples of Spamming

Symantec provides a monthly report, titled "The State of Spam: A Monthly Report." In the report, it provides examples of current popular scams, categories of spam, originating countries, volume, and much more.

Spyware

Spyware is computer software that is installed surreptitiously on a personal computer to intercept or take partial control over the user's interaction with the computer, without the user's knowledge or consent. Although the term *spyware* suggests software that secretly monitors the user's behavior (Chapter 8), the functions of spyware extend well beyond simple monitoring. Spyware programs can collect various types of personal information, such as Internet surfing habits and sites that have been visited, which violate your privacy,

spyware
Software that gathers user information over an Internet connection without the user's knowledge.

CASE 9.1
EC Application
INTERNET STOCK FRAUD AIDED BY SPAM

A study reported by Lerer (2007) concluded that stock spam moves markets. The researchers found that the average investor who buys a stock during a spam promotion and then sells after the campaign ends up losing about 5.5 percent of his or her investment. In contrast, the spammer who buys stock before the spam campaign and sells during the campaign makes a 5.79 percent return.

The federal government made headlines on March 8, 2007, by cracking down on dozens of penny stocks whose prices have been manipulated. The success of *Operation Spamalot*, conducted by the Securities and Exchange Commission (SEC), still will not end spam. There are two reasons spam won't go away: It works and it's profitable. Despite increased enforcement, warnings, and federal laws, spam is not only continuing but flourishing. And there's no reason to think the SEC will be able to do much to stop it.

Stock spam has gotten much worse in the last few years. Stock spam messages rose 120 percent during the 6-month period ending March 2007. In total, stock-related messages make up about 20 percent of all e-mail spam. The SEC estimates that 100 million stock spam messages are sent each week.

If you are not so lucky, you can end up in jail. Ralsky and Bradley sent billions of illegal e-mail advertisement to inflate the price of Chinese penny stocks and then reaped the profit. Both were sentenced, together with their accomplices, to several years in prison.

Secure Computing Research saw a 50 percent increase in spam. Spam now accounts for nearly 90 percent of all e-mail. The amount of image spam, which today accounts for 30 percent of all spam, tripled during the last two years.

Sources: Compiled from Lerer (2007) and Secure Computing (2011).

Questions

1. Why might people buy the penny stocks promoted in an e-mail message from an unknown source?

2. Use Google or Bing to find out what can be done to filter image spam.

---

but they can also interfere with user control of the computer in other ways, such as installing additional (even malicious) software and redirecting Web browser activity. Spyware is known to change computer settings, resulting in slow surfing speeds and/or loss of functionality of other programs. In an attempt to increase the understanding of spyware, a more formal classification includes software types that are captured under the term *privacy-invasive software*. Although spyware is used mainly by advertisers, it may also be used by criminals.

For more on spyware, see Chapter 14.

SOCIAL NETWORKING MAKES SOCIAL ENGINEERING EASY

Social engineering tactics have been diversified. In the past, social engineers used cleverly worded e-mails and face-to-face conversations to get information from their victims to launch attacks. But now, social networking sites that contain goldmines of information are major targets for new attack methods. Social engineering tactics or scams that depended on user interaction to execute an attack against them rose dramatically as of 2006. As more users take advantage of Web 2.0 applications like social networking sites, blogs, wikis, and RSS feeds, malware authors, identity thieves, and other criminals are going to exploit the weak points there. With the rise of Web 2.0 and more social interactions on social network sites, security experts warn of an increase in the incidence of hackers inserting malicious code into dynamically generated Web pages. The most popular sites such as Facebook and Twitter are attacked most frequently.

Social networking sites are creating a means for hackers and con artists to worm their way into the confidence of users, which leaves Internet users and businesses at a greater risk of attack, according to a study by Danish security firm CSIS.

The CSIS Example. Dennis Rand, a security researcher at CSIS, created a fictitious entry on the LinkedIn network before inviting random and unknown users to LinkedIn to join his private network. By posing as an ex-employee of "targeted" firms, he was able to prompt real workers from these firms into establishing connections. Within a few weeks, Rand created a network of 1,340 trusted connections. In a research paper, Rand explains how information gleaned through this network might be used to harvest e-mail addresses to send messages containing links to malicious codes that are more likely to be accepted because they come from a "trusted" source (Rand 2007).

How Hackers Are Attacking Social Networks

Hackers are manipulating the trusted nature of Facebook, MySpace, and other social networks to launch exploits and spread malware attacks. One reason is that social networks are designed to facilitate sharing of personal information, and the more data a person discloses, the more valuable he or she is to the site (see Chapter 7). Unfortunately, these sites have poor track records for security controls. They do not even encourage users to select strong passwords, and passwords on these sites never expire.

Here are some examples of security problems in social networking:

▶ Upon downloading an application, an unsuspecting user can inadvertently insert malicious code onto his or her profile page, computer, and potentially network of friends.

▶ Users received "buddy" requests from fake profiles. Traditional antispam solutions cannot differentiate between these requests and genuine ones; so bad guys can get specific, private information about users and potentially gather enough information to formulate a targeted attack.

▶ Big name social networking sites offer users attractive applications to enhance their profile pages. Often times these applications are built by third parties where the security is lax.

▶ One popular scammers' approach is to create a fake profile on a social networking site and use it to post malicious links and to phish other users.

▶ A scammer obtains your friends' user names and log-ins via password stealing or phishing. Then sends you a message on Facebook that your friends are stranded someplace and desperately need you to wire them money (to the scammer account, of course).

▶ Researchers at NetWitness uncovered a 75,000-strong botnet that infected companies around the world with the Zeus Trojan. Among its targets were Facebook, Yahoo!, and other sites. According to security pros, the botnet is part of a growing trend to use social networking sites as a stepping stone to steal valuable financial data.

▶ Messages left on Facebook users' walls (message area) urge them to view a superb video that portends to be hosted on Google's website. Clicking on the link leads users to a site that tries to entice them into downloading a program to watch the movie. The program is the Troj/Dloadr-BPL Trojan horse, which in turn downloads malicious code detected as Troj/Agent-HJX and displays an image of a court jester poking out his tongue.

Spam in Social Networks and in the Web 2.0 Environment

Social networks attracted spammers due to the large number of potential recipients and the less secured Internet platforms. Spammers like Facebook in particular despite the heavy fines imposed on them by the courts. Another area is blog spam.

Automated Blog Spam. Bloggers have found hundreds of automatically generated comments with links to herbal Viagra and gambling vendors on their pages. Software bots that trawl the Internet looking for suitable forms to fill in automatically generate the majority of blog spam. Blog owners can use tools to ensure that humans—and not an automated system—enter comments on their blogs.

Search Engine Spam and Splogs

Although content spam impacts media users, a greater concern to ethical e-commerce sites is **search engine spam**, which Yahoo! defines as "pages created deliberately to trick the search engine into offering inappropriate, redundant, or poor-quality search results." Those pages, called **spam sites**, use techniques that deliberately subvert a search engine's

search engine spam
Pages created deliberately to trick the search engine into offering inappropriate, redundant, or poor-quality search results.

spam site
Page that uses techniques that deliberately subvert a search engine's algorithms to artificially inflate the page's rankings.

splog

Short for *spam blog*. A site created solely for marketing purposes.

algorithms to artificially inflate the page's rankings. A similar tactic involves the use of splogs (short for *spam blog sites*), which are blogs created solely for marketing purposes. Spammers create hundreds of splogs that they link to the spammer's site to increase that site's search engine ranking. For information on search engine algorithms and page rankings, see google.com/corporate/tech.html.

Sploggers work on the principle that once Web surfers arrive at their site, a few will click on one of the linked advertisements. Each of these clicks earns a few cents for the splogger. And because any one splogger can run many millions of splogs, the spam can be very profitable.

Examples. Some examples of spam attacks in social networks are:

- In January 2009, Facebook won $1.3 billion from spammers in Canada who falsely obtained log-in information for Facebook users and then sent spam to those users' friends, violating the CAN-SPAM Act. In 2008, MySpace was awarded $230 million in a similar case (in both cases, the companies were unable to collect).

- In January 2009, Twitter became a hot target for hackers who hijacked the accounts of several high-profile users including that of President Obama (now users are protected).

- Instant messaging in social networks was found to be very vulnerable to hackers and other cybercriminals.

- Phishing for authentic social networking accounts lets spammers post comments on other members' pages and send messages from the phished accounts. These messages are often used to distribute spam. A link within a message could redirect the browser to a page that, say, purportedly hosts a video. The user is directed to install a new codec, but downloads malicious software.

- Hackers are posting content loaded with malicious software that is difficult to detect on YouTube, Facebook, MySpace, and other social network sites. Other methods are frequently invented.

- VoIP is used extensively in social networks, yet it is vulnerable to many attacks (products such as VoIPguard can help).

The discussion so far has concentrated on attacks. Defense mechanisms, including those related to spam and other unsolicited ads, are provided in Sections 9.6 through 9.10. First, let's examine what is involved in assuring information security.

Data Breach (Leak)

data breach

A security incident in which sensitive, protected, or confidential data is copied, transmitted, viewed, stolen, or used by an individual unauthorized to do so.

A data breach is a security incident in which sensitive, protected, or confidential data is copied, transmitted, viewed, stolen or used by an individual unauthorized to do so. Other terms for this phenomenon include *unintentional information disclosure, data leak,* or *data loss.* Incidents range from concerted attack by cybercriminals with the backing of national governments to careless disposal of used computer equipment or data storage media. Data breaches may involve financial information such as credit card or bank details, personal health information, personally identifiable information (PII), trade secrets of corporations, or intellectual property. According to en.wikipedia.org/wiki/Data_breach, a total of 227,052,199 individual records containing sensitive personal information were involved in security breaches in the United States between January 2005 and May 2008, excluding incidents where sensitive data was apparently not actually exposed. The number today is much higher. Data leaks received lots of publicity in 2010/2011 with the case of Wikipedia where one person used a USB to download extremely secret information. Furthermore, the leaked information was posted on the Internet.

Incidentally this is a good example of freedom of speech on the Internet versus national security (Chapter 14). For how to protect against data leaks, see Section 9.7.

Section 9.4 ▶ REVIEW QUESTIONS

1. Define phishing.
2. Describe the relationship of phishing to financial fraud.
3. Briefly describe some phishing tactics.
4. Describe spam and its methods.
5. Define splogs and explain how sploggers make money.
6. Why and how are social networks being attacked?

9.5 THE INFORMATION ASSURANCE MODEL AND DEFENSE STRATEGY

The *information assurance (IA) model* provides a framework for protection of information systems against unauthorized access to or modification of information that is stored, processed, or sent over a network. The importance of the IA model to EC is that it represents the processes for protecting information by insuring its *confidentiality, integrity,* and *availability.* This model is known as the CIA security triad. These elements are discussed next.

CONFIDENTIALITY, INTEGRITY, AND AVAILABILITY

The success and security of EC can be measured by these components: confidentiality, integrity, and availability of information at the business website.

1. **Confidentiality** is the assurance of data privacy. The data or transmitted message is encrypted so that it is readable only by the person for whom it is intended. Encryption strength can vary. Depending on the strength of the encryption method, intruders or eavesdroppers might not be able to break the encryption to read the data or text.

2. **Integrity** is the assurance that data are accurate or that a message has not been altered. It means that stored data has not been modified without authorization; a message that was sent is the same message that was received. The integrity function detects and prevents the unauthorized creation, modification, or deletion of data or messages.

3. **Availability** is the assurance that access to data, the website, or other EC service is timely, available, reliable, and restricted to authorized users.

Three concepts related to the IA model are *authentication, authorization,* and *nonrepudiation.*

AUTHENTICATION, AUTHORIZATION, AND NONREPUDIATION

All the CIA functions depend on authentication. *Authentication* requires evidence in the form of credentials, which can take a variety of forms, including something known (e.g., a password), something possessed (e.g., a smart card), or something unique (e.g., a signature or fingerprint). *Authorization* requires comparing information about the person or program with access control information associated with the resource being accessed. *Nonrepudiation* is the concept of ensuring that a party in a dispute cannot repudiate or refute the validity of a statement or contract. Although this concept can be applied to any transaction, by far the most common application is in verification and trust of signatures. One nonrepudiation method is the use of a *digital signature* (Section 9.6) that makes it difficult for people to dispute that they were involved in an exchange.

CIA security triad (CIA triad) Three security concepts important to information on the Internet: confidentiality, integrity, and availability.

confidentiality Assurance of data privacy and accuracy. Keeping private or sensitive information from being disclosed to unauthorized individuals, entities, or processes.

integrity Assurance that stored data has not been modified without authorization; a message that was sent is the same message as that which was received.

availability Assurance that access to data, the website, or other EC data service is timely, available, reliable, and restricted to authorized users.

New or improved methods to ensure the confidentiality of credit card numbers, integrity of entire messages, authentication of the buyer and seller, and nonrepudiation of transactions are being developed as older ones become ineffective.

E-COMMERCE SECURITY STRATEGY

An EC security strategy needs to address the IA model and its components. In Exhibit 9.7, an EC security framework is presented that defines the high-level categories of assurance and their controls. The major categories are regulatory, financial, marketing, and operations. Only the key areas are listed in the exhibit, but there is overlap in requirements in each category.

The Objective of Security Defense

The following are the major objectives of defense strategies:

1. **Prevention and deterrence.** Properly designed controls may prevent errors from occurring, deter criminals from attacking the system, and better yet, deny access to unauthorized people.

2. **Detection.** Like a fire, the earlier an attack is detected, the easier it is to combat, and the less damage is done. Detection can be performed in many cases by using special diagnostic software, at a minimal cost.

3. **Containment (contain the damage).** This objective is to minimize or limit losses once a malfunction has occurred. It is also called *damage control*. This can be accomplished, for example, by including a *fault-tolerant system* that permits operation in a degraded mode until full recovery is made. If a fault-tolerant system does not exist, a quick (and possibly expensive) recovery must take place. Users want their systems back in operation as fast as possible.

4. **Recovery.** A recovery plan explains how to fix a damaged EC system as quickly as possible. Replacing rather than repairing components is one route to fast recovery.

5. **Correction.** Correcting the causes of damaged systems can prevent the problem from occurring again.

6. **Awareness and compliance.** All organization members must be educated about the hazards and must comply with the security rules and regulations.

EXHIBIT 9.7   E-Commerce Security Strategy Framework

E-Commerce Security Strategy

Regulatory (External)	**Financial** (Internal)	**Marketing & Operations** (Internal)
Control: Database and network security	**Control:** Fraud; embezzlement, bad debt expense	**Control:** Website functions, customer transactions, electronic documents, intellectual property
Assurance metrics: Confidentiality, integrity, authorization	**Assurance metrics:** Authentication and integrity	**Assurance metrics:** Availability, nonrepudiation.
Protect against: Unauthorized access by hackers, former employees, malware, and crimeware Privacy violations	**Protect against:** Transactions using stolen identities, debit or credit cards, and checks. Unauthorized transactions and overrides Pretexting	**Protect against:** Phishing Spoofing Denial-of-service attacks Industrial espionage

Security Spending Versus Needs Gap

A major concern in information security management is how to match the security defense efforts (money, labor, time) against the major security threats. This is a difficult task since the EC threat landscape is constantly changing. For this reason, many companies cannot align their spending with the most dangerous threats.

Therefore in any defense strategy one should explore the following issues (examples are available in Chickowski 2008):

1. What are the greatest current data security issues?
2. What are the greatest risks of exposure?
3. Where do you spend the money? How is spending matched with risk exposure?
4. What are the benefits (including intangible) that you can get from money spent on security project tools?
5. What are the losses due to security incidents (in your organization and in general)?
6. What are the top security technologies that reduce security losses (e.g., firewall and antivirus are usually at the top)?
7. What will be the guidelines for the upcoming security budget?

In Sections 9.9 and 9.10 we discuss the implementation of this approach.

Assessing Security Needs

Another key item in security strategy is to find out what is missing from the current strategies and solutions. This is part of the risk assessment (Section 9.9). This can be done in different ways. Here are two representative suggestions:

▶ Conduct a vulnerability assessment of your EC systems. A **vulnerability assessment** is the process of identifying, quantifying, and prioritizing the vulnerabilities in a system. In EC we concentrate on the networks, database, fraud protection, etc. In general, the most critical information security vulnerabilities are those that can shut down the business. They could be network based, hardware based, or software based. Whatever the cause, the result is data or performance loss. The assessment will determine the need for the defense mechanisms described in Sections 9.6 through 9.8.

vulnerability assessment
The process of identifying, quantifying, and prioritizing the vulnerabilities in a system.

▶ Conduct penetration (pen) tests (possibly by ex-hackers). These are designed to simulate outside (external) attacks. This is called "black-box" testing. In contrast, software development companies conduct intensive "white-box" testing, which involves a careful inspection of the system—both hardware and software.

For more information, see Strom (2009).

Penetration Test

A **penetration test (pen test)** is a method of evaluating the security of a computer system or a network by simulating an attack from a malicious source (e.g., a cracker). The process involves an active analysis of the system for any potential vulnerabilities and attacks. This analysis is carried out from the position of a potential attacker, and can involve active exploitation of security vulnerabilities. Any security issues that are found will be presented to the system owner, together with an assessment of their impact and often with a proposal for mitigation including a technical solution. The intent of a penetration test is to determine feasibility of an attack and the amount of business impact of a successful exploit, if discovered. A pen test is a component of a full security audit. For details, see en.wikipedia.org/wiki/Penetration_test.

penetration test (pen test)
A method of evaluating the security of a computer system or a network by simulating an attack from a malicious source, (e.g., a cracker).

There are several methodologies to execute such assessment (some are proprietary to consultants). Also, there are many software tools for this purpose. Many universities, consultants, and vendors provide training and information on Internet and computer security.

EC Security and Life Cycle Management

EC security programs
All the policies, procedures, documents, standards, hardware, software, training, and personnel that work together to protect information, the ability to conduct business, and other assets.

computer security incident management
The monitoring and detection of security events on a computer or computer network, and the execution of proper responses to those events. The primary purpose of incident management is the development of a well understood and predictable response to damaging events and computer intrusions.

EC security management programs have a life cycle, and throughout that life cycle the EC security requirements must be continuously evaluated and adjusted. An EC security program is the set of controls over security processes to protect organizational assets.

Information Systems Security Life Cycle Management. Information systems security life cycle management refers to maintaining the security posture of an information system from its conception to design, implementation, release, and retirement through the integration of information. It includes sound information assurance practices. Several vendors provide the tools for each stage (e.g., see microsoft.com/security/sdl/adopt/tools.aspx).

Note that the life cycle process includes incident response plan and management. Computer security incident management involves the monitoring and detection of security events on a computer or computer network, and the execution of proper responses to those events. The primary purpose of incident management is the development of a well understood and predictable response to damaging events and computer intrusions. For details, see en.wikipedia.org/wiki/Computer_security_incident_management.

The major high-level stages in the life cycle of an EC security management program are shown in Exhibit 9.8.

THE DEFENSE SIDE OF EC SYSTEMS

We organize the defense into six categories:

1. **Defending access to computing systems, data flow, and EC transactions.** Here we present three topics: Access control (including biometrics), encryption of content, and public key infrastructure (PKI). These are presented in Section 9.6.

   This line of defense protects data, applications, and computing facilities within organizations. Intruders that circumvent access control will face encrypted material even if they pass a firewall.

2. **Defending EC networks.** Here we recognize first and foremost the protection provided by firewalls. The firewall isolates the corporate network and computing devices from the public networks, mostly the Internet. To make the Internet more secure we can use virtual private networks. On top of all these measures we can use intrusion detecting systems. When networks are protected, we can protect the incoming (usually not encrypted e-mail). Also, we protect against viruses and other malware that come over the networks. Note that these can be installed inside organizations, as well. These are discussed in Section 9.7.

3. **General, administrative, and application controls.** These are safeguards of a variety of types that are intended to protect computing assets by establishing guidelines, check procedures, etc. They are discussed in Section 9.8.

4. **Protection against social engineering and fraud.** Here we describe protection against spam, phishing, and spyware, all in Section 9.8. In Chapter 14 we also discuss the administrative and legal aspects of fraud protection.

5. **Disaster preparation, business continuity, and risk management.** These topics are managerial issues that are supported by software. Their essentials are described in Section 9.9.

6. **Implementing enterprisewide security programs.** Here we place all the items previously mentioned under the implementation umbrella in Section 9.10.

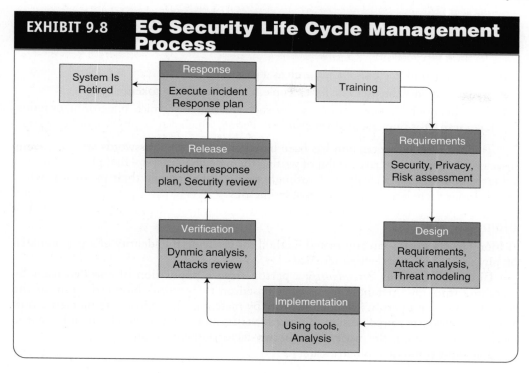

EXHIBIT 9.8   EC Security Life Cycle Management Process

Section 9.5 ▶ REVIEW QUESTIONS

1. What is information assurance? List its major components.
2. Define confidentiality, integrity, and availability.
3. Define authentication, authorization, and nonrepudiation.
4. List the six objectives of EC strategy.
5. Discuss the gap between security spending and a company's security needs gap.
6. Describe vulnerability assessment.
7. List the six categories of defense in EC systems.

9.6   THE DEFENSE I: ACCESS CONTROL, ENCRYPTION, AND PKI

In this section we describe three topics that deal with protection of EC information assets inside organizations, mostly the data computing facilities and documentation from outside and inside attacks.

ACCESS CONTROL

Network security depends on access control. **Access control** determines who (person, program, or machine) can legitimately use a network resource and which resources he, she, or it can use. A resource can be anything—Web pages, text files, databases, applications, servers, printers, or any other information source or network component. Typically, access control lists define which users have access to which resources and what rights they have with respect to those resources (i.e., read, view, write, print, copy, delete, execute, modify, or move).

access control
Mechanism that determines who can legitimately use a network resource.

Authorization and Authentication

Access control involves *authorization* (having the right to access) and *authentication*, which is also called *user identification* (proving that the user is who he or she claims to be).

   Authentication. After a user has been *identified*, the user must be *authenticated*. *Authentication* is the process of verifying that the user is who he or she claims to be (see VeriSign 2008). Verification usually is based on one or more characteristics that distinguish the individual from others.

Authentication methods include:

▶ Something only the user *knows*, such as a password.

▶ Something only the user *has*, for example, a smart card or a token.

▶ Something only the user *is*, or possesses, such as a signature, voice, fingerprint, or retinal (eye) scan. It is implemented via *biometric controls*, which can be physical or behavioral.

Traditionally, authentication has been based on passwords. Passwords are notoriously insecure because people have a habit of writing them down in easy-to-find places, choosing values that are guessed easily, and willingly telling other people their passwords when asked. Today there is an increased use of biometrics.

Biometric Systems

A **biometric control** is an automated method for verifying the identity of a person based on physical or behavioral characteristics.

Biometric systems can *identify* a person from a population of enrolled users by searching through a database for a *match* based on the person's biometric trait, or the system can *verify* a person's claimed identity by matching the individual's biometric trait against a previously stored version. Biometric verification is much simpler than biometric identification, and it is the process used in two-factor authentication.

The most common biometrics are:

▶ **Thumbprint or fingerprint.** Each time a user wants access, a thumb- or fingerprint (finger scan) is matched against a template containing the authorized person's fingerprint to identify him or her.

▶ **Retinal scan.** A match is attempted between the pattern of the blood vessels in the retina that is being scanned and a prestored picture of the retina.

▶ **Voice scan.** A match is attempted between the user's voice and the voice pattern stored on templates.

▶ **Signature.** Signatures are matched against the prestored authentic signature. This method can supplement a photo-card ID system.

Other biometrics are:

▶ Facial recognition
▶ Facial thermograph
▶ Hand geometry
▶ Hand veins
▶ Keystrokes
▶ DNA test
▶ Iris

For details, comparisons with regard to human characteristics, and cost–benefit analyses, see en.wikipedia.org/wiki/Biometrics.

To implement a biometric authentication system, the physiological or behavioral characteristics of a participant must be scanned repeatedly under different settings. The scans are then averaged to produce a biometric template, or identifier. The template is stored in a database as a series of numbers that can range from a few bytes for hand geometry to several thousand bytes for facial recognition. When a person uses a biometric system, a live scan is conducted, and the scan is converted to a series of numbers that is then compared against the template stored in the database.

biometric control
An automated method for verifying the identity of a person based on physical or behavioral characteristics.

biometric systems
Authentication systems that identify a person by measurement of a biological characteristic, such as fingerprints, iris (eye) patterns, facial features, or voice.

ENCRYPTION AND THE ONE-KEY (SYMMETRIC) SYSTEM

Encryption is the process of transforming or scrambling (encrypting) data in such a way that it is difficult, expensive, or time-consuming for an unauthorized person to unscramble (decrypt) it. All encryption methods have five basic parts (refer to Exhibit 9.9): *plaintext, ciphertext*, an *encryption algorithm*, the *key*, and *key space*. **Plaintext** is a human-readable text or message. **Ciphertext** is not human-readable because it has been encrypted. The **encryption algorithm** is the set of procedures or mathematical functions used to encrypt or decrypt a message. Typically, the algorithm is not the secret piece of the encryption process. The **key (key value)** is the secret value used with the algorithm to transform the message. The **key space** is the large number of possible key values (keys) created by the algorithm to use when transforming messages. Both encryption and trying to break the encryption codes are done today by powerful computers. However, the trick is to decide what data to encrypt, how to best manage encryption, and how to make the process as transparent as possible.

The major benefits of encryption are:

▶ Allows users to carry data on their laptops, PDAs, and flash drives.
▶ Protects backup media while they are offsite.
▶ Allows for highly secure virtual private networks.
▶ Enforces policies regarding who handles what corporate data.
▶ Ensures compliance with privacy laws and regulations, and reduces the risk of lawsuits.
▶ Protects the organization's reputation and secrets.

Encryption is the foundation for two major security systems: the *symmetric system*, with one secret key, and the *asymmetric system*, with two keys. The second method is the basis for the PKI system (described in the next section).

Symmetric (Private) Key Encryption

In a **symmetric (private) key encryption**, the same key is used to encrypt and decrypt the plaintext (see Exhibit 9.10). The sender and receiver of the text must share the same key without revealing it to anyone else—making it a so-called *private* system.

encryption
The process of scrambling (encrypting) a message in such a way that it is difficult, expensive, or time-consuming for an unauthorized person to unscramble (decrypt) it.

plaintext
An unencrypted message in human-readable form.

ciphertext
A plaintext message after it has been encrypted into a machine-readable form.

encryption algorithm
The mathematical formula used to encrypt the plaintext into the ciphertext, and vice versa.

key (key value)
The secret code used to encrypt and decrypt a message.

key space
The large number of possible key values (keys) created by the algorithm to use when transforming the message.

EXHIBIT 9.9   Encryption Components

Component	Description	Example or Description
Plaintext	The original message or document is created by the user, which is in human-readable form.	Credit card number 5342 8765 3652 9982
Encryption algorithm	The set of procedures or mathematical functions to encrypt or decrypt a message. Typically, the algorithm is not the secrete piece of the encryption process.	Add a number (the key) to each number in the card. If the resulting number is greater than 9, wrap around the number to the beginning (i.e., modulus arithmetic). For example, add 4 to each number so that 1 becomes 5, 9 becomes 3, etc.
Key or key value	The secret value used with the algorithm to transform the message.	The key dictates what parts (functions) of the algorithm will be used, in what order, and with what values.
Key space	The large number of possible key values (keys) created by the algorithm to use when transforming the message.	The larger the key space, the greater the number of possibilities for the key, which makes it harder for an attacker to discover the correct key.
Ciphertext	Message or document that has been encrypted into unreadable form.	The original 5342 8765 3652 9982 becomes 9786 2109 7096 3326.

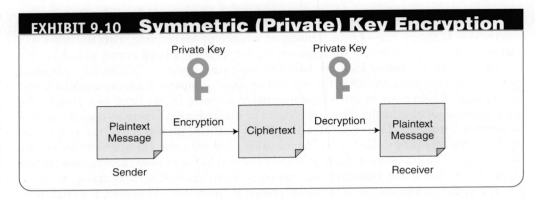

EXHIBIT 9.10   Symmetric (Private) Key Encryption

symmetric (private) key encryption
An encryption system that uses the same key to encrypt and decrypt the message.

Data Encryption Standard (DES)
The standard symmetric encryption algorithm supported by the NIST and used by U.S. government agencies until October 2000.

public key infrastructure (PKI)
A scheme for securing e-payments using public key encryption and various technical components.

public (asymmetric) key encryption
Method of encryption that uses a pair of matched keys—a public key to encrypt a message and a private key to decrypt it, or vice versa.

public key
Encryption code that is publicly available to anyone.

private key
Encryption code that is known only to its owner.

The Data Encryption Standard (DES) was at one time the standard symmetric encryption algorithm supported by U.S. government agencies. However, DES became too susceptible to attacks. In 2000, the National Institute of Standards and Technology (NIST) replaced DES with *Rijndael*, the new advanced encryption standard for encrypting sensitive but unclassified government data. Because the algorithms used to encrypt a message are well known, the confidentiality of a message depends on the key. It is possible to guess a key simply by having a computer try all the encryption combinations until the message is decrypted. High-speed and parallel processing computers can try millions of guesses in one second. This is why the length of the key (in bits) is the main factor in securing a message. If a key were 4 bits long (e.g., 1011), there would be only 16 possible combinations (i.e., 2 raised to the fourth power). However, a 64-bit encryption key would take 58.5 years to be broken using parallel processing (at 10 million keys per second). There are 2 raised to the 64th power possible combinations!

PUBLIC KEY INFRASTRUCTURE (PKI)

Public key infrastructure (PKI) is a scheme for securing e-payments using public key encryption and various technical components. It overcomes some of the shortcomings of the one-key system. The symmetric one-key encryption requires the movement of a key from the writer of a message to its recipient. Imagine trying to use one-key encryption to buy something offered on a particular Web server. If the seller's key was distributed to thousands of buyers, then the key would not remain secret for long. If the transfer of the key is intercepted, the key may be stolen or changed. The PKI solution uses two keys, public and private, and additional features that create a powerful system, which is very secure. In addition to the keys, PKI includes *digital signatures*, hash digests (function), and digital certificates. Let's see how PKI works.

Public (Asymmetric) Key Encryption

Public (asymmetric) key encryption uses a pair of matched keys—a public key that is publicly available to anyone and a private key that is known only to its owner. If a message is encrypted with a public key, then the associated private key is required to decrypt the message. If, for example, a person wanted to send a purchase order to a company and have the contents remain private, he or she would encrypt the message with the company's public key. When the company received the order, it would decrypt it with the associated private key, being the *only one able* to read the purchase order.

A most common public key encryption algorithm is RSA (rsa.com). RSA uses keys ranging in length from 512 bits to 1,024 bits. The main problem with such public key encryption is speed. Symmetrical algorithms are significantly faster than asymmetrical key algorithms. Therefore, public key encryption cannot be used effectively to encrypt and decrypt large amounts of data. In practice, a combination of symmetric and asymmetric encryption is used to encrypt messages. Public key encryption is supplemented by digital signature and certificate authority.

EXHIBIT 9.11 Digital Signatures

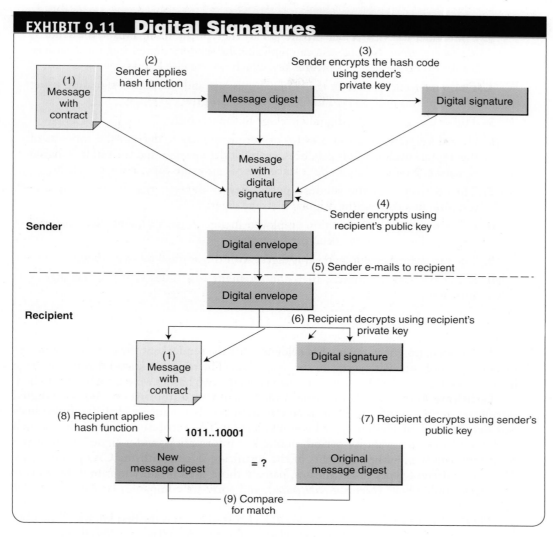

The PKI Process: Digital Signatures and Certificate Authorities

Digital signatures are the electronic equivalent of personal signatures that cannot be forged. Digital signatures are based on public keys for authenticating the identity of the sender of a message or document. They also can ensure that the original content of an electronic message or document is unchanged. Digital signatures have additional benefits in the online world. They are portable, cannot be easily repudiated or imitated, and can be time-stamped. According to the U.S. Federal Electronic Signatures in Global and National Commerce Act of 2000, digital signatures in the United States have the same legal standing as a signature written in ink on paper.

Exhibit 9.11 illustrates how the PKI process works. Suppose a person wants to send a draft of a financial contract to a company with whom he or she plans to do business as an e-mail message. The sender wants to assure the company that the content of the draft has not been changed en route and that he or she really is the sender. To do so, the sender takes the following steps:

1. The sender creates the e-mail message with the contract in it.
2. Using special software, a secured mathematical algorithm called a **hash function** is applied to the message, which results in a special summary of the message, converted into a string of digits that is called a **message digest (MD)**.

digital signature
Validates the sender and time stamp of a transaction so it cannot be later claimed that the transaction was unauthorized or invalid.

hash function
A mathematical computation that is applied to a message, using a private key, to encrypt the message.

message digest (MD)
A summary of a message converted into a string of digits after the hash has been applied.

3. The sender uses his or her private key to encrypt the hash. This is the sender's *digital signature.* No one else can replicate the sender's digital signature because it is based on the sender's private key, which no one else knows.

4. The sender encrypts both the original message and the digital signature using the recipient's public key. This couple forms a digital envelope.

5. The sender e-mails the digital envelope to the receiver.

6. Upon receipt, the receiver uses his or her private key to decrypt the contents of the digital envelope. This produces a copy of the message and the sender's digital signature. No one else can do it since there is only one copy of the private key.

7. The receiver uses the sender's public key to decrypt the digital signature, resulting in a copy of the original message digest.

8. Using the same hash function employed in step 2, the recipient then creates a message digest from the decrypted message.

9. The recipient then compares this digest with the original message digest.

10. If the two digests match, then the recipient concludes that the message is authentic.

digital envelope
The combination of the encrypted original message and the digital signature, using the recipient's public key.

In this scenario, the company has evidence that the sender sent the e-mail because the sender is the only one with access to the private key. The recipient knows that the message has not been tampered with because if it had been, the two hashes would not have matched.

Certificate Authority. Third parties called certificate authorities (CAs) issue digital certificates or SSL certificates. This is an electronic file that uniquely identifies individuals and websites and enables encrypted communication. The certificate contains things such as the holder's name, validity period, public key information, and a signed hash of the certificate data (i.e., hashed contents of the certificate signed with the CA's private key). There are different types of certificates, namely those used to authenticate websites (*site certificates*), individuals (*personal certificates*), and software companies (*software publisher certificates*).

certificate authorities (CAs)
Third parties that issue digital certificates.

There are several third-party CAs. VeriSign (verisign.com) is the best known of the CAs (see VeriSign 2008). VeriSign issues three classes of certificates: Class 1 verifies that an e-mail actually comes from the user's address. Class 2 checks the user's identity against a commercial credit database. Class 3 requires notarized documents. Companies such as Microsoft offer systems that enable companies to issue their own private, in-house certificates.

Secure Socket Layer (SSL)

PKI systems are further secured with SSL—the protocol for e-commerce. If the average user had to figure out how to use encryption, digital certificates, digital signatures, and the like, there would be few secure transactions on the Web. It is clever but difficult. Fortunately, Web browsers and Web servers handle many of these activities in a transparent fashion. Given that different companies, financial institutions, and governments in many countries are involved in e-commerce, it is necessary to have generally accepted protocols for securing e-commerce. One of the major protocols in use today is Secure Socket Layer (SSL), now renamed as Transport Layer Security (TLS). For further details, see en.wikipedia.org/wiki/Transport_Layer_Security.

In the next section, the focus is on the company's digital perimeter—the network.

Section 9.6 ▶ REVIEW QUESTIONS

1. Define access control.
2. What are the basic elements of an authentication system?
3. Define biometric systems and list five of their methods.
4. Define a symmetric (one-key) encryption.

5. List some of the disadvantages of the symmetric system.

6. What are the key elements of PKI?

7. Describe the PKI process.

8. What role does a certificate authority play?

9.7 THE DEFENSE II: SECURING E-COMMERCE NETWORKS

Several technologies exist that ensure that an organization's network boundaries are secure from cyber attack or intrusion and that if the organization's boundaries are compromised, the intrusion is detected quickly and combated. A slew of cyber attack techniques can arrive on the network, most known are viruses and other malware, DoS, botnet attacks, and more. The selection and operation of defense mechanisms against these attack technologies should be based on certain design concepts, as described at perimeterusa.com/solution.html. The major components for protecting internal information resources inside organizations from outside attackers are described next.

FIREWALLS

Firewalls are barriers between an internal trusted network, or a PC, and the untrustworthy Internet. Technically, it is a network node consisting of both hardware and software that isolates a private network from a public network. On the Internet, the data and requests sent from one computer to another are broken into segments called packets. Each packet contains the Internet address of the computer sending the data, as well as the Internet address of the computer receiving the data. Packets also contain other identifying information that can distinguish one packet from another. A firewall examines all data packets that pass through it and then takes appropriate action—to allow or not to allow. Firewalls can be designed mainly to protect against remote log-in, access via backdoors, spam, and different types of malware (e.g., viruses or macros). Firewalls can come in several shapes and forms and there can be a single one or several. For details, see Online File W9.4. A popular defense system is the one that includes two firewalls. It is known as the DMZ architecture.

firewall
A single point between two or more networks where all traffic must pass (choke point); the device authenticates, controls, and logs all traffic.

packet
Segment of data sent from one computer to another on a network.

The Dual Firewall Architecture: The DMZ

In the simple one firewall case, there is a firewall between the Internet and the internal users (usually sitting on the corporate intranet). In the DMZ architecture (DMZ stands for demilitarized zone), there are two firewalls between the Internet and the internal users. The area between the two firewalls is referred to as the DMZ and it is dedicated as the one for business partners. The architecture is shown in Exhibit 9.12

In this architecture, there are two firewalls: one between the Internet and the DMZ (border firewall) and another internal firewall between the DMZ and the internal network. All public servers are placed in the DMZ. With this setup, it is possible to have firewall rules that allow trusted partners access to the public servers but the interior firewall can restrict all incoming connections. By having the DMZ, the public servers are still provided more protection than if they were just placed outside a single firewall site.

Using internal firewalls at various intranet boundaries can also help limit damage from *internal threats* and things like worms that have managed to traverse the border firewalls.

Personal Firewalls

The number of users with high-speed broadband (cable modem or digital subscriber lines [DSL]) has increased the number of Internet connections to homes or small businesses. These "always-on" connections are much more vulnerable to attack than simple dial-up connections. With these connections, the home owner or small business owner runs the risk of information being stolen or destroyed, of sensitive information (e.g., personal or business financial information) being stolen, and of the computer being used in a DoS attack against others.

Personal firewalls protect desktop systems by monitoring all the traffic that passes through the computer's network interface card. They operate in one of two ways. With the

personal firewall
A network node designed to protect an individual user's desktop system from the public network by monitoring all the traffic that passes through the computer's network interface card.

EXHIBIT 9.12   The Two Firewalls: DMZ Architecture

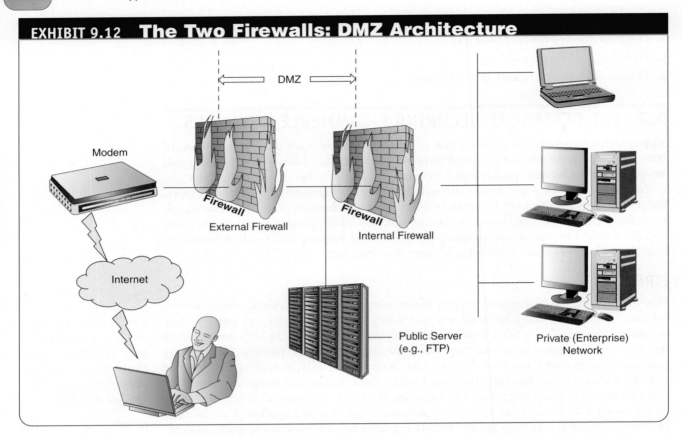

first method, the owner can create filtering rules (much like packet filtering) that the firewall uses to permit or delete packets. With the second method, the firewall can learn, by asking the user questions, how it should handle particular traffic. For a detailed comparison of several of these products, see firewallguide.com/software.htm.

Additional Virus, Malware, and Botnet Protection

Firewalls can protect against some but not all viruses. Your Windows operating system includes a firewall, but it may not be updated for all new viruses—the same goes for applications such as Microsoft Office. Thus, it is a good idea to subscribe to antivirus software such as from McAfee, Norton, or Windows Live One Care. Be very careful when you select antivirus software; some of them include malware. Using industry standard software is safe. For details about viruses including how to remove them, see microsoft.com/protect/computer/basics/virus.mspx, and microsoft.com/protect/computer/viruses/remove.mspx. All major vendors offer many products that can protect against different types of malware.

VIRTUAL PRIVATE NETWORKS (VPNS)

Suppose a company wants to establish a B2B application, providing suppliers, partners, and others access not only to data residing on its internal website, but also to data contained in other files (e.g., Word documents) or in legacy systems (e.g., large relational databases). Traditionally, communications with the company would have taken place over a private leased line or through a dial-up line to a bank of modems or a remote access server (RAS) that provided direct connections to the company's LAN. With a private line, (value-added line, VAL) the chances of a hacker eavesdropping on the communications between the companies would be minimal, but it is an expensive way to do business. A VPN allows a computer user to access a network via an IP address other than the one that actually connects the computer to the Internet. This is a less expensive solution. For details, see en.wikipedia.org/wiki/Virtual_private_network.

A **virtual private network (VPN)** uses the public Internet to carry information but remains private by using a combination of encryption to scramble the communications and authentication to ensure that the information has not been tampered with and comes from a legitimate source. A VPN verifies the identity of anyone using the network. In addition, a VPN can also support site-to-site communications between branch offices and corporate headquarters and the communications between mobile workers and their workplace.

VPNs can reduce communication costs dramatically. The costs are lower because VPN equipment is cheaper than other remote solutions; private leased lines are not needed to support remote access; remote users can use broadband connections rather than make long-distance calls to access an organization's private network; and a single access line can be used to support multiple purposes.

The main technical challenge of a VPN is to ensure the confidentiality and integrity of the data transmitted over the Internet. This is where protocol tunneling comes into play. With **protocol tunneling**, data packets are first encrypted and then encapsulated into packets that can be transmitted across the Internet. A special host or router decrypts the packets at the destination address. Cisco provides several types of VPNs including for wireless networks and smartphones. For details, see en.wikipedia.org/wiki/Virtual_private_network.

INTRUSION DETECTION SYSTEMS (IDS)

Even if an organization has a well-formulated security policy and a number of security technologies in place, it still is vulnerable to some attacks. For example, most organizations have antivirus software, yet most are subjected to virus attacks as was shown in the opening case. This is why an organization must continually watch for attempted, as well as actual, security breaches. This can be done by using intrusion detectors.

An **intrusion detection system (IDS)** is software and/or hardware designed to detect illegal attempts to access, manipulate, and/or disable computer systems through a network. An IDS is used to detect several types of malicious behaviors that can compromise the security and trust of a computer system. This includes network attacks against vulnerable services, data-driven attacks on applications, host-based attacks such as privilege escalation, unauthorized log-ins, access to sensitive files, and malware (viruses, Trojan horses, and worms).

The IDS checks files on a regular basis to see if the current signatures match the previous signatures. If the signatures do not match, security personnel are notified immediately. Some examples of commercial host-based systems are Symantec's Intruder Alert (symantec.com), Tripwire Security's Tripwire (tripwire.com), and McAfee's Entercept Desktop and Server Agents (mcafee.com).

Dealing with DoS attacks

As seen in the opening case it usually takes time to deal with a DoS attack. Early intrusion detecting can help. Since there are several types of DoS attacks (e.g., DDoS), there are several defense methods. For examples, see fxtechsupport.forumotion.com/t27-how-to-prevent-dos-ddos-attacks, and learn-networking.com/network-security/how-to-prevent-denial-of-service-attacks.

Cloud Computing Prevents DoS Attacks. In 2011, cyber attacks have demonstrated that cloud computing (Online Tutorial T7) can handle distributed denial-of-service (DDoS) attacks that crash traditional servers—for instance, when WikiLeaks briefly hosted its latest disclosure on Amazon Web Services (AWS). The three main ingredients in cloud computing that make it more resilient against cyber attacks are elasticity, bandwidth, and redundancy. While there is evidence that cloud computing can prevent DoS attacks, there were cases in 2010 and 2011 where DoS attacks occurred.

HONEYNETS AND HONEYPOTS

Honeynets are another technology that can detect and analyze intrusions. A **honeynet** is a network of honeypots designed to attract hackers like honey attracts bees. In this case, the **honeypots** are information system resources—firewalls, routers, Web servers, database

---

virtual private network (VPN)
A network that uses the public Internet to carry information but remains private by using encryption to scramble the communications, authentication to ensure that information has not been tampered with, and access control to verify the identity of anyone using the network.

protocol tunneling
Method used to ensure confidentiality and integrity of data transmitted over the Internet by encrypting data packets, sending them in packets across the Internet, and decrypting them at the destination address.

intrusion detection system (IDS)
A special category of software that can monitor activity across a network or on a host computer, watch for suspicious activity, and take automated action based on what it sees.

honeynet
A network of honeypots.

honeypot
Production system (e.g., firewalls, routers, Web servers, database servers) that looks like it does real work, but that acts as a decoy and is watched to study how network intrusions occur.

servers, files, and the like—that look like production systems but they do not do real work. The main difference between a honeypot and the real thing is that the activities in a honeypot come from intruders attempting to compromise the system. In this way, security experts watching the honeynet can gather information about why hackers attack, when they attack, how they attack, what they do after the system is compromised, and how they communicate with one another during and after the attack.

The Honeynet Project is a worldwide, not-for-profit research group of security professionals (see honeynet.org). The group focuses on raising awareness of security risks that confront any system connected to the Internet and teaching and informing the security community about better ways to secure and defend network resources. The project runs its own honeynets. They simply connect the honeypots to the Internet and wait for attacks to occur. They can advise companies about how to set up honeynets.

Before a company deploys a honeynet, it needs to think about what it will do when it becomes the scene of a cybercrime or contains evidence of a crime and about the legal restrictions and ramifications of monitoring legal and illegal activity. Online File W9.5 discusses these issues. A similar technique is the *penetration test* discussed earlier.

E-Mail Security

E-mail brings many of the security problems we have discussed. To begin with, we get viruses from e-mail attachments (we can get them of course from software downloads). Spam arrives via e-mail and so do social engineering attacks. Unfortunately firewalls may not be so effective in protecting e-mail, and therefore one should use antivirus as well as antispam software (available from dozens of vendors). E-mail encryption is advisable and it also available from many vendors. Finally, a technique called *outbound filtering* may be used. A brief description of each of these methods follows:

▶ **Antivirus and antispam.** Detect and quarantine messages that contain viruses, worms, spam, phishing attacks, or other unwanted content.

▶ **E-mail encryption.** Scrambles sensitive data in messages and attachments so they can be read only by intended recipients.

▶ **Outbound filtering.** Scan for unauthorized content, such as a customer's Social Security number, included in outgoing e-mail or other communications.

Note that e-mail is related to IM and chats that can be subject to attacks as well. For Google's e-mail security, see google.com.postini. Companies can beef up e-mail security by adding additional layers of defense, use only authorize e-mail servers, scan e-mail logs, and most of all educate people about e-mail dangers. For defense suggestions, see gfi.com/emailsecuritytest/ and Wiens (2010). For other guidelines, visit messagelab.com.

Cloud Computing May Help. As of 2008 there has been an increased interest in using cloud computing to improve e-mail security. Furthermore, this can be done by cutting costs 50 to 80 percent (per Habal 2010). There is growing support for moving e-mail to the cloud environment as well as moving e-mail archiving to the cloud. Despite the benefits, the adoption of cloud-based e-mail security solutions is still a very gradual process for most companies. It can be hard to cut through the marketing hype when nearly every vendor seems to be making a cloud claim. To help companies deciding on cloud-based e-mail security adoption and vendor selection, Habal (2010) provides some key questions enterprise EC buyers should ask when evaluating cloud-based e-mail security services.

Section 9.7 ▶ REVIEW QUESTIONS

1. List the basic types of firewalls and briefly describe each.
2. What is a personal firewall? What is DMZ architecture?
3. How does a VPN work; what are its benefits to users?
4. Briefly describe the major types of IDSs.
5. What is a honeynet? What is a honeypot?
6. Describe e-mail security.
7. How can cloud computing help?

EXHIBIT 9.13   Major Defense Controls

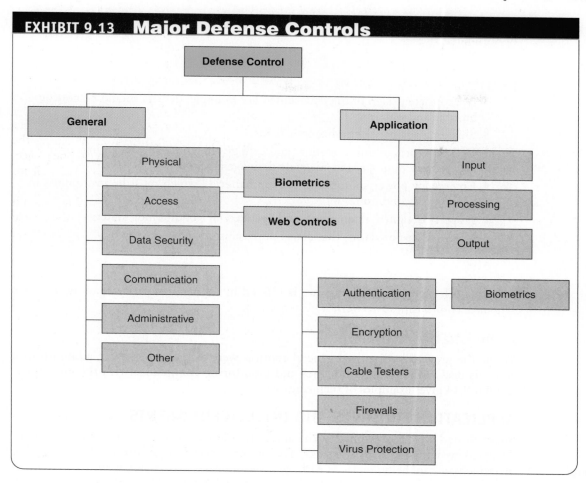

9.8   THE DEFENSE III: GENERAL CONTROLS, INTERNAL CONTROLS, COMPLIANCE, AND OTHER DEFENSE MECHANISMS

The objective of IT security management practices is to defend all the components of an information system, specifically data, software applications, hardware, and networks. A defense strategy requires several controls, as shown in Exhibit 9.13. General controls are established to protect the system regardless of the specific application. For example, protecting hardware and controlling access to the data center are independent of the specific application. Application controls are safeguards that are intended to protect specific applications. In this and the following sections, we discuss the major types of these two groups of information systems controls. Later in the section we cover spam and fraud mitigation.

GENERAL, ADMINISTRATIVE, AND OTHER CONTROLS

The major categories of general controls are physical controls, administrative controls, and other controls. A brief description of general controls is provided next

Physical Controls

Physical security refers to the protection of computer facilities and resources. This includes protecting physical property such as computers, data centers, software, manuals, and networks. It provides protection against most natural hazards as well as against some

general controls
Controls established to protect the system regardless of the specific application. For example, protecting hardware and controlling access to the data center are independent of the specific application.

application controls
Controls that are intended to protect specific applications.

human hazards. Appropriate physical security may include several controls, such as the following:

> ▶ Appropriate design of the data center. For example, the site should be noncombustible and waterproof.
> ▶ Shielding against electromagnetic fields.
> ▶ Good fire prevention, detection, and extinguishing systems, including sprinkler system, water pumps, and adequate drainage facilities.
> ▶ Emergency power shutoff and backup batteries, which must be maintained in operational condition.
> ▶ Properly designed, maintained, and operated air-conditioning systems.
> ▶ Motion detector alarms that detect physical intrusion.

Network access control software is offered by all major security vendors (e.g., see symantec.com/business/network-access-control).

Administrative Controls

While the previously discussed general controls were technical in nature, administrative controls deal with issuing guidelines and monitoring compliance with the guidelines. Exhibit 9.14 gives examples of such controls.

APPLICATION CONTROLS AND INTELLIGENT AGENTS

intelligent agents
Software applications that have some degree of reactivity, autonomy, and adaptability—as is needed in unpredictable attack situations. An agent is able to adapt itself based on changes occurring in its environment.

Sophisticated attacks are aimed at the application level, and many applications were not designed to withstand such attacks. For better survivability, information processing methodologies are being replaced with agent technology. **Intelligent agents**, also referred to as *softbots* or *knowbots*, are highly intelligent applications. The term *intelligent agents* generally means applications that have some degree of reactivity, autonomy, and adaptability—as it is used in unpredictable attack situations. An agent is able to adapt itself based on changes occurring in its environment, as shown in Exhibit 9.15.

PROTECTING AGAINST SPAM

Sending spam that disguises a sales pitch to look like a personal e-mail to bypass filters violates the U.S. Controlling the Assault of Non-Solicited Pornography and Marketing (CAN-SPAM) Act of 2003. However, many spammers hide their identity to escape detection by

EXHIBIT 9.14 Representative Administrative Controls

- Appropriately selecting, training, and supervising employees, especially in accounting and information systems
- Fostering company loyalty
- Immediately revoking access privileges of dismissed, resigned, or transferred employees
- Requiring periodic modification of access controls (such as passwords)
- Developing programming and documentation standards (to make auditing easier and to use the standards as guides for employees)
- Insisting on security bonds or malfeasance insurance for key employees
- Instituting separation of duties, namely, dividing sensitive computer duties among as many employees as economically feasible in order to decrease the chance of intentional or unintentional damage
- Holding periodic random audits of the system

EXHIBIT 9.15 Intelligent Agents

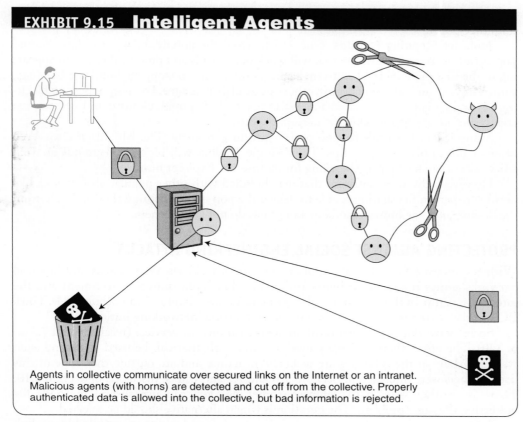

Agents in collective communicate over secured links on the Internet or an intranet. Malicious agents (with horns) are detected and cut off from the collective. Properly authenticated data is allowed into the collective, but bad information is rejected.

Source: Courtesy of Sandia Labs.

using hijacked PCs, or spam zombies, to send spam. For protecting your system against botnet attacks, which also spread a huge volume of spam, see MessageLabs (2009).

The **Controlling the Assault of Non-Solicited Pornography and Marketing Act (CAN-SPAM Act)** makes it a crime to send commercial e-mail messages with false or misleading message headers or misleading subject lines. The following are other provisions of the law:

▶ Requires marketers to identify their physical location by including their postal address in the text of the e-mail messages.

▶ Requires an opt-out link in each message, which must also give recipients the option of telling senders to stop all segments of their marketing campaigns.

▶ Allows for suits to be brought by ISPs, state attorneys general, and the federal government.

▶ Carries penalties of up to $250 per spammed e-mail message, with a cap of $2 million, which can be tripled for aggravated violations. There is no cap on penalties for e-mail sent with false or deceptive headers.

▶ Carries other penalties—those found guilty of violating the law may face up to 5 years in prison.

For more details, see spamlaws.com/federal/can-spam.shtml.

To protect users of e-mail, most e-mail providers introduce fairly successful filters that direct spam e-mails to junk folders. However, several spam e-mails still get into your in-box and several nonspam e-mails may end up in the junk folder. For more on protection against spam and spam blogs, see Online File W9.6. Spam is closely related to pop-up ads.

Controlling the Assault of Non-Solicited Pornography and Marketing (CAN-SPAM) Act
Law that makes it a crime to send commercial e-mail messages with false or misleading message headers or misleading subject lines.

PROTECTING AGAINST POP-UP ADS

As discussed in Chapter 4, the use of pop-ups and similar advertising programs is exploding. Sometimes it is even difficult to close these ads when they appear on the screen. Some of these ads may be part of a consumer's permission marketing agreement, but most are unsolicited. What can a user do about unsolicited pop-up ads? The following tools help minimize pop-ups.

Tools for Stopping Pop-Ups. One way to avoid the potential danger lurking behind pop-up ads is to install software that will block pop-up ads and prevent them from appearing in the first place. Several software packages offer pop-up stoppers. Some are free (e.g., panicware.com and adscleaner.com); others are available for a fee. For a list of pop-up blocking software, visit snapfiles.com/Freeware/misctools/fwpopblock.html and netsecurity. about.com/od/popupadblocking/a/aafreepopup.htm.

Many ISPs offer tools to stop pop-ups from appearing. The Mozilla Firefox Web browser does not allow pop-ups. The Google Toolbar will block pop-up ads as well. Microsoft offers free pop-up blocking for its Internet Explorer browser.

However, adware or software that gets bundled with other popular applications like person-to-person file sharing is able to deliver the pop-up ads because they originate from the desktop, not the browser, and blocking tools do not govern them.

PROTECTING AGAINST SOCIAL ENGINEERING ATTACKS

With the increased number of social engineering attacks via Web attacks and in social networks comes the need for better protection. The open source environment and the interactive nature of the technology also create risks (see Chapter 7 and Section 9.4). Thus, EC security becomes a necessity for any successful social networking initiative.

Social networking spans many different applications and services (recall Exhibit 7.3 on p. 340). Therefore, there are many methods and tools that can be used to defend such systems. Many of the solutions are technical in nature and are outside the scope of this book. Others were discussed in Sections 7.6 and 7.7 and will be discussed in Section 9.10. There is another issue with defense—sometimes you can use several methods for protecting the same problem. The question is which alternative should be selected.

Example. An impostor became a user's Facebook friend and then e-mailed him a link to a malware site. Security approaches that could be involved in countering this include: e-mail filtering, Web filtering, and desktop antimalware. DLP (data loss prevention) and network monitoring can also play a role. For further discussion, see Sarrel (2010) and Greengard (2010).

Protecting Against Phishing

Because there are many phishing attack methods, there are many defense methods as well. Illustrative examples are provided by Symantec (2009), ftc.gov, and en.wikipedia.org/wiki/Phishing. For analytical fraud protection, see sas.com/solutions/fraud/index.html and also IBM's ZTIC.

Protecting Against Malvertising

Microsoft combats malvertising by filing civil lawsuits against companies who allegedly create these fake ads. For more information about lawsuits, see stopmalvertising. com/news/microsoft-going-after-malvertising-threats.html and digwin.com/microsoft-advertising-and-internet-safety-enforcement-team-to-fight-malvertisers.

To help protect yourself against malvertising or scareware, you can:

▶ Install a firewall and keep it turned on.
▶ Use *automatic updating* to keep your operating system and software up to date.
▶ Install antivirus and antispyware software such as *Microsoft Security Essentials* and keep it updated.
▶ If your antivirus software does not include antispyware software, you should install a separate antispyware program such as *Windows Defender* and keep it updated. (Windows Defender is available as a free download for Windows XP and is included in Windows Vista and Windows 7.)
▶ Use caution when you click links in e-mail messages or on social networking websites.
▶ Familiarize yourself with common *phishing scams*.

PROTECTING AGAINST SPYWARE

In response to the emergence of spyware, a large variety of antispyware software exists. Running antispyware software has become a widely recognized element of computer security best practices for Microsoft Windows desktop computers. A number of jurisdictions have passed antispyware laws, which usually target any software that is surreptitiously installed to control a user's computer. The U.S. Federal Trade Commission (ftc.gov) has placed on the Internet a page of advice to consumers about how to lower the risk of spyware infection, including a list of dos and don'ts.

Using Policies and Training

Because successful social engineering attacks depend, in effect, on the cooperation of the victims, stopping social engineering attacks also depends on the victims. Certain positions within an organization are clearly vulnerable, such as those with access to private and confidential information or those that interact with customers or vendors. In the acceptable use policy (AUP) and employee training programs, all users should learn how to avoid becoming a victim of manipulation. Specific policies and procedures need to be developed for securing confidential information, guiding employee behavior with respect to confidential information, and taking the steps needed to respond to and report any social engineering breaches. For an overview of consumer and seller protection in EC, see Chapter 14.

Section 9.8 ▶ REVIEW QUESTIONS

1. What are general controls? List the various types.
2. What are administrative controls?
3. Define application controls.
4. How does one protect against spam?
5. How does one protect against pop-ups?
6. How does one protect against phishing, spyware, and malvertising?

9.9 BUSINESS CONTINUITY, DISASTER RECOVERY, SECURITY AUDITING, AND RISK MANAGEMENT

A major building block in EC security for large companies or companies where EC plays a critical role (e.g., banks, airlines, stock brokerages, e-tailers) is to prepare for natural or man-made disasters. Disasters may occur without warning. The best defense is to be prepared. Therefore, an important element in any security system is the *business continuity plan*, mainly consisting of a disaster recovery plan. Such a plan outlines the process by which businesses should recover from a major disaster. Destruction of all (or most) of the computing facilities can cause significant damage. Therefore, it is difficult for many organizations to obtain insurance for their computers and information systems without showing a satisfactory disaster prevention and recovery plan. The comprehensiveness of a business recovery plan is shown in Exhibit 9.16.

BUSINESS CONTINUITY AND DISASTER RECOVERY PLANNING

Disaster recovery is the chain of events linking the business continuity plan to protection and to recovery. The following are some key thoughts about the process:

▶ The purpose of a business continuity plan is to keep the business running after a disaster occurs. Each function in the business should have a valid recovery capability plan.

▶ Recovery planning is part of *asset protection*. Every organization should assign responsibility to managers to identify and protect assets within their spheres of functional control.

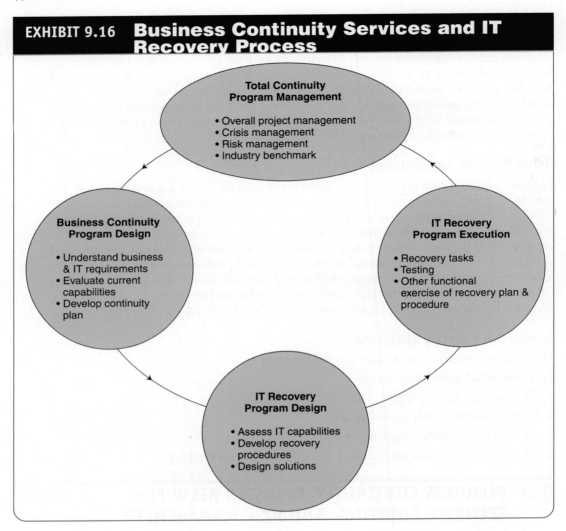

EXHIBIT 9.16   Business Continuity Services and IT Recovery Process

Total Continuity Program Management

- Overall project management
- Crisis management
- Risk management
- Industry benchmark

Business Continuity Program Design

- Understand business & IT requirements
- Evaluate current capabilities
- Develop continuity plan

IT Recovery Program Execution

- Recovery tasks
- Testing
- Other functional exercise of recovery plan & procedure

IT Recovery Program Design

- Assess IT capabilities
- Develop recovery procedures
- Design solutions

> ◗ Planning should focus first on recovery from a total loss of all capabilities.
>
> ◗ Proof of capability usually involves some kind of what-if analysis that shows that the recovery plan is current.
>
> ◗ All critical applications must be identified and their recovery procedures addressed in the plan.
>
> ◗ The plan should be written so that it will be effective in case of disaster, not just in order to satisfy the auditors.
>
> ◗ The plan should be kept in a safe place; copies should be given to all key managers, or it should be available on the intranet. The plan should be audited periodically.

disaster avoidance

An approach oriented toward prevention. The idea is to minimize the chance of avoidable disasters (such as fire or other human-caused threats).

Disaster recovery planning can be very complex, and it may take several months to complete. Using special software, the planning job can be expedited. See Case 9.2 for a discussion of the importance of business continuity and the ability to recover from a disaster.

Disaster Avoidance. Disaster avoidance is an approach oriented toward *prevention*. The idea is to minimize the chance of avoidable disasters (such as fire or other human-caused threats). For example, many companies use a device called *uninterrupted power supply (UPS)*, which provides power in case of a power outage.

CASE 9.2

EC Application

BUSINESS CONTINUITY AND DISASTER RECOVERY

Ninety-three percent of companies that suffer a significant data loss go out of business within 5 years, according to Freeman Mendel, the chair of the FBI's 2006 InfraGard National Conference. Even though business continuity/ disaster recovery (BC/DR) is a business survival issue, many managers have dangerously viewed BC/DR as only an IT security issue or as a "necessary evil." According to Marks (2008), the top barriers to a BC plan are: cost (89%), complexity (57%), low priority (56%), lack of top manage-ment support (42%), and lack of internal skills (21%).

Disasters teach the best lessons for both IT managers and corporate executives who *have not* implemented BC/DR processes. The success or failure of those processes depends on IT, as the following case indicates.

The city of Houston, Texas, and Harris County swung into action by turning Reliant Park and the Houston Astrodome into a "temporary city" with a medical facility, pharmacy, post office, and town square to house more than 250,000 Hurricane Katrina evacuees. Coast Guard Lt. Commander Joseph J. Leonard headed up the operation, drawing on his knowledge of the National Incident Command System. As Leonard explained, ineffective communication between the command staff and those in New Orleans, who could have informed Houston authorities about the number and special needs of the evacuees, caused a serious problem. In addition, agencies and organizations with poor on-scene decision-making authority hampered and slowed efforts to get things done.

Now businesses in hurricane alleys, earthquake corridors, and major cities are deploying BC/DR plans supported with software tools that allow them to replicate, or back up, their mission-critical IT applications to sites away from their primary data centers. In case of a disaster, companies can transmit vital accounting, project management, or transactional systems and records to their disaster recovery facilities, limiting downtime and data loss despite an outage at the primary location.

Globally, regulators are increasingly paying closer attention to business continuity and recovery times, which are now measured in hours rather than days. The Australian Prudential Regulation Authority (APRA) released its prudential standard on business continuity in April 2005. APRA gave Australian firms only 12 months to fix their compliance gaps.

Sources: Compiled from Fagg (2006), *Fiber Optics Weekly* (2006), and *infragardconferences.com* (accessed January 2011).

Questions

1. Why might a company that had a significant data loss not be able to recover?

2. Why are regulators requiring that companies implement BC/DR plans?

For BC guidelines, see Marks (2008) and the BC report at dataprotection.infor-mationweek.com. For a practical guide, see CA (2007). A major related activity of business continuity is auditing (see Online File W9.7).

RISK-MANAGEMENT AND COST–BENEFIT ANALYSIS

It is usually not economical to prepare protection against every possible threat. Therefore, an EC security program must provide a process for assessing threats and deciding which ones to prepare for and which ones to ignore or provide only reduced protection.

According to en.wikipedia.org/wiki/Information_security, a risk management process consists of:

1. Identification of assets and estimating their value. Include: people, buildings, hardware, software, data (electronic, print, others), and supplies.

2. Conduct a threat assessment. Include: acts of nature, acts of war, accidents, and malicious acts originating from inside or outside the organization.

3. Conduct a vulnerability assessment, and for each vulnerability calculate the probability that it will be exploited. Evaluate policies, procedures, standards, training, physical security, quality control, and technical security.

4. Calculate the impact that each threat would have on each asset. Use qualitative analysis or quantitative analysis.

5. Identify, select, and implement appropriate controls. Provide a proportional response. Consider productivity, cost effectiveness, and value of the asset.

Risk-Management Analysis

Risk-management analysis can be enhanced by the use of analytical software packages. A simplified computation is shown here:

$$\text{Expected loss} = P_1 \times P_2 \times L$$

where:
P_1 = probability of attack (estimate, based on judgment)
P_2 = probability of attack being successful (estimate, based on judgment)
L = loss occurring if attack is successful

Example:

$$P_1 = .02, P_2 = .10, L = \$1,000,000$$

Then, expected loss from this particular attack is:

$$P_1 \times P_2 \times L = 0.02 \times 0.1 \times \$1,000,000 = \$2,000$$

The amount of loss may depend on the duration of a system being out of operation. Therefore, some add duration to the analysis. The example calculation is not detailed. Next, we offer a more detailed calculation.

Calculating the Cost of a Fraud-Prevention System

Baseline offers a spreadsheet form for calculating the cost of a fraud prevention system. Two types are considered: start up (mostly fixed) and annual upkeep (mostly variable).

Examples of Fixed Cost.

▶ **Software and Services**
  ▶ Security tokens
  ▶ Server software
  ▶ Surveillance service
  ▶ Spam software
▶ **Hardware**
  ▶ Authentication server
  ▶ Development server
▶ **Labor**
  ▶ Project management
  ▶ Business and security analysts
  ▶ Development and integration
  ▶ Network and security
▶ **Training**
  ▶ Staff
  ▶ Trainers
▶ **Start-up Cost**

Examples of Annual Variable Operating Cost.
Operations: Annual Items.

▶ **Software and Services**
  ▶ Software fees
  ▶ Surveillance service
  ▶ Spam software
▶ **Hardware**
▶ **Labor**
  ▶ Management and analysis
  ▶ Development and integration
  ▶ Network and security

▶ **Customer Support**
  ▶ Staff
  ▶ Security leads
▶ **Operating Costs**

For a comprehensive discussion, examples, and research findings, see Sumner (2009).

Ethical Issues

Implementing security programs raises several ethical issues. First, some people are against monitoring any individual's activities. Imposing certain controls is seen by some as a violation of freedom of speech or other civil rights. A Gartner Group study showed that even after the terrorist attacks of September 11, 2001, only 26 percent of Americans approved a national ID database. Using biometrics is considered by many a violation of privacy.

Handling the privacy versus security dilemma is tough. There are other ethical and legal obligations that may require companies to "invade the privacy" of employees and monitor their actions. In particular, IT security measures are needed to protect against loss, liability, and litigation. Losses are not just financial, but also include the loss of information, customers, trading partners, brand image, and ability to conduct business due to the actions of hackers, malware, or employees.

Section 9.9 ▶ REVIEW QUESTIONS

1. Why do organizations need a business continuity plan?
2. List three issues a business continuity plan should cover.
3. Identify two factors that influence a company's ability to recover from a disaster.
4. What types of devices are needed for disaster avoidance?
5. How can you calculate expected loss?
6. List two ethical issues associated with security programs.

9.10 IMPLEMENTING ENTERPRISEWIDE E-COMMERCE SECURITY

Now that you have learned about both the threats and the defenses, we can discuss some implementation issues starting with the reasons why it is difficult, or even impossible, to stop computer crimes and information systems' malfunction. However, it is possible to contain many threats. However, it is necessary to get organized and well managed. We discuss here only a few topics.

THE DRIVERS OF EC SECURITY MANAGEMENT

The explosive growth of EC and SC together with an increase in the ever-changing strategies of cybercriminals (Jaishankar 2011), combined with regulatory requirements and demands by insurance companies, drive the need for comprehensive EC security management (see Steele 2009). Additional drivers are:

▶ Proliferating worldwide laws and regulations created in response to consumer and government concerns about identity theft and the privacy and security of personal information
▶ The complexity of global organizations due to outsourcing
▶ An ever-increasing emphasis on the value of intangible information assets and such valuation's impact on financial statements and accurate risk management
▶ New and faster technologies to transmit, store, and share information
▶ The often brutal competition in the global marketplace and associated pressure to reduce costs

EXHIBIT 9.17   Enterprisewide EC Security and Privacy Model

Senior Management Commitment & Support	Security Policies & Training	Security Procedures & Enforcement	Security Tools: Hardware & Software

SENIOR MANAGEMENT COMMITMENT AND SUPPORT

The success of an EC security strategy and program depends on the commitment and involvement of senior management. This is often called the "tone at the top." A genuine and well-communicated executive commitment about EC security and privacy measures is needed to convince users that insecure practices, risky or unethical methods, and mistakes due to ignorance will not be tolerated. Many forms of security are unpopular because they are inconvenient, restrictive, time-consuming, and expensive. Security practices tend not to be a priority unless they are mandatory and there are negative consequences for noncompliance.

Therefore, an EC security and privacy model for effective enterprisewide security begins with senior management's commitment and support, as shown in Exhibit 9.17. The model views EC security (as well as the broader IT security) as a combination of commitment and support, policies and training, procedures and enforcement, and tools executed as a continuous process.

Unified Front

The bad guys have time and money, and they are in large numbers, scattered around the globe. The only hope in fighting them is to create a unified front that starts with top management and trickles through the enterprise as well. Risk management and security programs by themselves may not be so effective. According to Bataller (2011) only 10 percent of companies have excellent programs, and 32 percent have satisfactory ones. The other 58 percent are in fair or bad shape. Bataller (2011) suggests a unified, participatory process that includes everybody in the organization (unified front) to solve the security problem.

Master Security Plan. One task that you should start with is developing a master security plan, which like any master plan pulls all the organization's security functions and activities together. For how it is done, see infosectoday.com/Articles/Security_Master_Plan.htm or Giles (2008).

EC SECURITY POLICIES AND TRAINING

An important step is to develop a general EC security policy, as well as procedures that specify acceptable use of computers and networks, access control, enforcement, roles, and responsibilities. The policies need to be disseminated throughout the organization and necessary training provided to ensure that everyone is aware of and understands them. These policies are important because access control rules, access control lists, monitoring, and rules for firewalls and routers are derived from them. For example, to avoid violating privacy legislation when collecting confidential data, policies need to specify that customers:

▶ Know that data is being collected.
▶ Give permission, or opt-in, for data to be collected.
▶ Have some control over how the information is used.
▶ Know the data will be used in a reasonable and ethical manner.

Similarly, to protect against social networking crimes, you can:

▶ Develop policies and procedures that tap into opportunities but provide protection. It is best to seek input from different departments and constituencies within the organization.
▶ Educate employees and others about what is acceptable and what is not acceptable.

The greater the understanding of how security issues directly impact business process levels, customer and supplier relationships, revenue streams, and management's liability, the more security will be incorporated into business projects and proposals. It is essential to have a comprehensive and up-to-date **acceptable use policy (AUP)** that informs users of their responsibilities when using company networks, wireless devices, customer data, and so forth. To be effective, the AUP needs to define the responsibilities of every user by specifying both acceptable and unacceptable computer usage. Access to the company networks, databases, and e-mail should never be given to a user until after this process is completed.

EC SECURITY PROCEDURES AND ENFORCEMENT

EC security procedures require an evaluation of the digital and financial assets at risk—including cost and operational considerations. To calculate the proper level of protection, managers responsible for a digital asset need to assess its risk exposure.

Another assessment is the *business impact analysis.* **Business impact analysis (BIA)** is an exercise that determines the impact of losing the support of an EC resource (e.g., e-procurement, e-ordering) to an organization; estimates how that loss may escalate over time; identifies the minimum resources needed to recover from the loss; and prioritizes the steps in the recovery of the processes and supporting systems. After estimating the risk exposure of digital assets, the organization should focus its resources on the risks that are the greatest.

WHY IS IT DIFFICULT TO STOP INTERNET CRIME?

The following are the major reasons Internet crime is so difficult to stop.

Making Shopping Inconvenient

Strong EC security makes online shopping inconvenient and is demanding on customers. The EC industry does not want to enforce safeguards that add friction to the profitable wheels of online commerce. It is possible, for example, to demand passwords or PINs for all credit card transactions, but that could discourage or prevent customers from completing their purchases. It is also possible to demand delivery only to the billing address for a credit card, but that would eliminate an important convenience for gift senders.

Lack of Cooperation from Credit Card Issuers and ISPs

A second reason is the lack of cooperation from credit card issuers and local and especially foreign ISPs. If the source ISP would cooperate and suspend the hacker's access, it would be very difficult for hackers to do what they do. The hacker would not be able to hack from the comfort of home because that street address would be blacklisted by the ISP.

Shoppers' Negligence

The third reason pertains to customers. Online shoppers are to blame for not taking necessary precautions to avoid becoming a victim. Some shoppers rely too heavily on fraud protection provided by credit card issuers, ignoring the bigger risk of identity theft. Phishing is rampant because some people respond to it—making it profitable. Although phishing gets most of the media attention, users expose themselves to equally dangerous risks by using debit cards on online gambling sites or revealing themselves in online communities like MySpace, Facebook, and France's Skyblog.

Ignoring EC Security Best Practices

The fourth reason is that many companies of all sizes fail to implement basic IT security management, such as best security practices, business continuity plans, and disaster recovery plans. In its fourth annual study on information security and the workforce released in 2008, the **Computing Technology Industry Association (CompTIA)**, a nonprofit trade group, said that the most widespread threats in the United States stem from spyware, the lack of user awareness, and virus and worm attacks. Because of the

acceptable use policy (AUP)
Policy that informs users of their responsibilities when using company networks, wireless devices, customer data, and so forth.

business impact analysis (BIA)
An exercise that determines the impact of losing the support of an EC resource to an organization and establishes the escalation of that loss over time, identifies the minimum resources needed to recover, and prioritizes the recovery of processes and supporting systems.

Computing Technology Industry Association (CompTIA)
Nonprofit trade group providing information security research and best practices.

known role of human error in information security breaches, 60 percent of the more than 2,000 government, IT, financial, and educational organizations surveyed worldwide had mandatory security training. Nearly 33 percent of all U.S. firms made certification required in 2008, compared to only 25 percent in 2006 and 14 percent in 2005 (CompTIA 2008).

Design and Architecture Issues

A fifth reason arises from information systems (IS) design and security architecture issues. It is well known that preventing vulnerability during the EC design and preimplementation stage is far less expensive than mitigating problems later. The IS staff of a company needs to plan security at the design stage because simple mistakes, such as not ensuring that all traffic into and out of a network pass through a firewall, are often to blame for letting in hackers. If companies don't invest the resources needed to ensure that their applications are secure, they may as well forget about security elsewhere on the website. Security needs to be built into an EC site from the very beginning and also into the application level.

There's no doubt that Web applications are attackers' target of choice and that every component in an EC application is subject to some sort of security threat.

Lack of Due Care in Business Practices

standard of due care

Care that a company is reasonably expected to take based on the risks affecting its EC business and online transactions.

The final reason is the lack of due care in business or hiring practices, outsourcing, and business partnerships. The standard of due care comes from the law and is also known as the "duty to exercise reasonable care." Due care in EC is care that a company is reasonably expected to take based on the risks affecting its EC business and online transactions. If managers ignore the standard of due care in business practices, hire criminals, outsource to fraudulent vendors, or partner with unsecured companies, they put their EC business and confidential data at risk, exposing themselves to legal problems. See Online File W9.8 for a discussion of the impacts on ChoicePoint for its negligence in not following reasonable information security and privacy practices. For a description of the PCI standard and requirements, see pcistandard.com.

Section 9.10 ▶ REVIEW QUESTIONS

1. If senior management is not committed to EC security, how might that impact the e-business?
2. What is a benefit of using the risk exposure model for EC security planning?
3. Why should every company implement an acceptable use policy?
4. Why is training required?
5. List the six major reasons why it is difficult to stop computer crimes.

MANAGERIAL ISSUES

Some managerial issues related to this chapter are as follows.

1. **What is the best EC security strategy for my company?** The security strategy of your company should be to deter, prevent, and detect the potential threats in conducting EC whether it is intentional or unintentional. Evaluating the threats, vulnerabilities, and risks of potential criminal attacks and their impacts on business operation is a manager's task. Developing the defense mechanism and disaster recovery plan should be shared throughout the organization. Designing the EC security plan as a part of the overall IT security plan is necessary. Educating senior management about the consequences of poor network security and the best practices in network risk management is essential to the development of a good strategy.

2. **Is the budget for EC security adequate?** To evaluate the adequacy of the EC security budget, which is usually part of the IT budget, it will be useful to compare yours with the national average. If the budget of your company is too low or too high, you will need to seriously review the reasons why. It is reported that the average IT security budget is about 10 percent of the total IT budget, while awareness training is about 3 percent of the total IT budget. Review whether the outsourcing plan for security expertise is adequately

balanced with internal effort because about 40 percent of companies outsource some computer security.

3. What steps should businesses follow in establishing a security plan? Security risk management is an ongoing process involving three phases: asset identification, risk assessment, and implementation. By actively monitoring existing security policies and procedures, companies can determine which of them are successful or unsuccessful and, in turn, which should be modified or eliminated. However, it also is important to monitor changes in business requirements, changes in technology and in the way it is used, and changes in the way people can attack the systems and networks. In this way, an organization can evolve its security policies and measures, ensuring that they continue to support the critical needs of the business.

4. Should organizations be concerned with internal security threats? Except for malware, breaches perpetrated by insiders are much more frequent than those perpetrated by outsiders. This is true for both B2C and B2B sites. Security policies and measures for EC sites need to address these insider threats. Pay special attention to the prevention of social engineering schemes that may allure insiders, and educate the new insiders about such threats.

5. What is the key to establishing strong e-commerce security? Most discussions about security focus on technology, with statements like "firewalls are mandatory" or "all transmissions should be encrypted." Although firewalls and encryption can be important technologies, no security solution is useful unless it solves a business problem and is adopted by customers. Determining your business requirements is the most important step in creating a security solution. Business requirements, in turn, determine your information requirements. Once you know your information requirements, you can begin to understand the value of those assets and the steps that you should take to secure those that are most valuable and vulnerable.

SUMMARY

In this chapter, you learned about the following EC issues as they relate to the chapter's learning objectives.

1. The importance and scope of EC information security. For EC to succeed, it must be secured. Unfortunately this is not an easy task due to many unintentional and intentional hazards. Security incidents and breaches interrupt EC transactions and increase the cost of doing business online. Internet design is vulnerable, and the temptation to commit computer crime is increasing with the increased applications and volume of EC. Criminals are expanding operations, creating an underground economy of stolen valuable information. A strategy is needed to handle the costly defense operation, which includes training, education, project management, and ability to enforce security policy. EC security will remain an evolving discipline because threats change, e-business needs change, and Web-based technologies to provide greater service change. An EC security strategy is needed to optimize EC security programs for efficiency and effectiveness. There are several reasons why. EC security costs and efforts from reacting to crises and paying for damages are greater than if organizations had an EC security strategy. The Internet is still a fundamentally insecure infrastructure. There are many criminals, and they are intent on stealing information for identity theft and fraud. Without a strategy, EC security is treated as a project instead of an ongoing, never-ending process.

2. Basic EC security issues and terminology. The security issue can be viewed as a battleground between attackers and attacks and defenders and defense. There are many variations on both sides and many possible collision scenarios. Owners of EC sites need to be concerned with multiple security issues: authentication, verifying the identity of the participants in a transaction; authorization, ensuring that a person or process has access rights to particular systems or data; auditing, being able to determine whether particular actions have been taken and by whom; confidentiality, ensuring that information is not disclosed to unauthorized individuals, systems, or processes; integrity, protecting data from being altered or destroyed; availability, ensuring that data and services are available when needed; and nonrepudiation, the ability to limit parties from refuting that a legitimate transaction took place.

3. Threats, vulnerabilities, and technical attacks. EC sites are exposed to a wide range of attacks. Attacks may be nontechnical (social engineering), in which a perpetrator tricks people into revealing information or performing actions that compromise network security. Or they may be technical, whereby software and systems expertise are used to attack the networks, database, or programs. DoS attacks bring operations to a halt by sending a flood of data to target computers or to as many computers on the Internet as possible. Malicious code attacks include viruses, worms, Trojan horses, or some combination of these. Over the past couple of years, various trends in malicious code have emerged, including an increase in the speed and volume of attacks; reduced time between the discovery of a vulnerability and the release of an attack to exploit the vulnerability; the growing use of bots to launch attacks; an increase in attacks on Web applications; and a shift to profit-motivated attacks.

4. **Internet fraud, phishing, and spam.** A large variety of Internet crimes exist. Notable are identify theft and misuse, stock market frauds, get-rich-quick scams, and phishing. Phishing attempts to get valuable information from people by masquerading as a trustworthy entity. Personal information is extracted from people (stolen) and sold to criminals who use it to commit financial crimes such as transferring money to illegal accounts. A related area is the use of unsolicited advertising or sales via spam.

5. **Information assurance.** The importance of the information assurance model to EC is that it represents the processes for protecting information by ensuring its confidentiality, integrity, and availability. Confidentiality is the assurance of data privacy. Integrity is the assurance that data is accurate or that a message has not been altered. Availability is the assurance that access to data, the website, or other EC data service is timely, available, reliable, and restricted to authorized users.

6. **Securing EC access control and communications.** In EC, issues of communication among trading partners are paramount. EC partners do not know in many cases their counterparts so they need secured communication and trust building. Trust starts with the authentication of the parties involved in a transaction; that is, identifying the parties in a transaction along with the actions they can perform. Authentication can be established with something one knows (e.g., a password), something one has (e.g., a token), or something one possesses (e.g., a fingerprint). Biometric systems can confirm a person's identity. Fingerprint scanners, iris scanners, facial recognition, and voice recognition are examples of biometric systems. A special encryption system for EC is the PKI. Public key nfrastructure (PKI), which is the cornerstone of secure e-payments and communication, also can authenticate the parties in a transaction. PKI uses several methods of encryption (private and public) to ensure privacy and integrity, and digital signatures to ensure authenticity and nonrepudiation. Digital signatures are themselves authenticated through a system of digital certificates issued by certificate authorities (CAs). For the average consumer and merchant, PKI is simplified because it is built into Web browsers and services. Such tools are secured because security is based on SSL (TSL) communication standards.

7. **Technologies for protecting networks.** At EC sites, firewalls, VPNs, and IDSs have proven extremely useful. A firewall is a combination of hardware and software that isolates a private network from a public network. Firewalls are of two general types—packet-filtering routers or application-level proxies. A packet-filtering router uses a set of rules to determine which communication packets can move from the outside network to the inside network. An application-level proxy is a firewall that accepts requests from the outside and repackages a request before sending it to the inside network, thus, ensuring the security of the request. Individuals with broadband access need personal firewalls. VPNs are used generally to support secure site-to-site transmissions across the Internet between B2B partners or communications between a mobile and remote worker and a LAN at a central office. IDSs monitor activity across a network or on a host. The systems watch for suspicious activity and take automated actions whenever a security breach or attack occurs. In the same vein, some companies are installing honeynets and honeypots in an effort to gather information on intrusions and to analyze the types and methods of attacks being perpetrated.

8. **The different controls and special defense mechanisms.** The major controls are general (including physical, access controls, biometrics, administrative controls, application controls, and internal controls for compliance).

9. **Protecting from fraud.** Given the large number of fraud methods it is difficult to protect against all of them. Fraud protection is done by vendors, by government regulations, and perhaps most important by consumer education. Knowing the most common methods used by criminals is the first step of defense. Remember, criminals are very experienced and clever.

10. **Role of business continuity and disaster recovery planning.** Disaster recovery planning is an integral part of effective internal controls and security management. Business continuity planning includes backup sites and a plan for what to do when disaster strikes. Such plans are required by insurance companies and some lenders. It is necessary to conduct drills that will ensure that people know what to do if disaster strikes.

11. **Enterprisewide EC security.** EC security procedures are inconvenient, expensive, tedious, and never ending. A defensive in-depth model that views EC security as a combination of commitment, people, processes, and technology is essential. An effective program starts with senior management's commitment and budgeting support. This sets the tone that EC security is important to the organization. Other components are security policies and training. Security procedures must be defined with positive incentives for compliance and at least negative consequences for violations. The last stage is the deployment of hardware and software tools based on the policies and procedures defined by the management team.

12. Why is it impossible to stop computer crimes? Responsibility or blame for cybercrimes can be placed on criminals and victimized industries, users, and organizations. The EC industry does not want to enforce safeguards that add friction to the profitable wheels of online commerce. Credit card issuers try to avoid sharing leads on criminal activity with each other or law enforcement. Online shoppers fail to take necessary precautions to avoid becoming a victim. IS designs and security architectures are still incredibly vulnerable. Organizations fail to exercise due care in business or hiring practices, outsourcing, and business partnerships. Every EC business knows that the threats of bogus credit card purchases, data breaches, phishing, malware, and viruses never end—and that these threats must be addressed comprehensively and strategically.

KEY TERMS

Acceptable use policy (AUP)	537	Deterring measures	499	Message digest (MD)	521
Access control	517	Digital envelope	522	Nonrepudiation	498
Application controls	527	Digital signatures	521	Packet	523
Authentication	498	Disaster avoidance	532	Page hijacking	503
Authorization	498	Domain name system (DNS)	491	Penetration test (pen test)	515
Availability	513	EC security programs	516	Personal firewall	523
Banking Trojan	502	EC security strategy	499	Phishing	494
Biometric control	518	E-mail spam	509	Plaintext	519
Biometric systems	518	Encryption	519	Prevention measures	499
Botnet	503	Encryption algorithm	519	Private key	520
Business continuity plan	494	Exposure	494	Protocol tunneling	525
Business impact analysis (BIA)	537	Firewall	523	Public key	520
Certificate authorities (CAs)	522	Fraud	494	Public (asymmetric) key encryption	520
CIA security triad (CIA triad)	513	General controls	527	Public key infrastructure (PKI)	520
Ciphertext	519	Hacker	496	Risk	494
Computer security incident management	516	Hash function	521	Search engine spam	511
Computing Technology Industry Association (CompTIA)	537	Honeynet	525	Social engineering	494
		Honeypot	525	Spam	494
Confidentiality	513	Identity theft	508	Spam site	511
Controlling the Assault of Non-Solicited Pornography and Marketing (CAN-SPAM) Act	529	Information assurance (IA)	499	Splog	512
		Information security	488	Spyware	509
Cracker	496	Integrity	513	Standard of due care	538
CSI Computer Crime and Security Survey	488	Intelligent agents	528	Symmetric (private) key encryption	520
		Internet underground economy	492		
Cybercrime	494	Intrusion detection system (IDS)	525	Trojan horse	501
Cybercriminal	494	IP address	491	Virtual private network (VPN)	525
Data breach	512	Key (key value)	519	Virus	501
Data Encryption Standard (DES)	520	Key space	519	Vulnerability	495
Denial-of-service (DoS) attack	503	Keystroke logging (keylogging)	493	Vulnerability assessment	515
Detection measures	499	Macro virus (macro worm)	501	Worm	501
		Malware (malicious software)	494	Zombies	495

DISCUSSION QUESTIONS

1. Consider how a hacker might trick people into giving him or her user IDs and passwords to their Amazon.com accounts. What are some of the ways that a hacker might accomplish this? What crimes can be performed with such information?

2. B2C EC sites continue to experience DoS attacks. How are these attacks perpetrated? Why is it so difficult to safeguard against them? What are some of the things a site can do to mitigate such attacks?

3. How are botnets, identity theft, DoS attacks, and website hijackings perpetrated? Why are they so dangerous to e-commerce?

4. Discuss some of the difficulties of eliminating online financial fraud.

5. Some companies prefer not to have disaster recovery plans. Under what circumstances does this make sense? Discuss.

6. Enter idesia-biometrics.com and look at its product. Discuss these benefits over other biometrics.

7. Enter trendsecure.com and find a tool called HijackThis. Try the free tool. Find an online forum that deals with it. Discuss the benefits and limitations.

8. Find information about the Zeus Trojan. Discuss why it is so effective as a financial data stealer. Why is it so difficult to mitigate this Trojan? Hint: See Falliere and Chien (2009).

9. Find information about the scareware social engineering method. Why do you think it is so effective?

10. The National Vulnerability Database (NVD) is a comprehensive cybersecurity database that integrates all publicly available U.S. government vulnerability resources and provides references to industry resources. Visit nvd.nist.gov and review 10 of the recent CVE vulnerabilities. For each vulnerability, list its published date, CVSS severity, impact type, and the operating system or software with the vulnerability.

TOPICS FOR CLASS DISCUSSION AND DEBATES

1. Survey results on the incidence of cyber attacks paint a mixed picture; some surveys show increases, others show decreases. What factors could account for the differences in the reported results?

2. A business wants to share its customer account database with its trading partners, while at the same time providing prospective buyers with access to marketing materials on its website. Assuming that the business is responsible for running all these systems, what types of security components (e.g., firewalls, VPNs, etc.) could be used to ensure that the partners and customers have access to the account information and others do not? What type of network administrative procedures will provide the appropriate security?

3. Why is it so difficult to fight computer criminals? What strategies can be implemented by financial institutions, airlines, and other heavy users of EC?

4. All EC sites share common security threats and vulnerabilities. Do you think that B2C websites face different threats and vulnerabilities than B2B sites? Explain.

5. Why is phishing so difficult to control? What can be done? Discuss.

6. Debate: The best strategy is to invest very little and only in proven technologies such as encryption and firewalls.

7. Debate: Can the underground Internet marketplace be controlled? Why or why not?

8. Debate: Is taking your fingerprints or other biometrics to assure EC security a violation of your privacy?

9. A body scan at airports created a big debate. Debate both points of this issue and relate it to EC security.

INTERNET EXERCISES

1. Your B2C site has been hacked with a new, innovative method. List two organizations where you would report this incident so that they can alert other sites. How do you do this, and what type of information do you have to provide?

2. Connect to the Internet. Determine the IP address of your computer by visiting at least two websites that provide that feature. You can use a search engine to locate websites or visit ip-adress.com or whatismyip address.com. What other information does the search reveal about your connection? Based on this information, how could a company or hacker use that information?

3. Enter the site of Perimeter eSecurity and find the white paper "Institutional Identity Theft." Compare institutional identity theft with personal identity theft. How can a company protect itself against identity theft?

4. The National Strategy to Secure Cyberspace provides a series of actions and recommendations for each of its five national priorities. Search and download a copy of the strategy online. Selecting one of the priorities, discuss in detail the actions and recommendations for that priority.

5. The Symantec Annual Internet Security Threat Report provides details about the trends in attacks

and vulnerabilities in Internet security. Obtain a copy of the latest report and summarize the major findings of the report for both attacks and vulnerabilities.

6. Enter perimeterusa.com and look for the white paper "Top 9 Network Security Threats in 2009." Summarize these threats. Then look for the white paper "The ABC's of Social Engineering." Summarize the suggested defense in both cases.

7. Enter security firm finjan.com and find examples of underground Internet activities in five different countries. Prepare a summary.

8. Enter ftc.gov/bcp/edu/microsites/idtheft, identytheft.info, idtheftcenter.org, and identytheftprotection.org. Find information about: the prevention, protection against, cases about, and survival of identity theft. Write a report.

9. Enter verisign.com and find information about PKI and encryption. Write a report.

10. Enter gfi.com/emailsecuritytest and similar sites. Write some guidelines for protecting your e-mail, both on your PC and on a mobile device.

11. Enter hijackthis.com. Do a free scan of your computer. Comment on the report you received.

12. Enter blackhat.com. Find out what they are about. Summarize some of their activities.

13. Enter bsimm.com/community. Describe the activities of the community and how it helps to fight cybercrime.

TEAM ASSIGNMENTS AND PROJECTS

1. **Assignment for the Opening Case**

   Read the opening case and answer the following questions:

   a. What kind of attack was it?
   b. Why was it difficult to stop it and to recover?
   c. What do you think motivated Maxwell to conduct the attack?
   d. After the incident, the hospital added more layers of defense. Why did they not have it before?
   e. After reading Section 9.7, what do you think can be done on top of what has been done to prevent the incident?
   f. Is the punishment severe enough to deter others? Why or why not?

2. Assign teams to report on the latest major spam and scam threats. Look at examples provided by ftc.gov, the Symantec report on the state of spam (2009), and white papers from IBM, VeriSign, McAfee, Symantec, and other security firms.

3. Several personal firewall products are available. A list of these products can be found at firewallguide.com/software.htm. Assign each team three products from the list. Each team should prepare a detailed review and comparison of each of the products they have been assigned.

4. Enter symantec.com/business/security_response/whitepapers.jsp and find the white papers: (1) "The Risks of Social Networking" and (2) "The Rise of PDF Malware." Prepare a summary of both and find how they relate to each other.

5. Watch the video "Cyber Attacks and Extortion" at searchsecurity.techtarget.com/video/0,297151,sid14_gci1345344,00.html. Answer the following questions:

   a. Why are there more extortions online today? How are they accomplished?
   b. What is involved in targeted e-mail attacks?
   c. What is an SQL injection attack?

6. Data leaks can be a major problem. Find all the major defense methods. Check all major security vendors (e.g., Symantec). Find white papers and Webinars on the subject.

7. Each team is assigned to one method of fighting against online fraud. Each method should deal with a different type of fraud (e.g., banking [try IBM's ZTIC], identify suspicious e-mails, dealing with cookies in Web browsers, credit card protection, securing wireless networks, installing antiphishing protection for your browser with phishing filter, and so forth).

Closing Case

HOW TWO BANKS STOPPED SCAMS, SPAMS, AND CYBERCRIMINALS

The nature of cybercriminals is changing from committing crimes just to see if they can and having fun doing it, moving to committing crimes for financial gain. Some say that as much as 90 percent of phishers are targeting financial institutions.

City National Bank (CNB) and Trust of Oklahoma

The bank expanded rapidly since 2006 and also branched out into Walmart supercenters. With the explosive growth came a bombardment of malware, which threatened the network, and unprecedented volumes of spam, which increased processing overhead on some systems. The existing controls were insufficient as the threats became more serious and dangerous. One concern was that power users would inadvertently download malicious software from the Web or open an e-mail attachment that contained a virus.

Previous solutions included limiting access to the Internet, and recording the security breaches, but they were not too successful at the gateway; they worked only at the desktop antivirus layer. The bank constantly made small policy changes. These included accepting a sender as friendly and blocking or adding a specific website to the blocked list. It was necessary to protect the employees from receiving offensive e-mail, and to block access to websites that contained illegal or offensive content. Moreover, the bank had a responsibility to the stakeholders to prevent offensive material from leaving the facility, which could open the company to lawsuits. A technical solution was found in a vendor called Marshal that offered several products that successfully protected the bank from e-mail, Web-based malware, and offensive content.

Next, the bank introduced a policy-based standard across the board. For example, a policy to block e-mail messages with attached batch, executable, and .zip files was established. Also employees were stopped from downloading potentially dangerous files and blocked access to offensive websites. Thus, Internet users are prevented from accidentally downloading malware. The software also helps to comply with Sarbanes-Oxley guidelines. Furthermore, the software allows the bank to hone its sensitive information policy to enforce the use of encryption.

In addition to several layers of antivirus protection, the system provides better protection against *zero-day malware*, for which there are no e-mail antivirus solutions in existence yet.

There have been numerous times when antivirus definitions did not catch a threat, but WebMarshal's policy engine and content scanning did catch it. This system has seen the bank through huge virus outbreaks on the Internet in which the bank was inundated by thousands of malware messages in a day.

Watching the Web

The main reason the bank chose WebMarshal was because of its capabilities. For example, if an employee accessed a website that has not been classified as pornographic, the software scans all the content on the site and looks for characteristics that would indicate it is pornographic. If the site has those characteristics, access is blocked immediately, and the site is blacklisted.

Since installing the Marshal system, the bank has doubled the number of users, quadrupled the size of the bank's website, and gone from receiving 1.5 million e-mail messages a month to 5 million messages a month. Because it is a centralized system, the bank can easily extend the Web and internal and external e-mail protection to new branches and implement security policies that protect the entire organization all from one centralized management console.

The ability to filter content in real time at the e-mail and Web gateway, as well as to set and change granular security policies on the fly, provides the bank with unprecedented security, protecting the network, employees, customers, and the company as a whole.

BankWest of South Dakota

Helping customers and communities achieve financial success is a primary focus of the bank. As a privately owned organization, the bank is free to make decisions based on long-term values rather than short-term profits. No bank in South Dakota offers more customer care and educational programs. During the last few years, the bank's customers were faced with social engineering and phishing problems. A few typical examples are:

▸ **Sweetheart schemes.** An online relationship between a customer and an overseas user that can last up to six months. Over the course of the relationship, the overseas user convinces the customer to wire funds, share bank account information, and open accounts.

▸ **Letters, postal service or e-mail.** A bank customer is notified that he or she has won the lottery or sweepstakes.

▸ **Phone scams.** A customer is asked to provide information from a government check and receives repeated phone calls, with each call asking for a different bit of personal information—Social Security number, birth date, etc. Phone scams usually target elderly customers and depend on the social engineer's ability to develop a rapport with the customer.

▸ **Cell phone scam.** A customer is told that his or her debit card has been compromised and the customer is asked to provide card details for replacement.

To combat the problem the bank had trained customer service and frontline staff to quickly target the latest social engineering schemes, and then work with customers to identify suspicious e-mails, phone calls, or in-person visits from third parties. The training resulted in the launch of the Information Security Employee Rewards Program, which honors staff for efforts to reduce the bank's risk. The program started in 2008 after the bank learned about the potential damage of social engineering. These schemes can shatter customer confidence in financial security, even when the institution is not to blame.

In June 2008, BankWest spearheaded its educational effort that focused on a training and rewards program. The bank's information security team regularly attends workshops and participates in forums related to social engineering and other fraud schemes. The information is immediately shared with the entire staff. All staff members also are required to complete online training in scheme detection that is designed by the bank.

The training program includes:

▶ How to identify phone scams, such as *vishing attempts*, which rely on automated phone call messages that lure customers into giving personal information, and pretext calls.

▶ How to identify *phishing e-mails* and use caution when clicking on links or opening file attachments.

▶ Conduct monthly training sessions and employee-oriented demonstrations on how to spot face-to-face, personal, social engineering schemes.

The bank also provides information about social engineering schemes on its websites. Employees are encouraged to point and direct customers to the site, as well as provide information about fraudulent schemes, when customers visit the branch.

Employee Rewards

The reward program is simple and inexpensive. Employees who identify suspicious schemes are given certificates and small monetary rewards. When an employee is given a certificate, his or her immediate supervisor is notified and encouraged to further reward the employee. BankWest has found that employees take pride in the program, prominently displaying their certificates for others in the branch to see.

The Results

Social engineering schemes have not decreased as a result of the education and rewards program, but reports of schemes have dramatically increased. Tracking the success of the program has been difficult, but based on the reported incidents, management estimates that employees are catching more than they are missing.

Sources: Compiled from Meason (2009), *cnbok.com* (accessed March 2011), Kitten (2010), and *bankwest-sd.com/index.asp?page=4072* (accessed March 2011).

Questions

1. List the major security problems of CNB of Oklahoma and relate them to the attack methods described in Section 9.2 through 9.4.

2. In what ways has CNB solved the e-mail problems? (List specific problems and solutions).

3. Given the problems of CNB and its solutions, what is an even better defense mechanism? (Use Sections 9.6 through 9.10, and what you can find on the Web.)

4. List the major security problems faced by BankWest and relate them to the attack methods described in Sections 9.2 through 9.4.

5. In what ways has BankWest solved the fraud schemes?

6. Given the problems of BankWest and its solutions, what is an even better defense mechanism?

ONLINE RESOURCES
available at pearsonglobaleditions.com/turban

Online Files

W9.1 Application Case: Hackers Profit from TJX's Corporate Data

W9.2 Top Cybersecurity Areas in 2011

W9.3 Examples of Internet Fraud

W9.4 What Firewalls Can Protect

W9.5 Application Case: Honeynets and the Law

W9.6 Protecting Against Spam and Splogs

W9.7 Auditing Information Systems

W9.8 Application Case: Impacts of ChoicePoint's Negligence in Information Security

Comprehensive Educational Websites

cbintel.com/auctionfraudreport.htm: A comprehensive list of Internet auction fraud statistics.

cert.org/computer_security: Comprehensive site, full of resources.

csrc.nist.gov: Computer Security Resource Center.

drj.com: Disaster Recovery Journal.

eseminarslive.com: Webinars, events, news on security.

ic3.gov/crimeschemes.aspx: A comprehensive list of Internet crime schemes and how to deal with them.

itworld.com/security: Comprehensive collection of papers on security.

nvd.nist.gov: A comprehensive cybersecurity database.

sans.org/security: Resources, glossary, research.

spamlaws.com: News, cases, legal information, and much more; spam, scams, security.

stateofsecurity.informationweek.com: Detailed security reports.

technet.microsoft.com/en-us/security/default.aspx: Comprehensive collection of papers on security.

technologyevaluation.com: White papers, etc.; look for security.

techsupportalert.com/best_computer_security_sites.htm: A detailed directory.

thebci.org: Business Continuity Institute.

verisignsecured.com: A major security vendor; tutorials.

webbuyersguide.com/resource/rllibrary.aspx?sitename= webbuyersguide: Look for security topic

zmicrosoft.com/technet/security/secnews/newsletter.htm: Comprehensive periodical newsletter.

REFERENCES

Bataller, E. "Risk Avengers." *Informationweek.com*, January 31, 2011.

Bradley, T. "Twitter Continues to Battle DDoS Attack." August 8, 2009. pcworld.com/businesscenter/article/169897/twitter_continues_to_battle_ddos_attack.html (accessed March 2011).

Brooks, J. "Conficker: What It Is, How to Stop It and Why You May Already Be Protected." *eWeek*, March 31, 2009. eweek.com/c/a/Security/Conficker-What-It-Is-How-To-Stop-It-and-Why-You-May-Already-Be-Protected-741288 (accessed March 2011).

CA. "Practical Disaster Recovery Planning: A Step-by-Step Guide." White paper, #MP310390107, 2007.

Chickowski, E. "Closing the Security Gap." *Baseline*, June 2008.

CompTIA. "Trends in Information Security: A CompTIA Analysis of IT Security and the Workforce." 2008. informationweek.com/whitepaper/ government/security/trends-in-information-security -a-comptia-analysi-wp1223489141665;jsessionid= L3YEJVF2MUVWVQE1GHRSKH4ATMY32JVN (accessed March 2011).

Dickey, C., R. M. Schneiderman, and B. Dehghanpisheh. "The Shadow War." *Newsweek*, December 13, 2010.

Eisenmann, C. "When Hackers Turn to Blackmail." *Harvard Business Review* (October 2009).

Fagg, S. "Continuity for the People." *Risk Management Magazine*, March 2006.

Falliere, N., and E. Chien. "Zeus: King of the Bots." White paper, Symantec, November 2009.

Fiber Optics Weekly. "Telstra Uses NetEx Gear." January 13, 2006.

Gage, D. "Bank of America Seeks Anti-Fraud Anodyne." *Baseline*, May 10, 2006. baselinemag.com/article2/0,11040,1962470,00.asp (accessed March 2011).

Giles, T. *How to Develop and Implement a Security Master Plan*. New York: Auerbach Pub., 2008.

Greengard, S. "Weaving a Web 2.0 Security Strategy." *Baseline*, September/October 2010.

Habal, R. "How to Assess Cloud-Based E-Mail Security Vendors." *eWeek*, September 28, 2010. eweek.com/ c/a/Cloud-Computing/How-to-Assess-CloudBased-EMail-Security-Vendors (accessed March 2011).

Jaishankar, K. *Cyber Criminology: Exploring Internet Crimes and Criminal Behavior*. New York: Auerbach Pub., 2011.

Jagatic, T., N. Johnson, M. Jakobsson, and F. Menczer. "Social Phishing." *Communication of the ACM*, 50, no. 10 (October, 2007).

Kawamoto, D. "California Man Pleads Guilty to Bot Attack." *CNET News*, May 5, 2006. news.cnet.com/California-man-pleads-guilty-to-bot-attack/2100-7348_3-6069238.html (accessed March 2011).

Kitten, T. "SD Bank Trains, Rewards Employees for Spotting Fraud Schemes." July 14, 2010. bankinfo-security.com/articles.php?art_id=2748&pg=2 (accessed March 2011).

Lerer, L. "Why the SEC Can't Stop Spam." *Forbes*, March 8, 2007. forbes.com/2007/03/08/sec-spam-stock-tech-security-cx_ll_0308spam.html (accessed March 2011).

Marketing Charts. "Fraudsters Filch $4B Online; Record Losses for U.S. E-Commerce." 2009. marketingcharts.com/interactive/fraudsters-filch-4b-online-record-losses-for-us-e-commerce-7144/cybersource-order-reject-rates-online-segment-fall-2008jpg (accessed March 2011).

Marks, H. "Practical Disaster Recovery." *Informationweek.com*, December 22–29, 2008.

McAfee. "Global Energy Cyberattacks: Night Dragon." White paper. Santa Clara, CA: McAfee Labs, February 10, 2011. mcafee.com/us/resources/white-papers/wp-global-energy-cyberattacks-night-dragon.pdf (accessed March 2011).

McCormick, J., and D. Gage. "Web Mob." *Baseline*, March 2005.

McMillan, R. "90 Percent of E-Mail Is Spam, Symantec Says." *PCWorld*, May 26, 2009a. pcworld.com/article/165533/90_percent_of_e-mail_is_spam_symantec_says.html (accessed March 2011).

McMillan, R. "FBI: Internet Fraud Complaints Up 33 Percent in 2008." *IDG News*, March 30, 2009b. network-world.com/news/2009/033009-fbi-internet-fraud-complaints-up.html?page=1 (accessed March 2011).

Meason, M. "Bank Protects More Than Money." *Baseline*, May 2009.

MessageLabs. "How to Defend Against New Botnet." White paper, 1011979.

Murphy, M. P. "Information Warfare: The NATO Cyber War Agreement." strategypage.com/htmw/htiw/articles/20100501.aspx (accessed March 2011).

O'Hagan, M. "Three Accused of Inducing Ill Effects on Computers at Local Hospital." *Seattle Times*, February 22, 2006. seattletimes.nwsource.com/html/localnews/2002798414_botnet11m.html (accessed March 2011).

Palgon, G. "Simple Steps to Data Security." *Security Management*, June 2008.

Prince, B. "How Attack Toolkits Impact the Cyber-Underground." January 18, 2011a. eweek.com/c/a/Security/How-Attack-Toolkits-Impact-the-CyberUnderground-438145 (accessed March 2011).

Prince, B. "Massive Check Fraud Run by Hackers Revealed at Black Hat." *eWeek*, July 28, 2010. eweek.com/c/a/Security/Massive-Check-Fraud-Operation-Run-by-Hackers-Revealed-at-Black-Hat-762787 (accessed March 2011).

Prince, B. "RSA Conference: The Fog of Cyber-War." February 17, 2011b. eweek.com/c/a/Security/RSA-Confernece-The-Fog-of-CyberWar-521201 (accessed March 2011).

Rand, D. "Threats When Using Online Social Networks." CSIS Security Group, May 16, 2007. csis.dk/dk/forside/LinkedIn.pdf (accessed March 2011).

Richardson, R. "2010 CSI Computer Crime and Security Survey." Computer Security Institute, 2010. gocsi.com/survey (accessed March 2011).

Roberts, P. F. "Webroot Uncovers Thousands of Stolen Identities." *InfoWorld*, May 8, 2006. infoworld.com/article/06/05/09/78139_HNTrojanrebery_1.html (accessed March 2011).

Sarrel, M. "Stay Safe, Productive on Social Networks." *eWeek*, April 5, 2010.

Secure Computing. "How to Protect Your Company and Employees from Image Spam." securecomputing.com/image_spam_WP.cfm (accessed March 2011).

Steele, B. "Due Diligence." *Baseline*, March 2009.

Strom, D. "Assessing Your Endpoint Security Needs." *Baseline*, January/February 2009.

Sullivan, D. "Business Security Measures Using SSL." White paper, Real-Time Publisher, 2011.

Sumner, M. "Information Security Threats: A Comparative Analysis of Impact, Probability, and Preparedness." *Information Systems Management* (Winter, 2009).

Symantec. "Symantec Report on Attack Kits and Malicious Websites." White paper, #1/2011/21169171. Symantec Corp., 2010.

Symantec. *Symantec Report on the Underground Economy: July 07–June 08*. Symantec Corp., November 2008, Report #14525717.

Symantec. "Web-Based Attacks." White paper, #20016955, February 2009.

Taipei Times. "Hacker Accused of Big Data Theft." August 19, 2009. taipeitimes.com/News/world/archives/2009/08/19/2003451473 (accessed March 2011).

VeriSign. "Fraud Alert: Phishing—the Latest Tactics and Potential Business Impact." White paper, #00027133-4411, 2009.

VeriSign. "Security and Trust: The Backbone of Doing Business over the Internet." White paper, #00026491-0920, 2008.

Wagley, J. "Fraud and Small Business." *Technofile*, January 2010.

Wiens, J. "You've Got (Secure) Mail." *Informationweek.com*, January 18, 2010.

Wong, G. "Chinese Police Shut Down Hacker Training Business." February 8, 2010. msnbc.msn.com/id/35297007/ns/technology_and_science-security (accessed March 2011).

ELECTRONIC COMMERCE PAYMENT SYSTEMS

Learning Objectives

Upon completion of this chapter, you will be able to:

1. Understand the shifts that are occurring with regard to online payments.

2. Discuss the players and processes involved in using credit cards online.

3. Discuss the different categories and potential uses of smart cards.

4. Discuss stored-value cards and identify under what circumstances they are best used.

5. Describe the situations where e-micropayments are used and the alternative ways for handling these situations.

6. Describe the processes and parties involved in e-checking.

7. Understand the major types of mobile payments.

8. Describe payment methods in B2B EC, including payments for global trade.

Content

PAY-PER-VIEW PAGES: THE NEXT ITUNES

The Problem

The e-book market is booming. In August 2010, Amazon.com released the third version of its popular Kindle e-book reader. This was preceded by the release of the first version of Barnes & Noble's Nook e-book reader in early 2009 and followed by the opening of Google's much awaited e-book service at the end of 2010. In 2010 the Kindle became Amazon.com's best-selling product of all time. That year, the sales of Kindle books exceeded its online sales of hardcover and paperback books. For every 100 paperbacks Amazon.com sells, it sells 115 Kindle e-books. For hardcover books, the ratio is three to one in favor of the Kindle editions (Tsotsis 2011). The same is true for Barnes & Noble where its sales of digital books now exceeds its online sales of traditional books.

For the most part, e-books are sold as "exact digital replicas" of their print counterparts. In other words, e-books are not sold a page or chapter at a time. Instead the buyer has to purchase the whole book. A slight variation on this theme is offered by Shortcovers.com, which is owned by the Canadian firm Indigo Books and Music Inc. and caters to consumers who read books online or on mobile devices (CBCNews 2009). Shortcovers.com focuses on providing "bite-sized" chunks of about 5,000 words such as individual chapters, short stories, blogs, magazines, newspaper articles, and pieces written and uploaded by users. Free and paid content can be viewed online or transferred to mobile devices using mobile apps that are distributed through iTunes and the Shortcovers.com website. For most of the books in its online catalog, Shortcovers.com provides the first chapter for free, sells the next two chapters for 99¢, or offers the entire e-book at a discount of up to half the publisher's list price. This works fine for works of fiction. Most fiction readers are primarily interested in purchasing the entire book, not individual pages or chapters. This isn't the case for nonfiction readers.

Plenty of nonfiction readers do not need nor want the complete book. For example:

- A reader is traveling to Rome, Italy, on his or her next vacation and only wants a couple of chapters from Fodor's holiday travel guide to Italy not the whole guide.

- A software programmer faces a perplexing problem and discovers a solution in a particular chapter of a well-known programming book. The book sells for $80, but the programmer only needs 5 pages from the 600-page edition.

- A professor wants to assign his or her students a series of chapter from a list of textbooks. Without violating copyright laws or requiring the students to spend a small fortune purchasing the texts, this really isn't feasible.

A few years ago, Amazon.com and Random House tried to remedy this problem. Amazon announced a plan called "Amazon Pages" that would allow readers to purchase parts of books online. The plan never came to fruition. Instead, it released the Kindle and opened the Kindle online store. Similarly, in February 2008 Random House began testing the idea of selling individual chapters online for $2.99. To date, the first, and only, title offered was Chip and Dan Heath's *Made to Stick*.

Selling books online—either hardcopy or electronic—is straightforward. Selling pages, chapters, or any other sections of a book or journal online for under $5 is another story. The barrier is not technical, it is financial. In the online world, the vast majority of consumers use credit cards to make purchases. The financial institutions issuing credit cards charge a fixed percentage for each credit card purchase, as well as a fixed fee. For a purchase under $5, it is difficult for a vendor to break even. It is the same problem faced by merchants in the offline world. Fortunately, the credit card companies, as well as electronic payment companies, such as PayPal, are well aware of the issues associated with small-value purchases and have begun to address the problem.

The Solution

Purchases under $5 are called *micropayments*. In the offline world, these small purchases are usually made with cash because credit card companies charge merchants too much in fees to make the transactions profitable. Cash does not work in the online world. In the online world, virtually every attempt to disintermediate cash and credit cards has failed. Yet, ample evidence suggests that consumers are willing to use their credit cards for micropayments.

In the online world, Apple's iTunes has clearly been a success. Originally, iTunes sold individual songs for 99¢. In 2009 Apple announced a multi-tier pricing scheme for iTunes: 69¢, 99¢, or $1.29, depending on a song's age and popularity. In February 2010, Apple announced its 10 billionth song download. In the same vein, Apple has been extremely successful in selling iPod, iPhone, and iPad applications through its App Store. Many of these applications cost $1.99. In January 2011, the company announced its 10 billionth application download.

Apple has overcome the costs associated with credit and debit card fees for low-cost items by having consumers set up accounts. The purchases of single items are aggregated until the total purchase amount makes it cost-effective to submit the payment to the credit or debit card issuer. Systems that aggregate purchases are also called "closed-loop" systems. The credit card companies are not enamored with these systems and prohibit merchants from aggregating purchases directly. However, they are currently reconsidering their stance because more and more consumers want to use their cards for small purchases.

The credit and debit card companies, as well as e-payment vendors (e.g., PayPal), are well aware of the difficulties associated with using cards for online micropayments. In response, they have lowered their fees in an effort to entice online (and offline) vendors to permit credit and debit card micropayments. Even with the new fee structure, purchases of less than $2 are still cost-prohibitive for the average merchant. Small-value payments are much less prohibitive for larger vendors, whose large card-purchase volumes enable them to negotiate with the card issuers for even smaller fees.

The Results

To date, companies such as Amazon.com and Random House have been unsuccessful with their pay-per-page or chapter plans. Clearly, Amazon.com is in a position to negotiate for smaller credit card fees. Like iTunes, it also has the ability to aggregate purchases for individual buyers. However, Random House does not sell directly to the public. Instead, it relies on other vendors, such as Amazon.com, to do the selling for it. Even with a viable micropayment system, there is no guarantee that pay-per-page or pay-per-chapter will interest consumers, especially given the usual restrictions placed on purchases of this sort.

Consider, for a moment, a few of the restrictions Random House has placed on its viewing programs:

- Books will be available for full indexing, search, and display.
- No downloading, printing, or copying will be permitted.
- Encryption and security measures must be applied to ensure protection of the digital content and compliance with the prescribed usage rules and territorial limitations.

In essence, the only thing the purchaser can do is view the page or chapter online. This is much more onerous than the restrictions placed on music or video downloads, which at least permit the purchaser to copy the content to their PCs or multimedia players. Unless these restrictions are loosened or eliminated, they will likely lead to the long-run failure of the Random House effort and other similar ones.

Sources: *CBCNews* (2009) and Tsotsis (2011).

WHAT WE CAN LEARN . . .

The overwhelming majority of B2C purchases are paid for by credit card. For merchants, the costs of servicing card payments are high. Transaction costs, potential chargeback fees for fraudulent transactions, and the costs of creating and administering a secure EC site for handling card payments are steep. Over the years, a number of less costly e-payment alternatives to credit cards have been proposed. Digital Cash, PayMe.com, Bank One's eMoneyMail, Flooz, Beenz, Wells Fargo's and eBay's Billpoint, and Yahoo!'s PayDirect are examples of alternatives that failed to gain a critical mass of users and subsequently folded. For a variety of reasons, PayPal is one of the few alternatives to credit cards that has succeeded against significant odds. The same can be said for the world of B2B e-payments. Although a number of diverse payment methods have been proposed, few have survived. This chapter discusses various e-payment methods for B2C and B2B and the underlying reasons why some have been adopted and others have not.

10.1   THE PAYMENT REVOLUTION

The year 2003 was a turning point in the use of cash, checks, and credit cards for in-store purchases. In that year, the combined use of credit and debit cards for the first time exceeded the combined use of cash and checks. Since that date, debit and credit cards have accounted for over 50 percent of in-store payments, with cash and checks making up the rest. The growth in the use of plastic is attributable to the substantial growth in the use of debit cards and the decline in the use of cash. In recent years, debit card use has been spurred by a change in the U.S. Electronic Funds Transfer Act, which eliminated the requirement for merchants to issue receipts for debit purchases of $15 or less.

Similar trends have occurred in noncash payments of recurring bills. In 2001, over 75 percent of all recurring bills were paid by paper-based methods (e.g., paper checks), whereas less than 25 percent of these payments were made electronically. Now, the percent of recurring bills paid electronically is over 50 percent.

For decades people have been talking about the cashless society. Although the demise of cash and checks is certainly not imminent, many individuals can live without checks and nearly without cash. In the online B2C world, they already do. Throughout the world, the overwhelming majority of online purchases are made with credit cards, although there are some countries where other payment methods prevail. For instance, consumers in Germany prefer to pay with either direct debit or bank cards, whereas those in China rely on debit cards.

For online B2C merchants, the implications of these trends are straightforward. In most countries, it is hard to run an online business without supporting credit card payments, despite the costs. It also is becoming increasingly important to support payments by debit card. Eventually, the volume of debit card payments may surpass credit card payments in the online world, as they have for offline purchases. For merchants who are interested in international markets, there is a need to support a variety of e-payment mechanisms, including bank transfers, COD, electronic checks, private-label cards, gift cards, instant credit, and other noncard payment systems, such as PayPal. Merchants who offer multiple payment types have lower shopping cart abandonment rates and higher order conversion, on average, resulting in increased revenues.

The short history of e-payments is littered with the remains of companies that have attempted to introduce nontraditional payment systems. One of the more recent attempts is Bitcoin (bitcoin.org). Bitcoin is a peer-to-peer, encrypted digital currency created in 2009 by Satoshi Nakamoto. The name also refers to the software that uses it and the network across which Bitcoin transactions occur. The currency can only be spent by the person that owns them, and they can never be used more than once. Supposedly the currency is growing. However, as some writers have noted, just like its predecessors this is still in its infancy and difficult to determine if it will have any success (O'Brien 2010).

It takes years for any payment system to gain widespread acceptance. For example, credit cards were introduced in the 1950s but did not reach widespread use until the 1980s. A crucial element in the success of any e-payment method is the "chicken-and-egg" problem: How do you get sellers to adopt a method when there are few buyers using it? And, how do you get buyers to adopt a method when there are few sellers using it? A number of factors come into play in determining whether a particular method of e-payment achieves critical mass. Some of the crucial factors include the following:

▶ **Independence.** Some forms of e-payment require specialized software or hardware to make the payment. Almost all forms of e-payment require the seller or merchant to install specialized software to receive and authorize a payment. Those e-payment methods that require the payer to install specialized components are less likely to succeed.

▶ **Interoperability and Portability.** All forms of EC run on specialized systems that are interlinked with other enterprise systems and applications. An e-payment method must mesh with these existing systems and applications and be supported by standard computing platforms.

▶ **Security. How safe is the transfer?** What are the consequences of the transfer being compromised? Again, if the risk for the payer is higher than the risk for the payee, then the payer is not likely to accept the method.

▶ **Anonymity.** Unlike credit cards and checks, if a buyer uses cash, there is no way to trace the cash back to the buyer. Some buyers want their identities and purchase patterns to remain anonymous. To succeed, special payment methods, such as e-cash, have to maintain anonymity.

▶ **Divisibility.** Most sellers accept credit cards only for purchases within a minimum and maximum range. If the cost of the item is too small—only a few dollars—a credit card will not do. In addition, a credit card will not work if an item or set of items costs too much (e.g., an airline company purchasing a new airplane). Any method that can address the lower or higher end of the price continuum or that can span one of the extremes and the middle has a chance of being widely accepted.

▶ **Ease of Use.** For B2C e-payments, credit cards are the standard due to their ease of use. For B2B payments, the question is whether the online e-payment methods can supplant the existing offline methods of procurement.

▶ **Transaction Fees.** When a credit card is used for payment, the merchant pays a transaction fee of up to 3 percent of the item's purchase price (above a minimum fixed fee). These fees make it prohibitive to support smaller purchases with credit cards, which leaves room for alternative forms of payment.

▶ **International Support.** EC is a worldwide phenomenon. A payment method must be easily adapted to local buying patterns and international requirements before it can be widely adopted.

▶ **Regulations.** A number of international, federal, and state regulations govern all payment methods. Even when an existing institution or association (e.g., Visa) introduces a new payment method, it faces a number of stringent regulatory hurdles. PayPal, for instance, had to contend with a number of lawsuits brought by state attorneys general that claimed that PayPal was violating state banking regulations.

Section 10.1 ▶ REVIEW QUESTIONS

1. What types of e-payments should B2C merchants support?
2. What is the "chicken-and-egg" problem in e-payments?
3. Describe the factors that are critical for an e-payment method to achieve critical mass.

10.2 USING PAYMENT CARDS ONLINE

payment cards
Electronic card that contains information that can be used for payment purposes.

Payment cards are electronic cards that contain information that can be used for payment purposes. They come in three forms:

▶ **Credit cards.** A credit card provides the holder with credit to make purchases up to a limit fixed by the card issuer. With each purchase, the credit card holder receives a loan from the credit card issuers. Credit cards rarely have an annual fee. Instead, holders are charged high interest—the annual percentage rate—on their average daily unpaid balances. Visa, MasterCard, and EuroPay are the predominant credit cards.

▶ **Charge cards.** The balance on a charge card is supposed to be paid in full upon receipt of the monthly statement. Technically, holders of a charge card receive a loan for 30 to 45 days equal to the balance of their statement. Such cards usually have annual fees. American Express's Green Card is the leading charge card, followed by the Diner's Club card.

▶ **Debit cards.** With a debit card, the money for a purchased item comes directly out of the holder's checking account (called a demand-deposit account). The actual transfer of funds from the holder's account to the merchant's takes place within 1 to 2 days. MasterCard, Visa, and EuroPay are the predominant debit cards.

authorization
Determines whether a buyer's card is active and whether the customer has sufficient funds.

settlement
Transferring money from the buyer's to the merchant's account.

PROCESSING CARDS ONLINE

The processing of card payments has two major phases: authorization and settlement. **Authorization** determines whether a buyer's card is active and whether the customer has sufficient available credit or funds. **Settlement** involves the transfer of money from the buyer's to the merchant's account. The way in which these phases actually are performed varies somewhat depending on the type of payment card. It also varies by the configuration of the system used by the merchant to process payments.

There are three basic configurations for processing online payments. The EC merchant may:

> ▶ **Own the payment software.** A merchant can purchase a payment-processing module and integrate it with its other EC software. This module communicates with a payment gateway run by an acquiring bank or another third party.
>
> ▶ **Use a point-of-sale system (POS) operated by an acquirer.** Merchants can redirect cardholders to a POS run by an acquirer. The POS handles the complete payment process and directs the cardholder back to the merchant site once payment is complete. In this case, the merchant system only deals with order information. In this configuration, it is important to find an acquirer that handles multiple cards and payment instruments. If not, the merchant will need to connect with a multitude of acquirers.
>
> ▶ **Use a POS operated by a payment service provider.** Merchants can rely on servers operated by third parties known as payment service providers (PSPs). In this case, the PSP connects with the appropriate acquirers. PSPs must be registered with the various card associations they support.

payment service provider (PSP)
A third-party service connecting a merchant's EC system to the appropriate acquiring bank or financial institution. PSPs must be registered with the various card associations they support.

For a given type of payment card and processing system, the processes and participants are essentially the same for offline (card present) and online (card not present) purchases. Exhibit 10.1 compares the steps involved in making a credit card purchase both online and offline. As the exhibit demonstrates, there is very little difference between the two.

EXHIBIT 10.1 Credit Card Purchases: Online Versus Offline

Online Purchase	Offline Purchase
1. The *customer* decides to purchase a CD on the Web, adding it to the electronic shopping cart and going to the checkout page to enter his or her credit card information.	1. The *customer* selects a CD to purchase, takes it to the checkout counter, and hands his or her credit card to the sales clerk.
2. The *merchant* site receives the customer's information and sends the transaction information to its *payment processing service (PPS)*.	2. The *sales clerk* swipes the card and transfers transaction information to a *point-of-sale (POS)* terminal.
3. The PPS routes information to the *processor* (a large data center for processing transactions and settling funds to the merchant).	3. The POS terminal routes information to the *processor* via a dial-up connection.
4. The processor sends information to the *issuing bank* of the customer's credit card.	4. The processor transmits the credit card data and sales amount with a request for authorization of the sale to their *issuing bank* of the customer's credit card.
5. The issuing bank sends the transaction to the processor, either authorizing the payment or not.	5. If the cardholder has enough credit in his or her account to cover the sale, the issuing bank authorizes the transaction and generates an authorization code; if not the sale is declined.
6. The processor routes the transaction result to the PPS.	6. The processor sends the transaction code back through the processor to the POS.
7. The PPS passes the results to the merchant.	7. The POS shows the outcome to the merchant.
8. The merchant accepts or rejects the transaction.	8. The merchant tells the customer the outcome of the transaction.

Sources: PayPal (2004) and Lamond and Whitman (1996).

Based on the processes outlined in Exhibit 10.1, the key participants in processing card payments online include the following:

> ▶ **Acquiring bank.** Offers a special account called an *Internet Merchant Account* that enables card authorization and payment processing.
> ▶ **Credit card association.** The financial institution providing card services to banks (e.g., Visa and MasterCard).
> ▶ **Customer.** The individual possessing the card.
> ▶ **Issuing bank.** The financial institution that provides the customer with a card.
> ▶ **Merchant.** A company that sells products or services.
> ▶ **Payment processing service.** The service provides connectivity among merchants, customers, and financial networks that enable authorization and payments. Usually these services are operated by companies such as CyberSource (cybersource.com).
> ▶ **Processor.** The data center that processes card transactions and settles funds to merchants.

Periodically, the news covers stories about a serious data breach against one of the firms processing credit card transactions. For example, in January 2009 Heartland Payment Systems reported that cybercriminals had compromised its computer network, gaining access to customer information associated with the 100 million credit card transactions it handles monthly (Worthen 2009). For some consumers, reports of this sort confirm their fears about using credit cards online. In these cases, there was a way to avoid the problem—"one-time credit cards." Basically, most of the major credit card companies, as well as PayPal, offer the means to generate a temporary, one-time credit card number. Once the temporary number is used for a purchase, it is no longer valid. In this way, even if the number is breached, it is useless.

FRAUDULENT CARD TRANSACTIONS

Although the processes used for authorizing and settling card payments offline and online are very similar, there is one substantial difference between the two. In the online world, merchants are held liable for fraudulent transactions. In addition to the lost merchandise and shipping charges, merchants who accept fraudulent transactions can incur additional fees and penalties imposed by the card associations. However, these are not the only costs. There also are the costs associated with combating fraudulent transactions. These include the costs of tools and systems to review orders, the costs of manually reviewing orders, and the revenue that is lost from rejecting orders that are valid. In their 12th annual survey of fraudulent online card transactions, CyberSource (2011) indicated that "managing online fraud continues to be a significant and growing cost for merchants of all sizes." However, for the past two years merchants have improved their fraud management performance.

For the past 12 years, CyberSource has sponsored a survey to address the detection, prevention, and management of fraud perpetrated against online merchants. CyberSource's 2010 survey of 334 merchants documented the following trends (CyberSource 2011):

> ▶ Online fraud peaked in 2008 when survey respondents reported $4.0 billion in revenue losses. Total losses declined to $3.3 billion in 2009 and $2.7 billion in 2010. Likewise, the percentage of revenue lost to fraud declined from 1.4 percent of revenue in 2008 to 0.9 percent in 2010.
> ▶ In 2010, merchants declined to accept 2.7 percent of online orders because of a suspicion of payment fraud. This is a slight increase from the 2.4 percent that were declined in 2009 but well below the 4 percent average rejection rate prior to 2008. This represents a 1.3 percent increase in total orders accepted.

▶ The combined reduction in rejected orders and the decline in losses due to payment fraud imply that merchants are focusing less on sales conversions and reducing order rejection rates due to suspicion of fraud and more on reducing losses from fraud.

▶ In 2010, fraud risk from international orders averaged 2.1 percent, which is similar to the 2009 levels. This is approximately two times the percent for domestic orders. For this reason, the rejection rates for international orders are substantially higher than the rate for domestic orders, hovering near 7 percent on average.

▶ Certain merchants were more susceptible to fraud than others. This was due to a number of factors: the merchant's visibility on the Web, the steps the merchant had taken to combat fraud, the ease with which the merchant's products could be sold on the open market, and the merchant's size. Medium-sized merchants continue to be a prime target because they have a large enough order volume to allow multiple fraud attempts and less secure environments than larger firms to detect or prevent fraud.

▶ In 2010, merchants spent about 0.2 percent of their online revenues to manage online payment fraud. This is about the same level of expenditure over the past couple years. As in the past, merchants continue to allocate the bulk of their fraud management budget to order review staff. As the number of online orders continues to increase, manual review is not a viable long-term strategy for merchants.

In addition to tracking cyberfraud trends, the CyberSource surveys also have monitored the steps taken by merchants to combat fraud. In 2010, merchants continued to use more fraud detection tools than in earlier years. In 2010, the median number of tools used by merchants was 4.6, compared with an average of 3.0 for the years leading up to 2008. Merchants are also spending more to combat fraud. The median amount spent to combat fraud in 2010 was 0.2 percent of online revenues. Most of the money was spent on review staff (47 percent), followed by third-party tools and services (31 percent) and internally developed tools (22 percent). The key tools used in combating fraud were:

▶ **Address verification.** Approximately 80 percent of all merchants use the Address Verification System (AVS), which compares the address entered on a Web page with the address information on file with the cardholder's issuing bank. This method results in a number of false positives, meaning that the merchant may reject a valid order. Cardholders often have new addresses or simply make mistakes in inputting numeric street addresses or zip codes. AVS is only available in the United States and Canada.

▶ **Manual review.** In 2010, over 70 percent of all merchants used the manual review method, which relies on staff to manually review suspicious orders. For small merchants with a small volume of orders, this is a reasonable method. For larger merchants, this method does not scale well, is expensive, and impacts customer satisfaction. Over the past few years, large merchants have begun to recognize the limitations of this method and have substantially reduced the percentage of orders that are manually reviewed.

▶ **Fraud screens and automated decision models.** Larger merchants (those generating over $25 million in revenue) often use fraud screens and automated decision models. These tools are based on automated rules that determine whether a transaction should be accepted, rejected, or suspended. A key element of this method is the ability of the merchant to easily change the rules to reflect changing trends in the fraud being perpetrated against the company.

▶ **Card verification number (CVN).** Approximately 75 percent of all merchants use the card verification number (CVN) method, which compares the verification number printed on the signature strip on the back of the card with the information on file with the cardholder's issuing bank. However, if a fraudster possesses a stolen card, the number is in plain view.

Address Verification System (AVS)
Detects fraud by comparing the address entered on a Web page with the address information on file with the cardholder's issuing bank.

card verification number (CVN)
Detects fraud by comparing the verification number printed on the signature strip on the back of the card with the information on file with the cardholder's issuing bank.

▶ **Card association payer authentication services.** In the last couple of years, the card associations have developed a new set of payer identification services (e.g., Verified by Visa and MasterCard SecureCode). These services require cardholders to register with the systems and merchants to adopt and support both the existing systems and the new systems. In 2004, it was estimated that over 55 percent of merchants would be using this method by 2005. In reality, only 23 percent of merchants in the 2010 survey indicated that they had adopted this method.

▶ **Negative lists.** Approximately 40 percent of all merchants use negative lists. A negative list is a file that includes a customer's information (IP address, name, shipping/billing address, contact numbers, etc.) and the status of that customer. A customer's transaction is matched against this file and flagged if the customer is a known problem.

The overall impact of these tools is that merchants are still rejecting a significant number of orders due to a suspicion of fraud. The problem with these rejection rates is that a number of the rejected orders are valid, resulting in lost revenue.

Section 10.2 ▶ REVIEW QUESTIONS

1. Describe the three types of payment cards.
2. What options does a merchant have in setting up an e-payment system?
3. List the major participants in processing cards online.
4. What costs does an online merchant incur if it submits a fraudulent card transaction?
5. Describe the major trends in fraudulent orders perpetrated against online merchants.
6. What steps are often taken by online merchants to combat fraudulent orders?

10.3 SMART CARDS

smart card
An electronic card containing an embedded microchip that enables predefined operations or the addition, deletion, or manipulation of information on the card.

A **smart card** looks like a plastic payment card, but it is distinguished by the presence of an embedded microchip (see Exhibit 10.2). The embedded chip may be a microprocessor combined with a memory chip or just a memory chip with nonprogrammable logic. Information on a microprocessor card can be added, deleted, or otherwise manipulated; a memory-chip card is usually a "read-only" card, similar to a credit card. Although the microprocessor is capable of running programs like a computer does, it is not a stand-alone computer. The programs and data must be downloaded from and activated by some other device (such as an ATM machine).

EXHIBIT 10.2 Smart Card

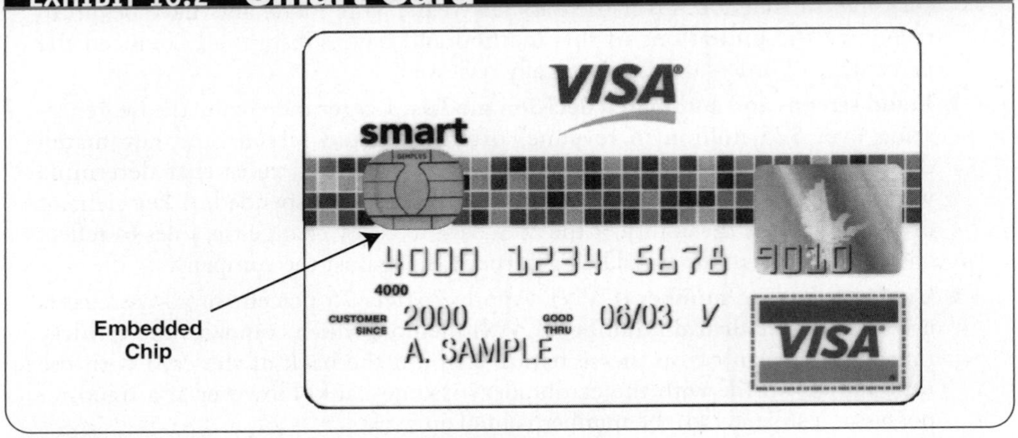

Source: Courtesy of Visa International Service Association.

TYPES OF SMART CARDS

There are two distinct types of smart cards. The first type is a **contact card**, which is activated when it is inserted into a smart card reader. The second type of card is a **contactless (proximity) card**, meaning that the card only has to be within a certain proximity of a smart card reader to process a transaction. *Hybrid cards* combine both types of cards into one.

Contact smart cards have a small gold plate about one-half inch in diameter on the front. When the card is inserted into the smart card reader, the plate makes electronic contact and data are passed to and from the chip. Contact cards can have electronically programmable, read-only memory (EPROM) or electronically erasable, programmable, read-only memory (EEPROM). EPROM cards can never be erased. Instead, data are written to the available space on the card. When the card is full, it is discarded. EEPROM cards are erasable and modifiable. They can be used until they wear out or malfunction. Most contact cards are EEPROM.

In addition to the chip, a contactless card has an embedded antenna. Data and applications are passed to and from the card through the card's antenna to another antenna attached to a smart card reader or other device. Contactless cards are used for those applications in which the data must be processed very quickly (e.g., mass-transit applications, such as paying bus or train fares) or when contact is difficult (e.g., security-entering mechanisms to buildings). Proximity cards usually work at short range, just a few inches. For some applications, such as payments at highway tollbooths, the cards can operate at considerable distances.

With *hybrid* and *dual-interface* smart cards, the two types of card interfaces are merged into one. A hybrid smart card has two separate chips embedded in the card: contact and contactless. In contrast, a dual-interface, or combi, smart card has a single chip that supports both types of interfaces. The benefit of either card is that it eliminates the need to carry multiple cards to support the various smart card readers and applications.

With both types of cards, *smart card readers* are crucial to the operation of the system. Technically speaking, a smart card reader is actually a read/write device. The primary purpose of the **smart card reader** is to act as a mediator between the card and the host system that stores application data and processes transactions. Just as there are two basic types of cards, there are two types of smart card readers—*contact* and *proximity*—which match the particular type of card. Smart card readers can be transparent, requiring a host device to operate, or stand alone, functioning independently. Smart card readers are a key element in determining the overall cost of a smart card application. Although the cost of a single reader is usually low, the cost can be quite high when hundreds or thousands are needed to service a large population of users (e.g., all the passengers traveling on a metropolitan mass transit system).

Like computers, smart cards have an underlying operating system. A **smart card operating system** handles file management, security, input/output (I/O), and command execution and provides an application programming interface (API). Originally, smart card operating systems were designed to run on the specific chip embedded in the card. Today, smart cards are moving toward multiple and open application operating systems such as MULTOS (multos.com) and Java Card (http://www.oracle.com/technetwork/java/javacard/overview/index.html). These operating systems enable new applications to be added during the life of the card.

APPLICATIONS OF SMART CARDS

In many parts of the world, smart cards often are used in place of or in addition to traditional credit and debit cards. Within EC, smart cards are used in the place of standard credit cards for general retail purchases and for transit fares. They also are used to support nonretail and nonfinancial applications. A general discussion of all types of smart card applications can be found at the GlobalPlatform website (globalplatform.org).

In 2010, the global market for smart cards grew to record levels, with North America showing the biggest gains. Approximately 6 billion smart cards were shipped in 2010, as compared to 4 billion in 2008. The biggest driver underlying the growth remains its application in the financial services market where smart cards are used as banking cards, ATM, and payment cards. The largest demand for smart cards continues to come from the Asia-Pacific region.

contact card
A smart card containing a small gold plate on the face that when inserted in a smart card reader makes contact and passes data to and from the embedded microchip.

contactless (proximity) card
A smart card with an embedded antenna, by means of which data and applications are passed to and from a card reader unit or other device without contact between the card and the card reader.

smart card reader
Activates and reads the contents of the chip on a smart card, usually passing the information on to a host system.

smart card operating system
Special system that handles file management, security, input/output (I/O), and command execution and provides an application programming interface (API) for a smart card.

Retail Purchases

The credit card associations and financial institutions are transitioning their traditional credit and debit cards to multiapplication smart cards. In many parts of the world, smart cards have reached mass-market adoption rates. This is especially true in Europe, where the goal was to have all bank cards be smart cards with strong authentication and digital signature capabilities by 2010.

In 2000, the European Commission established an initiative known as the Single Europe Payment Area (SEPA), encompassing 33 European countries. To bring this initiative to fruition, all the EU banks agreed to use the same basic bank card standard, enabling the use of credit and debit cards throughout the EU. The standard, EMV, is named after the three card associations that developed it (Europay, MasterCard, and Visa). It is based on smart cards with a microprocessor chip. The chip is capable of storing not only financial information, but other applications as well, such as strong authentication and digital signatures. The 33 countries have agreed to shift all their magnetic strip cards to EMV smart cards by December 2010. By April 2010, over 70 percent of the cards, 77 percent of the point of sale (POS) terminals, and 93 percent of ATM machines have been migrated (CapGemini 2010).

One benefit of smart cards versus standard cards is that they are more secure. Because they are often used to store more valuable or sensitive information (e.g., cash or medical records), smart cards often are secured against theft, fraud, or misuse. If someone steals a standard payment card, the number on the card is clearly visible, as is the owner's signature and security code. Although it may be hard to forge the signature, in many situations only the number (and security code) is required to make a purchase. The only protection cardholders have is that there usually are limits on how much they will be held liable for (e.g., in the United States it is $50). If someone steals a stored-value card (or the owner loses it), the original owner is out of luck.

However, if someone steals a smart card, the thief is usually out of luck (with the major exception of contactless, or "wave and go," cards used for retail purchases). Some smart cards show account numbers, but others do not. Before the card can be used, the holder may be required to enter a PIN that is matched with the card. Theoretically, it is possible to "hack" into a smart card. Most cards, however, now store information in encrypted form. The smart cards can also encrypt and decrypt data that is downloaded or read from the card. Because of these factors, the possibility of hacking into a smart card is classified as a "class 3" attack, which means that the cost of compromising the card far exceeds the benefits.

The other benefit of smart cards versus standard payment cards is that they can be extended with other payment services. In the retail arena, many of these services are aimed at those establishments where payments are usually made in cash and speed and convenience are important. This includes convenience stores, gas stations, fast-food or quick-service restaurants, and cinemas. Contactless payments exemplify this sort of value-added service.

A few years ago, the card associations began piloting contactless payment systems in retail operations where speed and convenience are crucial. All these systems utilize the existing POS and magnetic strip payment infrastructure used with traditional credit and debit cards. The only difference is that a special contactless smart card reader is required. To make a purchase, a cardholder simply waves his or her card near the terminal, and the terminal reads the financial information on the card. Data supplied by Bank of America supports the contention that contactless credit cards speed things along. The data indicate, for example, that the average contactless fast-food restaurant transaction takes 12.5 seconds, versus 26.7 seconds for the traditional credit card swipe and 33.7 seconds for cash.

In spite of their convenience, the overall uptake of contactless payment cards has been relatively slow. As an example, consider MasterCard PayPass (mastercard.com/aboutourcards/paypass.html). This is an EMV-compatible card that supports both magnetic strip and contactless payments. It was introduced in 2003 in a market trial in Orlando, Florida, and rolled out worldwide in 2005. In 2009, MasterCard issued around 66 million PayPass cards, which is approximately 20 percent of the total number of credit and debit MasterCards issued in that year. Visa's payWave and American Express's ExpressPay have had the same kind of uptake. Again, it is the same chicken-and-egg problem facing any new payment system.

Transit Fares

In major U.S. cities, commuters often have to drive to a parking lot, board a train, and then change to one or more subways or buses to arrive at work. If the whole trip requires a combination of cash and multiple types of tickets, this can be a major hassle. For those commuters who have a choice, the inconvenience plays a role in discouraging the use of public transportation. To eliminate the inconvenience, most major transit operators in the United States have implemented smart card fare-ticketing systems. In addition, the U.S. federal government has provided incentives to employers to subsidize the use of public transportation by their employees. In the United States, the transit systems in Washington, D.C.; Baltimore; San Francisco; Oakland; Los Angeles; Chicago; San Diego; Seattle; Minneapolis; Houston; Boston; Philadelphia; Atlanta; and the New York/New Jersey area have all instituted smart card payment systems. These systems have enabled metropolitan transit operators to move away from multiple, nonintegrated fare systems to systems that require only a single contactless card regardless of how many modes of transportation or how many transportation agencies or companies are involved.

The U.S. smart card transit programs are modeled after those used in Asia (Online File W10.1 provides an example). Like their Asian counterparts, some U.S. transit operators are looking to partner with retailers and financial institutions to combine their transit cards with payment cards to purchase goods and services such as snacks, bridge tolls, parking fees, or food in restaurants or grocery stores located near the transit stations.

In addition to handling transit fares, smart cards and other e-payment systems are being used for other transportation applications. For instance, Philadelphia has retooled all its 14,500 parking meters to accept payment from prepaid smart cards issued by the Philadelphia Parking Authority (philapark.org). Similarly, many of the major toll roads in the United States and elsewhere accept electronic payments rendered by devices called transponders that operate much like contactless smart cards.

Section 10.3 ▶ REVIEW QUESTIONS

1. What is a smart card? Contact card? Contactless card?
2. What is a smart card operating system?
3. Describe the use of smart cards in metropolitan transportation systems.

10.4 STORED-VALUE CARDS

What looks like a credit or debit card, acts like a credit or debit card, but isn't a credit or debit card? The answer is a **stored-value card**. As the name implies, the monetary value of a stored-value card is preloaded on the card. From a physical and technical standpoint, a stored-value card is indistinguishable from a regular credit or debit card. It is plastic and has a magnetic strip on the back, although it may not have the cardholder's name printed on it. The magnetic strip stores the monetary value of the card. This distinguishes a stored-value card from a smart card. With smart cards, the chip stores the value. Consumers can use stored-value cards to make purchases, offline or online, in the same way that they use credit and debit cards—relying on the same networks, encrypted communications, and electronic banking protocols. What is different about a stored-value card is that anyone can obtain one without regard to prior financial standing or having an existing bank account as collateral.

Stored-value cards come in two varieties: *closed loop* and *open loop*. Closed-loop, or single-purpose, cards are issued by a specific merchant or merchant group (e.g., a shopping mall) and can only be used to make purchases from that merchant or merchant group. Mall cards, store cards, gift cards, and prepaid telephone cards are all examples of closed-loop cards. Among closed-loop cards, gift cards have traditionally represented the strongest

stored-value card
A card that has monetary value loaded onto it and that is usually rechargeable.

growth area, especially in the United States. Until 2008, spending in the United States on gift cards was growing at a rapid rate. In 2008, spending retreated to 2006 levels. In 2010, the estimated amount spent on gift cards in the United States during the holiday season was around $25 billion. This was slightly higher than the previous two holiday seasons.

In contrast to a closed-loop card, an open-loop, or multipurpose, card can be used to make debit transactions at a variety of retailers. Open-loop cards also can be used for other purposes, such as receiving direct deposits or withdrawing cash from ATM machines. Financial institutions with card-association branding, such as Visa or MasterCard, issue some open-loop cards. They can be used anywhere that the branded cards are accepted. Payroll cards, government benefit cards, and prepaid debit cards are all examples of open-loop cards.

Stored-value cards may be acquired in a variety of ways. Employers or government agencies may issue them as payroll cards or benefit cards in lieu of checks or direct deposits. Merchants or merchant groups sell and load gift cards. Various financial institutions and nonfinancial outlets sell preloaded cards by telephone, online, or in person. Cash, bank wire transfers, money orders, cashiers' checks, other credit cards, or direct payroll or government deposits fund preloaded cards.

Stored-value cards have been and continue to be marketed heavily to the "unbanked" and "overextended." Approximately 100 million adults in the United States do not have credit cards or bank accounts—people with low incomes, young adults, seniors, immigrants, minorities, and others. Among those with credit cards, 40 percent are running close to their credit limits. The expectation is that these groups will be major users of prepaid cards in the future.

For example, every year individuals in the United States transferred billions of dollars to individuals in Mexico. Instead of sending money orders or cash, programs like the EasySend card from Branch Banking and Trust (BB&T) provide a secure alternative to transferring money to relatives and friends. With the EasySend program, an individual establishes a banking account, deposits money in the account, and mails the EasySend card to a relative or friend, who can then withdraw the cash from an ATM machine. When it was introduced in 2004, EasySend was focused primarily on the Hispanic community. Today, it is used by immigrant populations all over the world.

In a slightly different vein, the MasterCard MuchMusic and Visa Buxx cards provide young people with a prepaid, preloaded card alternative to credit cards or cash. Among other things, these alternatives provide a relatively risk-free way to teach kids fiscal responsibility.

Employers who are using payroll cards as an extension of their direct deposit programs are driving the growth of the prepaid, preloaded card market. Like direct deposit, payroll cards can reduce administrative overhead substantially. Payroll cards are especially useful to companies in the health care and retail sectors and other industries where the workforce is part time or transient and less likely to have bank accounts.

Section 10.4 ▶ REVIEW QUESTIONS

1. What is a closed-loop stored-value card? What is an open-loop card?
2. Identify the major markets for stored-value cards.

10.5 E-MICROPAYMENTS

Consider the following online shopping scenarios:

▶ A customer goes to an online music store and purchases a single song that costs 99¢.
▶ A person goes online to a leading newspaper or news journal (such as *Forbes* or *BusinessWeek*) and purchases (downloads) a copy of an archived news article for $1.50.
▶ A person goes to an online gaming company, selects a game, and plays it for 30 minutes. The person owes the company $3 for the playing time.
▶ A person goes to a website selling digital images and clip art. The person purchases a couple of images at a cost of 80¢.

These are all examples of **e-micropayments**, which are small online payments, usually under $10. From the viewpoint of many vendors, credit and debit cards do not work well for such small payments. Vendors who accept credit cards typically must pay a minimum transaction fee that ranges from 25¢ to 35¢, plus 2 to 3 percent of the purchase price. The same is true for debit cards, where the fixed transaction fees are larger even though there are no percentage charges. These fees are relatively insignificant for card purchases over $5, but can be cost-prohibitive for smaller transactions. Even if the transaction costs were less onerous, a substantial percentage of micropayment purchases are made by individuals younger than 18, many of whom do not have credit or debit cards.

e-micropayments
Small online payments, typically under $10.

Regardless of the vendor's point of view, there is substantial evidence, at least in the offline world, that consumers are willing to use their credit or debit cards for purchases under $5, as evidenced by the number of micropayment purchases made at convenience stores, quick-service restaurants, and coffee shops or were for subway or other transportation tolls.

In the online world, the evidence suggests that consumers are interested in making small-value purchases, but the tie to credit or debit card payments is less direct. For example, as noted in the opening cases, Apple's iTunes music store celebrated its 10 billionth download in 2010. A substantial percentage of these were downloads of single songs at 99¢ a piece. Although most of iTunes' customers paid for these downloads with a credit or debit card, the payments were not on a per-transaction basis. Instead, iTunes customers set up accounts and Apple then aggregates multiple purchases before charging a user's credit or debit card. Other areas where consumers have shown a willingness to purchase items under $5 are cell phone ringtones and ring-back tones and online games. The market for ringtones and ring-back tones is in the billions of dollars. The download of both types of tones is charged to the consumer's cell phone bill. Similarly, the market for online games is in the billions of dollars. Like songs and tones, the download of a game is usually charged to the consumer's account, which is, in turn, paid by credit or debit card.

As far back as 2000, a number of companies have attempted to address the perceived market opportunity by providing e-micropayment solutions that circumvent the fees associated with credit and debit cards. For the most part, the history of these companies is one of unfulfilled promises and outright failure. Digicash, First Virtual, Cybercoin, Millicent, and Internet Dollar are some of the e-micropayment companies that went bankrupt during the dot-com crash. A number of factors played a role in their demise, including the fact that early users of the Internet thought that digital content should be free.

More recently, Bitpass declared on January 2007 that it was going out of business. As late as fall 2006, Bitpass launched a digital wallet service that enabled consumers to store online downloads of digital content and the payment method used to fund their accounts (i.e., credit cards, PayPal, or Automated Clearing House debits). Bitpass succeeded in partnering with a large number of smaller vendors, as well as a number of larger companies, such as Disney Online and ABC, Inc. However, it purposely focused on the sale of digital content rather than branching out into other markets. Its narrow focus was probably a major factor in its demise.

Currently, there are five basic micropayment models that do not depend solely or directly on credit or debit cards and that have enjoyed some amount of success. Some of these are better suited for offline payments than online payments, although there is nothing that precludes the application of any of the models to the online world. The models include the following (D'Agostino 2006):

▷ **Aggregation.** Payments from a single consumer are batched together and processed only after a certain time period has expired (20 business days) or a certain monetary threshold (e.g., $10) is reached. This is the model used by Apple's iTunes. This model is well suited for vendors with a lot of repeat business.

▷ **Direct payment.** Micropayments are added to a monthly bill for existing services, such as a phone bill. This is the model used by the cellular companies for ringtone downloads. The payment service provider PaymentOne (paymentone.com) provides a network and e-commerce platform that enable consumers to add purchases of any size to their phone bills. They also support other micropayment options. A similar service called Boku is offered by Paymo (paymo.com) in 50 countries around the world. Boku enables purchases via your mobile phone number and account.

▶ **Stored value.** Up-front payments are made to a debit account from which purchases are deducted as they are made. Offline vendors (e.g., Starbucks) often use this model, and music-download services use variants of this model.

▶ **Subscriptions.** A single payment covers access to content for a defined period of time. Online gaming companies often use this model, and a number of online newspapers and journals (e.g., *Wall Street Journal*) also use it.

▶ **À la carte.** Vendors process purchases as they occur and rely on the volume of purchases to negotiate lower credit and debit card processing fees. The Golden Tee Golf video game uses this model, and quick-service restaurants (QSRs) such as McDonald's and Wendy's also use it.

In the past few years, micropayments have come to represent a growth opportunity for the credit card companies, because credit cards are being used increasingly as a substitute for cash. In response, both Visa and MasterCard have lowered their fees, especially for vendors such as McDonald's with high transaction volumes. In August 2005, PayPal also entered the micropayment market when it announced a new alternative fee structure of 5 percent plus 5¢ per transaction. This is in contrast to its standard fees of 1.9 to 2.9 percent plus 30¢ per transaction. If a PayPal vendor is being charged at a rate of 1.9 percent plus 30¢, then the alternative fee of 5 percent plus 5¢ will be cheaper for any item that costs $7 or less (you can do the math). It is $12 or less for 2.9 percent plus the 30¢ rate. Overall, the movement of the credit card companies and PayPal into the micropayment market does not bode well for those companies that provide specialized software and services for e-micropayments. In the long run, the credit card companies and PayPal will dominate this market. One exception, which is discussed in this chapter's closing case, is the online social gaming world. Here, there are a number of new micropayment entrants focused solely on social networks, not the broader micropayment market.

Section 10.5 ▶ REVIEW QUESTIONS

1. What is a micropayment?
2. List some of the situations where e-micropayments can be used.
3. Outside of using credit or debit cards, what are some of the alternative ways that an online merchant can handle micropayments?

10.6 E-CHECKING

As noted in Section 10.1, in the United States paper checks are the only payment instrument that is being used less frequently now than 5 years ago. In contrast, e-check usage is growing rapidly. In 2009, the use of online e-checks grew by 9 percent over the previous year, reaching 2.4 billion transactions. Web merchants hope that e-checks will raise sales by reaching consumers who do not have credit cards or who are unwilling to provide credit card numbers online. According to a CyberSource survey (2008), online merchants that implement e-checks experience a 3 to 8 percent increase in sales, on average.

e-check
A legally valid electronic version or representation of a paper check.

An **e-check** is the electronic version or representation of a paper check. E-checks contain the same information as a paper check, can be used wherever paper checks are used, and are based on the same legal framework. An e-check works essentially the same way a paper check works, but in pure electronic form with fewer manual steps. With an online e-check purchase, the buyer simply provides the merchant with his or her account number, the nine-digit bank ABA routing number, the bank account type, the name on the bank account, and the transaction amount. The account number and routing number are found at the bottom of the check in the magnetic ink character recognition (MICR) numbers and characters.

E-checks rely on current business and banking practices and can be used by any business that has a checking account, including small and midsize businesses that may not able to afford other forms of electronic payments (e.g., credit and debit cards). E-checks or their equivalents also can be used with in-person purchases. In this case, the merchant takes a paper check from the buyer at the point of purchase, uses the MICR information and the check number to complete the transaction, and then voids and returns the check to the buyer (see Case 10.1 for a complete description of the process).

CASE 10.1
EC Application

TO POP OR BOC: DIGITAL CHECKS IN THE OFFLINE WORLD

Check usage at the retail point of sale is declining rapidly, accounting for just 4 percent of POS transactions in 2010. In spite of this fact, two methods for converting paper checks into ACH transactions have been on the rise in the past few years. First, there is a special NACHA system known as Purchase Order Processing (POP). POP requires that checks be converted to an e-check at the checkout counter, then immediately handed back to the customers. Although POP was introduced in 1999, it wasn't until much later that it began to be employed by retailers. Today, POP accounts for about 480 million ACH network transactions per year. Second, there is another NACHA system called Back-Office Order Conversion (BOC). With this system, which became effective in March 2007, paper checks are collected at the checkout counter and converted later into an e-check. While BOC only accounts for 160 million ACH transactions per year, it is growing much more rapidly than POP.

The traditional processes used in handling paper checks written by consumers to make purchases in a store involve a number of steps and intermediaries (as many as 28). At a minimum, the checks taken by cashiers are collected periodically throughout the day. After collection, back office personnel process them. Once this is done, an armored car usually takes them from the store and delivers them to the store's bank. The store's bank processes them and sends them to a clearinghouse. From the clearinghouse, they move to the customer's bank. Not only is this time consuming, but it is also costly. Statistics show that it costs companies $1.25 to $1.55 to handle a paper check. This is in comparison to the administrative costs for an e-check, which can be as low as 10¢ per transaction. Based on these figures, any sized company stands to save a substantial amount of money by streamlining these traditional processes. This is where POP and BOC come into play.

Walmart, Old Navy, Office Depot, and Midwest grocery supercenter operator Meijer Inc. are some of the companies that have instituted POP. With POP, consumer checks are converted to ACH transactions at the time of the sale. When a customer writes a check for a purchase at a POS device, an MICR reader scans the check to capture the check details. The reader either keys or inserts the payment amount and the payee name at the time of purchase. At this point, the customer signs a written authorization. The casher then voids the check and returns it to the customer with a signed receipt. Eligible transactions pass through the ACH system, and a record of payment appears on the customer's bank statement.

POP has a number of benefits:

▶ Back-office and check-handling costs are substantially reduced.
▶ Consumer payments are received more quickly.
▶ Availability of funds is improved.
▶ Notification of insufficient funds happens sooner.

Although POP saves money, it also has a number of costs and limitations including:

▶ It requires specialized readers for each checkout counter.
▶ Cashiers need special training to convert the checks to ACH transactions at the POS.
▶ The authorization process can be cumbersome and confusing to consumers.
▶ It slows down the purchase process.

For these reasons, critics have indicated that BOC is a better alternative for the average merchant.

With BOC, the customer experience is similar to the traditional process. The customer writes a check for a purchase. The clerk either accepts or rejects the check after the merchant's verification service or guarantee provider verifies it. This does not require explicit customer authorization to convert the check to an electronic form. Once the checks are collected and moved to the back office, they are scanned into an ACH file and processed electronically. In this way, a merchant only needs one or two scanners and a few personnel to handle the process.

Walgreens, Target, Recreational Equipment Inc. (REI), and Kohl's are all examples of companies that have embraced BOC. Walgreens, for example, began implementing BOC in September 2008 (Geisen 2008). Its implementation is based on an outsourced solution called SPIN from Solutran (*solutran.com*). The solution eliminates all manual-based check deposits. Solutran provides the facilities required to convert a check to a form of electronic settlement, create and maintain images of the check, generate an electronic deposit file, and submit it to a financial institute. None of these processes requires specialized equipment at the POS. The solution has been rolled out to over 6,000 Walgreens stores. Walgreens has estimated that BOC reduces 50 to 70 percent of the costs of handling paper checks and saves them $3 million annually.

Sources: Compiled from Geisen (2008) and Ross (2009).

Questions

1. What does POP stand for and how does it work?
2. What does BOC stand for and how does it work?
3. What are the advantages and disadvantages of POP?

Most businesses rely on third-party software to handle e-check payments. Fiserv (fiserv.com), Chase Paymentech (paymentech.com), and Authorize.Net (authorize.net) are some of the major vendors of software and systems that enable an online merchant to accept and process electronic checks directly from a website. For the most part, these software offerings work in the same way regardless of the vendor.

The system shown in Exhibit 10.3 is based on Authorize.Net and is typical of the underlying processes used to support e-checks. Basically, it is a seven-step process. First, the merchant receives written or electronic authorization from a customer to charge his or her bank account (step 1). Next, the merchant securely transmits the transaction information to the Authorize.Net Payment Gateway server (step 2). The transaction is accepted or rejected based on criteria defined by the Payment Gateway. If accepted, Authorize.Net formats the transaction information and sends it as an ACH transaction to its bank (called the Originating Depository Financial Institution, or ODFI) with the rest of the transactions received that day (step 3). The ODFI receives transaction information and passes it to the ACH Network for settlement. The Automated Clearing House (ACH) Network uses the bank account information provided with the transaction to determine the bank that holds the customer's account (which is known as the Receiving Depository Financial Institution, or RDFI) (step 4). The ACH Network instructs the RDFI to charge or refund the customer's account (the customer is the receiver). The RDFI passes funds from the customer's account to the ACH Network (step 5). The ACH Network relays the funds to the ODFI (Authorize.Net's bank). The ODFI passes any returns to Authorize.Net (step 6). After the funds' holding period, Authorize.Net initiates a separate ACH transaction to deposit the e-check proceeds into the merchant's bank account (step 7).

As Exhibit 10.3 illustrates, the processing of e-checks in the United States relies quite heavily on the **Automated Clearing House (ACH) Network**. The ACH Network is a nationwide batch-oriented electronic funds transfer (EFT) system that provides for the interbank clearing of electronic payments for participating financial institutions. The Federal Reserve and Electronic Payments Network act as ACH operators, which transmit and receive ACH payment entries. ACH entries are of two sorts: credit and debit. An ACH credit entry credits a receiver's account. For example, when a consumer pays a bill sent by a company, the company is the receiver whose account is credited. In contrast, a debit entry debits a receiver's account. For instance, if a consumer preauthorizes a payment to a company, then the consumer is the receiver whose account is debited. In 2009, the ACH Network handled an estimated 18 billion transactions worth $30 trillion (NACHA 2010).

Automated Clearing House (ACH) Network
A nationwide batch-oriented electronic funds transfer system that provides for the interbank clearing of electronic payments for participating financial institutions.

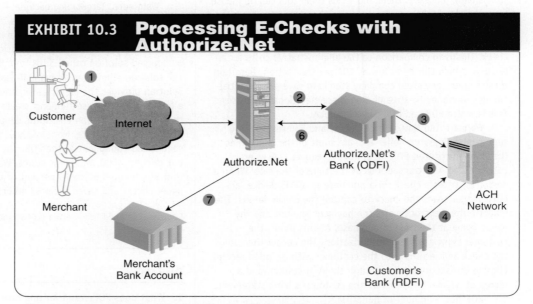

EXHIBIT 10.3 Processing E-Checks with Authorize.Net

Source: Authorize.Net. "eCheck.Net Operating Procedures and Users Guide." October 28, 2004. Authorize.net/files/echecknetuserguide.pdf. Copyright 2004. Authorize.Net and eCheck.Net are registered trademarks of Lightbridge, Inc.

The vast majority of these were direct payment and deposit entries (e.g., direct deposit payroll). Only 2.4 billion of these entries were Web-based ones, although this represented a 20 percent increase from 2008 to 2009.

E-check processing provides a number of benefits:

▶ It reduces the merchant's administrative costs by providing faster and less paper-intensive collection of funds.

▶ It improves the efficiency of the deposit process for merchants and financial institutions.

▶ It speeds the checkout process for consumers.

▶ It provides consumers with more information about their purchases on their account statements.

▶ It reduces the float period and the number of checks that bounce because of nonsufficient funds (NSFs).

Section 10.6 ▶ REVIEW QUESTIONS

1. What is an e-check?
2. Briefly describe how third-party e-check payment systems work.
3. What is the ACH?
4. List the benefits of e-checking.

10.7 MOBILE PAYMENTS

The term *mobile payment* refers to payment transactions initiated or confirmed using a person's cell phone or smartphone. Instead of paying with cash, check, or a credit or debit card, a buyer uses a mobile phone to pay for a range of services and digital or physical goods such as:

▶ Music, videos, ringtones, online game subscriptions, or other digital goods

▶ Transportation fares (bus, subway, or train), parking meters, and other services

▶ Books, magazines, tickets, and other hard goods

Among the wireless carriers, smartphone vendors, and mobile operators, there is a strong belief that mobile payments will emerge as a primary way to pay, potentially eliminating dependence on credit and debit cards, as well as cash. A recent study by *Juniper Research* (2010) appears to support this belief. The study estimated that the value of mobile payments for digital and physical goods, money transfers, and near-field communications (NFC) transactions will reach approximately $630 billion by 2014, which is a 37 percent increase from last year's estimate for 2013. While the bulk of the market involves the sale of digital goods (e.g., music, tickets, and games), the growth of mobile payments for physical goods is strong and will reach $100 billion by 2014. The rapid growth in mobile payments is the result of the widespread adoption of smartphones, the increased use of apps stores (like Apple's App Store), the increasing use of mobile payments for railway and other transportation tickets, and shopping at stores such as Amazon Mobile.

Overall, the study concluded that:

▶ The top three regions for mobile payments (Far East and China, Western Europe and North America) will represent nearly 70 percent of the global mobile payment gross transaction value by 2014.

▶ Vendors, retailers, merchants, content providers, mobile operators, and banks are all actively establishing new services and programs.

▶ However, in some areas such as NFC for example, greater collaboration is required to establish a widely accepted business model that translates easily into tangible services.

Mobile payments come in a variety of flavors including mobile proximity, remote, and POS payments. Each of these is described in the sections that follow.

MOBILE PROXIMITY PAYMENTS

Mobile proximity payments are used for making purchases in physical stores or transportation services. Proximity payments involve a special mobile phone equipped with an integrated chip or smart card, a specialized reader that recognizes the chip when the chip comes within a short distance of the reader, and a network for handling the payment. Essentially, a buyer waves the specially equipped mobile phone near a reader to initiate a payment. For this reason, proximity payments are also called contactless payments. Rarely, is additional authentication (e.g., a pin number) required to complete a contactless transaction. The payment could be deducted from a prepaid account or charged directly to a mobile phone or bank account.

In the United States, mobile proximity payments have only been used in a handful of pilot projects. For instance, from January 2008 to May 2008, a select group of riders of the San Francisco Bay Area Rapid Transit (BART) were able to pay their fares using their mobile phones (Feig 2008). The BART project utilized near-field (wireless) communication (NFC). Basically, the riders' phones were outfitted with NFC-enabled chips. Likewise, NFC readers were installed at the BART turnstiles. In this way, the riders simply tapped their phones on the NFC readers to gain entrance through the turnstiles. The fare was then deducted via the phone from their prepaid account. These same riders could also use their phones to pay for meals at local Jack in the Box fast-food restaurants.

Like many other experimental EC payment systems, the BART system relied on specialized chips, readers, and networks to handle payments. For this reason, the chances against widespread adoption of this particular system are overwhelming, even though the pilot was deemed a success. However, this doesn't mean that NFC won't form the basis of systems going forward. In fact, recent announcements suggest that NFC may play a major role in mobile payments in the next couple of years.

In November 2010, three major U.S. wireless carriers, Verizon, AT&T, and T-Mobile USA, announced a joint venture called Isis to allow their customers to pay for goods and services with their handsets. The mobile payment network uses Discover Financial Services' (DFS) payment network. For details, see online.wsj.com/article/SB10001424052748704740604576301482470575092.html. This announcement was followed a month later by an announcement from Google that its Android phones will be supporting NFC. Finally, in January 2011 Apple announced that the next versions of its iPhones and iPads will incorporate NFC chips.

While there seems to be agreement among many U.S. firms that NFC will play a major role in the future of EC mobile payments, there is still disagreement about the specific readers and networks to be used. In order to make payments via NFC, an entire ecosystem of players must cooperate. That includes network operators, handset and reader makers, banks, credit card companies, application developers, and the like. At the moment, few of these participants seem to be on the same page. Additionally, MasterCard and Visa are said to be developing their own systems. About the only thing they all agree on is that mobile payments are the wave of the future.

Outside the United States, adoption of mobile contactless payments has been much broader. For example, in Japan approximately 50 million customers of NTT DOCOMO use mobile phones for debit card transactions. In the future, they will also use them as credit cards. Interestingly, taxis in Japan, Germany, and other countries are starting to install wireless systems for receiving payments.

MOBILE REMOTE PAYMENTS

A number of initiatives have been launched to support mobile remote payments. These initiatives offer services that enable clients and consumers to use their mobile devices to pay their monthly bills, to shop on the Internet, to transfer funds to other individuals (P2P payments), and to "top off" their prepaid mobile accounts without having to purchase prepaid phone cards.

Case 10.2 provides an example of how mobile remote payments are being used in developing countries like India to service loans to those on the economic margins of the country.

CASE 10.2
EC Application

CLOSING THE DIGITAL DIVIDE WITH MOBILE MICROFINANCE IN BANGALORE (INDIA)

digital divide
Gap between people with effective access to digital and information technology and those without.

The term **digital divide** refers to the gap between people with effective access to digital and information technology and those without (see *en.wikipedia.org/wiki/digital_divide*). The gap is both a symptom and product of the larger issues of poverty and inequality. In underdeveloped and developing countries, the divide has widened as more of everyday life has moved to the digital arena across the globe. This is especially true in the financial arena. Although many of these countries do not have money to implement countrywide wireline phone systems, they can afford wireless wide area networks WWANs. This provides the opportunity to utilize mobile devices to narrow the widening technology gap.

The vast majority of the inhabitants in developing countries such as India are "unbanked." Some estimates put the worldwide number of unbanked at 70 percent of the world's population. Basically, they lack access to some of the basic financial services needed to live their daily lives, much less lift them out of poverty. As a consequence, they often turn to local moneylenders who charge exorbitant interest rates (sometimes more than 10 percent per month) in order to handle personal emergencies, life cycle needs (such as weddings and funerals), or to take advantage of investment opportunities (such as buying cars, homes, land, or equipment).

The world of microfinance is aimed at addressing some of

microfinance
Provision of financial services, in small amounts of money, to poor or low-income clients, including consumers and the self-employed.

these needs. **Microfinance** refers to the provision of financial services, in small amounts of money, to poor or low-income clients, including consumers and the self-employed. Microfinance is also a social movement predicated on the belief that access to a range of financial services will help lift the poor out of poverty. Obviously, financing can come from a variety of sources, both institutional and noninstitutional. However, the term *microfinance* is usually applied to formal financial institutions (such as banks).

A few years back, it was estimated that there were more than 3,000 financial institutions worldwide, serving the needs of some 665 million poor clients. About a fourth of those serviced were classified as microfinance. In 2007, it was estimated that these institutions were providing more than $25 billion in microfinance loans. Most of these individual loans were for amounts less than US$200.

Example: Grameen Koota Bank

Grameen Koota, one of these microfinance institutions, is located in Bangalore, India, and is part of a much larger financial institution, Grameen Bank. In 2009, it had more

than half a million clients and a loan portfolio of more than US$33 million. Sometime in early 2011, it planned to double its client base and increase its portfolio to US$150 million. In order to service its microfinance loans, the bank maintains a large staff of loan officers. In 2011 it planned to double the staff, as well as increase the number of branches from 150 to 250.

One of the primary jobs of these loan officers is to attend weekly client meetings held within the local communities in order to physically collect repayments. This is a high-risk process, plagued by theft, fraud, and embezzlement. Potentially, mobile banking and remote payments could be used to address some of the problems surrounding the collection of loans at Grameen Koota and other microfinance lending institutions. At least this is what Grameen Koota and the founders of start-up mChek, as well as mChek's financial backers at Draper Fisher Juvetson, believe.

As in the rest of India, cell phone use is growing rapidly among Grameen Koota's customers. In countries like India, China, and the Philippines, the penetration of cell phones, even among the poor is skyrocketing. In part, this is a result of rapidly declining costs of owning and using a cell phone. More than 1 billion people live in India; this is more than 17 percent of the world's population. The World Bank estimates that more than 450 million of these people live under the global poverty line—they live on less than US$1.25 per day. Current estimates put the number of cell phone subscribers in India around 740 million. By 2013, India is projected to have approximately 1.2 billion subscribers. This makes India the fastest growing cell phone market in the world and by 2013 the largest cell phone market in the world.

Even though most of the phones owned by the poor inhabitants in India have minimal functionality, they still offer SMS capabilities (which are cheaper than voice calls). These capabilities, in combination with mChek's software, provide Grameen Koota with the mobile means to make loans and receive payments without the need to send loan officers into the local community. In mid-2009 mChek got a boost when Bharti Airtel (India's leading provider of cell phones) announced it had decided to incorporate mChek's software directly into its SIM cards— the device inside a mobile phone that identifies the user and the telephone number.

MChek is not the only Indian company focused on providing mobile microfinance capabilities. Obopay India (a branch of the U.S.-based Obopay) has also developed a microfinance mobile platform. Obopay is working with Grameen Solutions, one of the organizations created by Muhammad Yunus, who received the Nobel Peace Prize in 2006 along with Grameen Bank for his work with microcredit.

Note that mobile banking can help the world's poor in other ways. For example, the State Bank of India offers savings accounts by using mobile phones (for about

(*continued*)

CASE 10.2 (continued)

36 percent of India's population). India has ambitious plans for the program, which is designed to be as convenient and user-friendly as possible. All a customer of this program has to do is go to the local grocery, mobile recharge agent, or a pharmacy to get a zero balance account. Following that, the user can deposit, withdraw, remit, and check balances all by just clicking a few buttons on the mobile phone.

Together with the rise in international microlending to those in developing countries, wider use of mobile banking and finance software has the potential to make a difference in the lives of citizens of India and elsewhere. Anything mobile finance can do to spur greater participation in the banking systems of these countries has a tangible, immediate impact on those countries by increasing the funds available to local entrepreneurs and businesses.

For further discussion, see *mint.com/blog/trends/the-future-of-mobile-finance*.

Sources: Compiled from Talbot (2008), Mitra (2008), and Shevock (2010).

Questions

1. What is microfinance?
2. What problem is Grameen Koota trying to solve by adopting mobile loans and payments?
3. How will mobile loans and payments work for organizations like Grameen Koota?
4. What are the social and economic impacts of the program?

Making Mobile Payments

A number of initiatives have been launched to support mobile remote payments. These initiatives offer services that enable clients and customers to pay their monthly bills, shop on the Internet, transfer funds to other individuals (P2P payments), and "top off" their prepaid mobile accounts without having to purchase prepaid phone cards. In each of these cases, the underlying processes are basically the same and include the following steps:

1. The payer initiating the payment sets up an account with a mobile payment service provider (MPSP).
2. The user selects an item to purchase. The merchant asks for a payment.
3. To make the payment, the payer sends a text message (or a command) to the MPSP that includes the dollar amount and the receiver's mobile phone number.
4. The MPSP receives the information and sends a message back to the payer, confirming the request and asking for the customer's PIN.
5. The payer receives the request on his or her mobile device and enters the PIN.
6. After the MPSP receives the payer's PIN, money is transferred to the receiver's account (credit card or bank account). The payer's account is debited.
7. After the transaction occurs, the payment information is sent to the payer's mobile device and his or her account at MPSP is debited.

MOBILE POS PAYMENTS

Similar steps are used to enable merchants or service providers the opportunity to conduct POS transactions without the need for special POS terminals. These payments have been labeled *mobile POS (mPOS)* transactions. With mPOS, the merchant utilizes a special mobile service to send a payment request from his or her mobile device to the customer's phone number. Once the request is received, the customer enters his or her PIN. At this point, the service sends a confirmation to both the merchant and the customer. The transactions are completed by debiting the customer's account and crediting the merchant's account. Even though the merchant is charged transaction and communication fees by the service operator, the cost is substantially less than a POS credit card–based transaction. These services are aimed at small businesses and independent operators such as doctors, dentists, delivery companies, taxis, and plumbers.

Section 10.7 ▶ REVIEW QUESTIONS

1. Discuss proximity-based wireless payments. How have they been used in the transportation arena?
2. What are the basic processes used in handling mobile remote payments?

10.8 B2B ELECTRONIC PAYMENTS

B2B payments usually are much larger and significantly more complex than the payments made by individual consumers. The dollar values often are in the hundreds of thousands, the purchases and payments involve multiple items and shipments, and the exchanges are much more likely to engender disputes that require significant work to resolve. Simple e-billing or EBPP (i.e., electronic bill presentment and payment) systems lack the rigor and security to handle these B2B situations. This section examines the processes by which companies present invoices and make payments to one another over the Internet.

CURRENT B2B PAYMENT PRACTICES

B2B payments are part of a much larger financial supply chain that includes procurement, contract administration, fulfillment, financing, insurance, credit ratings, shipment validation, order matching, payment authorization, remittance matching, and general ledger accounting. From a buyer's perspective, the chain encompasses the procurement-to-payment process. From the seller's perspective, the chain involves the order-to-cash cycle. Regardless of the perspective, in financial supply chain management the goal is to optimize accounts payable (A/P) and accounts receivable (A/R), cash management, working capital, transaction costs, financial risks, and financial administration.

Unlike the larger (physical) supply chain, inefficiencies still characterize the financial supply chains of most companies. A number of factors create these inefficiencies, including:

- The time required to create, transfer, and process paper documentation
- The cost and errors associated with manual creation and reconciliation of documentation
- The lack of transparency in inventory and cash positions when goods are in the supply chain
- Disputes arising from inaccurate or missing data
- Fragmented point solutions that do not address the complete end-to-end processes of the trade cycle

These inefficiencies are evident especially with A/P and A/R processes where payments are still made with paper.

The world of B2B payments continues to be slow to change. The vast majority of B2B payments are still made by check, and the barriers to electronic payments remain essentially the same—IT and constraints posed by the difficulty of integrating various systems, the inability of trading partners to send and receive automated remittance information, and difficulty in convincing customers and suppliers to adopt electronic payments. However, there is some evidence that companies are beginning to move to B2B e-payments. For example, in 2009 the number of B2B transactions on the ACH network increased 3 percent from the year before to 2 billion payments.

ENTERPRISE INVOICE PRESENTMENT AND PAYMENT

The process by which companies present invoices and make payments to one another through the Internet is known as **enterprise invoice presentment and payment (EIPP)**. For many firms, presentment and payment are costly and time consuming. It can cost up to $15 to generate a paper invoice and between $25 and $50 to resolve a disputed invoice. On the payment side, it takes 3 to 5 days for a check to arrive by mail. This means that millions of dollars of B2B payments are tied up in floats. This reduces the recipients' cash flow and increases the amount they must borrow to cover the float. In the same vein, manual billing and remittance can result in errors, which in turn can result in disputes that hold up payments. Given that most firms handle thousands of invoices and payments yearly, any reduction in time, cost, or errors can result in millions of dollars of savings. Improved cash flow, customer service, and data quality, along with reduced processing costs, are the primary reasons companies turn to EIPP.

enterprise invoice presentment and payment (EIPP)
Presenting and paying B2B invoices online.

EIPP Models

EIPP automates the workflow surrounding presentment and payment. Like EBPP, there are three EIPP models: seller direct, buyer direct, and consolidator.

Seller Direct. This solution links one seller to many buyers for invoice presentment. Buyers navigate to the seller's website to enroll in the seller's EIPP program. The seller generates invoices on the system and informs the appropriate buyers that they are ready for viewing. The buyers log into the seller's website to review and analyze the invoices. The buyers may authorize invoice payment or communicate any disputes. Based on predetermined rules, disputes may be accepted, rejected, or reviewed automatically. Once payment is authorized and made, the seller's financial institution processes the payment transaction.

This model typically is used when there are preestablished relationships between the seller and its buyers. If a seller issues a large number of invoices or the invoices have a high value, then there can be a substantial payoff from implementing an EIPP. For this reason, firms in the manufacturing, telecommunication, utilities, health care, and financial services industries use this model often.

Buyer Direct. In this model, there is one buyer for many sellers. Sellers enroll in the buyer's EIPP system at the buyer's website. Sellers post invoices to the buyer's EIPP, using the buyer's format. Once an invoice is posted, the buyer's staff will be notified. The buyer reviews and analyzes the invoices on the system. The buyer communicates any disputes to the appropriate seller. Based on predetermined rules, disputes may be accepted, rejected, or reviewed automatically. Once an invoice is approved, the buyer will authorize payment, which the buyer's financial institution will process. This is an emerging model based on the buyer's dominant position in B2B transactions. Again, it is used when the buyer's purchases result in a high volume of invoices. Companies such as Walmart are in a strong position to institute buyer-direct EIPPs.

Consolidator. This is a many-to-many model with the consolidator acting as an intermediary, collecting or aggregating invoices from multiple sellers and payments from multiple buyers. Consolidators are generally third parties who not only provide EIPP services but also offer other financial services (e.g., insurance, escrow). In this model, the sellers and buyers register with the consolidator's EIPP system. The sellers generate and transfer invoice information to the EIPP system. The consolidator notifies the appropriate buyer organization that the invoice is ready. The buyer reviews and analyzes the invoice. Disputes are communicated through the consolidator EIPP. Based on predetermined rules, disputes may be accepted, rejected, or reviewed automatically. Once the buyer authorizes the invoice payment, the consolidator initiates the payment. Either the buyer's or the seller's financial institution processes the payment.

The consolidator model eliminates the hassles associated with implementing and running an EIPP. The model has gained ground in those industries where multiple buyers rely on the same suppliers. The JPMorgan Chase Xign Business Settlement Network (jpmorgan.com/xign) and the Global eXchange Services (GXS) Trading Grid (gxs.com) are both third-party consolidators linking thousands of suppliers and buyers. Xign has more than 100,000 active suppliers in its network. GSX's Trading Grid supports online trading among 100,000 customers in over 50 countries. Each of these networks eliminates the need for point-to-point connections between suppliers and buyers; automates core functions of the A/P process, including invoice receipt, validation, routing, dispute management, approval, and payment; and complements and integrates with the suppliers' and buyers' existing purchasing and procurement systems. Online File W10.2 provides a good example of the benefits of the consolidator model.

EIPP Options

A variety of online options are available for making payments in an EIPP system. They differ in terms of cost, speed, auditability, accessibility, and control. The selection of a particular mechanism depends on the requirements of the buyers and sellers. Some frequently used B2B payment options follow.

ACH Network. The ACH Network is the same network that underlies the processing of e-checks (described in Section 12.6). The difference is that there are three types of B2B payments, which vary by the amount of remittance information that accompanies the payments. The remittance information enables a buyer or seller to examine the details of a particular invoice or payment. The three types of ACH entries for B2B transactions are: Cash Concentration or Disbursement (CCD), which is a simple payment, usually for a single invoice, that has no accompanying remittance data and is typically initiated by the buyer who credits the seller's account; Cash Concentration or Disbursement with Addenda (CCD+), which is the same as a CCD payment except that it has a small amount of remittance data (up to 80 characters); and Corporate Trade Exchange (CTX), which generally is used to pay multiple invoices and has a large amount of accompanying remittance data (up to a maximum of 9,999 records of 80 characters each).

The ACH Network does not require any special hardware. The cost of the software needed to initiate ACH transactions depends on the volume of CTX transactions. High volumes of CTX transactions require a much larger investment. In addition to hardware and software costs, the buyer's and the seller's financial institutions also charge file, maintenance, transaction, and exception handling fees for ACH transactions.

Purchasing Cards. Although credit cards are the instrument of choice for B2C payments, this is not the case in the B2B marketplace. In the B2B marketplace, the major credit card companies and associations have encouraged businesses and government agencies to rely on *purchasing cards* instead of checks for repetitive, low-value transactions. **Purchasing cards (p-cards)** are special-purpose payment cards issued to a company's employees. They are used solely for the purpose of paying for nonstrategic materials and services (e.g., stationery, office supplies, computer supplies, repair and maintenance services, courier services, and temporary labor services) up to a limit (usually $1,000 to $2,000). These purchases often represent the majority of a company's payments but only a small percentage of the dollars spent. Purchasing cards operate essentially the same as any other charge card and are used for both offline and online purchases. The major difference between a credit card and a purchase card is that the latter is a nonrevolving account, meaning that it needs to be paid in full each month, usually within 5 days of the end of the billing period.

> **purchasing cards (p-cards)**
> Special-purpose payment cards issued to a company's employees to be used solely for purchasing nonstrategic materials and services up to a preset dollar limit.

Purchasing cards enable a company or government agency to consolidate the purchases of multiple cardholders into a single account and, thus, issue a single invoice that can be paid through EDI, EFT, or an e-check. This has the benefit of freeing the purchasing department from day-to-day procurement activities and from the need to deal with the reconciliation of individual invoices. With a single invoice, accounts can be settled more quickly, enabling a company or agency to take advantage of discounts associated with faster payment. A single invoice also enables a company or agency to more easily analyze the spending behavior of the cardholders. Finally, the spending limits make it easier to control unplanned purchases. Some estimates suggest that efficiencies resulting from the use of purchasing cards can reduce transaction costs from 50 percent to 90 percent. To learn more about purchasing cards, see the National Association of Purchasing Card Professionals (napcp.org) and Purchasing Card News (purchasingcardnews.co.uk).

Fedwire or Wire Transfer. Among the forms of online B2B payments, Fedwire is second only to ACH in terms of frequency of use. Fedwire, also known as wire transfer, is a funds transfer system developed and maintained by the U.S. Federal Reserve system. It typically is used with larger dollar payments where time is the critical element. The settlement of real estate transactions, the purchase of securities, and the repayment of loans are all examples of situations where Fedwire is likely to be used. When Fedwire is used, a designated Federal Reserve Bank debits the buyer's bank account and sends a transfer order to the seller's Federal Reserve Bank, which credits the seller's account. All Fedwire payments are immediate and irrevocable.

Letters of Credit for Global Payments. *Letters of credit* often are used when global B2B payments need to be made, especially when there is substantial risk associated with the payment. A **letter of credit (L/C)**, also called a *documentary credit*, is issued by a bank on behalf of a buyer (importer). It guarantees a seller (exporter) that payment for goods or services will be made, provided the terms of the L/C are met. Before the credit is issued, the buyer and seller agree on all terms and conditions in a purchase and sale contract. The buying company then instructs its bank to issue a documentary credit in accordance with the contract. A credit can be payable at sight or at term. *At sight* means that payment is due upon presentation of

> **letter of credit (L/C)**
> A written agreement by a bank to pay the seller, on account of the buyer, a sum of money upon presentation of certain documents.

documents after shipment of the goods or after a service is provided. Alternatively, if the seller allows the buyer an additional period, after presentation of documents, to pay the credit (30, 60, 90 days, etc.), then the credit is payable *at term*. L/C arrangements usually involve a series of steps that can be conducted much faster online than offline.

For sellers the main benefit of an L/C is reduced risk—the bank assures the credit-worthiness of the buyer. For those global situations where the buyer is a resident in a country with political or financial instability, the risk can be reduced if the L/C is confirmed by a bank in the seller's country. Reduced risk also is of benefit to buyers who may use this fact to negotiate lower prices.

Section 10.8 ▶ REVIEW QUESTIONS

1. Describe the financial supply chain.
2. Describe the current state of B2B e-payments.
3. What is electronic invoice presentment and payment (EIPP)?
4. Describe the three models of EIPP.
5. Describe the basic EIPP options.
6. What is a purchasing card?

MANAGERIAL ISSUES

Some managerial issues related to this chapter are as follows.

1. **What payment methods should your B2C site support?** Most B2C sites use more than one payment gateway to support customers' preferred payment methods. Companies that only accept credit cards rule out a number of potential segments of buyers (e.g., teenagers, non–U.S. customers, and customers who cannot or do not want to use credit cards online). EFT, e-checks, stored-value cards, and PayPal are some possible alternatives to credit cards. The e-check is not used at all in Asia, because it is not an efficient method in the electronic era; thus, selecting the globally acceptable payment method is important for the globalization of EC.

2. **What e-micropayment strategy should your e-marketplace support?** If your EC site deals with items priced less than $10, credit cards are not a viable solution. Many digital-content products cost less than $1. For small-value products, e-micropayments should be supported. Fees may be taken from a prepaid account that is tied to the buyer's bank account or credit card, or the fee may be charged to the buyer's cell phone bill. The use of stored-value smart cards on the Internet has emerged, but has not widely penetrated the market because buyers need to install the card reader/writer. Your company should support multiple options so that customers can choose their preferred payment method.

3. **What payment methods should the C2C marketplace support?** In C2C sites like eBay, an e-mail payment method such as PayPal is popular. An alternative secure payment service is the escrow service. A buyer pays the e-market operator, and the e-market operator pays the seller once the delivery is confirmed by the buyer.

The Internet Auction Corporation site, the leading auctioneer in Korea, which was acquired by eBay, supports an escrow service for the payment of successful bids. The reason it provides the service is because PayPal restricts Korean customers from making purchases with PayPal. However, PayPal does allow Koreans to receive payment for goods they have sold. The bottom line is that it is important to understand popular payment methods in particular markets.

4. **Should we outsource our payment gateway service?** It takes time, skill, money, software, and hardware to integrate the payment systems of all the parties involved in processing any sort of e-payment. For this reason, even a business that runs its own EC site outsources the e-payment service. Many third-party vendors provide payment gateways designed to handle the interactions among the various financial institutions that operate in the background of an e-payment system. Also, if a website is hosted by a third party (e.g., Yahoo! Store), an e-payment service will be provided.

5. **How secure are e-payments?** Security and fraud continue to be major issues in making and accepting e-payments of all kinds. This is especially true with regard to the use of credit cards for online purchases. B2C merchants are employing a wide variety of tools (e.g., address verification and other authentication services) to combat fraudulent orders. These and other measures that are employed to ensure the security of e-payments have to be part of a broader security program that weighs risks against issues such as the ease of use and the fit within the overall business context.

6. **What B2B payment methods should we use?** Keep an open mind about online alternatives. When it comes to paying suppliers or accepting payments from partners, most large businesses have opted to stick with the tried-and-true methods of EFT or checks over other methods of electronic payment. For MROs, consider using purchasing cards. For global trade, electronic letters of credit are popular. The use of e-checks is another area where cost savings can accrue. With all these methods, a key factor is determining how well they work with existing accounting and ordering systems and with business partners.

SUMMARY

In this chapter, you learned about the following EC issues as they relate to the chapter's learning objectives.

1. **Payment revolution.** Cash and checks are no longer kings. Debit and credit cards now rule—both online and offline. This means that online B2C businesses need to support debit and credit card purchases. In international markets outside of Western Europe, buyers often favor other forms of e-payment (e.g., bank transfers). With the exception of PayPal, virtually all the alternatives to charge cards have failed. None have gained enough traction to overcome the "chicken-and-egg" problem. Their failure to gain critical mass has resulted from the confluence of a variety of factors (e.g., they required specialized hardware or setup or they failed to mesh with existing systems).

2. **Using payment cards online.** The processing of online card payments is essentially the same as it is for brick-and-mortar stores and involves essentially the same players and the same systems—banks, card associations, payment processing services, and the like. This is one of the reasons why payment cards predominate in the online world. The major difference is that the rate of fraudulent orders is much higher online. Surveys, such as those conducted annually by CyberSource, indicate that merchants have adopted a wide variety of methods over the past few years to combat fraudulent orders, including address verification, manual review, fraud screens and decision models, card verification numbers, card association authentication services, and negative files. In the same vein, some consumers have turned to virtual or single-use credit cards to avoid using their actual credit card numbers online.

3. **Smart cards.** Smart cards look like credit cards but contain embedded chips for manipulating data and have a large memory capacity. Cards that contain microprocessor chips can be programmed to handle a wide variety of tasks. Other cards have memory chips to which data can be written and from which data can be read. Most memory cards are disposable, but others—smart cards—can hold large amounts of data and are rechargeable. Smart cards have been and will be used for a number of purposes, including contactless retail payments, paying for mass transit services, identifying cardholders for government services, securing physical and network access, and storing health care data and verifying eligibility for health care and other government services. Given the sensitive nature of much of the data on smart cards, public key encryption and other cryptographic techniques are used to secure their contents.

4. **Stored-value cards.** A stored-value card is similar in appearance to a credit or debit card. The monetary value of a stored value card is housed in a magnetic strip on the back of the card. Closed-loop stored-value cards are issued for a single purpose by a specific merchant (e.g., a Starbucks gift card). In contrast, open-loop stored-value cards are more like standard credit or debit cards and can be used for multiple purposes (e.g., a payroll card). Those segments of the population without credit cards or bank accounts—people with low incomes, young adults, seniors, and minorities—are spurring the substantial growth of stored-value cards. Specialized cards, such as EasySend, make it simple for immigrant populations to transfer funds to family members in other countries. Similarly, specialized cards, such as MasterCard's MuchMusic, provide teens and preteens with prepaid debit cards that function like standard credit or debit cards while helping parents monitor and maintain control over spending patterns.

5. **E-micropayments.** When an item or service being sold online costs less than $5, credit cards are too costly for sellers. A number of other e-payment systems have been introduced to handle these micropayment situations. For the most part, they have failed. Yet, ample evidence indicates that consumers are interested in using their credit and debit cards for small-value online purchases (e.g., songs on iTunes, online games, and ringtone sales). In response, a number of newer micropayment models, such as aggregated purchases, have been developed to reduce the fees associated with credit and debit cards.

6. **E-checking.** E-checks are the electronic equivalent of paper checks. They are handled in much the same way as paper checks and rely quite heavily on the ACH Network. E-checks offer a number of benefits, including

speedier processing, reduced administrative costs, more efficient deposits, reduced float period, and fewer "bounced" checks. These factors have resulted in the rapid growth of e-check usage. The rapid growth is also being spurred by the use of e-checks for in-store purchases. Purchase Order Processing (POP) and Back-Office Order Conversion (BOC) are two systems, established by the NACHA, that enable retailers to convert paper checks used for in-store purchases to ACH debits (i.e., e-checks) without the need to process the checks using traditional procedures.

7. **Mobile payments.** The wireless and smartphone companies are rapidly enabling their customers to initiate or confirm payments and other financial transactions via their cell phones and smartphones. These transactions are one of two types: mobile proximity payments or mobile remote payments. With mobile proximity payments, also known as "contactless" payments, a cell phone or smartphone is outfitted with a special chip that allows users to swipe their phones near a payment device (e.g., POS reader), much like a contactless smart card or credit card. With mobile remote payments, the mobile handset can be used to make person-to-person, person-to-business, and business-to-business payments.

The uptake of mobile proximity payments is currently hindered because the vendors cannot agree on the chip, reader, or network standards to be employed.

8. **B2B electronic payments.** B2B payments are part of a much larger financial supply chain that encompasses the range of processes from procurement to payment and order to cash. Today, the vast majority of B2B payments are still made by check, although many organizations are moving to enterprise invoice presentment and payment (EIPP). There are three models of EIPP: seller direct (buyers go to the seller's website), buyer direct (sellers post invoices at the buyer's website), and consolidator (many buyers and many sellers are linked through the consolidator's website). Two of the largest consolidators are Xign Payment Services and GSX Trading Grid. In addition to these models, there are several EIPP payment options, including the ACH Network, purchasing cards, wire transfers, and letters of credit (L/C). The move to EIPP is being inhibited by the shortage of IT staff, the lack of integration of payment and account systems, the lack of standard formats for remittance information, and the inability of trading partners to send or receive electronic payments with sufficient remittance information.

KEY TERMS

Address Verification System (AVS)	555	Digital divide	567	Payment service provider (PSP)	553
Authorization	552	E-check	562	Purchasing cards (P-cards)	571
Automated Clearing House (ACH) Network	564	E-micropayments	561	Settlement	552
		Enterprise invoice presentment and payment (EIPP)	569	Smart card	556
Card verification number (CVN)	555	Letter of credit (L/C)	571	Smart card operating system	557
Contact card	557	Microfinance	567	Smart card reader	557
Contactless (proximity) card	557	Payment cards	552	Stored-value card	559

DISCUSSION QUESTIONS

1. Boku (boku.com) provides a system call Paymo (for pay mobile) that enables buyers to charge purchases to their cell phone accounts. How does the system work? Who are some of the companies supporting Paymo? Do you think the Paymo system will succeed? What factors will play a major role in its success or failure?

2. A textbook publisher is interested in selling individual book chapters on the Web. What types of e-payment methods would you recommend to the publisher? What sorts of problems will the publisher encounter with the recommended methods?

3. Recently, a merchant who accepts online credit card payments has experienced a wave of fraudulent orders. What steps should the merchant take to combat the fraud?

4. A retail clothing manufacturer is considering e-payments for both its suppliers and its buyers. What sort of e-payment method should it use to pay for office supplies? How should it pay suppliers of raw materials? How should its customers—both domestic and international clothing retailers—pay?

5. A metropolitan area wants to provide riders of its public transportation system with the ability to pay transit fares, as well as make retail purchases, using a single contactless smart card. What sorts of problems will it encounter in setting up the system, and what types of problems will the riders encounter in using the cards?

TOPICS FOR CLASS DISCUSSION AND DEBATES

1. If you were running an online retail store would you permit purchases with e-checks? Why or why not?

2. Why is the marketplace for electronic payment systems so volatile? Is there a need for some other form of electronic payment?

3. Besides e-books and online music, what are some of the other places where e-micropayments could be used?

4. Which would you prefer, paying for goods and services with a physical debit or credit card or paying with your cell phone? What are some of the benefits and limitations of each?

5. Several companies have entered the e-book business. At the moment, Amazon.com has the lead, although Google is trying to make inroads. Debate which of these two companies has the best chance of dominating this market in the long run. Barnes & Noble? Explain.

INTERNET EXERCISES

1. A number of years ago, eBay offered a payment system called Billpoint. It was a head-to-head competitor with PayPal. Use online sources to research why PayPal succeeded and Billpoint failed. Write a report based on your findings.

2. Select a major retail B2C merchant in the United States and one outside of North America. Detail the similarities and differences in the e-payment systems they offer. According to CyberSource's "Insider's Guide to ePayment Management" (cybersource.com/resources/collateral/Resource_Center/whitepapers_and_reports/insiders_guide.pdf), what other payment systems could the sites offer?

3. Download "Transit and Contactless Financial Payments" from smartcardalliance.org/pages/publictions-transit-financial. What are the key requirements for an automated fare-collection system? Based on the report, what type of payment system did the MTA New York City Transit pilot? What factors helped determine the type of system to be piloted? How did the pilot work?

4. Go to nacha.org. What is NACHA? What is its role? What is the ACH? Who are the key participants in an ACH e-payment?

5. Both Walgreens and Kohl's utilize Solutran's SPIN for their BOC systems. Based on information provided at Solutran's website (solutran.com) and information found in online articles about the system, what kinds of capabilities and benefits does the system provide? What is unique about the system? If you were running a large retail operation would you focus on POP or BOC?

TEAM ASSIGNMENTS AND PROJECTS

1. **Assignment for the Opening Case**

   Read the opening case and answer the following questions. Suppose Amazon decided to resurrect its Amazon Pages program.

   a. What sort of micropayment system should it use in order to run this business profitably?

   b. What types of business and legal issues would it encounter in this business?

   c. Besides the book and music businesses, describe some other online business where micropayments are or would be critical to its success.

2. Select some B2C sites that cater to teens and others that cater to older consumers. Have team members visit these sites. What types of e-payment methods do they provide? Do the methods used differ based on the target market? What other types of e-payment would you recommend for the various sites and why?

3. Write a report comparing smart card applications in two or more European and/or Asian countries. In the report, discuss whether those applications would succeed in North America.

4. Have one team represent MasterCard PayPass and another represent Visa payWave. The task of each team is to convince a company that its product is superior.

5. Have each team member interview three to five people who have made a purchase or sold an item via an online auction. Find out how they paid. What security and privacy concerns did they have regarding the payment? Is there an ideal payment method?

6. AT&T, Verizon, T-Mobile, and Discovery Financial Services announced a project called Isis that will result in a new cell phone–powered payment system. How will this system work? What are some of the competing systems that have been proposed? Which system has the best chance of success and why?

7. Go to the NACHA site for the Council on Electronic Billing and Payment (cebp.nacha.org). On the site it provides information (see the "initiatives" section) on various forms of EIPP and EBPP. Compare and contrast two of the forms it details.

Closing Case

FREEMIUMS IN THE SOCIAL GAMING WORLD

Social games played on sites like Facebook and MySpace are the hottest part of the game industry.

The Problem

In the early phase of the market for social games, the market was dominated by three companies: Zynga (zynga.com), Playdom (playdom.com), and Playfish (playfish.com). In November 2009, Electronic Arts (ea.com) acquired Playfish for $300 million in cash and stock and guaranteed another $100 million in bonus payouts if certain milestones were met by 2012. A short time later in December 2009, Digital Sky Technologies (dst-global.com), a Russian firm with offices in Moscow and London, bought a $180 million stake in Zynga.

Today, the social game market has shifted. Zynga is the clear market leader followed by RockYou (rockyou.com) and Crowdstar (crowdstar.com). In fact, Zynga is now estimated to be valued at US$5.5 billion up from an estimated US$2.5 billion a few years ago. Indeed, its estimated worth has surpassed the traditional game leader Electronic Arts, whose stock market value is approximately US$5.2 billion.

To the casual observer, these valuations seem astounding. It is the case that social games are simpler than the average video game and take much less time to play. It is also the case that they have expanded the game audience beyond traditional video gamers who tend to be young males. Yet, from an economic standpoint, the major difference between social games and video games is that the former are free. If players don't have to pay, where does the return on investment (ROI) for companies like Electronic Arts and investors like DST come from? The answer lies in micropayments.

The Solution

In 2007, Facebook launched a platform that enabled software developers to create applications for the site. Currently, the site has tens of thousands of applications. Today the most popular application category for social networks is social gaming. On Facebook, for example, there are 14 games that have more than 12 million active players per month. This is more than the number of monthly players for World of Warcraft, the most popular online game. Of course, they pay to play. Among the top 10 most popular social games on Facebook, Zynga has six offerings—Farmville, Café Word, TexasHoldem, Mafia Wars, Fishville, and Petville—with a combined audience of over 180 active players per month, while Playfish has two offerings—Pet Society and Restaurant City—which have 60 million active users per month.

If it doesn't cost anything to play a social game, then how does the game company make its money? One way is with advertising. Either continually or at various times during the game, ads can be displayed. Just as the advertising firms do with the search engine companies or other websites, the game companies can either be paid for "impressions" or "clicks." Historically, advertising revenues have been very low for all kinds of applications on Facebook or any other of the social networks. It is especially true for social games because advertising firms like to pay when a user clicks on an advertisement rather than paying for simply displaying the advertisement. Obviously, clicking on an advertisement while the game is in progress is disrupting to the flow of the game.

Increasingly, application developers of all sorts are turning toward a new model, which has been called "freemium" in the United States. The "freemium" has its roots in Asia and is built on the concept of providing a service for free and charging either for virtual goods or premium features. For example, in China the most popular instant messenger service is Tencent's QQ. Tencent is not a household name, except in Asia. In 2010, the company generated over US$1 billion in revenue with operating profits over US$300 million. Around 10 percent of the revenue came from ads. Seventy percent came from Internet services like games and digital goods: "gifts" such as virtual flowers, background music for users' profiles, and virtual pets. Some of the most popular items involve QQ Show, which is like Yahoo! Avatars. However, unlike Yahoo! Avatars, QQ avatars can be customized and personalized for a price. You can buy new clothes, hairstyles, accessories, and backgrounds. QQ users can also create a living space for their avatars, furnishing it with digital plants, couches, and the like. All of this can be done for a few RMBs here and a few RMBs there. RMB stands for renminbi, the Chinese currency, which is about US$.15. Pretty soon all of those RMBs add up to millions of dollars.

In the case of social games, the freemium model is built on the notion of giving away the games but charging players a small amount for virtual goods that enhance the game experience. One example is Mob Wars, a Zynga Facebook application in which players rise through the ranks of a gangster organization by committing crimes and fighting other players. Mob Wars costs nothing to play. Players are given a certain amount of virtual currency to spend on recruiting and equipping their mobs. To earn more, you have to perform certain tasks—or sidestep the process by paying with real money instead. According to TechCrunch, Mob Wars is generating US$1 million per month from these microtransactions.

The question is: How should these microtransactions be handled? It's the same micropayment issue that was raised in this chapter's opening case. However, in this instance there a number of start-ups that have arisen to address the issue, such as Spare Change (*sparechangeinc.com*), Zong (*zong.com*), and PayByCash (*paybycash.com*).

Among these, Spare Change seems to have the most traction. Spare Change, which was bought by PlaySpan (*store.playspan.com*), is used by the developers of Mob Wars and 700 other Facebook, MySpace, and Bebo applications. It takes three lines of code to add the Spare Change micropayment system to an application. Spare Change is processing $2.5 million micropayments per month, which is approximately $30 million a year. The Spare Change system handles payments as low as 10¢. In order to use the system, players need to register and tie their accounts to a credit card, a PayPal account, a Spare Change account, or a mobile phone bill. Once registered, the player is given a PIN number that can be used to purchase the virtual goods or service. Spare Change charges 8 percent for each transaction, which is much cheaper than the credit card companies or PayPal.

The Results

At this point it is difficult to tell what will happen to the companies developing social games and the companies developing the micropayment systems designed to support the games. It appears that they both have substantial momentum. But, we've seen this pattern before only to have the various companies meet their demise, especially the companies selling the micropayment systems. For the micropayment companies, one potential threat is the social network companies themselves. A couple of years ago, both Facebook and MySpace were working on payment systems for their application development platforms. Over time, both these efforts faded into the background. Even, if the social networks eventually provide their own systems, it does not mean that they will capture the market. Remember what happened to eBay in its battle with PayPal. Of course, while it lost the battle, it also won the war when it purchased PayPal.

Sources: May (2009), TechCrunch (2009), Fletcher (2010), and ZeroDegrees (2009).

Questions

1. What does the term *freemium* refer to? Give some examples.
2. On the social networks, why is it difficult to generate revenue through advertising? Why is it particularly hard for social games?
3. How does the Zong system differ from the Spare Change system?
4. What is the long-term prognosis for companies like Zong and Spare Change?

ONLINE RESOURCES
available at pearsonglobaleditions.com/turban

Online Files

W10.1   Application Case: Taiwan Money Card
W10.2   Application Case: The Check Is in the Network

Comprehensive Educational Websites

afponline.org: Association for Financial Professionals' website.

cardtechnology.com: Source for news about smart cards and such related payment and identification technologies as biometrics, PKI, mobile commerce, physical access control, and computer network security. Keep track of upcoming smart card conferences and find smart card vendors.

cybersource.com: CyberSource is focused on services that optimize business results through active management of the payment process from payment acceptance and order screening, through reconciliation and payment security.

globalplatform.org: Driven by its member organizations, with cross-industry representation from all world continents, GlobalPlatform is the worldwide leader in smart card infrastructure development.

nacha.org: NACHA—The Electronic Payments Association.

paymentsnews.com: Website maintained by Glenbrook Partners. For many years, the payment professionals at Glenbrook have monitored the news of the day across the wide-ranging field of electronic payments including mobile payments. Using a number of techniques, it continuously scans for news stories that payments professionals might find interesting—and share them here.

smartcardalliance.org: The Smart Card Alliance is a nonprofit, multi-industry association working to stimulate the under- standing, adoption, use, and widespread application of smart card technology.

REFERENCES

CapGemini. "World Payments Report 2010." 2010. scribd. com/doc/42705942/Capgemini-World-Payments- Report-2010 (accessed January 2011).

CBCNews. "Indigo Books Targets E-Book Market Chapter by Chapter." March 2, 2009. cbc.ca/arts/books/story/ 2009/03/02/tech-shortcovers.html (accessed January 2011).

CyberSource. "12th Annual 2011 Online Fraud Report." 2011. now.eloqua.com/e/f2.aspx (accessed January 2011).

CyberSource. "Insider's Guide to ePayment Management." 2008. cybersource.com/cgi-bin/pages/prep.cgi?page=/ promo/InsidersGuide2008/index.html (accessed January 2011).

D'Agostino, D. "Pennies from Heaven." *CIO Insight*, January 2006. allbusiness.com/company-activities- management/financial-performance/13443526- 1.html (accessed January 2011).

Feig, N. "BART Pilot Allows Users to Pay for Mass Transit Fares with Mobile Phones." February 21, 2008. banktech. com/articles/206801045 (accessed January 2011).

Fletcher, O. "China's Tencent, QQ Operator, Profits Rise 52%." November, 10, 2010. online.wsj.com/article/ SB10001424052748703805004575606001085011236. html (accessed January 2011).

Geisen, L. "BOC Budget-Beater." *NRF Store,* September 2008. stores.org/stores-magazine-september-2008/ boc-budget-beater (accessed January 2011).

Juniper Research. "Mobile Payment Transaction Values for Digital and Physical Goods to Exceed $300bn Globally Within 5 Years, According to Juniper Research." January 30, 2011. juniperresearch.com/viewpressrelease.php?id=128& pr=97 (accessed January 2011).

May, T. "The Nanopayment Plan." *Netmag*, July 2009. sparechange.s3.amazonaws.com/homepage/NET19 0.f_nano.pdf (accessed January 2011).

Mitra, S. "Mobile Microfinance." *Forbes*, June 6, 2008. forbes.com/home/2008/06/05/mitra-mobile-micro- finance-tech-wire-cx_sm_0606mitra.htm (accessed January 2011).

NACHA. "NACHA Reports 18.76 Billion in ACH Payments in 2009." NACHA press release. April 7, 2010. nacha.org/news/newsDetail.cfm/RecentBusinessNew sID/140 (accessed January 2011).

O'Brien, D. "Imagine Your Computer as a Wallet Full of Bitcoins." *Irish Times*, November 26, 2010. irishtimes. com/newspaper/finance/2010/1126/1224284180416. html (accessed January 2011).

Ross, J. "BOC, POP on a Roll." *Transaction Trends*, February 2009. electran.org/trends/2009/February09/ ISO_Corner_BOC-POP.pdf (accessed January 2011).

Shevock, J. "Microcapital Brief: Indian Microfinance Institution Grameen Koota Plans to Raise $21M." August 13, 2010. microcapital.org/microcapital-brief- indian-microfinance-institution-grameen-koota- plans-to-raise-21m (accessed January 2011).

Talbot, D. "Upwardly Mobile." *Technology Review*, November–December 2008. technologyreview.com/ business/21533 (accessed January 2011).

TechCrunch. "Spare Change on Track to Process $30 Million in Micropayments." December 2009. spare change.s3. amazonaws.com/homepage/Spare_Change_ On_Track_To_Process_$30_Million_In_ Micropayments.pdf (accessed January 2011).

Tsotsis, A. "Kindle Books Overtake Paperback Books to Become Amazon's Most Popular Format." January 27, 2011. techcrunch.com/2011/01/27/kindle-books- overtake-paperback-books-to-become-amazons- most-popular-format (accessed January 2011).

Worthen, B. "Credit Data Breached, Firm Says." *Wall Street Journal*, January 20, 2009. online.wsj.com/article/ SB123249174099899837.html (accessed January 2011).

ZeroDegrees. "QQ: Master of the Micropayment." December 2009. zerosocialmedia.com/2009/08/qq-master-of-the- micropayment (accessed January 2011).

CHAPTER 11

ORDER FULFILLMENT ALONG THE SUPPLY CHAIN AND OTHER EC SUPPORT SERVICES

Content

Learning Objectives

Upon completion of this chapter, you will be able to:

1. Describe the role of support services in electronic commerce (EC).

2. Define EC order fulfillment and describe the EC order fulfillment process.

3. Describe the major problems of EC order fulfillment.

4. Describe various solutions to EC order fulfillment problems.

5. Describe RFID supply chain applications.

6. Describe collaborative planning and the CPFR model.

7. Describe other EC support services.

8. Discuss the drivers of outsourcing support services.

HOW AMAZON.COM FULFILLS ORDERS

The Problem

With traditional retailing, customers go to a physical store and purchase items that they then take home. Large quantities are delivered to each store or supermarket; there are not too many delivery destinations. With e-tailing, customers want the goods quickly and to have them shipped to their homes. Deliveries of small quantities need to go to a large number of destinations. Also, items must be available for immediate delivery. Therefore, maintaining an inventory of items becomes critical. Maintaining inventory and shipping products cost money and take time, which may negate some of the advantages of e-tailing. Let's see how Amazon.com, the "king" of e-tailing, handles the situation.

When Amazon.com launched in 1995, its business model called for virtual retailing—no warehouses, no inventory, no shipments. The idea was to take orders and receive payments electronically and then let others fill the orders. It soon became clear that this model, although appropriate for a small company, would not work for the world's largest e-tailer.

The Solution

Amazon.com decided to change its business model and handle its own inventory and logistics. The company spent close to $2 billion to build warehouses around the country and became a world-class leader in warehouse management, warehouse automation, packaging, and inventory management. Amazon.com outsources the actual shipment of products to UPS and the U.S. Postal Service (USPS).

How is Amazon.com able to efficiently fulfill many millions of orders every month?

- **Step 1.** When a customer places an order online, a computer program checks the location of the item. It identifies the Amazon.com distribution center that will fulfill the order. Alternatively, it may identify the vendor that will fulfill the order in those cases where Amazon.com acts only as an intermediary. The program transmits the order automatically and electronically to the appropriate distribution center or vendor. Here, we describe what happens in Amazon.com's distribution centers, such as the 800,000 square-foot facility in Fernley, Nevada.

- **Step 2.** A "flowmeister" at the distribution center receives all orders and assigns them electronically to specific employees.

- **Step 3.** The items (such as books, games, and CDs) are stocked in bins. Each bin has a red light and a button. When an order for an item is assigned, the red light turns on automatically. Pickers move along the rows of bins and pick up the items from the bins with red lights; they press the button to reset the light. If the light returns, they pick another unit until the light goes off.

- **Step 4.** The picked items are placed into a crate moving on a conveyor belt, which is part of a winding belt system that is more than 10 miles long in each warehouse. Each crate can reach many destinations; bar code readers (operated automatically or manually) identify items in the crate at 15 different points in the conveyor maze. This tracks the location of an item at any given time and reduces errors to zero.

- **Step 5.** All crates arrive at a central location where bar codes are matched with order numbers. Items are moved from the crates to chutes, where they slide into cardboard boxes. Sophisticated technology allows items picked by several people in different parts of the warehouse to simultaneously arrive in the same chute and be packed in one box.

- **Step 6.** If gift wrapping was selected, this is done by hand.

- **Step 7.** Boxes are packed, taped, weighed, labeled, and routed to one of 40 truck bays in the warehouse. From there, they go to UPS or the USPS. The items are scanned continuously.

Note: Amazon buys the items from its suppliers in large quantities using the methods described in Chapter 4 (e-procurement). Thus, the items travel along the supply chain from the suppliers to Amazon.com (the e-tailer) and then to the customers.

Amazon.com also rents out space in its warehouse and provides logistics services to other companies. It takes orders for them, too. How does it work?

1. Sellers label and ship items in bulk to Amazon.com.

2. When Amazon.com receives sellers' items, it stores them until an order is placed.

3. When an order is placed, Amazon.com will pick, pack, and ship the items to individual customers and may combine several items in the same order.

4. Amazon.com manages after-ordering customer service and handles returns as needed.

The Results

Each warehouse can deliver 200,000 or more pieces a day. All five warehouses must handle more than 3 million pieces a day during the busiest part of the holiday season. (In 2004, the warehouses were able to deliver only 1 million pieces a day, creating some delays during peak periods). Amazon.com leases space to other retailers with online businesses, such as Target and Toys "R" Us. The system gives Amazon.com the ability to offer lower prices and stay competitive, especially because the company is becoming a huge online marketplace that sells thousands of items. As of 2007, profitability has been increasing steadily and so has the stock price.

To increase efficiency, Amazon.com combines several items into one shipment if they are small enough. Shipping warehouses

do not handle returns of unwanted merchandise—the Altrec.com warehouse in Auburn, Washington, handles returns.

Sources: Compiled from news items at *amazon.com* (accessed March 2011), Heizer and Render (2010), and LaMonica (2006).

WHAT WE CAN LEARN . . .

The Amazon.com case illustrates the complexity of order fulfillment by a large e-tailer and some of the solutions employed. Order fulfillment is a major EC support service, and it is the major topic of this chapter. A core element in order fulfillment is the supply chain, where problems and delays may occur. This chapter examines the topics mentioned in the opening case as well as some other support services, primarily acquisition of products and services, finance and accounting services, and customer service.

11.1 ORDER FULFILLMENT AND LOGISTICS: AN OVERVIEW

The implementation of most EC applications requires the use of support services. The most obvious support services are security (Chapter 9), payments (Chapter 10), infrastructure and technology (Chapters 2 and 13), and order fulfillment and logistics (this chapter). Most of the services are relevant for both B2C and B2B. Exhibit 11.1 summarizes the major services described in these chapters, which organizes services into the following categories, as suggested by the Delphi Group (delphigroup.com): e-infrastructure, e-process, e-markets, e-content, e-communities, and e-services. The exhibit shows representative topics in each category.

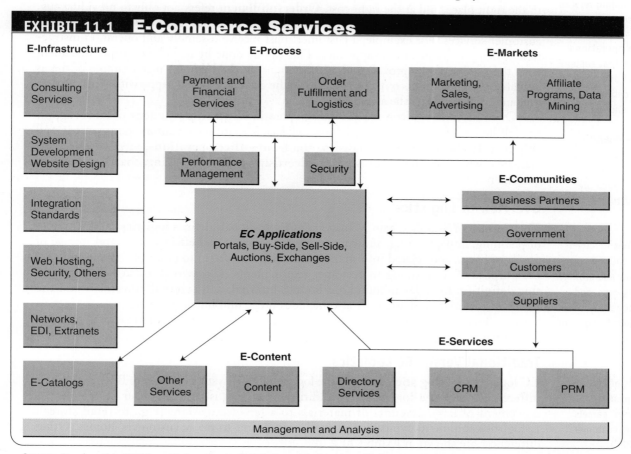

EXHIBIT 11.1 E-Commerce Services

Sources: Based on Chio (1997), p. 18, from Murphy (2004), Natural Fusion (*naturalfusion.com*, accessed May 2011), and author's experience.

Taking orders over the Internet could well be the easy part of B2C. Fulfillment and delivery to customers' doors can be the tricky parts. Many e-tailers have experienced fulfillment problems, especially during the 1990s. Amazon.com, for example, which initially operated as a totally virtual company, added physical warehouses with thousands of employees in order to expedite deliveries and reduce order fulfillment costs.

ACQUIRING GOODS AND SERVICES

Sellers need to acquire what they sell. They make products if they are manufacturers. They buy products if they are retailers, or they just refer buyers to sellers if they are intermediaries. In either case, efficient and effective acquisition needs to be done.

Deliveries to retailers and customers may be delayed for several reasons. These range from an inability to accurately forecast products' demand to ineffective e-tailing supply chains. Many of the same problems affect offline businesses. One issue typical to EC is that EC is based on the concept of "pull" operations that begin with an order, frequently a customized one. This is in contrast with traditional retailing, which usually begins with production to inventory that is then "pushed" to customers (see Online Tutorial T6). In the EC pull case, it is more difficult to forecast demand because of lack of experience and the potential changing consumer tastes. Another reason for delays is that in a B2C pull model, many small orders need to be organized to be delivered to the customers' doors, whereas in brick-and-mortar retailing, the goods are shipped in large quantities to retail stores where customers pick them up.

Before we analyze the order fulfillment problems and describe some solutions, we need to introduce some basic order fulfillment and logistics concepts.

Basic Concepts of Order Fulfillment and Logistics

The key objectives of order fulfillment are delivery of materials or services at the right time, to the right place, and at the right cost. **Order fulfillment** refers not only to providing customers with what they have ordered and doing so on time, but also to providing all related customer services. For example, a customer must receive assembly and operation instructions when purchasing a new appliance. This can be done by including a paper document with the product or by providing the instructions on the Web. (A nice example of this is available at safemanuals.com.) In addition, if the customer is not happy with a product, an exchange or return must be arranged.

Order fulfillment involves **back-office operations**, which are the activities that support the fulfillment of orders, such as packing, delivery, accounting, inventory management, and shipping. It also is strongly related to the **front-office operations**, or *customer-facing activities*, which are activities, such as advertising and order taking, that are visible to customers.

Overview of Logistics

The Council of Supply Chain Management Professionals defines **logistics** as "the process of planning, implementing, and controlling the efficient and effective flow and storage of goods, services, and related information from point of origin to point of consumption for the purpose of conforming to customer requirements" (*Logistics World* 2011). Note that this definition includes inbound, outbound, internal, and external movement and the return of materials and goods. It also includes order fulfillment. However, the distinction between logistics and order fulfillment is not always clear, and the terms are sometimes used interchangeably, as we do in this text.

Traditional Versus EC Logistics

EC logistics, or **e-logistics**, refers to the logistics of EC systems mainly in B2C. The major difference between e-logistics and traditional logistics is that the latter deals with the movement of large amounts of materials to a few destinations (e.g., to retail stores). E-logistics shipments typically are small parcels sent to many customers' homes. Other differences are shown in Exhibit 11.2.

order fulfillment
All the activities needed to provide customers with their ordered goods and services, including related customer services.

back-office operations
The activities that support fulfillment of orders, such as packing, delivery, accounting, and logistics.

front-office operations
The business processes, such as sales and advertising, which are visible to customers.

logistics
The operations involved in the efficient and effective flow and storage of goods, services, and related information from point of origin to point of consumption.

e-logistics
The logistics of EC systems, typically involving small parcels sent to many customers' homes (in B2C).

EXHIBIT 11.2 How E-Logistics Differ from Traditional Logistics

Characteristic	Traditional Knowledge	EC Logistics
Type, quantity	Bulk, large volume	Small, parcels
Destinations	Few	Large number, highly dispersed
Demand type	Push	Pull
Value of shipment	Very large, usually more than $1,000	Very small, frequently less than $50
Nature of demand	Stable, consistent	Seasonal (holiday season), fragmented
Customers	Business partners (in B2B), usually repeat customers (B2C), not many	Usually unknown in B2C, many
Inventory order flow	Usually unidirectional, from manufacturers	Usually bidirectional
Accountability	One link	Through the entire supply chain
Transporter	Frequently the company, sometimes outsourced	Usually outsourced, sometimes the company
Warehouse	Common	Only very large shippers (e.g., Amazon.com) operate their own

THE EC ORDER FULFILLMENT PROCESS

In order to understand why there are problems in order fulfillment, it is beneficial to look at a typical EC fulfillment process, as shown in Exhibit 11.3. The process starts on the left, when an order is received and after verification that it is a real order, several activities take

EXHIBIT 11.3 Order Fulfillment and the Logistics Process

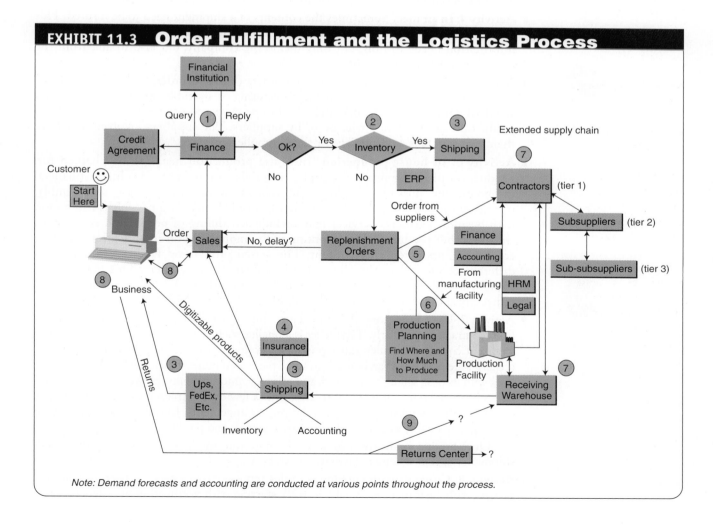

Note: Demand forecasts and accounting are conducted at various points throughout the process.

place, some of which can be done simultaneously; others must be done in sequence. These activities include the following steps:

▶ **Activity 1: Making sure the customer will pay.** Depending on the payment method and prior arrangements, the validity of each payment must be determined. In B2B, the company's finance department or a financial institution (i.e., a bank or a credit card issuer, such as Visa) may do this. Any holdup may cause a shipment to be delayed, resulting in a loss of goodwill or a customer. In B2C, in many countries, the customers usually prepay, frequently by credit card or by using services such as PayPal (Chapter 10). In other countries the customer may go to a payment station (e.g., a convenience store) and prepay there.

▶ **Activity 2: Checking for in-stock availability.** Regardless of whether the seller is a manufacturer or a retailer, as soon as an order is received, an inquiry needs to be made regarding stock availability. Several scenarios are possible that may involve the material management and production departments, as well as outside suppliers and warehouse facilities. In this step, the order information needs to be connected to the information about in-stock inventory availability or manufacturing capability.

▶ **Activity 3: Arranging shipments.** If the product is readily available, and it is paid for, it can be shipped to the customer right away (otherwise, go to activity 5). Products can be digital or physical. If the item is physical and it is readily available, packaging and shipment arrangements need to be made. It may involve both the packaging and shipping department and internal shippers or outside logistics services. Digital items are usually available because their "inventory" is not depleted. However, a digital product, such as software, may be under revision, and unavailable for delivery at certain times. In either case, information needs to flow among several partners.

▶ **Activity 4: Insurance.** Sometimes the contents of a shipment need to be insured. This could involve both the finance department and an insurance company, and again, information needs to flow, not only inside the company, but also to and from the customer and insurance agent.

▶ **Activity 5: Replenishment.** Customized orders (build-to-order, Online Tutorial T6) will always trigger a need for some manufacturing or assembly operation. Similarly, if standard items are out of stock, they need to be produced or procured. In both cases, production can be done in-house or by suppliers. The suppliers involved may have their own suppliers (subsuppliers or tier-2 suppliers).

▶ **Activity 6: In-house production.** In-house production needs to be planned for. Production planning involves people, materials, components, machines, financial resources, and possibly suppliers and subcontractors. In the case of assembly, manufacturing, or both, plant services may be needed, including possible collaboration with business partners. Services may include scheduling of people and equipment, shifting other products' plans, working with engineering on modifications, getting equipment, and preparing content. The actual production facilities may be in a different country than the company's headquarters or retailers. This may further complicate the flow of information and communication. All this needs to be done efficiently and effectively, as described in Online Tutorial T5.

▶ **Activity 7: Use contractors.** A manufacturer may opt to buy products or subassemblies from contractors. Similarly, if the seller is a retailer, such as in the case of Amazon.com or Walmart.com, the retailer must purchase products from its manufacturers. Several scenarios are possible. Warehouses can stock purchased items, which is what Amazon.com does with its best-selling books, toys, and other commodity items. However, Amazon.com does not stock books for which it receives only a few orders. In such cases, the publishers or intermediaries must make special delivery arrangements. In either case, appropriate receiving and quality assurance of incoming materials and products must take place.

Once production (activity 6) or purchasing from suppliers (activity 7) is completed, shipments to the customers (activity 3) can be arranged.

▶ **Activity 8: Contacts with customers.** Sales representatives need to keep in constant contact with customers, especially in B2B, starting with notification of orders received and ending with notification of a shipment or a change in delivery date. These contacts are usually done via e-mail and are frequently generated automatically (e.g., using RFID). For typical services that customers need, see Online File W11.1.

▶ **Activity 9: Returns.** In some cases, customers want to exchange or return items. Such returns can be a major problem, as billions of dollars in North American goods are returned each year for both online and offline situations. The movement of returns from customers back to vendors is called **reverse logistics**.

reverse logistics
The movement of returns from customers to vendors.

Order fulfillment processes may vary, depending on the product and the vendor. The order fulfillment process also differs between B2B and B2C activities, between the delivery of goods and of services, and between small and large products. Furthermore, certain circumstances, such as in the case of perishable materials or foods, require additional steps and administrative activities.

Such a complex process may have problems (see Section 11.2); automating the various steps can minimize or eliminate several of these problems.

The Administrative Activities of Order Taking and Fulfillment

The administrative activities of order taking and fulfillment may involve (according to en.wikipedia.org/wiki/Order_fulfillment) the following:

> ▶ **Product inquiry.** Initial inquiry about offerings, visit to the website, catalog request
> ▶ **Sales quote.** Budgetary or availability quote
> ▶ **Order configuration.** Where ordered items need a selection of options or order lines need to be compatible with each other
> ▶ **Order booking.** The formal order placement or closing of the deal
> ▶ **Order acknowledgment or confirmation.** Confirmation that the order is booked or received
> ▶ **Order sourcing or planning.** Determining the source or location of item(s) to be shipped
> ▶ **Order changes.** Changes to orders, if needed
> ▶ **Shipment release.** Process step where the warehouse/inventory stocking point starts the shipping process; may be comprised of picking, packing, and staging for shipment
> ▶ **Shipment.** The shipment and transportation of the goods
> ▶ **Delivery.** The delivery of the goods to the consignee or customer
> ▶ **Settlement.** The payment of the charges for goods, services, and delivery
> ▶ **Returns.** In case the goods are unacceptable or not required

Order Fulfillment and the Supply Chain

The nine-activity order fulfillment process previously described, as well as order taking, are integral parts of the supply chain. The flows of orders, payments, information, materials, and parts need to be coordinated among all the company's internal participants, as well as with and among external partners. The principles of supply chain management (SCM) must be considered when planning and managing the order fulfillment process, which due to its complexity may have problems.

Section 11.1 ▶ REVIEW QUESTIONS

1. Define order fulfillment and logistics.
2. Compare traditional logistics with e-logistics.
3. List the nine steps of the order fulfillment process.
4. Compare logistics with reverse logistics.

11.2 PROBLEMS IN ORDER FULFILLMENT ALONG SUPPLY CHAINS

During the 1999 holiday season, logistics problems plagued the B2C e-tailers, especially those that sold toys. Price wars boosted demand, and neither the e-tailers nor the manufacturers were ready for it. As a result, supplies were late in coming from manufacturers. Toys "R" Us, for example, had to stop taking orders around December 14. The manufacturers, warehouses, and distribution channels were not in sync with the e-tailers. As a result, many customers did not get their holiday gifts on time. Although most of these problems were solved, some still exist for certain sellers.

TYPICAL SUPPLY CHAIN PROBLEMS

The inability to deliver products on time is a typical problem in both offline and online commerce. Several other problems have been observed along the supply chain: Some companies grapple with high inventory costs; quality problems exist due to misunderstandings; shipments of wrong products, materials, and parts occur frequently; and the cost to expedite operations or shipments is high. The chance that such problems will occur in EC is even higher due to the lack of appropriate infrastructure and the special characteristics of EC. For example, most manufacturers' and distributors' warehouses are designed to ship large quantities to several stores; they cannot optimally pack and ship many small packages to many customers' doors. Improper inventory levels are typical in EC, as are poor delivery scheduling and mixed-up shipments.

Another major activity related to the supply chain problem is the difficulty in demand forecasting. In the case of standard or commodity items, such as toys, a demand forecast must be done in order to determine appropriate inventories of finished goods at various points in the supply chain. Such a forecast is difficult in the fast-growing field of online ordering. In the case of customized products, it is necessary to forecast the demand for the components and materials required for fulfilling customized orders. Demand forecasting must be done with business partners along the supply chain, as described in Online Tutorial T5. Supply chain problems jeopardize order fulfillment. The major management issues in supply chain management are: Distribution network configuration, inventory control, supply contracts, distribution strategies, strategic partnership, outsourcing and procurement, product design, information technology, and customer value.

WHY SUPPLY CHAIN PROBLEMS EXIST

Many problems along the EC supply chain stem from uncertainties and from the need to coordinate several activities, internal units, and business partners.

A major source of uncertainty in EC, as noted earlier, is the demand forecast. Factors such as consumer behavior, economic conditions, competition, prices, weather conditions, technological developments, and consumer taste and confidence influence demand. Any one of these factors may change quickly. The demand forecast should be conducted frequently, in conjunction with collaboration among business partners along the supply chain, in order to correctly gauge demand and make plans to meet it. Companies attempt to achieve accurate demand forecasts by methods such as information sharing using collaborative commerce (Chapter 5).

Pure EC companies are likely to have more problems because they do not have a logistics infrastructure already in place and are forced to use external logistics services rather than in-house departments for these functions. These external logistics services are often called **third-party logistics suppliers (3PL)**, or *logistics service providers*. Outsourcing such services can be expensive, and it requires more coordination and dependence on outsiders who may not be reliable. For this reason, large virtual retailers such as Amazon.com have or are developing their own physical warehouses and logistics systems. Other virtual retailers are creating strategic alliances with logistics companies or with experienced mail-order companies that have their own logistics systems.

third-party logistics suppliers (3PL)
External, rather than in-house, providers of logistics services.

Inefficient Financial Supply Chains Can Grind Businesses to a Halt

Note that supply chain problems and improvements refer not only to the flow of goods but also to the flow of information and money (Online Tutorial T5). Money flow includes invoicing, payment, collection, and so forth.

Suppliers and producers have implemented strategies to streamline operational efficiency by reducing or eliminating manual processes that are time-consuming and costly. But despite many impressive strides toward automation, the vast majority of financial transactions for many businesses are still paper-based.

Because of these manual processes and a lack of integration among trading partners, companies are finding it increasingly difficult to turn sales into cash promptly. Financial supply chains clogged with large amounts of aging and uncollected receivables can cause business operations to slow to a crawl while waiting for the financial pipeline to get moving. In a global economy where many other business processes are being transitioned from manual to computer-based, inefficient financial processes can put a company at a significant competitive disadvantage. To succeed in today's fast-paced global marketplace, companies need to take advantage of technological advances to optimize their financial supply chains. For solutions to such problems, see Crossgate Inc. (2010).

The Need for Information Sharing Along the Supply Chain

Information systems are the links that enable communication and collaboration along the supply chain. They represent one of the fundamental elements that link the organizations of the supply chain into a unified and coordinated system. In today's competitive business climate, EC and information technology are keys to the success, and perhaps even the survival, of any SCM initiative.

Case studies of some world-class companies, such as Walmart, Dell, and FedEx, indicate that these companies have created very sophisticated information systems, exploiting the latest technological developments, and creating innovative solutions. However, even world-class companies, such as Nike, may suffer from inappropriate information sharing resulting in poor forecasting and then severely underestimating the complexity of automating aspects of the supply chain.

In addition to uncertainties, lack of coordination and an inability or refusal to share information among business partners also creates EC supply chain fulfillment problems. One of the most persistent order fulfillment problems is the bullwhip effect (see Online File W11.2).

EC (and IT) can provide solutions to these order fulfillment problems, as the next section will show.

Section 11.2 ▶ REVIEW QUESTIONS

1. List some problems along the EC supply chain.
2. Explain how uncertainties create order fulfillment problems. List some of these problems.
3. What problems may exist in financial supply chains?
4. Describe the role of 3PLs.
5. Why is information sharing needed?

11.3 SOLUTIONS TO ORDER FULFILLMENT PROBLEMS ALONG SUPPLY CHAINS

Many EC logistics problems are generic; they can be found in the non-Internet world as well. Therefore, many of the solutions that have been developed for these problems in brick-and-mortar companies also work for e-tailers. IT and EC technologies facilitate most of these solutions. They also provide for automation of various operations along the supply chain that usually improve its operation. In this section, we will discuss some of the specific solutions to EC order fulfillment problems along the supply chain.

IMPROVEMENTS IN THE ORDER-TAKING ACTIVITY

One way to improve order fulfillment is to improve the order-taking activity and its links to fulfillment and logistics. Order taking can be done via e-mail or on a webstore and it may be automated. For example, in B2B, orders can be generated and transmitted automatically to suppliers when inventory levels fall below a certain threshold. It is a part of the *vendor-managed inventory* (VMI) strategy described in Chapter 5. The result is a fast, inexpensive, and more accurate (no need to rekey data) order-taking process. In B2C, Web-based ordering using electronic forms expedites the process, makes the process more accurate (e.g., intelligent agents can check the input data and provide instant feedback), and reduces processing costs for sellers. When EC order taking can interface or integrate with a company's back-office system, it shortens cycle times and eliminates errors.

Order-taking improvements also can take place within an organization, for example, when a manufacturer orders parts from its own warehouse. When delivery of such parts runs smoothly, it minimizes disruptions to the manufacturing process, reducing losses from downtime. For example, as detailed in Online File W11.3, Dell has improved the flow of parts in its PC repair operations, resulting in greater efficiency and cost savings.

Electronic Payments in E-Commerce

Implementing linkages between order-taking and payment systems also can be helpful in improving order fulfillment and money flows in the supply chains. Electronic payments can expedite both the order-taking phase and the payment delivery period. With such systems, payment processing can be significantly shorter and less expensive, and fraud can be better controlled. For details, see Chapter 10.

WAREHOUSING AND INVENTORY MANAGEMENT IMPROVEMENTS

warehouse management system (WMS)
A software system that helps in managing warehouses.

A popular EC inventory management solution is a **warehouse management system (WMS)**. WMS refers to a software system that helps in managing warehouses. It has several components. For example, in the case of Amazon.com, the system supports item pickers as well as packaging. Amazon.com's B2C WMS can handle hundreds of millions of packages. In Case 11.1, we describe a B2B WMS at Schurman Fine Papers, which demonstrates several applications.

Other Warehousing and Inventory Management Improvements

WMS is useful in reducing inventory and decreasing the incidence of out-of-stocks. Such systems also are useful in maintaining an inventory of repair items so repairs can be expedited (e.g., Dell, see Online File W11.3); picking items out of inventory in the warehouse (e.g., Amazon.com and Schurman); communicating (e.g., Schurman); managing product inventory (e.g., Schurman); receiving items at the warehouse (e.g., Schurman); and automating the warehouse (e.g., Amazon.com). For example, introducing a make-to-order (pull) production process and providing fast and accurate demand information to suppliers can minimize inventories. Allowing business partners to electronically track and monitor inventory levels and production activities can improve inventory management and inventory levels, as well as minimize the administrative expenses of inventory management. In some instances, the ultimate inventory improvement is to have no inventory at all; for products that can be digitized (e.g., software), order fulfillment can be instantaneous and can eliminate the need for inventory. Two methods of inventory improvements are VMI (Chapter 5) and the use of RFID (Online Tutorial T3 and Section 11.4). Next, we describe some other methods.

Automated Warehouses

Automated warehouses may include robots and other devices that expedite the pickup of products. An example of a company that uses such warehouses is Amazon.com (see the opening case).

CASE 11.1
EC Application

HOW WMS HELPS SCHURMAN IMPROVE ITS INTERNAL AND EXTERNAL ORDER FULFILLMENT SYSTEM

Schurman Fine Papers (*papyrusonline.com*) is a manufacturer and retailer of greeting cards and related products. It sells through its own 170 specialty stores (Papyrus), as well as through 30,000 independent retail outlets.

Using RedPrairie (*redprairie.com*) integrated logistics software solutions, Schurman improved its demand forecast and minimized both out-of-stocks and overstocking. The system also allows physical inventory counts to be conducted without the need to shut down the two central warehouses for a week three times a year.

The central warehouses receive shipments from about 200 suppliers worldwide (500 to 1,000 orders per day). Until 2003, all inventory and logistics management was done manually. One problem solved by the software is picking products from multiple stock-keeping unit (SKU) locations. Picking is faster now, with a minimum of errors.

Customers' orders come directly from the EDI and ignite the fulfillment and shipment process. This system automatically generates an advanced shipping notice (replacing the lengthy process of manual scanning). The new system also automates the task of assessing the length, width, height, and weight of each item before it goes into a box (to determine which item goes into what box). The system also improved inventory replenishment allocations. In the past, the list of items to be picked up included items not available in the primary location. Pickers wasted time looking for these items, and unfound items had to be picked up later from the reserve storage center, resulting in delays. The WMS simultaneously created two lists, expediting

fulfillment. This tripled the number of orders fulfilled per picker per day. The system also generates automatic replenishment orders for items falling below a minimum level at any storage location.

In addition, special software provides Schurman's customer service department with real-time access to inventory and distribution processes, allowing the department to track the status of all orders. The WMS also tracks the status of all orders and sends alerts when an order problem occurs (e.g., delay in downloading). An e-mail goes to all necessary parties in the company so they can fix the problem. Finally, information collected about problems can be analyzed so remedies can be made quickly. All this helps to reduce both overstocks and out-of-stocks.

Sources: Compiled from Parks (2004), *papyrusonline.com* (accessed March 2011), Maloney (2006), and *redprairie.com* (accessed January 2011).

Questions

1. Identify what the WMS automates, both in receiving and shipping.
2. In the future, RFID tags (Online Tutorial T3) could replace the bar codes that are currently used. What would be the advantages of using RFID? Where can it be used?
3. How has inventory management been improved?

Companies such as (fosdickfulfillment.com) and E-Fulfillment Services (efulfillment-service.com) provide order fulfillment services not only for themselves, but other companies too. The keys to successful inventory management, in terms of order fulfillment, are efficiency and speed, which wireless devices can facilitate.

Using Wireless Technologies

Wireless technologies have been used in warehouses for more than a decade. We discussed several applications in Chapter 6. For more, see Motorola (2007b) and the references there, the videos listed in Chapter 6, and motorola.com/supplychainmobility.

Using RFID to Improve WMS. In Chapter 6, we introduced the potential uses of RFID in supply chains. We provided an example of how RFID can track items as they move from the manufacturers' to the customers' warehouses. Once inside a customer's warehouse, RFID can track the whereabouts of the items. This can facilitate inventory counts and save pickers' trips.

CHANGING THE STRUCTURE AND PROCESS OF THE SUPPLY CHAIN

An efficient solution to many supply chain problems is to change the supply chain structure from a linear to a hub structure as illustrated in Exhibit 11.4. Notice that in a hub structure connection between supply chain partners and elements is much shorter. Also coordination and control is done at the center of the hub, making the management more

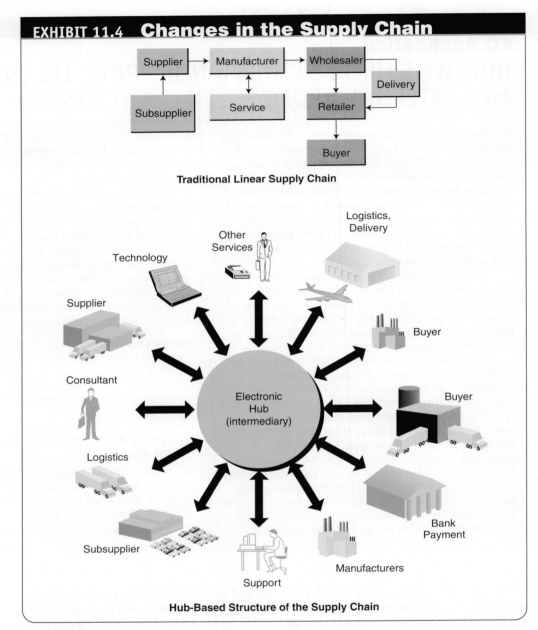

EXHIBIT 11.4   Changes in the Supply Chain

Traditional Linear Supply Chain

Hub-Based Structure of the Supply Chain

efficient, and the structure increases visibility. Long supply chains are usually more amenable to problems. Also, the hub structure management is usually fully digital, making order fulfillment faster, less expensive, and less problematic.

SPEEDING DELIVERIES

In 1973, an innovative, then tiny company initiated the concept of "next-day delivery." It was a revolution in door-to-door logistics. A few years later, that company, FedEx, introduced its "next-morning delivery" service. In 2010, FedEx moved more than 8 million packages with the help of over 280,000 employees, each day, all over the globe, using several hundred airplanes and several thousand vans. Incidentally, by one report, 70 percent of these packages were the result of EC (see en.wikipedia.org/wiki/fedex).

Same-Day, Even Same-Hour, Delivery

In the digital age, however, even the next morning may not be fast enough. Today, we talk about same-day delivery, and even delivery within an hour. Deliveries of urgent materials to and from hospitals are an example of such a service. Two of the newcomers to this area are eFulfillment Service (efulfillmentservice.com) and OneWorld Direct (owd.com). These companies have created networks for the rapid distribution of products, mostly EC-related ones. They offer national distribution systems across the United States in collaboration with shipping companies, such as FedEx and UPS.

Delivering groceries is another area where speed is important, as discussed in Chapter 3. Quick pizza deliveries have been available for a long time (e.g., Domino's Pizza). Today, many pizza orders can be placed online. Also, many restaurants deliver food to customers who order online, a service called "dine online." Examples of this service can be found at dineonline.com and gourmetdinnerservice.com.au. Some companies even offer aggregating supply services, processing orders from several restaurants and then making deliveries (e.g., dialadinner.com.hk in Hong Kong).

Supermarket Deliveries

Supermarket deliveries are done same day or next day. Arranging and making such deliveries may be difficult, especially when fresh or perishable food is to be transported, as discussed in Chapter 3. Buyers may need to be home at certain times to accept the deliveries. Therefore, the distribution systems for such enterprises are critical. For an example of an effective distribution system, see Online File W11.4 about Woolworths of Australia.

One of the most comprehensive delivery systems is that of GroceryWorks, now a subsidiary of Safeway USA. The original system is not available anymore, but it has very important lessons to teach us. It is described in a case study by Cisco-Eagle (2011) and in Online File W11.5.

PARTNERING EFFORTS AND OUTSOURCING LOGISTICS

An effective way to solve order fulfillment problems is for an organization to partner with other companies. For example, several EC companies partner with UPS or FedEx.

Logistics-related partnerships can take many forms. For example, marketplaces may be managed by one of many freight forwarders (forwarders.com) such as A & A Contract Customs Brokers, a company that helps other companies find "forwarders"—the intermediaries that prepare goods for shipping. Forwarders can find the best prices on air carriers, and the carriers bid to fill the space with forwarders' goods that need to be shipped.

SkyMall (skymall.com), now a subsidiary of Gemstar-TV Guide International, is a retailer that sells from catalogs on airplanes, over the Internet, and by mail order. It relies on its catalog partners to fill the orders. For small vendors that do not handle their own shipments and for international shipments, SkyMall contracts distribution centers owned by fulfillment outsourcer Sykes Enterprise. As orders come in, SkyMall conveys the data to the appropriate vendor or to a Sykes distribution center. A report is then sent to SkyMall.

Comprehensive Logistics Services

Major shippers, notably UPS and FedEx, offer comprehensive logistic services. These services are for B2C, B2B, G2B, and other types of EC. See Case 11.2 for a description of the broad EC services that UPS offers.

Outsourcing Logistics

Instead of a joint venture or equity ownership with partners, many companies simply outsource logistics. One advantage of outsourcing is that it is easy to change the logistics provider. Outsourcing is especially appealing to small companies.

INTEGRATED GLOBAL LOGISTICS SYSTEMS

An increase in global trading created a need for an effective global logistics system. Order fulfillment problems described earlier tend to be even larger in longer supply chains that cross country borders. The number of partners in such situations is usually larger (e.g., custom brokers, global carriers), and so is the need for coordination, communication, and collaboration. Furthermore, such systems require a high level of security, especially when the Internet is the centric technology platform. Integrating separate segments of the supply chain can be very beneficial for minimizing problems in long global chains.

CASE 11.2
EC Application
UPS PROVIDES BROAD EC SERVICES

United Parcel Service (UPS) is not only a leading transporter of goods sold on the Internet, but it also is a provider of expertise, infrastructure, and technology for managing global commerce—synchronizing the flow of goods, information, and funds for its customers.

UPS has a massive infrastructure to support these efforts. For example, it has the world's largest DB2 relational database that contains customer information and shipping records. UPS owns Worldport, which is the company's central air hub (located at Louisville International Airport). Worldport can handle almost 10 million packages a day in a facility of 5.2 million square feet. Periodically, UPS is approached by documentary producers about featuring its complex global operations on their shows. The most well-known is an episode of the History Channel's series "Modern Marvels." The episode showcases man's epic struggle against nature, high-tech gadgetry, international big business, and a nation's army on the move (see Mangeot 2010). More than 120,000 UPS customers have incorporated UPS's online tools into their own websites to strengthen their customer service. In addition, UPS offers the following EC applications:

▶ Electronic supply chain services for corporate customers, by industry. This includes a portal page with industry-related information and statistics.
▶ Calculators for computing shipping fees.
▶ Helping customers manage their electronic supply chains (e.g., expediting billing and speeding up accounts receivable).
▶ Improved inventory management, warehousing, and delivery.
▶ A shipping management system that integrates tracking systems, address validation, service selection, and time-in-transit tools with Oracle's ERP application suite (similar integration with SAP exists).
▶ Notification of customers by e-mail about the status and expected arrival time of incoming packages.

Representative Tools

UPS's online tools—a set of seven transportation and logistics applications—let customers do everything from tracking packages to analyzing their shipping history using customized criteria to calculate exact time-in-transit for shipments between any two postal codes in the continental United States.

The tools, which customers can download to their websites, let customers query UPS's system to get proof that specific packages were delivered on schedule. For example, if a company is buying supplies online and wants them delivered on a certain day, a UPS customer can use an optimal-routing feature to ensure delivery on that day, as well as automatically record proof of the delivery in its accounting system.

UPS offers logistics services tailored for certain industries. For example, the UPS Logistics Group provides supply chain reengineering, transportation network management, and service parts logistics to vehicle manufacturers, suppliers, and parts distributors in the auto industry worldwide. UPS Autogistics improves automakers' vehicle delivery networks. For example, Ford reduced the time to deliver vehicles from plants to dealers in North America from an average of 14 days to about 6 days. UPS Logistics Group offers similar supply chain and delivery tracking services to other kinds of manufacturers.

UPS also is expanding into another area important to e-business—delivery of digital documents. The company was the first conventional package shipper to enter this market in 1998 when it launched UPS Document Exchange. This service monitors delivery of digitally delivered documents and provides instant receipt notification, encryption, and password-only access.

UPS offers many other EC-related services. These include allowing customers to enter the UPS system from wireless devices; helping customers configure and customize services; and providing for electronic bill presentation and payment (for B2B), EFT, and processing of COD payments.

Sources: Compiled from Violino (2000), Farber (2003), and *ups.com* (accessed March 2011).

Questions

1. Why would a shipper, such as UPS, expand to other logistics services?
2. Why would shippers want to handle payments?
3. Why does UPS provide software tools to customers?
4. What B2B services does UPS provide? (Note: Check *ups.com* to make sure that your answers are up-to-date.)

ORDER FULFILLMENT IN MAKE-TO-ORDER AND MASS CUSTOMIZATION

As you may recall from Chapter 1, one of the advantages of EC is the ability to easily customize products and personalize services. Although taking customized orders is easily done online (recall the Dell case, Online File W11.3), the fulfillment of such orders may not be simple. Mass production enabled companies to reduce the price per unit. Customization may cost lots of money, since each item must be handled separately. Consumers, on the other hand, want customized products at a price that is not much higher than that of similar products produced by mass production. Another problem is the time frame. Customized products, especially big ones such as cars, may take a long time to produce. Customers are not willing to wait.

The question is how to deliver large numbers of customized products (mass customization, or build-to-order, see Online Tutorial T6, and en.wikipedia.org/wiki/mass_customization) at a reasonable cost and in a reasonable time.

Large companies such as Dell and Walmart can order goods on demand and get them quickly. Thus, these companies are in a better position to meet customer demand of build (or ship) to order. For how Walmart manages its logistics and order fulfillment, see Online File W11.6.

Fulfilling Orders

The pioneering approach by Dell was to produce the components of computers via mass production and to offer customization in the manner in which they were assembled. This solution has been adopted by many other manufacturers (e.g., see the closing case of this chapter regarding customized refrigerators). Most customized cars, shoes, toys, textbooks, and wedding rings are made this way. Of course, when you talk about millions of computers at Dell, the supply chain, the logistics, and the delivery of components become critical (see the Dell case [Online File W11.3] and the Dell example later in this chapter). You also need to closely collaborate with your suppliers. In addition, you need to have flexible production lines where changes are made quickly and inexpensively (e.g., painting cars at Toyota), and you need tools that enable quick and not-so-expensive changes (usually driven by computerized systems). This is usually a part of *intelligent factories* or production lines.

For sources on intelligent factories and mass customization, see the International Institute on Mass Customization & Personalization (iimcp.org), the *International Journal of Mass Customization* (inderscience.com/ijmassc), The Smart Factory KL (smartfactory.eu), and Managing Change (managingchange.com/masscust/overview.htm).

Here, we present an example of how customization is accomplished by these methods.

Example 1: Intelligent Factories. These factories work on a totally integrated automation that enables mass customization to be executed at a reasonable cost and speed. Major developers are Siemens AG, IBM, and General Electric. Selectron Corp. developed a virtual factory floor—MyFactory@SLR.com—which helps to manage its worldwide trading partners. Another company that develops intelligent factories is Anterus (see sciantaanalytics.com/resources/productspecs/PS-TheIntelligenceFactory.pdf).

Example 2: Distributed Mass Customization. Etsy (etsy.com) is a market maker for handmade goods, many of which are customized and sold online. Thousands of small producers custom produce on demand. Etsy aggregates them into one electronic marketplace. For details, see en.wikipedia.org/wiki/Etsy. For an example of how a global company handles its online orders for appliances, see this chapter's closing case about Multibras in Brazil.

HANDLING RETURNS (REVERSE LOGISTICS)

Allowing for the return of unwanted merchandise and providing for product exchanges are necessary to maintaining customers' trust and loyalty. The Boston Consulting Group (2001) found that the "absence of a good return mechanism" was the number two reason shoppers cited for refusing to buy on the Web frequently. A good return policy is a must in EC.

Dealing with returns is a major logistics problem for EC merchants. Several options for handling returns exist:

▸ **Return the item to the place of purchase.** This is easy to do with a purchase from a brick-and-mortar store, but not a virtual one. To return a product to a virtual store, a customer needs to get authorization, pack everything up, pay to ship it back, insure it, and wait up to two billing cycles for a credit to show up on his or her statement. The buyer is not happy and neither is the seller, who must unpack, check the paperwork, and resell the item, usually at a loss. This solution is workable only if the number of returns is small or the merchandise is expensive (e.g., Blue Nile).

▶ **Separate the logistics of returns from the logistics of delivery.** With this option, returns are shipped to an independent returns unit and are handled separately. This solution may be more efficient from the seller's point of view, but it does not ease the returns process for the buyer.

▶ **Completely outsource returns.** Several outsourcers, including UPS and FedEx, provide logistics services for returns. The services deal not only with delivery and returns but also with the entire logistics process. FedEx, for example, offers several options for returning goods (see fedex.com).

▶ **Allow the customer to physically drop the returned item at a collection station.** Offer customers locations (such as a convenience store or the UPS Store) where they can drop off returns. In Asia and Australia, returns are accepted in convenience stores and at gas stations. For example, BP Australia Ltd. (gasoline service stations) teamed up with wishlist.com.au, and Caltex Australia is accepting returns at the convenience stores connected to its gasoline stations. The accepting stores may offer in-store computers for ordering and may also offer payment options, as at Japanese 7-Elevens (7dream.com). In Taiwan and some other countries, you can order merchandise (e.g., books) pay, pick up the item ordered, and return unwanted items, at a 7-Eleven store. Click-and-mortar stores usually allow customers to return merchandise that was ordered from the online outlet to their physical stores (e.g., walmart.com and eddiebauer.com).

▶ **Auction the returned items.** This option can go hand-in-hand with any of the previous solutions.

For strategy and guidelines on returns, see Ellis (2006). The Reverse Logistics Executive Council (rlec.org) is a major portal on reverse logistics.

ORDER FULFILLMENT IN B2B

For an overview of B2B fulfillment, see *Supplychainer.com* (2006). B2B fulfillment may be more complex than that of B2C because it has at least six dimensions of complexity (versus two in B2C): shipment size, multiple distribution channels, more variety of shipment frequency, uneven breadth of carrier services, fewer carrier EC offerings, and complex EC transaction paths.

Using BPM to Improve Order Fulfillment

B2B order fulfillment commonly uses business process management (BPM) software to automate various steps in the process, as done by Daisy Brand (Case 11.3). The case also demonstrates how customers pressure suppliers to improve the order fulfillment process.

Online File W11.7 lists some representative B2B fulfillment players and challenges.

Using E-Marketplaces and Exchanges to Ease Order Fulfillment Problems in B2B

In Chapter 4, we introduced a variety of e-marketplaces and exchanges. One of the major objectives of these entities is to improve the operation of the B2B supply chain. Let's see how this works with different business models.

▶ A company-centric marketplace can solve several supply chain problems. For example, CSX Technology developed an extranet-based EC system for tracking cross-country train shipments as part of its supply chain initiative and was able to effectively identify bottlenecks and more accurately forecast demand.

CASE 11.3
EC Application
HOW DAISY BRAND FULFILLS B2B ORDERS

Daisy Brand (*daisybrand.com*), a large U.S. producer of dairy products, is known for its quality products. Its major customers are supermarkets that operate in a very competitive environment. Many of Daisy's customers require that Daisy Brand provide certain services that will improve the efficiency of the customers' operations—for example, vendor-managed inventory, collaborative planning, and forecasting. The customers pressured Daisy Brand to improve its services along the supply chain; order processing became a prime target for improvement.

The Daisy Brand information systems (IS) team uses technology to improve the efficiency of its order fulfillment process. Customers submit orders electronically. Every order that Daisy Brand handles travels through multiple applications: Customers submit orders through an electronic data interchange (EDI) transaction. From there, orders flow to an Invensys Protean enterprise resource planning (ERP) system and various other systems for fulfillment and ultimately to shipping. The company sought to implement a workflow solution that could integrate and automate this order-to-delivery process.

Using TIBCO's business integration and business process management (BPM) solution (see *tibco.com*), the EC team designed, developed, tested, and deployed a workflow that manages order processing from inception all the way to the point of delivery to ensure that orders move forward within the set time frame. The company can also send notifications about shipping activity back to the customer.

If an order is to ship within a certain number of hours, but it hasn't shipped, TIBCO's solution can trace the order and get it moving faster. TIBCO's solution also helps stop problems before they start by auditing customer order information before it enters the ERP system.

In addition to improving the efficiency of order processing at Daisy Brand, TIBCO's solution also enables the company to more flexibly accommodate customer needs. For example, a retail customer might change an order after the order is sent to the warehouse—perhaps to request that the order ship on a different day or with a different amount. In these cases, the TIBCO-based system sends an alert to the logistics management workbench to immediately notify the warehouse that the order has been modified. Thus, the logistics team can quickly implement the change, ensuring minimum impact on the order cycle time.

The workflow software is part of TIBCO's BPM software suite, which includes other applications for control of business processes and to improve agility. Future projects include automation of new customer entry; integration of plant control systems; support for collaborative planning, forecasting, and replenishment (CPFR) and vendor-managed inventory (VMI); and implementation of a real-time electronic order-arrival board.

Sources: Compiled from TIBCO (2006) and Smith (2006a).

Questions

1. Describe the steps in order fulfillment at Daisy Brand.
2. How does the automation of order fulfillment work?
3. How can supermarkets benefit from introducing electronic processing by Daisy Brand?
4. Enter *tibco.com* and find information about its BPM and workflow products. How can they support order fulfillment?
5. How can Daisy Brand improve its agility?

Note: A video supporting this case is available at *tibco.com*.

▶ Using an extranet, Toshiba America provides an ordering system for its dealers to buy replacement parts for Toshiba's products. The system smooths the supply chain and delivers better customer service.

▶ Supplychainer.com (2006) suggested taking into consideration the following seven elements (per High Jump Software) for optimal order fulfillment:

1. Integrate your systems.
2. Automate your pickings.
3. Incorporate automated shipment planning (ASP).
4. Automate shipment verification.
5. Reduce or eliminate paperwork.
6. Source orders based on facility workloads.
7. Incorporate sales and marketing into the process.

For additional discussion on how fulfillment is done in B2B, see fedex.com, ups.com, and supplychainer.com.

Order Fulfillment in Services

Thus far, we have concentrated on order fulfillment with physical products. Fulfilling service orders (e.g., buy or sell stocks, process insurance claims) may involve more information processing, which requires more sophisticated EC systems. Case 11.4 describes a reservation system used by Sundowner Motor Inns.

OTHER SOLUTIONS TO SUPPLY CHAIN PROBLEMS

visibility

The knowledge about where materials and parts are at any given time, which helps in solving problems such as delay, combining shipments, and more.

▶ *Visibility* increases along the supply chain. It is critical to know where materials and parts are at any given time. This is referred to as **visibility**. Such knowledge can help in solving problems such as delays, combining shipments, and more. Visibility is provided by several tools, such as bar codes, RFID, collaborative devices, and collaborative portals. Visibility implies creating information transparency through effective integration of information flows across the multiple e-marketplaces that comprise the chain. Such visibility allows organizations to coordinate supply chain interactions efficiently in dynamic market conditions.

▶ *Order fulfillment* can become instant if the products can be digitized (e.g., software). In other cases, EC order taking interfaces with the company's back-office systems, including logistics. Such an interface, or even integration, shortens cycle time and eliminates errors.

▶ *Managing risk* to avoid supply chain breakdown can be done in several ways. Carrying additional inventories is effective against the risk of stock-outs, and hence poor customer service, but it can be expensive. Also, in certain cases the risk increases because products may become obsolete. (Managing inventories was described in Chapter 4).

CASE 11.4

EC Application

HOW SUNDOWNER MOTOR INNS FULFILLS ITS ONLINE RESERVATIONS

Based in Shepparton, Victoria, Australia, Sundowner Motor Inns (*sundownerhotels.com.au.*) owns and franchises 24 large motels throughout rural Australia. Sundowner Motor Inns initiated a customer supply chain system to automate the management of room inventory. Software was developed to enable two existing systems to "talk" to each other: (1) the online booking system and (2) the offline property management system (PMS). The system has worked successfully since then and is continuously being improved.

Here is how the system fulfills orders:

1. Customers make a reservation inquiry at the company's website (*constellationhotels.com.au/sundowner*) or at independent online reservation portals (e.g., *wotif.com*, *expedia.com*).
2. Customers are connected automatically to a Web server, and the PMS provides graphic files, pricing, and room availability information.
3. In real time, the customer reviews room details.
4. The customer confirms the reservation by submitting his or her credit card details via the secure Web page.
5. Upon confirmation of the reservation, the PMS is updated automatically for room availability.
6. The company sends an automatic e-mail confirmation to the customer.

A significant internal process change was the shifting of a large network of rural motel managers from manually interacting with customers over the Internet to allowing an automated system to do it for them. Sundowner Motor Inns plans to continually deliver more customer value using the website as a central transaction platform. "Packaged" online deals are now available, offering a whole range of customized offers.

Sources: Compiled from Multimedia Victoria (2004) and from *constellationhotels.com.au/sundowner* (accessed March 2011).

Questions

1. Once you automate order fulfillment and your data are online, you can generate additional revenue. How?
2. What are the criteria for good order fulfillment in online hotel reservations?
3. Why is it advantageous to integrate the front-end and back-end systems?

▶ *Inventories can be minimized* by introducing a build-to-order manufacturing process as well as by providing fast and accurate information to suppliers. By allowing business partners to electronically track and monitor orders and production activities, inventory management can be improved and inventory levels and the expense of inventory management can be minimized. Inventories can be better managed if we know exactly where parts and materials are at any given time (e.g., by using RFID). Retailers' inventories can be managed electronically by their suppliers.

▶ *Self-service* can reduce supply chain problems and costs. Some activities can be done by customers, business partners, or employees. For example, customers can self-track the status of their orders (e.g., at FedEx, UPS, USPS, etc.); using FAQs customers and business partners may solve small problems by themselves. Customers can self-configure details of orders (e.g., for a computer at HP, Dell, and Apple), and finally employees can update personal data online.

▶ *Collaborative commerce* among members of the supply chain can be done in many areas ranging from product design to demand forecasting (see Chapter 5). The results are shorter cycle times, minimal delays and work interruptions, lower inventories, and lower administrative costs. A variety of tools exist ranging from collaborative hubs and networks to collaborative planning.

INNOVATIVE E-FULFILLMENT STRATEGIES

Several innovative e-fulfillment strategies exist. For example, supply chain partners can move information flows and hold off shipping actual physical goods until a point at which they can make more-direct shipments. Two examples of logistics postponement are (1) merge-in-transit and (2) rolling warehouses.

Merge-in-transit is a model in which components for a product may come from two different physical locations. For example, in shipping a desktop PC, the monitor may come from the East Coast of the United States and the CPU from the West Coast. Instead of shipping the components to a central location and then shipping both together to the customer, the components are shipped directly to the customer and merged into one shipment by the local deliverer (so the customer gets all the parts in one delivery), reducing unnecessary transportation.

With a **rolling warehouse**, products on the delivery truck are not preassigned to a destination, but the decision about the quantity to unload at each destination is made at the time of unloading. Thus, the latest order information can be taken into account, assisting in inventory control and lowering logistics costs (by avoiding repeat delivery trips). The rolling warehouse method also works in the ocean shipping industry, where it is called a *floating warehouse*.

Example: A World-Class Supply Chain and Order Fulfillment System Works at Dell

One of the most sophisticated order fulfillment systems is at Dell Computer. On one hand, Dell needs to fulfill both orders from individual customers and from businesses. On the other hand, Dell's suppliers need to fulfill Dell's orders for components and subassemblies. Here is how it is done.

Dell has completely automated its ability to take thousands of orders, translate them into millions of component requirements, and work directly with its suppliers to build and deliver products to meet customer requirements. More than 90 percent of Dell's component purchases now are handled online: Suppliers use an Internet portal to view Dell's requirements and changes to forecasts based on marketable activity and to confirm their ability to meet Dell's delivery requirements. Then, as Dell factories receive orders and schedule assemblies, a "pull" signal to the supplier triggers the shipment of only the materials required to build current orders, and suppliers deliver the materials directly to the appropriate Dell assembly lines.

Using Web Services, Dell now schedules every line in every factory around the world every 2 hours, and only brings 2 hours' worth of materials into the factory. This has

merge-in-transit
Logistics model in which components for a product may come from two (or more) different physical locations and are shipped directly to the customer's location.

rolling warehouse
Logistics method in which products on the delivery truck are not preassigned to a destination, but the decision about the quantity to unload at each destination is made at the time of unloading.

decreased the cycle time at Dell's assembly factories and reduced warehouse space—space that has been replaced by more manufacturing lines.

The project has produced more than just enhanced supply chain efficiencies and accelerated, highly reliable order fulfillment. At any given time, there is less than 4 days of inventory in the entire Dell operation, whereas many competitors routinely carry 30 days or more. In addition, automation has helped Dell react more quickly to correct potentially out-of-balance situations, made it much easier to prevent components from becoming obsolete, and improved response times across the supply chain by providing a global view of supply and demand at any specific Dell location at any time.

Integration and Enterprise Resource Planning

If you review Exhibit 11.3 for the order fulfillment process, you will notice that certain activities involve interfacing with other information systems, such as finance, inventory management, production schedule, vendor and customer contact, and logistics. Most of these interfaces are internal, but some are external (most with suppliers and customers). For the sake of effectiveness and efficiency, such interfaces need to be done quickly and without errors. The fewer manual interfaces we need to make, the better. How wonderful it would be if we used only one interface, and if it was automated! This is exactly what an enterprise resource planning (ERP) system does. For details, see Online Tutorial T5.

The Supply Chains of Tomorrow

According to a comprehensive study done at MIT, the supply chains of tomorrow must deliver varying degrees of the following six outcomes (per Melnyk, et al. 2010), each with a corresponding set of specific design traits. The outcomes that drive the supply chains are:

- Monitoring cost, quality, and delivery on time
- Safety and security of goods delivered
- Eliminating waste, reducing pollution, improving the environment
- Resilience, quick recovery from disruptions of all kinds
- Responsiveness—change quickly to adapt to changing conditions
- Innovation—using the supply chain as a source of new processes and products, both internally and with business partners

These outcomes will assure effective and efficient order fulfillment.

Section 11.3 ▶ REVIEW QUESTIONS

1. List the various order-taking solutions.
2. List solutions for improved delivery.
3. Describe same-day shipments.
4. Describe some innovative e-strategies for order fulfillment.
5. Describe how to effectively manage the return of items.
6. Describe issues in B2B fulfillment.
7. List three outcomes of tomorrow's supply chain.

11.4 RFID AND CPFR AS KEY ENABLERS IN SUPPLY CHAIN MANAGEMENT

Two major technologies were found effective for improving supply chains and reducing problems along it: RFID and CPFR.

THE ESSENTIALS OF RFID

One of the newest and most revolutionary solutions to supply chain problems is RFID. We introduce the concept of RFID in Online Tutorial T3. (Also see en.wikipedia.org/

wiki/RFID.) For an introductory video, see "RFID in Plain English" at youtube.com/watch?v= ffTbpmYapHo&feature=related.

Radio frequency identification (RFID) tags can be attached to or embedded in objects, animals, or humans; these tags use radio waves to communicate with a reader for the purpose of uniquely identifying the object, transmitting data, storing information about the object, or locating an item. Eventually, RFID tags will be attached to every item in the supply chain. Tags are like bar codes, but they contain much more information. Also, they can be read from a longer distance (up to 50 feet). This can be done due to the tag's relatively small size (although they are mostly still too large for some small items) and relatively low cost. Cost has been a real issue, and one inhibitor of the uptake of RFID technology. However, the cost of RFID technology is coming close to reaching a point where companies will be willing to invest in RFID because they can be more certain of achieving an ROI on their RFID investments. RFID tags for the 2008 Olympics and for the 2010 World Trade Fair have been produced at about 3¢ each. However, cost is just one factor. Organizations still need to learn exactly how to effectively use the capabilities of RFID technology in their supply chains with the back-office systems and how business processes may need to be redesigned and retooled so that solid business benefits accrue from the use of this technology (for benefits, see Loebbecke 2006).

Given these developments, what effect will RFID have on supply chains? Let's look at Exhibit 11.5, which shows the relationship between a retailer (Walmart), a manufacturer (such as P&G), and P&G's suppliers. Note that the tags are read as merchandise travels from the supplier to the retailer (steps 1 and 2). The RFID transmits real-time information on the location of the merchandise. Steps 3–6 show the use of the RFID at the retailer, mainly to confirm arrivals (step 3) and to locate merchandise inside the company, control inventory, prevent theft, and expedite processing of relevant information (steps 4–6). It is no longer necessary to count inventories, and all business partners are able to view inventory information in real time. This transparency can go several tiers down the supply chain. Additional applications, such as rapid checkout, which eliminates the need to scan each item, will be provided by RFID in the future.

According to Reyes (2011), RFID can help in improving supply chain visibility, asset visibility and capital goods tracking, returnable asset tracking, work-in-process tracking, as well as managing internal supply chains. Examples of several applications are presented next.

radio frequency identification (RFID) Tags that can be attached to or embedded in objects, animals, or humans and use radio waves to communicate with a reader for the purpose of uniquely identifying the object or transmitting data and/or storing information about the object.

RFID APPLICATIONS IN THE SUPPLY CHAIN AROUND THE GLOBE

Many potential and actual applications exist in enterprises using RFID (e.g., see *RFID Journal*). The following are examples of how RFID is used in the supply chain. For a comprehensive presentation and 32 case studies, see Reyes (2011) and Niederman, et al. (2007).

RFID at Metro AG-Germany

Metro, a huge retailer from Germany, is using RFID tags in an attempt to speed the flow of goods from manufacturers in China to their arrival in Europe at the Port of Rotterdam to distribution centers in Germany. Passive tags (see Online Tutorial T3) are being applied to cartons and cases of goods; active tags are also being applied to the containers in which those goods are packed for shipping. At various points en route to Germany, the active tags are read and record the arrival of the cargo, enabling a record to be kept of where goods are located at any point in time. This gives Metro greater insights into the flow of goods along its supply chain, with bottlenecks or points that slow the delivery of goods becoming quickly evident. This allows for a review of business processes and work practices to ensure speedier handling and delivery. In addition, these RFID tags are equipped with intrusion sensors, which give an indication of whether any attempt has been made to open the sealed containers during the journey. If the container is tampered with, the tags can trigger flashing lights or a siren to alert staff. Thus, Metro is able to detect any attempts to tamper with or pilfer stock (see Heinrich 2005).

The benefits of the RFID system to Metro are substantial. It is calculated that eliminating a single day from the supply chain will save Metro hundreds of thousands of dollars annually by reducing the amount of stock held in inventory. Estimates are that for large

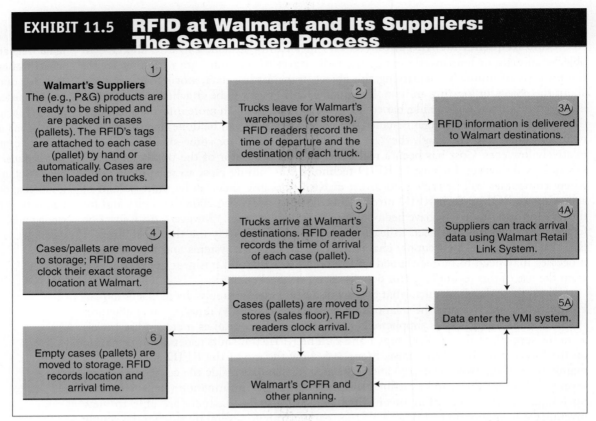

EXHIBIT 11.5   RFID at Walmart and Its Suppliers: The Seven-Step Process

1. Walmart's Suppliers
The (e.g., P&G) products are ready to be shipped and are packed in cases (pallets). The RFID's tags are attached to each case (pallet) by hand or automatically. Cases are then loaded on trucks.

2. Trucks leave for Walmart's warehouses (or stores). RFID readers record the time of departure and the destination of each truck.

3A. RFID information is delivered to Walmart destinations.

3. Trucks arrive at Walmart's destinations. RFID reader records the time of arrival of each case (pallet).

4. Cases/pallets are moved to storage; RFID readers clock their exact storage location at Walmart.

4A. Suppliers can track arrival data using Walmart Retail Link System.

5. Cases (pallets) are moved to stores (sales floor). RFID readers clock arrival.

5A. Data enter the VMI system.

6. Empty cases (pallets) are moved to storage. RFID records location and arrival time.

7. Walmart's CPFR and other planning.

Source: Drawn by E. Turban.

retailers (in excess of $1 billion in sales annually) each 1-day reduction in inventory can free up to $1 million in working capital (Sullivan 2006). For details, see future-store.org.

RFID at Starbucks

As Starbucks expands its range of fresh foods (such as salads, sandwiches, and the like) available at its outlets, the complexity and demands of managing this supply chain increase. Keeping the food fresh depends on keeping it at a steady cool state and in ensuring timely delivery. Starbucks is requiring its distributors to employ RFID tags to measure the temperature at the delivery trucks. These tags are programmed to record the temperature inside the truck every few minutes, and on return to the depot this temperature data can be downloaded and analyzed carefully. If there are unacceptable readings (e.g., the temperature is deemed to have risen too high), efforts are made to determine the cause and remedy the problem. This can then cause a redesign of critical business processes with regard to the transportation and handling of food (*RFID Journal* 2006). As RFID technology matures, it is conceivable, that in the future, the tags themselves will be able to detect variations in temperature and send a signal to a thermostat to activate refrigeration fans within the truck.

RFID at Deutsche Post (Germany)

Deutsche Post owns 6 million shipping containers that it uses to hold and transport about 70 million letters and other items that pass through its distribution centers daily. In order to process these crates, Deutsche Post prints in excess of 500 million thick paper labels, all of which are thrown away after a single use. It was environmental concerns, rather than purely economic ones, that drove Deutsche Post's RFID initiative.

Deutsche Post uses passive RFID tags with a bi-stable display, meaning that the text displayed remains on-screen after power is removed and does not change until power is restored and the text is rewritten by an RFID interrogator. Tags on the crates must be readable from all angles and in all types of weather, requiring a robust tag. Furthermore, the tags need to last about 5 years in order for the application to be financially viable.

Deutsche Post developed a custom tag and RFID reader, and uses specialized software in this innovative application. Several other post offices around the world use RFID (e.g., Canada). For other applications and more details, refer to Loebbecke (2006) and Reyes (2011).

RFID in the Federal Government (U.S. Department of Defense)

Inventory tracking is a logistical challenge throughout the armed services and federal agencies. At the same time, there is an urgent need to ensure the safety of military personnel and improve security worldwide. The end result is that RFID-based applications in the federal government and defense sectors are growing exponentially. RFID technology offers a viable solution with reliable, secure identification and tracking that integrates with existing enterprise mobility systems. For example, the U.S. Marine Corps uses RFID to improve flows in their supply chains.

RFID at Atlantic Beef Products (Ontario, Canada)

Cow's ears are tagged with RFID tags. After a cow is killed, its ear tags are scanned for food traceability. The carcass goes onto two leg hooks, each equipped with an RFID chip. They are synced to each animal's database record. The RFIDs replace bar codes, which could get contaminated with E. coli on the slaughter floor. The RFID helps track the movement of each cow and the meat produced at any time. The system won a gold medal from the Canadian IT organization.

RFID at Yodobashi Camera Handles Inventory of About 1 Million Items (Japan)

Yodobashi Camera launches a new product every day. In an extremely competitive environment, the company requires a system that responds to customer demands promptly and efficiently. Yodobashi carries a diverse range of products supplied by hundreds of manufacturers and distributors, and the complexity is compounded by a huge inventory that needs to be regularly tracked. The company required a solution that would make its warehouse management process seamless and more efficient.

Yodobashi Camera's warehouse management needs were solved by Motorola, which deployed an RFID-based Motorola inventory management solution that improved Yodobashi Camera's efficiency and real-time stock visibility. In addition, Yodobashi Camera has dramatically reduced workloads in the warehouse by automating the stock-taking process, which, in turn, has enabled better decision making. For details, see the Yodobashi Camera case study (Motorola 2007a).

RFID in Pharmaceuticals

MIT and SAP are examining the use of RFID in various industries, including pharmaceuticals and health care delivery, as well as the necessary IT architecture to support such use. The goal is to be able to know where everything or anything is at any given time. The challenge, however, is in determining how such a scenario would play out—what the actual network would look like once companies up and down the supply chain collaboratively start exchanging information among trading partners and their partners' partners.

The Food and Drug Administration (FDA), for example, is interested in using RFID to find counterfeit drugs in the supply chain. An RFID chip with patient information (called *SurgiChip*, approved by the FDA) goes with the patient into surgery to help prevent errors. RFID tags are also used for patient identification throughout hospitals. Finally, many hospitals use RFID tags to find the whereabouts of pieces of portable equipment.

Jeweler Gains Efficiency and Improves Customer Service with RFID (India)

Indian jewelry retailer Bhima & Brothers Jewelers (B&BJ) is tracking its high-value inventory and providing customers with immediate information regarding its jewelry, with an RFID system deployed first at one of its five stores. The system has reduced the amount of time the store requires to take inventory from 36 man-hours down to 1, and has decreased the time necessary to complete a sales transaction from between 6 to 8 minutes, to less than 1 minute. Not only does RFID provide the company with faster and more accurate inventory tracking, it also helps the retailer improve customer service. For details, see Swedberg (2009).

Theoretically, RFID can be read in many places along the supply chain, as illustrated in Exhibit 11.6.

For more examples of applications, see Online Tutorial T3 and Roberti (2007).

Other Uses

▶ RFID embedded in cell phones is beginning to replace credit cards, cash, train passes, keys to your car and home, business cards, and more (see Kharif 2006). DOCOMO of Japan introduced such a cell phone in 2004, and its use is growing rapidly.

▶ RFID can be used in sensor networks (see Chapter 6).

COLLABORATIVE PLANNING, FORECASTING, AND REPLENISHMENT

collaborative planning, forecasting, and replenishment (CPFR)
Project in which suppliers and retailers collaborate in their planning and demand forecasting to optimize flow of materials along the supply chain.

As you may recall, a major problem in order fulfillment is the demand forecast. A related problem is the bullwhip effect. A possible solution to both problems is CPFR.

Collaborative planning, forecasting, and replenishment (CPFR) is a business practice in which suppliers and retailers collaborate in planning and demand forecasting in order to ensure that members of the supply chain will have the right amount of raw materials and finished goods when they need them. The goal of CPFR is to streamline product flow from manufacturing plants all the way to customers' homes. Large manufacturers of consumer goods, such as P&G, have superb supply chains resulting from their use of CPFR.

EXHIBIT 11.6 Digital Supply Chains

Shipping

RFID

RFID

Transformed Store

Visibility Data Network

Retail Distribution Center

RFID

Object Naming Service (ONS)

Shipping

Retailer Headquarters

Logistics Company

Collaborative Business Network

Raw Materials Headquarters

CPG Headquarters

RFID

CPG Warehouse

Raw Materials Warehouse

Logistics Company

Global Data Synch

RFID

RFID

Shipping

Shipping

RFID

RFID

Finished Goods Factory

RFID

Source: Intel, "Building the Digital Supply Chain: An Intel Perspective." Intel Solutions White Paper, January 2005, Figure 5, p. 9. Reprinted with permission from Intel Corporation.

The essentials of CPFR are shown in Exhibit 11.7. The process is discussed in Online File W11.8. Note that this is a cyclical process in which sellers, buyers, and end customers are considered. The process starts with strategy and planning, followed by demand and supply management, which results in execution. The results are analyzed, leading to a reexamination of the strategy.

An interesting application of CPFR is that of West Marine, presented in Case 11.5. CPFR can be used with a company-centric B2B and with sell-side or buy-side marketplaces. For more on the benefits of CPFR, see cpfr.org/cpfr_pdf/index.html. Also, see en.wikipedia.org/wiki/CPFR. CPFR is one example of collaborative commerce, which was discussed in Chapter 5.

Section 11.4 ▶ REVIEW QUESTIONS

1. What is RFID?
2. How can RFID improve supply chain visibility?
3. Describe three RFID supply chain applications.
4. What is CPFR?
5. How can CPFR improve supply chain operations of an e-commerce retailer?

EXHIBIT 11.7   CPFR Model

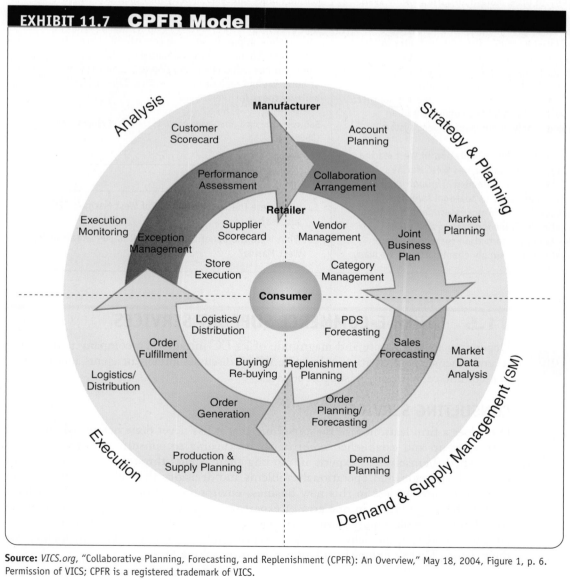

Source: *VICS.org*, "Collaborative Planning, Forecasting, and Replenishment (CPFR): An Overview," May 18, 2004, Figure 1, p. 6. Permission of VICS; CPFR is a registered trademark of VICS.

CASE 11.5
EC Application
WEST MARINE: A CPFR SUCCESS STORY

West Marine (*westmarine.com*) is the largest boating-supply company in the United States. It has 400 stores and annual sales of $690 million. The company sells more than 50,000 different products, ranging from stainless-steel propellers and anchors to life jackets and wetsuits, through its stores, website, catalog, and commercial sales arm.

West Marine has a dramatic story when it comes to its effective supply chain, which was guided and directed through its deep, intensive, and effective implementation of CPFR. West Marine is now regarded as having a showcase CPFR implementation; however, it wasn't always that way.

In 1997, West Marine acquired its East Coast competitor E&B Marine. As a result of the challenges of integrating the two companies, sales fell by almost 8 percent, and during the peak season out-of-stock situations rose by more than 12 percent over the previous year. Income dropped from $15 million in 1997 to little more than $1 million in 1998.

The situation was quite different when in 2003 West Marine purchased its largest competitor, BoatUS. West Marine successfully integrated BoatUS's distribution center in just 30 days. BoatUS's in-store systems were integrated into West Marine in just under 60 days. Further, supply chain performance and the bottom line were not affected.

So why was this second acquisition so much smoother? The difference was that by 2003 the company had an effective IT-enabled supply chain management system driven by CPFR.

In reviewing the CPFR implementation in West Marine, it is clear that a key success factor was West Marine's commitment to technology enablement. Through the CPFR information systems, data such as seasonal forecasts, promotional stock levels, and future assortment changes are calculated automatically. Joint forecasting and order fulfillment are enabled by information systems that are suitably integrated between supply chain partners. As many

similar case studies attest, such information sharing through integrated supply chain systems is one factor in successful supply chain management.

However, West Marine's successful CPFR implementation was not simply about the technology. Significant energy and resources were devoted to collaboration among the key supply chain personnel in West Marine and its supply chain partners. Joint skills and knowledge were developed along with the key elements of trust and joint understanding. These elements were built through joint education and training sessions as well as through the standard CPFR joint planning and forecasting sessions.

West Marine's CPFR program now involves 200 suppliers and more than 20,000 stock items, representing more than 90 percent of West Marine's procurement spending. Further, more than 70 of West Marine's top suppliers load West Marine's order forecasts directly into their production planning systems. In-stock rates at West Marine stores are well over 90 percent, forecast accuracy stands at 85 percent, and on-time shipments are now consistently better than 80 percent. Summing up West Marine's collaborative supply chain journey using CPFR, Larry Smith, senior vice president of planning and replenishment, states, "The results, we believe, speak for themselves."

Sources: Compiled from Ayers and Odegaard (2007) and Smith (2006b).

Questions

1. What were the major elements of West Marine's CPFR success?

2. What were the benefits of the CPFR implementation for West Marine?

11.5 OTHER E-COMMERCE SUPPORT SERVICES

Depending on the nature and magnitude of its EC initiatives, a company may require several other support services. Online File W11.9 discusses intelligent agents and their role in e-commerce, especially in support services.

CONSULTING SERVICES

How does a firm learn how to do something that it has never done before? Many firms, both start-up and established companies, are turning to consulting firms that have established themselves as experts in guiding their clients through the maze of legal, technical, strategic, and operational problems and decisions that must be addressed in order to ensure success in this new business environment. Some of these firms have established a reputation in one area of expertise, whereas others are generalists. Some consultants even take equity (ownership) positions in the firms they advise. Some consultants will build, test, and deliver a working website and may even host it and maintain it for their clients. There are three broad categories of consulting firms.

The first type of consulting firm includes those that provide expertise in the area of EC but not in traditional business. Some of the consultants that provide general EC expertise are Agency.com (agency.com), Virtusa (virtusa.com), Sun Microsystems (sun.com), Inforte (inforte.com), Sapient (sapient.com), Autonomy (autonomy.com), and WebTrends (webtrends.com).

The second type of consulting firm is a traditional consulting company that maintains divisions that focus on EC. These include the so-called Big Four U.S. accounting firms and the large established U.S. national management consulting firms. These firms leverage their existing relationships with their corporate clients and offer EC value-added services. Representative companies are Accenture, Computer Service Corporation, Cambridge Technology Partners, Boston Consulting Group, Booz Allen Hamilton, Deloitte & Touche, Ernst & Young, EDS, KPMG, McKinsey, and PricewaterhouseCoopers.

The third category of consulting firms is EC hardware and software vendors that provide technology-consulting services. These include SAP, IBM, Oracle, Microsoft, Cisco, Intel, and many more.

Online Consulting

Guideline (guideline.com) sells instant consulting. For an ad hoc fee starting at $500 or an annual fee of up to $10,000, clients can reach more than 70 consultants for phone or Web-based queries. Answers to business questions are produced within 24 hours, with backup documents. Experts give advice on product launches, market segmentation, and potential competitors' moves. A Web-only service to small and medium enterprises (SMEs) is available.

It is imperative that any firm seeking help in devising a successful online strategy select not only an experienced and competent consulting firm but also one with sufficient synergies with the client firm. For a discussion of vendor selection and management, see Chapter 13.

DIRECTORY SERVICES, NEWSLETTERS, AND SEARCH ENGINES

The EC landscape is huge, with hundreds of thousands of companies selling products and services online. How can a buyer find all the suitable sellers? How can a seller find all the suitable buyers? In B2B, vertical exchanges can help with this matching process, but even vertical exchanges include only a limited number of potential partners, usually located in one country. To overcome the problem of finding buyers or sellers online, a company may use directory services.

Directory Services

There are several types of *directory services*. Some simply list companies by categories; others provide links to companies. In many cases, the data are classified in several different ways for easy search purposes. In others, special search engines are provided. Finally, value-added services, such as matching buyers and sellers, are available. The following are some popular directories:

▸ B2Business.net (b2business.net) is a major resource for B2B professionals. It includes listings of business resources in about 30 functional areas, company research resources (e.g., credit checks, customs research, and financial reviews), information on start up (business plans, domain names, recruiting, patents, incubators, and even a graveyard), general EC information (e.g., books, articles, reports, events, and research), e-marketplace directories (e.g., enablers and builders, services, support services, and major markets), and infrastructure resources (e.g., security, connectivity, catalogs, content, portal builders, and ASPs).

▸ B2BToday.com (b2btoday.com) is a directory that contains listings of B2B services organized by type of service (e.g., website creation, B2B marketing, and B2B software) and product category (e.g., automotive and books). Each part of the directory highlights several companies at the start of the list that pay extra fees to be listed on the top; after the premium slots, the directory is organized in alphabetical order.

The directory listings are hyperlinked to the companies' websites. Many of the sites are involved in B2C.

- ▶ A2Z of B2B (a2zofb2b.com) is a directory of B2B companies organized in alphabetical order or industry order. It specifies the type and nature of the company, the venture capital sponsor of the B2B, and the stock market ticker (if the company's stock is listed on a publicly traded stock exchange).
- ▶ i-Stores (revolutionwebdesign.com) is a directory that targets online stores. The company provides website design and creation with emphasis on e-commerce solutions affordable for small businesses.
- ▶ Websters (webstersonline.com) is a large business directory organized by location and by product or service. In addition, it provides listings by industry and subindustry (according to SIC and NAICS codes).
- ▶ ThomasNet (thomasnet.com) provides a directory of several hundred thousands of manufacturers of industrial products and services in about 70,000 categories.
- ▶ Yahoo! Small Business (smallbusiness.yahoo.com/index) provides business directories. As of 2011, it listed more than 600,000 companies (dir.yahoo.com/Business_and_Economy).

Newsletters

There are many B2B newsletters to choose from. Several are e-mailed to individuals free of charge. Examples of B2B newsletters are shown at emarketer.com/newsletters (look for B2B Weekly) and Line56.com. Many companies (e.g., Ariba, Intel) issue corporate newsletters and e-mail them to people who request them. Also, companies can use software from onlinepressreleases.com to send online press releases to thousands of editors.

Directories and newsletters are helpful, but they may not be sufficient. Therefore, one may need specialized search engines.

Search Engines and News Aggregators

Several search engines can be used to discover B2B-related information. Some of these are embedded in the directories. Here are some examples:

- ▶ Moreover (moreover.com) is a search engine that locates information and aggregates B2B (and other business) news.
- ▶ Google offers a directory of components for B2B and B2C websites. These range from currency exchange calculators to server performance monitors (see directory.google.com).
- ▶ iEntry (ientry.com) provides B2B search engines, targeted "niche engines," and several industry-focused newsletters. IEntry operates a network of websites and e-mail newsletters that reaches more than 2 million unique opt-in subscribers. Newsletters are available in each of the following categories: Web Developers, Advice, Technology, Professional, Sports & Entertainment, Leisure & Lifestyles, and Web Entrepreneurs. Click on a newsletter to get a brief description and view sample content.

MORE EC SUPPORT SERVICES

Many other service providers support e-commerce in different ways. Each service provider adds a unique value-added service. This section describes only several representative examples.

Trust Services. Chapter 8 introduced the role of trust in B2C. Trust also is important in B2B because one cannot touch the seller's products and because buyers may not be known to sellers. Trust-support services such as TRUSTe, BBBOnline, and Ernst & Young's trust service are used both in B2C and B2B.

Trademark and Domain Names. A number of domain name services are available. Examples are verisign.com, mydomain.com, register.com, easyspace.com, and whois.net.

Digital Photos. Companies such as IPIX (ipix.com) provide innovative pictures for websites.

Global Business Communities. The e-commerce portal from Wiznet (wiznet.net) is a global, Web-based "business community" that supports the unique requirements of buying organizations, including cross-catalog searches, RFQ development and distribution, and decision support, while simultaneously enabling suppliers to dictate the content and presentation of their own product catalogs.

Access to Commercial Databases. Subscribers to Thomson Dialog (dialog.com) can access about 900 databases, including those containing patents, trademarks, government reports, and news articles.

Knowledge Management. Lotus Domino, a major knowledge management and collaboration company, offers the capability to manage Web content with its Domino product (see Online Tutorial T10).

Client Matching. TechRepublic (techrepublic.com) matches business clients with firms that provide a wide variety of IT services. It works like a matchmaking service. Clients define what they want, and TechRepublic performs the searching and screening, checking against some general parameters and criteria. This reduces the risk of clients making bad choices. Buyers also save time and have greater exposure to a larger number of IT service providers.

E-Business Rating Sites. A number of sites are available for businesses to research rankings of potential partners and suppliers. Bizrate.com, forrester.com, gomez.com, and consumersearch.com all provide business ratings.

Security and Encryption Sites. VeriSign (verisign.com) provides valuable encryption tools for all types of EC organizations. It provides domain site registration and several security mechanisms.

Web Research Services. A number of Web research providers help companies learn more about technologies, trends, and potential business partners and suppliers. Some of these are IDC (idc.com), ZDNet (zdnet.com), and Forrester (forrester.com).

Coupon-Generating Sites. A number of vendors help companies generate online coupons. Some of these are Q-pon.com (q-pon.com), CentsOff (centsoff.com), and TheFreeSite.com (thefreesite.com).

Exhibit 11.8 presents additional services available for B2B operations.

EXHIBIT 11.8 Other B2B Services

Category	Description	Examples
Marketplace concentrator (aggregator)	Aggregates information about products and services from multiple providers at one central point. Purchasers can search, compare, shop, and sometimes complete the sales transaction.	InternetMall, DealerNet, Insweb, Industrial Marketplace
Information brokers (infomediaries)	Provide product, pricing, and availability information. Some facilitate transactions, but their main value is the information they provide.	PartNet, Travelocity, Autobytel
Transaction brokers	Buyers can view rates and terms, but the primary business activity is to complete the transaction.	E*TRADE, Ameritrade
Digital product delivery	Sells and delivers software, multimedia, and other digital products over the Internet.	Regards.com, PhotoDisc, SonicNet
Content provider	Creates revenue by providing content. The customer may pay to access the content, or revenue may be generated by selling advertising space or by having advertisers pay for placement in an organized listing in a searchable database.	*Wall Street Journal* Interactive, Tripod
Online service provider	Provides service and support for hardware and software users.	CyberMedia, TuneUp.com
Specialized directories	Provide leads to a variety of B2B services categories.	Business.com, KnowledgeStorm, Searchedu.com

OUTSOURCING EC SUPPORT SERVICES

Most companies do not maintain in-house support services. Instead, they outsource many of these services.

Why Outsource EC Services?

Historically, early businesses were vertically integrated—they owned or controlled their own sources of materials, manufactured components, performed final assembly, and managed the distribution and sale of their products to consumers. Later, nearly all firms began to contract with other firms to execute various activities along the supply chain, from manufacturing to distribution and sales, in order to concentrate their activities on their *core competency*. This contracting practice is known as *outsourcing*.

When EC emerged, it became obvious that it would be necessary to outsource some of the support services involved in its deployment. Many companies prefer to do this due to:

- A desire to concentrate on the core business
- The need to have services up and running rapidly
- Lack of expertise (experience and resources) for many of the required support services
- The inability to have the economies of scale enjoyed by outsourcers, which often results in high costs for in-house options
- The inability to keep up with rapidly fluctuating demands if an in-house option is used
- The number of required services, which usually are simply too many for one company to handle

To show the importance of outsourcing, we will look briefly at the typical process of developing and managing EC applications (the e-infrastructure). The process includes the following major steps:

1. EC strategy formulation
2. Application design
3. Building (or buying) the systems
4. Hosting, operating, and maintaining the EC site

Each of these steps may include several activities, as shown in Exhibit 11.9. A firm may execute all the activities of this process internally, or it may outsource some or all of them.

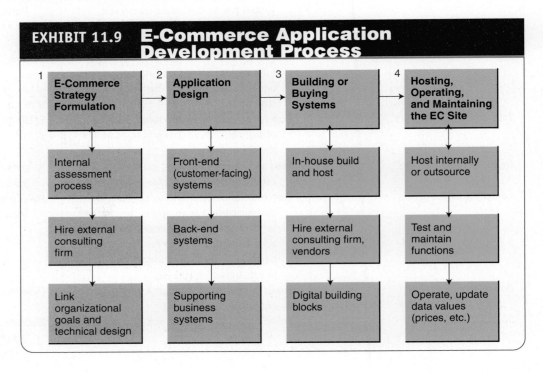

EXHIBIT 11.9 E-Commerce Application Development Process

1 E-Commerce Strategy Formulation	2 Application Design	3 Building or Buying Systems	4 Hosting, Operating, and Maintaining the EC Site
Internal assessment process	Front-end (customer-facing) systems	In-house build and host	Host internally or outsource
Hire external consulting firm	Back-end systems	Hire external consulting firm, vendors	Test and maintain functions
Link organizational goals and technical design	Supporting business systems	Digital building blocks	Operate, update data values (prices, etc.)

In addition to design and maintenance of technical systems, many other system design issues and business functions related to using a website also must be addressed. For example, a firm doing EC must design and operate its order fulfillment system and outbound logistics (delivery) functions; it must provide dynamic content on the site; and it must also provide services to its customers and partners.

IT Outsourcing and Application Service Providers

IT is the most frequently outsourced business activity. Most enterprises engaged in EC practice a very large degree of IT outsourcing. While concentrating on core competencies, they develop strategic alliances with partner firms in order to provide activities such as payment processing, order fulfillment, outbound logistics, website hosting, and customer service.

Outside contractors best serve SMEs with few IT staff and smaller budgets. Outside contractors also have proven to be a good choice for large companies wanting to experiment with EC without a great deal of up-front investment. In addition, outsourcing allows them to protect their own internal networks or to rely on experts to establish sites over which they will later assume control. Some of the best-known B2C sites on the Web (e.g., eddiebauer.com and 1800flowers.com) are run by third-party vendors.

Several types of providers offer services for creating and operating electronic storefronts.

One of the most interesting types of EC outsourcing is the use of application service providers. An **application service provider (ASP)** is an agent or vendor who assembles the functions needed by enterprises and packages them with outsourced development, operation, maintenance, and other services (see en.wikipedia.org/wiki/Application_service_provider for details).

application service provider (ASP)
An agent or vendor who assembles the functions needed by enterprises and packages them with outsourced development, operation, maintenance, and other services.

Section 11.5 ▶ REVIEW QUESTIONS

1. Describe the role of EC consultants and list their major types.
2. Describe the value offered by directory services. Provide three examples of what value they add.
3. Explain why specialized search engines are needed.
4. List some other EC support services.
5. List the major reasons why companies outsource EC support services.
6. Which types of services are outsourced the most?
7. Define ASPs.

MANAGERIAL ISSUES

Some managerial issues related to this chapter are as follows.

1. **If you are an EC vendor, what is the bottleneck in the order fulfillment process?** Order fulfillment is a critical task, especially for virtual EC vendors. The problem is not only the physical shipment but also the efficient execution of the entire order fulfillment process, which may be complex along a long supply chain. To enhance the order fulfillment process, the vendor needs to identify the bottleneck that needs improvement. Potential issues are the delayed delivery date, high return rate, high inventory cost, high shipping cost, and poor integration along the supply chain and demand chain. The EC vendor should identify its own problem first.

2. **For which items should we keep our own inventory?** As Amazon.com has experienced, online vendors try to avoid keeping inventory because it is expensive. However, we should not neglect the fact that retailing with appropriate inventory is a source of extra profit as well. In addition, for certain items, it is not possible to assure on-time delivery without having controllable inventory; the no-inventory policy is not always the best policy. A company has to design the portfolio plan of inventory and distribution centers for the items that have a positive effect of having inventory. A CPFR program may be adopted to minimize the burden of holding inventories. The plan for distribution centers must

be balanced with the plan of outsourced items through partners.

3. **What is the alliance strategy in order fulfillment?** Partnerships and alliances can improve logistics and alleviate supply chain problems. We need to decide in which part of order fulfillment we should count on partners. The typical activities that may be outsourced are shipping, warehousing, inventory holding, return management, and so on. Decide on the appropriate third-party logistics supplier that can provide reliable service for these activities. For certain items that you cannot supply well, a partner may take care of the entire merchandising as well as order fulfillment, especially if you have leverage on the online brand image. An example is Amazon.com's software corner, which is handled by Egghead.com.

4. **How should we manage returns?** Dealing with returns can be a complex issue. Reverse logistics is very costly, and most companies cannot continue online business if the return rate is too high. Use the CRM system to identify the items with higher return rates and resolve the reason or stop the online sales of such items. A company should estimate its percentage of returns and plan a process for receiving and handling them. The logistics of returns may be executed through an external logistic service provider.

5. **What logistics information should we provide to customers?** Customers, particularly business customers, want to know the availability of inventory and delivery date at the time of order. To meet these needs, the EC system should be integrated with the back-end information system. Customers may also want to trace the status of order processing, which should be managed by more than one company along the order fulfillment process. To provide seamless information beyond the boundary of the vendor, the partners should collaborate while developing their information systems.

6. **Should we use RFID for the order fulfillment?** If your buyer requires you to use RFID tags, there is no choice but to follow the request; however, the experts and equipment on RFID are not always available within a company. Some third-party logistics service providers support the tagging service. One question is who pays for the cost and who gets the benefit.? So far, big buyers such as Walmart and the Department of Defense get the benefit, while the suppliers pay the cost. In the long run, suppliers may be able to share the benefit in inventory management. However, it will take time until the cost of RFID chips becomes cost-effective and the penetration becomes pervasive enough to maximize the benefit of RFID technology.

7. **Can we use CPFR in SMEs?** CPFR is a conceptual model for working with business partners and is usually effective and efficient with large organizations. However, since it is basically a conceptual model of collaborative planning, it may work in some SMEs where collaborative planning is critical. A visit to *vics.org* and an examination of some of the applications there can help identify places where CPFR can help SMEs.

SUMMARY

In this chapter, you learned about the following EC issues as they relate to the chapter's learning objectives.

1. **The role of support services in EC.** Support services are essential to the success of EC. They range from order fulfillment to providing customer service. They can be done by the companies or they can be outsourced.

2. **The order fulfillment process.** Large numbers of support services are needed for EC implementation. Most important are payment mechanisms and order fulfillment. On-time delivery of products to customers may be a difficult task, especially in B2C. Fulfilling an order requires several activities ranging from credit and inventory checks to shipments. Most of these activities are part of back-office operations and are related to logistics. The order fulfillment process varies from business to business and also depends on the product. Generally speaking, however, the following steps are recognized: payment verification, inventory checking, shipping arrangement, insurance, production (or assembly), plant services, purchasing, customer contacts, and return of products.

3. **Problems in order fulfillment.** It is difficult to fulfill B2C orders due to uncertainties in demand and potential delays in supply and deliveries. Problems also result from lack of coordination and information sharing among business partners.

4. **Solutions to order fulfillment problems.** Automating order taking (e.g., by using forms over the Internet) and smoothing the supply chain are two ways to solve order fulfillment problems. Several other innovative solutions exist, most of which are supported by software that facilitates correct inventories, coordination along the supply chain, and appropriate planning and decision making.

5. **RFID tags.** Replacing bar codes with RFID can greatly improve locating items along the supply chain quickly. This technology has many other benefits and few limitations.

   The major applications are improving supply chain visibility, expediting tracking, speeding inventory counting, expediting deliveries, and reducing errors.

6. **Collaborative planning and CPFR.** Collaborative planning concentrates on demand forecasting and on resource and activity planning along the supply chain. Collaborative planning tries to synchronize partners' activities. CPFR is a business strategy that attempts to develop standard protocols and procedures for collabo-ration. Its goal is to improve demand forecasting by collaborative planning in order to ensure delivery of materials when needed.

7. **Other support services.** EC support services include consulting services, directory services, infrastructure providers, and many more. One cannot practice EC without some of them. These support services need to be coordinated and integrated. Some of them can be done in-house; others must be outsourced.

8. **Outsourcing EC services.** Selective outsourcing of EC services usually is a must. Lack of time and expertise forces companies to outsource, despite the risks of doing so. Using ASPs is a viable alternative, but they are neither inexpensive nor risk-free.

KEY TERMS

Application service provider (ASP)	609	Front-office operations	582	Rolling warehouse	597
Back-office operations	582	Logistics	582	Third-party logistics suppliers (3PL)	586
Collaborative planning, forecasting, and replenishment (CPFR)	602	Merge-in-transit	597	Visibility	596
		Order fulfillment	582		
E-logistics	582	Radio frequency identification (RFID)	599	Warehouse management system (WMS)	588
		Reverse logistics	585		

DISCUSSION QUESTIONS

1. Discuss the problem of reverse logistics in EC. What types of companies may suffer the most?

2. Explain why UPS defines itself as a "technology company with trucks" rather than as a "trucking company with technology."

3. Under what situations might the outsourcing of EC services not be desirable?

4. UPS and other logistics companies also provide financial services. Discuss the logic behind this.

5. Differentiate order fulfillment in B2C from that of B2B.

6. Discuss the motivation of suppliers to improve the supply chain to customers.

7. Discuss how CPFR can lead to more accurate forecasting and how it can resolve the bullwhip effect.

8. Describe the advantages of RFID over a regular bar code in light of supply chain management.

9. Discuss the need to integrate EC with partners' systems.

10. Discuss the need for intelligent and software agents. (Hint: See Online File W11.9.)

11. Investigate and discuss how artificial intelligence can be used to pick and pack orders faster and more accurately. Begin with McGown (2010).

TOPICS FOR CLASS DISCUSSION AND DEBATES

1. Discuss the need for intelligent software agents in order fulfillment and supply chain management.

2. Chart the supply chain portion of returns to a virtual store. Check with an e-tailer to see how it handles returns. Prepare a report based on your findings.

3. Discuss how CPFR can solve order fulfillment problems along the supply chain. Use Exhibit 11.7 to relate the elements of the figure to your proposed solutions.

4. Identify the major concerns about using RFID by companies. Discuss the validity of these concerns.

5. Should a B2B EC company outsource its delivery of ordered goods?

6. Some say outsourcing B2B services may hurt the competitive edge. Others disagree. Discuss.

7. Which activities are most critical in order fulfillment of B2C (check Exhibit 11.3)? For B2B? Discuss the differences.

8. Debate the issue of outsourcing EC order fulfillment. Consult Johnson (2010).

9. Debate: Should companies use RFID or not?

INTERNET EXERCISES

1. The U.S. Postal Service is also in the EC logistics field. Examine its services and tracking systems at usps.com/shipping. What are the potential advantages of these systems for EC shippers?

2. Enter redprairie.com and find its order fulfillment–related products and services. Prepare a list. Also, review the RFID products that can be used for order fulfillment.

3. Visit ups.com and find its recent EC initiatives. Compare them with those of fedex.com. Then go to wwwapps.ups.com/ctc/request and simulate a purchase. Report your experiences.

4. Visit freightquote.com and the sites of one or two other online freight companies. Compare the features offered by these companies for online delivery.

5. Enter efulfillmentservice.com. Review the products you find there. How does the company organize the network? How is it related to companies such as FedEx? How does this company make money?

6. Enter cerqa.com and find information about products that can facilitate order fulfillment. Write a report.

7. Enter kewill.com. Find the innovations offered there that facilitate order fulfillment. Compare it with shipsmo.com. Write a report.

8. Enter b2byellowpages.com and a2zofb2b.com. Compare the information provided on each site. What features do both sites share? How do the sites differ?

9. Visit b2btoday.com. Go to the B2B Communities area and identify the major vendors there. Then select three vendors and examine the services they provide to the B2B community.

10. Enter fulfillmentconcepts.com and find the solutions they offer for digital procurement. Also review their literature on fulfillment.

11. Enter support.dell.com and examine all the services available. Examine the tracking services Dell provides to its customers. Finally, examine Dell's association with bizrate.com. Write a report about customer service at Dell.

12. Investigate the status of CPFR. Start at vics.org/committees/cpfr, google.com, and yahoo.com. Also enter supply-chain.org and find information about CPFR. Write a report on the status of CPFR.

13. Enter future-store.org and find the progress on the use of RFID and other tools in supply chain improvements in retailing.

14. Enter the Market Lodge app at Facebook facebook.com/apps/application.php?id=7274648061 and bsocial networks.com/market-lodge-benefits.php. Summarize all the capabilities and benefits related to this chapter.

15. Enter rlec.org and summarize the differences between reverse and forward logistics. Also include returns management.

16. Enter autocart.biz and review the different classifications (options) available. Write a summary report.

17. Enter chainanalytics.com and find how it can improve logistics and solve supply chain and other fulfillment difficulties. Write a report.

18. Discuss the difficulties in fulfilling orders for fresh food. Start with Thau (2010).

19. Enter freshdirect.com and examine the methods it uses to improve order fulfillment of online grocery items. Also explain how to do an eco-friendly fulfillment.

20. Enter sifycorp.com and study their enterprise services. Specifically find what support services they provide. Write a report.

TEAM ASSIGNMENTS AND PROJECTS

1. **Assignment for the Opening Case**

   Read the opening case about Amazon.com and answer the following questions:

   a. What were the drivers of the centralized warehousing?

   b. Amazon.com is using third-party companies for the delivery. Can you guess why?

   c. Can Amazon.com use RFID in its warehouses. If yes, where and when? If no, why not?

   d. Find how Amazon.com handles returned merchandize.

   e. Draw Amazon.com's supply chain for books.

   f. Where do you think there are intelligent (software) agents in Amazon.com's order fulfillment/logistics?

2. Each team should investigate the order fulfillment process offered at an e-tailer's site, such as **barnes-and-noble.com**, **staples.com**, or **landsend.com**. Contact the company, if necessary, and examine any related business partnerships. Based on the content of this chapter, prepare a report with suggestions for how the company can improve its order fulfillment process. Each group's findings will be discussed in class. Based on the class's findings, draw some conclusions about how companies can improve order fulfillment.

3. FedEx, UPS, the U.S. Postal Service, DHL, and others are competing in the EC logistics market. Each team should examine one such company and investigate the services it provides. Contact the company, if necessary, and aggregate the team's findings into a report that will convince classmates or readers that the company in question is the best. (What are its best features? What are its weaknesses?)

4. Enter Ingram Micro's resources site (**ingrammicro.com/ext/0,,23344_23343_23345_21943,00.html**). Use the case studies and articles there to write a report on the importance and benefits of Web fulfillment. Include both order fulfillment and reverse logistics.

5. Watch RFID-Technology Video **youtube.com/watch?v=4Zj7txoDxbE** and answer the following questions:

   a. What are the quality control applications?

   b. What are the applications in the supply chain?

   c. What are the relationships to storage?

   d. How can the business process be improved?

   e. To where are data transferred?

   f. How do the RFID readers work?

   g. What is the merchandise management system?

   h. What are some future applications of RFID?

6. Read about SAP's Warehouse Management System at **prospectasoftware.com/Resources/sap_wm.pdf** and answer the following:

   a. What supply chain processes are supported and how?

   b. What are the benefits of the system?

   c. How is quality achieved?

   d. What is the role of mobility?

   e. How is this report related to this chapter?

Closing Case

HOW MASS CUSTOMIZED EC ORDERS ARE FULFILLED—MULTIBRAS OF BRAZIL

Introduction

Multibras S.A. is a subsidiary of the Whirlpool Corporation in Brazil. It manufactures and sells a variety of household appliances. Brastemp is the leading brand name of the company, and it is a pioneer of EC in Brazil (see *brastemp.com.br*).

Multibras has had an e-commerce department since 2001, providing customer service and selling its commodity-type products. In a very competitive global market, new marketing ideas are a must. Multibras became the first company in the world to sell made-to-order refrigerators on the Internet under the Brastemp name. You can see photos of these products at *flickr.com/photos/brastempyou*.

The Customized Product

The Brastemp "You" refrigerator is a niche product, built to order and available in only one size. It is a product that serves to strengthen the brand in terms of superior quality, and as one that launches market trends.

It also serves to reinforce the brand with frost-free functionality: The company chose this basic model for *You* as the model that sells most among the large refrigerator models. From the basic model, the consumer can configure a series of accessories, such as color, external opening of the doors, outer accessories (water dispenser, external electronic control), and internal accessories (door bottle, can and goblet cooler), with a total of 19,000 possible combinations. It is a highly profitable product.

The purchase can be made only on the company's website. There, the consumer chooses each item and adds it to the product, and that adds to the final price, which varies between R$3,200 and R$4,800 (US$1,923 to US$2,884 in March 2011), nearly 10 to 15 percent higher than for similar refrigerators in the series. It is not necessary to conclude the whole purchase in one step. The consumer can store his or her "creation" and return to it to make alterations. If there are any doubts about color (on the computer screen, the shades are not always very true), Brastemp will send small samples of painted steel to the consumer's home.

Fulfilling the Orders

Problems arose on the factory floor: In an automated mass-assembly line, with a production capacity of 20,000 units a day, would it be possible to manufacture a specific refrigerator without hindering the other products' production flow? That is, when an order for a *You* arrives on the production floor, the refrigerator enters and leaves the assembly line on the orders of a quality auditor. At each point, the auditor indicates to the assembler what items have been ordered by the customer—some, like wine bottle shelves and vegetable separators, are only available on the *You* refrigerator—and so on, until the end of the process, in a kind of parallel handcrafted assembly line. The customized refrigerator is identified by a name chosen by the customer when buying it, and this is the name by which it will be recognized, even at the customer call center.

After placing a buy order, the consumer can check the manufacturing status on the website in real time and monitor what is happening with regard to the production of both the product and its instruction manual (because the latter is also customized).

With this model of sales of customized products via the Internet, Multibras is seeking to achieve two strategic objectives. The first is to increase profitability through innovation (the website already serves to measure consumer preferences and strengthen Brastemp's image as a brand that launches new trends). The second is to reach the end customer without depending fully on the traditional distribution channels—the company sells refrigerators in several countries as well.

There used to be a myth that no one would buy items that were expensive without seeing and touching these products. Because the *You* line sold via the website consists of products with relatively high prices, this myth was dispelled the moment the site went live. Today it not only sells, it also ensures that Brastemp provides its buyers with a service that lives up to its name.

For Brastemp, it does not matter how buyers acquire a product—whether it is online or in a retail outlet—what matters is that they want a Brastemp product. The site is not meant to compete with the retail area, but rather to complement it. The Internet is used to help in those more remote locations where retailers do not operate; thus, the company avoids channel conflict with its distributors.

In addition to the presale and sales areas, the site also offers an after-sales service; in a private chat room, the user can use live chat with Brastemp's contact center employees via the website without the need to use a 1-800 number. Because the contact center and the service team are basically the same, customer service is available 24/7, and a large number of consumers' problems are solved in this way.

Sources: Compiled from Zilber and Nohara (2009) and from *brastemp.com.br* (accessed March 2011).

Questions

1. What are the drivers of the make-to-order project?
2. How are orders taken?
3. How are orders handled on the assembly line?
4. How are channel conflicts eliminated?
5. How is customer service provided?
6. How is make-to-order practiced?

ONLINE RESOURCES
available at pearsonglobaleditions.com/turban

Comprehensive Educational Websites

rfid.org: News, videos, cases.
rfidjournal.com: Comprehensive collection of articles, cases, videos.
vics.org: Business guidelines, collaboration (CPFR).
apics.org: Association for Operations Management.
cscmp.org: Council of supply chain management.

asuscma.org: Supply Chain Management Association.
reverselogisticstrends.com: News, trade shows, cases, etc.
agents.umbc.edu: Large collection of information about intelligent agents.
silicon.com/white-papers: See enterprise planning, supply management.

REFERENCES

Ayers, J. B., and M. A. Odegaard. *Retail Supply Chain Management.* London, UK: Auerbach Publications, 2007.

Boston Consulting Group. "Winning the Online Consumer: The Challenge of Raised Expectations." 2001. **bcg.com/impact_expertise/publications/files/Winning_Online_Consumer_Jun_01_ofa.pdf** (accessed March 2011).

Chio, S. Y., et al. *The Economics of Electronic Commerce.* Indianapolis, IN: Macmillan Technical Publishing, 1997.

Cisco-Eagle. "Grocerwork.com Delivers Fast, Efficient Online Grocery with Cisco-Eagle Order Picking System." 2011. **cisco-eagle.com/case-studies/Distribution-Case-Studies/GroceryWorks** (accessed March 2011).

Crossgate Inc. "Crossgate Reducing Aging Account Receivables with E-Invoicing," White paper. 2010. **crossgate.com/index.php?id=97&paperID=86&no_cache=1** (accessed March 2011).

Ellis, D. "Seven Ways to Improve Returns Processing." *Multichannelmerchant.com*, January 4, 2006. **multi-channelmerchant.com/opsandfulfillment/returns/improve_returns_processing_01042006** (accessed March 2011).

Farber, D. "UPS Takes Wireless to the Next Level." *ZDNet.com*, April 25, 2003. **zdnet.com/news/ups-takes-wireless-to-the-next-level/296395** (accessed March 2011).

Hayes-Weier, M. "Airbus' Sky-High Stakes on RFID." *InformationWeek*, April 18, 2008.

Heinrich, C. *RFID and Beyond.* Indianapolis, IN: Wiley & Sons, 2005.

Heizer, J., and B. Render. *Operations Management*, 10th ed. Upper Saddle River, NJ: Prentice Hall, 2010.

Johnson, R. "Three Reasons to Outsource Fulfillment." May 25, 2010. **infifthgear.com/clientuploads/Press/3_Reasons_to_Outsource_Fulfillment.pdf** (accessed May 2011).

Kharif, O. "What's Lurking in That RFID Tag?" *BusinessWeek Online*, March 16, 2006. **businessweek.com/technology/content/mar2006/tc20060316_117677.htm** (accessed March 2011).

LaMonica, M. "Amazon: Utility Computing Power Broker." *CNET News*, November 16, 2006. **news.com.com/Amazon+Utility+computing+powe+broker/2100-7345_3-6135977.html** (accessed March 2011).

Loebbecke, C. "RFID in the Retail Supply Chain." In M. Khosrow-Pour (Ed.). *Encyclopedia of E-Commerce, E-Government, and Mobile Commerce.* Hershey, PA: Idea Group Reference, 2006.

Logistics World. "What Is Logistics?" 2011. **logisticsworld.com/logistics.htm** (accessed March 2011).

Maloney, D. "More Than Paper Savings." *DC Velocity*, January 2006. **dcvelocity.com/articles/20060101/pdfs/06_01techreview.pdf** (no longer available online).

Mangeot, M. "Behind the Scenes Commentary: UPS Worldport History Channel's Modern Marvels." April 15, 2010. **blog.ups.com/2010/04/15/behind-the-scenes-commentary-worldport-on-history-channels-modern-marvels** (accessed March 2011).

Manufacturing Executive. "Webcase: Flying by Wire: Airbus Digitally Managed Supply Chain." **managing-automation.com/webcastview.aspx?content_id=228218** (no longer available online).

McGown, A. "Artificial Intelligence." *Retail Merchandiser*, February 1, 2010. **retail-merchandiser.com/featured-retail-reports/featured-supplier-reports/944-kiva-systems-artificial-intelligence.html** (accessed May 2011).

Melnyk, S., et al. "Outcome-Driven Supply Chains." *MIT Sloan Management Review* (Winter 2010).

Motorola. "Case Study: Yokobashi Camera." 2007a. **motorola.com/web/Business/Solutions/_ChannelDetails/_Documents/static_files/Yodobashi_case_study_eng_new.pdf** (accessed March 2011).

Motorola. "Synchronizing the Distribution Supply Chain with Mobility." White paper, #WP-SUPPLYCHAIN, December 2007b.

Multimedia Victoria. "Sundowner Motor Inns." eCommerce Case Studies. Victoria Government, Australia, 2004. **mmv.vic.gov.au/Search** (accessed March 2011).

Murphy, J. V. "Advanced Order Fulfillment Requires Warehouses with 'On Demand' Capability." *Global Logistics and Supply Chain Strategies*, June 2004. scvisions.com/articles/advanced_order4.pdf (accessed March 2011).

Niederman, F., et al. "Examining RFID Applications in Supply Chain Management." *Communications of the ACM*, July 2007.

Parks, L. "Schurman Fine Papers Rack Up Labor Savings." *Stores*, February 2004.

Reyes, P. *RFID in the Supply Chain.* New York: McGraw-Hill Professional, 2011.

RFID Journal. "Airbus to Present Case Study at RFID Journal Live! Europe 2007." September 5, 2007. rfidjournal.com/article/articleview/3596/1/1/definitions_off (accessed March 2011).

RFID Journal. "Starbucks Keep Fresh with RFID." December 13, 2006. rfidjournal.com/article/articleprint/2890/-1/1 (accessed March 2011).

Roberti, M. "Kimberly-Clark Gets an Early Win." *RFID Journal* (March/April 2007).

Smith, A. "Daisy Brand Uses BPM to Improve Agility." 2006. staffware.com/resources/customers/successstory_daisybrand.pdf (no longer available online).

Smith, L. "West Marine: A CPFR Success Story." *Supply Chain Management Review,* 10, no. 2 (2006b).

Sullivan, L. "Metro Moves Tagging Up the Supply Chain." *RFID Journal*, December 6, 2006. rfidjournal.com/article/articleprint/2873/-1/1 (accessed March 2011).

Supplychainer.com. "Seven Ways to Immediately Increase Fulfillment Speed." June 22, 2006. supplychainer.com/50226711/seven_ways_to_immediately_increase_order_fulfillment_speed.php (accessed March 2011).

Swedberg, C. "Indian Jeweler Gains Efficiency, Customer Service." *RFID Journal*, April 14, 2009.

Thau, B. "Out-of-the-Box Solution." *Stores*, January/February, 2010. stores.org/stores-magazine-february-2010/out-box-solution (accessed May 2011).

TIBCO. "Daisy Brand Uses TIBCO's Solution to Deliver Fresh Services." 2006. tibco.ru/multimedia/ss-daisy-brand_tcm70-758.pdf (accessed March 2011).

Violino, B. "Supply Chain Management and E-Commerce." *InternetWeek*, May 4, 2000.

Zilber, N. S., and J. J. Nohara. "Mass Customization and Strategic Benefits: A Case Study in Brazil." *Electronic Journal Information Systems in Developing Countries*, 36, no. 5 (2009).

CHAPTER 12

Part 5 E-Commerce Strategy and Implementation

EC STRATEGY, GLOBALIZATION, AND SMEs

Content

Learning Objectives

Upon completion of this chapter, you will be able to:

1. Describe the strategic planning process.
2. Describe the purpose and content of a business plan and a business case.
3. Understand how e-commerce impacts the strategic planning process.
4. Understand how to formulate, justify, and prioritize EC applications.
5. Describe strategy implementation and assessment, including the use of metrics.
6. Evaluate the issues involved in global EC.
7. Analyze the impact of EC on small and medium-sized business.

NEW EC STRATEGIES ENABLE TRAVELOCITY TO MOVE AHEAD IN THE ONLINE TRAVEL MARKET

Travelocity (*travelocity.com*) owned by Sabre Holdings Corporation, a world leader in travel marketing and distribution, was the first online travel company. However Travelocity's top e-strategists have had to work hard to put the company ahead of its competition. During the company's history, its initial strategy was to concentrate on airline ticketing and hotel bookings, and selling advertising on its website. This business model worked very well initially, making the company the early leader in online travel. However, this business model soon became ineffective when the airlines reduced, and then eliminated, travel agents' commissions and competitors entered the market successfully.

In 2002, Expedia (*expedia.com*) emerged as the new market leader and reported almost 500 percent more revenue than Travelocity. The losses in market share resulted in mounting financial losses for Travelocity and it was clear that its current e-strategies were no longer working.

The Opportunity

Guided by rigorous study of consumer behavior, the company developed new strategies in business and revenue models. First, Travelocity moved toward selling customized packages that incorporated more hotel bookings and car rentals. By buying blocks of airline tickets and hotel rooms, it moved from being a commission-based intermediary. Another strategy was to create a fast and effective search engine so that its customers could find the lowest prices for their travel needs. In response to

corporate customer requests for a means to track policy compliance and business performance, on August 8, 2010, Travelocity Business—Travelocity's business travel division—announced the release of a proprietary dashboard reporting solution that allowed its corporate customers to thoroughly and easily analyze their total travel programs. This newest EC strategy offered Travelocity Business customers a combination of best-in-class automation combined with traditional travel management services.

The Results

To better understand customer behavior and set performance standards for its EC strategy, the company used business analysis through its operations research department at Sabre Holdings, Travelocity's parent company. The results of the research pointed out a need for better customer service. By the first quarter of 2006, revenue grew to almost half of Expedia's (versus 20 percent in 2002), a 300 percent improvement over its performance in 2002. The strategic acquisition of Lastminute.com, a leader in European online travel, in 2005, and the later acquisition of ZUJI, a leader in Asia-Pacific online travel, contributed in part to its growth as a global distribution system. Using three performance metrics—brand impact index, conversion impact index, and customer satisfaction with the website—Travelocity® ranked first in satisfaction with rental car reservations and second in converting customers from browsing to purchasing by 2008. This strategy worked for a short period of time. However, additional market research led Travelocity to realize that it needed to offer more services to its corporate customers based on their need to better track travel policy compliance and overall business performance.

Through the new dashboards' visual representation of data, Travelocity Business customers can more easily view large data sets in a more meaningful and useful manner to help them compare a variety of vital travel metrics, ranging from adoption rates and travel spent by business unit to last savings and in-use tickets. According to Travelocity Business's president, Yannis Karmis, "the easy-to-navigate dashboards will not only give a clearer top-level view analysis, but will also allow sites to drill down for additional, important reporting information."

The 14 dashboards currently made available by Travelocity Business, offer its corporate clients customizable views that allow them to drill down into reports where data can be viewed

for various time periods or compared side-by-side. These reports include:

- Overall adoption by month or by quarter domestically and internationally
- Purchase spending by individual company units
- Analysis on areas of lost travel savings within a company
- Differences between the company's overall number of travel nights compared with number of missed hotel nights to show potential loss of savings from the supplier
- Nonrefundable versus refundable tickets purchased
- Purpose of trip in a variety of categories, including a customer-facing client meeting, internal noncustomer meeting, sales meeting, consultant travel, training, convention/conference travel, and customer service visits

And even more e-strategies are in the planning stage. In 2011, Travelocity Business hopes to offer business customers the option to choose a more advanced dashboard reporting system that will allow for more than 30 different dashboards and a "what if?" analysis capability, together with dashboards customized specifically for company and travel arranger needs. Clearly, Travelocity is committed to being the traveler's champion.

These constantly evolving e-strategies that include a customer-driven focus, 24/7 live phone support, competitive prices, and powerful technology have made Travelocity one of the largest travel companies in the world with annual gross bookings of more than US$10 billion.

Sources: Compiled from Keynote Competitive Research (2008), Travelocity (2008), Travelocity (2010), and HotelInteractive (2010).

WHAT WE CAN LEARN . . .

Recognizing that appropriate strategy, including IT and EC strategies, can help companies survive and excel is an important part of doing business online. For pure-play companies such as Travelocity, it may be even more important to be able to change strategies quickly in response to changing market conditions. Strategies are based on performance indices, which are used as targets as well as measures of success as demonstrated in the opening case. Once performance targets are set, including quantitative measures, improvement plans can be put into place and the strategy can be implemented. Then progress must be assessed and monitored, and changes put into place as appropriate.

The main focus of this chapter is on the basic steps in planning for, creating, implementing, and evaluating an EC strategy. The chapter also presents and discusses issues related to creating an e-strategy to engage in global EC and the opportunities that EC creates for small and medium-sized enterprises (SMEs).

12.1   ORGANIZATIONAL STRATEGY: CONCEPTS AND OVERVIEW

An organizational **strategy** is a broad-based framework for expressing how a business is going to accomplish its mission, what its goals should be, and what plans and policies it will need to accomplish these goals. An organization's strategy (including EC and IT strategies) starts with understanding where the company is today and where it wants to go in the future. The economic/financial crisis of 2008–2011 makes it even more important to have an effective EC and IT strategy as sales continue to grow and global competition increases.

strategy
A broad-based formula for how a business is going to accomplish its mission, what its goals should be, and what plans and policies will be needed to carry out those goals.

STRATEGY IN THE WEB ENVIRONMENT

Strategy is more than deciding what a company should do next. Strategy also is about making tough decisions about what not to do. Strategic positioning is making decisions about trade-offs, recognizing that a company must abandon or not pursue some products, services, and activities in order to excel at others. How are these trade-offs determined? Not merely with a focus on growth and increases in revenue, but also on profitability and increases in shareholder value over the long run. How is this profitability and economic value determined? By establishing a unique value proposition and the configuration of a tailored value chain that enables a company to offer unique value to its customers. Therefore, strategy has been, and remains, focused on questions about organizational fit, trade-offs, profitability, and value (Porter 2001).

Any contemporary strategy-setting process must include the Internet. Strategy guru Michael Porter (2001) argues that a coherent organizational strategy that includes the Internet is more important than ever before: "Many have argued that the Internet renders strategy obsolete. In reality, the opposite is true . . . it is more important than ever for companies to distinguish themselves through strategy. The winners will be those that view the Internet as a complement to, not a cannibal of, traditional ways of competing" (p. 63).

Porter's Competitive Forces Model and Strategies

Porter's competitive forces model has been used to develop strategies for companies to increase their competitive edge in their industry. It also demonstrates how IT and EC can enhance competitiveness.

The model recognizes five major forces that could endanger a company's position in a given industry. Other forces, such as those cited in Chapter 1, including the impact of government, affect all companies in the industry, and therefore may have less impact on the relative success of a company within its industry. Although the details of the model differ from one industry to another, its general structure is universal. The five major forces in an industry that affect the degree of competition and, ultimately, the degree of profitability are:

1. Threat of entry of new competitors
2. Bargaining power of suppliers
3. Bargaining power of customers or buyers
4. Threat of substitute products or services
5. Rivalry among existing firms in the industry

The strength of each force is determined by the industry's structure. Existing companies in an industry need to protect themselves against the forces; alternatively, they can use the forces to improve their position or to challenge the leaders in the industry. The relationships are shown in Exhibit 12.1. The definitions and details are provided by Porter (1980).

While implementing Porter's model, companies can identify the forces that influence competitive advantage in their marketplace and then develop a strategy. Porter (1985) proposed three such strategies: cost leadership, differentiation, and niche strategies.

In Exhibit 12.2, we first list Porter's three classical strategies, plus nine other general strategies, for dealing with competitive advantage. Each of these strategies can be enhanced by EC, as shown throughout the book.

The Impact of the Internet

Porter (2001) has identified several ways that the Internet impacts each of the five forces of competitiveness—bargaining power of consumers and suppliers, threats from substitutes and new entrants, and rivalry among existing competitors—that were originally described in one of his seminal works on strategy (Porter 1980). These five forces and associated Internet impacts are shown in Exhibit 12.3.

The impact of the Internet on strategic competitiveness and long-term profitability will differ from industry to industry. Accordingly, many businesses are taking a focused look at the impact of the Internet and EC on their future. For these firms, an **e-commerce strategy (e-strategy)** is the formulation and execution of a vision of how a new or existing company intends to do business electronically. The process of building an EC strategy is explained in detail later in this chapter. First, though, we continue our overview of organizational strategy and IT strategy, of which e-commerce strategy is a component.

e-commerce strategy (e-strategy)
The formulation and execution of a vision of how a new or existing company intends to do business electronically.

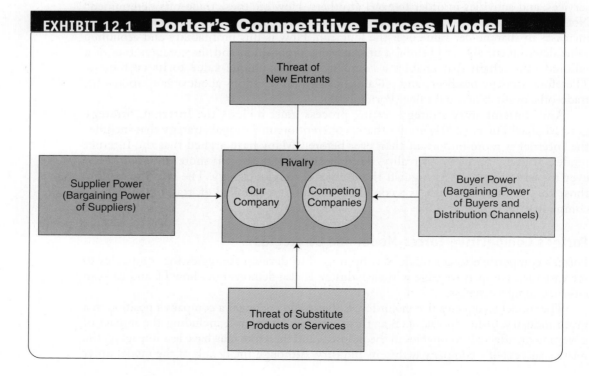
EXHIBIT 12.1 Porter's Competitive Forces Model

EXHIBIT 12.2 Strategies for Competitive Advantage

Strategy	Description
Classic Strategies	
Niche	Select a narrow-scope segment (market niche) and be the best in quality, speed, or cost in that segment.
Growth	Increase market share, acquire more customers, or sell more types of products.
Alliance	Work with business partners in partnerships, alliances, joint ventures, or virtual companies.
Innovation	
Time	Treat time as a resource, then manage it and use it to the firm's advantage.
Entry barriers	Create barriers to entry. By introducing innovative products or using EC business models to provide exceptional service, companies can create entry barriers to discourage new entrants.
Customer or supplier lock-in	Encourage customers or suppliers to stay with you rather than going to competitors. Reduce customers' bargaining power by locking them in.

EXHIBIT 12.3 Impacts of E-Commerce and Social Commerce on Industry Competition

Competitive Force	Impacts
Bargaining power of suppliers	**Decreases.** Due to e-procurement, availability of more suppliers (global), increase use of e-auctions, Internet procurement tends to give all buyers equal access to suppliers. There is more standardization of products and reduction of differentiation among suppliers. Not much difference in prices.
Bargaining power of customers	**Increases.** Due to the ability to compare prices, buy online, use group buying and daily deals (Groupon), use more recommendations (including from friends), get more power due to social network membership, customers are more knowledgeable and have more information. Customers can buy in global markets, reducing switching costs for customers. Customers can negotiate via new models (e.g., Priceline's name-your-own-price model).
Barriers to entry	**Decreases.** Due to ease of opening online businesses, there is faster access to more accurate information, reduced start-up and fixed costs, and new business reputation can spread fast online with word of mouth. It gets easier to clone competitors. Many new start-ups appear online.
Threat of substitute products, services	**Increases.** New products/services can be developed rapidly and advertised quickly on a global basis. Customers (also B2B) can find substitutes faster and easier and get reviews and recommendations fast. EC and SC facilitate new business models that can create alternative products/services.
Rivalry among existing competitors	**Increases.** Markets are more efficient, and it is easy to get timely information. But there are more competitors to deal with and less localization advantage. Global players gain access. More SMEs are competing. Increased online business facilitates competition.

EXHIBIT 12.4   E-Commerce Challenges

Technological	Nontechnological
Software Standards: Lack of universally accepted standards for quality, security, and reliability	**Distrust:** Skeptical buyers and sellers. Lack of trust in "virtual" companies
Integration: Difficult to integrate new e-commerce applications and software with existing applications and databases	**Regulations:** Lack of national and international government regulations and industry standards
Cost: Expensive and/or inconvenient Internet access in some areas.	**Measurement:** Immature methodologies for measuring benefits of and justifying e-commerce
	Legal: Unresolved legal issues
	Security: Perception that e-commerce locations are not secure

Strategic Planning for IT and EC

Unfortunately, you can't buy an EC strategy in a box. It takes creativity, planning, resources, and good technology skills to create a good EC strategy, and approaches vary from company to company. In addition, associated technological and nontechnological challenges that can plague e-commerce must be considered. The main difference between technical and nontechnical limitations is that technical limitations frequently can be solved by spending enough money, whereas nontechnical limitations are things that are more difficult to change since they involve things that cannot be changed easily—like people's attitude, lack of trust, resistance to change, faceless transactions, and more. As time passes, the limitations, especially the technological ones, are becoming less of an issue. In addition, careful planning can minimize the negative impact of some of them, and hopefully the information provided in this chapter will help you avoid some of the pitfalls associated with e-commerce. The major challenges associated with developing an EC strategy are shown in Exhibit 12.4.

Despite its limitations, e-commerce is a boon to an increasing number of companies. As companies become more experienced with e-commerce and technology continues to improve, the benefits will far outweigh the limitations, and we'll see an even greater rate of e-commerce adoption and increased customer satisfaction. On Cyber Monday during Thanksgiving weekend 2010, online sales topped $1 billion—the largest single-day take in Web history, and IT research firm Forrester Research predicts that annual online retail sales in the United States will more than double from $155 billion in 2009 to $249 billion by 2014. In 2014, total online retail sales are estimated to account for 8 percent of total retail sales in the United States. Forrester Research also predicts that by that time, 53 percent of total retail sales in the United States will be influenced by EC as consumers increasingly use the Internet to find and research products before buying. Thus, companies need to have some EC strategy to be able to compete. In the next section, we will discuss the systematic process, tools, and techniques that companies typically use to effectively plan their strategy (Schonfeld 2010).

strategic information systems planning (SISP)
A process for developing a strategy and plans for aligning information systems (including e-commerce applications) with the organization's business strategies.

Strategic information systems planning (SISP) refers to a process that is commonly used for developing a strategic plan to align information systems (including e-commerce applications) with the business strategies of an organization. It has been suggested that greater planning success can be achieved by using more extensive SISP in an uncertain environment. The SISP process is discussed next.

THE STRATEGIC PLANNING PROCESS

A strategy is important, but the process of developing a strategy is even more important. No matter how large or how small the organization, the strategic planning process forces corporate executives, a company's general manager, or a small business owner to assess the current position of the firm, where it should be, and how to get from here to there. The process also involves primary stakeholders, including the board of directors, employees,

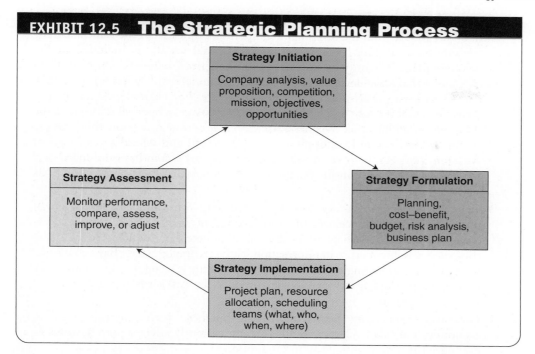

EXHIBIT 12.5   The Strategic Planning Process

and strategic partners. This involvement ensures that stakeholders buy into the strategy and reinforces stakeholder commitment to the future of the organization.

Strategy development will differ depending on the type of strategy, the implementation method, the size of the firm, and the approach that is taken. Nevertheless, any strategic planning process has four major phases, *initiation, formulation, implementation,* and *assessment,* as shown in Exhibit 12.5. (Note that the phases in Exhibit 12.5 correspond to section numbers in this chapter.) The major phases of the strategic planning process, and some identifiable activities and outcomes associated with each phase, are discussed briefly in the following text. The phases are then discussed more extensively as part of the e-commerce strategic planning process in Sections 12.3 through 12.6. Note that the process is cyclical and continuous. A brief description of the four phases follows.

Strategy Initiation

In the **strategy initiation** phase, the organization examines itself and its environment. The principal activities include setting the organization's mission and goals, examining organizational strengths and weaknesses, assessing environmental factors impacting the business, and conducting a competitor analysis. As emphasized throughout this chapter, this includes an examination of the potential contribution that the Internet and other emerging technologies can make to the business.

Specific outcomes from this phase include:

strategy initiation
The initial phase of strategic planning in which the organization examines itself and its environment.

▶ **Company analysis and value proposition.** The *company analysis* includes the vision, mission, value proposition, goals, capabilities, constraints, strengths, and weaknesses of the company. Questions typically asked in a company analysis are: What business are we really in? Who are our future customers? Do our mission statement and our goals adequately describe our intended future? What opportunities, and threats, do our business and our industry face? One key outcome from this analysis should be a clear statement of the company's **value proposition**—the benefit that a company's products or services provide to a company and its customers. Value proposition is actually a statement that summarizes the customer segment, competitor target, and the core differentiation

value proposition
The benefit that a company's products or services provide to a company and its customers.

of one's product from the offering of competitors. It describes the value added by the company (or the e-commerce projects), and usually is included in the business plan. It is only by knowing what benefits a business is providing to customers that chief-level executives can truly understand "what business they are in" and who their potential competitors are. For example, Amazon.com recognizes that it is not just in the book-selling business, but that it also is in the information-about-books business. Amazon.com's strategists know this is where customers find value in shopping at Amazon.com and where a great deal of Amazon.com's competitive advantage lies. So Amazon.com has introduced new services such as "search inside the book" to deliver on that value proposition to its customers.

▶ **Core competencies.** A *core competency* refers to the unique combination of the resources and experiences of a particular firm. It takes time to build these core competencies, and they can be difficult to imitate. For example, Google's core competency is its expertise in information search technology, and eBay's core competency is in conducting online auctions. A company is using its core competency to deliver a product or service. Google's products are AdWords and AdSense, and Intel produces chips.

▶ **Forecasts.** *Forecasting* means identifying business, technological, political, economic, and other relevant trends that are currently affecting the business or that have the potential to do so in the future.

▶ **Competitor (industry) analysis.** *Competitor analysis* involves scanning the business environment to collect and interpret relevant information about direct competitors, indirect competitors, and potential competitors. Several methodologies are available to conduct such an analysis, including a strengths, weaknesses, opportunities, and threats (SWOT) analysis and competitor analysis grid.

Strategy Formulation

strategy formulation
The development of strategies to exploit opportunities and manage threats in the business environment in light of corporate strengths and weaknesses.

Strategy formulation is the development of strategies to exploit opportunities and manage threats in the business environment in light of corporate strengths and weaknesses. In an EC strategy, the end result is likely to be a list of EC applications or projects to be implemented.

Specific activities and outcomes from this phase include:

▶ **Business opportunities.** If the strategy initiation has been done well, a number of scenarios for future development of the business will be obvious. How well these scenarios fit with the future direction of the company are assessed. Similarly, the first phase may also have identified some current activities that are no longer relevant to the company's future and are candidates for divestiture, outsourcing, or elimination.

▶ **Cost–benefit analysis.** Each proposed opportunity must be assessed in terms of the potential costs and benefits to the company in light of its mission and goals. These costs and benefits may be financial or nonfinancial, tangible or intangible, or short-term or long-term. More information about conducting a cost–benefit analysis is included in Chapter 13.

▶ **Risk analysis, assessment, and management.** The risks of each proposed EC initiative (project) must be analyzed and assessed. If a significant risk is evident, then a risk management plan is required. Of particular importance in an EC strategy are business risk factors such as transition risk and partner risk, which are discussed in Section 12.4.

> **Business plan.** Many of the outcomes from these first two phases—goals, competitor analysis, strategic opportunities, risk analysis, and more—come together in a business plan. As described in Section 12.2, every business—large or small, new or old, successful or not—needs a business plan to acquire funding and to ensure that a realistic approach is being taken to implement the business strategy. According to Access e-Commerce (2006), a business plan for EC is likely to include these activities: introduction, technology audit, check out the competition, set goals, identify the audience, build a team, create a budget, locate resources, use a website planning checklist, try a website promotion checklist, send a press release, evaluate the plan, prepare appendices to the plan, and identify related resources. The value proposition part of a business plan includes, these four phases: (1) value definition, (2) value development, (3) value measurement, and (4) value communication (see en.wikipedia.org/wiki/Value_proposition for details).

Strategy Implementation

In this phase, the emphasis shifts from "what do we do?" to "how do we do it?" In the **strategy implementation** phase, detailed, short-term plans are developed for carrying out the projects agreed on in strategy formulation. Specifically, decision makers evaluate options, establish specific milestones, allocate resources, and manage the projects.

Specific activities and outcomes from this phase include:

strategy implementation
The development of detailed, short-term plans for carrying out the projects agreed on in strategy formulation.

> **Project planning.** Inevitably, strategy implementation is executed through an EC project or a series of projects. Project planning includes setting specific project objectives, creating a project schedule with milestones, and setting measurable performance targets. Normally, a project plan would be set for each project and application.

> **Resource allocation.** Organizational resources are those owned, available to, or controlled by a company. They can be human, financial, technological, managerial, or knowledge based. This phase includes business process outsourcing (BPO) consideration and use.

> **Project management.** This is the process of making the selected applications and projects a reality—hiring staff; purchasing equipment; licensing, purchasing, or writing software; contracting vendors; and so on.

Strategy Assessment

Just as soon as implementation is complete, assessment begins. **Strategy assessment** is the continuous evaluation of progress toward the organization's strategic goals, resulting in corrective action and, if necessary, strategy reformulation. In strategy assessment, specific measures called *metrics* (discussed in Section 12.7) assess the progress of the strategy. In some cases, data gathered in the first phase can be used as baseline data to assess the strategy's effectiveness. If not, this information will have to be gathered. For large EC projects, business performance management tools can be employed (see oracle.com/us/corporate/Acquisitions/hyperion/index.html).

strategy assessment
The continuous evaluation of progress toward the organization's strategic goals, resulting in corrective action and, if necessary, strategy reformulation.

What happens with the results from strategy assessment? As shown in Exhibit 12.5, the strategic planning process starts over again, immediately. Note that a cyclical approach is required—a strategic planning process that requires constant reassessment of today's strategy while preparing a new strategy for tomorrow is demonstrated in Case 12.1.

EC Application

FOCUSING ON QUALITY OVER QUANTITY AT WARNER MUSIC GROUP

In 2008, Warner Music Group Corp. (WMG) announced a leadership transition of its digital strategy team. Michael Nash became the executive vice president of digital strategy and business development. Nash became responsible for the company's worldwide digital strategy and business development activity, including key initiatives driving Internet, mobile commerce, social commerce, and new music-based products and services.

The Opportunity

Since joining WMG in 2000, Nash had overseen WMG's new media projects, strategic relationships, and business development activities. "It has never been clearer that digital opportunities are key to the music industry's future growth," said Nash. He has also played a key role in building WMG's distribution footprint and partnership portfolio, including important initiatives with AT&T, Amazon.com, Google, Microsoft, Motorola, Verizon, and Sony Ericsson.

As an independent company that was spun off from AOL, WMG was aggressive on the Web. It was one of the first labels to strike a deal with YouTube and led the way in licensing other subscription and ad-supported music services. According to Nash, "The perspective initially was, 'Wow the Internet gives us vast distribution. Let's license a whole bunch of partners, they will sell it and we will collect a lot of little checks and some big checks.'"

Using this initial strategy, WMG aggressively developed new product and distribution opportunities in the mobile and online music spaces. As of 2009, WMG announced an ad-sales pact with video company Outrigger, a small group spun off the video site Veoh. The objective is that Outrigger will sell advertising on WMG videos across the Web, whether on YouTube or through other distributors, such as social networks, blogs, or the artists' own sites. Rather than negotiate licenses with distributors such as YouTube or AOL, WMG is seeking revenue-sharing deals in the hope that brands will embrace music videos as a high-end advertising vehicle. The strategy is that instead of collecting a royalty each time a video is played, WMG—through Outrigger—will sell advertising and share revenue with the world's largest video site.

The Results

In 2005, WMG had virtually no digital revenue, but by the second quarter of 2009, its digital revenues had climbed to $173 million (26 percent of the company's total revenue), while digital sales made up 31 percent of its worldwide recorded-music revenue and 41 percent of its total U.S. recorded-music revenue. WMG has consistently maintained its digital leadership showing the greatest U.S. digital album share advantage over physical album share of any of the major music companies since 2005.

The longer-range plan is for Outrigger to be phased out of ad sales duties and for WMG to produce its own ad sales in-house. The new strategy is the result of a retrenchment at WMG, as it rethinks the way music videos can be distributed on the Web. Referred to as version 2.0 of WMG's digital strategy, this time Nash stressed that WMG is planning for "quality over quantity" when it comes to music video distribution.

Sources: Compiled from Learmonth (2009), RedOrbit.com (2008), and *wmg.com* (accessed February 2011).

Questions

1. Why did WMG's strategy shift to quality?
2. Why did it develop a deal with YouTube? Is this a strategic alliance?
3. Why did WMG start its digital-oriented strategy?
4. Explore the ad arrangement with Outrigger. Does it make sense? Why?

STRATEGIC PLANNING TOOLS

To complete their strategic plans, strategists have devised a number of strategic planning tools and techniques. This section describes a few of the most popular tools. A strategic management textbook or handbook can provide more detailed information about these and other strategic planning tools.

Representative Strategic Planning Tools

strategy map
A tool that delineates the relationships among the key organizational objectives for all four BSC perspectives.

A useful strategic planning tool that graphically tells the story of how value is created in a business is a *strategy map*. A **strategy map** is a graphical representation of the strategy of an organization. It illustrates how an organization plans to achieve its mission and vision by means of a linked chain of continuous improvements. It does this by delineating the relationships among the key organizational objectives across four corporate perspectives: financial, internal, external, and learning/growth of the company. And, the strategy map displays the cause and effect relationships among these objectives. For example, Ontario Systems, a leading provider of accounts receivable and revenue cycle management solutions for the legal and health care industries, with headquarters in Muncie, Indiana, uses a strategy map to guide its mission to empower its customers to manage receivables and revenue cycles to maximize cash flow and profits and its vision to maximize shareholder value (see ontariosystems.com/download/Strategy_Map.pdf).

A strategy map begins at the top with a statement of the mission and vision of the company or a focus area within the company. This is followed by the company's financial objective (i.e., achieve breakthrough financial results). This objective is driven by the customer objective (i.e., provide a uniquely engaging customer experience). In turn, the customer objective is the result of an internal (i.e., process) objective (i.e., execute the strategic processes). The strategy map then continues down to the bottom of the hierarchy, where the learning and growth objectives are set out (e.g., a positive culture enables our people). Examples of strategy maps can also be found at: thepalladiumgroup.com/Knowledge-ObjectRepository/Sample_Strategy_Maps.pdf and smartdraw.com/examples/strategy—planning/strategy-maps.

Each objective that appears in a strategy map has an associated measure, target, and initiative. For example, the objective "provide a uniquely engaging customer experience" might be measured by customer satisfaction. For this measure, we might be targeting a 15 percent improvement over last year's figure in our customer service index. One of the ways of accomplishing this improvement is by implementing the customer feedback database.

Overall, strategy maps represent a hypothetical model of a business or one of the focus areas of the business. When specific names (of people or teams) are assigned to the various initiatives, the model serves to align the bottom-level actions of the organization with the top-level strategic objectives. When actual results are compared with targeted results, a determination can be made about whether the entire strategy should be called into question or whether the actions of those responsible for various parts of the strategy need to be adjusted.

SWOT analysis is a methodology that surveys the opportunities (O) and threats (T) in the external environment and relates them to the organization's internal strengths (S) and weaknesses (W) (see en.wikipedia.org/wiki/SWOT_analysis). SWOT analysis diagrams are available at smartdraw.com/specials/swotanalysis.htm.

A **competitor analysis grid** is another strategic planning tool that highlights points of differentiation between competitors and the target firm. The grid is a table with the company's most significant competitors entered in the columns and the key factors for comparison entered in the rows. Factors might include mission statements, strategic partners, sources of competitive advantage (e.g., cost leadership, global reach), customer relationship strategies, and financial resources. An additional column includes the company's data on each factor so that significant similarities and differences (i.e., points of differentiation) will be obvious. A competitor analysis grid template is available in Online Tutorial T2 on this textbook's website.

Scenario planning offers an alternative to traditional planning approaches that rely on straight-line projections of current trends. These approaches fail when low-probability events occur that radically alter current trends. The aim of scenario planning is to generate several plausible alternative futures, giving decision makers the opportunity to identify actions that can be taken today to ensure success under varying future conditions (see en.wikipedia.org/wiki/Scenario_planning).

The basic method in scenario planning is that a group of analysts generates simulation games for policy makers (see en.wikipedia.org/wiki/Scenario_planning). The games combine projected factors about the future, such as demographics, geography, military, political, and industrial information, with plausible alternative social, technical, economic, and political (STEP) trends, which are key driving forces. Scenario planning can include anticipatory thinking (future) elements that are difficult to formalize, such as subjective interpretations of facts, shifts in values, new regulations, or inventions.

Balanced scorecard is a tool that assesses organizational progress toward strategic goals by measuring performance in a number of different areas. Originally proposed by

SWOT analysis
A methodology that surveys external opportunities and threats and relates them to internal strengths and weaknesses.

competitor analysis grid
A strategic planning tool that highlights points of differentiation between competitors and the target firm.

scenario planning
A strategic planning methodology that generates plausible alternative futures to help decision makers identify actions that can be taken today to ensure success in the future.

balanced scorecard
A management tool that assesses organizational progress toward strategic goals by measuring performance in a number of different areas.

Kaplan and Norton (1996) as an alternative to narrowly focused financial assessments, the balanced scorecard seeks more balance by measuring organizational performance in four areas: finance, customers' assessments, internal business processes, and learning and growth. For more information about the balanced scorecard, see Hannabarger, et al. (2007), en.wikipedia.org/wiki/Balanced_scorecard, and Section 12.6.

Business Plan and Business Case

Two almost inevitable outcomes of strategy setting are a business plan and a business case. These concepts are covered in Online Chapter 15 and Online Tutorial T2. A **business plan** is a written document that identifies the company's goals and outlines how the company intends to achieve those goals. A **business case** is a business plan for a new initiative or large, new project inside an existing organization.

Section 12.1 ▶ REVIEW QUESTIONS

1. What is strategy?
2. Describe the strategic planning process.
3. Describe the four phases of strategic planning.
4. Why is a cyclic approach to strategic planning required?
5. Describe four tools that can be used for strategic planning.
6. What is a strategy map and how does it help in the strategic planning process?
7. What is a business case and how is it different from a business plan?

business plan

A written document that identifies a company's goals and outlines how the company intends to achieve the goals and at what cost.

business case

A business plan for a new initiative or large, new project inside an existing organization.

12.2 E-COMMERCE STRATEGY: CONCEPTS AND OVERVIEW

The Internet is playing an increasingly important part in organizational strategy. Strategy setting begins with the business strategy—determining an organization's vision, mission statement, and overall goals (see Exhibit 12.6). Then the information systems (IS) strategy is set, primarily by determining what information and associated information systems are required to carry out the business strategy. The information and communications technology (ICT) strategy is decided based on how to deliver the information and information systems via technology. An e-strategy is a derivative of both the IS strategy and the ICT strategy. The solid downward pointing arrows in Exhibit 12.6 depict the top-down portion of the process. The broken line indicates possible bottom-up activities, which means that lower-level strategies cause adjustments in higher-level strategies.

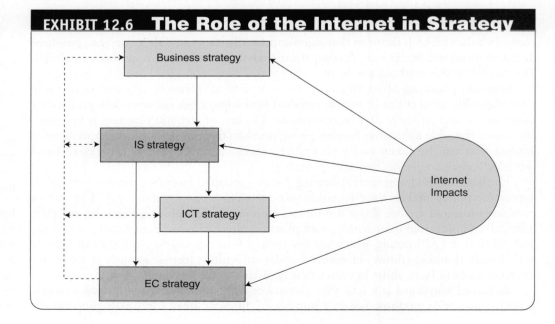

EXHIBIT 12.6 The Role of the Internet in Strategy

The Internet impacts all levels of organizational strategy setting, as shown by the shaded boxes in Exhibit 12.6. Business strategists need to consider the Internet's role in creating or innovating products, in product and service delivery, in supplier and customer relationships, and its impact on competition in the marketplace. Generally, strategic planners need to view the Internet as a complement to traditional ways of competing, not as a source of competitive advantage in and of itself (Porter 2001). IS strategists need to consider the Internet as a tool for collecting information and distributing it to where it is required. ICT planners will need to plan the integration of the Internet-based technologies into the existing ICT infrastructure. Thinking about and planning for the Internet should be subsumed into each of the four strategy levels.

Using the process just described, businesses continue to evolve their own e-commerce strategies, defined as the formulation and execution of a vision of how a new or existing company intends to do business electronically.

Consider the following examples of e-strategies in the public and private sectors that impact all of us—health care, and government.

Example: Health Care. In June 2010, Geisinger Health in Pennsylvania, HarborView Medical in Washington State, and Beth Israel Deaconess Medical Center in Massachusetts embarked on an observational study designed to improve patient access to medical records. In all, 100 primary care physicians volunteered to enable an estimated 25,000 to 30,000 patients to access their doctors' notes online. Under the Open Notes pilot study, participating patients are connected to their doctors via e-mail or through their health care provider's Web portal and are invited to view their doctors' notes after each visit and again before the subsequent visit (per Harpham 2010).

Example: Government. The City of Pittsburgh, Pennsylvania, recently sought to increase constituent satisfaction with public services. In response to increasing negative public sentiment concerning general road and neighborhood conditions, it developed a new iPhone app that allows people to submit photographs of potholes, dilapidated properties, and missing street signs and attach a description of the problem and submit it for action. In cooperation with YinzCam, a Pittsburgh-based company that is a Carnegie-Mellon University spinoff iPhone app developer, location information is now automatically located and submitted along with the complaint. Other municipalities have followed suit, including New York City that allows constituents to complete city forms from their phones (McGee, et al. 2009).

The following sections explain in detail the process of building an EC strategy.

Section 12.2 ❱ REVIEW QUESTIONS

1. Describe the process of deriving an EC strategy.
2. Describe the role of the Internet in setting EC strategy.
3. How should business strategic planners, IS strategists, and ICT planners consider the Internet and EC?

12.3   E-COMMERCE STRATEGY INITIATION

In the strategy initiation phase, the organization prepares the initial steps needed for starting the cycle, such as collecting information about itself, its competitors, and its environment. EC can make two fundamental contributions to the business: (1) facilitate value creation or value enhancement for company stakeholders and (2) lower the cost of providing goods and services to the marketplace. The steps in strategy initiation are to review the organization's vision and mission; to analyze its industry, company, and competitive position; and to consider various initiation issues.

REPRESENTATIVE ISSUES IN E-STRATEGY INITIATION

With company, competitor, and trend data in hand, the company faces a number of questions about its approach to and operation of its EC strategy that need to be explored prior to strategy formulation. These include the following.

First-Mover Advantage

The business, IT, and e-commerce worlds all have examples of companies that succeeded with first-mover advantage, companies that failed despite first-mover advantage, and late movers that are now success stories. Generally, the advantages of being first include an opportunity to make a first and lasting impression on customers, to establish strong brand recognition, to lock in strategic partners, and to create switching costs for customers. For example, Amazon.com was the first major online bookstore seizing a head start on later entrants. Established book retailers Barnes & Noble and Borders were quick to follow in Amazon.com's footsteps to develop their own websites. Amazon maintained its first-mover advantage in two ways; by partnering with Borders and continuing to extend its product offerings into apparel, electronics, toys, and housewares. This guarded against any customer preference for purchasing from Barnes & Noble by becoming a much larger, one-stop-shopping destination. Company strategists need to decide if they are likely to benefit from being first, or whether it would be better to wait and follow the leader. For more information, see referenceforbusiness.com/management/Ex-Gov/First-Mover-Advantage.html#ixzz18s5Eu0uO.

In some cases, being the first mover can have some disadvantages. The risks of being a first mover include the high cost of pioneering EC initiatives, making mistakes, the chance that a second wave of competitors will eliminate a first mover's lead through lower cost and innovation, and the risk that the move will be too early. Although the importance of a speedy market entry cannot be dismissed, over the long run first movers are often substantially less profitable than followers.

Examples. One of the first large-scale social networks was Geocities. It was closed (by Yahoo!) after 10 years of huge losses. Facebook was not a first mover, but it succeeded and replaced MySpace as a leader. LinkedIn, on the other hand is a successful first mover and so are Groupon and Foursquare.

So what determines whether a first mover succeeds or fails? It has been suggested that the following factors are important determinants of EC marketplace success: (1) the size of the opportunity (i.e., the first-mover company must be big enough for the opportunity, and the opportunity must be big enough for just one company); (2) the nature of the product (i.e., first-mover advantage is easier to maintain in commodity products in which later entrants have a hard time differentiating their products); and (3) whether the company can be the best in the market.

Given the uncertainty about when first-mover advantages occur, companies need to carefully consider the following questions when deciding on their strategy.

- Does the firm want to invest in seeking opportunities to be first?
- If opportunities arise, what is the best approach to market timing?
- Which of the three types of benefits are likely to be available to the first entrant in this market?
- Does the firm have the resources to sustain any initial benefits they gain from being first?
- If someone else enters first, how difficult will it be to follow?
- What advantages might later entry provide in better or lower-cost technology, or better adaptation to customer needs?

Carefully considering the answers to these questions helps company strategists decide which approach has the highest potential for long-term profits given their resources and market characteristics.

Managing Channel Conflict

As discussed in Chapters 2 and 3, channel conflict may arise when an existing company adds an online distribution channel. It is an aspect of e-commerce that has received a lot of attention because of its ability to bring the buyer and seller into closer contact through the elimination of one or more middlemen or intermediaries in the distribution channel.

Disintermediation is the term used to describe the process by which the consumer bypasses the services of an intermediary or intermediaries in the chain of distribution to purchase products directly from those who supply or produce them. Since the process of disintermediation is usually not instantaneous, managers find themselves caught in the uncomfortable position of needing to appease business partners in the distribution chain while in the process of eliminating existing relationships, and careful management of this process is essential. Several options exist for handling channel conflict:

disintermediation
The process by which the consumer bypasses the services of an intermediary or intermediaries in the chain of distribution to purchase products directly from those who supply or produce them.

- Let the established distributors handle e-business fulfillment, as the auto industry is doing. Buyers can order online, or they can provide directions to distributors online.
- Provide online services to intermediaries (e.g., by building portals for them) and encourage them to reintermediate themselves in other ways.
- Sell some products only online, such as LEGO (lego.com) is doing. Other products may be advertised online but sold exclusively offline. Avoid channel conflict entirely by not selling online. In such a case, a company could still have an EC presence by offering promotion and customer service online, as BMW (bmw.com) is doing.

The problem of channel conflict is further complicated by the need to add new intermediaries into the distribution chain to address the added requirements of e-commerce. Delivery, for example, becomes a critical part of overall customer satisfaction with online sales.

Separating Online and Offline Operations

Separating a company's online operations into a new company makes sense when: (1) the volume of anticipated e-business is large, (2) a new business model needs to be developed apart from the constraints of current operations, (3) the subsidiary can be created without dependence on current operations and legacy systems, and (4) the online company is given the freedom to form new alliances, attract new talent, set its own prices, and raise additional funding. Barnes & Noble, Halifax in the United Kingdom (online banking), and the ASB Bank in New Zealand are a few examples of companies that have established separate companies or subsidiaries for online operations.

The advantages of creating a separate company include reduction or elimination of internal conflicts; more freedom for the online company's management in pricing, advertising, and other decisions; the ability to create a new brand quickly (see the next section); the opportunity to build new, efficient information systems that are not burdened by the legacy systems of the old company; and an influx of outside funding if the market likes the e-business idea and buys the company's stock. The disadvantages of creating an independent division are that it may be very costly, risky, or both, and the new company will not benefit from the expertise and spare capacity in the business functions (marketing, finance, distribution) unless it gets superb collaboration from the parent company.

Brand Independence

A company faces a similar decision when deciding whether to create a separate brand for its online offerings. Generally, companies with strong, mature, international brands will want to retain and promote those brands online. Google has chosen extensions or variations of its strong brand name—Google Desktop, Google Print, Gmail, Google Maps—in introducing new products and services.

However, existing firms with a weak brand or a brand that does not reflect the intent of the online effort may decide to create a new brand. An analysis from an e-commerce strategic planning effort identified an opportunity to deliver an integrated e-commerce solution in the marketplace (see Case 12.2). To capitalize on this opportunity and retain its reputation, Axon created a new division and launched a new brand, Quality Direct, to distinguish the effort within the parent company.

CASE 12.2
EC Application
MEASURING PROFIT ON THE WEB: AXON OF NEW ZEALAND

Axon (*axon.co.nz*) is an IT solutions company with locations in New Zealand's four largest cities. Axon's goal is "to be New Zealand's most recommended IT Services Company."

In 2002, as part of an examination of the success of its Quality Direct service, Axon issued a white paper that examined business profitability on the Web. Specifically the white paper listed four areas of potential profits from Web activities and the metrics that Axon used to assess the impact of the Web on business profits. This case provides a real example of a small business that is profiting from its Web-based delivery of services and has collected some quantitative data to demonstrate its EC success.

Metrics were applied in four areas. Here we describe each of the four areas, followed by some of the metrics (a partial list) Axon used to assess goal achievement.

Cost Avoidance and Reduction
Web technologies can enhance profitability by reducing or eliminating transaction costs (e.g., product purchase) or inter-action costs (e.g., a meeting, a phone call). Cost avoidance and reduction happens through activities such as improved access to information, customer self-help, and error reduction.

The following metrics demonstrated cost avoidance and reduction by Axon:

▶ Selling costs were reduced by 40 percent for each dollar of margin generated.
▶ Call volume to sales support increased at less than 50 percent of the traditional rate.
▶ Warehouse space was reduced by 40 percent, while volume increased by 40 percent.
▶ Obsolete stock write-offs as percentage of revenue were reduced by 93 percent.

Customer Service Enhancements
Delivering information to customers on all aspects of their transactions helps make the product or service more visible. Increased visibility generates increased value from a customer's perspective.

The following metrics demonstrated customer service enhancements by Axon:

▶ Average days to delivery were reduced by 20 percent over 2 years.
▶ Satisfaction with the delivery process is consistently greater than 80 percent.

New Market Opportunities
New market opportunities include new services to existing clients, changing the value proposition for existing clients, and targeting new markets.

The following metrics demonstrated new market oppor-tunities by Axon:

▶ Product revenue increased over 40 percent in the first 12 months of full operation.

▶ New customers were added at twice the rate that previously was being achieved.

New Media Options
"New media" includes improved communication, advertising, and marketing efforts through lower collateral costs, improved target marketing, subscriber lists, and sold advertising space.

The following metrics demonstrated the use of new media options by Axon:

▶ Cost per item for e-mail was less than 1 percent of the cost per item for postal mail.
▶ Response rate to e-mail was five times the response rate to postal mail.
▶ Expenditures on brochure design and production were reduced by 45 percent.

IT Best Investment Opportunities
The following were identified as the best EC-related investment opportunities for the future:

▶ Application management and access to applications
▶ Desktop and server management
▶ Information collaboration
▶ Mobile and convergence technologies
▶ Server and storage consolidation
▶ Service optimization

In May 2010, Axon achieved its strategic objective when it was purchased by top New Zealand IT service provider Integral Technology Group for NZ$18 million and Integral Axon was formed. Then, on November 1, 2010, with its gross assets standing at NZ$37,964,699, Axon surpassed its original goals when Integral Axon was acquired for an undisclosed sum by Datacraft (*datacraft. co.nz*), a US$4 billion global IT services provider, which operates in 49 countries across five continents. This moved Axon (Integral Axon) into a top spot in the global IT services arena.

Sources: Compiled from Green (2002), *axon.co.nz*, and *nbr.co.nz/article/integral-buys-axon-18-million-deal-122457* (both accessed January 2011).

Questions

1. List four areas in which Axon demonstrates increased profitability through the use of the Web.

2. Describe the characteristics of the metrics listed here (e.g., financial, customer service, quantitative, time based).

3. What other metrics might apply? (Hint: Consult Section 12.6.)

STRATEGY IN THE WEB 2.0 ENVIRONMENT AND IN SOCIAL NETWORKING

Social networks, blogs, wikis, social TV, discussion forums, and mashups are examples of Web 2.0 applications. A 2009 online global study conducted by McKinsey & Company reported that 69 percent of the 1,700 responding executives had gained measurable benefits from the use of Web 2.0 technologies. Reported benefits included the ability to provide more innovative products and services, more effectively market their products and services, gain better access to knowledge, lower costs, and raise revenues. And, surprisingly, in light of the current recession, the survey respondents indicated that they will continue to invest heavily in Web 2.0 (*McKinsey Quarterly* 2009). This use of Web 2.0 tools and technologies to help employees, partners, suppliers, and customers work together to build networks of like-minded people and share information in the enterprise is called *Enterprise 2.0* (see Chapters 2 and 7).

Many companies are using Web 2.0 tools throughout their enterprises to allow employees to create profiles and connect with one another in ways similar to LinkedIn, Facebook, and MySpace (see Sections 7.7 in Chapter 7). Shuen (2008) offers four major reasons why companies should enable the use of internal social networks: (1) quick access to knowledge, know-how, and know-who; (2) expansion of social connections and broadening of affiliations; (3) self-branding and expression of a personal digital identity and reputation; and (4) viral distribution of knowledge through referrals, testimonials, benchmarking, and RSS updating. Deloitte, IBM, and Best Buy are three early adopters of internal social networking. All three companies believe that the easier and faster connections among employees facilitate cross-division collaboration and greater innovation (see Chapter 7).

In Chapter 7, Section 7.11, a strategy was suggested for companies to start small so that they can observe how people react to the tools, learn how to manage the process, and develop a social system. For instance, companies can start with a small internal project that addresses a real business problem around knowledge sharing. Blogs or wikis are self-contained tools with content management, structure, and tagging capability built right in. They can also start in one department by providing blogs to employees to share ideas around a particular project, such as customer development in sales, competitive analysis in marketing, and so forth. After the companies complete the internal "beta" project, they can expand the effort to include other Enterprise 2.0 tools, as well as to bring other departments onboard and even move outside the organization to involve customers, partners, and suppliers. For example, Dell first launched internal blogs before creating IdeaStorm, which is offered to external customers.

An internal social media site can evolve into a global site to support employees, customers, partners and suppliers.

Marketers are increasingly using social networking tools in a wide range of activities, including advertising, public relations, customer service, and product development. For example, Brewtopia (brewtopia.com.au) initially invited 140 of its friends to describe their ideal beer. Within weeks, more than 10,000 people from over 20 countries joined the community and voted for their favorite beer's style, color, and alcohol content; the shape of the bottle; and the color printed on the label. In 2007, the company offered a platform for its customers to discuss and create their own beers, and in 2011 these offerings have grown to include the ability to create personalized wine and customized bottled water.

Example. At Arizona State University, students use CarePass, a new health care service introduced in January 2010, to check in for appointments by texting the health center or logging into its website. Then they can opt to wait in their dorm room or elsewhere until they receive a text or e-mail to come in for their appointment. This enables the Campus Health Service to better manage the more than 250 patients it sees daily and reduces time that contagious patients are in the health center. In addition, CarePass offers a simple opt-in process that allows ASU employees to specify their health and wellness interests so they get the information (e.g., fitness classes) they want, as it becomes available through their mobile devices.

As of April 2010, CarePass had helped to double employee attendance for general health and hearing screenings and increased attendance for diet and fitness programs by 85 percent (*Alliviant.com* 2010).

The importance of including social media in an EC strategy was recently emphasized by GoECart (goecart.com), an e-commerce vendor that provides retailers of all sizes with innovative, on-demand e-commerce solutions Using customer information available through social networks, it is possible to develop an individual customer relationship strategy. For example, send an e-mail and a small promotional gift to celebrate a customer's birthday or develop a contest to generate interest in merchants' brands. An example is the highly successful April 2010 citywide treasure hunts in New York and London set up by Jimmy Choo, a popular luxury shoe company, to launch its athletic shoe collection; see (thestylepa.com/2010/04/shoes-jimmy-choo-trainer-hunt.html).

It is important to consider the following important issues when planning a successful online EC strategy that includes social media (*GoECart.com* 2010):

- Develop an overall e-commerce strategy with clearly defined business goals.
- Effectively market to existing customers.
- Sell globally as well as locally.
- Develop a consistent online and offline brand strategy.
- Create business profiles and allow customers to post reviews by leveraging free resources available to merchants on sites such as Yahoo!, Bing, Google Places, Facebook, Twitter, YellowPages.com, etc.
- Create surveys and two-way communication mechanisms to solicit feedback from customers.

Shuen (2008) provides a comprehensive guide to Web 2.0 strategy, and Gold (2009) provides a strategic guide for m-commerce. Other hints on how to develop a business-aligned social media and social networking strategy are provided at ddmcd.com/strategy_alignment.html. For the 2011 "17 Digital Marketing Trends," see econsultancy.com/us/blog/7014-digital-marketing-trends-2011-by-econsultancy-ceo-ashley-friedlein.

Section 12.3 ▶ REVIEW QUESTIONS

1. Describe the advantages, risks, and success factors that first movers face.
2. What are the advantages and disadvantages of creating a separate online company?
3. Why would an existing company want to create a new brand for its e-commerce initiative?
4. What strategic benefits are associated with using social networks?

12.4 E-COMMERCE STRATEGY FORMULATION

The outcome of the strategy initiation phase should be a number of potential EC initiatives that exploit opportunities and manage threats in the business environment in light of corporate strengths and weaknesses. In the strategy formulation phase, the firm must decide which initiatives to implement and in what order. Strategy formulation activities include evaluating specific EC opportunities and conducting cost–benefit and risk analyses associated with those opportunities. Specific outcomes include a list of approved EC projects or applications, risk management plans, pricing strategies, and a business plan that will be used in the next phase of strategy implementation. The following are the major activities in this phase.

SELECTING E-COMMERCE OPPORTUNITIES

More productive strategy selection approaches can be used when compelling internal or external forces drive the strategy selection process. A problem-driven strategy may be best when an organization has a specific problem that an EC application can solve. For example, the use of forward e-auctions using e-auctioneers such as Liquidation.com (liquidation.com) may be the best solution to dispose of excess equipment. A *technology-driven strategy* can occur when a company owns technology that it needs to use. A *market-driven strategy* can occur when a company waits to see what competitors in the industry do. As noted earlier, this late-mover strategy can be effective if the company can use its brand, technology, superior customer service, or innovative products and strategies to overcome any lost first-mover advantage.

Most times, however, it is best to use a systematic methodology that determines which initiatives to pursue and when, namely the application portfolio mix.

DETERMINING AN APPROPRIATE EC APPLICATION PORTFOLIO MIX

For years, companies have tried to find the most appropriate portfolio (group) of projects among which an organization should share its limited resources. The classic portfolio strategy attempts to balance investments with different characteristics. For example, the company would combine long-term speculative investments in new potentially high-growth businesses with short-term investments in existing profit-making businesses.

The BCG Model and an Internet Portfolio Map

One well-known framework of this strategy is the Boston Consulting Group's (BCG) growth-share matrix with its star, cash cow, wild card, and dog opportunities. In the 1970s, BCG created the popular "growth-share" matrix to assist corporations in deciding how to allocate cash among its business units and projects. The matrix has two dimensions: "Market growth rate," which can be low or high, and relative "market share," which can be low or high. This results in four cells: stars (high growth, high share), cash cows (high share, low growth), question marks (high growth, low share), and dogs (low growth, low share). The corporation would then categorize its business units (or projects) as stars, cash cows, question marks, and dogs, and allocate budgets accordingly, moving money from cash cows to stars and to question marks that had higher market growth rates, and hence higher upside potential (see en.wikipedia.org/wiki/Boston_Consulting_Group#BCG_growth-share_matrix for details).

Tjan (2001) adapted the BCG approach to create what he calls an "Internet portfolio map." Instead of evaluating market potential and market share, the Internet portfolio map is based on company fit and project viability, both of which can be either low or high. Various criteria, including market value potential, time to positive cash flow, time to implementation, and funding requirements, can be used to assess viability. Similarly, metrics such as alignment with core capabilities, alignment with other company initiatives, fit with organizational structure, and ease of technical implementation can be used to evaluate fit. Together, these create an Internet portfolio map (see Exhibit 12.7).

Each company will want to determine for itself the criteria used to assess viability and fit. Senior managers and outside experts evaluate each proposed EC initiative (e.g., a B2B procurement site, a B2C store, an enterprise portal) on each of these criteria, typically on a quantitative (e.g., 1 to 100) or qualitative (e.g., high, medium, low) scale. If some criteria are more important than others, these can be weighted appropriately. The scores are combined, and average fit and viability scores are calculated for each initiative. Initiatives in which there is high agreement on rankings can be considered with more confidence.

The various initiatives are then mapped onto the Internet portfolio map, which can be an invaluable guide for navigating an e-commerce strategy through uncharted waters. If both viability and fit are low, the project is rejected. If both are high, the project is adopted. If fit is high but viability is low, the project is redesigned (to get higher viability). Finally, if the fit is low but the viability is high, the project is not adopted, or sold. Senior management must also consider factors such as cost–benefit (discussed in Chapter 13) and risk (discussed next) in making the final decision about what initiatives get funded and in what order.

EXHIBIT 12.7   The Internet Portfolio Map

Company Fit with EC Project

	Low	High
High	Do not consider new project, sell if possible	Accept project, infuse cash
Low	Reject the project	Redesign project for higher viability

Viability of Projects

Sources: Compiled from A. K. Tjan. "Finally, a Way to Put Your Internet Portfolio in Order." *Harvard Business Review* (February 2001); J. Sons. "Resolving the Complexity Dilemma in E-Commerce Firms Through Objective Organization." *Logistics Information Management* (January 2001); and author's experience.

RISK ANALYSIS IN STRATEGY FORMULATION

e-commerce (EC) risk
The likelihood that a negative outcome will occur in the course of developing and operating an electronic commerce strategy.

While Web 2.0 enables new business opportunities, it also may create substantial risks because of the open and interactive nature of the technology. **E-commerce risk** is the likelihood that a negative outcome will occur in the course of developing and operating an e-commerce initiative. Risk on the Internet and in EC environments is different from those faced by offline companies. For example, an online company faces particular Internet security threats and vulnerabilities. As a result, a robust Web 2.0 security strategy is essential for success.

The most dangerous risk to a company engaged in e-commerce is business risk—the possibility that developing and operating an e-commerce strategy could negatively impact the well-being of the organization itself. In Online File W12.1, attention is given to business and EC risks.

SECURITY ISSUES TO CONSIDER DURING STRATEGY FORMULATION

Some security issues that need to be considered when setting an EC strategy include:

- Fraudulent and malicious acts committed by either employees or third parties against the company's computer systems
- Computer virus attacks that hinder or even close down the company's operations
- Accidental alterations to or destruction of electronic information and records
- Loss of intellectual property when trade secrets are copied or recorded
- Extortion
- Business interruption and extra expense caused by a computer virus or other malicious acts
- Accidental or malicious destruction of electronic information
- Costs to mitigate a covered loss
- Multimedia liability, such as libel, slander, invasion of privacy, infringement of copyright, plagiarism, and false advertising
- Liability for damage to a third-party's computer system

OTHER ISSUES IN E-COMMERCE STRATEGY FORMULATION

A variety of issues exist in e-strategy formulation, depending on the company, industry, nature of the applications, and so forth. This section discusses some representative issues.

Managing Conflict Between the Offline and Online Businesses

In a click-and-mortar business, the allocation of resources between offline and online activities can create difficulties. Especially in sell-side projects, the two activities can be viewed as competitors. In this case, personnel in charge of offline and online activities may behave as competitors. This conflict may cause problems when the offline side needs to handle the logistics of the online side or when prices need to be determined. For example, Sears lessened this conflict by offering a sales commission to its retail stores on all online sales based on the zip code of the online customers.

Corporate culture, the ability of top management to introduce change properly, and the use of innovative processes that support collaboration will all determine the degree of collaboration between offline and online activities in a business. Clear support by top management for both the offline and online operations and a clear strategy of "what and how" each unit will operate are essential.

Pricing Strategy

Traditional methods for determining price are the cost-plus and competitor models. **Cost-plus** means adding up all the costs involved—material, labor, rent, overhead, and so forth—and adding a percentage markup as profit. The competitor model determines price based on what competitors are charging for similar products in the marketplace.

Pricing products and services for online sales changes these pricing strategies in subtle ways:

> **cost-plus**
> Adding up all the costs involved, such as material, labor, rent, overhead, etc., and adding a percentage mark-up as profit.

▶ **Price comparison is easier.** In traditional markets, either the buyer or, more often, the seller has more information than the other party, and this situation is exploited in determining a product's price. By facilitating price comparison, the Internet helps create what economists call a perfect market—one in which both the buyer and the seller have ubiquitous and equal access to information, usually in the buyer's favor. On the Internet, search engines, price comparison sites (e.g., mysimon.com, kelkoo.co.uk), infomediaries, and intelligent agents make it easy for customers to find who offers the product at the best price.

▶ **Buyers sometimes set the price.** Name-your-own-price models such as Priceline. com and auction sites mean that buyers do not necessarily just take the price; sometimes they make the price.

▶ **Online and offline goods are priced differently.** Pricing strategy may be especially difficult for a click-and-mortar company. Setting prices lower than those offered by the offline business may lead to internal conflict, whereas setting prices at the same level will hurt competitiveness.

▶ **Differentiated pricing can be a pricing strategy.** For decades, airline companies have maximized revenues with yield management—charging different prices for the same product. In the B2C EC marketplace, one-on-one marketing can extend yield management from a class of customer (e.g., buying an airline seat early or later) to individual customers. In the B2B EC marketplace, extranets with customized pricing pages present different prices to different customers based on purchasing contracts, the customer's buying history, and other factors. Versioning, which is selling the same goods but with different selection and delivery characteristics, is especially effective in selling digitized goods. For example, time-critical information such as stock market prices can be sold at a higher price if delivered in real time rather than with a 20-minute delay. As with all forms of differentiated pricing, versioning information is based on the fact that some buyers are willing to pay more to receive some additional advantage.

> **versioning**
> Selling the same good, but with different selection and delivery characteristics.

Internet technologies tend to provide consumers with easier access to pricing information, which increases their bargaining power. To remain competitive and profitable, sellers will have to adopt smarter pricing strategies. Specifically, businesses will have to look at ways of using the Internet to optimize prices, primarily through greater precision in setting prices, more adaptability in changing prices, and new ways of customer segmentation for differentiated pricing.

Section 12.4 ▶ REVIEW QUESTIONS

1. Describe how a company should and should *not* select EC applications.
2. Explain Tjan's Internet portfolio map.
3. List four sources of business risk in EC. What questions exemplify each source of risk?
4. Discuss three strategies for smarter pricing online.

12.5 E-COMMERCE STRATEGY IMPLEMENTATION

The execution of the strategic plan takes place in the strategy implementation phase, in which detailed, short-term plans are developed for carrying out the projects agreed on in e-strategy formulation. Decision makers evaluate options, establish specific milestones, allocate resources, and manage the projects.

In this section, we examine some of the topics related to this implementation process.

E-COMMERCE STRATEGY IMPLEMENTATION PROCESS

Typically, the first step in e-strategy implementation is to find a champion and establish a Web team, which then initiates and manages the execution of the plan. As EC implementation continues, the team is likely to introduce changes in the organization. Thus, during the implementation phase, it also becomes necessary to develop an effective change management program, including the possibility of business process management.

Find a Champion

project champion
The person who ensures the EC project gets the time, attention, and resources required and defends the project from detractors at all times.

Every Web project and every Web team requires a project champion. The **project champion** is the person who ensures that the project gets the time, attention, and resources required and defends the project from detractors at all times. The project champion may be the Web team leader or a senior executive. In his study of e-strategy in 43 companies, Plant (2000) found, "In every successful e-commerce project studied, a strong project champion was present in the form of a senior executive or someone in a position to demonstrate to a senior executive the potential added value such a project could bring to the organization" (pp. 34–35). Similarly, "top management championship" was identified as a critical factor for organizational assimilation of Web technologies.

In creating a Web (project) team, the organization should carefully define the roles and responsibilities of the team leader, team members, the Webmaster, and the technical staff. The purpose of the Web team is to align business goals and technology goals and to implement a sound EC plan with available resources.

Start with a Pilot Project

Implementing EC often requires significant investments in infrastructure. Therefore, a good way to start is to undertake one or a few small EC pilot projects. Pilot projects help uncover problems early, when the plan can easily be modified before significant investments are made.

General Motors' pilot program (GM BuyPower) is an example of the successful use of a pilot project. On its website (gm.com/vehicles) shoppers can choose car options, check local dealer inventory, schedule test drives, arrange financing, and get best-price quotes by e-mail or telephone. GM BuyPower started as a pilot project in four western U.S. states before expanding to all states. Similarly, when Home Depot decided to go online in 2000 it started in six stores in Las Vegas, then moved to four other cities in the western United States, and eventually went nationwide.

Allocate Resources

The resources required for EC projects depend on the information requirements and the capabilities of each project. Some resources—software, computers, warehouse capacity, staff—will be new and unique to the EC project. Even more critical for the project's success is effective allocation of infrastructure resources that many applications share, such as databases, the intranet, and possibly an extranet.

Manage the Project

A variety of tools can assist in resource allocation. Project management tools, such as Microsoft Project, assist with determining specific project tasks, milestones, and resource requirements. Standard system design tools (e.g., data flow diagrams) can help in executing the resource-requirement plan.

E-COMMERCE STRATEGY IMPLEMENTATION ISSUES

There are many e-strategy implementation issues, depending on the circumstances. Here we describe some common ones.

Build, Buy, or Rent EC Elements

Implementation of an EC application requires access to the construction of the website and integration of the site with the existing corporate information systems (e.g., front end for order taking, back end for order processing). At this point, a number of decisions of whether to build, buy, or outsource various construction aspects of the application implementation process face the company. Some of these decisions include the following:

▶ Should site development be done internally, externally, or by a combination of internal and external development?

▶ Should the software application be built or will commercially available software be satisfactory?

▶ If a commercial package will suit, should it be purchased from the vendor or rented from an application service provider (ASP)? Should it be modified?

▶ Will the company or an external ISP (Internet service provider) host the website?

▶ If hosted externally, who will be responsible for monitoring and maintaining the information and system?

Each option has its strengths and weaknesses, and the correct decisions will depend on factors such as the strategic nature of the application, the skills of the company's technology group, and the need to move fast or not.

Outsource: What? When? To Whom?

Outsourcing can create strategic advantages for firms in that it provides access to highly skilled, low-cost labor and provides potential market opportunities. **Outsourcing** is generally defined as the process of contracting out the company's products or services to another organization that agrees to provide and manage these products/services for a set fee over a set period (Kern and Willcocks 2002). These services could be otherwise carried out in-house by the company's own employees. In the context of EC, outsourcing means the use of external vendors to acquire EC applications.

outsourcing
The use of an external vendor to provide all or part of the products and services that could be provided internally.

Successful implementation of EC projects often requires careful considerations of outsourcing strategies, which involve: (1) evaluating when outsourcing should take place; (2) deciding which part(s) to outsource and which to keep in-house; and (3) choosing an appropriate vendor(s).

Software-as-a-Service. In considering outsourcing, a company should look at both software-as-a-service and cloud computing (see Online Tutorial T7) as outsourcing options.

Outsourcing decisions for organizations, both large and small, are often made during EC project implementation. Large companies may choose outsourcing when they want to experiment with new EC technologies without a great deal of up-front investment.

Outsourcing also allows large firms to protect their internal networks and to gain expert advice. Small firms with limited IT expertise and tight budgets also find outsourcing advantageous.

Example: British Airways. British Airways (britishairways.com) wanted to offer special promotions to its customers based on their status (gold, silver, or bronze) in its customer loyalty program. To achieve this business objective, British Airways (BA) made a strategic decision to outsource its FAQ (Frequently Asked Questions) Web pages. RightNow Technologies, an application service provider, was chosen to automatically develop, manage, and post different sets of FAQs for BA's loyalty program. The new Web pages were successfully developed and implemented and are facilitating BA's e-strategy by allowing it to create customized marketing programs tailored to its individual customer needs.

Depending on the availability of cutting-edge resources and facilities, organizations may decide to develop EC applications in-house or work with external vendors or consultants. A comparison of the in-house and outsourcing approaches is provided in Exhibit 12.8. Sometimes, after an evaluation of both approaches, a hybrid approach is taken to leverage the benefit of both. Organizations may choose to outsource part or all of the EC implementation process or keep parts of the process in-house. For example, a company may have an external ISP host a website that is developed internally.

ISPs, ASPs, and consultants are external vendors (business partners) that are commonly involved in EC application developments:

▶ ISPs offer website design, Web hosting, and maintenance service for a monthly or yearly fee. It can be more cost-effective to host websites with heavy traffic with an ISP.

▶ ASPs offer application development service. They write programs and lease them to clients. ASPs can be an attractive alternative for small businesses with small technology budgets.

▶ Consultants offer consulting services in various aspects (e.g., security, system integration) that aim to streamline and smoothen the EC implementation process.

It is important not to overestimate the advantages of outsourcing since it also can involve a number of risk factors such as: shifts in the political stability and legal environment of the outsourcing host country; lack of experience with outsourcing and contract negotiations; dependency on the external provider; and hidden costs, to name a few.

 Online Chapter 15 discusses in more detail many of these options—build or buy, in-house or outsource, host externally or internally. In many such decisions, one needs to consider partners' strategy and business alliances as described in Online File W12.2.

Redesigning Business Processes and BPR

An internal issue many firms face at the implementation stage is the need to change business processes to accommodate the changes an EC strategy brings. Sometimes these changes are incremental and can be managed as part of the project implementation process. Sometimes the changes are so dramatic that they affect the manner in which the organization operates. In this instance, business process reengineering is usually necessary.

EXHIBIT 12.8 In-House Development Versus Outsourcing

Criteria	In-House Development	Outsourcing
Accessibility to the project	Greater	Limited
Knowledge of the systems and its development	More	Less
Retention of knowledge and skills in staff	Higher	Lower
Ownership cost	Higher	Lower
Self-reliance for maintenance, update, and expansion	Greater	Lower
Development times	Longer	Shorter
Experienced staff with technical know-how and specialized areas	Less	More

Business process reengineering (BPR) is a methodology for conducting a one-time comprehensive redesign of an enterprise's processes. BPR may be needed for the following reasons:

business process reengineering (BPR)
A methodology for conducting a comprehensive redesign of an enterprise's processes.

▶ To fix poorly designed processes (e.g., processes are not flexible or scalable)

▶ To change processes so that they will fit commercially available software (e.g., ERP, e-procurement)

▶ To produce a fit between systems and processes of different companies that are partnering in e-commerce (e.g., e-marketplaces, ASPs)

▶ To align procedures and processes with e-services such as logistics, payments, or security

As a company that based its reputation on personal contacts in door-to-door visits and home parties, e-commerce would seem to be the last thing Mary Kay would benefit from. In reality, the opposite proved to be true. Since it first introduced Web and e-commerce capabilities in 2000, more than 95 percent of Mary Kay's independent sales people currently place orders via the Internet. Online selling, resulting from its implementation of this evolving e-business strategy, has resulted in major changes in the way that Mary Kay interacts with its customers and is helping to make its original business model even more effective, as described in Online File W12.3.

Business Process Management

The term **business process management (BPM)** refers to activities performed by businesses to improve their processes. While such improvements are hardly new, software tools called business process management systems have made such activities faster and cheaper. BPM systems monitor the execution of the business processes so that managers can analyze and change processes in response to analysis rather than just a hunch. BPM differs from BPR in that it deals not just with one-time change to the organization but rather long-term-consequences and repetitive actions. The activities that constitute business process management can be grouped into three categories: design, execution, and monitoring. For details, see en.wikipedia.org/wiki/business_process_management.

business process management (BPM)
Method for business restructuring that combines workflow systems and redesign methods; covers three process categories—people-to-people, systems-to-systems, and systems-to-people interactions.

Section 12.5 ▶ REVIEW QUESTIONS

1. Describe a Web (project) team and its purpose.
2. What is the role of a project champion?
3. What is the purpose of a pilot project?
4. Discuss the major strategy implementation issues of application development and BPR.
5. Describe BPM and the need for it in EC development.

12.6 E-COMMERCE STRATEGY AND PROJECT PERFORMANCE ASSESSMENT

The last phase of EC strategy begins as soon as the implementation of the EC application or project is complete. Strategy assessment includes both the continual assessment of EC metrics and the periodic formal evaluation of progress toward the organization's strategic goals. Based on the results, corrective actions are taken and, if necessary, the strategy is reformulated.

THE OBJECTIVES OF ASSESSMENT

Strategic assessment has several objectives. The most important ones are:

▶ Measure the extent to which the EC strategy and ensuing projects are delivering what they were supposed to deliver. If they are not delivering, apply corrective actions to ensure that the projects are able to meet their objectives.

> ▶ Determine if the EC strategy and projects are still viable in the current environment.
> ▶ Reassess the initial strategy in order to learn from mistakes and improve future planning.
> ▶ Identify failing projects as soon as possible and determine why they failed to avoid the same problems on subsequent projects.

Web applications often grow in unexpected ways, expanding beyond their initial plan. For example, Genentec Inc., a biotechnology giant, wanted merely to replace a homegrown bulletin-board system. It started the project with a small budget but soon found that the intranet had grown rapidly and had become very popular in a short span of time, encompassing many applications. For a guideline and framework for performance management, see Gosselin (2010).

MEASURING RESULTS AND USING METRICS

key performance indicator (KPI)
A quantifiable measurement, agreed to beforehand, that reflects the critical success factors of a company, department or project.

The rapid growth of e-commerce has resulted in a lot of poor online selling where companies have enjoyed ever-increasing sales with little effort on their part to monitor online activity. Then, this growth has slowed but the number of e-commerce companies has increased resulting in greater competition between online companies and a bust for many of them. This new e-commerce environment has made the measuring of success a critical activity. However, the trick is to measure the right key performance indicators. A **key performance indicator (KPI)** is a quantifiable measurement, agreed to beforehand, that reflects the critical success factors of a company, department, or projects. Different companies measure success or failure by a different set of KPIs. For example, eCommera (eCommera.com), a provider of intelligent e-commerce trading solutions that enable brand owners and retailers to sell efficiently and intelligently across multiple channels, recently conducted a survey to identify the most used KPIs for e-commerce. Exhibit 12.9 lists the measurement concerns that companies are facing and Exhibit 12.10 demonstrates the gap that currently exists between the KPIs that e-commerce companies consider important and the extent to what is actually measured.

In measuring KPIs, some companies may realize that their goals were unrealistic, that their Web servers are inadequate to handle demand, or that expected cost savings have not been realized. Others may experience so much success that they have to respond to numerous requests for additional EC applications from various functional areas in the company.

Assessing EC is difficult because of the many configurations and impact variables involved and the somewhat intangible nature of what is being measured. However, a review of the requirements and design documents should help answer many of the

EXHIBIT 12.9 2011 E-Strategy Measurement Challenges

Description	% of Companies Concerned
Attracting new customers or clients to the site	40
Improving online marketing effectiveness	38
Retaining existing customers and clients	31
Finding the right staff	25
Managing technology innovation	16
Analytics and understanding how to optimize performance	13
Planning an international strategy	7
Engaging social medical channels	5

Sources: Compiled from Wyse (2010) and Econsultancy (2010).

EXHIBIT 12.10 E-Strategy KPI Measurement Gap

E-Strategy KPI	% of Companies Measuring KPI
Customer satisfaction	59
Average order value (AOV)	50
Conversion	48
Gross profit per order	36
Lost demand due to customer cancellations	29
Return on inventory	28
Track lost demand from customers declined and/or charge backs	25
Lost demand caused by lack of inventory	24
Lost profit through fraud	21
Lost demand caused by inefficient order processing	20

Sources: Compiled from Wyse (2010) and Econsultancy (2010).

questions raised during the assessment. It is important that the Web team develop a thorough checklist to address both the evaluation of project performance and the assessment of a changing environment. One way to measure a project's performance is to use *metrics*.

E-Commerce Metrics

A **metric** is a specific, measurable standard against which actual performance is compared. Metrics assist managers in assessing progress toward goals, communicating the strategy to the workforce through performance targets and identifying where corrective action is required. Exhibit 13.2 (p. 667) lists a number of tangible and intangible metrics for various EC users. An example of a company that has implemented a comprehensive EC metrics approach is Axon, as described in Case 12.2 (p. 632).

metric
A specific, measurable standard against which actual performance is compared.

Corporate (Business) Performance Management and Balanced Scorecards

Corporate (business) performance management (CPM, BPM) is a closed-loop process that links strategy to execution in order to optimize business performance. The major steps of the process are:

1. Setting goals and objectives
2. Establishing initiatives and plans to achieve those goals
3. Monitoring actual performance against the goals and objectives
4. Taking corrective action

corporate (business) performance management (CPM, BPM)
Advanced performance measuring and analysis approach that embraces planning and strategy.

It is a real-time system that alerts managers to potential opportunities, impending problems and threats, and then empowers them to react through models and collaboration. Strategic planning in CPM includes the following eight steps:

1. Conduct a current situation analysis.
2. Determine the planning horizon.
3. Conduct an environment scan.
4. Identify critical success factors.
5. Complete a gap analysis (performance versus goals).
6. Create a strategic vision.
7. Develop a business strategy.
8. Identify strategic objectives and goals.

This provides an answer to the question "Where do we want to go?" The CPM tells the company "how to get there." Then the firm monitors its performance, usually using the balanced scorecard. This answers the question "How are we doing?" Finally, by comparing actual performance to the strategy and goal, the company can decide "what needs to be done differently," and then act and adjust plans and execution.

Balanced Scorecards. One of the best-known and most widely used performance management system is the balanced scorecard (see en.wikipedia.org/wiki/Balanced_scorecard). Kaplan and Norton first articulated this methodology in their 1992 *Harvard Business Review* article "The Balanced Scorecard: Measures That Drive Performance." For an overview, see Person (2009).

From a high-level viewpoint, the balanced scorecard is both a performance measurement and a management methodology that helps an organization translate its financial, customer, internal process, learning, and growth objectives and targets a set of actionable initiatives. As a measurement methodology, the balanced scorecard is designed to overcome the limitations of systems that are financially focused. It does this by translating an organization's vision and strategy into a set of interrelated financial and nonfinancial objectives, measures, targets, and initiatives. The nonfinancial objectives fall into one of three perspectives:

- ▶ **Customer.** These objectives define how the organization should appear to its customers if it is to accomplish its vision.
- ▶ **Internal business process.** These objectives specify the processes the organization must excel at in order to satisfy its shareholders and customers.
- ▶ **Learning and growth.** These objectives indicate how an organization can improve its ability to change and improve in order to achieve its vision.

With the balanced scorecard approach, the term *balance* arises because the combined set of measures is supposed to encompass indicators that are:

- ▶ Financial and nonfinancial
- ▶ Leading and lagging
- ▶ Internal and external
- ▶ Quantitative and qualitative
- ▶ Short term and long term

Balanced Scorecards and Metrics. The balanced scorecard can be viewed as a method for evaluating the overall health of organizations and projects (including EC ones) by looking at metrics in four areas: finance, customer satisfaction, learning and growth for employees, and internal business processes (see en.wikipedia.org/wiki/balanced_scorecard). It is an advanced method for EC justification. Each of the four areas can be defined by organizational goals and corresponding measurable metrics (e.g., see Beasley, et al. 2008).

Aligning Strategies and Actions. As a strategic management methodology, the balanced scorecard enables an organization to align its actions with its overall strategies and with risk analysis (e.g., see Beasley, et al. 2008). It accomplishes this task through a series of interrelated steps. The specific steps that are involved vary from one book to the next. In our case, the process can be captured in five steps:

1. Identify strategic objectives for each of the perspectives (about 15 to 25 in all).
2. Associate measures with each of the strategic objectives; a mix of quantitative and qualitative should be used.
3. Assign targets to the measures.
4. List strategic initiatives to accomplish each of the objectives (i.e., responsibilities).
5. Link the various strategic objectives through a strategy map.

Web Analytics

One large and growing area of EC strategy assessment is **Web analytics**, the analysis of clickstream data to understand visitor behavior on a website. (See Chapter 8 and Online Tutorial T8 for details.) Web analytics begins by identifying data that can assess the effectiveness of the site's goals and objectives (e.g., frequent visits to a site map may indicate site navigation problems). Next, analytics data are collected, such as where site

Web analytics
The analysis of clickstream data to understand visitor behavior on a website.

visitors are coming from, what pages they look at and for how long while visiting the site, and how they interact with the site's information. The data can reveal the impact of search engine optimization or an advertising campaign, the effectiveness of website design and navigation, and, most important, visitor conversion. Because the goal of most EC websites is to sell product, the most valuable Web analytics are those related to step-by-step conversion of a visitor to a customer down the so-called purchase funnel.

Information about Web analytics is available from Sostre and LeClaire (2007), emetrics.org, and jimnovo.com. Two of many Web analytics tools include WebTrends (webtrends.com) and ClickTracks (clicktracks.com).

Compete for Web Analytics. Compete (compete.com) specializes in competitive analysis via Web analytics. It provides its customers with: A profile of competitors with competitive analysis, traffic data and analysis, identification of new threats, and a detailed blog.

Section 12.6 ▶ REVIEW QUESTIONS

1. Describe the need for assessment.
2. Define metrics and describe their contribution to strategic planning.
3. Describe the corporate performance management approach to strategy assessment.
4. What is a balanced scorecard?
5. Define Web analytics.

12.7 A STRATEGY FOR GLOBAL E-COMMERCE

The decision of whether to "go global" is a strategic issue. In a June 30, 2010, report on world Internet use, Miniwatts Marketing Group reported that nearly 2 billion people worldwide are regular Internet users. Of these, approximately 248 million people are in North America, more than 800 million are in Asia, and nearly a half billion are in Europe (internetworldstats.com/stats.htm). These statistics illustrate the huge potential that exists for companies to expand their market share through the use of EC.

The decision to go global is made for many reasons, both reactive and proactive. Reactive reasons include competitors are selling internationally, customers demand global access, cultural differences, and trade barriers. Proactive reasons include seeking economies of scale, realization of new international markets, gaining access to sufficient or new resources, cost savings, and local government incentives. Regardless of the reasons, expanding globally to realize a company's strategic objectives requires rational planning and a quick response to opportunities.

A global electronic marketplace is an attractive thrust in a corporate EC strategy. Going global means access to larger markets, mobility (e.g., to minimize taxes), and flexibility to employ workers anywhere. However, going global is a complex and strategic decision process due to a multiplicity of issues. Geographic distance is the most obvious dimension of conducting business globally, but, frequently, it is not the most important dimension. Instead cultural, political, legal, administrative, and economic dimensions are equally likely to threaten a firm's international ambitions. This section briefly examines the opportunities, problems, and solutions for companies using e-commerce to go global.

BENEFITS AND EXTENT OF GLOBAL OPERATIONS

A major advantage of EC is the ability to do business at any time, from anywhere, and at a reasonable cost. These are also the drivers behind global EC, and there have been some incredible success stories in this area. For example:

▶ EBay conducts auctions in hundreds of countries worldwide.
▶ Alibaba.com (Chapter 4) provides B2B trading services to thousands of companies in hundreds of countries.

▶ Amazon.com sells books and hundreds of other items to individuals and organizations in over 190 countries.

▶ Small companies, such as ZD Wines (zdwines.com), sell to hundreds of customers worldwide. HOTHOTHOT.com (hothothot.com) reported its first international trade only after it went online; within 2 years global sales accounted for 25 percent of its total sales. From its beginnings in 1997, when it reported an average of 500 hits per day, in 10 years the company reported over 10,000 hits per day and its annual growth rate is over 125 percent, selling more than 100 brands of hot sauce and salsa to customers in 45 countries.

▶ Major corporations, such as GE and Boeing, have reported an increasing number of out-of-the-country vendors participating in their electronic RFQs. These electronic bids have resulted in a 10 to 15 percent cost reduction and more than a 50 percent reduction in cycle time.

▶ Many international corporations have considerably increased their success in recruiting employees for foreign locations when they use online recruiting (see xing.com and linkedin.com).

BARRIERS TO GLOBAL E-COMMERCE

Despite the benefits and opportunities offered by globalization, there are several barriers to global EC. Some of these barriers face any EC venture but become more difficult when international impacts are considered. These barriers include authentication of buyers and sellers (Chapter 9), generating and retaining trust (Chapter 8), order fulfillment and delivery (Chapter 11), security (Chapter 9), and domain names. Others are unique to global EC. We will use the culture, administration, geography, economics (CAGE) distance framework proposed by Ghemawat (2001) to identify areas in which natural or manmade barriers hinder global EC.

Cultural Differences

The Internet is a multifaceted marketplace made up of users from many cultures. The multicultural nature of global EC is important because cultural attributes determine how people interact with companies, agencies, and each other based on social norms, local standards, religious beliefs, and language. Cultural and related differences include spelling differences (e.g., American versus British spelling), information formatting (e.g., dates can be mm/dd/yy or dd/mm/yy), graphics and icons (e.g., mailbox shapes differ from country to country), measurement standards (e.g., metric versus imperial system), the use of color (e.g., European websites tend to use brighter and bolder colors than U.S. sites do), protection of intellectual property (e.g., Chinese tolerance of copyright infringement has Confucian roots), time standards (e.g., local time zones versus Greenwich Mean Time), styles of navigation (e.g., people in the Middle East tend to scan from right to left rather than left to right), and information density on homepages (e.g., Asian homepages tend to have a higher density of information than U.S. homepages). Solutions for overcoming cultural barriers begin with an awareness of cultural identities and differences in the target markets. Many companies are globalizing their websites by creating different sites for different cultural groups, taking into account site design elements, pricing and payment infrastructures, currency conversion, customer support, and language translation.

Language Translation

Of the earth's 6.5 billion population, less than 1 billion people speak English as their native or a second language. In contrast, slightly more than 1 billion people speak Mandarin Chinese. In their study of 1,000 top websites, Sargent and Kelly (2010) reported that more than 72 percent of consumers say they would be more likely to buy a product with information in their own language and 56.2 percent say that the ability to obtain information in their own language is more important than price. Given that it takes 83 of the world's 6,912 languages to reach 80 percent of the world's population, it follows that websites offered in only one language can address no more than 30 percent of the total online population. Clearly, these single language websites are severely limiting their customer base. It is not surprising then, that language translation is one of the most obvious and most important aspects of creating and maintaining global websites. The top 25 global websites support an average of 58 languages. Byte Level Research reviewed 250 corporate global websites, to identify the top 25 "amazing global gateways"—leaders, laggards, and best practice companies were identified (Yunkers 2011). The "Top 10 Global Websites of 2011" are listed in Exhibit 12.11.

The number one global website in 2011 was Facebook. It replaced Google, who had held the top spot for a number of years. Facebook's recent innovations (see the closing case in Chapter 7) include multilingual plug-ins, an improved global gateway, and multilingual user profiles. Sargent and Kelly (2010) also reported that 23 is the average number of languages supported by the 250 sites who participated in the survey. The primary problems with language translation are speed and cost. It may take a human translator a week to translate a medium-sized website into another language. For large sites, the cost can be upwards of $500,000, depending on the complexity of the site and languages for translation, and it may take a long time. Some companies address the cost and time problems by translating their Web pages into different languages through so-called *machine translators*. A list of free translator programs can be found at humanitas-international.org/newstran/more-trans.htm and websearch.about.com/od/internetresearch/a/translate.htm. To read about how one organization is successfully using machine translation, see Online File W12.4. Recently, more and more companies are using globalization management systems or language service providers (LSPs) that provide "native" translators and use modern translation software to keep previously translated content in a translation memory so as to cut costs and increase consistency. For a directory of LSPs, consult proz.com/translation-agencies or lspzone.com/en/community/directory.

Legal Issues

One of the most contentious areas of global EC is the resolution of international legal issues (Chapter 14). A number of national governments and international organizations are working together to find ways to avoid uncoordinated actions and encourage uniform legal standards. An ambitious effort to reduce differences in international law governing EC is the United Nations Commission on International Trade Law (UNCITRAL) Model Law on Electronic Commerce. Its purpose is to offer national legislators a set of internationally acceptable rules that detail how a number of legal obstacles to the development of e-commerce may be removed and how a more secure legal environment may be created

EXHIBIT 12.11 Top 10 Global Websites of 2011

Rank	Company Name	Industry Sector	Website Address
1	Facebook	Web Services	facebook.com
2	Google	Web Services	google.com
3	Cisco	Enterprise Technology	cisco.com
4	3M	Diversified	3m.com
5	LG	Consumer Technology	lg.com/global/index.jsp
6	Philips	Diversified	philips.com/global/index.page
7	Samsung	Consumer Technology	samsung.com/global/business/telecomm/aboutus/AboutUs_BusinessOverview.html
8	NIVEA	Consumer Goods	nivea.com//gateway/
9	Symantec	Consumer Technology	symantec.com
10	Hewlett-Packard	Consumer Technology	welcome.hp.com/country/us/en/wwwelcome.html

Sources: Compiled from Yunker (2011) and Acclaro.com (2011).

through the formulation of modern, fair, and harmonized rules on commercial transactions (see uncitral.org). The Model Law has been adopted in some form in many countries and legal jurisdictions, including Singapore, Australia, Canada, Hong Kong, and some American states (e.g., California, Colorado, Iowa, and Kentucky).

International trade organizations, such as the World Trade Organization (WTO) and the Asia-Pacific Economic Cooperation (APEC) forum, have working groups that are attempting to reduce EC trade barriers in areas such as pricing regulations, customs, import/export restrictions, tax issues, and product specification regulations.

Geographic Issues and Localization

The geographic issues of shipping goods and services across international borders are well known. Barriers posed by geography differ based on the transportation infrastructure between and within countries and the type of product or service being delivered. For example, geographic distance is almost irrelevant with online software sales.

Example: Clarins Group. Clarins Group (clarins.com), a major player in the skin care, makeup, and fragrance business sector, is significantly increasing its global online presence and its e-commerce analytics to optimize online performance of its trading platform. From a single platform, with the help of eCommera's Intelligent Trader, the Clarins group will deliver the sites for each of its brands including Clarins, Thierry Mugler, and Azzaro perfumes, in more than 15 countries, while addressing the challenges of multichannel, multilanguage and multicurrency.

Localization. Many companies use different names, colors, sizes, and packaging for their overseas products and services. This practice is referred to as *localization*. In order to maximize the benefits of global information systems, the localization approach should also be used in the design and operation of the supporting information systems. For example, many websites offer different language or currency options, as well as special content. Europcar (europcar.com), for example, offers portals in 118 countries, each with an option for 1 of 10 languages.

Economic Issues

Economic and financial issues encompassing global EC include government tariffs, customs, and taxation. In areas subject to government regulation, tax and regulatory agencies have attempted to apply the rules used in traditional commerce to electronic commerce, with considerable success. Exceptions include areas such as international tariff duties and taxation. Software shipped in a box would be taxed for duties and tariffs when it arrives in the country. However, software downloaded online relies on self-reporting and voluntary payment of tax by the purchaser, something that does not happen very often.

The key financial barrier to global EC is electronic payment systems. To sell effectively online, EC firms must have flexible payment methods that match the ways different groups of people pay for their online purchases. Although credit cards are used widely in the United States, many European and Asian customers prefer to complete online transactions with offline payments. Even within the category of offline payments, companies must offer different options depending on the country. For example, French consumers prefer to pay with a check, Swiss consumers expect an invoice by mail, Germans commonly pay for products only upon delivery, and Swedes are accustomed to paying online with debit cards.

Pricing is another economic issue. A vendor may want to price the same product at different prices in different countries in consideration of local prices and competition. However, if a company has one website, differential pricing will be difficult or impossible. Similarly, what currency will be used for pricing? What currency will be used for payment?

E-Commerce in Developing Countries. Economic conditions determine the degree of the development of countries. Some developing countries are using EC as a springboard to improve their economies (e.g., China, Malaysia, India). Other developing countries are making strides. For a discussion. see Sanayei (2011).

BREAKING DOWN THE BARRIERS TO GLOBAL E-COMMERCE

A number of international organizations and experts have offered suggestions on how to break down the barriers to global EC. Some of these suggestions include the following:

> ▶ **Be strategic.** Identify a starting point and lay out a globalization strategy. Remember that Web globalization is a business-building process. Consider what languages and countries it makes sense for the company to target and how the company will support the site for each target audience.
>
> ▶ **Know your audience.** Carefully consider the target audience. Be fully informed of the cultural preferences and legal issues that matter to customers in a particular part of the world.
>
> ▶ **Localize.** As much as practical and necessary, offer websites in national languages; offer different sites in different countries (e.g., "Yahoo! Japan" is at yahoo.co.jp); price products in local currencies; and base terms, conditions, and business practices on local laws and cultural practices.
>
> ▶ **Think globally, act consistently.** An international company with country websites managed by local offices must make sure that areas such as brand management, pricing, corporate information, and content management are consistent with company strategy.
>
> ▶ **Value the human touch.** Trust the translation of the website content only to human translators, not machine translation programs. Involve language and technical editors in the quality assurance process. One slight mistranslation or one out-of-place graphic can turn off customers forever.
>
> ▶ **Clarify, document, explain.** Pricing, privacy policies, shipping restrictions, contact information, and business practices should be well documented and located on the website and visible to the customer. To help protect against foreign litigation, identify the company's location and the jurisdiction for all contract or sales disputes.
>
> ▶ **Offer services that reduce barriers.** It is not feasible to offer prices and payments in all currencies, so link to a currency exchange service (e.g., xe.com) for the customer's convenience. In B2B e-commerce, be prepared to integrate the EC transaction with the accounting/finance internal information system of the buyer.

Section 12.7 ▶ REVIEW QUESTIONS

1. Describe globalization in EC and the advantages it presents.
2. Describe the major barriers to global EC in each dimension of the CAGE framework.
3. What can companies do to overcome the barriers to global EC?
4. Discuss the pros and cons of a company offering its website in more than one language.

12.8 E-COMMERCE STRATEGY FOR SMALL AND MEDIUM-SIZED ENTERPRISES

E-commerce can be one of the most effective business tactics for SMEs. The potential for SMEs to expand their markets and compete with larger firms through EC is enormous. Some of the first companies to take advantage of Web-based electronic commerce were small and medium-sized enterprises (SMEs). While larger, established, tradition-bound companies hesitated, some forward-thinking SMEs moved onto the Web because they realized there were opportunities in marketing, business expansion, business launches, cost-cutting, and tighter partner alliances. Some examples are: virtualvine.com, hothothot.com, and philaprintshop.com.

Yet, many appear to be unaware of the strategic benefits of EC, and its use remains a largely untapped resource in SMEs. For example, a June 2010 survey of small business success found that 67 percent of the participating 500 U.S.-based SMEs reported they currently have a website or were likely to have a website within the next 2 years, but only 37 percent said they were currently advertising online, and this number was only expected to rise to 48 percent by 2012. When asked about how important their websites were in helping them market their brand, serve their customers, and run their business, only one-third of SMEs felt that their websites were "extremely important," while 35 percent felt that websites were "somewhat important," and 31 percent felt that they were not "at all important" to their business success. Interestingly, less than one-fifth of the SMEs rated themselves as "highly competitive" (Smith 2010).

Clearly, SMEs are still finding it difficult to formulate or implement an EC strategy, mainly because of the inability to handle large volumes of business, limited use of EC by suppliers, lack of knowledge or IT expertise in the SME, and limited awareness of the associated opportunities and risks. As a result, many SMEs create static websites that are not used to market or expand their business and do not use EC to interactively sell their products or services. However, there is a growing number of SMEs that are blazing the EC strategy trail. Online File W12.5 describes one of these success stories.

Choosing an EC approach is a strategic decision that must be made in the context of the company's overall business strategy. On the positive side, the nature of EC lowers the barriers to entry, and it is a relatively inexpensive way of reaching a larger number of buyers and sellers who can more easily search for, compare prices, and negotiate a purchase. However, there are also some inherent risks associated with the use of EC in SMEs. Exhibit 12.12 provides a list of major advantages and disadvantages of EC for SMEs.

EXHIBIT 12.12 Advantages and Disadvantages of EC for Small and Medium-Sized Businesses

Advantages/Benefits	Disadvantages/Risks
▶ Inexpensive sources of information. A Scandinavian study found that over 90 percent of SMEs use the Internet for information search (OECD 2001). ▶ Inexpensive ways of advertising and conducting market research. Banner exchanges, newsletters, chat rooms, and so on are nearly zero-cost ways to reach customers. ▶ Competitor analysis is easier. The Scandinavian study found that Finnish firms rated competitor analysis third in their use of the Internet, after information search and marketing. ▶ Inexpensive ways to build (or rent) a storefront. Creating and maintaining a website is relatively easy and cheap (see Online Chapter 15). ▶ SMEs are less locked into legacy technologies and existing relationships with traditional retail channels. ▶ Image and public recognition can be generated quickly. A Web presence makes it easier for a small business to compete against larger firms. ▶ An opportunity to reach worldwide customers. No other medium is as efficient at global marketing, sales, and customer support. ▶ Other advantages for SMEs include increased speed of customer payments, closer ties with business partners, reduced errors in information transfer, lower operating costs, and other benefits that apply to all businesses.	▶ Lack of financial resources to fully exploit the Web. A transactional website may entail relatively high up-front fixed costs in terms of cash flow for an SME. ▶ Lack of technical staff or insufficient expertise in legal issues, advertising, etc. These human resources may be unavailable or prohibitively expensive to an SME. ▶ Less risk tolerance than a large company. If initial sales are low or the unexpected happens, the typical SME does not have a large reserve of resources to fall back on. ▶ When the product is not suitable or is difficult for online sales (e.g., experiential products such as clothes or beauty products; perishable products, such as certain foods), the Web opportunity is not as great. ▶ Reduced personal contact with customers represents the dilution of what is normally a strong point for a small business. ▶ Inability to afford entry to or purchase enough volume to take advantage of digital exchanges.

GLOBALIZATION AND SMEs

In addition to increasing their domestic market, EC opens up a vast global marketplace for SMEs, but only a small percentage of them conduct a significant part of their business globally. However, a growing number is beginning to use EC to tap into the global marketplace in some way, but even then SMEs are more likely to purchase globally than to sell globally. In the 2010 "Survey of Small Business Success," the incidence of global purchasing by SMEs showed an increase in the first 6 months of 2010 from 11 percent to 18 percent. On the other hand, global selling of products and services by SMEs decreased in the same time period. Despite this, SMEs doing business globally report that EC has a "major impact" on their ability to operate on a broader scale. EC activities that SMEs engage in globally include communicating with global customers (41%), buying supplies (31%), and selling their products globally online (27%).

RESOURCES TO SUPPORT SMEs

SME owners often lack strategic management skills and consequently are not always aware of changes in their business environment with respect to emerging technologies. Fortunately, SMEs have a variety of support options. Almost every developed country in the world has a government agency devoted to helping SMEs become more aware of and able to participate in electronic commerce (e.g., sba.gov, business.gov.au).

In addition, vendors realize the opportunity represented by thousands of businesses going online, and many have set up a variety of service centers that typically offer a combination of free information and fee-based support. Examples are IBM's Small Business Center (ibm.com/businesscenter/smb/us/en) and Microsoft's Small Business Center (microsoft.com/business/en-us/default.aspx). Professional associations, Web resource services (e.g., smallbusiness.yahoo.com, lounge.verticalresponse.com), and small businesses that are in the business of helping other small businesses go online, sponsor other small business support centers.

Resources to assist SMEs in going global are also emerging as helpful tools for SMEs that want to expand their horizons. For example, the Global Small Business Blog (GSBB) (borderbuster.blogspot.com) was created in 2004 by Laurel Delaney, founder of GlobeTrade, an international management consulting and marketing solutions company to help entrepreneurs and small business owners expand their businesses internationally.

A good source regarding SMEs' use of e-markets to do international business is emarketservices.com/start/Case-studies-and-reports/index.html.

SMEs AND SOCIAL NETWORKS

One of the fastest growing EC technologies being adopted by SMEs is social commerce. Social networking sites are growing in popularity across the board, so it is no surprise that SMEs also view social networking as a means to improve customer relationships, build community, and create feedback loops regarding their products and services.

Social networking sites are a particularly good fit for smaller businesses because SMEs often do not have a peer group nearby with which to discuss relevant topics. On the Internet, SMEs can turn to sites that cater to small businesses and provide them with access to peers, information on starting up, and e-strategy advice (see Weston 2008). In addition to using these sites to make contacts and get advice (e.g., at LinkedIn), they can be very useful in a B2B context as a way to build relationships with partners or build contact networks with other small businesses.

It has always been the case that business success is intimately linked to how well an organization taps into its relationships across employees, customers, partners, and suppliers. Social networking is just a means to that end—it helps humanize the organization and enables people to establish relationships and participate from a community perspective. Exhibit 12.13 lists 10 steps to success when using social media in SMEs. For tips on how to use YouTube to promote SMEs, see masternewmedia.org/online_marketing/youtube-promote-content-viral-marketing/youtube-video-marketing-10-ways-20070503.htm.

Although there is no doubt that the use of social networking among small businesses will grow, managing expectations is key. SMEs have to live up to the anticipated outcomes

EXHIBIT 12.13 10 Steps to a Successful Social Media Strategy

Step	Description
1	Understand what social media is and the benefits of using it.
2	Identify the audience you want to reach.
3	Identify the resources you currently have available.
4	Identify most appropriate technologies to use.
5	Start a blog to foster a sense of community around your business.
6	Build social media profiles on Facebook, LinkedIn, Twitter, and You Tube.
7	Make your blog social-media friendly—include buttons, widgets, badges, RSS icon, good share-friendly content.
8	Build relationships with your target market—it's all about the people!
9	Turn friends and followers into clients and customers—build an e-mail list.
10	Decide how you will monitor and measure the success of your social media initiative.

Sources: Compiled from Gallagher (2010) and Ward (2009).

people have when they participate in such social networks; it must be bidirectional. If it seems like just another marketing or PR ploy, or if the company exploits the community, then the results will be worse than having not participated at all. For more details and statistics, see Maddox (2008).

Section 12.8 ▶ REVIEW QUESTIONS

1. What are the advantages or benefits of EC for small businesses?
2. What are the disadvantages or risks of EC for small businesses?
3. What are the advantages and disadvantages for small businesses online?
4. How can social networks help SMEs become more competitive?

MANAGERIAL ISSUES

Some managerial issues related to this chapter are as follows:

1. **What is the strategic value of EC to the organization?** It is important for management to understand how EC can improve marketing and promotions, customer services and sales, and the supply chain and procurement processes. More significantly, the greatest potential of EC is realized when management views EC from a strategic perspective, not merely as a technological advancement. Management should determine the primary goals of EC, such as new market creation, cost avoidance and reduction, and customer service enhancement.

2. **How do you relate the EC activities with business objectives and metrics?** Companies first must choose objectives and design appropriate metrics to measure the goals and actual achievement. The companies need to exercise this with caution because the metrics may accidentally lead employees to behave in the opposite direction of the intended objectives. The balanced scorecard is a popular framework adopted to define objectives, establish performance metrics, and then map them. EC planning needs to identify

what the role of EC is in achieving the goals in BSC metrics.

3. **Should the EC activities be spun off as a separate company?** This is a debatable issue. Sometimes it is useful in eliminating conflicts of prices and strategy. Also, using the spin-off as an IPO can be rewarding. Lotte Department Store in Korea has spun off Lotte.com because of its unique growth. However, it created the *lotteshopping.com* site to assist traditional shopping. In other cases, the spin-off can create problems and administrative expenses. Walmart, Barnes & Noble, and Sears have suffered from their spin-offs and have merged them into the offline part of their companies.

4. **How should the e-business scope evolve?** As Amazon.com experienced, a company may handle a certain item in the beginning stage. But the number of items will expand to include many kinds. As the scope of items expands, the order fulfillment plan has to evolve accordingly considering the alliance

strategy with partners who have strong sourcing capability. The key competitors will be changed as the scope of business evolves. Management has to envision the prospect of e-business that can create justifiable revenue and profit so that investors can join the funding and patiently wait. The community in the social network needs to be linked with the revenue creation eventually.

5. **What are the benefits and risks of EC?** Strategic advantage has to be carefully weighed against potential risks. Identifying CSFs for EC and doing a cost–benefit analysis is an important step in developing an EC strategy. Benefits can be derived not only from the adoption of EC, but also from the reengineering of traditional business processes. Benefits often are difficult to quantify, especially because gains tend to be strategic. In such an analysis, risks should be addressed with contingency planning (deciding what to do if problems arise).

6. **Why do we need an EC planning process?** A strategic plan is both a document and a process. Dwight D. Eisenhower, former U.S. president, once said "Plans are nothing, planning is everything." A planning process that includes management, employees, business partners, and other stakeholders not only produces a planning document that will guide the business into the future but also achieves buy-in among the participants about where the company is going and how it intends to get there. The same can be said for e-business planning—the process is as important as the plan itself.

7. **How can EC go global?** Going global with EC is a very appealing proposition for companies of all sizes, but it may be difficult to do, especially on a large scale or for SMEs that lack the necessary resources. Companies need to identify, understand, and address the barriers to globalization such as culture, language, and law as well as customers and suppliers. The e-business needs to decide on a localization strategy. Some companies, such as eBay, acquire or establish local companies to support local customers, whereas other companies, such as Amazon.com, only support the English site. In B2B, one may create collaborative projects with partners in other countries.

8. **How do you manage the EC project?** Forming an effective team is critical for EC project success. The team's leadership, the balance between technical and business staff, getting the best staff representation on the team, and having a project champion are essential for success. Reconciling the business objectives and system design is critical. IT sourcing needs to be considered, particularly for SMEs.

SUMMARY

In this chapter, you learned about the following EC issues as they relate to the chapter's learning objectives:

1. **The strategic planning process.** Four major phases compose this cyclical process: initiation, formulation, implementation, and assessment. A variety of tools are available to carry out this process.

2. **Writing a business plan and a business case.** A business plan is an essential outcome of a strategic planning process. Writing the business plan may produce more significant outcomes than the plan itself. The purpose of the plan is to describe the operation of the business, and its content includes revenue sources, business partners, and trading procedures. A business case is a distinctive type of business plan. It refers to a business plan for a new initiative or large, new project inside an existing organization.

3. **The EC strategic process.** Considering e-commerce in strategy development does not radically change the process, but it does impact the outcome. Move-to-the-Net firms must approach the process differently than born-on-the-Net firms, but both types of firms must recognize the way electronic technologies, such as the Internet, make an e-difference. Because of the comprehensiveness of EC, formal strategic planning is a must.

4. **E-strategy initiation and formulation.** The strategy initiation phase involves understanding the company, the industry, and the competition. Companies must consider questions such as "Should we be a first mover?" "Should we go global?" and "Should we create a separate company or brand?" With the proliferation of the Web 2.0 tools, companies should also consider strategies related to Web 2.0 and social networking. In strategy formulation, specific opportunities are selected for implementation based on project viability, company fit, cost–benefit, risk, and pricing.

5. **E-strategy implementation and assessment.** Creating an effective Web team and ensuring that sufficient resources are available initiate the implementation phase. Other important implementation issues are whether to outsource various aspects of development and the need to redesign existing business processes. Immediately after implementation, assessment begins.

Metrics provide feedback, and management acts by taking corrective action and reformulating strategy, if necessary.

6. **Issues in global EC.** Going global with EC can be done quickly and with a relatively small investment. However, businesses must deal with a number of different issues in the cultural, administrative, geographic, legal, and economic dimensions of global trading.

7. **Small and medium-sized businesses and EC.** Depending on the circumstances, innovative small companies have a tremendous opportunity to adopt EC with little cost and to expand rapidly. Being in a niche market provides the best chance for small business success, and a variety of Web-based resources are available that small and medium-sized business owners can use to help ensure success.

KEY TERMS

Balanced scorecard	627	Cost-plus	637	Strategy	619
Business case	628	Disintermediation	631	Strategy assessment	625
Business plan	628	e-commerce (EC) risk	636	Strategy formulation	624
Business process management (BPM)	641	e-commerce strategy (e-strategy)	620	Strategy implementation	625
		Key performance indicator (KPI)	642	Strategy initiation	623
Business process reengineering (BPR)	641	Metric	643	Strategy map	626
		Outsourcing	639	SWOT analysis	627
Competitor analysis grid	627	Project champion	638	Value proposition	623
Corporate (business)		Scenario planning	627	Versioning	637
performance management		Strategic information systems		Web analytics	644
(CPM, BPM)	643	planning (SISP)	622		

DISCUSSION QUESTIONS

1. How would you identify competitors for your small business that wants to launch an EC project?

2. How would you apply Porter's five forces and Internet impacts in Exhibit 12.3 to the Internet search engine industry?

3. Why must e-businesses consider strategic planning to be a cyclical process?

4. How would you apply the SWOT approach to a small, local bank that is evaluating its e-banking services?

5. Offer some practical suggestions as to how a company can include the impact of the Internet in all levels of planning.

6. Amazon.com decided not to open physical stores, whereas First Network Security Bank (FNSB), which was the first online bank, opened its first physical bank in 1999. Compare and discuss the two strategies.

7. Discuss the pros and cons of going global with a physical product.

8. For each part of the CAGE framework, briefly discuss one barrier that may negatively impact e-commerce companies doing business globally.

9. Find some SME EC success stories and identify the common elements in them.

10. Submit three questions regarding EC strategy for small business to the Small Business Expert (free) at **smallbusinessanswers.yahoo.com/?fr=bps737888**. Summarize your experience.

11. After viewing the video "FiftyOne Global Ecommerce Demo" (**youtube.com/watch?v=2YazivwAm2o&feature=related**) consider the following: "Fifty-One" claims to address all the issues associated with currency conversion, fraud screening, payment processing, customer brokering, international freight forwarding, destination country delivery, and in-country returns management.

   a. Discuss how a company embarking on global e-commerce would approach each of these challenges without the assistance of a company like Fifty-One.

   b. Would these challenges be insurmountable? For each challenge, explain why or why not.

   c. Would the type or size of a business affect whether it could successfully navigate these challenges to global e-commerce? Explain your conclusions.

TOPICS FOR CLASS DISCUSSION AND DEBATES

1. Has the availability of EC affected the way we assess industry attractiveness? Consider whether Porter's five forces still apply in an EC setting and develop new criteria for assessing the attractiveness of online industries.

2. Consider the challenges of a brick-and-mortar company manager who wants to create an integrated (online/offline) business. Discuss the challenges that he or she will face.

3. As the principles in a small business that already has an effective Web presence, you are considering taking your company global. Discuss the main issues that you will have to consider in making this strategic decision.

4. Examine the seven strategies of Facebook and Twitter at **socialmediatoday.com/christinegallagher/165536/ top-7-facebook-and-twitter-strategies** and comment on them.

5. Debate: Is Google Translate good for the translation of websites?

6. Is Amazon eBay's biggest challenge? (See Ackerman 2008.) What about Walmart.com?

7. Debate whether you think that the Internet has changed (or will change) the strategy of organizations that deliver distance education. Discuss the new value that is created for them by EC. How can organizations offering *e-learning opportunities* capture this value? Develop a list of examples.

8. Debate whether group members think that the customer gains more value from EC than the company. Discuss both sides of the issue of whether companies profit by the use of EC to the same extent that customers do. Support your side of the debate by providing some examples.

9. Debate: Will Facebook Places crush Foursquare in the location-based competition? Why or why not?

INTERNET EXERCISES

1. Survey several online travel agencies (e.g., **travelocity. com**, **orbitz.com**, **cheaptickets.com**, **priceline.com**, **expedia.com**, **bestfares.com**) and compare the business strategies of three of them. How do they compete against physical travel agencies?

2. Enter **digitalenterprise.org** and go to Web analytics. Read the material on Web analytics and prepare a report on the use of Web analytics for measuring advertising success.

3. Check the music CD companies on the Internet (e.g., **cduniverse.com**, **silverdisc.com**). Do any of these companies focus on specialized niche markets as a strategy?

4. Enter **ibm.com/procurement** and go to the e-procurement section. Prepare a report on how IBM's Supplier Integration Strategy can assist companies in implementing an EC strategy.

5. Compare the following search engines: **google.com**, **search.yahoo.com**, **ask.com**, and **mooter.com**. Conduct a comparative search (i.e., search for the same term at each site), learn more about how each search engine works (e.g., click on "about us" or similar link), and look for comparative articles at websites such as **search enginewatch.com**. Consider the strengths and weaknesses of each site, when one would be more useful than another, and what special features distinguish it in the

search engine marketplace. Prepare a report based on your findings.

6. One of the most global companies is Amazon.com (**amazon.com**). Find stories about its global strategies and activities (try **google.com** and **forbes.com**). What are the most important lessons you learned?

7. Visit **business.com/guides/startup** and find some of the EC opportunities available to small businesses. Also, visit the website of the Small Business Administration (SBA) office in your area. Summarize recent EC-related topics for SMEs.

8. Enter **alloy.com** and **boltagain.ning.com**. Compare the sites on functionality, ease of use, message boards, homepage layout, and so on. Prepare a report based on your findings.

9. Find out how websites such as **tradecard.com** facilitate the conduct of international trade over the Internet. Prepare a report based on your findings.

10. Conduct research on small businesses and their use of the Internet for EC. Visit sites such as **microsoft. com/smallbusiness/hub.mspx** and **uschamber. org**. Also, enter **google.com** or **yahoo.com** and type "small businesses + electronic commerce." Use your findings to write a report on current small business EC issues.

11. Enter businesscase.com and review its products. What are the benefits of case builders to people conducting e-commerce strategy development?

12. Enter languageweaver.com and locate its product for language translation for multinational corporations. Write a report.

13. Enter compete.com and identify all the services it provides, all lists, ranking, marketing performance, and competitive intelligence reports it provides. Prepare a list of the services and comment on their value to the merchants.

TEAM ASSIGNMENTS AND PROJECTS

1. **Assignment for the Opening Case**

Read the opening case and answer the following questions.

   a. List and discuss the factors that are driving Travelocity to change its e-strategy.
   b. Considering the 14 dashboards that Travelocity has already created, come up with two or three other dashboards that would be useful.
   c. Share your experiences of using Travelocity with the group and discuss the extent to which its e-strategy meets your personal needs.

2. Have three teams represent the following units of one click-and-mortar company: (1) an offline division, (2) an online division, and (3) top management. Each team member represents a different functional area within the division. The teams will develop an EC strategy in a specific industry (a group of three teams will represent a company in one industry). Teams will present their strategies to the class.

3. The relationship between manufacturers and their distributors regarding sales on the Web can be very strained. Direct sales may cut into the distributors' business. Review some of the strategies available to handle such channel conflicts. Each team member should be assigned to a company in a different industry. Study the strategies, compare and contrast them, and derive a proposed generic strategy.

4. Each team needs to find the latest information on one global EC issue (e.g., cultural, administrative, geo-graphic, economic). Each team prepares a report based on their findings.

5. Enter strassmann.com and find 10 entries related to EC strategy (including videos). Prepare summaries of them relating to this chapter.

6. Compare the services provided by Yahoo!, Microsoft, and Website Pros Inc. to SMEs in the e-commerce area. Each team should take one company and make a presentation.

7. Enter buzzle.com/editorials/9-21-2004-59556.asp and execute the three exercises related to strategic e-commerce.

Closing Case

CATCHOFTHEDAY SEIZES THE MARKET

When two brothers Garry and Hezi Leibovich started a small company operating out of their garage, little did they know that it would make them millionaires five years later. Founded in 2006, CatchOfTheDay (COTD) is modelled on the simple idea of selling a discounted product every day via online means. The concept is similar to the American website *Woot.com* but different from group buying sites such as *Groupon.com* and *LivingSocial.com*, which only offer discounts on products and services if a large group of people are willing to buy the same product. COTD also has a sister site called Scoopon, which mimics *Groupon.com*.

The Business Opportunity and Growth

Australians are shopping online more than ever before according to data collated by PricewaterhouseCoopers (PwC) and Frost & Sullivan. Revenue from online shopping increased to $13.6 billion in 2011, up more than 13 percent since 2010. This contributed to a decline in traditional sales as reported by the Australian Bureau of Statistics in 2011, which forced the downsizing of many traditional retailers who were unable to compete due to high rent and poor sales. Examples include the book-selling chain Borders and the apparel store chain Premier.

Online customers are increasingly becoming value and price conscious. It is easy for them to browse the web and compare prices and reviews of a particular product at their convenience. The uncertainty of employment and increasing household costs due to the global financial crisis also make online deals more attractive to consumers.

There has been plenty of growth in this market. In the last year more than a dozen similar online retail sites like COTD have been launched in Australia. To counter this, COTD has put several strategies in place to stay in business. In order to ensure a steady stream of products, COTD sources them from over 600 suppliers including L'Oréal, Toshiba, and Samsung (see *catchoftheday.com.au/ suppliers.php* for further details) who want to get rid of their end-of-line stock. This way it can acquire products cheaply and therefore sell them cheaply. It also pays its suppliers within 24 hours. This has been one of its key competitive advantages resulting in 109 percent growth since 2006.

However, to be successful in the online retail market one needs a good customer base. It is every online retailer's dream to have a strong and loyal customer base. A strong customer base facilitates widespread social marketing, which enables the fast spread of information about products leading to increased sales. To achieve this, COTD relies on Google and Web 2.0 tools.

Employing Web 2.0 Tools

Web 2.0 tools can quickly disseminate information forming viral marketing campaigns. COTD has a strong presence on Facebook, YouTube, Twitter, and iPhone (via an app). COTD runs quick and short social marketing campaigns through these Web 2.0 mediums to encourage strong sales (see *facebook.com/CatchAustralia*). One campaign resulted in COTD selling AUD1 million worth of Samsung TV units in an hour. It is estimated that every day over 130,000 people receive COTD's Facebook message containing the deal of the day while 250,000 people receive a push notification via their iPhone application. This excludes its 14,000 daily followers on Twitter.

In total, COTD has approximately 550,000 subscribers, and they are remarkably loyal. Eighty percent of its customers are known to visit the site four times a week. Despite this, COTD does not handle its clients personally. All communication is through e-mail.

The Results

Having a strong customer base due to its Web 2.0 presence, wide range of supplies, and cheap pricing has made COTD stand out in the Australian online retail market.

Sources: Compiled from Cain (2011), Johnston (2011), Kaplan (2011), and Lahiff (2011).

Questions

1. What makes CatchOfTheDay so successful?
2. Discuss the challenges facing CatchOfTheDay in the future.
3. Should CatchOfTheDay use other Web 2.0 tools to attract customers? If so, why?

ONLINE RESOURCES
available at pearsonglobaleditions.com/turban

Online Files

Comprehensive Educational Websites

bizauto.com/net.htm: Business Automation five-step approach to success on the Internet.

net-strat.com/portfolio.htm: Company offering website design, Internet strategy, online marketing, and search engine optimization.

monitus.com/internet.htm: Company offering Web design and Internet strategy.

sazbean.com/2008/10/06/creating-an-internet-business-strategy-implementation: Comprehensive coverage about developing an Internet strategy and implementation.

tutorialized.com/tutorials/eCommerce/Strategy/1: Tutorials on how e-commerce affects businesses, hosting packages, shopping cart software, marketing, strategies, and more.

e-commerce-digest.com/strategies.html: A detailed guide to successful online strategy and implementation.

informationweek.com/news/206902611: Seven social networking strategies for small businesses.

macnewsworld.com/story/64639.html: Article on why social networking strategies fail.

seoincreasetraffic.com/648865-Simple-Social-Networking-Strategies-to-Increase-Traffic-to-Your-Site.html: Simple social networking strategies to increase traffic to your website.

REFERENCES

Access eCommerce. "Developing Your Internet Business Plan." 2006. **access-ecom.info/section.cfm?sid=bp&%20xid=MN** (accessed March 2009).

Acclaro.com. "The 2011 Website Globalization Report Card." **acclaro.com/translation-localization-blog/the-2011-website-globalization-report-card-121** (accessed February 2011).

Akerman, E. "Amazon Is eBay's Biggest Challenge." *Maui News*, August 28, 2008.

Allviant.com. "CarePass Technology Drives Dramatic Increase in Employee Engagement in Wellness Screening Programs at Arizona State University." April 21, 2010. **allviant.com/2010/04/21/allviant-carepass-technology-drives-dramatic-increase-in-employee-engagement-in-wellness-screening-programs-at-arizona-state-university** (accessed February 2011).

Beasley, M., A. Chen, K. Nunez, and L. Wright. "Working Hand in Hand: Balanced Scorecards and Enterprise Risk Management." *Strategic Finance*, March 2008.

Cain, A. "Big Fish in a Growing Pond." *theage.com.au*, July 1, 2011. **theage.com.au/business/key-leaders/big-fish-in-a-growing-pond-20110630-1gsog.html** (accessed August 2011).

Econsultancy. "New eCommera Report Unveils Inconsistent Measurement of E-Commerce Profitability Across the Board." November 9, 2010. **econsultancy.com/us/press-releases/5274-new-ecommera-report-unveils-inconsistent-measurement-of-ecommerce-profitability-across-the-board** (accessed February 2011).

Flanagan, C. "Enterprise 2.0: It's No Field of Dreams." June 21, 2010. **cflanagan.wordpress.com/2010/06/21/enterprise-2-0-its-no-field-of-dreams** (accessed December 2010).

Gallagher, S. "Small Business Social Media—6 Steps to Success." 2010. **socialmediatoday.com/SMC/178322** (accessed December 2010).

Ghemawat, P. "Distance Still Matters: The Hard Reality of Global Expansion." *Harvard Business Review* (September 2001).

GoECart.com. "GoECart CEO Provides Social Networking Tips for Online Merchants During WGCH Radio Interview." September 28, 2010. **blog.goecart.com/index.php/goecart-ceo-provides-social-networking-tips-during-interview** (accessed February 2011).

Gold, J. E. "E-Guide: A Strategic Approach to Enabling Mobile Business Applications." Sponsored by BlackBerry. **searchmobile_computing.com** (accessed December 2010).

Gosselin, M. "Designing and Implementing a Performance Measurement System." *CMA Management*, November 2010.

Green, S. *Profit on the Web*. Auckland, New Zealand: Axon Computertime, 2002.

Hannabarger, C., F. Buchman, P. Economy, and P. Hesse-Hujber, M. *Balanced Scorecard Strategy for Dummies*. Hoboken, NJ: Wiley & Son, 2007.

Harpham, W. S. "Why OpenNotes and Access to Medical Chart Is Important." *KevinMD.com*, August 2010. **kevinmd.com/blog/2010/08/opennotes-access-medical-chart-important.html** (accessed February 2011).

HotelInteractive. "Travelocity Business Expands Reporting Suite." August 11, 2010. **hotelinteractive.com/article.aspx?articleid=17836** (accessed February 2011).

Johnston, C. "Trading Web Is Winning Big Business." *theage.com.au*, January 8, 2011. **theage.com.au/technology/technology-news/trading-web-is-winning-big-business-20110107-19iwh.html** (accessed August 2011).

Kaplan, M. "Online Discounter Catchoftheday.com.au Is Enjoying a Great Success." *The Australian*, May 1, 2010. **theaustralian.com.au/business/opinion/online-discounter-catchofthedaycomau-is-enjoying-a-great-success/story-e6frg9n6-1225860811308** (accessed August 2011).

Kaplan, R. S., and D. P. Norton. *The Balanced Scorecard: Translating Strategy into Action*. Boston: Harvard Business School Press, 1996.

Kern, T., and L. Willcocks. "Exploring Relationships in Information Technology Outsourcing: The Interaction Approach." *European Journal of Information Systems*, 11 (2002).

Keynote Competitive Research. "Airline Travel Study." 2008. **keynote.com/docs/kcr/KCR_Airlines.pdf** (accessed February 2011).

Lahiff, K. "Australians' Love Affair with Online Stores." *Switzer.com*, August 4, 2011, switzer.com.au/technology/feature/australians-love-affair-with-online-stores (accessed August 2011).

Learmonth, M. "Warner Music Group Launches Web Strategy 2.0." *Advertising Age*, October 8, 2009. adage.com/print?article_id=139539 (accessed February 2011).

Maddox, K. "Looking for Small-Business Owners? Try Advertising on Social Networks." *B2B Magazine*, June 9, 2008.

McGee, M., A. Conry-Murray, and J. Foley. "The Customer Web." *InformationWeek,* October 5, 2009.

McKinsey Quarterly. "Economic Conditions Snapshot, June 2009: McKinsey Global Survey Results." mckinsey-quarterly.com/Economic_conditions_snapshot_June_2009_McKinsey_Global_Survey_Results_2378 (accessed February 2011).

Nash, K. S. "Fresh Catch: Web Auctions Net Lost Customers for Fish Exchange." *CIO Magazine*, September 1, 2009.

OECD (Organization for Economic Cooperation and Development). Enhancing SME Competitiveness: The OECD Bologna, Italy, Ministerial Conference, 2001.

Person, R. *Balanced Scorecards and Operational Dashboards with Microsoft Excel*. Hoboken, NJ: Wiley & Sons, 2009.

Plant, R. T. *E-Commerce: Formulation of Strategy*. Upper Saddle River, NJ: Prentice Hall, 2000.

Porter, M. E. *Competitive Strategy: Techniques for Analyzing Industries and Competitors*. New York: The Free Press, 1980.

Porter, M. E. *Competitive Advantage: Creating and Sustaining Superior Performance*. New York, The Free Press, 1985.

Porter, M. E. "Strategy and the Internet." *Harvard Business Review* (March 2001).

RedOrbit.com. "Warner Music Group Announces Transition in Digital Strategy Team." February 25, 2008. redorbit.com/news/entertainment/1267802/warner_music_group_announces_transition_in_digital_strategy_team/index.html# (accessed February 2011).

Sanayei, A. (Ed.). *E-Business in Developing Countries*. London: Koros Press Ltd., 2011.

Sargent, B., and N. Kelly. *Gaining Global Presence: Common Practices from 10,000 Top Websites*. Lowell, MA: Common Sense Advisory Inc. 2010. commonsenseadvisory.com/Portals/_default/Knowledgebase/ArticleImages/101130_R_Global_Web_Presence_Preview.pdf (accessed January 2011).

Schonfeld, E. "Forrester Forecast: Online Retail Sales Will Grow by $250 Billion by 2014." *TechCrunch*, March 8, 2010. techcrunch.com/2010/03/08/forrester-forecast-online-retail-sales-will-grow-to-250-billion-by-2014 (accessed February 2011).

Shuen, A. *Web 2.0: A Strategy Guide: Business Thinking and Strategies Behind Successful Web 2.0 Implementations*. Sebastopol, CA: O'Reilly, 2008.

Smith, R. H. "The State of Small Business Report." June 16, 2010. rhsmith.umd.edu/ces/pdfs_docs/SBSI_July_2010.pdf (accessed February 2011).

Sostre, P., and J. LeClaire. *Web Analytics for Dummies*. Hoboken, NJ: Wiley & Sons, 2007.

Tjan, A. K. "Finally, a Way to Put Your Internet Portfolio in Order." *Harvard Business Review* (February 2001).

Travelocity. "Travelers Find Doing Good More Difficult with Tighter Budgets." December 22, 2008. Press release. phx.corporate-ir.net/phoenix.zhtml?c=75787& p=irol-newsArticle&ID=1238477 &highlight= (accessed January 2011).

Travelocity. "Travelocity Launches Major Fall and Holiday Travel Savings with the 'Fall for Fall' Sale." September 30, 2010. businesswire.com/news/home/20100930005308/en/Travelocity-Launches-Major-Fall-Holiday-Travel-Savings (accessed February 2011).

Ward, A. S. "5 Steps to a Successful Social Media Strategy." August 18, 2009. amysampleward.org/2009/08/18/5-steps-to-a-successful-social-media-strategy (accessed February 2011).

Wyse, B. "Ecommerce Research Findings: How Are We Measuring Online Profitability?" *Trading Intelligence Quarterly*, October 2010. scribd.com/doc/41517888/The-Trading-Intelligence-Quarterly-Issue-2 (accessed January 2011).

Yunker, J. *The 2011 Web Globalization Report Card*. Pacific Northwest: Byte Level Research LLC, 2011. bytelevel.com/reportcard2011 (accessed January 2011).

CHAPTER 13

IMPLEMENTING EC SYSTEMS: FROM JUSTIFICATION TO SUCCESSFUL PERFORMANCE

Learning Objectives

Upon completion of this chapter, you will be able to:

1. Describe the major components of EC.

2. Describe the need for justifying EC investments.

3. Understand the difficulties in measuring and justifying EC investments.

4. Recognize the difficulties in establishing intangible metrics.

5. List and describe traditional and advanced methods of justifying EC investments.

6. Describe some examples of EC justification.

7. Describe the role of economics in EC evaluation.

8. Discuss the steps in developing an EC system.

9. Describe the major EC development strategies.

10. List the various EC development methods along with their benefits and limitations.

11. Discuss the major outsourcing strategies.

12. Describe the criteria used in selecting software vendors and packages.

13. Describe EC organizational structure, business process management, and change management.

14. Understand how product, industry seller, and buyer characteristics impact the success of EC.

Content

VODAFONE ESSAR OF INDIA

Vodafone Essar is a subsidiary of Vodafone Group Plc., a global mobile telephony company. Vodafone Essar operates in India, and in February 2011 it had about 131 million subscribers, about 23 percent of India's total mobile base, and was growing at 25 to 30 percent annually. The company needed an enabled Web platform to provide EC services to customers, employees, and partners.

The Problem

The rapid growth of the company, the size of the country served, the large number of subscribers, and the intense competition in the mobile telecommunications industry forced the company to develop a superb communication system with its customers and business partners. The old Web presence (static, HTML pages) was inadequate. A study pointed to a need for an e-commerce-enabled interactive portal that would care for customers, employees, and partners. The requirements of this EC application were many and diversified, since the company wanted to offer new services that would provide competitive advantage. The need for more functionality, speed, ease of use, and so forth became a necessity as well as the need for quick implementation of any attempted solution.

The project was a very large-scale one since it required robustness, scalability, high availability, flexibility, and security. Also integration with back-end systems was needed to facilitate order fulfillment.

The company wanted to revamp its website, envisioning a Web portal that could enhance its website and extend value-added service functionalities on the Web; integrate with the telecommunication systems to offer content optimized for mobile phones; and integrate with the B2B extranet and/or its partners' websites. E-commerce functionality was an integral and integrated part of this service enablement and customer-care goals.

There was no formal justification for needing the portal and no quantitative analysis. Competitive and market forces and the rapid growth were considered qualitatively in the decision to undertake the project.

The Solution

Since the company's IT team was unable to build such a project by themselves in time, the company decided to outsource the system development. The company contacted three leading vendors. Discussions with all three companies, proposals to meet the needs rapidly, integration considerations, reputation of the vendors and their employees, and more factors were weighted in the vendor selection process. Furthermore, a mapping of the system requirements against the vendors' product offering was also done. The winner was Microsoft.

The solution implemented by the Microsoft team was a customer-focused, e-commerce-enabled Internet platform that is flexible enough to grow with the rapid growth of the company's business. The platform enables self-care by customers—they are able to buy services, download content, and transact with Vodafone on their own. The solution also integrates seamlessly with the company's mobile platform and with hosted services and external service providers—a strategic direction of the corporation's "Software as a Service" (SaaS) initiative.

The portal's back end was based on Microsoft Customer Care Framework (CCF) 2006, Microsoft Office SharePoint Server 2007, and Microsoft Commerce Server 2007. The middle tier utilized SQL Server 2008 and Microsoft Connected Services Framework 3.0. The portal interfaces with Vodafone's line-of-business applications, which provides for service-oriented architecture (SOA).

Microsoft Office SharePoint Server 2007 provides advantages such as comprehensive content management and enterprise search, accelerating shared business processes,

and it facilitates information-sharing across the organization's boundaries. Commerce Server 2007 enables the creation of full-featured Web business applications, extension of business across communication networks, and integration of e-commerce solutions within the existing IT infrastructure.

Microsoft Customer Care Framework (CCF) is an enterprise software solution for contact and self-care centers that delivers a unified corporate agent desktop system that consolidates data from core business systems such as billing, CRM, and order management applications to the customer service agent desktop. CCF enables dramatic improvements in the contact centers' efficiency by delivering an improved, consistent customer experience.

The platform promises high availability, security, performance efficiency, and faster deployment of new services. Partner management is more efficient; and third-party applications and services can be acquired and integrated quickly. It has support for multiple end-user devices, such as desktops, mobile phones, Xbox, or Zune.

Implementation took about 6 months. Given the scale of the project, it could have taken double that time in other organizations. This speed was the result of superb planning and the expertise of the corporate IT team and the Microsoft experts.

The first phase of the solution enables a high-end and feature-rich corporate website for Vodafone. Customers can register themselves, log in, browse the catalogs of value-added services and order or download their choices, pay their bills, and manage their subscriptions. New connections can also be bought via the portal. The portal supports third-party payment gateways from multiple providers to provide flexibility in payment and billing mechanisms. The portal houses other business applications as well. For instance, prospective employees can upload their résumés for Vodafone's HR team. For partners, the portal acts as a publishing platform. They can view their transaction and billing details and access Vodafone's CRM.

In the second phase, the mobile platform was integrated with the extranet network and portal. This enables the availability of e-commerce services on mobile phones; business partner employees can use their mobile phones for nearly all the transactions that they can perform on the offline Web portal.

The Results

The portal offers a secure and user-friendly platform and good response time. All the functionalities that were desired are fully supported. About 12 million subscribers regularly used the portal as of 2009.

Specifically, the portal provides five benefits:

1. **Robustness, scalability, and security.** The robustness and performance efficiency of the portal translates to higher consumer satisfaction. The portal provides high availability for all services; assures a highly secure environment for user registration, e-commerce transactions, and subscription management; and is scalable to meet the growing needs of Vodafone, as it foresees exponential future growth.

2. **E-commerce customer support.** The support for e-commerce transactions (the biggest factor in deciding to rebuild the portal) enables flexible payment mechanisms and value-added services in an easy-to-use, user-friendly format.

3. **Integration with other applications.** The portal integrates seamlessly with Microsoft products and applications and content that Vodafone uses in other applications; thus, Vodafone's partners can easily use the portal interface to access those applications.

4. **Good response time.** The portal enables users to conduct transactions quickly.

5. **Reduced time-to-market.** The platform enables Vodafone to create and deploy new services quickly. Third-party or hosted applications and services can also be acquired and integrated in a short period of time.

In 2009, Vodafone was voted as the most admired marketer in India in a country-wide survey.

Sources: Compiled from Microsoft (2008), *vodafone./pages/index.aspx,* and *en.wikipedia.org/wiki/Vodafone_Essar* (both accessed March 2011).

WHAT WE CAN LEARN . . .

Many organizations need to replace manual or outdated computerized systems with a Web-based EC one, which is exactly what happened to Vodafone Essar. The first step was to envision the new system and its capabilities and to justify it. Justification can be quantitative and/or qualitative. In this case, there was a strategic need to do so, and the justification was qualitative due to the intangible benefits and the competitive need. This is usually the first step in developing EC systems as described first in this chapter.

From this point on, Vodafone followed a typical EC development process, which is described later in this chapter. The major activities, after the EC requirements were articulated, were: selecting a vendor to plan and implement the EC. (Most organizations today, use vendor(s) for at least some of the development activities). Next, Vodafone selected the system components and the development tools from the vendor. A joint vendor-company team was established to manage the implementation. Once the system was completed, its success was measured. The process described in this case is suitable to a large company that needed B2C and B2B capabilities on a large scale. This chapter also presents several alternative development options that can be fitted to different companies including SMEs, under different circumstances.

13.1 THE IMPLEMENTATION LANDSCAPE

Now that you know all about e-commerce benefits and applications, you wonder what to do next. Now is the time you should ask yourself: "Do I need it?" and "How am I going to do it?" The answers to these two questions can be very complex, since they depend on many factors that we will discuss in this chapter. We refer to these factors as *implementation factors*.

THE MAJOR IMPLEMENTATION FACTORS

Many factors may determine the need and success of e-commerce projects. We organize them in the following categories.

Justification/Economics

The first issue is to find out if you need to get involved in EC project(s). This issue can be very complex for large-scale projects. We call it EC project justification. This issue is covered in Sections 13.2 through 13.6.

Acquire or Develop Your E-Commerce System

This issue is not simple either, especially when medium- and large-scale projects are involved. We cover this issue in Sections 13.7 through 13.9.

Organizational Readiness and Impacts of E-Commerce

How to organize your EC unit within the organization and how to deal with changing business processes and other changes brought by e-commerce are all part of the implementation considerations. In addition, potential impacts on marketing, manufacturing and people need to be addressed. Also, some technical issues such as connecting to other information systems need to be considered. These are all described in Section 13.10.

How to Succeed?

The last part of this chapter (Section 13.11) deals with some of the critical success factors of implementing EC projects.

We organized these factors in a framework, which is shown in Exhibit 13.1.

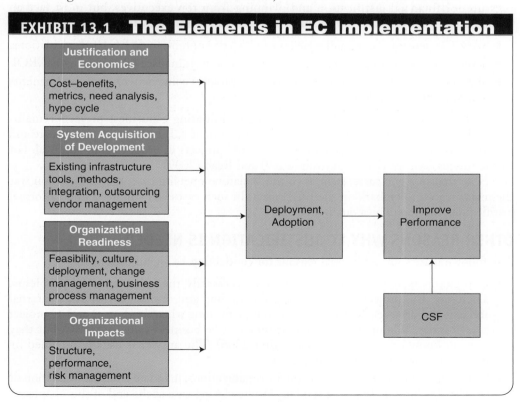

EXHIBIT 13.1 The Elements in EC Implementation

- **Justification and Economics**
  Cost–benefits, metrics, need analysis, hype cycle

- **System Acquisition of Development**
  Existing infrastructure tools, methods, integration, outsourcing vendor management

- **Organizational Readiness**
  Feasibility, culture, deployment, change management, business process management

- **Organizational Impacts**
  Structure, performance, risk management

→ Deployment, Adoption → Improve Performance ← CSF

On the left side of the exhibit we placed the major factors that impact implementation. They all may affect the adoption and deployment of the EC projects. A successful deployment and adoption will lead to improved performance.

Section 13.1 ❯ REVIEW QUESTIONS

1. Why is the implementation of EC so complex?
2. What are the major elements of EC implementation? (Consult Exhibit 13.1.)
3. What factors determine deployment and adoption? (Consult Exhibit 13.1.)

13.2 WHY JUSTIFY E-COMMERCE INVESTMENTS? HOW CAN THEY BE JUSTIFIED?

Companies need to justify their EC investments for a number of different reasons.

INCREASED PRESSURE FOR FINANCIAL JUSTIFICATION

Once upon a time, or so the story goes, the beggars of New York City decided to conduct a competition as to who could collect the most money in one day. Many innovative ideas were employed, and several beggars collected almost $1,000 each. The winner, however, collected $5 million. When asked how he did it, the beggar replied: "I made a sign that said 'EC experts need funding for an innovative electronic marketplace' and put the sign in front of the New York Stock Exchange."

This story symbolizes what happened from 1995 through 2000, when EC projects and start-up companies were funded with little or no analysis of their business viability or finances. The result of the rush to invest was the 2001 to 2003 "dot-com bust," when hundreds of EC start-ups went out of business and the stock market crashed. Some companies and individual investors lost more than 90 to 100 percent of their investments! Furthermore, many companies, even large ones such as Disney, Merrill Lynch, and Sears, terminated EC projects after losing considerable amounts of money and realizing few benefits from huge investments. The positive result of the crash was the "back-to-basics" movement, namely, a return to carefully checking and scrutinizing any request for EC funding.

Today, companies are holding the line on IT and EC budgets. IT executives feel the pressure for financial justification and planning from top executives, but most face an uphill battle to address this new accountability, as demonstrated by the following statistics:

❯ Sixty-five percent of companies lack the knowledge or tools to do EC ROI calculations.
❯ Seventy-five percent have no formal processes or budgets in place for measuring EC ROI.
❯ Sixty-eight percent do not measure how EC projects coincide with promised benefits 6 months after completion.

At the same time, demand for expanding or initiating e-business projects remains strong. In order to achieve the optimal level of investment, CIOs will need to calculate and effectively communicate the value of proposed EC projects in order to gain approval. For further discussion, see Keen and Joshi (2009) and Read (2009).

Note that in some cases, such as in the Vodafone opening case, the competition was the major reason to embark on the EC project. In such cases you still need to do a formal justification, but it will be a qualitative one.

OTHER REASONS WHY EC JUSTIFICATION IS NEEDED

The following are some additional reasons for conducting EC justification:

❯ Companies now realize that EC is not necessarily the solution to all problems. Therefore, EC projects must compete for funding and resources with other internal and external projects. Analysis is needed to determine when funding of an EC project is appropriate. Companies know that they receive business value from EC, but they want to know *how much value* (see Alter 2006). The answer is usually provided by ROI, which we discuss in Section 13.4.
❯ Some large companies, and many public organizations, mandate a formal evaluation of requests for funding (e.g., see the Del Monte closing case at the end of this chapter).

> Companies are required to assess the success of EC projects after completion and later, on a periodic basis.

> The success of EC projects may be assessed in order to pay bonuses to those involved with the project.

Reasons for IT and EC justification reported by *CIO Insight* (2004) are as follows: pressure from top management, internal competition for funding, the large amount of money involved (if relevant), and weak business conditions. The same study found that justification forces EC and IT into better alignment with the corporate business strategy. Finally, justification increases the credibility of EC projects. Similar reasons exist for justifying new EC start-ups.

EC INVESTMENT CATEGORIES AND BENEFITS

Before we look at how to justify EC investments, let's examine the nature of such investments. One basic way to categorize different EC investments is to distinguish between investment in infrastructure and investment in specific EC applications.

IT infrastructure provides the foundation for EC applications in the enterprise. IT infrastructure includes servers, intranets, extranets, data centers, data warehouses, knowledge bases, etc. In addition there is a necessity to integrate with many applications throughout the enterprise that share the infrastructure. Infrastructure investments are made for the long term.

EC applications are specific projects and programs for achieving certain objectives—for example, the Vodafone portal is taking customer orders online and providing e-procurement. The number of EC applications can be large. They may be in one functional department or several departments may share them, which makes assessment of their costs and benefits more complex.

The major reasons that companies invest in IT and EC are to improve business processes, lower costs, increase productivity, increase customer satisfaction and retention, increase revenue and market share, reduce time-to-market, and gain a competitive advantage.

HOW IS AN EC INVESTMENT JUSTIFIED?

Justifying an EC investment means comparing the costs of each project against its benefits in what is known as a **cost–benefit analysis**. To conduct such an analysis, it is necessary to define and measure the relevant EC benefits and costs. Cost–benefit analysis is frequently assessed by *return on investment (ROI)*, which is also the name of a specific method for evaluating investments.

cost–benefit analysis
A comparison of the costs of a project against the benefits.

A number of different methods are available to measure the *business value* of EC and IT investments. Traditional methods that support such analyses are *net present value (NPV)* and ROI (see Online File W13.1).

Cost–Benefit Analysis and the Business Case

The cost–benefit analysis and the business value are part of a *business case* (see Online Chapter 15). Several vendors provide templates, tools, guidelines, and more for preparing the business case in specific areas. For example, itbusinessedge.com provides an SOA Business Case Resource Kit (the templates are in Microsoft Word). ROI is calculated with Excel's templates (see itbusinessedge.com/premiumtools/0069-soabizcase-0002.aspx). For further details, see Online Chapter 15.

WHAT NEEDS TO BE JUSTIFIED? WHEN SHOULD JUSTIFICATION TAKE PLACE?

Not all EC investments need to be formally justified. In some cases, a simple one-page qualitative justification will do. The following are cases where formal evaluation may not be needed:

> When the value of the investment is relatively small for the organization

> When the relevant data are not available, are inaccurate, or are too volatile

> When the EC project is mandated—*it must* be done regardless of the costs involved (e.g., as in the opening case)

However, even when formal analysis is not required, an organization should conduct at least some qualitative analysis to explain the logic of investing in the EC project.

USING METRICS IN EC JUSTIFICATION

metric
A specific, measurable standard against which actual performance is compared.

A **metric** is a specific, measurable standard against which actual performance is compared. Metrics are used to describe costs, benefits, or the ratio between them. They are used not only for justification but also for other economic activities (e.g., to compare employee performance in order to reward specific employees). Metrics can produce very positive results in organizations by driving behavior in a number of ways. Metrics can:

> ▶ Be the basis for specific goals and plans.
> ▶ Define the value proposition of business models (Chapter 1).
> ▶ Communicate a business strategy to the workforce through performance targets.
> ▶ Increase accountability when metrics are linked with performance appraisal programs and rewards.
> ▶ Align the objectives of individuals, departments, and divisions to the enterprise's strategic objectives.
> ▶ Track the performance of EC systems, including usage, types of visitors, page visits, conversion rate, and so forth.
> ▶ Assess the health of companies by using tools such as balanced scorecards and performance dashboards (see Person 2009).

EC metrics can be tangible or intangible; see Exhibit 13.2 for examples.

Metrics, Measurements, and Key Performance Indicators

Metrics need to be defined properly with a clear way to measure them. For example, revenue growth can be measured in total dollars, in percentage change over time, or in percentage growth as compared to that of the entire industry. *Cost avoidance*, for example, can be achieved in many ways, one of which may be "decrease obsolete stock write-offs as percentage of revenue." Defining the specific measures is critical; otherwise, what the metrics actually measure may be open to interpretation. Exhibit 13.3 shows the process of using metrics. The cyclical process begins with setting up goals and objectives for organizational and EC performance, which is then expressed by a set of metrics. The

key performance indicators (KPIs)
The quantitative expression of critically important metrics.

metrics are expressed by a set of **key performance indicators (KPIs)**, which are the quantitative expression of critically important metrics (known as *critical success factors*). Metrics that deal directly with organizational performance and the contribution of EC to such performance are used frequently, and often one metric has several KPIs.

The KPIs are continuously monitored by the organization, (e.g., via Web analytics, financial reports, marketing data, and so forth. As shown in Exhibit 13.3, the KPIs that reflect actual performance are compared to the desired KPIs and planned metrics. If a gap exists, corrective actions take place and then goals, objectives, and metrics are adjusted up or down.

Examples. In Australia, the government of Victoria is one of the leaders in exploiting the Internet to provide a one-stop service center called "Do It Online." It employs many metrics (see vic.gov.au). In the United States, CA.gov (my.ca.gov) offers many services for the citizens of California. In both cases, the metrics of "travel" and "wait time" for citizens who would otherwise have to visit a physical office was used in justifying offering the EC service of renewing driver's licenses.

Another example of metrics is shown in the *balanced scorecard method* (see Chapter 12 and en.wikipedia.org/wiki/balanced_scorecard). This method uses four types of metrics: *customer*, *financial*, *internal businesses processes*, and *learning growth* (see Person 2009).

We limit our discussion here mainly to individual EC projects or initiatives. EC projects deal most often with the automation of business processes, and as such, they can be viewed as capital investment decisions. Online Chapter 15 discusses investment in a start-up company.

EXHIBIT 13.2 Sample EC Metrics for Various Entities of Users

EC User	Tangible Metrics	Intangible Metrics
Buyer (B2C)	• Cost/price of the product • Time in executing the transaction • Number of available alternatives	• Ease of use of EC • Convenience in purchasing • Information availability • Reliability of the transaction • Privacy of personal data
Seller (B2C)	• Profit per customer • Conversion rate of visitors • Customer retention rate • Inventory costs • Profit per item sold • Market share	• Customer satisfaction • Customer loyalty • Transaction security
Net-enhanced organization (B2B)	• From design-to-market (time) • Cash-to-cash cycle • Percentage of orders delivered on time or early • Profit per item sold	• Flexibility in changing purchase orders • Agility to sustain unplanned production increase • Risk reduction • Improved quality of products/services
Government (G2C)	• Reduction in cost of transactions • Reduction in licensing fees • Increase in participation in government programs • Lower tax rates	• Citizen satisfaction • Reelection of candidates • Choice of interacting with elected officials • Promoting democratic principles • Disseminating more information quickly

Additional Examples of Measurements Made with Metrics

- More than one-third of consumers use the same password for online banking as they do for other online activities.
- More than 50 brands were targeted by phishing scams in November 2004.
- More than half of consumers say they are less likely to respond to an e-mail from their bank because of phishing threats.
- Experts say that 80 percent of the infrastructures of large industries are likely to be hit by cyber attacks.
- Some consumers of financial products say phishing has turned them away from Web transactions.
- Consumers are slightly more likely to receive permission-based e-mails from online merchants than other retail businesses.
- Two-thirds of computers have spyware on them.
- Spam messages are considerably shorter than legitimate e-mails.
- EBay tops the list of online destinations on Black Friday (the day after Thanksgiving).
- Spam takes up volume, but not bandwidth.

Sources: Compiled from *cio.com/topic/1406/Metrics* (accessed December 2004–March 2009) and Borenstein, et al. (2005).

There are many tools that help in the performance monitoring and measurement of e-commerce and the application of metrics (as shown in Exhibit 13.3). One of the most useful tools for EC is Web analytics, which was briefly introduced in Chapter 12. Web analytics is closely related to metrics (e.g., via Google Analytics, see Clifton 2010).

Web Analytics

Web analytics is the measurement, collection, analysis, and reporting of Internet data for purposes of understanding and optimizing Web usage. Web analytics is not just a tool for measuring website traffic; it can be used as a tool for EC market research as well as for performance evaluation. Web analytics applications can also help companies measure the results of traditional print advertising campaigns. It helps one estimate how the traffic to

Web analytics
(1) The analysis of click-stream data to understand visitor behavior on a website. (2) The measurement, collection, analysis, and reporting of Internet data for the purposes of understanding and optimizing Web usage.

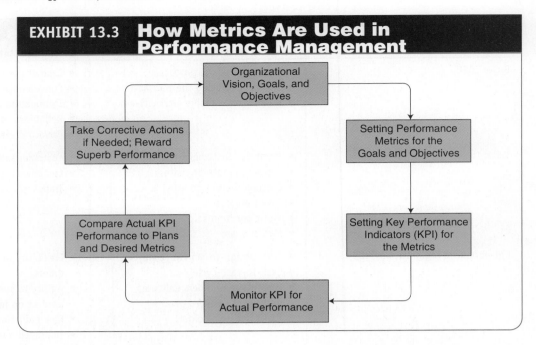

EXHIBIT 13.3 How Metrics Are Used in Performance Management

the website changed after the launch of an EC-based advertising campaign. Web analytics provides data on the number of visitors, page views, etc., to gauge the traffic and popularity trends that help in doing the market research. Similarly, the technology can be used to measure website performance prior to the introduction of EC projects and then compare it for results of a pilot EC project. For additional information, see en.wikipedia.org/Web_analytics and Kaushik (2009).

Now that we understand the need for conducting EC justification and the use of metrics, let's see why EC justification is so difficult to accomplish.

Section 13.2 ▶ REVIEW QUESTIONS

1. List some of the reasons for justifying an EC investment.
2. Describe the risks of not conducting an EC justification study.
3. Describe how an EC investment is justified.
4. List the major EC investment categories.
5. When is justification of EC investments unnecessary?
6. What are metrics? What benefits do they offer?
7. Describe KPI.
8. Describe the cyclical use of metrics as it relates to organizational performance.
9. What is Web analytics, and what role does it play in the justification of EC projects?

13.3 DIFFICULTIES IN MEASURING AND JUSTIFYING E-COMMERCE INVESTMENTS

Justifying EC (and IT) projects can be a complex and, therefore, difficult process. Let's see why.

THE EC JUSTIFICATION PROCESS

The EC justification process varies depending on the situation and the methods used. However, in its extreme, it can be very complex. As shown in Exhibit 13.4, five areas must be considered in the justification of IT projects. In this section, we discuss the intangible and tangible areas. In Chapter 12, we discussed some strategic and tactical considerations.

In addition to the complex process, one may face other difficulties in conducting justifications.

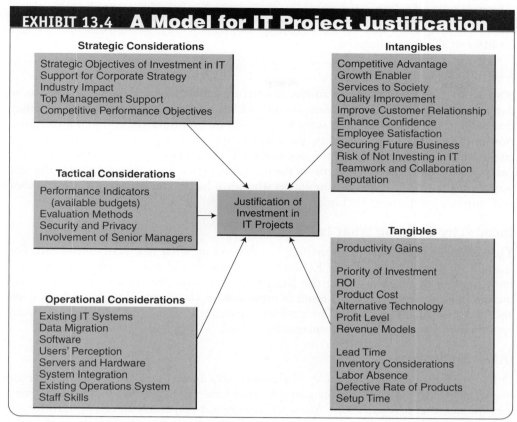

EXHIBIT 13.4   A Model for IT Project Justification

Strategic Considerations

Strategic Objectives of Investment in IT
Support for Corporate Strategy
Industry Impact
Top Management Support
Competitive Performance Objectives

Intangibles

Competitive Advantage
Growth Enabler
Services to Society
Quality Improvement
Improve Customer Relationship
Enhance Confidence
Employee Satisfaction
Securing Future Business
Risk of Not Investing in IT
Teamwork and Collaboration
Reputation

Tactical Considerations

Performance Indicators
   (available budgets)
Evaluation Methods
Security and Privacy
Involvement of Senior Managers

Justification of Investment in IT Projects

Tangibles

Productivity Gains

Priority of Investment
ROI
Product Cost
Alternative Technology
Profit Level
Revenue Models

Lead Time
Inventory Considerations
Labor Absence
Defective Rate of Products
Setup Time

Operational Considerations

Existing IT Systems
Data Migration
Software
Users' Perception
Servers and Hardware
System Integration
Existing Operations System
Staff Skills

Sources: Compiled from *International Journal of Information Management*, March 2001; A. Gunasekaran, P. Love, F. Rahimi, and R. Miele. "A Model for Investment Justification in Information Technology Projects," and P. Misra. "Evolution of the Philosophy of Investments in IT Projects." *Issues in Informing Sciences and Information Technology*, 3 (2006).

DIFFICULTIES IN MEASURING PRODUCTIVITY AND PERFORMANCE GAINS

One of the major benefits of using EC is increased productivity. However, productivity increases may be difficult to measure for a number of different reasons.

Data and Analysis Issues

Data, or the analysis of the data, may hide productivity gains. Why is this so? For manufacturing, it is fairly easy to measure outputs and inputs. For example, Toyota produces motor vehicles—a relatively well-defined product that shows gradual quality changes over time. It is not difficult to identify the inputs used to produce these vehicles with reasonable accuracy. However, in service industries, such as finance or health care delivery, it is more difficult to define what the products are, how they change in quality, and how they may be related to corresponding benefits and costs.

For example, banks now use EC to handle a large portion of deposit and withdrawal transactions through ATMs. The ability to withdraw cash from ATMs 24/7 is a substantial benefit for customers compared to the limited hours of the physical branch. But, what is the value of this to the bank in comparison with the associated costs? If the incremental value exceeds the incremental costs, then it represents a productivity gain; otherwise, the productivity impact is negative.

EC Productivity Gains in One Area May Be Offset by Losses in Other Areas

Another possible difficulty is that EC gains in certain areas of the company may be offset by losses in other areas. For example, increased online sales may decrease offline sales, a situation known as *cannibalism*. Or consider the situation where an organization installs a new EC system that makes it possible to increase output per employee. If the organization reduces its production staff but has to increase its IT staff, the productivity gains from EC could be small, or even negative.

Hidden Costs and Benefits

Some costs and benefits are less visible, or even are completely hidden. These need to be determined and considered. Examples of hidden costs or benefits include currency fluctuations; the need to upgrade software or hardware over time; the cost of underestimation or overestimation of benefits; the cost of supporting changes; the cost of paying employees who were forced to retire due to the EC project (e.g., pension, health care); the cost of headcount reduction; the cost of the transition period for employees used to the "old way"; and the cost of displaced employees who leave before the EC project is completed and temporary employees are hired.

Incorrectly Defining What Is Measured

The results of any investment justification depend on what is actually measured. For example, to assess the benefits of EC investment, one should usually look at productivity improvement in the area where the EC project was installed. However, productivity increase may not necessarily be a result of profitable improvements (e.g., due to large costs and/or losses in other areas). The problem of definitions can be overcome by using appropriate metrics and key performance indicators.

Other Difficulties

Other performance measurement difficulties also have been noted. A number of researchers have pointed out, for example, that time lags may throw off productivity measurements (e.g., Misra 2006). Many EC investments, especially those in e-CRM, take 5 to 6 years to show significant positive results, but many studies do not wait that long to measure productivity changes. For a list of other factors that impact performance, see Devaraj and Kohli (2002).

RELATING EC AND IT EXPENDITURES TO ORGANIZATIONAL PERFORMANCE

Exhibit 13.5 shows some of the difficulties in finding the relationship between EC investment and organizational performance. The exhibit shows that the relationship between investment and performance is indirect; factors such as shared EC and IT assets and how they are used can impact organizational performance and make it difficult to assess the value of an IT (or EC) investment.

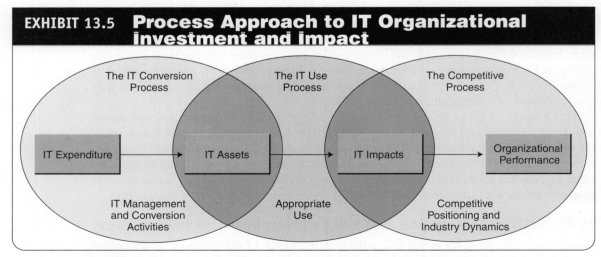

EXHIBIT 13.5 Process Approach to IT Organizational Investment and Impact

The IT Conversion Process — The IT Use Process — The Competitive Process

IT Expenditure → IT Assets → IT Impacts → Organizational Performance

IT Management and Conversion Activities — Appropriate Use — Competitive Positioning and Industry Dynamics

Source: C. Soh and L. M. Markus, "How IT Creates Business Value: A Process Theory Synthesis," *Proceedings of the 16th International Conference on Information System*, Amsterdam, December 1995. Used with permission of the authors.

Furthermore, changes in organizational performance may occur years after installing an EC application. Thus, proper evaluation must be done over the entire life cycle of the system. Unfortunately, the duration of the life cycle is usually not known. This requires forecasting, which may be difficult. In EC, it is even more difficult because investors often require that risky and fast-changing EC systems pay for themselves within 3 to 5 years. For further discussion, see Keystone Strategy, Inc. (2006). For difficulties in measuring intangible costs and benefits, see Online File W13.2.

In many cases, EC projects generate intangible benefits, such as faster time-to-market, increased employee and customer satisfaction, easier distribution, greater organizational agility, and improved control. These are very desirable benefits, but it is difficult to place an accurate monetary value on them. For example, many people would agree that e-mail improves communications, but it is not at all clear how to measure the value of this improvement. Managers are very conscious of the bottom line, but no manager can prove that e-mail is responsible for so many cents per share of the organization's total profits.

INTANGIBLE COSTS AND BENEFITS

Broadly speaking, EC costs and benefits can be classified into two categories: tangible and intangible. *Tangible* costs and benefits are easier to measure. For example, the cost of software (cost) and the amount of labor saved (benefit) are easy to determine. *Intangible* costs and benefits are usually more difficult to measure.

Tangible Costs and Benefits

The costs involved in purchasing hardware, software, consulting, and support services usually are tangible, as are the costs of telecommunication services, maintenance, and labor. These costs can be measured through accounting information systems (e.g., from the general ledger). Similarly, tangible benefits, including increased profitability, improved productivity, and greater market share, can be measured with relative ease.

Intangible Costs and Benefits

When it comes to *intangible* costs and benefits, organizations must develop innovative metrics to track these as accurately as possible. Intangible costs may include some vague cost such as that of the learning curve of the firm's customer service employees to incorporate an EC system to respond to customer inquiries. Another intangible cost may involve having to change or adapt certain business processes or information systems, such as processing items returned by customers or building and operating an inventory tracking system. An additional difficulty is separating EC costs from the costs of routine maintenance of inventory and other relevant IT systems.

An analyst could ignore intangible benefits, but doing so implies that their value is zero, which may lead an organization to reject EC investments that could indirectly increase revenues and profitability. Therefore, it is necessary to consider intangible benefits in a way that reflects their potential impact. The question is how to do it (see Hubbard 2007).

Handling Intangible Benefits

The first step in dealing with intangible benefits is to define them and, if possible, specify how they are going to be measured.

The most straightforward solution to the problem of evaluating intangible benefits in cost–benefit analysis is to make *rough estimates* of the monetary values of all the intangible benefits and then conduct an ROI or similar financial analysis. The simplicity of this approach is attractive, but in many cases the simplification assumptions used in these estimates are debatable. If an organization acquires the EC technology because decision makers assigned too high a value to intangible benefits, the organization could find that it has wasted some valuable resources. On the other hand, if the valuation of intangible benefits is too low, the organization may reject the EC investment and later find itself losing market share to competitors who did implement the technology.

Intangible costs and benefits may be approached in a number of different ways. Several of the methods presented in Section 13.4 also can be used to evaluate intangible benefits. For more on intangible costs and benefits, see Online File W13.2.

One way to deal with intangible benefits is to develop a balanced scorecard (Chapter 12) for the proposal investment. This approach requires listing both tangible and intangible goals and their measures. For an example of how this works, see Person (2009).

THE PROCESS OF JUSTIFYING EC AND IT PROJECTS

Justifying large-scale investments is not only about selecting a method; it is also about how to execute it. The appropriate process is not simple. The major steps of this process, according to *Baseline* (2006) and the authors' experience are:

> ▶ Lay an appropriate foundation for analysis with your vendor, and then conduct your ROI.
> ▶ Conduct a good research on metrics (including internal and external metrics) and validate them.
> ▶ Justify and document the cost and benefit assumptions.
> ▶ Document and verify all figures used in the calculation. Clarify all assumptions.
> ▶ Do not leave out strategic benefits, including long-term ones. Is the project really bolstering the company's competitive and strategic advantage?
> ▶ Be careful not to underestimate cost and overestimate benefits (a tendency of many managers).
> ▶ Make figures as realistic as possible and include risk analysis.
> ▶ Commit all partners, including vendors and top management.

These difficulties cause many companies not to measure the value of IT and EC projects (Alter 2006). This can be a risky approach. For those companies that like to try a formal justification, we present a number of methods in Sections 13.4 and 13.5.

THE USE OF GARTNER'S HYPE CYCLE

Before we introduce the specific methods used in justification, we present the concept of the hype cycle. Organizations can use this topic to assess specific EC technologies and tools so they can develop a strategy before they invest efforts and money in cost–benefit and justification.

What Is Gartner's Hype Cycle?

hype cycle
A graphic representation of the maturity, adoption, and social application of specific IT tools.

A **hype cycle** is a graphic representation of the maturity, adoption, and social application of specific IT tools. The term was coined by Gartner Inc. The hype cycle provides a snapshot of the relative maturity of different categories of technologies, IT methodologies, and management-related disciplines. They highlight overhyped areas versus those technologies that are high impact, and provide estimates of how long technologies and trends will take to reach maturity.

Each hype cycle has five stages that reflect the basic adoption path any technology follows, starting with a trigger point, through overblown hype, and then enduring disillusionment, before finally becoming more mainstream and accepted. The five stages are:

1. **Technology trigger.** A breakthrough, public demonstration, product launch, or other event that generates significant media and industry interest.
2. **Peak of inflated expectations.** A phase of overenthusiasm and unrealistic projections during which a flurry of publicized activity by technology leaders may result in

some successes but more failures as the technology is pushed to its limits. The only enterprises making money at this stage are conference organizers, consultants, and magazine publishers.

3. **Trough of disillusionment.** The point at which the technology becomes unfashionable and the media abandons the topic, because the technology did not live up to its inflated expectations.

4. **Slope of enlightenment.** Focused experimentation and solid hard work by an increasingly diverse range of organizations lead to a true understanding of the technology's applicability, risks, and benefits. Commercial off-the-shelf methodologies and tools become available to ease the development process.

5. **Plateau of productivity.** The real-world benefits of the technology are demonstrated and accepted. Tools and methodologies are increasingly stable as they enter their second and third generation. The final height of the plateau varies according to whether the technology is broadly applicable or benefits only a niche market.

Application of the Hype Cycle

Gartner Inc. provides an annual report that covers about 80 different hype cycles evaluating over 1,800 different technologies across 75 industries. For information including a video, see gartner.com/it/page.jsp?id=1447613. Of course, Gartner charges for providing its reports, which include technology trends. The 2009 and 2010 reports cover many EC technologies such as mobile commerce and devices, microblogging, green IT in data centers, social analytics, cloud computing, context-aware computing, virtual worlds, location-based applications, security, RFID, video telepresence, and collective intelligence.

An example of how EC technologies are placed in August 2010 on the hype cycle is available at gartner.com/it/page.jsp?id=1447613. The site provides an interesting discussion on several emerging EC technologies. Examination of the hype cycle can be useful to any organization that seriously considers the emerging tools of e-commerce.

Section 13.3 ❭ REVIEW QUESTIONS

1. How do organizations measure performance and productivity? What are the difficulties in measuring performance and productivity?

2. Why is it difficult to relate EC (IT) investments to organizational performance? List the major reasons.

3. Define tangible costs and benefits.

4. Define intangible costs and benefits and explain why they must be considered when justifying an IT investment.

5. How should management handle the intangibles and uncertainties of benefits?

6. Define hype cycle and describe its five stages.

7. Describe how the hype cycle is used in e-commerce.

13.4 METHODS AND TOOLS FOR EVALUATING AND JUSTIFYING E-COMMERCE INVESTMENTS

At their core, all economic justification approaches attempt to account for the costs and benefits of investments. They differ in their ability to account for the tangible and intangible costs and benefits of EC, particularly when compared to other corporate investments.

OPPORTUNITIES AND REVENUE GENERATED BY EC INVESTMENT

In preparing the business case for EC investment, as we will describe later, one should examine the potential *additional revenues* created by the EC investments. Chapter 1 presented the typical revenue models generated by EC and the Web. Additional examples are:

> ▶ Companies that allow people to play games for a fee, or watch a sports competition in real time for a fee (e.g., see espn.com)
> ▶ Increased revenues via products or services from a larger global market because of more effective product marketing on the Web
> ▶ Increased margins attained by using processes with lower cost
> ▶ Increased revenues as a consequence of becoming an online portal
> ▶ Increased value-added content from selling searches, access to data, and electronic documents
> ▶ Commission generated from affiliated marketing

Companies use commercially available tools or develop in-house tools. And as with the economic justification of non-EC investments, a number of different methods can be applied to EC investments.

METHODOLOGICAL ASPECTS OF JUSTIFYING EC INVESTMENTS

Before presenting the specific methods for EC justification, let's examine one methodological issue that is common to most of these methods.

Types of Costs

Although costs may appear to be the simple side of a cost–benefit analysis, they may be fairly complex at times. Here are a few things to consider:

> ▶ **Distinguish between initial (up-front) costs and operating costs.** The initial costs may be a one-time investment or they may spread over several months or years. In addition, system operating costs needs to be considered.
> ▶ **Direct and indirect shared costs.** Direct costs can be related directly to a specific project. Indirect costs usually are shared infrastructure-related costs. In addition, the costs may be related to several EC and IT projects. Therefore, one needs to allocate these costs to the specific projects. Such allocation may not be easy to perform; a number of approaches to cost allocation are available (consult an accountant).
> ▶ **In-kind costs.** Although it is easy to track monetary payments, costs also may be in kind; for example, contributions of a manager, contribution of machine time, and so on. These frequently are indirect shared costs (e.g., overhead), which complicates their calculation.

TRADITIONAL METHODS FOR EVALUATING EC INVESTMENTS

The following are the most popular methods for evaluating IT and EC investments. For details, see Online File W13.1 and Wattemann (2007).

The ROI Method

The *ROI method* uses a formula that divides the total net benefits (revenues less costs, for each year) by the initial cost. The result is a ratio that measures the ROI for each year or for an entire period; also, see Keen and Joshi (2009). Online File W13.1 provides the ROI formula and an example. In calculating ROI, one should consider the following techniques.

Payback Period

With the payback-period method, the company calculates how long it will take for the net benefits to pay back the entire initial investment. Online File W13.1 also provides the details of this method.

NPV Analysis

In an *NPV analysis*, analysts convert future values of benefits to their present-value equivalents by discounting them at the organization's cost of funds. This requires that analysts determine a discount rate, which can be the average or the marginal interest rate paid by a company to obtain loans. Then the analyst can compare the present value of the future benefits with the present value of the costs required to achieve those benefits to determine whether the benefits exceed the costs. A project with estimated NPV greater than zero may be a candidate for acceptance. One with an estimated NPV less than zero would probably be rejected. One needs to consider the intangible benefits. For more specific guidelines and decision criteria on how NPV analysis works, consult a financial management textbook and Online File W13.1.

Internal Rate of Return (IRR)

For an investment that requires and produces a number of cash flows over time, people use the *internal rate of return (IRR)* method. The IRR is the discount rate that makes the NPV of those cash flows equal to zero. Some companies set a minimum acceptable IRR (or hurdle rate) based on their own cost of capital and the minimum percentage return they'd like to see from their investments.

Break-Even Analyses

A *break-even point* is the point at which the benefits of a project are equal to the costs. Firms use this type of analysis to determine the point at which the EC investment starts to pay for itself.

The Total Costs and Benefits of Ownership

The costs of an IT system may accumulate over many years. An interesting approach for IT cost evaluation is the *total cost of ownership*. **Total cost of ownership (TCO)** is a formula for calculating the cost of owning, operating, and controlling an IT system, even one as simple as a PC. The cost includes acquisition costs (hardware and software), operations costs (maintenance, training, operations, evaluation, technical support, installation, downtime, auditing, virus damage, and power consumption), and control costs (standardization, security, central services). The TCO may be 100 percent higher than the cost of the hardware, especially for PCs.

> **total cost of ownership (TCO)**
> A formula for calculating the cost of owning, operating, and controlling an IT system.

By identifying these various costs, organizations can make more accurate cost–benefit analyses. David, et al. (2002) offer a methodology for calculating TCO. They also provide a detailed example of the items to include in TCO calculations. For further discussion, see Bothama (2006). For comprehensive information about TCO, see en.wikipedia.org/wiki/Total-cost-of-ownership. For calculations in an open-source environment, see Spector (2006).

A similar concept is **total benefits of ownership (TBO)**. This calculation includes both tangible and intangible benefits. By calculating and comparing TCO and TBO, one can compute the payoff of an IT investment (i.e., payoff = TBO – TCO).

> **total benefits of ownership (TBO)**
> Benefits of ownership that include both tangible and intangible benefits.

Economic Value Added

Economic value added (EVA) attempts to quantify the net value added by an investment. It is the return on invested capital (i.e., after-tax cash flow) generated by a company minus the cost of the capital used in creating the cash flow. For example, if the earnings per share are 10 percent and the cost of capital is 12 percent per share, the investment reduces rather than adds economic value.

For a comparison of some of these methods, see Exhibit 13.6 and Pisello (2006).

EXHIBIT 13.6   Evaluating EC and IT Traditional Investments Methods

Method	Advantages	Disadvantages
Internal rate of return (IRR)	Brings all projects to common footing. Conceptually familiar.	Assumes reinvestment at same rate. Can have multiple roots. No assumed discount rate.
Net present value (NPV) or net worth (NW)	Very common. Maximizes value for unconstrained project selection.	Difficult to compare projects of unequal lives or sizes.
Payback period	May be discounted or nondiscounted. Measure of exposure.	Ignores flows after payback is reached. Assumes standard project cash flow profile.
Benefit-to-cost analysis or ratio	Conceptually familiar.	May be difficult to classify outlays as expenses or investments.
Economic value added	Measures net value created for the stakeholder.	The true benefits can be difficult to measure.

Using Several Traditional Methods for One Project

Some companies use several traditional methods to be on the safe side. Each of these methods, provides us with a different aspect of the analysis.

The ROI is measured over 3 to 5 years. It is expressed as a percentage and helps assess the net benefits of a project relative to the initial investment. The NPV indicates the magnitude of the project and whether it generated a profit. It is expressed in terms of a currency (e.g., dollars, pounds, yuan). The payback period provides information about the risk. The longer the projected period, the longer the risk of obsolescence. It also measures the positive cumulative cash flow. The IRR is frequently used to decide whether to commit to an investment. In many cases, an investment is accepted when the IRR is greater than the opportunity cost.

Business ROI Versus Technology ROI

When implementing ROI, one should look both at the business side and the technology side of the project to be justified. For details, see Online File W13.3. Related to this is the issue of measuring the quality of EC projects (see Smith 2006).

IMPLEMENTING TRADITIONAL METHODS

When implementing traditional methods, one may encounter some difficulties. Therefore, the methods discussed earlier are frequently implemented by using calculators.

ROI CALCULATORS

The traditional methods of calculating ROI involve fairly simple formulas and are available as Excel functions or other calculators. Calculators are also available for complex and proprietary formulas.

ROI calculator
Calculator that uses metrics and formulas to compute ROI.

Vendors and consulting companies have accumulated quite a bit of experience in developing metrics and tools called **ROI calculators** to evaluate investments. Recently, companies specializing in ROI also have developed ROI calculators, some of which are in the public domain.

The Offerings from *Baseline* Magazine

One of the major sources of simple calculators is *Baseline* (baselinemag.com). It offers several dozen Excel-based calculators (for free or for a fee). Examples of calculators they offer include:

- ▶ Calculating ROI (*Baseline* 2006)
- ▶ Figuring the ROI of RFID

▶ Comparing smartphones and laptops
▶ Figuring the ROI of application performance management
▶ Determining your true total cost of ownership (TCO)
▶ Calculating the ROI of VoIP
▶ Determining the cost of videoconferencing solutions

In addition, *Baseline* offers tutorials, guides, statistical data, and more related to these calculators.

Other Calculators

Nucleus Research Inc. (nucleusresearch.com), a research and advisory company, uses several ROI calculators in helping businesses evaluate IT investments. Nucleus Research argues that if a company must make frequent justifications for EC and has unique intangible costs and benefits, it may be necessary to custom build an ROI evaluation tool. ROI calculators for e-services are also available. For instance, Streaming Media (streamingmedia.com) provides an ROI calculator to measure the costs and benefits of telecommunication bandwidth for videoconferencing, streaming video, and video file servers.

Few organizations have attempted to assess the ROI on e-learning, perhaps because it is so difficult to calculate and justify. However, Learnativity.com (learnativity.com) provides resources such as ROI calculators, methodologies, a bibliography, and online communities to support the assessment of e-learning (see learnativity.com/roi-learning.html).

ROI calculators also are available from various other companies, such as Phoenix Technologies (phoenix.com), Citrix's XenDesktop (citrix.com/English/ps2/products/product.asp?contentID=163057&ntref=3_nav), and Alinean, Inc. (alinean.com). CovalentWorks Corporation (covalentworks.com) specializes in B2B calculators. For more examples of ROI calculators, see roi-calc.com, gantrygroup.com, and phormion.com.

ADVANCED METHODS FOR EVALUATING IT AND EC INVESTMENTS

According to Sidana (2006), traditional methods that are based only on tangible financial factors may not be sufficient for many IT and EC justifications. Therefore, new methods have evolved with time and now include intangible factors such as customer satisfaction (e.g., see Smith and Laurent 2008). These methods may supplement the ROI traditional methods or replace them.

Renkema (2000) presents a comprehensive list of more than 60 different appraisal and justification methods for IT investments. For details of some of these and other methods, see McKay and Marshall (2004). Most justification methods can be categorized into the following four types:

1. **Financial approaches.** These appraisal methods consider only those impacts that can be valued monetarily. They focus on incoming and outgoing cash flows as a result of the investment made. Traditional methods with modifications are examples of financial approach methods.

2. **Multicriteria approaches.** These methods consider both financial impacts and nonfinancial impacts that cannot be (or cannot easily be) expressed in monetary terms. These methods employ quantitative and qualitative decision-making techniques. Examples include information economics, balanced scorecard, and value analysis (see Online File W13.4). For a further description, see Borenstein, et al. (2005).

3. **Ratio approaches.** These methods use several ratios to assist in EC investment evaluation (e.g., EC expenditures versus total turnover). The metrics used usually

are financial in nature, but other types of metrics can be used as well. An example of this would be EC expenditures divided by annual sales or EC expenditures as a percentage of the operating budget.

4. **Portfolio approaches.** These methods apply portfolios (or grids) to plot several investment proposals against decision-making criteria. Portfolio methods are more informative than multicriteria methods and generally use fewer evaluation criteria. These are very complex.

Exhibit 13.7 summarizes representative advanced methods useful in evaluating EC investments.

Unfortunately, none of these methods is perfect or universal. Therefore, you need to look at the advantages and disadvantages of each. Exhibit 13.8 shows the popularity (or use) of the major methods.

Justification methods are usually included in a business plan or business case (see Online Chapter 15 and Online Tutorial T2). Business case software for EC is available from bplans.com and paloalto.com.

Section 13.4 ▶ REVIEW QUESTIONS

1. Briefly define ROI, NPV, payoff period, IRR, and break-even methods of evaluation.
2. What are ROI calculators?
3. Describe the four major justification approaches.

EXHIBIT 13.7 Advanced Methods for EC Justification and Evaluation

- **Value analysis.** With the value analysis method, the organization evaluates intangible benefits using a low-cost, trial EC system before deciding whether to commit a larger investment in a complete system.

- **Information economics.** Using the idea of critical success factors, this method focuses on key organizational objectives and the potential impacts of the proposed EC project on each of them.

- **Scoring methodology.** This method assigns weights and scores to various aspects of the evaluated project (e.g., weights to each metric) and then calculates a total score. Information economics methods are used to determine the aspects to include in the scoring.

- **Benchmarks.** This method is appropriate for evaluating EC infrastructure. Using industry standards, for example, the organization can determine what the industry is spending on e-CRM. Then the organization can decide how much it should spend.

  Benchmarks may be industry metrics or best practices recommended by professional associations or consultants.

- **Management by maxim.** An organization may use this method to determine how much it should invest in large EC (and IT) infrastructures. It is basically a combination of brainstorming and consensus-reaching methodologies.

- **Real-options valuation.** This is a fairly complex assessment method, and it is used only infrequently. It can be fairly accurate in certain situations. The idea behind this method is to look at future opportunities that may result from the EC investment and then place monetary values on them.

- **Balanced scorecard.** This method evaluates the health or performance of the organization by looking at a broad set of factors, not just financial ones. It is becoming a popular tool for assessing EC projects. (See Beasley, et al. 2006 and Pearlson and Sounders 2006.)

- **Performance dashboard.** This is a variant of the balanced scorecard that is used widely in e-business situations. A dashboard is a single view that provides the status of multiple metrics. (See Pearlson and Sounders 2006.)

- **Activity-based costing and justification.** This managerial accounting concept was adapted for assessing EC investments in recent years and has been proven to be fairly successful. (See Peacock and Tanniru 2005.)

EXHIBIT 13.8 Popularity of the Various Justification Methods

Technique	Percentage Who Use It (2004)	Percentage Who Use It (2006)
ROI	44	52
Internal ROI	40	47
Activity-based costing	37	32
Company-specific measure	36	57
Net present value	35	33
Economic value added	29	31
Balanced scorecard	24	NA
Return on assets	24	35
Return on equity	18	19
Portfolio management	16	NA
Applied information economics	9	9
Real options	6	NA
Time to payback	NA	60

NA = Not available

Sources: Compiled from *CIO Insight* (2004) and Alter (2006).

13.5 EXAMPLES OF E-COMMERCE METRICS AND PROJECT JUSTIFICATION

The methods and tools described in the previous section can be used alone, in combination, or with modifications to justify different EC projects. Here, we provide a few examples of how these methods and tools can be used to justify different types of EC projects.

JUSTIFYING E-PROCUREMENT

E-procurement (see Chapter 4) is not limited to just buying and selling; it also encompasses the various processes involved in buying and selling: selecting suppliers, submitting formal requests for goods and services to suppliers, getting approval from buyers, processing purchase orders, fulfilling orders, delivering and receiving items, and processing payments.

Given the diversity of activities involved in e-procurement, the metrics used to measure the value of e-procurement must reflect how well each process is accomplished. However, the focus on the metrics used will differ for buyers and sellers. For example, *buyers* will be interested in metrics such as how quickly they can locate a seller; *sellers* will be most interested in click-to-release time (i.e., the time that elapsed from when the customer clicked to buy an item online until the warehouse staff had a ticket to pick and pack the order). Setting metrics for e-procurement is especially difficult when procurement is done in B2B exchanges. An example of e-procurement metrics is given next.

Example: E-procurement Metrics. Measuring the success of e-procurement is in many ways similar to measuring the success of the purchasing department. Some direct measures involve the company's ability to secure quality, cost-effective materials, and supplies that are delivered on time. The following metrics indicate excellence in e-procurement:

- ▶ Increased order fulfillment rate
- ▶ Increased on-time deliveries
- ▶ Decreased number of rejects received from suppliers
- ▶ Decreased purchase order processing time

> ▶ Decreased prices due to increased supplier visibility and order aggregation
> ▶ Decreased ratio of freight costs to purchases
>
> **Indirect metrics include minimizing costs, such as:**
>
> ▶ Reduced inventory costs
> ▶ Reduced raw material costs
> ▶ Reduced rework costs
> ▶ Reduced operating costs
> ▶ Reduced freight costs

E-procurement can directly or indirectly affect these metrics. Measuring and monitoring e-procurement activities is crucial to identifying both problematic and successful areas. It provides insight into what an organization is doing right and wrong so that it can pinpoint which activities it needs to investigate and adjust.

The evolution from simple online buying of supplies and materials to full-scale involvement in e-marketplaces is shown in Online File W13.5.

JUSTIFYING A PORTAL

In making the case for investing in a Web portal, you need to employ a business case that contains the internal and external perspectives of the business. The internal payoff must result in productivity improvements, whereas revenue generation determines the external value. Although several commercial portal development environments are available, large companies may consider building theirs in-house. Metrics and ROI analysis can serve as a prerequisite to the build-versus-buy decision.

Some of the tangible benefits from investment in portal technology include revenue growth, call center productivity increases, and increased customer loyalty and retention. Adopters also report much improved trading relationships with suppliers and other business partners. However, most of the benefits of portals are intangible. For example, employee portals have the potential to fundamentally change and improve employer–employee relationships—a desirable benefit, although somewhat difficult to measure. Portals offer the following benefits, which are difficult to quantify:

▶ They offer a simple user interface for finding and navigating content via a browser.

▶ They improve access to business content and increase the number of business users who can access information, applications, and people.

▶ They offer access to common business applications from anywhere in a geographically distributed enterprise and beyond. Using Web-enabled mobile or wireless devices, content can be accessed from anywhere.

▶ They offer the opportunity to use platform-independent software (Java) and data (XML).

For examples of ROI of portals, see *Baseline* (2006).

JUSTIFYING SOCIAL NETWORKING AND THE USE OF WEB 2.0 TOOLS

Justifying social networking initiatives and the use of Web 2.0 can be difficult due to the intangible benefits and the potential risks (Chapters 7 and 9). However, in many cases the cost is relatively low and so companies embark on such projects without formal justification, especially in cases of experiments. The major issue could be that of risk assessment. Some of the tools are available for free or are being added by vendors to communication and collaboration tools.

JUSTIFYING AN INVESTMENT IN MOBILE COMPUTING AND IN RFID

Justifying the cost of mobile computing may be difficult due to cost sharing infrastructure and the many intangible benefits. *Baseline* (baselinemag.com) offers tutorials and several calculators to help companies do the following:

▶ Calculate the return on the wireless workforce
▶ Calculate the return on outsourcing mobile device management
▶ Calculate the cost of the wireless networks

Vendors of wireless and mobile hardware, software, and services offer tutorials and calculators, as well (e.g., Symbol Technology—now a Motorola company, Sybase, and Intel). For a comprehensive discussion of the justification of mobile computing, see *MobileInfo.com* (2011).

Many medium and large corporations are considering implementing RFID systems to improve their supply chain operations (see Chapter 11). Although such systems offer many tangible benefits that can be defined, many measures cannot be developed due to the fact that the technology is new and that legal requirements (for privacy protection) are still evolving. For a discussion of RFID, see Online Tutorial T3. For a fee, baselinemag.com offers an RFID justification calculator.

An example of justifying an investment in wireless computing is provided in Online File W13.6.

JUSTIFYING SECURITY PROJECTS

More than 85 percent of viruses enter business networks via e-mail. Cleaning up infections is labor intensive, but antivirus scanning is not (see Chapter 9). ROI calculators are available (e.g., at baselinemag.com) to judge the cost of using an expert to decontaminate a system versus the use of software to keep the system virus free.

Employee security training is usually poorly done. Companies tell employees what to do, with little or no time devoted to why specific security rules are in place. ROI calculators are available to estimate the cost for training sessions with enough time to explain "why," allowing workers to understand the consequences of ignoring or misusing security procedures.

Section 13.5 ▶ REVIEW QUESTIONS

1. List five success factors for e-procurement.
2. List five performance metrics for e-procurement.
3. List some metrics that can justify an EC portal.
4. List some metrics for justifying the installation of a wireless network in a restaurant (consult Online File W13.6).

13.6 THE ECONOMICS OF E-COMMERCE

The economic environment of e-commerce is broad and diversified. In this section, we present only representative topics that relate to the traditional microeconomic theory and formula.

REDUCING PRODUCTION COSTS

Production costs are the costs to produce the product or service a company is selling. E-commerce makes a major contribution to lowering production costs. For example, e-procurement may result in cost reductions. Much of intrabusiness EC deals with cost reductions. The following economic principles express these reductions.

Product Cost Curves

The *average variable cost (AVC)* represents the behavior of average costs as quantity changes. The AVC of many physical products and services is U shaped (see Exhibit 13.9).

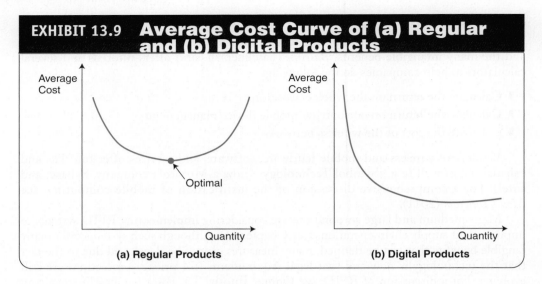

EXHIBIT 13.9   Average Cost Curve of (a) Regular and (b) Digital Products

(a) Regular Products

(b) Digital Products

This curve indicates that, at first, as quantity increases, the average cost declines (part a). As quantity increases still more, the cost goes back up due to increasing variable costs (especially marketing costs) and fixed costs (more management is needed) in the short run. However, the variable cost per unit of digital products is very low (in most cases) and almost fixed (once the initial investment is recovered), regardless of the quantity. Therefore, as Exhibit 13.9 shows, with digital products the average cost per unit (part b) declines as quantity increases because the fixed costs are spread (prorated) over more units. This relationship results in increasing returns with increased sales. It provides competitive advantage because EC users can sell at lower prices.

Production Function

production function
An equation indicating that for the same quantity of production, Q, companies either can use a certain amount of labor or invest in more automation.

The **production function**, shown in Exhibit 13.10 (part a), represents a mathematical formula that indicates that for the same quantity of production, Q, companies either can use a certain amount of labor or invest in more automation (e.g., they can substitute IT capital for labor). For example, for a quantity $Q = 1,000$, the lower the amount of labor needed the higher the required IT investment (capital costs). When EC enters the picture, it *shifts* the function inward (from L_1 to L_2), lowering the amount of labor and/or capital needed to produce the same $Q = 1,000$. Again, EC provides competitive advantage, allowing companies to sell at lower prices than the competition.

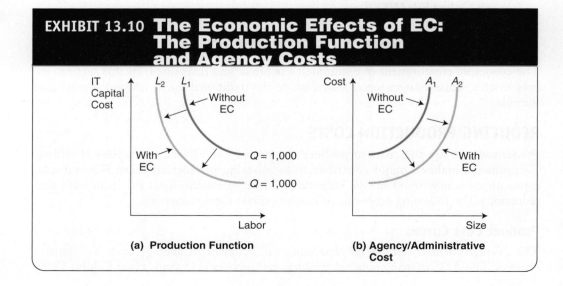

EXHIBIT 13.10   The Economic Effects of EC: The Production Function and Agency Costs

(a) Production Function

(b) Agency/Administrative Cost

Agency Costs

Exhibit 13.10 (part b) shows the economics of the firm's **agency costs** (or *administrative costs*). These are the costs incurred in ensuring that certain support and administrative tasks related to production are performed as intended (e.g., by an agent). In the "old economy," agency costs (A_1) grew with the size (and complexity) of the firm, reaching a high level of cost quickly and frequently preventing companies from growing to a very large size. In the digital economy, the agency costs curve shifts outward, to A_2. This means that as a result of EC, companies can significantly expand their business without too much of an increase in administrative costs. Again, this is a competitive advantage for the rapidly growing companies.

agency costs
Costs incurred in ensuring that the agent performs tasks as expected (also called *administrative costs*).

Transaction Costs

Transaction costs cover a wide range of costs that are associated with the distribution (sale) and/or exchange of products and services. Most economists (e.g., Chen 2005) divide these costs into the following six categories:

transaction costs
Costs that are associated with the distribution (sale) or exchange of products and services including the cost of searching for buyers and sellers, gathering information, negotiating, decision making, monitoring the exchange of goods, and legal fees.

1. **Search costs.** Buyers and sellers incur costs in locating each other and in locating specific products and services.
2. **Information costs.** For buyers, this includes costs related to learning about the products and services of sellers and the basis for their cost, profit margins, and quality. For sellers, this includes costs related to learning about the legitimacy, financial condition, and needs of the buyer, which may lead to a higher or lower price.
3. **Negotiation costs.** Buyers and sellers need to agree on the terms of the sale (e.g., quantity, quality, shipments, financing, etc.). Negotiation costs result from meetings, communication-related expenses, exchanges of technical data or brochures, entertainment, and legal fees.
4. **Decision costs.** For buyers, decision costs result from the evaluation of sellers and their internal processes, such as purchasing approval, to ensure that they meet the buyers' policies. For sellers, decision costs arise in the determination of whether to sell to one buyer instead of another buyer, or not at all.
5. **Monitoring costs.** Buyers and sellers need to ensure that the goods or services purchased translate into the goods or services exchanged. In addition, they need to make sure that the exchange proceeds according to the terms under which the sale was made. This may require transaction monitoring, inspection of goods, and negotiations over late or inadequate deliveries or payments.
6. **Legal-related costs.** Buyers and sellers need to ensure that they remedy unsatisfied terms. Legal-related costs include costs that arise from fixing defects and providing substitutions and agreeing on discounts and other penalties. They also include litigation costs in the event of a legal dispute.

As we have seen throughout the book, e-commerce can reduce all these costs. Reducing transaction cost benefits mostly customers by providing competitive advantage through better customer service. For example, search engines and comparison bots can reduce search costs and information costs. EC also can drastically reduce the costs of monitoring, collaborating, and negotiating.

Exhibit 13.11 reflects one aspect of transaction costs. As seen in the exhibit, there is a trade-off between transaction cost and size (volume) of business. Traditionally, in order to reduce transaction costs, firms had to grow in size (as depicted in curve T_1). In the digital economy, the transaction cost curve shifts downward to position T_2. This means that EC makes it possible to have low transaction costs even with smaller firm size and to enjoy much lower transaction costs as firm size increases.

INCREASED REVENUES

Throughout the text, we have demonstrated how an organization can use EC to increase revenues through webstores, auctions, cross-selling opportunities, multichannel distribution arrangements, and so on. EC can also be used to increase revenues by improving reach and richness.

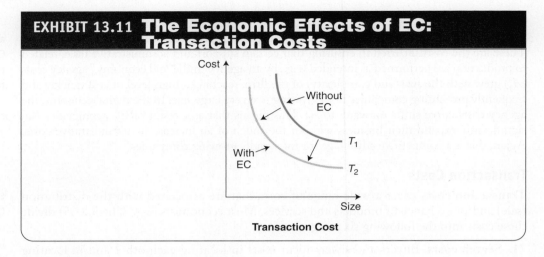

EXHIBIT 13.11 The Economic Effects of EC: Transaction Costs

Reach Versus Richness

Another economic impact of EC is the trade-off between the number of customers a company can reach (called *reach*) and the amount of interactions and information services it can provide to them (*richness*). According to Evans and Wurster (2000), for a given level of cost (resources), there is a trade-off between reach and richness. The more customers a company wants to reach, the fewer services it can provide to them for a given amount of money used in the transaction cost. Exhibit 13.12 depicts this economic relationship.

The case of stockbroker Charles Schwab illustrates the implementation of the reach versus richness trade-off. Initially, Schwab attempted to increase its reach. To do so, the company went downward along the curve (see Exhibit 13.12), reducing its richness. However, with its website (schwab.com), Schwab was able to drastically increase its reach (moving from point A to B) and at the same time provide more richness in terms of customer service and financial information to customers, moving from point B to point C. For example, Schwab's Mutual Fund Screener allows customers to design their own investment portfolios by selecting from an array of mutual funds. Providing such services (richness) allows Schwab to increase the number of customers (reach), as well as charge higher fees than competitors that provide few value-added services. In summary, the Internet pushes the curve outward toward the upper right-hand corner of the chart, allowing more reach with the same cost. For additional details, see Jelassi and Enders (2008).

Other Ways to Increase Revenues

EC can also increase revenues by:

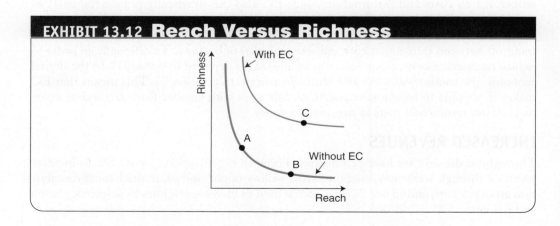

EXHIBIT 13.12 Reach Versus Richness

> ◗ Providing products or services from a larger global market because of more effective product marketing on the Web
> ◗ Allowing customers to order anytime from any place via the use of m-commerce and l-commerce
> ◗ Using processes with lower internal cost (e.g., using lower cost computers) and with higher prices because of value-added services to the customer (e.g., information attached to product)
> ◗ Becoming an online portal
> ◗ Creating value-added content from selling searches, access to data, and electronic documents

The remainder of this section deals with some other issues related to the economics of EC.

REDUCING TRANSACTION FRICTION OR RISK

Allowing the customer to utilize an EC-based calculator and avoid potentially embarrassing situations can reduce psychological risks. For example, online tracking tools reduce psychological concerns by allowing customers to check the status of a package. By publishing specifications and providing product comparison engines, EC can help reduce a customer's risk of purchasing an unwanted product or one of poor quality. EC also has been instrumental in providing customers with an accurate picture of product availability, helping them to avoid the risk of unexpected delays. Proper explanations can mitigate customer concerns over the security of EC transactions. Finally, linking the transaction to third-party security providers, such as the Better Business Bureau or VeriSign, can address customer concerns over privacy and security. In this way, EC can provide value by lowering the transaction friction or risk and providing the customer with *economic value*.

FACILITATING PRODUCT DIFFERENTIATION

Organizations can use EC to provide **product differentiation**—products with special features. For example, McAfee allows users of its VirusScan virus-detection software to automatically update the latest security patches online, differentiating itself from those that require manual upgrades. Differentiation does not necessarily require a physical product; services also can be differentiated. EC can provide differentiation through better product information, informing users on how to use the product, how to replenish it, and how to provide feedback.

EC INCREASES AGILITY

EC can provide firms with the **agility** to monitor, report, and quickly respond to changes in the marketplace and the business environment. Companies with agile systems can respond to customer requests quickly, improving customer service. FedEx, UPS, and other delivery companies can provide location information because they use EC to connect with customers and make available package tracking information. EC systems enable companies to learn more about customers and understand their buying habits. This enables a company to better predict trends for better planning and quickly introduce changes when needed. Similarly, e-procurement has given firms the ability to quickly locate sellers and place orders. Sellers, in turn, use e-fulfillment to quickly locate products in their warehouses and fill customer orders.

VALUATION OF EC COMPANIES

Valuation is the process of trying to determine the value or worth of a company. It is done for the purpose of selling a company or determining its value for going public (an IPO) or for a proposed merger. In the EC context, valuation often is conducted to determine a reasonable IPO price when a start-up company goes public.

product differentiation
Special features available in products that make them distinguishable from other products. This property attracts customers that appreciate what they consider an added value.

agility
An EC firm's ability to capture, report, and quickly respond to changes happening in the marketplace and business environment.

valuation
The fair market value of a business or the price at which a property would change hands between a willing buyer and a willing seller who are both informed and under no compulsion to act. For a publicly traded company, the value can be readily obtained by multiplying the selling price of the stock by the number of available shares.

Many valuation methods exist (e.g., see Smith and Laurent 2008). The three most common ones, according to Rayport and Jaworski (2004), are the *comparable method*, the *financial performance method*, and the *venture capital method*:

▶ **The comparable method.** With this method, analysts compare the company with similar companies on as many factors as possible (e.g., size, industry, customer base, products, growth rate, book value, debt, sales, financial performance). In addition, they may look at performance trends, management teams, and other features. A major difficulty with this method is finding such information for privately held companies.

▶ **The financial performance method.** This method uses projections of future earnings (usually 5 years), cash flows, and so on to find the NPV of a company. With this method, the analyst needs to discount future cash flows using a discount or interest rate. The major problem with this method is in determining the discount rate, which is based on future interest rates. Analysts may use pro forma income statements, free cash flow values, and the company's terminal value (the value of the company, if sold, 3 to 5 years in the future) to generate a valuation.

▶ **The venture capital method.** Venture capital (VC) firms (Online Chapter 15) invest in start-ups and usually take them through to their IPOs. They may use combinations of the first two methods, concentrating on terminal value. The VC firm then discounts the terminal value of the company, using a very high discount rate (e.g., 30 percent to 70 percent). When companies pay using their stocks, they have high valuation so they can afford to buy a high-valuation EC company. An example is IAC/Interactive Corp., which purchased AskJeeves in March 2005 in an all-stock acquisition. This compensates the company for the high risk it assumes.

Let's look at one of the most successful IPOs of an EC company—Google. Google floated its IPO in fall 2004, targeting it at $85 per share. Within a few weeks, the share price more than doubled, reaching more than $450 in late 2005, $500 in 2006, and more than $700 in 2007, giving Google a market capitalization of $200 billion a year. The increase in share price indicated that investors were willing to pay huge premiums for anticipated future performance and valuation. Many acquisitions and mergers from 1996 through 2001 involved unrealistically high valuations, and so did the acquisition of social networks from 2005 to 2007. For example, Google paid $1.65 billion for YouTube.com in 2006. Note that when EC companies acquire other EC companies, they frequently pay in the form of stock, not cash, so such high valuations are more appropriate. Google uses this same strategy to acquire other companies. In 2010, Google offered to buy Groupon for $6 billion. Groupon declined the offer. It plans to go to the stock market and then the valuation of the company may reach $20 billion.

In summary, the economics of EC enable companies to be more competitive and more profitable. It also enables them to grow faster, collaborate better, provide superb customer service, and innovate more quickly. As in any economic environment, here, too, those that capitalize on these opportunities will excel; the rest are doomed to mediocrity or failure.

Once EC projects are justified, these systems need to be developed.

Section 13.6 ▶ REVIEW QUESTIONS

1. How does EC impact the production cost curve?
2. Define transaction costs. List the major types and explain how EC can reduce such costs.
3. How can EC increase revenues?
4. How can EC increase the competitive advantage for a firm?
5. What are the benefits of increasing reach? How can EC help?
6. Explain the impact of EC on product differentiation and agility.
7. Define valuation. Why is it so high for some EC start-ups?

13.7 A FIVE-STEP APPROACH TO DEVELOPING AN E-COMMERCE SYSTEM

Once it has been determined that a business can benefit from an online presence, the business type, the product line, the business's organization, and the budget dictate what functionality the EC system should have and how the website should be developed. Companies can choose from a number of different types of websites, and projects including B2C, B2B, exchanges, e-procurement, portal (see the opening case), and the like. Sites of a particular type (e.g., retailer, provider of business services, manufacturer, distributor/wholesaler, media, travel/entertainment) usually use the same underlying applications and provide similar sorts of functionality. Although this simplifies the task of creating the underlying application architecture, the site requirements must still be considered carefully. Before discussing the best approach to developing a site, it would be useful to review previous chapters to consider the major characteristics, functionalities, and requirements of the EC system being developed. Some typical capabilities needed by a webstore are shown in Exhibit 13.13.

A well-developed website not only adds to the value of products or services being offered, but it also enhances the worth of the company. Therefore, once you have a clear understanding of the e-commerce system requirements and consider all the elements of the e-commerce system including people, procedures, and so forth (see Exhibit 13.14), it is important that a firm choose the correct development strategy to obtain the greatest return on its investment. The diversity of e-business models and applications, which vary in size from small stores to global exchanges, requires a variety of development methodologies and approaches.

For example, webstores with a few key components can be developed with HTML, Java, Web 2.0, or another programming language. They also can be implemented with existing commercial packages, purchased or leased from an application service provider (ASP), or from a site builder. Larger or special EC applications can be developed in-house or outsourced (see the opening case). Building medium to large applications requires extensive integration with

EXHIBIT 13.13 Capabilities Needed by Webstore Users	
Buyers Need the Ability to:	**Sellers Need the Ability to:**
• Discover, search for, evaluate, and compare products for purchase using e-catalogs. • Select products to purchase and negotiate or determine their total price. • Place an order for desired products using a shopping cart. • Pay for the ordered products, usually through some form of credit. • Confirm an order, ensuring that the desired product is available. • Track orders once they are shipped.	• Provide access to a current catalog of product offerings, allowing prospective buyers to analyze and evaluate the offerings. • Provide an electronic shopping cart in which buyers can assemble their purchases. • Verify a customer's credit and approve the customer's purchase. • Process orders (back-end services). • Arrange for product delivery. • Track shipments to ensure that they are delivered. • Provide the means for buyers and visitors to register at the site, to make comments, or to request additional information. • Answer customers' questions or pass queries and requests to a Web-based call center. • Analyze purchases in order to customize buyers' experiences. • Provide Web-based postsale support. • Create the capability for cross-selling and up-selling. • Provide language translation if needed. • Measure and analyze the traffic at the site to modify and maintain the various applications.

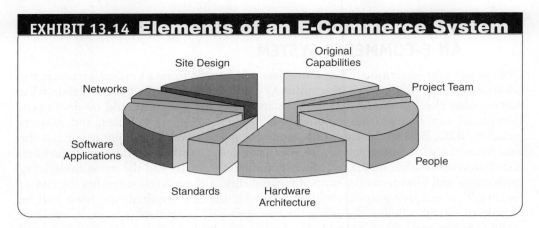

EXHIBIT 13.14 Elements of an E-Commerce System

existing information systems, such as corporate databases, intranets, enterprise resource planning (ERP), and other application programs. Therefore, although the process of building EC systems can vary, in many cases, it tends to follow a fairly standard format.

The traditional *systems development life cycle (SDLC)* systematically leads developers through six analysis and design stages: problem identification, analysis, logical design, physical design, implementation, and maintenance. The SDLC is the basis for development of the majority of traditional business systems (see Kendall and Kendall [2011] for more details on this approach). However, innovative new software and hardware are enabling a move to a more streamlined approach to e-commerce development, as discussed in Online File W13.6. Exhibits 13.15 and 13.16 show the major steps needed to develop a typical e-commerce application.

STEP 1: IDENTIFYING, JUSTIFYING, AND PLANNING EC SYSTEMS

EC applications, like all other information systems, are usually built to enable one or more business processes. Consequently, their planning must be aligned with that of the organization's overall business plan and the specific processes involved. Always remember that

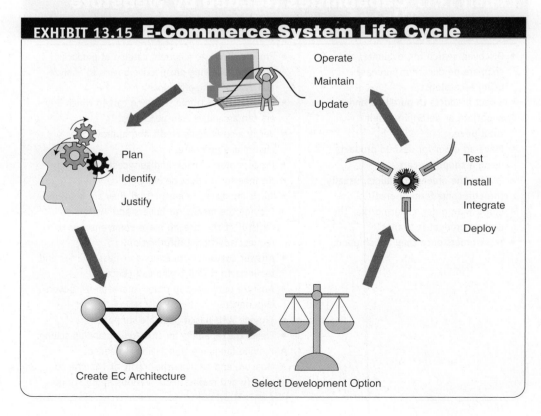

EXHIBIT 13.15 E-Commerce System Life Cycle

EXHIBIT 13.16 The EC Application Development Process

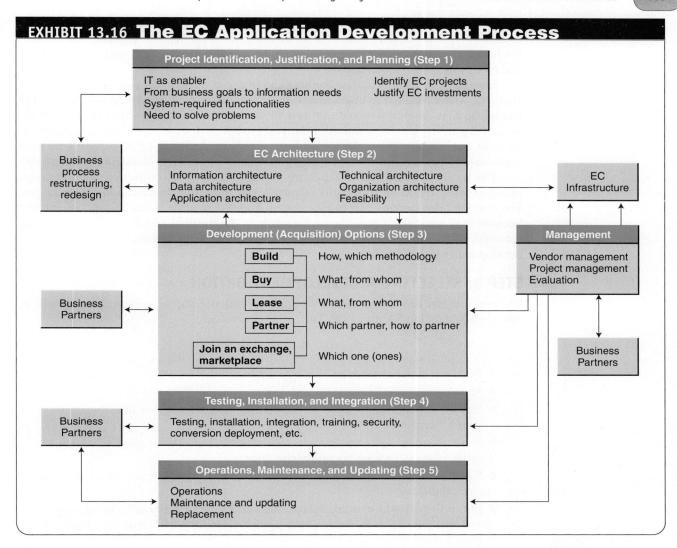

existing processes may need to be restructured to take full advantage of the benefits of the supporting IT and EC projects (see BPM, Section 13.10). Furthermore, each application must be carefully analyzed, using possibly different methods, to ensure that it will have the needed functionality to meet the requirements of the business processes and the users, and assure that the EC project benefits will justify its cost. Both of these activities may be complex, but they are necessary, especially for systems that require high investment to acquire, operate, and maintain. The output of this step is a decision to go with a specific application, with a timetable, budget, and assigned responsibility or not to go. This first step is typically performed in-house (with consultants if needed). All other steps can be completed either in-house or outsourced.

STEP 2: CREATING AN EC ARCHITECTURE

An **EC architecture** is a plan for organizing the underlying infrastructure and applications of a site. The plan specifies the following:

EC architecture
A plan for organizing the underlying infrastructure and applications of a site.

- Information and data required to fulfill the business goals and vision
- Application modules that will deliver and manage the information and data
- Specific hardware and software on which the application modules will run
- Necessary security, scalability, and reliability required by the applications
- Human resources and procedures for implementing the architecture

Various IT tools and methodologies can be used to support the creation of an application architecture. Because the creation of an architecture is an iterative process, collaborative methodologies, such as *joint application development (JAD)*, are especially useful in identifying and modifying system requirements.

Example. TD Bank, a leading banking and financial services company headquartered in Portland, Maine, wanted to upgrade its online customer service to provide information fast enough so that customers would not have to send e-mails or make phone calls. With the help of RightNow's on-demand solutions and professional services, TD Bank increased its 24-hour maximum response rate to customer e-mails from a mediocre 90 percent level to an impressive 97 percent and lowered e-mail volume by 55 percent, to about 35 messages a day.

The results obtained from step 2 are routed to a steering committee at the strategic planning level. Based on the results of step 2, the application portfolio may be changed. For example, the steering committee may discourage or scale down the specific project because it is too risky. Once the architecture is determined and the project gets final approval, a decision about *how* to develop the specific EC application must be made and a development option chosen.

STEP 3: SELECTING A DEVELOPMENT OPTION

EC applications can be developed through several alternative approaches that will be discussed in detail in Section 13.8. The major options are:

- ▶ Build the system in-house.
- ▶ Have a vendor build a customized system.
- ▶ Buy an existing application and install it, with or without modifications, by yourself or through a vendor.
- ▶ Lease standard software from an application service provider (ASP), lease as a service (SaaS), or lease via utility computing.
- ▶ Enter into a partnership or alliance that will enable the company to use someone else's application.
- ▶ Join a third-party e-marketplace, such as an auction site, a bidding (reverse auction) site, or an exchange, that provides needed capabilities to participants (e.g., Yahoo! Store).
- ▶ Use cloud computing (see Online Tutorial T7).
- ▶ Use a combination of approaches.

Once the development option is chosen, the system can be developed. At the end of this step, an application is ready to be installed and made available. No matter what option is chosen, it is important to keep in mind that all the different applications that support the various capabilities of the website must be coordinated and considerable collaboration between developers and users is necessary. In addition, there is a strong possibility that the firm will work with vendor(s) and/or software provider(s). In this case, the firm will need to manage its vendor relationships (see Section 13.9).

STEP 4: INSTALLING, TESTING, INTEGRATING, AND DEPLOYING EC APPLICATIONS

Once a system has been developed, the next step involves getting the application up and running in the selected hardware and network environment. One of the steps in installing an application is connecting it to back-end databases, to other applications, and often to other websites. For example, if a prospective customer orders a product from a site, it would be helpful if the site could determine if the product is in stock. To do this, the ordering system would need to be connected to the inventory system. This step can be done in-house or outsourced.

At this point, the modules that have been installed need to be tested using a series of different tests:

- **Unit testing**. Test each module one at a time.
- **Integration testing**. Test the combination of modules acting in concert.
- **Usability testing**. Test the quality of the user's experience when interacting with the site.
- **Acceptance testing**. Determine whether the site meets the firm's original business objectives and vision.

Once all the website applications pass all the tests, they can be made available to the end users. At this stage, developers may need to address issues such as conversion strategies, training, and resistance to change.

STEP 5: OPERATIONS, MAINTENANCE, AND UPDATES

It typically takes more time, effort, and money to operate and maintain an EC or EC project site than it does to build and install it in the first place. To enjoy continual usage, a site needs to be updated frequently. For example, at a B2C site, new products need to be added to the catalog, prices need to be changed, and new promotions need to be run. These changes and updates need to undergo the same testing procedures used during the installation process. Additionally, usage patterns and performance need to be studied (e.g., using Web analytics) to determine which parts of the underlying applications should be modified or eliminated from the site.

MANAGING THE DEVELOPMENT PROCESS

The development process can be fairly complex and must be managed properly. For medium-to-large applications, a project team is usually created to manage the process and the vendors. Collaboration with business partners also is critical. Some e-business failures are the result of a lack of cooperation by business partners. For example, a firm can install a superb e-procurement system, but if its vendors do not use it properly, the system will collapse. Projects can be managed with project management software (see examples of various project management software at en.wikipedia.org/wiki/Comparison_of_project_management_software). Best practice management also includes periodic evaluations of system performance. Standard project management techniques and tools are useful for this task. Finally, do not rule out the possibility that implementing an EC project may require restructuring one or more business processes.

Section 13.7 ▶ REVIEW QUESTIONS

1. Examine 10 different websites and choose your 5 favorites. Explain why you like each site. Relate your answers to the content of this chapter.
2. Go to the website of each of the developers/Webmasters of your five favorite websites. What expertise do they profess to have? What projects have they completed? Would you feel comfortable hiring their services?
3. List the major steps in developing an EC application.
4. Define the various types of testing used during the EC development process.

13.8 DEVELOPMENT STRATEGIES FOR E-COMMERCE PROJECTS

If the desired website is relatively simple, a firm may decide to build the website in-house. To do so the firm must ask a few questions: Is the firm capable of developing the site (e.g., qualified staff)? Does the firm have access to the proper tools to create the pages, and so forth? If the firm does not have these capabilities, it is usually best to turn over the task to a professional developer. The ideal developer is one who can design a site with the correct look and feel, who has an in-depth knowledge of both EC and the business it is supposed to support, as well as the industry the company is in and who is able to correctly handle any complex coding that may be required. A useful site for finding an experienced website designer is WebDesigners-Directory (webdesigners-directory.com). Other resources for

unit testing
Testing application software modules one at a time.

integration testing
Testing the combination of application modules acting in concert.

usability testing
Testing the quality of the user's experience when interacting with a website.

acceptance testing
Determining whether a website meets the original business objectives and vision.

developing a website are available at Sell It! (sellitontheweb.com). The Microsoft Small Business Center (microsoft.com/smallbusiness/resources/technology/ecommerce/5_common_e_commerce_site_mistakes.mspx) offers some tips for avoiding five common e-commerce mistakes associated with overall site design and infrastructure. Regardless of the complexity of the site, four basic options for developing an EC website are available:

1. **Develop the site in-house** either from scratch or with off-the-shelf components.
2. **Buy a packaged application** designed for a particular type of EC site.
3. **Outsource system development.**
4. **Lease the application** from a third party: cloud computing.

Each of these approaches has its benefits and limitations, and it is important to remember that the development options are not mutually exclusive. A combination of hard and soft project and change management methodologies can guide successful in-house development of enterprisewide information systems. Each of these development options is discussed in detail next.

IN-HOUSE DEVELOPMENT: INSOURCING

insourcing
In-house development of applications.

The first generation of EC development was accomplished largely through proprietary programming and in-house development that is widely referred to as **insourcing**. Using this approach, the Internet browser serves as the development platform. The programmers write EC systems using a combination of HTML and script languages such as HTX, CGI, IDC, and JavaScript. Databases developed on top of a database management system (DBMS) usually serve as the information repository to store EC data. Although this first generation of EC development has built up valuable experience and achieved industrial momentum, the lack of **reusability** (i.e., the likelihood a segment of source code can be used again to add new functionalities with slight or no modification) in current EC applications and the lack of **interoperability** (i.e., the ability to connect people, data, diverse systems, and standards) created a great barrier to widespread application of EC.

reusability
The likelihood a segment of source code can be used again to add new functionalities with slight or no modification.

interoperability
Connecting people, data, and diverse systems; the term can be defined in a technical way or in a broad way, taking into account social, political, and organizational factors.

Although insourcing can be time-consuming and costly, it may lead to EC applications that best fit an organization's strategy and vision and differentiate it from the competition. Companies that have the resources to develop their e-business application in-house may follow this approach in order to differentiate themselves from the competition, which may be using standard applications that can be bought or leased. The in-house development of EC applications, however, is a challenging task, because most applications are novel, have users from outside the organization, and involve multiple organizations. Furthermore, the system maintenance and updating may require considerable resources in the future. Insourcing options including build from scratch, build from components, and enterprise application integration are discussed in Online File W13.7.

Insourcing is a challenging task that requires specialized IT resources. For this reason, most organizations usually rely on packaged applications or completely outsource the development and maintenance of their EC sites.

Note: In-house development is frequently done with the help of vendors. Sometimes it is completely outsourced to a professional system developer.

BUY THE APPLICATIONS (OFF-THE-SHELF APPROACH)

turnkey approach
Ready to use without further assembly or testing; supplied in a state that is ready to turn on and operate.

A number of commercial packages provide standard features required by EC applications. These packages are ready to turn on and operate. This option is also known as a **turnkey approach**; the package is ready to use without further assembly and it requires only minimum testing.

The turnkey approach involves buying a commercial package, installing it as is, and starting it up. Buying a commercial package requires much less time and money than in-house development. When selecting a particular package, the package should not only satisfy current needs, but it must also be flexible enough to handle future ones; otherwise, the package may quickly become obsolete. Additionally, because one package can rarely meet all of an organization's requirements, it is sometimes necessary to acquire multiple packages. In this case, the packages need to be integrated with each other and with other software and data.

The following are the major advantages of purchasing EC systems:

▶ Many different types of off-the-shelf software packages are available.
▶ It saves time and money (compared to in-house development).
▶ The company need not hire programmers specifically dedicated to an EC project.
▶ The company knows what it is getting before it invests in the product.
▶ The company is neither the first nor the only user.
▶ The price is usually much lower than the in-house option.
▶ The vendor updates the software frequently.

This option also has some major disadvantages:

▶ Software may not exactly meet the company's needs.
▶ Software may be difficult or impossible to modify, or it may require huge process changes.
▶ The company may experience loss of control over improvements and new versions.
▶ Off-the-shelf applications can be difficult to integrate with existing systems.
▶ Vendors may drop a product or go out of business.

For a directory of vendors of EC turnkey systems, see softwaresearch.us/search.aspx? keywords=E+commerce+turnkey. The buy option is especially attractive if the software vendor allows for modifications. However, the option may not be as attractive in cases of high obsolescence rates or high software cost. In such cases, leasing may be a more appealing option.

OUTSOURCING EC SYSTEMS DEVELOPMENT AND APPLICATIONS

The use of outside contractors or external organizations (often software vendors) to acquire EC applications is called outsourcing. This option has been described in Chapter 12. It is a method of transferring the management and/or day-to-day execution of an entire business function to a third-party service provider. In many cases, systems need to be built quickly, and the special expertise of outside contractors and software vendors is necessary.

outsourcing
A method of transferring the management and/or day-to-day execution of an entire business function to a third-party service provider.

Large companies may choose outsourcing when they want to experiment with new EC technologies without a great deal of up-front investment. Outsourcing also allows large firms to protect their internal networks and to gain expert advice. Small firms with limited IT expertise and tight budgets also find outsourcing advantageous.

Outsourcers can perform any or all tasks in EC applications development. For example, they can plan, program, and build applications and integrate, operate, and maintain them. It is useful for firms to develop good relationships with outsourcers.

Types of Outsourcing Options

Several types of vendors offer services for creating and operating EC applications:

▶ **Software houses.** Many software companies, from IBM to Oracle, offer a range of outsourcing services for developing, operating, and maintaining EC applications.
▶ **Outsourcers and others.** IT outsourcers, such as EDS (now HP Enterprise Services at hp.com), offer a variety of services. Also, the large CPA companies and management consultants (e.g., Accenture) offer some outsourcing services.

> ▸ **Telecommunications companies.** Increasingly, the large telecommunications companies are expanding their hosting services to include the full range of IT and EC solutions. MCI, for example, offers Web Commerce services for a monthly fee.

The benefits of outsourcing are listed in Exhibit 13.17.

Although the trend to outsource is rising, so is the trend to conduct outsourcing offshore—mainly in India and China. This approach is not without risks. For example, although outsourcing offshore may lead to substantial dollar savings, offshore labor skills may be inferior to those found onshore, and the resultant quality of the website development may be unacceptable.

LEASING EC APPLICATIONS: CLOUD COMPUTING AND SOFTWARE-AS-A-SERVICE

A recent trend in EC acquisition is to lease systems rather than to buy them. This includes ready to use applications and tools/components for system development. In the old days of computing during the mainframe era, leasing used to be a popular strategy. In recent years it become very popular appearing under several variations and names. Most known are *utility computing*, *software-as-a-service*, and *on-demand computing*. Lately, it is bundled under the concept of *cloud computing*.

EXHIBIT 13.17 Benefits of Outsourcing

The major benefits are:

Financial
- Avoidance of heavy capital investment, thereby releasing funds for other uses
- Improved cash flow
- Improved cost–benefit ratios due to economies of scale and from sharing hardware, software, and personnel
- Less need for expensive office space

Technical
- Access to emerging EC technologies
- Ability to achieve technological improvements more easily
- Faster application development and placement of EC apps into service

Management
- Concentration on developing and running core business activity; improved company focus
- Delegation of EC development (design, production, and acquisition) and operational responsibility to vendors
- Reduced risk of bad software

Human Resources
- Less IT/EC employees are needed
- Elimination of need to recruit and retain competent IT staff
- Opportunity to draw on specialist skills available from an external pool of expertise, when needed
- Enriched career development and opportunities for remaining staff

Quality
- Clearly defined *service levels*
- Improved performance accountability

Flexibility
- Quick response to business demands (agility)
- Ability to handle EC peaks and valleys activities and demands more effectively (flexibility)

Cloud Computing

Cloud computing refers to the provision of computational resources on demand via a computer network. You pay only for actual usage. Cloud computing can be compared to the supply of electricity and gas, or the provision of other utilities. All of these shared services are presented to the users in a simple way that is easy to understand without the users needing to know how the services are created. Therefore, cloud computing includes the concept of utility computing. Similarly, cloud computing offers computer application developers and users an abstract view of services that simplifies and ignores much of the details and inner workings.

cloud computing
The provision of computational resources on demand via a computer network. You pay only for actual usage.

Cloud computing is an on-demand Internet structure that is broken up into multiple segments including: cloud infrastructure, cloud platforms, cloud application, cloud storage, and more. For details, see Online Tutorial T7.

Cloud computing is related to this chapter in two ways. First, one can lease several e-commerce applications (e.g., e-CRM, e-procurement, e-payment, e-order fulfillment); second, it provides developers with easy to use tools and methodologies. The name *cloud* refers to the Internet since services are available on the Internet by using the browser. For further details, see wikipedia.org/wiki/Cloud_computing.

Software-as-a-Service (SaaS). This is basically the cloud application service that delivers software (including EC packages) as a service over the Internet, eliminating the need to install and run the application on the customer's own computers and simplifying maintenance and support. People tend to use the terms "*SaaS*" and "*cloud*" interchangeably, when in fact they are two different things. Key characteristics of SaaS include:

- Network-based access to, and management of, commercially available standard software
- Activities that are managed from central locations rather than at each customer's site, enabling customers to access applications remotely via the Web
- Application delivery that typically is closer to a one-to-many model (single instance, multitenant architecture) than to a one-to-one model, including architecture, pricing, partnering, and management characteristics
- Centralized feature updating, which obviates the need for downloadable patches and upgrades

Advantages of Cloud Applications

The major advantages for the users are:

- Accessible from anywhere with an Internet connection
- No local server installation—saves time and money
- Pay per use or subscription-based payment methods
- Rapid scalability—provides strategic advantage
- System maintenance (back up, updates, security, etc.) often included in service
- Possible security improvements, although users with high security requirements (e.g., large corporations) may find SaaS itself a security concern
- Reliability of systems incorporating the technology
- Reduced time-to-market

For other benefits, see Online Tutorial T7.

OTHER DEVELOPMENT OPTIONS

Besides the previously mentioned major options for developing EC applications, several other options are currently available and are appropriate under certain circumstances:

▶ **Join an e-marketplace.** With this option, the company "plugs" itself into an e-marketplace. For example, a company can place its catalogs in Yahoo!'s marketplace. Visitors to Yahoo!'s store will find the company's products and will be able to make purchases. The company pays Yahoo! monthly space-rental fees. In such a case, Yahoo! is a hosting service for the company as well. As for development, the company will use templates to build its webstore, and it can start to sell after only a few hours of preparation work.

▶ **Join a consortium.** This option is similar to the previous one, except that the company will be one of the e-market owners. Thus, the company may have more control over the market architecture.

▶ **Join an auction or reverse auction third-party site.** Joining a third-party site is another alternative. Again the plug-in can be done quickly. Many companies use this option for certain e-procurement activities.

▶ **Form joint ventures.** Several different joint-venture partnerships may facilitate e-business application development. For example, four small banks in Hong Kong developed a joint e-banking system. In some cases, a company can team up with another company that already has an application in place.

▶ **Use a hybrid approach.** A hybrid approach combines the best of what the company does internally with an outsourced strategy to develop contracted partnerships. Hybrid models work best when the outsourced partner offers a higher level of security, faster time-to-market, and good service-level agreements.

SELECTING A DEVELOPMENT OPTION

Before choosing an appropriate development option, you need to consider a number of issues in order to generate a list of requirements and capabilities. The following is a list of representative questions that need to be addressed when defining requirements:

▶ **Customers.** Who are the target customers? What are their needs? What kind of marketing tactics should a business use to promote the webstore and attract customers? How can a business enhance customer loyalty? How can a business engage the customers to make them happy and return?

▶ **Merchandising.** What kinds of products or services will the business sell online? Are soft (digitized) goods or hard goods sold? Are soft goods downloadable?

▶ **Sales service.** Can customers order online? How? Can they pay online? Can they check the status of their orders online? How are customer inquiries handled? Are warranties, service agreements, and guarantees available for the products? What are the refund procedures?

▶ **Promotion.** How are the products and services promoted? How will the site attract customers? Are coupons, manufacturer's rebates, or quantity discounts offered? Is cross-selling possible?

▶ **Transaction processing.** Is transaction processing in real time? How are taxes, shipping and handling fees, and payments processed? Are all items taxable? What kinds of shipping methods will the site offer? What kinds of payment methods, such as checks, credit cards, or cybercash, will the site accept? How will the site handle order fulfillment?

> **Marketing data and analysis.** What information, such as sales, customer data, and advertising trends, will the site collect? How would the site use such information for future marketing?

> **Branding.** What image should the webstore reinforce? How is the webstore different from those of the competition?

The initial list of requirements should be as comprehensive as possible. It is preferable to validate the identified requirements through focus-group discussions or surveys with potential customers. The business can then prioritize the requirements based on the customers' preferences. The final list of prioritized requirements serves as the basis for selecting and customizing the appropriate package or designing a webstore from scratch.

Vendor and software selection are discussed in Online File W13.8.

Section 13.8 ▶ REVIEW QUESTIONS

1. List the major e-commerce development and acquisition options.
2. Define insourcing.
3. List some of the pros and cons of using packaged EC applications.
4. Compare the buy option against the lease option. What are the benefits and risks associated with each option?
5. Compare the other development options. If you were the owner of a small company trying to establish a new webstore, which would you choose?
6. How can cloud computing be used as an option for acquiring a system?
7. What is SaaS?
8. What are the advantages of building with templates? What are the disadvantages?
9. List the typical features of a webstore.
10. What are some of the selection criteria for a software option?
11. Describe cloud computing technologies as a leasing option.

13.9 ORGANIZATIONAL IMPACTS OF E-COMMERCE

Only limited statistical data or empirical research on the full organizational impact of EC is available because of the relative newness of the field. Therefore, the discussion in this section is based primarily on experts' opinions, logic, and only some actual data.

Existing and emerging Web technologies are offering organizations unprecedented opportunities to rethink strategic business models, processes, and relationships. These e-opportunities can be divided into three categories: e-marketing (Web-based initiatives that improve the marketing of existing products; see Zimmerman 2007); e-operations (Web-based initiatives that improve the creation of existing products); and e-services (Web-based initiatives that improve service industries and customer service). The discussion here is also based in part on the work of Bloch, et al. (1996), who approached the impact of e-marketplaces on organizations from a value-added point of view. Their model, which is shown in Exhibit 13.18, divides the impact of e-marketplaces into three major categories: *improving direct marketing, transforming organizations*, and *redefining organizations*. This section examines each of these impacts.

IMPROVING MARKETING AND SALES

Traditional direct marketing is done by mail order (catalogs) and telephone (telemarketing). According to the Direct Marketing Association, actual sales generated by direct mail

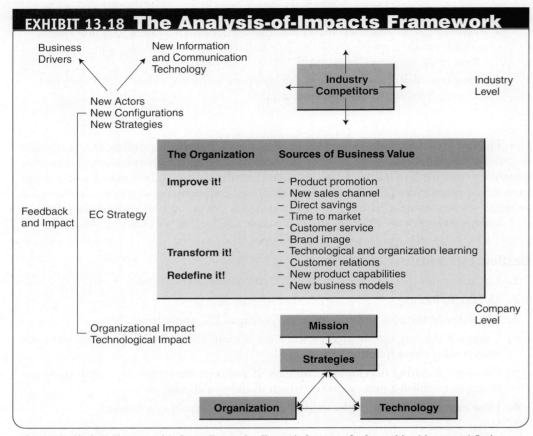

EXHIBIT 13.18 The Analysis-of-Impacts Framework

Source: M. Bloch, Y. Pigneur, and A. Segev. "Leveraging Electronic Commerce for Competitive Advantage: A Business Value Framework." Proceedings of the Ninth International Conference on EDI-IOS, Bled, Slovenia, June 1996. Reprinted by permission of Yves Pigneur.

totaled $960 billion in 2007. This figure is small, but growing rapidly. Zimmerman (2007), Zappala, and Gray (2006), and others, describe the impacts of e-marketplaces on B2C direct marketing.

For digital products—software, music, and videos—the changes brought by e-markets is dramatic. Already, these are delivered over the Internet. The ability to deliver digitized products electronically affects (eliminates) packaging and greatly reduces the need for specialized distribution models.

New sales models for digitized goods such as downloading music, videos and software, shareware, freeware, social shopping, and pay-as-you-use are emerging. Although these models currently exist only within particular sectors, such as the software and publishing industries, they will eventually pervade other sectors.

The impacts of e-marketplaces on marketing and sales are summarized in Exhibit 13.19.

All of these impacts of EC on direct marketing provide companies, in some cases, with a competitive advantage over those that use only traditional direct-sales methods, as illustrated in the Blue Nile case in Chapter 2 (p. 87). Furthermore, because the competitive advantage is so large, e-markets are likely to replace many nondirect marketing channels. Some people predict the "fall of the shopping mall," and many retail stores and brokers of services (e.g., stocks, real estate, and insurance) are labeled by some as soon-to-be-endangered species.

TRANSFORMING ORGANIZATIONS AND WORK

A second impact of e-marketplaces is the transformation of organizations. Here, we look at four key topics: *organizational learning, changing the nature of work*, and *disintermediation and reintermediation*, and the *structure of the EC unit*.

EXHIBIT 13.19 The Changing Face of Marketing

	Old Model—Mass and Segmented Marketing	New Model—One-to-One and Customization
Relationships with customers	Customer is mostly a passive recipient.	Customer is an active coproducer. Target marketing is to individuals.
Customer needs	Articulated.	Articulated and inferred.
Segmentation	Mass market and target segments.	Segments looking for customized solutions and segmented targets; one-to-one targets.
Product and service offerings	Product line extensions and modification.	Customized products, services, and marketing; personalization.
New product development	Marketing and R&D drive new product development.	R&D focuses on developing the platforms that allow consumers to customize based on customer inputs.
Pricing	Fixed prices and discounting.	Customer influencing pricing (e.g., Priceline.com; auctions); value-based pricing models, e-auctions, e-negotiations (i-offer).
Communication	Advertising and PR.	Integrated, interactive, and customized marketing communication, education, and entertainment; use of avatars.
Distribution	Traditional retailing and direct marketing.	Direct (online) distribution and rise of third-party logistics services.
Branding	Traditional branding and co-branding.	The customer's name as the brand (e.g., My Brand or Brand 4 ME).
Basis of competitive advantage	Marketing power.	Marketing finesse and "capturing" the customer as "partner" while integrating marketing, operations, R&D, and information.
Communities	Discount to members in physical communities.	Discounts to members of e-communities; social networking.
Advertising	TV, newspapers, billboards.	Innovative, viral, on the Web, wireless devices.

Sources: Compiled from Wind (2001), Kioses, et al. (2006), and Singh (2006).

Technology and Organizational Learning

Rapid progress in EC will force a Darwinian struggle: To survive, companies will have to learn and adapt quickly to the new technologies. This struggle will offer them an opportunity to experiment with new products, services, and business models, which may lead to strategic and structural changes. An example is the newspaper industry where losses, bankruptcies, and consolidations are regular events. For example, the *New York Times* is developing its electronic version and products to compensate for the reduction in advertisement income of its printed version. These changes may transform the way in which business is done. We believe that as EC progresses, it will have a large and durable impact on the strategies of many organizations and industries. New technologies will require new organizational structures and procedures. For instance, the structure of the organizational unit that handles online marketing might be different from the conventional sales and marketing departments. Problems in traditional bookstores and record stores and the struggle of companies such as Borders and Blockbuster to survive illustrate what is going on in some industries.

In summary, corporate change must be planned and managed. Before getting it right, organizations may have to struggle with different experiments and learn from their mistakes.

The Changing Nature of Work

The nature of some work and employment will be restructured in the digital age; it is already happening before our eyes. For example, driven by increased competition in the global marketplace, firms are reducing the number of employees to a core of essential staff and outsourcing whatever work they can to countries where wages are significantly lower. The upheaval brought on by these changes is creating new opportunities and new risks and is forcing people to think in new ways about jobs, careers, and salaries.

Digital age workers will have to be very flexible. Few will have truly secure jobs in the traditional sense, and many will have to be willing and able to constantly learn, adapt, make decisions, and stand by them. Many others will work from home (see Chapter 14).

The digital age company will have to view its core of essential workers as its most valuable asset. It will have to constantly nurture and empower them and provide them with every means possible to expand their knowledge and skill base (Anandarajan, et al. 2006). One area where work is changing is intermediation.

Disintermediation and Reintermediation

Intermediaries are agents that mediate between sellers and buyers. Usually, they provide two types of services: (1) They provide relevant information about demand, supply, prices, and requirements and, in doing so, help match sellers and buyers; (2) They offer value-added services such as transfer of products, escrow, payment arrangements, consulting, or assistance in finding a business partner. In general, the first type of service can be fully automated and thus is likely to be assumed by e-marketplaces, infomediaries, and portals that provide free or low-commission services. The second type requires expertise, such as knowledge of the industry, the products, and technological trends, and it can only be partially automated.

disintermediation
Elimination of intermediaries between sellers and buyers.

Intermediaries that provide only (or mainly) the first type of service may be eliminated; this phenomenon is called **disintermediation**. An example is travel agents in the airline industry. The airlines are pushing electronic tickets. As of 2004, most airlines require customers to pay $5 or more per ticket if they buy the ticket from an agent or by phone, which is equivalent to the agent's commission. This is resulting in the *disintermediation* of travel agents from the purchasing process. In another example, discount stockbrokers that only execute trades manually are disappearing. However, brokers who manage electronic intermediation are not only surviving but may also be prospering (e.g., E*TRADE). This phenomenon, in which disintermediated entities or newcomers take on new intermediary roles, is called *reintermediation* (see Chapters 3 and 4).

Disintermediation is more likely to occur in supply chains involving several intermediaries, as illustrated in the Blue Nile case in the jewelry industry (Chapter 2, p. 87).

Restructuring Business Processes

As stated in step 2 of the system development process, business processes may need to be restructured to take full advantage of EC projects. Several methods exist for doing just that. We will briefly introduce some of them here.

Restructuring Business Processes and the Use of Business Process Reengineering. By using technology and reorganization tools, a company can prepare a current work analysis of its clients and, accordingly, provide organizational structure solutions that are an alternative to the existing processes.

Such solutions consist of new job definitions, work flows, and responsibilities and competencies of the employees in full compliance with the restructuring process.

The first step when considering how to better organize a process is to ask, "What is the final goal of this process?" For example, a final goal of delivery can be to get the invoice paid. The second step is to plan out the process step by step, looking for inefficiencies and the use of manual labor. Mapping out all the steps reveals bottlenecks that can be eradicated and manual steps that can easily be automated. This makes it easy to create a faster and more predictable process.

A formal approach to restructuring is called *business process reengineering* (BPR).

business process reengineering (BPR)
A methodology for conducting a comprehensive redesign of an enterprise's processes.

Business Process Reengineering. Business process reengineering (BPR) is the analysis and design of workflows and processes within an organization. A business process is a set of logically related tasks performed to achieve a defined business outcome. Reengineering involves restructuring and it can be done in many ways.

Business process reengineering is also known as *business process redesign*, *business transformation*, or *business process change management*. For the cyclical process of BPR and details and discussion, see en.wikipedia.org/wiki/Business_process_reengineering.

Business Process Management. **Business process management (BPM)** is a holistic management approach focused on aligning all aspects of an organization with the wants and needs of clients. It promotes business effectiveness and efficiency while striving for innovation, flexibility, and integration with technology. BPM attempts to improve processes continuously. It can therefore be described as a "process optimization process." It is argued that BPM enables organizations to be more efficient, more effective, and more capable of adaptation to change. For details, see en.wikipedia.org/wiki/Business_process_management and Jeston and Nelis (2008).

REDEFINING ORGANIZATIONS

Following are some of the ways in which e-markets redefine organizations.

New and Improved Product Capabilities

E-markets allow for new products to be created and for existing products to be customized in innovative ways. Such changes may redefine organizations' missions and the manner in which they operate. Customer profiles, as well as data on customer preferences, can be used as a source of information for improving products or designing new ones.

Personalization and Mass Customization

Mass customization enables manufacturers to create specific products for each customer based on the customer's exact needs (see Online Tutorial T6). For example, Motorola gathers customer needs for a pager or a cellular phone, transmits the customer's specifications electronically to the manufacturing plant where the device is manufactured, and then sends the finished product to the customer within a day. Dell pioneered this approach in building its products. Many other companies are following Dell's lead: Mattel's My Design lets fashion-doll fans custom build a friend for Barbie at Mattel's website; the doll's image is displayed on the screen before the person places an order. Nike allows customers to customize shoes, which can be delivered in a week. Lego.com allows customers to configure several of its toys. Finally, De Beers and Blue Nile allow customers to design their own engagement rings. The automobile industry is starting to customize its products and expecting to save billions of dollars in inventory reduction alone every year by producing made-to-order cars. You can design your own T-shirt, Swatch watch, and many other products and services. Configuring the details of the customized products, including the final design, ordering, and paying for the products, is done online. Also known as *build-to-order*, customization can be done on a large scale, in which case it is called *mass customization*. For a historical discussion of the development of the idea of mass customization, see en.wikipedia.org/wiki/mass_customization. With the use of mass-customization methods, the cost of customized products is at or slightly above the comparable retail price of standard products. Exhibit 13.20 shows how customers can order customized Nike shoes.

Impacts on Manufacturing

EC is changing manufacturing systems from mass-production lines to demand-driven, just-in-time manufacturing. These production systems are integrated with finance, marketing, and other functional systems, as well as with business partners and customers. Using Web-based ERP systems (supported by software such as SAP R/3), companies can direct customer orders to designers and/or to the production floor within seconds. Production cycle time can be cut by 50 percent or more in many cases, even if production is done in a different country from where the designers and engineers are located.

CHANGE MANAGEMENT

Deploying an EC project, especially if it involves major restructuring, introduces changes to organizations that must be properly managed.

business process management (BPM)
A holistic management approach focused on aligning all aspects of an organization with the wants and needs of clients. It promotes business effectiveness and efficiency while striving for innovation, flexibility, and integration with technology.

mass customization
A method that enables manufacturers to create specific products for each customer based on the customer's exact needs.

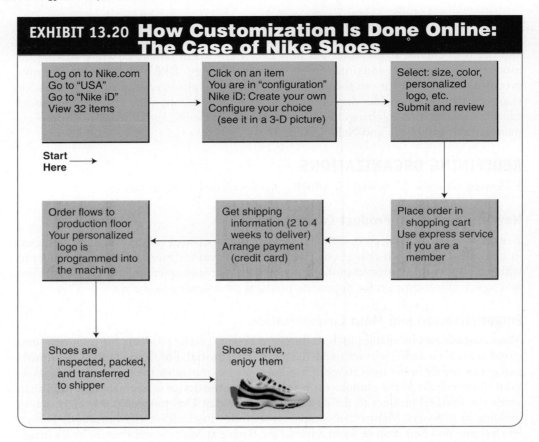

EXHIBIT 13.20 How Customization Is Done Online: The Case of Nike Shoes

---

change management

A structured approach to shifting/transitioning individuals, teams, and organizations from a current state to a desired future state. It is an organizational process aimed at empowering employees to accept and embrace changes in their current business environment.

Change management is a structured approach to shifting/transitioning individuals, teams, and organizations from a current state to a desired future state. It is an organizational process aimed at empowering employees to accept and embrace changes in their current business environment.

A formal organizational *change management* begins with a systematic diagnosis of the current situation in order to determine both the need for change and the capability to change. The objectives, content, and process of change should all be specified as part of a change management plan.

According to en.wikipedia.org/wiki/Change_management, successful change management is more likely to occur if the following are included:

▶ Benefits management and realization to define measurable stakeholder aims, create a business case for their achievement (which should be continuously updated), and monitor assumptions, risks, dependencies, costs, return on investment, benefits, and cultural issues affecting the progress of the associated work.

▶ Effective communications that informs various stakeholders of the reasons for the change (Why?), the benefits of successful implementation (What is in it for us, and you?) as well as the details of the change (When? Where? Who is involved? How much will it cost? etc.).

▶ Devise an effective education, training, and/or skills upgrading program for the organization.

▶ Counter resistance from the employees of companies and align them with the organization's overall strategic direction.

▶ Provide personal counseling (if required) to alleviate any change-related fears.

▶ Monitor the implementation and fine-tuning as required.

HOW TO ORGANIZE AN EC UNIT IN A COMPANY

If a company is engaged in EC, it will have employees in this area. The question is how to organize the EC unit doing it. The best organizations depend on many variables such as:

- The absolute and relative side of the EC workforce
- The nature of the EC projects (e.g., e-tailing, e-procurement, e-training)
- The existing organizational structure of the company
- Is the company pure-play EC?
- The nature of the products/services sold by the company
- The internal politics of the organization
- How many EC projects exist
- The budget of the EC workforce

These factors need to be considered. The major options available are discussed next.

Options for Organizing the EC Workforce

The major options are as follows.

Report to the Marketing Department. This is a viable solution for the case where e-tailing is the major EC activity

Report to the Finance Department. This happens in cases where EC involves repeated RFQ, outsourcing, and other finance-related activities.

Report to the Chief Operating Officer. This could be a good solution if the major EC activity is e-procurement.

Distribute the EC Workforce in Several Departments. This can be a suitable solution when EC activities are fairly independent of each other and closely related to specific departments.

Report to the IT Department. This makes sense when EC is continuously engaged in the technical aspects of EC.

Create a New, Autonomous EC Department. This solution can vary for a large EC workforce, and when top management wants to give EC special visibility.

No Formal Structure for EC. Should the EC unit be a separate entity or part of the IT department?

Create an Autonomous Division or a Separate Online Company

When the volume of e-business is large, the temptation to create a separate company increases, especially if you take it to an IPO. Barnes & Noble did just that.
The advantages of creating a separate company are:

- Reducing or eliminating internal conflicts
- Providing more freedom for the online company's management in pricing, advertising, and other decisions
- Creating a new brand quickly
- Taking the e-business to an IPO, and if successful, making a fortune

The disadvantages of creating an independent division are:

- It may be very costly and risky.
- Collaboration with the offline business may be difficult.
- You lose the expertise of the business function (marketing, finance, distribution), unless you get superb collaboration.

Note that some spin-offs of this nature, such as barnesandnoble.com, were not doing so well, and grainger.com has merged back into its parent company. However, several spin-off online companies have succeeded as independent entities.

Section 13.9 ▶ REVIEW QUESTIONS

1. List the major parts of Bloch, et al.'s value-added model.
2. Describe how EC improves direct marketing.

3. Describe how EC transforms organizations.

4. Describe how EC redefines organizations.

5. Define process restructuring and BPR.

6. Define BPM and explain its relationship to change management.

7. Discuss the need for change management in deploying EC projects to e-business.

8. Describe the position and structure of the EC unit in organizations.

13.10   OPPORTUNITIES FOR SUCCESS IN E-COMMERCE AND AVOIDING FAILURE

Now that EC has been around for several years, it is possible to observe certain patterns and success stories that contribute to its success or failure of EC projects. By examining these patterns, one can find indications of the opportunities that lie ahead and how to avoid pitfalls along the way. This section examines EC failures, the key factors to EC success, and some strategies that are needed to enable EC success.

FACTORS THAT DETERMINE E-COMMERCE SUCCESS

The economic capabilities of EC described earlier influence some industries more than others. The success factors of EC depend on the industry, the sellers and buyers, and the products sold. Furthermore, the ability of sellers to create economic value for consumers will also determine EC success. When deciding to sell online, looking at the major factors that determine the impact of EC can assist in evaluating the chances for success.

 Four categories of e-market success factors commonly exist: *product*, *industry*, *seller*, and *consumer* characteristics. These factors are discussed in Online File W13.9.

E-Commerce Failures

By examining the economic history of previous innovations, the failure of EC initiatives and EC companies (see discussions in Chapters 1 through 4) should come as no surprise. Three economic phenomena suggest why this is the case:

1. At a macroeconomic level, technological revolutions, such as the railroad and the automobile industries, have had a boom-bust-consolidation cycle. For example, between 1904 and 1908, more than 240 companies entered the then-new automobile manufacturing business in the United States. In 1910, the shakeout began. Today, there are only three major U.S. automakers, but the size of the auto industry has grown several hundred times.

   Arthur (1996) compared the Internet revolution with the railroad revolution and found that both followed a similar pattern. First, there was the excitement over the emerging technology, then irrational euphoria followed by inflated market values of anything related to the new technology, and then the bust. However, Arthur notes that following the bust, the railroads saw their golden period, in which railroad activities in England grew tenfold. Why was this the case? Arthur believes that the real benefits of a technology come when organizations structure their activities around the cluster of technologies (e.g., after railroads emerged, steel rails, track safety systems, traffic control systems, and so on were needed). Similarly, businesses relocated to where the cost and availability of raw materials were favorable along the railroad lines.

2. At a mid-economic level, the bursting of the dot-com bubble from 2000 through 2003 is consistent with periodic economic downturns that have occurred in real estate, precious metals, currency, and stock markets.

3. At a microeconomic level, the "Web rush" reflected an overallocation of scarce resources—venture capital and technical personnel—and too many advertising-driven business models. This is analogous to the influx of people and resources to specific places during a "gold rush."

Chapters 3 and 12 provide some of the specific reasons for failure in B2C EC: lack of profitability, excessive risk exposure, the high cost of customer acquisition, poor performance, and static website design. Two additional financial reasons are lack of funding and incorrect revenue models. An example is the Webvan case, an express delivery company that lost $1.2 billion—the largest of any other bankrupt dot.com. Another company is Kozmo whose story is available in Online File W13.10. With EC, B2B businesses have been trying to improve interfirm operations and customer service by allowing customers and partners to interact directly with the websites providing self-service.

E-COMMERCE SUCCESSES

Despite the failure of hundreds of start-ups and thousands of EC projects, EC is alive and well and continues to grow rapidly after a short pause from 2000 through 2002, as discussed throughout the text.

EC success stories abound, primarily in specialty and niche markets. One example is Puritan's Pride (puritan.com), a successful vitamin and natural health care product store. Another is Campusfood (campusfood.com), which allows college students to order takeout food online (Chapter 1). Also doing very well are employment sites, such as Monster (monster.com). Alloy (alloy.com) is a successful shopping and entertainment portal for young adults. As pointed out in Chapter 3, online services such as stock trading, travel reservations, online banking, and more are commanding a major part of the business in their industries. For a comparison of how these and other thriving online businesses have translated critical success factors (CSFs) from the old economy into EC success, see Exhibit 13.21.

EC companies such as Priceline, Netflix, Amazon.com, Facebook, and Google are becoming major players in their industries, making their shareholders very rich.

Following are some of the reasons for EC success and suggestions from EC experts and consultants on how to succeed in EC.

Strategies for EC Success

Thousands of brick-and-mortar companies are adding online marketing and/or procurement channels with great success. Examples are uniglobe.com, staples.com, homedepot.com, walmart.com, clearcommerce.com, 1800flowers.com, and iflyswa.com (Southwest Airlines). Existing firms can use organizational knowledge, brand recognition, infrastructure, and other "morphing strategies" to migrate from the offline marketplace to the online marketspace. The following are strategies and critical success factors that can help EC succeed.

▶ Kauffman, et al. (2006) assert strategies that include moving to higher-quality customers, changing products or services in their existing market, and establishing an

EXHIBIT 13.21 Critical Success Factors: Old Economy and EC

Old Economy CSFs	EC CSFs
Vertically integrate or do it yourself.	Create new partnerships and alliances; stay with core competency.
Deliver high-value products.	Deliver high-value service offerings that encompass products.
Build market share to establish economies of scale.	Optimize natural scale and scope of business; look at mass customization.
Analyze carefully to avoid missteps.	Approach with urgency to avoid being locked out; use proactive strategies.
Leverage physical assets.	Leverage intangible assets, capabilities, and relationships—unleash dormant assets.
Compete to sell product.	Compete to control access and relationships with customers; compete with websites.

offline presence (e.g., moving from pure-play dot-com to click-and-mortar). The authors provide guidelines for understanding successful e-business strategy.

▶ Pavlou and Gefen (2004) found that institutional-based trust, which is derived from buyers' perceptions that effective third-party institutional mechanisms are in place, is critical to EC success. These mechanisms include (1) feedback mechanisms, (2) third-party escrow services, and (3) credit card guarantees. This helps explain why, despite the inherent uncertainty that arises when buyers and sellers are separated in time and in space, online marketplaces are proliferating.

▶ A group of Asian CEOs recommend the following EC CSFs: select robust business models, anticipate the dot-com future, foster e-innovation, carefully evaluate a spin-off strategy, co-brand, employ ex-dot-com staffers, and focus on the e-generation, as alloy.com and bolt.com have done. Kambil and van Heck (2002) found that for an EC exchange to be successful, it has to create value for *all* participants, not just the sellers, the market maker, or the buyers. The issue of value in an online exchange is the subject of debate among the many suppliers in the electronic marketplace. These authors also recommend that for EC to be successful, it should support and enrich human interactions through technologies such as virtual reality (i.e., increase richness).

▶ Pricing in EC has continued to be a challenge for sellers because of handling and shipping costs. Often the seller and market maker will see the potential for profits and ignore the fact that the buyers will subscribe to EC only if they see the benefit in price or product variety. For example, HP, Amazon.com, and other e-tailers decided to absorb delivery costs for orders above a certain level (e.g., $25). Free shipping is also available at Dell, Newegg, and many other e-tailers.

▶ New technologies can boost the success of EC. For example, RFID has great potential for improving the supply chain (Chapter 11); however, it will take a large investment in EC infrastructure and applications to realize its full potential.

Guidelines for success in the following areas are provided by en.wikipedia.org/wiki/Electronic_commerce and others:

▶ Technical and organizational aspects of good management
▶ Customer-oriented approach
▶ Handling problems properly and quickly
▶ Product suitability for online sale (especially digital products)
▶ Consumer acceptance of electronic shopping
▶ Peters (2006) offered 15 steps to EC success at websitecm.com. Peters supports several of Wikipedia's guidelines.
▶ Veneeva (2006) suggests that the current improvements in Internet services and their inherent characteristics, like improved security, reliability, user-friendliness, two-way communication, low costs, accessibility, and customizability, have been the driving forces for successful e-commerce.

Additional Guidelines for EC Success. A number of experts and consultants have proposed many more keys to success. Several studies identified the following factors that contributed to the successful implementation of B2C and B2B EC projects:

▶ The top three factors for successful B2C e-commerce are effective marketing management, an attractive website, and building strong connections with the customers.
▶ The top three factors for successful B2B e-commerce are the readiness of trading partners, information integration inside the company and in the supply chain, and the completeness of the EC system.
▶ The top three factors for the overall success of an e-business are a proper business model, readiness of the firm to become an e-business, and internal enterprise integration.

At this still-early stage of the EC revolution, success cannot be assured, and failure rates will remain high. However, if companies learn from the mistakes of the past and follow the guidelines offered by experts and researchers, their chances for success are greatly enhanced.

In the remaining parts of this section, we will discuss important strategies and factors that should be considered to assure EC success.

CULTURAL DIFFERENCES IN EC SUCCESSES AND FAILURES

Chapter 1 mentioned culture as a possible barrier to the use of EC. In Chapter 12, we discussed the need to understand cultural issues such as differences in social norms, measurement standards, and nomenclature. Here, we raise the issue of cultural differences so that appropriate metrics can be developed.

One of the strengths of EC is the ease with which its adopters can reach a global population of consumers or suppliers. However, EC-driven businesses must consider the cultural differences in this diverse global consumer base because without the broad acceptance of the EC channel, consumers may choose not to participate in online transactions. Critical elements that can affect the value of EC across cultures are perceived trust, consumer loyalty, regulation, and political influences. Even the content of online ads can mean different things in different cultures. Due to these differences, the transaction costs, including coordination costs, may vary among the consumer base.

EC success factors differ among countries and so do adoption strategies (see Online File W13.11).

Can EC Succeed in Developing Economies?

Similar to cultural differences, developed and developing economies vary in how EC is used and whether the economics favor this channel of commerce. Developing economies struggle with various issues taken for granted in developed economies, such as the United States or Singapore.

Developing economies often face power blackouts, unreliable telecommunications infrastructure, undependable delivery mechanisms, and the fact that only a few customers own computers and credit cards. Such limitations make it difficult for firms to predict whether EC investments will pay off, and when. However, developing economies, such as China and India, represent a significant opportunity for EC to connect businesses to customers, as well as other businesses. The potential volume of transactions in developed countries can make EC investments more attractive for established firms. This is because much of the cost of EC systems development would have already been recovered because EC initiatives frequently can use existing IT infrastructures.

The traditional EC assumption is that every computer user has the investment capacity to own a computer and maintain a dedicated Internet connection, as is the case in developed economies. In developing economies, the assumption will have to be revised to incorporate low-cost access, pay for use only, a community of users, and mass coverage. The payoffs from EC use in developing countries are likely to go beyond financial returns. Enabling people to take advantage of EC technology without disrupting their traditions may be the most valuable, yet intangible, return.

A major booster for EC in developing countries is the increasing use of low-cost laptop computers in a wireless environment. With computer cost less than $150 (in 2011 and declining) and the widespread use of cell phones with Internet access and free access in public places, it is likely that EC use will increase significantly in developing countries. For comprehensive coverage of e-commerce in developing countries, see Sanayei (2010).

Section 13.10 ▶ REVIEW QUESTIONS

1. Describe product characteristics in EC.
2. What are industry characteristics in EC?
3. What are seller characteristics in EC?
4. What are consumer characteristics in EC?
5. List three reasons why EC failure should not come as a surprise.
6. What are some reasons for EC success?
7. Relate EC to cultural differences.
8. Discuss some factors of implementation in developing countries.

MANAGERIAL ISSUES

Some managerial issues related to this chapter are as follows:

1. **How should the value of EC investment be justified?** EC investments must be measured against their contribution to business objectives. The best justification may come from the behavior of competitors. If EC has a strategic value to customers, there is no choice but to invest as long as competitors provide EC services. EC investments will involve direct and indirect costs as well as tangible and intangible benefits. The impact of EC on reengineering the existing processes and systems must not be ignored.

   Automated transactions in EC may replace human roles in sales, procurement, and services. However, in some applications like customer service and knowledge management, EC may supplement rather than replace the human element. The measurement of EC value, including both tangible and intangible benefits, should occur against the backdrop of metrics that define business performance and success. To identify the intangible benefits, refer to the business performance indicators in the balanced scorecard, which may not be easily measured in tangible metrics.

2. **Which investment analysis method should we adopt for EC justification?** The precise estimation of total cost of ownership is a good starting point for financial investment analysis. If an intangible benefit is the primary source of benefit, such as enhanced customer services and quality assurance of purchased material, management has to judge the tangible cost with an intangible benefit. However, if the tangible benefit can be precisely measured, such as creation of new revenue and/or reduced purchase cost, the net present value and ROI can be computed with tangible benefits and costs. Based on the investment analysis, the intangible factors may be considered additionally for managers' multicriteria judgments. Since there is high uncertainty in estimating the future revenue creation, the best or worst case analysis may supplement the most-likely analysis.

3. **Who should conduct the justification?** For small projects, the project team possibly in cooperation with the finance department can do the analysis. For a large or complex project, we may use the unbiased outside consultant although it may be expensive. The justification should include both tangible and intangible benefits and costs. However, some vendors may provide ROI calculators as a part of a proposal that may fit with your application without extra charge.

4. **Should we use the hype cycle?** The hype cycle can be extremely useful in determining EC strategy. Small organizations may use some of the free material (e.g., one year old; no details). For specific advice it may be worth it to pay Gartner for the detailed charts and analysis.

5. **What is the outsourcing strategy?** Many large-scale enterprises are capable of building and running their own EC websites. However, EC websites may require complex integration, security, and excellent performance. Outsourcing has become the major trend in order to reduce the large development investment. These services enable companies to start small and evolve to full-featured functions through the use of ASPs, Internet malls, and software vendors that offer merchant server and EC applications. Outsourcing is strongly recommended, particularly for small companies. Nevertheless, some parts should be built in-house (insourced) to secure more direct control over data management. Thus, the integration of internal systems and outsourced systems is a challenging issue.

6. **Should we embark on cloud computing products for our EC initiatives?** According to the hype cycle, you probably should wait for awhile. However, companies do report successful implementation in EC system development, security, e-CRM, and e-procurement. Given that it takes only a few years to move from hype to maturity, it is wise to at least experiment with some projects.

7. **Which strategy should we choose for vendor selection: the inside-out or outside-in approach?** Because most EC applications are built from packaged applications and components, or are outsourced to a third party, the success of the EC application rests on choosing the right vendor and package. Two approaches are the inside-out approach (e.g., an ERP package provided by a vendor that expands its scope to encompass the e-business components like e-procurement and e-CRM) and the outside-in approach (the best-of-the-breed of e-business components can be integrated within an ERP package). Recently, the solution of inside-out tends to win in the market because design by a single vendor provides a more consistent architecture.

8. **What kinds of organizational changes may be needed?** Companies should expect organizational changes in all functional areas once e-commerce reaches momentum. Change is particularly evident in the financial services sector, where services can broadly be replaced by the Internet. Social marketing and shopping is another area with major potential changes (especially f-commerce). Electronic procurement changes the purchasing business processes, and affiliate programs change the paradigm of marketing and business partnerships. Finally, the trends toward build-to-order and demand-driven manufacturing will continue to expand and may require restructuring of some business processes.

9. **Is it possible to predict EC success?** The more comprehensive the analysis, the more accurate the justification of the EC project; its chances for success and approval will be greater even though management cannot precisely know the future success of the project. Procurement innovation using EC is almost risk free in achieving the goals. Refer to the fee strategy of iMarketKorea (iMK) for its procurement services in

the closing case in Chapter 4. IMK does not charge a fee, but shares the discount effect with its customers. This kind of project is almost risk free. However, using EC for sales increases is uncertain. Opening new independent e-marketplaces may require high investment and is very risky because the entry barriers may be already very high. This kind of EC investment may fail. The risk depends on the type of EC being used.

SUMMARY

In this chapter, you learned about the following EC issues as they relate to the chapter's learning objectives.

1. **The major components of EC implementation.** Four major categories exist for implementation: justification and economics (cost–benefit); acquiring and/or developing the EC systems; assurance of organizational readiness and performance of necessary restructuring, training, and so forth; and cultivating the necessary success factors while avoiding the mistakes.

2. **The need for EC justification.** Like any other investment, EC investment (unless it is small) needs to be justified. Many start-up EC companies have crashed because of no or incorrect justification. In its simplest form, justification looks at revenue minus all relevant costs. Analysis is done by defining performance and comparing actual performance to the planned one's metrics and KPI related to organizational goals.

3. **The difficulties in justifying EC investment.** The nature of EC makes it difficult to justify due to the presence of many intangible costs and benefits. In addition, the relationship between investment and results may be complex, extending over several years. Also, several projects may share both costs and benefits; several different or organizational areas may feel the impacts (sometimes negatively).

4. **Difficulties in established intangible metrics.** Intangible benefits may be difficult to define. Some of these benefits change rapidly; others have different values to different people or organizational units. Therefore, metrics that are based on intangible benefits have qualitative measures that are difficult to compare. One solution is to quantify the qualitative measures. Scoring methodology, value analysis, and other advanced methods, as described in Online File W13.4, can be used.

5. **Traditional methods for evaluating EC investments.** Evaluating EC involves a financial analysis, usually the ROI analysis, as well as an assessment of the technology and its architecture. Future costs and benefits need to be discounted, using the NPV method, especially if the costs and benefits will extend over several years. A payback period describes how long it will take to

recover the initial investment. However, financial ROI alone can lead to an incomplete and misleading evaluation. Tools to integrate the various ROI aspects of EC investment include the balanced scorecard (BSC), which also focuses on the internal business processes and learning and growth perspective of the business. EC ROI should take into account the risk of reducing possible failures or adverse events that can drain the financial ROI. No method is universal or perfect, so selecting a method (or a mix of methods) is critical.

6. **Describe the justification of representative EC projects.** The justification of an EC project starts with a need analysis and then involves listing all the cost and the benefits. Examples are the justification of e-procurement and m-commerce. All EC projects include intangible and tangible benefits and costs that must be identified. Then, a method(s) must be selected to match the particular characteristics of the EC application.

7. **EC economic evaluation.** Economic fundamentals must be kept in mind when evaluating an EC investment. With nondigital products, the cost curve shows that average per unit costs decline as quantity increases. However, with digital products, the variable cost per unit usually is low, and thus, the evaluation will differ. Similar differences are evident in EC's ability to lower transaction costs, agency costs, and transaction risks. EC can also enable the firm to be agile in responding faster to changing market conditions and ensure increasing returns to scale regardless of the volume involved. Finally, EC enables increased reach with multimedia richness at a reasonable cost.

8. **The major steps in developing an EC system.** Because of their cost and complexity, EC sites need to be developed in a systematic fashion. The development of an EC site should proceed in steps. First, an EC application portfolio is defined based on an organization's strategy. Second, the EC architecture is created. Next, a decision is made whether to build, buy,

or outsource the development. Third, the system is installed, tested, and deployed. Finally, the system goes into maintenance mode, with continual changes being made to ensure the system's continuing success.

9. **The major EC development strategies, along with their advantages and disadvantages.** EC sites and applications are rarely built from scratch. Instead, enterprises buy a packaged EC suite and customize it to suit their needs, or they outsource the development to a third party. A new generation of Web tools is taking the programmer out of the development process and empowering more users to develop their own websites. The selection of one option over another should be based on a systematic comparison of a detailed list of requirements that examines important considerations such as flexibility, information needs, user-friendliness, hardware, and software resources.

10. **The varied EC application development methods, along with their benefits and limitations.** Once a strategy has been determined, numerous development methods can be used to develop an EC system. These include Web 2.0, software as a service (SaaS), utility computing, cloud computing, and many others listed and detailed within the chapter. Depending on the resources available to the organization developing the EC system and the requirements of the system, one or more of the different development methods will be chosen to create the most efficient and effective solution.

11. **EC application outsourcing strategies.** Many enterprises elect to outsource the development and maintenance of their EC sites and applications. The most common type of EC applications outsourcing is the use of software as a service (SaaS). Utility computing is another popular option, and the emerging concept of cloud computing is growing in popularity. An enterprise can also rely on an existing e-marketplace or exchange. A webstore can be hosted by an Internet mall. Or an enterprise could enter into a joint development agreement with a venture partner or a consortium. Again, the choice depends on the functional requirements of the EC site or application, the costs involved, the time frame, and the available IT resources.

12. **Criteria used in selecting software vendors and packages.** A systematic process should be used in selecting a third-party tool or an outsourcing company. Among the key steps in making the selection are (1) identifying potential vendors and packages, (2) detailing the evaluation criteria, (3) using the criteria to produce a short list of possible vendors, (4) choosing a candidate from the short list, (5) negotiating the deal and modifications needed to meet overall application needs, and (6) establishing an SLA to define who is responsible for specific aspects of the development and maintenance, and what quality metrics will be used for the services to be rendered.

13. **The impact of e-markets on organizations.** All functional areas of an organization can be affected by e-markets. Broadly, e-markets improve direct marketing and transform and redefine organizations. Direct marketing (manufacturers to customers) and one-to-one marketing and advertising are becoming the norm, and mass customization and personalization are taking off. Production is moving to a build-to-order model, changing supply chain relationships and reducing cycle time. Business process management (BPM) enables organizations to be more efficient, more effective, and more capable of adaptation to change. Change management is an organizational process aimed at empowering employees to accept and embrace changes in their current business environment. Both these processes are crucial to organizational growth.

14. **Reasons for EC success and failure.** Products, industry, seller, and consumer characteristics require different metrics of EC value. With the growing worldwide connectivity to the Internet, EC economics will play a major role in supporting buyers and sellers. Like other innovations, EC is expected to go through the cycle of enormous success, followed by speculation, and then disaster before the reality of the new situation sets in. Some EC failures were the result of problematic website design, lack of sustained funding, and weak revenue models. Success in EC has come through automating and enhancing familiar strategies, such as branding, morphing, trust building, and creating value for all trading partners by enriching the human experience with integrated and timely information. EC investments can go beyond the traditional business models by creating digital options. To ensure success, complementary investments must be made in managing change and responding to cultural differences among EC users.

KEY TERMS

Acceptance testing	691	EC architecture	689	Reusability	692
Agency costs	683	Hype cycle	672	ROI calculator	676
Agility	685	Insourcing	692	Total benefits of ownership	
Business process management		Integration testing	691	(TBO)	675
(BPM)	701	Interoperability	692	Total cost of ownership (TCO)	675
Business process reengineering		Key performance indicator (KPI)	666	Transaction costs	683
(BPR)	700	Mass customization	701	Turnkey approach	692
Change management	702	Metric	666	Unit testing	691
Cloud computing	695	Outsourcing	693	Usability testing	691
Cost–benefit analysis	665	Product differentiation	685	Valuation	685
Disintermediation	700	Production function	682	Web analytics	667

DISCUSSION QUESTIONS

1. Your state government is considering an online vehicle registration system. Develop a set of EC metrics and discuss how these metrics differ from that of the existing manual system.

2. Discuss the advantage of using several methods (e.g., ROI, payback period) to justify investments.

3. Enter businesscase.com and find material on ROI analysis. Discuss how ROI is related to a business case.

4. A craftsperson operates a small business making wooden musical instruments in a small U.S. town. The business owner is considering using EC to increase the business's reach to the nation and the world. How can the business owner use EC to increase richness to make the products more attractive to consumers?

5. A company is planning a wireless-based CRM system for its customers. Almost all the benefits are intangible. How can you justify the project to top management?

6. A large company with a number of products wants to start selling on the Web. Should it use a merchant server or an EC application suite? Assuming it elects to use an EC application suite, how would you determine whether the company should outsource the site or run it in-house?

7. An enterprise wants to modify its EC site so that it conforms more closely with the company's overall business strategies. What sorts of online data are available for this purpose? How can these data be collected? What types of business strategy questions can be addressed by these data?

8. Discuss product and industry characteristics as effecting EC success.

9. Discuss the need to restructure business processes and how to do it.

TOPICS FOR CLASS DISCUSSION AND DEBATES

1. Discuss the logic of outsourcing the combined Web hosting and site construction. What are some of the disadvantages?

2. Enter clearvale.com and find the free enterprise product for businesses looking for a simple way to offer social networking functionalities for employees. Examine the capabilities provided and discuss the cases for which such an offer could be attractive. When would it be unattractive?

3. Debate: A cost–benefit analysis may be inaccurate, so why should we conduct it?

4. Debate the use of utility computing (leasing) against the purchase of a merchant suite by a retailer.

5. Debate: An airline offers extensive travel services online including hotels, car rentals, vacations, and so forth all over the globe. Its online business should be autonomous.

INTERNET EXERCISES

1. Enter **idc.com** and find how it evaluates ROI on intranets, supply chains, and other EC and IT projects. Enter **nucleusresearch.com**. Go to "Research," "Latest Research," and then click "View ROI Scorecards." Open the PDF file titled "Market ROI Scorecard: Hosted CRM" for a review of hosted CRM vendors. Summarize your findings in a report. (Note: Use Google to find this information.)

2. Enter **schwab.com**. Examine the list of online services available for planning and retirement, and advised investment services. Relate them to *richness* and *reach*.

3. Go to **google.com** and search for articles dealing with the ROI of RFID. List the key issues in measuring the ROI of RFID.

4. Go to **alinean.com/salesenablement.aspx** and follow the walk-through of the calculators. Find the capabilities of the calculators. Calculate the ROI of a project of your choice as well as the TCO.

5. Enter **sas.com**, **corvu.com**, **balancedscorecard.org**, and **cio.com**. Find demos and examples of how to use the various tools and methods to evaluate EC projects. Write a report.

6. Enter **solutionmatrix.com** and find information about ROI, metrics, and cost–benefit tools. Write a report based on your findings.

7. Enter **roi-calc.com**. View the demos. What investment analysis services does the company provide?

8. Enter **zebra.com** and find its ROI calculators (go to resource library). What analysis do the calculators provide?

9. Enter **timberland.com** and design a pair of boots. Design a pair of shoes at **nike.com** and **zappos.com/shoe.zhtml**. Compare all three.

10. Enter **sap.com** and use the "casebuilder calculator" for a hypothetical (or real) EC project. Write a report on your experience.

11. Enter **searchcio.techtarget.com** and find free ROI analysis tools. Download a tool of your choice and identify its major components. Write a report.

12. Enter **peaksalesconsulting.com/CRM-ROI.htm** and use its free calculator to examine a CRM project of your choice.

TEAM ASSIGNMENTS AND PROJECTS

1. **Assignment for the Opening Case**

   Read the opening case and answer the following questions:

   a. What were the drivers of the EC project?

   b. Why was there no formal justification and need analysis?

   c. Describe the outsourcing and vendor selection process (consult Section 13.8).

   d. The core of the system was based on SaaS. Today it is changed to cloud computing (Online Tutorial T7). Explain how cloud computing can improve the EC system.

   e. The SharePoint server was an integral part of the system. Consider adding Chatter (**salesforce.com/chatter**). Is it worth it? Why or why not?

   f. E-CRM was a major component in the system. Consult Online Tutorial T1 and explain why it was absolutely necessary to use e-CRM as a component.

2. Download and then read the ROI case study "Venda Xerox Document Supplies (Case Study E11)" from the Nucleus Research (**nucleusresearch.com**) website. While you are connected to the Internet, click "ROI Help Tutorial" in the NR_Standard_ROI_Tool.xls file and read modules 1 through 4. Enter your assumptions of costs and benefits into the calculator and examine how they impact the overall ROI, payback period, NPV, and average yearly cost of ownership (under the Summary tab).

   Answer the following questions based on the Venda Xerox Document Supplies ROI case study.

   a. What were the key reasons why Xerox developed an EC system?

   b. What were the areas in which Xerox could benefit from EC?

   c. How did Xerox calculate the ROI of the EC system?

3. Explore the business value of EC. Each member enters a different site (e.g., **nicholasgcarr.com**, **baselinemag.com**, **strassmann.com**, etc.). Prepare a presentation on issues, value, and directions.

4. Select a series of websites that cater to the same type of buyer and product/service (e.g., several websites that offer CDs or computer hardware). Divide the sites among several teams and ask each team to prepare an analysis of the different sorts of functions

provided by the sites, along with a comparison of the strong and weak points of each site from the buyer's perspective.

5. Several vendors offer products for creating webstores. The websites of these vendors usually list those online stores that currently use their software (customer success stories). Assign each team a number of vendors. Each team should prepare reports comparing the similarities and differences among the vendors' sites and evaluating the customers' success stories. Do the customers take advantage of the functionality provided by the various products?

6. Read the Alliance Insurance case in Online File W13.12. Answer all the questions in the case.

7. Enter youtube.com/watch?v=qh1drAg1jdg and watch the video titled "Gartner Hype Cycle." Write a summary of the major points. Then do the assignment provided there.

8. The class will set up a store in Facebook. You can use the application from payment.com or from support.bigcommerce.com/questions/1172. Have several members place products there while others do some shopping. Write a report on your experience.

Closing Case

DEVELOPING A WEB 2.0 PLATFORM TO ENABLE INNOVATIVE MARKET RESEARCH AT DEL MONTE

The Problem

Utilizing the latest innovations in technology can often give companies a competitive advantage, particularly if they are the first to use that technology in the marketplace. Even if a company is not the first to market, keeping up with technology trends and capabilities often becomes a necessity to thrive in the business world. One key to using technology to create a competitive advantage is to observe what strides are being made in various industries or sectors, and then develop that idea or tool to be applicable to the business at hand.

One major trend in today's society is social networking. Sites such as Facebook and MySpace have caused a phenomenon—especially among teenagers and young adults. Social networks are powerful tools that allow people to build or maintain relationships with others around the world. Now the idea has evolved to incorporate social networking into businesses (Chapter 7). One such company to introduce social networking into its business environment is Del Monte.

Del Monte is known mostly for manufacturing canned fruits and vegetables. In addition to these products, Del Monte also produces pet food such as 9Lives, Gravy Train, Meow Mix, Milk-Bone, as well as other products. Once Del Monte made the decision to experiment with social networking, it had to decide how to best implement it to support its diverse product line.

The Solution

Even though Del Monte executives were able to see the value of a social networking system, the IT department was not equipped to handle the implementation of a social network. So, Del Monte recruited MarketTools, a firm that specializes in market research and data analysis, and also has experience with Web 2.0 capabilities.

With the help of MarketTools, Del Monte's website now offers a platform for customers to chat and blog about products, or share tips and recipes. MarketTools monitors millions of blogs in order to recognize key ideas among consumers and identify trends. The information that customers share with each other is collected and analyzed by MarketTools. Del Monte then teamed up with Umbria (a division of J.D. Power and Associates and a pioneer in drawing market intelligence from the online community), to assist it in further analyzing and profiling the information collected and stored in a data warehouse. By utilizing social networks, Del Monte can conduct market research much more efficiently. Focus groups have become a thing of the past. All that is required now is to sift through the vast amount of customer information that is collected in cyberspace. The information collected helps Del Monte plan its marketing, advertising, and customer service applications. It also helps in evaluating the success of EC projects and justifying similar investments.

The Result

Del Monte used this method of market research when developing a dog treat, Snausages Breakfast Bites. By paying attention to customer blogs and by posting questions to customers, Del Monte concluded that owners of small dogs would be the major purchasers of Snausages Breakfast Bites. Del Monte depended on the dog lovers group for guidance in the development of this product. By doing so, a smaller treat was produced, packaging decisions were revised, product cycle time was reduced to 6 months, and Del Monte was able to cut costs.

Sources: Compiled from Steel (2008), Greengard (2008), and *marketools.com/solution* (accessed April 2011).

Questions

1. What motivated Del Monte to use social networks?

2. Relate the capabilities of the social network sites to the market research activities (be specific on a one-to-one basis).

3. Compare the methods used here to both computerized and noncomputerized focus groups.

4. How can the data collected be used for EC justification?

ONLINE RESOURCES
available at pearsonglobaleditions.com/turban

WWW

Online Files

W13.1   Nucleus Research's ROI Methodology

W13.2   Handling Intangible Benefits

W13.3   Issues in Implementing Traditional Justification Methods

W13.4   Advanced Methods for Justifying EC and IT Investments Value Analysis

W13.5   E-Procurement Complexities in Marketplaces

W13.6   Application Case: Cost–Benefit Justification of Wireless E-Commerce at Paesano Restaurant of Australia

W13.7   Insourcing Options

W13.8   Vendor and Software Selection

W13.9   Categories of E-Market Success Factors

W13.10   Application Case: The Rise and Fall of Kozmo.com

W13.11   Application Case: The Success Story of E-Choupal

W13.12   Application Case: Alliance Insurance Exercise

Comprehensive Educational Websites

mmv.vic.gov.au/ecommerce: Case studies.

nucleuresearch.com: Metrics, ROI.

roi-calc.com: Calculators, metrics.

baselinemag.com: Calculators, metrics.

strassmann.com: ROI, justification.

ecommercedevelopmentcenter.com/services.asp: E-Commerce Development Center resources and links.

fstc.org: Financial Services Technology Consortium.

webbuyersguide.com/resource/brief.aspx?id=13626&category= 92&sitename=webbuyersguide&kc=newseditors022809&src= newseditors022809: The Gartner Magic Quadrant for E-Commerce.

wiki.secondlife.com/wiki/video_tutorials: Video tutorials for d-learning providers.

vectec.org/resources: Research resources into the various aspects of e-business.

allthingsweb2.com: Open directory of Web 2.0 tools and so forth.

REFERENCES

Alter, A. "The Bitter Truth About ROI." *CIO Insight*, July 2006.

Anandarajan, M., et al. (Eds.). *The Internet and Workplace Transformation.* Armonk, NY: M.E. Sharpe, Inc., 2006.

Arthur, W. B. "Increasing Returns and the New World of Business." *Harvard Business Review*, 74, no. 4 (1996).

Baseline. "How to Calculate ROI." September 6, 2006. baselinemag.com/article2/0,1540,2012723,00.asp (accessed April 2011).

Beasley, M., A. Chen, K. Nunez, and L. Wright. "Balanced Scorecard and Enterprise Risk Management." *Strategic Finance*, March 2006.

Bloch, M., Y. Pigneur, and A. Segev. "Leveraging Electronic Commerce for Competitive Advantage: A Business Value Framework." *Proceedings of the Ninth International Conference on EDI-IOS*, June 1996, Bled, Slovenia.

Borenstein, D., P. Betencourt, and R. Baptista. "A Multi-Criteria Model for the Justification of IT Investments." *INFOR*, February 2005.

Bothama, H. "State of the Art in TCO." SAP white paper with ASUG, January 2006.

Chen, S. *Strategic Management of E-Business*, 2nd ed. West Sussex, England: John Wiley & Sons, Ltd., 2005.

CIO Insight. "Top Trends for 2005." December 2004.

Clifton, B. *Advanced Web Metrics with Google Analytics*, 2nd ed. Hoboken, NJ: Sybex, 2010.

David, J. S., D. Schuff, and R. St. Louis. "Managing Your IT Total Cost of Ownership." *Communications of the ACM*, 45, no. 1 (2002).

Devaraj, S., and R. Kohli. *The IT Payoff: Measuring Business Value of Information Technology Investment.* Upper Saddle River, NJ: Prentice Hall, 2002.

Evans, P., and T. S. Wurster. *Blown to Bits: How the New Economics of Information Transforms Strategy.* Boston, MA: Harvard Business School Press, 2000.

Greengard, S. "Del Monte Gets Social." *Baseline*, July 30, 2008.

Hubbard, D. W. *How to Measure Anything: Finding the Value of Intangible in Business.* Hoboken, NJ: Wiley & Sons, 2007.

Jelassi, T., and A. Enders. *Strategies for E-Business.* 2nd ed. Harlow, England: Prentice Hall, 2008.

Jeston, J., and Nelis, J. *Business Process Management: Practical Guides to Successful Implementation*, 2nd ed. Burlington, MA: Butterworth-Heinemann, 2008.

Kambil, A., and E. van Heck. *Making Markets: How Firms Can Design and Profit from Online Auctions and Exchanges.* Boston, MA: Harvard Business School Press, 2002.

Kauffman, R. J., T. Miller, and B. Wang. "When Internet Companies Morph: Understanding Organizational Strategy Changes in the 'New' New Economy." *Special Issue: Commercial Applications of the Internet*, July 2006.

Kaushik, A. *Web Analytics 2.0: The Art of Online Accountability and Science of Customer Centricity.* Hoboken, NJ: Sybex, 2009.

Keen, J. M., and R. Joshi. *Making Technology Investment Profitable: ROI Roadmap to Better Business Cases*, 2nd ed. Hoboken, NJ: Wiley & Sons, 2009.

Kendall, K. E., and J. E. Kendall, *Systems Analysis and Design*, 8th ed. New Jersey: Prentice Hall, 2011.

Keystone Strategy, Inc. *Enterprise IT Capabilities and Business Performance Study.* March 16, 2006.

Kioses, E., K. Pramatari, and G. Doukidis. "Factors Affecting Perceived Impact of E-Marketplaces." *Proceedings of the 19th Bled eConference*, Bled, Slovenia, June 5–7, 2006.

McKay, J., and P. Marshall. *Strategic Management of E-Business.* Milton, Australia: Wiley & Sons, 2004.

Microsoft. "Case Study: Vodafone Essar. Limited." June 25, 2008. microsoft.com/india/CustomerEvidence/details. aspx?casestudyid=472&type=C (accessed February 2011).

Misra, R. "Evolution of the Philosophy of Investments in IT Projects." *Issues in Informing Sciences and Information Technology*, 3 (2006).

MobileInfo.com. "Mobile Computing Business Cases." mobileinfo.com/business_cases.htm (accessed January 2011).

Pavlou, P. A., and D. Gefen. "Building Effective Online Marketplaces with Institution-Based Trust." *Information Systems Research*, 15, no. 1 (2004).

Peacock, E., and M. Tanniru. "Activity-Based Justification of IT Investments." *Information Management*, March 2005.

Pearlson, K. E., and C. S. Sounders. *Managing and Using Information Systems.* Hoboken, NJ: Wiley & Sons, 2006.

Person, R. *Balanced Scorecards and Operational Dashboards with Microsoft Excel.* Hoboken, NJ: Wiley & Sons, 2009.

Peters, J. "15 Steps to E-Commerce Success." *WebsiteCM. com*, August 1, 2006. websitecm.com/ articles/15-steps-to-e-commerce-success-part-1 (accessed April 2011).

Pisello, T. "Metrics: ROI, IRR, NPV, Payback, Discounted Payback." *Techtarget*, September 15, 2006. searchcrm. techtarget.com/expert/KnowledgebaseAnswer/ 0,289625,sid11_gci1216028,00.html (accessed April 2011).

Rayport, J., and B. J. Jaworski. *Introduction to E-Commerce*, 2nd ed. New York: McGraw-Hill, 2004.

Read, T., *The IT Value Network: From IT Investment to Stakeholder Value*, Hoboken, NJ: Wiley & Sons, 2009.

Renkema, T. J. W. *The IT Value Quest: How to Capture the Business Value of IT-Based Infrastructure.* Chichester (UK) and New York: Wiley & Sons, 2000.

Sanayei, A. *E-Commerce in Developing Countries.* London, UK: Press Ltd., 2010.

Sidana, N. "The ROI on IT Investment." *Network Magazine*, December 2006. networkmagazineindia.com/200612/analyst'scorner01.shtml (accessed April 2011).

Singh, A. M. "Evolution of Marketing to E-Marketing." In M. Khosrow-Pour (Ed.), *Encyclopedia of E-Commerce, E-Government, and Mobile Commerce.* Hershey, PA: Idea Group Reference, 2006.

Smith, R. "Are You Meeting Quality Goals?" *Baseline*, October 2006.

Smith, A. C., and J. Laurent. "Allocating Value Among Different Classes of Equity." *Journal of Accountancy* (March 2008).

Soh, C., and L. M. Markus. "How IT Creates Business Value: A Process Theory Synthesis." *Proceedings of the 16th International Conference on Information Systems*, Amsterdam, Netherlands, December 10–13, 1995.

Spector, D. H. M. "Calculating TCO and ROI in Open Source Platforms." *TechRepublic*, April 6, 2006. techrepublic.com/downloads/calculating-tco-and-roi-on-open-source-platforms/172973 (accessed April 2011).

Steel, E. "The New Focus Groups: Online Networks." *Wall Street Journal Digital Network*, January 14, 2008. online.wsj.com/article/SB120027230906987357.html?mod=hpp_us_inside_today (accessed April 2011).

Veneeva, V. "E-Business: Success or Failure?" *Ezinearticles. com*, June 29, 2006. ezinearticles.com/?E-Business:-Successof-Failure?&id=232635 (accessed April 2011).

Wattemann, R. "ROI 101: Making the Business Case for Technology Investment." *CIO.com*, Analyst Report #1344 (by Nucleus Research). cio.com/analyst/report1344.html (no longer available online).

Wind, Y. "The Challenge of Customization in Financial Services." *Communications of the ACM* (2001).

Zappala, S., and C. Gray. *Impact of E-Commerce on Consumers and Small Firms.* Surrey, UK: Ashgate Publishing Co., 2006.

Zimmerman, J. *Web Marketing for Dummies.* Indianapolis, IN: Wiley & Sons, 2007.

CHAPTER 14

E-COMMERCE: REGULATORY, ETHICAL, AND SOCIAL ENVIRONMENTS

Content

Learning Objectives

Upon completion of this chapter, you will be able to:

1. Understand the foundations for legal and ethical issues in EC.

2. Describe intellectual property law and understand its adjudication.

3. Explain privacy and free speech issues and their challenges.

4. Describe types of fraud on the Internet and how to protect against them.

5. Describe the needs and methods to protect both buyers and sellers.

6. Describe EC-related societal issues.

7. Describe Green EC and IT.

WHY IS DISNEY FUNDING CHINESE PIRATES?

Disney's funding arm, Steamboat Ventures, invested $10 million in a popular Chinese video- and file-sharing site called 56.com (*56.com*). The site had 33 million registered members in 2009. Note that the words for "*56*" in Chinese sound similar to "I'm happy."

The Problem

In May 2008, The Walt Disney Company released its animated film *Wall-E*; the film was released on DVD in November 2008. However, immediately after the movie release in May, the robot love story was available for free on the Chinese video site 56.com. In other words, Disney is funding a Chinese site that bootlegs it own work.

The problem is that pirated movies are difficult to detect because they appear under different names. Although 56.com managed to remove some of the full-length bootlegged copies,

many others remain. The 56.com site is often referred to as a Chinese version of YouTube. But unlike YouTube, 56.com and similar sites like Toudou and Youku don't impose 10-minute limits on uploaded videos. And that makes them a haven for illegally uploaded videos, including full-length movies and TV episodes.

If 56.com were in any country but China, we'd expect the Recording Industry Association of America (RIAA) and similar organizations to put pressure on the company to remove copyrighted materials. But China doesn't have a very strong record of enforcing Western copyright laws.

The Solution

One reason that Disney invested in 56.com was that it hoped that Steamboat Ventures, as a major investor, would influence 56.com to take action against copyright violators. In other words, Steamboat Ventures is trying to help 56.com curb pirated videos.

In the United States, you can take legal action against companies such as 56.com for copyright violations. For example, media giant Viacom is suing Google's YouTube for $1 billion, requesting access to users' IP addresses and the video identifiers

for the entire YouTube database to see whether users are watching infringing videos more than noninfringing videos. The court ruled in favor of Google and no punitive damages were awarded. The judge determined that since 2005, Viacom, owner of iFilm.com, appears to have infringed copyrighted videos in the same manner as it had claimed YouTube was harming Viacom's interests (Albanesius 2008). However, that is not an option (yet) in China. At best, the Chinese government will provide a warning to violators.

The Results

Although 56.com is still facilitating free movies, video games, and the like, Disney seems not to be too concerned with these actions. Its investment provides the company a distribution channel for its products that may provide a strategic advantage to Disney in China. In March 2009, Disney allowed YouTube to run short videos as well as full episodes of its ABC (a television station) and ESPN (Internet and television sports channel) networks under an ad-revenue sharing arrangement.

In August 2009, 56.com launched 56KanKan, a fee-based innovative video content platform that provides user-paid benefits to original video authors, video makers, and copyright owners in exchange for video sharing. 56KanKan obtains highly valued and original video resources (uploaded by the original makers of the works) and then sets a price according to the quality of the videos.

Sources: Compiled from *56.com* (2009), Albanesuis (2008), McBride and Chao (2008), and *wikipedia.org/wiki/56.com* (accessed March 2011).

WHAT WE CAN LEARN . . .

Violation of copyrights on computers, as well as on the Internet, is a major problem for creators and distributors of intellectual property such as software, movies, music, and books. The problem arises not only because it is difficult to monitor millions of users and their postings, but also because in many countries there is not much legal protection of copyright, and even if there is, it is difficult and very expensive to enforce. Protection of intellectual property is one of the major EC legal issues presented in this chapter. An overview of other intellectual property topics, and especially piracy, are also presented. A full analysis of the legal and ethical issues is far beyond the scope of one chapter. For a comprehensive treatment and case studies, see Mann and Winn (2008). This chapter also deals with several societal issues related to EC, especially the potential environmental impacts known as "*Green EC*," and how the societal issues impact individual privacy and lifestyle enjoyment.

14.1 ETHICAL CHALLENGES AND GUIDELINES

Ethics describes how individuals choose to interact with one another. It is the branch of philosophy that deals with what is considered to be right and wrong. Ethics define the nature of duties that people owe themselves and one another. For example, one duty is to not intrude on a person's **privacy**, which is the right to be left alone and free of unreasonable personal intrusions.

Issues of privacy, ownership, control, and security must be confronted in understanding the ethical challenges of EC. The following are some of the daily concerns that confront ethical officers in a company: *Does information's availability justify its use? How much effort and expense should managers incur in considering questions of data access and privacy? What can employers expect from employees with regard to nondisclosure when going to work for another firm? What part of an information asset belongs to an organization and what is simply part of an employee's general knowledge? Do employees know the degree to which behavior is monitored? Does data gathered violate employee privacy rights? Is accuracy an explicit part of someone's responsibility? Have the implications of potential error been anticipated? Have systems been reviewed for the most likely sources of security breach? What's the liability exposure of managers and the organization?* For details, see Relkin (2006).

ETHICAL PRINCIPLES AND GUIDELINES

Law (that is, public law) embodies ethical principles, but the two are not the same. Acts that are generally considered unethical may not be illegal. Lying to a friend may be unethical, but it is not illegal. Conversely, the law is not simply the coding of ethical norms, and not all ethical codes are incorporated into public law.

A common agreement in a society as to what is right and wrong determines ethics, but they are not subject to legal sanctions except when they overlap with activities that also are illegal.

Online File W14.1 shows a framework for ethical issues.

An example of one ethical issue is the Facebook fiasco of 2009, described next.

Example: Who Owns User-Generated Content?

In February 2009, Facebook casually slipped into its terms of service an updated clause that users must sign before joining, announcing that users give Facebook an irrevocable, perpetual, nonexclusive, transferable, fully paid, worldwide license to use, retain, and display content posted to the site. In other words, anything you upload to Facebook can be used by Facebook in any way it deems fit, forever, no matter what you do later. Consumer watchdog groups and privacy experts immediately cried foul.

The objective of this change was to enable Facebook to sell customer data to marketers: Facebook needed more revenue sources. As a result, Facebook pointed out that the company would not use information in a way that goes against the privacy settings outlined by users, but retaining rights to content after the user has left is unprecedented for a social media site.

A November 2009 lawsuit, filed in U.S. District Court for the Northern District of California, alleged that the modifications have in reality reduced privacy protections for Facebook users rather than increasing it, as the company had claimed it would (Vijayan 2010). Facebook did not do a good enough job of communicating the changes to the terms of service, privacy experts say. Rather than asking users to agree to the new terms, or even sending an e-mail alert to all users, the company quietly added this line to its terms: Your continued use of the Facebook Service after any such changes constitutes your acceptance of the new terms. That may not be good business practice, but is it unethical?

BUSINESS ETHICS

Business ethics is a form of applied ethics that examines ethical principles and moral or ethical problems that arise in a business environment. In the increasingly conscience-focused marketplaces of the twenty-first century, the demand for more ethical business

---

ethics
The branch of philosophy that deals with what is considered to be right and wrong.

privacy
The right to be left alone and free of unreasonable personal intrusions.

business ethics
A form of applied ethics that examines ethical principles and moral or ethical problems that arise in a business environment.

processes and actions (known as *ethicism*) is increasing. Simultaneously, pressure is being applied on industries to improve business ethics through new public initiatives and laws (e.g., higher UK road tax for higher-emission vehicles). For example, today most major corporate websites emphasize a commitment to promoting noneconomic social values under a variety of headings (e.g., ethics codes, social responsibility charters).

Business ethics defines how a company integrates the core values of honesty, trust, respect, and fairness into its policies and practices—and complies with legal standards and regulations. The scope of business ethics has expanded to encompass a company's actions with regard not only to how it treats employees and obeys laws but to the nature and quality of the relationships with shareholders, customers, business partners, suppliers, the community, the environment, and even future generations, as well. European companies especially have embraced this expanded definition of ethics. Under recent clarifications of the U.S. Federal Sentencing Guidelines (ussc.gov/Guidelines), companies with credible ethics programs, as opposed to merely *paper* programs such as that of Enron, may reduce penalties or avoid prosecution for crimes committed by managers or employees.

Because of the worldwide scope and universal accessibility of the Internet, there are serious questions as to which ethical rules and laws apply. Since there are no U.S. federal or state statutes that currently prohibit employers from monitoring their electronic workplace, these questions involve an appreciation of the law that is constantly changing. Lawsuits and criminal charges are very disruptive, expensive, and may damage customer relations (see whitepapers.technologyevaluation.com/search/for/corporate-e-mail-lawsuits.html).

The Issues of Internet Abuse in the Workplace

In 2009, the 24/7 Wall St. Company conducted a workplace study about how people spend time online, and the actual wasted time and productivity losses turned out to be staggering. The survey found that while most workers spend about 22 hours online each week, about a quarter of that is time spent on personal matters, or approximately about 5 hours of lost productivity each week. In general, workers spent more than an hour per week on social media, followed by online games and e-mail. A majority of companies have banned access to social networks, such as Facebook, Twitter, MySpace, and LinkedIn. Last year, a study released by Robert Half Technology, an IT staffing company, found that 54 percent of companies were banning the use of social networking sites like Facebook, Twitter, MySpace, and LinkedIn. The top 10 "time wasters" were: social networks (1.24 hrs/wk); online games (0.56 hr/wk); personal e-mail (0.45 hr/wk); portals (0.24 hr/wk); instant messaging (0.22 hr/wk); fantasy football and gambling (0.12 hr/wk); pornography (0.13 hr/wk); video/movies (0.21 hr/wk); search (0.19 hr/wk), and online shopping (0.15 hr/wk) (24/7 Wall St. 2010).

Dealing with Internet Abuse. Instead of banning social networks at work, some employers are following less draconic measures by setting the following in place: employees are encouraged to check their social networks only once or twice a day, employees are encouraged to consolidate their social networking streams, develop a clear social networking policy, and utilize technology made for consolidation. The social networking policy should communicate clear guidelines from employers to employees stressing that employees do not waste more than 20 minutes per day of company time on social networks (Nutshell Mail 2010).

Monitoring Employees—Is It Ethical?

Google and several other software application providers have incorporated new spyware on smartphones that enable employers to spy on the whereabouts of their employees using the built-in GPS tracking systems. Latitude by Google will collect personal information of its users' travels by sending personal data to Google mainframes for the employers to log on, monitor, and observe employee travel. The ethical question is whether by giving Google the ability to monitor people's whereabouts does it tempt Google too much—in that this new power to exploit the privacy of the individual's real-time whereabouts will be given

EXHIBIT 14.1   Safeguards to Minimize Exposure to Risk of Criminal or Civil Charges

1. Does the website clearly post shipment policies and guarantees? Can the company fulfill those policies and guarantees? Does the website explain what happens in case of a missed deadline? Does it comply with Federal Trade Commission (FTC) rules?
2. Does the website clearly articulate procedures for customers to follow when returning gifts or seeking a refund for services not received?
3. Has the company checked backgrounds before entering agreements with third-party vendors and supply chain partners? Do those agreements with vendors and partners indemnify (i.e., protect) the company against their failure to deliver goods or process transactions on time and correctly?
4. If a third-party ISP or Web-hosting service is used, are there safeguards if the site crashes, is infected by malware, or if bandwidth is insufficient to meet all of your customers' needs?
5. Is there sufficient customer support staff, and are they knowledgeable and adequately trained to process inquiries from customers?

over to government and its requests for such information without proper warrant (Coursey 2009). In other words, businesspeople engaging in EC need guidelines as to what behaviors are reasonable and what risks are foreseeable under a given set of circumstances. Two major risks are a criminal charge and lawsuit (civil charge). Exhibit 14.1 lists examples of safeguards to minimize exposure to those risks. (Also see Yamamura and Grupe 2008.)

EC ETHICAL ISSUES

There are many EC- and Internet-related ethical issues that are related to legal issues (Himma and Tavani 2008). These issues are often categorized into intellectual property rights, privacy, free speech versus censorship, and consumer and merchant protection against fraud.

- **Intellectual property rights.** Ownership and value of information and intellectual property. Rights to intellectual property are easy to violate on the Internet, resulting in billions of dollars of losses to the owners of the rights (Section 14.2).
- **Privacy.** The collection, storage, and dissemination of information about individuals. Internet users in many countries rate privacy as their first or second top concerns. Specifically, Internet users are concerned with broad government intrusion of privacy (Section 14.3).
- **Free speech versus censorship.** The issue of attempting to control offensive, illegal, and potentially dangerous information on the Internet is controversial. This collides with rights of free speech (Section 14.4).
- **Consumer and merchant protection against fraud.** It is easy to reach millions on the Internet and to conduct different types of e-commerce-related fraud. The success of e-commerce depends on the protection provided to consumers and merchants (Section 14.5).

For further discussion, see wiki.media-culture.org.au/index.php/ECommerce_-_Legal_and_Ethical_Issues.

Examples of ethical issues discussed elsewhere in this book are channel conflict (Chapter 3), pricing conflict (Chapter 3), disintermediation (Chapters 3, 4, and 8), and trust (Chapter 8). Two additional EC-related ethical issues are nonwork-related use of the Internet and codes of ethics. See also en.wikipedia.org/wiki/Ethical_code.

Nonwork-Related Use of the Internet

As described earlier, a majority of employees use e-mail and surf the Web for nonwork-related purposes. The use of company property (i.e., computers, networks) for e-mail and Internet use creates risk and wastes time. The degree of risk depends on the extent to which the company has implemented policies and procedures to prevent and detect illegal uses. For example, companies may be held liable for their employees' use of e-mail to harass another employee, participate in illegal gambling, or distribute child pornography (Gray 2010).

Codes of Ethics

A practical and necessary approach to limiting nonwork-related Internet surfing is an Internet-acceptable use policy (AUP) to which all employees must conform. It includes EC, social networks, and any IT-related topics. Without a formal AUP, it is much more difficult to enforce acceptable and eliminate unacceptable behaviors and punish violators. Whenever a user signs on to the corporate network, the user should see a reminder of the AUP and be notified that online activities are monitored. Such notification should be a part of a code of ethics.

Corporate *codes of ethics* state the rules and expected behaviors and actions. Typically, the ethics code should address the use of offensive content and graphics, as well as, proprietary information. It should encourage employees to think about who should and who should not have access to information before they post it on the website. The code should specify whether the company allows employees to set up their own Web pages on the company intranet and state policies regarding private e-mail usage and nonwork-related surfing during working hours. A company should formulate a general idea of the role it wants websites to play in the workplace. This should guide the company in developing an AUP and provide employees with a rationale for that policy. Finally, do not be surprised if the code of ethics looks a lot like simple rules of etiquette; it should. Exhibit 14.2 lists several useful guidelines for a corporate Web policy. For a list of website quality guidelines, see Online File W14.2. For ethics case studies, see harpercollege. edu/~tmorris/ekin/resources.htm.

Section 14.1 ▶ REVIEW QUESTIONS

1. List seven ethical issues related to EC.
2. List the major principles of ethics.
3. Define business ethics.
4. Give an example of an EC activity that is unethical but not illegal.
5. How can employees abuse the Internet? How do small companies deal with this?
6. Describe the employee monitoring issue.
7. List the major issues that should be included in a code of ethics.

EXHIBIT 14.2 Corporate Web Policy Guidelines

- Issue written AUP guidelines about employee use of the Internet and communication systems including e-mail and instant messaging.
- Make it clear to employees that they cannot use copyrighted or trademarked material without permission.
- Post disclaimers concerning content, such as sample code, that the company does not support.
- Post disclaimers of responsibility concerning content of online forums and chat sessions.
- Make sure that Web content and activity comply with the laws in other countries, such as those governing contests and privacy.
- Make sure that the company's Web content policy is consistent with other company policies.
- Appoint someone to monitor Internet legal and liability issues and have that person report to a senior executive or legal counsel.
- Have attorneys with cyberlaw expertise review Web content to make sure that there is nothing unethical or illegal on the company's website and that all required statements and disclaimers are properly included.

14.2 INTELLECTUAL PROPERTY LAW

The legal system is faced with the task of maintaining a delicate balance between preserving social order and protecting individual rights. Keep in mind that the term *individual* when used in law is broadly defined to mean a person, group of people, or other legal entity, such as an organization or corporation. In this section, we explain the various types of intellectual property laws and the issues arising from EC.

INTELLECTUAL PROPERTY IN E-COMMERCE

Intellectual property (IP) refers to creations of the mind: inventions, literary and artistic works, and symbols, names, images, and designs used in commerce. IP is divided into two categories: (1) *industrial property*, which includes inventions (patents), trademarks, industrial designs, and geographic indications of source; and (2) *copyright*, which includes literary and artistic works such as novels, poems and plays, films, musical works, artistic works such as drawings, paintings, photographs and sculptures, and architectural designs (see wipo.int/about-ip/en). **Intellectual property law** refers to the area of the law that includes *patent law*, *copyright law, trademark law, trade secret law,* and other relevant branches of the law, such as licensing and unfair competition.

Intellectual property law may also be concerned with the regulation of mental products, including creativity. It affects such diverse subjects as the visual and performing arts, electronic databases, advertising, and video games. Creativity is an integral part of the entire business world, as is the protection of innovation. Visit Online File W14.3 for related intellectual property websites.

There are various intellectual property law specialties as shown in Exhibit 14.3. Those specialty laws are interrelated and may even overlap.

Copyright Infringement and Protection

Numerous high-profile lawsuits already have been filed regarding online copyright infringement. A **copyright** is an exclusive right of the author or creator of a book, movie, musical composition, or other artistic property to print, copy, sell, license, distribute, transform to another medium, translate, record, perform, or otherwise use. In the United States, as soon as a work is created in a tangible form, such as through writing or recording, the work automatically has federal copyright protection. A copyright does not last forever; it is good for a fixed number of years after the death of the author or creator (e.g., 50 years in the United Kingdom). In the United States in 1998, copyright was extended to 70 years after the death of the author by the Sonny Bono Copyright Extension Act. After the copyright expires, the work reverts to the public domain. Copyrights are owned in many cases by corporations

intellectual property (IP)
Creations of the mind, such as inventions, literary and artistic works, and symbols, names, images, and designs, used in commerce.

intellectual property law
Area of the law that includes patent law, copyright law, trademark law, trade secret law, and other branches of the law such as licensing and unfair competition.

copyright
An exclusive right of the author or creator of a book, movie, musical composition, or other artistic property to print, copy, sell, license, distribute, transform to another medium, translate, record, perform, or otherwise use.

EXHIBIT 14.3	Intellectual Property Laws and Their Protections	
Laws	**Protection Provided by the Law**	
Intellectual property law	Protects creations of the human mind	
Patent law	Protects inventions and discoveries	
Copyright law	Protects original works of authorship, such as music and literary works, and computer programs	
Trademark law	Protects brand names and other symbols that indicate the source of goods and services	
Trade secret law	Protects confidential business information	
Law of licensing	Enables owners of patents, trademarks, copyrights, and trade secrets to share them with others on a mutually agreed-upon basis	
Law of unfair competition dealing with counterfeiting and piracy	Protects against those who try to take a free ride on the efforts and achievements of creative people	

infringement
Use of the work without permission or contracting for payment of a royalty.

(e.g., the copyrights to this book). In such a case, the copyrights will potentially last forever unless legally reassigned. The legal term for the use of the work without permission or contracting for payment of a royalty is infringement.

Legal Aspects of Infringement. In November 2010, the U.S. Senate Judiciary Committee approved a controversial Copyright Enforcement Bill that would give the authorities dramatic new copyright enforcement powers allowing it to take down entire domains "dedicated to online piracy" rather than just targeting files that actually infringe copyright law. The Combating Online Infringement and Counterfeits Act (COICA) gives U.S. law enforcement the right to shut down websites without trial or defense if it finds the central reason for the site is to distribute copyrighted information illegally. The act allows both civil and criminal forfeitures of property used to commit copyright infringement and the potential impact is on content creators, music or movie distributors and publishers. The problem is that under this bill, most business websites are considered publishers since they post static or dynamic content (e.g., blogs) or sales brochures. Under this act, there is significant risk of IT disruption during the enforcement activities allowed. In the worst-case scenario, a disgruntled employee posts copyrighted material on the company website, unbeknownst to the directors of the company, just before being terminated. The FBI, once alerted by an anonymous whistle-blower, could, after discovering the online distribution of possible copyrighted material, shut down the domain name and confiscate the company's server as evidence, even if no charges are filed for months thereafter. More practically, problems may occur should office workers innocently share songs or videos outside the company firewall, or should an employee's PowerPoint presentation contain copyrighted quotes or movie clips, and are subsequently distributed to branch offices across the WAN or Internet (Gross 2008 and Fogarty 2011).

Examples of Infringement

To protect its interests, the Recording Industry Association of America (RIAA), the recording industry's trade group, uses selective lawsuits to stamp out rampant music piracy on the Internet. More than 7 years ago, the RIAA began its massive litigation campaign that now includes more than 20,000 lawsuits targeting alleged copyright scofflaws on peer-to-peer networks. However, during this period RIAA has spent more than $58 million in pursuit of targeted infringers yet has received awards of less than $1.4 million (less than about 2 percent) (Thomson 2010).

Example 1. The file-sharing software company LimeWire lost a long-running court battle to the major recording companies in May 2010. A judge with the U.S. District Court in New York ruled that the company and its chairman, Mark Gorton, were liable for inducing copyright infringement. Besides the file-sharing companies and Internet service providers, RIAA targeted the elderly, students, children, and even the dead. No one in the United States who used Kazaa, LimeWire, or other file sharing networks was immune from the RIAA's investigators, and fines under the Copyright Act go up to $150,000 per purloined music track (Nakashima 2010b).

Example 2. On November 5, 2010, the RIAA won a major victory over defendant Jammie Thomas-Rasset, who lost her retrial. Rasset was the woman who was ordered to pay a heavy fine for downloading MP3s using Kazaa, a file sharing network. She was ordered to pay $1.5 million, or $62,500 fine per shared song, for 24 songs she shared via Kazaa in 2006. The appeals court reaffirmed the judgment that the RIAA was awarded in 2006 by a Minneapolis jury. Thomas-Rasset's legal team has already announced that they will file a new appeal (Madrak 2010).

However, since 2009, court records show that new federal copyright infringement lawsuits plummeted to a six-year low. This follows the year after the RIAA abandoned its litigation campaign "sue 'em all" against file sharers. In July 2010, the U.S. District Court judge reduced the jury's award from $675,000, or $22,500 per infringed work, on a student convicted of illegal file-sharing, to $67,500, or $2,250 per infringed work, on due process grounds, holding that the jury's award was unconstitutionally excessive. See en.wikipedia.org/wiki/RIAA_v._Tenenbaum and Bambauer (2010).

Furthermore, legal shields are frustrating copyright infringement lawsuits. In June 2010, a federal judge handed Google a major victory. Google rebuffed media company Viacom's attempt to collect more than $1 billion in damages for the alleged copyright abuses of Google's popular YouTube service. The ruling by U.S. District Judge Louis Stanton in New York embraces Google's interpretation of a 12-year-old law that shields Internet services from claims of copyright infringement, as long as they promptly remove illegal content when notified of a violation since YouTube had gone way beyond what is required by law to protect copyright owners. In 2007, YouTube proved that it introduced a file screening software program utilizing video recognition technology, which recognizes copyrighted video and shuts down the streaming service in about 1 minute (Townsend 2010). Finally, pending copyright infringement lawsuits are not favored because they are lengthy and very costly. As an alternative to lawsuits, the entertainment industry led primarily by the Motion Picture Association of America (MPAA) and RIAA is actively pursuing digital rights management policy initiatives through federal legislation and the courts.

Digital Rights Management (DRM)

Digital rights management (DRM) is an umbrella term for any of several arrangements that allow a vendor of content in electronic form to control the material and restrict its usage. These arrangements are technology-based protection measures. Typically, the content is a copyrighted digital work to which the vendor holds rights. In the past, when content was analog in nature, it was easier to buy a new copy of a copyrighted work on a physical medium (e.g., paper, film, tape) than to produce such a copy independently. The quality of most copies often was inferior. Digital technologies make it possible to produce and distribute a high-quality duplicate of any digital recording with minimal effort and cost. The Internet virtually has eliminated the need for a physical medium to transfer a work, which has led to the use of DRM systems for protection.

digital rights management (DRM)
An umbrella term for any of several arrangements that allow a vendor of content in electronic form to control the material and restrict its usage.

However, DRM systems may restrict the *fair use* of material by individuals. In law, **fair use** refers to the use of copyrighted material for *noncommercial* purposes. Several DRM technologies were developed without regard for privacy protection. Many systems require the user to reveal his or her identity and rights to access protected content. Upon authentication of identity and rights to the content, the user can access the content for free (see epic.org/privacy/drm).

fair use
The legal use of copyrighted material for noncommercial purposes without paying royalties or getting permission.

All is not well with DRM system applications, however, especially if it has to do with Apple's controlled ecosystem. In July 2010, the Library of Congress ruled in favor of the Electronic Frontier Foundation, who argued that jail breaking one's iPhone should be allowed as "fair use," even though it required one to bypass some DRM and then to reuse a small bit of Apple's copyright firmware code. In Apple's losing argument, it claimed that jail breaking was not "fair use" but "terrible, ridiculous, and illegal" and that Apple's controlled ecosystem was of great value to consumers (Kravets 2010).

Patents

A **patent** is a document that grants the holder exclusive rights to an invention for a fixed number of years (e.g., 17 years in the United States and 20 years in the United Kingdom). Patents serve to protect tangible technological inventions, especially in traditional industrial areas. They are not designed to protect artistic or literary creativity. Patents confer monopoly rights to an idea or an invention, regardless of how it may be expressed. An invention may be in the form of a physical device or a method or process for making a physical device. In addition, some business methods are also patentable.

patent
A document that grants the holder exclusive rights to an invention for a fixed number of years.

Certain patents granted in the United States deviate from established practices in Europe. For example, Amazon.com successfully obtained a U.S. patent for its "One-Click" ordering and payment procedure. Using this patent, Amazon.com sued Barnes & Noble in 1999 and 2000, alleging that its rival had copied its patented technology. Barnes & Noble was enjoined by the courts from using the procedure. However, on May 12, 2006, the USPTO ordered a re-examination of the "One-Click" patent. In November 2007, Amazon.com responded by amending the broadest claims (1 and 11) to restrict them to a "shopping cart model" of commerce. In March 2010, the revised patent was confirmed. See en.wikipedia.org/wiki/1-Click. For a sample of EC patents, see Online File W14.4.

In August 2010, the U.S. Supreme Court unanimously rejected the machine-or-transformation test as the sole test for process patent eligibility. However, the Court declined to offer an alternative to its June 2010 vague ruling of the Bilski vs. Kappos case, leaving to the U.S. Court of Appeals for the Federal Circuit the task of developing new criteria for patentability. The upcoming decision may have a wide-ranging effect on the patenting practices of e-commerce companies and may call into question the validity of thousands of patents granted on business methods since the 1990s. For more details, see Roberts (2010).

In December 2010, Internet Licensing LLC amended a lawsuit in District Court in Seattle, against Apple, eBay, Facebook, Google, and nine other companies for violating four of its patents.

In April 2009, Bank of America, MasterCard, Visa, and 20 other firms were sued by Actus, a Texas-based patent-holding company, over alleged infringements of four patents on an electronic payment system for e-commerce. The patents in question relate to "methods and apparatus for conducting e-commerce using electronic tokens," where digital currency is used by customers for online payments. In March 2011, the case was still pending (Finextra 2010). In November 2009, an addition made to the congressional budget bill attempted to reduce the risk that companies' business practices are violating someone's patent. The addition allows companies a limited right to continue using business methods, without paying royalties, if they provide proof that they utilized the business methods prior to learning that they had been patented. See en.wikipedia.org/wiki/Patent.

The business methods patent is meant to protect new ways of doing business. In 2010, the Supreme Court ruled that patents cannot cover abstract ideas. In January 2011, Senator Leahy introduced a bill designed to reform the U.S. patent process. Senator Schumer introduced an amendment to the bill that would authorize a pilot program to review business method patents (Smith 2011).

Oracle Versus Google. In following its legal right of enforcement, Oracle has been mining its newly acquired patent portfolio and has been actively seeking and suing infringers. Oracle has taken on Google over its Android product for using Oracle's Java technology (copying Java code) without a license. Over the last 5 years, Google has aggressively developed cloud computing products for business, relying on Java technology to enhance mobile software applications. Google claims the suit is baseless. The courts will decide. For details, see Krazit (2010).

Trademarks

Similar to a patent is a *trademark*, which is a symbol businesses use to identify their goods and services; government registration of the trademark confers exclusive legal right to its use.

A **trademark** is a distinctive sign or indicator used to identify products or services to consumers. A trademark is used by individuals, business organizations, or other legal entities to notify consumers of a unique source, and to distinguish its products or services from those of other entities. Trademarks protect words, names, symbols, sounds, smells, or colors that distinguish goods and services from those manufactured or sold by others and to indicate the source of the goods. **Trademark dilution** is the use of famous trademarks in public that diminishes the capacity of the mark to distinguish goods or services, or tarnishes the mark in the eyes of the consumer. In 2004, the Federal Trademark Dilution Act (FTDA) was enacted to protect famous trademarks from third-party uses, which, while not likely to confuse, nonetheless diminish the capacity of the mark to distinguish goods or services, or tarnishes the mark.

Trademarks, unlike patents, can be renewed forever as long as they are being used in commerce. The owner of a registered trademark may commence legal proceedings under statutory law for trademark infringement to prevent unauthorized use of that trademark. For example, use of a trademark without permission can be considered infringement of the trademark holder's rights. However, because registration is not required, the owner of a common law trademark may also file suit. One drawback to common law trademarks is that an unregistered mark is generally not protectable outside the geographical area within which it has been used or in geographical areas into which it may be reasonably expected to expand (see en.wikipedia.org/wiki/Trademark and en.wikipedia.org/wiki/United_States_trademark_law).

In 2008, eBay won a landmark trademark case against Tiffany, a leading jewelry retailer, who had sued eBay alleging that many of the items being advertised on eBay as Tiffany merchandise were actually fakes. Tiffany argued that eBay's action constituted deliberate

trademark
A symbol used by businesses to identify their goods and services; government registration of the trademark confers exclusive legal right to its use.

trademark dilution
The use of famous trademarks in public that diminishes the capacity of the mark to distinguish goods or services, or tarnishes the mark in the eyes of the consumer.

trademark infringement, false advertising, and trademark dilution. EBay responded that eBay cannot be held responsible for policing the millions of customer listings on its site for potential misuse of Tiffany's trademark. The U.S. District judge ruled that eBay cannot be held liable for trademark infringement "based solely on their generalized knowledge that trademark infringement might be occurring on their websites" (Savitz 2008).

FAN AND HATE SITES

Fan and hate websites are part of the Internet self-publishing and UGC phenomena that includes blogging (see Chapters 2 and 7). Fan sites may violate intellectual property rights. For example, some people get advanced copies of new movies or TV programs and create sites that compete with the legal sites of the movie or TV producer, even before the legal site is activated. Although the producers can get a court order to close such sites, new sites can appear the next day. Although the intention of the fans may be good, they may cause damage to the creators of the intellectual property. Philosophically opposed to fan websites are hate websites, which disseminate negative comments and can cause problems for corporations, as well as for individuals.

Many hate sites are directed against large corporations (e.g., Walmart, Microsoft, Nike). Associated with hate sites is the idea of **cyberbashing**, which is the registration of a domain name that criticizes an organization or person (e.g., paypalsucks.com, walmartblows.com). As long as these websites contain legitimate complaints that are not libelous, defamatory in character, sponsored by competitors, or do not infringe on trademark rights by confusing consumers, they are protected because they fall within the protections of the First Amendment. Material published on fan sites, hate sites, and newsgroups may also violate the copyrights of the creators or distributors of intellectual property. This issue is another example of the conflict between protection of intellectual property and free speech, as discussed in Section 14.3.

cyberbashing
Domain name that criticizes an organization or person.

Section 14.2 ▶ REVIEW QUESTIONS

1. What is intellectual property law? How is it helpful to creators and inventors?
2. Define DRM. Describe one potential impact on privacy and one drawback.
3. What is meant by "fair use"? How does the "jail breaking" of iPhones fall under "fair use"?
4. Define trademark infringement and discuss why trademarks need to be protected from dilution.
5. Describe fan and hate sites. How do they benefit society? Should they be more regulated?
6. Define cyberbashing. Should attempts to expose unscrupulous corporate activities be banned?

14.3 PRIVACY RIGHTS, PROTECTION, AND FREE SPEECH

Privacy means different things to different people. In general, privacy is the right to be left alone and the right to be free of unreasonable personal intrusions. (For other definitions of privacy, see the Privacy Rights Clearinghouse at privacyrights.org.) Privacy has long been a legal, ethical, and social issue in most countries.

Privacy rights protection is one of the most debatable and frequently emotional issues in EC and SC. Here we explore the major aspects of the problem.

SOCIAL NETWORKS CHANGING THE LANDSCAPE OF PRIVACY AND ITS PROTECTION

What are your privacy rights and what constitutes invasion of privacy? The explosion in online communications technologies has created complex new ethical dilemmas for both businesses and government agencies. As transaction costs for processing, storing, and transmitting data drop dramatically and sophisticated tracking and monitoring software become widespread, concerns arise around online consumer privacy, free speech, and defamation.

Social media appears to be causing an evolution of privacy issues online. Yet, today's young people are less concerned about privacy—having a different standard of privacy than their parents. They are connected with blogs, photos, and SMS messages. As a consequence, there is a major cultural shift taking place that appears to redefine the barriers that marketers need to overcome to reach customers. Thought to be creepy just 10 years ago, new opportunities for privacy intrusion by marketers exist to offer potential customers better personalized experiences. See Bharvaga (2010) for a discussion.

Global View

Note that privacy is treated differently in different countries. For example, back in November 2009, Google was sued in Switzerland over privacy concerns regarding its Street View application. Even though Google blurs the faces and license plates that appear in Street View, users of the service can also request that certain images, like their homes, be removed or blurred. The Swiss government still has concerns about the application (Pfanner 2009).

PRIVACY RIGHTS AND PROTECTION

Today, virtually all U.S. states and the federal government, either by statute or by common law, recognize the right to privacy, but few government agencies actually follow all these statutes (e.g., citing reasons of national security for their malfeasance). The definition of privacy can be interpreted quite broadly. However, the following two rules have been followed fairly closely in past U.S. court decisions: (1) the right of privacy is not absolute. Privacy must be balanced against the needs of society; (2) the public's "right to know" is superior to the individual's right of privacy. These two rules show why it is sometimes difficult to determine and enforce privacy regulations, and gives government a legitimate and plausible denial for conducting illegal activity in direct violation of statutes or common law.

With regard to EC, Section 5 of the Federal Trade Commission Act prohibits unfair or deceptive practices and gives the Federal Trade Commission (FTC; a regulatory agency) authority to take action against companies whose lax security practices could expose the personal financial information of customers to theft or loss; it also protects privacy. For an explanation of the FTC Act, see ftc.gov/privacy/privacyinitiatives/promises.html. Those practices extend to individual privacy, free speech, and defamation if a company does not fulfill its duty to protect the rights of others.

Federal regulations under "Obamacare," passed in December 2009, stipulate that the electronic health records of all Americans be provided on a national exchange. However, are privacy standards strong enough to push electronic health record legislation onto health care providers? That is, if providers give the data, they violate the privacy right; if they do not, they violate Obamacare. The new regulations appear to be one of the first steps toward the government's goal of universal adoption of electronic health records (EHRs) by 2014, as outlined in the 2009 economic stimulus law. One solution to this and other privacy situations is to get people's permission (The Moral Liberal 2010). One mechanism for this is discussed next.

Opt-In and Opt-Out

opt-out
Business practice that gives consumers the opportunity to refuse sharing information about themselves.

To some extent, privacy concerns have been overshadowed by post–September 11 counter-terrorism efforts, but consumers still expect and demand that companies behave as responsible custodians of their personal data. One way to manage this issue is *opt-in* and *opt-out* information practices. Opt-out is a business practice that gives consumers the opportunity to refuse to share information about themselves. Offering opt-out is a good customer practice, but it is difficult to opt out in some industries either because consumer demand for opt-out is low or the value of the customer information is high. For example, to thwart identity theft, Facebook suggests that users take advantage of the "Facebook list" to help organize friends by groups, so that individual privacy policies can be applied to the groups for safer public use. In addition, Facebook's new privacy position now forces users to opt out of sharing activities on other sites, ranging from what movies they've seen to where they shopped online. See Collins (2010) and facebook.com/help/?page=839 for details.

In contrast, opt-in is based on the principle that information sharing should not occur unless customers affirmatively allow it or request it.

opt-in
Agreement that requires computer users to take specific steps to allow the collection of personal information.

Providing privacy protection for data as it flows through the Internet requires a careful reconsideration of the business community's interest in promoting commerce, the government's interests in fostering economic growth and protecting its citizens, and the interest of individuals in protecting themselves from intrusive overreach by government and merchants in the private sector. Protecting privacy in the digital age requires the use of all of the tools available: legislation, self-regulation, public education, and the technology itself. See cdt.org/privacy/guide/protect.

According to IBM (2008), a successful online privacy project should include the following six practices:

1. **Get organized.** Form a cross-functional privacy team to help guide your endeavor.

2. **Define requirements.** Define the requirements of your privacy project and identify the types of applications/hardware/data that must be protected.

3. **Perform data inventory.** Analyze and catalog your data stores, flows, processes, dependencies, and business rules to help simplify the scope of your privacy project.

4. **Select solution.** Choose and implement a data privacy solution that provides the techniques needed to protect privacy in all environments.

5. **Test, test, test.** Develop a prototype and methodology for your project and then test the prototype for validation.

6. **Widen the scope.** Expand your data privacy project to encompass other applications across your organization.

For further information on privacy protection, see privacyassociation.org.

Some Measures of Privacy Protection

Several government agencies, communities, and security companies specialize in privacy protection. Representative examples in the USA include consumerprivacyguide.org/law, privacyprotect.org/about-privacyprotection, and firewallguide.com/privacy.htm.

FREE SPEECH ONLINE VERSUS PRIVACY PROTECTION

Internet regulation at a federal level is authorized by the Free Speech and Commerce clause, Communications Decency Act, Federal Computer Fraud and Abuse Act, CAN-SPAM, Lanham Act, and the Anti-Cybersquatting Consumer Protection Act of 1999. As with all rights, the right of free speech is not unlimited. Free speech does not mean any speech. Some of the traditional restrictions on what may be freely said or published are defamation laws (including privacy violation), contempt of court, and national security. For example, it is illegal to scream "fire" in a crowded theater or make bomb threats in an airport, but there is no law against taking pictures in public places. Free speech often clashes with privacy, protection of children, indecency, and so forth.

Even in the United Kingdom there is an increasing risk of personal privacy invasion from police for the taking of photographs in a public place. Police have arrested its local citizenry under the charge of "antisocial behavior" (e.g., filming police), especially when the video of an arrest is placed on the Internet for public viewing (Lewis and Domokos 2010).

Example. A U.S. motorcyclist, who filmed his own arrest for speeding by a nonuniformed police officer in an unmarked car with his helmet camera, now faces up to 5 years in prison for posting his arrest on YouTube in April 2010. The felony charge levied is "illegal monitoring" for not getting permission to record the undercover arresting officer's voice; however, the motorcyclist admitted the speeding but vows to fight the charge of illegal monitoring using freedom of speech as a defense. See youtube.com/watch?v=QNcDGqzAB30&feature=related.

Free Speech Online Versus Child Protection Debate

The conflict over free speech versus child protection erupted after the *Children's Internet Protection Act (CIPA)* was signed into law in December 2000. CIPA mandated the use of filtering technologies in schools and libraries that receive certain types of U.S. federal funding. CIPA was immediately challenged in court, so it did not go into effect at that time. Opponents of the law relied on earlier court cases (that is, a legal precedent), saying that government-imposed limitations on the public's right to freely read and learn at public libraries violated the free speech protections of the First Amendment. A **legal precedent** is a judicial decision that may be used as a standard in subsequent similar cases. For details of the debate, see ACLU (2006). It was a major victory for proponents of free speech online in May 2002 when a district court declared the CIPA as unconstitutional. The district court judges ruled that the CIPA was overbroad and would violate the First Amendment rights of library patrons, both adults and minors. That court ordered that the CIPA not be enforced. The conflict did not end there. The district court's decision was appealed to the Supreme Court. In June 2003, Supreme Court judges declared that the CIPA was constitutional. Their review represented the third time justices had heard arguments pitting free speech against attempts to protect children from offensive online content. The CIPA went into effect in 2004, but efforts to defeat it still continue and, of course, the issue of enforcing it is debatable, too.

legal precedent
A judicial decision that may be used as a standard in subsequent similar cases.

In May 2010, by a 6 to 3 majority, the Washington State Supreme Court ruled that public libraries can filter pornography—or subjects banned by library policy, including guns, violence, and other Web content—for the purpose of protecting children. The court concluded that a library can under the CIPA, subject to the limitations set forth in the opinion, filter Internet access for all patrons, including adults, without violating article I, section 5 of the Washington State Constitution. An example of protecting children versus privacy can be seen in Online File W14.5. An example that involved digital images is provided next.

Example. In June 2010, New York Attorney General Andrew Cuomo spearheaded the creation of a database of "*digital fingerprints*" to flag child pornography and keep it off social networks.

With the hash values of over 8,000 known child-porn images stored in the database, Cuomo hopes its intended clients—social-networking, file-sharing, and photo-storage sites—will start to use it "immediately."

Facebook and MySpace have already signed on as partners in the new initiative. Here is how it works: the collection of "digital fingerprints," compiled through law enforcement efforts over the years, can be used as a filter by a partner social network. So when a photo is uploaded, it can be checked against the contents of the database. If there is a match, the photo is not permitted to be uploaded. Use of the database is also available to law enforcement authorities.

THE PRICE OF PROTECTING AN INDIVIDUAL'S PRIVACY

In the past, the complexity of collecting, sorting, filing, and accessing information manually from several different government agencies was a built-in protection against misuse of private information. It was simply too expensive, cumbersome, and complex to invade a person's privacy. The Internet, in combination with powerful computers and targeting algorithms with access to large-scale databases, has, in all practical terms, eliminated those barriers.

In the fight against terrorism and the promotion of public safety, child privacy protection laws in Europe, like the United States, also appear to be losing ground as British authorities have made it mandatory for travelers to submit to the "naked body" scanners. Specifically, airport security personnel have been caught printing out and circulating digital images of full naked body scans of airline travelers and set alarm bells ringing, especially in light of the fact that some images were of minors (breaking the UK child pornography laws). For refusing to be digitally scanned, the travelers are not allowed to travel and often face further questioning and explicit verbal humiliation (Watson 2010). Today's technology enables monitoring people's activities from a distance, violating their privacy, as shown in Case 14.1.

CASE 14.1
EC Application

HEY TEACHER, LEAVE THEM KIDS ALONE! ACTIVATING LAPTOP WEBCAMS TO SPY ON STUDENTS AT HOME

Unbeknownst to the students in the class, and without their authorization, Pennsylvania high school administrators have been spying on the activities of underage children by indiscriminately using the ability to remotely activate the webcams built into each laptop issued to students by the Lower Merion School District, and intentionally intercepting their private webcam images in possible violation of federal and state laws.

The continued surveillance of the students even while they are at home by the assistant principal at Harriton High School revealed that a minor (student) was engaged in improper behavior in his home. The assistant principal, Linda Matsko, later punished the student for his "improper behavior in his home," using a webcam shot from the student's computer as evidence. On November 11, 2009, the parents of the minor were shown photographic images of their son in the bedroom (from the webcam embedded in the minor's personal laptop issued by the school district), and, for the first time, made aware that the school district had the ability to capture webcam images inside their home from any location in which the personal laptop computer was kept. It appears that the school district was not just monitoring their webcams—it was allegedly tracking *all* of their activities on the computer (although the webcam watching is the most disturbing aspect). Pennsylvania high school student, Blake Robbins, filed a class action lawsuit against the Lower Merion School District on behalf of all 1,800 students provided with laptops, for invasion of privacy, theft of private information, and unlawful interception of personal information (in violation of the Electronic Communications Privacy Act), among other claims. The case is still pending.

Sources: Compiled from Hill (2010), Schreiber (2010), Lattanzio (2010), and *courthousenews.com/2010/02/18/Eyes.pdf* (accessed March 2011).

Questions

1. What legitimate excuse could be made to justify this behavior? Why must it be stopped?

2. What federal laws were broken? What rights in the U.S. Constitution were violated?

3. What precedent will be set by the upcoming decision? Can you see a way that schools will be allowed to continue this behavior for a narrowly construed purpose?

4. Find the status of the legal case.

Here is another example of freedom of speech on the Internet colliding with public safety.

Example: Sheriff Sues Craigslist to Curb Prostitution. The Sheriff of Cook County, Illinois, filed a federal lawsuit in March 2009, alleging that Craigslist had become the top provider of prostitution services in the United States and claiming that missing children, runaways, abused women, and women trafficked in from foreign countries are routinely forced to have sex with strangers because they are being pimped on Craigslist.

The sheriff wanted Craigslist to shut down the erotic services category of its website and to compensate his department for the cost of prosecuting website-related prostitution cases. But Web free speech advocates argue that existing laws insulate Craigslist from any illegal activities related to its ads, and they predict defeat for the sheriff's legal efforts. For details, see San Miguel (2009). Nonetheless, in May 2009, Craigslist decided to eliminate its "erotic services" category and screen all submissions to a new "adult services" section before they are posted. Sheriff Dart said his lawsuit would stay on file until he sees changes online. In September 2010, Craigslist closed all sex-related classified ads on its site (Miller 2010).

HOW INFORMATION ABOUT INDIVIDUALS IS COLLECTED AND USED ONLINE

The Internet offers a number of opportunities to collect private information about individuals. Representative examples of the ways that the Internet can be used to find information about an individual are provided next; the last three are the most common ways of gathering information on the Internet.

> ▶ By reading an individual's blogs or newsgroup postings
> ▶ By looking up an individual's name and identity in an Internet directory
> ▶ By reading an individual's e-mail, IM, or text messages
> ▶ By monitoring and conducting surveillance on employees
> ▶ By wiretapping wireline and wireless communication lines
> ▶ By asking an individual to complete a registration form on a website
> ▶ By recording users' actions as they navigate the Web with a browser, usually using cookies
> ▶ By using spyware, keystroke loggers, and similar methods

Website Registration

Virtually all B2C sites, marketing websites, online magazines, vendors, government sites, and social networks ask visitors to fill out registration forms. During the process, individuals voluntarily provide their names, addresses, phone numbers, e-mail addresses, hobbies and likes or dislikes, and other personal information in order to participate, receive a download, win a lottery, or receive some other benefit in exchange. There are few restraints on the ways in which the site can use this information. The site might use it to improve customer service. Or the site could just as easily sell the information to another company, which could use it in an inappropriate or intrusive manner.

Internet users are skeptical of the necessity of giving such information to online businesses. Most people dislike registering at websites they visit; 15 percent refuse to register at all. Many do not trust companies and do not share their personal information. This may all change. In February 2010, the UN International Telecommunications Union Secretary General, Hamadoun Toure, told the World Economic Forum in Davos that global treaties need to be enacted in the name of stopping cyberwarfare. (Government security expert Richard Clarke defines cyberwarfare as "actions by a nation-state to penetrate another nation's computers or networks for the purposes of causing damage or disruption" [Clarke 2010]). Craig Mundie, chief research and strategy officer for Microsoft, told fellow globalists at the summit that the Internet needed to be policed by means of introducing licenses similar to driver's licenses—in other words government permission to use the Web. It is possible that with a license you will not have to register (Watson, et al. 2010). In July, Germany sued Facebook over violations of its data privacy laws. Facebook in Germany was accused of saving private information of individuals who do not use the site and have not granted the site access to their details. Many people who had been contacted by Facebook after it obtained their names and e-mail addresses through friends listing them as contacts in Facebook accounts filed several complaints. Facebook faces several thousand euros in fines (Albanesius 2010).

Cookies

A popular way that a website can gather information about an individual is by using cookies. As described in Chapter 8, a *cookie* contains data that are passed back and forth between a website and an end user's browser as the user navigates the site. Cookies enable sites to keep track of users without having to constantly ask the users to identify themselves.

Originally, cookies were designed to help with personalization and market research; however, cookies can also be used to invade an individual's privacy. Cookies allow websites to collect detailed information about a user's preferences, interests, and surfing patterns. The personal profiles created by cookies often are more accurate than self-registration because users have a tendency to falsify information in a registration form. Now, algorithms can scan as many as 30,000 links per second. That makes it possible for Webmasters to stealthily gobble up huge amounts of information within seconds of those visiting their sites and can gain access to a user's browser history and information. For details, see *E-Commerce Journal* (2010).

Although the ethics of the use of cookies are still being debated, concerns about cookies reached a pinnacle in 1997 at the U.S. FTC hearings on online privacy. Following those hearings, Netscape and Microsoft introduced options enabling users to *block cookies*. Since that time, the uproar has subsided because most users accept cookies rather than fight them. The problem with deleting or disabling cookies is that the user will have to keep reentering information and, in some instances, may be blocked from viewing useful pages.

Cookies can be successfully deleted by informed users with programs such as: Cookie Monster, Cookienator, and CCleaner. By setting the privacy levels on Web browsers very high, new cookies can be blocked.

Spyware as a Threat to Privacy and Intellectual Property

In Chapter 9, we discussed *spyware* as a tool that some merchants use to spy on users without their knowledge. Spyware infections are a major threat to privacy and intellectual property. Spyware, also known as *crimeware*, refers to all unwanted software programs designed to steal proprietary information, or that target data stores containing confidential information.

Spyware may enter the user's computer as a virus or as a result of the user's clicking an option in a deceptive pop-up window. Sometimes when users download and install legitimate programs, they get spyware as well. Spyware is very effective in tracking users' Web surfing habits. It can scan computer hard drives for sensitive files and send the results to hackers or spammers. Spyware use is clearly a violation of the computer user's privacy. It can also slow down computer performance. Spyware writers are getting more innovative and are trying to avoid detection. As described in Chapter 9, a *keystroke logger* runs in the background of the user's computer and records every keystroke the user makes. A hacker can then identify confidential information and then steal the user's social security number, bank account number, and password, all of which can be used in identify theft.

While specific spyware can harvest data, it can also be used to take pictures from an infected computer's Webcam and send the photos over the Internet to criminals and perverts for illegal purposes (see Case 14.1).

Thus, many IT professionals realize that a fast-growing business on the Internet today is the business of spying on Internet users. The broad array of new types of cookies and other surveillance technologies that companies are now deploying on Internet users is staggering. The tracking of consumers has grown both far more pervasive and far more intrusive than is realized by all but a handful of people in the vanguard of the industry. Without warning, sophisticated tracking technology is being installed onto the computers of innocent Internet users. While most are innocuous, some tools include evil malware, which can surreptitiously regenerate even after users try to delete them. The information collected on individuals is being refreshed and then bought and sold on the underground Internet market (Chapter 9).

The new technologies are transforming the Internet economy. Before, advertisers primarily bought ads on specific Web pages, but now advertisers are paying a premium to follow people around the Internet, 24 hours per day—wherever they go. There are now more than 100 middlemen or tracking companies, data brokers, and advertising networks that are competing to meet the growing demand for surreptitious data on individual behavior and interests (Angwin 2010).

Unfortunately, antivirus software and Internet firewalls cannot always "see" most spyware; special protection is needed. Many free and low-cost antispyware software packages are on the market. Representative free antispyware programs are Ad-Aware, Spybot, SpyKiller, and PestPatrol. For-fee programs include SpySubtract, Spy Sweeper, Ad-Aware Plus, and SpyWasher. Spyware protection is provided also by Symantec and other companies that provide Internet security software.

Even if you use antispyware, your smartphone and public Wi-Fi connection may be giving up personal information on you by transmitting your location back to your cell phone/Internet provider about every 7 seconds. Government supercomputers are capable of reading every e-mail sent, listening to every mobile conversation, reading every text

spyware
All unwanted software programs designed to steal proprietary information, or that target data stores containing confidential information.

message, knowing every user location (e.g., GPS), and following every credit card purchase besides tracking every website visited by Internet users around the globe. In fact, every day, collection systems at the National Security Agency intercept and store 1.7 billion e-mails, phone calls, and other types of communications. Records about when you are at church, school, work, a political rally, or a hospital or clinic are stored for months or even years. That is a treasure trove of information about your private life that's not just interesting to companies, but also to the government, which uses the information to follow many thousands of people a year. The problem is that collecting these data is needed for national security. But, it violates our privacy. Technology behind the new smartphones can allow government agencies to surreptitiously record your conversations, take pictures of your surroundings, and report your GPS coordinates even without you turning on your phone (Greenwald 2010).

RFID's Threat to Privacy

Although several states have mandated or are considering legislation to protect customers from a loss of privacy due to RFID tags, as mentioned in Online Tutorial T3 and in Chapter 11, privacy advocates fear that the information stored on RFID tags or collected with them may be used to violate an individual's privacy. RFID tag awareness reached a tipping point with Walmart's announcement in August 2010 that the retailer will place removable "smart tags" on clothing so that the RFID tags could be read by handheld scanners to track inventory levels and keep a better eye on loss prevention. Since the cost of RFID chips has been dropping, affordable RFID technology now allows for real-time tracking of the whereabouts of citizens wearing clothes with RFID, who have no idea they are being tracked. RFID chips are already embedded into passports (Chapter 9) and other everyday items and can be the size of a dust speck (Smith 2010).

Other Methods

Other methods of collecting data about people are:

> ▶ **Site transaction logs.** These logs show the usage patterns of people surfing the Internet.
> ▶ **EC ordering systems and shopping carts.** These features permit others to know what you ordered, when, from whom, and how much you paid for the item.
> ▶ **Search engines.** Search engines can be used to collect information about your searches. Also, specialized searches (e.g., maps), blogging, chatting, and Web conferences are sources of privacy information.
> ▶ **Behavioral targeting.** Behavioral targeting uses tools for collaborative filtering and analysis of user-entered data.
> ▶ **Polling and surveys.** Personal data may be revealed by participating in online voting, completing questionnaires, and so forth.
> ▶ **Payment information and e-wallets.** These may include information that can be leaked or sold to others.

For details, see en.wikipedia.org/wiki/Payment_Card_Industry_Data_Security_Standard.

Privacy of Employees

There are several issues concerning employee privacy. In addition to wasting time online, employees may disclose trade secrets and possibly make employers liable for defamation based on what they do on the corporate website. In response to these concerns, many companies monitor their employees' usage of e-mail and Web surfing activities. One tool that allows companies to spy on their employees is Google's Latitude, which works in combination with a GPS/cell phone (see Coursey 2009).

Personal Internet use during working hours can significantly impact productivity according to the Maricopa County Internal Audit Department that monitors Internet usage. They postulate that if each county employee with Internet access spends 5 work-time minutes each weekday on personal Web activities, the resulting productivity cost to the county could exceed $3.4 million annually so they implemented Internet monitoring programs to (1) increase management's awareness of employee usage, (2) promote acceptable usage, (3) limit abuse of county resources, and (4) provide useful information (Scott and Ross 2010).

Example: The Ontario Versus Quon Case. At issue is whether the City of Ontario Police Department in California violated an officer's constitutional right to privacy when it reviewed personal text messages sent and received on a government-issued pager. When the department issued pagers to officers, it had a formal policy covering computer, Internet, and e-mail usage stating the systems were for official use only. The policy allowed for "light personal communications" but warned employees should have no expectation of privacy. There was no specific policy for text messaging; however, the police found that less than 15 percent of messages sent and received by officer Quon involved police business. Many of the private messages were sexually explicit.

Quon and three others sued the city of Ontario in 2004, claiming their Fourth Amendment rights against unreasonable searches and seizures had been violated. They believed the informal policy created a reasonable expectation of privacy for their personal activities. Nevertheless, the Ninth Circuit Court of Appeals in San Francisco found in favor of Quon. In June 2010 the U.S. Supreme Court unanimously held that the City of Ontario's review of Jeff Quon's, and others', text messages sent on City-issued pagers did not constitute an unreasonable search and did not violate the Fourth Amendment to the Constitution (Supreme Court of the United States 2010).

The issue of how to monitor employees is complex and debatable because the possibility of invasion of privacy. For comprehensive coverage, see Stanton and Stam (2006). One of the issues there that relates to *Ontario vs. Quon* is the "employees policing themselves."

For more about Internet usage monitoring, see acespy.com/employee.html.

PRIVACY PROTECTION BY INFORMATION TECHNOLOGIES

Can social network users retain their privacy while still benefiting from these websites services? Yes, but only through using NOYB, a software encryption program that provides privacy while preserving some of the functionality of the social network. NOYB, short for *none of your business*, is based on the observation that some online services, notably social networking websites, can operate on "fake" data. Thus, privacy can be preserved by restricting the ability to recover the real data from the fake data to authorized users only. This observation naturally leads to the privacy issue solution: user data is first encrypted, and the ciphertext encoded to look like legitimate data. The online service can then operate on the ciphered data; however, only authorized users can decode and decrypt the result (Guha 2009).

Dozens of software programs and IT procedures are available to protect your privacy. Some were defined in Chapter 9. Representative examples are:

▶ **Platform for Privacy Preferences Project (P3P).** Software that communicates privacy policies (described later in this chapter).

▶ **Encryption.** Software programs such as PKI for encrypting e-mail, payments transactions, and other documents.

▶ **Spam blocking.** Built into browsers and e-mail; blocks pop-up and unwanted mail.

▶ **Spyware blocking.** Detects and removes spyware and adware; built into some browsers.

▶ **Cookie managers.** Prevents the computer from accepting cookies; disables cookies.

▶ **Anonymous e-mail and surfing.** Allows you to send e-mail and surf without a trace.

PRIVACY ISSUES IN WEB 2.0 TOOLS AND SOCIAL NETWORKS

The explosion of social networks raises some special issues in privacy and free speech. Here are a few examples.

Presence, Location-Based Systems, and Privacy

Establishing real time connections (presence) in the social networking world is an important activity. For example, Facebook added instant messaging (IM) to its website, enabling users to know when friends are online. In May 2010, Skype announced and released the Skype-on-TV setup, the Webcam, which is compatible with Panasonic or Samsung Internet-enabled HDTV. Now, Skype offers Skype video chat for more than two people to exploit the video conferencing experience for consumers (Wilhelm 2010).

IBM Lotus also supports presence capabilities tied into "Connections," while Microsoft offers similar capabilities with SharePoint. Apple's FaceTime and CoreMotion APIs in iOS allow developers to make use of the gyroscope for ultimate location awareness by measuring true roll, pitch, and yaw, making the iPhone sensitive to motion on six total axes (Northcott 2010).

What happens when LinkedIn, Facebook, Twitter, or MySpace provides the ability for a GPS-enabled mobile device or the 4G gyroscope of the new iPhone to dynamically share its location status with others? Will or how will businesses begin to take advantage of these same capabilities to build applications to enable GPS tracking of field sales and support personnel by leveraging the location status capabilities already present in their mobile devices or surreptitious monitoring of their texting and e-mail (see Chapter 7 for LBS)? What are the privacy implications? Who will be held responsible or legally liable for unforeseen harm resulting from so much awareness and connectivity?

It looks as if clear rules for social networks are needed to govern what social networks can do with the massive amount of personal data they collect and how they inform their users about their practices. Senator Charles Schumer (NY) asked the FTC to articulate a set of guidelines. Facebook claims it offers users "powerful" privacy tools, but the Privacy Rights Clearinghouse organization suggested consumers need a PhD to understand these privacy rules.

Free Speech via Wikis and Social Networks

Free speech and privacy rights collide in a world populated by anonymous critics and cyberbullies. But the attacks are not always from competitors or others outside the company. The nature of the Internet ensures that we may become our own worst enemies personally and professionally, based on the content or images we post on blogs, or the friends we keep on social networking pages.

PRIVACY PROTECTION BY ETHICAL PRINCIPLES

The ethical principles commonly applied to the collection and use of personal information also apply to information collected in e-commerce. These principles include the following:

▶ **Notice or awareness.** Consumers must be given notice of an entity's information practices prior to the collection of personal information. Consumers must be able to make informed decisions about the type and extent of their disclosures based on the intentions of the party collecting the information.

▶ **Choice or consent.** Consumers must be made aware of their options as to how their personal information may be used, as well as any potential secondary uses of the information. Consent may be granted by the consumers through opt-out clauses.

▶ **Access or participation.** Consumers must be able to access their personal information and challenge the validity of the data.

▶ **Integrity or security.** Consumers must be assured that their personal data are secure and accurate. It is necessary for those collecting the data to take whatever precautions are required to ensure that they protect data from loss, unauthorized access or alteration, destruction, and fraudulent use, and to take reasonable steps to gain information from reputable and reliable sources. For an example of where the protection of personal data has been questioned, see Case 14.2.

▶ **Enforcement or redress.** A method of enforcement and remedy must be available. Otherwise, there is no real deterrent or enforceability for privacy issues.

The broadest law in scope is the Communications Privacy and Consumer Empowerment Act (1997), which requires, among other things, that the FTC enforce online privacy rights in EC, including the collection and use of personal data. For representative U.S. federal privacy legislation, see Online File W14.6. For the status of pending legislation in the United States, visit the Center for Democracy and Technology at cdt.org/privacy/guide/protect.

Online Privacy Clarification

Consumers think that online privacy policies mean that the website will not sell or use data in specific ways. But there may be a disconnect between business practices and consumer expectations. Consumers think privacy notices mean certain default protections; they do not understand that privacy policies are just notices. They do not guarantee any rights.

Customers are willing to share all kinds of information when they see firms using that information to enhance their experience. But some data-driven interactions can easily

---

CASE 14.2

EC Application

OCTOPUS CARD USED EVERYWHERE AND TRACKED EVERYWHERE

Smart cards are being used across the world as a form of electronic payment. The Octopus Card is a contactless stored-value smart card which has been in service since 1997 in Hong Kong. It was first used as a convenient alternative way of paying public transportation fares. Since then, the variety of services the Octopus Card can be used for is getting larger. Not only is it used as a stored-value card in shops, restaurants, car parks, etc., it is also used for office sign-in, as well as for access control in commercial and residential buildings.

In terms of popularity, the Octopus Card is a great success—as of August 2011, more than 24 million cards are in circulation in Hong Kong, which is more than Hong Kong's population of 7 million. There are over 60,000 readers used by over 4,000 service providers. Ninety-five percent of people between the ages of 16 and 65 have an Octopus Card and it is virtually the sole provider. Conceptually, it can also be used for personal identification. The "card usage" data is stored on the card and therefore, the locations, rides, and purchases of the card holders may be traced.

One incident involving the use of card data has caused the Federation of Trade Unions in Hong Kong to file a complaint against the Octopus Card company claiming it is breaching the privacy of personal data. The complaint was triggered by the success of police in tracking down a suspected acid-thrower in January 2010. The suspect threw a corrosive liquid onto his victim with intent to cause grievous bodily harm, leaving a bag at the scene which was later spotted on CCTV recordings at a nearby station. The police said that they were able to find the suspect by using CCTV recordings as well as Octopus Card usage data to find holders of Octopus cards used in the station around the time of the attack. The incident unveiled that data stored on the Octopus Card can be traced. A representative of the Federation expressed the potential risk of information leaks to third parties, which could lead to unfair commercial activities toward customers. For example, it is possible that customers' data could be sold to other merchants for commercial gain without customers' awareness. An Octopus Card spokesperson explained however, that the company provides information to the police only upon the provision of a search warrant and court order as required by law. It is clear therefore, that the protection of personal data is a contentious issue.

Sources: The Standard (2010), Octopus (2009), and MacManus (2009).

Questions

1. What are the potential uses of the collected data?
2. What is the Federation of Trade Unions' main concern?

cross the line from customer delight into customer despair, and oftentimes this despair is caused by the following pitfalls:

1. Asking customers for data and then neglecting to use it for the customer's benefit or expectation.

2. Failing to protect the data collected; losing customer data in a security breach quickly drives despair.

3. Customers perceiving that their data was somehow used to harm them, either by wasting their time with an avalanche of unwanted solicitations or by cornering them with hidden costs or restrictions.

Therefore, clarification of how data will be used and protected is necessary for a good EC relationship.

The USA PATRIOT Act Versus Privacy

The USA PATRIOT Act (officially, Uniting and Strengthening America by Providing Appropriate Tools Required to Intercept and Obstruct Terrorism) was passed in October 2001, in the aftermath of the September 11 terrorist attacks. Its intent is to give law enforcement agencies broader range in their efforts to protect the public. However, the American Civil Liberties Union (ACLU), the Electronic Freedom Foundation (EFF), and other organizations have grave concerns, including (1) expanded surveillance with reduced checks and balances, (2) overbreadth with a lack of focus on terrorism, and (3) rules that would allow U.S. foreign intelligence agencies to more easily spy on Americans.

On March 9, 2007, the U.S. Department of Justice (DOJ) said that the FBI had improperly used provisions of the USA PATRIOT Act to obtain thousands of telephone, business, and financial records without prior judicial approval (Johnson and Lipton 2007). The report is available on the DOJ's website at justice.gov/oig/new.htm. The result of this report is that the government may restrain some parts of the act that allow expanded surveillance in the following areas:

▶ E-mail and Internet searches
▶ Nationwide roving wiretaps
▶ Requirement that ISPs hand over more user information
▶ Expanded scope of surveillance based on new definitions of terrorism
▶ Government spying on suspected computer trespassers with no need for a court order
▶ Wiretaps for suspected violations of the Computer Fraud and Abuse Act
▶ Dramatic increases in the scope and penalties of the Computer Fraud and Abuse Act
▶ General expansion of Foreign Intelligence Surveillance Act (FISA) authority
▶ Increased information sharing between domestic law enforcement and intelligence
▶ FISA detours around federal domestic surveillance limitations; domestic surveillance detours around FISA limitations

In April 2010, President Obama signed a 1-year extension of several provisions of the PATRIOT Act. Three sections of the PATRIOT Act that stay in force will: (1) authorize court-approved roving wiretaps that permit surveillance on multiple phones; (2) allow court-approved seizure of records and property in antiterrorism operations; and (3) permit surveillance against a so-called lone wolf, a non-U.S. citizen engaged in terrorism who may not be part of a recognized terrorist group (see also *Fox News* [2010]). For details and discussions, see **en.wikipedia.org/wiki/USA_PATRIOT_ACT**.

Government Spying on Its Citizenry

On September 28, 2010, the Obama administration asked for legislation that would require social networking companies and voice-over-Internet service providers to adapt their technology so law enforcement agents could monitor users' communications during criminal and terrorism investigations. At issue is the proper balance between personal privacy and national security, whereby innovation and commerce is not stifled. The claim is that social networking sites have technology that has outpaced government law enforcement capabilities. The laws on the books do not cover the new communication (i.e., texting and social networking). Opponents see this as nothing more than unbridled government eavesdropping (Nakashima 2010a).

P3P Privacy Platform

The **Platform for Privacy Preferences Project (P3P)** is a protocol allowing websites to declare their intended use of information they collect about browsing users. It is designed to give users more control of their personal information when browsing by communicating a website's privacy policies to its users, allowing them to compare the policies to their preferences or to other standards. P3P was developed by the World Wide Web Consortium (W3C) in April 2002.

> **Platform for Privacy Preferences Project (P3P)**
> A protocol allowing websites to declare their intended use of information they collect about browsing users.

P3P is a mechanism that helps to express a website's data management practices. P3P manages information through privacy policies. When a website uses P3P, it sets up a set of policies that allows it to state its intended uses of personal information that may be gathered from its site visitors.

P3P provides a standard XML format that websites can use to encode their privacy policies. Sites also provide XML "policy reference files" to indicate which policy applies to which part of the site. Sites can optionally provide a "compact policy" by configuring their servers to issue a special P3P header when cookies are set.

The Purpose of P3P. As the Web became an acceptable medium in which to sell products and services, electronic commerce, websites tried to collect more information about the people who purchased their merchandise. Some companies used controversial practices such as tracker cookies to ascertain the users' demographic information and buying habits, using this information to provide specifically targeted advertisements. Users who saw this as an invasion of privacy would sometimes turn off the cookies or use proxy servers to keep their personal information secure. P3P was designed to give users more precise control over the kind of information that they are sharing. According to the W3C, the main goal of P3P is to increase user trust and confidence in the Web through technical empowerment.

When users decide to use P3P, they set their own policies and state what personal information they will allow to be seen by the sites that they visit. For information on how to create and publish your company's P3P policy, see w3.org/P3P/details.html.

The process of P3P is shown in Exhibit 14.4. It is based on the following five points: (1) request P3P policy files, (2) send P3P policy files, (3) request Web page, (4) send Web page, and (5) display page and policy to user (Department of Commerce 2009).

PRIVACY PROTECTION IN COUNTRIES OTHER THAN THE UNITED STATES

In 1998, the European Union passed a privacy directive (EU Data Protection Directive) reaffirming the principles of personal data protection in the Internet age. This directive protects privacy more than U.S. protection laws. Member countries are required to put this directive into effect by introducing new laws or modifying existing laws in their respective countries. The directive aims to regulate the activities of any person or company that controls the collection, storage, processing, or use of personal data on the Internet.

In many countries, the debate continues about the rights of the individual versus the rights of society. In some countries, like China, there is little privacy protection.

Section 14.3 ▶ REVIEW QUESTIONS

1. Define privacy and free speech. Do your definitions depend on technology?
2. List some of the ways that the Internet can collect information about individuals.

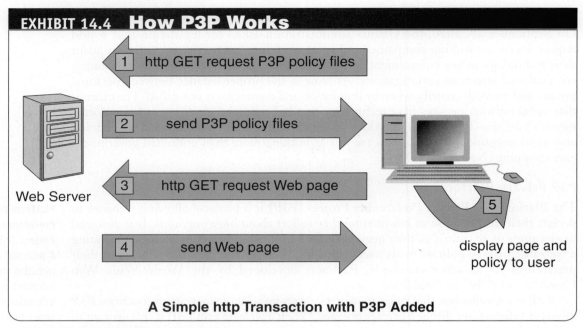

EXHIBIT 14.4   How P3P Works

1. http GET request P3P policy files
2. send P3P policy files
3. http GET request Web page
4. send Web page
5. display page and policy to user

Web Server

A Simple http Transaction with P3P Added

Source: U.S. Department of Commerce (2009).

3. What are cookies and spyware, and what do they have to do with online privacy?
4. List four common ethical principles related to the gathering of personal information.
5. Describe privacy issues in social networks. What are the dangers?
6. Define P3P and describe its objectives and procedures.
7. How has the reauthorized USA PATRIOT Act expanded the government's reach?

14.4 OTHER EC LEGAL ISSUES

During the last 10 years, a large number of laws dealing with EC and the Internet have been enacted. Representative major issues are listed in Exhibit 14.5.

Note that some of these issues were discussed in previous sections. Note also that legal issues are country or even state dependent. For a comprehensive coverage of these, see Davidson (2009), Mallor, et al. (2009), Cheeseman (2008), Volonino, et al. (2007), and Mann and Winn (2008). You can find a comprehensive e-commerce law blog at ecommercelaw.typepad.com.

THE LEGAL AND REGULATORY ENVIRONMENT

The open information environment in which we live has overwhelmed existing legal and technical mechanisms intended to protect privacy, copyrights, and trade secrets. To some, privacy is simply the claim of individuals, groups, and institutions to determine for themselves when, how, and to what extent information about them is used lawfully and appropriately by others. However, advances in communication and information technology and the ease of data searching have left this vulnerable group unaware of stealth discovery, privacy invasion, unfair misuse of personal information, copyright infringement, and identity theft. Information flow policies restricting movement cannot stop the threat of identity theft or privacy invasion alone. Contemporary information systems should be built to encourage compliance and maximize the possibility of accountability for violations (see Weitzner, et al. 2008).

Example. Arvest, a financial service provider, provides its customers with a comprehensive privacy policy and notice statement to earn their trust and confidence. The company recognizes a customer's expectation of privacy and outlines how customer information is collected. It discloses to what affiliates and third-party companies that this information is shared with. It maintains confidentiality of customer information and will

EXHIBIT 14.5   Summary of Important EC Legal Issues

Issue	Description
E-filings in court	Litigation means a large quantity of paper. Some courts allow electronic filing of such documents.
Evidence, electronic evidence (e-evidence)	Some electronic documents can be used as evidence in court. The State of New York, for example, allows e-mails to be used as evidence. For an overview of electronic evidence, see Volonino, et al. (2007).
Jurisdiction	Ability to sue in other states or countries: Whose jurisdiction prevails when litigants are in different states or countries? Who can sue for Internet postings done in other countries?
Liability	The use of multiple networks and trading partners makes the documentation of responsibility difficult. How can liability for errors, malfunctions, or fraudulent use of data be determined?
Defamation	Is the ISP liable for material published on the Internet because of services it provides or supports? (Usually not.) Who else is liable for defamation? What if the publisher is in another country?
Identity fraud	The Identity, Theft, and Assumption Deterrence Act of 1998 makes identity fraud a federal felony carrying a 3- to 25-year prison sentence.
Computer crime	The Information Infrastructure Protection Act (IIP Act, 1996) protects information in all computers.
Digital signature	Digital signatures are recognized as legal in the United States and some other countries, but not in all countries (see Chapter 9).
Regulation of consumer databases	The United States allows the compilation and sale of customer databases; the European Union Directive on Data Protection prohibits this practice.
Encryption technology	Export of U.S. encryption technology was made legal in 1999. (Countries still restricted from export are Iran, Syria, Sudan, North Korea, and Cuba.)
Time and place	An electronic document signed in Japan on January 5 may have the date January 4 in Los Angeles. Which date is considered legal if disputes arise?
Location of files and data	Much of the law hinges on the physical location of files and data. With distributed and replicated databases, it is difficult to say exactly where data are stored at any given time.
Electronic and clickwrap contracts	If all the elements to establish a contract are present, an electronic contract is valid and enforceable.
E-communications privacy	The Electronic Communications Privacy Act (ECPA) of 1986 makes it illegal to access stored e-mail or e-mail in transmission.
IPOs online	Websites with the necessary information on securities offerings are considered a legal channel for selling stock in a corporation.
Antitrust	*U.S. DOJ v. Microsoft* found that (1) Microsoft used predatory and anticompetitive conduct to illegally maintain the monopoly in Windows OS; (2) Microsoft illegally attempted to monopolize the market for Internet browsing software; and (3) Microsoft illegally bundled its Web browser with Windows OS, engaging in a tying arrangement in violation of the Sherman Act.
Taxation	Taxation of sales transactions by states is on hold in the United States and some (not all) countries, but the issue will be revised.
Money laundering	How can money laundering be prevented when the value of the money is in the form of a smart card?
Miscellaneous	Domain names, Internet gambling, e-mail, SMS, cyberbullying, and national electronic surveillance.

Sources: Compiled from Cheeseman (2008), FTC.gov, Volonino, et al. (2007), and Volonino and Robinson (2004).

respond quickly to questions of privacy. It also has a "do not call" list for consumers and customers, should that service be desired. See arvestblog.com/Privacy.aspx.

We now discuss only two issues: e-discovery and cyberbullying.

E-DISCOVERY

Electronic discovery (e-discovery) refers to any process in which electronic data is sought, located, secured, and searched with the intent of using it as evidence in a civil or criminal legal case. E-discovery can be carried out offline on a particular computer or it can

electronic discovery (e-discovery)
Discovery in civil litigation that deals with information in electronic format; also referred to as *electronically stored information* (ESI).

be done in a network. Court-ordered or government sanctioned hacking for the purpose of obtaining critical evidence is also a type of e-discovery. For details, see en.wikipedia. org/wiki/Electronic_discovery.

Types of Data E-Discovery

In the process of electronic discovery, data of all types can serve as evidence. This can include text, images, calendar files, databases, spreadsheets, audio files, animation, websites, and computer programs. Even malware such as viruses, Trojans, and spyware can be secured and investigated. E-mail can be an especially valuable source of evidence in civil or criminal litigation, because people are often less careful in these exchanges than in hard copy correspondence such as written memos and postal letters.

How Electronic Discovery Is Used

Even law firms are going green by saving paper, especially on discovery. In this context, an *electronic form* is the representation of information as binary numbers. Electronic information is different from paper information because of its intangible form, volume, transience, and persistence. Also, electronic information is usually accompanied by *metadata* (data about data), which is never present in paper information unless manually coded. E-discovery poses new challenges and opportunities for attorneys, their clients, technical advisors, and the courts, as electronic information is collected, reviewed, and produced.

Also included in e-discovery is "raw data," which forensic investigators can review for hidden evidence.

E-discovery deals frequently with e-mail archives. According to Conry-Murray (2008), e-mail is the prime target of e-discovery requests, and it must have features such as full-content index, keyword search, and metadata index.

E-Discovery and Social Networks

Speaking of discovery, should families of the newly deceased get access to their dead loved one's social network after they die? For how long and how much information of the dearly departed do they need to know? How do you manage privacy in the afterlife?

Facebook has developed a policy for its deceased users. If next of kin asks to have a profile taken down, then Facebook will comply. It will not hand over a user's password even to let family members read private messages. Yahoo! Mail's rule is to keep accounts private, even after a person's death. Asset Lock and Deathswitch are firms that offer an encrypted space for people to store their passwords and other digital information. Deathswitch will assume you are dead after sending a series of unanswered prompts. Legacy Locker will manage your Web domains after your death, verifying, of course, from two independent sources that you have actually died. Facebook now provides friends and relatives, after proof of death, of course, the option to "memorialize" the profile pages of friends and relatives who have died (see Gaelle 2009).

CYBERBULLYING

cyberbullying
The use of information and communication technologies to support deliberate, repeated, and hostile behavior by an individual or group, that is intended to harm others.

Cyberbullying is the use of information and communication technologies to support deliberate, repeated, and hostile behavior by an individual or group, that is intended to harm others. Cyberbullies use the Internet, cell phones, or other devices or post text or images intended to hurt or embarrass another person. Cyberbullying can be as simple as continuing to send e-mail to someone who has said they want no further contact with the sender, but it may also include threats, sexual remarks, pejorative labels (i.e., hate speech), ganging up on victims by making them the subject of ridicule in forums, and posting false statements as fact aimed at humiliation.

Cyberbullying Versus CyberStalking

The practice of cyberbullying is not limited to children and, while the behavior is identified by the same definition in adults, the distinction in age groups is sometimes referred to as cyberstalking or cyberharassment when perpetrated by adults toward adults. Common tactics used by cyberstalkers are to vandalize a search engine or encyclopedia, to threaten a victim's earnings, employment, reputation, or safety. A repeated pattern of such actions against a target by an adult constitutes cyberstalking.

The Possible Damage of Cyberbulllying

In 2007, Debbie Heimowitz, a Stanford University master's student, created Adina's Deck, a film based on Stanford accredited research. She worked in focus groups for 10 weeks in three different schools to learn about the problem of cyberbullying in Northern California. The findings determined that over 60 percent of students had been cyberbullied and were victims of cyberbullying.

A survey carried out by the trade union Amicus in the United Kingdom reported that one fifth of employees in the United Kingdom were being bullied electronically. While cyberbullying includes e-mails, it also extends to social networking sites; the overall effect can be seriously detrimental to morale within an organization. Amicus estimates that bullying costs the UK economy over £2 billion (US$325 billion) per annum in sick pay, staff turnover, and productivity loss. Often, a cybervictim's only recourse is to secure or remove his or her profile from a social network, or change his or her e-mail.

As cyberbullying has become more common in society, particularly among young people, legislation and awareness campaigns have arisen to combat it. (e.g., cyberbullying.us and stopcyberbullying.org).

Example. In 2008, a jury convicted a mom of the lesser charges for her role in a mean-spirited Internet hoax that apparently drove a 13-year-old girl to suicide. In effect it was a kind of cyberbullying. Lori Drew created a fictitious 16-year-old boy on MySpace and then sent flirty messages from him to a teenage neighbor, Megan Meier, who had said mean things about Drew's daughter, causing her to suffer from depression. After 4 weeks of flirting, the fictitious boy dumped the unsuspecting 13-year-old, who later committed suicide. According to the prosecution, this was a clear case of "cyberbullying," but the case hinged on an unprecedented and highly questionable application of the Computer Fraud and Abuse Act. The jury chose not to extend the law. As a result, felony conspiracy charges were dropped and only the minor misdemeanor charges were upheld. See en.wikipedia.org/wiki/United_States_v._Lori_Drew.

Section 14.4 ▶ REVIEW QUESTIONS

1. List some of the issues that EC will face in the coming years that will affect your daily life.
2. Define cyberbullying. What can be its damage?
3. Define e-discovery. How is it related to the law? To e-commerce?

14.5 CONSUMER AND SELLER PROTECTION FROM ONLINE FRAUD

An FBI report released in March 2009 revealed that the number of EC fraud complaints reached 304,000 in 2010 at a price tag of hundreds of millions of dollars (Internet Crime Complaint Center 2011). Therefore, it is necessary to defend EC consumers.

CONSUMER (BUYER) PROTECTION

Consumer protection is critical to the success of any commerce, especially electronic, where buyers do not see sellers. The FTC enforces consumer protection laws in the United States (see ftc.gov). The FTC provides a list of 10 scams that are most likely to arrive by bulk e-mail (see onguardonline.gov/spam.html). In addition, the European Union and the United States are attempting to develop joint consumer protection policies. For details, see the Trans Atlantic Consumer Dialogue website at tacd.org.

Representative Tips and Sources for Your Protection

Protecting consumers is an important topic for government agencies, vendors, professional associations, and consumer protection organizations. They provide many tips on how to protect consumers online. A representative list follows.

- Users should make sure that they enter the real website of well-known companies, such as Walmart, Disney, and Amazon.com, by going directly to the site, rather than through a link, and should shop for reliable brand names at those sites.
- Check any unfamiliar site for an address and telephone and fax numbers. Call and quiz a salesperson about the seller.
- Check out the seller with the local chamber of commerce, Better Business Bureau (bbbonline.org), or TRUSTe (truste.com).
- Investigate how secure the seller's site is and how well it is organized.
- Examine the money-back guarantees, warranties, and service agreements before making a purchase.
- Compare prices online with those in regular stores—too-low prices may be too good to be true.
- Ask friends what they know. Find testimonials and endorsements.
- Find out what redress is available in case of a dispute.
- Consult the National Consumers League Fraud Center (fraud.org).
- Check the resources available at consumerworld.org.

In addition to these tips, consumers also have shopper's rights on the Internet, as described in the following list of sources:

- The FTC (ftc.gov): Abusive e-mail should be forwarded tospam@uce.gov; ftc.gov/bcp/menus/consumer/tech/online.shtm provides tips for online shopping and Internet auctions.
- National Consumers League Fraud Center (fraud.org).
- Federal Citizen Information Center (pueblo.gsa.gov).
- U.S. Department of Justice (usdoj.gov).
- The FBI's Internet Crime Complaint Center (ic3.gov/default.aspx).
- The American Bar Association provides online shopping tips at safeshopping.org.
- The Better Business Bureau (bbbonline.org).
- The U.S. Food and Drug Administration for buying medicine and medical products online (fda.gov/oc/buyonline).
- The Direct Marketing Association (the-dma.org).

Disclaimer: This is general information on consumer rights. It is not legal advice on how any particular individual should proceed. If you require specific legal advice, consult an attorney.

Third-Party Assurance Services

Several public organizations and private companies attempt to protect consumers. The following are just a few examples.

Protection by Third-Party Intermediary. Intermediaries who manage electronic markets try to protect buyers and sellers there. A good example is eBay, which provides an extensive protection program (see pages.ebay.com/coverage/index.html).

TRUSTe's "Trustmark." TRUSTe (truste.org) is a nonprofit group whose mission is to build users' trust and confidence in the Internet by promoting the policies of disclosure and informed consent. TRUSTe certifies and monitors website privacy and e-mail policies and practices, and resolves thousands of consumer privacy problems every year (see truste. com/about_TRUSTe). Sellers who become members of TRUSTe can add value and increase consumer confidence in online transactions by displaying the TRUSTe

Advertising Affiliate "Trustmark" (a seal of quality). This mark identifies sites that have agreed to comply with responsible information-gathering guidelines. In addition, the TRUSTe website provides its members with a "privacy policy wizard," which helps companies create their own privacy policies. The site offers several types of seals such as privacy, children, e-health, safe harbor, wireless, e-mail services, and international services.

The TRUSTe program is voluntary. The licensing fee for use of the Trustmark ranges from $500 to $10,000, depending on the size of the online organization and the sensitivity of the information it is collecting. Many websites are certified as TRUSTe participants, including AT&T, CyberCash, Excite, IBM, Buena Vista Internet Group, CNET, Google, Infoseek, the *New York Times*, and Yahoo!. However, there still seems to be a fear that signing with TRUSTe could expose firms to litigation from third parties if they fail to live up to the letter of the TRUSTe pact, and that fear is likely to deter some companies from signing up.

In an attempt to build online trust between consumers and businesses, TRUSTe and Adgregate Markets announced a joint venture to develop the world's first privacy standards to distributed commerce ads and applications for online, mobile, and social networks. Under this partnership, TRUSTe has certified Adgregate Web privacy practices and verified that the customer data management practices of Adgregate's distributed commerce platform and Adgregate's platform of products, including ShopFans, ShopAds, and SecureAds uphold Adgregate's privacy commitment. For details, see TRUSTe (2010).

Better Business Bureau. The Better Business Bureau (BBB), a private nonprofit organization supported largely by membership, provides reports on businesses that consumers can review before making a purchase. The BBB responds to millions of inquiries each year. Its BBBOnLine program (bbbonline.com) is similar to TRUSTe's Trustmark. The goal of the program is to promote confidence on the Internet through two different seals. Companies that meet the BBBOnLine standards for the Reliability Seal are members of the local BBB and have good truth-in-advertising and consumer service practices. Those that exhibit the BBBOnLine Privacy Seal on their websites have an online privacy protection policy and standards for handling consumers' personal information. In addition, consumers are able to click on the BBBOnLine seals and instantly get a BBB report on the participating company.

Which?. Supported by the European Union, Which? (which.co.uk) gives consumers protection by ensuring that online traders under its Which? Web Trader scheme abide by a code of proactive guidelines. These guidelines outline issues such as product information, advertising, ordering methods, prices, delivery of goods, consumer privacy, receipting, dispute resolution, and security.

Web Trust Seal and Others. The Web Trust seal program is similar to TRUSTe. The American Institute of Certified Public Accountants (cpawebtrust.com) sponsors it. Another program, Gomez (gomez.com), monitors customer complaints and provides merchant certification.

Evaluation by Consumers. A large number of sites include product and vendor evaluations offered by consumers. For example, Deja.com, now part of Google, is home to many communities of interest whose members trade comments about products at groups.google.com. In addition, epubliceye.com allows consumers to give feedback on reliability, privacy, and customer satisfaction. It makes available a company profile that measures a number of elements, including payment options.

The Computer Fraud and Abuse Act (CFAA)

The **Computer Fraud and Abuse Act (CFAA)** was passed in 1984 and amended several times and is an important milestone in EC legislation. Initially, the scope and intent of CFAA was to protect government computers and financial industry computers from criminal theft by outsiders. In 1986, the CFAA was amended to include stiffer penalties for violations, but it still only protected computers used by the federal government or financial institutions. Then, as the Internet expanded in scope, so did the CFAA. In 1994 and in 1996, there were significant revisions of CFAA that added a civil law component and civil charges to this criminal law. In 2001 it was amended by the USA PATRIOT Act (Section 14.3), which provides for counterterrorism activities.

Computer Fraud and Abuse Act (CFAA)
Major computer crime law to protect government computers and other Internet-connected computers.

SELLER PROTECTION

The Internet makes fraud by customers or others easier because of user anonymity. It must protect sellers against:

▶ Customers who deny that they placed an order
▶ Customers who download copyrighted software and/or knowledge and sell it to others
▶ Customers who give false payment (credit card or bad check) information in payment for products and services provided
▶ Use of their name by others (e.g., imposter sellers)
▶ Use of their unique words and phrases, names, and slogans and their Web addresses by others (trademark protection)

Sellers also can be attacked illegally or unethically by competitors.

Example 1. A class action lawsuit was filed against McAfee in the United States District Court for the Northern District of California (Case No. 10-1455-HRL) alleging that after customers buy McAfee software from McAfee's website, a deceptive pop-up ad appears that looks like the rest of the McAfee page that thanks customers for their product purchase, and, then asks them to click a "Try it Now" button, which they claim tricks them into subscribing to Arpu, Inc. McAfee apparently transmits customer credit/debit card and billing information to Arpu for an undisclosed fee for each customer signing up with Arpu (*ClassActionLawSuitsInTheNews* 2010). See also courthousenews.com/2010/04/08/McAfee.pdf.

Example 2. LVMH is leading the fashion sector's battle to protect luxury brands online as well as jewelers, watch manufacturers, and other luxury item vendors. When it comes to the virtual world, counterfeiters, nonapproved vendors, and freeloaders are not the problem, but the idea about the freedom of the Internet itself. There is tension between the Internet and intellectual property rights. Perhaps because of this, LVMH has come to the conclusion that continuing to sue people and companies will not solve the problem. Instead LVMH is working with the Internet Market Commission in Brussels to try to craft an agreement to cover luxury distribution online.

What Can Sellers Do?

Cardcops.com provides a database of credit card numbers that have had chargeback orders recorded against them. Sellers who have access to the database can use this information to decide whether to proceed with a sale. In the future, the credit card industry is planning to use biometrics to deal with electronic shoplifting. Also, sellers can use PKI and digital certificates, especially the SET protocol, to help prevent fraud (see Chapter 9).

Other possible solutions include the following:

▶ Use intelligent software to identify questionable customers (or do this identification manually in small companies). One technique, for example, involves comparing credit card billing and requested shipping addresses.
▶ Identify warning signals—that is, red flags—for possible fraudulent transactions.
▶ Ask customers whose billing address is different from the shipping address to call their bank and have the alternate address added to their bank account. Retailers agree to ship the goods to the alternate address only if this is done.

For further discussion of what merchants can do to protect themselves from fraud, see OnGuard Online at onguardonline.gov/spam.html.

PROTECTING BUYERS AND SELLERS: ELECTRONIC AND DIGITAL SIGNATURES

One method to help distinguish between legitimate and fraudulent transactions is electronic signatures. Electronic signature legislation is designed to accomplish two goals: (1) to remove barriers to e-commerce and (2) to enable and promote the desirable public policy goal of e-commerce by helping to build trust and predictability needed by parties doing business online.

A signature, whether electronic or on paper, is a symbol that signifies intent to be bound to the terms of the contract or transaction. Thus, the definition of *signed* in the Uniform Commercial Code includes "any symbol" so long as it is "executed or adopted by a party with present intention to authenticate writing."

An **electronic signature** is a generic term that refers to the various methods by which one can "sign" an electronic record (see Chapter 9). Although all electronic signatures are represented digitally (i.e., as a series of ones and zeroes), many different technologies can create them. Examples of electronic signatures include a name typed at the end of an e-mail message by the sender; a digitized image of a handwritten signature attached to an electronic document; a secret code or PIN to identify the sender to the recipient; a code or "handle" that the sender of a message uses to identify him- or herself; a unique biometrics-based identifier, such as a fingerprint or a retinal scan; and a digital signature created through the use of public key cryptography (see Chapter 9). Digital signatures have generated the most business and technical usage, as well as legislative initiatives.

> **electronic signature**
> A generic, technology-neutral term that refers to the various methods by which one can "sign" an electronic record.

Authentication and Biometric Controls

In cyberspace, buyers and sellers do not see each other. Even when videoconferencing is used, the authenticity of the person on the other end must be verified unless the person has been dealt with before. However, if one can assure the identity of the person on the other end of the line, one can imagine improved and new EC applications. For example, students will be able to take exams online from any place without the need for proctors. Fraud among recipients of government entitlements and transfer payments will be reduced to a bare minimum. Buyers will be assured who the sellers are, and sellers will know who the buyers are, with a very high degree of confidence. Arrangements can be made so that only authorized people in companies can place (or receive) purchasing orders. Interviews for employment and other matching applications will be accurate because it will be almost impossible for imposters to represent other people. Overall, trust in online transactions and in EC in general will increase significantly.

As discussed in Chapter 9, the solution for such authentication is provided by *biometric controls*. Biometric controls provide access procedures that match every valid user with a *unique user identifier (UID)*. They also provide an authentication method that verifies that users requesting access to the computer system are really who they claim to be. Authentication and biometric controls are valid for both consumer and merchant protection.

Fraud Detecting Systems

There is a large number of fraud detection systems. Well known is the use of data mining for credit card fraud. For other methods, see Parks (2010). CyberSource developed several tools for detecting fraud. For details, see CyberSource (2011) and **authorize.net/files/fdswhitepaper.pdf**.

GOVERNMENT REGULATION OF E-COMMERCE

Governments are regulating EC activities in order to protect both buyers and sellers.

Example. Marketers and brands using social networks find their activities in those spaces regulated by the UK's Advertising Standard Authority (ASA). The regulations extend the regulatory framework currently in place for paid online ads to all other online marketing communications. As a result, claims from marketers on their own websites and third-party sites like social networks are now subject to the UK scrutiny, as they are in TV, print, and other forms of online advertising. The code is designed to ensure that ads do not offend or mislead, and that they respect specific laws relating to the online marketing of alcohol, gambling, auto, health, and financial products. For details, see **clickz.com/3639734**.

Section 14.5 ▶ REVIEW QUESTIONS

1. Describe consumer protection measures.
2. Describe assurance services.

3. What must a seller do to protect itself against fraud? How?
4. Describe types of electronic signatures. Who is protected? Why?
5. Describe authentication and biometric controls.

14.6 PUBLIC POLICY AND POLITICAL ENVIRONMENTS

We include in this chapter four topics that relate to public policy and are closely related to e-commerce.

NET NEUTRALITY APPROVED BY THE FCC

Internet neutrality (also *network neutrality*, *net neutrality*, or *NN*) has been a hotly debated topic that will shape the future of the Internet (see en.wikipedia.org/wiki/Net_ neutrality). It became a high-profile topic when telecommunications network operators (telcos) AT&T and Verizon stated that they should have the right to charge extra for premium placement on their network to recoup vast investments in their infrastructure. Currently, all Internet traffic is being treated equally (or "neutrally") by telecommunication providers. In response, numerous grassroots campaigns emerged to try to stop such a practice. That means that 5 percent of Internet consumers are using up to 90 percent of the available bandwidth because of the "peer-to-peer" (P2P) explosion. See p2p-security. com/about-p2p/the-bandwidth-hog.

On December 21, 2010, the Federal Communications Commission (FCC) approved net neutrality, the principle that Internet service providers cannot discriminate against certain services or applications. Net neutrality puts in place three high-level rules for service providers (i.e., cable and telecommunications companies). The first, dubbed "Robust Transparency," calls for providers of both fixed and mobile broadband to clearly disclose their bandwidth management policies to consumers and application developers. The second, called the "No Blocking Rule," prohibits fixed broadband providers from blocking content but allows "reasonable network management." Mobile broadband providers get a lighter version of the policy. They are simply forbidden from blocking competing voice and videoconferencing services. The third rule appears to overlap with the second. It says that fixed broadband providers can't levy "unreasonable discrimination" against outside applications (Coffey 2010).

Note that implementation of net neutrality is not simple; it involves Web companies, fiber-optics owners, content providers, mobile carriers, and consumers. For details, see en.wikipedia.org/wiki/Network_neutrality. Opponents are fighting the authority of the FCC to enforce net neutrality.

TAXATION OF EC TRANSACTIONS

taxation

The process whereby charges are imposed on individuals or property by the legislative branch of the federal government and by many state governments to raise funds for public purposes.

The process whereby charges are imposed on individuals or property by the legislative branch of the federal government and by many state governments to raise funds for public purposes is called **taxation**. A tax that is directly imposed by the law-making body of a government on merchandise, products, or certain types of transactions is an *excise tax*, which includes carrying on a profession or business, obtaining a license, or transferring property. Excise taxes are a fixed and absolute charge that is independent from the taxpayer's financial status or the value that the taxed property has to the taxpayer. A tax that takes the taxpayer's wealth into account, as represented by the taxpayer's income or the property he or she owns, is a *property tax*. A property tax that is assessed and levied upon the taxpayer's income is called an *income tax*. These types of tax can be related to e-commerce.

In addition to taxing individuals and companies, the government taxes products and services sold. The most common tax is the "sales tax." A *value-added tax* is an indirect tax that is paid on the value added to the product at each stage of production, distribution, and sales. See en.wikipedia.org/wiki/Internet_taxes.

From the inception of the Internet until the late 1990s, the Internet was free of regular taxation by government in the United States at all levels (federal, states, cities) and also free of any specially targeted tax levies, duties, imposts, or license fees. However, in 1992, a

U.S. Supreme Court ruling stated that states can only require sellers to collect taxes if they have a physical presence in the *same state* as the consumer. The Court in *Quill Corp. v. North Dakota,* 504 U.S. 298 112 S. Ct. 1904, 119 L. Ed. 2d 91, stated that the current system taxing thousands of jurisdictions across the country makes it too complicated for online retailers to collect sales taxes fairly and efficiently (see taxfoundation.org/blog/show/963.html).

By 1996, that began to change as several U.S. states and municipalities began to see Internet services as a potential source of state tax revenue. The 1998 Internet Tax Freedom Act halted the expansion of direct taxation of the Internet. However, the act did not affect sales taxes applied to online purchases.

Today, nearly all online transactions are subject to one form of tax or the other. The Internet Tax Freedom Act merely precludes states in the United States from imposing their sales tax, or any other kind of gross receipts tax, on certain online services. For example, a state may impose an income or franchise tax on the net income earned by the provider of online services, while the same state may be precluded from imposing its sales tax on the gross receipts of that provider. In addition, as noted previously, the Internet Tax Freedom Act does not prevent taxation of the sale of goods through the Internet.

The question of whether states should be able to tax sales conducted over the Internet has generated increased interest as states scramble for additional funding in the wake of budget deficits. Technically, these transactions are taxable (en.wikipedia.org/wiki/Internet_taxes and lawbrain.com/wiki/Taxation). Several states are facing severe budget deficits. Budget and taxing authorities have placed the issue of collecting Internet taxes high on their list to generate state revenues. For example, in 2009, Lawrence County, Pennsylvania, joined a growing number of local governments nationwide seeking class action redress over online hotel reservation companies, for tax avoidance. It appears that there is a consensus forming among state lawmakers that Internet taxes are inevitable. Yet, there is consumer resistance. On January 11, 2010, a class action lawsuit was filed against AT&T alleging that it improperly charged sales tax to access the Internet in violation of Connecticut law and the Internet Tax Freedom Act.

Under President Obama's direction, the Federal Communication Commission (FCC) has also been active in promoting an Internet tax. In April 2010, the FCC put forth the National Broadband Plan, which contains Internet tax-increase proposals. It states that a tax upon telecommunications service providers, created by the FCC in 1997, "should broaden the universal service contribution base" (*Washington Times* 2010).

In July 2010, in a move to legalize Internet gambling, the House Financial Services Committee approved a bill that lays the groundwork for a multibillion-dollar online tax. A vote is expected in Congress soon. Internationally, the UN's World Health Organization (WHO) also desires funding. The WHO proposed, at the UN Summit Copenhagen 2010, a program to generate $30 billion in annual revenue from a global indirect tax in the form of "digital" taxes on the global Internet "hits," and a "financial" tax on all online financial transactions (Russell 2010).

INTERNET CENSORSHIP BY COUNTRIES

The control or suppression of the publishing or accessing of information on the Internet is called **Internet censorship**. Any government can try to prevent its citizens from viewing these websites even if it has no control over the websites themselves. Filtering can be based on a blacklist of offensive website content providers or be dynamic with full-blown written biometrics to identify potential blacklist candidates. To be blacklisted, a website will have all or part of its content censored by a government agency that sees its content as disruptive to the populace. The legal issues of Internet censorship are similar to offline censorship, however, because the national borders are more permeable online; residents of a country that bans certain information can sometimes find it on ancillary websites hosted outside the country.

Internet censorship
The control or suppression of the publishing or accessing of information on the Internet.

More than three dozen states around the world take part in censoring what their citizens can see and do on the Internet. This practice is increasingly widespread, with extensive filtering regimes in place in China, Iran, Burma (Myanmar), Syria, Uzbekistan, and Egypt during 2011. Censorship using technological filters is often coupled with restrictive laws related to what the press can publish, opaque surveillance practices, and severe penalties for people who break the state's rules of using the Internet. This trend has been emerging since at least 2002. See lawprofessors.typepad.com/media_law_prof_blog/2010/09/filtering-worldwide.html. The United States is fast becoming one to censor the Internet. In early 2009, Obama appointed Cass Sunstein as the White House's Regulatory Czar. Sunstein is an advocate for Internet censorship, having written several white papers promoting the subject. In his writings, Sunstein has advocated everything from regulating the content of personal e-mail communications to forcing nonprofit groups to publish information on their websites that is counter to their beliefs and mission (*WorldNetDaily* 2009). For details on censorship in the United States, China, and other countries, see Online File W14.7.

REGULATORY COMPLIANCE

regulatory compliance
Systems or departments in an organization whose job is to ensure that personnel are aware of and take steps to comply with relevant laws, standards, policies, and regulations.

Regulatory compliance refers to systems or departments in an organization whose job is to ensure that personnel are aware of and take steps to comply with relevant laws, standards, policies, and regulations of its government. These laws can be found both in domestic and international rules and standards, each having criminal and/or civil penalties. Unfortunately, the definition of what constitutes an effective compliance plan has been elusive due to legal ambiguity, complexity, and convolution.

In general, *compliance* means conforming to a rule, such as a specification, policy, standard, or law. *Regulatory compliance* describes the activities that corporations or public agencies are conducting in their efforts to comply with relevant laws and regulations.

Due to the increasing number of regulations and need for operational transparency, organizations are increasingly adopting the use of consolidated and harmonized sets of compliance controls. This approach is used to ensure that all necessary governance requirements can be met without the unnecessary duplication of effort and activity from resources.

International Compliance

The International Organization for Standardization (ISO) produces international standards such as ISO17799. The International Electrotechnical Commission (IEC) produces international standards in the electrotechnology area.

Compliance in the United States

Corporate scandals and breakdowns such as the Enron case of reputational risk in 2001 have highlighted the need for stronger compliance and regulations for publicly listed companies. The most significant regulation in this context is the Sarbanes-Oxley Act developed by two U.S. congressmen, Senator Paul Sarbanes and Representative Michael Oxley in 2001, which defined significant personal responsibility of corporate top management for the accuracy of reported financial statements.

Compliance in the United States generally means compliance with laws and regulations. These laws can have criminal or civil penalties or can be regulations. The definition of what constitutes an effective compliance plan has been elusive. Most authors, however, continue to cite the guidance provided by the United States Sentencing Commission in Chapter 8 of the Federal Sentencing Guidelines (see ussc.gov/orgguide.htm).

On October 12, 2006, the U.S. Small Business Administration relaunched Business.gov (business.gov), which provides a single point of access to government services and information that helps businesses comply with government regulations.

As a result of the recent global economic recession of 2007–2010 following the collapse of major investment banks and the unprecedented loss of trillions of investment capital, the Dodd-Frank Wall Street Reform and Consumer Protection Act was signed into law by President Obama on July 21, 2010, in order to promote the financial stability of the United States. The Dodd-Frank Act sought to improve accountability and transparency in the financial system, to end "too big to fail," to protect the American taxpayer by ending bailouts, and to protect consumers from abusive financial services practices. For compliance in other countries, see en.wikipedia.org/wiki/Regulatory_compliance.

To help with compliance issues, you can use EC software, especially to manage *compliance data*. **Compliance data** is defined as all data belonging or pertaining to enterprise or included in the law, which can be used for the purpose of implementing or validating compliance. Compliance software is available from all major software companies (e.g., Oracle, IBM, EMC, Agilent Technologies, and Computer Associates).

Here is an indirect issue of regulatory compliance.

compliance data
Data pertaining to the enterprise included in the law that can be used for the purpose of implementing or validating compliance.

Equal Opportunity and Discrimination

As described in Chapters 3 and 7 there is an increased tendency to use social networks for finding a job and for recruiters to fulfill positions. However, recruiting companies may face an interesting problem.

Recruiting Online: Is It a Possible Discrimination? HR departments and heads of departments are googling candidates and looking them up on Facebook, Twitter, and LinkedIn just to get a clearer sense of what they are like before they come for interviews.

About 77 percent of hiring managers now use social media sites to check out job candidates, according to a recent poll by executive career site ExecuNet. This practice comes with a few legal risks that recruiters need to keep in mind. One pitfall has to do with the concept of "disparate impact." To avoid the appearance of *racial discrimination*, the pool of candidates who can apply for a job should be made up of a mix of ethnic groups that roughly reflects the workforce as a whole. Relying too heavily on social media sites makes this difficult. Consider: The U.S. population is 13 percent African American and 15 percent Hispanic, but both groups are underrepresented on LinkedIn. Only 2 percent of LinkedIn members are Hispanic and 5 percent are African American. Therefore, there is a possibility of racial discrimination. The issue of disparate impact is particularly sensitive for defense contractors and other employers whose main customer is the government, since the Office of Federal Contract Compliance Programs requires contractors to be transparently nondiscriminatory in hiring or lose its business.

The solution could be to advertise job openings through multiple channels, and get candidates from a variety of different sources, including employee referral programs. Social media sites are tremendously useful, but they should be only one part of your information-gathering process. Another legal risk you take when you check someone out online is that you may discover information that you would not be allowed to ask about in a job interview. Conclusion: Consult a legal expert.

Section 14.6 ▶ REVIEW QUESTIONS

1. What is net neutrality and how will it affect the Internet?
2. Why is net neutrality such a hotly debated issue? Find the legal status of this issue.
3. Describe how taxes relate to e-commerce.
4. Describe e-discovery. Relate it to e-commerce.
5. Why are regulatory compliance laws subject to broad interpretation?
6. What is Internet censorship?
7. Discuss the potential for discrimination when recruiting online. What is a possible solution?

14.7 SOCIETAL ISSUES AND GREEN EC

At this point in the chapter, our attention turns to several societal issues of EC. Rising energy prices, a lingering recession, and evolving public attitudes have altered the way businesses view energy-efficient technology. Savvy enterprises now recognize the benefits of going green. The first societal topic is one of concern to many—the digital divide.

THE DIGITAL DIVIDE

Despite the factors and trends that contribute to future EC growth, since the inception of the Internet, and e-commerce in particular, a gap has emerged between those who have

digital divide
The gap that has emerged between those who have and those who do not have the ability to use the technology.

and those who do not have the ability to use the technology. This gap is referred to as the **digital divide**. The gap exists both *within* and *between* countries. The U.S. federal and state governments are attempting to close this gap within the country by encouraging training and supporting education and infrastructure. In the United States, a recent phone survey of U.S. households found 20 million households are still without Internet access (Duffy 2008). The gap among countries, however, may be widening rather than narrowing. For an overview and statistics, see en.wikipedia.org/wiki/Digital_divide. Many government and international organizations are trying to close the digital divide, including the United Nations and Citizens Online. It was predicted that by 2008, developing countries would have a broadband penetration rate of only 3 percent. However, with the use of mobile phone technology, developing countries reached nearly 50 percent in 2008 (*American Free Press* 2008). According to an October 2010 survey, the number of mobile broadband connections in developing countries of the Asia-Pacific region will increase to 27.2 million by 2015. Australia leads the market in mobile broadband penetration (*GSMA News* 2010).

Overcoming the Digital Divide

Governments, companies, and not-for-profit organizations are trying to reduce the digital divide. (See detailed coverage at en.wikipedia.org/wiki/Digital_divide.) One example is the One Laptop per Child project (laptop.org/en/laptop) because it fosters competition for the provision of cheaper equipment, relying heavily on open standards and free open source software. For example, the *OLPC XO-1* is an inexpensive laptop computer intended to be distributed to children in developing countries around the world, to provide them with access to knowledge. Programmer and free software advocate Richard Stallman has highlighted the importance of free software among groups concerned with the digital divide such as the World Summit on the Information Society. Notwithstanding, these efforts to provide individual access or shared access, such as through telecenters, desktop virtualizations and multiseat configurations, are probably the most simple and common ways to affordable information and communication technology (ICT) access today.

For a short video, see laptop.org/en/video/brand/index.html. The cost of the computer is around $100. However, in 2011, China was developing a similar computer that will cost around $50.

In Case 10.2 (p. 567), we provided an example of how poor farmers in India use cell phones to make payments on bank loans and receive information.

TELECOMMUTING

telecommuting
Working at home using a PC and the Internet.

One spinoff of increased broadband penetration is **telecommuting**: working at home using a PC and the Internet. Telecommuting is on the rise in the United States and in several developing countries. With the rise of information technology and communications technology, more and more employees are doing jobs that used to require being in the office from their own homes. Telecommuting can reduce the number of cars on our highways and thereby reduce per capita energy consumption and traffic congestion—both of which are sustainable. For a list of potential benefits, see Exhibit 14.6.

In 2009, 1.7 million more employees worked at home than in 2000. This represents a 31 percent increase in market share, from 3.3 percent to 4.3 percent of all employment. However, it can also lead to decreased social capital as society advances deep into the cyberspace world of communicating via text messaging, Skype, Facebook, Twitter, and other social networks instead of face-to-face communication. For those living in the suburbs, telecommuting is great because it saves them their 1- to 2-hour commute to work every day (Enviro Boys 2010).

Example. Ascend One, a consumer-debt counseling call center business, was forced to change networking strategies in order to grow. Ascend One's success was substantially burdened by having to provide its agents with daily cumbersome support and application updates on their desktop computers. By combining virtualization and teleworking, Ascend One was able to increase customer satisfaction and improve the productivity and morale of its call center employees by allowing them to work at home and to run tier-hosted applications from servers in the data center instead of their desktops. Call agent productivity

EXHIBIT 14.6 Potential Benefits of Telecommuting or Virtual Work

Individuals	Organizational	Community and Society
▶ Reduces or eliminates travel-related time and expenses ▶ Improves health by reducing stress related to compromises made between family and work responsibilities ▶ Allows closer proximity to and involvement with family ▶ Allows closer bonds with the family and the community ▶ Decreases involvement in office politics ▶ Increases productivity despite distractions	▶ Reduces office space needed ▶ Increases labor pool and competitive advantage in recruitment ▶ Provides compliance with the Americans with Disabilities Act ▶ Decreases employee turnover, absenteeism, and sick leave usage ▶ Improves job satisfaction and productivity	▶ Conserves energy and lessens dependence on foreign oil ▶ Preserves the environment by reducing traffic-related pollution and congestion ▶ Reduces traffic accidents and resulting injuries or deaths ▶ Reduces the incidence of disrupted families when people do not have to quit their jobs if they need to move because of a spouse's new job or family obligations ▶ Increases employment opportunities for the homebound ▶ Allows the movement of job opportunities to areas of high unemployment

increased by 10 percent. Regional weather conditions did not impact attendance. Extending remote access enhanced employee job satisfaction and resulted in lower attrition rates. Business continuity and disaster recovery capabilities were improved. The technology also allowed the company to maintain extraordinary levels of contact with remote employees. Training programs were accessible 24 hours per day with one click. Ascend One recognizes that technology is only a means to an end and the real challenge in managing virtualization and telecommuting is managing people (Park 2009).

GREEN EC AND IT

There are many opportunities to go EC green, and here we present the major ones.

Operating Greener Businesses, Eco-Friendly Data Centers, and Cloud Computing

The growing power consumption of computing technology and high energy costs are having a direct negative impact on business profitability. Enterprises are trying to reduce energy costs and increase the use of recyclable materials. **Green computing** is the study and practice of eco-friendly computing resources (e.g., see en.wikipedia.org/wiki/Green_computing). In this section, we focus on how EC is *going green* by adopting environmentally friendly practices.

With an increased awareness about the damage to the physical environment and ecosystem, organizations and individuals are looking at potential improvements and savings that can be made in the EC and IT industry. These efforts are known as **Green IT**. For example, energy use in data centers (facilities used to house computer systems and associated components, such as storage) is a major concern to corporations. Green EC/IT is a growing movement (see Nelson 2008). According to Gartner Inc., Green IT is expanding to many areas (see enterpriseinnovation.net; a blog by John Phelps). For guidelines on how to go green, see Exhibit 14.7.

In 2009, the American Recovery and Reinvestment Act (AARA) was signed into legislation by President Obama. AARA allocates over $70 billion to be invested in green initiatives (renewable energy, smart grids [Online Tutorial T4], energy efficiency, etc.). In January 2010, the U.S. Energy Department granted $47 million of the AARA money toward projects that aim to improve the energy efficiency of data centers, such as: optimizing

Green computing
The study and practice of eco-friendly computing resources; is now a key concern of businesses in all industries—not just environmental organizations.

Green IT
Begins with manufacturers producing environmentally friendly products and encouraging IT departments to consider more friendly options like virtualization, power management, and proper recycling habits.

EXHIBIT 14.7 Turning IT Green: Guidelines for Saving Computing Power

- Using the computer's power management options, set all computers to hibernate and use standby.
- Train all personnel to turn off monitors when not in use.
- Power down all computers automatically after hours or when not in use.
- Embrace telecommuting and support employees who wish to stay home to work.
- Configure IT data center equipment by recommended operating temperatures. Use air conditioning only for temperature sensitive equipment operations.
- Embrace cloud computing. Replace existing servers with virtualization, as money permits.

Increase Cooling Efficiency

- Optimize airflow in the data center to reduce the mean gradient temperature and reduce cooling requirements.
- Use a hot/cold aisle configuration, in which equipment racks are arranged in alternating rows of hot and cold aisles.
- Rely on air handlers to better control airflow within the data center and enable more efficient cooling.
- Deploy smart cooling energy-management systems with sensors to reduce energy consumption by as much as 40 percent.
- Increase cooling temperature targets to slightly above the data center baseline temperature. Every added degree results in an estimated 4 percent reduction in energy consumption.
- Install renewable cooling sources such as outside air during the winter—where practicable—to minimize usage of internal cooling systems.

data center hardware and software, improving the power supply chain, and funding new data center cooling technologies (see en.wikipedia.org/wiki/Green_computing). For a company with 10,000 PCs, just leaving most of them on overnight can cost up to US$165,000 in electricity bills, while spewing more than 1,380 tons of carbon dioxide into the air per year. Company data center servers are also known to be both power hungry and heat generating. PC monitors consume about 80 to 100 billion kilowatt hours of electricity every year in the United States. Both Intel and AMD are producing new chips aimed at reducing this amount of energy usage. Turning off PCs when not in use can save a company's bottom line and add to good corporate social behavior by reducing the damage caused by excess carbon dioxide release. Finally, discarded PCs and other computer equipment can cause serious waste disposal problems. An important issue is how to recycle old equipment and whose responsibility it is to take care of the problem (the manufacturers? the users?). *Green software* refers to software products that help companies save energy or comply with EPA requirements.

How to Operate Greener Businesses, Data Centers, and Supply Chains

Chief information officers (CIOs) who are looking to operate greener businesses, data centers, and supply chains should focus on: (1) virtualization, (2) software management, and (3) harnessing the "cloud." Virtualization brings uptake of energy saving solutions to drive down energy consumption, thus ticking both environmental and money-saving boxes by reducing their physical inventory. Companies seeking advice, tools, and processes can turn to software management outsourcing to help them achieve their software estate and licensing management needs. Finally, cloud computing is predicted to gather 45 percent of all IT applications in the "cloud" by 2017. See Online Tutorial T7.

In 2011, and in the future, is eco-friendly computing and business growth compatible with high unemployment rates and continued global financial uncertainty? Yes, they are, according to Gartner Group, which claims that 80 percent of the world's data centers are constrained by heat, space, and power requirements. In addition to the demand on processing capability to satisfy the growth of the business, there is enormous demand on power consumption and space requirements for computing platforms. Data center configurations are no longer based on one dimension (e.g., price or performance)—meaning that factors other than affordability or performance must be considered. The equation is much more complicated. For a discussion, see Gibson (2009).

Installation and unmanaged proliferation of this high-density IT equipment can lead to unexpected problems with power density capabilities and cooling infrastructure problems including overheating, overloads, and loss of redundancy. To ensure predictable performance and optimize use of the physical infrastructure resource, the data center must have the ability to measure and predict power and cooling capability at the rack enclosure level (Rasmussen 2007).

An enterprise may cut energy costs in half, double space efficiency, and increase server utilization levels to as high as 85 percent with some investment and it may take a few years. Gaining these efficiencies requires dealing with these four issues: the desktop, data center computing power, data center power/cooling, and data center storage. According to an October 2010 survey, 25 percent of organizations expect server spending to grow by 5 percent to 10 percent. Many organizations are turning to server virtualization, such as cloud computing, to cut energy costs, double space efficiency, and increase server utilization (reported by Washburn 2010). For more details on green computing, see Online File W14.8.

Example 1. Wells Fargo is a large financial institution that offers a wide range of services, including consumer and corporate banking, insurance, investments, and mortgages. Its revenue in 2008 exceeded $42 billion. The company is data-dependent and known for its eco-friendliness. In 2007, with the increase in energy costs, the company decided to go "green" in its two new data centers. Data centers must ensure security and availability of their services, and when they are planned from scratch, they can be energy efficient with low power consumption. The two new facilities have more than 8,000 servers that consume considerable power and generate heat.

Several energy-saving features were introduced, including water-based economizers that regulate energy usage and cool the physical environment, a computer-controlled central fan system for cooling the floors, direct air to cool specific hot spaces, and semiconductor chips that automatically shut off power until it is needed. With increasing volumes of data, Wells Fargo constantly expands and renovates its data centers, taking environmental concerns into consideration. The company experimented with a solar system for making hot water, with motion-detector lights, and with variable-speed fans. Data analysis from July 2010 revealed that the average server within the Wells Fargo data center environments now uses 150 watts of power, compared with 300 watts just one year ago, and the storage being provisioned by the financial services giant also uses roughly half what the arrays previously required (Clancy 2010).

Example 2. During the 2010 GreenNet conference in San Francisco, Google's Green Energy Czar Bill Weihl spoke of Google's strategies for cutting energy consumption to reduce its average data center power consumption by 30 percent. The most significant gains for Google were achieved by reducing its overhead costs associated with running a data center, including cooling, power infrastructure, and lighting. Weihl urged that its data center managers check their manufacturer-recommended inlet temperatures on their IT equipment and adjust the thermostat accordingly.

On top of that, Weihl stated that Google, whenever possible, embraced free cooling— such as cooling towers and outside air to supplement costly CRAC operations. Besides the use of energy-efficient technologies, Weihl stressed the importance of measuring and monitoring the utilization levels of servers and using power management server capabilities. Additionally, he noted that monitoring performance of both infrastructure and IT gear helped Google track and address its performance inefficiencies. Google is also pursuing more flexibility in purchasing clean energy from alternative sources (Samson 2010).

Global Green Regulations

Global regulations also are influencing green business practices. Sustainability regulations such as RoHS (rohs.eu and rohs.gov.uk) in the European Union (EU) will increasingly impact how supply chains function regardless of location. The RoHS directive stands for "the restriction of the use of certain hazardous substances in electrical and electronic equipment." For example, EU member states ensured that beginning in July 2006, new electrical and electronic equipment put on the market would not contain any of six banned substances—lead, mercury, cadmium, hexavalent chromium, poly-brominated biphenyls (PBB), and polybrominated diphenyl ethers (PBDE)—in quantities exceeding maximum concentration values.

Eco-friendly practices reduce costs and improve public relations in the long run. Not surprisingly, demand for green computers is on the rise. A tool to help companies find such hardware is the Electronic Product Environmental Assessment Tool (EPEAT).

The Electronic Product Environmental Assessment Tool

Electronic Product Environmental Assessment Tool (EPEAT)
A searchable database of computer hardware that meets a strict set of environmental criteria.

Maintained by the Green Electronics Council (GEC), the **Electronic Product Environmental Assessment Tool (EPEAT)** is a searchable database of computer hardware that meets a strict set of environmental criteria. Among other criteria, products registered with EPEAT comply with the U.S. government's Energy Star 4.0 rating (see energystar.gov); have reduced levels of cadmium, lead, and mercury; and are easier to upgrade and recycle. Energy Star–qualified products use less energy. Depending on how many criteria they meet, products receive a gold, silver, or bronze certification rating.

EPEAT rates computers and monitors on a number of environmental criteria, including energy efficiency, materials used, product longevity, take-back programs, and packaging. Twenty-two percent of the 109 million computers shipped worldwide in 2007 were registered on EPEAT (epeat.net). In August 2009, the Green Electronics Council went global when it announced the availability of an international EPEAT purchasing registry, enabling the world's leading electronics manufacturers to list green computers and monitors in 40 countries across the globe (LaMonica 2009).

Telecommuting, which was discussed earlier, also offers several green benefits, including reducing rush-hour traffic, improving air quality, improving highway safety, and even improving health care (see Exhibit 14.6 on p. 753).

OTHER SOCIETAL ISSUES

Many other societal issues can be related to EC. Three in which EC has had a generally positive impact are mentioned here: education, public safety, and health.

Education

E-commerce has had a major impact on education and learning, as described in Chapter 5. Virtual universities are helping to reduce the digital divide. Companies can use the Internet to retrain employees much more easily, enabling them to defer retirement if they so choose. Homebound individuals can get degrees from good institutions, and many vocational professions can be learned from home.

Public Safety, Criminal Justice, and Homeland Security

With increased concerns about public safety after September 11, 2001, many organizations and individuals have started to look at technologies that will help to deter, prevent, or detect criminal activities of various types. Various e-commerce tools can help increase our safety at home and in public. These include e-911 systems; global collaborative commerce technologies (for collaboration among national and international law enforcement units); e-procurement (of unique equipment to fight crime); e-government efforts at coordinating, information sharing, and expediting legal work and cases; intelligent homes, offices, and public buildings; and e-training of law enforcement officers.

Today, public surveillance is a reality. It is a double-edged sword, and the government edge is sharper—they are the watchers and we are the helpless targets. The United States, Canada, and Britain are now heavy users of cameras—Britain being the largest with over 4.2 million, about one camera for every 14 people. London alone has about 500,000 cameras hovering over the city. Camera systems are on street corners, in public bathrooms, in residential neighborhoods, and even in parks and forests. The proliferation of citywide surveillance cameras is spreading across America, the merits of which remain debatable.

The issue is whether the financial, functional, and social impact of these systems is worth the intrusion on privacy. The fact remains that most cities use the surveillance cameras more for retrieval of images rather than for active monitoring. Thus, as a crime suppressant, these cameras make little financial sense since one person can only actively monitor 10 cameras at one time. The City of Chicago has installed more than 10,000 cameras inside the city limits. For active monitoring, it would need to hire an additional 1,000 city employees—an impractical dream with budget overruns, lower tax revenues, and high unemployment (Gallio 2010).

Health Aspects

Is EC a health risk? Generally speaking, it is probably safer and healthier to shop from home than in a physical store. However, some believe that exposure to cellular mobile communication radiation may cause health problems. It may take years before the truth of this claim is known. Even if communication radiation does cause health problems (e.g., brain tumors), the damage could be insignificant due to the small amount of time most people spend on wireless shopping and other wireless activities. However, given the concern of some about this issue, protective devices may soon be available that will solve this problem.

EC technologies such as collaborative commerce can help improve health care. For example, using the Internet, the approval process of new drugs has been shortened, saving lives and reducing suffering. Pervasive computing helps in the delivery of health care. Intelligent systems facilitate medical diagnoses. Health care advice can be provided from a distance. Finally, intelligent hospitals, doctors, and other health care facilities use EC tools (see Europe's Information Society 2009).

Section 14.7 ❱ REVIEW QUESTIONS

1. Define the digital divide.
2. Describe the One Laptop per Child project.
3. Describe how EC can improve education.
4. Describe how EC can improve safety and security.
5. Describe the impact of EC on health services.
6. What is green computing?
7. List three ways in which green computing can help protect the environment or conserve resources.
8. What is a green supply chain? Give one example.
9. How do the new data centers help us "go green?"
10. How does telecommuting or virtual work conserve the environment?

MANAGERIAL ISSUES

Some managerial issues related to this chapter are as follows:

1. **What legal and ethical issues should be of major concern to an EC enterprise?** Key issues to consider include the following: (1) what type of proprietary information should we allow and disallow on our site? (2) Who will have access to information that visitors post to our site? (3) Do the content and activities on our site comply with laws in other countries? (4) What disclaimers do we need to post on our website? (5) Are we using trademarked or copyrighted materials without permission? Regardless of the specific issues, an attorney should periodically review the content on the site, and someone should be responsible for monitoring legal and liability issues.

2. **What are the most critical ethical issues?** Negative or defamatory articles published online about people, companies, or products on websites or blogs can lead to charges of libel—and libel can stretch across countries. Issues of privacy, ethics, and legal exposure may seem tangential to running a business, but ignoring

them puts the company at risk of fines, customer anger, and disruption of the operation of an organization. Privacy protection is a necessary investment.

3. **How can intellectual property rights be protected when it comes to digital content?** To protect intellectual property rights such as video, music, and books online, we need to monitor what copyrights, trademarks, and patents are infringed upon over the Internet. Portal sites that allow pirated video and music files should be monitored. This monitoring may require a vast amount of work, so software agents may be employed to continually inspect the pirated material. The risk to the business that can be caused by the infringement and the possibility of legal protection as well as technical protection by current regulation and potential new common law should be analyzed. Consider settling any suit for damages by negotiation. If the violator is not controllable, consider owning the origin of the challenge by acquiring it as Disney did in China.

4. **How can patent costs be monitored effectively?** Some people claim that patents should not be awarded to business or computer processes related to EC (as is the case in Europe). Therefore, investing large amounts of money in developing or buying patents may be financially unwise in cases where patents may not hold. Some companies that own many business model patents have been unable to create business value out of the patents.

5. **What is the ethical principle of protecting the privacy of customers?** To provide personalized services, companies need to collect and manage customers' profile data. In practice, the company has to decide whether it would use spyware to collect data. This process may easily cross the line from customer delight into customer despair (as is the case in Google Street View or Facebook privacy settings). The company needs a well-established principle of protecting customer privacy: Notify customers before collecting their personal information; inform and get consent on the type and extent of disclosures; allow customers to access their personal data and make sure the data are accurate and securely managed; and apply some method of enforcement and remedy to deter privacy breaches. In this manner, the company can avoid legal suits and gain the long-term trust of customers.

6. **How can a company create opportunities in the global trend toward green EC?** Reducing carbon emissions and saving energy are global issues that can be serious threats but can also provide opportunities for businesses during the next decade. (1) EC can save carbon emission by reducing physical transportation. This is a generic contribution of EC. (2) EC can provide the exchange platform that trades the CO_2 emission rights with the clean development mechanism projects conducted in developing countries. This is a new business opportunity. (3) The IT hardware platform for EC is vying for the Energy Star Excellence Award from the Environmental Protection Agency to prove that their products are contributing to the protection of the environment and to gain consumer preference. This is a threat and an opportunity for platform manufacturers.

SUMMARY

In this chapter, you learned about the following EC issues as they relate to the chapter's learning objectives.

1. **Understanding legal and ethical challenges and how to contain them.** The global scope and universal accessibility of the Internet create serious questions as to which ethical rules and laws apply. Ignoring laws exposes companies to lawsuits or criminal charges that are disruptive, expensive, and damaging to customer relations. The best strategy is to avoid behaviors that expose the company to these types of risk. Important safeguards are a corporate code of ethics stating the rules and expected behaviors and actions and an Internet acceptable use policy.

2. **Intellectual property law.** EC operations are subject to various types of intellectual property (IP) laws—some of which judges create in landmark court cases. IP law provides companies with ways to get compensated for damages or misuse of their property rights. IP laws passed by Congress are being amended to better protect EC. These protections are needed because it is easy and inexpensive to copy or steal intellectual works on the Internet (e.g., music, photos, movies) and to distribute or sell them without the permission of the owner. These actions violate or infringe upon copyrights, trademarks, and patents. Although the legal aspects seem fairly clear, monitoring and catching violators remains difficult.

3. **Privacy, free speech, defamation, and their challenges.** B2C companies use CRM and depend on customer information to improve products and services. Registration and cookies are two of the ways used to collect this information. The key privacy issues are who controls this information and how private it should remain. Strict privacy laws have been passed recently that carry harsh

penalties for any negligence that exposes personal or confidential data. There is ongoing debate about censorship on the Internet. The proponents of censorship feel that it is up to the government and various ISPs and websites to control inappropriate or offensive content. Others oppose any form of censorship; they believe that control is up to the individual. In the United States, most legal attempts to censor content on the Internet have been found unconstitutional. The debate is not likely to be resolved.

4. **Fraud on the Internet and how to protect consumers against it.** Protection is needed because there is no face-to-face contact; there is great possibility for fraud; there are insufficient legal constraints; and new issues and scams appear constantly. Several organizations, private and public, attempt to provide the protection needed to build the trust that is essential for the success of widespread EC. Of special importance are electronic contracts (including digital signatures), the control of gambling, and what taxes should be paid to whom on interstate and international transactions. Although the trend is not to have a sales tax or a value-added tax, this may not be the case for too much longer.

5. **Protection of buyers and sellers.** Many procedures are used to protect consumers. In addition to legislation, the FTC tries to educate consumers so they know the major scams. The use of seals on sites (such as TRUSTe) can help, as well as tips and measures taken by vendors. Sellers can be cheated by buyers and by other sellers or thieves. Protective measures include using contacts and encryption (PKI, Chapter 10), keeping databases of potential criminals and sharing the information with other sellers, educating employees, and using intelligent software.

6. **Societal impacts of EC.** EC brings many societal benefits, ranging from improved security, transportation, and education to better health care delivery and international collaboration. Although the digital divide still exists between developed and developing countries, the advent of mobile computing, especially through cell phones, is beginning to close the gap.

7. **Green EC.** EC requires large data centers that waste energy and create pollution. Other environmental concerns are also caused by the use of EC. There are several ways to make EC greener, including working from home (telecommuting).

KEY TERMS

DISCUSSION QUESTIONS

1. What can EC websites and social networks do to ensure the safeguarding of personal information?

2. Privacy is the right to be left alone and free of unreasonable personal intrusions. What are some intrusions that you consider "unreasonable?"

3. Who should control minors' access to "offensive" material on the Internet—parents, the government, or ISPs? Why?

4. Discuss the conflict between freedom of speech and the control of offensive websites.

5. Discuss the possible insufficient protection of opt-in and opt-out options. What would you be happy with?

6. Clerks at 7-Eleven stores enter data regarding customers (gender, approximate age, and so on) into the computer. These data are then processed for improved decision making. Customers are not informed about this, nor are they being asked for permission. (Names are not keyed in.) Are the clerks' actions ethical? Compare this with the case of cookies.

7. Why do many companies and professional organizations develop their own codes of ethics? After all, ethics are ethics.

8. Cyber Promotions, Inc., attempted to use the First Amendment in defense of its flooding of AOL subscribers with junk e-mail. AOL tried to block the junk e-mail. A federal judge agreed with AOL that unsolicited e-mail is annoying, a costly waste of Internet time, and often inappropriate and, therefore, should not be sent. Discuss some of the issues involved, such as freedom of speech, how to distinguish between junk and nonjunk e-mail, and the analogy with regular mail.

9. Find the status of the Sarbanes-Oxley Act (SOX). Discuss the impact of e-commerce on small online businesses.

10. Through the continual reauthorization of the controversial PATRIOT Act and other draconian laws in support of its "never-ending" war on terror, is the federal government weakening the protection of individual civil liberties and constitutionally guaranteed inalienable rights?

11. Does afterlife privacy concern you? Compare and contrast the option for users to control family member access to social networks and passwords.

TOPICS FOR CLASS DISCUSSION AND DEBATES

1. Discuss what the RIAA hopes to achieve by using lawsuits against college students for copyright infringement. How will the proposed Copyright Enforcement Bill, if enacted, support further RIAA lawsuits?

2. The proposed Copyright Enforcement Bill defines everyone that posts a website as a publisher and liable under the act. Enforcement under this proposed bill for unintentional use or distribution of copyrighted content on business websites could result in the confiscation of a company's domain name or server, which in turn could potentially disable the company's e-mail capability—substantially killing commerce. What steps should a business take to minimize the risk? Discuss.

3. The IRS buys demographic market research data from private companies. These data contain income statistics that could be compared with tax returns. Many U.S. citizens feel that their rights within the realm of the Electronic Communications Privacy Act (ECPA) are being violated; others say that this is an unethical behavior on the part of the government. Discuss.

4. Many hospitals, health maintenance organizations, and federal agencies are converting, or plan to convert, all patient medical records from paper to electronic storage (using imaging technology) in compliance with the Patient Protection and Affordable Care Act (PPAC), also known as "Obamacare." The PPAC mandates that all medical records shall be freely disseminated to insurance companies, besides the U.S. government and government-approved third-party venders. Once completed, electronic storage will enable quick access, any time and from any place, to most records. However, the availability of these records in a database or on networks or smart cards may allow people, some of whom are unauthorized, to view another person's private medical data. To protect privacy fully may cost too much money or may considerably slow the speed of access to the records. What policies could health care administrators use to prevent unauthorized access? Discuss.

5. The Communications Decency Act, which was intended to protect children and others from pornography and other offensive material online, was approved by the U.S. Congress but then was ruled unconstitutional by the courts. Discuss the importance and implications of this incident.

6. Erotic services advertising on Craigslist amounted to a significant portion of the total revenue before being taken down following national publicity over the robbery and murder of a Boston masseuse, who had advertised on Craigslist. Under the 1996 Federal Communications Act, Craigslist claimed innocence and immunity for content in which it had no role in creating. Following the murder, it complied with authorities' wishes and voluntarily removed listings geared toward escort services, sensual massage, exotic dancing, and so forth. Address the following topics in a class discussion:

    a. Craigslist may have chosen to voluntarily remove its erotic-related advertising for politics, even though no laws were being broken. Discuss free speech versus public safety. Take an issue and support the pro and con of Craigslist's action.

    b. Do you agree that self-governing Web content to be the most effective means of providing public safety or should the federal government step in to enact tougher laws?

    c. Take the position of the erotic dancer. Determine an argument in favor of reversing the Craigslist decision to remove "erotic services" advertising using free speech and right to contract.

    d. Are there any privacy issues present? Could Craigslist succeed in a lawsuit based on the premise that it had the right to respect the privacy of adults and that it should be allowed to provide advertising for such services on the Web, when only adults make or read the listings?

7. Debate the issue of trusting social networks to keep your information private. Companies that mine data regarding doctors' drug prescription habits and then sell it to pharmaceutical firms are suing to block laws barring the practice in three states. They argue that data mining offers valuable benefits, such as tracking side effects and flagging other potential safety issues. Their opponents maintain the data is used to steer doctors toward more expensive drug choices.

8. Debate the issue of ownership of user-generated content (the Facebook example). One group should be for and one against.

9. Address the following topics in class debates:

   a. Is net neutrality good for EC?
   b. Should the exchange of songs between individuals be allowed over the Internet?
   c. Is the USA PATRIOT Act too loose or too tight?
   d. It may be too expensive for some companies to "go green." If they "go green," they may not be able to compete against companies in countries that do not practice green EC. Should the government subsidize green EC?
   e. Who should own content created by employees during their regular work hours?
   f. Are privacy standards tough enough to protect electronic health records?

INTERNET EXERCISES

1. You want to set up an ethical blog. Using sites such as CyberJournalist.net: A Bloggers' Code of Ethics at **cyberjournalist.net/news/000215.php**, review the suggested guide to publishing on a blog. Make a list of the top 10 ethical issues for blogging.

2. You want to set up a personal website. Using legal sites such as **cyberlaw.com**, prepare a report summarizing the types of materials you can and cannot use (e.g., logos, graphics, etc.) without breaking copyright law.

3. Use **google.com** to search for industry and trade organizations involved in various computer privacy initiatives. One of these groups is the World Wide Web Consortium (W3C). Describe its Privacy Preferences Project (**w3.org/tr/2001/wd-p3p-20010928**). Prepare a table with 10 initiatives and describe each briefly.

4. Enter **pgp.com**. Review the services offered. Use the free software to encrypt a message.

5. Enter **calastrology.com**. What kind of community is this? Check the revenue model. Then enter **astrocenter.com**. What kind of site is this? Compare and comment on the two sites.

6. Enter **nolo.com**. Try to find information about various EC legal issues. Find information about international EC issues. Then go to **legalcompliance.com** or **cyber**

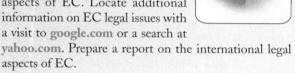

triallawyer.com. Try to find information about international legal aspects of EC. Locate additional information on EC legal issues with a visit to **google.com** or a search at **yahoo.com**. Prepare a report on the international legal aspects of EC.

7. Find the status of the latest copyright legislation. Try **fairuse.stanford.edu**. Is there anything regarding the international aspects of copyright legislation? Write a report.

8. Enter **ftc.gov** and identify some of the typical types of fraud and scams on the Internet. List 10 of them.

9. Enter **usispa.org** and **ispa.org.uk**, two organizations that represent the ISP industry. Identify the various initiatives they have undertaken regarding topics discussed in this chapter. Write a report.

10. Visit **consumers.com**. What protection can this group give that is not provided by BBBOnLine?

11. Download freeware from **brothersoft.com/downloads/unsolicited-email.html** and learn how to prohibit unsolicited e-mail. Describe how your privacy is protected.

12. Enter **scambusters.com** and identify and list its antifraud and antiscam activities.

TEAM ASSIGNMENTS AND PROJECTS

1. **Assignment for the Opening Case**

   Read the opening case and answer the following questions:

   a. Discuss the issue of preventing movies and TV shows from being streamed online for free.
   b. Was it ethical for Disney to invest in 56.com?
   c. What are the business benefits to Disney if it is not fighting with 56.com?
   d. Discuss the global considerations of this case.
   e. Find the status of the $1 billion lawsuit Viacom brought against YouTube.

2. The number of lawsuits in the United States and elsewhere involving EC has increased. Have each team prepare a list of five recent EC legal cases on each topic in this chapter (e.g., privacy, digital property, defamation, domain names). Prepare a summary of the issues of each case, the parties, the courts, and dates. What were the outcomes of these cases? What was (or might be) the impact of each decision?

3. Form three teams. Have a debate on free speech versus protection of children between two teams. The third team acts as judges. One team is for complete freedom of speech on the Internet; the other team advocates protection of children by censoring offensive and pornographic material. After the debate, have the judges decide which team provided the most compelling legal arguments.

4. It is legal to monitor employees' Internet activity, e-mail, and instant messages. At the same time, it is illegal to open letters addressed to individuals and sent to the company's address. Why is that necessary? To what extent is it ethical? Are employees' rights being violated? Have two teams debate these issues.

5. Amazon.com is disputing several states that trying to force the company to collect state taxes. Amazon cancelled its affiliation program in California when the sales tax for online retailing was imposed. Furthermore the company supports a referendum to repeal the California law. Check the status of this law and its relationship to Federal law. Start at **geekwire.com**.

Closing Case

PIRATE BAY AND THE FUTURE OF FILE SHARING

What had triumphantly been hailed as a landmark 2009 copyright law case of the Motion Picture Association of America (MPAA) against illegal file sharing in Sweden appears to have not significantly deterred online file sharing. In fact, just the opposite has occurred.

An Overview

The Pirate Bay (TPB) site was launched in 2003 as a commercial enterprise offering free access to most media content (including copyrighted material) using BitTorrent peer-to-peer file-hosting protocol (see *en.wikipedia.org/wiki/BitTorrent(Protocol)*) services. The offering includes movies, TV shows, e-books, live sport games, software, and more. TPB had been ranked as the 86th most popular website in the world and 17th in Sweden (January 2011). In May 2006, Swedish police raided the website's servers in Stockholm, confiscating their equipment but kept the website down for only 3 days. In March 2011, TPB boasted that it had more than 3 million unique peers over 4.5 million registered users, even though registration is not required to be able to download BitTorrent files. The site generates revenue by advertisements, donations, and sales of merchandise.

The Legal Situation

Pirate Bay has been involved in a number of lawsuits, both as a defendant and a plaintiff. The Pirate Bay trial in Sweden charged four individuals with promoting copyright infringement by facilitating other people's breach of copyright law by using TPB's BitTorrent technology. For 34 cases of copyright infringement, the damage claims could exceed US$12 million. The trial started on February 16, 2009, and ended on March 3, 2009, with a guilty verdict, which carried a one-year prison sentence and a fine of US$3.5 million. The four founders lost on appeal in 2010

and succeeded in getting reduced prison time, but the copyright infringement fine was increased, likely a result of TPB's continued operation and facilitation of copyright infringement. The site is now blocked by several countries. The U.S. government considers TPB (together with Chinese sites Baidu and Taobao) as top markets for pirated and counterfeit goods.

Current Operation

As of March 2011, TPB continues to offer BitTorrent file sharing. In fact, much public support was noted. The Piratbyrån ("The Pirate Bureau"), a Swedish organization, was established by TPB followers to support people opposed to current ideas about intellectual property. In addition to protests against the intellectual property bill as a whole, the Pirate Party has created and called for noncommercial file sharing to be legalized in the United Kingdom. Formed in 2009, the party entered candidates in the 2010 UK general election and won a seat in Parliament. The Pirate Party advocates copyright and patent law reform and a reduction in government surveillance. TPB's founders have worked on several other decentralized peer-to-peer file-sharing websites, which have flourished in filling the enormous global demand for file sharing.

All along, file-sharing technology has been one step ahead of enforcement. For example, in December 2007, TPB moved from a custom Linux-based server, called Hypercube, to Opentracker so that its BitTorrent tracking software could enable the use of UDP tracker protocol. In June 2008, TPB adapted its servers to support SSL encryption in response to Sweden's new wiretapping law. In January 2009, TPB launched IPv6 support for its tracker system.

Even after losing its November 2010 appeal, TPB kept growing. In 2011, TPB's founders launched a new website, called IPREDator, offering IP address anonymity to registered users by tunneling traffic into a secure server, which reassigns fake IP addresses to registered users so that they may access TPB or other BitTorrent tracking sites on the Web for file sharing without revealing their true IP addresses. Although TPB continues to thrive today, as one of the most popular websites on the Internet, many countries are enacting new tougher copyright protection laws aimed directly at stopping this illegal activity. Note that Facebook blocks all shared links to TPB in both public and private messages.

Discussion

Pirate Bay is one of a hundred websites that specialize in pirated and counterfeit content. Pirate Bay does not host content in contrast to sites like *justin.tv* that allows people to upload videos, included pirated ones. Pirate Bay only links to illegal material. Only torrent files are saved at the server. This means that no copyrighted and/or illegal materials are stored by the company. It is therefore, according to TPB, not possible to hold the people behind Pirate Bay responsible for the material that is being spread using the tracker. The Swedish Supreme Court will decide the issue.

The Pirate Bay case is only one part of a much broader issue of protecting intellectual property on the Internet. An interesting related issue is the hosting of content by sites such as YouTube and Justin.tv, which is more complicated (e.g., see Stone 2011).

Note that one aspect in this case is that the U.S. government is pushing the Swedish government to take a tougher stand against pirating.

Sources: Compiled from Stone (2011), *en.wikipedia.org/wiki/ The_Pirate_Bay,en.wikipedia.org/wiki/The_Pirate_Bay_trial,* and *en.wikipedia.org/wiki/Legal_aspects_of_file_sharing* (all accessed March 2011).

Questions

1. Compare TPB's legal problems to that of Napster between 2000 and 2005, and to that of Kazaa (see *computer.howstuffworks.com/Kazaa4.htm*).

2. Debate the issue of freedom of speech on the Internet against the need to protect intellectual property.

3. What is Pirate Bay's business model? What are its revenue sources? (Find more information.)

4. Explore the international legal aspects of this case. Can one country persuade another country to introduce tougher laws?

5. Read the Stone (2011) article and identify all the measures used to battle piracy in the live games case. Which of these measures can be used in the Pirate Bay case? Which cannot? Why?

ONLINE RESOURCES
available at pearsonglobaleditions.com/turban

Online Files

W14.1 Framework for Ethical Issues
W14.2 Website Quality Guidelines
W14.3 Intellectual Property Websites—International Sites
W14.4 Representative EC Patents
W14.5 Application Case: Protection Pitted Against Privacy
W14.6 Representative U.S. Federal Privacy Legislation
W14.7 Censorship in the United States, China, and Around the Globe
W14.8 How to Go Green in a Data Center and the Related Supply Chain

Comprehensive Educational Websites

ftc.gov: Major source on consumer fraud and protection.
dmoz.org/society/issues/fraud/Internet: Comprehensive resources on fraud.
fraud.org: The National Consumers League Fraud Center.
ic3.gov: The FBI's Internet crime complaint center.
fda.gov/oc/buyonline: Food and Drug Administration center for buying medicine and medical products online.
regulatorycompliance.com: A private company with a comprehensive collection.
business.gov: A single point of access to government services.

sba.gov/advo/laws/law_modeleg.html: Small Business Administration's advocacy site to stay current with federal regulations.
law.com: A comprehensive legal collection.
lawbrain.com: A comprehensive collection of Internet law–related material.
litmanlaw.com: A patent search law firm.
privacy.org: A comprehensive source of privacy information.
epic.org: A privacy watchdog site.
privacyrights.org: An educational clearinghouse.
itworld.com/green-it: A comprehensive source for IT-related issues, including green EC and IT.
digitaldivide.org: A comprehensive collection of related material.
greenit.net: A comprehensive collection of related material.
techworld.com/green-it: A comprehensive collection of related material.
epolicyinstitute.com: A comprehensive collection of related EC policy material.
eff.org/issues/bloggers/legal: A comprehensive collection of blogging resources.
tinyurl.com/dy75tf: A comprehensive resource for energy-saving initiatives, with white papers, calculators, guides, and other tools and resources.

REFERENCES

24/7 Wall St. "The Top Ten Ways Workers Waste Time Online." September 30, 2010. 247wallst.com/2010/09/30/the-top-ten-ways-workers-waste-time-online (accessed March 2011).

56.com. "56.com Launch Content C-C Platform '56 Kan Kan.'" August 18, 2009. 56.com/v/about/en/intro_press_en.html (accessed March 2011).

ACLU. "Libraries, the Internet, and the Law: Adults Must Have Unfiltered Access." November 16, 2006. aclu-wa.org/news/libraries-internet-and-law-adults-must-have-unfiltered-access (accessed March 2011).

Albanesius, C. "Report: Germany Investigating Facebook Privacy." July 7, 2010. appscout.com/2010/07/report_germany_investigating_f.php (accessed March 2011).

Albanesius, C. "Viacom Will Know What You Have Watched on YouTube." *PCMag.com*, July 3, 2008. pcmag.com/article2/0,2817,2324635,00.aspml (accessed March 2011).

American Free Press. "Digital Divide Widens Gap Between Rich Versus Poor Nations: UN." February 7, 2008. services.inquirer.net/print/print.php?article_id=20080207-117406 (accessed March 2011).

Angwin, J. "The New Gold Mine: Your Secrets." July 30, 2010. online.wsj.com/article/SB10001424052748703940904575395073512989404.html?mod=what_they_know (accessed March 2010).

Bambauer, D. "Tenebaum and Statutory Damages." July 11, 2010. blogs.law.harvard.edu/infolaw/2010/07/11/tenenbaum-and-statutory-damages (accessed March 2011).

Bharvaga, R. "Social Media and the Axe Murderer: How Privacy Is Evolving Online." February 7, 2010. social-mediatoday.com/SMC/172786 (accessed March 2011).

Boyle, M. "*sex.com*, Drugs, and a Rocky Road." *Fortune*, December 12, 2005. money.cnn.com/magazines/fortune/fortune_archive/2005/12/12/8363122/index.htm (accessed March 2011).

Cheeseman, H. R. *Business Law*, 7th ed. Upper Saddle River, NJ: Prentice Hall, 2008.

China Daily. "Microsoft Wins Piracy Lawsuit." July 20, 2009. chinaipmagazine.com/en/news-show.asp?id=958 (accessed March 2011).

China Post. "Microsoft Wins China Piracy Lawsuit." July 21, 2009. chinapost.com.tw/china/c_business/2009/07/21/217168/Microsoft-wins.htm (accessed March 2011).

China.org. "Microsoft Likely to Face Anti-Monopoly Lawsuit in China." July 31. 2008. china.org.cn/business/highlights/2008-07/31/content_16109635.htm (accessed March 2011).

Clancy, H. "Virtualization Core to Wells Fargo Green IT Initiative." July 6, 2010. zdnet.com/blog/green/virtualization-core-to-wells-fargo-green-it-initia-tive/12852 (accessed March 2011).

ClassActionLawSuitsInTheNews. "McAfee Class Action Lawsuit Filed over Arpu Pop Up Advertisements." April 9, 2010. classactionlawsuitsinthenews.com/class-action-lawsuits/mcafee-class-action-lawsuit-filed-over-arpu-pop-up-advertisements (accessed March 2011).

Coffey, B. "FCC Tips Net Neutrality Passage but Questions Remain." December 20, 2010. blogs.forbes.com/elizabethwoyke/2010/12/20/fcc-tips-net-neutrality-passage-but-questions-remain/?boxes=Homepagetopnews (accessed March 2011).

Collins, J. C. "Fortify Your Facebook Privacy Settings." *Journal of Accountancy* (June 2010).

Conry-Murray, A. "IT Fought the Law." *Information-Week*, June 23, 2008.

Coursey, D. "Spy on Your Workers with Google Latitude." *PCWorld*, February 5, 2009.

Davidson, A. *The Law of Electronic Commerce.* Melbourne, Australia: Cambridge University Press, 2009.

Department of Commerce. "How Does P3P Work?" 2009. osec.doc.gov/webresources/P3P_user_Admin_files/TextMostly/Slide7.html (accessed March 2011).

Duffy, J. "20% of U.S. Has Never Sent an E-Mail." May 17, 2008. pcworld.com/businesscenter/article/146019/20_of_us_has_never_sent_e-mail.html (accessed March 2011).

E-Commerce Journal. "Any Internet Browser Exposes Your Personal Data: Online Privacy Is a Myth Now." May 21, 2010. ecommerce-journal.com/node/28170 (accessed March 2011).

Enviro Boys. "Is Telecommuting on the Rise?" November 15, 2010. enviroboys.com/2010/11/telecommuting-onrise.html (accessed March 2011).

Europe's Information Society. "Telemedicine for the Benefit of Patients, the Healthcare System, and Society." 2009. ec.europa.eu/information_society/activities/health/policy/telemedicine/index_en.htm (accessed March 2011).

Expatica.com. "Microsoft Boss Decries Software Piracy by China Firms." August 10, 2010. expatica.com/es/news/spanish-news/microsoft-boss-decries-software-piracy-by-china-firms_101826.html (accessed March 2011).

Finextra. "BoA, MasterCard, Visa Sued Over E-Commerce Payment Patents." April 17, 2009. finextra.com/news/fullstory.aspx?newsitemid=19929 (accessed March 2011).

Fogarty, K. "Copyright Infringement Bill Could Bring the FBI to Your Intranet." 2011. itworld.com/legal/128550/copyright-infringement-bill-could-bring-fbi-your-intranet?page=0%2C0.

Fox News. "Obama Signs One-Year Extension of PATRIOT Act." February 27, 2010. foxnews.com/politics/2010/02/27/obama-signs-year-extension-patriot-act (accessed March 2011).

Gaelle, F. "Managing Your Afterlife." *Time*, September 2009.

Gallio, L. "Surveillance Cameras: Big Brother and Big Sis Are Watching." August 29, 2010. examiner.com/homeland-security-in-houston/surveillance-cameras-big-brother-and-big-sis-are-watching (accessed March 2011).

Gibson, S. "Data Center Waste Watch." *Smarter Technology*, October 2009.

Gray, B. R. "Bullying and Harassment in the Workplace." 2010. ezinearticles.com/?Bullying-And-Harassment-In-The-Workplace&id=5200849 (accessed March 2011).

Greenwald, G. "The Government's One-Way Mirror." December 20, 2010. salon.com/news/opinion/glenn_greenwald/2010/12/20/surveillance/index.html (accessed March 2011).

Gross, G. "House Passes Copyright Enforcement Bill." May 8, 2008. macworld.com/article/133379/2008/05/copyright.html (accessed March 2011).

GSMA News. "Asia Pacific LTE Connections to Surpass 120 Million by 2015." November 16, 2010. mobile-businessbriefing.com/article/asia-pacific-lte-connections-to-surpass-120-million-by-2015 (accessed March 2011).

Guha, S. "NOYB: Privacy in Social Networks." 2009. saikat.guha.cc/paper.php?id=wosn08-guha:noyb (accessed March 2011).

Hill, K. "Lawsuit of the Day: Hey Teacher, Leave Them Kids Alone!" February 18, 2010. abovethelaw.com/2010/02/lawsuit-of-the-day-hey-teacher-leave-them-kids-aloneor-activating-laptop-webcams-to-spy-on-students-at-home-is-not-cool (accessed March 2011).

Himma, K. E., and H. T. Tavani. *The Handbook of Information and Computer Ethics.* Hoboken, NJ: Wiley & Sons, 2008.

IBM. "Data Privacy Best Practices: Time to Take Action." White paper, *IBM Information Management Software*, September 2008.

Internet Crime Complaint Center. "2010 IC3 Report." March 2011. ic3.gov/media/annualreport/2010_IC3Report.pdf (accessed March 2011).

Johnson, D., and E. Lipton. "Justice Department Says F.B.I. Misused Patriot Act." *New York Times*, March 9, 2007.

Kravets, D. "U.S. Declares iPhone Jailbreaking Legal, Over Apple's Objections." July 26, 2010. wired.com/threatlevel/2010/07/feds-ok-iphone-jailbreaking (accessed March 2011).

Krazit, T. "Oracle Sues Google over Android and Java." August 12, 2010. news.cnet.com/8301-30684_3-20013546-265.html (accessed March 2011).

LaMonica, M. "Green Electronics EPEAT Registry Goes Global." August 10, 2009. news.cnet.com/8301-11128_3-10306132-54.html (accessed March 2011).

Lattanzio, V. "2nd Lawsuit Filed Over WebcamGate." nbcphiladelphia.com/news/politics/2nd-Lawsuit-Filed-Over-WebcamGate-99368474.html (accessed March 2011).

Lewis, P., and J. Domokos. "Caught on Camera: Lancashire Police Arrest Amateur Photographer." February 21, 2010. guardian.co.uk/uk/video/2010/feb/21/police-arrest-photographer (accessed March 2011).

MacManus, R. "Hong Kong's Octopus Card: Utility Outweighs Privacy Concerns." *ReadWriteWeb*, September 2, 2009. readwriteweb.com/archives/hong_kongs_octopus_card.php (accessed September 2009).

Madrak, S. "When Single Moms Are Fined $1.5M, It's Time to Take a New Look at Copyright Protection in the Digital Age." November 6, 2010. crooksandliars.com/susie-madrak/when-single-moms-are-fined-15m-its-ti (accessed March 2011).

Mallor, J., et al. *Business Law: The Ethical, Global and E-Commerce Environment*, 14th ed. New York: McGraw-Hill, 2009.

Mann, R. J., and J. K. Winn. *Electronic Commerce (Law in Commerce)*, 3rd ed. New York: Aspen Publishers, 2008.

McBride, S., and L. Chao. "Disney Battles Pirates at China Affiliate." *Wall Street Journal-Asia*, November 24, 2008.

McCarthy, K. "*sex.com* Thief Arrested." *The Register* (UK), October 28, 2005. theregister.co.uk/2005/10/28/sexdotcom_cohen_arrested (accessed March 2011).

Miller, C. C. "Craigslist Says It Has Shut Its Section for Sex Ads." *New York Times*, September 15, 2010. nytimes.com/2010/09/16/business/16craigslist.html (accessed March 2011).

The Moral Liberal. "Protect Our Right to Opt Out of Electronic Healthcare Systems." July 21, 2010. themoralliberal.com/2010/07/21/protect-our-right-to-opt-out-of-electronic-health-records-systems (accessed March 2011).

Nakashima, E. "U.S. Seeks Ways to Wiretap the Internet." September 28, 2010a. washingtonpost.com/wp-dyn/content/article/2010/09/27/AR2010092706637.html (accessed March 2011).

Nakashima, R. "LimeWire Loses RIAA Case over Copyright Infringement." May 12, 2010b. huffingtonpost.com/2010/05/12/limewire-loses-riaa-case-_n_574338.html (accessed March 2011).

Nelson, N. "How to Estimate Energy Efficiency." *eWeek*, July 7, 2008.

Northcott, S. "iPhone 4: Impressions Part 2." July 1, 2010. touchreviews.net/iphone-4-initial-impressions-part-2-imovie-gyroscope (accessed March 2011).

Nutshell Mail. "Free Your Employees from Wasting Time on Social Networks and E-Mail." January 25, 2010. blog.nutshellmail.com/2010/01/25/free-your-employees-from-wasting-time-on-social-networks-and-email (accessed March 2011).

Oates, J. "Microsoft Faces Second 'Black Screen' Lawsuit." *The Register*, October 28, 2008. theregister.co.uk/2008/10/28/ms_wga_china (accessed March 2011).

Oates, J. "Microsoft's WGA Changes Today." *The Register*, February 20, 2007. theregister.co.uk/2007/02/20/wga_changes_today (accessed March 2011).

Octopus. "Key Statistics at a Glance." octopus.com.hk/octopus-for-businesses/benefits-for-your-business/en/index.html.

Park, H. S. "Empowering Employees with Technology." *Baseline*, May 27, 2009. baselinemag.com/c/a/IT-Management/Empowering-Employees-With-Technology-586442 (accessed March 2011).

Parks, L. "Just the Ticket: Detection System Helps New Era Virtually Eliminate Online Fraud." *Stores*, April 2010.

Pfanner, E. "Swiss Say Google's Street View Is Too Revealing." *New York Times*, November 13, 2009. nytimes.com/2009/11/14/technology/companies/14google.html (accessed March 2011).

Posner, J. "*sex.com* Settles Monumental Case Against VeriSign/Network Solutions." *CircleID*, April 20, 2004. circleid.com/posts/sexcom_settles_monumental_case_against_verisign_network_solutions (accessed March 2011).

Rasmussen, N. "Power and Cooling Capacity Management for Data Centers." 2007. apcmedia.com/salestools/NRAN-6C25XM_R0_EN.pdf (accessed March 2011).

Relkin, J. "10 Ethical Issues Confronting IT Managers." *TechRepublic.com*, August 15, 2006. techrepublic.com/article/10-ethical-issues-confronting-it-managers/6105942 (accessed March 2011).

Roberts, K. L. "'Machine-or-Transformation Test' Rejected as Sole Test for Process Patents." August 13, 2010. abanet.org/litigation/litigationnews/top_stories/081310-supreme-court-patents-bilski.html

Russell, G. "U.N.'s World Health Organization Eying Global Tax on Banking, Internet Activity." January 15, 2010. foxnews.com/world/2010/01/15/uns-world-health-organization-eyeing-global-tax-banking-internet-activity (accessed March 2011).

Samson, T. "GreenNet 2010: Google Shares Its Green Data Center Secrets." April 29, 2010. infoworld.com/d/green-it/greennet-2010-google-shares-its-green-data-center-secrets-328?page=0,1 (accessed March 2011).

San Miguel, R. "Sheriff Sues Craigslist to Curb Prostitution." *E-Commerce Times*, March 6, 2009.

Savitz, E. "eBay Wins Tiffany Trademark Case." July 14, 2008. blogs.barrons.com/techtraderdaily/2008/07/14/ebay-wins-tiffany-trademark-case (accessed March 2011).

Schreiber, J. "Big Brother Is Here, Families Say." February 18, 2010. abovethelaw.com/2010/02/lawsuit-of-the-day-hey-teacher-leave-them-kids-aloneor-activating-laptop-webcams-to-spy-on-students-at-home-is-not-cool (accessed March 2011).

Scott, L., and T. Ross. "Monitoring Internet Usage." Spring 2010. governmentauditors.org/index.php?option=com_content&view=article&id=594:monitoring-Internet-usage-spring-2010&catid=47:accounts&Itemid=123 (accessed March 2011).

Smith, J. "Schumer Circulates Amendment to Leahy Patent Bill." *National Journal*, January 26, 2011. techdailydose.nationaljournal.com/2011/01/schumer-circulates-amendment-t.php (accessed March 2011).

Smith, M. "The Next Big Privacy Concern: RFID 'Spychips.'" July 27, 2010. networkworld.com/community/node/64181 (accessed March 2011).

Stanton, J. M., and K. Stam. "Visible Employee: Using Work Place Monitoring and Surveillance to Protect Information Assets." *Information Today, Inc.*, 2006.

Supreme Court of the United States. "City of Ontario, CA et al. v. Quon." June 17, 2010. supremecourt.gov/opinions/09pdf/08-1332.pdf (accessed May 2011).

Techrights. "Microsoft Hopes to Make Money from Lawsuits in China." July 26, 2009. techrights.org/2009/07/26/msft-lawsuits-in-china (accessed March 2011).

The Standard. "Privacy Fears Emerge over Tentacles of Octopus Card." March 31, 2010. thestandard.com.hk/news_detail.asp?pp_cat=11&art_id=96486&sid=27584770&con_type=1".

Thomson, I. "RIAA Spent $58 Million Suing File-Sharers, Got 2% Back." July 15, 2010. dslreports.com/forum/remark,24521964?hilit=riaa (accessed March 2011).

Townsend, K. "Google's Qualification for Safe Harbor Protection from Copyright Liability Provides Guidance for Responding To and Sending DMCA Notices." 2010. kilpatricktownsend.com/~/media/Ryan_T_Bricker_Googles_Qualifications_for_Safe_Harbor_Protecion.ashx (accessed March 2011).

TRUSTe. "TRUSTe and Adgregate Markets Partner Up." April 19, 2010. truste.com/about_TRUSTe/pressroom/news_truste_adgregate_facebook_shopping.html (accessed March 2011).

Vijayan, J. "Facebook Hit with Class Action over Privacy Changes." February 17, 2010. macworld.com/article/146481/2010/02/facebook_lawsuit.html (accessed March 2011).

Volonino, L., and S. Robinson. *Principles and Practices of Information Security.* Upper Saddle River, NJ: Prentice Hall, 2004.

Volonino, L., R. Anzaldua, and J. Godwin. *Computer Forensics: Principles and Practices.* Upper Saddle River, NJ: Prentice Hall, 2007.

Washburn, D. "Forrester: Ways to Cut Data Center Energy Costs." *Computerworld*, October 20, 2010. computerworld.com/s/article/9192058/Forrester_Ways_to_Cut_Data_Center_Energy_Costs?taxonomyId=12 (accessed March 2011).

Washington Times. "Internet Taxation Is on the Way." April 2, 2010. washingtontimes.com/news/2010/apr/02/Internet-taxation-is-on-the-way (accessed March 2011).

Watson, P. J. "Exposed: Naked Body Scanner Images of Film Star Printed, Circulated by Airport Staff." February 9, 2010. infowars.com/exposed-naked-body-scanner-images-of-film-star-printed-circulated-by-airport-staff (accessed March 2011).

Watson, P. J., A. Jones, and S. Watson. "Enemies of Free Speech Call for Internet Licensing." February 1, 2010. prisonplanet.com/enemies-of-free-speech-call-for-Internet-licensing.html (accessed March 2011).

Weitzner, D. J., H. Abelson, T. Berners-Lee, J. Feigenbaum, J. A. Hendler, and G. J. Sussman. "Information Accountability." *Communications of the ACM* (June 2008).

Wilhelm, A. "Skype on Your TV Is Now Possible—Check Out How." May 18, 2010. thenextweb.com/apps/2010/05/18/skype-on-your-tv-is-now-possible-check-out-how (accessed March 2010).

WorldNetDaily. "U.S. Regulatory Czar Nominee Wants Net 'Fairness Doctrine.'" April 27, 2009. wnd.com/index.php?fa=PAGE.view&pageId=96301 (accessed March 2011).

Yamamura, J. H., and F. Grupe. "Ethical Considerations for Providing Professional Services Online." *CPA Journal* (May 2008).

CHAPTER **15**

LAUNCHING A SUCCESSFUL ONLINE BUSINESS AND EC PROJECTS

Content

Learning Objectives

Upon completion of this chapter, you will be able to:

1. Understand the fundamental requirements for initiating an online business.

2. Describe the process of initiating and funding a startup e-business or large e-project.

3. Understand the process of adding EC initiatives to an existing business.

4. Describe the issues and methods of transforming an organization into an e-business.

5. Describe the process of acquiring websites and evaluate building versus hosting options.

6. Understand the importance of providing and managing content and describe how to accomplish this.

7. Evaluate websites on design criteria, such as appearance, navigation, consistency, and performance.

8. Understand how search engine optimization may help a website obtain high placement in search engines.

9. Understand how to provide some support e-services.

10. Understand the process of building a webstore.

11. Know how to build a webstore with templates.

A complete version of this chapter is available on the textbook's website.

GLOSSARY

Note: Page references with W represent Web (online) pages.

acceptable use policy (AUP) Policy that informs users of their responsibilities when using company networks, wireless devices, customer data, and so forth. 537

acceptance testing Determining whether a website meets the original business objectives and vision. 691

access control Mechanism that determines who can legitimately use a network resource. 517

ad views The number of times users call up a page that has a banner on it during a specific period; known as *impressions* or *page views*. 453

Address Verification System (AVS) Detects fraud by comparing the address entered on a Web page with the address information on file with the cardholder's issuing bank. 555

advergaming The practice of using computer games to advertise a product, an organization, or a viewpoint. 464

affiliate marketing A marketing arrangement by which an organization refers consumers to the selling company's website. 472

affiliate network A network that acts as an intermediary between publishers (affiliates) and merchant affiliate programs. 472

agency costs Costs incurred in ensuring that the agent performs tasks as expected (also called *administrative costs*). 683

agility An EC firm's ability to capture, report, and quickly respond to changes happening in the marketplace and business environment. 685

angel investor A wealthy individual who contributes personal funds and possibly expertise at the earliest stage of business development. W15-9

application controls Controls that are intended to protect specific applications. 527

application service provider (ASP) An agent or vendor who assembles the functions needed by enterprises and packages them with out-sourced development, operation, maintenance, and other services. 609

attractors Website features that attract and interact with visitors in the target stakeholder group. W15-15

auction A competitive process in which a seller solicits consecutive bids from buyers (forward auctions) or a buyer solicits bids from sellers (backward auctions). Prices are determined dynamically by the bids. 98

audit An important part of any control system. Auditing can be viewed as an additional layer of controls or safeguards. It is considered as a deterrent to criminal actions especially for insiders. W9-10

augmented reality (AR) A live direct or indirect view of a physical, real-world environment whose elements are *augmented* by computer-generated sensory input, such as sound or graphics. 464

authentication Process to verify (assure) the real identity of an individual, computer, computer program, or EC website. 498

authorization (1) Determines whether a buyer's card is active and whether the customer has sufficient funds. (2) Process of determining what the authenticated entity is allowed to access and what operations it is allowed to perform. 498, 552

Automated Clearing House (ACH) Network A nationwide batch-oriented electronic funds transfer system that provides for the interbank clearing of electronic payments for participating financial institutions. 564

automated question-answer (QA) A system that locates, extracts, and provides specific answers to user questions expressed in natural language. 258

automatic vehicle location (AVL) A means for automatically determining the geographic location of a vehicle and transmitting the information to a request. 309

availability Assurance that access to data, the website, or other EC data service is timely, available, reliable, and restricted to authorized users. 513

avatars Animated computer characters that exhibit humanlike movements and behaviors. 119, W8-12

B2B marketing Marketing by manufacturers and wholesalers along the sell-side of the supply chain. 219

B2B portals Information portals for businesses. 210

back end The activities that support online order fulfillment, inventory management, purchasing from suppliers, payment processing, packaging, and delivery. 86

back-office operations The activities that support fulfillment of orders, such as packing, delivery, accounting, and logistics. 582

balanced scorecard A management tool that assesses organizational progress toward strategic goals by measuring performance in a number of different areas. 627

balanced scorecard method Analysis of a variety of matrices (finance, internal operation, agility, customer opinions) for evaluating the overall health of an organization. W13-7

banking Trojan A Trojan that comes to life when computer owners visit one of a number of online banking or e-commerce sites. 502

banner On a Web page, a graphic advertising display linked to the advertiser's Web page. 455

bartering The exchange of goods and services. 103

bartering exchange An intermediary that links parties in a barter; a company submits its surplus to the exchange and receives points of credit, which can be used to buy the items that the company needs from other exchange participants. 103, 205

behavioral targeting Targeting that uses information collected about an individual's Web-browsing behavior, such as the pages they have visited or the searches they have made, to select an advertisement to display to that individual. 442

benchmarks An approach to evaluating infrastructure that focuses on *objective* measures of performance. W13-6

best-practice benchmarks Benchmarks that emphasize how information system activities are actually performed rather than on numeric measures of performance. W13-6

biometric control An automated method for verifying the identity of a person based on physical or behavioral characteristics. 518

biometric systems Authentication systems that identify a person by measurement of a biological characteristic, such as fingerprints, iris (eye) patterns, facial features, or voice. 518

biometrics An individual's unique physical or behavioral characteristics that can be used to identify an individual precisely (e.g., fingerprints). 451

blog A personal website that is open to the public to read and to interact with; dedicated to specific topics or issues. 104

Bluetooth A set of telecommunications standards that enables wireless devices to communicate with each other over short distances. 288

botnet A huge number (e.g., hundreds of thousands) of hijacked Internet computers that have been set up to forward traffic, including spam and viruses, to other computers on the Internet. 503

brick-and-mortar (old economy) organizations Old-economy organizations (corporations) that perform their primary business offline, selling physical products by means of physical agents. 38

brick-and-mortar retailers Retailers who do business in the non-Internet, physical world in traditional brick-and-mortar stores. 144

business case (1) A business plan for a new initiative or large, new project inside an existing organization. (2) A document that justifies the investment of internal, organizational resources in a specific application or project. 628, W15-7

business continuity plan A plan that keeps the business running after a disaster occurs. Each function in the business should have a valid recovery capability plan. 494

business ethics A form of applied ethics that examines ethical principles and moral or ethical problems that arise in a business environment. 719

business impact analysis (BIA) An exercise that determines the impact of losing the support of an EC resource to an organization and establishes the escalation of that loss over time, identifies the minimum resources needed to recover, and prioritizes the recovery of processes and supporting systems. 537

business model A method of doing business by which a company generates revenue to sustain itself and achieves its goals. 60, 141

business plan A written document that identifies a company's goals and outlines how the company intends to achieve the goals and at what cost. 628, W15-7

business process management (BPM) (1) Method for business restructuring that combines workflow systems and redesign methods; covers three process categories—people-to-people, systems-to-systems, and systems-to-people interactions. (2) A holistic management approach focused on aligning all aspects of an organization with the wants and needs of clients. It promotes business effectiveness and efficiency while striving for innovation, flexibility, and integration with technology. 641, 701, W15-13

business process reengineering (BPR) A methodology for conducting a comprehensive redesign of an enterprise's processes. 641, 700

business social network A social network whose primary objective is to facilitate business connections and activities. 373

business-oriented social networks A social network whose major interest is business topics. Members are professional people. Such networks are used mostly for creating contacts, providing requirements, and enlisting members' support for problem solving and knowledge sharing. 115

business-to-business (B2B) E-commerce model in which all of the participants are businesses or other organizations. 42

business-to-business e-commerce (B2B EC) Transactions between businesses conducted electronically over the Internet, extranets, intranets, or private networks; also known as eB2B (electronic B2B) or just B2B. 205

business-to-business-to-consumer (B2B2C) E-commerce model in which a business provides some product or service to a client business that maintains its own customers. 42

business-to-consumer (B2C) E-commerce model in which businesses sell to individual shoppers. 42

business-to-employees (B2E) E-commerce model in which an organization delivers services, information, or products to its individual employees. 43

button A small banner that is linked to a website; may contain downloadable software. 453

buy-side e-marketplace (1) A corporate-based acquisition site that uses reverse auctions, negotiations, group purchasing, or any other e-procurement method. (2) A private e-marketplace in which one company makes purchases from invited suppliers. 88, 196

Captcha tool Completely Automated Public Turing test to tell Computers and Humans Apart, which uses a verification test on comment pages to stop scripts from posting automatically. W9-8

card verification number (CVN) Detects fraud by comparing the verification number printed on the signature strip on the back of the card with the information on file with the cardholder's issuing bank. 555

card-not-present (CNP) transaction A credit card transaction in which the merchant does not verify the customer's signature. W15-34

certificate authorities (CAs) Third parties that issue digital certificates. 522

change management A structured approach to shifting/transitioning individuals, teams, and organizations from a current state to a desired future state. It is an organizational process aimed at empowering employees to accept and embrace changes in their current business environment. 702

channel conflict Situation in which an online marketing channel upsets the traditional channels due to real or perceived damage from competition. 169

chatterbot A program that attempts to simulate a conversation, with the aim of at least temporarily fooling customers into thinking they are conversing with a human. W8-12

CIA security triad (CIA triad) Three security concepts important to information on the Internet: confidentiality, integrity, and availability. 513

ciphertext A plaintext message after it has been encrypted into a machine-readable form. 519

click (ad click) A count made each time a visitor clicks on an advertising banner to access the advertiser's website. 453

click-and-mortar (click-and-brick) organizations Organizations that conduct some e-commerce activities, usually as an additional marketing channel. 39

click-and-mortar retailers Brick-and-mortar retailers that offer a transactional Web site from which to conduct business. 144

click-through rate/ratio (CTR) The percentage of visitors who are exposed to a banner ad and click on it. 453

clickstream behavior Customer movements on the Internet. 449

clickstream data Data that occur inside the Web environment; they provide a trail of the user's activities (the user's clickstream behavior) in the website. 450

cloud computing The provision of computational resources on demand via a computer network. You pay only for actual usage. 695

co-opetition Two or more companies cooperate together on some activities for their mutual benefit, even while competing against each other in the marketplace. W12-2

collaboration hub (c-hub) The central point of control for an e-market. A single c-hub, representing one e-market owner, can host multiple collaboration spaces (c-spaces) in which trading partners use c-enablers to exchange data with the c-hub. 261

collaborative commerce (c-commerce) The use of digital technologies that enable companies to collaboratively plan, design, develop, manage, and research products, services, and innovative EC applications. 43, 260

collaborative filtering A market research and personalization method that uses customer data to predict, based on formulas derived from behavioral sciences, what other products or services a customer may enjoy; predictions can be extended to other customers with similar profiles. 442

collaborative planning, forecasting, and replenishment (CPFR) Project in which suppliers and retailers collaborate in their planning and demand forecasting to optimize flow of materials along the supply chain. 602

collaborative portals Portals that allow collaboration. 213

collaborative website A site that allows business partners to collaborate. W15-15

collective intelligence (CI) The capacity of human communities to evolve toward higher order complexity and harmony, through such innovation mechanisms as variation-feedback-selection, differentiation-integration-transformation, and competition-cooperation-coopetition. 386

communal shopping A method of shopping where the shoppers enlist others to participate in the purchase decision. 344

company-centric EC E-commerce that focuses on a single company's buying needs (many-to-one, or buy-side) or selling needs (one-to-many, or sell-side). 181

competitor analysis grid A strategic planning tool that highlights points of differentiation between competitors and the target firm. 627

compliance data Data pertaining to the enterprise included in the law that can be used for the purpose of implementing or validating compliance. 751

Computer Fraud and Abuse Act (CFAA) Major computer crime law to protect government computers and other Internet-connected computers. 745

computer security incident management The monitoring and detection of security events on a computer or computer network, and the execution of proper responses to those events. The primary purpose of incident management is the development of a well understood and predictable response to damaging events and computer intrusions. 516

Computing Technology Industry Association (CompTIA) Nonprofit trade group providing information security research and best practices. 537

confidentiality Assurance of data privacy and accuracy. Keeping private or sensitive information from being disclosed to unauthorized individuals, entities, or processes. 513

consortium trading exchange (CTE) An exchange formed and operated by a group of major companies in an industry to provide industry-wide transaction services. 209

consumer-to-business (C2B) E-commerce model in which individuals use the Internet to sell products or services to organizations or individuals who seek sellers to bid on products or services they need. 42

consumer-to-consumer (C2C) E-commerce model in which consumers sell directly to other consumers. 43, 265

contact card A smart card containing a small gold plate on the face that when inserted in a smart card reader makes contact and passes data to and from the embedded microchip. 557

contactless (proximity) card A smart card with an embedded antenna, by means of which data and applications are passed to and from a card reader unit or other device without contact between the card and the card reader. 557

content The text, images, sound, and video that make up a Web page. W15-20

content management The process of adding, revising, and removing content from a website to keep content fresh, accurate, compelling, and credible. W15-24

context-aware computing Application's ability to detect and react to a set of environmental variables that is described as context (which can be sensor information or other data including users' attitudes). 312

Controlling the Assault of Non-Solicited Pornography and Marketing (CAN-SPAM) Act Law that makes it a crime to send commercial e-mail messages with false or misleading message headers or misleading subject lines. 529

conversion rate The percentage of clickers who actually make a purchase. 453

cookie A data file that is placed on a user's hard drive by a remote Web server, frequently without disclosure or the user's consent, which collects information about the user's activities at a site. 441

copyright An exclusive right of the author or creator of a book, movie, musical composition, or other artistic property to print, copy, sell, license, distribute, transform to another medium, translate, record, perform, or otherwise use. 723

corporate (business) performance management (CPM, BPM) Advanced performance measuring and analysis approach that embraces planning and strategy. 643

corporate (enterprise) portal A major gateway through which employees, business partners, and the public can enter a corporate website. 54, 211

cost–benefit analysis A comparison of the costs of a project against the benefits. 665

cost-plus Adding up all the costs involved, such as material, labor, rent, overhead, etc., and adding a percentage mark-up as profit. 637

CPM (cost per mille, i. e., thousand impressions) The fee an advertiser pays for each 1,000 times a page with a banner ad is shown. 453

cracker A malicious hacker, such as Maxwell, in the opening case, who may represent a serious problem for a corporation. 496

cross-selling Offering similar or complementary products and services to increase sales. W15-21

crowdsourcing The act of outsourcing tasks, traditionally performed by an employee or contractor, to an undefined, large group of people or community (a "crowd"), through an open call. 384

CSI Computer Crime and Security Survey Annual security survey of U. S. corporations, government agencies, financial and medical institutions, and universities conducted by the Computer Security Institute. 488

customer loyalty A deep commitment to repurchase or repatronize a preferred product/service continually in the future, thereby causing repetitive same-brand or same brand-set purchasing, despite situational influences and marketing efforts that have the potential to cause switching behavior. 434

customer relationship management (CRM) A customer service approach that focuses on building long-term and sustainable customer relationships that add value both to the customers and the merchants. 369

cyberbashing Domain name that criticizes an organization or person. 727

cyberbullying The use of information and communication technologies to support deliberate, repeated, and hostile behavior by an individual or group, that is intended to harm others. 742

cybercrime Intentional crimes carried out on the Internet. 494

cybercriminal A person who intentionally carries out crimes over the Internet. 494

data breach A security incident in which sensitive, protected, or confidential data is copied, transmitted, viewed, stolen, or used by an individual unauthorized to do so. 512

Data Encryption Standard (DES) The standard symmetric encryption algorithm supported by the NIST and used by U. S. government agencies until October 2000. 520

denial-of-service (DoS) attack An attack on a website in which an attacker uses specialized software to send a flood of data packets to the target computer with the aim of overloading its resources. 503

desktop purchasing Direct purchasing from internal marketplaces without the approval of supervisors and without the intervention of a procurement department. 204

desktop search Search tools that search the contents of a user's or organization's computer files, rather than searching the Internet. The emphasis is on finding all the information that is available on the user's PC, including Web browser histories, e-mail archives, and word-processed documents, as well as in all internal files and databases. 95

detection measures Ways to determine whether intruders attempted to break into the EC system; whether they were successful; and what they may have done. 499

deterring measures Actions that will make criminals abandon their idea of attacking a specific system (e.g., the possibility of losing a job for insiders). 499

digital divide Gap between people with effective access to digital and information technology and those without. 567, 752

digital economy An economy that is based on digital technologies, including digital communication networks, computers, software, and other related information technologies; also called the *Internet economy*, the *new economy*, or the *Web economy*. 52

digital enterprise A new business model that uses IT in a fundamental way to accomplish one or more of three basic objectives: reach and engage customers more effectively, boost employee productivity, and improve operating efficiency. It uses converged communication and computing technology in a way that improves business processes. 52

digital envelope The combination of the encrypted original message and the digital signature, using the recipient's public key. 522

digital products Goods that can be transformed to digital format and delivered over the Internet. 86

digital rights management (DRM) An umbrella term for any of several arrangements that allow a vendor of content in electronic form to control the material and restrict its usage. 725

digital signature or **digital certificate** Validates the sender and time stamp of a transaction so it cannot be later claimed that the transaction was unauthorized or invalid. 521

direct marketing Broadly, marketing that takes place without intermediaries between manufacturers and buyers; in the context of this book, marketing done online between any seller and buyer. 142

direct materials Materials used in the production of a product (e.g., steel in a car or paper in a book). 184

disaster avoidance An approach oriented toward prevention. The idea is to minimize the chance of avoidable disasters (such as fire or other human-caused threats). 532

disintermediation The process by which the consumer bypasses the services of an intermediary or intermediaries in the chain of distribution to purchase products directly from those who supply or produce them. 87, 168, 631, 700

distance learning Formal education that takes place off campus, usually, but not always, through online resources. 244

domain name A name-based address that identifies an Internet-connected server. Usually it refers to the portion of the address to the left of .com and .org, etc. W15-19

Domain Name System (DNS) (1) A hierarchical naming system for computers, services, or any resource participating in the Internet; it is like a directory. (2) Translates (converts) domain names to their numeric IP addresses. 491, W15-20

double auction An auction in which multiple buyers and their bidding prices are matched with multiple sellers and their asking prices, considering the quantities on both sides. 101

dynamic pricing A rapid movement of prices over time and possibly across customers, as a result of supply and demand matching. 98, 209

dynamic Web content Content that must be kept up-to-date. W15-21

e-bartering (electronic bartering) Bartering conducted online, usually in a bartering exchange. 103

e-business A broader definition of EC that includes not just the buying and selling of goods and services, but also servicing customers, collaborating with business partners, and conducting electronic transactions within an organization. 38

e-check A legally valid electronic version or representation of a paper check. 562

e-commerce (EC) risk The likelihood that a negative outcome will occur in the course of developing and operating an electronic commerce strategy. 636

e-commerce strategy (e-strategy) The formulation and execution of a vision of how a new or existing company intends to do business electronically. 620

e-distributor An e-commerce intermediary that connects manufacturers with business buyers (customers) by aggregating the catalogs of many manufacturers in one place—the intermediary's website. 94

e-government E-commerce model in which a government entity buys or provides goods, services, or information to businesses or individual citizens. 43, 232

e-grocer A grocer that takes orders online and provides deliveries on a daily or other regular schedule or within a very short period of time. 162

e-learning The online delivery of information for purposes of education, training, or knowledge management. 241

e-logistics The logistics of EC systems, typically involving small parcels sent to many customers' homes (in B2C). 582

e-loyalty Customer loyalty to an e-tailer or loyalty programs delivered online or supported electronically. 435

e-mail advertising Adding advertisements to e-mail messages sent to customers. 456

e-mail marketing A form of direct marketing which uses e-mail as a means of communicating commercial messages to an audience. 456

e-mail spam A subset of spam that involves nearly identical messages sent to numerous recipients by e-mail. 509

e-mall (online mall) An online shopping center where many online stores are located. 90

e-marketplace An online market, usually B2B, in which buyers and sellers exchange goods or services; the three types of e-marketplaces are private, public, and consortia. 85

e-micropayments Small online payments, typically under $10. 561

e-newsletter A collection of short, informative articles sent at regular intervals by e-mail to individuals who have an interest in the newsletter's topic. W15-24

e-procurement (electronic procurement) The electronic acquisition of goods and services for organizations via the Internet, EDI, etc. 197

e-sourcing The process and tools that electronically enable any activity in the sourcing process, such as quotation/tender submittance and response, e-auctions, online negotiations, and spending analyses. W4-5

e-tailers Retailers who sell over the Internet. 42, 136

EC architecture A plan for organizing the underlying infrastructure and applications of a site. 689

EC security programs All the policies, procedures, documents, standards, hardware, software, training, and personnel that work together to protect information, the ability to conduct business, and other assets. 516

EC security strategy A strategy that views EC security as the process of preventing and detecting unauthorized use of the organization's brand, identity, website, e-mail, information, or other asset and attempts to defraud the organization, its customers, and employees. 499

electronic auctions (e-auctions) Auctions conducted online. 99

electronic (online) banking or **e-banking** Various banking activities conducted from home or the road using an Internet connection; also known as cyberbanking, virtual banking, online banking, and home banking. 158

electronic book (e-book) A book in digital form that can be read on a computer screen or on a special device. 250

electronic catalogs (e-catalogs) The presentation of product information in an electronic form; the backbone of most e-selling sites. 94

electronic commerce (EC) The process of buying, selling, or exchanging products, services, or information via computer. 38

electronic discovery (e-discovery) Discovery in civil litigation that deals with information in electronic format; also referred to as *electronically stored information* (ESI). 741

electronic market (e-marketplace) An online marketplace where buyers and sellers meet to exchange goods, services, money, or information. 39

Electronic Product Environmental Assessment Tool (EPEAT) A searchable database of computer hardware that meets a strict set of environmental criteria. 756

electronic retailing (e-tailing) Retailing conducted online, over the Internet. 136

electronic shopping cart An order-processing technology that allows customers to accumulate items they wish to buy while they continue to shop. 97

electronic signature A generic, technology-neutral term that refers to the various methods by which one can "sign" an electronic record. 747

encryption The process of scrambling (encrypting) a message in such a way that it is difficult, expensive, or time-consuming for an unauthorized person to unscramble (decrypt) it. 519

encryption algorithm The mathematical formula used to encrypt the plaintext into the ciphertext, and vice versa. 519

enterprise application integration (EAI) Class of software that integrates large systems. W13-13

enterprise invoice presentment and payment (EIPP) Presenting and paying B2B invoices online. 569

enterprise search The practice of identifying and enabling specific content across the enterprise to be indexed, searched, and displayed to authorized users. 95

ethics The branch of philosophy that deals with what is considered to be right and wrong. 66, 719

event shopping A B2C model in which sales are done to meet the needs of special events (e.g., a wedding, black Friday). 146

exchanges (trading communities, trading exchanges) Many-to-many e-marketplaces, usually owned and run by a third party or a consortium, in which many buyers and many sellers meet electronically to trade with each other. 181

expert location systems (ELS) Interactive computerized systems that help employees find and connect with colleagues who have expertise required for specific problems—whether they are across the country or across the room—in order to solve specific, critical business problems in seconds. 258

exposure The estimated cost, loss, or damage that can result if a threat exploits a vulnerability. 494

extranet A network that uses the Internet to link multiple intranets. 39

f-commerce (1) E-commerce activities conducted on Facebook or influenced by the site. (2) The ability to execute transactions in Facebook without leaving the network or leveraging the open graph by integrating Facebook into traditional site-based e-commerce platforms. It ties each transaction to the social graph. 45, 417

fair use The legal use of copyrighted material for noncommercial purposes without paying royalties or getting permission. 725

firewall A single point between two or more networks where all traffic must pass (choke point); the device authenticates, controls, and logs all traffic. 523

folksonomy (collaborative tagging, social tagging) The practice and method of collaboratively creating, classifying, and managing tags to annotate and categorize content. 110

forward auction An auction in which a seller entertains bids from buyers. Bidders increase price sequentially. 100

fraud Any business activity that uses deceitful practices or devices to deprive another of property or other rights. 494

front end The portion of an e-seller's business processes through which customers interact, including the seller's portal, electronic catalogs, a shopping cart, a search engine, and a payment gateway. 86

front-office operations The business processes, such as sales and advertising, which are visible to customers. 582

general controls Controls established to protect the system regardless of the specific application. For example, protecting hardware and controlling access to the data center are independent of the specific application. 527

geographical information system (GIS) A computer system capable of integrating, storing, editing, analyzing, sharing, and displaying geographically referenced (spatial) information. 307

geolocation The process of automatically identifying a Web user's physical location without that user having to provide any information. 306, 357

geosocial networking A type of social networking in which geographic services and capabilities such as geocoding and geotagging are used to enable additional social dynamics. 357

global positioning system (GPS) A worldwide satellite-based tracking system that enables users to determine their position anywhere on the earth. 306

Government 2.0 How government makes use of Web 2.0 technologies to interact with citizens and provide government services. 238

government-to-business (G2B) E-government category that includes interactions between governments and businesses (government selling to businesses and providing them with services and businesses selling products and services to the government). 235

government-to-citizens (G2C) E-government category that includes all the interactions between a government and its citizens. 232

government-to-employees (G2E) E-government category that includes activities and services between government units and their employees. 237

government-to-government (G2G) E-government category that includes activities within government units and those between governments. 236

green computing The study and practice of eco-friendly computing resources; is now a key concern of businesses in all industries—not just environmental organizations. 753

green IT Begins with manufacturers producing environmentally friendly products and encouraging IT departments to consider more friendly options like virtualization, power management, and proper recycling habits. 753

group purchasing The aggregation of orders from several buyers into volume purchases so that better prices can be negotiated. 204

hacker Someone who gains unauthorized access to a computer system. 496

hash function A mathematical computation that is applied to a message, using a private key, to encrypt the message. 521

hit A request for data from a Web page or file. 453

honeynet A network of honeypots. 525

honeypot Production system (e. g., firewalls, routers, Web servers, database servers) that looks like it does real work, but that acts as a decoy and is watched to study how network intrusions occur. 525

horizontal marketplaces Markets that concentrate on a service, material, or a product that is used in all types of industries (e.g., office supplies, PCs). 184

hype cycle A graphic representation of the maturity, adoption, and social application of specific IT tools. 672

identity theft Fraud that involves stealing an identity of a person and then the use of that identity by someone pretending to be someone else in order to steal money or get other benefits. 508

incubator A company, university, or nonprofit organization that supports businesses in their initial stages of development. W15-9

indirect materials Materials used to support production (e.g., office supplies or light bulbs). 184

infomediaries Electronic intermediaries that provide and/or control information flow in cyberspace, often aggregating information and selling it to others. 92

information architecture How the site and its Web pages are organized, labeled, and navigated to support browsing and searching throughout the website. W15-28

information assurance (IA) The protection of information systems against unauthorized access to or modification of information whether in storage, processing, or transit, and against the denial of service to authorized users, including those measures necessary to detect, document, and counter such threats. 499

information economics An approach similar to the concept of critical success factors in that it focuses on key organizational objectives, including intangible financial benefits, impacts on the business domain, and impacts on IT itself. W13-4

information portals Portals that store data and enable users to navigate and query these data. 213

information security Protecting information and information systems from unauthorized access, use, disclosure, disruption, modification, perusal, inspection, recording or destruction. 488

informational website A website that does little more than provide information about the business and its products and services. W15-14

infringement Use of the work without permission or contracting for payment of a royalty. 724

insourcing In-house development of applications. 692

integration testing Testing the combination of application modules acting in concert. 691

integrity Assurance that stored data has not been modified without authorization; a message that was sent is the same message as that which was received. 513

intellectual property (IP) Creations of the mind, such as inventions, literary and artistic works, and symbols, names, images, and designs, used in commerce. 723

intellectual property law Area of the law that includes patent law, copyright law, trademark law, trade secret law, and other branches of the law such as licensing and unfair competition. 723

intelligent agents (IA) Software applications that have some degree of reactivity, autonomy, and adaptability—as is needed in unpredictable attack situations. An agent is able to adapt itself based on changes occurring in its environment. 528, W11-9

interactive marketing Online marketing, facilitated by the Internet, by which marketers and advertisers can interact directly with customers, and consumers can interact with advertisers/vendors. 452

interactive video A technique used to blend user interaction and videos. 463

interactive voice response (IVR) A voice system that enables users to request and receive information and to enter and change data through a telephone to a computerized system. 287

interactive website A website that provides opportunities for the customers and the business to communicate and share information. W15-14

intermediary A third party that operates between sellers and buyers. 86

internal procurement marketplace The aggregated catalogs of all approved suppliers combined into a single internal electronic catalog. 203

Internet censorship The control or suppression of the publishing or accessing of information on the Internet. 749

Internet underground economy E-markets for stolen information made up of thousands of websites that sell credit card numbers, social security numbers, other data such as numbers of bank accounts, social network IDs, passwords, and much more. 492

interoperability Connecting people, data, and diverse systems; the term can be defined in a technical way or in a broad way, taking into account social, political, and organizational factors. 692

intrabusiness EC E-commerce category that includes all internal organizational activities that involve the exchange of goods, services, or information among various units and individuals in an organization. 42

intranet An internal corporate or government network that uses Internet tools, such as Web browsers, and Internet protocols. 39

intrusion detection system (IDS) A special category of software that can monitor activity across a network or on a host computer, watch for suspicious activity, and take automated action based on what it sees. 525

IP address An address that uniquely identifies each computer connected to a network or the Internet. 491

ISP hosting service A hosting service that provides an independent, stand-alone website for small and medium-sized businesses. W15-19

key (key value) The secret code used to encrypt and decrypt a message. 519

key performance indicator (KPI) A quantifiable measurement, agreed to beforehand, that reflects the critical success factors of a company, department or project. 642, 666

key space The large number of possible key values (keys) created by the algorithm to use when transforming the message. 519

keystroke logging (keylogging) A method of capturing and recording user keystrokes. 493

keyword banners Banner ads that appear when a predetermined word is queried from a search engine. 455

knowledge management (KM) The process of capturing or creating knowledge, storing it, updating it constantly, disseminating it, and using it whenever necessary. 253

learning agents Software agents that have the capacity to adapt or modify their behavior—that is, to learn. W11-12

learning management system (LMS) Software applications for the administration, documentation, tracking, and reporting of training programs, classroom and online events, e-learning programs, and training content. 249

learning on-demand Learning provided to an employee while the work is being done (in terms of troubleshooting or performance support). In a learning on-demand environment, courses, references, help files, documents, Webcasts, audios, videos, books, and presentations are all made available when and where a worker needs them. 249

legal precedent A judicial decision that may be used as a standard in subsequent similar cases. 730

letter of credit (L/C) A written agreement by a bank to pay the seller, on account of the buyer, a sum of money upon presentation of certain documents. 571

live banners A banner ad that is created dynamically (or whose content is created dynamically) at the time of display, instead of being preprogrammed with fixed content. 455

localization The process of converting media products developed in one environment (e.g., country) to a form culturally and linguistically acceptable in countries outside the original target market. 474

location-based commerce (l-commerce) Delivery of e-commerce transactions to individuals in a specific location, at a specific time. 146, 304

location-based service (LBS) An information service accessible from and to mobile devices through a mobile network utilizing the ability to make use of the geographical position of the mobile device to deliver a service to the user. 308

logistics The operations involved in the efficient and effective flow and storage of goods, services, and related information from point of origin to point of consumption. 582

macro virus (macro worm) A macro virus or macro worm is executed when the application object that contains the macro is opened or a particular procedure is executed. 501

malware (malicious software) A generic term for malicious software. 494

management by maxim A five-step process that brings together corporate executives, business-unit managers, and IT executives in planning sessions to determine appropriate infrastructure investments. W13-7

market segmentation The process of dividing a consumer market into logical groups for conducting marketing research and analyzing personal information. 438

marketspace A marketplace in which sellers and buyers exchange goods and services for money (or for other goods and services), but do so electronically. 86

mashup Combination of two or more websites into a single website that provides the content of both sites (whole or partial) to deliver a novel product to consumers. 110

mass customization A method that enables manufacturers to create specific products for each customer based on the customer's exact needs. 701

maverick buying Unplanned purchases of items needed quickly, often at non-prenegotiated higher prices. 196

merchant brokering Deciding from whom (from what merchant) to buy a product. 432

merge-in-transit Logistics model in which components for a product may come from two (or more) different physical locations and are shipped directly to the customer's location. 597

message digest (MD) A summary of a message converted into a string of digits after the hash has been applied. 521

metric A specific, measurable standard against which actual performance is compared. 643, 666

metric benchmarks A method that provides numeric measures of performance. W13-6

microblogging A form of blogging that allows users to write messages (usually up to 140 characters) and publish them, either to be viewed by anyone or by a restricted group that can be chosen by the user. These messages can be submitted by a variety of means, including text messaging, instant messaging, e-mail, MP3, or just on the Web. 107

microfinance Provision of financial services, in small amounts of money, to poor or low-income clients, including consumers and the self-employed. 567

mirror site An exact duplicate of an original website that is physically located on a Web server on another continent or in another country. W15-18

mobile advertising (m-advertising) Ads sent to and presented on mobile devices. 467

mobile agents Software agents that move to other systems, performing tasks there. A *mobile agent* can transport itself across different system architectures and platforms. W11-11

mobile banking Performing banking activities such as balance checks, account transactions, payments, credit applications, etc., via a mobile device. 291

mobile browser (microbrowser) Web browser designed for use on a mobile device optimized to display Web content most effectively for small screens on portable devices. 285

mobile commerce (m-commerce; m-business) Any business activity conducted over a wireless telecommunications network or from mobile devices. 277

mobile enterprise Application of mobile computing inside the enterprise (e.g., for improved communication among employees). 293

mobile entertainment Any type of leisure activity that utilizes wireless telecommunication networks, interacts with service providers, and incurs a cost upon usage. 300

mobile government (m-government) The wireless implementation of e-government mostly to citizens but also to businesses. 239

mobile marketing Conducting marketing on or with a mobile device. 466

mobile portals Portals accessible via mobile devices, especially cell phones and PDAs. 92, 213, 286

mobile social networking Members converse and connect with one another using cell phones or other mobile devices. 117, 342

mobile worker Any employee who is away from his or her primary work space at least 10 hours a week or 25 percent of the time. 294

mobility The degree to which the agents themselves travel over the network. Some agents are very mobile; others are not. W11-11

MRO (maintenance, repair, and operation) Indirect materials used in activities that support production. 184

multiagent systems (MASs) Computer systems in which there is no single designer who stands behind all the agents; each agent in the system can be working toward different, even contradictory, goals. W11-12

multichannel business model A business model where a company sells in multiple marketing channels simultaneously (e.g., both physical and online stores). 142

multimedia messaging service (MMS) The emerging generation of wireless messaging; MMS is able to deliver rich media. 287

name-your-own-price model Auction model in which a would-be buyer specifies the price (and other terms) he or she is willing to pay to any willing and able seller. It is a C2B model that was pioneered by Priceline.com. 100

network-based positioning Relies on base stations to find the location of a mobile device sending a signal or sensed by the network. 306

nonrepudiation Assurance that online customers or trading partners cannot falsely deny (repudiate) their purchase or transaction. 498

on-demand delivery service Express delivery made fairly quickly after an online order is received. 162

one-to-one marketing Marketing that treats each customer in a unique way. 439

online intermediary An online third party that brokers a transaction online between a buyer and a seller; may be virtual or click-and-mortar. 183

online trust The belief that an online website or other digital entities can deliver what they promise so that the recipient trusts them. 437

opt-in Agreement that requires computer users to take specific steps to allow the collection of personal information. 729

opt-out Business practice that gives consumers the opportunity to refuse sharing information about themselves. 728

order fulfillment All the activities needed to provide customers with their ordered goods and services, including related customer services. 582

outsourcing (1) A method of transferring the management and/or day-to-day execution of an entire business function to a third-party

service provider. (2) The use of an external vendor to provide all or part of the products and services that could be provided internally. 639, 693

packet Segment of data sent from one computer to another on a network. 523

page An HTML (Hypertext Markup Language) document that may contain text, images, and other online elements, such as Java applets and multimedia files; may be generated statically or dynamically. 453

page hijacking Creating a rogue copy of a popular website that shows contents similar to the original to a Web crawler. Once there, an unsuspecting user is redirected to malicious websites. 503

partner relationship management (PRM) Business strategy that focuses on providing comprehensive quality service to business partners. 187

patent A document that grants the holder exclusive rights to an invention for a fixed number of years. 725

pay per click (PPC) A popular Internet advertising payment model where advertisers pay their host only when the ad is clicked on. 473

payment card Electronic card that contains information that can be used for payment purposes. 552

payment service provider (PSP) A third-party service connecting a merchant's EC system to the appropriate acquiring bank or financial institution. PSPs must be registered with the various card associations they support. 553

penetration test (pen test) A method of evaluating the security of a computer system or a network by simulating an attack from a malicious source (e.g., a cracker). 515

penny auction A formal auction in which participants pay a non-refundable small fee for each bid. Bid level changes by small increments. 101

permission advertising Advertising (marketing) strategy in which customers agree to accept advertising and marketing materials (known as *opt-in*). 471

person-to-person lending Lending done between individuals circumventing the bank's traditional role in this process. W7-1

personal area network (PAN) A wireless telecommunications network for device-to-device connections within a very short range. 288

personal digital assistant (PDA) A stand-alone handheld computer principally used for personal information management. 284

personal firewall A network node designed to protect an individual user's desktop system from the public network by monitoring all the traffic that passes through the computer's network interface card. 523

personalization The matching of services, products, and advertising content with individual consumers and their preferences. 441

personalized content Web content that matches the needs and expectations of the individual visitor. W15-23

pervasive computing Computing capabilities embedded in the environment but typically not mobile. 311

phishing A crimeware technique to steal the identity of a target company to get the identities of its customers. 494

plaintext An unencrypted message in human-readable form. 519

Platform for Privacy Preferences Project (P3P) A protocol allowing websites to declare their intended use of information they collect about browsing users. 739

podcast A media file that is distributed over the Internet using syndication feeds for playback on mobile devices and personal computers. As with the term *radio*, it can mean both the content and the method of syndication. A collection of audio files in MP3 format. W15-23

pop-under ad An ad that appears underneath the current browser window, so when the user closes the active window the ad is still on the screen. 456

pop-up ad An ad that appears in a separate window before, after, or during Internet surfing or when reading e-mail. 456

prevention measures Ways to help stop unauthorized users (also known as "intruders") from accessing any part of the EC system. 499

privacy The right to be left alone and free of unreasonable personal intrusions. 719

private key Encryption code that is known only to its owner. 520

private shopping club A members-only shopping club, where members can buy goods at large discounts. 146

procurement management The planning, organizing, and coordinating of all the activities relating to purchasing goods and services needed to accomplish the organization's mission. 196

product brokering Deciding what product to buy. 432

product differentiation Special features available in products that make them distinguishable from other products. This property attracts customers that appreciate what they consider an added value. 685

production function An equation indicating that for the same quantity of production, Q, companies either can use a certain amount of labor or invest in more automation. 682

project champion The person who ensures the EC project gets the time, attention, and resources required and defends the project from detractors at all times. 638

protocol tunneling Method used to ensure confidentiality and integrity of data transmitted over the Internet by encrypting data packets, sending them in packets across the Internet, and decrypting them at the destination address. 525

public (asymmetric) key encryption Method of encryption that uses a pair of matched keys—a public key to encrypt a message and a private key to decrypt it, or vice versa. 520

public e-marketplaces Third-party exchanges open to all interested parties (sellers and buyers). 182

public key Encryption code that is publicly available to anyone. 520

public key infrastructure (PKI) A scheme for securing e-payments using public key encryption and various technical components. 520

purchasing cards (p-cards) Special purpose payment cards issued to a company's employees to be used solely for purchasing nonstrategic materials and services up to a preset dollar limit. 571

radio frequency identification (RFID) (1) A short-range radio frequency communication technology for remotely storing and retrieving data using devices called *RFID tags* and *RFID readers*. (2) Tags that can be attached to or embedded in objects, animals, or humans and use radio waves to communicate with a reader for the purpose of uniquely identifying the object or transmitting data and/or storing information about the object. 316, 599

random banners Banner ads that appear at random, not as the result of the user's action. 455

Really Simple Syndication (RSS) A family of Web-feed formats used to publish frequently updated digital content. W15-22

real-time location system (RTLS) Systems used to track and identify the location of objects in real time. 305

referral economy The effect upon sales of consumers receiving a referral or recommendation from other consumers. 166

regulatory compliance Systems or departments in an organization whose job is to ensure that personnel are aware of and take steps to comply with relevant laws, standards, policies, and regulations. 750

reintermediation The process whereby intermediaries (either new ones or those that had been disintermediated) take on new intermediary roles. 168

relationship marketing Marketing method that focuses on building a long-term relationship with customers. 439

reputation-based systems Systems used to establish trust among members of online communities where parties with no prior knowledge of each other use the feedback from their peers to assess the trustworthiness of the peers in the community. 437

request for proposal (RFP) Notice sent to potential vendors inviting them to submit a proposal describing their software packages and how it would meet the company's needs. W13-14

request for quote (RFQ) The "invitation" to participate in a tendering (bidding) system. 201

resident agents Software agents that stay in the computer or system and perform their tasks. W11-11

reusability The likelihood a segment of source code can be used again to add new functionalities with slight or no modification. 692

reverse auction (bidding or **tendering system)** Auction in which the buyer places an item for bid (tender) on a request for quote (RFQ) system, potential suppliers bid on the job, with the price reducing sequentially, and the lowest bid wins; primarily a B2B or G2B mechanism. 100

reverse logistics The movement of returns from customers to vendors. 585

risk The probability that a vulnerability will be known and used. 494

ROI calculator Calculator that uses metrics and formulas to compute ROI. 676

rolling warehouse Logistics method in which products on the delivery truck are not preassigned to a destination, but the decision about the quantity to unload at each destination is made at the time of unloading. 597

scenario planning A strategic planning methodology that generates plausible alternative futures to help decision makers identify actions that can be taken today to ensure success in the future. 627

scoring methodology A method that evaluates alternatives by assigning weights and scores to various aspects and then calculating the weighted totals. W13-5

search advertising A method of placing online advertisements on Web pages that show results from search engine queries. 457

search engine A computer program that can access databases of Internet resources, search for specific information or key words, and report the results. 96

search engine optimization (SEO) The application of strategies intended to position a website at the top of Web search engines. 459, W15-34

search engine spam Pages created deliberately to trick the search engine into offering inappropriate, redundant, or poor-quality search results. 511

self-hosting When a business acquires the hardware, software, staff, and dedicated telecommunications services necessary to set up and manage its own website. W15-19

sell-side e-marketplace A Web-based marketplace in which one company sells to many business buyers from e-catalogs or auctions, frequently over an extranet. 88, 188

Semantic Web An evolving extension of the Web in which Web content can be expressed not only in natural language, but also in a form that can be understood, interpreted, and used by intelligent computer software agents, permitting them to find, share, and integrate information more easily. 122

sensor network A collection of nodes capable of environmental sensing, local computation, and communication with its peers or with other higher performance nodes. 316

service-level agreement (SLA) A formal agreement regarding the division of work between a company and a vendor. W13-15

settlement Transferring money from the buyer's to the merchant's account. 552

shopping portals Gateways to e-storefronts and e-malls; may be comprehensive or niche oriented. 164

shopping robots (shopping agents, shopbots) Tools that scout the Web on behalf of consumers who specify search criteria. 165

short message service (SMS) A service that supports the sending and receiving of short text messages on mobile phones. 286

signature file A simple text message an e-mail program automatically adds to outgoing messages. W15-34

site navigation Aids that help visitors find the information they need quickly and easily. W15-28

smart card An electronic card containing an embedded microchip that enables predefined operations or the addition, deletion, or manipulation of information on the card. 556

smart card operating system Special system that handles file management, security, input/output (I/O), and command execution and provides an application programming interface (API) for a smart card. 557

smart card reader Activates and reads the contents of the chip on a smart card, usually passing the information on to a host system. 557

smart grid An electricity network managed by utilizing digital technology. 313

smartphone A mobile phone with PC-like capabilities. 584

social bookmarking Web service for sharing Internet bookmarks. The sites are a popular way to store, classify, share, and search links through the practice of folksonomy techniques on the Internet and intranets. 110

social capital A sociological concept that refers to connections within and between social networks. The core idea is that social networks have value. Just as physical capital or human capital can increase productivity (both individual and collective), so do social contacts affect the productivity of individuals and groups. 336

social commerce (SC) The delivery of e-commerce activities and transactions through social networks and/or via Web 2.0 software. 50, 339

social computing An approach aimed at making the human–computer interface more natural. 48

social CRM (SCRM) A customer engagement strategy in support of companies' defined goals and objectives toward optimizing the customer experience. Success requires a focus on people, processes, and technology associated with customer touchpoints and interactions. 369

social customer Members of social networks who do social shopping and understand their rights and how to use the wisdom and power of crowdsourcing and communities to their benefit. 369

social engineering A type of nontechnical attack that uses some ruse to trick users into revealing information or performing an action that compromises a computer or network. 494

social game A video game played in a social network. 401

social graph A term coined by Mark Zuckerberg of Facebook, which originally referred to the social network of relationships between users of the social networking service provided by Facebook. The idea was for Facebook to benefit from the social graph by taking advantage of the relationships between individuals that Facebook provides, to offer a richer online experience. This definition was expanded to refer to a social graph of all Internet users. 338

social learning Learning, training, and knowledge sharing in social networks and by using social software tools for learning. 246

social location-based marketing Marketing activities that are related to social behavior and are related to social networking activities. 310

social marketing A combination of social policy and marketing practices to achieve a set of social behavioral goals within a target audience. 335

social marketplace The term is derived from the combination of *social networking* and *marketplace*. An online community that harnesses the power of one's social networks for the introduction, buying, and selling of products, services, and resources, including one's own creations. Also may refer to a structure that resembles a social network but is focused on individual members. 352

social media The online platforms and tools that people use to share opinions, experiences, insights, perceptions, and various media, including photos, videos, and music, with each other. 335

social media marketing (SMM) A term that describes use of social media platforms such as networks, online communities, blogs, wikis, or any other online collaborative media for marketing, market research, sales, CRM, and customer service. It may incorporate ideas and concepts from social capital, Web 2.0, social media, and social marketing. 336

social network A category of Internet applications that help connect friends, business partners, or individuals with specific interests by providing free services such as photo presentation, e-mail, blogging, and so on using a variety of tools. 49

social networking The creation or sponsoring of a social network service and any activity, such as blogging, done in a social network (external or internal). 49

social networking service (SNS) A service that builds online communities by providing an online space for people to build free homepages and that provides basic communication and support tools for conducting different activities in the social network. 49

social shopping A method of e-commerce where shoppers' friends become involved in the shopping experience. Social shopping attempts to use technology to mimic the social interactions found in physical malls and stores. 343

social software A software product that enables people to rendezvous, connect, and collaborate through computer-mediated communication. 104

social-oriented website A site that provides users online tools for communication and sharing information on common interests. W15-15

software agents Autonomous software programs that carry out tasks on behalf of users. W11-10

spam The electronic equivalent of junk mail. 494

spam site Page that uses techniques that deliberately subvert a search engine's algorithms to artificially inflate the page's rankings. 511

spamming Using e-mail to send unwanted ads (sometimes floods of ads). 471

splog Short for *spam blog*. A site created solely for marketing purposes. 512

spot buying The purchase of goods and services as they are needed, usually at prevailing market prices. 183

spyware Software that gathers user information over an Internet connection without the user's knowledge. 449, 509, 733

standard of due care Care that a company is reasonably expected to take based on the risks affecting its EC business and online transactions. 538

stickiness Characteristic that influences the average length of time a visitor stays in a site. 454

storebuilder service A hosting service that provides disk space and services to help small and microbusinesses build a website quickly and cheaply. W15-17

stored-value card A card that has monetary value loaded onto it and that is usually rechargeable. 559

strategic information systems planning (SISP) A process for developing a strategy and plans for aligning information systems (including e-commerce applications) with the organization's business strategies. 622

strategic (systematic) sourcing Purchases involving long-term contracts that usually are based on private negotiations between sellers and buyers. 183

strategy A broad-based formula for how a business is going to accomplish its mission, what its goals should be, and what plans and policies will be needed to carry out those goals. 619

strategy assessment The continuous evaluation of progress toward the organization's strategic goals, resulting in corrective action and, if necessary, strategy reformulation. 625

strategy formulation The development of strategies to exploit opportunities and manage threats in the business environment in light of corporate strengths and weaknesses. 624

strategy implementation The development of detailed, short-term plans for carrying out the projects agreed on in strategy formulation. 625

strategy initiation The initial phase of strategic planning in which the organization examines itself and its environment. 623

strategy map A tool that delineates the relationships among the key organizational objectives for all four BSC perspectives. 626

supplier relationship management (SRM) A comprehensive approach to managing an enterprise's interactions with the organizations that supply the goods and services it uses. 187

SWOT analysis A methodology that surveys external opportunities and threats and relates them to internal strengths and weaknesses. 627

symmetric (private) key encryption An encryption system that uses the same key to encrypt and decrypt the message. 520

syndication The sale of the same good (e.g., digital content) to many customers, who then integrate it with other offerings and resell it or give it away free. W15-22

tags A nonhierarchical key word or term assigned to a piece of information (such as an Internet bookmark, digital image, video clip, or any computer document). 109

taxation The process whereby charges are imposed on individuals or property by the legislative branch of the federal government and by many state governments to raise funds for public purposes. 748

telecommuting Working at home using a PC and the Internet. 752

tendering (bidding) system Model in which a buyer requests would-be sellers to submit bids; the lowest bidder wins. 63

terminal-based positioning Calculating the location of a mobile device from signals sent by the device to base stations. 306

third-party logistics suppliers (3PL) External, rather than in-house, providers of logistics services. 586

total benefits of ownership (TBO) Benefits of ownership that include both tangible and intangible benefits. 675

total cost of ownership (TCO) A formula for calculating the cost of owning, operating, and controlling an IT system. 675

trademark A symbol used by businesses to identify their goods and services; government registration of the trademark confers exclusive legal right to its use. 726

trademark dilution The use of famous trademarks in public that diminishes the capacity of the mark to distinguish goods or services, or tarnishes the mark in the eyes of the consumer. 726

transaction costs Costs that are associated with the distribution (sale) or exchange of products and services including the cost of searching for buyers and sellers, gathering information, negotiating, decision making, monitoring the exchange of goods, and legal fees. 683

transaction log A record of user activities at a company's website. 449

transactional website A website that sells products and services. W15-15

Trojan horse A program that appears to have a useful function but that contains a hidden function that presents a security risk. 501

trust The psychological status of willingness to depend on another person or organization. 436

turnkey approach Ready to use without further assembly or testing; supplied in a state that is ready to turn on and operate. 692

tweet Text-based posts up to 140 characters in length posted to Twitter. 107

Twitter A free microblogging service that allows its users to send and read other users' updates. 107

ubiquitous computing (ubicom) Computing capabilities that are being embedded into the objects around us, which may be mobile or stationary. 311

unique visit A count of the number of visitors entering a site, regardless of how many pages are viewed per visit. 454

unit testing Testing application software modules one at a time. 691

up-selling Offering an upgraded version of the product in order to boost sales and profit. W15-21

usability (of website) The quality and usefulness of the user's experience when interacting with the website. W15-32

usability testing Testing the quality of the user's experience when interacting with a website. 691

user profile The requirements, preferences, behaviors, and demographic traits of a particular customer. 441

user-generated media Various kinds of media content, that are produced by end users and are publicly available. 333

valuation The fair market value of a business or the price at which a property would change hands between a willing buyer and a willing seller who are both informed and under no compulsion to act. For a publicly traded company, the value can be readily obtained by multiplying the selling price of the stock by the number of available shares. 685

value proposition (1) The benefit that a company's products or services provide to a company and its customers. (2) The benefits a company can derive from using EC. 62, 623

vendor-managed inventory (VMI) A system in which retailers make their suppliers fully responsible for determining when to order and possibly how much to order. 262

venture capital (VC) Money invested in a business by an individual, a group of individuals (venture capitalists), or a funding company in exchange for equity in the business. W15-9

versioning Selling the same good, but with different selection and delivery characteristics. 637

vertical marketplaces Markets that deal with one industry or industry segment (e. g., steel, chemicals). 184

viral blogging Viral (word-of-mouth) marketing done by bloggers. 356

viral marketing (viral advertising) Word-of-mouth marketing by which customers promote a product or service by telling others about it (frequently their friends). 356, 461

viral video A video clip that gains widespread popularity through the process of Internet sharing, typically through e-mail or IM messages, blogs, and other media-sharing websites. 359, 463

virtual community A group of people with similar interests who interact with one another using the Internet. 111

virtual (pure-play) e-tailers Firms that sell directly to consumers over the Internet without maintaining a physical sales channel. 143

virtual (pure-play) organizations Organizations that conduct their business activities solely online. 39

virtual corporation (VC) An organization composed of several business partners sharing costs and resources for the production or utilization of a product or service. W12-2

virtual private network (VPN) A network that uses the public Internet to carry information but remains private by using encryption to scramble the communications, authentication to ensure that information has not been tampered with, and access control to verify the identity of anyone using the network. 525

virtual university An online university from which students take classes from home or other offsite locations, usually via the Internet. 244

virtual world A user-defined world in which people can interact, play, and do business. The most publicized virtual world is Second Life. 50, 119

virus A piece of software code that inserts itself into a host, including the operating systems, in order to propagate; it requires that its host program be run to activate it. 501

visibility The knowledge about where materials and parts are at any given time, which helps solving problems such as delay, combining shipments, and more. 596

visit A series of requests during one navigation of a website; a pause of a certain length of time ends a visit. 453

vlog (or video blog) A blog with video content. 104

voice portal (1) A portal accessed by telephone or cell phone. (2) A website with an audio interface that can be accessed through a telephone call. 92, 287

vortal B2B portals that focus on a single industry or industry segment; "vertical portals." 210

vulnerability Weakness in software or other mechanism that threatens the confidentiality, integrity, or availability of an asset (recall the CIA model). It can be directly used by a hacker to gain access to a system or network. 495

vulnerability assessment The process of identifying, quantifying, and prioritizing the vulnerabilities in a system. 515

warehouse management system (WMS) A software system that helps in managing warehouses. 588

Web 2.0 The second generation of Internet-based services that lets people collaborate and share information online in new ways, such as social networking sites, wikis, communication tools, and folksonomies. 48

Web 3.0 A term used to describe the future of the World Wide Web. It consists of the creation of high-quality content and services produced by gifted individuals using Web 2.0 technology as an enabling platform. 121

Web 4.0 The Web generation after Web 3.0. It is still an unknown entity. However, it is envisioned as being based on islands of intelligence and as being ubiquitous. 123

Web analytics (1) The analysis of clickstream data to understand visitor behavior on a website. (2) The measurement, collection, analysis, and reporting of Internet data for the purposes of understanding and optimizing Web usage. 644, 667, W15-34

Web bugs Tiny graphics files embedded in e-mail messages and in websites that transmit information about users and their movements to a Web server. 449

Web hosting service A dedicated website hosting company that offers a wide range of hosting services and functionality to businesses of all sizes. W15-18

Web mining Data mining techniques for discovering and extracting information from Web documents; explores both Web content and Web usage. 450

Web portal A single point of access, through a Web browser, to critical business information located inside and outside (via Internet) an organization. 90

Web syndication A form of syndication in which a section of a website is available for other sites to use. W15-22

Webcasting A free Internet news service that broadcasts personalized news and information, including seminars, in categories selected by the user. 473

Webstore (storefront) A single company's website where products or services are sold and usually has an online shopping cart associated with it. Many Webstores target a specific industry and find their own unique corner of the market. 89

Wi-Fi (wireless fidelity) The common name used to describe the IEEE 802.11 standard used on most WLANs. 288

wiki (wikilog) A blog that allows everyone to participate as a peer; anyone may add, delete, or change content. 109

WiMAX A wireless standard (IEEE 802.16) for making broadband network connections over a medium-size area such as a city. 289

wireless local area network (WLAN) A telecommunications network that enables users to make short-range wireless connections to the Internet or another network. 288

wireless mobile computing (mobile computing) Computing that connects a mobile device to a network or another computing device, anytime, anywhere. 282

wireless wide area network (WWAN) A telecommunications network that offers wireless coverage over a large geographical area, typically over a cellular phone network. 289

worm A software program that runs independently, consuming the resources of its host in order to maintain itself, that is capable of propagating a complete working version of itself onto another machine. 501

zombies Computers infected with malware that are under the control of a spammer, hacker, or other criminal. 495

Index

Note: Page references with E represent exhibits; those with W represent Web pages.